MOON

COSTA RICA

CHRISTOPHER P. BAKER

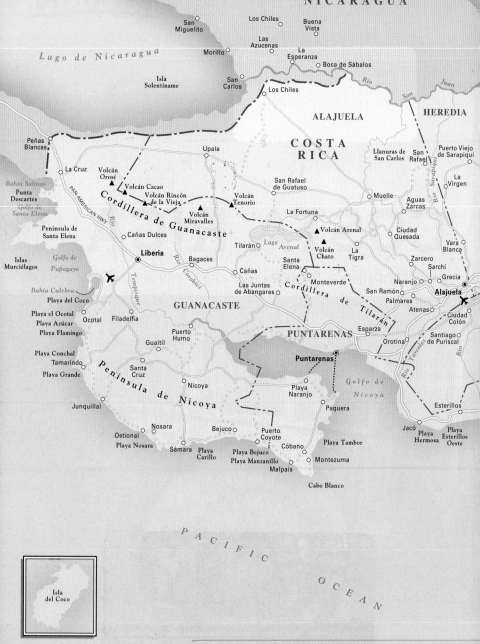

Contents

DISCOVER
Costa Rica

O n my first visit to Costa Rica, I performed yoga in a crisply cool cloud forest with accommodations in a Swiss-style hotel amid the pines. The next day I participated in dawn calisthenics on a Pacific beach within sight of marine turtles and monkeys. Therein lies Costa Rica's beauty.

Despite its diminutive size, Costa Rica is a kind of microcontinent unto itself—one sculpted to show off the full potential of the tropics. The diversity of terrain is remarkable. You can journey from the Amazon to a Swiss alpine forest simply by starting on the coastal plains and walking uphill. The tableau changes from dense rainforest, dry deciduous forests, open savanna, and lush wetlands to montane cloud forest swathing the upper slopes of volcanoes. Along the Pacific and Atlantic Oceans, dozens of inviting beaches run the gamut from frost-white to chocolate, and islands and offshore coral reefs open up a world more beautiful than a casket of gems.

The nation's 12 distinct ecological zones are home to an astonishing array of flora and fauna—approximately 5 percent of all known species on earth—and include more butterfly species than in all of Africa, and more than twice the number of bird species in the whole of the United States. Stay here long enough and

Clockwise from top left: church in La Fortuna with Arenal Volcano in the background; the plaza at Zarcero; violet sabrewing hummingbird; red-lored Amazon; basilisk or "Jesus Christ" lizard; pachira flowering on Playa Santa Teresa.

you'll begin to think that with luck, you might see examples of all the creatures on earth.

Unlike many destinations, where humans have driven animals into the deepest seclusion, Costa Rica's wildlife loves to put on a song and dance. Animals and birds are prolific and relatively easy to spot: sleek jaguars on the prowl; sloths moving languidly among the high branches; scarlet macaws launching from their perches to fly away squawking.

Since my first visit, the country has also exploded as a world-class venue for active adventures—scuba diving, sportfishing, white-water rafting, surfing, and horseback riding. The adrenaline rush never stops, be it ATV tours or zip-line adventures.

Plus, the nation boasts a huge choice of fantastic resorts, boutique hotels, rustic lodges, surfer camps, and budget *cabinas*. And while its neighbors have been racked by turmoil, Costa Rica has enjoyed remarkable normalcy—few extremes of wealth and poverty, no standing army, a proud history as Central America's most stable democracy, and a quality of life among the highest in the western hemisphere.

Clockwise from top left: oxen harvesting African date palms; lovers embracing at sunset in Tamarindo; mountain stream at Nectandra; traditional painted oxcart wheel.

Planning Your Trip

Where to Go

San José

The bustling capital city is a handy hub for forays farther afield. Pre-Columbian artifacts are exhibited at three small yet excellent **museums;** a handful of **galleries** satisfy art enthusiasts; and souvenir shoppers are well served by quality **crafts stores.** The city boasts superb **restaurants,** thriving **nightlife,** and great **hotels.**

Central Highlands

Wrapped by volcanoes and rugged mountains, the densely populated highlands are tremendously scenic, with a springlike climate. The scenery is best enjoyed by ascending the **Poás** or **Irazú volcanoes,** with stops at **Café Britt** or **Doka Estate;** or to explore the nation's major pre-Columbian site at **Monumento Nacional Guayabo.** Two of the nation's premier white-water runs cascade from these mountains.

The Caribbean Coast

This humid zone is notable for its Afro-Caribbean culture. Offbeat **Cahuita** and **Puerto Viejo** draw surfers and backpackers and serve as departure points for treks into indigenous reserves. Wildlife-rich **Parque Nacional Cahuita** and **Parque Nacional Tortuguero** are easily accessed—the latter by canal from waterfront nature lodges. Marine turtles lay eggs up and down the coast. Anglers are gung-ho about **Barra del Colorado.**

The Northern Zone

The northern lowland is a center for active adventures focused around **Parque Nacional Volcán Arenal.** Hiking, hot springs, horseback riding,

Arenal Volcano

The Northern Zone

Guanacaste and the Northwest

Central Highlands

The Nicoya Peninsula

Central Pacific

Caribbean Sea

The Caribbean Coast

San José

South-Central Costa Rica

Golfo Dulce and the Osa Peninsula

PACIFIC OCEAN

© AVALON TRAVEL

and zip-line adventures are popular. **Laguna de Arenal** draws windsurfers and freshwater anglers, while the **Caño Negro** wildlife refuge is a nirvana for bird-watchers. Nature lodges grant access to rugged **Parque Nacional Braulio Carrillo,** and the **Volcán Tenorio** region is evolving as a new frontier for active adventures.

Guanacaste and the Northwest

The northwest is distinct for its dry climate and deciduous tropical forests: Bird-watching is superb at **Parque Nacional Palo Verde** and **Parque Nacional Santa Rosa,** which boasts historical sites. This is also cowboy country; numerous ranches double as eco-oriented activity centers at the base of volcanoes. A big draw is **Monteverde,** a mountain idyll boasting attractions and activities that will hold your attention for days.

The Nicoya Peninsula

This region is known for its white-sand beaches linked by an unpaved coastal road that may require fording rivers. Scuba diving, surfing, and sportfishing are key draws. **Playa Grande** and **Ostional** are important nesting sites for marine turtles. Inland, **Guaitíl** preserves its indigenous pottery tradition, and nearby **Barra Honda** is the nation's major speleological site.

Accommodations range from surf camps to sublime high-end resorts, concentrated at **Playa Tamarindo** and **Bahía Culebra.**

Central Pacific

Forest-clad mountains hem a narrow coastal plain fringed by beaches. **Jacó,** Costa Rica's most developed resort, is popular with the party crowd. **Tárcoles** is great for crocodile safaris; **Parque Nacional Carara** offers world-class bird-watching; and **Manuel Antonio** combines wildlife encounters with a huge selection of fine lodging and dining. Nearby **Quepos** is a center for sportfishing. Whale-watching draws visitors to the **Costa Ballena.**

Golfo Dulce and the Osa Peninsula

Soaking rains nurture the forests of **Parque Nacional Corcovado.** The humble port of **Golfito** is a base for sportfishing and forays to remote rainforest lodges. Kilometer-long waves wash up at surf capital **Pavones.** Tucked-away **Drake Bay** is good for diving and whale-watching excursions and trips to **Isla del Caño,** an erstwhile indigenous ceremonial site. Some 500 kilometers (300 miles) southwest of mainland Costa Rica, **Isla del Coco** is off-limits to all but experienced divers.

South-Central Costa Rica

The nation's Cinderella region draws birders and nature lovers to **Los Cusingos** and **Wilson Botanical Garden.** Hale and hearty adventure seekers follow the trail up **Chirripó,** the nation's highest mountain; the trailhead is accessed by one of several Shangri-la valleys that lead into the rugged **Parque Internacional La Amistad.** Indigenous communities exist in isolation, but the easy-to-reach village of **Boruca** offers an initiation.

When to Go

Costa Rica has two distinct seasons: **dry season** (Dec.-Apr.) and **wet season** (May-Nov.). Although regional distinctions exist, rainy season is typified by brief afternoon showers or downpours. As the season progresses, more sustained rains occur, often lasting for days. Prices are usually lower in rainy season, and it is easier to find vacant rooms in popular destinations.

The Caribbean and Osa Peninsula can be rainy year-round.

Peak-season rates usually apply for Christmas, New Year's, and Easter, when many accommodations and car rentals are booked months in advance.

My favorite time to visit is **May through early June,** when crowds have departed and the first rains have greened up the scenery.

Before You Go

Passports and Visas

Citizens of the United States, Canada, and most European nations traveling to Costa Rica need a **passport** valid for at least six months beyond their intended length of stay, plus a ticket for onward travel. Stays of up to 90 days are permitted without a visa.

Vaccinations

Officially, **no vaccinations** are required for entry into Costa Rica, but it's a good idea to be up-to-date on tetanus, typhoid, and hepatitis shots. If you plan on taking preventive medications against malaria, start taking them a few weeks before potential exposure.

Transportation

Most visitors fly into San José's **Juan Santamaría International Airport.** Travelers planning on visiting only Nicoya and Guanacaste might consider flying in and out of Liberia's **Daniel Oduber International Airport.** Many people choose to travel around Costa Rica on inexpensive domestic flights. It's also easy to get between popular destinations on cheap public buses and tourist shuttle vans. Car rental agencies are located at every major tourist destination, but it's wise to book ahead. **A 4WD vehicle is essential;** most main roads are paved, but many popular spots are accessed only by rutted dirt roads.

Don't Miss:

squirrel monkey at Manuel Antonio National Park

- **Museo del Oro Precolombino:** This San José museum is chock-full of gold artifacts, jade ornaments, and other indigenous relics (page 43).

- **Poás Volcano National Park:** Costa Rica's most visited national park stars an active volcano (page 97).

- **La Paz Waterfall Gardens:** Explore a butterfly enclosure, walk-through aviary, snake and frog exhibits, and a wildcat zoo that has the only captive jaguar in Costa Rica. Cloud forest trails lead to the namesake waterfalls (page 94).

- **Tortuguero National Park:** Time your visit to witness green turtles nesting on the beach (page 158).

- **Manuel Antonio National Park:** The wildlife's not shy at this park, where you're practically guaranteed to spot monkeys and sloths in the trailside trees, almost at fingertip distance (page 413).

- **Cahuita:** Come to this laid-back Afro-Caribbean community to chill in a hammock, savor *rondón* (fish cooked and seasoned in coconut milk), and jive to "Don't Worry About a Thing" (page 172).

- **Arenal Volcano National Park:** Hike along lava trails surrounding the youngest and most regularly active of Costa Rica's volcanoes (page 214).

- **San Gerardo de Dota:** This retreat offers premier cloud-forest terrain that is unparalleled for the quetzal viewing (page 133).

- **Casa Orquídeas:** The birding is exceptional at this rainforest resort, reachable solely by boat (page 459).

- **Jewels of the Rainforest Insect Museum:** Costa Rica's showcase insect exhibit astounds, plus adjacent facilities at Selvatura activity center include zip line and hanging bridge trails (page 260).

Best of Costa Rica

Few visitors have time to explore Costa Rica from tip to toe, but the following itinerary takes in half a dozen of the best national parks, a potpourri of active adventures, and many of the best sights.

Day 1

Arrive in San José. Take the afternoon to visit the **Museo del Jade** and **Museo del Oro Precolombino,** then dinner at **Hotel Grano de Oro.**

Day 2

An early-morning visit to **Parque Nacional Volcán Poás** is followed by a visit to the **La Paz Waterfall Gardens.** In the late afternoon, get a feel for Costa Rica's coffee culture with a tour at **Café Britt** or **Doka Estate.**

Days 3-4

Head to **La Fortuna** and fill your days with hiking at **Parque Nacional Volcán Arenal;** a ride

on the **Sky Tram,** including the zip line; and a soak at **Balneario Tabacón** hot springs. A traditional meal at **Choza de Laurel** is a good way to end the day.

Day 5

Transfer via Laguna de Arenal and Tilarán to **Monteverde,** where the **Monteverde Lodge** makes a fine base. After lunch, head to **Selvatura** for a canopy adventure.

Day 6

Rise early for a guided hike in **Monteverde Cloud Forest Biological Reserve** or **Santa Elena Cloud Forest Reserve.** In the afternoon, visit **Herpetarium Adventures** and the **Frog Pond.** In the evening, take a guided twilight walk at **Bajo del Tigre.**

Day 7

Transfer to **Parque Nacional Rincón de la**

hikers amid dwarf cloud forest atop Poás Volcano

Best Beaches

Costa Rica boasts glorious beaches, virtually all backed by rainforest. Swim with caution; many beaches are known for riptides.

THE CARIBBEAN

Tortuguero: This silvery beach backed by lush rainforest is the most important green turtle nesting site in the Caribbean (page 158).

Playa Blanca, Parque Nacional Cahuita: With several beautiful golden-sand beaches broken by rocky headlands, Cahuita is a great place to sunbathe or snorkel amid the offshore coral reef (page 172).

THE NICOYA PENINSULA

Playa Conchal: This sometimes crowded beach of tiny seashells changes from bleached white to gray, depending on tidal and weather conditions. The calm turquoise waters host a coral reef (page 318).

Playa Grande at dawn

Playa Flamingo: Perhaps the most magnificent white-sand beach in the nation, this gently curving scimitar is bookended by rugged headlands but has few services (page 320).

Playa Grande: This miles-long beach has vast views across the bay toward Tamarindo. It's also the nation's prime nesting site for leatherback turtles (page 332).

Playa Montezuma: Stretching east from the eponymous village, this coral-colored beach is washed by crashing surf (page 368).

Playa Naranjo: Surrounded on two sides by swampy estuaries, this golden-sand beach provides access to Parque Nacional Santa Rosa. See big cats, crocodiles, tamanduas, and scarlet macaws (page 364).

Playa Ostional: Time your visit for an *arribada*, when thousands of olive ridley turtles crawl ashore here to lay their eggs (page 343).

Playa Güiones, Nosara: Studded with rocky islets and tide pools, this ruler-straight expanse can be 200 meters (660 feet) deep at low tide (page 345).

Playa Santa Teresa: Rugged headlands and isles, tropical forest, and fearsome surf make this one of the nation's most dramatic beaches (page 372).

CENTRAL PACIFIC

Playa Manuel Antonio: Curling around a sheltered bay like a shepherd's crook, this beach has it all: calm turquoise waters, rocky headlands, rainforest, and views toward distant mountains (page 413).

Playas Esterillos: Palm-fringed with gray sands, four beaches in one run along some 20 kilometers (12 miles) of shoreline (page 396).

GOLFO DULCE AND THE OSA PENINSULA

Playa Platanares: East of Puerto Jiménez, Platanares abuts both rainforest and mangrove, is an important nesting site for marine turtles, and offers whale and dolphin viewing (page 447).

Playa Zancudo: Washed by surf and littered with tree trunks, this beach has stupendous views across the Golfo Dulce (page 464).

aerial view of Nicoya looking north from Sámara

Vieja. After settling in at one of the nature lodges that double as activity centers, you'll want to visit the bubbling mud pools and fumaroles and partake of canopy tours, horseback riding, and hikes.

Day 8

Today, it's the Nicoya Peninsula and **Tamarindo,** arriving in time for lunch at a beachfront restaurant. This evening, head to **Playa Grande** to witness marine turtles laying eggs (in season)—you'll need to make reservations.

Day 9

Head south to **Nosara** via **Ostional National Wildlife Refuge.** If you're driving, the coast road will prove an adventure. With good timing and prior planning, you can visit the turtle *arribada* at Ostional.

Days 10-11

Travel to **Manuel Antonio** for wildlife-viewing, snorkeling, and relaxing in and around Parque Nacional Manuel Antonio. The resort hotels here offer superb accommodations, and there are plenty of excellent restaurants and a lively night scene.

Days 12-13

Transfer to the Osa Peninsula for more rugged adventure. A guided hike along coastal and rainforest trails in **Parque Nacional Corcovado** leads to waterfalls and offers phenomenal wildlife sightings.

Day 14

Return to San José for your homeward flight, or extend your trip and fly to Tortuguero, where you can explore **Parque Nacional Tortuguero** by canoe or boat.

Consider a stay at a mountain or rainforest lodge, an aerial tree house, or even a working farm. Most have naturalist guides and activities such as canoeing and hiking. Some offer luxury fit for a king; others are basic, although no less endearing.

CENTRAL HIGHLANDS

Xandari: Stunning views, divinely designed and decorated villas, a superb spa, plus hikes through bamboo forests and a coffee estate—what more could you ask for? Food? Yes, even that is gourmet and organic (page 96).

Villablanca Cloud Forest Hotel & Nature Reserve: Mists drift ethereally around this old hacienda atop the Continental Divide. Converted into a chic hotel, it combines cozy chalets, a gourmet restaurant, and fabulous hiking (page 108).

Finca Rosa Blanca Coffee Plantation & Inn: Settle into this boutique hotel in the hills above Heredia and you may never leave. Couples in the one-of-a-kind honeymoon suite may never want to come up for air (page 116).

Pacuare Jungle Lodge: This sumptuous eco-lodge in thick mountain rainforest is reached solely by river, offering a jaw-dropping end to a thrilling day of white-water rafting (page 143).

THE CARIBBEAN COAST

Almonds & Corals Lodge Tent Camp: Imagine a deluxe East African safari lodge dropped into the rainforest beside the shore (page 190).

THE NORTHERN ZONE

Rancho Margot: Plaudits go to the visionary owners of this sustainable farm and eco-lodge on the shores of Laguna de Arenal. Choose a budget bunkhouse or a romantic bungalow (page 220).

The Springs Resort & Spa: Combine sumptuous suites with grand views of Volcán Arenal, plus hot-spring pools and cascades, an outdoor activity center, a wildlife rescue center—no wonder *The Bachelor* was filmed here (page 212).

THE NICOYA PENINSULA

Tree Tops Bed & Breakfast: It's just you and friendly owners Jack and Karen at this simple bed-and-breakfast suspended over a lovely beach. Gourmet meals and fabulous conversation are part of the bargain (page 342).

Anamaya Resort: With its coastal setting, inspired aesthetic, and events like fire-dancing and Zumba, this upscale hotel appeals to gregarious travelers who appreciate something quirky (page 370).

CENTRAL PACIFIC

Hacienda Barú: With its own wildlife reserve, this long-established eco-retreat has modest accommodations but first-rate activities, from horseback riding to tree-rappels (page 418).

Kurà Design Villas: Wow—this architectural stunner offers all-glass villas with stunning coastal views from on high (page 427).

GOLFO DULCE AND THE OSA PENINSULA

Lapa's Nest Costa Rica Tree House: See eye-to-eye with the monkeys and macaws at this one-of-a-kind tree house surrounded by rainforest (page 447).

Lapa Ríos: Speaking of tree houses, this deluxe eco-lodge rises over the rainforest of Cabo Matapalo; you can watch the wildlife while lounging on your deck, or opt for guided excursions (page 452).

SOUTH-CENTRAL COSTA RICA

Casa Mariposa: Budget backpackers intent on hiking Chirripó stay at this simple mountain retreat just steps from the trailhead (page 484).

Monte Azul: Boutique Hotel + Center for Art and Design: The yang to Casa Mariposa's yin (or is it vice versa?), this deluxe boutique lodge at the base of Chirripó doubles as an artists' retreat (page 485).

Ecoadventure

Escape the madding crowds and experience the *real* Costa Rica—these truly fascinating places and experiences that many visitors miss.

Ecotours

At Maderas Rainforest Conservancy on the Caribbean Coast, **La Suerte Biological Field Station Lodge** has 10 kilometers (6 miles) of rainforest trails open to ecotourists, along with ecology workshops.

Finca Luna Nueva Lodge is an organic, biodynamic herbal farm in the Northern Zone that welcomes visitors for hikes, tours, and classes on sustainable living.

The **Santa Juana Rural Mountain Adventure Tour** offers a chance to interact with a Central Pacific mountain community, integrated into an ecotourism project that is a model for how things should be done.

Part of the Punta Río Claro National Wildlife Refuge in the Golfo Dulce region, the **Punta Marenco Lodge** welcomes ecotourists and serves as a center for scientific research.

Cultural Immersion

A resurgence of cultural pride, assisted by tourism efforts, is opening the indigenous reserves to respectful visitation and an interest in traditional crafts.

In the Central Highlands, visit the **Beneficio Coopedota,** which handles the coffee beans for 700 local producers. The visit includes a plantation tour, a video, and tasting.

The **Reserva Indígena Kèköldi,** on the Caribbean Coast, is home to some 200 Bribrí and Cabecar people. Reforestation and other conservation projects are ongoing; visitors are educated on indigenous history and traditions. Reserva Indígena Talamanca-Bribrí and **Reserva Indígena Talamanca-Cabecar** protect the traditional lifestyle of the indigenous people. **Reserva Indígena Yorkin** welcomes visitors and leads hikes.

American crocodile

A naturalist guide demonstrates leaf ecology.

The three indigenous communities of the **Reserva Indígena Malekú,** in the Northern Zone, provide traditional music and dance performances, cultural presentations, and a museum on indigenous culture. A volunteer and study program at **Rustic Pathways** contributes to and learns from the Malekú culture. **Sarapiquís Rainforest Lodge** is a scientific research and educational center with a Museum of Indigenous Culture, an archaeological dig, and a reconstruction of an indigenous village.

Reserva Indígena Boruca, in South-Central Costa Rica, welcomes visitors keen to see traditional balsa masks being made.

Reforestation Projects

On the Caribbean Coast, **ANAI** works to protect the forest and to evolve a sustainable livelihood through reforestation and other earth-friendly methods; sign up for one of its Talamanca Field Adventures trips.

Hacienda Lodge Guachipelín, a century-old working cattle ranch, offers activities on more than 1,000 hectares (2,470 acres) in Guanacaste, plus a 1,200-hectare (3,000-acre) tree-reforestation project.

From Buenos Aires in South-Central Costa Rica, you can take a Jeep taxi to **Durika Biological Reserve,** a well-run commune deep in the mountains on the edge of Parque Internacional La Amistad. The rugged drive is not for the faint-hearted, but once there you can participate in a reforestation project, and even help milk the goats.

Volunteer Opportunities

Sea Turtle Conservancy needs volunteers to assist in research at Tortuguero, including during its twice-yearly turtle tagging and monitoring programs. Volunteers are also needed on the Caribbean Coast for the **Marine Turtle Conservation Project,** which conducts research and protects the turtles from predators and poachers. Pacuare is now the most important leatherback site in Costa Rica; the **Asociación Salvemos las Tortugas de Parismina** protects the eggs of leatherback turtles during nesting season. The **Asociación de Desarrollo Integral de Ostional,** on the Nicoya Peninsula,

Top Wildlife Spots

National parks, wildlife refuges, and biological reserves are found throughout the country. They range from swampy wetlands to dry-forest environments and from lowland rainforests to high-mountain cloud forests. Sign up for guided natural-history excursions or hire a local naturalist guide. You'll see many times more critters in the company of an eagle-eyed guide.

- **Asociación Salvemos las Tortugas de Parismina:** Leatherback, green, and hawksbill turtles come ashore at this private sanctuary (page 158).

- **Corcovado National Park:** This remote and dense rainforest is one place you may be able to spot tapirs and jaguars, and scarlet macaws are a dime a dozen (page 453).

- **Curú National Wildlife Refuge:** Three species of turtles come ashore at this private refuge (page 366).

- **Gandoca-Manzanillo National Wildlife Refuge:** Turtle lovers are sure to spot leatherbacks (Apr.-May), greens (July-Sept.), and hawksbills (Mar.-Aug.) (page 191).

- **Crocodile Safari on the Río Tárcoles:** Guaranteed close-up sightings of giant crocodiles (page 386).

- **La Paz Waterfall Gardens:** This splendid park has a fabulous aviary, plus snake, butterfly, hummingbird, and frog exhibits (page 94).

- **Manuel Antonio National Park:** This popular park offers easy wildlife-viewing from wide-open trails (page 413).

- **Monteverde Cloud Forest Biological Reserve:** Monteverde draws bird-watchers keen to spot a quetzal (page 255).

poison dart frog at La Paz Waterfall Gardens

- **Ostional National Wildlife Refuge:** This 248-hectare (613-acre) refuge protects the major nesting site of olive ridley turtles (page 343).

- **Palo Verde National Park:** This national park is known for its vast flocks of waterfowl and migratory birds (page 275).

- **Playa Camaronal:** Olive ridleys nest year-round and leatherbacks nest in March and April (page 358).

- **Los Quetzales National Park:** Your chances of seeing quetzals are vastly improved at this national park (page 133).

- **Tortuguero National Park:** This is my favorite place for wildlife-viewing. You may see river otters, caimans, and even manatees. Turtle-viewing at night is icing on the cake (page 158).

oversees turtle welfare and accepts volunteers to assist with turtle programs. And the **Programa Restauración de Tortugas Marinas** in Pavones has freed more than 100,000 turtle hatchlings to the sea. Volunteers are needed. **Rancho Mastatal Environmental Learning Center and Lodge,** in the Central Highlands, welcomes volunteers. This 89-hectare (219-acre) farm and private wildlife refuge offers environmental workshops and language courses.

Spend the day at **Aiko-Logi-Tours,** a 135-hectare (330-acre) sustainable farm and rainforest on the Caribbean coast. Volunteers are welcome to work on various eco-oriented projects. **Punta Mona Center for Sustainable Living and Education,** a communal organic farm and environmental center near the Gandoca-Manzanillo National Wildlife Refuge, accepts volunteers and internships. It teaches traditional and sustainable farming techniques and other environmentally sound practices.

Also on the Caribbean, volunteers are needed at the **Jaguar Rescue Center** for animals. It focuses on education as well as rehabilitation of animals on a rainforest plot linked to the Reserva Indígena Kèköldi.

La Gran Vista Agroecological Farm teaches sustainable agricultural practices and relies on volunteer labor. At **Three Seeds Eco-Education Camp,** volunteers teach English to local children while learning about organic farming and sustainable living practices.

Surf's Up

For many, the search for the perfect wave has ended in Costa Rica, the "Hawaii of Latin American surf." You're spoiled for choice, with dozens of world-class venues and no shortage of surf camps, surf schools, and rental outlets.

The Caribbean Coast

The Caribbean has fewer breaks than the Pacific but still offers great surfing. Waves are short yet powerful rides, sometimes with Hawaiian-style radical waves. The best times are summer (late May-early Sept.) and winter (Dec.-Mar.), when Atlantic storms push through the Caribbean, creating three-meter (10-foot) swells.

A 20-minute boat ride from Puerto Limón is **Isla Uvita,** with a strong and dangerous left. Farther south, there are innumerable short breaks at **Cahuita.** Still farther south, **Puerto Viejo** has the biggest rideable waves in Costa Rica. Immediately south, **Playa Cocles** is good for beginners.

Guanacaste and the Northwest

Surfing is centered on **Parque Nacional Santa Rosa,** and **Witch's Rock** at Playa Naranjo, one of the best beach breaks in the country. While many of the hot spots require a 4WD vehicle for access, surf excursions from nearby Nicoya beach resorts make them more accessible. The best time is during the rainy season (May-Nov.).

The Nicoya Peninsula

Nicoya offers more than 50 prime surf spots, more than anywhere else in the nation. Just north of Tamarindo is **Playa Grande,** with a five-kilometer-long (3-mile-long) beach break acclaimed as Costa Rica's most accessible and consistent. **Tamarindo** is an excellent jumping-off point for a surf safari south to more isolated beaches, including at **Playa Avellanas** and **Playa Negra** (definitely for experts only), **Nosara** and **Playas Sámara, Coyote, Manzanillo,** and **Malpaís.** All have good surf, lively action, and several surf camps.

Central Pacific

Central Pacific surfing centers on **Jacó,** where the waves appeal to beginners and intermediates. Farther south are **Playa Hermosa,** which has

surfer at sunset on Playa Grande

expert beach breaks and an international contest every August, and **Playas Esterillos Este and Oeste.** Farther south, what **Manuel Antonio** lacks in consistency it more than makes up for in natural beauty. **Dominical** has "militant" sandbars and long point waves in an equally beautiful tropical setting. The best conditions are July to December.

Golfo Dulce and the Osa Peninsula

The cognoscenti head to **Pavones,** on the southern shore of the Golfo Dulce. On a decent day, the fast, nearly one-kilometer (0.6-mile) left break is one of the longest in the world. The waves are at their grandest in rainy season, when the long left point can offer a three-minute ride. **Cabo Matapalo,** on the Osa Peninsula, is another top spot.

Family Fun

Combining educational options with fun keeps children (and parents) enthralled.

Birds and Butterflies

In San José, more than 30 species flit about in **Spirogyra Butterfly Garden.**

A visit to **La Paz Waterfall Gardens,** in the Central Highlands, includes an optional guided tour through the gardens and laboratory, where young tykes can learn about each stage of a butterfly's life cycle.

El Castillo, in the Northern Zone, is home to **The Butterfly Conservancy,** a butterfly garden and insect museum. **Selva Verde** is renowned for its birdlife and has a small butterfly garden.

In Guanacaste, the **Monteverde Butterfly Garden** features three habitats filled with hundreds of tropical butterflies. At Islita, in Nicoya, visit **The Ara Project,** a breeding program for endangered green and scarlet macaws; reservations are a must.

The Central Pacific region is home to **Manuel**

Antonio Nature Park and Wildlife Refuge. Here, explore a butterfly garden, a crocodile and caiman lagoon, and exhibits on poison dart frogs.

Culture Vultures

San José's **Pueblo Antiguo and Parque de Diversiones** is a Costa Rican Disney, with locales that dramatize the events of Costa Rican history.

Café Britt, in the Central Highlands, is a fun theatrical learning experience about the production and processing of coffee.

Sample fruit and learn about chocolate production at **Finca la Isla Botanical Garden,** on the Caribbean Coast.

At **Guaitíl,** in Nicoya, Chorotega artisans permit kids to make their own ceramics, fire them in a kiln, then paint them.

Parks and Reserves

Travel to the Caribbean Coast to ride the **Rainforest Aerial Tram,** an educational trip through the forest canopy. Or take an open-air tram through the canopy at **Veragua Rainforest Research and Adventure Park**

before checking out the butterfly, snake, and frog exhibits.

The **Monteverde Cloud Forest Biological Reserve** in Guanacaste protects hundreds of species of mammals, birds, amphibians, and reptiles. Kids helped create the **Bosque Eterno de Los Niños,** the largest private reserve in Central America. There's a Children's Nature Center, a self-guided interpretive trail, an arboretum, and a visitors center. The highlight at **Selvatura** is exploring the canopy along treetop walkways and suspended bridges, and you'll be bugged out by the incredible **Jewels of the Rainforest Insect Museum.**

On the Nicoya Peninsula, at **El Viejo Wildlife Refuge and Wetlands,** you can ride in amphibious vehicles and take a boat or a zip-line canopy tour. Viewing turtles nesting at night at **Parque Nacional Marino Las Baulas** is well worth keeping the kids up late.

Safaris and Tours

Take a dolphin safari into **Gandoca-Manzanillo National Wildlife Refuge** on the Caribbean Coast.

Glasswing butterfly, Monteverde Butterfly Garden

scarlet macaw

Visit the Northern Zone's **Arenal Theme Park** for phenomenal volcano views enjoyed from an aerial Sky Tram.

Africa Safari Adventure Park, a private wildlife reserve in Guanacaste, features elands, camels, ostriches, zebras, antelopes, giraffes, and warthogs.

The catamaran journey to the Nicoya Peninsula's **Isla Tortuga** thrills, and once you arrive, you get to snorkel and kayak.

A guided canoe or boat trip through **Parque Nacional Tortuguero** with naturalist guide Karla Taylor gets you up close and personal with crocodiles, caimans, river otters, and—if you're lucky—manatees.

At Tárcoles, in the Central Pacific, take a **Crocodile Safari** to view crocs close up and personal.

Wildlife Wonders

At La Garita de Alajuela, take the kids to **Zoo Ave,** where they'll get to see animals and birds typical of Costa Rica; and, in Grecia, to the **World of Snakes,** where the kids can hold snakes.

On the Caribbean Coast, the **Sloth Sanctuary** is a great place for a précis on everything you didn't know about cuddly sloths.

Guanacaste is home to **The Bat Jungle,** where kids can watch bats flit, feed, and mate. Saving and raising big cats is the mission at **Centro de Rescate Las Pumas,** where ocelots, jaguars, cougars, margays, jaguarundis, and "tiger" cats are on view.

Parque Reptilandia, in the Central Pacific region, is one of the best-laid-out parks in the country, with turtles, crocodiles, and snakes.

Adrenaline Rush

Hiking, white-water rafting, and zip-line canopy tours—here are the best of the countless adrenaline-charged experiences, from A to Z.

Autogiro

Worth the trip to Playa Sámara, in Nicoya, an open-cockpit flight in an autogiro at **Flying Crocodile Flying Center** is the ultimate high. Hover, swoop, and plunge over the coast and mountains.

Hiking

Having previously made a reservation through the National Park Service, allow two or three days for hiking in **Parque Nacional Chirripó**, with an overnight near the mountain summit. The second day, you'll be on the trail well before dawn for the final hike to the summit of Costa Rica's highest mountain.

You can hike to the summit of **Rincón de la Vieja** volcano in one day, but set off well before dawn, as no overnighting is allowed. It's a great workout, rewarded with spectacular views.

Kite-Surfing

The adrenaline kick of whizzing across or over wind-whipped **Laguna de Arenal** on a sailboard or a kite at **Tico Wind Surf Center** is boosted by signs warning that crocodiles have been spotted here.

Scuba Diving

Beginners take the plunge at the **Islas Murciélagos,** off northwest Nicoya, to commune with manta rays, whale sharks, and giant groupers. Trips are offered by scuba outfitters at Playas del Coco, Playa Ocotal, and Playa Hermosa.

For the ultimate rapture of the deep, experienced divers should take a 10-day trip aboard the *Okeanos Aggressor* to **Isla del Coco,** where hundreds of hammerhead sharks await your arrival.

Tree Climbing

On the Osa Peninsula, **Everyday Adventures**

hiking in Rincón de la Vieja National Park

National Geographic Sea Lion in Golfo Dulce

zip-lining at Sky Trek, Arenal

in Puerto Jiménez challenges you to a rope climb up a giant strangler fig for a 20-meter (66-foot) free-fall plunge to the ground.

In the northern lowlands, you can also play like Spider-Man by climbing inside a hollow strangler fig, or haul yourself up a giant ceiba tree, courtesy of **Serendipity Adventures.**

White-Water Rafting

A trip down either the **Río Reventazón** or **Río Pacuare,** both accessed from Turrialba, guarantees more white-water sizzle than seltzer. Between the rapids, calm spots allow for swimming and wildlife spotting. Plan an overnight trip with **Aventuras Naturales** and a night at their deluxe Pacuare Jungle Lodge.

Zip Lines

Choose more than three dozen zip lines throughout Costa Rica. **Sky Trek,** at Arenal in the northern lowlands, is one of the best, with four kilometers (2.5 miles) of cables, including a 750-meter-long (2,460-foot-long) span.

San José

Look for ★ to find recommended
sights, activities, dining, and lodging.

Highlights

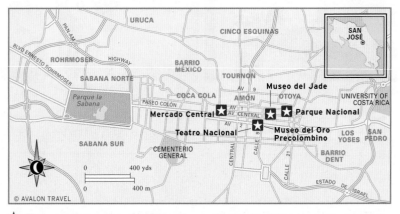

★ **Museo del Oro Precolombino:** The highlight of the Museos Banco Central de Costa Rica, this splendid collection of pre-Columbian gold and jade displays a cornucopia of indigenous ornaments and artifacts. Also here is an excellent numismatic museum (page 43).

★ **Teatro Nacional:** San José's architectural pride and joy gleams after a recent restoration. See it by day, then dress up for an evening classical performance in season (page 43).

★ **Museo del Jade:** The world's largest

collection of pre-Columbian jade ornamentation is exhibited in creative displays in a new facility (page 46).

★ **Parque Nacional:** A breath of fresh air in the crowded city, this leafy park is the setting for the Monumento Nacional (page 47).

★ **Mercado Central:** Tuck your wallet safely away to explore this tightly packed warren of stalls and stores selling everything from pig's heads to saddles. This is a great place to eat for pennies in true Tico fashion (page 50).

S an José, the nation's capital, squats on the floor of the Meseta Central, a fertile upland basin 1,150 meters (3,773 feet) above sea level in the heart of Costa Rica. Surrounded by mountains, it's a magnificent setting. The city's central position

makes it an ideal base for forays into the countryside, applying the hub-and-spoke system of travel—almost every part of the country is within a four-hour drive.

San José—or "Chepe," as Ticos call it—dominates national life. Two-thirds of the nation's urban population live in greater San José, whose 1.4 million people represent 30 percent of the nation's population. San José is congested, bustling, and noisy. Its commercial center is dominated by hotels, offices, ugly modern high-rises, and shops. Uncontrolled growth in recent years has spread the city's tentacles until the suburban districts have begun to blur into the larger complex. Although the city is not without its share of homeless people and beggars, there are few of the ghoulish *tugurios* (slums) that scar the hillsides of so many other Latin American cities. The modest working-class barrios (neighborhoods) are mostly clean and well ordered,

and the tranquil residential districts such as Sabana Sur, San Pedro, and Rohrmoser have gracious houses with green lawns. Many streets in the older neighborhoods are still lined with one- and two-story houses made of wood or even adobe with ornamental grill-work. What few older structures remain are of modest interest, however: The city is almost wholly lacking the grand colonial structures of, say, Havana or Mexico City. If it's colonial quaintness you're seeking, skip San José.

Nonetheless, the city offers several first-rate museums and galleries. Despite its working-class tenor, the city is large enough, and its middle-class component cosmopolitan enough in outlook, to support a vital cultural milieu, which has surged in recent years. There are scores of accommodations for every budget, including backpacker hostels and one of the world's preeminent boutique hotels. The restaurant scene is impressive, with dozens of

Previous: lobby of the Teatro Nacional; *Edificio Correo* (Post Office). **Above:** gold pendant of an eagle in the Museo del Oro Precolombino.

Greater San José

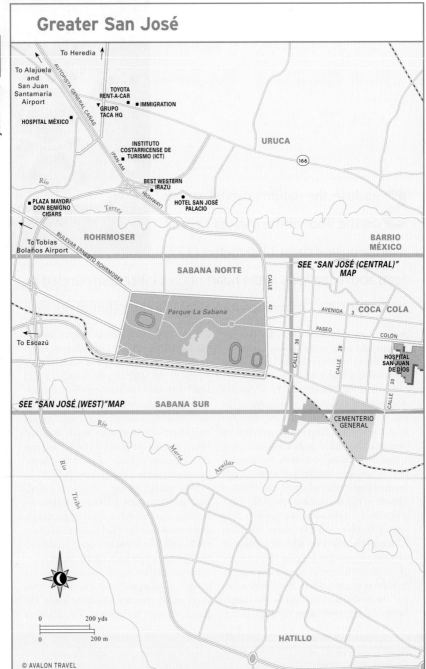

To Heredia

To Alajuela and San Juan Santamaría Airport

AUTOPISTA GENERAL CAÑAS

TOYOTA RENT-A-CAR

GRUPO TACA HQ

■ IMMIGRATION

HOSPITAL MÉXICO

(PAN-AM)

INSTITUTO COSTARRICENSE DE TURISMO (ICT)

URUCA

166

Rio

BEST WESTERN IRAZU

HIGHWAY)

Torres

PLAZA MAYOR/ DON BENIGNO CIGARS

HOTEL SAN JOSÉ PALACIO

BULEVAR ERNESTO ROHRMOSER

ROHRMOSER

BARRIO MÉXICO

To Tobias Bolaños Airport

SABANA NORTE

SEE "SAN JOSÉ (CENTRAL)" MAP

CALLE 42

Parque La Sabana

AVENIDA 3 COCA COLA

PASEO

To Escazú

CALLE 36

CALLE 28

COLÓN

HOSPITAL SAN JUAN DE DIOS

CALLE 20

SEE "SAN JOSÉ (WEST)" MAP

SABANA SUR

Rio

CEMENTERIO GENERAL

Maria

Aguilar

Rio

Tiribi

0   200 yds

0   200 m

HATILLO

© AVALON TRAVEL

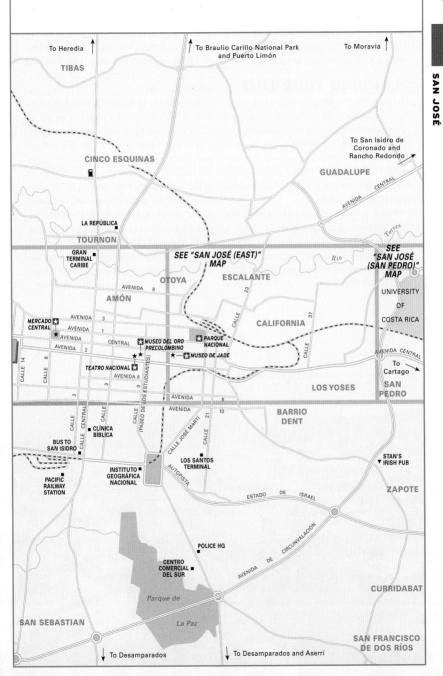

To Heredia ↑

To Braulio Carillo National Park
and Puerto Limón ↑

To Moravia ↑

TIBAS

CINCO ESQUINAS

GUADALUPE

To San Isidro de
Coronado and
Rancho Redondo →

AVENIDA CENTRAL

LA REPÚBLICA

TOURNON

Torres

Río

GRAN
TERMINAL
CARIBE

OTOYA

SEE "SAN JOSÉ (EAST)"
MAP

ESCALANTE

SEE
"SAN JOSÉ
(SAN PEDRO)"
MAP

AVENIDA 9

CALLE 23

UNIVERSITY
OF
COSTA RICA

AMÓN

AVENIDA 3

MERCADO
CENTRAL

AVENIDA 1

AVENIDA

CENTRAL

AVENIDA 2

CALLE 14

CALLE 8

MUSEO DEL ORO
PRECOLOMBINO

PARQUE
NACIONAL

CALIFORNIA

CALLE 37

AVENIDA CENTRAL

To
Cartago →

MUSEO DE JADE

TEATRO NACIONAL

AVENIDA 6

CALLE 2

AVENIDA 9

CALLE (PASEO DE LOS ESTUDIANTES)

AVENIDA 8

LOS YOSES

SAN
PEDRO

AVENIDA

CLÍNICA
BÍBLICA

CALLE 1

CALLE CENTRAL

CALLE 3

CALLE 5

CALLE JOSÉ MARTÍ

AVENIDA 10

CALLE 21

BARRIO
DENT

BUS TO
SAN ISIDRO

PACIFIC
RAILWAY
STATION

INSTITUTO
GEOGRÁFICA
NACIONAL

LOS SANTOS
TERMINAL

AUTOPISTA

STAN'S
▼ IRISH PUB

ZAPOTE

ESTADO DE ISRAEL

POLICE HQ

CENTRO
COMERCIAL
DEL SUR

AVENIDA DE CIRCUNVALACIÓN

CURRIDABAT

Parque de

La Paz

SAN SEBASTIAN

SAN FRANCISCO
DE DOS RÍOS

↓ To Desamparados

↓ To Desamparados and Aserrí

globe-spanning eateries, including some exciting nouvelle options. Night owls will appreciate San José's vivacious nightlife, from modest casinos to raging discos with Latin music hot enough to cook the pork.

PLANNING YOUR TIME

The majority of visitors to the country spend one or two days in the capital city, whose bona fide visitor attractions can be counted on two hands. After a day or two, it is time to move on. You'll appreciate basing yourself in a leafy residential district to escape the noise and bustle of downtown, where the major sights of interest are located.

Avoid driving in San José—despite the city's grid system of one-way streets, finding your way around can be immensely frustrating. Downtown is compact and ideal for walking, with everything of interest within a few blocks of the center. Watch out for potholes, tilted flagstones, and gaping sewer holes. Be wary when crossing streets—Tico drivers give no mercy to those still in the road when the light turns green. Don't take your eyes off the traffic for a moment. Stand well away from the curb, especially on corners, where buses often mount the curb.

San José has a high (and worsening) crime rate. Be especially wary in and around the Coca-Cola bus terminal (avoid the area altogether at night) and the red-light district south of Avenida 2 (especially between Calles Central and 10) and the sleazy zone northwest of the Mercado Central. Give a wide berth to Barrio Lomas, in the extreme west of Pavas; this is the city's desperately poor slum area and the domain of violent gangs. Also avoid parks, especially Parque Nacional, at night. Don't use buses at night, and be alert if you use them by day. Never walk around with a camera or purse slung loose over your shoulder.

San José has a compact core, as seen from above Parque Morazán.

Sights

ORIENTATION

Streets (*calles*) run north to south; avenues (*avenidas*) run east to west. Downtown San José is centered on Calle Central and Avenida Central (which is closed to traffic between Calles 14 and 7), although the main thoroughfare is Avenida 2. To the north of Avenida Central, *avenidas* ascend in odd numbers (Avenida 1, Avenida 3, and so on); to the south they descend in even numbers (Avenida 2, Avenida 4, etc.). West of Calle Central, *calles* ascend in even numbers (Calle 2, Calle 4, etc.); to the east they ascend in odd numbers (Calle 1, Calle 3, and so on).

West of downtown, Paseo Colón runs 2.5 kilometers (1.5 miles) to Parque la Sabana (Paseo Colón is closed to traffic on Sunday). East of downtown, Avenida 2 merges into Avenida Central, which runs through the Los Yoses and San Pedro districts en route to Cartago.

Josefinos (as San José residents are called) rarely refer to street addresses by *avenida* and *calle*. Very few streets have street numbers, there are no postal codes, and an amazing number of Josefinos have no idea what street they live on. Costa Ricans use landmarks, not street addresses, to find their way around. They usually refer to a distance in meters (*metros*) from a particular landmark. *Cien metros* (100 meters, about 330 feet) usually refers to one block; *cincuenta metros* (50 meters, about 165 feet) is used to mean half a block. A typical address might be "200 meters east and 425 meters south of the gas station, near the church in San Pedro."

These landmarks have passed into local parlance, so that Josefinos will immediately know where is meant by "100 meters north and 300 meters west of Auto Mercado," for example, although many reference landmarks disappeared years ago. For example, the Coca-Cola factory near Avenida Central and Calle 14 disappeared long ago, but the reference is still to "Coca-Cola."

And no wonder: The city didn't even have street signs until September 27, 2012, when San José Mayor Johnny Araya unveiled the first sign. The municipal authorities are slated to erect some 22,000 signs and plaques. By the time you read this, hopefully all the signs will be up. Note, however, that many streets will be renamed after illustrious political and intellectual figures from Costa Rican history. Stage Two will be to give every building a number. Don't hold your breath that Costa Ricans will actually use them: They're emotionally wed to the "landmark" system.

Addresses are still given by the nearest street junction. Thus, Restaurante Tin Jo, on Calle 11 midway between Avenidas 6 and 8, gives its address as "Calle 11, Avenidas 6/8." In phone directories and advertisements, *calle* may be abbreviated as "c," and *avenida* as "a."

To get your bearings, take a walking tour with **ChepeCletas** (tel. 506/2222-7548, www. chepecletas.com), which offers daytime tours and NoctUrbano tours by night focused on architecture and neighborhoods.

PLAZA DE LA CULTURA

San José's unofficial focal point is the **Plaza de la Cultura,** bordered by Calles 3 and 5 and Avenidas Central and 2. Musicians, jugglers, and marimba bands entertain the crowds. Travelers gather on the southwest corner to absorb the colorful atmosphere while enjoying a beer and food on the open-air terrace of the venerable Gran Hotel, fronted by a little plaza named **Parque Mora Fernández.** Note too the historic **Cine Diversiones** (Calle 5, Ave. Central/2), with a beautiful metal filigree facade.

The **Costa Rican Tourist Board** has a tiny tourist information office in the Centro de Conservación (Ave. Central, Calles 1/3,

San José (West)

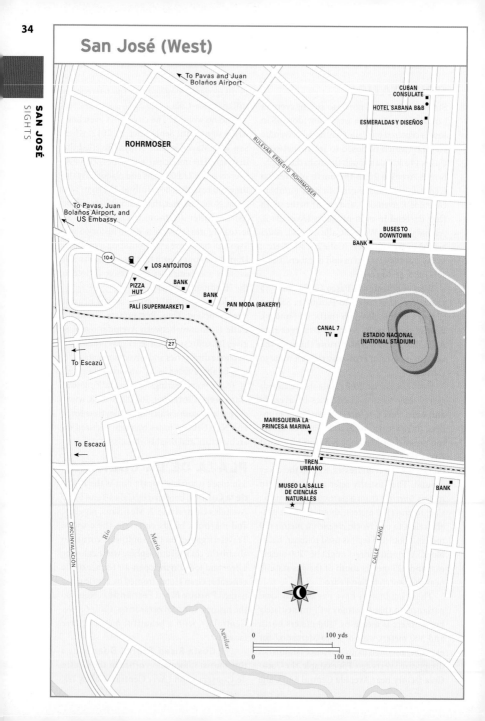

To Pavas and Juan
Bolaños Airport

CUBAN
CONSULATE

HOTEL SABANA B&B

ESMERALDAS Y DISEÑOS

ROHRMOSER

BULEVAR ERNESTO ROHRMOSER

To Pavas, Juan
Bolaños Airport, and
US Embassy

BUSES TO
DOWNTOWN

BANK

104

LOS ANTOJITOS

PIZZA
HUT

BANK

BANK

PALÍ (SUPERMARKET)

PAN MODA (BAKERY)

CANAL 7
TV

ESTADIO NACIONAL
(NATIONAL STADIUM)

27

To Escazú

MARISQUERIA LA
PRINCESA MARINA

To Escazú

TREN
URBANO

BANK

MUSEO LA SALLE
DE CIENCIAS
NATURALES

CIRCUNVALACIÓN

Río

Marita

Aguilar

CALLE LANG

0   100 yds

0   100 m

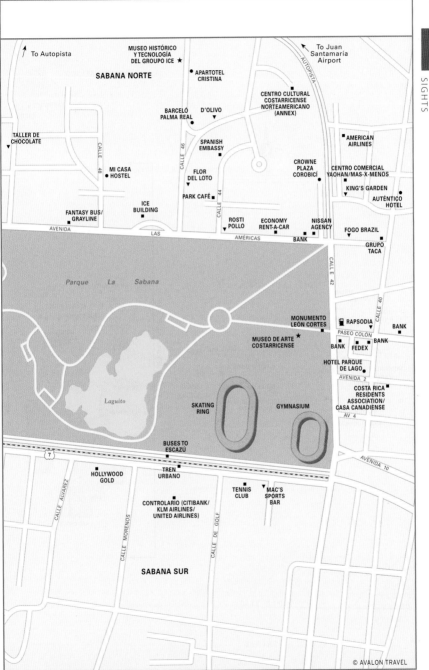

To Autopista

To Juan Santamaría Airport

MUSEO HISTÓRICO Y TECNOLOGÍA DEL GROUPO ICE ★

SABANA NORTE

APARTOTEL CRISTINA

CENTRO CULTURAL COSTARRICENSE NORTEAMERICANO (ANNEX)

BARCELÓ PALMA REAL

D'OLIVO

AMERICAN AIRLINES

TALLER DE CHOCOLATE

CALLE 48

CALLE 46

SPANISH EMBASSY

CROWNE PLAZA COROBICÍ

CENTRO COMERCIAL YAOHAN/MAS-X-MENOS

MI CASA HOSTEL

FLOR DEL LOTO

KING'S GARDEN

AUTÉNTICO HOTEL

CALLE 44

PARK CAFÉ

FANTASY BUS/ GRAYLINE

ICE BUILDING

ROSTI POLLO

ECONOMY RENT-A-CAR

NISSAN AGENCY

FOGO BRAZIL

AVENIDA

LAS

AMÉRICAS

BANK

GRUPO TACA

Parque   La   Sabana

CALLE 42

CALLE 40

MONUMENTO LEÓN CORTES

RAPSODIA

BANK

Laguito

MUSEO DE ARTE COSTARRICENSE ★

PASEO COLÓN

BANK

FEDEX

BANK

HOTEL PARQUE DE LAGO

AVENIDA 2

SKATING RING

GYMNASIUM

COSTA RICA RESIDENTS ASSOCIATION/ CASA CANADIENSE

AV 4

BUSES TO ESCAZÚ

AVENIDA 10

7

HOLLYWOOD GOLD

TREN URBANO

CALLE ALVAREZ

CALLE MORENOS

CONTROLARIO (CITIBANK/ KLM AIRLINES/ UNITED AIRLINES)

TENNIS CLUB

MAC'S SPORTS BAR

CALLE DE GOLF

SABANA SUR

© AVALON TRAVEL

San José (Central)

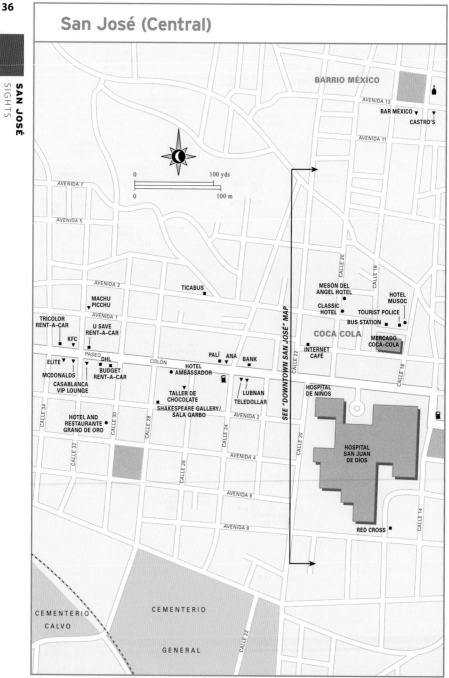

BARRIO MÉXICO

AVENIDA 13

BAR MÉXICO ▼
CASTRO'S ▼

AVENIDA 11

AVENIDA 7

AVENIDA 5

0   100 yds
0   100 m

AVENIDA 3

TICABUS ■

MACHU
PICCHU ▼

AVENIDA 1

CALLE 20
CALLE 18

MESÓN DEL
ANGEL HOTEL ■

HOTEL
MUSOC ■

CLASSIC
HOTEL ●   TOURIST POLICE
BUS STATION ■ ■ ●

COCA COLA

MERCADO
COCA-COLA

TRICOLOR
RENT-A-CAR
■   KFC ▼

U SAVE
RENT-A-CAR ■

PASEO

PALÍ ANA
■ ▼   BANK ■

CALLE 22

CALLE 16

INTERNET
CAFÉ

ELITE ▼ ▼
■
MCDONALDS

DHL ■
BUDGET
RENT-A-CAR

COLÓN

HOTEL
AMBASSADOR ●
■

CASABLANCA
VIP LOUNGE

TALLER DE
CHOCOLATE ■

▼ ▼
LUBNAN
TELEDOLLAR

HOSPITAL
DE NIÑOS

SHAKESPEARE GALLERY/
SALA GARBO

AVENIDA 2

CALLE 20

CALLE 24

CALLE 28

SEE "DOWNTOWN SAN JOSÉ" MAP

HOTEL AND
RESTAURANTE ●
GRANO DE ORO

CALLE 24

CALLE 34

CALLE 32

CALLE 30

CALLE 28

CALLE 26

AVENIDA 4

HOSPITAL
SAN JUAN
DE DÍOS

AVENIDA 6

CALLE 14

AVENIDA 8

RED CROSS ■

CEMENTERIO
CALVO

CEMENTERIO

GENERAL

CALLE 22

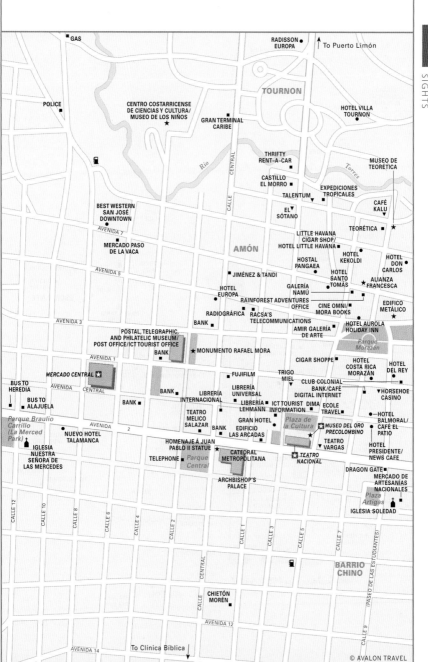

GAS

POLICE

RADISSON EUROPA

↑ To Puerto Limón

TOURNON

CENTRO COSTARRICENSE DE CIENCIAS Y CULTURA/ MUSEO DE LOS NIÑOS ★

GRAN TERMINAL CARIBE

HOTEL VILLA TOURNON

Río

CENTRAL

CALLE

Torres

THRIFTY RENT-A-CAR

MUSEO DE TEORÉTICA

CASTILLO EL MORRO ■

TALENTUM ▼

EXPEDICIONES TROPICALES ■

CAFÉ KALU

EL SÓTANO ▼

TEORÉTICA ★

BEST WESTERN SAN JOSÉ DOWNTOWN ■

AVENIDA 7

AMÓN

LITTLE HAVANA CIGAR SHOP/ HOTEL LITTLE HAVANA ■

MERCADO PASO DE LA VACA ■

HOTEL KEKOLDI ■

HOTEL DON CARLOS ●

AVENIDA 5

JIMÉNEZ & TANDI ■

HOSTAL PANGAEA ■

HOTEL SANTO TOMÁS ●

ALIANZA FRANCESCA ★

HOTEL EUROPA ■

GALERÍA NAMÚ ■

RAINFOREST ADVENTURES OFFICE ■

CINE OMNI/ MORA BOOKS ■

EDIFICIO METÁLICO ■

RADIOGRÁFICA ■

RACSA'S TELECOMMUNICATIONS

AVENIDA 3

BANK ■

AMIR GALERÍA DE ARTE ■

HOTEL AUROLA HOLIDAY INN ■

Parque Morazán

POSTAL, TELEGRAPHIC, AND PHILATELIC MUSEUM/ POST OFFICE/ICT TOURIST OFFICE ■

BANK ■

AVENIDA 1

★ MONUMENTO RAFAEL MORA

CIGAR SHOPPE ■

HOTEL COSTA RICA MORAZÁN ■

HOTEL DEL REY ■

MERCADO CENTRAL ✚

CENTRAL

AVENIDA 1

FUJIFILM ■

TRIGO MIEL ▼

CLUB COLONIAL ■

BANK/CAFÉ DIGITAL INTERNET

▼ HORSEHOE CASINO

BUS TO HEREDIA ■

BUS TO ALAJUELA ■

BANK ■

LIBRERÍA INTERNACIONAL ■

LIBRERÍA UNIVERSAL ■

LIBRERÍA LEHMANN ■

ICT TOURIST INFORMATION ■

DIMA ■

ECOLE TRAVEL ■

● HOTEL BALMORAL/ CAFÉ EL PATIO

Parque Braulio Carrillo (La Merced Park)

AVENIDA CENTRAL

BANK ■

TEATRO MELICO SALAZAR ■

GRAN HOTEL ■

EDIFICIO LAS ARCADAS ■

Plaza de la Cultura

★ MUSEO DEL ORO PRECOLOMBINO

TEATRO VARGAS ▼

NUEVO HOTEL TALAMANCA ●

AVENIDA 2

BANK ■

HOMENAJE A JUAN PABLO II STATUE ★

HOTEL PRESIDENTE/ NEWS CAFE ■

IGLESIA NUESTRA SEÑORA DE LAS MERCEDES ▲

TELEPHONE ■

Parque Central

CATEDRAL METROPOLITANA ✚

✚ TEATRO NACIONAL

DRAGON GATE ▬

ARCHBISHOP'S PALACE

MERCADO DE ARTESANÍAS NACIONALES

Plaza Artigas

IGLESIA SOLEDAD

CALLE 12
CALLE 10
CALLE 8
CALLE 6
CALLE 4
CALLE 2
CALLE 1
CALLE 3
CALLE 5
CALLE 7
CALLE 9
PASEO DE LAS ESTUDIANTES

BARRIO CHINO

CHIETÓN MORÉN ■

CALLE

CENTRAL

AVENIDA 12

AVENIDA 14

To Clínica Bíblica ↓

© AVALON TRAVEL

San José (East)

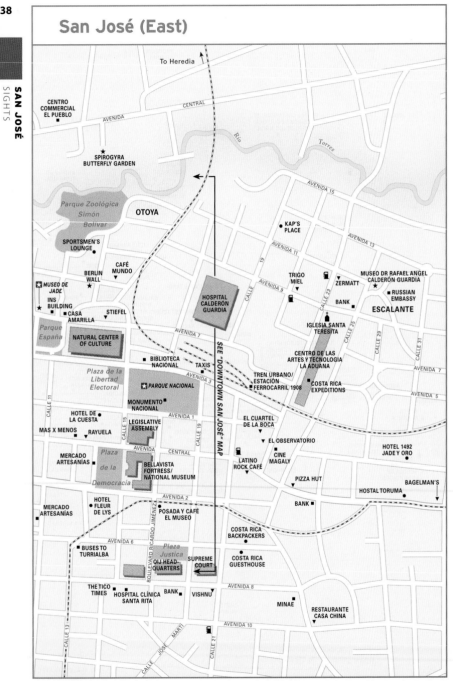

To Heredia

CENTRO COMMERCIAL EL PUEBLO

CENTRAL

AVENIDA

Río

Torres

★ SPIROGYRA BUTTERFLY GARDEN

AVENIDA 15

Parque Zoológica Simón Bolivar

OTOYA

KAP'S PLACE

AVENIDA 13

SPORTSMEN'S LOUNGE

AVENIDA 11

CALLE 19

CAFÉ MUNDO

BERLIN WALL

★ MUSEO DE JADE

INS BUILDING

CASA AMARILLA

STIEFEL

HOSPITAL CALDERÓN GUARDIA

AVENIDA 9

TRIGO MIEL

ZERMATT

MUSEO DR RAFAEL ANGEL CALDERÓN GUARDIA ★

CALLE 23

BANK

RUSSIAN EMBASSY

ESCALANTE

CALLE 25

CALLE 29

CALLE 31

IGLESIA SANTA TERESITA

Parque España

NATURAL CENTER OF CULTURE

AVENIDA 7

CALLE 11

Plaza de la Libertad Electoral

BIBLIOTECA NACIONAL

TAXIS

AVENIDA 3

★ PARQUE NACIONAL

CENTRO DE LAS ARTES Y TECNOLOGIA LA ADUANA

AVENIDA 7

AVENIDA 5

MONUMENTO NACIONAL

AVENIDA 1

TREN URBANO/ ESTACIÓN FERROCARRIL 1908

COSTA RICA EXPEDITIONS

HOTEL DE LA CUESTA

CALLE 15

LEGISLATIVE ASSEMBLY

CALLE 19

EL CUARTEL DE LA BOCA

MAS X MENOS

RAYUELA

AVENIDA

CENTRAL

EL OBSERVATORIO

HOTEL 1492 JADE Y ORO

MERCADO ARTESANÍAS

Plaza de la Democracia

BELLAVISTA FORTRESS/ NATIONAL MUSEUM

LATINO ROCK CAFÉ

CINE MAGALY

BAGELMAN'S

PIZZA HUT

HOSTAL TORUMA

HOTEL FLEUR DE LYS

AVENIDA 2

BANK

MERCADO ARTESANÍAS

POSADA Y CAFÉ EL MUSEO

BOULEVARD RICARDO JIMÉNEZ

AVENIDA 6

COSTA RICA BACKPACKERS

BUSES TO TURRIALBA

Plaza Justicia

OIJ HEAD-QUARTERS

SUPREME COURT

COSTA RICA GUESTHOUSE

THE TICO TIMES

HOSPITAL CLÍNICA SANTA RITA

BANK

VISHNU

AVENIDA 8

MINAE

RESTAURANTE CASA CHINA

CALLE 13

CALLE JOSÉ MARTI

CALLE 21

AVENIDA 10

SEE "DOWNTOWN SAN JOSÉ" MAP

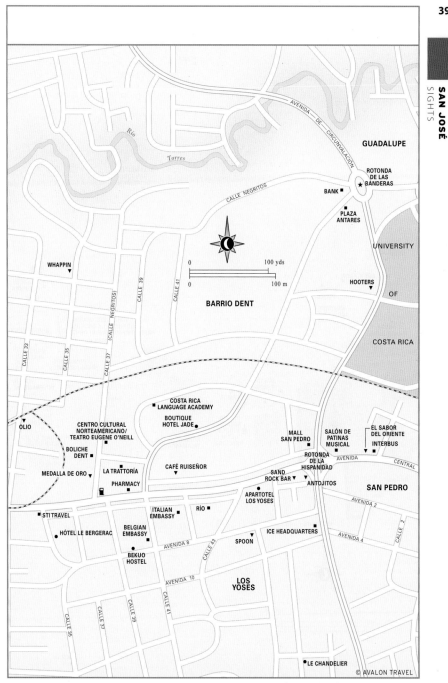

GUADALUPE

AVENIDA — DE — CIRCUNVALACIÓN

Río Torres

CALLE NEGRITOS

ROTONDA DE LAS BANDERAS

BANK

PLAZA ANTARES

UNIVERSITY

WHAPPIN

CALLE 39

CALLE 41

HOOTERS

OF

BARRIO DENT

0   100 yds

0   100 m

COSTA RICA

CALLE 33

CALLE 35

CALLE 37

(CALLE NEGRITOS)

COSTA RICA LANGUAGE ACADEMY

OLIO

CENTRO CULTURAL NORTEAMÉRICANO/ TEATRO EUGENE O'NEILL

BOUTIQUE HOTEL JADE

SALÓN DE PATINAS MUSICAL

EL SABOR DEL ORIENTE

INTERBUS

MALL SAN PEDRO

BOLICHE DENT

ROTONDA DE LA HISPANIDAD

AVENIDA

CENTRAL

MEDALLA DE ORO

LA TRATTORÍA

CAFÉ RUISEÑOR

SAND ROCK BAR

ANTOJITOS

SAN PEDRO

PHARMACY

ST TRAVEL

ITALIAN EMBASSY

RÍO

APARTOTEL LOS YOSES

AVENIDA 2

CALLE 2

HÓTEL LE BERGERAC

BELGIAN EMBASSY

AVENIDA 8

CALLE 43

ICE HEADQUARTERS

AVENIDA 4

BEKUO HOSTEL

SPOON

AVENIDA 10

LOS YOSES

CALLE 41

CALLE 39

CALLE 37

CALLE 35

LE CHANDELIER

© AVALON TRAVEL

Downtown San José

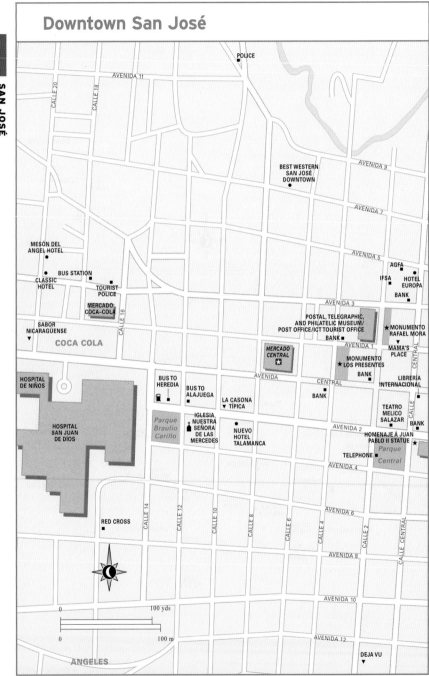

POLICE

AVENIDA 11

CALLE 20
CALLE 18

BEST WESTERN
SAN JOSÉ
DOWNTOWN

AVENIDA 9

AVENIDA 7

AVENIDA 5

MESÓN DEL
ANGEL HOTEL

AGFA

IFSA   HOTEL
EUROPA

BUS STATION

CLASSIC
HOTEL

TOURIST
POLICE

BANK

MERCADO
COCA-COLA

CALLE 16

AVENIDA 3

POSTAL, TELEGRAPHIC,
AND PHILATELIC MUSEUM/
POST OFFICE/ICT TOURIST OFFICE

★ MONUMENTO
RAFAEL MORA

SABOR
NICARAGÜENSE

BANK

AVENIDA 1

MAMA'S
PLACE

COCA COLA

MERCADO
CENTRAL

MONUMENTO
★ LOS PRESENTES

CENTRAL

HOSPITAL
DE NIÑOS

BUS TO
HEREDIA

AVENIDA

BANK

LIBRERÍA
INTERNACIONAL

BUS TO
ALAJUEGA

CENTRAL

BANK

TEATRO
MELICO
SALAZAR

HOSPITAL
SAN JUAN
DE DÍOS

Parque
Braulio
Carillo

LA CASONA
▼ TÍPICA

IGLESIA
NUESTRA
SEÑORA
DE LAS
MERCEDES

NUEVO
HOTEL
TALAMANCA

AVENIDA 2

BANK

HOMENAJE Á JUAN
PABLO II STATUE

Parque
Central

TELEPHONE

AVENIDA 4

CALLE 14
CALLE 12
CALLE 10
CALLE 8
CALLE 6
CALLE 4
CALLE 2

CALLE CENTRAL

RED CROSS

AVENIDA 6

AVENIDA 8

0   100 yds

0   100 m

AVENIDA 10

AVENIDA 12

ANGELES

DEJA VU
▼

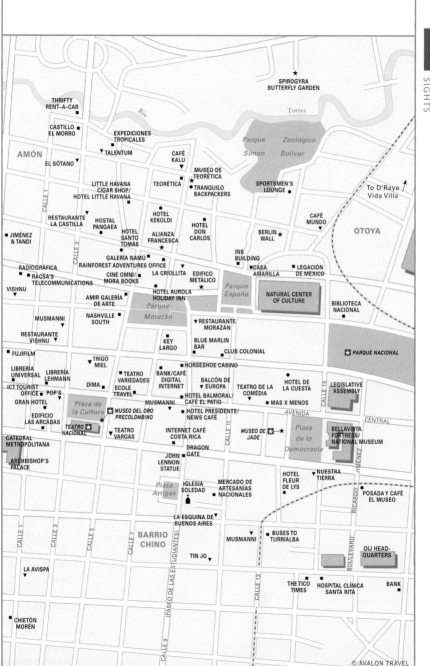

SPIROGYRA
BUTTERFLY GARDEN

Río Torres

Parque
Simón Zoológico
Bolívar

THRIFTY
RENT-A-CAR

CASTILLO
EL MORRO

EXPEDICIONES
TROPICALES

AMÓN

EL SÓTANO

TALENTUM

CAFÉ
KALU

MUSEO DE
TEORÉTICA

To D'Raya
Vida Villa

LITTLE HAVANA
CIGAR SHOP/
HOTEL LITTLE HAVANA

TEORÉTICA

TRANQUILO
BACKPACKERS

SPORTSMEN'S
LOUNGE

CAFÉ
MUNDO

OTOYA

RESTAURANTE
LA CASTILLA

HOSTAL
PANGAEA

HOTEL
KEKOLDI

HOTEL
DON
CARLOS

BERLIN
WALL

JIMÉNEZ
& TANDI

HOTEL
SANTO
TOMÁS

ALIANZA
FRANCESCA

RADIOGRÁFICA

GALERÍA NAMÚ

INS
BUILDING

RACSA'S
TELECOMMUNICATIONS

RAINFOREST ADVENTURES OFFICE

CINE OMNI/
MORA BOOKS

LA CRIOLLITA

EDIFICO
METÁLICO

CASA
AMARILLA

LEGACIÓN
DE MEXICO

VISHNU

AMIR GALERÍA
DE ARTE

HOTEL AUROLA
HOLIDAY INN

Parque
España

NATURAL CENTER
OF CULTURE

BIBLIOTECA
NACIONAL

MUSMANNI

NASHVILLE
SOUTH

Parque
Morazán

RESTAURANTE
VISHNU

RESTAURANTE
MORAZÁN

KEY
LARGO

BLUE MARLIN
BAR

CLUB COLONIAL

PARQUE NACIONAL

FUJIFILM

TRIGO
MIEL

HORSESHOE CASINO

LIBRERÍA
UNIVERSAL

LIBRERÍA
LEHMANN

TEATRO
VARIEDADES

BANK/CAFÉ
DIGITAL
INTERNET

BALCÓN DE
EUROPA

TEATRO DE LA
COMÉDIA

HOTEL DE
LA CUESTA

LEGISLATIVE
ASSEMBLY

ICT TOURIST
OFFICE

POP'S

DIMA

ECOLE
TRAVEL

HOTEL BALMORAL/
CAFÉ EL PATIO

MAS X MENOS

GRAN HOTEL

MUSMANNI

AVENIDA

CENTRAL

EDIFICIO
LAS ARCADAS

MUSEO DEL ORO
PRECOLOMBINO

HOTEL PRESIDENTE/
NEWS CAFÉ

Plaza de
la Cultura

TEATRO
NACIONAL

TEATRO
VARGAS

INTERNET CAFÉ
COSTA RICA

MUSEO DE
JADE

Plaza
de la
Democracia

BELLAVISTA
FORTRESS/
NATIONAL MUSEUM

CATEDRAL
METROPOLITANA

DRAGON
GATE

ARCHBISHOP'S
PALACE

JOHN
LENNON
STATUE

Plaza
Artigas

IGLESIA
SOLEDAD

MERCADO DE
ARTESANÍAS
NACIONALES

HOTEL
FLEUR
DE LYS

NUESTRA
TIERRA

POSADA Y CAFÉ
EL MUSEO

LA ESQUINA DE
BUENOS AIRES

CALLE 1

CALLE 3

CALLE 5

CALLE 7

BARRIO
CHINO

TIN JO

MUSMANNI

BUSES TO
TURRIALBA

OIJ HEAD-
QUARTERS

LA AVISPA

THE TICO
TIMES

HOSPITAL CLÍNICA
SANTA RITA

BANK

CHIETÓN
MORÉN

(PASEO DE LAS ESTUDIANTES)

CALLE 9

CALLE 13

CALLE 11

CALLE 15

RICARDO

JIMÉNEZ

BOULEVARD

© AVALON TRAVEL

San José (San Pedro)

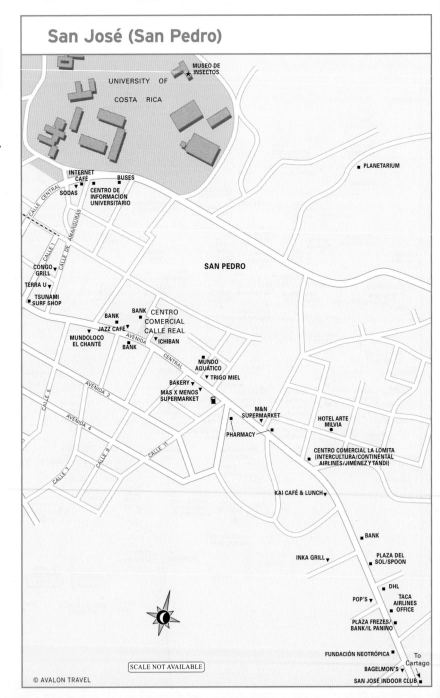

MUSEO DE INSECTOS

UNIVERSITY OF COSTA RICA

PLANETARIUM

CALLE CENTRAL

INTERNET CAFÉ
BUSES
SODAS
CENTRO DE INFORMACÍON UNIVERSITARIO

CALLE 1

CALLE DE MARGURAS

SAN PEDRO

CONGO GRILL
TERRA U
TSUNAMI SURF SHOP

BANK
BANK
CENTRO COMERCIAL CALLE REAL
JAZZ CAFÉ
MUNDOLOCO EL CHANTÉ
AVENIDA
ICHIBAN
BANK

AVENIDA CENTRAL

MUNDO AQUÁTICO
TRIGO MIEL

CALLE 5

AVENIDA 2

BAKERY
MAS X MENOS SUPERMARKET

M&N SUPERMARKET

HOTEL ARTE MILVIA

AVENIDA 4

PHARMACY

CENTRO COMERCIAL LA LOMITA (INTERCULTURA/CONTINENTAL AIRLINES/JIMÉNEZ Y TANDI)

CALLE 9
CALLE 11

CALLE 7

KAI CAFÉ & LUNCH

BANK

INKA GRILL
PLAZA DEL SOL/SPOON

DHL

POP'S
TACA AIRLINES OFFICE

PLAZA FREZES/ BANK/IL PANINO

FUNDACIÓN NEOTRÓPICA

To Cartago

BAGELMON'S

SAN JOSÉ INDOOR CLUB

SCALE NOT AVAILABLE

© AVALON TRAVEL

9am-5pm Mon.-Fri.), 50 meters (165 feet) northwest of the plaza.

★ Museo del Oro Precolombino

The world-class **Museo del Oro Precolombino** (Pre-Columbian Gold Museum, tel. 506/2243-4221, www.museosdelbancocentral.org, 9:15am-5pm daily, $11, students $8), in the triple-tiered former bank vaults beneath the plaza (the entrance is on Calle 5), is the highlight of the Museos Banco Central de Costa Rica, run by the state-owned Banco Central. The more than 2,000 glittering pre-Columbian gold artifacts displayed weigh in at over 22,000 troy ounces. Highlights include displays on early metallurgy and a gold-adorned life-size cacique (chieftain), plus there's a large collection of pre-Columbian metates and more. A collection of old coins is displayed in the adjoining **Museo de Numismática** (Numismatic Museum), while a small exhibit hall features works from the bank's art collection.

Guided **tours** (tel. 506/2243-4223, 1-15 people, $60) are given with 48 hours' notice; bring identification for entry.

★ Teatro Nacional

The nation's architectural showpiece, the **Teatro Nacional** (National Theater, Ave. 2, Calles 3/5, tel. 506/2010-1110, ticket office tel. 506/2010-1111, www.teatronacional.go.cr, 9am-4pm Mon.-Sat., guided tours $7), on the south side of Plaza de la Cultura, is justifiably a source of national pride. The theater was conceived in 1890, when a European opera company featuring the prima donna Adelina Patti toured Central America but was unable to perform in Costa Rica because there was no suitable theater. Jilted, the ruling *cafeteleros* (coffee barons) voted a tax on coffee exports to fund construction of a theater, and craftspeople from all over Europe were imported. It was inaugurated on October 21, 1897, with a performance of *Faust* by the Paris Opera.

Outside, the classical Renaissance facade is topped by statues (they're replicas; the originals are inside) symbolizing Dance, Music, and Fame; note the figures of Beethoven and Spanish dramatist Calderón de la Barca to each side of the entrance. Inside, the vestibule, done in pink marble, rivals the best of ancient Rome, with allegorical figures of Comedy and Tragedy, stunning murals depicting themes in Costa Rican life and commerce, and a triptych ceiling supported by six-meter-tall

figure of a jaguar in the Museo del Oro Precolombino

(20-foot-tall) marble columns topped with bronze capitals; a ceiling mural to the rear by Italian artist Aleardo Villa shows an allegorical coffee and banana harvest.

Art and good taste are lavishly displayed on the marble staircase, with its gold-laminated ornaments sparkling beneath bronze chandeliers and in the upstairs foyer. A grandiose rotunda, painted in Milan in 1897 by Arturo Fontana, highlights the three-story auditorium, designed in a perfect horseshoe and seating 1,040 in divine splendor. The auditorium floor was designed to be raised to stage level by a manual winch so the theater could be used as a ballroom.

PARQUE CENTRAL

This small palm-shaded park, laid out in 1880 between Calles Central and 2 and Avenidas 2 and 4, is San José's main plaza. The unassuming park has a fountain, a bronze statue, hardwood sculptures, and a large domed structure where the municipal band plays concerts on Sunday. The bandstand rests over the **Carmen Lyra Children's Library,** named for a Costa Rican writer famous for her children's stories.

Across Avenida 2, the **Teatro Melico Salazar** (tel. 506/2257-6005 or 506/2222-5424, www.teatromelico.go.cr, by appointment, free), dating to the 1920s and named for a famous Costa Rican tenor, is a study in understated period detail.

The area immediately southwest of the square is best avoided for safety reasons.

Catedral Metropólitana

Dominating the east side of Parque Central is the city's modest Corinthian-columned **Catedral Metropólitana** (Metropolitan Cathedral, tel. 506/2221-3826, 6am-noon and 3pm-6pm Mon.-Sat., 6am-9pm Sun.), with a Greek Orthodox-style blue domed roof. The original cathedral was toppled by an earthquake in 1821; the current structure dates from 1871. The interior is unremarkable, barring its lofty barrel-arched ceiling supported by fluted columns. Outside, at the corner of Avenida Central, is the **Homenaje a Juan Pablo II,** the *Homage to Pope John Paul II* statue inaugurated in 2006.

Tucked in the cathedral's shadow to the south is the **Curía** (Archbishop's Palace), dating from 1887.

Teatro Nacional

PARQUES ESPAÑA AND MORAZÁN

Parque Morazán is tucked between Calles 5 and 9 and Avenidas 3 and 5. The park's four quadrants surround the domed **Temple of Music,** supposedly inspired by Le Trianon in Paris. The park has busts of various South American heroes. It's also the site of a cultural fair (10am-5pm Sat.) intended to revive folkloric traditions.

Parque Morazán merges east into diminutive **Parque España,** a secluded place to rest beneath tall and densely packed trees. Note the busts that form a pantheon of national figures. A life-size statue of conquistador Juan Vásquez de Coronado stands on the southwest corner. On the north side of the park the old ornately stuccoed, ocher-colored colonial **Casa Amarilla,** dating from 1917, once housed the Court of Justice. Today it's the Chancellery, or foreign affairs department. Guided tours are offered by appointment (tel. 506/2223-7555, 8am-4pm Mon.-Fri.). A huge chunk of the Berlin Wall is displayed in the northeast corner of the grounds.

The **Edificio Metálico** (tel. 506/2221-0026), between Parque Morazán and Parque España, is one of San José's more intriguing buildings. It's made entirely of prefabricated metal. Designed by the French architect Victor Baltard, the structure was shipped piece by piece from Belgium in 1892 and welded together in situ. The facade is dressed with a bust of Minerva, the goddess of wisdom. The building is now a school.

Centro Nacional de Cultura

On the east side of Parque España, the erstwhile Fábrica Nacional de Licores (Liquor Factory) now houses the multifaceted **Centro Nacional de Cultura** (National Center of Culture, CENAC, tel. 506/2221-2022, 10:30am-5:30pm Tues.-Sat., free). The building dates to 1887, and though it's drained of alcohol, relics of the distilling days linger. The **Museo de Arte y Diseño Contemporáneo** (Museum of Contemporary Art and Design, tel. 506/2257-7202, www.madc.ac.cr) shows revolving displays by leading Costa Rican artists. Note the old sun clock and decorative stonework on the southeast side. The National Dance Company, National Theater Company, and Museum of Iberoamerican Culture are housed here.

nave of the Catedral Metropólitana

Cultural Walking Tours

The past few years have seen a blossoming of cultural appreciation for San José and the corresponding launch of several walking tours and regular cultural events. Here's the pick of the litter:

- **Enamorate de tu Ciudad** (Love Your City, tel. 506/2257-1214 or 506/8655-1793, www. enamoratedetuciudad.com), sponsored by the Ministry of Culture and Youth, is held 9am-5pm every Saturday in Parque Morazán, Parque España, and Parque Merced, with traditional crafts, musicians, and other performers.

- The *GAM Cultural* guide sponsors a monthly **Art City Tour** (www.gamcultural.com/tours, 5:30pm-9pm)—a nighttime event called "Noche en Blanco" (White Night), when museums, galleries, and other cultural venues offer free admission and the parks and streets host myriad artistic and cultural events. Choose from five routes with the option of a free electric bus, cycling, or walking. Expat resident Molly Keeler also offers the **Costa Rica Art Tour** (tel. 506/2288-0896, www.costaricaarttour.com) with visits to five artists' studios.

- For a private guided tour, call U.S. expat Stacey Corrales, who runs **Barrio Bird Tours** (tel. 506/6050-1952, www.toursanjosecostarica.com), with five walking tours: One is an overview tour ($22); others focus on art and the culinary scene, bar life for night owls, and one for photography buffs. Stacey also arranges custom tours.

- You don't have to speak Spanish, but it sure helps to best appreciate a cycling tour or **NoctUrbano** nighttime walking tour with **ChepeCletas** (tel. 506/2222-7548, www. chepecletas.com). Check the website for upcoming tours, in addition to a weekly free walking tour (9:30am Thurs., reservations required) from Parque Nacional.

- By night, join a pub crawl with **Carpe Chepe** (tel. 506/8326-6142, www.carpechepe.com, 7pm Thurs. and Sat.), popular with young locals.

PLAZA DE LA DEMOCRACÍA

This square, between Avenidas Central and 2 and Calles 13 and 15, was built in 1989 to receive visiting presidents attending the Hemispheric Summit. Dominating the plaza on the east side is the crenellated 1870 **Cuartel Bellavista** (Bellavista Fortress), which today houses the National Museum. On the west side is a bronze statue of Don "Pepe" Figueres. Remodeled in 2009, the formerly unkempt, dreary plaza has become a pleasant place to hang out. Two blocks south are the buildings of the Judicial Circuit, including the Supreme Court and OIJ (criminal investigation) buildings. The National Museum and modernist **Corte Suprema** (Supreme Court), on Plaza de la Justicia, are linked by a pedestrian precinct, **Bulevar Ricardo Jiménez,** known colloquially as Camino de la Corte, with shade trees, wrought-iron lampposts, and benches.

Two blocks to the southwest of the plaza, a

Dragon Gate (Ave. 2, Calle 9) opens to pedestrian-only Paseo de los Estudiantes and **Plaza Artigas,** presided over by the classical **Iglesia Soledad.** The church's arched nave is painted like the night sky, with stars. The highlight, however, is the park's life-size bronze **statue of John Lennon** by Cuban artist José Ramón Villa—an exact copy of the statue in Havana's Parque Lennon. Plaza Artigas has several other sculptures of note and is at the heart of the recently revived **Barrio Chino** (Chinatown). It spans Calle 7 to 9 and Avenidas 2 to 14 along newly cobbled and pedestrianized Paseo de los Estudiantes.

★ Museo del Jade

In May 2014 the fabulous **Museo del Jade Marco Fidel Tristán** (Calle 13, Ave. Central/2, tel. 506/2287-6034, 10am-5pm daily, $15) moved to a custom-designed five-story building on the northwest side of Plaza de la Democracía. It displays the largest presents. The **Edificio Central** (main building), built in 1937, houses the nation's legislative assembly.

Guided visits are offered 9am-2:45pm Monday-Thursday and 10am-noon Friday. A dress code applies: no sandals, shorts, or miniskirts. Cameras are permitted, without flash.

Museo Nacional

A superb collection of pre-Columbian art (pottery, stone, and gold) and an eclectic mix of colonial-era art, furniture, costumes, and documents highlight the **Museo Nacional** (National Museum, Plaza de la Democracía and Aves. Central/2, tel. 506/2257-1433, www. museocostarica.go.cr, 8:30am-4:30pm Tues.-Sat., 9am-4:30pm Sun., adults $8, students $4), in the old Cuartel Bellavista on the east side of Plaza de la Democracía. Separate exhibition halls deal with history, archaeology, geology, religion, and colonial life. Only a few exhibits are translated into English. The towers and walls of the fortress are pitted with bullet holes from the 1948 civil war. The museum surrounds a landscaped courtyard featuring colonial-era cannons and ancient stone spheres.

You enter and exit off the plaza via a butterfly garden. Note the pre-Columbian sphere inside a giant glass dome shaped like a Fresnel lens outside the entrance.

Parque España

collection of jade in the Americas, including pre-Columbian carved adzes and pendants, backlit to show off the beautiful translucence. The museum also displays pre-Columbian ceramics and gold miniatures organized by culture and region. It has excellent signage in English.

Asamblea Legislativa

The **Asamblea Legislativa** (Legislative Assembly, tel. 506/2243-2000, www.asamblea.go.cr, free) occupies three buildings on the north side of the plaza on Calle 15. The blue building—the **Castillo Azul**—to the east was originally the presidential palace, built in 1911 by presidential candidate Máximo Fernández in anticipation of victory in the 1914 elections. He lost, and then lent his home to president-elect Alfredo González Flores as his official residence. Later it served as the U.S. Diplomatic Mission. Behind it, the **Casa Rosada** (Pink House), dating from 1833, has two rooms with galleries of paintings and photographs of past Costa Rican

★ PARQUE NACIONAL

Parque Nacional, the largest and most impressive of the city's central parks, graces a hill that rises eastward between Calles 15 and 19 and Avenidas 1 and 3. At the park's center is the massive **Monumento Nacional** (National Monument), one of several statues commemorating the War of 1856. The statue depicts the spirits of the Central American nations defeating the American adventurer William Walker. The monument was made in the Rodin studios in Paris. The park is not safe at night.

On the north side of the square, note the impressive modernist **Biblioteca Nacional** (tel. 506/2257-4814, www.abinia.org/costarica), built in 1971. Immediately northeast of the park, the ornate art nouveau **Antiguo Estación Ferrocarril** was built in 1907 as the Atlantic Station. Today, it is the main station for the commuter train to Heredia and Cartago. To the rear are vintage rolling stock and an old steam locomotive, Locomotora 59 (or Locomotora Negra), imported from Philadelphia in 1939.

Immediately to the northeast, the huge redbrick building houses the **Centro de las Artes y Tecnología La Aduana,** colloquially called the Antigua Aduana (Old Customs), a former customs building and later the national mint, converted into a 15,000-square-meter (161,000-square-foot) exhibition and performing-arts space.

BARRIO AMÓN AND BARRIO OTOYA

Barrio Amón and Barrio Otoya, north of Parques Morazán and España, form an aristocratic residential neighborhood founded at the end of the 19th century by a French immigrant, Amón Fasileau Duplantier, who arrived in 1884 to work for a coffee enterprise owned by the Tournón family. The area, full of grand historic homes, is worth an exploratory walk.

Of particular note is the **Castillo el Moro** (Ave. 11, Calle 3), the ornate, Moorish-style, turreted former home of Archbishop Don Carlos Humberto Rodríguez Quirós.

Avenida 9, between Calles 7 and 3, is lined with beautiful ceramic wall murals depicting traditional Costa Rican scenes. Check out the home with a life-size figure of a campesino at Calle 11 number 980.

TeoréTica (Calle 7, Aves. 9/11, tel. 506/2233-4881, www.teoretica.org, 9am-5pm Mon.-Tues. and Thurs.-Fri., 9am-7pm Wed., 10am-4pm Sat.) is a local artists foundation that offers workshops. Its art gallery, **Museo de TeoréTica** (same hours, donation), is across the street with various galleries displaying avant-garde exhibitions in a 1934 art deco building that hosts a contemporary art collection, assembled by curator Virginia Pérez-Ratton in the 1980s.

Centro Costarricense de Ciencias y Cultura

The castle-like hilltop structure on the west side of Barrio Amón, at the north end of Calle 4, served as the city penitentiary from 1910 until 1979. Today it houses the **Centro Costarricense de Ciencias y Cultura** (Costa Rican Science and Cultural Center,

young Ticos playing marimbas by the John Lennon statue, Plaza Artigas

tel. 506/2258-4929, www.museocr.org, 8am-4:30pm Tues.-Fri., 9:30am-5pm Sat.-Sun., free), comprising a library and auditorium (note the fantastic sculptures outside) as well as the **National Gallery** (not to be confused with the National Gallery of Contemporary Art), dedicated to contemporary art displayed in airy exhibition halls conjured from former jail cells. Also here is the **Museo de los Niños** (Children's Museum, adults $2, children $1.50), which lets children reach out and touch science and technology with exhibits that include a planetarium and rooms dedicated to astronomy, the earth, Costa Rica, ecology, science, human beings, and communications. A taxi is recommended, as the surrounding area is dicey for walking.

Parque Zoológico

The six-hectare (14-acre) **Simón Bolívar Zoo** (Calle 7, Ave. 11, tel. 506/2256-0012, www.fundazoo.org, 8am-3:30pm Mon.-Fri., 9am-4:30pm Sat.-Sun., adults $4.50, children $2) has steadily improved, although conditions for many animals still fall short. The native species on display include spider and capuchin monkeys, amphibians and reptiles, most of the indigenous cats, and a small variety of birds, including toucans and tame macaws.

The Nature Center has a video room, a library, and a work area for schoolchildren.

BARRIO TOURNÓN

This district lies north of Barrio Amón, north of the Río Torres, and a hilly 20-minute walk from the city center. Its main draw for visitors is **Centro Comercial El Pueblo** (Ave. 0, tel. 506/2221-9434, 9am-5am daily), an entertainment and shopping complex designed to resemble a Spanish colonial village. El Pueblo's warren of alleys harbors art galleries, crafts stores, restaurants, and nightclubs. The Calle Blancos bus departs from Avenida 5 and Calles 1/3. Use a taxi at night. Taxis to and from El Pueblo often overcharge, so settle on a fee before getting into a cab. There's free parking and 24-hour security.

Also worth a browse is the **Spirogyra Butterfly Garden** (Ave. 0, tel. 506/2222-2937, www.butterflygardencr.com, 8am-4pm daily, adults $7, children $5), a small butterfly farm and botanical garden 50 meters (165 feet) east and 150 meters (500 feet) south of El Pueblo. More than 30 species flutter about in the netted garden and are raised for export; hummingbirds abound. Bilingual tours are offered every half hour, or you can opt for a

The Museo Nacional is housed in the former Cuartel Bellavista.

30-minute self-guided tour; an educational video is shown.

WEST-CENTRAL DOWNTOWN

★ Mercado Central

The warren-like **Mercado Central** (Central Market, 6am-8pm Mon.-Sat.) between Avenidas Central and 1 and Calles 6 and 8 is San José's most colorful market and heady on atmosphere. There are flower stalls, saddle shops, and booths selling medicinal herbs purported to cure everything from sterility to common colds. The annex has booths selling octopus and seafood, plus butchers' booths with oxtails and pigs' heads. Pickpockets thrive in crowded places like this—watch your valuables.

Museo Postal, Telegráfico y Filatélico

Overlooking a grassy plaza, the exquisite **Edificio Postal** (Calle 2, Aves. 1/3), the main post office, dates from 1911 in a dramatic eclectic style with Corinthian pilasters adorning the facade. On the second floor, the **Museo Postal, Telegráfico y Filatélico** (Postal, Telegraphic, and Philatelic Museum, tel. 506/2223-9766, ext. 219, 8am-5pm Mon.-Fri., $0.35) features old phones, philatelic history displays, and postage stamps, including Costa Rica's oldest stamp, dating from 1863. Buy your ticket—a prepaid postcard—at the downstairs counter. The museum hosts a stamp exchange the first Saturday of every month.

Parque Braulio Carrillo

Tiny **Parque Braulio Carrillo,** between Avenidas 2 and 4 and Calles 12 and 14, is also known as La Merced Park. The park is pinned by a monument honoring the astronomer Copernicus and a statue of the namesake former president of Costa Rica. Rising over the park's east side is **Iglesia Nuestra Señora de las Mercedes,** completed in 1907 in Gothic style. The interior is intriguing for its slender columns painted with floral motifs.

WEST OF DOWNTOWN

Parque la Sabana

This huge 72-hectare (178-acre) park, 1.6 kilometers (1 mile) west of the city center, at the west end of Paseo Colón, used to be the national airfield. Today, it's a focus for sports and recreation, with baseball diamonds, basketball courts, jogging and walking trails, soccer fields, tennis and volleyball courts,

Mercado Central

an inline-skating track, and an Olympic-size swimming pool (noon-2pm daily, $3). Sabana's trails provide a peaceful environment for running beneath the shade of eucalyptus and native trees, although it should be avoided at night. The Sabana-Cementerio bus, which leaves from Calle 7 and Avenida Central, will bring you here.

Dominating the park to the northwest, the **Estadio Nacional** (National Stadium) was completed in March 2011 to much fanfare. Funded and built by the Chinese government with Chinese workers, the 35,000-seat multi-purpose stadium has a retractable roof.

The **Museo de Arte Costarricense** (Contemporary Art Museum, tel. 506/2256-1281, www.musarco.go.cr, 9am-4pm Tues.-Sun., free), located in an old airport terminal, faces Paseo Colón on the east side. The recently rehabilitated museum houses a permanent collection of important works by Costa Rica's leading artists, including a diverse collection of woodcuts, wooden sculptures, and 19th- and 20th-century paintings. Revolving exhibitions of contemporary artists are also shown. The Salón Dorado (Golden Hall), on the second floor, depicts the nation's history from pre-Columbian times through the 1940s; done in stucco and bronze patina, the resplendent mural was constructed by French sculptor Louis Féron. A highlight is the sculpture garden to the rear, combining magnificent contemporary and pre-Columbian pieces.

Museo La Salle de Ciencias Naturales (La Salle Museum of Natural Sciences, tel. 506/2232-1306, 7:30am-4pm Mon.-Sat., 9am-5pm Sun., adults $2, children $1), in the Colegio La Salle on the southwest corner of Parque la Sabana, displays a comprehensive collection of Central American flora and fauna (mostly stuffed animals and mounted insects), plus geological specimens and other exhibits covering zoology, paleontology, archaeology, and entomology. Some of the stuffed beasts are a bit moth-eaten (others are so comic, you wonder if the taxidermist was drunk), but the overall collection is impressive. The foyer contains life-size dinosaurs (well, facsimiles). The Sabana-Estadio bus, which departs from the Catedral Metropólitana on Avenida 2, passes Colegio La Salle.

Towering over the north side of the park is the headquarters of **ICE** (Instituto Costarricense de Electricidad). Technicians on a busman's holiday might visit the **Museo Histórico y Tecnológico del Grupo**

interior of Iglesia Nuestra Señora de Las Mercedes

ICE (200 meters/660 feet north of ICE, tel. 506/2220-6054, 7am-4pm Mon.-Fri., free), with various exhibits relating to electricity and phones. Signs are in Spanish only.

Pueblo Antiguo and Parque de Diversiones

The splendid five-hectare (12-acre) Disney-style attraction **Pueblo Antiguo** (tel. 506/2242-9200, www.puebloantiguo.co.cr, 9am-7pm Fri.-Sun., free), 200 meters (660 feet) northeast of Hospital México in La Uruca, is the Colonial Williamsburg of Costa Rica. It recreates the locales and dramatizes the events of Costa Rican history. Buildings in traditional architectural styles include a replica of the National Liquor Factory, Congressional Building, a church, a market, a fire station, and the Costa Rican Bank. The place comes alive with oxcarts, horse-drawn carriages, live music, folkloric dances, and actors dramatizing the past. The park has three sections: the capital city, the coast, and the country (with original adobe structures, including a sugar mill, a coffee mill, and a milking barn). There are crafts shops, and a restaurant serves typical Costa Rican cuisine.

Pueblo Antiguo is part of a theme park, **Parque de Diversiones** (www. parquediversiones.com), that features roller coasters, bumper cars, and waterslides.

EAST OF DOWNTOWN

The relatively upscale barrios of Los Yoses and San Pedro sprawl eastward for several kilometers. Although they offer few sightseeing attractions, the barrios have boomed in recent years as hubs for dining and entertainment, particularly in Barrio Dent—the zone between Rotonda de la Bandera and Rotonda de la Hispanidad, west of the University of Costa Rica.

Universidad de Costa Rica

The **Universidad de Costa Rica** (University of Costa Rica, tel. 506/2511-0000, www.ucr. ac.cr), in San Pedro, about two kilometers (1.2 miles) east of downtown, is a fine place to take in Costa Rica's youthful bohemianism. The Facultad de Artes Musicales (School of Music) basement houses the **Museo de Insectos** (Insect Museum, tel. 506/2207-5647, www.miucr.ucr.ac.cr, 1pm-4:45pm Mon.-Fri., adults $2, children $0.50), displaying an immense collection of Costa Rican and Central American insects, including a spectacular display of butterflies. Knowledgeable guides are available, but call ahead.

Parque la Sabana is popular with cyclists.

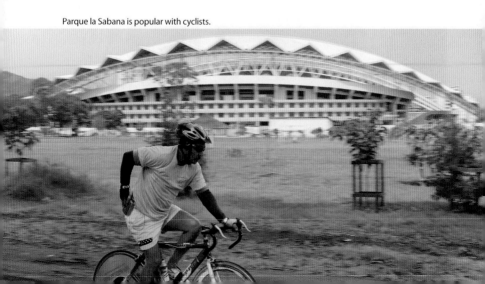

Entertainment and Events

Whatever your nocturnal craving, San José has something to please. The *Tico Times* and the "Viva" section of *La Nación* have listings of what's on in San José. Also pick up a copy of *GAM Cultural What's Going On,* a fold-out pamphlet issued free at tourist venues, which includes events and a handy map. **TeoréTica** (Calle 7, Aves. 9/11, tel./fax 506/2233-4881, www.teoretica.org), a local artists foundation and gallery, hosts *tertulias* (get-togethers). An events calendar is listed on its website.

NIGHTLIFE
Bars

Bars aimed at tourists are concentrated in "Gringo Gulch" (Calles 5/9, Aves. Central/3), but many are salacious, and muggings on the street are frequent. Bars in San Pedro are more bohemian, catering to the university crowd and upscale Ticos. Most of the other class acts are in Escazú, about five kilometers (3 miles) west of town. Avoid the spit-and-sawdust working-class bars, where patrons often fight. Smoking in bars has been banned since 2012.

DOWNTOWN

Housed in a remodeled colonial building, **Bar Morazán** (Ave. 3, Calle 9, tel. 506/2256-5110, 11am-2am Mon.-Fri., 5pm-3am Sat.) draws an eclectic crowd for its warm ambience within redbrick walls adorned with traffic signs. It has a jukebox and serves meals. The house drink is a *guaro melón*—sugarcane liquor with fruit juice.

Catercorner, the slightly salacious **Key Largo** (Calle 7, Aves. 1/3, tel. 506/2257-7800, 11am-3am daily), now run by the Hotel Del Rey, draws a Latin clientele with dancing to live music (pop on Tues.-Wed. and Fri., tropical music Thurs., 1960s hits Sat.). Local prostitutes have always been an abiding presence.

Local bohemians prefer the laid-back **El Cuartel de la Boca del Monte** (Ave. 1, Calles 21/23, tel. 506/2221-0327, 11:30am-2pm and 6pm-2am Mon.-Wed. and Fri., 6pm-midnight Thurs., 6pm-2am Sat., men $4, women free), a popular hangout for young Josefinos and the late-night after-theater set. The brick-walled bar is famous for its 152 inventive cocktails, often served to wild ceremony and applause. It has live music on Monday, Wednesday, and Friday and doesn't get in the groove until around 10pm.

Around the corner from El Cuartel, **El Observatorio** (Calle 23, Aves. Central/1, tel. 506/2223-0725, www.elobservatorio.tv, 6pm-2am Mon.-Sat.) plays up the movie theme (the Cine Magaly is across the road), with movie posters and occasional screenings. High ceilings lend an airy ambience. It has live music most nights, with something for every taste.

The *farandula* (bohemian in-crowd) gravitates to **Rayuela** (Ave. Central, Calles 13/15, tel. 506/8376-1409, www.enrayuela.blogspot. com, 6pm-2am daily), a dark cozy bar where folk singers and poets host *peñas*. Nearby **Stiefel** (Ave. 7, Calles 13/15, tel. 506/8854-4824, 6pm-1am Mon.-Sat.), in Barrio Amón, caters to Costa Rica's recent explosion in microbrews and bills itself as an eco-brewery. Start with a flight of four miniature samplers before graduating to a pint of Praying Nun or Maldita Vida. It has a great pub ambience.

WEST OF DOWNTOWN

The **Shakespeare Bar** (Ave. 2, Calle 28, tel. 506/2258-6787, 5pm-2am Tues.-Sat.) serves an intellectual crowd, drawn to the adjoining Teatro Laurence Olivier and Sala Garbo cinema. It has a piano bar and sometimes hosts live jazz. On Sabana Sur, **Mac's American Bar** (tel. 506/2231-3145, 9am-2am daily) is a TV bar popular with gringos. There's a pool table upstairs.

As close as you can get to Miami or New York in Costa Rica, **Rapsodía Lounge** (Paseo Colón, Calle 40, tel. 506/2248-1720, www.rapsodiacr.com, 5pm-2:45am Tues.-Sat.)

Gay San José

Costa Rica is a conservative country and the gay and lesbian scene is somewhat closeted. The hot clubs and other venues change frequently.

ACCOMMODATIONS

A U.S. travel agency, Colours Destinations, operates **Colours Oasis Hotel** (tel. 506/2296-1880, U.S./Canada tel. 866-517-4390, www.coloursoasis.com, $79-179 s, $89-189 d year-round, lower with Internet specials), a small gay-owned colonial-style property in the quiet residential Rohrmoser district. It has exquisite contemporary decor. There's a pool, a whirlpool tub, and a TV room, plus a café, a restaurant, and a bar.

Other gay-friendly hotels include **Hotel Fleur de Lys, Hotel Kekoldi,** and **Hotel Santo Tomás.**

MEETING PLACES

Gay-friendly spots include **Café Mundo** (Ave. 9, Calle 15, tel. 506/2222-6190) and **Café La Esquina,** in Colours Oasis Hotel. The latter has gay theme parties monthly.

Joseph Itiel, author of *¡Pura Vida!: A Travel Guide to Gay & Lesbian Costa Rica,* strongly advises against "cruising" the parks, where "you can get yourself into real trouble."

ENTERTAINMENT AND EVENTS

You gotta hand it to Costa Rica's gays: They run some of the best dance clubs in San José. They're straight-friendly too, which explains why there are usually lots of women and couples on weekends.

La Avispa (Calle 1, Aves. 8/10, tel. 506/2223-5343, www.laavispa.com) has long been *the* gay and lesbian fixture and is the hottest venue in town. Passing through its unassuming doors in a low-class barrio, you'll be amazed to find a top-notch disco on two levels playing mostly techno and Latin music. There's also a pool room, a bar, and a big-screen TV upstairs. It draws fashionistas, both gay and straight, and drag queens flock on show night.

Most gay clubs are located in a rough part of town south of downtown; whatever you do, take a taxi.

is one of the chicest lounge bars in the city with its minimalist decor and retro lava-lamp videos. It has multiple levels and spaces, including outdoors, with DJs and dancing.

Sophisticates also head to the **Casablanca VIP Lounge** (Paseo Colón, Calle 32, tel. 506/8394-5458, noon-5am Mon.-Sat.), looking like a chic transplanted piece of Miami's South Beach, with its parachute drapes, open-air lounge, and neon lighting. It serves Mediterranean tapas and has nightly themes, including live music on Friday and an electronic DJ on Saturday.

EAST OF DOWNTOWN

Nova Río (Calle 41, tel. 506/2283-1548, 8pm-3am Mon.-Sat.), on Avenida Central in Los Yoses, is a chill-out lounge with TVs showing music videos. A hip young crowd gathers for schmoozing to a background of eclectic sounds, from electronic to current hits. Nearby, **Sands Rock Bar** (tel. 506/2281-0307, 5pm-5am daily) is rock-and-roll central, with live concerts and some heavy metal thrown in for good measure.

For a pint of Guinness, head to **Stan's Irish Pub** (tel. 506/2253-4360, 4pm-2am Mon.-Fri., 4pm-3am Sat., 11am-11pm Sun.), 125 meters (400 feet) west of the Casa Presidential, in the southeasterly district of Zapote. Owner Stanley Salas sells more than 60 types of beers from around the world. Stan's has live music and comedy nights.

Discos and Clubs

El Pueblo (www.centrocomercialpueblo. com), in Barrio Tournon, boasts a fistful of discos plus a dozen shoulder-to-shoulder bars tucked into a warren of alleyways, featuring everything from salsa to Bolivian folk music.

For electronica, techno, and rave-style partying, hit the energized **Vértigo** (tel. 506/2257-8424, www.vertigocr.com, 8pm-6am Mon.-Sat.), in Edificio Colón on Paseo Colón. This cavernous space has a VIP lounge section that has mellower fare, such as reggae; otherwise electronica rules.

In Barrio Mexico, **Castro's** (Ave. 13, Calle 22, tel. 506/2256-8769, 8pm-6am Fri. & Sat.) is an immensely popular dance club with a shifting mood: On any night expect to hear *bachata,* merengue, reggae, and salsa. It has a variety of rooms on two levels.

East of downtown, local DJ and musician Bernal Monestel recently opened the cool and casual **Mundoloco El Chante** (Ave. Central, tel. 506/8318-3000, 4pm-2am Mon-Thurs., 3pm-2am Fri.-Sat., 1pm-noon Sun.), in San Pedro. Live bands can run the gamut from reggae to rock.

THE ARTS
Live Music and Dance

Big-time artists occasionally hit Costa Rica and typically perform at the **Teatro Nacional** (tickets tel. 506/2010-1111, www. teatronacional.go.cr), **Teatro Melico Salazar** (tel. 506/2222-5424, www.teatromelico.go.cr), or **Auditorio Nacional** (tel. 506/2222-7647), in the Museo de los Niños. Look for advertisements in the local newspapers.

CLASSICAL

The **Orquesta Sinfónica Nacional** (National Symphony Orchestra, tel. 506/2240-0333, www.osn.go.cr) performs at the Teatro Nacional (tickets tel. 506/2010-1100, www. teatronacional.go.cr), with a variable schedule February-December. The orchestra posts an annual calendar on its website.

The **Centro Cultural Costarricense-Norteamericano** (Costa Rican-North American Cultural Center) hosts concerts in its Eugene O'Neill Theater (tel. 506/2207-7500, www.centrocultural.cr).

JAZZ

The nascent Tico jazz scene is fairly robust. Venues include the **Shakespeare Gallery** (Calle 28, Ave. 2, tel. 506/2258-6787, 5pm-2am Tues.-Sat.), but the big enchilada is the **Jazz Café** (Ave. Central, tel. 506/2253-8933, www. jazzcafecostarica.com, 6pm-midnight daily, cover $5 pp) in a venerable redbrick building in San Pedro. It hosts big names from around the globe and has all the ambience one could hope for in a classic jazz club.

El Sótano (Calle 3, Ave. 11, tel. 506/2221-2302, 8pm-2am daily) is well-named for its cellar jazz club. At the breaks between sets, head upstairs to check out the art galleries and mingle with the *farandula* (in-crowd).

Theater

The **Little Theater Group** (tel. 506/8858-1446, www.littletheatregroup.org) presents English-language musicals and comedies throughout the year at the Teatero Laurence Olivier (Ave. 2, Calle 28).

FESTIVALS AND EVENTS

The city hosts the **International Festival of Cinema** (tel. 506/2256-0620, www.costaricafilmfestival.org) each July-August, usually in La Aduana (Calle 23, Aves. 3/7).

The **International Arts Festival** in November is launched with a street parade. Henry Bastos leads the **San José Art City Tour** (tel. 506/8817-3136, bastoshenry@gmail. com, www.gamcultural.com) once every other month.

The **Oxcart Festival** (Festival de las Carretas), along Paseo Colón in November, celebrates traditional rural life with a parade of dozens of oxcarts (*carretas*).

The **Festival de la Luz** (Festival of Light, mid-Dec.) is a Christmas parade along Calle 42 highlighted by floats trimmed with colorful Christmas lights (6pm-10pm). The lighting of the Museo de los Niños (Calle 4, Ave. 13, tel. 506/2238-4929, www.museocr.org) in early December is an annual tradition, with fireworks and thousands of lights.

The annual **running of the bulls** occurs during Christmas and New Year's at the fairground in Zapote with a *tope* (horse parade) and bull riding and taunting. There's a special tourist-only section with fireworks. It coincides with a massive *tope* each December 26, when as many as 3,000 men and women ride down Paseo Colón and downtown.

Shopping

Shop hours are typically 8am-6pm Monday-Saturday. Many places close at noon for a siesta; a few stay open until late evening.

ARTS AND CRAFTS

San José is replete with arts and crafts, such as reproduction pre-Columbian gold jewelry, hammocks, wood carvings, Panamanian *molas,* and miniature oxcarts. **Mercado de Artesanías Nacionales** (Calle 11, Aves. 4/6, Mon.-Sat.), in Plaza Artigas, teems with colorful stalls. The plaza hosts an open-air art exhibition (*Pintura al aire libre*) 10am-4pm every Saturday March-July. The **Mercado Central,** on Avenida Central, has a panoply of leatherwork and other artisans' stalls.

Specialty handicraft stores concentrate near Parque Morazán and include **Gallery Amir** (Calle 5, Ave. 5, tel. 506/2221-9128, www.amirart.net), which sells top-quality wood carvings and furniture. **Centro Comercial El Pueblo** (Ave. 0, tel. 506/2221-9434, www.centrocomercialelpueblo.com, 9am-5am daily) also has many high-quality art galleries and crafts stores.

My favorite store is **Galería Namú** (Ave. 7, Calles 5/7, tel. 506/2256-3412, www.galerianamu.com), where the superb indigenous art and crafts include Boruca masks and weavings and jewelry from Panamá and elsewhere. **Chieton Moren** (Calle 1, Aves. 10/12, tel. 506/2267-6716, www.chietonmoren.org), located behind the Iglesia de la Dolorosa, sells indigenous crafts direct from the artists—and the earnings return to the artists (*chieton moren* means "fair deal").

Another excellent gallery is **Arte** **Contemporáneo Andrómeda** (Ave. 9, Calle 9, tel. 506/2223-3529, 9am-7pm Mon.-Fri., noon-6pm Sat.).

BOOKS

Librería Internacional (tel. 800-542-7374, www.libreriainternacional.com), Costa Rica's answer to Barnes & Noble, has stores on Avenida Central (tel. 506/2257-2563), in Rohrmoser (tel. 506/2290-3331), in San Pedro (tel. 506/2253-9553), and outside town in Escazú (tel. 506/2201-8320). **LibroMax** (tel. 800-542-7662, www.libromax.com) has outlets in Mall San Pedro and Multiplaza (in Escazú); and **Librería Universal** has an outlet at Avenida Central and Calles Central and 1 (tel. 506/2222-2222, www.universalcr.com).

Mora Books (Calle 5, Ave. 5/7, tel. 506/8383-8385, www.morabooks.com, 11am-7pm Mon.-Sat.), on the west side of the Holiday Inn, sells used books as well as magazines and maps.

COFFEE

Every souvenir store sells premium packaged coffee. Make sure the package is marked *puro*—otherwise the coffee may be laced with enough sugar to make even the most ardent sugar lover turn green. You can also buy whole beans—albeit not the finest export quality—roasted before your eyes at the **Mercado Central** (Ave. Central, Calle 6). Ask for whole beans (*granos*), or you'll end up with superfine grounds. One pound of beans costs about $1.

The **Café Britt** stores in the airport departure lounge are well stocked.

CLOTHING

If you admire the traditional Tico look, check out the **Mercado Central** (Ave. 1, Calle 6), where you'll find embroidered *guayabero* shirts and blouses and cotton campesino hats. Shoemakers also abound, many selling cowboy boots, including dandy two-tones.

The best place for upscale brand-name boutiques is **Mall San Pedro** (Ave. Central at Rotonda de la Hispanidad, San Pedro, tel. 506/2283-7540). You can buy hiking, climbing, and adventure gear at **Mundo Aventura** (Ave. 3, Calle 36, tel. 506/2221-6934, www.maventura.com).

JEWELRY

Artisanal markets sell attractive indigenous-style earrings and bracelets. Much of what you'll see on the street is actually gold-washed, not solid gold. Most upscale hotel gift stores sell Colombian emeralds and semiprecious stones, 14-karat-gold earrings and brooches, and fabulous pre-Columbian re-creations: Try **Esmeraldas y Diseños** (tel. 506/2231-4808, www.esmeraldasydisenos.com) in Sabana Norte. The **Gold Museum Shop** (tel. 506/2243-4317, 9:30am-5pm daily), beneath the Plaza de la Cultura, sells quality gold reproductions.

One of my favorite stores, **Kiosco SJO** (Ave. 7, Calle 11, tel. 506/2258-1829, 11am-6pm Mon., 11am-10pm Tues.-Sat.) has some of the hippest handmade creations by Latin American artisans, including jewelry and handcrafted leather bags and boots, all of top quality.

Accommodations

San José's accommodations run the gamut from budget hovels to charming boutique hotels and large name-brand options. San José is noisy; it is always wise to ask for a room away from the street.

DOWNTOWN
Under $25

Among budget dorm options, the best is ★ **Costa Rica Backpackers** (Ave. 6, Calles 21/23, tel. 506/2221-6191, www.costaricabackpackers.com, dorm from $12 pp, private room $17 pp), run by two friendly and savvy French guys, Stefan and Vincent. This spotless, secure backpacker pad is in a large house with a small kidney-shaped swimming pool and garden with hammocks and swing chairs. It offers male, female, and mixed dorms with shared baths, plus private rooms (one is a lovely space with a king bed), all with heaps of hot water. All dorms have lockers. A huge TV lounge has leather sofas. It has cooking facilities, laundry, storage, and a tour-planning room, as well as free 24-hour Internet and coffee, plus an airport shuttle. Movies are shown nightly.

Their Mochila Bar, next door, is a great spot for draft beer, games, and grooving to sounds from electronica to salsa.

★ **Pangea Hostel** (Ave. 7, Calles 3/5, tel. 506/2221-1992, www.hostelpangea.com, dorm $14 pp, private room $45-55), in a converted old home in Barrio Amón, receives raves—and no wonder: Splashed with colorful murals throughout, this thoughtfully prepared hostel offers splendid services, including a kitchen, a TV lounge, a pool table, a lovely pool with a whirlpool tub, and a wet bar. It even has its own shuttle, and the open-air restaurant upstairs has a licensed bar that knows how to throw a wild party. There are six clean dorms and 26 basically furnished private rooms, all with shared baths with hot water, as well as five suites. It offers free storage, free Internet access, free international calls, and free breakfast.

$25-50

The owners of Costa Rica Backpackers run the slightly more upscale **Costa Rica Guesthouse** (tel./fax 506/2223-7034, www.

costa-rica-guesthouse.com, $15-38 pp) across the road, with 23 dorms and rooms, some with private baths. Lodging options vary markedly and include three upstairs rooms with glass walls and king beds. One room has a kitchen, and all have free Wi-Fi. A lovely patio and a TV room are highlights.

The more eccentric **Hotel de la Cuesta** (Ave. 1, Calles 11/13, tel. 506/2256-7946, www.pensiondelacuesta.com, dorm $10-12, private room from $27 s, $33 d) is a cozy, offbeat charmer. This 1930s house, full of antiques and potted plants, is adorned with the works of the former owners, local artists Dierdre Hyde and Otto Apuy. There are a mixed dorm and a female dorm, nine rooms (from standard to "deluxe"), plus a furnished apartment for up to six people. The shared baths are clean. There's a TV room and self-service laundry; guests get use of the kitchen and Wi-Fi.

$50-100

The colorful and gay-friendly **Hotel Kekoldi** (Ave. 9, Calles 5/7, tel. 506/2240-0804, www.kekoldi.com, from $55 s, $65 d), in a two-story 1950s house in Barrio Amón, offers 10 spacious rooms with hardwood floors, tropical pastels, heaps of light, and lovely wrought-iron furnishings along with cable TV, Wi-Fi, fans, and safes. Breakfasts are served in a beautiful garden in Japanese style.

If you don't mind its somewhat institutional style, the **Hotel Balmoral** (Ave. Central, Calles 7/9, tel. 506/2222-5022, www.balmoral.co.cr, from $76 s/d, including breakfast) is a great a steps-to-everything option one block east of Plaza de la Cultura. Its 112 small, air-conditioned, contemporary-themed rooms in five room types have Wi-Fi (for a fee) and safes. It has an excellent outdoor café and a casino. A near carbon copy across the street, the **Hotel Presidente** (tel. 506/2010-0000, www.hotel-presidente.com, from $83 s/d, including breakfast) will appeal to travelers who like the services of a large-scale hotel. A highlight of its 110 spacious air-conditioned bedrooms (all with Wi-Fi) is the travertine-clad

baths. It has a rooftop whirlpool and sauna, a casino, and a bar, plus a wonderful street-front café-restaurant.

For Old World charm, consider the American-run **Hotel Santo Tomás** (Ave. 7, Calles 3/5, tel. 506/2255-0448, www.hotelsantotomas.com, from $53 s/d), an intimate bed-and-breakfast with 19 nonsmoking rooms in an elegant turn-of-the-20th-century plantation home with high vaulted ceilings and lovely hardwood and colonial tile floors. Rooms vary in size, but all have antique reproduction furniture and all the necessary amenities; larger deluxe rooms away from road noise are worth paying a little extra for. It has TV lounges, a full-service tour-planning service, a solar-heated swimming pool, and the delightful Restaurant El Oasis, but the best part is its handy access to the city's downtown sights.

Nearby, the homey, well-run **Hotel Don Carlos** (Calle 9 bis, Aves. 7/9, tel. 506/2221-6707, www.doncarloshotel.com, from $70 s, $80 d, including breakfast) also occupies a wood-paneled colonial mansion replete with Sarchí oxcarts, magnificent wrought-iron work, stained-glass windows, stunning art, and bronze sculptures. It has 36 rooms and suites, all with cable TV, safes, blow-dryers and free Wi-Fi. Unique pluses are its tremendous gift shop, a sundeck with a water cascade and a plunge pool, plus an espresso bar and a restaurant lit by an atrium skylight.

A similarly quaint and gracious alternative, the well-run Swiss-owned **Hotel Fleur de Lys** (Calle 13, Aves. 2/4, tel. 506/2223-1206, www.hotelfleurdelys.com, low season from $78 s, $86 d, high season from $88 s, $96 d, including breakfast) has 31 individually styled rooms and suites in a restored colonial mansion. All have sponge-washed pastel walls and wrought-iron or wicker beds with crisp linens. A wood-paneled restaurant serves Italian cuisine, and live music is offered twice weekly in the bar. There's on-site parking.

With a superb location on Plaza de la Cultura, the **Gran Hotel** (Ave. 2, Calle 3, tel. 506/2221-4000, www.grandhotelcostarica.

com, from $57 s/d) has two great restaurants and a coffee lounge. Still, dating from 1899 and named a national landmark, its 102 modestly furnished rooms are a bit dowdy, despite a recent refurbishing and Wi-Fi; take a more elegant junior suite. Rooms facing the plaza can be noisy. It has a basement casino.

$100-150

Dominating the downtown skyline, and the biggest hotel in town, is the sophisticated **Hotel Aurola Holiday Inn** (Ave. 5, Calle 5, tel. 506/2523-1000, www.aurolahotels.com, from $108 s/d). The modern high-rise overlooking Parque Morazán offers 201 spacious, hermetically sealed, and regally furnished rooms with Wi-Fi. The 11th floor is smoke-free, and an executive floor caters to business travelers. Topping off the hotel's attractions is the 17th floor mirador restaurant, adjacent to the casino. It has an indoor pool.

WEST OF DOWNTOWN
Under $25

A shining star among San José's hostels is ★ **Mi Casa Hostel** (Calle 48, tel. 506/2231-4700, www.micasahostel.com, dorm $13 pp, private room $30-34 s/d, including breakfast), a beautiful 1950s modernist home with a pool table and Internet access in the exquisite stone-faced TV lounge, opening through a wall of glass to a stone patio and a quaint garden. It has a communal kitchen and laundry. A superb coed dorm upstairs gets heaps of light; a women's dorm is simpler. Four private rooms have foam mattresses and vary in size. It's 150 meters (500 feet) north and 50 meters (165 feet) west of ICE, in Sabana Norte.

Gaudy's Backpackers (Ave. 5, Calle 36/38, tel. 506/2248-0086, www.backpacker.co.cr, dorm from $12 pp, private rooms from $16 pp) is in a beautiful and spotless home in a peaceful residential area. You enter to a lofty-ceilinged TV lounge with sofas and a pool table. It opens to a courtyard with hammocks. There are two coed dorms (one with 8 bunk beds, another with 12 bunk beds) and 13 small private rooms. Guests get use of a full kitchen, and there's laundry service, plus free Internet access.

$50-100

Focusing on a business clientele, the **Tryp San José Sabana Hotel** (Ave. 3, Calle 38, tel. 506/2547-2323, www.tryphotels.com, from $84 s/d), in the Centro Colón tower, will please city sophisticates with its stylish aesthetic. The 98 carpeted, nonsmoking rooms (including 42 suites) are furnished in rich chocolate, taupe, and tropical tones, with king beds, Wi-Fi, flat-screen TVs, and CD and iPod stations. Some rooms have volcano views, suites have kitchenettes, and there's an executive floor with a business center, the classy Sepia Lounge Bar & Restaurant, a casino, a small gym, and a nightclub-bar.

A delightful alternative nearby, **Auténtico Hotel** (Ave. 5, Calle 40, tel. 506/2222-5266, www.autenticohotel.com, from $88 s/d, including breakfast), formerly the Hotel Torremolinos, was recently redone in a chic style that city sophisticates will adore. A highlight is a lush garden with shade umbrellas and a pool. Its 80 rooms and 12 suites are modest in size but handsomely furnished in stylish chocolates, orange, and white. All have Wi-Fi. Suites have glassed-in balconies. It offers a pool and a whirlpool tub, plus a courtesy bus and a beautiful restaurant.

I'm fond of the modern four-story **Parque del Lago Boutique Hotel** (Paseo Colón, Calles 40/42, tel. 506/2247-2000, www.parquedellago.com, from $75 s/d) for the hip contemporary style and to-die-for mattresses of its 33 beautifully decorated air-conditioned rooms, plus six suites with kitchenettes; and for its fabulous café-restaurant and bar. It has a spa.

$100-150

Perfect for and popular with businesspeople, the stylish **Barceló Palma Real** (tel. 506/2290-5060, www.hotelpalmareal.com, from $154 s/d) enjoys a quiet residential locale in Sabana Norte. This upscale contemporary boutique hotel, full of marble and autumnal colors, has 65 tastefully decorated rooms with handsome wooden floors, orthopedic mattresses, and spacious travertine-lined baths. There's a state-of-the-art gym, a whirlpool tub, a business center, and an elegant restaurant.

The ★ **Hotel Grano de Oro** (Calle 30, Ave. 2, tel. 506/2255-3322, www.hotelgranodeoro.com, from $158 s/d) is indisputably the city's finest hotel (and a great bargain). A member of the Small Distinctive Hotels of Costa Rica, the gracious turn-of-the-20th-century mansion is in a quiet residential neighborhood off Paseo Colón. Congenial hosts Eldon and Lori Cooke have overseen the creation of a world-class hotel that combines traditional Old World Costa Rican style with contemporary elegance. Ascending its glass-covered staircase to a stylish lobby makes a dramatic entry, and the superlative restaurant is indisputably San José's finest. Orthopedic mattresses guarantee contented slumber in 41 faultlessly decorated guest rooms done up in a variety of sophisticated color combinations and featuring black rattan and hand-crafted iron furniture, plus canopied king beds in some rooms. Flat-screen TVs, safes, minibars, and phones are standard, and all rooms are air-conditioned. Extravagant baths boast torrents of very hot water. The sumptuous rooftop Vista de Oro suite has a plate-glass wall providing views of three volcanoes. There's a gift shop and a rooftop solarium with two whirlpool tubs. No request is too much for the ever-smiling staff.

Nearby, and a total contrast, is the **Crowne Plaza Corobicí** (tel. 506/2232-8122, www.crowneplaza.com, $102-415 s/d), on the northeastern corner of Parque la Sabana, best suits business and convention travelers. Its angled exterior is ungainly, but its soaring atrium, with a surfeit of marble and tier upon tier of balconies festooned with ferns, is impressive. The 213 spacious rooms and suites boast handsome furnishings and modern accoutrements. Suites have kitchenettes. It has a nightclub, a casino, a 24-hour cafeteria, and Italian and Japanese restaurants.

EAST OF DOWNTOWN
Under $25

Backpackers have always raved about the **Hostel Toruma** (Ave. Central, Calles 29/31, tel. 506/2234-8186, www.hosteltoruma.com, $14 pp dorm, $20 pp shared bath, $40 s, $55 d private bath, including breakfast), a sister to Hostel Pangea. In a beautiful old colonial-style structure, formerly the home of a Costa

Hotel Grano de Oro

Rican president, it has segregated dorms in 17 well-kept rooms, plus seven private rooms with double beds, folding couches, flat-screen TVs, and private baths. It has laundry facilities, a restaurant, Internet access, a swimming pool, parking, and airport shuttles.

If I were a backpacker, there's no doubt I'd opt for ★ **Hostel Bekuo** (Ave. 8, Calles 39/41, tel. 506/2234-1091, www.hostelbekuo. com, $11 pp dorm, from $16 pp private rooms), an awesome conversion of a beautiful 1950s modernist home with shiny hardwood floors, clean modern baths, a breeze-swept Internet and TV lounge, plus a pool table and a communal kitchen. Walls of glass open to a garden. It has male, female, and mixed dorms, plus private rooms.

$25-50

★ **Kap's Place** (Calle 19, Aves. 11/13, tel. 506/2221-1169, www.kapsplace.com, $25-90 s, $45-100 d) has been an acclaimed institution among budget travelers as long as I've been coming to Costa Rica. This clean, charming guesthouse has 23 rooms, including 6 hostel-type rooms, 3 with shared baths and 12 with full kitchens, in various adjoining buildings, on a tranquil street in Barrio Aranjuéz, a 20-minute walk from downtown. Although rooms vary widely, all are decorated in lively colors and have cable TV and phones, and there's free Internet and Wi-Fi access. A lovely covered patio garners sunlight and has hammocks. No meals are served, but guests have kitchen privileges, and there's a kids playroom.

$50-100

The lovely and unpretentious **Hotel Le** **Bergerac** (Calle 35, Ave. Central, tel. 506/2234-7850, www.bergerachotel.com, from $87 s/d, including breakfast) is a peaceful and intimate bed-and-breakfast with yesteryear decor. Although English-owned, this pretty mansion-hotel in Los Yoses, with views south toward the Cordillera Talamanca, plays up a French theme. Some of the 19 rooms in three buildings have tiny patio gardens; all have Wi-Fi and glistening hardwood floors. It boasts the Cyrano Restaurant. Light sleepers might find noise from a nearby disco a problem on weekend nights.

Even more intimate, the **Hotel 1492 Jade y Oro** (Ave. 1 no. 2985, Calles 31/33, tel. 506/2225-3752, www.hotel1492.com, $50 s, $60 d), in the quiet residential neighborhood of Barrio Escalante, exudes a family home ambience, thanks not least to a handsome lounge with a fireplace. This beautiful colonial-style residence has 10 handsomely appointed rooms (three are junior suites) with hardwood floors. Most rooms have windows that open to small gardens, and there's a patio garden where a happy hour of wine and cheese is hosted nightly. Rates include Tico breakfast.

Over $100

The low-rise **Boutique Hotel Jade** (tel. 506/2224-2455, www.hotelboutiquejade.com, from $126 s, $136 d), in Los Yoses, has a classy contemporary ambience. It has 30 spacious, carpeted, executive-style rooms with spacious showers. Junior suites are truly classy. Murals adorn the corridor walls. There's a small lounge, a garden with a beautiful swimming pool, and the sophisticated Jürgen's Restaurant.

Food

Many of the best restaurants can be found in San Pedro, east of downtown. *Sodas*—cheap snack bars serving typical Costa Rican food—serve working-class fare, such as tripe soup or chicken with rice-and-bean dishes. You can usually fill up for $2-4.

DOWNTOWN
Breakfast

La Criollita (Ave. 7, Calles 7/9, tel. 506/2256-6511, 7am-9pm Mon.-Fri., 7am-4pm Sat.), a clean and atmospheric favorite of the business crowd, serves full American breakfasts ($5) and Tico breakfasts ($5), as well as soups, salads, sandwiches, tempting entrées such as garlic shrimp ($8) and roast chicken ($5), plus natural juices. You can choose an airy, skylighted indoor setting with contemporary decor, or a shaded patio.

The artsy Argentinean-run **Café de la Posada** (Ave. 2, Calle 17, tel. 506/2258-1027, 7am-7pm Mon.-Thurs., 7am-11pm Fri.-Sun.) appeals to a bohemian crowd and is a good spot for a quiet breakfast. It offers jazz and classical music and serves espressos and cappuccinos, plus quiches, omelets, sandwiches (all from $1.50), Argentinean empanadas, and tempting desserts.

Cafés and Sodas

One of the best coffee shops in town is the **Alma de Café** (tel. 506/2233-2178, 9am-7pm Mon.-Fri., 9am-4pm Sat.) inside the foyer of Teatro Nacional. Tempting sandwiches, snacks, and desserts complement the lovely neoclassical Parisian ambience.

Bohemians will also appreciate **Talentum** (Ave. 11, Calles 3/3A, tel. 506/2256-6346, www.galeriatalentum.com, 11:30am-6:30pm Mon.-Fri., 9am-4pm Sat.), a new art space with live music, screenings, and other cultural events. The cozy café serves salads and light dishes plus cappuccinos.

★ **Spoon** (tel. 506/2217-2600, www. spooncr.com) has burgeoned over the past decade from a small takeout bakery into a chain with outlets throughout the city, including Avenida Central, Calle 5/7 (tel. 506/2255-2480), and Mall Pedro in Los Yoses (tel. 506/2283-4538). In addition to desserts, Spoon serves sandwiches, salads, lasagna, soups, empanadas (pastries stuffed with chicken and other meats), and *lapices,* the Costa Rican equivalent of submarine sandwiches, all at bargain prices in a spick-and-span environment. I also like the chain **Trigo Miel** (Calle 3, Aves. Central/1, tel. 506/2221-8995, www.trigomiel.com, 7am-8pm Mon.-Sat., 8am-6pm Sun.) for set lunches, sandwiches, and desserts. It has outlets at Avenida 9 at Calle 21, and Avenida Central at Calle 29 (tel. 506/2253-7157).

The **Mercado Central** (Aves. Central/1, Calles 6/8) has dozens of inexpensive *sodas.* My favorite *soda* is **Mama's Place** (Ave. 1, Calles Central/2, tel. 506/2223-2270, 8am-8pm Mon.-Fri., 8am-4pm Sat.), a mom-and-pop restaurant run by an Italian couple and serving huge portions heavy on the spaghetti. Go for the *casado* (set lunch, $6) with choice of fish, chicken, or pork.

Asian

For more than two decades **Tin Jo** (Calle 11, Aves. 6/8, tel. 506/2221-7605, www.tinjo.com, 11:30am-3pm and 5:30pm-10pm Mon.-Thurs., 11:30am-3pm and 5:30pm-10pm Fri.-Sat., and 11:30am-10pm Sun.) has been one of my faves, and also a favorite of locals for its budget-priced pan-Asian fare: tasty Mandarin and Szechuan specialties, plus sushi, satay ($4), samosas ($3), curries ($9), and a pretty good pad thai ($9).

Costa Rican

The Centro Comercial El Pueblo, in Barrio Tournón, has several restaurants known for traditional Costa Rican fare. The most popular is **La Cocina de Leña** (tel. 506/2222-1883, 11:30am-10pm Sun.-Thurs., 11am-11:30pm Fri.-Sat., entrées from $10) for its cozy ambience of a rural farmhouse. Dishes include creole chicken; *olla de carne* soup; and square tamales made with white cornmeal, mashed potatoes, and beef, pork, or chicken, wrapped tightly in a plantain leaf.

Also done up in rustic yesteryear fashion, **Nuestra Tierra** (Ave. 2, Calle 15, tel. 506/2258-6500, 24 hours daily) serves traditional dishes served with a flourish. Try the superb corvina in mango sauce. It hosts traditional folkloric shows; call for times. I experienced excellent service, but pushy attempts to extract extra tips can spoil the experience.

The 24-hour **Café 1930** (tel. 506/2221-4000), the terrace café fronting the Gran Hotel, serves simple but filling Costa Rican fare—you might find me here eating a lunch of *arroz con pollo* (rice with chicken, $4). It has an excellent buffet until 10am. A pianist entertains.

Italian

The **Balcón de Europa** (Calle 9, Aves. Central/1, tel. 506/2221-4841, 11am-11pm Tues.-Sun., under $15) is a revered culinary shrine. The late chef Franco Piatti was a local institution who presented moderately priced cuisine from central Italy in an appropriately warm, welcoming setting with wood-paneled walls festooned with historic photos and framed proverbs. New chef Jean Pierre has tilted the menu toward French-Italian.

Nouvelle

Perhaps my favorite for unpretentious yet superb dining when I'm downtown is ★ **Kalú** (Calle 7, Ave. 11, tel. 506/2253-8426, www.kalu.co.cr, noon-6pm Mon., noon-9:30pm Tues.-Sat.), the brainchild of world-renowned local Chef Camille Ratton. This avant-garde restaurant doubles as a lounge-bar and gallery. It's the kind of place you look forward to hanging out with friends on the open-air deck or chilling in leather sofas in the lounge.

The fantastic and eclectic menu spans salads, burgers, paninis, and pizzas, plus an incredible gnocchi malbec ($15). Soups range from cream of *ayote* ($6) and ceviche ($10.50) to chicken mole ($8). Superb desserts include cheesecake and a fabulous cherry tart.

Spanish and South American

Another favorite gem is ★ **La Esquina de Buenos Aires** (Calle 11, Ave. 6, tel. 506/2223-1909, www.laesquinadebuenosaires.com, 11:30am-3pm and 6pm-10:30pm Mon.-Fri., 12:30pm-11pm Sat., noon-10pm Sun., $5-20), a genuine Argentinean restaurant with tremendous atmosphere. The wide-ranging menu of gourmet dishes is supported by a vast wine list heavy with malbecs. The onion soup is excellent, and I enjoyed a fillet of sole in blue cheese with boiled potatoes ($9).

Meat eaters will salivate at **Fogo Brasil** (Ave. de las Américas, Calles 40/42, tel. 506/2248-1111, www.fogobrasilcr.com, 11:30am-11:30pm daily, $6-25), a classy Brazilian steak house where waiters dressed as Argentinean gauchos serve charcoal-roasted meats. It also has a pasta bar and excellent buffet, and the wide-ranging menu even has sushi. And the caipirinhas are great! It offers free hotel transfers.

WEST OF DOWNTOWN
Cafés and *Sodas*

I like **Sabor Nicaragüense** (Calle 20, Aves. Central/1, tel. 506/2248-2547, 7am-9pm daily), a clean simple family *soda* with heaps of light and both inside and outside dining. It serves *gallo pinto*, enchiladas, and Nicaraguan specialties.

Coffee and Snacks

Chocoholics should sniff out the **Taller de Chocolate** (tel. 506/2231-4840, www.tallerdelchocolate.com, 10am-6pm Mon.-Fri., 10am-3pm Sat.), 100 meters (330 feet) north of Torre la Sabana, on Sabana Norte. It sells delicious homemade chocolates, plus cappuccinos and espressos.

Asian

Flor del Loto (Calle 46, tel. 506/2232-4652, 11am-3pm and 6pm-11pm Mon.-Fri., 11am-11pm Sat., 11am-9:30pm Sun., $7), in Sabana Norte, is the place if you like your Chinese food hot and spicy. Mouth-searing specialties include Shi Chuen-style pork as well as vegetables, bamboo shoots, and tofu stir-fried in sizzling hot-pepper oil.

Another good option is **King's Garden** (tel. 506/2255-3838, 11am-1am daily), adjoining the Centro Comercial Yaohan. The head chef is from Hong Kong; the menu features many favorites from the city as well as Cantonese and Szechuan dishes.

Italian

You could be in Milan or Rome at the elegant **L'Olivo** (tel. 506/2220-9440, noon-3pm and 6:30pm-10:30pm Mon.-Sat., $4-15), next to Hotel Palma Real on Sabana Norte. Serving superb pastas and seafood, some folks consider it the city's best Italian restaurant.

Mexican

Costa Rican families flock to inexpensive yet classy **Los Antojitos** (11:30am-10pm Mon.-Tues., 11:30am-11pm Wed.-Thurs., 11:30am-11:30pm Fri.-Sat., 11:30am-10pm Sun.). Meals start at $4, and a grilled tenderloin costs $10. It has four outlets in San José: west of Parque la Sabana in Rohrmoser (tel. 506/2231-5564); east of downtown in Los Yoses (tel. 506/2225-9525); in Centro Comercial del Sur in San Pedro (tel. 506/2227-4160); and north of town on the road to Tibas (tel. 506/2235-3961).

Middle Eastern

Acclaimed as one of the city's hippest restaurants, **Sash** (tel. 506/2230-1010, noon-midnight Mon.-Thurs., noon-3am Fri.-Sat.), in Centro Comercial Plaza Mema off Bulevar Rohrmoser, plays up a trendy take on Levantine decor and menu. Try the *mesa Lebanese* assortment of meats, salads, and veggies. I love its cozy arched alcoves with sofas. The place is usually full.

Nouvelle

Don't leave town without trying the ★ **Restaurante Grano de Oro** (Calle 30, Aves. 2/4, tel. 506/2255-3322, www.hotelgranodeoro.com, 7am-10pm daily), an elegant wood-paneled restaurant where French-born chef Francis Canal has successfully merged Costa Rican ingredients into an exciting fusion menu, heavy on surf and turf. The menu changes regularly and features such dishes as poached mahimahi with leeks, tenderloin in green peppercorn sauce, a superb salmon soufflé, and sweet curry chicken sprinkled with coconut. Try the specialty cocktails, and leave room for the sublime Pie Grano de Oro dessert. Huge windows open to an outdoor patio popular with hotel guests and local businesspeople for breakfasts and lunch. The superb Gringo breakfast—a large bowl of granola and bananas along with thick slices of freshly baked whole-wheat toast—should see you through the day.

Nearby at the chic **Iconos Café Bar** (tel. 506/2247-2000, 5am-10pm daily) at Hotel Parque del Lago, sophisticated decor is matched by gourmet Costa Rican dishes that include cream of sweet corn soup ($5.50), mahimahi with green plantain crunch ($14), and pumpkin cheesecake with honey ($5.50). It's also a great breakfast spot.

★ **Park Café** (Calle 44, tel. 506/2290-6324, www.parkcafecostarica.blogspot.com, 5:30pm-9pm Tues.-Sat.), off Sabana Norte, ranks among the finest restaurants in the country. Set in an antique store with a courtyard garden, its contemporary styling (not to mention the setting) is bold and exciting. Michelin-starred English chef Richard Neat (with his wife, Louise) conjures up divine tapas and globe-spanning dishes. Lunch might include a roasted tuna fillet with ginger chutney and artichoke salad under the shade of the flowering orchid tree, while candlelit dinner might be *ballotine* of foie gras with grilled sweet corn.

Seafood and Steaks

For a cheap meal, check out **Marisquería La**

Princesa Marina (tel. 506/2296-7667, 11am-10:30pm Mon.-Sat., 11am-9pm Sun., $1-9), on Sabana Oeste. This canteen-like seafood spot is a favorite of Ticos at lunch. It serves from a wide menu and wins no gourmet prizes, but at least it will fill you up.

Spanish and South American

One of my favorite restaurants is ★ Machu Picchu (Calle 32, Aves. 1/3, tel. 506/2283-3679, www.restaurantemachupicchu.com, 10am-10pm Mon.-Sat., 11am-6pm Sun.), for authentic Peruvian seafood. Try the superb ceviche ($2.50-5) or the *picante de mariscos* (seafood casserole with onions, garlic, olives, and cheese). The menu is moderately priced (some potato entrées are less than $4; garlic octopus is $6), and the *pisco* sours are powerful. For a refreshing equivalent to lemonade, try the delicious *chicha morada*, made with boiled pineapple and other fruits.

Vegetarian

The superb ★ Restaurante Vishnu (Ave. 1, Calles 1/3, tel. 506/2223-4434, 7am-9:30pm Mon.-Sat., 9am-8pm Sun.) serves health-food breakfasts, lunches, and dinners. Meals are generous in size and low in price (a *casado* costs $4); the menu includes veggie lasagna, veggie burgers, and fruit salads. Vishnu has 10 other outlets around town, including at Calle 14, Avenida Central/2; and at Calle 1, Avenida 4.

EAST OF DOWNTOWN
Cafés and *Sodas*

One of the best spots is Bagelmen's (Ave. 2, Calle 33, tel. 506/2224-2432, www.bagel-menscr.com, 7am-9pm daily), in Barrio La California; it also has an outlet in eastern San Pedro. The Costa Rican equivalent of Starbucks, it combines a hip ambience with a simple yet appealing menu featuring Reuben, tuna, smoked ham, and other sandwiches ($2-5), plus bagels (onion, pumpernickel), muffins, brownies, cinnamon rolls, and breakfast specials, from *gallo pinto* to scrambled eggs.

In Los Yoses I'm fond of Café Ruisenor (Ave. Central, Calles 41/43, tel. 506/2225-2562,

7am-8pm Mon.-Fri., 8am-6pm Sat., 10am-6pm Sun.), a classy, trendy spot serving a range of coffee drinks that include lattes ($1.75) as well as soups, salads, sandwiches, and entrées such as curried chicken, sea bass with herbs and white wine, and pepper steak. Desserts include banana splits, German apple tart, and parfaits.

Costa Rican

Not many restaurants in San José serve Caribbean fare. An exception, and a fantastic one at that, is Whapin' (Calle 35, Ave. 13, tel. 506/2283-1480, 8am-10pm Mon.-Fri., 11am-10pm Sat.), in Barrio Escalante, serving up delicious Caribbean cooking in no-frills surroundings. Many dishes are cooked in coconut milk, such as *rondon* stew, and even classic chicken, rice, and beans.

French and Mediterranean

Exuding romantic ambience with its dark wainscoting and soft lighting, the bistro-style Olio (Calle 33, Ave. 3/5, tel. 506/2281-0541, 11:30am-11pm Mon.-Wed., 11:30am-11:45pm Thurs., 11:30am-12:30am Fri., 5:30pm-12:30am Sat., $5-12), 200 meters (660 feet) north of Bagelmen's in Barrio Escalante, specializes in Spanish tapas and Mediterranean fare, such as a Greek meze plate. Meat lovers should try the *arrollado siciliano*—a fillet of steak stuffed with sun-dried tomatoes, spinach, and mozzarella. Olio has a large wine list and a small patio.

Latin American

I love the combination of ambience and cuisine at Chancay (tel. 506/2225-4046, www.chancay.info, noon-3:30pm and 6:30pm-10:30pm Mon.-Thurs., noon-11pm Fri.-Sat., noon-9:30pm Sun.), located in Plaza Antares in the Monte de Oca district. The venue is a sleek 21st-century building with heaps of plate glass and stainless steel. Live musicians play Peruvian tunes. I've enjoyed appetizers of thin-sliced potato in cheese sauce and hot pepper ($6.25) and a great corvine *limeña* entrée—sea bass with mashed white beans and red pepper sauce ($15).

Information and Services

INFORMATION

ICT, the Costa Rican Tourist Board (beside the expressway in the La Uruca district, tel. 506/2299-5800), operates a visitor information booth (tel. 506/2443-2883) at Juan Santamaría Airport. It has a tiny office in the Centro de Conservación (Ave. Central, Calles 1/3, 9am-5pm Mon.-Fri.), 50 meters (165 feet) northwest of Plaza de la Cultura.

Travel Agencies

There are dozens of English-speaking travel agencies in San José. They can arrange city tours, one-day and multiday excursions, beach resort vacations, air transportation, and more. I recommend American-run **Costa Rica Expeditions** (Ave. 3, Calles 25/29, tel. 506/2521-6099, www.costaricaexpeditions.com), in the Antigua Aduana.

Emergencies

The privately run **Hospital Clínica Bíblica** (tel. 506/2522-1000, www.clinicabiblica.com) is the best hospital in town and accepts U.S. Medicare. Most foreigners head to the impressive **Hospital Cima** (tel. 506/2208-1000, www.hospitalcima.com), beside the *autopista* in Escazú, west of San José.

The public **Hospital Dr. Calderón Guardia** (tel. 506/2257-7922) and **Hospital México** (tel. 506/2242-6700) are alternatives, as is the public **Hospital San Juan de Díos** (Paseo Colón, Calle 16, tel. 506/2257-6282), the most centrally located medical facility. They provide free emergency health care on the social security system. The **Hospital Nacional de Niños** (Children's Hospital, Paseo Colón, tel. 506/2222-0122, www.hnn.sa.cr) cares for children. Women are served by the **Hospital de la Mujer** (Calle Central, Ave. 22, tel. 506/2257-9111).

The **Policía Turística** (tel. 506/2227-4866, http://policiaturisticacr.blogspot.com) patrol downtown on bicycles and are based out of a small office at the Coca-Cola bus terminal (Ave. 3, Calle 16).

Mail

The main post office, or **Correo Central** (Calle 2, Aves. 1/3, tel. 506/2223-9766, www.correos.go.cr, 8am-5pm Mon.-Fri., 7:30am-noon Sat.), has a 24-hour stamp machine. You can also buy stamps and post your mail at the front desks of upscale hotels. **FedEx** (Paseo Colón, Calle 40, tel. 506/2239-0576, http://fedex.com/cr_english) and **DHL** (Paseo Colón, Calles 30/32, tel. 506/2209-6000, www.dhl.co.cr/en.html) offer courier services.

Money

San José has dozens of **banks.** Most have a separate foreign exchange counter, will give cash advances against your Visa card (and in some cases, your MasterCard), and have **ATMs** that issue cash from your checking account or advances against credit cards.

Edificio Correo (Post Office)

Outside banking hours, head to **Teledolar Casa de Cambio** (Paseo Colón, Calle 24, tel. 506/2248-1718, 8:30am-4pm Mon.-Sat., 8:30am-2pm Sun.), which changes foreign currency.

Credomatic (Calle Central, Aves. 3/5, tel. 506/2295-9898, www.credomatic.com) will assist you with card replacement for Visa and MasterCard.

Transportation

GETTING THERE AND AWAY
Air
Juan Santamaría International Airport (SJO, tel. 506/2437-2400, www.aeris.cr) is on the outskirts of Alajuela, 17 kilometers (11 miles) west of San José. There is a **ICT Visitor Information Booth** (tel. 506/2443-2883, 9am-5pm Mon.-Fri.) in the baggage-claim area. There's a bank in the departure terminal and exchange bureaus in the baggage claim area, but they offer lousy rates and take 10 percent more than the bank and hotel exchange rates; in any event, there's no urgency to change money here as you can operate with dollars virtually anywhere in Costa Rica. Taxis accept dollars, but you'll need local currency for public buses into San José.

Tobías Bolaños Airport (SYQ, tel. 506/2232-2820), in Pavas, about four kilometers west of town, is used for domestic flights, including by Nature Air, small charter planes, and air taxis. Bus 14B runs from Avenida 1, Calles 16/18, and stops in Pavas, a short walk from the airport.

The airline **Grupo TACA** (tel. 506/2299-8222, 8am-8pm Mon.-Fri., 8am-5pm Sat., 8am-5pm Sun.) has a reservations center at Calle 40 and Avenida de las Américas.

Car
Westbound from downtown San José, **Paseo Colón** feeds right onto the **Pan-American Highway** (Hwy. 1, or Autopista General Cañas), which leads to the Pacific coast, Guanacaste, and Nicaragua. A tollbooth just east of Juan Santamaría Airport charges 60

colones ($0.12) per vehicle for westbound traffic only.

Carretera Prospero Fernández runs west from Parque Sabana past Escazú, becoming a toll expressway—**Autopista San José-Caldera** (Autopista del Sur), leading to the Pacific lowlands. Alas, the 77-kilometer-long (48-mile-long) highway was badly conceived with one-lane bridges and poorly constructed, and it is subject to landslides. There are several toll booths; the total cost to drive the entire distance is about $3.50.

Calle 3 leads north from downtown and becomes the **Guápiles Highway** (Hwy. 32) for Puerto Limón and the Caribbean and Northern Zone. **Avenida 2** leads east via San Pedro to Cartago and the southern section of the **Pan-American Highway** (Hwy. 2), bound for Panamá; there's a tollbooth (60 colones/$0.12) about three kilometers (2 miles) east of the suburb of San Pedro.

Bus
San José has no central terminal. Buses for Puerto Limón and the Caribbean depart from the **Gran Terminal del Caribe** (Calle Central, Aves. 15/17). Most buses to other destinations leave from the area referred to as **Coca-Cola** (centered on Ave. 3, Calles 16/18, but encompassing many surrounding streets); there's a 24-hour **police station,** tel. 506/2257-3096. Other buses leave from the bus company office or a street-side bus stop (*parada*). Many street departure points are unmarked, so ask locals.

A Safe Passage/Viaje Seguro (tel. 506/8365-9678 or 506/2440-2414, www.costaricabustickets.com) will make your bus

San José Bus Terminals

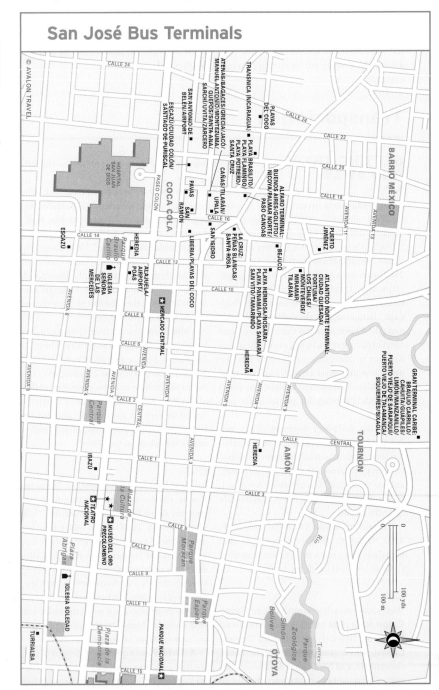

© AVALON TRAVEL

CALLE 24

TRANSNICA (NICARAGUA)

PLAYAS DEL COCO

ATENAS/BAGACES/GRECIA/JACO/
MANUEL ANTONIO/MONTEZUMA/
QUEPOS/SANTA ANA/
SARCHI/UVITA/ZARCERO

SAN ANTONIO DE BELEN/AIRPORT

ESCAZU/CIUDAD COLON/
SANTIAGO DE PURISCAL

PLAYA BRASILITO/
PLAYA FLAMINGO/
PLAYA POTRERO/
SANTA CRUZ

CANAS/TILARAN/
UPALA

PAVAS

SAN RAMON

LIBERIA/PLAYAS DEL COCO

SAN ISIDRO

HOSPITAL SAN JUAN DE DIOS

COCA COLA

PASEO COLON

ESCAZU

CALLE 14

HEREDIA

BRAULIO CARRILLO

Parque
Braulio
Carrillo

IGLESIA SEÑORA DE LAS MERCEDES

ALAJUELA/ AIRPORT/ POAS

CALLE 12

CALLE 16

CALLE 10

CALLE 8

CALLE 6

CALLE 4

CALLE 2

CALLE 24

CALLE 22

CALLE 20

CALLE 18

BARRIO MÉXICO

AVENIDA 13

AVENIDA 11

ALFARO TERMINAL:
BUENOS AIRES/GOLFITO/
NICOYA/PALMAR NORTE/
PASO CANOAS

BEJUCO

PUERTO JIMENEZ

LA CRUZ/
PEÑAS BLANCAS/
SANTA ROSA

PLAYA HERMOSA/NOSARA/
PLAYA PANAMA/PLAYA SAMARA/
SAN VITO/TAMARINDO

ATLANTICO NORTE TERMINAL:
CIUDAD QUESADA/
FORTUNA/
LOS CHILES/
MONTEVERDE/
MIRAMAR/
TILARAN

HEREDIA

MERCADO CENTRAL

AVENIDA 6

AVENIDA 8

AVENIDA 4

AVENIDA 2

CENTRAL

AVENIDA 5

AVENIDA 7

AVENIDA 9

Parque Central

IRAZU

CALLE 1

CALLE 3

HEREDIA

CENTRAL

AMÓN

TOURNON

GRAN TERMINAL CARIBE:
BRAULIO CARRILLO/
CAHUITA/GUAPILES/
LIMON/MANZANILLO/
PUERTO VIEJO DE SARAPIQUI/
PUERTO VIEJO DE TALAMANCA/
SIQUIERRES/SIXAOLA

CALLE
CENTRAL

Río

Plaza de la Cultura

TEATRO NACIONAL

MUSEO DEL ORO PRECOLOMBINO

CALLE 5

CALLE 7

Parque Morazán

CALLE 9

CALLE 11

IGLESIA SOLEDAD

Plaza Abrigas

Parque España

Parque
Simón
Bolívar

Zoológica

OTOYA

Torres

TURRIALBA

Plaza de la Democracia

PARQUE NACIONAL

CALLE 15

0   100 yds
0   100 m

reservations and buy your tickets for you in advance. Tickets cost $25 single, $45-55 for a pair to anywhere in the nation. The company also offers airport transfers and a pickup and drop-off service to bus stops and stations in San José. The ICT publishes a bus schedule, including the companies and phone numbers.

GETTING AROUND
To and From the Airport
TAXI
Taxi Aeropuerto (tel. 506/2222-6865, www.taxiaeropuerto.com) operates taxis between Juan Santamaría Airport and downtown and accepts reservations 24 hours daily; they're orange (local San José taxis are red). The legally sanctioned fare into downtown San José adjusts according to gasoline prices; at press time was $23 by day and night ($5 to Alajuela); you pay in advance at an official booth immediately outside the arrivals lounge and are given a ticket.

BUS
Red buses run by **Tuasa** (tel. 506/2222-5325) operate between downtown San José (Ave. 2, Calles 12/14) and Alajuela every five minutes via Juan Santamaría Airport, 5am-10pm daily, and then every 30 minutes 10pm-5am Monday-Saturday. The fare is 400 colones ($0.80). The driver will make change, but you'll need small bills or coins. The journey takes about 30 minutes. Luggage space is limited. A second company, **Station Wagon** (tel. 506/2442-3226), offers similar service using yellow buses, 4am-midnight daily.

SHUTTLE
Interbus (tel. 506/2283-5573, www.interbusonline.com) offers a 24-hour airport shuttle for $15 pp to and from San José by reservation. **Grayline** (tel. 506/2220-2126, www.graylinecostarica.com) operates an Airline Express ($12) linking Juan Santamaría Airport and downtown San José every 30 minutes. Some hotels offer free shuttles.

CAR RENTAL
Several car rental companies have offices as you exit customs at Juan Santamaría Airport; additional offices are within one kilometer (0.6 miles) east of the airport, in Río Segundo de Alajuela. If you plan on spending a few days in San José before heading off to explore the country, you'll be better off using taxis and local buses. Make your car reservations before leaving home.

Car
Car rental agencies in San José are concentrated along Paseo Colón. But don't even think about using a rental car for travel within San José; it entails too many headaches. Most places are quickly and easily reached by taxi, by bus, or on foot. Note that **Paseo Colón,** normally with two-way traffic, is one-way only—eastbound—6:30am-8:30am weekdays. A **peripheral highway** (*circunvalación*) passes around the south and east sides of San José.

Costa Rica implemented a *pico y placa* ("rush hour and license plate") law in 2005 as a way of reducing traffic congestion. All noncommercial private vehicles are banned from metropolitan San José 6am-7pm weekdays, based on the last number of their vehicle license plate, as follows: Monday 1 and 2; Tuesday 3 and 4; Wednesday 5 and 6; Thursday 7 and 8; Friday 9 and 0. Foreign visitors are not exempt. However, exemptions are made for cars owned by individuals with disabilities, buses, taxis, and motorcycles. Fines are currently about $13, but violators can supposedly be fined as often as they are pulled over on any given day.

Private **parking lots** offer secure 24-hour parking; you must leave your ignition key with the attendant. Never park in a no-parking zone, marked "Control por Grúa" (controlled by tow truck). Regulations are efficiently enforced.

Break-ins and **theft** are common; rental cars are especially vulnerable. Never leave anything of value in your car, even in the trunk.

Bus

San José has an excellent network of privately owned local bus services. Most buses operate 5am-10pm daily, with frequency of service determined by demand. Downtown and suburban San José buses operate every few minutes. Buses to the suburbs often fill up, so it's best to board at their principal downtown *parada*, designated by a sign, "Parada de Autobuses," showing the route name and number.

A sign in the windshield tells the route number and destination. Fares are marked by the doors and are collected when you board. Drivers provide change and tend to be honest. Buses cost 125-250 colones ($0.25-0.50) downtown and less than 100 colones elsewhere within the metropolitan area.

From the west, the most convenient bus into town is the **Sabana-Cementerio** service (route 2), which runs counterclockwise between Sabana Sur and downtown along Avenida 10, then back along Avenida 3 (past the Coca-Cola bus station) and Paseo Colón. The **Cementerio-Estadio** service (route 7) runs in the opposite direction along Paseo Colón and Avenida 2 and back along Avenida

12. Both take about 40 minutes to complete the circle.

Buses to **Los Yoses** and **San Pedro** run east along Avenida 2 and, beyond Calle 29, along Avenida Central. Buses to **Coronado** begin at Calle 3, Avenidas 5/7; to **Guadalupe** at Avenida 3, Calles Central/1; to **Moravia** from Avenida 3, Calles 3/5; and to **Pavas** from Avenida 1, Calle 18. Buses to **Escazú** depart Ave. 6, Calles 14/16 and also from Calle 16, Avenidas 1/3 every 30 minutes or so.

Be wary of pickpockets on buses.

Train

A great way to beat the cross-town traffic is to hop on the ~~Tren Interurbano~~ commuter train that links Pavas (on the west side of town) with San Pedro (on the east side). Trains depart the **Estación Ferrocarril Pacífico** (Pacific Station, Ave. 20, Calle Central/7, tel. 506/2257-6161, www.incofer.go.cr) and operate six times daily Monday-Friday and three times daily Saturday-Sunday ($0.25) in each direction, stopping at or near the U.S. Embassy, La Salle (south side of Parque la Sabana), and Universidad de Costa Rica (University of Costa Rica). Another service

traffic around Mall San Pedro

links the **Estación Ferrocarril Atlántico** (Atlantic Station, Ave. 3, Calle 21, no tel.) to Heredia, with 15 daily departures; a third service leaves the same station three times daily for Cartago.

Taxi

Licensed taxis are red (taxis exclusively serving Juan Santamaría Airport are orange); if it's any other color or lacks the inverted yellow triangle on the doors, it's a "pirate" taxi operating illegally. You can travel anywhere within the city for less than $8. The official rate at press time was 605 colones ($1.15) per kilometer. By law, taxi drivers (who must display a business card with their name, license plate, and other details) must use their meters (*marias*) for journeys of less than 12 kilometers (7.5 miles), but few do. Always demand that the taxi driver use the meter; otherwise you're going to get ripped off. A 20 percent surcharge is allowed at night. You do not normally tip taxi drivers in Costa Rica, but you can give your taxi driver any small change remaining after you pay the fare.

Finding a taxi is usually not a problem, except during rush hour and when it's raining. One of the best places is Parque Central, where they line up on Avenida 2, and in front of the Gran Hotel and Teatro Nacional, two blocks east. Avoid hailing a taxi on the street, as many drivers work in cahoots with robbers who hop into the cab. For a taxi, call **Coopetaxi** (tel. 506/2235-9966) or **Coopetico** (tel. 506/2224-7979).

There are reports of taxi drivers making sexual advances toward single women; this is more likely to happen with pirate taxis, which you should always avoid. Few taxis have functioning seat belts.

Bicycle

Fearless travelers might consider renting a bicycle. Until now, the city has not been bicycle-friendly, but in 2012 plans were announced to create a downtown bicycle path. Meanwhile, **ChepeCletas** (tel. 506/8849-8316, www.chepecletas.com) arranges bicycle get-togethers.

Estación Ferrocarril Atlántico

The Central Highlands

Themed beauty of the Central Highlands owes much to the juxtaposition of valley and mountain. The large, fertile central valley—sometimes called the Meseta Central (Central Plateau)—is a tectonic depression about 20 kilometers (12 miles) wide and 70 kilometers (43 miles) long. The basin is held in the cusp of verdant mountains that rise on all sides, their slopes quilted with dark-green coffee and pastures as bright as fresh limes. Volcanoes of the Cordillera Central frame the valley to the north, forming a smooth-sloped meniscus. To the south lies the massive blunt-nosed bulk of the Cordillera Talamanca. The high peaks are generally obscured by clouds for much of the "winter" months (May-Nov.). When clear, both mountain zones offer spectacularly scenic drives, including the chance to drive to the very crest of two active volcanoes, Poás and Irazú.

The Meseta Central is really two valleys in one, divided by a low mountain ridge—the Fila de Bustamente (or Cerro de la Carpintera)—which rises immediately east of San José. West of the ridge is the larger valley of the Río Poás and Río Virilla, with flanks gradually rising from a level floor. East of the ridge, the smaller Valle de Guarco (containing Cartago) is more tightly hemmed in and falls away to the east, drained by the Río Reventazón.

Almost 70 percent of the nation's populace lives here, concentrated in the four colonial cities of San José, Alajuela, Cartago, and Heredia, plus lesser urban centers that derive their livelihood from farming. Sugarcane, tobacco, and corn smother the valley floor, according to elevation and microclimate. Dairy farms rise up the slopes to more than 2,500 meters (8,200 feet). Small coffee fincas are also everywhere on vale and slope. Pockets of natural vegetation remain farther up the slopes and in protected areas such as Parque Nacional Braulio Carrillo, Parque Nacional Tapantí-Macizo de la Muerte, and other havens of untamed wildlife.

Although variations exist, an invigorating

Previous: blue morpho butterfly; Finca Rosa Blanca Coffee Plantation & Inn. **Above:** topiary in the plaza at Zarcero.

Look for ★ to find recommended
sights, activities, dining, and lodging.

Highlights

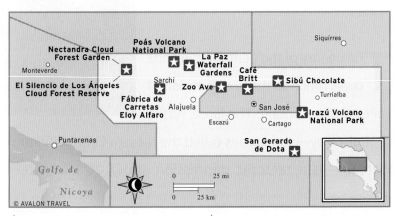

© AVALON TRAVEL

★ **La Paz Waterfall Gardens:** The world's largest butterfly enclosure, an aviary, snake and frog exhibits, hiking trails, and spectacular waterfalls highlight a visit to this nature theme park. It also has a fine restaurant and luxurious accommodations (page 94).

★ **Poás Volcano National Park:** Imagine—a drive-in volcano! You can park near the summit, then walk to the crater rim of this steaming volcano. As a bonus, you're provided with stupendous views (page 97).

★ **Fábrica de Carretas Eloy Alfaro:** At this astonishing workshop, traditional *carretas* (oxcarts) are made in traditional fashion, with power supplied by a waterwheel (page 102).

★ **Zoo Ave:** A Noah's Ark-ful of critters is displayed at this well-run zoo offering close-up encounters with animals you may not want to meet in the wild. All the favorites are here, from monkeys to the big cats (page 105).

★ **Nectandra Cloud Forest Garden:** This exquisitely manicured botanical garden amid a cloud forest is a perfect place to learn about montane ecology (page 107).

★ **El Silencio de Los Ángeles Cloud Forest Reserve:** Sloths, monkeys galore, and countless bird species inhabit this mist-shrouded, mountain-crest forest with nature trails, an INBio station, and a fantastic hotel (page 108).

★ **Café Britt:** Workers in campesino outfits provide an entertaining introduction to the world of coffee, beginning with theatrical skits and ending with your favorite beverage (page 112).

★ **Sibú Chocolate:** Watch artisans handcrafting delicious chocolates and thrill to a tasting that includes fascinating insight into the world of cacao and chocolate (page 121).

★ **Irazú Volcano National Park:** The drive up Irazú Volcano is a scenic switchback made more fun by the anticipation of magnificent views from the summit (page 124).

★ **San Gerardo de Dota:** Here you'll find a paradisiacal valley with a magnificent climate, a choice of delightful accommodations, and birdwatching—including quetzal-viewing—as good as anywhere in the nation (page 133).

and salubrious climate is universal. In the dry season, mornings are clear and the valley basks under brilliant sunshine. In the wet ("green") season, clouds typically form over the mountains in the early afternoon, bringing brief downpours. Temperatures average in the mid-20s Celsius (mid-high 70s Fahrenheit) year-round in the valley and cool steadily as one moves into the mountains, where coniferous trees lend a distinctly alpine feel.

PLANNING YOUR TIME

You could well spend two weeks touring the highlands, but for most folks three or four days should prove sufficient. Ideally you'll want your own car, although tour operators in San José offer excursions. Don't underestimate the time it can take to move between destinations: Roads are convoluted and signage is poor. Touring the highlands en route to another region makes sense; choose your destinations accordingly. The area has several superb boutique hotels, which make perfect bases for exploring on the hub-and-spoke principle. Seasonality is not a factor in deciding when to visit, as the area has year-round springlike temperatures, with a propensity to afternoon downpours in wet season (May-Oct.).

Northwest of San José, must-sees are **Parque Nacional Volcán Poás,** where you can peer into the bowels of a living volcano, **La Paz Waterfall Gardens**, and a visit to a coffee estate. You'll want a second base hotel if planning to visit the Cartago and Orosi or Turrialba region.

bromeliads in the Nectandra Cloud Forest Garden

Central Highlands

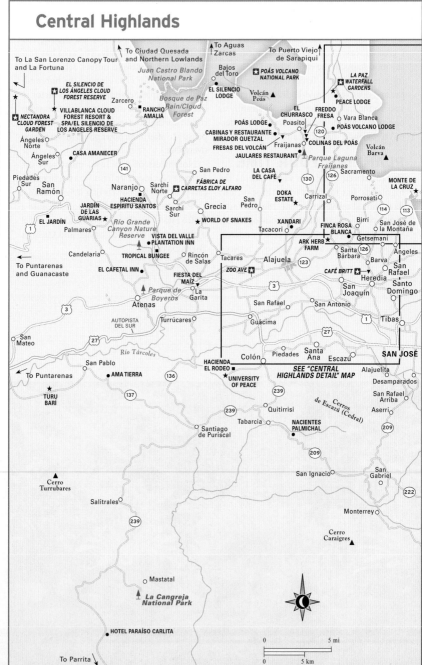

To La San Lorenzo Canopy Tour and La Fortuna

To Ciudad Quesada and Northern Lowlands

To Aguas Zarcas

To Puerto Viejo de Sarapiquí

Juan Castro Blando National Park

Bajos del Toro

★ POÁS VOLCANO NATIONAL PARK

LA PAZ WATERFALL GARDENS

EL SILENCIO DE LOS ÁNGELES CLOUD FOREST RESERVE

Zarcero

EL SILENCIO LODGE

Volcán Poás

PEACE LODGE

Bosque de Paz Rain/Cloud Forest

RANCHO AMALIA

VILLABLANCA CLOUD FOREST RESORT & SPA/EL SILENCIO DE LOS ÁNGELES RESERVE

EL CHURRASCO

FREDDO FRESA

NECTANDRA CLOUD FOREST GARDEN

Poasito

Vara Blanca

POÁS VOLCANO LODGE

Ángeles Norte

POÁS LODGE

Ángeles Sur

CASA AMANECER

CABINAS Y RESTAURANTE MIRADOR QUETZAL

(120)

COLINAS DEL POÁS

Fraijanas

Volcán Barva

Piedades Sur

San Ramón

(141)

San Pedro

FRESAS DEL VOLCÁN

JAULARES RESTAURANT

Parque Laguna Fraijanes

Sacramento

LA CASA DEL CAFÉ

(130)

(126)

MONTE DE LA CRUZ

FÁBRICA DE CARRETAS ELOY ALFARO

Naranjo

Sarchí Norte

San Pedro

DOKA ESTATE

Carrizal

Porrosatí

(114)

(113)

JARDÍN DE LAS GUARIAS

HACIENDA ESPÍRITU SANTOS

Sarchí Sur

Grecia

WORLD OF SNAKES

Birrí

San José de la Montaña

EL JARDÍN

(1)

Palmares

Río Grande Canyon Nature Reserve

XANDARI

Tacacori

FINCA ROSA BLANCA

Getsemaní

VISTA DEL VALLE PLANTATION INN

ARK HERB FARM

Santa Bárbara

(126)

Ángeles

Candelaria

Rincón de Salas

Tacares

Alajuela

(123)

Barva

San Rafael

To Puntarenas and Guanacaste

TROPICAL BUNGEE

EL CAFETAL INN

FIESTA DEL MAÍZ

ZOO AVE

CAFÉ BRITT

Heredia

Santo Domingo

Parque de Boyeros

La Garita

San Joaquín

Atenas

Turrúcares

AUTOPISTA DEL SUR

ZOO AVE

San Rafael

San Antonio

Guácima

(1)

Tibas

(3)

(27)

San Mateo

(27)

Río Tárcoles

Colón

Piedades

Santa Ana

Escazú

SAN JOSÉ

San Pablo

AMA TIERRA

(136)

HACIENDA EL RODEO

UNIVERSITY OF PEACE

SEE "CENTRAL HIGHLANDS DETAIL" MAP

Alajuelita

Desamparados

To Puntarenas

TURU BARÍ

(137)

(239)

Cerros de Escazú (Cedral)

San Rafael Arriba

Aserrí

(209)

(239)

Quitirrisí

Tabarcia

NACIENTES PALMICHAL

Santiago de Puriscal

(209)

San Ignacio

San Gabriel

(222)

Salitrales

(239)

Monterrey

Cerro Caraigres

Mastatal

La Cangreja National Park

HOTEL PARAÍSO CARLITA

To Parrita

Cerro Turrubares

0   5 mi

0   5 km

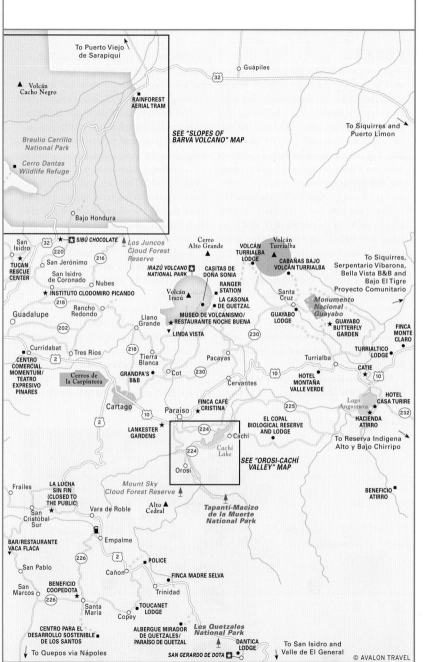

To Puerto Viejo
de Sarapiquí

○ Guápiles

32

▲ Volcán
Cacho Negro

■ RAINFOREST
AERIAL TRAM

SEE "SLOPES OF
BARVA VOLCANO" MAP

To Siquirres and
Puerto Limón

Braulio Carrillo
National Park

Cerro Dantas
Wildlife Refuge

○ Bajo Hondura

San
Isidro   32   ★ ■ SIBÚ CHOCOLATE   ▲ Los Juncos
220   Cloud Forest
★   ○ San Jerónimo   216   Reserve
TUCAN
RESCUE   San Isidro
CENTER   de Coronado   ○ Nubes
          ★ INSTITUTO CLODOMIRO PICANDO
218   Rancho
Guadalupe Redondo
          202
          ○ Curridabat ○ Tres Ríos
■ ★
CENTRO
COMERCIAL 2
MOMENTUM/
TEATRO
EXPRESIVO Cerros de
PINARES   la Carpintera
           218
Cartago   Tierra
           Blanca   ○ Cot
           GRANDPA'S
           B&B
           10
           2   Paraíso ○
           LANKESTER
           GARDENS   224

Cerro
Alto Grande
▲   VOLCÁN   Volcán
           TURRIALBA Turrialba
IRAZÚ VOLCANO ■   LODGE   CABAÑAS BAJO
NATIONAL PARK CASITAS DE   VOLCÁN TURRIALBA
               DOÑA SONIA
               RANGER
Volcán ▲   STATION   Santa
Irazú   LA CASONA   Cruz
               • DE QUETZAL
Llano   MUSEO DE VOLCANISMO/   GUAYABO
Grande ★ RESTAURANTE NOCHE BUENA   LODGE
         ▼ LINDA VISTA
                    230

To Siquirres,
Serpentario Vibarona,
Bella Vista B&B and
Bajo El Tigre
Proyecto Comunitario

■ Monumento
Nacional
Guayabo   GUAYABO
             BUTTERFLY   FINCA
             GARDEN   MONTE
                           CLARO
                           ■

Pacayas

230   Cervantes

FINCA CAFÉ
★ CRISTINA

○ Cachí

225

Cachí
Lake

Turrialba   TURRIALTICO
                LODGE ■
10
                ★ CATIE
HOTEL   10
MONTAÑA
VALLE VERDE

Lago   HOTEL
Angostura   CASA TURIRE
             HACIENDA   232
             ATIRRO

To Reserva Indígena
Alto y Bajo Chirripó

EL COPAL
BIOLOGICAL RESERVE
AND LODGE

SEE "OROSI-CACHÍ
VALLEY" MAP

○ Frailes
          LA LUCHA
          SIN FIN
          (CLOSED TO
          THE PUBLIC)   Vara de Roble ○
San   ★
Cristóbal   Alto ▲
Sur   Cedral
BAR/RESTAURANTE
VACA FLACA
▼
○ San Pablo
                226   ○ Empalme
                         2
○ San   BENEFICIO
Marcos   COOPEDOTA
            226   ★
            Santa   Cañón ○
            María
            ○ Copey
CENTRO PARA EL
DESARROLLO SOSTENIBLE ■
DE LOS SANTOS

↓ To Quepos via Nápoles

Mount Sky
Cloud Forest Reserve ▲

Tapantí-Macizo
de la Muerte
National Park

224   Orosi ○

BENEFICIO
ATIRRO ■

■ POLICE

FINCA MADRE SELVA ●

○ Trinidad

TOUCANET
LODGE ●

ALBERGUE MIRADOR   Los Quetzales
DE QUETZALES/   National Park
PARAÍSO DE QUETZAL ▲   DANTICA
                                   LODGE
SAN GERARDO DE DOTA ■ ○

To San Isidro and
Valle de El General ↓

© AVALON TRAVEL

Escazú and Vicinity

ESCAZÚ

Beginning only four kilometers (2.5 miles) west of San José's Parque Sabana, Escazú is officially part of metropolitan San José. However, it is divided from the capital by a hill range and river canyon and is so individualistic that it functions virtually as a sister city. The town is accessed by the Carretera Próspero Fernández (Hwy. 27), an expressway that passes north of Escazú and continues via Ciudad Colón to the Pacific lowlands.

There are actually three Escazús, each with its own church, patron saint, and character. **San Rafael de Escazú** is the ultramodern, congested lower town, nearest the expressway. A beautiful old church—**Iglesia Jiménez y Tandi**—stands surrounded by chic restaurants, shopping plazas, and condominium towers that have drawn scores of English-speaking expatriates. This is the classiest address in the entire country, as the many million-dollar homes and upscale condos attest.

San Rafael merges uphill and south to **San Miguel de Escazú,** the heart of old Escazú.

San Miguel was originally a crossroads on trails between indigenous villages. The indigenous people gave it its name, Itzkatzu (Resting Place). A small chapel constructed in 1711 became the first public building. Here, time seems to have stood still for a century. The occasional rickety wooden oxcart weighed down with coffee beans comes to town, pulled by stately oxen. Cows wander along the road. There are still a few cobblestone streets with houses of adobe, including those around the village plaza with its red-domed church, built in 1799 and painted with a traditional strip of blue color at the bottom to ward off witches. The church has a new frontage in a modern style with twin towers and overlooks the **Parque República de Colombia.**

Above San Miguel, the road climbs steadily to **San Antonio de Escazú,** a dairy and agricultural center beyond which the steep slopes are clad in coffee bushes and cloud forest. Farther uphill rises Monte La Cruz (topped by an imposing 15-meter-tall/50-foot-tall iron cross), Piedra Blanca, Cerro Rabo de Mico

colonial-era church in San Rafael de Escazú

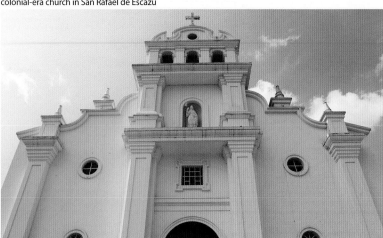

Rafael de Escazú, wildlife rescue center **Refugio Herpetológico de Costa Rica** (tel. 506/2282-4614, www.refugioherpeto-logico.com, 9am-4pm Tues.-Sun., adults $14, students $11, children $7) cares for animals and birds seized by the Ministry of the Environment from poachers and illegal captivity. Although it mostly exhibits snakes, it also has crocodiles, turtles, monkeys, and toucans. Guided tours are offered.

Entertainment and Events

Escazú is a happening spot for young Josefinos with cash to throw around. Hip-hoppin' **Centro Comercial Trejos Montealegro** has several clubs, such as **Órale** (tel. 506/2228-6436, 5:30pm-1am Mon.-Tues., 5:30pm-2am Wed., 5:30pm-4am Thurs., 5:30pm-6am Fri.-Sat.), with lively music and an outdoor bar that claims the "best margaritas south of Mexico." The most sophisticated disco is **Luxe** (tel. 506/2288-4849, 9pm-6am Thurs.-Sat.), on the north side of the expressway in San Rafael and perfect for dancing till dawn.

Jazz-loving bohemians head to the **Jazz Café** (tel. 506/2288-4740, www.jazzcafecos-tarica.com), about 400 meters (0.25 miles) east of Plaza Itzkazú. The lineup features everyone from hot locals to Cuban superstar Chucho Valdés.

On Christmas Day, a hydraulic engine is employed to move singular figures—including a headless priest, the devil spinning a Ferris wheel, the corpse who opens his coffin, and a carousel, all elements of a Nativity celebration—in front of Iglesia San Antonio (in San Antonio de Escazú).

The **Día de los Boyeros** festival (second Sun. in Mar.) pays homage to *boyeros,* the men who guide the traditional oxcarts to market. More than 100 *boyeros* from around the country trim their colorful carts and gather for this celebration, which includes an oxcart parade helped along by a supporting cast of women and children in traditional garb, plus a musical accompaniment of *ci-marronas,* the traditional instrument mandatory for popular feasts.

Parroquia San Miguel de Escazú

(the tallest, at 2,455 meters/8,054 feet), and Cerro de Escazú, fluted with waterfalls.

The real estate boom here has been ferocious, typified by the 2010 opening of **Avenida Escazú** (tel. 506/2288-0101, www.avenidaescazu.com), an upscale multifunction development of 12 high-rise buildings housing boutiques, hotels, offices, medical facilities, and even an IMAX theater.

Sights

In the hills of Bello Horizonte, **Barry Biesanz Woodworks** (tel. 506/2289-4337, www.biesanz.com, 8am-5pm Mon.-Fri., 9am-3pm Sat.) is the workshop of one of Costa Rica's leading wood designers and craftspeople. Barry Biesanz and his workers turn native hardwoods into beautiful bowls, boxes, and furniture. His boxes and bowls grace the collections of three U.S. presidents, Pope John Paul II, and assorted European royalty.

On the old road to Santa Ana, about four kilometers (2.5 miles) west of San

Escazú

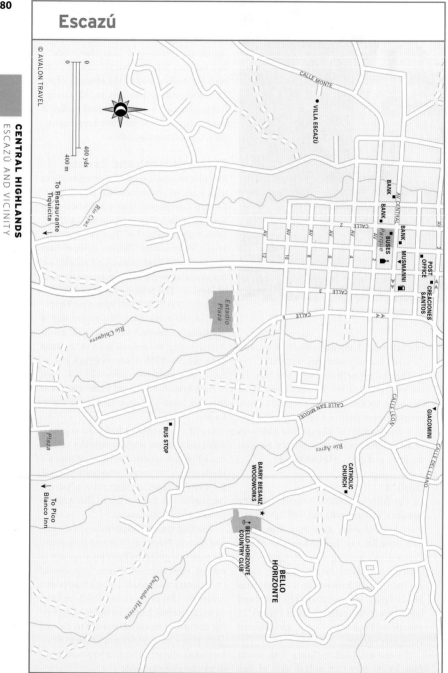

© AVALON TRAVEL

0   400 yds
0   400 m

To Restaurante
Tiquicia

CALLE MONTE

VILLA ESCAZÚ

Río Chiquero

Estadio
Plaza

Plaza

BUS STOP

To Pico
Blanco Inn

Quebrada Herrera

Río Agres

CALLE SAN MIGUEL

BARRY BIESANZ
WOODWORKS

CATHOLIC
CHURCH

GIACOMINI

CALLE LEÓN

CALLE DEL LLANO

BELLO HORIZONTE
COUNTRY CLUB

BELLO
HORIZONTE

BANK

BANK

BANK

BUSES

MUSMANNI

Parque

AV CENTRAL

POST
OFFICE

CREACIONES
SANTOS

CALLE

AV

CALLE

CALLE

AV

AV

AV

12

10

8

6

4

2

3

5

3

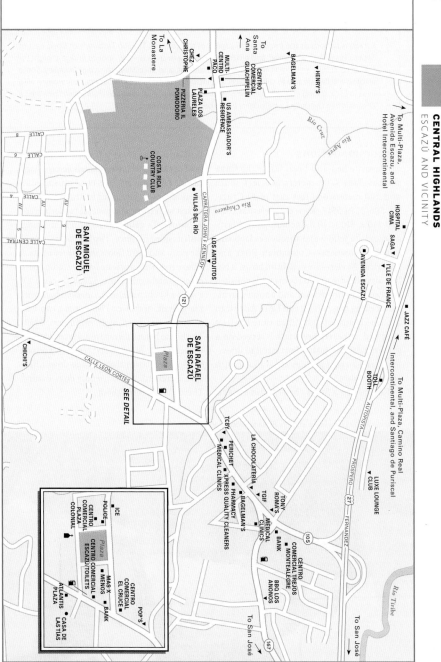

To Santa Ana

To La Monastere

To Multi-Plaza, Avenida Escazú, and Hotel Intercontinental

BAGELMAN'S

HENRY'S

CHEZ CHRISTOPHE

MULTI CENTRO PACO

CENTRO COMERCIAL GUACHIPELIN

PIZZERIA IL POMODORO

PLAZA LOS LAURELES

US AMBASSADOR'S RESIDENCE

COSTA RICA COUNTRY CLUB

VILLAS DEL RIO

LOS ANTOJITOS

CARRETERA JOHN F KENNEDY

Río Cruz

Río Agres

HOSPITAL CIMA

SAGA

ÎLE DE FRANCE

AVENIDA ESCAZÚ

JAZZ CAFÉ

CALLE 8

CALLE 6

CALLE 4

AV 5

AV 7

AV 9

CALLE CENTRAL

SAN MIGUEL DE ESCAZÚ

Río Chiquero

121

SAN RAFAEL DE ESCAZÚ

Plaza

CALLE LEON CORTES

CHICH'S

SEE DETAIL

To Multi-Plaza, Camino Real Intercontinental, and Santiago de Puriscal

TOLL BOOTH

LUXE LOUNGE CLUB

AUTOPISTA

PROSPERO

27

FERNANDEZ

TCBY

PERICHET

XPRESS QUALITY CLEANERS

MEDICAL CLINICS

LA CHOCOLATERIA

BAGELMAN'S

PHARMACY

TONY ROMA'S

TGIF

MEDICAL CLINICS

BANK

CENTRO COMERCIAL MONTEALEGRE

105

BBQ LOS ANONOS

To San José

Río Tiribe

ICE

POLICE

CENTRO COMERCIAL PLAZA COLONIAL

Plaza

CENTRO COMERCIAL ESCAZÚ/TOILETS

MAS X MENOS

BANK

CENTRO COMERCIAL EL CRUCE

POP'S

ATLANTIS PLAZA

CASA DE LAS TIAS

To San José

167

Witch Capital of Costa Rica

Escazú is famous as the *bruja* (witch) capital of the country. The Río Tiribí, which flows east of Escazú, is said to be haunted, and old men still refuse to cross the Los Anonos Bridge at night for fear of La Zegua, an incredibly beautiful enchantress, and Mico Malo, the magic monkey. Some 60 or so witches are said to still live in Escazú, including Doña Estrella, who says, "Any woman who lives in Escazú long enough eventually becomes a *bruja*." Amorous travelers should beware La Zegua: When the unlucky suitor gets her to bed, she turns into a horse.

Accommodations

My favorite bed-and-breakfast is the **Casa de Las Tías** (200 meters/660 feet south and 200 meters/660 feet east of El Cruce, tel. 506/2289-5517, www.casadelastias.com, $90-110 s, $100-110 d, including breakfast), an exquisite yellow-and-turquoise clapboard home. Its owners—Colombian Pilar and American Xavier—are delightful hosts. It has five airy wood-paneled rooms with polished hardwood floors, wicker and antique furniture, ceiling fans, Wi-Fi, and Latin American art. The beautiful light-filled suite boasts a king bed. A hearty breakfast is served on a garden patio. It's just a short stroll to downtown, and airport pickups are available with advance notice.

Resembling a Swiss chalet, **Villa Escazú**

Bed and Breakfast (off Calle Monte, tel./fax 506/2289-7971, www.hotels.co.cr/villaescazu, 2-night minimum, $49-65 s/d, including breakfast) boasts stunning hardwood interiors mixed with rustic and tasteful modern decor. A "minstrel's gallery" overhangs the lounge with its stone fireplace. Two bedrooms on both the main and third floors share three baths. A deluxe room has a private bath; a studio apartment (5-night minimum, $225) has cable TV, a sofa, a kitchenette, and a modern bath with a large walk-in shower. There's also a two-bedroom apartment (5-night minimum, $250). The house boasts a wraparound veranda with wicker chairs. Breakfast is served on a terrace overlooking lawns that cascade downhill to a fruit orchard. Guest-friendly dogs abound. There's Wi-Fi throughout.

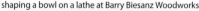

shaping a bowl on a lathe at Barry Biesanz Woodworks

Rhett and Scarlett would feel at home at the ★ **Grand Tara** (tel. 506/2288-6362, www. grandtaracostarica.com, low season from $80-130 s/d), high in the hills above Escazú. The Greek Revival plantation mansion (built in 1978 for Shah Mohammad Reza Pahlavi of Iran) has the most sensational views of any hotel around, and the 15 bedrooms boast antique rosewood tester beds and plenty of Old World charm. It also has 26 two-bedroom villas in classical style, all with fax machines, printers, and computers with Internet access. A penthouse suite offers a 360-degree view. Facilities include a gym, a pool, a cigar bar, a casino, and a restaurant. Health nuts will love the Garden Spa.

Alta (tel. 506/2282-4160, U.S. tel. 888-388-2582, www.thealtahotel.com, $105-142 s/d) is located on a hillside three kilometers (1.8 miles) west of Escazú on the old road to Santa Ana. This five-story hotel is lent a monastic feel by its hand-forged ironwork, whitewashed narrow corridors, and cathedral ceilings, but there's nothing ascetic about it's awesome decor. The 23 deluxe rooms (including four suites and a three-bedroom penthouse suite) display a fine contemporary aesthetic, and all have high-speed Internet or Wi-Fi. Some rooms hug the oval glass-tiled swimming pool in the shade of a spreading *guanacaste* tree. The acclaimed La Luz restaurant serves creole-fusion cuisine. There's a full-service spa.

The large-scale and deluxe **Intercontinental Costa Rica at Multipalza Mall** (tel. 506/2208-2100, www.ichotelsgroup.com/intercontinental, $207-541 s/d), off the Carretera Próspero Fernández expressway at Bulevár Camino Real, two kilometers (1.2 miles) west of Escazú, exudes contemporary opulence. It's perfect for travelers who want to have heaps of restaurants, shops, and entertainment options nearby. Each of the 372 air-conditioned rooms has a king bed with an orthopedic mattress, plus magnificent marble baths. The hotel—centered on a five-story atrium lobby—has many facilities, including four restaurants and an awesome clover-shaped pool with swim-up bar. Rates include breakfast, but Wi-Fi costs extra.

Food

Escazú is a center for fine dining, with dozens of great options. The scene is ever-changing.

A splendid breakfast or lunch option is **Bagelmen's** (tel. 506/2228-4460, www.bagelmenscr.com, 7am-9pm daily), 100 meters (330 feet) north of El Cruce, resembling Starbucks but also serving bagels (onion, pumpernickel, and others), muffins, brownies, and cinnamon rolls, plus breakfast specials such as *gallo pinto* and scrambled eggs. You can sit in the air-conditioned café or outside on a shady patio. It also has an outlet 200 meters (660 feet) north of Centro Comercial Guachipelín.

My favorite breakfast spot, however, is ★ **Chez Christophe** (tel. 506/2224-1773, 7am-7pm Tues.-Sat., 8am-6pm Sun.), a French bakery in Plaza de la Paco. It makes delicious croissants, waffles, omelets, quiches, and pastries, plus french toast that is out of this world. Go on Sunday for the social scene.

At ★ **La Luz** (tel. 506/2282-4160, www.thealtahotel.com, 6:30am-10pm daily, $7-25), in the Alta hotel, three kilometers (1.8 miles) west of Escazú on the old road to Santa Ana, chef Carlos Zuñiga's quality fusion cuisine melds Costa Rican ingredients with spicy creole influences. The setting is classy, the views splendid, and the service exemplary. Try the macadamia nut-crusted chicken in *guaro*-chipotle cream, or fiery garlic prawns in tequila-lime-butter sauce, followed by a chocolate macadamia tart. Sunday brunch (9am-4pm) is a special treat; there's live jazz on Saturday night.

Reservations are essential at **Le Monastère** (tel. 506/2228-8515, www.monastere-restaurant.com, 6:30pm-11pm Mon.-Sat.), which has been called a "religious dining experience," not for the cuisine but for the venue—a restored chapel amid gardens in the hills west of town off the Santa Ana road. The waiters dress like monks, and Gregorian chants provide background music. The French menu includes grilled lamb chops and vol-au-vent of asparagus. Expect to pay $30 pp.

For a far less pretentious hillside option, head up the mountain to the rustic **Restaurante Tiquicia** (tel. 506/2289-5839, www.miradortiquicia.com, noon-midnight Tues.-Thurs., noon-2am Fri.-Sat., noon-9pm Sun.), which entertains diners with folkloric dances (noon Tues.-Sun.) and live music (Fri.-Sat.). The food is simple, tasty, and traditional Costa Rican—and what a view!

★ **Saga** (Ave. Escazú, tel. 506/2208-6615, www.sagarestaurant.com, 11am-11pm Mon.-Sat., 11am-6pm Sun., $35), 100 meters (330 feet) east of CIMA hospital on the *autopista,* is a hip fusion restaurant that I love for its minimalist decor, leather banquette chairs, and glass walls. The dishes are works of art. Try the Oriental sea bass carpaccio or portobello mushroom cream soup ($9), followed by New Zealand lamb chops ($32) or duck breast.

For French cuisine I prefer the chic ambience of ★ **L'Ile de France** (Ave. Escazú, tel. 506/2289-7533, www.liledefrance.net, noon-11:30pm Mon.-Sat., 11:30am-7pm Sun. Mar.-Dec. 24), catercorner to Saga and with hip 21st-century decor. Chef Jean Claude works inspired magic, with such dishes as terrine de shrimp ($15), seafood bisque with cognac ($13.50), and coq au vin ($22).

For fresh seafood in an unpretentious setting, I head to ★ **Product C** (Edificio IMAX, Ave. Escazú, Escazú, tel. 506/2288-5570, www.product-c.com, noon-11pm Mon.-Sat., noon-6pm Sun.), where Canadian chef Damien Geneau delivers on a brilliant concept: 100 percent sustainable seafood dishes (all fish are hand-caught in the waters around Isla Chira). I savored marinated octopus ($7.25), ceviche ($6), carpaccio of trout with capers, and a fabulous sashimi. Daily specials might include blackened mackerel ($11) and fish tacos ($10). The restaurant doubles as a fish market, which provides the setting.

There are two chocolate specialty shops: **La Chocolatería** (tel. 506/2289-9637, www.lachocolatier.net, 8am-7pm Mon.-Fri., 10am-7pm Sat.), above El Cruce; and **Giacomini** (Calle de Llano, tel. 506/2288-3381, www.pasteleriagiacomin.com, 10am-7pm Mon.-Sat.), a superb coffee shop with a garden patio and waterfalls, in Belo Horizonte. It serves paninis ($5), croissants, salads, pastries, cappuccino, and espresso in addition to chocolate delights.

Getting There

Buses depart San José for Escazú from Avenida 1, Calle 18, every 15 minutes. The "Bebedero" bus departs San José from Calle 14, Avenida 6, for San Antonio de Escazú. A bus for San Rafael de Escazú departs Calle 16, Avenidas Central/1.

SANTA ANA TO CIUDAD COLÓN

Santa Ana, about five kilometers (3 miles) west of Escazú, is a sleepy town set in a sunny mountain valley. The church dates from 1870, and there are still many old adobe and wooden houses clad in bougainvillea. Today it is famous for ceramics; there are some 30 independent pottery shops in the area, many still using old-fashioned kick-wheels to fashion the pots. However, the area all around the town itself (especially north toward San Antonio de Belén) is the fastest-growing (and trendiest) area in the nation: a center for high-tech service industries, new shopping malls, hip new hotels—and traffic jams.

Continuing west you reach **Piedades,** about five kilometers (3 miles) west of Santa Ana. This peaceful village has a beautiful church. The road gradually rises to **Ciudad Colón,** a neat little town about eight kilometers (5 miles) west of Santa Ana and where the **Julia and David White Artists Colony** (tel. 506/2249-1414, www.forjuliaanddavid.org) offers residential courses for artists.

Reserve Forestal el Rodeo, in the hills about five kilometers (3 miles) southwest of Ciudad Colón and part of a cattle estate called **Hacienda el Rodeo** (tel. 506/2249-1013, www.haciendaelrodeo.com, 10am-6pm Sat.-Sun. and holidays)—protects the largest remaining tract of virgin forest in the Meseta Central. It's a popular place to go horseback riding and draws local families en masse on weekends. A rustic restaurant serves Tico fare. One kilometer (0.6 miles) beyond Hacienda el Rodeo is the **University for Peace** (tel. 506/2205-9000, www.upeace.org, 8am-4:30pm Mon.-Fri.), charged with the mission of global education and research in support of the peace and security goals of the United Nations and contributing to building a culture of peace. The 303-hectare (749-acre) facility includes botanical gardens containing busts of famous figures, such as Gandhi and Henry Dunant (founder of the Red Cross). Visitors are welcome (8am-4pm daily, $0.75); follow the road that passes the entrance gate and you'll arrive at the **Monument for Disarmament, Work, and Peace**, set around a lake full of geese.

Accommodations

You'll enjoy lovely views from **Hotel El Marañon** (tel. 506/2249-1271, www.cultourica.com, $45 s, $60 d), a few kilometers west of Piedades in the hillside hamlet of La Trinidad. This understated German-owned retreat is popular for its Spanish-language courses, on-site. It has 14 rooms done up in lovely tropical pastels. There's also a three-room apartment with a kitchen ($75). Hammocks are slung beneath *ranchitos* in the orchard garden.

Hotel Posada Canal Grande (tel. 506/2282-4089, www.hotelcanalgrande. com, $58 s, $78 d) is on an old coffee finca 800 meters (0.5 miles) north of the church in Piedades. A Florentine art collector operates the two-story villa-hotel, which boasts an old terra-cotta tile floor, antique furnishings, plump leather chairs, and a fireplace that transport you to Tuscany. The 12 bedrooms have parquet wood floors, exquisite rattan-framed queen beds with Guatemalan bedspreads, and wide windows offering views toward the Golfo de Nicoya. Italian taste is everywhere, from the chic furniture to the classical vases overflowing with flowers. There's a large pool in grounds mantled in coffee and fruit trees.

Bohemians who like things eclectic and eccentric might consider **Corteza Amarilla Art Lodge & Spa** (tel. 506/2203-7350, www.cortezaamarillalodge.com, junior suite $142 s/d, suite $181 s/d), five kilometers (3 miles) west of Santa Ana on the main San José-Colón road. This rambling offbeat charmer has 12 spacious air-conditioned rooms and suites with

bust of Mahatma Gandhi at the University for Peace, Ciudad Colón

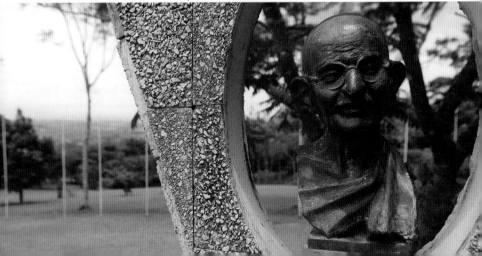

stone-walled showers set amid a tropical fantasia. Wi-Fi, blow-dryers, and coffeemakers are standard. However, some rooms get hot.

When I want to be pampered, I opt for ★ **Casa Bella Rita Boutique B&B** (tel. 506/2249-3722, www.casabellarita.com, low season $109-139 s/d, high season $119-139 s/d), at Brasil de Santa Ana. Owners Steve and Rita bring 50 years of restaurant experience to their intimate bed-and-breakfast as well as a lovely (and very colorful) aesthetic to the six individually styled rooms and public lounges. The Canopy Room, the largest, has a king and a queen bed and heaps of light; the Mariposa Room boasts a garden shower. All have air-conditioning, ceiling fans, iPod stations, and cable TV. Steve and Rita are fabulous hosts who serve amazing breakfasts and provide such thoughtful touches as bathrobes and a free airport shuttle. There's a lovely patio garden with a small pool and lounge chairs overlooking the canyon of the Río Virilla.

Food

Corteza Amarilla Fine Dining (tel. 506/2203-7350, www.cortezaamarillalodge.com, 7am-10pm daily), at the Corteza Amarilla Art Lodge & Spa, five kilometers (3 miles) west of Santa Ana on the main San José-Colón road, is known for its artfully presented gourmet fusion cuisine, such as gravlax of salmon ($6), Mediterranean octopus carpaccio ($10), and penne pasta with shrimp and scallops ($20). The menu displays a Hindu influence. Meals are delicious and artfully presented.

The in-vogue place to dine is ★ **Bacchus** (Calle Lajas at Calle 6, tel. 506/4001-5418, www.bacchus.cr, noon-3pm and 6pm-11pm Mon.-Fri., noon-11pm Sat., noon-9pm Sun.), a Mediterranean-themed, Italian-run restaurant and pizzeria considered one of the best restaurants in the country. Housed in a converted colonial home furnished in contemporary style, this classy eatery delivers consistently excellent nouvelle dishes. I enjoyed a tuna tartare appetizer ($11.50), three-mushroom soup ($10), and gnocchi *de espinaca* (spinach, $13). This is sophisticated dining at its best.

Getting There

Empresa Comtrasuli (tel. 506/2258-3903) buses to Ciudad Colón and Santiago de Puriscal depart San José from Calle 20, Avenidas 3/5, every 30 minutes 5am-10:30pm Monday-Saturday. Driving, take the Santa Ana exit off the Carretera Próspero Fernández expressway. From Escazú, take the road west from El Cruce in San Rafael.

SANTIAGO DE PURISCAL

Beyond Ciudad Colón the road snakes into the mountains and the town of Santiago de Puriscal, an important agricultural town 20 kilometers (12 miles) west of Ciudad Colón and gateway to the **Reserva Indígena Quitirrisí** (Quitirrisí Indigenous Reserve), protecting the land of the Quitirrisí indigenous community on the slopes of Cerro Turrubares. They sell fine baskets and other weavings at roadside stalls.

From Santiago you can follow a paved road southwest to **Salitrales,** 18 kilometers (11 miles) west of Santiago. Due west from Santiago, another road snakes through the mountains and descends to Orotina via San Pablo de Turrubares. By continuing south 11 kilometers (7 miles) beyond Salitrales and turning east, you arrive at **Rancho Mastatal Environmental Learning Center and Lodge** (tel. 506/2416-6263, www.ranchomastatal.com), an 89-hectare (219-acre) farm and private wildlife refuge. Rancho Mastatal has seven kilometers (4 miles) of wilderness trails leading through pristine forest replete with wildlife. It offers environmental workshops and languages courses, and welcomes volunteers. Horses can be rented ($10, with a guide). You can overnight by camping or staying in an eclectic assortment of cabins.

Seeking a healthful spa retreat? Head to **Ama Tierra** (tel. 506/2419-0110, U.S. tel. 866-659-3805, www.amatierra.com, low season $140 s, $185 d, high season $165 s, $210 d), two kilometers (1.2 miles) east of San Pablo de

Turrubares and 19 kilometers (12 miles) west of Santiago de Puriscal, set in a 3.2-hectare (8-acre) estate with trails. Run by Colorado expats Bob and Jill Ruttenberg, it has 10 endearing albeit sparsely furnished duplex casita "junior suites" with whirlpool tubs. Health-conscious meals are served on a veranda with magnificent views. It specializes in yoga retreats and has an open-air dojo, plus a full-service spa.

Getting There and Around

The Ciudad Colón bus from San José continues to Santiago de Puriscal. The **Empresa Comtrasuli** (tel. 506/2258-3903) buses to Ciudad Colón depart San José from Calle 20, Avenidas 3/5, every 30 minutes 5am-10:30pm Monday-Saturday. **Jeep taxis** line the square in Santiago.

Cariari to La Guácima

CIUDAD CARIARI AND SAN ANTONIO DE BELÉN

Ciudad Cariari is centered on an important junction on the Autopista General Cañas, 12 kilometers (7.5 miles) west of San José and about five minutes' drive from Juan Santamaría Airport. Here are San José's leading conference center, a major shopping mall, a golf course, and three of the nation's longest-standing premium hotels. The 18-hole championship **Cariari Country Club** (tel. 506/2293-3211 or 506/2293-5585, www.clubcariari.com, 6am-5pm daily) golf course, open to public play, was designed by George Fazio; it charges $60 weekdays, $100 weekends.

From Ciudad Cariari, the road west leads five kilometers (3 miles) to **San Antonio de Belén**, a small unassuming town that has taken on new importance since the opening of Intel's microprocessor assembly plant in 1997, employing almost 3,000 people. The road system hereabouts is convoluted.

Accommodations

The gringo-owned **Belén Trailer Park** (tel. 506/2239-0421, RVs $16, camping $14 s/d), about one kilometer (0.6 miles) east of Belén Plaza, is Costa Rica's only fully equipped RV and camper site. It has hookups with electricity and water, plus laundry, hot showers, and secure parking.

Popular with tour groups and conventioneers, the **Wyndham Plaza Herradura** (tel. 506/2209-9800, http://wyndhamherradura.com, from $120 s/d), at Ciudad Cariari, adjoins the Cariari Convention Center. Recently remodeled, it now has chic 21st century styling in its 229 spacious air-conditioned rooms (including 28 suites) accented with dark hardwoods. As expected for a convention hotel, it's loaded with facilities, including a spa, large outdoor swimming pool, 10 night-lit tennis courts, and impressive entertainment facilities, including a casino. A shuttle runs to downtown.

Immediately south of the Herradura is the **Doubletree Cariari by Hilton** (tel. 506/2239-0022, http://doubletree1.hilton.com, from $129 s/d), offering similar contemporary styling and a similar range of amenities, including a championship golf course, tennis courts, and an Olympic-size pool. The 220 spacious air-conditioned rooms and 24 suites (all with Wi-Fi) are handsomely appointed. There are also two restaurants and a casino.

It's lovely setting amid a coffee plantation with a panoramic mountain vista is reason enough to choose the colonial-style **Costa Rica Marriott Hotel & Resort** (tel. 506/2298-0000, U.S. tel. 888-236-2427, www.marriotthotels.com, from $139 s/d), at Ribera de Belén, one kilometer (0.6 miles) northeast of San Antonio. This jewel has 290 rooms and nine suites, all with regal furnishings and Internet modems (but not Wi-Fi) plus French

Central Highlands Detail

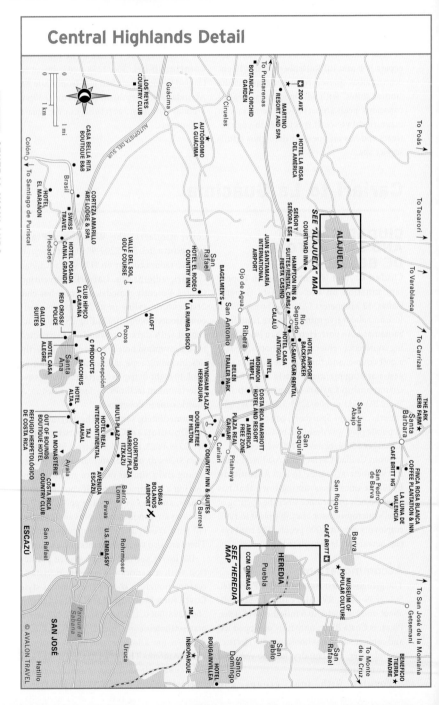

© AVALON TRAVEL

doors opening to a patio or balcony. It offers a golf practice range, an infinity swimming pool, three restaurants, tennis courts, a gym, and more.

Food

For traditional Costa Rican fare and charmingly rustic ambience, head to **El Rodeo** (tel. 506/2293-3909, www.elrodeohotel.com, noon-10pm Mon.-Sat., noon-4:45pm Sun.), two kilometers (1.2 miles) south of San Antonio de Belén on the road to Santa Ana. Decorated in traditional hacienda style and adorned with saddles and other rodeo-themed miscellany, it serves a wide-ranging menu that includes sliced tongue on a corn tortilla ($1), ceviche, and hot jalapeño cream tenderloin ($9).

Sakura (tel. 506/2209-9800, ext. 706, noon-3pm and 6pm-11pm Mon.-Sat., noon-10pm Sun.), in the Wyndham Plaza Herradura, at Ciudad Cariari adjoining the Cariari Convention Center, offers superb *teppan*-style Japanese cooking and an excellent sushi bar.

"Divine" sums up the artisanal chocolates and truffles at **Chocolate Nahua** (tel. 506/2293-3058, noon-7pm daily), an elegant boutique café and store in Centro Comercial Plaza Cariari, next to the Doubletree Cariari hotel. Indulge with locally made Sibu chocolates and a cappuccino or espresso.

Getting There

Buses depart San José for San Antonio de Belén from Avenida 1, Calles 20/22, hourly on the half hour, and every 15 minutes on weekends. Buses also depart Alajuela from Calle 10, Avenida Central.

LA GUÁCIMA

The road west from San Antonio de Belén continues to La Guácima, where local residents have painted buildings throughout the village with butterfly murals—art in the streets at its best. The art was the inspiration of Joris Brinkerhoff, founder of the Butterfly Farm, a local butterfly breeding center (the larvae are exported) now closed to the public.

In 2015, **Parque Viva** (tel. 506/4107-8482, http://parqueviva.com) opened as the nation's foremost entertainment and events center, with a performance amphitheater, plazas, and a race circuit that is an enhancement of the **Autódromo La Guácima**, the nation's main auto race track.

For La Guácima, buses depart hourly (less frequently Sun.) from Avenida 4, Calles 10/12, behind the Merced church in San José. Take the bus until the last stop (about one hour), from where you walk—follow the signs—about 400 meters (0.25 miles). From Alajuela, buses marked "La Guácima Abajo" depart from Calle 10, Avenida 2, seven times daily.

Alajuela and Vicinity

ALAJUELA

Alajuela (pop. 51,000) sits at the base of Volcán Poás, 20 kilometers (12 miles) northwest of San José and two kilometers (1.2 miles) north of Juan Santamaría Airport and the Pan-American Highway. First named La Lajuela in 1657, the town is known locally as La Ciudad de los Mangos for the mango trees around the main square. Today, Costa Rica's second city is a modestly cosmopolitan town with strong links to the coffee industry. Saturday is market day.

At the heart of town is **Parque Central,** officially called Plaza del General Tomás Guardia, with various busts of important locals from decades past. Twice weekly, music is played in the domed bandstand. Pretty 19th-century structures with fancy iron grilles surround the park. The square is backed by the red-domed colonial-era **Parroquia Nuestra Señora de Pilar** cathedral, where ex-presidents Tomás Guardia and León Cortés Castro are buried. It has some impressive religious statuary, including

Alajuela

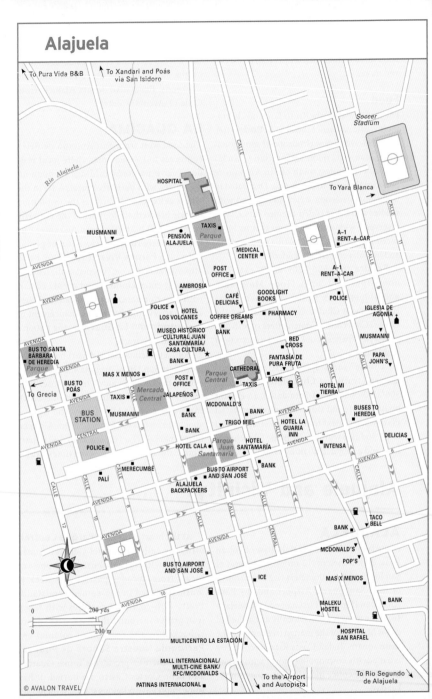

To Pura Vida B&B

To Xandari and Poás
via San Isidoro

Soccer
Stadium

Río Alajuela

HOSPITAL

To Yara Blanca

MUSMANNI

TAXIS
Parque

PENSIÓN
ALAJUELA

A-1
RENT-A-CAR

MEDICAL
CENTER

POST
OFFICE

A-1
RENT-A-CAR

AVENIDA

AMBROSIA

CAFÉ
DELICIAS

GOODLIGHT
BOOKS

POLICE

AVENIDA

POLICE
HOTEL
LOS VOLCANES

COFFEE DREAMS

PHARMACY

IGLESIA DE
AGONIA

MUSEO HISTÓRICO
CULTURAL JUAN
SANTAMARÍA/
CASA CULTURA

BANK

RED
CROSS

MUSMANNI

AVENIDA

BUS TO SANTA
BÁRBARA
DE HEREDIA
Parque

FANTASIA DE
PURA FRUTA

PAPA
JOHN'S

AVENIDA

MAS X MENOS

BANK

POST
OFFICE

Parque
Central

CATHEDRAL

TAXIS

BANK

HOTEL MI
TIERRA

To Grecia

BUS TO
POÁS

JALAPEÑOS

Mercado
Central

MCDONALD'S

BANK

HOTEL LA
GUARIA
INN

BUSES TO
HEREDIA

TAXIS

MUSMANNI

BANK

TRIGO MIEL

DELICIAS

BUS
STATION

CENTRAL

BANK

INTENSA

POLICE

HOTEL CALA

Parque
Juan
Santamaría

HOTEL
SANTAMARÍA

AVENIDA

MERECUMBE

BANK

PALÍ

BUS TO AIRPORT
AND SAN JOSÉ

ALAJUELA
BACKPACKERS

BANK

TACO
BELL

AVENIDA

BANK

MCDONALD'S

POP'S

BUS TO AIRPORT
AND SAN JOSÉ

AVENIDA

ICE

MAS X MENOS

BANK

MALEKU
HOSTEL

0   200 yds
0   200 m

HOSPITAL
SAN RAFAEL

AVENIDA

MULTICENTRO LA ESTACIÓN

MALL INTERNACIONAL/
MULTI-CINE BANK/
KFC/MCDONALDS

To the Airport
and Autopista

To Río Segundo
de Alajuela

© AVALON TRAVEL

PATINAS INTERNACIONAL

Parroquia Nuestra Señora de Pilar cathedral, Alajuela

a glass cabinet full of eclectic and macabre offerings to La Negrita. **Iglesia de Agonía,** in Greek Orthodox-meets-baroque style, is five blocks east.

Memories of Juan Santamaría, or "Erizo" (Hedgehog, referring to Santamaría's bristly hair), the homegrown drummer-boy hero of the Battle of 1856, figure prominently in Alajuela, notably in the **Museo Histórico Cultural Juan Santamaría** (Ave. 1, Calles Central/2, tel. 506/2441-4775, www.museo-juansantamaria.go.cr, 10am-5:30pm Tues.-Sun., free), housed in the former colonial city jail on the northwest corner of the Parque Central. This small museum tells the story of the War of 1856 against the no-good American adventurer William Walker. Call ahead to arrange a screening of an English-language film. Guided tours are given 9am-4:30pm Tuesday-Friday.

Two blocks south of Parque Central is **Parque Juan Santamaría** (Calle 2, Aves. 2/4), a tiny concrete plaza with a statue of the national hero rushing forward with a flaming torch and a rifle to defend the country against William Walker's ragtag army.

Entertainment and Events

The **Fiesta Casino** (tel. 506/2431-1455, www.fiesta.cr), by the Hampton Inn, 400 meters (0.25 miles) east of the airport, has slots and roulette, plus U.S. sports on the big screen and Las Vegas-style cabarets nightly. Happy hour runs 4pm-7pm daily.

For roller-skating, head to **Patines Internacional** (tel. 506/2443-8087, 7pm-10pm Mon.-Sat., 5pm-10pm Sun., $2.50), behind Mall Internacional on the airport boulevard.

Every April 11, **Juan Santamaría Day** is cause for celebration, with parades, bands, dancing, and arts and crafts fairs. The town also hosts the annual nine-day **Mango Festival** in July.

Soccer fans might join local fanatics at a **Liga Deportivo Alajuelense** (tel. 506/2443-1617, www.ida.cr) game at Estadio Alejandro Morera (Calle 9, Ave. 9).

Shopping

Señor & Señora Ese (2 kilometers/1.2 miles west of Alajuela, tel. 506/2441-8333, www.srysraese.com, free tours 8am-5:30pm daily), at Villa Bonita de Alajuela, is more than a mega souvenir store and factory; it's an experience: More than 280 employees craft everything from key rings to placemats from precious hardwoods. Stay for a traditional lunch ($6).

Accommodations

Alajuela does not lack for backpackers. Although it hardly looks like a hostel—it seems too upscale—the four-story **Alajuela Backpackers Boutique Hostel** (Ave. 4, Calle 4, tel. 506/2441-7149, www.alajuelabackpackers.com, dorm $14-19 pp, private room $55-70 s/d) is one of the fanciest backpackers' digs in Costa Rica. It has 21 rooms, most of them serene four-bed dorms. For privacy, opt for a king bed in a private room with a flat-screen TV. The fourth-floor beanbag Sky

Lounge is a cool place to sup some suds. It's one block west of Parque Juan Santamaría.

Of Alajuela's dozen or so budget hotels, I prefer the bargain-priced **Hotel Santamaría** (Ave. 4, Calle Central, tel. 506/2442-8388, www.santamariacr.com, $35 s, $40 d), a lovely yet simple hotel kept impeccably clean. It has a great location on the south side of Parque Juan Santamaría. Guest rooms have colorful bedspreads, cable TV, and private baths.

Another charmer is **Hotel Los Volcanes** (Ave. 3, Calles Central/2, tel. 506/2441-0525, www.hotellosvolcanes.com, shared bath $35 s, $46 d, private bath $46-64 s, $60-74 d), facing the museum. Housed in a fully restored 1920s home with lofty paneled ceilings and polished hardwoods, it offers six large well-lit bedrooms with ceiling fans and pleasing furnishings (wrought-iron and hardwood beds), cable TV, and handsome baths. Two more elegant rooms are to the rear, where there's a patio with hammocks. It has a small TV lounge, plus laundry and secure parking. Rates include full breakfast and airport transfers.

A mere 400 meters (0.25 miles) from the airport, the **Hampton Inn and Suites** (tel. 506/2436-0000, U.S. tel. 800-426-7866, www.hamptoninn.com, from $90 s/d) is perfect if you have tight flight transfers and don't mind charmless motel-style Americana. It's clean and has all the amenities you'll need for a one-night stay, and the Fiesta Casino is a stone's throw away. Rates include continental breakfast and airport transfers but are vastly overpriced.

In the northern suburbs, **Pura Vida Hotel** (off the road to Tuetal, tel. 506/2430-2929, www.puravidahotel.com, low season $79-125 s/d, high season $95-165 s/d) is an intimate B&B run by Californians Nhi and Bernie. Set in a beautiful 0.4-hectare (1-acre) garden, this handsome old timber-beamed home has a contemporary aesthetic that hints at Santa Fe. Its seven rooms and self-contained bungalows are all themed. The Orchid Room, for example, is done up in whites and reds with a black four-poster metal bed. It offers Internet access and has a garden restaurant serving gourmet dishes (by reservation). There are lots of guest-friendly dogs, plus secure parking; excursions are offered.

Food

Jalapeños (Calle 1, Aves. 3/5, tel. 506/2430-4027, 11:30am-9pm Mon.-Sat., 11:30am-8pm Sun.) is a cheerful place to spice up your diet with great Tex-Mex bargains on eggs

cannon in Parque Juan Santamaría, Alajuela

rancheros, omelets, and nachos (made with fresh corn flautas). I recommend the spicy *sopa Azteca*. The hosts, Norman and Isabel, are delightful.

Ambrosia (Ave. 5, Calle 2, tel. 506/2201-5057, 10am-9pm Mon.-Sat.) offers a pleasantly airy ambience for enjoying Costa Rican fare and Italian dishes, including four types of lasagna. The *batidos* (milk shakes) are great. You don't need to be vegetarian to delight in **El Chante Vegano** (Ave. 5, Calles Central/1, tel. 506/8911-4787, www.elchantevegano.com, 11am-8pm Tues.-Sat.,11am-4pm Sun.), a new mom-and-son restaurant serving vegan organic treats such as pizza, a portobello burger, and *sopa Azteca* in a delightfully cozy ambiance with hand-painted murals.

Seeking a delightful little coffee spot? Head to the clean and airy **Trigo Miel** (Ave. 2, Calles Central/2, tel. 506/2442-2263, www.trigomiel.com, 7am-8pm Mon.-Sat., 8am-6pm Sun.), which has Wi-Fi along with delicious sandwiches and desserts.

Information and Services

Goodlight Books (Ave. 3, Calles 1/3, tel. 506/2430-4083, rosacarballov@gmail.com, 10am-6pm daily), run by amiable expat Larry and his silent sidekick Clea (she's a bewigged mannequin), has more than 10,000 books and serves espressos and pastries on the patio. The many Internet cafés include **Café Net** (Ave. 9, Calles 1/3, tel. 506/2441-1210).

Hospital San Rafael (Ave. 12, tel. 506/2436-1000) is a full-service facility. The **police station** (tel. 506/2440-8889) is at Avenida 3, Calle 7, and at Calle 2, Avenidas 3/5; for the local traffic police, call tel. 506/2441-7411; for criminal investigation, call the OIJ (tel. 506/2437-0442).

Getting There

TUASA (tel. 506/2222-5325) buses depart San José from Avenida 2, Calles 10/12, every 10 minutes 4am-10pm daily. Return buses (tel. 506/2442-6900) depart from Calle 8, Avenidas Central/1, in Alajuela. The buses run past Juan Santamaría Airport.

Major car rental companies have offices in Río Segundo de Alajuela. **A-1 Rentacar** (tel. 506/2443-8109, www.a1cr.com) is at Avenida 3, Calle 7.

THE SLOPES OF POÁS VOLCANO

Above Alajuela, the scenic drive up Volcán Poás takes you through quintessential coffee country, with rows of shiny dark-green bushes creating artistic patterns on the slopes. Farther up, coffee gives way to fern gardens and fields of strawberries grown under black shade netting, then dairy pastures separated by forests of cedar and pine.

Routes to Poás Volcano National Park

There are three routes to Parque Nacional Volcán Poás: via Carrizal, San Isidro, or San Pedro. All lead via **Poasito,** the uppermost village on the mountain and a popular way station for hungry sightseers.

CARRIZAL ROUTE

From Alajuela, Avenida 7 exits town and turns uphill via Carrizal and Cinco Esquinas to **Vara Blanca,** a village nestled just beyond the saddle between the Barva and Poás volcanoes on the edge of the Continental Divide about 25 kilometers (16 miles) north of Alajuela. At Vara Blanca, turn west for Parque Nacional Volcán Poás.

North from Vara Blanca the road snakes through the valley of the Río Sarapiquí via Cinchona, the epicenter of a magnitude 6.1 earthquake that struck on January 8, 2009, devastating the area and claiming 40 lives. The village was completely destroyed.

SAN ISIDRO ROUTE

From downtown Alajuela, Calle 2 leads north through the heart of coffee country via **San Isidro de Alajuela**, about seven kilometers (4.5 miles) above Alajuela, and **Fraijanes,** beyond which it continues steeply uphill two kilometers (1.2 miles) to Poasito. **Colinas del Poás** (tel. 506/2482-1212, www.

colinasdelpoas.com, 8am-4pm daily), at Fraijanes, offers trout fishing plus a two-hour canopy tour ($50) that ends with an astonishing two-kilometer (1.2-mile) zip-line run.

SAN PEDRO ROUTE

A more common route to Poás is via San José de Alajuela, San Pedro, and Sabana Redondo. San José de Alajuela, about three kilometers (2 miles) west of Alajuela, is a village at a major junction: west (Hwy. 3) for La Garita and northwest to Grecia, Sarchí, and San Ramón. The road to Poás begins at Cruce de Grecia y Poás, one kilometer (0.6 miles) along the Alajuela-Grecia road. From here it's uphill all the way via the pretty hamlet of San Pedro. The road merges with the road via San Isidro at Fraijanes.

★ La Paz Waterfall Gardens

Splendid nature and wildlife park **La Paz Waterfall Gardens** (tel. 506/2482-2720, www.waterfallgardens.com, 8am-5pm daily, adults $38, children $22) is at Montaña Azul, about four kilometers (2.5 miles) north of Vara Blanca. It features trails through a soaring hangar-size aviary with a separate climate-controlled butterfly cage. There's also a hummingbird garden, a serpentarium

(snakes), a walk-through ranarium (frogs), a monkey exhibit, plus a trout lake and orchid houses. A highlight is the vast walk-in aviary, with everything from macaws and toucans to guans (don't wear earrings, which the macaws like to swoop down and seize). The Jungle Cat Exhibit is worth the price of admission alone and offers a rare chance to see ocelots, margays, jaguarundis, pumas, and even a jaguar. All have been placed here by the Ministry of the Environment (MINAE) because they were old or injured or had been exposed to humans too long to be released back into the wild.

The various exhibits are accessed by riverside concrete trails that eventually lead steeply downhill to four waterfalls. Standing on the viewing platform at the Templo Fall, you're pummeled by spray blasted from the base of the fall. Continuing downriver, a metal staircase that clings to the side of the cliff descends to the Magía Blanca (the largest cascade), Encantada, and the La Paz falls—a pencil-thin roadside fall that attracts Ticos en masse on weekends. It's a daunting climb back, but shuttles back to the hotel are offered from the roadside trail exit. The Casita de la Paz recreates a traditional farmhouse. The restaurant has a superb buffet plus marvelous views. Bird-watching tours are offered.

orange-billed nightingale-thrush, La Paz Waterfall Gardens

La Paz Waterfall

and gift store, an open-air restaurant with magnificent views, and a traditional *trapiche* (sugarcane mill), with vats for boiling and evaporating. Eighteen species of butterflies flap around inside a walk-through netted garden. Also here: a bonsairetum, or bonsai farm. The same family, which sells its coffee under the Café Tres Generaciones label, also runs **La Casa del Café La Luisa** (tel. 506/2482-1535, 7am-5pm Mon.-Thurs., 7am-7pm Fri.-Sun.), a lovely café perched above the coffee fields three kilometers (2 miles) north of San Isidro de Alajuela.

Accommodations
Drawing yoga and good-living fanatics for health-themed packages in the pure mountain air, the **Pura Vida Health Spa** (U.S. tel. 770-403-0238 or 888-767-7375, www.puravidaspa.com, low season from $150 s, $230 d, high season from $175 s, $250 d, including meals), at Pavas de Carrizal, seven kilometers (4 miles) northeast of Alajuela, offers 50 villas, cabanas, and luxury carpeted chalet tents ("tentalows") with shared baths amid enchanting gardens with pools, plus two suites with king beds in the main house. When driving from Alajuela, take a sharp left at Salon Apolo 15, and Pura Vida is one kilometer (0.6 miles) up the dirt road.

I adore the all-new ★ **Poás Volcano Lodge** (tel. 506/2482-2194, www.poasvolcanolodge.com, low season $115-245 s/d, high season $145-295 s/d), on a dairy farm about one kilometer (0.6 miles) west of Vara Blanca. The magnificent rough-stone mountaintop farmhouse lodge, stunningly situated amid emerald-green pastures between the Poás and Barva volcanoes, was rebuilt in an exciting combination of old and new since being badly damaged by the January 2009 earthquake. The exciting minimalist motif features glazed concrete floors and a combo of modern and period furnishings. The five spacious bedroom suites in the lodge feature glazed hardwood floors, thick down comforters, Wi-Fi, and stylish modern baths with slate floors and large walk-in showers; some retain

Last admission is 3pm. The entrance fee includes a huge buffet lunch. Guided tours are offered by reservation only, including the Behind-the-Scenes Animal Encounters Tour ($45) and guided tours that include transportation from and back to San José (adults $65, children $55).

Doka Estate
At San Isidro de Alajuela a turn-off from the highway leads four kilometers (2.5 miles) west to **Doka Estate** (tel. 506/2449-5152, www.dokaestate.com, 8am-5pm Mon.-Fri., 8am-4pm Sat.-Sun.), at Sabanilla de Alajuela, a great place to learn about coffee production and processing. This privately owned coffee plantation and century-old mill, which still operates entirely by hydraulic power, offers the Doka Coffee Tour (9am, 10am, 11am, 1:30pm, 2:30pm, and 3:30pm daily, no 3:30pm tour Sun., $18; an optional breakfast costs $4, and lunch costs $7), where visitors are taught the age-old techniques of coffee growing, milling, and roasting. There's a coffee-tasting room

old roof beams and original stone walls. Eight rooms furnished in simpler fashion are in an adjacent block. Horseback rides and mountain bikes are offered along forest trails good for spotting quetzals. Filling breakfasts are included in the rates, and dinner is served by request.

For a Tolkien-meets-Disney treat, check into the ★ **Peace Lodge** (tel. 506/2482-2720, www.waterfallgardens.com, low season $335-710 s/d, high season $375-770 s/d) at the La Paz Waterfall Gardens, at Montaña Azul, about four kilometers (2.5 miles) north of Vara Blanca. Imagine natural stone, huge hemispheric stone fireplaces, rough-hewn four-poster king beds with canopy netting, tables of diced timbers, hardwood floors, lofty ceilings, and stone balconies with stone whirlpool tubs and awesome views toward Volcán Poás. The mammoth skylighted baths resemble caverns and have natural stone whirlpool tubs and separate all-stone waterfall showers. Every need is catered to, from umbrellas for rainy days to flashlights for electricity blackouts. Excellent buffet meals are served by day, and the elegant guests-only upstairs restaurant offers three-course dinners ($28).

★ **Xandari** (tel. 506/2443-2020, U.S. tel. 866-363-3212, www.xandari.com, low season $195-450 s/d, high season $265-570 s/d) is a contemporary stunner perched amid the hotel's own coffee fields in the hills above Tacacori, five kilometers (3 miles) north of Alajuela. Xandari has been named among the top 10 resorts in Central and South America by both *Condé Nast Traveler* and *Travel + Leisure*. The 24 villas are furnished with dark hardwoods and explosively colorful works of art, poured-concrete sofas with heaps of cushions, plus sponge-washed walls, Guatemalan bedspreads, and plump down pillows; rippling hardwood ceilings and voluptuously curving walls and stained-glass windows echo the theme in the public lounge. Each room has a kitchenette, its own expansive terrace with a shady *ranchito,* and a cavernous walk-in shower with a wall of glass facing onto a private courtyard garden. The restaurant serves health-conscious meals. There are three swimming pools with whirlpool tubs, a soundproofed TV lounge, a studio for artists and yoga practitioners, a gym, and an electric car to transport guests to and from the full-service **Xandari Spa Village** (spa@xandari.com). Xandari has a goat farm, an orchid house, a medicinal plant tour, and trails that lead through a bamboo forest to waterfalls. Rates include airport transfers and breakfast.

shoveling coffee beans at Doka Estate

Food

The gourmet **Restaurante Colbert** (tel. 506/2482-2776, www.colbert.co.cr, 7am-9pm daily), at Vara Blanca, is a bakery and café with an airy, well-lit hillside restaurant with magnificent views. It offers set breakfasts, plus croissants, crêpe suzette, sandwiches, and French-Tico fusion cuisine such as tilapia in tomato sauce ($7) from gifted, toque-wearing French chef Joël Suire.

La Paz Waterfall Gardens, at Montaña Azul, about four kilometers (2.5 miles) north of Vara Blanca, has a superb buffet restaurant (tel. 506/2482-2720, 8am-4pm daily) that's worth the visit here alone for lunch (adults $13, children $7).

On the San Pedro road below Fraijanes, I love the atmospheric and rustic ★ **Jaulares** (tel. 506/2482-2155, 7am-9pm Mon.-Thurs., 7am-midnight Fri.-Sat., 7am-8pm Sun.), serving meals cooked on an open wood-burning stove. The black bean soup ($2) is superb, as is the jalapeño steak ($10). It also serves *casados* (set lunches, $5), plus an open buffet ($12). It's favored by locals on Saturday night, when it has live music.

Just up the hill from Jaulares, **Freddo Fresa** (tel. 506/2482-1495, 7am-10pm daily) is hewn of cypress timbers and has a fantastic rustic ambience. It serves homemade goodies such as tortillas, grilled-chicken sandwiches with fresh bread, and *picadilla* of potatoes, corn, sweet red pepper, and cilantro—all with ingredients from Emilio's organic garden. The food is prepared on an old stove, and there are fresh strawberry shakes to die for.

At Poasito, the **Steak House El Churrasco** (tel. 506/2482-2135, www.el-churrascocr.com, 9am-5pm Tues.-Sun.) is a popular spot for tenderloins, *lengua en salsa,* and other meat dishes (from $4). Try the bean dip with tortillas and jalapeños, followed by tiramisu.

Getting There

Buses (tel. 506/2449-5141) for Poasito depart Alajuela from Avenida Central, Calle 10, hourly 9am-5pm Saturday-Sunday. Monday-Friday, buses depart four times daily 9am-6:15pm.

★ POÁS VOLCANO NATIONAL PARK

There are few volcanoes where you can drive all the way to the rim. At **Parque Nacional Volcán Poás** you can—well, at least to within 300 meters (1,000 feet), where a short stroll puts you at the very edge of one of the world's

guest suite at Poás Volcano Lodge

largest active craters, 1.5 kilometers (0.9 miles) wide. The viewing terrace gives a bird's-eye view not only 320 meters (1,050 feet) down into the hellish bowels of the volcano, but also down over the northern lowlands.

Poás (2,708 meters/8,885 feet) is a restless giant with a 40-year active cycle. It erupted moderately in the early 1950s and has been intermittently active ever since. The park is frequently closed to visitors because of sulfur gas emissions. Over the millennia it has vented its anger through three craters. Two now slumber under a blanket of vegetation; one even cradles a lake. But the main crater bubbles persistently with active fumaroles and a simmering sulfuric pool that frequently changes hues and emits a geyser up to 200 meters (660 feet) into the steam-laden air. The water level of the lake has gone down about 15 meters (50 feet) during the past decade, one of several indications of a possible impending eruption; after 12 years of silence, in March 2006 a series of explosions caused the park to close temporarily. In the 1950s a small eruption began to push up a new cone on the crater floor: The **Cono Von Frantzius** is now 80 meters (260 feet) high and still puffing.

A walk of 600 meters (2,000 feet) on the **Sendero Sombrilla de Pobre** connects the parking lot to the crater lookout. The 800-meter (0.5-mile) **Botos Trail,** just before the viewing platform, leads via a surreal dwarf forest to an extinct crater filled with a cold-water lake called Botos. This trail and the 530-meter (1,700-foot) **Escalonia Trail,** which begins at the picnic area, provide for pleasant hikes and are wheelchair accessible. The dense forests are home to emerald toucanets, coyotes, resplendent quetzals, sooty robins, hummingbirds, frogs, and the Poás squirrel, which is endemic to the volcano.

As often as not, it is foggy up here, and mist floats like an apparition through the dwarf cloud forest draped with bromeliads and mosses. Clouds usually form mid-morning. Plan an early-morning arrival to enhance your chances of a cloud-free visit. On a sunny day it can be 21°C (70°F). On a cloudy day, it is normally bitterly cold and windy at the crater rim; dress accordingly. Poás is popular on weekends with local Ticos, who arrive by the busload. Visit midweek if possible.

Information and Services

Parque Nacional Volcán Poás (tel. 506/2482-2424 or 506/2482-1227, www.sinac.go.cr, adults $10, children $1) has a **visitors center** (tel. 506/2482-2424, 8am-3:30pm

the main crater at Poás Volcano

daily) with restrooms, a souvenir store, and a café, plus an exhibit hall and an auditorium where audiovisual presentations are given on Sunday. The park has no accommodations, and camping is not permitted. Parking costs $2.50.

Getting There

TUASA (tel. 506/2222-5325) buses depart San José ($5) at 8:30am daily from Avenida 2, Calles 12/14, via Alajuela. The journey takes 90 minutes. Return buses depart at 2:30pm daily. **TUASA** (tel. 506/2442-6900) buses also leave from Alajuela at 8:30am daily. Tour operators in San José offer day trips to Poás (half-day about $35, full-day $55).

Grecia to Zarcero

Highway 141 leads west from Alajuela, snaking through scenic coffee country and then climbing into an alpine setting—a marvelous drive.

GRECIA

Grecia, on Highway 141, some 18 kilometers (11 miles) northwest of Alajuela, is an important market town famous for its rust-red twin-spired metal church, **Iglesia de Nuestra Señora de las Mercedes,** made of steel plates imported from Belgium in 1897. An all-marble altar rises fancifully like one of Emperor Ludwig's fairy-tale castles. The church is fronted by a pretty park with tall palms, an obelisk erected to commemorate the foundation of Grecia in July 1864, fountains, and a domed music temple.

World of Snakes

Just east of Grecia, on the main Sarchí road, the Austrian-run **World of Snakes** (tel./fax 506/2494-3700, www.theworldofsnakes.com, 8am-5pm daily, adults $11, children and students $6) displays a collection of more than 150 snakes from around the world, including many of Costa Rica's most beautiful critters. The facility breeds 70 different species for sale and for reintroduction to the wild. It educates visitors to dispel the negative image of snakes with a clear message—don't harm snakes. The critters live behind glass windows

Iglesia de Nuestra Señora de las Mercedes, Grecia

in re-creations of their natural habitats. You can handle nonvenomous species. There are also caimans, snapping turtles, and poison dart frogs. The last guided tour is at 4pm.

Getting There

Buses (tel. 506/2258-2004) depart San José from Avenida 3, Calles 18/20, every 30 minutes 5:35am-10:10pm Monday-Saturday, less frequently Sunday. The bus station in Grecia is at Avenida 2, Calles 4/6, two blocks west of the plaza, where taxis congregate on the north side.

SARCHÍ

Sarchí, set amid coffee fields 29 kilometers (18 miles) northwest of Alajuela, is Costa Rica's crossroads of crafts—famous for the intricately detailed, hand-painted oxcarts that originated here in the middle of the 19th century. The town celebrates them on the first week of February with bull-riding, amusement rides, and, of course, a parade of oxcarts. Handcrafted souvenirs—including chess sets, salad bowls, leather sandals, rockers, and miniature oxcarts decorated in traditional geometric designs—are sold at shops all along the road of Sarchí Sur (you can order

custom-made furniture from any of dozens of workshops, or *talleres*), which sits atop a steep hill about one kilometer (0.6 miles) east of Sarchí Norte, the town center. Many white-washed buildings are painted with the town's own floral motif trim.

Sarchí Norte's **church**, on the plazas, is one of the most beautiful in the nation and has a vaulted hardwood ceiling and carvings. Note the humongous oxcart in the plaza.

At **Fábrica de Carretas Joaquín Chaverri** (tel. 506/2454-4411m 8am-5pm daily), in Sarchí Sur, you can see souvenirs and oxcarts being painted in workshops at the rear of the huge souvenir store.

The **Else Kientzler Botanical Gardens** (tel. 506/2454-2070, www.elsegarden.com, 8am-4pm daily, adults $10, children and students $7, guided tour $25 by reservation), 800 meters (0.5 miles) north of the stadium in Sarchí Norte, displays 2,000 species of flora on seven hectares (17 acres) of gardens. It's superb for bird-watching. Almost three kilometers (2 miles) of trails wind through the gardens, which represent plants from throughout the tropical world and even feature a small maze. A portion of the garden features a trail for blind visitors.

maze at Else Kientzler Botanical Gardens, Sarchí

Sarchí

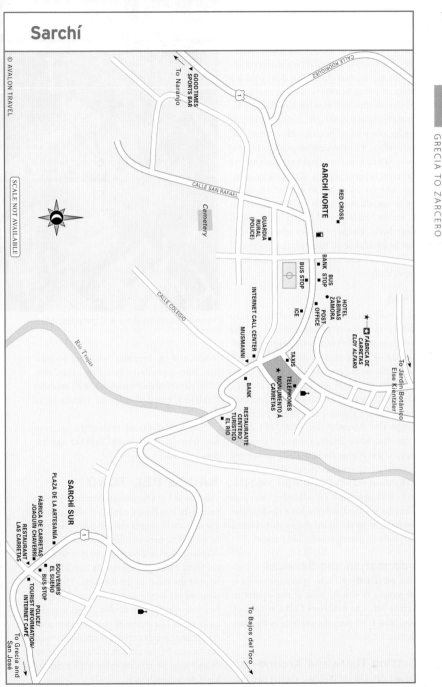

© AVALON TRAVEL

SCALE NOT AVAILABLE

To Naranjo

GOOD TIMES
SPORTS BAR

CALLE RODRIGUEZ

CALLE SAN RAFAEL

Cemetery

SARCHÍ NORTE

RED CROSS

GUARDIA
RURAL
(POLICE)

CALLE COLEGIO

BANK
STOP

BUS
STOP

BUS STOP

ICE

INTERNET CALL CENTER

MUSMANN

HOTEL
CABINAS
ZAMORA

POST
OFFICE

FÁBRICA DE
CARRETAS
ELOY ALFARO

TAXIS

TELEPHONES

MONUMENTO A
CARRETAS

BANK

RESTAURANTE
CENTRO
TURÍSTICO
EL RÍO

Río Trojas

To Jardín Botánico
Else Kientzler

SARCHÍ SUR

PLAZA DE LA ARTESANÍA

FÁBRICA DE CARRETAS
JOAQUÍN CHAVERRIA

RESTAURANT
LAS CARRETAS

SOUVENIRS
EL SUEÑO

BUS STOP

POLICE/
TOURIST INFORMATION/
INTERNET CAFÉ

To Grecia and
San José

To Bajos del Toro

★ Fábrica de Carretas Eloy Alfaro

Fábrica de Carretas Eloy Alfaro (tel. 506/2454-4131, www.fabricadecarretaseloyalfaro.com, 6am-6pm Mon.-Fri., free) is a piece of living history—the only workshop in the country still making Costa Rica's famous *carretas* (oxcarts) featuring the 16-pie-wedge-piece wheel bound with a metal belt. Justifiably, it's now a national historic treasure. Witness workers making yokes and 11 different types of oxcarts in traditional manner, with the lathes and tools all still powered by an age-old waterwheel. Go just after dawn to see the red-hot metal frames being put on the wheels. You can wander around at will, but be careful of all the whizzing belts and pulleys! You enter via a huge souvenir store (open daily).

Food

In Sarchí Sur there are several eateries in the Plaza de la Artesanía, including the small, homey **Restaurant Helechos** (tel. 506/2454-4560, 10am-6pm daily), which serves tacos, burgers, and such tantalizing dishes as tongue in salsa and garlic shrimp, along with desserts, natural juices, and cappuccinos. On the east side of the plaza, **La Troja del Abuelo** (tel. 506/2454-4973, 11am-6pm Mon.-Thurs., 11am-midnight Fri.-Sun.) offers a large menu of *típico* dishes (try the sea bass in mushroom sauce).

Restaurant Las Carretas (tel. 506/2454-1633, 9am-6pm daily, $5), adjoining Fábrica de Carretas Joaquín Chaverri, has a shaded patio out back; it serves *típico* dishes plus chicken parmigiana, pastas, salads, and burgers.

Information and Services

The **post office** (7am-5pm Mon.-Fri.) is 50 meters (165 feet) west of the square in Sarchí Sur. The **Internet Call Center** (tel. 506/2454-1133) is on the west side of the plaza in Sarchí Norte.

Getting There and Around

Buses (tel. 506/2258-2004) depart San José

miniature oxcarts at Fábrica de Carretas Eloy Alfaro, Sarchí

from Calle 18, Avenidas 5/7, every 30 minutes 5am-10pm daily. Buses (tel. 506/2494-2139) depart Alajuela from Calle 8, Avenidas Central/1, every 30 minutes 5:30am-10pm daily.

Taxis wait on the west side of the square in Sarchí Norte, or call **Sarchí Taxi Service** (tel. 506/2454-4028).

BAJOS DEL TORO

From Sarchí, at a turnoff 100 meters (330 feet) east of the Río Trojas, a road climbs north up the mountain slopes via Luisa and Ángeles to the saddle between the Poás and Platanar volcanoes before dropping sharply to Bajos del Toro, a tranquil Shangri-la hamlet at the head of the valley of the Río Toro. The route is incredibly scenic, and at times daunting, as you weave along a road that clings precariously to the face of the often cloud-shrouded mountains. An alternative route is the road that begins by the church in Zarcero; it's an often-foggy 30-minute drive with a dauntingly steep switchback.

The 400-hectare (990-acre) **Bosque de Paz Rain/Cloud Forest Biological Reserve** (tel. 506/2234-6676, www.bosquedepaz.com), accessed via a solitary valley west of Bajos del Toro, boasts 22 kilometers (14 miles) of hiking trails leading to waterfalls, a botanical garden, hummingbird gardens, and lookout points. The forests are replete with exotic wildlife, including howler, capuchin, and spider monkeys as well as cats and—according to the owner—more bird species than anywhere else in the nation.

El Remanso de las Mariposas (tel. 506/2241-5840) is a butterfly garden at the north end of the hamlet.

About seven kilometers (4.5 miles) north of Bajos del Toro is a 200-meter (660-foot) waterfall—**Catarata del Toro** (tel. 506/2761-0861, www.catarata-del-toro.com, 8am-5pm daily, $10). Trails lead to the cascade, the bottom of which is reached by a 500-step staircase. Rappelling and guided hikes are available. Entrance costs $35, including lunch ($79 with transportation).

Accommodations and Food

Perfect for nature lovers, **Bosque de Paz** (tel. 506/2234-6676, www.bosquedepaz.com, $134-196 s, $188-286 d including breakfast) has a rustic stone and log lodge with a handsome restaurant serving *típico* food, plus 12 cozy rooms with wrought-iron beds, terracotta floors, and private baths with hot water. A one-day excursion from San José (for an additional fee) includes lunch. Reservations are required.

The relaxing ★ **El Silencio Lodge & Spa** (tel. 506/2761-0301, www.elsilenciolodge.com, $295 s, $325 d year-round) has a gorgeous 21st-century aesthetic that comes as a surprise for a conscientious eco-lodge. It operates on an all-inclusive principle. Spacious bungalows perched on the forested slopes have gleaming hardwood floors, peaked rattan ceilings, cast-iron hearths, divinely comfortable king beds with down duvets, and a wall of glass that slides open to put you closer to Mother Nature. Travertine-clad baths have huge walk-in showers, and there are whirlpool tubs on the wooden decks (which lack privacy). Thoughtful extras range from fluffy robes and slippers to umbrellas and a fully stocked fridge (on the house). A gas stove switches on automatically at night to keep things cozy. The luxurious, domed Zen-like spa in the forest is like something out of *Star Trek*, while the elegant restaurant (open to nonguests at the management's discretion) serves healthy

the plaza at Zarcero

gourmet meals. It offers prix-fixe dinners ($35), such as pan-grilled trout with green rice, almonds, and orange-rum sauce. I was served by the fireplace in a comfy leather chair while listening to Andrea Bocelli, Sibelius's *Finlandia,* and jazz. Awesome!

Getting There

Buses run from Sarchí (3pm daily, 1 hour, $1.50) and Jeep taxis run from both Sarchí and Zarcero.

ZARCERO

Naranjo, five kilometers (3 miles) west of Sarchí and three kilometers (2 miles) north of the Pan-American Highway, is an important agricultural center with a pretty twin-towered baroque church. North of Naranjo the main road that leads to Ciudad Quesada and the northern lowlands is one of the most scenic alpine drives in the country, with dairy cattle munching contentedly on emerald slopes. The road twists and coils to **Zarcero,** a pleasant mountain town with an impressive setting beneath green mountains.

Dominating the town is the whitewashed church fronted by **Parque Francisco Alvarado**—a veritable open-air museum of fantastic topiary. The work is that of Evangelisto Blanco, who has unleashed his wildest ideas in leafy splendor: a cat riding a motorcycle along the top of a hedge, an elephant with light bulbs for eyes, corkscrews whose spiral foliage coils up and around the trunks like serpents around Eden's tree, even a bullring complete with matador, a charging bull, and spectators.

At **Zapote,** eight kilometers (5 miles) north of Zarcero, you reach the Continental Divide, with sweeping vistas of the northern lowlands far below. Or you can follow the road that begins at the plaza and leads east downhill to Bajos del Toro.

For a fun adventure-filled break, stop at **Rancho Amalia** (tel. 506/2463-3335, www.ranchoamalia.com, 9am-4pm daily), one kilometer (0.6 miles) south of Zarcero, for as horseback tour ($10-20) on a coffee finca with a forest. It has two cozy cabins ($60 s/d).

Getting There

Buses (tel. 506/2255-4318) for Zarcero depart San José every 30 minutes 5am-7:30pm daily from Calle 12, Avenidas 7/9; and from San Ramón at 5:45am, 8:30am, noon, 2:30pm, and 5pm daily. Buses depart from the southwest corner of the park in Zarcero; the bus stop for San José faces the church.

La Garita to San Ramón

LA GARITA

La Garita, spanning the Pan-American Highway (Hwy. 1) about 12 kilometers (7.5 miles) west of Alajuela, is important for its location at the junction of Highway 3, which leads west for Atenas, Orotina, and Puntarenas (and east for Alajuela). The area boasts a salubrious climate, and La Garita is famed for ornamental-plant farms known as *viveros.*

The **Botanical Orchid Garden** (tel. 506/2487-8095, www.orchidgardencr.com, 8:30am-4:30pm Tues.-Sun., adults $12, children $6), about two kilometers (1.2 miles) west of the *autopista,* opened in 2011 after 30 years in the making. This lovely garden displays 75 native orchid species and about 75 exotics. Educational tours are fascinating; I was surprised to learn about how global warming is affecting orchid flowering patterns. And did you know that vanilla comes from a Mexican orchid? It also displays palms, heliconias, and bamboo species; there is an orchid reforestation program; and it breeds macaws and parrots. A lovely airy café serves salads, quesadillas, and the like.

★ Zoo Ave

Splendid **Zoo Ave** (tel. 506/2433-8989, http://rescateanimalzooave.org/en, 9am-5pm daily, adults $20, children under age 12 free), at Dulce Nombre, on Highway 3 about 3.5 kilometers (2 miles) east of the Pan-American Highway, comprises 59 hectares (146 acres) of landscaped grounds and is a wildlife rescue center for injured and confiscated wildlife. The fantastic bird collection (the largest in Central America) includes dozens of toucans, cranes, curassows, parrots, and more than 100 other Costa Rican species. Zoo Ave is one of only two zoos in the world to display resplendent quetzals. Macaws fly free. You'll also see crocodiles, deer, turtles, ostriches, tapirs, peccaries, pumas, and all four species of indigenous monkeys in large enclosures. The zoo has successfully bred the scarlet macaw, green macaw, curassow, guan, and about 50 other native bird species with the help of a human-infant incubator. The breeding center is off-limits. A visitors center shows video presentations and offers educational events. Plus, it recently added a canopy zip line and a botanic garden.

The Atenas and La Garita buses from Alajuela pass by the zoo.

Accommodations and Food

The Canadian-run **Hotel La Rosa de América** (tel./fax 506/2433-2741, www.larosadeamerica.com, low season $58-65 s, $69-75 d, high season $73-80 s, $83-90 d), in Barrio San José de Alajuela, is a charming mid-priced country-style option in a lushly landscaped garden. Don't expect luxury. Its 12 cabins are modestly appointed but quite comfortable. Tropical breakfasts are served in a homey restaurant. There's a small swimming pool, a day spa, a TV lounge, and free Wi-Fi throughout. Rates include breakfast and tax. It's 100 meters (330 feet) south of La Mandarina on the main Alajuela-La Garita road.

If you seek luxury, head to the gracious **Martino Resort and Spa** (tel. 506/2433-8382, www.hotelmartino.com, $140-180 s/d), an Italianate themed hotel on 2.4 hectares (6 acres) with lush manicured grounds full of classical statuary located 200 meters east of Zoo Ave. Lacquered hardwoods abound, as in the majestic columned lounge boasting plump sofas. It has 34 air-conditioned suites with tile floors, double doors for soundproofing, terraces (some facing a lake), spacious baths with monogrammed towels, and free Wi-Fi. Facilities include a huge swimming pool, an Italian restaurant, a bar, a casino, a tennis court, and a state-of-the-art gym and spa. Trails access a bird sanctuary.

For a genuine local experience, I head to ★ **Fiesta del Maíz** (tel. 506/2487-5757, 10am-8pm Mon. and Wed.-Thurs., 7am-9pm Fri.-Sun.), on Highway 3 about one kilometer (0.6 miles) west of the Pan-American Highway. This large cafeteria-style restaurant is famous for tasty corn meals that include *chorreadas* (corn fritters), tamales (corn pudding), corn on the grill, and tasty rice with corn and chicken. No plate costs more than $3.

Getting There

Buses for La Garita depart from Avenida 2, Calle 10, in Alajuela every 30 minutes 6am-9pm daily.

ATENAS AND VICINITY

Balmy Atenas, on Highway 3, five kilometers (3 miles) west of La Garita, is an agricultural town renowned for its perpetually spring-like climate (in 1994, *National Geographic* declared it the best climate in the world). A beautiful church built in 1908 stands over the plaza, two blocks south of Highway 3. The old *camino de carretas* (oxcart trail) ran through Atenas, and during the peak of coffee harvest, trains of 800-plus carts would pass by, carrying beans to Puntarenas. The **Monumento a los Boyeros** (Monument to the Oxcart Drivers) stands at the eastern entrance to town.

Railroad buffs may thrill to the **Museo Ferroviario** (Railroad Museum, tel. 506/2446-0091 or 506/8810-0660, 9am-6pm Sun. only, donation), four kilometers

(2.5 miles) southeast of town at Río Grande de Atenas. This excellent little museum displays several restored antique locomotives.

Bungee Jumping

Thrill seekers can leap off the 83-meter (272-foot) Puente Negro over the Río Colorado, one kilometer (0.6 miles) east of Rosario, just west of the Pan-American Highway, eight kilometers (5 miles) northeast of Atenas. **Tropical Bungee** (tel./fax 506/2248-2212, www.bungee.co.cr, 9am-3pm daily high season, 9am-3pm Sat.-Sun., by reservation Mon.-Fri. low season) offers bungee jumps from the bridge under the guidance of "jump masters" using an 11-meter (36-foot) bungee. The company charges $75 for the first jump, $110 for two jumps. Anyone with back, neck, or heart problems is advised not to jump. The San José-Puntarenas bus from Calle 12, Avenida 7, or the San José-Naranjo bus from Calle 16, Avenida 1, will drop you off at Salon Los Alfaro, from which it's a short walk north to the bridge.

Shopping

One of the best-stocked souvenir stores in the country is here: **Molas y Café Gift Shop** (tel. 506/2446-5155, molasycafe@racsa.co.cr), on the main highway on the east side of Atenas. It employs Kuna indigenous women from Panamá to make *molas* on-site; break out your camera!

Accommodations

El Cafetal Inn (tel. 506/2446-5785, www.cafetal.com, low season standard $60 s, $70 d, suites $75 s/d, bungalow $90 s/d, high season standard $65 s, $75 d, suites $85 s/d, bungalow $90 s/d) is an elegant bed-and-breakfast on a small coffee and fruit finca in Santa Eulalia, about five kilometers (3 miles) north of Atenas. El Salvadoran Lee Rodríguez, the friendly owner, runs this 10-bedroom hostelry. The lounge has marble floors and a cascade, and bay windows offer valley and mountain vistas. The upstairs rooms (some quite small) are modestly appointed, with thin

Monument to the Oxcart Drivers, Atenas

panel walls. For a touch of extra romance, take a Hansel-and-Gretel cottage with a king bed. There's a large clover-shaped swimming pool. Howler monkeys hang out in the trees nearby.

For a true splurge look to ★ **Vista del Valle Plantation Inn** (tel./fax 506/2451-1165, www.vistadelvalle.com, low season room $90 s/d, cottages $144-166 s/d, high season room $100 s/d, cottages $160-185 s/d), a serene bed-and-breakfast on a working citrus and coffee finca on the edge of the Río Grande Canyon Preserve. Lush lawns fall away into tall bamboo forest. The main lodge (with one room for rent) is a Frank Lloyd Wright-style architectural marvel in wood; floor-to-ceiling plate-glass windows flood Vista del Valle with light. Ten cottages are reached by stone trails; some have their own kitchens, and all have Wi-Fi. All boast tasteful yet minimalist decor and furnishings plus a private balcony or wraparound veranda, and lavish Oriental-style baths with granite tile work. Seven condo-villas have been added, but they're far less appealing.

Facilities include a beautiful pool and whirlpool tub fed by a water cascade, plus mountain bikes and a stable. Gourmet meals are served. Rates include breakfast.

Food

On the northeast side of the village square, **La Carreta Restaurant Café & Heladería** (tel. 506/2446-3156, 8am-8pm Mon.-Sat., 10am-6pm Sun.), housed in a venerable wooden building, offers an intimate atmosphere and tasty budget treats such as sandwiches and ice cream. It's also a great place to watch local life around the plaza.

Locals flock to **Restaurant La Trocha del Boyero** (tel. 506/2443-0533, 11:30am-8pm Thurs.-Tues.), on the east side of town, for *comida típica*, delicious seafood dishes, and the house special—grilled beef—to be enjoyed on an outdoor deck.

Getting There

Buses (tel. 506/2446-5767) for Atenas depart San José ($1.10) more or less every hour 5:40am-10pm Monday-Saturday, less frequently on Sunday, from Calle 16, Avenidas 1/3; and from Alajuela every 30 minutes 6am-10pm Monday-Saturday, less frequently on Sunday, from Avenida 2, Calles 8/10.

SAN RAMÓN AND VICINITY

San Ramón, about 12 kilometers (7.5 miles) due west of Naranjo and one kilometer (0.6 miles) north of Highway 1, is a gateway to the northern lowlands via a mountain road that crests the cordillera, then begins a long sinuous descent to La Tigra.

This agricultural and university town is known for its Saturday *feria del agricultor* (farmers market). The impressive **Parroquia de San Ramón Noñato** church on the main square is built of steel manufactured by the Krupp armament factory in Germany. It has a beautiful colonial tile floor and stained-glass windows. The **San Ramón Museum** (tel. 506/2437-7137, 9am-5pm Tues.-Sat., free) on the north side of the plaza, concentrates on local art exhibits; one room is dedicated to natural history. Curious to see a human embryo pickled in formaldehyde? It has one.

★ Nectandra Cloud Forest Garden

Nature lovers will thrill to hiking the trails at **Nectandra Cloud Forest Garden** (tel./fax 506/2445-4642, www.nectandra.org, 7am-5pm Tues.-Sun., $60, includes guided tour, deposit required), 15 kilometers (9.5

bungee jumping with Tropical Bungee

miles) north of San Ramón. It's surrounded by 104 hectares (257 acres) of forest reserve where quetzals can be seen while hiking its eight kilometers (5 miles) of superbly maintained trails. It has a visitors center and a café. Reservations are required.

★ El Silencio de los Ángeles Cloud Forest Reserve

The tourist-friendly **El Silencio de los Ángeles Cloud Forest Reserve,** an extension of the 800-hectare (2,000-acre) Los Ángeles Cloud Forest Reserve, begins at 700 meters (2,300 feet) elevation and tops out at 1,800 meters (5,900 feet). When the clouds clear, you can see Volcán Arenal. Three kilometers (2 miles) of manicured, well-signed trails lead into the cloud forest. Two short 1.5-kilometer (0.9-mile) and 2-kilometer (1.2-mile) trails have wooden walkways with nonslip surfaces. A third, hard-hiking trail (plan on 6-9 hours) descends past waterfalls and natural swimming pools. The calls of howler monkeys emanate from the shrouded interior, and capuchin and spider monkeys are often seen. Bird species include bellbirds, trogons, and aracaris, and laurel trees have been planted to lure quetzals (birding tours are offered at 6am and 8:15am daily, $26).

Other mammals such as ocelots, jaguars, and jaguarundis are present.

The reserve adjoins the **Villablanca Cloud Forest Hotel & Nature Reserve** (tel. 506/2461-0300, www.villablanca-costarica.com, 8am-3pm daily). Guided hikes (nonguests $26, hotel guests free) are compulsory for drop-in visitors, while hotel guests can take self-guided hikes. Don't miss the night walk at 6pm ($26). Bird-watching and nature hikes ($24-55) are offered. INBio has a research center here, specializing in butterflies, where visitors can view taxonomists studying butterflies and other insects. The tour of the hotel's organic greenhouses and compost production facility is fascinating. The *vivero* (hothouse) is especially interesting on a nocturnal tour, when you can spot dozens of frogs. The hotel's quaint **La Mariana Wedding Chapel** has a remarkable ceiling inlaid with painted ceramic tiles on the theme of Latin American religious virgins.

Recreation

The **San Lorenzo Canopy Tour** (tel. 506/2447-9331, www.canopysanlorenzo.com), 32 kilometers (20 miles) north of San Ramón, has two zip-line options: The first features 13 platforms, eight cables, and two hanging

studying a preserved specimen in the San Ramón Museum

bridges spanning two guided trails; or you can take the Adventure Cable Tour by zip line using six cables, the longest 850 meters (2,800 feet). The latter has two parallel cables, so you can race your best friend. Each costs $35 for 90 minutes, or $55 for both. There's also a canyoneering option involving a waterfall rappel ($50), plus an option to fly like Superman in a harness, guided hiking, river rafting, and a night tour.

Accommodations

Years ago I offered a ride to Habitat for Humanity volunteers Christopher Panzer and his Peruvian wife, Luisa. "You also signed a copy of my dog-eared Moon Handbook," he reminded me by email. The couple now operates a splendid B&B: Set on a hilltop with sensational views a few kilometers northeast of town, **Casa Amanecer Bed & Breakfast** (tel. 506/2445-2100, www.casa-amanecer-cr. com, $65 s, $75 d) is a family-friendly and holistic place. Constructed of teak with glazed concrete in minimalist style, its four colorful rooms are adorned with Latin American ethnic art. All rooms have spacious walk-in showers and covered verandas with rockers for enjoying the views. Vegetarian meals are served, massages are offered, and the lounge doubles as an art gallery. Guests are made to feel like family friends.

★ **Villablanca Cloud Forest Hotel & Nature Reserve** (tel. 506/2461-3800, www.

villablanca-costarica.com, low season from $170 s/d, high season from $189 s/d) sits atop the Continental Divide on the edge of the Los Ángeles reserve. The main lodge, once a colonial farmhouse, now boasts a hip contemporary face-lift. The 35 cozy chalets, which sleep 2 to 6 people, some wheelchair-accessible, are appointed with handmade hardwood pieces, small fireplaces, and both a bathtub and huge walk-in shower and (in suites) separate whirlpool tubs big enough for a *Playboy* party. The full-service spa is welcome after a day of hiking or horseback riding. The bar-lounge, with two huge hearths, flat-screen TVs, and plump leather sofas, is inviting, and there's even a sur-round-sound movie theater (a nature documentary is shown at 6pm daily, followed by a top movie at 8pm). This hotel prides itself on having earned five "leaves" in the Certification for Sustainable Tourism program. The hotel's **El Sendero Restaurant** serves gourmet Latin American fare in a classy ambience recalling the hotel's farm heritage.

Getting There and Around

Buses (tel. 506/2222-0064) for San Ramón depart San José ($1.60) every 45 minutes 5:50am-10pm daily from Calle 16, Avenidas 10/12. Taxis operate from the main plaza, or call **Taxis San Ramón** (tel. 506/2445-5966 or 506/2445-5110).

Heredia and Vicinity

HEREDIA

Heredia (pop. 32,000), 11 kilometers (7 miles) north of San José and colloquially known as La Ciudad de las Flores (City of Flowers), is surrounded by coffee fields. A pleasant atmosphere pervades the grid-patterned town despite its jostling traffic. The **National University** is here.

Heredia is centered around a weath-ered colonial cathedral—the **Basílica de**

la Inmaculada Concepción—containing beautiful stained-glass windows as well as bells delivered from Cuzco, Peru. Built in 1797, it is squat and thick-walled and has withstood many earthquakes. The church faces west onto lively **Parque Central,** shaded by large mango trees and with various busts and monuments. On the north side of the cathedral, across the street, is the bronze **Monumento Nacional a la Madre**

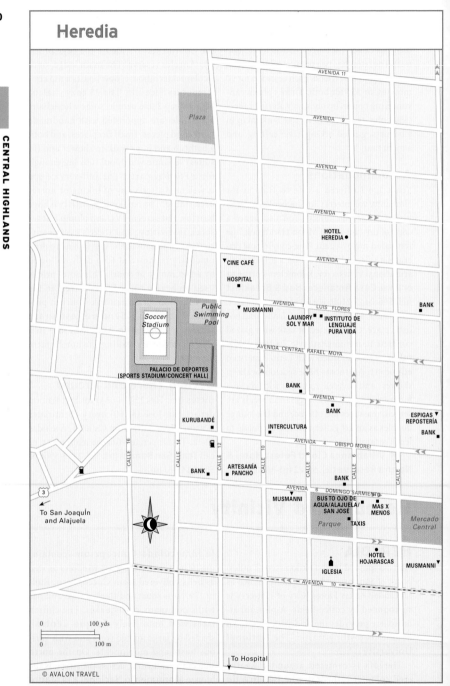

Heredia

AVENIDA 11

Plaza

AVENIDA 9

AVENIDA 7

AVENIDA 5

HOTEL
HEREDIA ●

AVENIDA 3

▼ CINE CAFÉ

HOSPITAL
■

AVENIDA 1   LUIS FLORES

BANK
■

▼ MUSMANNI

*Public
Swimming
Pool*

LAUNDRY ■   ■ INSTITUTO DE
SOL Y MAR   LENGUAJE
             PURA VIDA

*Soccer
Stadium*

AVENIDA CENTRAL RAFAEL MOYA

PALACIO DE DEPORTES
(SPORTS STADIUM/CONCERT HALL)

BANK
■

AVENIDA 2

BANK
■

KURUBANDÉ
■

INTERCULTURA
■

ESPIGAS ▼
REPOSTERÍA

BANK
■

AVENIDA 4   OBISPO MOREI

CALLE 16

CALLE 14

CALLE 12

CALLE 10

CALLE 8

CALLE 6

CALLE 4

BANK
■

ARTESANÍA
■ PANCHO

BANK
■

AVENIDA 6   DOMINGO SARMIENTO

▼ MUSMANNI

BUS TO OJO DE
AGUA/ALAJUELA/
SAN JOSÉ

MAS X
MENOS
■

Parque   TAXIS

*Mercado
Central*

3

To San Joaquín
and Alajuela

HOTEL
HOJARASCAS
■

MUSMANNI ▼

✝
IGLESIA

AVENIDA 10

| 0 | | 100 yds |
| 0 | | 100 m |

To Hospital →

© AVALON TRAVEL

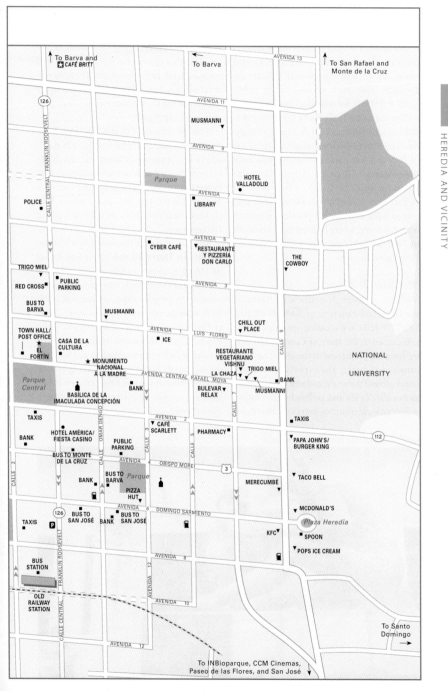

(National Monument to the Mother), by contemporary artist Francisco Zuñiga.

El Fortín, a circular fortress tower, borders the north side of the plaza. The gun slits widen to the outside, a curious piece of military ineptitude—they easily allowed bullets in but made it difficult for defenders to shoot out.

The **Casa de la Cultura** (tel. 506/2261-4485, casaheredia@cultura.cr, 9am-9pm daily, free), next to El Fortín, contains a small art gallery and historical exhibits. It was once the residence of President Alfredo González Flores (in office 1914-1917), who was exiled in 1917 after a coup d'état. He was later welcomed back and ran his political activities from his home, where he lived until his death in 1962. Refurbished, it is today a National Historic Monument.

★ Café Britt

Midway between Heredia and Barva is the finca and *beneficio* of **Café Britt** (tel. 506/2277-1600, www.coffeetour.com), where you can learn the story of Costa Rican coffee from the plantation to the cup. The company roasts, packs, and exports to specialty stores around the world and welcomes visitors to its coffee fields and garden by reservation only. Vastly entertaining tours are offered, led by staff in traditional country costumes and highlighted by a *Flavors of Costa Rica* multimedia presentation telling the history of coffee. There's a cinema for private events, and more in-depth private tours are offered by reservation. The factory store offers mail-order delivery to the United States. It has an elegant gourmet restaurant.

The 90-minute **Classic Coffee Tour** (9:30am, 11am, 12:45pm, and 3:15pm daily, adults $22, students/children $17) concludes in the tasting room, where you are shown how experts taste coffee. The four-hour Coffee & Nature Tour (11am Fri.-Sun., adults $68, children/students $68) includes a visit to INBioparque.

You can also visit the company's historic **Beneficio Tierra Madre,** above San Rafael de Heredia, about six kilometers (4 miles) northeast of Heredia; it is also open to individual visits by prior arrangement (tel. 506/2277-1600, www.beneficiotierramadre.com). Here, at Costa Rica's first certified organic-only *beneficio,* you can witness firsthand the processing of coffee in a facility adorned with exquisite murals by the nation's leading artists. A coffee-bush maze was being created at last visit, and an open-air coffee museum will have a live theater.

National Monument to the Mother, Heredia

El Fortín, Heredia

Entertainment

A *zona rosa*—a night-scene hot spot—has evolved around Avenida Central and Calle 7. Among the several bars popular with Heredia's many students are **La Choza** (tel. 506/2237-1553, 4pm-1am Mon.-Fri., 3pm-1am Sat.-Sun.), which packs 'em in nightly for music, from salsa to rock, and for U.S. football and Costa Rican soccer games on the big-screen TV; and lounge-bar-style **Chill Out Place** (Ave. 1, Calle 7, tel. 506/2560-5112, www.chilloutplacecr.com, 1pm-1:30am Tues.-Thurs., noon-2am Fri.-Sat., noon-midnight Sun.), the hippest place in town, with live music on Sunday and Reggae Roots Night on Wednesday.

The city's largest and most stylish disco is **Moon Nightlife** (tel. 506/2265-1078, 8pm-2:30am Fri.-Sun.), in a former warehouse with a fantastic light system and space for 2,500 patrons to dance to techno and salsa. It's in San Joaquín de Flores, on the road to Alajuela.

Accommodations

The modern **Hotel América** (Calle Central, Aves. 2/4, tel. 506/2260-9292, www.hotelamericacr.com, $60 s, $70 d), 50 meters (165 feet) south of Parque Central, is a good mid-range bargain. It features 50 air-conditioned rooms and suites, all with pleasing decor, phones, and private baths with hot water. It has a steak house and offers 24-hour room service, plus tours. Rates include breakfast.

Outside town, the superbly run Dutch-owned ★ **Hotel Bougainvillea** (tel. 506/2244-1414, www.bougainvillea.co.cr, $99-109 s, $109-119 d), about 800 meters (0.5 miles) east of Santo Domingo, is a splendid bargain and appeals for its fabulous setting in vast landscaped grounds (with a hedge maze) surrounded by a sea of coffee plants, with a beautiful view of the mountain ranges and San José. This gracious contemporary three-story hotel has 78 spacious rooms and four suites, a gift shop, a swimming pool, a tennis court, and an elegant restaurant. A shuttle runs to San José.

INBioparque

INBioparque (tel. 506/2507-8107, www.inbioparque.com, 8:30am-2pm Tues.-Fri., 9am-3:30pm Sat.-Sun., adults $25, students $19, children $15, includes guided tour) is an educational park two kilometers (1.2 miles) southwest of Santo Domingo, a historic village three kilometers (2 miles) southeast of Heredia and three kilometers (2 miles) north of San José. It's run by the Instituto Nacional de Biodiversidad, a nongovernmental organization devoted to cataloging Costa Rica's biodiversity. One exhibition hall focuses on the planet's biodiversity; the second lets you observe how Costa Rica was formed and inhabited. Interpretive trails lead through native habitats, with wildlife exhibits. Botanists will have a field day, and there are caimans, frogs, iguanas, and a butterfly garden. Visitors can opt for guided tours ($3 for 2 hours). Last admission is one hour before closing. Transfers cost $10.

San José-Heredia Commuter Train

The **Tren Interurbano** is a commuter train that connects San José and Heredia. Operated by TUASA (Transportes Unidos Alajuelenses, www.incofer.go.cr), which also operates local bus service, the route is served by four air-conditioned two-car diesel-powered trains along a 10-kilometer (6-mile) route between San José's Terminal Pacífico and the Terminal Heredia (Ave. 10, Calle Central).

The trains depart 15 times daily and make seven stops along the route: Calderón Guardia in Tibas, San Francisco, Colima, Cuatro Reinas, Santa Rosa de Santo Domingo, Miraflores, and Heredia Central, ending at Heredia's hospital.

The trip takes 30 minutes and costs a bargain 460 colones (US$0.85)—not bad for a service that has cost Costa Rica's INCOFER rail agency US$3.5 million to purchase and install. The trains make the commute oh-so-much easier—those commuting by car are often stuck for up to an hour in traffic on the congested roads linking the capital with the country's third-largest city.

Food

Outside town, at Santo Domingo, the **Hotel Bougainvillea** (tel. 506/2244-1414, www.hb.co.cr) is known for its excellent cuisine in a gracious restaurant. It offers a *plato fuerte* (entrée, dessert, and coffee) for $15—a good value. Don't miss the buffet brunch on Sunday. Also in Santo Domingo, **Ceviche del Rey** (tel. 506/2244-2985, www.ceviche-delreycr.com, 11:30am-3pm and 6pm-11pm Mon.-Thurs., 11:30am-11pm Fri.-Sun.) serves superb Peruvian dishes, such as appetizers of boiled potatoes with cheese cream or octopus salad with olives, and sea bass in mushroom sauce.

Downtown and good for filling up for pennies is **Spoon** (tel. 506/2263-2159, www.spooncr.com, 8am-9pm daily), in Plaza Heredia; this clean, well-run, air-conditioned café serves a wide range of value-priced set meals, salads, pastries, and desserts. I also like **Espigas Repostería** (Ave. 2, Calle 2, tel. 506/2237-3275, 7am-9:30pm daily), a well-run café and bakery with a pleasing ambience. It serves pastries, patties, and a value-priced lunchtime buffet ($4). **Trigo Miel** (Ave. 3 at Calle Central, tel. 506/2237-9696, www.trigomiel.com, 7am-8pm Mon.-Sat., 8am-6pm Sun.) has a pleasant Wi-Fi lounge and serves delicious fresh-baked goods and coffees and teas.

For vegetarian dishes, head to **Restaurante Vegetariano Vishnu Mango Verde** (Calle 7, Aves. Central/1, tel. 506/2237-2526, 8am-7pm Mon.-Sat.), serving pita sandwiches (from $2), veggie burgers ($2), and *batidos* ($1) in several cubicle-like rooms.

Information and Services

Hospital San Vicente (Calle 14, Ave. 16, tel. 506/2261-0091) and the **Red Cross** (Ave. 3, Calle Central) provide medical services. There's a **pharmacy** at Avenida 2, Calle 7. The **police station** is on Calle Central, Avenidas 5/7. Criminal investigation is handled by the **OIJ** (tel. 506/2262-1011). The **post office** is on the northwest corner of the plaza.

Heredia is known for its language schools, which include **Intercultura** (Ave. 4, Calle 12, tel. 506/2260-8480, www.interculturacostarica.com); and **Centro Panamericano de Idiomas** (tel. 506/2265-6306, www.cpi-edu.com), in San Joaquín de Heredia.

Getting There

Microbuses Rápido (tel. 506/2233-8392) offers bus service from San José ($0.55) every 10 minutes 5am-midnight daily, and every 30 minutes midnight-5am daily, from Calle 1, Avenidas 7/9; and on the same schedule from Avenida 2, Calles 12/14 (tel. 506/2222-8966). In Heredia, minibuses depart for San José from Calle 1, Avenidas 7/9, and buses from Avenida 2, Calles 10/12.

Basílica de Barva adorned for Independence Day

from 1885 and once owned by former president Alfredo González Flores; the house has been kept as it was when he died. It has exhibits on traditional Costa Rican architecture through the ages. Guided tours are offered for groups only. Sunday is family day, with clowns and shows for children.

Buses for Barva depart Heredia from Calle Central, Avenidas 1/3.

SANTA BÁRBARA DE HEREDIA

This lively and compact town with colonial-era adobe houses sits in the heart of coffee country, about five kilometers (3 miles) northwest of Heredia and three kilometers (2 miles) west of Barva.

A perfect alternative to Café Britt is the **Finca Rosa Blanca Organic Coffee Tour** (tel. 506/2269-9392, www.fincarosablanca. com), at a 14-hectare (35-acre) sustainable organic coffee estate one kilometer east of town. Tours are led by acclaimed barista Leo Vergnani, one of Costa Rica's most knowledgeable coffee experts. Leo is also a tremendous orator who infuses his presentations with vitality and fascinating lore. You can even participate in the coffee harvest (Oct.-Jan.). The finca has a stable for horseback rides.

The Ark Herb Farm (tel. 506/2239-2111, www.arkherbfarm.com, by appointment 8am-4pm Mon.-Sat., $12) covers seven hectares (17 acres) of tranquil gardens on the lower slopes of Barva, 2.5 kilometers (1.5 miles) above Santa Bárbara de Heredia. More than 400 varieties of medicinal herbs, shrubs, and trees from around the world are grown here, mostly for export to North America. Another 600 species are grown in the garden. Owners Tommy and Patricia Thomas offer fascinating one-hour tours (by appointment) that will leave you enthralled.

Accommodations and Food

If Gaudí and Frank Lloyd Wright had combined their talents, the result might be an architectural stunner as eclectic and

Taxis wait on the south side of Parque Central, or call tel. 506/2260-3300.

BARVA

Barva, about two kilometers (1.2 miles) north of Heredia, is one of the oldest settlements in the country. The **Basílica de Barva,** which dates to 1767, features a grotto on its northeast corner dedicated to the Virgin of Lourdes. The exquisite church faces a square full of contemporary sculptures and surrounded by red-tiled colonial-era adobe houses. Barva is famous as a center for huge *mascaras,* which even top the street signs. It hosts the **Feria de la Mascarada**—the Mask Festival—in late March, when locals don giant masks, many of which mock politicians and celebrities.

The **Museum of Popular Culture** (tel. 506/2260-1619, 8am-4pm Mon.-Fri., by appointment Sat., 10am-4pm Sun., $1), signed 1.5 kilometers (0.9 miles) southeast of Barva, at Santa Lucía de Barva, presents a picture of rural life at the turn of the 20th century. It is housed in a renovated adobe home dating electrifying as ★ **Finca Rosa Blanca Coffee Plantation & Inn** (tel. 506/2269-9392, www. fincarosablanca.com, low season $260-420 s/d, high season $320-565 s/d), one kilometer (0.6 miles) northeast of Santa Bárbara de Heredia. Inspired by Gaudí's architectonics and the Santa Fe style, the family-run Rosa Blanca is one of Costa Rica's preeminent boutique hotels. The ecologically sensitive hotel was the first in the nation to earn a perfect 100 percent in the Certification for Sustainable Tourism awards, which the owner was instrumental in founding. Its hillside position amid six hectares (15 acres) of coffee and orchards offers romantic vistas. The focal point is a circular atrium lounge with wraparound sofas and an open hearth. The place is like a museum, with imaginative and tasteful statuettes, prints, and New Mexican artifacts in every delightful nook and cranny. Tended by U.S. expat owners Glenn and Teri Jampol, it has 11 gorgeous junior suites, two master suites, and four villas, all with Wi-Fi. Each individually themed room is luxuriously appointed with pillow-top mattresses, down duvets, and a whirlpool tub; most are named for their trompe l'oeil landscapes. The honeymoon suite has a bath with walls painted to resemble a tropical rainforest, with water that tumbles down a rocky cascade into the fathoms-deep tub shaped liked a natural pool; and a hardwood spiral staircase twists up to a rotunda bedroom with a canopied bed and wraparound windows. There is an infinity swimming pool, a hot tub, a library, a stable for guided horseback rides (2-hour minimum, $45 pp), and the superb El Tigre Vestido restaurant, adjoined by a full-service spa.

★ **Restaurante El Tigre Vestido** (tel. 506/2269-9392, www.eltigrevestido.com, 6am-10pm daily), set above coffee fields at Finca Rosa Blanca Coffee Plantation & Inn, one kilometer (0.6 miles) northeast of Santa Bárbara de Heredia, serves gourmet four-course dinners using organic estate-grown produce. Breakfasts include tropical fruit *arepas* (pancakes, $8) and homemade granola ($5). Lunches such as Central American *pupusas* are served on a huge banana leaf. Leave room for the homemade ice cream. The Latin fusion menu, prepared by chef Rodrigo Nuñez, includes squash soup ($8), mountain trout on a ragout of saffron sweet corn ($15), and pork loin with crisp leeks and coffee sauce ($20). Choose to eat in the stylish indoors or on a lovely shaded deck with views over San José.

It could be the most fun you've had at

Finca Rosa Blanca Coffee Plantation & Inn

a restaurant in eons, so plan on dining at ★ **La Lluna de Valencia** (tel. 506/2269-6665, www.lallunadevalencia.com, 7pm-10pm Thurs., noon-10pm Fri.-Sat., noon-5pm Sun., mid-Jan.-mid-Dec.), an informal Spanish restaurant at San Pedro de Barva, between Barva and Santa Bárbara de Heredia. Its ebullient and eccentric Catalan owner, Vicente Aguilar, is a riot! The setting is a charming centenary building with a rustic thatched extension out back. It serves flavorful Spanish dishes. For appetizers, try the gazpacho ($6) or octopus in wine ($7.50). For a main course, you must order paella, especially the seafood paella ($9.50), accompanied by a carafe of killer sangria. End with a *carajillo* house café with various liqueurs. Go for the flamenco the first Sunday of every month, and live music every Friday and Saturday night. And boy, can Vicente sing!

Getting There

A bus for Santa Bárbara de Heredia departs Heredia from Avenida 1, Calles 1/3, every 15 minutes Monday-Friday. From Heredia, Calle Central leads north to Barva, where you turn left at the plaza and head straight (westward) for Santa Bárbara de Heredia.

THE SLOPES OF BARVA VOLCANO

The southern slopes of Volcán Barva are laced by narrow roads that ascend sharply to alpine retreats, most easily accessed from Barva.

Five hundred meters (0.3 miles) north of Barva, the road forks. The left fork leads via the village of **Birrí** to Carraizal and Volcán Poás. In Birrí, a road to the right at Restaurante Las Delicias leads east, steeply uphill, to the hamlet of **Porrosatí** (also known as Paso Llano), a true alpine setting with Swiss-style houses and where the air is decidedly chilly. The area below Porrosatí is known for its mountain resorts in the midst of pine forests. (The right fork at the Y junction north of Barva also leads uphill to Porrosatí, via **San José de la Montaña**.)

At Porrosatí, a turnoff to the left leads via the hamlet of Sacramento to the **Parque Nacional Braulio Carrillo** ranger station. The **Canopy Adventure** (tel. 506/2266-0782, www.canopycr.com), one kilometer (0.6 miles) below Porrosatí, has 13 platforms with zip lines (adults $45, children $35). The longest run is 200 meters (660 feet). Prefer to keep your feet on the ground? There are also trails, and two- to eight-hour guided hikes.

Centro Turístico Monte de la Cruz

Two kilometers (1.2 miles) northeast of Heredia and two kilometers (1.2 miles) east of Barva lies **San Rafael,** on the lower slopes of Volcán Barva. A medieval stonemason would be proud of the town's Gothic church, with its buttresses and magnificent stained-glass windows.

North of San Rafael, the road begins a progressive ascent, the temperatures begin to drop, and hints of the Swiss Tyrol begin to appear, with pine and cedar forests and emerald-green pastures grazed by dairy cattle. Remnants of ancient oaks and other primary forests carpet the higher reaches. Passing the upscale Club Campestre El Castillo, at a Y-fork two kilometers (1.2 miles) beyond head right to **Monte de la Cruz Reserve** (8am-4pm Mon.-Fri., 8am-5pm Sat.-Sun.). This 15-hectare (37-acre) private forest reserve, eight kilometers (5 miles) north of San Rafael, offers trails through pine forest and cloud forest good for spotting quetzals. It is often cloudy and usually cool, if not cold and wet.

The fork to the left north of El Castillo leads to the Parque Residencial del Monte, an exclusive residential area that includes the **Hotel Chalet Tirol** (tel. 506/2267-6222, www.hotel-chaleteltirol.com) within the 15-hectare (37-acre) private Tirol Cloud Forest on the upper reaches of Barva. Horseback rides cost $50, by reservation.

Events

The **Costa Rica Music Festival** (tel. 506/2282-7724, www.costaricamusic.com) is hosted at Hotel Chalet Tirol each July

The Slopes of Barva Volcano

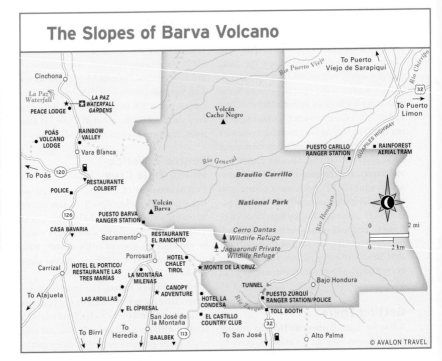

Cinchona

La Paz Waterfall
PEACE LODGE

LA PAZ WATERFALL GARDENS

To Puerto Viejo de Sarapiquí

To Puerto Limón

POÁS VOLCANO LODGE

RAINBOW VALLEY

Vara Blanca

To Poás 120

RESTAURANTE COLBERT

POLICE

126

PUESTO BARVA RANGER STATION

CASA BAVARIA

Sacramento

RESTAURANTE EL RANCHITO

Porrosatí

HOTEL EL PORTICO/RESTAURANTE LAS TRES MARIAS

Carrizal

LA MONTAÑA MILENAS

HOTEL CHALET TIROL

LAS ARDILLAS

CANOPY ADVENTURE

To Alajuela

EL CIPRESAL

San José de la Montaña

BAALBEK 113

To Birrí

To Heredia

Volcán Cacho Negro

PUESTO CARILLO RANGER STATION

GUÁPILES HIGHWAY

Río General

Braulio Carrillo

Volcán Barva

National Park

Cerro Dantas Wildlife Refuge

Jaguarundi Private Wildlife Refuge

MONTE DE LA CRUZ

TUNNEL

Bajo Hondura

HOTEL LA CONDESA

PUESTO ZURQUÍ RANGER STATION/POLICE

EL CASTILLO COUNTRY CLUB

TOLL BOOTH

32

To San José

Alto Palma

Rainforest Aerial Tram

To Puerto Limón

0   2 mi
0   2 km

© AVALON TRAVEL

and August in the Salzburg Café Concert Dinner Theater, which looks like a set for *The Sound of Music*. The hotel offers other events throughout the year.

Accommodations

For alpine rusticity amid the pines, you can't beat the **Las Ardillas Spa Resort** (tel. 506/2266-0015, www.grupoardillas.com, $85 s/d), with eight rustic log-and-brick cabins, each with a fireplace and kitchenette. The resort is two miles above Birrí, en route to Porrosatí. There's a game room, a bar and restaurant, a children's play area, and a simple spa with a whirlpool and a sauna. Hiking is offered. Rates include breakfast and tax, plus spa treatments on weekends.

For quaint charm, check into Tyrolean-themed **Hotel Chalet Tirol** (Centro Turístico Monte de la Cruz, tel. 506/2267-6222, www.hotelchaleteltirol.com, chalet $93-128 s/d, suites $93-155 s/d year-round), with 10 rustic yet charming twin-level alpine

cabins hand-painted in Swiss fashion. Or opt for one of 13 modern hotel rooms, each with a TV, fireplace, and furnishings from a Hansel-and-Gretel story. There's a pool, a sauna, a fitness room, two tennis courts, and Wi-Fi in the lodge, which has an excellent restaurant.

Food

For wonderful rustic mountain ambience, try **Las Ardillas** (tel. 506/2266-0015, www.grupoardillas.com, 7am-8pm Mon.-Thurs., 7am-9pm Fri., 7am-11pm Sat., 7am-9pm Sun., $4-10), centered on a stone hearth and serving steak in red wine, filet mignon, almond sea bass, and the like prepared on a wood-burning stove using organic homegrown produce. It's located two miles above Birrí, en route to Porrosatí.

The French **Restaurante Los Tiroleses** (tel. 506/2267-6222, noon-7pm Mon., noon-8:30pm Tues.-Wed., noon-10pm Thurs., noon-midnight Fri.-Sat., noon-6pm Sun.)

at Hotel Chalet Tirol (tel. 506/2267-6222, www.hotelchaleteltirol.com) is twinned, incongruously, with an Irish pub called the Green Dragon. Think escargots ($8) and chateaubriand with béarnaise and mushroom sauce ($18).

I love ★ **Baalbek Bar and Grill** (tel. 506/2267-6683, www.baalbekbaryrestaurante.com, noon-midnight Mon.-Thurs. and Sun., noon-1am Fri.-Sat.) at Los Ángeles de San Rafael, about five kilometers (3 miles) below Monte Cruz de la Montaña. This upscale Lebanese restaurant boasts sublime views as well as splendid Mediterranean food such as *mehshe* (chicken and rice rolled in cabbage leaves, with hummus and salad, $12) and baba ghanoush (grilled eggplant with tahini, $6.50). Choose from the elegant downstairs restaurant or more intimate booths with hookahs upstairs. It has live music, from blues to Arabian, plus belly dancers on Saturday night.

Getting There

Buses depart Heredia for San José de la Montaña, Porrosatí, and Sacramento from Calle 1, Avenidas Central/2, at 5:25am, 6:25am, noon, and 4pm Monday-Friday and 6:30am, 11am, and 4pm Saturday-Sunday. Buses from Porrosatí depart at 7:30am, 1pm, and 5pm daily.

Buses for San Rafael depart Heredia from the Mercado Central hourly 8am-8pm daily. Buses to El Castillo and Bosque de la Hoja depart Heredia from the Mercado Central hourly 8am-8pm daily. For Monte de la Cruz, take a bus departing at 9am, noon, or 4pm daily.

Braulio Carrillo National Park and Vicinity

Northeast from San José, the Guápiles Highway (Hwy. 32) climbs up the saddle between the Barva and Irazú volcanoes and enters Parque Nacional Braulio Carrillo (www.sinac.go.cr) before descending to the Caribbean lowlands.

En route, divert west off Highway 32 to **San Isidro de Heredia.** This otherwise sleepy town on the southwestern slope of the Volcán Barva is renowned for its multiple-spired Gothic church, looking like it belongs on the top of an iced wedding cake.

Nearby, in the community of San Josecito, midway between San Isidro and Highway 32, is **Toucan Rescue Ranch** (tel. 506/2268-4041, www.toucanrescueranch.org, donation), a licensed wild-animal rescue facility that offers a chance to see toucans, macaws, sloths, and other creatures in a farm-like setting. You can even stay at the charming colonial-era quinta (farm) with its red-tile rooms ($85 s/d, including breakfast). It's open by reservation only for "Breakfast with the Babies"

at 8am (adults $50, children $20), and two-hour tours at 2pm (adults $24, children $12). Custom tours can be arranged.

BRAULIO CARRILLO NATIONAL PARK

Rugged mountains, dormant volcanoes, deep canyons, swollen rivers, seemingly interminable clouds, torrential rains, and persistent drizzle characterize **Parque Nacional Braulio Carrillo,** which begins 20 kilometers (12 miles) northeast of San José. The 47,699-hectare (117,866-acre) park, 84 percent of which is primary forest, was established in 1978 and named in honor of the president who promoted the cultivation of coffee. It extends from 2,906 meters (9,534 feet) above sea level atop Volcán Barva down to 36 meters (118 feet) elevation at La Selva, in Sarapiquí in the Caribbean lowlands. This represents the greatest elevation range of any Costa Rican park. Temperature and rainfall vary greatly and are extremely unpredictable. Annual rainfall is between 400 and 800 centimeters (150-315 inches). Rains tend to diminish in March and April.

Encompassing five ecological zones ranging from tropical wet to cloud forest, Braulio Carrillo provides a home for 600 identified species of trees, more than 500 species of birds, and 135 species of mammals, including howler and capuchin monkeys, tapirs, jaguars, pumas, ocelots, peccaries, and the *tepezcuintle* (lowland paca), the park's mascot. The park provides excellent birding. Quetzals are common at higher elevations, and toucans, parrots, and hummingbirds are ubiquitous. Those elephant ear-size leaves common in Braulio Carrillo are *sombrilla del pobre* (poor man's umbrella).

There have been armed robberies in the park. Hike with a park ranger if possible. Theft from cars parked near trailheads has also been a problem.

sprawling roots in the rainforest

Entrances

The main entrance ($10) is the **Puesto Quebrada González** (tel. 506/2257-0922, 8am-4pm daily) ranger station, on Highway 32 approximately 42 kilometers (26 miles) northeast of San José on the lower northern slopes, 15 kilometers (9.5 miles) north of the Zurquí tunnel; ironically you pass through the park to get there. Northbound from San José, you first enter the park at Zurquí just west of the tunnel; there's a tollbooth ($0.50). Zurquí (tel. 506/2268-1039) is the administrative headquarters, but the trails here are closed to the public.

You can also enter the park at **Puesto Barva** ranger station (tel. 506/2266-1883, 8am-4pm Tues.-Sun.), three kilometers (2 miles) northeast of Sacramento and just three kilometers (2 miles) from the summit of Volcán Barva (2,906 meters/9,534 feet); access is via a very steep, deeply rutted rock road—a 4WD vehicle is essential, and you'll be in first gear.

Two other stations—**Puesto El Ceibo** and **Puesto Magsasay** (both 8am-5pm daily)— lie on the remote western fringes of the park,

reached by rough trails from just south of La Virgen, on the main road to Puerto Viejo de Sarapiquí.

Hiking

Three short and moderately easy trails lead from Quebrada González: **Sendero El Ceibo** is one kilometer (0.6 miles); **Sendero Las Palmas** is two kilometers (1.2 miles); and **Sendero Los Botarramas** is approximately three kilometers (2 miles). South of the ranger station is a parking area on the left (when heading north) with a lookout point and a trail to the Río Patria, where you can camp (no facilities). Another parking area beside the bridge over the Río Sucio (Dirty River) has picnic tables and a short loop trail.

Four trails are accessed from Puesto Barva. A loop trail leads to the summit from Porrosatí (the trail is marked as "BCNP Sector Barva") and circles back to the ranger station (4-5 hours of hiking round-trip). The trail leads up through cloud forest—good for spotting resplendent quetzals—to the crater and a lookout point. Fog, however, is usually the order of the day. From the summit, you can continue all the way downhill to La Selva in the northern lowlands. It's a lengthy and arduous hike that may take several days and is recommended only for experienced hikers with suitable equipment. Take an Instituto Geográfica map and a compass, plus high-quality waterproof gear and warm clothing, and—of course—sufficient food and water. You can camp beside the crater lake, behind the ranger station, or at two picnic areas with barbecue grills on the trail (no facilities). You can join this trail from Puesto El Ceibo and Puesto Magsasay; you can also drive in a short distance along a 4WD trail from Puesto Magsasay.

Bring sturdy rain gear, and preferably hiking boots. The trails will most likely be muddy. Several hikers have become lost for days in the fog and torrential rains. If you intend to do serious hiking, let rangers know in advance, and check in with them when you return.

Getting There

Buses for Guápiles and Puerto Limón depart several times per hour from San José's Gran Terminal Caribe, at Calle Central, Avenidas 15/17; they drop off and pick up at the Zurquí and Puesto Carrillo ranger stations.

Most tour operators in San José offer tours to Braulio Carrillo.

★ SIBÚ CHOCOLATE

Not to be missed while passing through Braulio Carrillo is a visit to **Sibú Chocolate** (tel. 506/2268-1335, www.sibuchocolate. com, $24), an artisanal chocolate producer and café adjoining the home of co-owners and master chocolatiers Julio Fernández and George Soriano, 200 meters west of Hwy 32 at the main turn-off for San Isidro de Heredia at the Restaurante Rancho Zurquí (the road instantly forks, with San Isidro to the left; take the right fork that parallels Highway 32, passing Los Filtros JSM company; Sibú is signed from here). A historian and former naturalist guide fluent in English, Julio gives spellbinding presentation on the history and ecology of cacao and chocolate-making to accompany a tasting of gourmet truffles, caramel, and pure dark chocolate tasting squares that are a pure gustatory delight. Surprise—chocolate was first made by Mesoamerican indigenous peoples. The name Sibú pays homage to the Bribrí and Cabecar creator god, and each individual

creations at Sibú Chocolate

handcrafted chocolate is made from 100 percent organic locally produced cacao and decorated in pre-Columbian designs. You can watch artisans tempering chocolate on marble slabs and decorate bonbons by hand. Linger for lunch in the café and explore the organic gardens. Reservations are essential, 48 hours in advance.

Cartago and Vicinity

East of San José, the Autopista Florencio del Castillo passes through the suburb of Curridabat, climbs over the ridge known as Cerros de la Carpintera, then drops steeply to Cartago, about 21 kilometers (12 miles) southeast of San José. Cartago is a gateway to Parque Nacional Volcán Irazú, the Orosi Valley, and Turrialba.

CARTAGO

The city of Cartago (pop. 120,000) was founded in 1563 by Juan Vásquez de Coronado, the Spanish governor, as the nation's first city. Cartago—a Spanish word for Carthage, the ancient North African trading center—reigned as the colonial capital until losing its status to San José in the violent internecine squabbles of 1823. Volcán Irazú looms over Cartago: In 1841 and again in 1910, earthquakes toppled much of the city.

A **statue of the Virgen de los Ángeles** by world-famous sculpture Jiménez Deredia greets visitors arriving from San José along Avenida 2.

Cartago's central landmark is the ruins of the **Iglesia de la Parroquia** (Ave. 2, Calle 2), alias Ruinas Santiago Apostól and colloquially called "Las Ruinas." Completed in 1575 to honor Saint James the Apostle, the church was destroyed by earthquakes and rebuilt a number of times before its final destruction in the earthquake of 1910. Today, only the walls remain.

The **Cartago Municipal Museum** (Ave. 6, Calle 2, tel. 506/2591-1050, 9am-4pm Tues.-Sat., 9am-3pm Sun., free) is housed in the handsome Comandancia de la Fuerza Pública de Cartago, the former army barracks. It has exhibits on the history of the city and hosts temporary art exhibitions and live concerts.

Basilica de Nuestra Señora de los Ángeles, Cartago

La Negrita Pilgrimage

Every August 2, hundreds of Costa Ricans walk from towns far and wide to pay homage to the country's patron saint, La Negrita, at Cartago's Basílica de Nuestra Señora de los Ángeles. The event attracts pilgrims from throughout Central America. Many start at dawn and *crawl* all the way from San José on their knees. Others carry large wooden crosses. On any day, you can see the devout crawling down the aisle, muttering their invocations, repeating the sacred names, oblivious (one hopes) to the pain.

Basílica de Nuestra Señora de los Ángeles

Cartago's imposing cupola-topped **Basílica de Nuestra Señora de los Ángeles** (Cathedral of Our Lady of the Angels, Aves. 2/4, Calles 14/16, tel. 506/2551-0465), 10 blocks east of the main plaza, faces onto Plaza de Santuario Nacional. There's a unique beauty to the soaring all-wood interior, with its marvelous stained-glass windows, ornate altar, various shrines, and columns and walls painted in floral motifs. The cathedral is home to Costa Rica's patron saint, La Negrita, or La Virgen de los Ángeles, and the destination of thousands of Costa Ricans during the annual La Romería pilgrimage. The 20-centimeter-tall (8-inch-tall) black statue of La Negrita is embedded in a gold- and jewel-encrusted shrine above the main altar. According to superstition, in 1635 a mulatto peasant girl named Juana Pereira found a small stone statue of the Virgin holding the Christ child. Twice Juana took the statue home and placed it in a box, and twice it mysteriously reappeared at the spot where it was discovered. The cathedral is said to mark the spot (the first cathedral was toppled by an earthquake in 1926).

Beneath the basilica (and entered from the northeast corner) is the **Cripta de la Piedra de Hellaza**—a crypt with the rock where Juana supposedly found La Negrita, plus fascinating displays of ex-votos or *promesas:* gold and silver charms and other offerings. On the southeast corner, a spring (*la fuente*) that emanates from the ground is said to have curative powers.

Accommodations and Food

The best option in the city is **Casa Mora B&B** (Calle 16, Aves. 4/6, tel. 506/2551-0324, www.casamoracr.com, $57-80 s, $75-98 d), Cartago's only boutique hotel. This converted wooden mansion, built in 1972 in traditional style, boasts five junior suites and suites furnished in antique fashion. It has free Wi-Fi.

Cartago Grill (Ave. 1, Calles 8/10, tel. 506/2551-5342, cartagogrill@gmail.com, 11am-2:30pm daily) specializes in meats and Argentinean-style grills and serves a *casado* ($3), or *almuerzo ejecutivo*, as does **Amadeus Café** (Calle 10, Aves. 2/4, tel. 506/2552-6262, 11am-7pm Mon.-Sat., $2-12), a small, pleasant conversion of a colonial home, now filled with contemporary art.

On the north side of the cathedral plaza, **La Puerta del Sol** (tel. 506/2551-0615, 8:30am-midnight daily) is good for *casados* ($5) and typical local dishes.

For a clean, pleasant coffee shop with Wi-Fi, head to **Trigo Miel** (Ave. 4, Calles 4/6, tel. 506/2552-2260; Ave. 5, Calles 3/5, tel. 506/2552-6303, 7am-8pm Mon.-Sat., 8am-6pm Sun.).

Information and Services

There are **banks** downtown. Medical clinics cluster around **Hospital Dr. Max Peralta** (Ave. 5, Calles 3/5, tel. 506/2550-1999, www.hmp.sa.cr). There are more **pharmacies** and **dentists** than you would care to count. The **police station** is at Avenida 6, Calle 2.

Getting There

Empresa Lumaca (tel. 506/2537-2320) buses depart San José ($0.70) from Avenida 10,

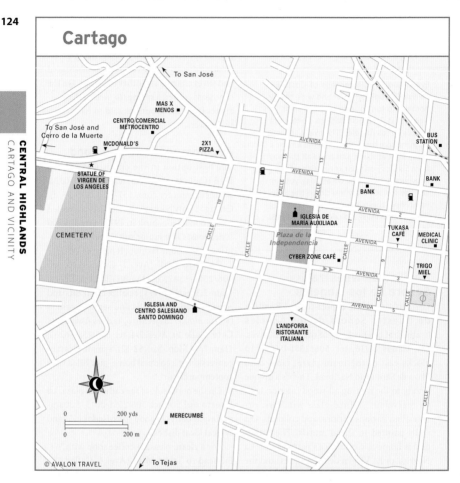

Cartago

Calle 5, every 10 minutes 4:45am-9pm daily, then less frequently until midnight. Buses will drop you along Avenida 2, ending at the Basílica. Buses depart Cartago for San José from Avenida 4, Calles 2/4; and for Turrialba from Avenida 3, Calles 8/10, every 30 minutes 6am-10:30am daily and hourly thereafter until 10:30pm.

An electric **commuter train** runs eight times daily each way between San José's Estación Atlántico and Cartago (Ave. 3, Calles 4/6, 40 minutes, $1.05), continuing to Paraíso.

Taxis hang out on the north side of Las Ruinas.

★ IRAZÚ VOLCANO NATIONAL PARK

The slopes north of Cartago rise gradually to the summit of Volcán Irazú; it's a 21-kilometer (13-mile) journey to the entrance to **Parque Nacional Volcán Irazú** (tel. 506/2200-5025, pnvolcanirazu@accvc.org, www.sinac.go.cr, 8am-3:30pm daily, $10). The slopes are dotted with tidy farming villages of pastel houses. Dairy farming is important, and the fertile fields around the village of Cot are veritable salad bowls—carrots, onions, potatoes, and greens are grown intensively.

Volcán Irazú (3,432 meters/11,260 feet)

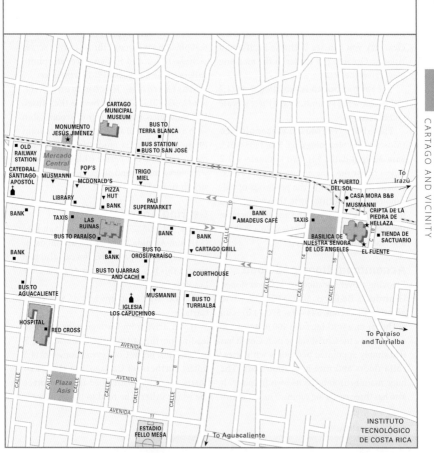

derives its name from two words from indigenous languages: *ara* (point) and *tzu* (thunder). The volcano has been ephemerally active, most famously on March 13, 1963, the day that U.S. president John F. Kennedy landed in Costa Rica on an official visit; Irazú broke a 20-year silence and began disgorging great columns of smoke and ash.

The windswept 100-meter-deep (330-foot-deep) Diego de la Haya crater contains a sometimes-pea-green, sometimes-rust-red mineral-tinted lake. A larger crater—one of five craters to be seen—is 300 meters (980 feet) deep. Two separate trails lead from the parking lot to the craters. Follow those signed with

blue-and-white symbols (don't follow other trails made by irresponsible folks whose feet destroy the fragile ecosystems). The crater rims are dangerously unstable; keep your distance.

A sense of bleak desolation pervades the summit, like the surface of the moon. It is often foggy. Even on a sunny day, expect a cold, dry, biting wind. Dress warmly. Little vegetation lives at the summit, though stunted dwarf oaks, ferns, lichens, and other species are making a comeback. The best time to visit is March or April.

Don't be put off if the volcano is shrouded in fog. Often the clouds lie below the summit of the mountain—there's no way of telling until you drive up there—and you'll emerge into brilliant sunshine as you ascend. On a clear day you can see both the Pacific and Atlantic Oceans. The earlier in the morning you arrive, the better.

The **ranger booth** is two kilometers (1.2 miles) below the summit, where there's a café and toilets.

The privately run **Museo Vulcanológico** (Museum of Volcanology, tel. 506/2305-8013, 8am-3:30pm daily, $4), two kilometers (1.2 miles) below the ranger station, offers an excellent introduction to the processes of volcanology and specifically to the geology and history of the Irazú volcano and its effects on the local community. Trails lead to a lookout and waterfalls.

Accommodations and Food

Enjoying a lovely location on the lower slopes, **Grandpa's B&B** (tel. 506/2536-7418, www. grandpashotel.com, $44-49 s, $70-74 d) is an old house on a working farm 400 meters (0.25 miles) above the Christ statue near Cot. It has five simply appointed bedrooms with terracotta floors and nice hardwood beds. The huge main bedroom has its own fireplace. It also has three rustic log cabins. The delightful

Restaurant 1910 (tel. 506/2536-6063, www. restaurant1910.com, 11:30am-9pm Mon.-Thurs., 11:30am-10pm Fri.-Sat., 11:30am-6:30pm Sun.) is a stone's throw away. It serves *comida típica* and has an excellent photo gallery of the namesake 1910 earthquake.

Restaurante Nochebuena (tel. 506/2503-8013, $25 pp), beside the Museo Vulcanológico, has a rustic three-room cabin with a fireplace and a kitchen. The restaurant (9am-4pm daily) is modestly elegant; the menu ranges from *pozole* (thick corn soup with pork, onions, and oregano, $4) to grilled sirloin steak ($8).

Getting There

Buses (tel. 506/2530-1064) depart San José ($3) from Avenida 2, Calles 1/3, at 8am daily, returning at 12:30pm daily. You can also hop aboard this bus in Cartago on Avenida 2, by Las Ruinas.

A **taxi** will cost upward of $25 from Cartago.

If you drive from Cartago, take the road leading northeast from the Basílica. At a Y junction just below Cot, seven kilometers (4.5 miles) northeast of Cartago, is a **statue of Jesus,** his arms outstretched as if to embrace the whole valley. The road to the right leads

main crater at Irazú Volcano

to Pacayas, Santa Cruz, and the Monumento Nacional Guayabo. The road to the left leads to Parque Nacional Volcán Irazú (turn right before Tierra Blanca; Irazú is signed).

PARAÍSO

Paraíso, a small town seven kilometers (4.5 miles) east of Cartago on Highway 10, is gateway to the Valle de Orosi-Cachí, to the southeast. Continue east six kilometers (4 miles), however, and you reach Birrisito de Paraíso, where Linda Mayher and Ernesto Carman run **Finca Cristina** (tel./fax 506/2574-6426, U.S. tel. 203-549-1945, www.cafecristina.com), a 12-hectare (30-acre) environmentally sound coffee farm. They welcome visitors by appointment for fascinating educational tours (adults $10, children $5) that give a total immersion in understanding the ecology of an organic coffee farm. Bring insect repellent. The sign on the highway is easy to miss; look for a white arch, then take the next dirt road to the east and go 500 meters (0.3 miles) to the unsigned red gate.

Buses (tel. 506/2574-6127) depart Cartago for Paraíso ($0.30) from the southeast side of Las Ruinas on Avenida 1 every 10 minutes 5am-11pm daily. Get off at the Camp Ayala electricity installation and walk approximately 600 meters (0.4 miles) to the south.

Jardín Botánico Lankester

Covering 10.7 hectares (26 acres) of exuberant forest and gardens, **Jardín Botánico Lankester** (tel. 506/2552-3247, www.jbl.ucr.ac.cr, 8:30am-4:30pm daily, adults $7.50, students and children $5.50), one kilometer (0.6 miles) west of Paraíso, is one of the most valuable botanical centers in the Americas, with about 1,000 native and exotic orchid species (best in Feb.-Apr.), plus bromeliads, heliconias, bamboo, cacti, and palms, plus a Japanese garden and a fern garden. You can pre-book guided tours.

The garden was conceived by an Englishman, Charles Lankester West, who arrived in Costa Rica in 1898 and established the garden in 1917 as an adjunct to his coffee plantation. After his death, the garden was donated to the University of Costa Rica in 1973.

OROSI-CACHÍ VALLEY

South of Paraíso, Highway 224 drops steeply into the Valle de Orosi, a self-contained world dedicated to raising coffee and centered on a huge artificial lake drained by the Río Reventazón. Highway 224 divides below

Oxen are still used to till the fields on Irazú Volcano.

Orosi-Cachí Valley

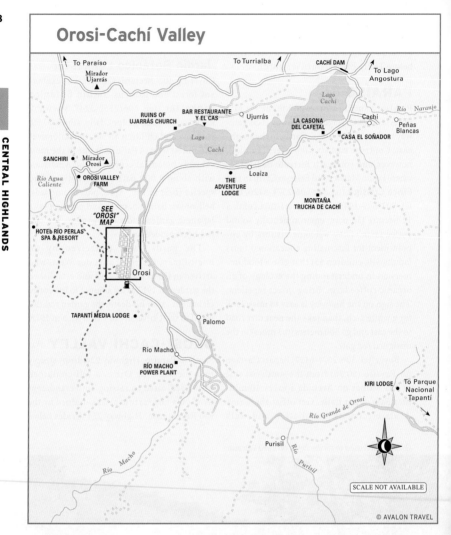

To Paraíso

Mirador Ujarrás

To Turrialba

CACHÍ DAM

To Lago Angostura

Lago Cachí

RUINS OF UJARRÁS CHURCH

BAR RESTAURANTE Y EL CAS

Ujurrás

LA CASONA DEL CAFETAL

Río Naranjo

Cachí

Peñas Blancas

Lago Cachí

CASA EL SOÑADOR

SANCHIRI

Mirador Orosi

OROSI VALLEY FARM

Río Agua Caliente

Loaiza

THE ADVENTURE LODGE

MONTAÑA TRUCHA DE CACHÍ

SEE "OROSI" MAP

HOTEL RÍO PERLAS SPA & RESORT

Orosi

TAPANTÍ MEDIA LODGE

Palomo

Río Macho

RÍO MACHO POWER PLANT

KIRI LODGE

To Parque Nacional Tapantí

Río Grande de Orosi

Purisil

Río Purísil

Río Macho

SCALE NOT AVAILABLE

© AVALON TRAVEL

Paraíso and loops around Lago Cachí: one way drops to Orosi, the other to Ujarrás; the valley, which is surrounded on all sides by mountains, thus makes a fine full-day circular tour.

For a fabulous view over the valley, call in at **Mirador Orosi** (tel. 506/2574-4688, 8am-4:30pm daily, free), two kilometers (1.2 miles) south of Paraíso. This park has lawns, topiary, and picnic tables.

If you're traveling to or from Turrialba, take the dramatically scenic road that links Ujarrás with the main highway about two kilometers (1.2 miles) east of Cervantes; this roller coaster snakes through boulder-strewn countryside farmed with chayote; it's awesome.

Orosi

The village of Orosi, eight kilometers (5 miles) south of Paraíso, is the center of the coffee-growing region. Its main claim to fame is its charming **Iglesia San José de Orosi,** built by the Franciscans in 1735 of solid adobe with a rustic timbered roof, terra-cotta tiled floor, and gilt altar. The restored church, adorned with gilt icons, has withstood earth tremors with barely a mark for almost three centuries. The church adjoins a small **religious art museum** (tel. 506/2533-3051, 1pm-5pm Tues.-Fri., 9am-5pm Sat.-Sun., $0.75) displaying furniture, religious statuary, paintings, and silver. Photography is not allowed.

Vivero Anita (tel. 506/2533-3307, www.viveroanita.com, 8:30am-5pm daily, $1), next to Orosi Lodge, raises orchids and welcomes visitors.

South of town, the road divides at Río Macho: The main road crosses the river (a small toll is collected on Sun.) and turns north to continue around the lake's southern shore via the village of Cachí. A side road continues south nine kilometers (5.5 miles) to Parque Nacional Tapantí via the Río Grande valley.

Around Lago Cachí

Lago Cachí (Lake Cachí) was created when the Instituto Costarricense de Electricidad (ICE) built the Cachí dam across the Río Reventazón to supply San José with hydroelectric power.

On the southern shore, just east of Cachí village, **Casa del Soñador** (Dreamer's House, tel. 506/2577-1186 or 506/8955-7779, qhermes@rocketmail.com, 9am-6pm daily, free) is the unusual home of brothers Hermes and Miguel Quesada, who carry on the tradition of their father, Macedonio, of carving crude figurines from coffee-plant roots; the carvings are offered for sale. The house—with carved figures leaning over the windows—is made entirely of rough-cut wood. Check out the *Last Supper* on one of the walls.

Ujarrás, on the north shore of the lake, seven kilometers (4.5 miles) southeast of Paraíso, is the site of **Las Ruinas de Ujarrás** (8am-4:30pm daily, free), the ruins of a church, Nuestra Señora de la Limpia Concepción, built out of limestone between 1681 and 1693 to honor La Virgen del Rescate de Ujarrás. The church owes its existence to

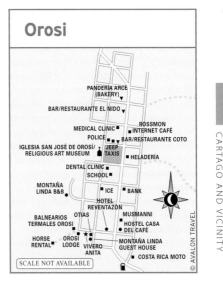

an imagined miracle. In 1666 the pirate Henry Morgan led a raiding party into the Valle de Turrialba to sack the highland cities. They were routed after the defenders prayed at Ujarrás. The ruins are set in a walled garden. Thousands of pilgrims from Paraíso flock here each Easter Sunday to honor the imagined intercession of the Virgin Mary in the pirate attack.

Sports and Recreation

Balnearios Termales Orosi (tel. 506/2533-2156, 7:30am-4pm Wed.-Mon., $2), two blocks west of the plaza, has 30°C (86°F) mineral hot-spring pools; it's clean and well run.

You can fish for trout at **Montaña Trucha de Cachí** (tel. 506/2577-1457), 1.5 kilometers (0.9 miles) south of Highway 224, near the village of Cachí.

Aventuras Orosi (tel. 506/2533-4000, www.aventurasorosicr.com) guarantees you white-water thrillws, offers a canopy zip-line tour, and also has a rope climb between treetops. You can book through **Orosi Tourist Info & Art Café** (OTIA, tel. 506/2533-3640, otiac@ice.go.cr) in the village center. It's the best source for information on local activities.

Accommodations

Choose a dorm, opt for more salubrious private digs, or arrange a homestay at **Montaña Linda** (tel. 506/2533-3640, www.montanalinda.com), one block north of Balnearios Termales Orosi. Run by Dutch couple Sara and Toine Verkuijlen, this rustic yet welcoming place has for years been a favorite of backpackers, and of language students at their Spanish school. The hostel (dorm $9 pp, private room $15 s, $22 d) has three dorms and eight private rooms with hot water; a separate guesthouse three blocks away has three upstairs rooms (two with double beds, one with a double and a bunk, $30 s, 40 d). Meals are served, and guests get kitchen privileges.

I frequently stay at the delightful **Orosi Lodge Cabinas y Cafetería** (tel./fax 506/2533-3578, www.orosilodge.com, low season $51 s/d, high season $58 s/d), next to Balneario Termales Orosi, three blocks south of the church. Inspired by local architecture, with clay lamps and locally crafted hardwoods, it has six simply furnished rooms in a charming two-story whitewashed structure. All have bamboo furnishings, colorful little baths with hot water, and a balcony with views. You can also choose a two-bedroom chalet (low season $75 s/d, high season $85 s/d). Its coffee shop is a delightful place to relax.

The most upscale place is the recently opened and lovely boutique ★ **La Casona del Cafetal** (tel. 506/2577-1414, www.lacasonadelcafetal.com, $150-250 s/d), long one of my favorite restaurants, but now with the addition of gorgeously furnished rooms overlooking the lake at this coffee-estate on the south side of Lago Cachí. Decor in spacious guest rooms blends contemporary and period styling, and I love the awesome travertine-clad baths with huge walk-in showers. The owners have added a spa, and Wi-Fi is free.

Food

The open-air **Bar/Restaurant Mirador Sanchiri** (Sanchiri Mirador and Lodge, tel. 506/2574-5454, www.sanchiri.com, 7am-9pm

Miguel Quesada at Casa del Soñador, Cachí

daily), above Orosi on the road from Paraíso, serves *comida típica* ($6-10), enjoyed with stunning vistas of the valley through plate-glass windows.

Orosi Lodge (tel./fax 506/2533-3578, www.orosilodge.com, 7am-7pm Mon.-Sat.) serves an excellent continental breakfast ($4), pizza ($3.50), sandwiches, croissants, bagels with salami and cheese, natural juices, and ice cream sundaes. On Sunday it's open to lodge guests only. It's a cool place to chill on rainy days with your laptop or a good book. Otherwise start your day at **Panadería Suiza** (tel. 506/8706-6777, 6am-5pm Tues.-Sat., 6am-3pm Sun.), where Swiss-born Franzisca serves a smile along with delicious pastries and hearty breakfasts.

I like the rusticity at the charming open-sided **Restaurante Coto** (tel. 506/2533-3032, 8am-midnight daily), on the north side of the soccer field. Come for the *casados* ($4), or oven-roasted fare cooked over coffee wood.

For an unbeatable view, the lakeside **La Casona del Cafetal** (tel. 506/2577-1414, www.lacasonadelcafetal.com, 11am-6pm daily) serves crepes, soups, salads, and Costa Rican dishes such as tilapia with mushrooms and fresh-caught trout with pesto sauce. On Sunday, a hearty international all-you-can-eat buffet costs $20. It's set in lush grounds on a coffee finca.

The **Panadería Arce** (tel. 506/2533-3244, 4am-6pm Mon.-Sat., 5am-noon Sun.) bakery is three blocks north of the soccer field in Orosi.

Information and Services
Sara and Toine Verkuijlen's **Orosi Tourist Info & Art Café** (tel. 506/2533-3640, otiac@ice.go.cr) is the best resource. It also has a Spanish language school (OTIAC).

A **medical clinic** (tel. 506/2374-8225 or 506/2552-0851) is 50 meters (165 feet) northeast of the soccer field. The **police station** is on the northwest corner of the soccer field.

Orosi Lodge (tel./fax 506/2533-3578, www.orosilodge.com, 7am-7pm daily) offers Internet access.

Getting There and Around
Autotransportes Mata Irola (tel. 506/2533-1916) buses depart Cartago for Orosi ($0.65) from Calle 4, Avenida 1, every 30 minutes 5:30am-10:35pm Monday-Saturday, less frequently on Sunday. Return buses depart from the soccer field in Orosi. Buses do not complete a circuit of Lago Cachí; you'll have to backtrack to Paraíso to visit Ujarrás and the Cachí dam by public bus. Buses depart Cartago for Cachí via Ujarrás from one block east and one block south of Las Ruinas.

Jeep taxis (tel. 506/2533-3087 or 506/8378-0357) await customers on the north side of the soccer field in Orosi; a tour around the lake will cost about $25.

TAPANTÍ-MACIZO DE LA MUERTE NATIONAL PARK
Parque Nacional Tapantí-Macizo de la Muerte (tel. 506/2200-0090 or 506/2206-5615, www.sinac.go.cr, 8am-4pm daily, $10), 27 kilometers (17 miles) southeast of Cartago, sits astride the northern slopes of the Cordillera Talamanca, which boasts more rain and cloud cover than any other region in the country. February, March, and April are the driest months. The many fast-flowing rivers and streams are excellent for fishing, permitted April to October.

The 58,328-hectare (144,131-acre) park, at the headwaters of the Río Reventazón, climbs

Las Ruinas de Ujarrás

from 1,200 to 2,560 meters (3,940-8,400 feet) elevation; it extends all the way up to Cerro de la Muerte. The park has several ecological zones, from lower montane rainforest to montane dwarf forest. Terrain is steep and rugged. It's a habitat for resplendent quetzals (often seen near the ranger station) and more than 260 other bird species, plus mammals such as river otters, tapirs, jaguars, ocelots, jaguarundis, howler monkeys, and multitudinous snakes, frogs, and toads.

Well-marked trails begin near the park-entrance ranger station, which has a small nature display. Sendero Oropendola leads to a deep pool by the Río Macho. There's a vista point, from where another short trail, Sendero La Catarata, leads to a waterfall viewpoint, about four kilometers (2.5 miles) along. A trailhead opposite the beginning of the Oropendola Trail leads into the mountains.

Accommodations and Food

There are no accommodations inside the park, and camping is not allowed. **Kirí Lodge** (tel. 506/2533-2272, www.kirilodge.net, $35 s, $45 d, including breakfast and tax), two kilometers (1.2 miles) west of the park, has six cabins with handsome stone-walled showers. Some rooms have bunk beds. The restaurant (7am-8pm daily, $4-15) specializes in trout culled from its own ponds.

Getting There

Buses depart Cartago at 6:30am, 11am, 1pm, and 4pm daily and travel via Orosi as far as Purisil, five kilometers (3 miles) from the park entrance; the 4pm bus goes only as far as Río Macho, nine kilometers (5.5 miles) from the park. You can hike or take a **Jeep taxi** from Orosi ($10 each way) or Purisil ($5 each way).

Cartago to Cerro de la Muerte

South of Cartago, the Pan-American Highway (Hwy. 2) begins a daunting ascent over the Talamanca Mountains, cresting the range at Cerro de la Muerte (Mountain of Death) at 3,491 meters (11,453 feet) before dropping down into the Valle de El General and the Pacific southwest. The vistas are staggering, and opportunities abound for hiking, trout fishing, and bird-watching—notably for resplendent quetzals, which are common hereabouts (especially Nov.-Mar.). The region is clad in native oak and cloud forest, and the climate is brisk.

Drive carefully: The **Association for Safe International Road Travel** (www.asirt.org) has named this the fourth most dangerous section of road in the world. The road is often fog-bound (it's best to head out early to mid-morning, before the clouds roll in), zigzags with sudden hairpin turns, is washed out in places, and is used by buses and trailer rigs with crazy drivers.

CARTAGO TO CAÑÓN

At **Enpalme,** 30 kilometers (19 miles) south of Cartago, a side road descends in a series of spectacular switchbacks to Santa María de Dota; while at **Vara de Roble,** two kilometers (1.2 miles) north of Enpalme, another road—known as Ruta de Los Santos (Route of the Saints)—leads west to San Cristóbal via La Lucha Sin Fin. You can also reach Santa María de Dota from **Cañón,** five kilometers (3 miles) south of Enpalme at Km. 58 via a dirt road that descends steeply to **Copey.** Copey is a small agricultural village at about 2,120 meters (6,960 feet) elevation, eight kilometers (5 miles) southwest of Cañón and five kilometers (3 miles) east of Santa María de Dota.

CAÑÓN TO CERRO DE LA MUERTE

At Trinidad, five kilometers (3 miles) south of Cañón, you pass through the **Parque Nacional Tapantí-Macizo de la Muerte.**

The Cuenca Queberi Trail, which begins at Km. 61, leads into the reserve.

At Km. 70, a side road leads to **Mirador de Quetzales** (tel. 506/2381-8456, www.elmiradordequetzales.com, 8am-5pm daily, $6 for trail access), also called Finca Eddy Serrano, the perfect spot for viewing quetzals. Up to 20 pairs of quetzals have been seen feeding in treetops near the finca. Serrano leads guided quetzal hikes for hotel guests (6:30am-4pm daily, $15 pp), and the Robledal Oak Forest Trail is open to self-guided hikes with a map and illustrated booklet.

Finally, at Km. 89, you crest **Cerro de la Muerte.** The name derives not from the dozens who have lost their lives through auto accidents, but from the many poor campesinos who froze to death in days of yore while carrying sacks of produce to trade in San José. The summit is marked by a forest of radio antennae. A dirt road leads up to the antennae, from where you'll have miraculous views, weather permitting. At 3,000 meters (9,800 feet) the stunted vegetation is Andean *páramo,* complete with wind-sculpted shrubs, peat bogs, and marshy grasses. Be prepared for high winds.

Los Quetzales National Park

Parque Nacional Los Quetzales (tel. 506/2200-5354, 8am-4pm daily, $10), created in 2005 and covering 5,000 hectares (12,360 acres) of cloud forest on the upper reaches of the Río Savegre, borders the Pan-American Highway between Km. 70 and Km. 80; the main entrance is opposite Restaurante Los Chesperitos, at Km. 76.5. It has trails and opens for bird-watchers at 6am by appointment; guides ($10 pp) can be hired with 24 hours' notice. The San José-San Isidro bus (hourly from Calle Central, Ave. 22, tel. 506/2222-2422) will drop you at the entrance.

★ San Gerardo de Dota

San Gerardo de Dota, nine kilometers (5.5 miles) west and sharply downhill from the Pan-American Highway at Km. 80, is an exquisite hamlet tucked at the base of a narrow wooded valley at 1,900 meters (6,200 feet) elevation—a true Shangri-la cut off from the rest of the world. It's a magnificent setting. The road is snaking, steep, and breathtakingly beautiful.

The Valle de Río Savegre is a center for apples and peaches; it also attracts resplendent quetzals, especially during the April-May nesting season. The Savegre Mountain Hotel hosts the **Quetzal Education Research Center** (tel. 506/2740-1010, www.qerc.org, 9am-5pm Mon.-Fri., free), a research entity with an exhibition hall operated in association with the religious Southern Nazarene University of Oklahoma. Also here is the **Savegre Biological Reserve** (www.savegre. co.cr), at Savegre Natural Reserve & Spa; there are trails, and it offers Jeep tours into the cloud forest. Perhaps the best spot for guaranteed quetzal spotting in season (Oct.-Feb.) is **Finca Luis Monge** (tel. 506/2740-1005, $5), about one kilometer (0.6 miles) above the village school.

The **Trogon Lodge Canopy Tour** offers a zip-line ride among five treetop platforms ($35), plus a waterfall hike and horseback ride ($35).

Accommodations

Renowned by birders, **Albergue Mirador de Quetzales** (tel. 506/2381-8456, $50 pp, including meals and tour), is set amid cloud forest at 2,600 meters (8,500 feet) at Km. 70 on the Pan-American Highway. This rustic yet cozy lodge has 11 A-frame log cabins boasting marvelous views, all with hot water. You can camp ($6 pp) under thatched roofs with tables and barbecue grills. Rates include three meals daily and a quetzal tour.

Popular with tour groups, **Trogon Lodge** (tel. 506/2293-8181, www.grupomawamba. com, standard $86 s, $106 d, junior suite $130 s, $150 d) enjoys a beautiful and secluded riverside setting at the head of the Valle de San Gerardo, in San Gerardo de Dota. It has 10 simply appointed two-bedroom hardwood cabins with tasteful fabrics, heaters, and verandas. Meals are served in a rustic lodge overlooking a trout pond. Fishing is available. Trails lead to waterfalls. Guided horseback rides, quetzal tours, a canopy tour, and mountain bike rentals are offered.

The classiest option (quite remarkable considering its humble beginning when I first visited two decades ago), and set amid beautifully landscaped grounds, is **Savegre Lodge Natural Reserve & Spa** (tel. 506/2740-1028, www.savegre.com, from $110 s/d), in San Gerardo de Dota. Its 20 original all-wood cabins (with heaters) are now complemented by 20 newer, more spacious, wood-paneled junior suites. It has trails, birding trips, cloud-forest hiking, guided horseback riding, and trout fishing. After a day's activity you can relax at a deluxe full-service spa.

One of my favorite hotels in Costa Rica, ★ **Dantica Cloud Forest Lodge & Gallery** (tel. 506/2740-1067, www.dantica. com, low season $98-248 s/d, high season $102-224), midway between the highway and valley bottom, is a dramatic modernist creation with walls of glass throughout. Run by a Danish-Colombian couple, it has seven one- and two-bedroom villas built in Colombian farmstead fashion with genuine antique doors and terra-cotta roof tiles, plus a suite tastefully furnished Ikea-style, with cozy down duvets, thermal blankets, and whirlpool tubs. Lovely details include teak and gray stone floors, halogen ceiling lights, and tasteful art pieces. Thoughtful extras include flashlights, ponchos, and walking sticks. Two-bedroom villas have fully equipped kitchens. Some rooms are a hilly 200-meter (660-foot) hike from reception. A gift store sells quality indigenous pieces and exhibits ethnic art. Massages are offered, and seven kilometers (4.5 miles) of trails lead through a private 20-hectare (49-acre) forest adjoining Parque Nacional Los Quetzales.

Food

All the lodges serve food, including ★ **Restaurante La Tapir** (7am-9pm daily, $2-20), at Dantica Cloud Forest Lodge, with its glass walls and cozy cast-iron stove. Look for such breakfast treats as European-style pancakes, and a bagel with smoked salmon, cream cheese, capers, and peppers. Lunch could include steak sandwiches with onions, mushrooms, and paprika. I enjoyed a gourmet dinner of grilled zucchini with tomato *pomodori* sauce ($4.50), a fillet of trout with fresh herbs ($9.50), and a hot banana with ice cream and chocolate sauce ($5).

For a truly Costa Rican treat, a 400-meter (0.25-mile) uphill hike from Dantica brings you to **Miriam's Quetzals** (tel. 506/2740-1049, 6am-8pm daily, $5-10), a local farmstead and *soda* where the charming Serrano family serves delicious, filling meals in a simple room heated by an old cast-iron stove. Miriam also rents out basic cabins with heaters ($35) and has trails good for spotting quetzals.

Restaurant Los Lagos (tel. 506/2740-1009, loslagoslodge@costarricense.cr, 6am-7pm Mon.-Thurs., 6am-9pm Fri.-Sun., $5-12), in the valley bottom opposite Cabinas El Quetzal, specializes in trout dishes and *casados* ($5); it also has lodging. Nearby, the trendy **Café Kahawa** (tel. 506/2740-1051, 7am-8pm daily) has a lovely open-air riverside setting for enjoying an eclectic range of dishes, from tacos to fresh trout (even fresh trout ceviche) with organic veggies.

Getting There

The San Isidro **bus** departs San José from Calle Central, Avenida 22, and will drop you or pick you up anywhere along Highway 2. Most hotel owners will pick you up at the bus stop on the highway with advance notice.

A **minibus** (tel. 506/8367-8141, $15) connects the Pan-American Highway with San Gerardo and meets the San José-San Isidro bus at Km. 80 at 7:40am daily; it departs San Gerardo for the highway at 6:50am daily.

There's a **gas station** at Enpalme.

Ruta de Los Santos

South of San José lies a little-touristed region of hidden valleys perfect for a full-day drive along the scenic Ruta de Los Santos (Route of the Saints), so called because most of the villages are named after saints. These villages can also be accessed by driving south from Cartago along the Pan-American Highway (Hwy. 2) and turning west at Enpalme or Cañón.

SAN JOSÉ TO SAN GABRIEL

From San José's southern suburb of Desamparados, Highway 209 climbs into the Fila de Bustamante mountains via **Aserrí,** a pretty hillside town famed for its handsome church. The grade increases markedly to the crest of the mountains just north of **Tarbaca.** En route you gain a breathtaking view of Volcán Irazú.

Three kilometers (2 miles) south of Tarbaca is a Y junction. The road to the right (Hwy. 209) drops westward to **San Ignacio de Acosta,** a charming little town nestled on a hillside. You can see its whitewashed houses

for miles around. The sun sets dramatically on its steep west-facing slopes. The road to the left (Hwy. 222) at the Y junction drops to **San Gabriel.**

SAN GABRIEL TO SANTA MARÍA DE DOTA

From San Gabriel, Highway 222 continues southeast, dropping and rising via Frailes to **San Cristóbal Sur,** a market town better known to Ticos for **La Lucha Sin Fin** (The Endless Struggle), two kilometers (1.2 miles) east of San Cristóbal, the finca of former president and national hero Don "Pepe" Figueres, who led the 1948 revolution from here.

East of La Lucha, the road clambers precipitously through pine forests three kilometers (2 miles) to the Pan-American Highway. Instead, turn south from San Cristóbal and follow a scenic route via **San Pablo de León Cortes** to **San Marcos de Tarrazú,** dramatically situated over coffee fields and dominated by a handsome white church with a domed roof. You can visit the local coffee mill, **Beneficio Coopetarrazú** (tel.

Parque Central, Santa María de Dota

506/2546-6098 or 506/8842-2269), by prior arrangement.

From San Marcos, the main road climbs southeast to **Santa María de Dota,** a tranquil village whose main plaza has a small but dramatic granite monument—the **Monumento Liberación Nacional**—honoring those who died in the 1948 revolution. This is a major coffee-producing area; indigenous people from as far away as Boca del Toro, in Panamá, provide the field labor. You can visit the **Beneficio Coopedota** (tel. 506/2541-2828, 9am-5pm Mon.-Fri., $10), which handles the beans for 700 local producers and accepts visitors by reservation, in season; the visit includes a plantation tour, a video, and tasting.

From Santa María, the roads east snake steeply to the Pan-American Highway, with dramatic views en route.

Accommodations
Cabinas Cecilia (tel./fax 506/2541-1233, www.cabinascecilia.net, from $35 s, $55 d), 400 meters (0.25 miles) south of the plaza in Santa María de Dota, is set in a lovely garden surrounded by coffee fields. It has nine simple cabins of rough-hewn timbers and stone floors (plus Wi-Fi) around a farmhouse-style open-air dining area serving food from a wood-fired stove. Cecilia also offers massages.

A true nature lodge of stone and polished timbers, **El Toucanet Lodge** (tel. 506/2541-3045, www.eltoucanet.com, low season standard $55 s, $73 d, junior suite $90 s, $108 d, high season standard $60 s, $80 d, junior suite $100 s, $120 d, including breakfast and tax), on a 40-hectare (100-acre) fruit farm one kilometer (0.6 miles) east of Copey, is perfect for bird-watchers—more than 170 species have been seen at the lodge. Quetzal sightings are virtually a daily occurrence, as the property adjoins Parque Nacional Los Quetzales. It has six simply furnished *cabinas,* a family cabin

for six people with a fireplace and kitchenette, and two suites with a wall of glass and a whirlpool tub. You can access hiking trails, or take a horseback or coffee tour. Guests get a free quetzal tour.

Food
The place to eat is **Soda La Casona** (tel. 506/2541-2258, 7am-7pm daily) in Santa María (take the first left after the bridge into town when approaching from Enpalme). This clean family restaurant serves filling meals. Take a peek in the kitchen to choose among the simmering pots. A filling *casado* costs about $6. It typically stays open until the last guest leaves. **Beneficio Coopedota** (tel. 506/2541-2828, 6am-6pm Mon.-Sat.), 100 meters northwest of the plaza, has a lovely café and bakery.

Hollywood couldn't have conceived a more rustic spot than **Restaurante Bar Vaca Flaca** (tel. 506/2546-3939, 11am-10pm daily), at Alto de Abajonal, near San Antonio. This Colorado-style place is very country, very cowboy (think cowhide seats and rifles on the walls), and serves a house special: chicken breast with mushrooms and broccoli ($4). The bar hosts live music and stays open until 2am.

Getting There
Buses (tel. 506/2410-0330) from San José to Aserrí ($0.75) depart from Calle 2, Avenidas 6/8, and for San Ignacio ($0.75) from Calle 8, Avenidas 12/14, hourly 5:30am-10:30pm daily. Buses (tel. 506/2410-0015) from San José to San Ignacio de Acosta depart from Calle 8, Avenidas 12/14, every 30 minutes 5:20am-10:30pm daily.

Empresa Los Santos (tel. 506/2546-7248) buses to San Marcos and Santa María ($2.15) depart San José from Avenida 16, Calles 19/21, seven times 6am-7:30pm daily. Return buses to San José depart Santa María six times 5:15am-6:15pm daily.

Turrialba and Vicinity

East of Cartago, Highway 230 falls eastward through the valley of the Río Reventazón before a final steep descent to the regional center of Turrialba. The route runs via **Cervantes.** An alternate, less-traveled mountain route from Cartago runs via **Pacayas,** where thrill-seekers might be tempted to stop at **Parque de Aventuras Paraíso de Volcanes** (tel. 506/2534-0272, www.paraisodevolcanes. com)—a comprehensive activity center with everything from ATVs to zip lines.

TURRIALBA

Turrialba, a small town 65 kilometers (40 miles) east of San José, was once an important stop on the old highway between San José and the Caribbean. The opening of the Guápiles Highway via Parque Nacional Braulio Carrillo stole much of its thunder, and the town was further insulated when train service to the Caribbean ended in 1991. The now-rusted tracks still dominate the town, which squats in a valley bottom on the banks of the Río Turrialba at 650 meters (2,130 feet) above sea level.

Turrialba is a base for white-water adventures on the **Ríos Reventazón** and **Pacuare.** At its heart is **Parque la Dominica,** undistinguished but for the dramatic modernist **Iglesia Parroquia San Buenaventura** on the south side. The U.S.-run **Serendipity Adventures** (tel. 506/2558-1000, U.S./Canada tel. 888-226-5050, www.serendipity-adventures.com) offers hot-air ballooning, rafting, hiking, kayaking, and other adventures. **Costa Rica Rios** (tel. 506/2556-8664, U.S./Canada tel. 888-434-0776, www.costaricarios.com) specializes in canoeing and kayaking; and **Explornatura** (tel. 506/2556-0111, www.explornatura.com) offers white-water trips and coffee tours.

CATIE

The **Centro Agronómico Tropical de Investigación y Enseñanza** (CATIE, Center for Tropical Agriculture Investigation and Learning, tel. 506/2558-2000, www.catie.ac.cr), four kilometers (2.5 miles) east of Turrialba, is one of the world's leading tropical agricultural research stations. It covers 1,036 hectares (2,560 acres) devoted to experimentation and research on livestock and tropical plants and crops, including more than 2,500 coffee varieties. Trails provide superb bird-watching, and the orchards, herbarium, and husbandry facilities are fascinating. CATIE also contains the largest library on tropical agriculture in the world. The grounds include the **Jardín Botánico** (Botanical Garden, 7am-4pm Mon.-Fri., 8am-4pm Sat.-Sun., $6), with a lake full of waterfowl; guided five-hour tours ($20 pp) are given, including a tour by bicycle. It has a café and a reception area with an exhibition. Weekend visits are offered by appointment.

Buses depart for CATIE from Avenida Central, Calle 2, in Turrialba. You can also catch the bus to Siquirres from Avenida 4, Calle 2, and ask to be dropped off.

Accommodations and Food

Beloved of international budget travelers, in town the American-run **Hotel Interamericano** (Ave. 1, Calle 1, tel. 506/2556-0142, www.hotelinteramericano.com, shared bath $12 s, $22 d, private bath $25 s, $30-35 d) offers 22 clean rooms in several categories, with cable TV and hot water. It has Internet access and laundry, plus a small bar and cafeteria. The best budget digs in town is the clean **Casa de Lis Hostel** (Ave. Central, Calle 2, tel. 506/2556-4933, www.hostelcasadelis.com, from $20 pp), in a converted middle-class home. Choose from dorms or private rooms.

You can fill up for less than $3 at **Restaurante La Garza** (tel. 506/2556-1073, 10am-11pm daily), on the plaza's northwest

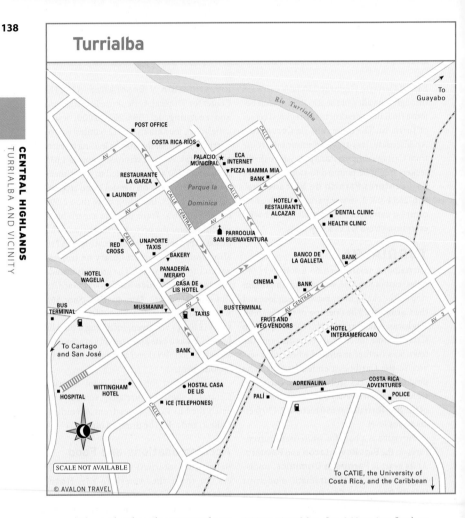

Turrialba

corner; it has set lunches, plus pastas and even Chinese fare.

To the south end of town, **Restaurant Betico Mata** (tel. 506/2556-8640, 11am-midnight daily) satisfies your meat craving with marinated grilled dishes. It has a drive-through service.

Information and Services

The **post office** (tel. 506/2556-1679) is on Calle Central, Avenida 8. You can make international calls from **Eca Internet** (tel. 506/2556-1586,

8:30am-10pm Mon.-Sat., 8:30am-1pm Sun.), on the east side of the square.

The **Hospital William Allen** (tel. 506/2556-4343) is on the west side of town. The **medical center** and a **dental clinic** are on Avenida 2, Calle 3. There's a **laundry** (tel. 506/2556-2194, 8am-4:45pm Mon.-Sat.) on Calle 2, Avenidas 6/8.

Spanish by the River (tel. 506/2556-7380, www.spanishatlocations.com), about three kilometers (2 miles) west of town, offers Spanish language instruction.

Getting There

Buses (tel. 506/2556-4233) depart San José ($2) from Calle 13, Avenidas 6/8, hourly 8am-8pm daily via Cartago. Buses depart Cartago for Turrialba from Avenida 3, Calle 8. **Taxis** (tel. 506/2556-3434) congregate around the square.

LAGO ANGOSTURA AND VICINITY

East of Turrialba, Highway 10 continues past CATIE two kilometers (1.2 miles) to a Y junction: The main highway descends to **Siquirres** and the Caribbean after switchbacking steeply uphill to tiny **Turrialtico,** eight kilometers (5 miles) east of Turrialba. The branch road off Highway 10 leads southeast to the valleys of the Río Atirro and, to the east, Río Tuis.

One kilometer (0.6 miles) east of CATIE, you cross the Río Reventazón (Exploding River). The river, which begins its life at the Lago Cachí dam, is dammed about two kilometers (1.2 miles) upstream of the bridge to create the 256-hectare (633-acre) **Lago Angostura.** The Proyecto Hidroeléctrico Angostura (Angostura Hydroelectric Project), the largest hydroelectricity-generating plant in the country, began humming in 2000.

Below Lago Angostura, the river cascades down the eastern slopes of the Cordillera Central to the Caribbean plains. On a good day it serves up Class III-IV rapids.

Hacienda Atirro dominates the flatlands south of the lake. The sugarcane-processing factory can be visited in harvest season as part of a plantation tour; you can book through **Hotel Casa Turire** (tel. 506/2531-1111, www.hotelcasaturire.com), on the south shore of Lago Angostura, which also offers horseback tours, mountain biking, and other activities. Nearby, the **Beneficio Grano de Oro** (tel. 506/2531-2008, www.goldenbean.net) coffee estate also welcomes visitors for the Golden Bean Coffee Tour.

Finca Monte Claro B&B (tel. 506/2538-1383, www.fincamonteclaro.com, $15 pp, including breakfast), an organic coffee and fruit farm with a reforestation program, offers tours; it's about 12 kilometers (7.5 miles) east of Turrialba, near Pavones.

Serpentario Viborana (tel. 506/2538-1510 or 506/8882-5406, viborana@racsa.co.cr, 9am-5pm daily, 1 hour $10, 2 hours $15) is a serpentarium near Pavones, about 3 km (2 miles) beyond Turrialtico. About 100 snakes are displayed in cages, including dozens of fer-de-lance and a huge cage full of eyelash vipers;

Lago Angostura and the lower Reventazón Valley

owner-herpetologist Minor Camacho Loiza is one of Costa Rica's leading experts in these deadly species. A visit begins in the open-air lecture room, and trails lead into the forest. Three different tours are offered.

With a 4WD vehicle, you can descend the gnarly track to the community of **Bajo del Tigre**, four kilometers (2.5 miles) from the highway; the turnoff is about 15 kilometers (9.5 miles) beyond Turrialtico. Here, Ríos Tropicales has funded a community project that now features a *serpentario* (snakes) and *orquideario* (orchids) at the **home of Juan Alberto González** (tel. 506/2554-1536, 7am-5pm daily, donation). There is also a butterfly farm nearby.

Accommodations and Food

Have an at-one-with-nature experience at **Finca Monte Claro B&B** (tel. 506/2538-1383, www.fincamonteclaro.com, $15 pp, including breakfast), where a former sheepfold on piles has been converted into an open and shaded deck where you can sleep with the elements on simple beds with mosquito nets. You get views of both the volcano and town of Turrialba, plus use of a kitchenette and a shared bath and toilets. There is no electricity. Horseback tours are available.

You can't beat the views at **Turrialtico Mountain Lodge & Restaurant** (tel. 506/2538-1111, www.turrialtico.com, low season $52-68 s/d, high season $58-75 s/d), amid landscaped grounds high above Turrialtico. Its 14 rooms are modern charmers, and the restaurant (7am-10pm daily) similarly combines rusticity and elegance. Rates include breakfast and taxes.

The most outstanding hotel for miles is ★ **Hotel Casa Turire** (tel. 506/2531-1111, www.hotelcasaturire.com, low season $168-452 s/d, high season $185-452 s/d), on the south shore of Lago Angostura, about 15 kilometers (9.5 miles) southeast of Turrialba. Relaxing and romantic, this hotel is infused with a Georgian England motif and is justifiably a member of the Small Distinctive Hotels of Costa Rica. You sense the sublime

the moment you arrive via a long palm-lined driveway and enter the atrium lobby of the plantation property, with its colonial-tiled floors, Roman pillars, and sumptuous leather sofas and chairs. The 12 spacious, lofty-ceilinged rooms have Wi-Fi and flat-screen TVs with cable and lovely marble-clad baths. Four suites have French doors opening onto private verandas; the master suite has a whirlpool tub. A wide wraparound veranda opens onto manicured lawns, a small figure-eight pool, and a sunning deck. There's an eco-farm (with water buffalo) and a stable, plus a spa, horse-and-carriage rides, and a fitness trail (with a guide and arranged in advance only). This is also the place to treat yourself to a meal. It boasts a coveted four leaves from the Certification for Sustainable Tourism.

The restaurant at **Hotel Casa Turire** (7am-10am, 11:30am-4pm, and 6pm-9:30pm daily) is worth the drive from Turrialba to enjoy gourmet treats using organic produce from the hotel's own gardens. A typical meal might include curried banana soup ($6), dorado with orange sauce, almonds, and mashed potatoes ($12), and hot chocolate cake with flambéed bananas ($5).

Getting There

Buses (tel. 506/2556-4233) for Siquirres depart Turrialba from Avenida 4, Calle 2, hourly 5:30am-6:30pm daily, passing Turrialtico.

GUAYABO NATIONAL MONUMENT

Monumento Nacional Guayabo (tel. 506/2559-0117, www.sinac.go.cr, 8am-3:30pm daily, adults $6, children $1), on the southern flank of Volcán Turrialba, 19 kilometers (12 miles) north of Turrialba, is the nation's only archaeological site of any significance. Don't expect anything of the scale or scope of the Mayan and Aztec ruins of Guatemala, Honduras, Mexico, or Belize. The society that lived here between 1000 BC and AD 1400, when the town was mysteriously abandoned, was far less culturally advanced than its northern neighbors. No record exists of the

Spanish having known of Guayabo. In fact, the site lay uncharted until rediscovered in the late 19th century. Systematic excavations—still underway—were begun in 1968.

The 218-hectare (539-acre) monument encompasses tropical wet forest on valley slopes surrounding the archaeological site. Trails lead to a lookout point, where you can surmise the layout of the pre-Columbian village. To the south, a wide cobbled pavement leads past ancient stone entrance gates and up a slight gradient to the village center, which at its peak housed an estimated 1,000 people. The pavement—*calzada*—is in perfect alignment with the cone of Volcán Turrialba. Conical bamboo living structures were built on large circular stone mounds (*montículos*), with paved pathways between them leading down to aqueducts and a large water tank.

About four hectares (10 acres) have been excavated and are open to the public via the **Mound Viewing Trail.** Note the monolithic rock carved with petroglyphs of an alligator and a jaguar.

The ranger booth has a free self-guided-tour pamphlet, but you can hire a guide from the **Asociación de Guias U-Suré** (tel. 506/8534-1063), opposite the ticket booth. Here, too, are the park administration office,

a miniature model of the site, and a hut with pre-Columbian finds. Many of the artifacts unearthed here are on display at the National Museum in San José.

Accommodations and Food

The ranger station offers eight **campsites** with shelters ($2 pp), plus flush toilets, cold-water showers, and barbecue pits.

The American-run eco-sensitive **Guayabo Lodge** (tel./fax 506/2538-8400, www.guayabolodge.com, low season $78-140 s, $94-140 d, high season $83-140 s, $104-140 d), 400 meters (0.25 miles) west of Santa Cruz, enjoys a hillside setting. This modern two-story structure has 23 uniquely decorated rooms with parquet floors and delightful decor that includes wrought-iron beds, gaily painted armoires, and indigenous inspired artwork. When not exploring the 80-hectare (198-acre) finca, settle yourself in a hammock and enjoy the views. The finca has its own dairy and cheese factory (tours are given), and it hosts a cooking school.

You can get a filling meal at **La Calzada** (tel. 506/2559-0437, 8pm-5pm Tues.-Thurs.), 400 meters (0.25 miles) below the park entrance. It serves local fare, plus trout fresh from its own pond.

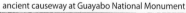

ancient causeway at Guayabo National Monument

Getting There

Transtuso (tel. 506/2556-0362) buses depart Turrialba for Guayabo village from Avenida 4, Calle 2, at 6:20am, 11:15am, 3:10pm, and 5:20pm Monday-Saturday and at 9am, 3pm, and 6:30pm Sunday. Return buses depart Guayabo at 5:15am, 7am, 12:30pm, and 4pm Monday-Saturday and 7am, 12:30pm, and 4pm Sunday. A taxi from Turrialba costs about $30 round-trip.

The paved road from Turrialba deteriorates to a rough dirt and rock path about four kilometers (2.5 miles) below Guayabo. You can approach Guayabo from the northwest, via Santa Cruz; it's about 10 kilometers (6 miles) by rough dirt road and is signed.

TURRIALBA VOLCANO NATIONAL PARK

In **Parque Nacional Volcán Turrialba** (www.sinac.go.cr), Volcán Turrialba, at 3,329 meters (10,922 feet) and the country's most easterly volcano, was very active during the 19th century, but slumbered peacefully until 2001, when it showed signs of activity after 135 years of dormancy. On January 6, 2010, *boom*—the volcano erupted and currently remains worrisomely active. By historical standards it wasn't an earth-shattering eruption, but the activity continues, and at press time, access was intermittently limited.

It can be very cold and rainy up here—bring sweaters and rain gear. There are no rangers posted at Parque Nacional Volcán Turrialba, so access is free. Contact **SINAC** (tel. 506/2268-8091) in San José.

A paved (but badly eroded) road winds steeply north from **Santa Cruz,** about 12 kilometers (7.5 miles) north of the town of Turrialba, to Finca Central; it's a rugged three-kilometer (2-mile) drive by 4WD vehicle from there. An alternate route for 4WD vehicles only is via the Parque Nacional Volcán Irazú road, signed for "Volcán Turrialba Lodge"; turn off two kilometers (1.2 miles) below the park ranger station.

You can also hike from the hamlet of **Santa Teresa,** reached by direct bus or car

from Cartago via Pacayas, on the southwestern slope. The trail climbs through cloud forest to the summit, which features three craters, a mirador (lookout point), and a guardhouse topped by an antenna. A trail at the summit leads to the crater floor; another circumnavigates the crater (there are active fumaroles on the western side).

Accommodations and Food

Perfect for bird-watchers and hikers, **Volcán Turrialba Lodge** (tel. 506/2273-4335, www. volcanturrialbalodge.com, $45 s/d, including breakfast and tax) is set magnificently in the saddle between the Irazú and Turrialba volcanoes at 2,800 meters (9,190 feet) elevation, about three kilometers (2 miles) north of Esperanza and eight kilometers (5 miles) northwest of Santa Cruz. The rustic lodge—on a working farm—has 18 simple yet comfy rooms with private baths. Meals are cooked over a wood fire and served in a cozy lounge heated by a woodstove. Guided hikes and horseback rides are offered.

Getting There

Buses depart Cartago for Pacayas and Santa Cruz from south of Las Ruinas, and from the bus center at Calle 2, Avenidas 2/4, in Turrialba. You can take a **Jeep taxi** from Santa Cruz or Pacayas.

LAGO ANGOSTURA TO MORAVIA DE CHIRRIPÓ

Heading east from Atirro through the valley of the Río Tuis via the tiny communities of **Tuis, Bajo Pacuare,** and **Hacienda Grano de Oro,** you find yourself in a fabulous alpine plateau not unlike parts of Colorado. You'll need a 4WD vehicle. A few kilometers beyond, about 30 kilometers (19 miles) east of Highway 10, the dirt road passes through the off-the-beaten-path hamlet of **Moravia de Chirripó** and peters out at **Hacienda Moravia,** from where trails filter into the Cordillera Talamanca and **Reserva Indígena Chirripó,** a remote reserve that receives few visitors. The indigenous presence is strong, in local faces and in bright traditional garb. Alas, evangelical Christians have made a serious dent in this region, eroding indigenous culture; many tourist businesses are evangelical-focused.

Sports and Recreation

Bajo Pacuare is a traditional starting point for white-water rafting trips on the **Río Pacuare,** a thrilling river that plunges through remote canyons and rates as a classic white-water run. **Tico's River Adventures** (tel. 506/2556-1231, www.ticoriver.com), based in Turrialba, is recommended, as is **Aventuras Naturales** (tel. 506/2225-3939, www.adventurecostarica. com) in San José.

Accommodations and Food

Several rafting companies have lodges in the Pacuare Canyon. In most cases, you have to be a participant on the companies' river trips to stay there. You'll need a rugged 4WD vehicle to reach the sublime ★ **Pacuare Jungle Lodge** (tel. 800-963-1195, www.pacuarelodge. com, 2-day package from $420 pp, including transportation and meals), set high on a lush rainforest hilltop overlooking the Pacuare River. This thatched rainforest retreat, owned by Aventuras Naturales, has a cozy lounge bar and a gourmet restaurant. The gorgeous, exquisitely appointed palm-thatched bungalows each boast a wall of glass, teak floors, handcrafted rattan wicker chairs, and a king canopy bed with a vast canyon view. There's even a honeymoon suite with an infinity pool fed by a natural waterfall; heck, it even has its own suspension bridge linked to a private treetop canopy. Most guests are white-water rafters partaking of fun on the river. You have to hike the last 300 meters (1,000 feet) to get here.

Rancho Naturalista (tel. 506/2100-1855, U.S. tel. 888-246-8513, www.ranchonaturalista.net, low season $140 pp, high season $170 pp, including meals), one kilometer (0.6 miles) beyond Tuis, is a hilltop hacienda-lodge run by American evangelists. It sits on a 50-hectare (124-acre) ranch surrounded by premontane rainforest at 900 meters (3,000 feet) elevation at the end of a steep dirt-and-rock road. The mountain retreat is popular with nature and bird-watching groups; guests have recorded more than 410 bird species. Though its 15 rooms vary, all are pleasant, with hardwood beams and down comforters. The upstairs has a lounge with a library. Rates include three meals, guided hikes, and horseback riding.

Getting There

Buses (tel. 506/2556-5155) for Tuis and Moravia depart from the bus center at Calle 2, Avenidas 2/4, in Turrialba.

The Caribbean Coast

Costa Rica's Caribbean coast extends some 200 kilometers (120 miles) from Nicaragua to Panamá. The zone—wholly within Limón Province—is divided into two distinct regions.

North of Puerto Limón, the port city midway down the coast, is a long, straight coastal strip backed by a broad alluvial plain cut through by the Tortuguero Canals, an inland waterway that parallels the coast all the way to the Nicaraguan border. Crocodiles, caimans, monkeys, sloths, and exotic birds can be seen from the tour boats that carry passengers through the rainforest-lined canals and freshwater lagoons culminating in Parque Nacional Tortuguero and Refugio Nacional de Vida Silvestre Barra del Colorado, a national wildlife refuge. A few roads penetrate to the northern frontier far inland of the coast, but they are often impassable except for brief periods in the dry season. For locals, motorized canoes (*cayucos* or *canoas*) and water taxis are the main means of getting around the swampy waterways.

South of Puerto Limón is the Talamanca coast, a narrow coastal plain broken by occasional headlands and coral reefs and backed by the looming Cordillera Talamanca. A succession of sandy shores leads the eye toward Panamá. The zone is popular with surfers.

The coast is sparsely settled, with tiny villages spaced far apart. Except for the coastal town of Puerto Limón, what few villages lie along the coast are ramshackle and beaten by tropical storms, though given a boost by booming tourism. Life along the Caribbean coast of Costa Rica is fundamentally different than in the rest of the country. Life is lived at an easy pace. It may take you a few days to get in the groove. Don't expect things to happen at the snap of your fingers.

The Afro-Caribbean *costeños* (coast dwellers), who form approximately one-third of Limón Province's population of 250,000, have little in common with the *sponyamon*—the "Spaniard man," or highland mestizo, who represents the conservative Latin American culture. More than anywhere else in Costa Rica, the peoples of the Caribbean coast

---

Previous: surfer riding bicycle in Cahuita; youth with fresh fish, Cahuita. **Above:** workers carrying bananas near Guápiles.

Look for ★ to find recommended
sights, activities, dining, and lodging.

Highlights

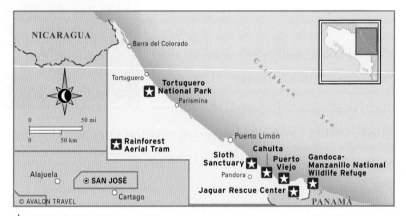

★ **Rainforest Aerial Tram:** A ride through the rainforest canopy on this ski lift-style tram provides a fabulous introduction to tropical ecology, while a serpentarium and other wildlife exhibits display some of the creatures you may be lucky enough to see on the ride (page 150).

★ **Tortuguero National Park:** Wildlife awaits in this watery world where everyone gets around by boat. The beach is a prime nesting site for marine turtles, the national park is tops for bird-watching and animal-viewing, and the village is a funky charmer (page 158).

★ **Sloth Sanctuary:** The world's only such reserve lets you get up close to these endearing Muppet-like creatures (page 169).

★ **Cahuita:** Popular with the offbeat crowd, this small village has heaps of character. Several eateries serve spicy local cuisine, and Parque

Nacional Cahuita offers great beaches, diverse wildlife, and a small coral reef (page 172).

★ **Puerto Viejo:** Drawing surfers and latter-day hippies, this somnolent village has tremendous budget accommodations. Activities include horseback riding and hikes to indigenous villages, and beautiful beaches run south for miles (page 178).

★ **Jaguar Rescue Center:** This well-run animal rescue center offers guided tours—a chance to hold a monkey in your hand and gain a greater appreciation for Costa Rica's embattled wildlife (page 185).

★ **Gandoca-Manzanillo National Wildlife Refuge:** This reserve spans several ecosystems teeming with animal life, from crocodiles to monkeys and manatees. Turtles also come ashore to lay eggs (page 191).

reflect a mingling of races and cultures. There are Creoles of mixed African and European descent; Caribs, whose ancestors were African and indigenous Caribbean; mestizos, of mixed Spanish and Amerindian blood; more Chinese than one might expect; and, living in the foothills of the Talamancas, approximately 5,000 Bribrí and Cabecar indigenous people.

The early settlers of the coast were British pirates, smugglers, log-cutters, and their slaves, who brought their own Caribbean dialects with words that are still used today. During the late 19th century, increasing numbers of English-speaking Afro-Caribbean families—predominantly from Jamaica—came to build and work the Atlantic Railroad and banana plantations, eventually settling and infusing the local dialect with the lilting parochial patois phrases familiar to travelers in the West Indies. Afro-Caribbean influences are also notable in the regional cuisine and in the Rastafarians one meets in Cahuita and Puerto Viejo. Some of the young Afro-Caribbean males here appear sullen and lackadaisical, even antagonistic; some seem to harbor a resentment of white visitors. But most locals have hearts of gold, and there's a strong, mutually supportive community that travelers may not easily see. (Paula Palmer's *What Happen: A Folk History of Costa Rica's Talamanca Coast* and *Wa'apin Man* provide insight into the traditional Creole culture of the area.)

The Caribbean coast is generally hot and exceedingly wet, averaging 300 to 500 centimeters (120-200 inches) of rain annually. Except for September and October, the region has no real dry season and endures a "wet season" in which the rainfall can exceed 100 centimeters (39 inches) per month. Rains peak from May to August and again in December and January, when sudden storms blow in, bowing down the coconut palms, deluging the Talamancas, and causing frequent flooding and closures of the road south of Limón.

PLANNING YOUR TIME

Most people stay at least one week to get in the groove and make the most of the southern Caribbean's offbeat offerings. Many visitors arrive with no schedule, intent on kicking it until the money runs out or they get an urge to move on. This is particularly so of the laidback hamlets of **Cahuita** and **Puerto Viejo,** budget havens popular with surfers, tie-dyed backpackers, and those seeking immersion in Creole culture.

Laguna Penitencia, Tortuguero

The Caribbean Coast

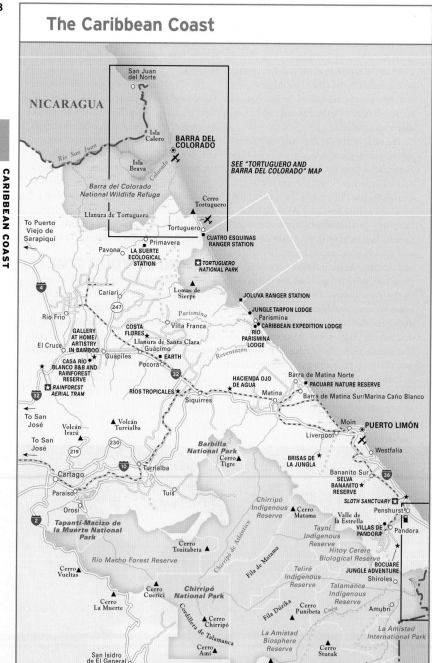

NICARAGUA

San Juan del Norte

Isla Calero

BARRA DEL COLORADO

Isla Brava

SEE "TORTUGUERO AND BARRA DEL COLORADO" MAP

Barra del Colorado National Wildlife Refuge

Cerro Tortuguero

Llanura de Tortuguero

Tortuguero

To Puerto Viejo de Sarapiquí

Primavera

Pavona

LA SUERTE ECOLOGICAL STATION

■ **CUATRO ESQUINAS RANGER STATION**

★ **TORTUGUERO NATIONAL PARK**

Cariari

Lomas de Sierpe

JOLUVA RANGER STATION

Río Frío

COSTA FLORES

Villa Franca

GALLERY AT HOME/ ARTISTRY IN BAMBOO

Parismina

JUNGLE TARPON LODGE
CARIBBEAN EXPEDITION LODGE
RÍO PARISMINA LODGE

El Cruce

Llanura de Santa Clara

Guácimo

■ **EARTH**

CASA RÍO BLANCO B&B AND RAINFOREST RESERVE

Guápiles

Pocora

RAINFOREST AERIAL TRAM

RÍOS TROPICALES

To San José

HACIENDA OJO DE AGUA

Siquirres

Matina

Barra de Matina Norte

■ **PACUARE NATURE RESERVE**

Barra de Matina Sur/Marina Caño Blanco

Volcán Irazú

Volcán Turrialba

To San José

Moín

PUERTO LIMÓN

Liverpool

Westfalia

Cartago

Turrialba

Barbilla National Park

Cerro Tigre

BRISAS DE LA JUNGLA

Bananito Sur

SELVA BANANITO RESERVE

Paraíso

Tuís

SLOTH SANCTUARY

Orosi

Tapantí-Macizo de la Muerte National Park

Chirripó Indigenous Reserve

Cerro Matama

Penshurst

Valle de la Estrella

VILLAS DE PANDORA

Pandora

Tayní Indigenous Reserve

Hitoy Cerere Biological Reserve

Cerro Tsuitabeta

Río Macho Forest Reserve

Teliré Indigenous Reserve

BOCUARÉ JUNGLE ADVENTURE

Shiroles

Cerro Vueltas

Chirripó National Park

Cerro Cuerici

Talamanca Indigenous Reserve

Amubri

Cerro La Muerte

Cerro Punibeta

La Amistad International Park

Cordillera de Talamanca

Cerro Chirripó

Fila Dúrika

San Isidro de El General

Cerro Amí

La Amistad Biosphere Reserve

Cerro Stutuk

Cerro Durika

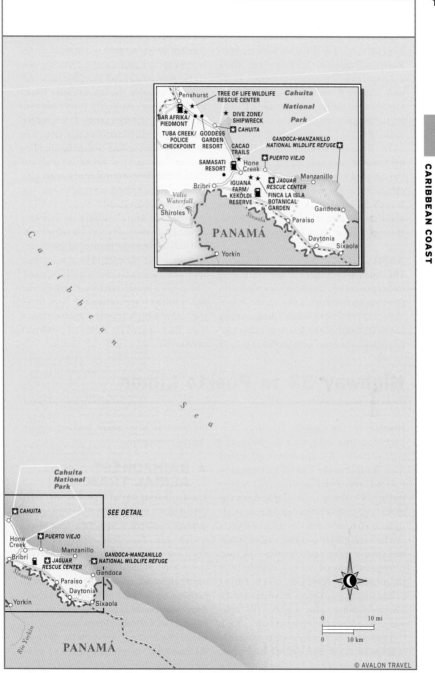

© AVALON TRAVEL

Surfers head to Puerto Viejo and the beaches that run south to the hamlet of **Manzanillo.** There's no shortage of options for viewing wildlife, but nowhere beats **Parque Nacional Tortuguero;** allow 2-3 days here. Tortuguero is famous as the most important nesting site in the western Caribbean for the Pacific green turtle. If viewing turtles is important, plan to visit from July to October.

You'll need to fly to Tortuguero (or Barra del Colorado), or take a boat. Buses serve Cahuita and Puerto Viejo, from where tour excursions to places of interest are offered. If you're driving, check weather conditions ahead, as the area frequently gets flooded, closing Highway 32 and the coast highway.

Safety Concerns

The region has witnessed a burgeoning drug trade in recent years and also has a reputation for crime against tourists. In Cahuita, Puerto Viejo, and Tortuguero (where a drug-running cartel is entrenched and drug trafficking happens under the noses of authorities) visitors may be pestered by young males trying to sell them drugs. Hoteliers in the region claim that the bad reputation is all a sad misrepresentation, but during my most recent visits, things seemed to have gotten worse, including several violent attacks and murders. In March 2013, for example, the U.S. Embassy issued a safety advisory for Puerto Viejo after a series of armed robberies against U.S. travelers, including two hotel invasion robberies. The negativity is more than counterbalanced by the scores of wonderful, welcoming souls and the fact that the vast majority of visitors have a fantastic time without any trouble. Still, you need to be on your guard.

Some local Afro-Caribbean men are very forward with their advances toward women, and judging from the number of young foreign women on the arms of local men, their approaches are sometimes warmly received. The "rent-a-Rasta" syndrome engendered has inspired a reputation for "free love" that other female travelers must contend with. Be prepared for subtle to persistent overtures.

Highway 32 to Puerto Limón

Highway 32, the Guápiles Highway, connects San José with the Caribbean and runs east-west 104 kilometers (65 miles) from the foot of the Cordillera Central to Puerto Limón. Drive carefully: The heavily trafficked highway coils steeply down the mountains and is often fog-bound, landslides are frequent, and Costa Rican drivers can be exceedingly reckless—all of which makes for a white-knuckle drive. The road is frequently closed due to landslides; call the *tránsitos* (tel. 506/2268-2157) in Zurquí before setting out. Things may improve if a Chinese-financed plan to widen the highway to four lanes comes to fruition.

The road spills onto the northern lowlands at **El Cruce,** at the junction with Highway 4, with a gas station and **Rancho Roberto's** (tel. 506/2711-0050), a huge, modestly elegant thatched restaurant.

★ RAINFOREST AERIAL TRAM

The **Rainforest Aerial Tram** (tel. 506/2257-5961, U.S./Canada tel. 305-704-3350, www.rainforestadventure.com, 9am-4pm Mon., 6:30am-4pm Tues.-Sun., adults $60, students and children $30), on a 475-hectare (1,174-acre) private nature reserve on the northeastern boundary of Parque Nacional Braulio Carrillo, is an unforgettable experience. Constructed at a cost of more than $2 million by Dr. Donald Perry, author of the fascinating book *Life Above the Jungle Floor,* the tram takes visitors on a guided 90-minute excursion through the rainforest canopy.

The mysteries of the lush canopy unfold with each passing tree. Your ride is preceded by an instructional video. Then it's 2.6 kilometers (1.6 miles) via cable car (each car holds six people, including a naturalist guide) in the manner of a ski lift, giving you a new vantage on the "spectacular hanging gardens of the rainforest roof." Birding excursions are also offered.

There's also a zip line with 10 cables and 14 platforms (adults $10), several trails, a butterfly and frog garden ($10), plus guided hiking and more (for extra fees). A "Six-in-One" fee (adults $99, children $65) includes all the facilities, plus as many tram rides as you want. On sunny days in high season, expect a wait of up to one hour, as the lines are long (coffee, fruit drinks, and cookies are served). It has a restaurant and accommodations, plus a nocturnal tour for overnight guests.

The tram is on Highway 32, four kilometers (2.5 miles) past the Braulio Carrillo ranger station and 15 kilometers (9.5 miles) west of Guápiles. The parking lot is on a dangerously fast bend. The bus between San José and Guápiles will drop you off at Chichorronera la Reserva or "El Teleférico" ($1.50), but be sure to tell the driver to drop you at the entrance to the tram. Many unfortunate guests have had to trek back uphill after the driver passed the entrance and kept going.

GUÁPILES TO SIQUIRRES
Guápiles

Guápiles, 14 kilometers (9 miles) east of Santa Clara, is a center for the Río Frío banana region that spreads for miles to the north. It's the largest town in the Caribbean lowlands, but there is no reason to visit.

Artist Patricia Erickson (tel./fax 506/2710-1958, pm_anatee@yahoo.com, by appointment only) welcomes visitors to her **Gallery at Home** studio on the west bank of the Río Blanco, south of the highway, six kilometers (4 miles) west of town. Her vibrant paintings dance with brilliant Caribbean colors, many of them portraying her trademark faceless Limonense women of color with floating limbs. Her husband, Brian, makes fabulously creative bamboo furniture at nearby **Artistry in Bamboo** (tel. 506/2710-1958, www.brieri.com, 8am-4pm Mon.-Fri., 8am-noon Sat.). He offers tours of his bamboo and sculpture garden by appointment ($25 for 1-2 people).

Nature lovers with a deep interest in conservation might divert off Highway 32 and head north about 35 kilometers (26 miles) to

Rainforest Aerial Tram

La Suerte Biological Field Station Lodge (tel. 506/2710-8005, U.S./Canada tel. 305-666-9932, www.maderasrfc.org), on the banks of the Río Suerte at La Primavera, near the southwestern border of Barra del Colorado and 20 kilometers (12 miles) inland from Parque Nacional Tortuguero. There are 10 kilometers (6 miles) of rainforest trails open to ecotourists (day visit $8 pp, including lunch) and teaching workshops in tropical ecology, from primate behavior to herpetology. It has rustic accommodations. A bus leaves Cariari, 15 kilometers (9.5 miles) north of Guápiles, at 6:30am and 10:30am daily.

ACCOMMODATIONS AND FOOD

The intimate, laid-back **Casa Río Blanco Ecolodge** (tel./fax 506/2710-4124, www.casa-rioblanco.com, $53 s, $77 d, including breakfast), is on the banks of the Río Blanco, seven kilometers (4.5 miles) west of Guápiles and one kilometer (0.6 miles) south of the bridge (and only 12 kilometers/7.5 miles from the Rainforest Aerial Tram). Delightful Dutch owners Herbie and Annette offer four charming wooden cabins with private baths with hot water, orthopedic mattresses, and a screened wall that opens to a spacious porch—perfect for relaxing with the river bubbling away

below. It's great for wildlife viewing, and the couple lead bird-watching and nature hikes.

In Guápiles, the resort-style **Hotel & Country Club Suerre** (tel. 506/2713-3000, www.suerre.com, from $80 s, $110), at the east end of town, is popular with Costa Rican families passing through. This elegant property has 55 spacious air-conditioned rooms appointed with hardwoods. Facilities include an Olympic-size pool, a restaurant, two bars and a disco, and a whirlpool tub and sauna.

There are dozens of wayside restaurants catering to the traffic. I'm partial to the handsome **Restaurante Río Danta** (tel. 506/2710-2626, 11am-1pm daily), five kilometers (3 miles) west of Guápiles. Like most restaurants along the highway, it serves *típico* dishes, including *casados* (set lunches, $5-9), but it also has short trails leading into the adjacent private forest reserve, good for spotting poison dart frogs.

Guácimo

Guácimo is a small town and important truck stop about 12 kilometers (7.5 miles) east of Guápiles and about 400 meters (0.25 miles) north of Highway 32. **EARTH** (Escuela de Agricultura de la Región Tropical Húmeda, tel. 506/2713-0000, tours tel. 506/2713-0248,

Patricia Erickson's Gallery at Home, Guápiles

ext. 5002, www.earth.ac.cr, 8am-4:30pm daily), the School of Tropical Humid Agriculture, one kilometer (0.6 miles) east of town, is a university that teaches agricultural techniques to students from Latin America. It specializes in researching ecologically sound or sustainable agriculture. EARTH has its own banana plantation and 400-hectare (990-acre) forest reserve with nature trails. Visitors are welcome. **Costa Rica Expeditions** (tel. 506/2257-0766, www.costaricaexpeditions. com) offers a full-day tour from San José.

Siquirres

Siquirres, 25 kilometers (16 miles) east of Guácimo and 49 kilometers (30 miles) west of Limón, is a major railroad junction, echoing to the clanging of locomotives working freight for the banana companies. Before 1949, blacks traveling west had to get off the train here due to apartheid laws. Those days are long gone, but this is where you truly transition into the Caribbean region; Spanish songs give way to reggae, and *gallo pinto* gives way to *rondón*.

Siquirres is two kilometers (1.2 miles) east of the Río Reventazón and one kilometer (0.6 miles) west of the Río Pacuare. White-water rafters traditionally take out at Siquirres.

About five kilometers (3 miles) east of Siquirres and 100 meters (330 feet) west of the Río Pacuarito, a dirt road leads south 17 kilometers (11 miles) to the remote 12,000-hectare (29,650-acre) **Parque Nacional Barbilla** (8am-4pm daily, $6), on the northeast flank of the Talamanca Mountains. Its creation in the face of heavy logging is a testament to the efforts of the Fundación Nairi, which has a small field station, Estación Biológica Barbilla. The park is administered by SINAC's **Amistad Caribe Conservation Area office** (tel. 506/2768-5341, aclac@minae. go.cr) in Siquirres. The **ranger station** (tel. 506/2768-8603 or 506/8396-7611, www.sinac. go.cr), at Las Brisas del Pacuarito, 10 kilometers (6 miles) from the highway, has restrooms and potable water. A 4WD vehicle is required to get there. A taxi from town will cost about $10.

Veragua Rainforest Research & Adventure Park

The superb **Veragua Rainforest Research & Adventure Park** (tel. 506/4000-0949, www.veraguarainforest.com, adults $66, students and children $55; with canopy tour adults $99, students and children $75) is the keystone of a private reserve protecting 1,300 hectares (3,200 acres) of primary and secondary rainforest at Las Brisas del Veragua; the turnoff is at Liverpool, about 12 kilometers (7.5 miles) west of Limón, and a 4WD vehicle is required. Highlights include butterfly, snake, and frog exhibits (including a walk-through nocturnal frog garden with misters) linked by elevated boardwalks over the forest. An open-air tram through the canopy whisks you steeply down to the riverside Trail of the Giants (good for spotting poison dart frogs), which leads to a fabulous waterfall. Thoughtful education signage is a bonus. This is also an active research facility, run in collaboration with INBio; you can watch biologists at work. Even the stylishly modern yet old-fashioned urinals offer forest views. The entrance fee includes a guided tour and lunch in a lovely open-air restaurant.

The **Original Canopy Tour** (tel. 506/2291-4465, www.canopytour.com, adults $55, students and children $45), at Veragua Rainforest Research & Adventure Park, offers a thrilling zip-line adventure through the rainforest canopy.

Getting There

Empresario Guápileños (tel. 506/2222-0610) buses from San José depart the Gran Terminal del Caribe on Calle Central, Avenidas 13/15, every hour 5:30am-7pm daily for Guápiles ($2.50), Guácimo ($2.75), and Siquirres ($3). **Transportes Caribeños** (tel. 506/2221-2596) buses also depart the same terminal hourly 5:30am-7pm daily, bound for Limón. Buses depart Guápiles for Puerto Viejo de Sarapiquí seven times daily.

Make sure the bus is a faster *directo* buses and not a slower *colectivo*, which makes stops en route.

Puerto Limón and Vicinity

PUERTO LIMÓN

Puerto Limón (pop. 65,000) is an important maritime port and gateway to all other points on the Caribbean. The harbor handles much of the sea trade for Costa Rica. Trucks hauling containers rumble along the main road day and night. Except for Carnival, when it gets in the groove, Puerto Limón is merely a jumping-off point for most travelers; there is little of interest to see. However, it throbs with vitality and is populated by colorful characters at a crossroad of cultures.

The 1991 earthquake dealt Puerto Limón a serious blow. The city has come a long way since, as reflected in the razing of decrepit buildings and a sense of newfound prosperity. A cruise ship port (tel. 506/2799-0215) draws cruise ships. However, the city has a bad reputation among Ticos and is often referred to as "Piedropolis" (Crack City), and crime (mostly between gangs) has resurged in recent years as drug trafficking has become more pernicious.

Orientation

Highway 32 from San José enters town from the west and becomes Avenida 1, paralleling the railroad track that runs to the cruise port. The *avenidas* (east-west) are aligned north of Avenida 1 in sequential order. The *calles* (north-south) are numbered sequentially and run westward from the waterfront. The street signs are not to be trusted. Most addresses and directions are given in direction and distance from the market or Parque Vargas.

The road leading south from the junction of Avenida 1 and Calle 9 leads to Cahuita and Puerto Viejo. Avenida 6 leads out of town to Moín and the JAPDEVA dock, where boats can be hired for the trip to Tortuguero.

Sights

There's not much to keep you in town, although the **Mercado Central** (Aves. Central/2, Calles 3/4), at the heart of town, is worth a browse. The unremarkable and slightly decayed **Parque Vargas,** at the east end of Avenidas 1 and 2, is literally an urban jungle, with palm promenades and a crumbling bandstand amid a tangle of vines. On the north side, a fading mural by Guadalupe

The Black Star Line in Puerto Limón was built in 1922.

Puerto Limón

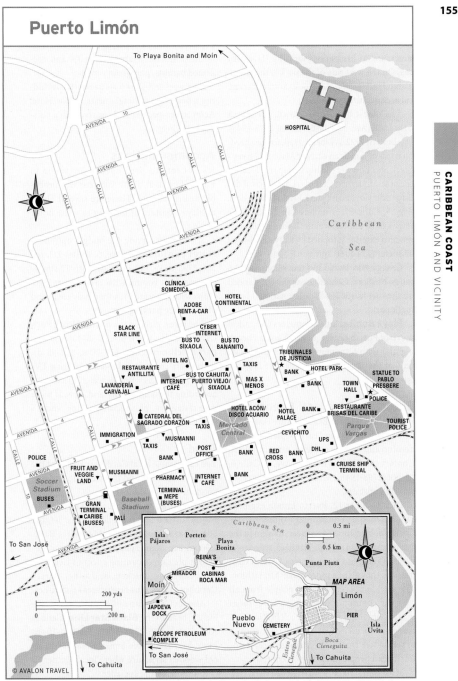

To Playa Bonita and Moín

HOSPITAL

Caribbean

Sea

AVENIDA 10

AVENIDA 9

AVENIDA 8

CALLE 3

CALLE 2

AVENIDA 7

CALLE 4

CALLE 5

CALLE 6

CALLE 7

AVENIDA 6

CLÍNICA
SOMEDICA

HOTEL
CONTINENTAL

ADOBE
RENT-A-CAR

CYBER
INTERNET

BLACK
STAR LINE

BUS TO
SIXAOLA

BUS TO
BANANITO

AVENIDA 6

HOTEL NG

TRIBUNALES
DE JUSTICIA

TAXIS

BANK

HOTEL PARK

RESTAURANTE
ANTILLITA

INTERNET
CAFÉ

BUS TO CAHUITA/
PUERTO VIEJO/
SIXAOLA

MAS X
MENOS

BANK

STATUE TO
PABLO
PRESBERE

TOWN
HALL

POLICE

LAVANDERÍA
CARVAJAL

AVENIDA 5

CATEDRAL DEL
SAGRADO CORAZÓN

HOTEL ACÓN/
DISCO ACUARIO

HOTEL
PALACE

BANK

RESTAURANTE
BRISAS DEL CARIBE

AVENIDA 4

IMMIGRATION

TAXIS

*Mercado
Central*

CEVICHITO

*Parque
Vargas*

TOURIST
POLICE

CALLE 3

TAXIS

MUSMANNI

UPS

POLICE

AVENIDA 3

BANK

POST
OFFICE

BANK

RED
CROSS

BANK

DHL

CRUISE SHIP
TERMINAL

FRUIT AND
VEGGIE LAND

MUSMANNI

PHARMACY

INTERNET
CAFÉ

BANK

CALLE 10

*Soccer
Stadium*

BUSES

AVENIDA 2

GRAN
TERMINAL
CARIBE
(BUSES)

TERMINAL
MEPE
(BUSES)

*Baseball
Stadium*

PALÍ

AVENIDA 1

To San José

To Cahuita

Caribbean Sea

0   0.5 mi

0   0.5 km

Isla
Pájaros

Portete

Playa
Bonita

Punta Piuta

REINA'S

MAP AREA

MIRADOR

CABINAS
ROCA MAR

Moín

Limón

PIER

JAPDEVA
DOCK

Pueblo
Nuevo

CEMETERY

Isla
Uvita

RECOPE PETROLEUM
COMPLEX

*Boca
Cieneguita*

To San José

To Cahuita

0   200 yds

0   200 m

© AVALON TRAVEL

Alvarea shows life in Limón since pre-Columbian days. A bronze bust of Christopher Columbus, erected in 1990 for the 500th anniversary of his party's landing, faces the sea. On the west side of the park is the stucco **Town Hall** (*alcaldía*), a fine example of tropical architecture.

The oldest building in town, the **Black Star Line** (Ave. 5, Calle 6, tel. 506/2798-1948), was built in 1922 as Liberty Hall, former headquarters of Jamaican activist Marcus Garvey's Black Star Line Steamship Company. Nearby, the post-Modernist Catholic **La Catedral del Sagrado Corazón** (Sacred Heart Cathedral, Ave. 3, Calle 7), completed in 2010, is the town's most impressive site. Its dramatic postmodern exterior is topped by a crystal-shaped 47-meter (154-foot) spire.

Craggy **Isla Uvita** lies one kilometer (0.6 miles) offshore. Columbus supposedly landed on the islet in 1502; it is now a national landmark park.

Playa Bonita, four kilometers (2.5 miles) north of Puerto Limón, boasts a golden beach popular with Limonenses. Swimming is safe only at the northern end. The surf is good, but unreliable.

Entertainment and Events

The **Día del Negro** (Black Culture Festival) is held in late August and early September, with domino and oratory contests, music, and art. Contact the Black Star Line (Ave. 5, Calle 6, tel. 506/2798-1948), which has a legendary social club upstairs.

Each October 12, Puerto Limón explodes in a bacchanal. The annual Columbus Day **Carnival** is celebrated with fervor akin to the bump-and-grind style of Trinidad, with street bands, floats, and every ounce of Mardi Gras passion, though in a more makeshift fashion. The weeklong event attracts people from all over the country, and getting a hotel room is virtually impossible. The celebrations include a Dance Festival—a rare opportunity to see dances from indigenous groups, Afro-Caribbean people, and calypso contests.

Most bars have a raffish quality. An exception is **Cevichito** (Ave. 2, Calles 2/3, tel. 506/2758-4976, from 10am daily), on the pedestrian strip. The bar, decorated with flags of the world, has a large-screen TV and one-armed bandits, plus groovy music.

The weekend **Disco Acuario** ($5, including a beer, free to hotel guests) in the Hotel Acón is jam-packed and sweaty, with a pulsing Latin beat.

Accommodations

It's not safe to park outside anywhere in Puerto Limón at night; your car will probably be broken into. There are several hotels at Playa Bonita, but nothing to write home about.

A standout among the budget options is **Hotel Continental** (Ave. 5, Calles 2/3, tel. 506/2798-0532, $12 s, $17 d), with 12 simple but spacious rooms with fans and private baths with hot water. It's spotlessly clean and offers secure parking.

The nicest place in town is the **Hotel Park** (Ave. 3, Calle 1, tel. 506/2758-4364, www.parkhotellimon.com, $58-70 s, $72-98 d), with 32 air-conditioned rooms featuring TVs and private baths with hot water. Prices vary according to room quality and view. It has a nice restaurant, plus secure parking, and it's well maintained.

Food

You can sample local Caribbean dishes at the open-air *sodas* around the Mercado Central, good for filling *casados* ($2).

More than a mere café, **Caribbean Kalisi Coffee Shop** (Calle 6, Aves. 3/4, tel. 506/2758-3249, 7am-8pm Mon.-Fri., 8am-7:30pm Sat., 8am-3pm Sun.) dishes out delicious plates of steaming coconut rice with red beans and chicken, and other purely Caribbean faves, plus hearty breakfast dishes.

Also for Caribbean dishes and heaps of ambience, head to the **Black Star Line** (Calle 5, Ave. 5, tel. 506/2798-1948, 7:30am-10pm Mon.-Sat., 11am-5pm Sun., *casado* $3), in an old wooden structure where locals gather to play dominoes and socialize.

Costa Rica's Aquatic Coastal Highway

Four canals link the natural channels and lagoons stretching north of Moín to Tortuguero and the Río Colorado. These canals form a connected "highway"—virtually the only means of getting around along the coast. One can travel from Siquirres eastward along the Río Pacuare, then northward to Tortuguero, and from there to the Río Colorado, which in turn connects with the Río San Juan, which will take you westward to Puerto Viejo de Sarapiquí.

The waterway is lined with rainforest vegetation in a thousand shades of green, making for a fascinating journey. Noisy flocks of parrots speed by doing barrel rolls in tight formation. Several species of kingfishers patrol the banks. In places the canopy arches over the canal, and howler monkeys sounding like rowdy teenagers may protest your passing. Keep a sharp eye out for mud turtles and caimans perched on logs to absorb the sun's rays.

At Playa Bonita, the open-air beachfront **Reina's** (tel. 506/2795-0879, 10am-11pm Mon.-Thurs., 8am-1am Fri.-Sun.) is the hip spot hereabouts and draws the party crowd (and local riffraff). It's a good place to hang and watch the surf pump ashore while savoring a shrimp cocktail ($9), ceviche ($6), snapper ($10), or Caribbean-style rice and beans ($6). Don't leave anything in your car in the parking lot.

Information and Services

The **Hospital Tony Facio** (tel. 506/2758-2222, emergency tel. 506/2758-0580) is on the seafront *malecón,* reached via Avenida 6. For private service, head to **Clínica Somedica** (Ave. 6, Calle 4, tel. 506/2798-4004, www.somedicacr.com). The **Red Cross** (tel. 506/2758-0125) is at Avenida 1, Calle 4.

The **police station** is on the northwest corner of Avenida 3, Calle 8. Criminal investigation is handled by the OIJ (tel. 506/2799-1437). The **post office** is at Calle 4, Avenida 2. The best Internet café is **Cyber Internet** (Ave. 4, Calle 4, tel. 506/2758-5061). **Immigration** (Dirección General de Migración y Extranjería) is on Avenida 3, Calles 6/7.

Getting There

Nature Air (tel. 506/2299-6000, U.S. tel. 800-235-9272, www.natureair.com) and **SANSA** (tel. 506/2229-4100, U.S./Canada tel. 877-767-2672, www.flysansa.com) offer regular service from San José to Limón's airport (LIO, tel. 506/2758-1379), two kilometers (1.2 miles) south of town.

Transportes Caribeños (tel. 506/2221-2596) runs double-decker buses that depart the Gran Terminal del Caribe (Calle Central, Aves. 13/15) in San José hourly 5am-7pm daily. The buses continue to Cahuita, Puerto Viejo, Bribrí, and Sixaola. Buses to San José ($4) depart Puerto Limón from Calle 2, Avenida 2.

Local buses depart Limón for Cahuita ($1.25), Puerto Viejo ($2), and Sixaola ($3.50) from opposite Radio Casino on Avenida 4 eight times 5am-6pm daily. Buses for Manzanillo ($2) leave at 6am, 2:30pm, and 6pm daily. Buy tickets in advance at the *soda* beside the bus stop, as buses get crowded. Around the corner on Calle 4 to the north is the bus stop for Playa Bonita and Moín.

Six kilometers (4 miles) north of Puerto Limón, at Moín, you can catch a boat to Tortuguero. The dock is north of the railroad tracks.

Getting Around

From Puerto Limón, the **bus** to Playa Bonita, Portrete, and Moín operates hourly from Calle 4, Avenida 4, opposite Radio Casino. **Taxis** await customers on the south side of the market.

PUERTO LIMÓN TO TORTUGUERO

Lagoons and swamps dominate the coastal plains north of Limón. Many rivers meander through this region, carrying silt that the coastal tides conjure into long, straight brown-sand beaches. The only community along the canals is **Parismina**, on the ocean-side spit at the mouth of the Río Parismina, 45 kilometers (28 miles) north of Moín. It is popular year-round with anglers.

Sea turtles come ashore to nest all along the coast, notably at **Barra de Matina**, midway between Moín and Parismina (see www. costaricaturtles.com). Here, **Asociación Salvemos las Tortugas de Parismina** (tel. 506/2798-2220, www.parisminaturtles. org), run by former Peace Corps volunteer Vicky Taylor, operates a nature reserve that exists primarily to protect the eggs of leatherback turtles from poachers during the nesting season. With the demise of the leatherback population at Playa Grande in Nicoya, the Parismina-Pacuare corridor is now the most important leatherback site in Costa Rica. Volunteers are needed to join biologists and hired guards to patrol the beach, tag and measure turtles, and relocate nests

(one-week minimum). **Conselvatur** (tel./fax 506/2253-8118, www.conselvatur.com) offers an eight-day Sea Turtle Research and Rainforest Exploration trip that features Reserva Pacuare.

The reserves can be accessed by road via **Matina**, a banana town on the banks of the Río Matina four kilometers (2.5 miles) north of Highway 32 (the turnoff is at Bristol, about 28 kilometers/17 miles east of Siquirres); and by boat from Moín ($20 pp) or **Caño Blanco Marina** (tel. 506/2206-5138), near Barra de Matina Sur.

Accommodations and Food

In Parismina, **Iguana Verde** (tel. 506/2798-0828, with fan $10 pp, with a/c $20 pp) is set in a lush garden with a resident parrot. English-speaking Ricky and Jendra Knowles offer three clean rooms with private baths, plus a relaxing café and a grocery.

Sportfishing enthusiasts are catered to at two dedicated sportfishing lodges at Parismina: **Río Parismina Lodge** (tel. 506/2229-7597, U.S./Canada tel. 800-338-5688, www.riop.com) and **Jungle Tarpon Lodge** (U.S. tel. 800-544-2261, www.jungle-tarpon.com). Both offer fishing packages and take in guests on an ad hoc basis.

Tortuguero and Barra del Colorado

★ TORTUGUERO NATIONAL PARK

Parque Nacional Tortuguero (www.sinac. go.cr) extends north along the coast for 22 kilometers (14 miles) from Jaloba, six kilometers (4 miles) north of Parismina, to Tortuguero village. The 19,000-hectare (47,000-acre) park is a mosaic of deltas on an alluvia plain nestled between the Caribbean coast on the east and low-lying volcanic hills to the west. The park protects the nesting beach of the green turtle, the offshore waters to a distance of 30 kilometers (19 miles), and the wetland forests extending inland for about 15 kilometers (9.5 miles).

The park—one of the most varied in Costa Rica—has 11 ecological habitats, from high rainforest to herbaceous marsh communities. Fronting the sea is the seemingly endless expanse of beach. Behind that is a narrow artificial canal, connected to the sea at one end and fed by a river at the other; it parallels the beach for its full 35-kilometer (22-mile) length. In back of the canal and the lagoon to its north is a coastal rainforest and swamp complex threaded by an infinite maze of serpentine channels and streams.

Tortuguero shelters more than 300 bird species, among them toucans, aracaris,

Tortuguero and Barra del Colorado

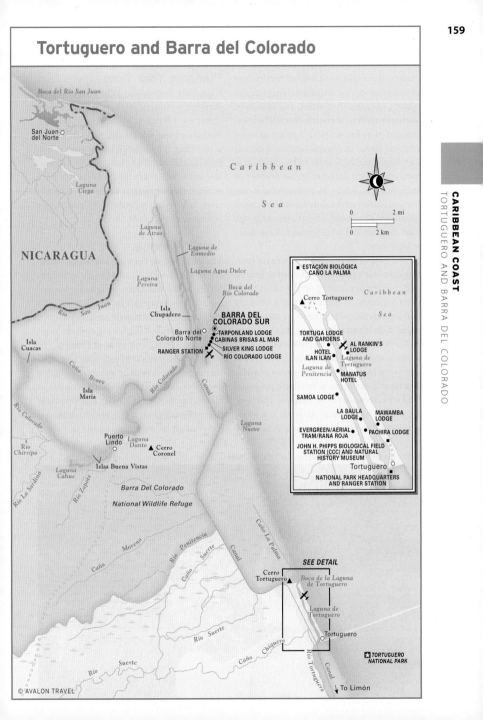

Boca del Río San Juan

San Juan
del Norte

Laguna
Ciega

NICARAGUA

Laguna
de Atras

Laguna de
Enmedio

Laguna Agua Dulce

Laguna
Pereira

Caribbean

Sea

0 — 2 mi
0 — 2 km

Isla
Chupadero

Boca del
Río Colorado

**BARRA DEL
COLORADO SUR**

Barra del
Colorado Norte

TARPONLAND LODGE
CABINAS BRISAS AL MAR
SILVER KING LODGE
RÍO COLORADO LODGE

RANGER STATION

Isla
Cuacas

Río   San Juan

Caño   Bravo

Isla
Maria

Río   Colorado

Canal

Río Colorado

Río
Chirripó

Puerto
Lindo

Laguna
Danto

▲ Cerro
Coronel

Islas Buena Vistas

Laguna
Nueve

Laguna
Cahue

Río La Sardina

Río Zapate

Barra Del Colorado

National Wildlife Refuge

Moreno

Caño

Río Penitencia

Caño   Suerte

Canal

Caño La Palma

Río   Suerte

Caño   Chiquero

Río   Suerte

Río

© AVALON TRAVEL

SEE DETAIL

Cerro
Tortuguero ▲

Boca de la Laguna
de Tortuguero

Laguna de
Tortuguero

Tortuguero

★ TORTUGUERO
NATIONAL PARK

Río Tortuguero

Canal

↓ To Limón

Detail inset:

■ ESTACIÓN BIOLÓGICA
CAÑO LA PALMA

▲ Cerro Tortuguero

Caribbean

Sea

TORTUGA LODGE
AND GARDENS

AL RANKIN'S
LODGE

HOTEL
ILAN ILAN

Laguna de
Tortuguero

Laguna de
Penitencia

MANATUS
HOTEL

SAMOA LODGE

LA BAULA
LODGE

MAWAMBA
LODGE

EVERGREEN/AERIAL
TRAM/RANA ROJA

PACHIRA LODGE

JOHN H. PHIPPS BIOLOGICAL FIELD
STATION (CCC) AND NATURAL
HISTORY MUSEUM

Tortuguero

NATIONAL PARK HEADQUARTERS
AND RANGER STATION

oropendolas, herons, kingfishers, anhingas, jacanas, and the great green macaw; 57 species of amphibians and 111 of reptiles, including three species of marine turtles; and 60 mammal species, including jaguars, tapirs, ocelots, cougars, river otters, and manatees. Tortuguero's fragile manatee population was thought to be extinct until a group of about 100 was found in remote lagoons a decade ago. Their numbers seem to be growing, as indicated by an increase in the number of collisions with boats. In 2005 several manatee sanctuaries were created, where boats are prohibited or velocity is restricted, although boat captains still whiz through these zones at high speed.

The wide-open canals are superb for spotting crocodiles, giant iguanas, basilisk lizards, and caimans luxuriating on the fallen raffia palm branches. At night you might even spy bulldog bats skimming the water and scooping up fish. It's an amazing sight.

The western half of the park is under great stress from logging and hunting, which have increased in recent years as roads intrude. The local community is battling a proposed highway sponsored by banana and logging interests. Rubbish disposal is a problem; leave no trash. The park is severely understaffed, and as a result, environmental abuses continue.

Planning Your Time

Rain falls year-round. The three wettest months are January, June, and July. The three driest are February, April, and November. Monsoon-type storms can lash the region at any time. The interior of the park is hot, humid, and windless. Take good rain gear, and note that it can be cool enough for a windbreaker or sweater while speeding upriver. Take insect repellent—the mosquitoes and no-see-ums can be fierce.

Turtle Viewing

The park protects the most important hatchery in the western Caribbean for green sea turtles, which find their way onto the brown-sand beaches every year June to October, with the greatest numbers arriving in September. Giant leatherback turtles arrive from mid-February to July, with greatest frequency in April and May, followed by female hawksbill turtles in July. Annually as many as 30,000 greens swim from their feeding grounds as far away as the Gulf of Mexico and Venezuela to lay their eggs on the beach. Each female arrives two to six times, at 10- to 14-day

spotting a green iguana in Tortuguero National Park

intervals, and waits two or three years before nesting again. The number of green turtles nesting has quadrupled during the last 25 years; that of leatherbacks continues to decline.

During the 1950s, the Tortuguero nesting colony came to the attention of biologist-writer Archie Carr, a lifelong student of sea turtles. His lobby—originally called the Brotherhood of the Green Turtle—worked with the Costa Rican government to establish Tortuguero as a sanctuary, established in 1963; the area was named a national park in 1970.

Local guides escort **Turtle Walks** (8pm-10pm and 10pm-midnight each evening in turtle-nesting season, $10, including guide; only guides can buy tickets to access the beach at night). No one is allowed on the 35-kilometer (22-mile) nesting sector without a guide after 6pm, and a maximum of 10 people per guide per night are allowed on the beach at night. Each of the five sectors has a guard post. No cameras or flashlights are permitted. Keep quiet—the slightest noise can send the turtle hurrying back to sea—and keep a discreet distance. You are asked to report any guide who digs up turtle hatchlings to show you: This is absolutely prohibited.

When hiring a guide, ensure that they have a formal accreditation sticker to give you prior to going to the beach. The cost of the sticker pays for turtle-spotters—*rastreadores*—who spot for nesting turtles and call in the position to guides. Unqualified guides without stickers ignore the accreditation process to offer cheaper guide services and undercut the competition.

Recreation

Trails into the forests—frequently waterlogged—begin at the park stations at both ends of the park; the number of people permitted at any one time is limited. The two-kilometer (1.2-mile) **El Gavilán Trail** leads south from the Cuatro Esquinas ranger station south of Tortuguero village and takes in both beach and rainforest. Rubber boots are compulsory in wet season (the trail is often closed due to flooding), when fer-de-lance snakes abound. Rent boots at Ernesto Tours (tel. 506/2709-8070, $1) or book a hiking tour ($15). A two-kilometer (1.2-mile) section of **Sendero Jaguar** is accessible with a guide; the other 16 kilometers (10 miles) are accessible at night for turtle viewing.

You can hire dugout canoes (*cayucos* or *botes*) at Ernest Tours ($10 pp for 3 hours, with

turtle conservation sign at Tortuguero

Volunteers for Conservation

Sea Turtle Conservancy (tel. 506/2297-6576; in the U.S.: 4424 NW 13th St., Suite A1, Gainesville, FL 32609, U.S. tel. 352-373-6441 or 800-678-7853, www.conserveturtles.org) needs volunteers to assist in research, including during its twice-yearly turtle tagging and monitoring programs. The group also invites volunteers to join its fall and spring bird-research projects at Tortuguero. No experience is needed. The fieldwork is complemented by guided hikes, boat tours, and other activities.

Numerous other organizations that seek volunteers for environmental, social, and developmental work include **Firsthand** (www.firsthand-costarica.com); **Planet Conservation** (tel. 506/2772-4720, www.planetconservation.com); and **Save the Turtles of Parisima Projects Abroad** (tel. 506/2798-2220, www.parisminaturtles.org, www.projects-abroad.org).

guide $15 pp). Check on local currents and directions, as the former can be quite strong, and it's easy to lose your bearings amid the maze of waterways. Skippered *pangas* (flat-bottomed boats with outboard motors) and *lanchas* (with inboard motors) can also be rented; try to rent one with an electric or nonpolluting four-stroke motor. Don't forget to pay your park entrance fee before entering Parque Nacional Tortuguero.

Guides and Tours

If you want to see wildlife, you absolutely need a guide. Even in the darkest shadows, they can spot caimans, birds, crocodiles, and other animals you will most likely miss. The **Asociación de Guía de Tortuguero** (tel. 506/2767-0836, www.asoprotur.com, 5am-7pm daily) is a local is a local cooperative of 40 trained guides; its office is by the water-taxi dock.

More than a dozen small-scale tour operators in Tortuguero village offer a similar nature-focused menu of canal trips, turtle-watching trips, and rainforest hikes. By far the best guide is Karla Taylor Martínez, of **Karla's Travel Experience** (tel. 506/2262-0383 or 506/8915-2386, libertad73@live.com). She is a fluent English speaker who specializes in canoe trips and gives a sensational presentation. Descended from the very first settler of the village, when it was known as Turtle Bogue, Karla knows the lagoons and channels of this water-bound world like the

back of her hand. What sets the "Karla Taylor Experience" apart from the others is her personal tale of why Tortuguero holds such importance to her, which grants you an entirely new appreciation for Tortuguero and for nature's healing potential.

Ross Ballard, a former field biologist, also specializes in interpretive tours with his **Ballard Excursions** (tel. 506/2709-8193 or 506/8320-5232, ballardross1@gmail.com), as does Mauricio Rodríguez Vargas of **Rainforest Life Tours** (tel. 506/2763-4072, mauricr86@yahoo.es).

You can also book guided trips at any of the lodges or through tour companies in San José. **Costa Rica Expeditions** (tel. 506/2257-0766, www.costaricaexpeditions.com) is recommended.

Information and Services

The park is open 6am-5:45pm daily; last entry is at 5pm. The $10 admission also includes access to Caño Palma, in the Barra del Colorado wildlife refuge. The fee is payable at the **Cuatro Esquinas** ranger station (tel./fax 506/2709-8086, 6am-noon and 1pm-5pm), at the southern end of Tortuguero village; at **Estación Jalova,** at the park's southern end (45 minutes by boat from Tortuguero village); or at **Aguas Frias** (tel. 506/8394-0203), on the western limit of the park and accessed by driving north from the Guápiles highway via Cariari and Pococi. No fee applies if you're in transit. Cuatro Esquinas has an excellent

Tortuguero

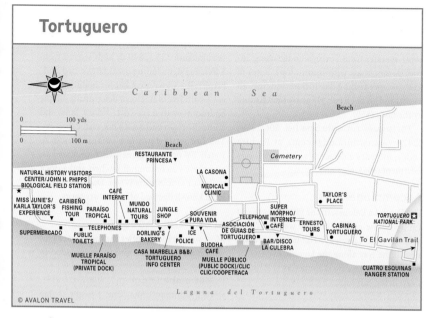

© AVALON TRAVEL

information center. You can camp ($2 pp) at Jalova, with outside showers and toilets. (Crocodiles are often seen sunning on the mud banks immediately south of Estación Jalova.)

TORTUGUERO VILLAGE AND LAGOON

Somnolent, funky Tortuguero village (pop. 550), on the northern boundary of Parque Nacional Tortuguero, sprawls over a thin strip of land at the northern end of the **Canal de Tortuguero** and the southern end of **Laguna del Tortuguero,** at the junction with **Laguna Penitencia,** a canal that leads to Barra del Colorado. Laguna del Tortuguero extends north six kilometers (4 miles) to the ocean, where the tannin-stained freshwater pours into the Caribbean; it is lined with nature lodges.

It's an 80-kilometer (50-mile), three-hour journey along the Canal de Tortuguero from Moín by high-powered water taxi; by small plane from San José, it's a 30-minute flight that sets you down on a thin strip of land with the ocean crashing on one side and the lagoon

and the rainforest on the other (the ocean here is not safe for swimming because of rip currents and sharks).

The village comprises a warren of narrow sandy trails (there are no roads) lined by rickety wooden houses and, increasingly, more substantial buildings spawned by the tourism boom. The south end of the village is best avoided after dark. In recent years, drug trafficking has escalated enormously.

The Sea Turtle Conservancy's **John H. Phipps Biological Field Station** (tel. 506/2709-8125, www.conserveturtles.org), about 500 meters (0.3 miles) north of the village, can be accessed by a trail behind the beach. It features a must-see **Natural History Visitors Center** (tel. 506/2709-8091, 10am-noon and 2pm-5pm daily, $2) with turtle exhibits and educational presentations on rainforest ecology, including a video about turtle ecology, and life-size models of turtles hatching and a female laying eggs.

The **TortuFest: Festival Cultural Tortuguero** (early Nov.) is a fun-filled, carnival-style event with boat floats.

Sports and Recreation

Eddie Brown Sportfishing (tel. 506/2252-4426 or 506/8834-2221, www.tortugalodge.com) operates from Tortuga Lodge using 26- and 28-foot boats with Bimini tops. Rates of $320-395 per fishing day include lodging, all meals, and an open bar. He also offers fishing by the hour ($50).

Tortuguero Jungle Spa (tel. 506/2256-2242, www.pachiralodge.com), at Pachira Lodge, includes a delectable chocolate body treatment ($95), plus massages.

Accommodations

The Disco La Paloma, in the village, belts out a top-volume racket into the wee hours, so only the dead can sleep. The noise reverberates all the way along the lagoon, even as far as Tortuga Lodge, two kilometers (1.2 miles) away. Bring earplugs.

IN THE VILLAGE

Tortuguero sometimes fills up; if you arrive without reservations, make it a priority to secure accommodations immediately.

There are at least two dozen budget options. Perhaps because I like its rustic restaurant with sand floor, I'm partial to **La Casona** (tel. 506/2709-8092, $18 s, $25 d), within a stone's throw of the beach on the north side of the soccer field. It has nine airy, well-kept cabins, with ceiling fans and modern baths (two rooms share a bath) in a garden, plus a three-bedroom *casona* (house). There's Wi-Fi, and a TV lounge was to be added. Andres is a licensed tour guide.

★ **Miss Junie's** (tel. 506/2709-8102, www.iguanaverdetours.com, downstairs $45 s, $50 d, upstairs $55 s, $60 d, including breakfast), at the north end of the village, has the nicest rooms in the village: 12 clean and simply furnished rooms in a two-story structure, each with a ceiling fan, screened windows, and a modern bath with hot water. The locale is great, and it has the best restaurant in the village. Karla Taylor Experience canoe trips operate from here, as does her brother's Iguana Verde Tours. The family is a delight.

Canadian owner Dale Roth runs the waterfront **Casa Marbella B&B** (tel. 506/2709-8011, http://casamarbella.tripod.com, low season from $35 s, $40 d, high season from $40 s, $45 d, including breakfast), a bed-and-breakfast—and a great bet for budget travelers—with five airy, clean, delightfully simple bedrooms with terra-cotta floors, fans, and clinically clean baths with hot-water showers. You can settle down in a common room to watch TV or enjoy games when rain strikes, and there's a communal kitchen and a dock with hammocks, plus Wi-Fi. Dale is a font of local knowledge and offers nature tours.

ALONG THE LAGOONS

Most nature lodges offer multiday packages with meals, transfers, and tours included in the rates below.

Mawamba Lodge (tel. 506/2709-8181, www.grupomawamba.com, 1-night, 2-day packages from $251 s or $420 d low season, $279 s, $460 d high season, including transportation and meals), about 800 meters (0.5 miles) north of Tortuguero on the east side of Laguna del Tortuguero, has 58 attractive all-wood rooms reached by canopied walkways. All have king beds, and four superior rooms have huge baths. There's an airy family-style restaurant and bar, a lovely swimming pool and sundeck, plus a whirlpool tub, a game room, and a nature trail.

Across the lagoon from Mawamba, and set in lush grounds, **Pachira Lodge** (tel. 506/2256-7080, www.pachiralodge.com, 1-night, 2-day packages from $249 s, $418 d low season, $279 s, $458 d high season) offers a similar alternative, with its 88 attractively furnished thatched cabins, handsome dining room serving buffet meals, and turtle-shaped pool. Thirty-two more upscale rooms are in newer A-frame stilt cabins connected by raised boardwalks; the aesthetic is lovely, and they get heaps of light. This section has an open-air full-service spa with steam baths.

Setting the standard to beat, and my favorite by far, ★ **Tortuga Lodge and Gardens** (tel. 506/2257-0766, www.

costaricaexpeditions.com, 1-night, 2-day packages from $528 pp), operated by Costa Rica Expeditions, offers the best food, the best guides, and the best overall experience. Pluses at this eco-sensitive lodge, facing the airstrip four kilometers (2.5 miles) north of town, include a sophisticated lounge bar, gourmet nouvelle Costa Rican cuisine in its torch-lit waterfront open-air restaurant, and a stone-lined gradual-entry swimming pool. The 24 spacious waterfront rooms are fronted by wide verandas with leather rockers. Each has queen beds, huge screened windows, ceiling fans, and modern baths with solar-heated water. The lodge sits amid 20 hectares (49 acres) of landscaped grounds and forest; muddy nature trails offer guaranteed sightings of poison dart frogs. Service is exemplary and includes a cold-towel welcome and turn-down service. It's the only fishing lodge in Tortuguero and also offers hikes and turtle walks plus multiday packages. Guests arriving by boat are greeted with a gourmet picnic lunch midway, and staff gather to wave as guests arrive and depart.

Food

Not to be missed for local fare is ★ **Miss Junie's** (tel. 506/2709-8102, 7:30am-2:30pm and 6:30pm-9:30pm daily), where $10 will buy you a platter of fish, chicken, or steak with rice and beans simmered in coconut milk, plus fruit juice and dessert. Reservations are recommended in high season. The enclosed restaurant has a fascinating photo display portraying the history of the village. Her son Ray also puts his culinary skills to work at **Taylor's Place** (no tel., 6pm-8:30pm daily), southwest of the soccer field. You dine under thatch in a garden, where Ray serves gourmet treats such as garlic grilled fish, beef in tamarind sauce, plus a veggie option.

The colorful thatched **Buddha Café** (tel. 506/2709-8084, www.buddacafe.com, noon-9pm daily, under $8), riverside in the village center, serves Italian cuisine that includes pizzas, crepes, and lasagna. Its urbane ambience, including an open-air lounge, has brought a touch of class to the village. The food is great.

La Casona (tel. 506/2709-8092, 8am-noon and 1pm-9pm daily), on the north side of the soccer field, serves pancakes with bananas as well as omelets and typical *casados*. I recommend the chicken in coconut ($8) or delicious lasagna de *palmito* (heart of palm).

At **Dorling's Bakery** (tel. 506/2709-8202, 5am-7pm daily), gracious Nicaraguan Dorling bakes delicious empanadas, cakes, apple pie,

relaxing at Tortuga Lodge and Gardens

and cheesecakes. You've got to try the raspberry truffle brownie. Dorling also has hearty breakfasts (including omelets and granola with fruit and yogurt), plus cappuccinos, milk shakes, and cheap lunches, including coconut chicken ($8.50).

To splurge, catch a ride to **Ara Macaw** (tel. 506/2709-8197, 7am-9am, noon-2pm, and 6:30pm-8:30pm daily), in the suave Manatus Hotel. Here you can woo your loved one in a romantic candlelit setting while enjoying gourmet Caribbean fusion cuisine. A three-course prix fixe dinner ($25) is offered for nonguests, by reservation.

Information and Services

Daryl Loth staffs the **Tortuguero Information Center** at Casa Marbella B&B (tel. 506/2709-8011, http://casamarbella.tripod.com) and is by far the best source of information. **Jungle Shop** (tel. 506/2709-8072, jungle@racsa.co.cr), in the village center, and **Paraíso Tropical** (tel. 506/2709-8095), about 50 meters (165 feet) farther north by the main dock, also offer visitor information services. Both sell souvenirs and phone cards.

The **medical clinic,** facing the dock, is open 8am-4pm Tuesday-Wednesday. There's a **pharmacy** 100 meters (330 feet) farther south, near the **police station** (tel. 506/2709-8188). There's a **Café Internet** (tel. 506/2709-8058, 9am-9pm daily) on the waterfront path.

Getting There

AIR

Both **Nature Air** (tel. 506/2299-6000, U.S. tel. 800-235-9272, www.natureair.com) and **SANSA** (tel. 506/2229-4100, U.S./Canada tel. 877-767-2672, www.flysansa.com) operate scheduled daily flights between San José and the landing strip four kilometers (2.5 miles) north of Tortuguero village. SANSA offers boat transfers to the village.

Costa Rica Expeditions (tel. 506/2257-0766, www.costaricaexpeditions.com) and other tour operators with lodges in Tortuguero operate private charter services; tour members get priority, but you may be

Fresh coconut water is a perfect way to beat the heat.

able to get a spare seat (about $75 one-way). You can arrange charter flights for about $500 one-way per four- or six-passenger plane.

BOAT

Locals prefer to use public *lanchas* (tel./fax 506/2709-8005 in Tortuguero), which leave from the end of the bus route at **La Pavona.** This requires taking two buses. First, take the 9am **Empresario Guápileño** (tel. 506/2222-2727 or 506/2710-7780, $2.50) bus to Cariari (15 kilometers/9.5 miles northeast of Guápiles) from San José's Gran Caribe bus terminal (tel. 506/2221-2596); buy your ticket in the Guápiles booth. (You could also take a 6am bus to Cariari.) Second, take the **Coopetraca** bus that leaves Cariari for La Pavona from the "old" bus station, five blocks north of the San José terminal, at 11:30am, arriving at La Pavona, 29 kilometers (18 miles) from Cariari, in time for the early-afternoon boat departure at about 1pm. Buy your boat ticket at La Pavona dock from **Inversiones Chavarría** (tel. 506/2767-6043 or 506/8812-3975), which has a restaurant and secure parking ($10 per day), rather than prepaid at the bus station. You can also take a bus from San José at 10:30am or 1pm, arriving Cariari in time for a 3pm bus to La Pavona; this should get you to the dock in time for the 4:30pm *lancha* to Tortuguero. However, this is cutting it close, as bad weather often delays in the buses. If you miss the boat, you can lodge at the pleasant **Hotel El Trópico** (tel. 506/2767-7070, from $25), about 500 meters north of the bus station in Cariari; it has a restaurant.

Return boats depart Tortuguero for La Pavona at 5:30am, 9am, 11am, and 2:45pm daily.

The route follows the Río Suerte through Parque Nacional Tortuguero and can be impassable in extreme high and low waters—you might even have to get out and help push the boat over sandbars, a good reason to choose the least full boat at La Pavona. The quickest way back to San José is to take the early boat, then a direct bus to Guápiles, then a bus to San José.

Water taxis also serve Tortuguero from the JAPDEVA dock in Moín (tel. 506/2795-0066), including **Rubén Viajes Bananero** (tel. 506/2709-8005, viajesbananero@yahoo.com, $30 one-way), departing Moín at 10am daily, return departures from Tortuguero at 10am daily. Francesca and Modesto Watson offer trips aboard the **Riverboat** *Francesca* (tel. 506/2226-0986, www.tortuguerocanals.com); prices for the boat-only transfer are negotiable depending on space available: Expect to pay $60-80 pp for four people round-trip, $220 pp for one or two people. Its one-night, two-day package is bargain-priced at $200 pp, including transfers from and to San José, the boat trip, and an overnight at Laguna Lodge. *Warning:* Touts will flag you down as you approach the JAPDEVA dock. Some touts and boat captains steer visitors toward specific lodgings and guides; most cannot be relied on.

Private boats for package-tour groups serve Tortuguero from **Caño Blanco Marina** (tel. 506/2206-5138), near Barra de Matina Sur. Tour operators in San José will accept reservations for these boat transfers on a space-available basis. A private skipper willing to take individuals without pre-booked group boat transfers can usually also be found here; a private charter to Tortuguero costs about $100 one-way, $180 round-trip per couple. Public water taxis depart about 10 minutes after the buses arrive. To get to the marina from San José, take a 9am bus (buses run 5am-7pm daily) from San José's Gran Caribe bus

boats to Tortuguero at La Pavona

terminal and get off at Siquirres, from where **Hermanos Caño Aguilar** (tel. 506/2768-8172) buses depart for Caño Blanco Marina at 4:30am and 12:30pm Monday-Friday and at 6am and 2pm Saturday-Sunday (return buses depart Caño Blanco at 7am and 1:30pm Mon.-Fri. and at 7:30am and 3pm Sat.-Sun.). Caño Blanco Marina has secure parking, 10 simple cabins with fans (with fan $25 s/d, with a/c $30 s/d), and a restaurant.

In Tortuguero, **Boletería** (tel. 506/2767-0390) has water taxis to anywhere you want to go.

BARRA DEL COLORADO NATIONAL WILDLIFE REFUGE

Refugio Nacional de Vida Silvestre Barra del Colorado (tel. 506/2710-1070, www.sinac.go.cr) protects 91,200 hectares (225,360 acres) of rainforest and wetlands extending north from the estuary of Lagunas del Tortuguero to the Río San Juan, the border with Nicaragua. About 30 kilometers (19 miles) from the sea, the Río San Juan divides, with the San Juan flowing northeast and the main branch—the Río Colorado—flowing southeast to the sea through the center of the reserve. Dozens of tributaries form a labyrinth of permanent sloughs and ephemeral waterways that have made the region inaccessible to all but boat traffic.

More remote and more isolated, Barra del Colorado is a replica of Parque Nacional Tortuguero—to which it is linked by canal—and protects a similar panoply of wildlife. Great green macaws wing screeching over the canopy, mixed flocks of antbirds follow advancing columns of army ants, and jabiru storks with two-meter (6-foot) wingspans circle above. Large crocodiles inhabit the rivers and can be seen basking on mud banks. However, there are virtually no facilities, and no ranger station.

Unexciting and ramshackle Barra del Colorado village sits astride the mouth of the 600-meter-wide (2,000-foot-wide) Río Colorado. **Barra del Norte,** on the north side of the river, has no roads, just dirt paths littered with trash and a broken concrete walkway down its center between slum cabins made of corrugated tin and wooden crates. The more pleasant **Barra del Sur** has an airstrip and most of the hamlet's few services. The village once prospered as a lumber center but went into decline during two decades of the Nicaraguan conflict, when the village became a haven for Nicaraguan refugees. Locals

American crocodile, Barra del Colorado

mainly rely on fishing or serve as guides for the half dozen sportfishing lodges, but drug trafficking is entrenched.

The few lodges here specialize in sportfishing, for which Barra is famous. Local tarpon are so abundant that a two-meter (6-foot) whopper might well jump into your boat. Gars—with an ancestry dating back 90 million years—are also common; growing up to two meters long (6 feet), these bony-scaled fish have long, narrow crocodile-like snouts full of vicious teeth. The Río San Juan is entirely Nicaraguan territory—when you are on the water, you are inside Nicaragua—but Costa Ricans have right of use.

Accommodations and Food

The sportfishing lodges rely on group business. When there are no groups, they can be lonely places. Only two places can be recommended.

Cabinas Brisas del Mar (tel. 506/2200-4993, $40 s/d, with 3 meals $70 d), on the east side of the airstrip, operates like a B&B and is run by a pleasant Tico couple. It has three rooms upstairs (with carpets) and two below, all with screened windows, local TV, ceiling fans, and clean baths with hot water. Seafood, Chinese, and local dishes are served in an open-air *soda*.

Sportfishers should choose **Silver King Lodge** (tel. 506/8381-1403, U.S. tel. 800-335-0755, www.silverkinglodge.net, minimum 3-night, 3-day package from $3,465 s, $5,500 d, all-inclusive). Although far from upscale, it offers 10 spacious, modestly furnished duplexes linked by covered catwalks. All have queen beds with orthopedic mattresses, ceiling fans, coffeemakers, plus large showers. You even get a small swimming pool, a huge whirlpool tub, a tackle shop, a bar, and a restaurant serving all-you-can-eat buffets. A heavy-duty offshore craft permits deep-sea fishing. The lodge closes mid-June to August and in December.

Information and Services

Local expat resident Diana Graves at **Diana's**

CyD Souvenirs (tel. 506/2200-0686, 8am-9pm daily) is the best source of visitor information; she has an Internet café.

The **police station** (tel. 506/2200-3536 or 506/2200-3435) is in the Salón Comunal.

Getting There

Both **Nature Air** (tel. 506/2299-6000, U.S. tel. 800-235-9272, www.natureair.com) and **SANSA** (tel. 506/2229-4100, U.S./Canada tel. 877-767-2672, www.flysansa.com) fly daily from San José if they get two or more passengers. You can also charter a light plane from San José.

A rough road leads from Puerto Viejo de Sarapiquí to Pavas (at the juncture of the Ríos Toro and Sarapiquí), where you can also charter a boat. Water taxis serve Barra del Colorado from the dock at La Pavona and from Tortuguero.

PUERTO LIMÓN TO CAHUITA

South of Puerto Limón, the shore is lined by brown-sand beaches fringed by palms. About 30 kilometers (19 miles) south of Limón, the road crosses the Río Estrella a few kilometers north of the village of **Penshurst,** where a branch road leads into the Valle del Río Estrella. The valley is blanketed by banana plantations of the Dole Standard Fruit Company, headquartered at **Pandora,** about six kilometers (4 miles) inland of Penshurst. The Río Estrella rises in the foothills of the steep-sided, heavily forested Talamanca massif, and it irrigates the banana plantations as it crosses the broad plains in search of the Caribbean. The river estuary forms a dense network of channels and lagoons that shelter birds, including great flocks of snow-white cattle egrets.

★ Sloth Sanctuary

The world's only **Sloth Sanctuary** (tel. 506/2750-0775, www.slothsanctuary.com), one kilometer (0.6 miles) north of the Río Estrella, is a 75-hectare (185-acre) wildlife sanctuary owned and run privately by Judy

Arroyo. It cares for injured sloths (or those confiscated as illegal pets) and rehabilitates them in its "slothpital" (more than 130 are in residence). The refuge has released more than 100 sloths back into the wild, and dozens can be viewed alongside agoutis and various other critters. It also serves as an educational and research center, and offers one of Costa Rica's most fulfilling experiences for visitors interested in learning about these adorable, famously slow-moving, and much misunderstood creatures.

Guided two-hour tours (hourly on the hour 8am-2pm Tues.-Sun., adult $25, ages 5-11 $15, under age 5 free) begin with an excellent video and include a one-hour canoe trip in the freshwater lagoons and marshes of the Estrella delta—a great place to spot caimans, river otters, monkeys, and other wildlife. A special behind-the-scenes Insider Tour costs $150, by reservation.

Selva Bananito Lodge & Reserve

The private 950-hectare (2,350-acre) **Selva Bananito Lodge & Reserve** (Conselvatur, tel. 506/2253-8118 in San José or tel. 506/8375-4419, www.selvabananito.com), 15 kilometers (9.5 miles) inland from Bananito Norte—five kilometers (3 miles) inland of the coast road—protects primary rainforest on the slopes of the Talamancas. Activities such as birdwatching, nature hikes, horseback riding, and waterfall rappels are offered.

The reserve is tough to reach, but worth the effort if you're seeking an off-the-beaten-track eco-focused adventure. A high-clearance 4WD is essential for the muddy track and for fording the river just before you arrive. Signs guide the way. During heavy rains or after a prolonged rainy season, you should arrange in advance to meet reserve guides at Salón Delia in Bananito. To get there, turn right off the main highway about one kilometer (0.6 miles) south of the Río Vizcaya (18 km/11 miles south of Limón) for Bananito. Beyond Salón Delia, cross the railroad track, then a creek, and take the left fork at a Y-junction, from where the lodge is signed. There are gates to be opened (and closed behind you), and a final river to cross, then a final rugged section to reach the lodge.

Hitoy-Cerere Biological Reserve

Undeveloped and off the beaten track, the 9,050-hectare (22,400-acre) **Reserva Biológica Hitoy-Cerere** (tel. 506/2795-1446,

Judy Arroyo with rescued sloths at the Sloth Sanctuary

www.sinac.go.cr, 8am-5pm daily, $10), part of the Parque Internacional La Amistad, is one of the nation's least-visited parks. It is surrounded by three reservations for indigenous people—Talamanca, Telire, and Estrella.

Take your pick of arduous trails or moderately easy walks from the ranger station along the deep valley of the Río Hitoy-Cerere to waterfalls with natural swimming holes. The park is a starting point for trans-Talamanca journeys to the Pacific via a trail that leads south to the village of San José Cabecar and up the valley of the Río Coén and across the saddle between Cerro Betsú (2,500 meters/8,200 feet) and Cerro Arbolado (2,626 meters/8,615 feet) to Ujarrás, in the Valle de El General. Large sections have not been explored, and trails into the interior are overgrown, unmarked, and challenging (indigenous guides are available for local hikes).

Rainfall is prodigious: 700 centimeters (275 inches) in a year is not unknown, and March, September, and October are usually the driest months. The result: one of the best specimens of wet tropical forest in the country.

You can reserve basic lodging at the ranger station; researchers get priority. Camping is permitted, and there are basic showers and toilets. The park is signed from Pandora. You'll need a 4WD vehicle if you're driving.

Accommodations and Food

Selva Bananito Lodge (Conselvatur, tel. 506/2253-8118, www.selvabananito.com, standard $85 s, $100 d, superior $125 s, $140 d, including breakfast), at Selva Bananito Reserve, has 11 elegant ridgetop wooden cabins on stilts, with solar-heated water (there's no electricity), and a deck with hammocks for enjoying the splendid views. More spacious superior cabins have terra-cotta floors, foldaway doors opening to verandas with hammocks, plus baths with high-tech fittings and picture windows. Dining is family style. It offers various packages, with a two-night minimum. See the cautions about getting here in the section above.

What a delight it is to stay with Judy Arroyo and the friendly sloths at **Sloth Sanctuary B&B** (tel. 506/2750-0775, www.slothsanctuary.com, $80-115 s/d, including breakfast). Choose from six rooms, all with queen or king beds.

Getting There

Cahuita-bound **Transportes Mepe** (tel. 506/2257-8129) buses depart the Gran Caribe terminal in San José at 6am, 10am, 2pm, and 4pm daily, all stopping in Estrella en route.

Local buses depart Puerto Limón (tel. 506/2758-1572, Ave. 4, Calles 3/4) for Pandora and the Dole banana plantation (10 kilometers/6 miles from the Hitoy-Cerere park entrance) and Cahuita every two hours 5am-6pm daily. Jeep-taxis from Finca 6 in the Valle la Estrella cost about $15 one-way. Jeep-taxis from Cahuita cost about $50 each way; you will need to arrange your return trip in advance if you stay overnight in the park.

Transportes Ferroviarios Costarricenses (TRANSFECO, tel. 506/2258-1765, transfeco@hotmail.com) operates sightseeing tours by train between Moín and the Valle la Estrella, with bus transfer from San José.

Cahuita and Vicinity

★ CAHUITA

This offbeat village (pop. 3,000), 45 kilometers (28 miles) south of Puerto Limón and one kilometer (0.6 miles) east of Highway 36, is an in-vogue destination for backpackers and escapist vacationers who like things simple. Cahuita is no more than two parallel dirt streets crossed by four rutted streets overgrown with grass, with ramshackle houses spread apart. The village is totally laid-back and not for those seeking luxuries. What you get is golden- and black-sand beaches backed by coconut palms, an offshore coral reef (now severely depleted), and an immersion in Creole culture, including Rastafarians, with their dreadlocks and a lifestyle that revolves around reggae, Rasta, and—discreetly—reefer. Bob Marley is God in Cahuita.

Despite its fascinating charm, Cahuita struggles to overcome a lingering negative perception fed by high crime, drug use, and the surly attitude displayed by many local Afro-Caribbean males. The police force has been beefed up (there's even a police checkpoint on the main road north of Cahuita;

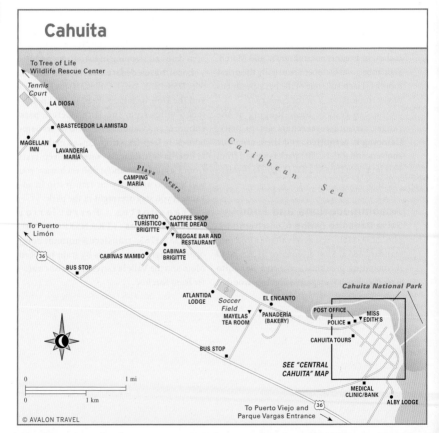

Cahuita

To Tree of Life
Wildlife Rescue Center

Tennis
Court

LA DIOSA

ABASTECEDOR LA AMISTAD

MAGELLAN
INN

LAVANDERÍA
MARÍA

CAMPING
MARÍA

Playa Negra

Caribbean Sea

CENTRO
TURÍSTICO
BRIGITTE

CAOFFEE SHOP
NATTIE DREAD

To Puerto
Limón

REGGAE BAR AND
RESTAURANT

CABINAS MAMBO

CABINAS
BRIGITTE

36

BUS STOP

ATLANTIDA
LODGE

Soccer
Field

EL ENCANTO

Cahuita National Park

POST OFFICE

MISS
EDITH'S

MAYELAS
TEA ROOM

PANADERÍA
(BAKERY)

POLICE

CAHUITA TOURS

BUS STOP

SEE "CENTRAL
CAHUITA" MAP

MEDICAL
CLINIC/BANK

ALBY LODGE

0   1 mi

0   1 km

To Puerto Viejo and   36
Parque Vargas Entrance

© AVALON TRAVEL

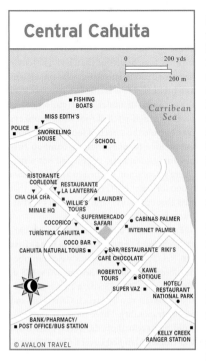

Central Cahuita

0   200 yds
0   200 m

FISHING BOATS

Carribean Sea

MISS EDITH'S

POLICE
SNORKELING HOUSE

SCHOOL

RISTORANTE CORLEONE   RESTAURANTE
CHA CHA CHA   LA LANTERNA
                WILLIE'S   LAUNDRY
MINAE HQ   TOURS
         SUPERMERCADO
COCORICO   SAFARI   CABINAS PALMER
TURÍSTICA CAHUITA   INTERNET PALMER
      COCO BAR
CAHUITA NATURAL TOURS   BAR/RESTAURANTE RIKI'S
              CAFÉ CHOCOLATE
          ROBERTO   KAWE
          TOURS   BOTIQUE
          SUPER VAZ   HOTEL/
                 RESTAURANT
                 NATIONAL PARK

BANK/PHARMACY/
POST OFFICE/BUS STATION

KELLY CREEK
RANGER STATION

© AVALON TRAVEL

& Botanical Gardens (tel. 506/2755-0014, www.treeoflifecostarica.com, 9am-3pm Tues.-Sun. Nov.-Apr. 20, $12; guided tour only 11am Tues.-Sun. July-Aug., $15), on Playa Negra, is a great place for a précis on some of the critters to look for in the wild. The monkeys, kinkajous, and peccaries were all rescued from injury or were illegal pets confiscated from their owners; many are nursed back to health for release to the wild. The center, which also has iguana- and turtle-breeding programs, is set in five hectares (12 acres) of lush gardens, arranged in well-signed groups such as bromeliads, heliconias, and palms.

Entertainment and Events

Look out for live performances by Walter Ferguson, a local and national legend for his calypso; in July 2010 Cahuita initiated the annual **Festival de la Cultura y el Ambiente Walter Ferguson** (http://acamcostarica.com/walterferguson).

There's plenty of night action in Cahuita, although it's an almost exclusively male affair (as far as locals go). The class act is **Café Cocorico** (50 meters/165 feet north of the plaza, tel. 506/2755-0324, 7am-2pm and 5pm-midnight Wed.-Mon.), which shows free movies nightly while you sip killer cocktails.

Coco's Bar (tel. 506/2755-0437, noon-11pm daily) is the livelier spot and is now preferred by the Latin set for salsa, soca, and reggae. Coco's goes head-to-head with **Ricky's Bar** (tel. 506/2755-0305), across the street; it hosts live calypso on Wednesday and Saturday.

Sports and Recreation

Cahuita Tours (tel. 506/2755-0101, www.cahuitatours.com) and **Willie's Tours** (tel. 506/2755-1024, www.williestourscostarica.com), in the village center, offer a panoply of tours and activities, including snorkeling trips, bird-watching, fishing, dolphin-watching, horseback rides, and trips farther afield. Willie's Tours (by far the best agency) even has a full-day tour to Bocas del Toro in Panamá ($95).

every vehicle is searched), but enforcement seems lax. Locals run a committee to police the community, keep the beaches clean, and generally foster improvements.

It now has a shopping mall and a bank, and the main street is paved, but otherwise Cahuita seems immune to the boom in nearby Puerto Viejo and to the upscale boutique revolution sweeping the rest of the country.

North of Cahuita village is a black-sand beach, **Playa Negra,** which runs for several miles. **Playa Blanca** (White Beach) is a two-kilometer (1.2-mile) scimitar of golden sand that stretches south from the village along the shore of the national park. Beware of riptides. A second pale-sand beach lies farther along, beyond the rocky headland of Punta Cahuita; it is protected by an offshore coral reef and provides safer swimming in calmer waters. Theft is a problem on the beach; do not leave your possessions unattended.

The **Tree of Life Wildlife Rescue Center**

Centro Turístico Brigitte (tel. 506/2755-0053, www.brigittecahuita.com) offers guided horseback rides. **Snorkeling House** (tel. 506/8361-1924) specializes in snorkeling tours ($25 pp), offered at 9am and 1pm daily.

Accommodations

Cahuita offers dozens of options; most are in the budget category. Hustlers hang around the bus stop with the intent of guiding you to a hotel where they receive a commission; they're not above lying, such as telling you that your preferred hotel has closed or is full. Many hoteliers are as laid-back as their clientele.

Budget travelers can't do better than **Centro Turístico Brigitte** (tel. 506/2755-0053, www.brigittecahuita.com, rooms $15 s, cabin $35 s, $40 d, bungalow with kitchen $50), 50 meters (165 feet) inland of Playa Negra. Run by Swiss-born Brigitte, this is rustic Cahuita at its best. It only has a one-person studio with a shared bath, plus two simple cabins (one with a kitchen), but health-conscious meals are served in a charming little restaurant with Wi-Fi, and Brigitte offers horseback tours. Brigitte also rents houses and is perhaps the best source of reliable information in the area.

A romantic gem where I often choose to lay my head, the private and peaceful Austrian-run ★ **Alby Lodge** (tel./fax 506/2755-0031, www.albylodge.com, $60 s/d) has four beautiful thatched Thai-style hardwood cabins sitting on stilts amid lawns and hibiscus. I love lazing in a hammock on the veranda, or under a mosquito net beneath the high-pitched roof while monkeys play outside the screened louvered window. Other nice touches include bamboo furnishings, safes, fans, Wi-Fi, and hot water. There's a common kitchen in an airy *rancho* (good for watching the howler monkeys that pass through daily), and a natural pond attracts frogs. Rates include tax.

For romantic ambience and a great bargain, choose **El Encanto Bed & Breakfast Inn** (tel. 506/2755-0113, www.elencantobedandbreakfast.com, low season $70 s, $75 d, high season $75 s, $85 d), a two-story bed-and-breakfast run by French Canadians and oozing tranquility. Three rooms in the main building have orthopedic queen mattresses and Guatemalan bed covers, Oriental carvings, ceiling fans, and pleasant baths. They also have cabins in a well-maintained garden, a fully furnished apartment, and a lovely house with balcony, plus a small but exquisite patio restaurant and secure parking. It has a

beach at Cahuita National Park

yoga center and an amoeba-shaped pool. Rates include breakfast (and taxes in low season).

A long-standing favorite, the equally romantic **Magellan Inn** (tel./fax 506/2755-0035, www.magellaninn.com, low season $65-105 s/d, high season $85-130 s/d, including continental breakfast) is set in lush landscaped grounds. Six spacious, sparsely furnished rooms feature plentiful hardwoods, tile floors, and French doors that open onto private patios. The garden, with a sunken swimming pool, is cut into a coral reef. All rooms have Wi-Fi. The open-air lounge, with Oriental rugs and sofas, is a lovely place to relax. Terry, the owner, will prepare gourmet table d'hôte meals.

Claiming its own little beach and ideal for yoga practitioners, **La Diosa** (tel. 506/2755-0055, www.hotelladiosa.com, low season $55-85 s, $65-95 d, high season $60-95 s, $70-105 d) is one of the most inviting lodgings in Cahuita. Adorned with river stones, the four lovely rooms and six inviting bungalows are painted in lively canary yellow and tropical blues, with divinely comfortable double beds (with batik spreads) on poured-concrete platforms, plus Wi-Fi and spacious modern baths. Two cabins have whirlpool tubs on raised platforms. It has a small pool and a lovely yoga space adorned with Asian art.

Food

There's excellent eating in Cahuita, but the scene is ever-changing. Some places are only open in season (Dec.-May), and most accept cash only.

My preferred breakfast spot in the village is **Café Chocolatte 100 Percent Natural** (tel. 506/2755-0010, 6:30am-3pm Tues.-Sun.), a delightful, airy café that serves granola with yogurt, *gallo pinto,* waffles, omelets, burritos, sandwiches, and veggie plates. Mellow music and a great ambience combine to make this the breakfast spot of choice.

The renowned ★ **Miss Edith's** (tel. 506/2755-0248 or 506/8782-4192, 11:30am-10pm Mon.-Sat., noon-10pm Sun., $6-10), 50 meters (165 feet) east of the police station, is a homey place that offers aromatic Caribbean specialties such as "rundown" (a spiced stew of fish, meat, and vegetables simmered in coconut milk) and lobster with curry and coconut milk ($15). Miss Edith also offers a vegetarian menu. Don't expect rapid service—or even a smile—but you'll love the genuine Caribbean experience, and the coconut curries are to die for.

Gourmands will find the best dining in town is the open-air **Cha Cha Cha** (tel. 506/2755-0476, noon-10pm daily, closed in low season, $5-15), an unpretentious place to savor

advertisements for hotels and activities in Playa Negra

Caribbean Spicy

One of the pleasures of the Caribbean coast is the uniquely spicy local cuisine, which owes much to the populace's Jamaican heritage. The seductive flavors are lent predominantly by coconut, ginger, chilies, and black pepper. Breadfruit, used throughout the Caribbean isles but relatively unknown in Costa Rica, is a staple, as are various tropical roots.

You'll even find ackee and salt fish (one of my favorite breakfasts), made of ackee fruit and resembling scrambled eggs in texture and color. It is often served with johnnycakes, fried sponge dumplings that make great fillers to accompany fish *en escabeche* (pickled), or "rundown," mackerel cooked in coconut milk. You must try highly spiced jerk chicken, fish, or pork, smoked at open-air grills and lent added flavor by tongue-searing pepper marinade.

Desserts include ginger cakes, puddin', *pan bon* (a kind of bread laced with caramelized sugar), banana brownies, and ice cream flavored with fresh fruits.

superb "cuisine of the world" with appetizers such as tapenade ($6) and grilled calamari salad ($7.50), entrées such as curried chicken ($10), and desserts such as banana flambé, all artfully presently on chic oversize plates. The rustic decor is romantic by candlelight, while world music adds just the right note.

Also for romantic atmosphere, head to **Cocorico** (tel. 506/2755-0409, 8am-2pm and 5pm-10pm Thurs.-Tues.) for its colorful decor and Arabian-style ceiling drapes. An Italian chef conjures gnocchi, pizzas, and crepes with homemade ice cream ($5). All dishes are less than $10.

Information and Services

Cahuita Tours (tel. 506/2755-0000, www.cahuitatours.com) acts as an informal visitor information office, as does **Centro Turístico Brigitte** (tel. 506/2755-0053), which also has laundry ($8 per basket). **MINAE** (tel. 506/2755-0060, 8am-4pm Mon.-Fri.) has a national parks office in the village.

There's a government **medical center** at the entrance to town, on the main road from Highway 36, plus a **private clinic** (tel. 506/2755-0345, cell 506/8352-6981) at Suizo Loco Lodge.

The **post office** (tel. 506/2755-0096, 8am-noon and 1:30pm-5:30pm Mon.-Fri.) is three blocks north of the plaza. The **police station** (Guardia Rural, tel. 506/2755-0217 or 911) is

next door. The **bank** (tel. 506/2284-6600) is open 8am-4pm Monday-Friday.

Centro Turístico Brigitte has Internet service (7am-7pm daily) for $1 per 30 minutes, as does **Willie's Tours** (tel. 506/8917-6982, www.willies-costarica-tours.com, 8am-noon and 2pm-8pm Mon.-Sat., 4pm-8pm Sun.), in the village center. **Internet Palmer** (tel. 506/2755-0435, 8am-5pm Mon.-Fri.) has Skype and Wi-Fi.

Getting There

Transportes Mepe (tel. 506/2257-8129) buses depart the Gran Caribe terminal in San José for Cahuita ($8) at 6am, 10am, 2pm, and 4pm daily. They continue to Puerto Viejo and Sixaola. Local buses depart Puerto Limón (tel. 506/2758-1572, 1 hour, $1.25) from Avenida 4, Calles 3/4, hourly 5am-6pm daily.

Buses depart Cahuita from 50 meters (165 feet) southwest of Coco Bar, for San José at 7:30am, 9:30am, 11:30am, and 4:30pm daily, and for Limón hourly 6:30am-8pm daily. The ticket office is open 7am-5pm daily.

Getting Around

For a taxi, call tel. 506/2755-0435, or contact **Cabinas Palmas** (tel. 506/2755-0046) or **Cahuita Tours** (tel. 506/2755-0000, www.cahuitatours.com).

Centro Turístico Brigitte rents bicycles ($6 daily).

CAHUITA NATIONAL PARK

Cahuita's 14 kilometers (9 miles) of beaches are shaded by palm trees, lush forests, marshlands, and mangroves. Together they make up 1,067-hectare (2,637-acre) **Parque Nacional Cahuita** (www.sinac.go.cr), created in 1970 to protect the 240 hectares (593 acres) of offshore coral reef that distinguish this park from its siblings. Animal life abounds in the diverse habitats—an ideal place to catch a glimpse of tamanduas, pacas, coatis, raccoons, sloths, agoutis, armadillos, iguanas, and troops of howler and capuchin monkeys, and to focus your binoculars on ibis, rufous kingfishers, toucans, parrots, and, in season (Dec.-Feb.), macaws. Cahuita's freshwater rivers and estuaries are also good places to spot caimans.

Gangs of capuchin monkeys may beg for tidbits, often aggressively. Many folks have been bitten. Feeding wild monkeys with human foodstuffs alters their habits and can adversely affect their health. Don't feed the monkeys!

The offshore reef lies between Puerto Vargas and Punta Cahuita. Smooth water here provides good swimming; it's possible to wade out to the edge of the coral with the water only at knee level. At the southern end of the park, beyond the reef, huge waves lunge onto the beach—a nesting site for three species of turtles—where tide pools form at low tide. Check with rangers about currents and where you can walk or snorkel safely. Snorkelers can try their luck near Punta Cahuita or Punta Vargas (you must enter the water from the beach on the Punta Vargas side and swim out to the reef). Snorkeling is only permitted with a guide or organized snorkeling tour.

Besides what remains of the coral, there are scant remains of two old shipwrecks about seven meters (23 feet) below the surface, both with visible ballast and cannons. One wreck has two cannons, and the second, a more exposed site, has 13. The average depth is six meters (20 feet). The best time for diving and snorkeling is during the dry season, February-April; water clarity during the rest of year is not good because of silt brought by the rivers.

Information and Services

A footbridge leads into the park from the **Kelly Creek Ranger Station** (tel. 506/2755-0461, 6am-5pm daily, donation), officially known as Puesto Playa Blanca, at the southern end of Cahuita village. A shady seven-kilometer (4.5-mile) nature trail leads from here to the **Puerto Vargas Ranger Station**

visitors spotting wildlife in Cahuita National Park

The Destruction of Cahuita's Coral Reefs

Corals are soft-bodied animals that secrete calcium carbonate to form an external skeleton that is built on and multiplied over thousands of generations to form fabulous and massive reef structures. The secret to coral growth is the symbiotic relationship with single-celled algae—zooxanthellae—that grow inside the cells of coral polyps and photosynthetically produce oxygen and nutrients, which are released as a kind of rent directly into the coral tissues. Coral flourishes close to the surface in clear, well-circulated tropical seawater warmed to a temperature between 21°C and 27°C (70-81°F).

Twenty years ago, Cahuita had a superb fringing reef—an aquatic version of the Hanging Gardens of Babylon. Today, much of it is dead following uplift during the 1991 earthquake and silt washing down from mainland rivers. Coral growth is hampered by freshwater runoff and by turbidity from land-generated sediments, which clog their pores so that zooxanthellae can no longer breathe. Along almost the entire Talamanca coast and the interior, trees are being logged, exposing the topsoil to the gnawing effects of tropical rains. The rivers bring agricultural runoff as well—poisonous pesticides used in the banana plantations and fertilizers ideal for the proliferation of seabed grasses and algae that starve coral of vital oxygen. It is only a matter of time before the reef is completely gone. Prospects for the reef at Gandoca-Manzanillo are equally grim.

Asociación Widecast (tel. 506/2236-0947, www.widecast.org) takes volunteers for its marine conservation project at Cahuita.

(tel. 506/2755-0302, 8am-4pm Mon.-Fri., 7am-5pm Sun., $10), the main park entrance, three kilometers (2 miles) south of Cahuita midway along the park; the trail takes about two hours with time to stop for a swim.

The Puerto Vargas entrance is 400 meters (0.25 miles) west of Highway 36, about three kilometers (2 miles) south of Cahuita (the Sixaola-bound bus will drop you off near the entrance). You can drive to Puerto Vargas from here; the entrance gate is locked after hours. Camping is not permitted.

Puerto Viejo and Vicinity

About 13 kilometers (8 miles) south of Cahuita, the road forks just after Hone Creek (also spelled Home Creek). The main road turns east toward **Bribrí;** a spur leads three kilometers (2 miles) to **Playa Negra,** a black-sand beach that curls east to Puerto Viejo, enclosing a small bay with a capsized barge in its center. The tiny headland of Punta Pirikiki at its eastern end separates Puerto Viejo from the sweep of beaches—**Playa Pirikiki, Playa Chiquita,** and others—that run all the way to **Manzanillo** and Panamá. You can walk along the beach from Cahuita at low tide.

★ PUERTO VIEJO

Puerto Viejo is one of the most happening spots in Costa Rica. The discos are hopping, and on peak weekends, you can't find a room to save your soul. Deluxe hotels have opened, as have malls—a mega change from the funky little hamlet I recall from two decades ago. Nonetheless, the surfer, backpacker, and counterculture crowds are firmly rooted here and dominate the scene, having settled and established bistros and restaurants alongside the locals. Drugs traded up the coast from Colombia find their way here, and the whiff of ganja (marijuana) drifts on the air. Violent

Puerto Viejo and Vicinity

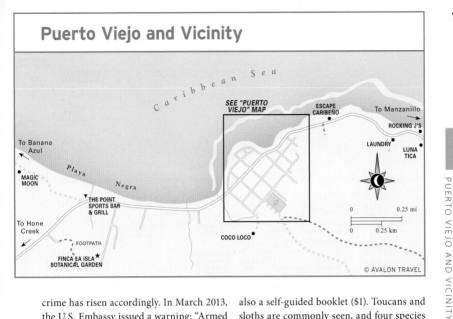

SEE "PUERTO VIEJO" MAP

Caribbean Sea

To Banana Azul

MAGIC MOON

Playa Negra

THE POINT SPORTS BAR & GRILL

To Hone Creek

FOOTPATH

FINCA LA ISLA BOTANICAL GARDEN

COCO LOCO

ESCAPE CARIBEÑO

To Manzanillo

ROCKING J'S

LAUNDRY

LUNA TICA

0   0.25 mi

0   0.25 km

© AVALON TRAVEL

crime has risen accordingly. In March 2013, the U.S. Embassy issued a warning: "Armed robbery continues to be the primary criminal threat facing tourists in the southern Caribbean coast of Costa Rica." The warning still holds.

Cacao Trails Museum & Wildlife Trail (tel. 506/2756-8186, www.cacaotrails.com, $25), at Hone Creek, is a cacao farm with a tiny chocolate museum. There are also crocodiles, a snake exhibit, a museum on indigenous culture, and a botanical garden, plus canoeing ($25) on canals through the cacao plantation. Stay a while and enjoy a meal at the thatched restaurant.

Finca la Isla Botanical Garden

The five-hectare (12-acre) **Finca la Isla Botanical Garden** (tel. 506/2750-0046, 10am-4pm Fri.-Mon., self-guided tour $6, guided tour for 3 or more people $8-10 pp), one kilometer (0.6 miles) west of town, is a treat for anyone interested in nature. Here, Lindy and Peter Kring grow spices, exotic fruits, and ornamental plants for sale, and even makes their own chocolate from cacao. You can sample the fruits and learn about chocolate production on a guided tour. There's

also a self-guided booklet ($1). Toucans and sloths are commonly seen, and four species of poison dart frogs make their homes in the bromeliads grown for sale. You're virtually guaranteed to see them hopping around underfoot even as you step from your car. The finca is 400 meters (0.25 miles) from the road and 200 meters (660 feet) west of El Pizote Lodge, and it's signed. Lunches are offered by arrangement.

Kèköldi Indigenous Reserve

The 3,547-hectare (8,765-acre) **Reserva Indígena Kèköldi,** in the hills immediately west of Puerto Viejo, extends south to the borders of the Gandoca-Manzanillo refuge. It is home to some 200 Bribrí and Cabécar people. Reforestation and other conservation projects are ongoing. Gloria Mayorga Balma, coauthor of *Taking Care of Sibo's Gift*, educates visitors on indigenous history and ways.

You can visit the **Iguana Farm** ($1.50) where green iguanas are raised; the turnoff is 400 meters (0.25 miles) south of Hone Creek, beside Abastacedor El Cruce, then 200 meters (660 feet) along the dirt road.

The **Talamanca Association for Ecotourism and Conservation** (ATEC,

Puerto Viejo

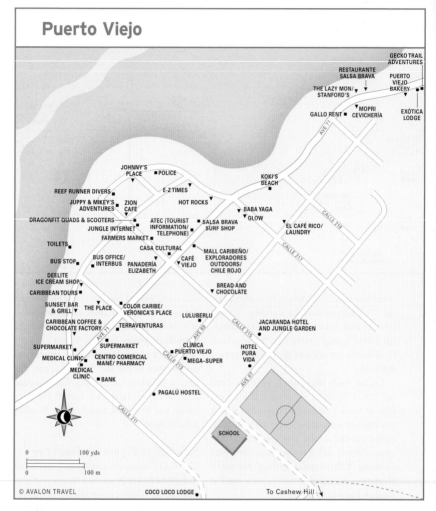

GECKO TRAIL
ADVENTURES

RESTAURANTE
SALSA BRAVA

PUERTO
VIEJO
BAKERY

THE LAZY MON/
STANFORD'S

GALLO RENT

MOPRI
CEVICHERÍA

EXÓTICA
LODGE

AVE 71

JOHNNY'S
PLACE

POLICE

KOKI'S
BEACH

REEF RUNNER DIVERS

E-Z TIMES

JUPPY & MIKEY'S
ADVENTURES

ZION
CAFÉ

HOT ROCKS

BABA YAGA
GLOW

CALLE 219

DRAGONFIT QUADS & SCOOTERS

JUNGLE INTERNET

ATEC (TOURIST
INFORMATION/
TELEPHONE)

SALSA BRAVA
SURF SHOP

EL CAFÉ RICO/
LAUNDRY

FARMERS MARKET

CALLE 217

TOILETS

CASA CULTURAL

MALL CARIBEÑO/
EXPLORADORES
OUTDOORS/
CHILE ROJO

BUS STOP

BUS OFFICE/
INTERBUS

PANADERÍA
ELIZABETH

CAFÉ
VIEJO

DEELITE
ICE CREAM SHOP

CARIBBEAN TOURS

BREAD AND
CHOCOLATE

SUNSET BAR
& GRILL

THE PLACE

COLOR CARIBE/
VERONICA'S PLACE

LULUBERLU

CALLE 215

JACARANDA HOTEL
AND JUNGLE GARDEN

CARIBBEAN COFFEE &
CHOCOLATE FACTORY

TERRAVENTURAS

AVE 69

SUPERMARKET

SUPERMARKET

CLÍNICA
PUERTO VIEJO

HOTEL
PURA
VIDA

MEDICAL CLINIC

CENTRO COMERCIAL
MANÉ/ PHARMACY

CALLE 213

MEGA-SUPER

AVE 67

MEDICAL
CLINIC

BANK

PAGALÚ HOSTEL

AVE 71

CALLE 211

SCHOOL

0   100 yds

0   100 m

© AVALON TRAVEL

COCO LOCO LODGE

To Cashew Hill

tel. 506/2750-0398, www.ateccr.org, 8am-9pm Mon.-Sat., 10am-6pm Sun.) arranges tours (from half-day $20, full-day $35). The **Costa Rican Association of Community-Based Rural Tourism** (tel. 506/2290-7514, www.actuarcostarica.com) also offers tours.

You can even spend a day at **Aiko-Logi-Tours** (tel. 506/2750-2084, www.aiko-logi-tours.com, $60 including transfers), a 135-hectare (334-acre) sustainable farm and rainforest four kilometers (2.5 miles) west of Hone Creek. It's a perfect locale for hiking,

swimming in crisp mountain pools, and engaging with nature. Volunteers are welcome to work on various eco-oriented projects. You can sleep here in tents on overnight tours ($99 pp, including transfers).

The **Kèköldi Scientific Center** (tel. 506/8362-3886, www.kekoldicr.com/scientific-center) works to safeguard the local environment through research projects. It welcomes volunteers and offers dorm accommodations ($20, including meals) with advance arrangement.

bromeliads at Finca La Isla Botanical Garden

Entertainment and Events

Puerto Viejo is known for its lively bars and discos. Folks travel from as far afield as Limón to bop.

The happening bar downtown is the open-air, hard-to-avoid **Tex-Mex** (6pm-2am daily), which epitomizes Puerto Viejo's laid-back philosophy and bills itself proudly as "the most dangerous bar in town." Its cocktail list runs from mojitos to *orgasmos;* its **Jungle Open-Air Cinema** shows movies at 6pm, 8pm, and 10pm nightly; and the bar has flat-screen TVs showing sports.

The coolest waterfront scene is at **Lazy Mon** (tel. 506/2750-0608, www.thelazymon. com, 1pm-late daily), at Stanfords. This music bar packs 'em in for and live reggae, calypso, and salsa music; DJs; and Xbox, darts, and pool.

Or, for a groovy disco-lounge scene, choose **Baba Yaga** (tel. 506/8388-4359), the reggae hot spot almost any night of the week.

Each fall, Puerto Viejo hosts the **ArteViva Festival** (tel. 506/8729-3888, www.

arteviva-puertoviejo.com), a three-day festival dedicated to Caribbean art and culture, with fireworks, live music, and art exhibits.

Sports and Recreation

The local community organization **ATEC** (tel. 506/2750-0398, www.ateccr.org, 8am-9pm Mon.-Sat., 10am-6pm Sun.) offers hiking and nature excursions, including into the Kèköldi reserve.

Terraventuras (tel. 506/2750-0750, www. terraventuras.com), on the main drag, and **Exploradores Outdoors** (tel. 506/2750-2020, www.exploradoresoutdoors.com), in Centro Comercial Puerto Viejo, offer a wide menu activities and excursions, from rainforest hikes to canopy zip lines and ocean kayaking.

For horseback-riding adventures, call **Caribe Horse Riding Club** (tel. 506/8705-4250, www.caribehorse.com) at Playa Negra.

Reef Runner Divers (tel. 506/2750-0480, www.reefrunnerdivers.com) offers guided dive tours (1 tank $50, 2 tanks $80, night dive $60), PADI certification ($325), and dolphin ($75) and snorkeling ($35) tours.

SURFING

Puerto Viejo is legendary among the surfing crowd. November through April, especially, the village is crowded with surfers, who come for a killer six-meter (20-foot) storm-generated wave called La Salsa Brava. Beach Break, at Playa Cocles, about three kilometers (2 miles) south of Puerto Viejo, is good for novices and intermediates. Snorkelers should use extreme caution in these waters, and never snorkel during rough weather.

Almost a dozen surf shops offer board rental and repair, including **Juppy & Mikey Adventures** (tel. 506/2750-0621), which also has kayak tours to Gandoca and rents kayaks and snorkeling gear. **Caribbean Surfing** (tel. 506/8357-7703) also offers lessons, and **Salsa Brava Surf Shop** (tel. 506/2750-0689) rents kayaks and snorkeling gear as well. For private lessons, call **Hershel Gordon** (tel. 506/8357-7703, $50 for 2 hours, including transportation and surfboard). He also offers a kayak tour on the Río Punta Uva.

Shopping

Color Caribe (tel. 506/2750-0075, 9am-8pm daily), on the main drag, stocks a great selection of clothing, jewelry, and souvenirs, including hand-painted and silk-screened clothing, plus hammocks and colorful wind chimes. **LuluBerlu** (tel. 506/2750-0394, 9am-9pm daily), one block east of the main drag, sells an original range of ceramics, jewelry, and miscellany.

Accommodations

Demand is high; make your reservation in advance or secure a room as soon as you arrive. Beware of touts who wait as the bus arrives and try to entice you to specific lodgings—they're known to tell lies to dissuade you from any specific place you may already have in mind. The following are the best of dozens of options, including at least two dozen beachfront hotels speckling the shore south of town.

Backpackers have great options. The best known, and long favored by backpacking surfers, is the well-run yet totally laid-back beachfront **Rocking J's** (tel. 506/2750-0665, www. rockingjs.com, hammocks $7, tents $8 s, $11 d, dorm $11 pp, private rooms from $26). Pitch your tent at a sheltered site beneath eaves, sleep outside in a hammock, or take a dorm room or even a private room in varying configurations with lofty bunks and desks below; rooms share two solar-heated showers and five cold-water showers. There's also a tree house, suites, and even a three-story house. Guests can use a communal kitchen, and there's laundry, a grill restaurant, free Wi-Fi, parking, and a bar with live music and wild theme parties. Maybe that's why it's called Rocking J's? Kayaks and bicycles can be rented.

A total contrast, the German-run ★ **Pagalú Hostel** (tel. 506/2750-1930, www. pagalu.com, dorm $12 pp, shared bath $23 s, $26 d, private bath $27 s, $30 d) elevates the concept of hostel accommodations to a new level with its beautiful contemporary design and Teutonic efficiency. It makes great use of space, with a huge open-air lounge with a kitchen. All rooms have ceiling fans, and very clean and tasteful baths with glass-brick walls and plenty of hot water, plus thoughtful extras such as bedside halogen reading lights and plenty of shelving. One room is wheelchair-accessible, and there's secure parking.

For charm and simplicity, I love **Jacaranda Hotel & Jungle Garden** (tel./

two-toed sloth hanging upside down in the rain

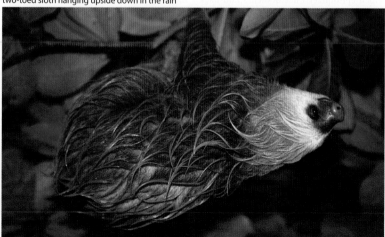

fax 506/2750-0069, www.cabinasjacaranda. net, low season $24-30 s, $32-40 d, high season $28-35 s, $35-55 d), where a wonderful hostess, Vera from Trinidad, offers 14 cabins with Wi-Fi set in an exquisite garden. Furnishings are basic but delightful, with subdued tropical walls and colorful mosaic floors throughout. Japanese paper lanterns, mats, Guatemalan bedspreads, hammocks, and mosquito nets are nice touches. Garden massages are offered, and there's a communal kitchen.

I always enjoy resting my head at **Coco Loco** (tel./fax 506/2750-0281, www.cocolocolodge.com, low season $45-63 s/d, high season $75-87 s/d), where eight simply furnished log-and-thatch Polynesian-style *cabinas* are raised on stilts amid lawns. They have mosquito nets over the beds, and hammocks on the porches. Simple breakfasts are served on a raised deck. Two two-room bungalows with kitchens are also available. The Austrian owners offer tours.

Kicking up the rainforest-lodge theme a notch, what's not to like about ★ **Banana Azul** (tel. 506/2750-2035, www.bananaazul. com, $89-144 d), a delightful 14-room guesthouse in an ocean-side palm-shaded garden at the north end of Playa Negra? Although simply furnished, all rooms have Wi-Fi, mosquito nets, and heaps of cozy warmth; suites verge on luxurious. An airy terrace serves as the restaurant. Cool off in the pool, steep in the jetted tub, or enjoy a massage on the beach. Owners Colin and Roberto do things right here. It's a great place to chill.

Food

Puerto Viejo has a cosmopolitan range of eateries, even gourmet cuisine. For breakfast and a cup of joe, I head to ★ **Bread and Chocolate** (tel. 506/2750-0723, 6:30am-6:30pm Tues.-Sat., 6:30am-2:30pm Sun.) for killer cinnamon-oatmeal pancakes ($4), crispy sautéed potatoes with jerk barbecue sauce, grilled sandwiches, and more. Competing in style and substance, **Café Rico** (tel. 506/2750-0510, 6am-2pm Fri.-Wed.) is a laid-back place serving food on a palm-fringed veranda; Roger, the English owner, serves huevos rancheros ($4), omelets ($4), granola with yogurt and fruit ($3.50), pancakes, and sandwiches. I recommend the Annarosa special: fried potatoes with cheddar cheese, fried eggs, and bacon ($4). Café Rico has a book exchange and bicycle rentals. Alternatively, the **Caribbean Coffee & Chocolate Factory** (tel. 506/2750-0850, 7am-9pm Mon.-Fri., 7am-9pm Sat.-Sun.) is a

surfers in the rain in Puerto Viejo

cool spot to enjoy home-baked muffins, macadamia cookies, multigrain breads, and veggie dishes, plus organic coffee and chocolate drinks. It has free Wi-Fi.

For a light lunch, **Sel et Sucre Crêperie & Fruit Bar** (tel. 506/2750-0636, noon-9:30pm Tues.-Sun.) serves delicious crepes. The clean, air-conditioned **Fruit & Veggie Land** (no tel., 8am-7pm Mon.-Sat., 8:30am-7pm Sun.) sells fresh salads plus fruit juices and *batidos* (milk shakes).

Justifiably popular by night, ★ **Chile Rojo** (tel. 506/2750-0025, www.bestchilerojo.com, 9am-10pm daily), upstairs in the Centro Comercial Puerto Viejo, packs in diners who come to savor Asian-inspired dishes. I recommend the veggie samosa with tamarind chutney ($3.50), Thai fish-and-coconut soup ($6), and the delicious green curry with coconut milk and veggies ($9). There is an all-you-can-eat sushi and Asian buffet ($12) on Monday nights.

To feel the Caribbean vibe, head to **Jammin'** (tel. 506/8826-4332, 9am-9pm daily), a small Rasta-styled *soda* with tree-trunk stools. Try the jerk chicken ($5) and roast fish ($3.50). It has tremendous rootsy Jamaican atmosphere. My fave for real local fare, however, is the charming ★ **Veronica's Place** (tel. 506/2750-0263, www.veronicasplacepv.com, 10am-8pm Sun.-Thurs., 10am-4pm Fri., 7am-10pm Sat.), above Color Caribe in a colorful Caribbean structure on the main drag. Veronica serves pancakes, omelets, and *gallo pinto* for breakfast, plus a large vegetarian menu with raw-food dishes using organic ingredients she grows herself. Veronica also offers cooking classes (and rents charming and simple rooms for $20 pp). She accepts volunteers for the kitchen and at her organic farm in Cocles.

The world's your oyster at **Stashu's Con Fusión** (tel. 506/2750-0530, 5pm-10pm Thurs.-Tues.), with an eclectic globe-spanning menu and nightly specials. How about spicy chicken chocolate chili with garlic roasted mashed potatoes? Or macadamia-crusted fillet of snapper in white chocolate and lemon cream sauce? Stashu's specializes in organic dishes, and has a groovy open-air ambience.

For an airy and barefoot, unbuttoned oceanfront setting, head to the offbeat Spanish-run **Salsa Brava** (tel. 506/2750-0241, noon-11pm Wed.-Sun., $4-15), with rainbow-hued furniture and a grandstand view of surfers licking the salsa brava wave. The menu includes tuna ceviche salad, caesar salad with chicken teriyaki, and grilled garlic fish, plus sangria and ice cream. Portions are huge and the fare is surprisingly good.

Information and Services

ATEC (tel. 506/2750-0398, www.ateccr.org, 8am-9pm Mon.-Sat., 10am-6pm Sun.) is the informal node of local activity and acts as a visitor information bureau. It has public phones (tel. 506/2750-0188) outside.

Dr. Pablo Brenes (Calle 213, Aves. 69/71, tel. 506/8333-7317) has a clinic and speaks English. There's also a **medical clinic** (tel. 506/2750-0079, emergency tel. 506/8870-8029, 10am-7pm Mon.-Fri., for emergencies Sat.-Sun.) at the entrance to town, plus a **dental clinic** (tel. 506/2750-0303, emergency tel. 506/2750-0389) 50 meters (165 feet) inland of the beachfront bus stop.

The **police station** (tel. 506/2750-0230) is next to Johnny's Place. There's a **bank** with an ATM plus a pharmacy in Centro Comercial Mané. Mall Caribeño, 50 meters (165 feet) south, has a **pharmacy** (tel. 506/2750-2109), a **laundry** (8am-7pm daily), and the **post office** (tel. 506/2750-0404). **Café Rico** (tel. 506/2750-0510, 6am-2pm Fri.-Wed.) also has laundry service and offers free coffee while you wait.

Getting There and Away

Transportes Mepe (tel. 506/2257-8129, www.mepecr.com) buses ($10 from San José, $2.50 from Limón) depart the Gran Caribe terminal in San José for Puerto Viejo five times daily 6am-4pm and run via Cahuita. Return buses depart Puerto Viejo (tel. 506/2750-0023) for San José at 7:30am, 9am,

11am, and 4pm daily, and for Limón hourly 7:30am-7:30pm daily. The Puerto Limón-Puerto Viejo buses are usually crowded; get to the station early.

Interbus (tel. 506/4100-0888, www.interbusonline.com) operates minibus shuttles from San José. **Caribe Shuttle** (tel. 506/2750-0626, www.caribeshuttle.com) also has a shuttle from San José, and shuttles to Bocas del Toro and Panamá City from Puerto Viejo ($32) twice daily. **Navi Tours** (tel. 506/7037-2458, navi.tours.costa.rica@gmail.com) also has a shuttle from San José ($35).

Getting Around

You can rent beach-cruiser bicycles from **Tienda Marcos** (tel. 506/2750-0303, $6 per day, $48 per week). For ATV and motorcycle rentals, head to **Dragonfly** (tel. 506/2750-0728, www.dragonfly-pv.com, ATVs $55 for 5 hours, $75 per day; scooters $15 for 1 hour, $40 for 6 hours, $50 per day, $250 per week). **Poás Rent-a-Car** (tel. 506/2750-0400, www.poasrentacar.com) has an outlet in Puerto Viejo.

PLAYA COCLES TO PUNTA UVA

South of Puerto Viejo, the paved road sidles past one lovely beach after another. Beginning immediately south of town, coral-colored **Playa Cocles**—popular with surfers—runs southeast for four kilometers (2.5 miles) to the rocky point of Punta Cocles, beyond which **Playa Chiquita** merges into **Playa Uva**, together unfurling south four kilometers (2.5 miles) to Punta Uva, about eight kilometers (5 miles) southeast of Puerto Viejo. Here, caimans can be seen in the swampy estuary of the Río Uva. Beyond the rugged headland, a five-kilometer (3-mile) gray-sand beach curls gently southeast to **Manzanillo,** a fishing village at the end of the road. Be cautious swimming: The riptides can be ferocious. Lifeguards are occasionally on duty (for information, visit www.cocles.org).

When you want a break from sunning or surfing, check out **Chocorart** (tel. 506/2750-0075 or 506/8866-7493, chocoart@ice.co.cr, by reservation only, 8am-5pm daily, $15 pp), at Playa Chiquita, where a Swiss couple offers tours and demos at their cocoa farm and chocolate "factory." You'll learn all about cacao production, from the bean to the chocolate bar, on their hilly farm. Similarly, **The Chocolate Forest Experience** (tel. 506/8836-8930, www.caribeanschocolate.com, $26), at Playa Cocles, has tours that show how "real" artisanal chocolate is made from cacao grown organically (10am Mon., 10am and 2pm Tues. and Thurs., 2pm Fri.-Sat.). It has a Chocolate Tasting Lounge (9am-6pm Mon.-Sat.).

The road is sprinkled its entire length with lodges, cozy inns, restaurants, and small-scale tour services. The beach zone is effectively an extension of Puerto Viejo and can be visited easily by walking or by bicycle, scooter, or *colectivo.*

★ Jaguar Rescue Center

At the nonprofit **Centro de Rescate Jaguar** (tel. 506/6061-7967 or 506/2750-0710, www.jaguarrescue.com, tours 9:30 and 11:30am Mon.-Sat., by reservation only, adults $18, children under 10 free) at Playa Chiquita, you can see all manner of wildlife—including caimans, monkeys, and all the venomous snake species in Costa Rica. Owners Encar and Sandro are trained biologists who work to rehabilitate injured or orphaned animals for reintroduction to the wild. They do a magnificent job, including their professionally led guided tours of the facility.

Rehabilitated animals are released at nearby **La Ceiba Reserva Natural** (La Ceiba Private Biological Reserve), protecting a 45-hectare (111-acre) plot of primary rainforest in the mountains inland of Punta Uva. The Centro de Rescate Jaguar offers guided tours of La Ceiba at 7am Mon.-Sat. (adults $55, children $10, including breakfast) and, for night owls, at 7pm Mon.-Sat. (adults $60, children $10, including dinner).

Playa Cocles to Manzanillo

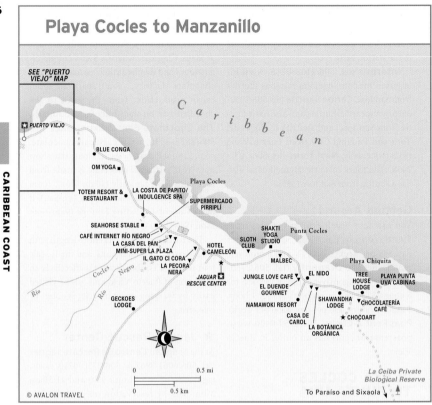

SEE "PUERTO VIEJO" MAP

PUERTO VIEJO

BLUE CONGA

OM YOGA

Caribbean

Playa Cocles

TOTEM RESORT & RESTAURANT

LA COSTA DE PAPITO/ INDULGENCE SPA

SUPERMERCADO PIRRIPLÍ

SEAHORSE STABLE

CAFÉ INTERNET RÍO NEGRO
LA CASA DEL PAN
MINI-SUPER LA PLAZA
IL GATO CI CORA
LA PECORA NERA

JAGUAR RESCUE CENTER

HOTEL CAMELEÓN

SHAKTI YOGA STUDIO

SLOTH CLUB

Punta Cocles

MALBEC

JUNGLE LOVE CAFÉ

EL NIDO

Playa Chiquita

TREE HOUSE LODGE

PLAYA PUNTA UVA CABINAS

EL DUENDE GOURMET

NAMAWOKI RESORT

SHAWANDHA LODGE

CHOCOLATERÍA CAFÉ

GECKOES LODGE

CASA DE CAROL

LA BOTÁNICA ORGÁNICA

CHOCOART

Rio Cocles Negro

Rio

0   0.5 mi
0   0.5 km

© AVALON TRAVEL

La Ceiba Private Biological Reserve

To Paraíso and Sixaola

Entertainment

Down at Playa Cocles, the thatched **Sloth Society Bar** (tel. 506/2750-0080) enlivens things at La Costa de Papito hotel with live music on Tuesday (Jim Vicks plays a "funka-jazza-bossa-bluesy-rock" mix) and Thursday (Junior's Calypso Trio). Nearer to town, **Totem Beach Bar** (tel. 506/2750-0758) has a Caribbean night with reggae vibes at 6pm every Wednesday.

Sports and Recreation

At **Seahorse Stables** (tel. 506/8859-6435, www.horsebackridingincostarica.com, by reservation, from $75), near the southern end of Playa Cocles, Edwin Salem, the gracious Argentinean owner, offers horseback rides and even arranges occasional polo matches on the beach. He also offers sailing lessons on

his 18-foot Hobie Cat as well as overnight turtle-watching tours ($150, including lodging), plus surfing trips.

Punta Uva Dive Center (tel. 506/2759-9191, www.puntauvadivecenter.com) has scuba trips to the reefs of Gandoca-Manzanillo. Herschel at **Quiet Kayak Tour** (tel. 506/8357-7703, $50 pp) will take you up the Uva River.

For an after-activity indulgence, treat yourself to a decadent chocolate body rub and cacao butter massage or similar sensual delight at the **Indulgence Spa** (tel. 506/2750-8413, www.purejunglespa.com), at La Costa de Papito at Playa Cocles.

Accommodations

A super chill place to bunk, the Dutch-run **Walaba Hostel** (Punta Uva, tel.

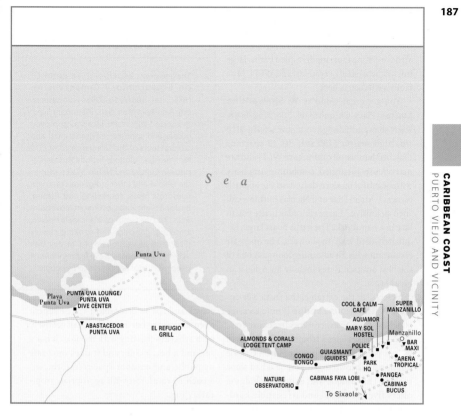

506/2750-0147, www.walabahostel.com, dorms from $13, private rooms from $25 s, $35 d), has a counterculture vibe and great open-air ambience. Choose from dorms or private cabins overlooking a lush garden. The alfresco lounge is a perfect place to laze in a hammock or watch a DVD on a large flat-screen.

At **La Costa de Papito** (Playa Cocles, tel. 506/2750-0080, www.lacostadepapito.com, low season from $54 s/d, high season from $59 s/d, including taxes), New York hotelier Eddie Ryan has conjured 10 simple yet tastefully decorated bungalows exuding a rainforest ambience within a lush palm-shaded garden. Ceiling fans are a nice touch, as are leopard- or zebra-pattern sheets, tiled baths, and shady porches with hammocks under thatch. Four smaller cabins have outside "rainforest" baths. There's a laundry and massages, plus bicycle,

surfboard, boogie-board, and snorkel rentals. Hearty breakfasts are served on your porch and in the restaurant. The pièce de résistance: a full-service spa.

Two of my favorite resort hotels recently merged to form the **Cariblue Beach and Jungle Resort** (Playa Cocles, tel. 506/2750-0035, www.cariblue.com, from $90 s/d), which offers a touch of chic sophistication in a lush Caribbean rainforest-garden setting. Choose from seven types of accommodations, which vary widely in style, although all have Wi-Fi, flat-screen TVs, and lovely ambience. The thatched restaurant oozes romance by night.

If it's color you want, look no farther than **Aguas Claras** (Punta Cocles, tel. 506/2750-0131, www.aguasclaras-cr.com, $70-220 s/d), with five adorable one- to three-bedroom Victorian-style cottages with gingerbread trim that look like they belong on a postcard. Set in a manicured garden, each is a different size, accommodating two to six people, and all have ceiling fans, modern tiled baths, large full kitchens, shady verandas, and Wi-Fi. Miss Holly's Kitchen is here.

You get great value at ★ **Shawandha Lodge** (Playa Chiquita, tel. 506/2750-0018, www.shawandhalodge.com, low season $110 s/d, high season $130 s/d). Its 12 spacious thatched hardwood cabins have Wi-Fi and are marvelously furnished, combining simplicity with beautiful modern decor that the Spanish owners—Maho Díaz and Nicolas Buffile—call "neo-primitive." Large verandas invite you to laze in a hammock. The baths boast large, exquisitely tiled walk-in showers. The open-air restaurant with an adjoining lounge is one of the best around. Rates include an American breakfast.

Eclectic in the extreme, the rustic yet upscale ★ **Tree House Lodge** (Punta Uva, tel. 506/2750-0706, www.costaricatreehouse.com, $177-345 s/d) exudes a fabulous Middle Earth feel, or perhaps something Robinson Crusoe might have thrown together if he'd had some money. This unique and endearing lodging offers five individual and irresistible hardwood units with forest or beach settings. The original all-wood two-story Tree House, for example, is built in and around a huge tree, with separate elements connected by a steel suspension bridge. The Beach Suite features a Tolkien-style dome bath (the owners claim it's the largest in the country) with stained-glass windows and a huge whirlpool tub. Yes, it has modern amenities such as iPod docks. This is a fantastic place.

The most upscale—and controversial—lodging option is the avant-garde **Le Caméléon** (Playa Cocles, tel. 506/2582-0140, www.lecameleonhotel.com, from $295 s/d), a chic retro-contemporary boutique hotel with all-white Ikea-style decor. The rooms, in four types, are gorgeous, although purists consider the place too urbane for a coast known for reggae, Rastas, and reefer. Amenities include Wi-Fi, air-conditioning (a first on this

ATEC: Grassroots Ecotourism

The grassroots **Asociación Talamanca de Ecoturismo y Conservación** (ATEC, tel. 506/2750-0398, www.ateccr. org, 8am-9pm Mon.-Sat., 10am-6pm Sun.), in Puerto Viejo, trains locals as approved guides and sponsors environmental and cultural tours of the Talamanca coast ($75 for a full day). Options include African-Caribbean Culture and Nature Walks, trips to the Kèköldi and other indigenous reserves, rainforest hikes, snorkeling and fishing, bird and night walks, overnight "adventure treks" into the Gandoca-Manzanillo reserve, kayaking, dancing, and cooking classes ($25), and an arduous 6- to 16-day trek over the Talamancas ($250 pp, minimum 4 people). All trips are limited to six people.

coast), and flat-screen cable TV. The superb open-air lounge-bar-restaurant can get lively with sybarites toasting with mojitos. It has a spa and a beach club, and it does integrate its public and outdoor spaces into the encroaching rainforest with appropriate tropical styling.

Food

Start the day with health food such as hempseed granola, whole-wheat pancakes, and lentil burgers at **La Botánica Orgánica** (Playa Chiquita, tel. 506/2750-0696, 8am-3pm Tues.-Fri., 9am-3pm Sat.-Sun.).

Savor the finest cuisine east of San José at ★ **La Pecora Nera** (south of Punta Cocles, tel. 506/2750-0490, pecoranera@racsa.co.cr, 5:30pm-11pm Tues.-Sun. high season only, $5-20, cash only), a genuine fine-dining experience in unpretentious surrounds at fair prices. Ilario Giannono, the young Italian owner, offers exquisitely executed bruschetta, spaghetti, pizzas, calzones, and a large selection of daily specials. I recommend the mixed starters plate, a meal in itself.

For a more urbane setting, opt for the open-air **Le Numu** (Playa Cocles, tel.

506/2582-0140, 7am-10pm daily), set in a lush garden at Le Caméléon. Menu highlights includes duck breast salad ($14), salmon and mushroom tart ($14), and Dijon-horseradish-crusted mahimahi ($15). The bar specializes in martinis and hosts live calypso on Saturday twice a month.

I like to kick back in a hammock at the beachfront **Punta Uva Lounge** (Punta Uva, tel. 506/2659-9048, 11am-5pm daily), with simple thatched dining areas amid lawns opening to the beach; it serves sandwiches and simple rice and fish dishes, plus ice cream and cocktails.

Manzanillo and Vicinity

MANZANILLO

This lonesome hamlet sits at the end of the road, 13 kilometers (8 miles) south of Puerto Viejo. The populace has lived for generations in what is now the wildlife refuge, living off the sea and using the land to farm cacao until 1979, when the *Monilinia* fungus wiped out the crop. Electricity arrived only in 1989, four years after the first dirt road linked it to the rest of the world. The hamlet has since become a darling of the offbeat, alternative-travel set.

From Manzanillo, a five-kilometer (3-mile) coastal trail leads to the fishing hamlet of **Punta Mona** (Monkey Point) and the heart of Refugio Nacional de Vida Silvestre Gandoca-Manzanillo.

Sports and Recreation

Coral reefs lie offshore, offering good snorkeling and diving.

Crazy Monkey Canopy Ride, at **Almonds & Corals Lodge Tent Camp** (tel. 506/2271-3000, www.almondsandcorals.com), has zipline rides ($40) at 8am and 2pm daily.

A local cooperative, **Guías Autóctonos Naturalistas de Manzanillo** (tel. 506/2759-9064), on the left as you enter Manzanillo, offers bird-watching, fishing, hiking, horseback riding, and snorkeling excursions, plus nocturnal turtle-nesting trips. Two that are recommended are **Carlos León Moya** (tel. 506/2759-9070, http://manzanillo-caribe.com/carlos/carlos.html) and **Abel**

palms and fishing boats at Manzanillo

Bustamante (tel. 506/2759-9043, http:// manzanillo-caribe.com/abel/abel.html).

Aquamor Talamanca Adventures (tel. 506/2759-9012 or 506/8835-6041, www.greencoast.com/aquamor.htm, 7am-6pm daily) is a full-service dive shop offering dives ($35-95), PADI certification courses ($350), snorkeling ($8-35) and snorkel-gear rental, kayak trips (from $35), and a dolphin observation safari ($40). It's also the best source of information. The staff at Aquamor can tell you where it's safe to snorkel; check out their Coral Reef Information Center. Simeon Creek, by the entrance to the Gandoca-Manzanillo refuge, is a great place to kayak; expect to see all manner of wildlife.

Local guide Peter Gascar will lead you to his lookout platform, the **Nature Observatorio Manzanillo** (tel. 506/8628-2663, http://natureobservatorio.com, $55), 25 meters (82 feet) high in a giant nispero tree. You ascend via a challenging rope climb (not for anyone suffering vertigo) to a two-story rainforest research platform claimed to be the largest in the world. The five-hour tour is led by an indigenous guide and includes nature study.

Accommodations and Food

No camping is permitted on the beach. You can camp under palms at **Camping Manzanillo** (tel. 506/2759-9008, $5 pp) and at the **Casa de Guías MANT** ($8 pp), which also has Internet access.

Budget travelers gravitate to **Cabinas Maxi** (tel. 506/2759-9073, standard $25 s/d, with fridge and TV $35 s/d), adjoining Restaurant/Bar Maxi. It has six modern, clean, simple concrete *cabinas* with TVs, fans, bamboo furnishings, and private baths.

The Dutch-run **Cabinas Faya Lobi** (tel. 506/2759-9167, www.cabinasfayalobi.com, $99 s/d) is a more upscale option in a modern two-story building with black stone highlights. It has four cross-ventilated rooms with stone floors and quaint baths with hot water and mosaics, plus Wi-Fi. They share a simple kitchen and an open-air lounge with hammocks. The owners also rent a "jungle house" called **Jungle Dreamz** (www.jungledreamz.com, from $180 s/d, 2-night minimum), a cozy two-bedroom bungalow in a lush garden setting.

Epitomizing laid-back tropical sophistication, the thatched ★ **Congo Bongo** (tel. 506/2759-9016, www.congo-bongo.com, from $145 s/d) is set in a former cacao plantation (now reverting to rainforest) 10 minutes' walk west of Manzanillo. Blending perfectly with its setting, it has an adorable, agreeably rustic mood and motif to each of its seven distinct cabins, billed as "vacation homes." All have batik fabrics, mosquito nets, kitchens, and broad shady patios with sofas and rockers. It's just you and the rainforest animals. A trail leads to the beach.

Part safari camp, part boutique hotel, **Almonds & Corals Lodge Tent Camp** (tel. 506/2271-3000 or 506/2759-9056, www.almondsandcorals.com, low season $145-245 s/d, high season $195-295 s/d), three kilometers (2 miles) north of Manzanillo, has a lonesome forest setting a few leisurely steps from the beach. Each of 24 tent "pavilions," connected by lamp-lit boardwalks, is raised on a stilt platform and features mosquito nets and a deck with a hammock—a touch of Kenya come to the Caribbean. Separate junior suites and suites are even nicer. Each cabin has its own shower and toilet in separate washhouses. Raised walkways lead to the beach, pool, snack bar, and restaurant serving Costa Rican food. You can rent kayaks, bicycles, and snorkeling gear.

The ultimate expression of rusticity, **Restaurant/Bar Maxi** (tel. 506/2759-9073, 11:30am-10pm daily, $5-15) serves *típico* dishes and seafood, such as *pargo rojo* (red snapper) and lobster. The gloomy disco-bar downstairs is enlivened by the slap of dominoes and the blast of Jimmy Cliff and Bob Marley, and the dancing spills out onto the sandy road. The upstairs has a breezy terrace and gets packed to the gills on weekends and holidays, even in the middle of the day. Service can be slow and indifferent.

Want something more personal? U.S. expats Andy and Molly will cook up delicious seafood—they'll even take you out to sea, or under it, to catch your own lobster or snapper—at **Cool & Calm Café** (tel. 506/2750-3151, www.coolandcalmcafe.com, 4pm-9pm Mon., 11am-9pm Wed.-Sun.), a cool little bamboo structure in Manzanillo village. You'll dine to reggae riffs.

Getting There
Buses depart Puerto Limón for Manzanillo (2 hours) via Cahuita and Puerto Viejo on an irregular, but more or less hourly, basis 6am-8pm daily.

★ GANDOCA-MANZANILLO NATIONAL WILDLIFE REFUGE

The 9,446-hectare (23,342-acre) **Refugio Nacional de Vida Silvestre Gandoca-Manzanillo** (tel. 506/2759-9001, www.sinac.go.cr, daily 8am-4pm) protects a beautiful brown-sand, palm-fringed nine-kilometer (5.5-mile) crescent-shaped beach where four species of turtles—most abundantly, leatherbacks—come ashore to lay their eggs January to April. Some 4,436 hectares (10,962 acres)

of the park extend out to sea. The ocean has riptides and is not safe for swimming. The reserve—which is 65 percent tropical rainforest—also protects rare swamp habitats, including the only mangrove forest on Costa Rica's Caribbean shores, two *jolillo* palm swamps, a 300-hectare (740-acre) *cativo* forest, and a live coral reef.

The freshwater **Laguna Gandoca,** one kilometer (0.6 miles) south of Gandoca village, is a lagoon with two openings into the sea. The estuary, full of red mangrove trees, is a complex world braided by small brackish streams and snakelike creeks. The mangroves shelter both a giant oyster bed and a nursery for lobsters and the swift and powerful tarpon. Manatees and a rare estuarine dolphin—the *tucuxi*—swim and breed here, as do crocodiles and caimans. The park is home to at least 358 species of birds (including toucans, red-lored Amazon parakeets, and hawk-eagles) as well as margays, ocelots, pacas, and sloths.

The hamlets of Punta Uva, Manzanillo (the northern gateway), Punta Mona, and Gandoca (the southern gateway) form part of the refuge. Because communities of indigenous people live within the park, it is a mixed-management reserve; the locals' needs are integrated into park-management policies. **Punta**

entering Gandoca-Manzanillo National Wildlife Refuge

The *Tucuxí* Dolphin

The *tucuxí* dolphin (*Sotalia fluviatilis*) is a rare species whose existence hereabouts, though known to local anglers for generations, only recently filtered out from the swamps of Manzanillo to the broader world. The little-known species is found in freshwater rivers, estuaries, and adjacent coastal areas of Central and South America from as far north as Laguna Leimus in Nicaragua to the upper reaches of the Amazon River. Pods of *tucuxí* (pronounced "too-KOO-shee") interact with pods of bottle-nosed dolphins, and interspecies mating has been observed.

The **Talamanca Dolphin Foundation** (tel. 506/2759-0612) is a nonprofit organization that conducts research into the dolphins and offers guided boating tours.

Mona Center for Sustainable Living and Education (no tel., www.puntamona.org) is a communal organic farm and environmental center. It teaches traditional and sustainable farming techniques and other environmentally sound practices. It accepts volunteers, internships are available, and day and overnight visitors are welcome ($40 pp, including boat transfers, guided tour, and kayaking). Kayaking, guided hikes, and yoga retreats are offered.

Exploring the Park

The park is easily explored simply by walking the beaches; trails also wind through the flat lowland rainforest fringing the coast. A coastal track leads south from the east side of Manzanillo village to Gandoca village (two hours), where you can walk the beach one kilometer (0.6 miles) south to Laguna Gandoca. Beyond the lagoon, a trail winds through the rainforest, ending at the Río Sixaola and the border with Panamá. A guide is recommended.

ANAI (Asociación Nacional de Asuntos Indígenas, tel. 506/2224-6090 or 506/2756-8120, www.anaicr.org) works to protect the forest and to evolve a sustainable livelihood through reforestation and other earth-friendly methods; it offers Talamanca Field Adventures trips throughout the southeast. Volunteers are needed for the Marine Turtle Conservation Project, which conducts research and protects the turtles from predators and poachers. Contact ANAI or ATEC (Asociación Talamanca de Ecoturismo y Conservación, tel./fax 506/2750-0398, www.ateccr.org) to see how you can help.

You can hire a guide and a boat in Sixaola to take you downriver to the mangrove swamps at the river mouth (dangerous currents and reefs prevent access from the ocean). The **Costa Rican Association of Community-Based Rural Tourism** (ACTUAR, tel. 506/2248-9470, www.actuarcostarica.com) offers eco-minded tours plus homestay accommodations with locals at El Yüe Eco-Agro Farm and other indigenous lodges.

The **MINAE ranger station** (tel. 506/2759-9001, 8am-4pm daily) is at the entrance to Manzanillo village; the MINAE headquarters (tel. 506/2759-9100) at Gandoca is 500 meters (0.3 miles) inland from the beach. Entrance costs $6, but there is rarely anyone to collect the fee.

Accommodations and Food

Camping is permitted in the park, but there are no facilities. The nearest accommodations are in the villages of Manzanillo and Gandoca, on the northern and southern entrances to the reserve, respectively.

The various accommodations at Gandoca are often closed in low season and include the breeze-swept **Cabinas Orquídeas** (tel. 506/2754-2392), run by a friendly older couple. They have 18 rooms. Four upstairs rooms have bunks and a shared bath with cold water only for $12 pp, $20 pp with meals. Others have private baths ($25 pp, $30 pp with meals). The best bet here is **Albergue Kaniki** (tel. 506/2754-1071, $18 pp), with three small dorm rooms with bunks and lots of light and cold-water baths. You can also camp on the lawns. Meals are served, and you can rent sea kayaks and take horseback rides, plus bird-watching, hiking, and dolphin tours.

Punta Mona Center for Sustainable Living and Education (tel. 506/2614-5735 or 506/8391-2116, www.puntamona.org, $40 pp, including meals) operates on a community living basis and has cabins. ANAI welcomes volunteers to its **Finca Loma** (tel. 506/2759-9100, www.anaicr.org), an ecotourism project beside the turtle hatchery. You need to sign up for a six-week minimum stay and may find yourself doing all kinds of physical chores. There is no electricity.

Getting There

You can drive to Gandoca village via a 15-kilometer (9.5-mile) dirt road that leads north from the Bribrí-Sixaola road; the turnoff is signed about three kilometers (2 miles) west of Sixaola. Keep left at the crossroads 1.5 kilometers (0.9 miles) down the road. If you get caught short of money, there's a roadside 24-hour ATM at Finca Sixaola, midway to Gandoca.

Río Sixaola Region

BRIBRÍ AND VICINITY

From Hone Creek, Highway 36 winds inland through the foothills of the Talamancas and descends to Bribrí, a small town 60 kilometers (37 miles) south of Puerto Limón and the administrative center for the region. It is surrounded by banana plantations spread out in a flat valley backed by tiers of far-off mountains. The indigenous influence is noticeable. Just before the Sixaola turnoff, stop in at the **Casa-Estudio de Fran Vázquez** (tel. 506/2751-0205), a well-known local artist.

The paved road ends in Bribrí, but a dirt road leads west through the gorge of the Río Sixaola and the village of Bratsi, where the vistas open up across the Valle de Talamanca, surrounded by soaring mountains—a region known as Alta Talamanca. The United Fruit Company once reigned supreme in the valley, and the history of the region is a sad tale (many of the indigenous people who opposed destruction of their forests at the turn of the 20th century were hunted down and murdered or jailed). You'll need a 4WD vehicle.

The only three reasons to visit this region are: to access Gandoca; to cross into Panamá; or to explore the indigenous reserves.

Talamanca Indigenous Reserves

The **Reserva Indígena Talamanca-Bribrí** and **Reserva Indígena Talamanca-Cabecar** are incorporated into Parque Internacional La Amistad (www.sinac.go.cr), the international peace park on the slopes of the Talamanca Mountains. The parks were established to protect the traditional lifestyle of the indigenous people, although the communities and their land remain under constant threat from loggers, squatters, and evangelicals.

The Cabecar indigenous people have no villages, as they prefer to live apart. Although the people speak Spanish and wear Western clothing, their philosophy that all living things are the work of Sibo, their god of creation, has traditionally pitted indigenous groups against pioneers. Government proposals to build a trans-Talamanca highway and a hydroelectric dam are being fought by the local people. The communities supplement their income by selling crafts and organically grown cacao. Amubri, eight kilometers (5 miles) west of Bratsi, is the main town and gateway to the reserve.

The main settlement of the Talamanca-Bribrí reserve is the hamlet of Shiroles, setting for **Finca Educativa Indígena** (tel. 506/8571-4722, redidigena1@gmail.com), an administrative center for the Bribrí people; it has a rustic 12-bedroom lodge ($10 pp, 3 days all-inclusive $133 pp).

If you go, enter with a sense of humility and respect. Do not treat the community members as a tourist oddity; you have as much to learn from the indigenous communities as to share.

Beyond Bribrí, a moderate 30-minute hike off the Bratsi road leads to the 20-meter (66-foot) Volio waterfall, popular with local tour guides; it has a pool that's good for swimming.

The **Reserva Indígena Yorkin** (tel. 506/8375-3372) welcomes visitors and leads hikes. Artisans of the Estibrawpa Women's Group display their traditional (rather crude) crafts. The reserve is accessed by canoe up the Río Yorkin from Bambú. The two-day, one-night trip includes lodging, transportation, and meals ($60 pp, extra day $25). However, it is extremely basic (no towels or toilet paper); choose to sleep either in simple bedrooms with basic private baths, or upstairs on a platform with mats beneath mosquito-net tents. Solar panels feed electricity in the common areas. Reports about the experience are mixed. The **Costa Rican Association of Community-Based Rural Tourism** (ACTUAR, tel. 506/2248-9470, www.actuarcostarica.com) and **Aventuras Naturales Yorkin** (tel. 506/2200-5211, www.aventurasyorkin.co.cr) offer tours.

Information and Services

Banco Nacional (10am-noon and 1pm-3:45pm Mon.-Fri.) in Bribrí is the only bank for miles. It gets crowded and can take hours to get money changed.

There's a **Red Cross** (tel. 506/2758-0125) evacuation center in Bribrí for emergencies. The **police station** (tel. 506/2758-1865) is opposite the Red Cross.

Getting There

The San José-Limón **bus** passes through Bribrí en route to Sixaola ($3.50 to Sixaola).

Buses depart Limón from opposite Radio Casino on Avenida 4 eight times 5am-6pm daily. Buses depart Bribrí for Shiroles at 8am, noon, and 5:30pm daily.

If **driving** from Puerto Viejo, you can take a dirt road that crosses the mountains, linking Punta Uva to Paraíso, about 10 kilometers (6 miles) west of Sixaola.

SIXAOLA: CROSSING INTO PANAMÁ

Sixaola, 34 kilometers (21 miles) southeast of Bribrí, is on the north bank of the 200-meter-wide (660-foot-wide) fast-flowing Río Sixaola. The only visitors to this dour border town (it's not a place to get stuck overnight) are typically crossing the river into Panamá en route to Boca del Toro (the equally dour Panamanian village of Guabito is on the south bank of the river). You can walk or drive across the border. Remember to advance your watch by one hour as you enter Panamá.

The **Costa Rican customs and immigration offices** (tel. 506/2754-2044, 7am-5pm daily) are on the west end of the bridge that links the two towns. The **Panamanian office** (tel. 507/759-7952), on the east end, is open 8am-6pm daily.

The basic **Hotel el Imperio** (tel. 506/2754-2289, $16 s/d) is on the left as you come into Sixaola. It faces the police checkpoint, so at least your room should be secure. There are a few other grim cabins and a fistful of uninspired eateries.

Buses depart Sixaola for San José at 5am, 7:30am, 9:30am, and 2:30pm daily, and for Limón six times 5am-5pm daily. The bus station, as such, is just one block from the border crossing; pedestrians arriving in Panamá have to buy a $15 bus ticket out of Panamá before passing to the customs office and then immigration for a tourist visa ($3).

There's a **gas station** about 10 kilometers (6 miles) east of Bribrí. You'll be stopped and possibly searched at the *comando* (police checkpoint, tel. 506/2754-2160) as you enter Sixaola.

The Northern Zone

Look for ★ to find recommended
sights, activities, dining, and lodging.

Highlights

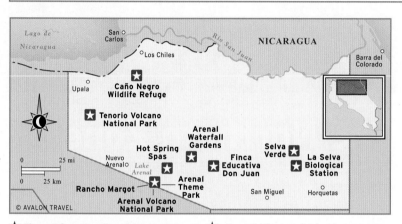

★ **Finca Educativa Don Juan:** Experience a fun and inspiring introduction to organic farming at this family-run farm (page 204).

★ **Hot Spring Spas:** At Balneario Tabacón, one of the enticing hot springs options, you can bathe in steaming waters that tumble from the Volcán Arenal and cascade through a landscaped garden (page 207).

★ **Arenal Waterfall Gardens:** This fantastic set of landscaped hot-springs cascades (and the setting for an episode of *The Bachelor*) also features a wildcat center (page 208).

★ **Arenal Volcano National Park:** With a symmetrical volcano at its heart, this national park has hiking trails over still-warm lava flows and open spaces for prime wildlife-viewing (page 214).

★ **Rancho Margot:** This ecologically self-sustaining farm and wildlife rescue center has rustic but endearing accommodations, plus hiking, rappelling, and horseback riding (page 220).

★ **Arenal Theme Park:** The aerial tram at this private reserve promises high-mountain rides and staggering vistas. Nature trails and canopy tours provide close-up encounters with wildlife (page 220).

★ **Caño Negro Wildlife Refuge:** This croc-infested swamp and forest ecosystem is a dream for bird-watchers, wildlife lovers, and anglers, who hook tarpon, garfish, and snook (page 226).

★ **Tenorio Volcano National Park:** Long off the tourist charts, this volcano is a newfound frontier for hikers. Trail destinations include the jade-colored Río Celeste (page 229).

★ **Selva Verde:** Enfolded by rainforest, this dedicated nature lodge offers instant access to wildlife-rich terrain. Options include guided hikes by day and night, plus canoeing on the Río Sarapiquí (page 234).

★ **La Selva Biological Station:** The wildlife viewing at this scientific research station is awesome. Expect to see peccaries close up on guided walks through the rainforest (page 237).

The northern lowlands constitute a 40,000-square-kilometer (15,400-square-mile) watershed drained by the Ríos Frío, San Carlos, and Sarapiquí and their tributaries, which flow north to the Río San Juan, forming the border with

Nicaragua. The rivers meander like restless snakes and flood in the wet season, when much of the landscape is transformed into swampy marshlands. The region is made up of two separate plains (*llanuras*): in the west, the Llanura de los Guatusos, and farther east, the Llanura de San Carlos. Today, travelers are flocking here thanks to the singular popularity of Volcán Arenal and the fistful of adventures based around nearby La Fortuna.

These plains were once rampant with tropical rainforest. During recent decades much of it has been felled as the lowlands have been transformed into farmland. But there's still plenty of rainforest extending for miles across the plains and clambering up the north-facing slopes of the cordilleras, whose scarp face hems the lowlands.

Today, the region is a breadbasket for the nation, and most of the working population is employed in agriculture. The land in the southern uplands area of San Carlos, centered on the regional capital of Ciudad Quesada, is almost 70 percent dedicated to dairy cattle. The lowlands are the realm of beef cattle and plantations of pineapples, bananas, and citrus.

The climate has much in common with the Caribbean coast: warm, humid, and consistently wet. Temperatures hover at 25-27°C (77-81°F) year-round. The climatic periods are not as well defined as those of other parts of the nation, and rarely does a week pass without a prolonged and heavy rain shower (it rains a little less from February to the beginning of May). Precipitation tends to diminish and the dry season grows more pronounced northward and westward.

PLANNING YOUR TIME

Allocate up to one week if you want to fully explore the lowlands. The region is a vast triangle, broad to the east and narrowing to the west. Much of the region is accessible only along rough dirt roads that turn to muddy

Previous: Arenal Volcano; coatimundi at Lake Arenal. **Above:** hikers at La Selva Biological Station.

The Northern Zone

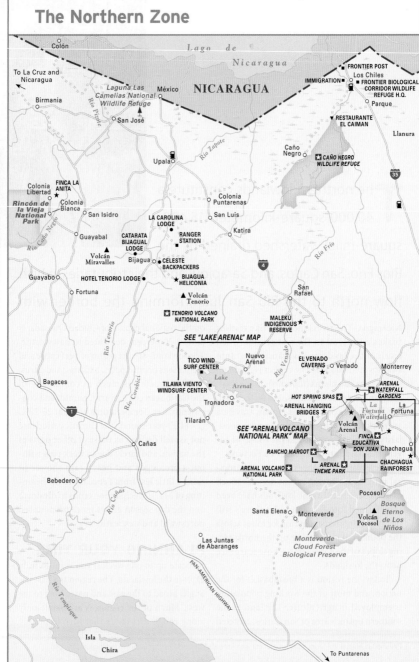

Lago de Nicaragua

Colón

To La Cruz and Nicaragua

Birmania

Laguna Las Camelias National Wildlife Refuge

Río Pizote

San José

México

NICARAGUA

Los Chiles

FRONTIER POST

IMMIGRATION

FRONTIER BIOLOGICAL CORRIDOR WILDLIFE REFUGE H.Q.

Parque

RESTAURANTE EL CAIMAN

Llanura

Upala

Río Zapote

Caño Negro

CAÑO NEGRO WILDLIFE REFUGE

35

Colonia Libertad

FINCA LA ANITA

Rincón de la Vieja National Park

Colonia Blanca

Colonia Puntarenas

San Luis

Río Caño Negro

San Isidro

Guayabal

LA CAROLINA LODGE

Katirá

Volcán Miravalles

CATARATA BIJAGUAL LODGE

RANGER STATION

Río Frío

Bijagua

CELESTE BACKPACKERS

Guayabo

HOTEL TENORIO LODGE

BIJAGUA HELICONIA

San Rafael

Fortuna

Volcán Tenorio

TENORIO VOLCANO NATIONAL PARK

MALEKÚ INDIGENOUS RESERVE

SEE "LAKE ARENAL" MAP

Bagaces

TICO WIND SURF CENTER

Nuevo Arenal

Río Venado

EL VENADO CAVERNS

Venado

Monterrey

TILAWA VIENTO WINDSURF CENTER

Lake Arenal

HOT SPRING SPAS

ARENAL HANGING BRIDGES

ARENAL WATERFALL GARDENS

La Fortuna Waterfall

La Fortuna

1

Tronadora

Tilarán

SEE "ARENAL VOLCANO NATIONAL PARK" MAP

Volcán Arenal

FINCA EDUCATIVA DON JUAN

Chachagua

Cañas

RANCHO MARGOT

ARENAL THEME PARK

CHACHAGUA RAINFOREST

Bebedero

ARENAL VOLCANO NATIONAL PARK

Pocosol

Río Cañas

Santa Elena

Monteverde

Volcán Pocosol

Bosque Eterno de Los Niños

Las Juntas de Abaranges

Monteverde Cloud Forest Biological Preserve

PAN-AMERICAN HIGHWAY

Río Tempisque

Isla Chira

To Puntarenas

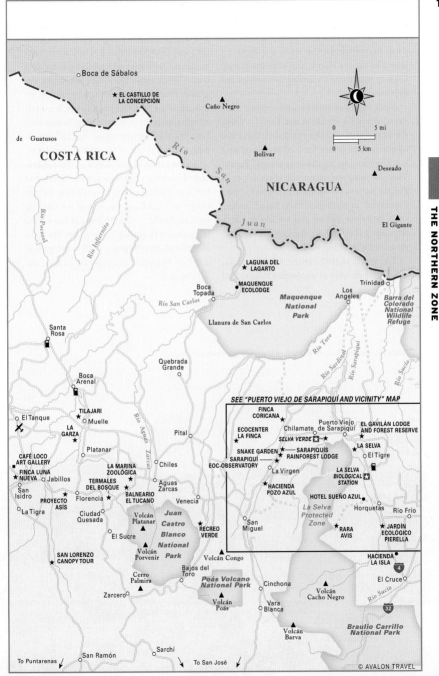

o Boca de Sábalos

★ EL CASTILLO DE
LA CONCEPCIÓN

▲ Caño Negro

de Guatusos

COSTA RICA

Bolívar

▲ Deseado

NICARAGUA

0   5 mi
0   5 km

El Gigante ▲

Río Pocosol

Río Infiernito

Río San

Juan

★ LAGUNA DEL
LAGARTO

★ MAQUENQUE
ECOLODGE

Boca
Topada

Río San Carlos

Llanura de San Carlos

*Maquenque
National
Park*

Los
Angeles

Trinidad o

*Barra del
Colorado
National
Wildlife
Refuge*

Santa
Rosa

Quebrada
Grande o

Río Toro

Río Sardinal

Río Sarapiquí

Río Sucio

Boca
Arenal

★ TILAJARI
o Muelle

o El Tanque

★ LA
GARZA

Platanar o

o Jabillos

CAFÉ LOCO
ART GALLERY

★ FINCA LUNA
NUEVA

San
Isidro

o La Tigra

PROYECTO
ASÍS ★

★ LA MARINA
ZOOLÓGICA

Florencia ★

Ciudad
Quesada o

El Sucre o

Río Aguas Zarcas

Pital o

Chiles o

Aguas
Zarcas

★ TERMALES
DEL BOSQUE

★ BALNEARIO
EL TUCANO

Venecia o

*Juan
Castro
Blanco
National
Park*

▲ Volcán
Platanar

▲ Volcán
Porvenir

★ RECREO
VERDE

★ SAN LORENZO
CANOPY TOUR

Cerro
Palmira ▲

Zarcero o

Bajos del
Toro

Volcán Congo ▲

*Poás Volcano
National Park*

▲ Volcán
Poás

Cinchona o

Vara
Blanca o

▲ Volcán
Cacho Negro

El Cruce o

Río Sucio

▲ Volcán
Barva

*Braulio Carrillo
National Park*

SEE "PUERTO VIEJO DE SARAPIQUÍ AND VICINITY" MAP

FINCA
CORICANA ★

★ ECOCENTER
LA FINCA

Chilamate ●

Puerto Viejo
de Sarapiquí o

EL GAVILÁN LODGE
AND FOREST RESERVE

SELVA VERDE ★ ● ★

★ LA SELVA

SNAKE GARDEN ★ ● ★ SARAPIQUÍS
SARAPIQUÍ ★ ● RAINFOREST LODGE
EOC-OBSERVATORY

La Virgen o

o El Tigre

*LA SELVA
BIOLOGICAL*
STATION

★ HACIENDA
POZO AZUL

HOTEL SUEÑO AZUL ●

o Horquetas

Río Frío

San
Miguel o

*La Selva
Protected
Zone*

★ RARA
AVIS

★ JARDÍN
ECOLÓGICO
PIERELLA

HACIENDA
LA ISLA ●

④

To Puntarenas ↓

o San Ramón

Sarchí o

↓ To San José ↓

© AVALON TRAVEL

San Miguel

quagmires in the wet season; a 4WD vehicle is essential. You can descend from the Central Highlands via any of half a dozen routes that drop sharply down the steep north-facing slopes of the cordilleras and onto the plains. Choose your route according to your desired destination.

Most sights of interest concentrate near the towns of **La Fortuna** and **Puerto Viejo de Sarapiquí.** For the naturalist, there are opportunities galore for bird-watching and wildlife-viewing, particularly around Puerto Viejo de Sarapiquí, where the lower slopes of Parque Nacional Braulio Carrillo provide easy immersion in rainforest from nature lodges such as **Selva Verde** and **La Selva.** Boat trips along the Río Sarapiquí are also recommended for spotting wildlife.

The main tourist center is La Fortuna, which has dozens of accommodations and restaurants, plus tour companies offering horseback riding, river trips, bicycle rides, and other adventure excursions. Its location at the foot of **Parque Nacional Volcán Arenal** makes it a great base for exploring; three days here is about right. The longer you linger, the greater your chance of seeing an eruption, although since 2010 the volcano has been relatively quiescent. Volcán Arenal looms over **Laguna de Arenal,** whose magnificent alpine setting makes for an outstanding drive.

To the far west, the slopes of the Tenorio and Miravalles volcanoes are less developed but worthwhile, with several new nature lodges around **Bijagua,** one of my favorite regions. To the north, the town of Los Chiles is a gateway to **Refugio Nacional de Vida Silvestre Caño Negro,** a wildlife refuge that is one of the nation's prime bird-watching and fishing sites.

Citrus plantations dominate much of the northern lowlands.

Ciudad Quesada and Vicinity

CIUDAD QUESADA

Ciudad Quesada (pop. 30,000), known locally as San Carlos, hovers above the plains at 650 meters (2,130 feet) elevation on the north-facing slope of the Cordillera de Tilarán, with the lowlands spread out at its feet. Despite its mountainside position, the bustling market town is the gateway to the northern region. It is surrounded by lush pasture grazed by prize-specimen dairy cattle.

The annual Feria del Ganado (Cattle Fair) in April is one of the largest in the country, with a horse parade (*tope*) and general merriment.

Termales del Bosque (tel. 506/2460-4740, www.termalesdelbosque.com, 8am-5pm daily, adults $22, children $12), about five kilometers (3 miles) east of Ciudad Quesada, is billed as an ecological park with hiking trails through botanical gardens, plus horseback rides ($15-45) and mineral hot springs (adults $12, children $6). It offers aromatherapy, mud applications, massages, and hikes into Parque Nacional Juan Castro Blanco.

Juan Castro Blanco National Park

Rising to the southeast of Ciudad Quesada are the still active Volcán Platanar (2,183 meters/7,162 feet) and Volcán Porvenir (2,267 meters/7,438 feet), at the heart of Parque Nacional Juan Castro Blanco. Covering 14,453 hectares (35,714 acres), it protects slopes extending from 700 meters elevation. It is replete with wildlife, including Baird's tapir and, at upper elevations, the resplendent quetzal. It can also be accessed from Bajos del Toro and El Silencio de Los Ángeles Cloud Forest Reserve, in the Central Highlands. The main access is now from El Sucre, about five kilometers (3 miles) south of Ciudad Quesada. A dirt road leads 10 kilometers (6 miles) to a new visitors center (tel. 506/8815-7094, apanajuca@gmail.com, daily 8am-4pm, by donation), from where trails lead through montane rainforest to sparkling lakes.

Restaurante El Congo (tel. 506/8872-9808, 9am-5pm Sat.-Sun.), one kilometer (0.6 miles) before the visitors center, caters to hikers with fresh-caught trout and *comida típica.*

La Marina Zoológica

Private zoo La Marina Zoológica (tel./fax 506/2474-2100, www.zoocostarica.com, 8am-4pm daily, adults $10, children $8), 12 kilometers (7.5 miles) east of Ciudad Quesada, beyond Termales del Bosque on the road to Aguas Zarcas (15 kilometers/9.5 miles east of Ciudad Quesada), houses jaguars, tapirs, agoutis, peccaries, badgers, monkeys, and other mammal species as well as birds from around the world. The Alfaro family has been taking in orphaned animals for three decades, and the zoo now has more than 450 species of birds and other animals, many confiscated by the government from owners who lacked permits to keep them. The zoo even has two lions and successfully breeds tapirs. The zoo is a nonprofit, and donations are appreciated.

Proyecto Asis

Animals lovers will likewise find pleasure at Proyecto Asis (tel. 506/2475-9121, www.institutoasis.com, adults $29, children $17), an animal rescue center at Florencia, about 20 kilometers (13 miles) northwest of Ciudad Quesada. It rehabilitates injured animals, but also serves to educate locates in the conservation ethic. You can even volunteer here.

Accommodations

There's no shortage of budget accommodations in town, most offering a choice of shared or private baths for around $10 pp. Favored by business travelers, Hotel Don Goyo (Calle 2, Ave. 4, tel. 506/2460-1780, $22 s, $33 d) offers 21 clean, modern rooms that stair-step down a hillside. Each has cable TV and a private bath

Ciudad Quesada

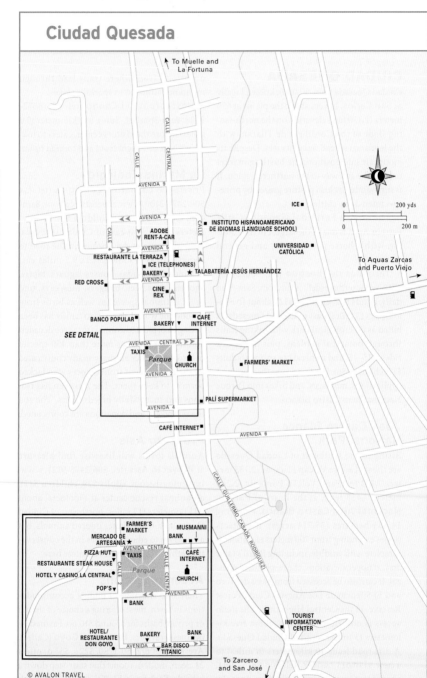

To Muelle and
La Fortuna

CALLE CENTRAL

CALLE 2

AVENIDA 9

ICE ■

0   200 yds
0   200 m

AVENIDA 7

CALLE

CALLE 4

INSTITUTO HISPANOAMERICANO
DE IDIOMAS (LANGUAGE SCHOOL)

ADOBE
RENT-A-CAR

UNIVERSIDAD ■
CATÓLICA

AVENIDA 5

To Aquas Zarcas
and Puerto Viejo

RESTAURANTE LA TERRAZA

ICE (TELEPHONES)

★ TALABATERÍA JESÚS HERNÁNDEZ

BAKERY ▼

AVENIDA 3

RED CROSS ■

CINE
REX ■

AVENIDA 1

BANCO POPULAR ■

BAKERY ▼

■ CAFÉ
INTERNET

SEE DETAIL

AVENIDA   CENTRAL ►►

TAXIS

Parque

CHURCH

■ FARMERS' MARKET

AVENIDA 2

AVENIDA 4

■ PALÍ SUPERMARKET

CAFÉ INTERNET ■

AVENIDA 6

(CALLE GUILLERMO CASADA RODRÍGUEZ)

FARMER'S
■ MARKET

MUSMANNI

MERCADO DE
ARTESANÍA ★

BANK

PIZZA HUT ■

AVENIDA CENTRAL

■ TAXIS

CAFÉ
INTERNET

RESTAURANTE STEAK HOUSE ▼

Parque

CHURCH

HOTEL Y CASINO LA CENTRAL ●

CALLE 2

CALLE CENTRAL

POP'S ▼

AVENIDA 2

■ BANK

HOTEL/
RESTAURANTE
DON GOYO ●

BAKERY
▼

BANK

AVENIDA 4

BAR DISCO
TITANIC

To Zarcero
and San José

TOURIST
INFORMATION
CENTER

© AVALON TRAVEL

with hot water; most have heaps of light. It has a pleasant restaurant.

The more upscale and nature-focused **Termales del Bosque** (tel. 506/2460-4740, www.termalesdelbosque.com, from $70 s, $95 d), on the road to Aguas Zarcas, has 44 attractive, albeit small, modern air-conditioned cabins and four deluxe bungalows amid landscaped grounds in an ecological park with hot springs. Rates include breakfast.

At **Hotel El Tucano Resort & Thermal Spa** (tel. 506/2460-6000, www.hoteltucano.com, from $110 s/d year-round), healing hot springs hiccup out of clefts in the rocks on which the hotel is built. Located eight kilometers (5 miles) east of Ciudad Quesada, the riverside hotel with a large open-air swimming pool is styled loosely as a Swiss chalet complex, with wrought-iron lanterns and window boxes. The 87 guest rooms are rather ho-hum in decor, despite beautiful hardwoods and king beds; master suites are wood-paneled. It has a restaurant, a casino, a full-service spa, forest trails, a gym, tennis, miniature golf, and horseback riding.

Food

The clean and modern **Restaurante Steak House Coca Loca** (tel. 506/2460-3208, 11am-11pm daily, $5-11), on the west side of the plaza, specializes in delicious *lomitos* (steaks), served with pickled jalapeños and black bean sauce.

For ambience head to **La Terraza** (Calle Central, Ave. 3, tel. 506/2460-5287, 11am-midnight daily), three blocks north of the plaza. The upstairs restaurant has a terrace, with an old cast-iron stove and lanterns. The menu is heavy on surf and turf ($4-10).

Information and Services

The **Costa Rica Tourist Board** (Calle del Hogar de Ancianos, tel. 506/2461-9102, ictsancarlos@ict.go.cr) operates a tourist bureau next to the Universidad Católica, on the northeast side of town. **CATUZON,** the Cámara de Turismo de la Zona Norte (Northern Zone Chamber of Tourism, tel.

506/2479-7512, 8am-5pm Mon.-Fri.) has an ill-stocked bureau two blocks south of the main square.

The **hospital** (tel. 506/2460-1080) is on Calle Central, about two kilometers (1.2 miles) north of the plaza. The **Red Cross** (tel. 506/2410-0599) is at Avenida 3, Calle 4. There are banks in the center of town.

Getting There

Buses (tel. 506/2255-4318 or 506/2460-5064) depart San José ($2.30) from Calle 12, Avenidas 7/9, every 45 minutes 5am-7:30pm daily; the trip takes three hours via Zarcero.

In Ciudad Quesada, the bus terminal is one block northwest of the plaza. Buses (tel. 506/2460-5032) run to La Fortuna at 6am, 10:30am, 1pm, 3:30pm, and 5pm daily; Los Chiles every two hours 5am-5pm daily; and Puerto Viejo at 6am, 10am, and 3pm daily.

You can rent cars from **Alamo Rent-a-Car** (Ave. 5, Calle Central, tel. 506/2460-0650).

CHACHAGUA

The village of Chachagua, about 20 kilometers (12 miles) west of Ciudad Quesada and 10 kilometers (6 miles) southeast of La Fortuna, is evolving as a center for ecotourism. About one kilometer (0.6 miles) east of the village, a dirt road leads to the **Chachagua Rainforest** (tel. 506/2468-1011, www.chachaguarainforesthotel.com), a 130-hectare (320-acre) private forest reserve, cattle ranch, and fruit farm nestled at the foot of the Tilarán mountain range. It has a lodge, along with a small butterfly garden and an orchid garden, and the forest is a great place for bird-watching and hiking.

Nearby, **Finca Luna Nueva Lodge** (tel. 506/2468-4006, www.fincalunanuevalodge.com) is an organic biodynamic herb farm that welcomes visitors for hikes and various tours ($20-60), plus classes ranging from the culinary arts to sustainable living. Wheelchair-accessible trails lead through a rainforest reserve, with a 15-meter-tall (50-foot-tall) observation tower. It's unsigned; take the dirt track on the south side of the highway 100 meters (330 feet) east of Restaurante Los

Piruchos del Volcán, at San Isidro de Peñas Blancas. You can overnight here.

You must visit **Coco Loco Art Gallery** (tel. 506/2468-0990, www.artedk.com, 8am-5pm Mon.-Sat.), five kilometers (3 miles) east of Chachagua. This exquisite German-run roadside bistro has galleries displaying the very finest Costa Rican crafts, including hammocks, exquisite marble carvings, and ceramics, plus owner Ruth Deiseroth-Kweton's own exotic, indigenous-infused art and masks.

Accommodations and Food

For chic, contemporary aesthetics in the midst of nature, check into **Chachagua Rainforest Lodge** (tel. 506/2468-1010, www.chachaguarainforesthotel.com, $160-240 s/d), three kilometers (2 miles) south of Chachagua. It has 22 spacious wooden cabins, each with two double beds, ceiling fans, Wi-Fi, gorgeous baths, and a deck with a picnic table and benches for enjoying the natural surroundings. The atmospheric natural-log restaurant looks out on a corral where *sabaneros* (cowboys) offer rodeo shows. There's a swimming pool, horseback riding, and nature and bird-watching hikes.

★ **Finca Luna Nueva Lodge** (south of Chachagua, tel. 506/2468-4006, www.fincalunanuevalodge.com, low season from $90 s, $102 d, high season from $102 s, $114 d) has a delightful eco-lodge with seven spacious air-conditioned rooms in two raised wooden structures with wraparound balconies; there are also two styles of bungalows, including family-size units. It has Wi-Fi, a spa and a solar-heated tub, and an ozonated swimming pool. The restaurant serves organic meals and will especially appeal to eco-conscious travelers.

La Fortuna to Tabacón and Arenal Volcano

The town of La Fortuna is the main gateway to Volcán Arenal, which looms to the southwest of town. Two decades ago La Fortuna was a dusty little agricultural town with potholed dirt streets. Today, it thrives on tourist traffic. In town there's not much to see except the church on the west side of the landscaped plaza, anchored by a sculpture of a volcano, but outside town the range of activities is the most concentrated in the nation, with enough to occupy visitors for a week.

West from La Fortuna, the main road begins a gradual, winding ascent to Laguna de Arenal around the northern flank of Volcán Arenal (1,670 meters/5,479 feet), some 15 kilometers (9.5 miles) from town. It's a stupendously scenic drive as you curve around Costa Rica's most active volcano. However, the volcano is often covered in clouds and getting to see an eruption is a matter of luck. The dawn hours are best, before the clouds roll in. You stand a reasonable chance in dry season, and less than favorable odds in rainy season.

MINAE's Comisión Nacional de Emergencias has set up four "safety zones" around the volcano and ostensibly regulates commercial development. It's highly arbitrary, however, and any cataclysmic eruption would devastate the entire area.

★ FINCA EDUCATIVA DON JUAN

Ebullient farmer, conservationist, educator, and former math teacher 'Don' Juan Bautista is the star of his own show at the **Finca Educativa Don Juan** (Don Juan Educational Farm, tel. 506/2479-8394, www.fincaeducativadonjuan.webs.com, $25 pp, by appointment), two kilometers (1.4 miles) southeast of La Fortuna at Jaúuri de Fortuna (turn south at the synthetic soccer fields, then right after 200 meters). Juan has dedicated himself to turning his one-hectare (2.5-acre) farm into

La Fortuna

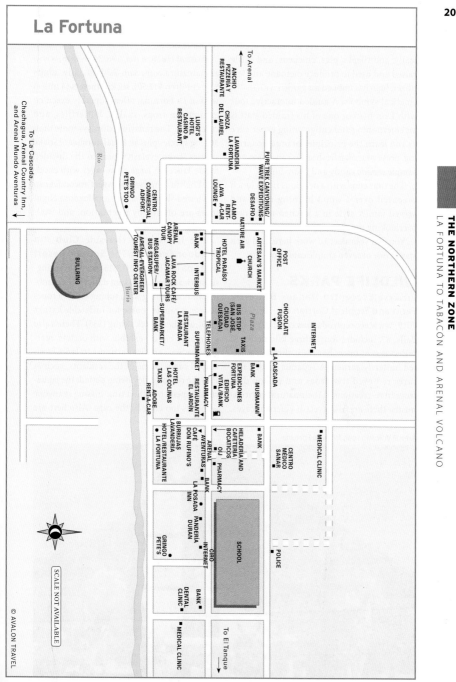

To Arenal

ANCHIO PIZERIA Y RESTAURANTE

CHOZA DEL LAUREL

LUIGI'S HOTEL CASINO & RESTAURANT

LAVANDERIA LA FORTUNA

LAVA LOUNGE

DESAFIO

PURE TREK CANYONING/ WAVE EXPEDITIONS

NATURE AIR

ALAMO RENT- A-CAR

ARTESAN'S MARKET

POST OFFICE

CHOCOLATE FUSION

GRINGO PETE'S TOO

CENTRO COMMERCIAL ADIFORT

ARENAL CANOPY TOUR

BANK

HOTEL PARAISO TROPICAL

CHURCH

MEGASUPER/ JACAMAR TOURS

ARENAL EVERGREEN TOURIST INFO CENTER

BUS STATION

INTERBUS

LAVA ROCK CAFE/ RESTAURANT LA PARADA

SUPERMARKET/ BANK

BULLRING

Plaza

BUS STOP (SAN JOSE, CIUDAD QUESADA)

TAXIS

TELEPHONES

SUPERMARKET

PHARMACY

EXPEDICIONES FORTUNA

BANK

MUSMANNI

LA CASCADA

INTERNET

HOTEL LAS COLINAS

TAXIS

ADOBE RENTA-CAR

RESTAURANTE EL JARDIN

EDIFICIO VITAL/BANK

BANK

HELADERIA AND CAFETERIA BOCATICOS

CENTRO MEDICO SANAR

MEDICAL CLINIC

BURRUJAS LAVANDERIA

HOTEL/RESTAURANTE LA FORTUNA

CAFE DON RUFINO'S

ARENAL AVENTURAS

OU PHARMACY

BANK

LA POSADA INN

PANDERIA DURAN

GRINGO PETE'S

CIRO INTERNET

SCHOOL

POLICE

DENTAL CLINIC

BANK

MEDICAL CLINIC

To El Tanque

To La Cascada, Arenal Country Inn, and Arenal Mundo Aventuras

To La Cascada, Chachagua, Arenal Country Inn, and Arenal Mundo Aventuras

Rio

Burío

SCALE NOT AVAILABLE

© AVALON TRAVEL

an educational center and model for sustainable agriculture.

More than 50 crops are produced organically, and tilapia, pigs, chickens, and cattle raised and used to produce methane and fertilizer. Juan has imbued his garden with mathematical symbols. A guided interactive tour with Don Juan or one of his trained staff is an entertaining and enlightening experience as you learn the principles of organic farming, press your own fresh sugar cane juice, and sample *sobado* candy and *guaro* liquor.

The tour ends with a delicious *típica* lunch prepared over a wood-burning stove and served family style in a kitchen-restaurant overlooking the river.

You can volunteer to work here, and even stay at one of seven simple cabins on-site.

WILDLIFE PARKS

Preserve **Ecocentro Danaus Butterfly Farm and Tropical Garden** (tel. 506/2479-7019, www.ecocentrodanaus.com, 8am-4pm daily, $7, includes tour), three kilometers (2 miles) east of town, has trails through a netted butterfly garden. A separate garden features red-eyed tree frogs and poison dart frogs in re-creations of their natural environments; there are also eyelash vipers in cages.

A small lake has caimans, turtles, and waterfowl. The 6pm night walk (by reservation) is recommended.

Arenal Natura (tel. 506/2479-1616, www.arenalnatura.com, 8am-7:30pm daily, adults $35, children $17.50), six kilometers (4 miles) west of La Fortuna, offers superbly executed exhibits on frogs, snakes, butterflies, and crocodiles. The ranarium displays more than 30 frog species plus an equal number of snake species (from eyelash vipers to the dreaded fer-de-lance) in large glass cages with excellent English-language signage. Crocodiles can be viewed sloshing about in a lagoon. Night tours are offered by reservation, and well-versed guides lead tours.

The landscaped riverside **Club Rio Outdoor Center** at **The Springs Resort and Spa** (tel. 506/2401-3313, www.thespringscostarica.com, 8am-11pm daily) has a climbing and rappelling wall, tubing ($25), a ropes course, a rapids course for inflatable kayaks ($35), and horseback riding ($35). There's also a fantastic big-cat exhibit, with ocelots, margays, pumas, and jaguarundis in large landscaped cages. Some of the residents, such as Pito the ocelot, enjoy being petted; the jaguarundis spend half their time hissing at anyone who gets too close to the cage. Also here are

Arenal Volcano seen from La Fortuna

Jaguar Island, an open puma exhibit, a walk-through sloth exhibit, Monkey Island, and a snake center. It has a riverfront restaurant and bar. An all-inclusive day-pass costs $99 adults, $75 under age 12.

THEME PARKS

Ecological tropical park **Arenal Mundo Aventura** (tel. 506/2479-9762, www.arenalmundoaventura.com, 8am-5pm daily), two kilometers (1.2 miles) south of La Fortuna on the Chachagua road, is a 552-hectare (1,364-acre) rainforest reserve that offers waterfall rappelling (adults $67, children $55), zip-line tours (adults $67, children $55), horseback rides (adults $50, children $42), and nature trails with guided hikes ($35), including a nocturnal walk and guided birding (adults $48, children $39). Indigenous Malekú people demonstrate their music and dance in a traditional village.

Reserva Ecológica Catarata La Fortuna (La Fortuna Waterfall Ecological Reserve, tel. 506/2479-8338, www.arenaladifort.com, 8am-5pm daily, closed during heavy rains, $10 with guide), about four kilometers (2.5 miles) south of town, is in the care of a local community development group—the Asociación de Desarrollo Integral de La Fortuna. The turnoff for the falls is two kilometers (1.2 miles) southeast of town, where a paved road leads uphill 2.5 kilometers (1.5 miles) to the entrance. You can view the falls in the distance from a mirador (lookout), where a slippery and precipitous trail (20 minutes' walk) leads down a steep ravine to the base of the cascade; there are steps and handrails for the steepest sections. Swimming is not advised.

Six kilometers (4 miles) west of La Fortuna, **Los Lagos Hotel Spa and Resort** (tel. 506/2479-1000, www.hotelloslagos.com, $10) has a quasi-theme park with 400 hectares (990 acres) of primary forest with trails and horseback riding, plus a ranarium (frog exhibit), crocodiles, a butterfly garden, and lush gardens with waterslides spiraling down to hot- and cold-water swimming pools. It also hosts the Canopy Tour Los Cañones.

★ HOT SPRING SPAS

Several entities make the most of the hot springs that pour from the base of the volcano. Most famous and largest of the *balnearios* (bathing resorts) is **Balneario Tabacón** (Tabacón Hot Springs, tel. 506/2519-1999, U.S. tel. 877-277-8291, www.tabacon.com, 10am-10pm daily, full-day pass with lunch or dinner

pressing sugarcane in a traditional press at Finca Educativa Don Juan

adults $85, children $30), 13 kilometers (8 miles) west of La Fortuna. It taps the steaming waters of the Río Tabacón tumbling from the lava fields to cascade alongside the road. This Spanish colonial-style *balneario* features five natural mineral pools fed by natural hot springs set in exotic, beautifully landscaped gardens, where steam rises moodily amid thick foliage. You can sit beneath waterfalls—like taking a hot shower—and lean back inside, where it feels like a sauna. The complex also has a restaurant and three bars, including a swim-up bar in the main pool. Towels, lockers, and showers are available. You'll fall in love with Tabacón by night too, when a dip becomes a romantic indulgence. I recommend the Temazcal treatment, based on an ancient indigenous steam room, at the deluxe full-service **Grand Spa** (tel. 506/2479-2028), perhaps the country's most sumptuous spa. It offers complete services in a gorgeous facility that includes open-air treatment rooms in the lush gardens. Note that Tabacón is in a high-risk zone. The former community of Tabacón was destroyed in 1968 by an eruption that killed 78 people, and in June 1975 an eruptive lava flow passed over the site of today's springs. Visitors assume their own risk.

Baldi Termae Spa (tel. 506/2479-2190, www.baldihotsprings.cr, 10am-10pm daily, day pass $31, with lunch and dinner $51), five kilometers (3 miles) west of La Fortuna, features 25 hot mineral pools, ranging 20°C to 35°C (69-95°F), lined with natural stone and landscaped with cascades and foliage. However, this Disneyesque success story can get packed—the huge spiral waterslide is a major draw, although several visitors report that it is too fast and risky. One pool has its own restaurant and deluxe hotel, two have bars, and there's a small snack bar and lockers.

I much prefer the more tranquil and tasteful **Titokú Hot Springs** (tel. 506/2479-1700, www.hotelarenalkioro.com, adults $43, children $15), immediately west of Baldi Termae. Its eight stone-lined pools vary in temperature. It has a full-service bar and buffet restaurant.

★ Arenal Waterfall Gardens

The fantastic **Arenal Waterfall Gardens,** at **The Springs Resort and Spa** (tel. 506/2401-3313, www.thespringscostarica.com, 8am-11pm daily, 24-hour pass $40, 2-day pass $50), five kilometers (3 miles) west of town, combines 19 hot spring river pools and cascades (15 more are in the works) fed by natural hot spring mineral water pumped up from 120

soaking in thermal pools at Balneario Tabacón

meters (400 feet) below ground. It uses state-of-the-art filtration to maintain water purity.

ENTERTAINMENT

The huge **Volcán Look Disco** (tel. 506/2479-9691, 8pm-3am Wed.-Sat., men $5, women free), four kilometers (2.5 miles) west of town, has a restaurant, pool tables, and Ping-Pong. Things don't stir until after 11pm.

The **Lava Lounge Bar & Grill** (tel. 506/2479-7365, www.lavaloungecostarica. com, 11am-midnight daily) is an atmospheric place to enjoy a cocktail, and also serves food. **The Springs Resort** (tel. 506/2401-3313, www.thespringscostarica.com), five kilometers (3 miles) west of town, has a tremendous game room, plus three fantastic hot spring-pool bars, accessible to nonguests with a pass (2-day pass $50).

SPORTS AND RECREATION

More than a dozen tour agencies in town offer a similar menu that includes fishing at Laguna de Arenal; trips to Volcán Arenal and Tabacón (check that the entrance fee is included in the tour price), Catarata La Fortuna, Caño Negro, and Cavernas de Venado; mountain biking; horseback trips; a safari float on the Río Peñas Blancas; and white-water rafting trips. You may be approached on the street by so-called guides, but the local chamber of commerce warns visitors "not to take tours or information off the street."

The best all-around company is **Desafío Adventure Company** (tel. 506/2479-0020, www.desafiocostarica.com), a one-stop shop for all kinds of adventures. It is particularly recommended for white-water rafting and horseback rides, as is **Don Tobias Cabalgata** (tel. 506/2479-1912, www.cabalgatadontobias. com) at Hotel Arenal Springs Resort. **Pure Trek Canyoning** (tel. 506/2479-1313, www. puretrekcostarica.com) specializes in waterfall rappelling.

Serendipity Adventures (tel. 506/2558-1000, U.S. tel. 888-226-5050, www.serendipityadventures.com, $345 pp) offers hot-air-balloon rides at dawn. Feeling flush? For a bird's-eye view of the area, take to the sky. You can rent ATVs and take ATV tours with **Powerwheels Adventures** (tel. 506/2479-1348, www.fourtraxadventure. com). **Bike Arenal** (tel. 506/2479-7150, www. bikearenal.com) offers bicycle tours.

Zip-Line Canopy Tours

For canopy tours, you're spoiled for choice.

ocelot at Arenal Waterfall Gardens

The **Arenal Canopy Tour** (tel. 506/2479-9769, www.canopy.co.cr, $45) offers a package that begins with a 40-minute horseback ride; you'll then whiz among 13 tree platforms using rappelling equipment. It takes two hours to traverse the circuit in a harness. Trips are offered four times daily. **Ecoglide Tarzan Swing** (tel. 506/2479-7120, www.arenalecoglide.com, adults $55, students and children $35), which has a 15-cable, 18-platform zip line, plus a Tarzan swing, offers trips four times daily.

Arenal **Paraíso Canopy Tour** (tel. 506/2460-5333, www.arenalparaiso.com, $45), at the Arenal Paraíso Hotel, has two-hour tours four times daily. Six kilometers (4 miles) west of La Fortuna, the Los Lagos Hotel (tel. 506/2479-1000, www.hotelloslagos.com) hosts the **Canopy Tour Los Cañones** ($25).

ACCOMMODATIONS

Every year several new hotels open. There are dozens to choose from; if they are omitted here, it does not necessarily indicate that they are not to be considered. Additional lodgings line the road between La Fortuna and El Tanque. They offer no advantages in location, however, being farther away from the volcano.

In La Fortuna

Penny-pinchers should head to **Gringo Pete's** (La Fortuna, tel. 506/2479-8521, www.gringopetes.com, dorms from $5 pp, private rooms from $6 pp), a rambling home-turned-hostel in lively color schemes with a choice of open-air and enclosed dorms, one with an en suite shower. Three private rooms share baths. There's a lounge with Wi-Fi, a communal kitchen, lockers, hammocks, and a barbecue grill outside. Tours are offered. It's a solid bargain. Gringo Pete also runs **Gringo Pete Too,** with six dorm rooms and 15 rooms with private baths.

The almost luxurious yin to Gringo Pete's yang is **Arenal Backpackers' Resort** (tel. 506/2479-7000, www.arenalbackpackers.com, dorm from $12 pp, camping $13, private rooms from $18 pp), with free Wi-Fi, a lovely swimming pool with a bar, and hammocks on spacious lawns. Orthopedic mattresses, silent air-conditioning, and flat-screen TVs are among the treats at this first-class budget option, three blocks west of the church.

Also setting a high standard for hostels, ★ **Arenal Hostel Resort** (tel. 506/2479-9222, http://arenalhostelresort.net, dorm $16 pp, private rooms $40 s, $50 d) is perhaps the nicest. Spotless, with eye-pleasing decor, it

main street in La Fortuna with Arenal Volcano in the distance

has a pool with a swim-up bar, a communal kitchen open 24-7, Wi-Fi throughout, fun activities, and even an ATM machine. It's on the main drag, one block west of the park.

In addition to the hostels above, the **Hotel Paraíso Tropical** (tel. 506/2479-9222, low season $40 s, $55 d, high season $45 s, $60 d), on the south side of the church, is one among several dozen almost identical *cabinas* in town it has 13 spacious, modestly furnished rooms with all the required amenities. Upstairs rooms are larger and have balconies with views. There's secure parking, a restaurant, a tour office, and Internet access.

Although rooms are nothing to write home about, its fine restaurant and a perfect center-of-town location are reasons enough to stay at **Luigi's Hotel & Casino** (tel. 506/2479-9636, www.luigishotel.com, low season $48 s/d, high season $60 s/d, including breakfast and tax), a two-story wooden lodge on La Fortuna's main drag. There's a pool, a whirlpool tub, Internet access, a gym, a casino, and a bar.

Outside La Fortuna
$25-50

Clean and comfortable, the well-run, no-frills **Hotel Arenal Rossi** (tel. 506/2479-9023, www.hotelarenalrossi.com, low season $36 s, $42 d, high season $40 s, $47 d, including tax and breakfast), about two kilometers (1.2 miles) west of La Fortuna, offers 25 simple but pretty *cabinas* with Wi-Fi. Rooms vary in size; one has a full kitchen. It has a steak house restaurant, plus a kids pool and swings.

$50-100

About a dozen cookie-cutter hotels in this category line the road to Tabacón. I'm partial to **Miradas Arenal** (tel. 506/2479-1944, www.miradasarenal.com, $96-125 s/d), about nine kilometers (5.5 miles) west of La Fortuna, not least for its volcano views. It has seven attractive wooden cabins amid broad lawns, and each has French doors that open to verandas.

With an enviable setting at a higher elevation than any other hotel in the region, the **Arenal Observatory Lodge & Spa** (tel.

506/2479-1070, reservations tel. 506/2290-7011, www.arenalobservatorylodge.com, $94-151 s/d) sits on the slopes of Cerro Chato—a smaller and extinct volcano immediately east of Volcán Arenal. Stay here for stupendous views over the lake and the volcano. It was built in 1987 as an observatory for the Smithsonian Institute and the University of Costa Rica. Today it has 40 rooms of three types in four widely dispersed buildings. The modestly furnished but comfortable standard rooms have twin beds and sliding glass doors that open to volcano-view balconies. Four observatory rooms have volcano views through vast picture windows, as do nine spacious superior rooms in the Smithsonian block, reached via a suspension bridge. Five luxury junior suites are more graciously furnished and have the best views. Five rooms are wheelchair-accessible. A converted farmhouse, **La Casona** ($63 s/d), 500 meters (0.3 miles) away, accommodates 14 more guests in four rooms with shared baths (only three rooms have volcano views). The **White Hawk Villa** accommodates 10 people (from $510). The lodge offers horseback rides, hikes, and free canoeing on Lake Chato. There's a splendid walk-in infinity swimming pool, plus a whirlpool tub, a kids pool, and a bar.

$100-150

For seclusion and great volcano views, you can't beat **Lomas del Volcán** (tel. 506/2479-9000, www.lomasdelvolcan.com, low season $120 s, $130 d, high season $130 s, $135 d), amid dairy pastures about one kilometer (0.6 miles) off the main road, four kilometers (2.5 miles) west of town. It has 13 spacious wooden stilt cabins, some with king beds, and all with glass-enclosed porches. Nature trails lead into the forest. Horses can be rented, and there's Wi-Fi in the reception area.

With its stone-faced reception area, **Volcano Lodge** (tel. 506/2479-1717, www.volcanolodge.com, low season $115 s/d, high season $150 s/d), about six kilometers (4 miles) west of town, offers 20 beautifully appointed two-bedroom cottages with large picture windows as well as porches with rockers for enjoying the volcano views beyond the gardens, which have a lovely swimming pool with swim-up bar. Choose a king bed or two queens. Facilities include a pool and a whirlpool tub, and intermittent Wi-Fi. The restaurant is one of the finest around.

Another of my near-identical faves is the hillside **Montaña de Fuego Resort & Spa** (tel. 506/2479-1220, www.montanadefuego.com, $150 s/d), with 66 handsome hardwood air-conditioned *cabinas* and bungalow suites with splendid volcano views through glass-enclosed verandas (many rooms face away from the volcano). The hotel has a glass-enclosed restaurant, a swimming pool, a spa, and a zipline canopy.

OVER $150

By far the most dramatic hotel is ★ **The Springs Resort & Spa** (tel. 506/2401-3313, www.thespringscostarica.com, low season from $445 s/d, high season from $490 s/d), five kilometers (3 miles) west of La Fortuna. This deluxe all-suite property (an episode of the TV series *The Bachelor* was filmed here) is particularly fun for families for its hot springs, wildlife draws, and riverside activities. The six-story main building is built on a hillside, with tiered hot springs landscaped into grottos, waterfalls, and pools. The suites, in separate blocks, all have wall-of-glass volcano views from raised king beds. Hallmarks that delight include huge flat-screen TVs, iPod docks, DVD players, luxurious furnishings, and sumptuous marble-clad baths with walk-in showers and separate his-and-hers whirlpool tubs. Plus you get direct access to its Arenal Waterfall Gardens for free.

The upscale, nonsmoking **Tabacón Lodge** (tel. 506/2479-2000, www.tabacon.com, from $255 s/d year-round), 200 meters (660 feet) uphill of Balneario Tabacón, is set amid lush well-maintained gardens. The property has 73 air-conditioned rooms, all with beautiful Georgian-inspired mahogany furnishings, king beds, 40-inch flat-screen TVs, marble-clad baths, and a patio affording a volcano view. Nine rooms are junior suites with private garden whirlpool tubs. There's a small gym, a gourmet restaurant, a swim-up bar in a hot spring pool, and the luxurious Grand Spa at the *balneario*. Rates include breakfast and unlimited access to the *balneario*.

Taking the prize for audacious locale is the all-suite **Arenal Kioro** (tel. 506/2479-1700, www.hotelarenalkioro.com, low season from $209 s, $239 d, high season from $335 s, $385 d), at the very base of the volcano. Its 53 spacious and graciously appointed air-conditioned suites have walls of glass, lush contemporary furnishings, marble-clad baths, and en-suite whirlpool tub with volcano views. There's a full-service spa, a gym, and two hot spring swimming pools, while the superb Restaurante Heliconias enjoys a grandstand view. If the volcano erupts, you might find yourself too close for comfort.

Earning laurels from major travel magazines, ★ **Arenal Nayara Hotel & Gardens** (tel. 506/2479-1600, www.arenalnayara.com, $280-590 s/d year-round), five miles west of La Fortuna, is perhaps the most romantic and stylish hotel for miles. It's inspired by Balinese architecture and makes tremendous use of Indonesian hardwood furnishings. The huge, gracious guest rooms have lively color schemes (lime green, tangerine) and a traditional feel melding with flat-screen TVs and other contemporary touches. Most rooms have king beds, many canopied, and all come with a panoply of modern amenities, plus raised bamboo ceilings and large glass French doors opening to balconies with whirlpool tubs. The stylish baths have indoor and outdoor showers. The restaurant is one of the best around. Arenal Nayara is truly lovely.

FOOD
In La Fortuna

The thatched-roof **Rancho La Cascada Restaurant** (tel. 506/2479-9145, 6am-11pm daily), on the north side of the plaza, serves filling breakfasts, plus *típico* and eclectic dishes, such as burgers and pastas ($2-6).

For traditional local fare, head to **Choza**

de Laurel (tel. 506/2479-7063, www.la-chozadelaurel.com, 6:30am-10pm daily), a rustic Tican country inn with cloves of garlic hanging from the roof and an excellent *plato especial*—a mixed plate of Costa Rican dishes. Grilled chicken ($2-6) and *casados* (set lunches, $4) are other good bets, served by waitresses in traditional costume.

For elegance, I opt for **Restaurante Luigi** (tel. 506/2479-9698, 6am-11pm daily), two blocks west of the plaza. This airy upscale option lists a large pasta and pizza menu, plus the likes of bruschetta ($5), cream of mushroom soup ($4), beef stroganoff ($10), and sea bass with shrimp ($15). It specializes in flambé and has a large cocktail list.

Some of the best eats in town are at ★ **Don Rufino** (tel. 506/2479-9997, www.donrufino. com, 7am-11pm daily), one block east of the plaza. Airy and elegant, it offers a wide menu that ranges from veggies on the grill ($6) to filet mignon ($15) or porterhouse with gorgonzola sauce ($18); the house special is *pollo al estilo de la abuela* (grandma's chicken). It serves great *bocas* at the bar and is the town's unofficial epicenter of social life.

The restaurant at **Arenal Observatory Lodge** (tel. 506/2479-1070, www.arenalobservatorylodge.com) is open to nonguests and serves breakfast (7am-8:30am daily), lunch (11:30am-4:30pm daily), and dinner (6pm-8:30pm daily). The food is tasty and filling, but you're here for the magnificent vantage point.

For ice cream, head to **Heladería Bocatico** (tel. 506/2479-9576), on the plaza's east side. This open-air restaurant has a hip, modern motif with a bamboo ceiling and stainless-steel chairs on a wooden deck.

Outside La Fortuna

The upscale **Los Tucanes Restaurant** (Tabacón Lodge, uphill from Balneario Tabacón, tel. 506/2479-2000, www.tabacon. com, 6:30am-10:30am and 5pm-10pm daily) offers magnificent volcano views. I like its chic contemporary styling and the views over a lovely swimming pool with a cascade. The menu spans the globe with such treats as sautéed escargots ($26) and roasted salmon with truffle-oil mashed potatoes ($28).

An upscale standout south of town, the elegant ★ **Restaurante Heliconias** (tel. 506/2479-1700, www.hotelarenalkioro.com, 6:30am-10pm daily), in the Arenal Kioro hotel, is right below the lava flows. Its position is spectacular, with a wall of glass that opens so you can even hear the lava while you dine. The cuisine also rates well. Begin, perhaps, with the octopus cocktail ($12) or *pejibaye* cream ($6) followed by sea bass in caper sauce ($16), and perhaps the seafood salad made at your table with 12 ingredients.

★ **Altamira** (tel. 506/2479-1600, www. arenalnayara.com, 6:30am-10am, 11am-2pm, and 5:30pm-10pm daily), at the Arenal Nayara Hotel, five miles west of La Fortuna, is no less stylish, blending a Balinese theme into a contemporary style. Gazpacho ($6), ceviche, mushroom gratin, beef jalapeño tenderloin ($16), and seafood Pernod ($18) exemplify the menu. Dine beneath a huge *palenque* roof hung with Chinese lanterns. The hotel also serves Latin fusion dishes plus sushi in its **Sushi Amor** restaurant, done up incongruously with traditional Costa Rican decor.

INFORMATION AND SERVICES

The **Clínica La Fortuna** (tel. 506/2479-9142, 7am-5pm Mon.-Fri., 7am-noon Sat.) is two blocks northeast of the gas station. The private **Clínica Médico Sanar** (tel. 506/2479-9420), two blocks east of the plaza, has an ambulance service. The **Arenal Dental Clinic** (tel. 506/2579-9696) is one block southeast of the school, with **Consultorio Médico** (tel. 506/2479-8911) opposite.

The **police station** (tel. 506/2479-9689) is on the north side of the school; for the **tourist police,** call tel. 506/2479-7257. The **OIJ** (criminal investigation, tel. 506/2579-7225) office is on the main drag, one block east of the plaza.

There are three **banks** in town, and more Internet cafés than you can shake a stick at, including **Ciro Internet** (tel. 506/2479-7769) on the main drag opposite the school. Head to **Lavandería La Fortuna** (tel. 506/2479-9547, 8am-9pm Mon.-Sat.), one block west of the plaza, or **Burruja Lavandería** (opposite Hotel Fortuna, tel. 506/2479-7115, 7am-10pm daily) for laundry.

GETTING THERE AND AROUND

Autotransportes San Carlos (tel. 506/2255-0567) buses depart San José ($3) from Calle 12, Avenidas 7/9, at 6:15am, 8:40am, and 11:30am daily. Return buses depart La Fortuna from the south side of the plaza at 12:45pm and 2:45pm daily. Buses (tel. 506/2460-3480) depart Ciudad Quesada for La Fortuna ($1.05) 13 times daily at irregular hours. **Interbus** (tel. 506/4100-0888, www.interbusonline.com) and **Grayline Costa Rica** (tel. 506/2220-2126, www.graylinecostarica.com) operate shuttles from San José ($35) and popular tourist destinations in Nicoya and Guanacaste.

Alamo (tel. 506/2479-9090, www.alamocostarica.com) has a car rental office on the main drag in La Fortuna. **Bike Rental Arenal** (tel. 506/2479-7150, www.bikearenal.com), seven kilometers (4.5 miles) south of town, rents mountain bikes ($22 daily, $132 weekly). **Segway Costa Rica** (tel. 506/2479-8736, www.segwaycostarica.com, over age 7, $39) offers tours of the town by Segway glider at 9am, 1pm, and 4pm daily.

★ ARENAL VOLCANO NATIONAL PARK

The 12,016-hectare (29,692-acre) **Parque Nacional Volcán Arenal** (tel. 506/8775-2943 or 506/2461-8499, www.sinac.go.cr, 8am-4pm daily, last entrance at 3pm except with local guide, $10) lies within the 204,000-hectare (500,000-acre) Arenal Conservation Area, a polyglot assemblage protecting 16 reserves in the region between the Guanacaste and Tilarán mountain ranges, and including Laguna de Arenal. The park has two volcanoes: extinct Chato (1,140 meters/3,740 feet),

Arenal Volcano

whose collapsed crater contains an emerald lagoon, and active Arenal (1,633 meters/5,358 feet), a picture-perfect cone.

Hiking too close to the volcano is not advisable. Heed the warning signs—the volcano is totally unpredictable, and there is a strong possibility of losing your life if you venture into restricted zones.

Arenal slumbered peacefully throughout the colonial era. On July 29, 1968, it was awakened from its long sleep with a fateful earthquake. The massive explosion that resulted wiped out the villages of Tabacón and Pueblo Nuevo. The blast was felt as far away as Boulder, Colorado. Thereafter its lava flows and eruptions were relatively constant, and on virtually any day you could see smoking cinder blocks tumbling down the steep slope from the horseshoe-shaped crater—or at night, watch a fiery cascade of lava spewing from the 140-meter-deep (460-foot-deep) crater. Some days the volcano blew several times in an hour, spewing house-size rocks, sulfur dioxide, chloride gases, and red-hot lava. The

Arenal Volcano National Park

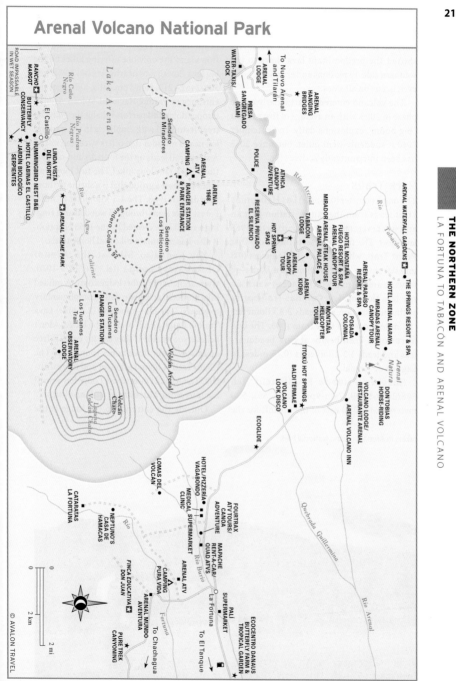

© AVALON TRAVEL

volcano's active vent often shifts location; for the past decade it has been on the northern side, but in 2008 a collapse at the crater rim shifted the predominant lava flows to the southern side. Explosions and eruptions, however, occur on all sides.

The volcano entered a particularly active phase in 2005, with an average of five to eight "big boom" explosions daily. In September 2010 it suddenly went quiet, but since 2013 has been intermittently active.

Park Trails

The one-kilometer (0.6-mile) **Las Heliconias Trail** leads from the ranger station past an area where vegetation is recolonizing the 1968 lava flow. The trail intersects the **Look-Out Point Trail**, which leads 1.3 kilometers (0.8 miles) from the ranger station to a mirador—a viewing area—from which you can watch active lava flowing. **Las Coladas Trail** begins at the intersection and leads 2.8 kilometers (1.7 miles) to a lava flow from 1993. The **Los Miradores Trail** begins at park headquarters and leads 1.2 kilometers (0.75 miles) to Laguna de Arenal.

Reserva Privada El Silencio (tel. 506/2479-9900, 7am-9pm daily, $5), 500 meters (0.3 miles) east of the turnoff for the national park, has a three-kilometer (2-mile) trail. You can even drive up to a lookout beneath the flow. The closest hiking to the lava flows (and the only one offering hikes on the big lava flows), is at nearby **Arenal 1968** (tel. 506/2462-1212, 8am-7pm daily, $15), near the entrance to Parque Nacional Volcán Arenal. Oropendolas and parrots inhabit the *guayaba* trees festooned with epiphytes in the parking lot, near a mirador that offers sweeping vistas. A steep trail leads up the four-decade-old lava flow. It's a fabulous hike! The full loop trail takes you past a grotto that is a shrine to those who died in 1968. The 4.5-kilometer (3-mile) Forest Hike leads through a wooded area ringing a small lake created by the 1968 eruption. It also has mountain bike and horse trails.

You can also hike at the **Arenal Observatory Lodge** (tel. 506/2479-1070, www.arenalobservatorylodge.com). A guided hike is offered at 8:30am daily (complimentary to guests). The four-kilometer (2.5-mile) Lava Trail (a tough climb back to the lodge—don't believe your guide if they say it's easy) is free and takes about three hours round-trip. The Chato Trail (4 hours) is longer and more difficult. The Arenal Observatory Lodge has a small but interesting **Museum of Volcanology.**

Outside the entrance to the lodge is the

hikers in Arenal Volcano National Park

trailhead for the private **Los Tucanes Trail** (self-guided, 8am-8pm daily, $4), which leads to the southernmost lava flows (1 hour one-way). **Arenal ATV** (tel. 506/2479-8643, www.origi-nalarenalatv.com), opposite the park entrance gate, has ATV tours ($89) at 7:30am, 11:30am, and 2:30pm daily.

No camping is allowed in the park. However, you can camp on land adjacent to the ranger station ($2.50 pp), with basic toilets and showers.

Getting There

The turnoff to the park entrance is 2.5 kilometers (1.5 miles) west of Tabacón and 3.5 kilometers (2 miles) east of the Laguna de Arenal dam. The dirt access road leads 1.5 kilometers (0.9 miles) to the ranger station, which gives a small informational pamphlet and has restrooms. A dirt road leads north from here 1.5 kilometers (0.9 miles) to a parking lot and hiking trails.

Laguna de Arenal

Picture-perfect Laguna de Arenal might have been transplanted from England's Lake District, surrounded as it is by emerald-green mountains. The looming mass of Volcán Arenal rises over the lake to the east. About 2 to 3 million years ago, tectonic movements created a depression that filled with a small lagoon. In 1973, the Costa Rican electric utility company, ICE, built an 88-meter-long (289-foot-long), 56-meter-tall (184-foot-tall) dam with an electricity-generating station at the eastern end of the valley, creating a narrow 32-kilometer-long (20-mile-long) reservoir covering 12,400 hectares (30,640 acres). High winds whip up whitecaps, providing thrills for wind- and kite-surfers, and powering the huge turbines that stud the mountain ridge southwest of the lake. Warning: Crocodiles have been seen in the lake in recent years. Don't ask me how they got there!

The only town is **Nuevo Arenal,** a small pueblo on the north-central shore, 32 kilometers (20 miles) northeast of Tilarán, immediately west of the Guanacaste-Alajuela provincial boundary. It was created in 1973 when the artificial lake flooded the original

Arenal Volcano from Laguna de Arenal

Laguna de Arenal

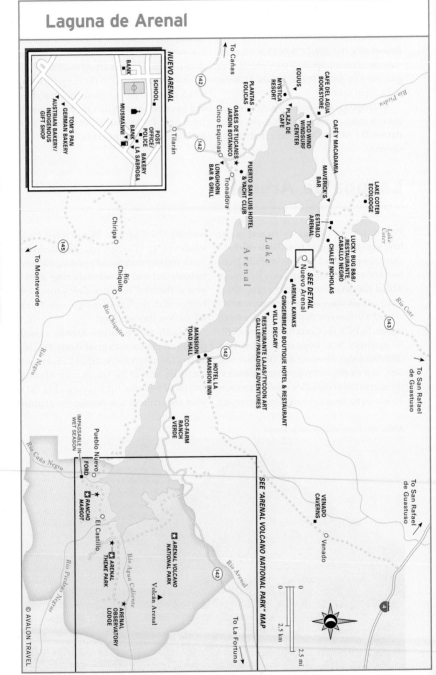

NUEVO ARENAL

BANK
SCHOOL
POST OFFICE
POLICE
BANK
BANK
BAKERY
LA SABROSA
MUSMANNI
TOM'S PAN
GERMAN BAKERY
AUSTRIAN BAKERY/
INDIGENOUS
GIFT SHOP

To Canas
To Canas

(142)

To Tilarán

(142)

Cinco Esquinas

PLANTAS
EOLICAS

MYSTICA
RESORT

EQUUS

CAFE DEL AGUA
BOOKSTORE

TICO WIND
WINDSURF
CENTER

PLAZA DE
CAFE

OASES DE TUCANES
JARDIN BOTÁNICO

Tronadora

LONGHORN
BAR & GRILL

PUERTO SAN LUIS HOTEL
& YACHT CLUB

CAFÉ MACADAMIA

MAVERICK'S
BAR

ESTABLO
ARENAL

Río Piedra

LAKE COTER
ECOLODGE

Lake
Coter

LUCKY BUG B&B/
RESTAURANTE
CABALLO NEGRO

CHALET NICHOLAS

SEE DETAIL
Nuevo Arenal

ARENAL KAYAKS

GINGERBREAD BOUTIQUE HOTEL & RESTAURANT

VILLA DECARY

RESTAURANTE LAJAS/TYCOON ART
GALLERY/PARADISE ADVENTURES

Chiripa

(145)

To Monteverde

Río Chiquito

Río Chiquito

Río
Chiquito

Lake
Arenal

Río Cote

(143)

To San Rafael
de Guastuso

MANSION
TOAD HALL

HOTEL LA
MANSION INN

(142)

ECO-FARM
RANCH
VERDE

Río Negro

Río Caño Negro

IMPASSABLE IN
WET SEASON

Pueblo Nuevo
FORD

RANCHO
MARGOT

El Castillo

Río Agua Caliente

Río Piedras Negras

ARENAL
THEME PARK

ARENAL
OBSERVATORY
LODGE

ARENAL VOLCANO
NATIONAL PARK

Volcán Arenal

SEE "ARENAL VOLCANO NATIONAL PARK" MAP

VENADO
CAVERNS

Venado

Río Arenal

To San Rafael
de Guastuso

(142)

To La Fortuna

0   2.5 km
0   2.5 mi

© AVALON TRAVEL

eyelash viper, Arenal Hanging Bridges

Coter, a small lake five kilometers (3 miles) northwest of Nuevo Arenal.

On the south side, the paved road continues east only as far as **Tronadora,** beyond which it turns to dirt and eventually peters out. You cannot get through to La Fortuna, or **El Castillo**—a community with accommodations and attractions on the lake's southeast. El Castillo is reached via the dirt road that passes the entrance to Parque Nacional Volcán Arenal. El Castillo was pretty badly shaken by the September 2012 earthquake, and many properties were badly damaged.

SIGHTS

Arenal Hanging Bridges (tel. 506/2290-0469, 8am-4:30pm daily, last entrance 3:30pm, adults $24, seniors $19, students $14), within a 250-hectare (618-acre) reserve immediately east of the dam, provides a marvelous introduction to forest ecology as you follow a three-kilometer (2-mile) self-guided interpretive trail with 15 sturdy bridges, some up to 100 meters (330 feet) long, suspended across ravines and treetops. Guided tours include an early-morning bird-watching tour (adults $47, seniors $42, students $37). You get great volcano views.

The Butterfly Conservancy (tel. 506/2479-1149, www.butterflyconservatory. org, 8:30am-4:30pm daily, adults $12, under age 8 and students $8) at El Castillo is a butterfly garden and insect museum with live scorpions, rhinoceros beetles, and lizards, among other creatures. About 30 species of butterflies are raised here and flit beneath seven netted arenas, claimed to be the largest in Costa Rica, while others are released to repopulate the wild. It also has a poison dart frog exhibit, a botanical garden with medicinal plants, and trails good for viewing monkeys. Next door, Victor Hugo Quesada's **Jardín Biológico y Serpientes del Arenal** (tel. 506/8358-6773, 8am-9pm daily, low season $12, high season $15) has an excellent snake exhibit with about 35 species, including pit vipers and fer-de-lance, plus poison dart frogs, lizards, turtles, and arachnids. The **Arenal Ecozoo**

settlement, and now occupies a ridge of prime real estate with gorgeous views. This is the only place to gas up and use an ATM.

The lake is easily reached from La Fortuna, 20 kilometers (12 miles) east of the dam, or from Cañas on the Pan-American Highway via Tilarán. The paved road swings around the north and west side of the lake, linking the two towns. The section east of Nuevo Arenal is backed by thick rainforest and is one of the prettiest drives in Costa Rica, with a fistful of eclectic restaurants and bed-and-breakfasts dotting the route. Animals such as coatis are often present, begging for food (don't feed the wildlife). I've even seen a peccary crossing the road. Landslides are a frequent occurrence and often close the road east of Nuevo Arenal for days at a time; at best, expect some washed-out sections.

A dirt road that begins just east of Hotel La Mansion Inn leads over the cordillera to Cavernas de Venado. Another road leads north from just west of Nuevo Arenal to San Rafael de Guatuso; a fork leads past Lago (tel. 506/2479-1059, www.arenalecozoo.com, 8am-7pm daily, adults $15, students and children $10), a stone's throw away, has hopped on the bandwagon and offers its own butterfly garden, serpentarium, insectarium, ranarium, and insect exhibits.

★ Rancho Margot

Rancho Margot (tel. 506/8302-7318, www.ranchomargot.com), on the banks of the Río Caño Negro, at the end of the dirt road west of El Castillo, is a fascinating self-sufficient organic farm, an ecological activity center, and a kibbutz-like teaching community based on sustainable rural tourism and conservation. Pigs and cattle are raised; prosciutto, cheeses, and other products are made on-site; and visitors can participate in farm activities. It's based around an ivy-clad farmstead in traditional colonial style. Educational tours are offered; you'll get to see the pig-waste compost heater, which provides the methane that heats a swimming pool, and learn why it doesn't stink. Activities include horseback riding ($35-50), kayaking ($40), rappelling ($55), and hiking ($20) on the property's 152 hectares (376 acres) of forest bordering the Children's Eternal Rainforest Reserve. It also hosts twice-daily yoga plus Spanish-language programs,

and has a wildlife rehabilitation center housing deer and monkeys. *Comida típica* meals are served hot from the stove. The ranch operates its own bus from the plaza in La Fortuna at 7am, noon, and 5:45pm daily.

★ Arenal Theme Park

Want to fly through the air with the greatest of ease while enjoying spectacular views? **Arenal Theme Park** (tel. 506/2479-4100, www.skyadventures.travel, 7:30am-5pm daily), immediately east of El Castillo, on the north-facing slopes of the Cordillera de Tilarán, offers phenomenal volcano vistas, to be enjoyed from an aerial **Sky Tram** (adults $44, students $38, children $28) that rises 236 meters (774 feet) to takes visitors up to a mirador (lookout) The mirador is the beginning of the **Sky Trek** (adults $77, students $61, children $48, including tram) zip-line circuit, with 2.8 kilometers (1.7 miles) of zip lines stretching across canyons and between treetops. There's also a **Sky Walk** by suspension bridges, and a white-water **Sky Drift.**

ENTERTAINMENT

Who'd have thought such a wild and wacky disco would be found here, but when Saturday comes around, don't miss

spider monkey with youngster, Arenal Hanging Bridges

the **Equus Disco,** an open-air stone-lined party palace surrounded by dense foliage and giant rocks. It's located one kilometer west of Mystica Resort. Even the local howler monkeys are known to howl to the music. It has a huge video screen.

SPORTS AND RECREATION

Hacienda Toad Hall (tel. 506/2692-8063, www.toadhallarenal.com), about six kilometers (4 miles) east of Nuevo Arenal, rents horses and offers horseback riding. **Rancho Margot** (tel. 506/8302-7318, www.ranchomargot.com), on the banks of the Río Caño Negro, at the end of the dirt road west of El Castillo, also rents horses, offers horseback riding, and has kayaking.

Windsurfing and Water Sports

In the morning the lake can look like a mirror, but the calm is short-lived. More normal are nearly constant 30- to 80-km/h (20-50 mph) winds, which whip up whitecaps and turn the lake into one of the world's top windsurfing spots. Swells can top one meter (3 feet). Forty km/h (25 mph) is the *average* winter day's wind speed. November, December, and January are the best months for windsurfing; September and October are worst.

Englishman Peter Hopley runs the **Tico Wind Surf Center** (western shore, tel. 506/2692-2002, www.ticowind.com, 9am-6pm daily Dec.-Apr.). Peter uses state-of-the-art equipment, has a great lineup of gear, and offers instruction in several languages. One-hour beginner lessons cost $50; a full nine-hour course costs $480. Board rentals are from $15 per hour, $42 half-day. You need a 4WD vehicle for access.

Paradise Adventures (tel. 506/8856-3618, www.paradise-adventures-costa-rica.com) spices up the experience with wakeboarding behind speedboats—it's like snowboarding on water. Owner Jonny T brings in world champs as instructors. **Fly Zone** (tel. 506/8339-5876, www.flyzone-cr.com) has similar offerings.

Arenal Kayaks (tel. 506/2694-4366, www.arenalkayaks.com), about one kilometer (0.6 miles) east of Nuevo Arenal, rents kayaks and has guided trips using handcrafted wooden kayaks made on-site.

Fishing and Lake Tours

The lake is stocked with game fish—*guapote, machaca,* and for lighter-tackle enthusiasts, *mojarra.* Most of the hotels hereabouts offer fishing tours, as does **Captain Ron's Laguna de Arenal Fishing Tours** (tel. 506/2694-4678, www.arenalfishing.com), in Nuevo Arenal. **Puerto San Luis Lodge & Yacht Club** (tel. 506/2695-5750, www.hotelpuertosanluiscr.com) rents out 8- and 20-passenger boats for fishing and lake tours.

The *Rain Goddess* (U.S. tel. 317-408-5942, www.arenalhouseboattours.com) is a deluxe 65-foot live-aboard vessel that operates three-hour lake tours (4 hours, $100 pp) at 4pm daily, with dinner optional. You can also charter the boat and customize your own program; it sleeps eight.

SHOPPING

The **Lucky Bug Gallery** (tel. 506/2694-4515, www.luckybugcr.net, 7am-5pm daily), two kilometers (1.2 miles) west of Nuevo Arenal, sells a fabulous array of quality custom crafts, from metal insects and naked fairy lamps to masks, exquisite hammered tin pieces, and ceramics. Many of the fabulous works are by owners Monica and Willy Krauskopf's triplets: Alexandra, Katherine, and Sabrina. They will ship oversize pieces.

Likewise, the venerable **Toad Hall** (tel. 506/2692-8063, www.toadhallarenal.com, 8:30am-6pm daily), six kilometers (4 miles) east of Nuevo Arenal, sells a huge range of quality souvenirs and has a top-notch café.

Casa Delagua (tel. 506/2692-2101, goodell50@gmail.com, 8am-sunset daily), on the northwest shore, hosts an art gallery selling superb works by, not least, artist Juan Carlos Ruiz, plus books and music DVDs.

ACCOMMODATIONS

Hotels are predominantly along the north shore. There are many more to choose from, but these are my pick of the litter.

El Castillo

One of few true budget options in the area, **Essence Arenal** (tel. 506/2479-1131, www.essencearenal.com, camping $5, tent $28, rooms $28-48 s/d), set on 22 hectares (54 acres) of forested grounds one kilometer (0.6 miles) south of El Castillo, is a backpackers hostel and tent resort. The tents are safari-style, on decks; deluxe tents have private baths. A huge hearth keeps things warm in the lounge, and there's a TV room, a pool, free Internet access, and movie nights. It also has double, triple, and quad rooms, all with orthopedic mattresses. Chef Isaac Weliver prepares gourmet vegetarian dishes.

For intimacy in El Castillo, opt for former Pan Am flight attendant Ellen Neely's lovely **Hummingbird Nest B&B** (tel. 506/8835-8711, www.hummingbirdnestbb.com, 2-night minimum, $55 s, $85 d, includes tax and breakfast), set in hilltop gardens. You get fabulous volcano views through picture windows in its two guest rooms; baths are a bit small. All rooms have ceiling fans, mini fridges, and homey decor such as frilly pillows. It has a patio whirlpool tub. Hummingbird Nest is a solid bargain.

Rancho Margot (tel. 506/8302-7318, www.ranchomargot.com, 2-night minimum, bunkhouse $70 pp, all-inclusive; bungalows $149 pp, including meals) has bunks in basic yet clean and well-thought-out dorm rooms with shared baths. There are 18 lovely bungalows at the forest's edge, nicely furnished and boasting terra-cotta floors, whitewashed walls, modern baths, and spacious decks. Prices include a tour, yoga, and some activities. The Sunday buffet draws locals from far and wide—no wonder, as a professional chef attends to the kitchen.

North and West Shore

American owners Jeff and Bill make you feel right at home in **Villa Decary** (tel. 506/2694-4330 or 800-556-0505, www.villadecary.com, low season $99-149 s/d, high season $109-164, cash only), a small country inn on a former fruit and coffee finca on three hilly hectares (7 acres) between Nuevo Arenal and the botanical gardens. The contemporary two-story structure glows with light. Hardwood furniture gleams. Five large bedrooms have bright Guatemalan covers, plus a balcony with a handy rail that serves as a bench and a table. Three new *cabinas* are perched farther up the hill. The gardens and surrounding forest are great for bird-watching. The hotel is gay-friendly and has Wi-Fi. No credit cards are accepted. Rates include full breakfast.

Gourmands will appreciate the Israeli-owned **Gingerbread Boutique Hotel & Restaurant** (tel. 506/2694-0039, www.gingerbreadarenal.com, low season $95 s/d, high season $110 s/d), three kilometers (2 miles) east of Nuevo Arenal. The stone-clad gourmet restaurant is the main reason to stay here. It has five exquisitely decorated air-conditioned rooms with cable TV, phones, Wi-Fi, and ceiling fans, plus colorful art and themed wall murals; the windowless air-conditioned wine cellar had blood-red walls and a garden shower.

Lovers of New Mexico styling will feel right at home at ★ **Hacienda Toad Hall** (tel. 506/2692-8063, U.S. tel. 800-796-0471, www.toadhallarenal.com, from $75 s/d), about eight kilometers (5 miles) east of Nuevo Arenal. The magnificent creation of Jeff and Lydia Van Mill from Arizona, it's done up in gorgeous sepia tones and has a breeze-swept pool and a sundeck with views. Choose from the two-bedroom hacienda, a two-bedroom bi-level villa, a single-bedroom *cabina,* or the Jungle Suite, all tastefully furnished with rustic antiques and flat-screen TVs. The couple offer horseback tours, plus you get the superb café-restaurant next door.

I love the hillside **Mystica Resort** (tel. 506/2692-1001, www.mysticacostarica.com, rooms $90 s, $120 d, villa $165), run by an Italian couple. Set in lush grounds on the west shore, it offers six large, simply furnished rooms in pastel earth tones with king beds, thick comforters, and luxurious linens. Sit on your veranda and admire the landscaped grounds cascading to the lake below and Volcán Arenal in the distance. Gourmet dinners are served in a high-ceilinged restaurant specializing in pizzas. It has a yoga deck, a landscaped swimming pool, and a massage room. A romantic private villa has a kitchen and a fireplace. Rates include breakfast.

Friendly Great Danes welcome guests to the delightful American-run ★ **Chalet Nicholas** (tel./fax 506/2694-4041, www. chaletnicholas.com, low season $67 s/d, high season $77 s/d, cash only), a splendid three-bedroom Colorado-style guesthouse two kilometers (1.2 miles) west of Nuevo Arenal. Run by live-in owners Catherine and John Nichola, it exudes charm and all the comforts of home. Two bedrooms are downstairs. A spiral staircase winds up to a larger semiprivate loft bedroom with a cozy sitting area boasting a deck good for bird-watching. All rooms have volcano views. It has a TV lounge, a fruit orchard, an orchid house, and hiking and horseback riding into an adjacent forest reserve. The organic meals get rave reviews. Rates include breakfast—perhaps Cathy's macadamia-nut pancakes served with fresh fruit. Smoking is not allowed, and credit cards are not accepted.

By far the most sumptuous hotel hereabouts is the hillside **Hotel La Mansion Inn** (tel. 506/2692-8018, www.lamansion-arenal.com, low season $135-595 s/d, high season $195-995 s/d), next to Toad Hall. Bougainvillea clambers over 16 *cabinas* with lake views, wrought-iron furniture, mezzanine bedrooms with king beds, and French doors that open to verandas with Sarchí rockers. Five luxury rooms take the decor to new heights. The luxe Royal Honeymoon Suite and Royal Cottage sleep up to six. An open-air bar is shaped like a ship's bow, and the restaurant is nautically themed. There's a spring-fed infinity pool, horseback riding, canoes, and rowboats. Rates include breakfast and horseback riding.

FOOD

At El Castillo, be sure to go for pizza or just a laugh from John DaVita, a former LA punk rocker who runs ★ **Pizza John's Jardín Escondido** (tel. 506/2479-1155, noon-9pm daily), tucked away off the road to Rancho Margot; keep an eye out for the sign. John loves to tell outrageous tales, but also cooks

photographing coatis near Lake Arenal

up a mean pizza and delicious homemade ice cream.

Moving along the north shore, for breakfast I head to ★ **Tom's Pan** (tel. 506/2694-4547, www.tomspan.com, 7:30am-4pm Mon.-Sat. low season, 7:30am-5:30pm daily high season), in Nuevo Arenal. This delightfully rustic German-run outdoor café is splendid for enjoying American breakfasts. It also has sandwiches, beef stew with veggies, dumplings with bacon, sauerkraut, chicken with rice, roast pork with homemade noodles, Tom's pastries, and other splendid baked goods. Competing next door, the **Austrian Bakery** (tel. 506/2694-4445, 8am-5pm daily) is more contemporary and serves fabulous bread, croissants, and cappuccinos, among other treats. It also has a tremendous crafts store.

In pizza mode, on the west shore the charming restaurant at **Mystica Resort** (tel. 506/2692-1001, noon-9pm daily) has a splendid Italian menu that includes 16 types of pizza (from $8), plus pastas, and a large Italian wine list, served in front of a cozy hearth.

Levantine dishes feature on the menu at the Tuscan-style ★ **Gingerbread** (Gingerbread Boutique Hotel, tel. 506/2694-0039, www.gingerbreadarenal.com, 5pm-9pm Tues.-Sat., $20), three kilometers (2 miles) east of Nuevo Arenal, with a daily menu that can also include filet mignon, jumbo shrimp with couscous and lentils, and tuna sashimi. Israeli owner-chef Eyal Ben-Menachem really knows how to deliver mouthwatering fare.

A more contemporary alternative, **Gallery y Restaurante Lajas** (tel. 506/2694-4780, lajasdesinet@racsa.co.cr, 8am-5pm daily), 300 meters (1,000 feet) east of Villa Decary, serves a great *gallo pinto*, sandwiches, salads, soups, seafood dishes, espressos, and cappuccinos on an open-air veranda. Carlos, the owner, excels at chess; take time to challenge him to a game.

The drive along the north shore is worth it to dine at **Toad Hall** (tel. 506/2692-8063, www.toadhallarenal.com, 8:30am-6pm daily), eight kilometers (5 miles) east of Nuevo

Arenal, where the ambience and lake views are sublime. Breakfast? Try a three-egg omelet or thick pancakes with fresh fruit ($7). Lunch? Perhaps a grilled chicken salad ($9) or fish taco ($10) washed down with a fresh fruit smoothie. Similar in style, **Restaurante Caballo Negro** (tel. 506/2694-4515, www.luckybugcr.net, 7am-8pm daily, $5-12), at Lucky Bug B&B, two kilometers (1.2 miles) west of Nuevo Arenal, offers an eclectic menu that includes schnitzel, chicken cordon bleu, eggplant parmigiana, and cappuccino. Dine overlooking a delightful garden and lake; you can even fish from a canoe and catch your own tilapia or bass. It has Wi-Fi.

For superb lake views, I head to the endearingly rustic **Café y Macadamia** (tel. 506/2692-2000, 7:30am-5pm daily), about six kilometers west of Nueva Arenal. The enthusiastic owners deliver tasty tilapia *campesina* ($10), beef chalupa ($9), and pasta tagliatelle ($9), plus macadamia muffins, blackberry cakes, and fruit shakes.

INFORMATION AND SERVICES

There's a **bank,** a **gas station,** and a **police station** (tel. 506/2694-4358) in Nuevo Arenal. **Lucky Bug Gallery** (tel. 506/2694-4515, www.luckybugcr.com), two kilometers (1.2 miles) west of Nuevo Arenal, and **Tom's Pan** (tel./fax 506/2694-4547), in the village of Nuevo Arenal, have Internet access.

GETTING THERE AND AROUND

Buses (Garaje Barquero, tel. 506/2232-5660) depart San José for Nuevo Arenal from Calle 16, Avenidas 1/3, at 6:15am, 8:40am, and 11:30am daily. Buses depart Cañas for Tilarán and Nuevo Arenal ($0.50) at 7:30am and 3pm daily; from Tilarán at 8am and 4:30pm daily; and from La Fortuna to Tilarán via Nuevo Arenal at 7am and 12:30pm daily.

An **express bus** departs Nuevo Arenal for San José via Ciudad Quesada at 2:45pm daily; additional buses depart for Ciudad Quesada at 8am and 2pm daily. A bus marked "Guatuso" also departs Arenal at 1:30pm daily for San Rafael, Caño Negro, and Upala in the northern lowlands.

Water taxis depart the dam at the east end of the lake and run to Nuevo Arenal, El Castillo, and Tronadora.

Los Chiles and Vicinity

LOS CHILES

Los Chiles, a small frontier town on the Río Frío, about 100 kilometers (60 miles) north of Ciudad Quesada and four kilometers (2.5 miles) south of the Nicaraguan border, is a gateway to Refugio Nacional de Vida Silvestre Caño Negro.

Los Chiles is reached by road via **Muelle,** an important crossroads village 21 kilometers (13 miles) north of Ciudad Quesada, at the junction of Highway 4 (running east-west between Upala and Puerto Viejo de Sarapiquí) and Highway 35 (north-south between Ciudad Quesada and Los Chiles). There's a gas station. Muelle is worth a visit to view the iguanas that reliably congregate in the treetops, seen at eye level from the bridge beside the Restaurante Iguana Azul.

The **Reserva Biológica La Garza** (tel. 506/2475-5222, www.hotellagarza.com) at Platanar, four kilometers (2.5 miles) south of the Muelle crossroads, protects wildlife on a 600-hectare (1,480-acre) working cattle and stud farm with forest trails. Horseback rides (from $10 for 90 minutes) and hikes are offered, and it has rappelling. Day visitors are welcome to use the pool and facilities.

The ruler-straight drive north from Muelle is modestly scenic, with the land rolling endlessly in a sea of lime-green pastures and citrus—those of the Ticofrut company, whose fincas stretch all the way to the Nicaraguan border. The colors are marvelous, the intense greens made more so by soils as red as lipstick. There are two civil-guard checkpoints on the road to Los Chiles.

Crossing into Nicaragua

As of 2014 it is possible to cross to or from Nicaragua at Tablillas, seven kilometers (4.5 miles) north of Los Chiles, and from there a new bridge crosses the Río San Juan and a new highway leads to Chontales in Nicaragua.

Foreigners can also cross into Nicaragua by a *colectivo* (shared water taxi, $10 pp) that departs Los Chiles for San Carlos de Nicaragua at 11am (it departs when full, which often isn't until 1:30pm) and 2:30pm daily. A private boat costs $150 for 5-7 passengers; call the public dock (tel. 506/2471-2277) or **Río Frío Tours** (tel. 506/2471-1090). The **immigration office** (tel. 506/2471-1233, 8am-6pm daily) is by the wharf.

Accommodations and Food

Los Chiles has only budget accommodations, most quite basic. The nicest place is **Hotel Wilson Tulipán** (tel./fax 506/2471-1414, www.hoteleswilson.com, $28 s, $41 d), opposite the immigration office, 50 meters (165 feet) from the dock. This clean, modern hotel features a pleasant country-style bar and restaurant. The 10 spacious, simply furnished air-conditioned rooms have private baths with hot water. There's secure parking, plus Wi-Fi, an Internet café, and a laundry; Óscar Rojas, the owner, arranges trips to Caño Negro.

Although billing itself as a convention hotel and social club for wealthy Ticos, American-run **Tilajari Resort Hotel** (tel. 506/2462-1212, www.tilajari.com, low season from $79 s/d, high season from $99 s/d), one kilometer (0.6 miles) west from the Muelle crossroads, is the best hotel for miles, with 76 spacious, nicely furnished air-conditioned rooms and junior suites, some with king beds; plus three tennis courts, a swimming pool, a children's pool, racquetball courts, a sauna, a gym, and a sensational whirlpool complex. There's an open-air riverside lounge bar, a disco, conference facilities, and the elegant Katira Restaurant, where chef Manuel Tuz conjures up gourmet nouvelle Costa Rican dishes. Ticos flock here on weekends. Crocodiles sun themselves on the banks of the Río San Carlos in plain view of guests, iguanas roost in the treetops, and hummingbirds emblazon the 16-hectare (40-acre) garden.

Information and Services

There's a **hospital** (tel. 506/2471-2000) 500 meters (0.3 miles) south of town and a **Red Cross** clinic on the northwest side of the plaza in Los Chiles. The **police station** (tel. 506/2471-1183) is on the main road as you enter town, and there's another by the wharf. There's a **bank** on the northeast side of the soccer field. **Hotel Rancho Tulipán** (tel./fax 506/2471-1414, 6am-11pm daily) has an Internet café.

Getting There

You can charter flights to Los Chiles airstrip. **Autotransportes San Carlos** (tel. 506/2255-4318) buses depart San José ($3.50) from Calle 12, Avenidas 7/9, at 5:30am and 3pm daily; return buses depart at 5am and 3:30pm daily. Buses run between Ciudad Quesada and Los Chiles throughout the day.

There's a gas station one kilometer (0.6 miles) south of town, and another 22 kilometers (14 miles) south of Los Chiles at Pavón.

★ CAÑO NEGRO WILDLIFE REFUGE

Refugio Nacional de Vida Silvestre Caño Negro (www.sinac.go.cr), southwest of Los Chiles, is a tropical everglade teeming with wildlife. The 9,969-hectare (24,634-acre) reserve protects a lush lowland basin of knee-deep watery sloughs and marshes centered on **Lago Caño Negro,** a seasonal lake fed by the fresh waters of the Río Frío. The region floods in wet season. In February-April, the area is reduced to shrunken lagoons; wildlife congregates along the watercourses, where caimans gnash and slosh out pools in the muck.

Caño Negro is a bird-watcher's paradise. The reserve protects the largest colony of neotropic cormorants in Costa Rica and the only permanent colony of Nicaraguan grackles. Cattle egrets, wood storks, anhingas, roseate spoonbills, and other waterfowl gather in the thousands. The reserve is also remarkable for its large population of caimans. Looking down into waters as black as Costa Rican coffee, you may see the dim forms of big snook,

male green iguana in orange mating color

silver-gold tarpon, and garish garfish. Bring plenty of insect repellent.

The hamlet of Caño Negro, 23 kilometers (14 miles) southwest of Los Chiles, nestles on the northwest shore of Lago Caño Negro. Locals make their living from fishing and guiding. The ranger station (tel. 506/2471-1309, 8am-5pm daily) is 400 meters (0.25 miles) inland from the dock and 200 meters (660 feet) west of the soccer field.

Local volunteers operate the Criadero de Tortugas (tel. 506/2876-1181, 8am-4pm daily, free), west of the soccer field and where turtles are bred for release to the wild. The village also has a butterfly garden: Mariposario La Reinita (tel. 506/2471-1301, 8am-4pm daily, $4), with 16 species flitting about within nets.

Sports and Recreation

Caño Negro's waters boil with tarpon, snook, drum, *guapote, machaca,* and *mojarra.* Fishing season is July-March (no fishing is allowed Apr.-June); licenses ($30) are required, obtainable from the ranger station in the village or through the various fishing lodges.

Hotel de Campo (tel. 506/2471-1012) and Natural Lodge Caño Negro (tel. 506/2471-1426, www.canonegrolodge.com) have fishing packages and lagoon tours, and you can rent canoes and kayaks. You can hire guides and boats at the dock. Try Joel Sandoval (tel. 506/8823-4026), or Manuel Castro of Pantanal Tours (tel. 506/8825-0193, $50 for up to 4 people for 4 hours).

Accommodations and Food

You can stay overnight in the Caño Negro ranger station if space is available ($6 pp).

You'll need a sleeping bag and a mosquito net. It has cold showers. Meals cost $5.

The Hotel de Campo (tel. 506/2471-1012, www.hoteldecampo.com, $79 s, $95 d), in Caño Negro village, stands lakeside amid landscaped grounds with a citrus orchard. Sixteen handsome, cross-ventilated, air-conditioned cabins have a choice of king or queen beds and have terra-cotta floors, lofty wooden ceilings with fans, and large modern baths with hot water. There's a bar and restaurant, a gift store, a tackle shop, and a swimming pool.

Fishing writer Jerry Ruhlow calls Bar y Restaurante El Caimán (tel. 506/2469-8200, 6:30am-7pm daily) "sort of a drive-in for boats." This unlikely find is beside the bridge at San Emilio; water vessels stop alongside it to order meals or cold beverages. It serves typical Tico fare. Canoe and boat trips are offered ($70 for 2 hours).

Getting There

A road from El Parque, 10 kilometers (6 miles) south of Los Chiles, runs 10 kilometers (6 miles) west to a bridge at San Emilio, from where you can reach Caño Negro village via a dirt road that continues south to Colonia Puntarenas, on the main La Fortuna-Upala road (Hwy. 4). A 4WD vehicle is recommended. Several companies in La Fortuna offer trips. Canoa Aventura (tel. 506/2479-8200, www.canoa-aventura.com) specializes in trips to Caño Negro.

Buses depart daily from Upala to Caño Negro village via Colonia Puntarenas at 11am and 3pm daily. You can rent a boat in Los Chiles ($70 for 2 people, $15 pp for 6 people or more).

Highway 4 to Upala

The mostly paved Carretera 4 (Hwy. 4) between La Fortuna (or, more precisely, Tanque, a major crossroads community eight kilometers/five miles east of La Fortuna) and Upala, has opened the extreme northwest of the Northern Zone as a new tourism frontier focused on the natural delights of Parque Nacional Volcán Tenorio.

Beyond Upala, the unpaved road leads via the community of San José to the hamlets of Brasilia and Santa Cecilia and, from there, by paved road to La Cruz, on the Pan-American Highway in the extreme northwest of Costa Rica.

SAN RAFAEL AND VICINITY

From Tanque, the highway shoots northwest to **San Rafael de Guatuso,** an agricultural town on the Río Frío, 40 kilometers (25 miles) northwest of Tanque. San Rafael (often called Guatuso) subsists largely on cattle ranching and rice farming. You can rent boats and guides here for trips down the Río Frío to the Caño Negro wildlife refuge, reached via dirt road from **Colonia Puntarenas,** 25 kilometers (16 miles) northwest of San Rafael.

Venado Caverns

At Jicarito, about 25 kilometers (16 miles) northwest of Tanque and 15 kilometers (9.5 miles) southeast of San Rafael de Guatuso, a paved road leads south seven kilometers (4.5 miles) to the mountain hamlet of Venado, nestled in a valley bottom and famous for the **Cavernas de Venado** (tel. 506/2478-9081 or 506/2478-8008, 9am-4pm daily, adults $22, children $12) two kilometers (1.2 miles) farther west. The limestone caverns, which extend 2,700 meters (8,860 feet) and feature stalactites, stalagmites, and underground streams, weren't discovered until 1945, when the owner of the farm fell into the hole. A guide will lead you on a two-hour exploration.

The admission cost includes use of a flashlight, a safety helmet, and rubber boots. Bats and tiny colorless frogs and fish inhabit the caves, which also contain seashell fossils and a luminous "shrine." Expect to get soaked—you'll wade up to your chest!—and covered with ooze (bring a change of clothes). The farm has a rustic *soda,* a swimming pool, and changing rooms with showers.

You can also reach Venado via a rough dirt road from the north shore of Laguna de Arenal. Tour operators in La Fortuna offer tours, as does **Cavernas de Venado Tours** (tel. 506/8344-2246, www.cavernasdevenado. com). A bus departs Ciudad Quesada for Venado at 1pm daily; it returns at 4pm.

Malekú Indigenous Reserve

Two kilometers (1.2 miles) east of San Rafael, a dirt road leads south to the 3,244-hectare (8,016-acre) **Reserva Indígena Malekú** (Malekú Indigenous Reserve, www.indigenasmalekus.com), in the foothills of the cordillera. Here, the **Centro Ecológico Malekú Araraf** (tel. 506/8888-4250, centroecologicomalekuararaf@yahoo.es, 8am-4pm daily) has trails and a cultural presentation. Competing **Eco-Adventure Tafa Malekú** (tel. 506/2464-0443, 7am-4pm daily, $1) has a museum on indigenous culture. **Rancho Típico Malekú Araraf** (tel. 506/8839-0540) has a traditional music and dance performance (by reservation only, $35 pp, including a tour). The three indigenous communities are gracious in the extreme—these lovely people, who speak Malekú Jaica, helped me immensely when I seriously injured myself falling through a rotten bridge.

Rustic Pathways (U.S. tel. 440-975-9691 or 800-321-4353, www.rusticpathways. com) offers a volunteer and study program for schoolchildren and students where you can contribute to and learn from the Malekú people.

The Malekú Culture

About 600 Malekú people survive on the Tongibe reservation (*palenque*) on the plains at the foot of Volcán Tenorio, near San Rafael de Guatuso, on land ceded to them by the government in the 1960s. While struggling to preserve their cultural identity, today they are mostly farmers who grow corn and a type of root called *tiquisqui*.

Until a few generations ago, Malekú (also known as Guatusos) strolled through San Rafael wearing clothes made of cured tree bark called *tana*. No one wears *tana* these days, but the Malekú take great pride in their heritage. Many continue to speak their own language. Radio Cultural Malekú (1580 AM, 88.3 FM) airs programs and announcements in Malekú, and Eliécer Velas Álvarez instructs the youngsters in Malekú at the elementary school in Tongibe.

The San Rafael area has many ancient tombs, and jade arrowheads and other age-old artifacts are constantly being dug up. Reconstructions of a typical Malekú village have been erected at Reserva Indígena Malekú and at Arenal Mundo Aventura, just south of La Fortuna.

Accommodations and Food

Nature Nirvana! That's **Leaves and Lizards** (tel. 506/2478-0023, U.S. tel. 888-828-9245, www.leavesandlizards.com, low season from $175 s/d, high season from $195 s/d, including breakfast), in the hills of Monterrey de Santo Domingo, 18 kilometers (11 miles) northwest of Tanque and three kilometers (2 miles) south of Highway 4. Run by Steve and Debbie Legg, an eco- and community-friendly couple from Florida, it has six simply furnished but delightful hillside cabins with decks for enjoying volcano views over 11 hectares (26 acres) of property. Meals are provided at the main lodge, which has Wi-Fi. Cabins have iPod docks, coffeemakers, and microwaves. A minimum three-night stay is required.

Getting There

Buses (tel. 506/2256-8914) for San Rafael de Guatuso depart San José ($4) from Calle 12, Avenidas 7/9, at 5am, 8:40am, and 11:30am daily. Buses also depart for San Rafael from Tilarán at noon daily.

TENORIO VOLCANO AND VICINITY

Upala, 40 kilometers (25 miles) northwest of San Rafael de Guatuso, is an agricultural town only 10 kilometers (6 miles) south of the Nicaraguan border. Dirt roads lead north to Lago de Nicaragua. From Upala, a paved road leads south via the saddle between the Tenorio and Miravalles volcanoes before descending to the Pan-American Highway in Guanacaste. The only town is **Bijagua,** a center for cheese-making (and, increasingly, for ecotourism) 38 kilometers (24 miles) north of Cañas, on the northwest flank of Volcán Tenorio.

Several private reserves abut Parque Nacional Volcán Tenorio and grant access via trails. For example, about 200 meters (660 feet) north of the park access road, a dirt road leads to the American-owned **La Carolina Lodge** (tel. 506/2466-6393, www.lacarolinalodge.com), a ranch and stables with trails for horseback rides into the park. Another dirt road leads east from the Banco Nacional in Bijagua two kilometers (1.2 miles) to **Albergue Heliconia Lodge & Rainforest** (tel. 506/2466-8483, www.heliconiaslodge.com), run by a local cooperative. The lodge sits at 700 meters (2,300 feet) elevation, abutting the park. Three trails lead into prime rainforest and cloud forest.

★ Tenorio Volcano National Park

Volcán Tenorio (1,916 meters/6,286 feet), rising southeast of Upala, is blanketed in montane rainforest and protected within 18,402-hectare (45,472-acre) **Parque Nacional Volcán Tenorio** (www.sinac.go.cr, $10, via the private reserves $1). Local hiking is superb, albeit often hard going on higher slopes. Cougars and jaguars tread the forests, where birds and beasts abound.

A rugged dirt road (4WD vehicle required) that begins five kilometers (3 miles) north of Bijagua, on the west side of Tenorio, leads 11 kilometers (7 miles) to the main park entrance at the **Puesto El Pilón ranger station** (tel. 506/2200-0135).

Three trails are open to the public. The main trail—Sendero Misterio del Tenorio—leads 3.5 kilometers (2 miles) to the Río Celeste and **Los Chorros** hot springs; this is the only place where swimming is permitted. Set amid huge boulders, the springs change gradually, from near boiling close to the trail to pleasantly cool near the river. The second trail leads to the **Catarata del Río Celeste** (Río Celeste Waterfall) and the **Pozo Azul,** a teal-blue lagoon. A third trail, accessible with a guide only, leads to three waterfalls. You cannot hike to the summit (where tapirs drink at **Lago Las Dantas,** Tapir Lake, which fills the volcanic crater); access is permitted solely to biologists.

Guided hikes are offered by the local guides association: try **Jonathon Ramírez** (tel. 506/2402-1330, from $20). The ranger station has a small butterfly and insect exhibit, plus horseback riding. No camping is permitted within the park.

Accommodations and Food

There are several backpacker and simple budget accommodations in Upala and Bijagua.

Set high on the mountainside, **Albergue Heliconias** (tel. 506/2466-8483, www.heliconiaslodge.com, rooms $70 s, $85 d, cottages $85 s, $95 d, including breakfast) is the simplest of the eco-lodges; it's signed in town. It has six no-frills rustic cabins (two have a double bed and a bunk; four have two bunks) with small baths and hot showers, and there are four more upscale octagonal cottages. Dining is family style.

Feeling very much like the horse ranch that it is, **La Carolina Lodge** (tel. 506/2466-6393, www.lacarolinalodge.com, low season

$90-105 s, $130-170 d, high season $100-115 s, $150-190 d, including 3 meals and a guided tour) occupies a charming farmstead on the north flank of Tenorio. It has four double rooms with solar-powered electricity and shared baths with hot water. There are also four private cabins with private baths. A wooden deck hangs over a natural river-fed pool, and a porch has rockers and hammocks. Rates include guided hikes and horseback riding.

The elegant hillside **Tenorio Lodge** (tel. 506/2466-8282, www.tenoriolodge.com, $115 s, $123 d), one kilometer south of Bijagua, offers great valley views from amid heliconia gardens. Its eight peak-roofed stylishly contemporary wooden bungalows have walls of glass, sponge-washed walls, glazed concrete floors, plus king beds, ceiling fans, and chic solar-powered designer baths. The glass-walled volcano-view restaurant (open to non-guests 7am-9pm daily for continental fare) is a class act and features live marimba music. At night, you can soak in either of two cedar hot tubs.

Avant-garde defines the French-run eco-conscious ★ **Celeste Mountain Lodge** (tel. 506/2278-6628, www.celestemountainlodge.com, $133 s, $168 d, including all meals and tax), enjoying a pristine and sensational location three kilometers (2 miles) northeast of Bijagua. Innovative and stylishly contemporary with its open-plan design, stone tile floor, gun-metal framework, glistening hardwood ceiling, and halogen lighting, this dramatic two-tier lodge boasts vast angled walls of glass plus glassless walls with panoramic volcano views from the restaurant and public areas. The 18 rooms, though small, are comfy, with king beds, lively fabrics, and stylish baths. Dining is gourmet (dishes here are "Tico fusion") and family-style. There's a wood-heated hot tub. Trails even accommodate disabled visitors, thanks to an innovative human-powered one-wheel rickshaw; packed lunches are prepared. I love this place, where everything is made of recycled materials, right down to biodegradable soaps.

A stunner by any standard, the non-smoking ★ **Río Celeste Hideaway** (tel. 506/2206-4000, www.riocelestehideaway. com, $190-259 s/d, includes breakfast), eight miles east of the entrance to Tenorio Volcano National Park, features gorgeous tropical architecture with dark hardwoods and rich Asian-inspired fabrics. Set in lush gardens, its 26 bungalows offer a king or two queen beds, luxurious linens, flat-screen TVs, iPod stations, CD/DVD players, private patios, and open-air showers. A free-form pool has a bar, and the Kantala Restaurant and blue-backlit Delirio bar are a dramatic space for enjoying cocktails and gourmet dishes.

Information and Services

A good resource for updates on this fast-evolving region is the **Cámara de Turismo Tenorio-Miravalles** (tel. 506/2466-7010, tenorio-miravalles@hotmail.com, 9am-3pm daily), the local Chamber of Tourism, on the south side of Bijagua.

There's a **hospital** (tel. 506/2470-0058) in Upala, plus a **bank** five blocks north of the bridge in Upala. The **police station** (Guardia Rural, tel. 506/2470-0134) is 100 meters (330 feet) north and west of the bridge.

Getting There

Buses (tel. 506/2221-3318 or 506/2470-0743) for Upala depart San José from Calle 12, Avenidas 3/5, four times daily 10:15am-7:30pm. Return buses depart Upala four times daily 4:30am-9:30pm. Buses also run between Cañas and Upala several times daily.

Puerto Viejo de Sarapiquí and Vicinity

The Llanura de San Carlos is the easternmost (and broadest) part of the northern lowlands. The Ríos San Carlos, Sarapiquí, and others snake across the landscape, vast sections of which are waterlogged for much of the year. The region today is dependent on the banana and pineapple industry, which has planted much of the land and woven a grid-work maze of dirt roads and railroad tracks linking towns.

Fortunately, swaths of rainforest still stretch north to the Río San Juan, linking Parque Nacional Braulio Carrillo with the rainforests of the Nicaraguan lowlands, much of which is protected within private reserves. Fishing is good, and there are crocodiles, river otters, and plenty of other wildlife to see while traveling on the rivers. Even manatees have been seen in the lagoons between the Río San Carlos and Río Sarapiquí.

There are two **routes to Puerto Viejo** from San José, forming a loop around Parque Nacional Braulio Carrillo. Both routes (western and eastern) over the mountains are subject to severe landslides.

PUERTO VIEJO DE SARAPIQUÍ

Puerto Viejo de Sarapiquís (not to be confused with Puerto Viejo de Talamanca, on the Caribbean coast), at the confluence of the Ríos Puerto Viejo and Sarapiquí, was Costa Rica's main shipping port in colonial times. It is still the main town in the region, with banks, a hospital, and other key services. Today, the local economy is dominated by banana and pineapples plantations, which stretch for miles around: You can take a tour of Dole's **Bananero La Colonia** (tel. 506/2768-8683 or 506/8383-4596, www.bananatourcostarica. com, $25), five kilometers (3 miles) southeast of Puerto Viejo, at 1:30pm Tuesday by appointment.

Accommodations and Food

The best option in Puerto Viejo is the simply furnished **Hotel Bambú** (tel. 506/2766-6005, www.elbambu.com, low season $65-74 s, $70-84 d, high season $72-82 s, $78-93 d, including breakfast), facing the soccer field. It has 40 clean, modern rooms with ceiling fans

Puerto Viejo de Sarapiquí and Vicinity

and air-conditioning, TVs, and hot water. It also has two self-sufficient apartments for six people, plus a large modern restaurant and a swimming pool in a thatch-fringed courtyard.

Information and Services

There are two banks near the soccer field. The **post office** is opposite Banco Nacional at the east end of Puerto Viejo. The **Red Cross** (tel. 506/2766-6212) adjoins the **police station** (tel. 506/2766-6575) at the west end of town, near the **hospital** (tel. 506/2766-6212).

Cafenet de Sarapiquí (tel. 506/2766-6223, 8am-10pm daily), at the west end of town, offers Internet access.

Getting There

Empresario Guapileños (tel. 506/2222-2727 or 506/2257-6859) buses depart the Gran Terminal Caribe in San José (2 hours, $2) 10 times 6:30am-6:30pm daily via the Guápiles Highway and Horquetas (do not take the Puerto Viejo de Talamanca bus—you want Puerto Viejo de Sarapiquís). **Taxis** wait on the north side of the soccer field, next to the bus stop, in Puerto Viejo.

WESTERN ROUTE VIA LA VIRGEN AND CHILAMATE

The less-trafficked western route to Puerto Viejo is via Vara Blanca, through the saddle of the Poás and Barva volcanoes, then dropping down to San Miguel (the junction westward for La Fortuna) and connecting to Puerto Viejo de Sarapiquís via La Virgen and Chilamate.

About 10 kilometers (6 miles) north of San

Sharks in the Río San Juan

If you see a shark fin slicing the surface of the Río San Juan, you will be forgiven for thinking you've come down with heatstroke. In fact, there *are* sharks in this freshwater river. The creatures, along with other species normally associated with salt water, migrate between the Atlantic Ocean and the murky waters of Lago de Nicaragua, navigating 169 kilometers (105 miles) of river and rapids en route. The sharks are classified as euryhaline species—they can cross from salt water to freshwater and back again with no ill effects.

For centuries, scientists were confounded by the sharks' presence in Lago de Nicaragua. The lake is separated from the Pacific by a 17-kilometer (11-mile) chunk of land, and since rapids on the Río San Juan seemingly prevent large fish from passing easily from the Caribbean, surely, the thinking went, the lake must have once been connected to one or the other ocean. Uplift of the Central American isthmus must have trapped the sharks in the lake.

Studies in the early 1960s, however, showed that there were no marine sediments on the lake bottom; thus the lake was never part of the Atlantic or the Pacific. It was actually formed when a huge block of land dropped between two fault lines; the depression then filled with water.

Then, ichthyologists decided to tag sharks with electronic tracking devices. It wasn't long before sharks tagged in the Caribbean turned up in Lago de Nicaragua, and vice versa. Incredibly, the sharks are indeed able to negotiate the rapids and move between lake and sea.

Miguel, the hamlet of La Virgen is the setting for several nature-related sites of interest, including the **Snake Garden** (tel. 506/2761-1059, snakegarden1@costaricense.co.cr, 9am-5pm daily, adults $15, students and children $10), which exhibits some 70 species of snakes, plus iguanas, turtles, and other reptiles. It also has night tours.

Hacienda Pozo Azul (tel. 506/2438-2616, U.S. tel. 877-810-6903, www.pozoazul.com), at La Virgen, raises Holstein cattle and doubles as an activity center offering horseback rides ($42-50), white-water trips ($58-84), a canopy tour ($53), river-canyon rappelling (from $40), and guided hikes ($27). A full-day, all-activity program costs $110, including transfers from San José.

Finca Corsicana (tel. 506/2761-1052, www.collinstreet.com/pages/finca_corsicana_home) offers two-hour tours of its organic pineapple farm (8am, 10am, noon, and 2pm daily, $15) at Llano Grande, seven kilometers (4.5 miles) northwest of La Virgen. It claims to be the largest such farm in the world.

Sarapiquí Eco-Observatory

Photographing birds is like shooting fish in a barrel at **Sarapiquí Eco-Observatory** (tel. 506/2761-0801 or 506/8346-7088, www.sarapiquieco-observatory.com, 7am-5pm daily, self-guided tour $20 adults, $10 children), a lodge at the edge of the Tirimbina Rainforest Reserve at La Virgen de Sarapiquí. Dedicated to birding, the lodge has a long shaded balcony and a second observation deck set up with scopes and feeders. Trails lead down through the rainforest to the river. Your bilingual host, David Lando Ramírez, is a font of knowledge, and a resident professional photographer offers photography workshops. Guided tours ($30) include nighttime walks. Tree-planting ($30) is a popular activity, as David and his dad also have a reforestation project with four types of habitats.

Sarapiquís Rainforest Lodge

Sarapiquís Rainforest Lodge (tel. 506/2761-1004, www.sarapiquis.com), formerly Centro Neotrópico Sarapiquís, on the banks of Río Sarapiquí about one kilometer (0.6 miles) north of La Virgen, is sponsored by the Belgian nonprofit Landscape Foundation and serves as a scientific research and educational center as well as an eco-lodge.

The **Museum of Indigenous Culture** (9am-5pm daily), with more than 400 pre-Columbian artifacts and a 60-seat movie theater, is a focal point of the center. There's an archaeological dig—**Alma Alta Archaeological Park**—of four indigenous tombs dating from 800 BC to AD 155, plus a reconstruction of an indigenous village. A farm grows fruits and vegetables based on ecological farming practices. There's an astronomical observatory, and you can wander the trails though **Chester's Field Botanical Garden,** with about 500 native species.

Visitors are welcomed on either of two mandatory tours led by indigenous guides ($15-20), providing an in-depth insight into Costa Rica's indigenous culture, including a display of pottery-making.

Tirimbina Rainforest Reserve

A 250-meter-long (820-foot-long) canopied bridge leads across the river gorge and into the **Tirimbina Rainforest Reserve** (tel. 506/2761-0333, www.tirimbina.org, 7am-5pm daily), adjoining Sarapiquís Rainforest Lodge. It has eight kilometers (5 miles) of trails, with suspension bridges and a 110-meter (360-foot) canopy walkway. A museum portrays life in the forest. Nature walks cost $15 self-guided, $25 guided, and there's also a World of Bats night walk ($22), a chocolate tour ($27), and bird-watching ($25). Students and children get discounts. Tirimbina hosts researchers and offers accommodations, from bunk rooms to private air-conditioned rooms.

★ Selva Verde

Selva Verde (tel. 506/2761-1800, U.S. tel. 800-451-7111, www.selvaverde.com, 7am-3pm daily, $5, free to hotel guests), on the banks of the Río Sarapiquí, about one kilometer (0.6 miles) east of Chilamate and eight kilometers (5 miles) west of Puerto Viejo, is a private reserve protecting some 192 hectares (474 acres) of primary rainforest adjacent to Parque Nacional Braulio Carrillo. At its heart is an internationally acclaimed nature lodge and the **Sarapiquí Conservation Learning Center** (Centro de Enseñanza), with a lecture room and a library. The reserve is renowned

for its birdlife, and it has a small butterfly garden. Trails lead through the forests (poison dart frogs abound), and the lodge has naturalist guides. Guided hiking is available (2 hours adults $22, children $11), including by night (adults $20, children $10), plus the reserve offers a wildlife boat ride (adults $30, children $15).

Recreation

The area is popular for waterborne nature-viewing or fishing trips on the Río Sarapiquí, as well as white-water rafting and kayaking. The most popular put-in point is at La Virgen, with Class II and III rapids below. A second put-in point is Chilamate, offering more gentle Class I and II floats. Companies that offer tours include **Costa Rica Expeditions** (tel. 506/2257-0766, www.costaricaexpeditions. com) and **Ríos Tropicales** (tel. 506/2233-6455, www.riostropicales.com). **Aguas Bravas** (tel. 506/2766-6524 or 506/2296-2072, www.aguasbravascr.com), at Chilamate, also specializes in white-water trips ($60) and has bird-watching tours, horseback riding, and other adventures.

You can explore the rainforest canopy at the **Sarapiquí Canopy Tour** (tel. 506/2290-6015, www.crfunadventures.com), which has 15 platforms, a suspension bridge, and one kilometer (0.6 miles) of zip line. It has a full-day nature-viewing river trip and canopy tour combo ($95).

Accommodations

Want to really feel as one with nature? **Hacienda Pozo Azul** (tel. 506/2761-1360, www.pozoazul.com, $80 s, $92 d, including breakfast), at La Virgen, makes it easy with its 30 roomy four-person tent-suites under tarps on raised platforms in the forest. Clean, well-maintained shared baths have hot water. There's even Wi-Fi. The hacienda also has **Magasay Jungle Lodge** ($60 s, $96 d, including all meals), bordering Parque Nacional Braulio Carrillo. This wooden lodge has 10 rooms with bunks, plus solar power and hot showers.

Perfect for birders, ★ Selva Verde (tel. 506/2766-6800, U.S. tel. 800-451-7111, www. selvaverde.com, low season $99-142 s, $117-205 d, high season $116-165 s, $134-225 d, including breakfast) has a 45-room lodge set in eight hectares (20 acres) of lush gardens and forest on the banks of the Río Sarapiquí, about one kilometer (0.6 miles) east of Chilamate. Thatched walkways lead between the spacious and airy hardwood cabins raised on stilts. Choose cabins with private baths at the River Lodge, or rooms with shared baths at the Creek Lodge; all are simply furnished and have ceiling fans, two single beds, screened windows, large baths with piping-hot water, and verandas with hammocks and rockers. Five more upscale bungalow rooms are air-conditioned. There's a swimming pool, and meals are served buffet-style. Selva Verde is popular with groups; book well in advance.

The Sarapiquí Rainforest Lodge (tel. 506/2761-1004, U.S./Canada tel. 866-581-0782, www.sarapiquis.org, $105 s/d year-round), one kilometer (0.6 miles) north of La Virgen, is centered on a thatched eco-lodge in pleasing ocher yellow and sienna. Each of three units has eight "deluxe" rooms shaped like pie slices arrayed in a circle around an atrium. There are 16 rooms in an adjunct wing. All feature lively fabrics, handmade furniture, natural stone floors, fans, large walk-in showers, and Wi-Fi. Eight rooms are air-conditioned. Although they lack windows, a glass door opens to a wraparound veranda overlooking the gardens or river. There's a splendid restaurant.

Food

If traveling the Vara Blanca-San Miguel route, do stop at Soda Galería de Colibrí (7am-5pm daily), which is all that remains of the former village of Cinchona, destroyed by the 2009 earthquake. The owner lost his entire family yet clings on. His simple *soda* serves typical Costa Rican dishes, including *cuajada,* homemade cheese in a tortilla wrap.

The restaurant at Selva Verde (7am-8pm daily, $10-15), about one kilometer (0.6 miles)

east of Chilamate, is open to nonguests, so pop in for filling and tasty home-style Costa Rican cooking. The elegant El Sereno Restaurant (7am-10pm daily), at Centro Neotrópico Sarapiquís, one kilometer (0.6 miles) north of La Virgen, offers gourmet dining.

Getting There

Buses (tel. 506/2257-6859) depart the Gran Terminal Caribe in San José 10 times 6:30am-6:30pm daily, via Puerto Viejo de Sarapiquí. Buses also connect San Miguel to La Fortuna.

EASTERN ROUTE VIA EL CRUCE AND HORQUETAS

The heavily trafficked eastern route between San José and Puerto Viejo de Sarapiquí traverses the saddle between the Barva and Irazú volcanoes via Highway 32 (Guápiles Hwy.), dropping down through Parque Nacional Braulio Carrillo and then north via Horquetas. At the base of the mountains, at El Cruce, is the junction with Highway 4, which runs due north for 34 kilometers (21 miles) to Puerto Viejo.

The only village between El Cruce and Puerto Viejo is Horquetas, exactly midway between the two. Horquetas is home to the Jardín Ecológico Pierella (tel. 506/8752-9154, www.pierella.com, by appointment, $15), a butterfly breeding center set in a manicured garden. Visitors also get to see animals such as peccaries, agoutis, and toucans. María Luz Jiménez gives a splendid 20-minute tour of her *palmito* plantation at Palmitours (tel. 506/2764-1495, tourpalmito@gmail.com, 9am-5pm daily, $35, including lunch), about five kilometers (3 miles) south of La Selva. Her roadside restaurant serves all things made of *palmito,* including a delicious lasagna, pancakes, ceviche, and muffins.

Isla Las Heliconias

Isla Las Heliconias (Heliconia Island, tel. 506/2764-5220, www.heliconiaisland.com, self-guided tour $12, guided tour $18), about five kilometers (3 miles) north of Horquetas, is indeed an island-turned-heliconia garden, created with an artist's eye and lovingly tended by naturalist Tim Ryan and now tended by Dutch owners Henk and Carolien Peters-van Duijnhoven. The exquisite garden was started in 1992 and today boasts about 80 species of heliconia, plus ginger and other plants, shaded by almond trees in which green macaws nest. The garden also includes palms, orchids, and bamboo from around the world. Needless to say, birds abound.

Nearby, **Frog's Heaven** (tel. 506/8891-8589, 8am-8pm daily, $35) is another tropical garden, this one a habitat for two dozen or so frog species to hop around or be discovered hiding beneath a leaf. Guided tours are offered by owner José.

Rara Avis

Rara Avis (tel. 506/2764-1111, www.rara-avis.com), a 1,280-hectare (3,163-acre) rainforest reserve abutting Parque Nacional Braulio Carrillo, 15 kilometers (9.5 miles) west of Horquetas, is one of the original sustainable projects in the country. It hosts a biological research station and several novel projects designed to show that a rainforest can be economically viable if left intact, not cut down. Projects include ecotourism and producing exportable orchids and philodendrons for wicker. There's a butterfly farm and an orchid garden. More than 360 bird species inhabit the reserve, along with jaguars, tapirs, monkeys, anteaters, coatimundis, and butterflies galore.

Visitors can view the canopy from two platforms ($35, including 2-hour guided hike), including one at the foot of a spectacular double waterfall: Rara Avis gets up to 550 centimeters (217 inches) of rain per year and has no dry months. The trails range from easy to difficult. Rubber boots are recommended (the lodge has boots to lend for those with U.S. shoe sizes 12 or smaller). Guided walks include night tours ($15).

Most people consider the experience of getting to Rara Avis part of the fun; others have stated that no reward is worth three hours of bumping around on the back of a canopied tractor-pulled trailer. Even the tractor (which leaves Horquetas at 9am) sometimes gets stuck. Rara Avis is not a place for a day visit, and a two-night minimum stay is required.

Rara Avis has two accommodations options. **Waterfall Lodge** ($84 s, $160 d) features eight rooms, each with a private bathtub with hot water and a wraparound balcony with great views. You can also opt for one of four simple two-room cabins with bunks ($70

welcome sign at Isla Las Heliconias, near Horquetas

Following the Great Green Macaw

The **Bird Route** (www.costaricanbirdroute.com), launched in 2010 to promote ecotourism, offers four bird-watching itineraries centered on 15 nature reserves that together are home to more than 500 bird species. The reserves encompass a wide range of habitats. The prime focus is on the Sarapiquí-San Carlos region, centered on Puerto Viejo de Sarapiquí and Los Chiles. This is one of the last remaining habitats of the endangered great green macaw (one of the four itineraries is called "On the Trail of the Great Green Macaw"). The idea behind this is to promote bird-watching as a stimulus to conserve bird habitat, not least by providing income for local landowners and communities. You can purchase a map ($13) online and explore on your own, but I highly recommend hiring a guide, which you can also book online.

s, $150 d). Reservations are essential. Rates include meals.

★ La Selva Biological Station

One of Costa Rica's premier birding sites, **Estación Biológica La Selva** (tel. 506/2766-6565, www.ots.ac.cr), four kilometers (2.5 miles) south of Puerto Viejo, is a biological research station run by the Organization of Tropical Studies (OTS). The station is centered on a 1,500-hectare (3,700-acre) reserve—mostly premontane rainforest but with varied habitats—linked to the northern extension of Parque Nacional Braulio Carrillo. More than 420 bird species have been identified here, as have more than 500 species of butterflies, 120 species of mammals, and 55 species of snakes. The arboretum displays more than 1,000 tree species.

Almost 60 kilometers (37 miles) of trails snake through the reserve. Some have boardwalks; others are no more than muddy pathways. Rubber boots or waterproof hiking boots are essential, as is rain gear. Guided nature walks ($30-40) are offered at 8am and 1:30pm daily, and an early-bird bird-watching tour ($30) departs at 5:30am. Visitors who overnight can take a nocturnal tour ($40). You cannot explore alone, and only 65 people at a time are allowed in the reserve; nonscientists are restricted to certain trails. Still, the wildlife viewing is phenomenal. On

Welcome to La Selva Biological Station.

two recent visits, I photographed peccaries almost within reach, plus saw lots of poison dart frogs, snakes, crocodiles, and several great curassows. It is often booked solid months in advance. Reservations are required.

You can even overnight in comfortable dormitory-style accommodations (reservations c/o OTS, tel. 506/2524-0627, $98 s, $194 d, including meals, tax, and guided hike) with four bunks per room and communal baths; some are wheelchair-accessible. Meals are served right on time, and latecomers get the crumbs.

The OTS operates a shuttle van from San José ($10) on Monday, space permitting (researchers and students have priority), and between La Selva and Puerto Viejo Monday-Saturday. **Transporte Caribe** (tel. 506/2221-7990) buses from San José will drop you off at the entrance, from where you'll need to walk two kilometers (1.2 miles) to La Selva.

Accommodations and Food

Farm-style rusticity rules at **Hotel Sueño Azul** (tel. 506/2764-1000, www.suenoazulresort.com, $90-142 s/d year-round), two miles northwest of Horquetas. Rattan and bamboo features enhance the 55 simply appointed rooms; suites have outdoor whirlpool tubs. There's a lagoon and trails into the adjacent forest, plus horseback riding, a canopy tour, a rodeo, a folkloric evening, and even a full-service spa and yoga studio. The highlight, though, is a delightful rustic restaurant occupying a former cattle corral (7am-10pm daily), overlooking a free-form pool with a cascade. It's adorned with saddles and farm implements hanging from the dark wood-beamed ceiling; it serves *típico* dishes.

Belgian expat Jean-Pierre Knockeart plays congenial host at the 19-room ★ **Hacienda La Isla** (tel. 506/2764-2576, www.haciendalaisla.com, low season standard $109 s/d, suite $146 s/d, high season standard $126 s/d, suite $165 s/d, including tax), a boutique hotel three kilometers (2 miles) north of El Cruce. Themed to Costa Rica's colonial past, this former hacienda exudes the feel of yesteryear and is set amid orchards and lush gardens. The rooms and one suite are exquisitely furnished, with hardwood pieces and ocher color schemes. The restaurant delivers gourmet fusion cuisine. It has rainforest trails, and horseback riding is a specialty.

Getting There

Empresario Guapileños (tel. 506/2222-2727 or 506/2257-6859) buses depart the Gran Terminal Caribe in San José (2 hours, $2) 10

peccary at La Selva Biological Station

Whose River Is It?

Nicaragua has disputed Costa Rica's territorial rights to free use of the Río San Juan, while Costa Rica disputes Nicaragua's claim that the river is entirely Nicaraguan territory. The 205-kilometer-long (127-mile-long) river, which flows from Lago de Nicaragua to the Caribbean, marks most of the border between these countries. When you are on the water, you are inside Nicaragua.

Costa Ricans have had right of commercial use of the Río San Juan, but since 2001 Nicaraguan authorities have boarded Costa Rican boats and fined foreigners aboard ($25) for using the river without Nicaraguan visas. This has primarily affected sportfishing boats from Costa Rican lodges in Barra del Colorado, and tour boats and water taxis operating from Los Chiles.

In 2009 the International Court of Justice adjudicated on access rights to the river. Essentially it reaffirmed an 1858 treaty that acknowledged Nicaragua's ownership of the river while guaranteeing Costa Ricans free access. The important proviso was that non-Costa Rican passengers aboard Costa Rican vessels using the river are not required to obtain Nicaraguan visas. Both countries accepted the verdict, which also granted Nicaragua the right to build an interoceanic canal if it compensated Costa Rica for the damage. However, Costa Rica's militarized police force will no longer be permitted to patrol the river, which is also an avenue for drug trafficking. The two nations actually came to blows over this issue in 1998. The ruling paved the way for increased tourism along the river, which is bordered by the Refugio de Vida Silvestre Corredor Fronterizo (Frontier Corridor National Wildlife Refuge).

Just as the dust settled, in November 2010, Nicaragua's leftist president, Daniel Ortega, decided to fan the nationalist flames by accusing Costa Rica of wanting to seize the river. This came after Costa Rica appealed to the Organization of American States (OAS) to intervene after Nicaraguan dredging of the river intruded onto Isla Calero, in Costa Rican territory, and Nicaraguan troops occupied Costa Rican soil.

times 6:30am-6:30pm daily via the Guápiles Highway and Horquetas (do not take the Puerto Viejo de Talamanca bus—you want Puerto Viejo de Sarapiquís).

To get to Rara Avis in time, you will need to take the 6:30am bus from San José. This will drop you at Horquetas in time for the tractor-hauled transfer to Rara Avis from Horquetas at 9am daily. If driving, you can leave your car in a parking lot at the Rara Avis office in Horquetas. Later arrivals can rent horses ($35) for the four-hour ride, but not after 2pm.

FRONTIER CORRIDOR NATIONAL WILDLIFE REFUGE

The **Refugio Nacional de Vida Silvestre Corredor Fronterizo** (www.sinac.go.cr) extends for a width of two kilometers (1.2 miles) along the entire border with Nicaragua, coast to coast. Boats ply the Río San Juan, connecting Puerto Viejo de Sarapiquí with Barra del Colorado and Tortuguero (and west with San Carlos in Nicaragua). The nature-viewing is fantastic, with birds galore, monkeys and sloths in the trees along the riverbank, and crocodiles and caimans poking their nostrils and eyes above the water.

You can even visit **El Castillo de la Inmaculada Concepción,** built by the Spanish in 1675 on a hill dominating the river and intended to repel pirates and English invaders. The ruins are in Nicaragua, three kilometers (2 miles) west of where the Costa Rican border moves south of the river (you'll need your passport).

The transborder park was created in 1985, when Nicaraguan president Daniel Ortega seized on the idea as a way to demilitarize the area, at the time being used by anti-Sandinista rebels. Ortega proposed the region be declared an international park for peace and gave it the name Sí-a-Paz—Yes to Peace. Efforts by the Arias administration to kick the rebels out of Costa Rica's northern zone led to demilitarization of the area, but lack of funding and political difficulties prevented the two countries from making much progress. The end of the Nicaraguan war in 1990 allowed the governments to dedicate more money to the project, encompassing heavily logged and denuded terrain between the Ríos Sarapiquí and San Carlos and extending northward from Parque Nacional Braulio Carrillo to the Reserva Biológica Indio Maíz, which protects nearly 500,000 hectares (1.2 million acres) of rainforest in the southeast corner of Nicaragua.

In 2003 the efforts led to formalization of the boundaries of the 30,000-hectare (74,000-acre) **Refugio Nacional de Vida Silvestre Maquenque** (www.sinac.go.cr), a vast wildlife refuge that incorporates several disparate ecosystems and reserves linking the Corredor Fronterizo reserve with the Corredor Ecológico San Juan-La Selva (San Juan-La Selva Biological Corridor), covering 340,000 hectares (840,000 acres) and 29 protected areas, including Parque Nacional Tortuguero and the Barra del Colorado reserve.

Maquenque incorporates Humedal Lacustrino de Tamborcito, a wetland reserve that is prime habitat for manatees and tapirs; and **Laguna del Lagarto** (tel. 506/2289-8163, www.lagarto-lodge-costa-rica.com),

a private reserve that protects 500 hectares (1,240 acres) of virgin rainforest and bayou swamps harboring crocodiles, caimans, turtles, and poison dart frogs, along with ocelots, sloths, and all kinds of colorful bird species, including the rare green macaw. Laguna del Lagarto also has a butterfly garden, forest trails for hiking, and horseback rides ($20 for 2 hours). Four-hour boat trips on the San Carlos and San Juan Rivers cost $26 pp (minimum 4 people). It offers transfers from San José and can be reached by road via the hamlet of Boca Topada—the gateway—from Aguas Zarcasa.

Accommodations and Food

Perfect for nature lovers, the delightfully rustic **Laguna del Lagarto Lodge** (tel. 506/2289-8163, www.lagarto-lodge-costa-rica.com, low season $45 s, $60 d, high season $51 s, $75 d) offers 20 comfortable rooms in two buildings (18 with private baths, 2 with a shared bath, and all with hot water). Each has a large terrace with a view overlooking the Río San Carlos and the forest. A restaurant serves hearty Costa Rican buffet meals and arranges transfers.

A virtual clone, **Maquenque Eco-Lodge** (tel. 506/2479-8200, www.maquenqueecolodge.com, low season $91 s, $113 d,

water taxis on the Río Sarapiquí, at Puerto Viejo de Sarapiquí

high season $101 s, $125 d) also has delight-ful cabins overlooking a lagoon at the heart of its own 60-hectare (148-acre) reserve. It has eight kilometers (5 miles) of trails for hiking and horseback riding, plus canoe trips (www.canoa-aventura.com).

Information

The **Ministro de Ambiente y Energía** (Ministry of Environment and Energy, tel. 506/2471-2191, refugio.fronterizo@sinac.co.cr, 8am-4pm Wed. and Fri. only), in Los Chiles, has responsibility for administering the wild-life refuge; call or visit for information.

Getting There

A **water taxi** ($5) departs the dock in Puerto Viejo at 1:30pm for Trinidad (on the east bank of the Río Sarapiquí at its junction with the Río San Juan). Water taxis are also for hire, from slender motorized canoes to canopied tour boats for 8-20 passengers. Trips cost

about $10 per hour for up to five people. A full-day trip to the Río San Juan and back costs from $100 per boat. Expect to pay $500 for a charter boat (for up to 20 people) all the way down the Río San Juan to Barra del Colorado and Tortuguero.

Oasis Nature Tours (tel. 506/2766-6260, www.oasisnaturetours.com) offers boat trips to El Castillo and into Nicaragua.

By road, Refugio Nacional de Vida Silvestre Maquenque can be reached via the agricultural town of Pital, about six kilo-meters (4 miles) northeast of Aguas Zarcas. A road leads due north from Pital via Boca Topada to Laguna del Lagarto. **Buses** (tel. 506/2258-8914) for Pital depart San José from Calle 12, Avenidas 7/9, four times daily 7:40am-7:30pm; and from Ciudad Quesada hourly 5:30am-9:30pm daily. From Pital, buses run to Boca Topada at 9am and 4:30pm daily; return buses depart Pital at 5am and noon daily.

Guanacaste and the Northwest

Guanacaste has been called Costa Rica's Wild West. The name Guanacaste derives from *quahnacaztlan,* a word from an indigenous language meaning "place near the ear trees," for the tall and broad *guanacaste* (free ear or ear pod) tree that spreads its gnarled branches long and low to the ground; during the hot summer, all that walks, crawls, or flies gathers in its cool shade in the heat of midday.

The lowlands to the west are a vast alluvial plain of seasonally parched rolling hills broadening to the north and dominated by giant cattle ranches interspersed with smaller pockets of cultivation. To the east rises a mountain meniscus—the Cordillera de Guanacaste and Cordillera de Tilarán—studded with symmetrical volcanic cones spiced with bubbling mud pits and steaming vents. These mountains are lushly forested on their higher slopes. Rivers cascade down the flanks, slow to a meandering pace, and pour into the Tempisque basin, an unusually arid region smothered by dry forest and cut through by watery sloughs. The coast is indented with bays, peninsulas, and warm sandy beaches that are some of the least visited, least accessible, and yet most beautiful in the country. Sea turtles use many as nurseries.

The country's first national park, Santa Rosa, was established here, the first of more than a dozen national parks, wildlife refuges, and biological reserves in the region. The array of ecosystems in the region ranges from pristine shores to volcanic heights, encompassing just about every imaginable ecosystem within Costa Rica.

No region of Costa Rica displays its cultural heritage as overtly as Guanacaste, whose distinct flavor owes much to the blending of Spanish and indigenous Chorotega cultures. The people who today inhabit the province are tied to old bloodlines and live and work on the cusp between cultures. Today one can still see deeply bronzed wide-set faces and pockets of Chorotega life.

Costa Rica's national costume and music emanate from this region, as does the *punto guanacasteco,* the country's official dance.

Previous: colonial-era architecture, Puntarenas; Monteverde Cloud Forest Reserve. **Above:** three-toed sloth, Monteverde.

Look for ★ to find recommended
sights, activities, dining, and lodging.

Highlights

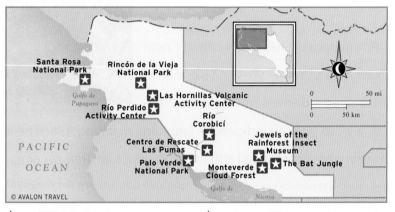

★ **Monteverde Cloud Forest:** This world-famous biological reserve is laced by fabulous nature trails for viewing quetzals and other wildlife (page 255).

★ **Jewels of the Rainforest Insect Museum:** This private insect collection is one of the nation's preeminent nature displays (page 260).

★ **The Bat Jungle:** Everything you learn about these amazing and ecologically imperative flying mammals will give you a whole new respect for them (page 261).

★ **Centro de Rescate Las Pumas:** At this rescue center, you're guaranteed eyeball-to-eyeball encounters with all the big cats you're unlikely to see in the wild (page 272).

★ **Río Corobicí:** A float trip on this relatively calm river is fun for the whole family (page 272).

★ **Las Hornillas Volcanic Activity Center:** This active walk-through crater has therapeutic mud pools you can actually bathe in (page 274).

★ **Río Perdido Activity Center:** This activity center on the lower slopes of Volcán Miravalles guarantees plenty of thrills, plus a sensational restaurant and spa (page 274).

★ **Palo Verde National Park:** Bird-watching par excellence is the name of the game at this watery world best explored by boat (page 275).

★ **Rincón de la Vieja National Park:** Magnificent scenery, bubbling mud pools, and trails to the volcano's summit are highlights of this national park (page 282).

★ **Santa Rosa National Park:** The finest of the dry-forest reserves offers unrivaled wildlife-viewing and top-notch surfing (page 286).

The region's heritage can still be traced in the creation of clay pottery and figurines. The campesino life here revolves around the ranch, and dark-skinned *sabaneros* (cowboys) are a common sight. Come fiesta time, nothing rouses so much cheer as the *corridas de toros* (bullfights) and *topes*, the region's colorful horse parades. Guanacastecans love a fiesta: The biggest occurs each July 25, when Guanacaste celebrates its independence from Nicaragua.

Guanacaste's climate is in contrast to the rest of the country. The province averages less than 162 centimeters (64 inches) of rain per year, though regional variation is extreme. For half the year (Nov.-Apr.) the plains receive no rain, it is hotter than Hades, and the sun beats down hard as a nail, although cool winds bearing down from northern latitudes can lower temperatures pleasantly along the coast December-February. The dry season usually lingers slightly longer than elsewhere in Costa Rica. The Tempisque basin is the country's driest region and receives less than 45 centimeters (18 inches) of rain in years of drought, mostly in a few torrential downpours during the six-month rainy season. The mountain slopes receive much more rain, noticeably on the eastern slopes, which are cloud-draped and deluged for much of the year.

PLANNING YOUR TIME

Guanacaste is a large region; its numerous attractions are spread out, and getting between any two major areas can eat up the better part of a day. The region is diverse enough to justify exploring it in its entirety, for which you should budget no less than one week. Monteverde alone requires a minimum of two days, and ideally three or four, to take advantage of all that it offers. Nor would you want to rush exploring Parque Nacional Rincón de la Vieja, requiring two or three nights.

The Pan-American Highway (Hwy. 1) cuts through the heart of lowland Guanacaste, ruler-straight almost all the way between the Nicaraguan border in the north and Puntarenas in the south. Juggernaut trucks frequent the fast-paced and potholed road, which since 2013 is now two lanes in both directions for most of its length. Drive cautiously! North of Liberia, the route is superbly scenic. Almost every sight of importance lies within a short distance of the highway, accessed by dirt side roads. If traveling by bus, sit on the east-facing side for the best views.

Touristy it might be, but Monteverde, the biggest draw, delivers in heaps. Its numerous attractions include canopy tours, horseback riding, and art galleries along with orchid, snake, frog, and butterfly exhibits, but most famous are its several cloud-forest reserves.

Recent years have seen a boost in regional tourism following expansion of the international airport at Liberia, now served with direct flights by most large U.S. carriers. The airport is well served by car rental companies. The town of Liberia is a gateway to both the Nicoya Peninsula and Parque Nacional Rincón de la Vieja, popular for hikes to the summit and for horseback rides and canopy tours from nature lodges outside the park. Liberia makes a good base for forays farther afield.

The Cámara de Turismo Guanacasteca (Guanacaste Chamber of Tourism, tel. 506/2690-9501, www.letsgoguanacaste.com), is a good resource.

Guanacaste and the Northwest

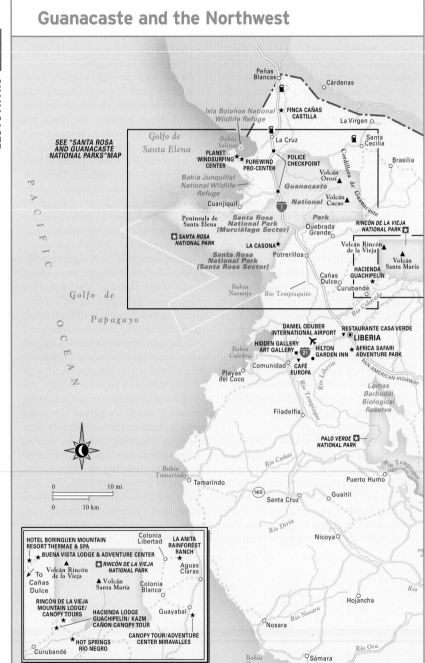

Peñas Blancas

Cárdenas

Isla Bolaños National Wildlife Refuge

★ FINCA CAÑAS CASTILLA

La Virgen

Golfo de
Santa Elena

La Cruz

Santa Cecilia

Bahía Salinas

Brasilia

PLANET WINDSURFING CENTER ★★ **PUREWIND PRO-CENTER**

POLICE CHECKPOINT

Volcán Orosí ▲

Cordillera de Guanacaste

Bahía Junquillal National Wildlife Refuge

Guanacaste

Volcán Cacao ▲

P A C I F I C

Cuanjiquil

National

Park

RINCÓN DE LA VIEJA NATIONAL PARK ★

Peninsula de Santa Elena

Santa Rosa National Park (Murciélago Sector)

Quebrada Grande

Volcán Rincón de la Vieja ▲

★ **SANTA ROSA NATIONAL PARK**

LA CASONA★

Potrerillos

Volcán Santa María

Santa Rosa National Park (Santa Rosa Sector)

Cañas Dulce

HACIENDA GUACHIPELÍN ★

Curubandé

Golfo de

Bahía Naranjo

Río Tempisquito

Río Colorado

Papagayo

DANIEL ODUBER INTERNATIONAL AIRPORT ✈

RESTAURANTE CASA VERDE
● **LIBERIA**

O C E A N

Bahía Culebra

HIDDEN GALLERY ART GALLERY ■

HILTON GARDEN INN

★ **AFRICA SAFARI ADVENTURE PARK**

Playas del Coco

Comunidad

CAFÉ EUROPA

Río Liberia

PAN-AMERICAN HIGHWAY

Río Tempisque

Lomas Barbudal Biological Reserve

Filadelfia

PALO VERDE ★ **NATIONAL PARK**

0 ———— 10 mi

0 ———— 10 km

Río Cañas

Río Tempisque

Puerto Humo

Bahía Tamarindo

Tamarindo

160

Santa Cruz

Guaitíl

Río Diriá

Nicoya

Río Tempisque

Hojancha

Río Nosara

Guayabal

Río

Nosara

Sámara

Río Ora

Bahía Garza

SEE "SANTA ROSA AND GUANACASTE NATIONAL PARKS" MAP

HOTEL BORINQUEN MOUNTAIN RESORT THERMAE & SPA
★ ★ **BUENA VISTA LODGE & ADVENTURE CENTER**

Colonia Libertad

LA ANITA RAINFOREST RANCH

To Cañas Dulce

Volcán Rincón de la Vieja

★ **RINCÓN DE LA VIEJA NATIONAL PARK**

Aguas Claras

▲ Volcán Santa María

RINCÓN DE LA VIEJA MOUNTAIN LODGE/ CANOPY TOURS ★

Colonia Blanca

★ **HACIENDA LODGE GUACHIPELÍN/ KAZM CAÑON CANOPY TOUR**

Guayabal

★ **HOT SPRINGS RÍO NEGRO**

CANOPY TOUR/ADVENTURE CENTER MIRAVALLES

Curubandé

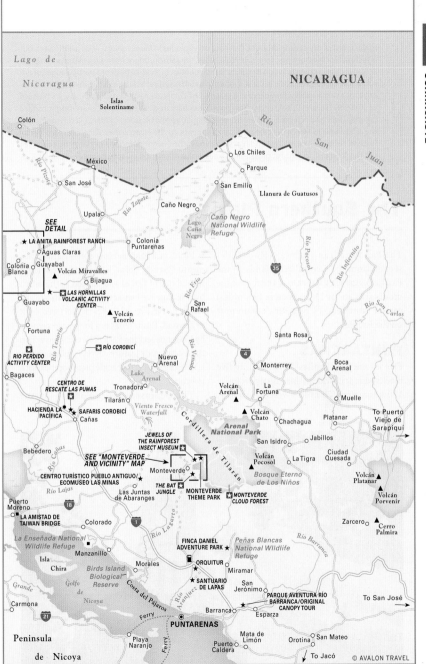

Lago de Nicaragua

NICARAGUA

Islas Solentiname

Colón

Río Pocosol

México

San José

Upala

Río Zapote

Los Chiles

Parque

San Emilio

Llanura de Guatusos

Caño Negro

Río San Juan

SEE DETAIL

★ LA ANITA RAINFOREST RANCH

Aguas Claras

Colonia Blanca Guayabal

Volcán Miravalles ▲

Bijagua

Guayabo

★ LAS HORNILLAS VOLCANIC ACTIVITY CENTER

Fortuna

▲ Volcán Tenorio

Colonia Puntarenas

Lago Caño Negro

Caño Negro National Wildlife Refuge

Río Pocosol

Río Infiernito

35

RÍO PERDIDO ACTIVITY CENTER

Bagaces

CENTRO DE RESCATE LAS PUMAS

Tronadora

HACIENDA LA PACÍFICA ★ SAFARIS COROBICÍ

Cañas

Tilarán

Viento Fresco Waterfall

Lake Arenal

Río Corobicí

Nuevo Arenal

San Rafael

Río Frío

Río Venado

Volcán Arenal ▲

La Fortuna

Santa Rosa

Monterrey

Boca Arenal

Muelle

To Puerto Viejo de Sarapiquí

Río San Carlos

4

Río Tenorio

Bebedero

Río Cañas

JEWELS OF THE RAINFOREST INSECT MUSEUM ★

SEE "MONTEVERDE AND VICINITY" MAP

CENTRO TURÍSTICO PUEBLO ANTIGUO/ ECOMUSEO LAS MINAS

Río Lajas

Puerto Moreno

LA AMISTAD DE TAIWAN BRIDGE

18

La Enseñada National Wildlife Refuge

Isla Chira

Grande

Golfo de Nicoya

Carmona

21

Peninsula de Nicoya

Cordillera de Tilarán

Monteverde

THE BAT JUNGLE

Las Juntas de Abaranges

Colorado

1

Río Lagarto

Manzanillo

Birds Island Biological Reserve

Morales

Costa del Pájaros

Playa Naranjo

Ferry

PUNTARENAS

Ferry

Arenal National Park

Volcán Chato ▲ Chachagua

San Isidro Jabillos

Volcán Pocosol La Tigra

Bosque Eterno de Los Niños

MONTEVERDE THEME PARK MONTEVERDE CLOUD FOREST

FINCA DANIEL ADVENTURE PARK ★

ORQUITUR

★ SANTUARIO DE LAPAS

Miramar

San Jerónimo

Barranca

Puerto Caldera

Mata de Limón

Peñas Blancas National Wildlife Refuge

Río Barranca

Platanar

Ciudad Quesada

Volcán Platanar ▲

Volcán Porvenir ▲

Zarcero Cerro Palmira

To San José

PARQUE AVENTURA RÍO BARRANCA/ORIGINAL CANOPY TOUR

Esparza

Orotina San Mateo

To Jacó

Río Aranjuez

© AVALON TRAVEL

A Palette in Bloom

In the midst of dry-season drought, Guanacaste explodes in Monet colors—not wildflowers, but a Technicolor blossoming of trees. In November, the saffron-bright flowering of the *guachipelín* sets in motion a chain reaction that lasts for six months. Individual trees of a particular genus are somehow keyed to explode in unison, often in a climax lasting as little as a day. Two or three bouquets of a single species may occur in a season. The colors are never static. In January, it's the turn of pink *poui* (savannah oak) and yellow *poui* (black bark tree). By February, canary-bright *corteza amarillo* (*Tabebuia ochracea*) and the trumpet-shaped yellow blossoms of *Tabebuia chrysantha* dot the landscape. In March delicate pink *curao* appears. As the *curao* wanes, *Tabebuia rosea* bursts forth in subtle pinks, whites, and lilacs. The *malinche*—royal poinciana or flame tree—closes out the six-month parade of blossoming trees with a dramatic display as bright as red lipstick.

The Southern Plains

The Pan-American Highway (Hwy. 1) descends from the Central Highlands to the Pacific plains via **Esparza,** at the foot of the mountains about 15 kilometers (9.5 miles) east of Puntarenas, Costa Rica's main port on the Pacific.

PUNTARENAS

Five kilometers (3 miles) long but only five blocks wide at its widest, this sultry port town, 120 kilometers (75 miles) west of San José, is built on a long narrow spit—Puntarenas means "Sandy Point"—running west from the suburb of **Cocal** and backed to the north by a mangrove estuary; to the south are the Golfo de Nicoya and a beach cluttered with driftwood. Puntarenas has long been favored by Josefinos seeking R&R. The old wharves on the estuary side feature decrepit fishing boats leaning against ramshackle piers popular with pelicans.

The peninsula was colonized by the

Catedral de Puntarenas

Spaniards as early as 1522. The early port grew to prominence and was declared a free port in 1847, a year after completion of an oxcart road from the Meseta Central. Oxcarts laden with coffee made the lumbering descent to Puntarenas in convoys; the beans were shipped from here via Cape Horn to Europe. It remained the country's main port until the Atlantic Railroad to Limón, on the Caribbean coast, was completed in 1890 (the railroad between San José and Puntarenas would not be completed for another 20 years). Earlier this century, Puntarenas also developed a large conch-pearl fleet. Some 80 percent of Porteños, as the inhabitants of Puntarenas are called, still make their living from the sea.

The town's main usefulness is as the departure point for day cruises to islands in the Golfo de Nicoya and for the ferries to Playa Naranjo and Paquera, on the Nicoya Peninsula. Cruise ships berth at the terminal opposite Calle Central.

Sights

The tiny **Catedral de Puntarenas** (Ave. Central, Calles 5/7), built in 1902, abuts the renovated **Antigua Comandancia de la Plaza,** a fortress-style building complete with tiny battlements and bars on its windows. It once served as a barracks and a city jail. Today it houses the refurbished **Museo Histórico Marino** (tel. 506/2661-0387, 9:45am-noon and 1pm-5:15pm Tues.-Sun., free), a history museum that has exhibits on city life from the pre-Columbian and coffee eras. Adjacent is the **Casa de la Cultura** (tel. 506/2661-1394, 10am-4pm Mon.-Fri., free), with an art gallery that doubles as a venue for literary, musical, and artistic events.

Everything of importance seems to happen along the **Paseo de los Turistas,** a boulevard paralleling the Golfo de Nicoya and abuzz with vendors, beachcombers, and locals flirting and trying to keep cool in the water. The boulevard's beachfront park is studded with contemporary statues.

On the north side of the peninsula, the sheltered gulf shore—the estuary—is lined with fishing vessels in various states of decrepitude. Roseate spoonbills, storks, and other birds pick among the shallows.

Entertainment and Events

Every mid-July the city honors Carmen, Virgin of the Sea, in the annual **Festival Perla del Pacífico** (Sea Festival), a boating regatta with boats decorated in colorful flags and banners. The local Chinese community

cannon outside the Museo Histórico Marino, Puntarenas

Puntarenas

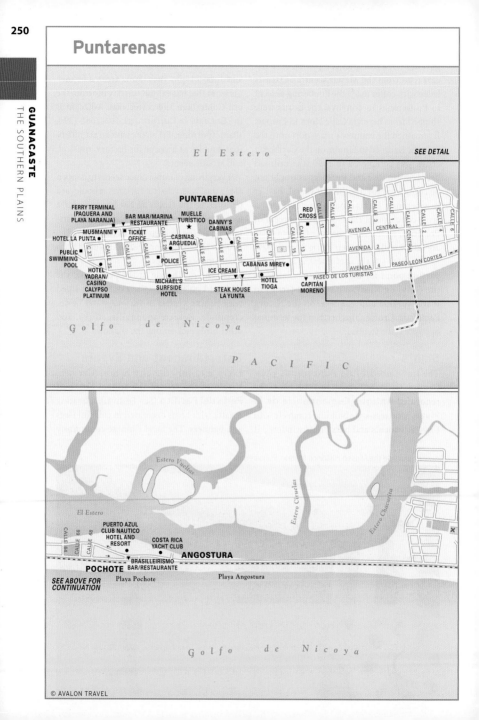

El Estero

SEE DETAIL

PUNTARENAS

FERRY TERMINAL
(PAQUERA AND
PLAYA NARANJA)

BAR MAR/MARINA
RESTAURANTE

MUELLE
TURÍSTICO

DANNY'S
CABINAS

RED
CROSS

HOTEL LA PUNTA

MUSMANNI

TICKET
OFFICE

CABINAS
ARGUEDIA

CALLE 7

CALLE 9

CALLE 11

CALLE 7

CALLE 5

CALLE 3

CALLE 1

CALLE CENTRAL

CALLE 2

CALLE 4

CALLE 6

AVENIDA CENTRAL

PUBLIC
SWIMMING
POOL

C. 37

CALLE 35

CALLE 33

CALLE 31

CALLE 29

CALLE 27

CALLE 25

CALLE 23

CALLE 21

CALLE 19

CALLE 17

CALLE 15

CALLE 13

AVENIDA 2

POLICE

ICE CREAM

CABANAS MIREY

AVENIDA 4

PASEO LEÓN CORTES

HOTEL
YADRAN/
CASINO
CALYPSO
PLATINUM

MICHAEL'S
SURFSIDE
HOTEL

STEAK HOUSE
LA YUNTA

HOTEL
TIOGA

CAPITÁN
MORENO

PASEO DE LOS TURISTAS

Golfo de Nicoya

PACIFIC

Estero Vueltas

Estero Ciruelas

Estero Chacarita

El Estero

CALLE 66

CALLE 68

CALLE 64

PUERTO AZUL
CLUB NAUTICO
HOTEL AND
RESORT

COSTA RICA
YACHT CLUB

ANGOSTURA

BRASILLEIRISMO
BAR/RESTAURANTE

POCHOTE

**SEE ABOVE FOR
CONTINUATION**

Playa Pochote

Playa Angostura

Golfo de Nicoya

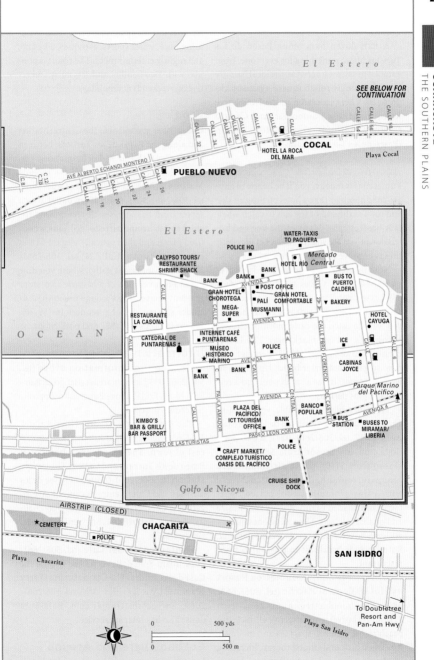

contributes dragon boats. In summer, concerts and plays are put on at the Casa de la Cultura.

A half-dozen bars along Paseo de los Turistas offers something for everyone, from karaoke to salsa. Otherwise, the local bars are overwhelmingly rough (guard against pickpockets). There's a casino in the Doubletree Resort by Hilton Puntarenas, and **Casino Calypso Platinum** is at the Hotel Yadran (Paseo de las Turistas, Calle 35).

Accommodations

Puntarenas is muggy; you'll be happy to have air-conditioning. Take a hotel on the gulf side and toward the end of the spit to catch whatever breezes exist. Many of the low-end hotels downtown are volatile refuges of ill repute; things improve west of downtown.

Now in French Canadian hands, **Hotel La Punta** (Ave. 1, Calles 35/37, tel. 506/2661-0696, www.hotellapunta.net, low season $60 s/d, high season $70 s/d) is a good choice if you want to catch the early-morning ferry to Nicoya; it's just one block away. The 12 air-conditioned rooms are pleasant enough and have spacious hot-water baths. Upper rooms have balconies. It has a small pool and a restaurant, plus parking.

The venerable, comfortable, yet undistinguished **Hotel Tioga** (Paseo de los Turistas, Aves. 15/17, tel. 506/2661-0271, www.hoteltioga.com, low season from $88 s/d, high season from $110) has 46 air-conditioned rooms surrounding a compact courtyard with a tiny swimming pool graced by its own palm-shaded island. Rooms vary in size and quality; all have TVs and phones but not all have hot water. There's secure parking. Rates include breakfast in the fourth-floor restaurant.

Perfect for families, **Doubletree Resort by Hilton Central Pacific** (tel. 506/2663-0808, http://doubletree1.hilton.com, from $218 all-inclusive) is an attractive all-inclusive beach resort with 230 spacious and modestly furnished air-conditioned rooms, including 87 junior suites and an opulent presidential suite, all with contemporary furnishings, including 27-inch flat-screen TVs. Heaps of facilities include an immense free-form swimming pool, water sports, activities, a casino, and nightly entertainment. The resort is popular with Tico families and gets noisy and active on weekends and holidays.

Food

Cheap *sodas* abound near the Central Market and along the Paseo de los Turistas, between Calles Central and 3. Recommended options along Paseo de los Turistas include **Matobe's** (Paseo de los Turistas, Calles 15/17, tel. 506/2661-3498, 11am-10pm daily), which serves fresh-baked pastas (I recommend the chicken fettuccine alfredo, $5) plus wood-fired pizza; and the rustically elegant **Steak House La Yunta** (Calle 21, tel. 506/2661-3216, 10am-midnight daily), where you dine on an open veranda of a historic two-story seafront house. It has a huge menu that includes shrimp, ceviche, tenderloin ($9-10), tongue in beet sauce ($8), and pork chops.

Information and Services

The city's **visitor information office** (tel. 506/2661-0337, ictpuntarenas@ict.go.cr, 8am-5pm Mon.-Fri.) is above Bancrédito, opposite the cruise-ship pier.

The **Monseñor Sanabria Hospital** (tel. 506/2630-8000) is eight kilometers (5 miles) east of town. There's a branch hospital at Paseo de los Turistas and Calle 9. The **police station** (tel. 506/2661-0740) is at Paseo de los Turistas and Calle Central; criminal investigation is handled by the **OIJ** (tel. 506/2630-0377). The **post office** is on Avenida 3, Calles Central/1.

Puntarenas Cyber Café (tel. 506/2661-4024, 10am-8pm daily) is tucked behind the Casa de la Cultura. The **Coonatramar ferry terminal** (Ave. 3, Calles 33/35, tel. 506/2661-1069, www.coonatramar.com, 8am-5pm daily) also has Internet service.

Getting There and Around

Empresarios Unidos (San José tel.

506/2222-8231, Puntarenas tel. 506/2661-3138) buses depart San José ($3) from Calle 16, Avenidas 10/12, every hour 6am-7pm daily. Buses also depart for Puntarenas from Monteverde (tel. 506/2645-5159) at 4:30am, 6am, and 3pm daily, and from Liberia (tel. 506/2663-1752) eight times 5am-3:30pm daily. Return buses depart the Puntarenas bus station (Calle 2, Paseo de los Turistas) for San José 4am-7pm daily; for Monteverde at 7:50am, 1:50pm, and 2:15pm daily; and Liberia 4:50am-8:30pm daily. **Interbus** (tel. 506/4100-0888, www.interbusonline.com) operates minibus shuttles from San José ($30) and popular tourist destinations in Nicoya and Guanacaste.

Buses ply Avenidas Central and 2. **Coopepuntarenas** (tel. 506/2663-1635) offers taxi service.

Car-and-passenger ferries for the Nicoya Peninsula leave the **Coonatramar ferry terminal** (Ave. 3, Calles 33/35, tel. 506/2661-9011, www.coonatramar.com, 8am-5pm daily). Buses marked "Ferry" operate along Avenida Central to the terminal ($2).

The **Costa Rica Yacht Club and Marina** (tel. 506/2661-0784, www.costaricayachtclub.com) has facilities for yachters.

COSTA DE PÁJAROS

At San Gerardo, on the Pan-American Highway, 40 kilometers (25 miles) north of Puntarenas, a paved road leads west to Punta Morales and the Golfo de Nicoya. There's fabulous bird-watching among the mangroves that line the shore—known as the Costa de Pájaros—stretching north to **Manzanillo,** the estuary of the Río Abangaritos, and beyond to the estuary of the Río Tempisque. The mangroves are home to ibis, herons, pelicans, parrots, egrets, and caimans. You can follow this coast road through cattle country to Highway 18, five kilometers (3 miles) east of the Tempisque bridge.

Refugio Nacional de Vida Silvestre La Enseñada (La Enseñada National Wildlife Refuge) is near Abangaritos, two kilometers (1.2 miles) north of Manzanillo, 17 kilometers (11 miles) from the Pan-American Highway. The 380-hectare (939-acre) wildlife refuge is part of a family-run cattle finca and salt farm, with nature trails and a lake replete with waterfowl and crocodiles.

The **Reserva Biológica Isla Pájaros** (Birds Island Biological Reserve) is about 600 meters (0.4 miles) offshore from Punta Morales. The 3.8-hectare (9.4-acre) reserve protects a colony of brown pelicans and other

cruise ship in Puntarenas

seabirds. Access is restricted to biological researchers.

A must-visit is **Santuario de Lapas el Manantial** (El Manantial Macaw Sanctuary, tel. 506/2661-5419 or 506/8823-2460, www.santuariolapas.com, 7am-5pm daily), a macaw-breeding center about six kilometers (4 miles) west of the Pan-American Highway at Aranjuez. Both scarlet and green macaws are raised here and fly free and unrestricted. There are also monkeys, tapirs, sloths, and other animals confiscated by the government from the illegal pet trade. Call ahead, as the entrance gate is usually locked.

Getting There
Buses depart Puntarenas for the Costa de Pájaros from Avenida Central, Calle 4.

LAS JUNTAS DE ABANGARES

Small it may be, but Las Juntas—at the base of the Cordillera Tilarán about 50 kilometers (31 miles) north of Esparza and six kilometers (4 miles) east of Highway 1 (the turnoff is at Km. 164, about 12 kilometers/7.5 miles north of the Río Lagarto and the turnoff for Monteverde)—figures big in the region's history. When gold was discovered in the nearby mountains in 1884, it sparked a gold rush. Hungry prospectors came from all over the world to sift the earth for nuggets, making Las Juntas a Wild West town. Inflated gold prices have lured many *oreros* (miners) back to the old mines and streams, and about 40 kilograms (88 pounds) of gold are recovered each week.

The *María Cristina,* a pint-size locomotive that sits in the town plaza, once hauled ore for the Abangares Gold Fields Company and dates from 1904. The *oreros* are honored with a **statue** in a triangular plaza on the northeast corner of town, which is splashed with colorful flowers and trim pastel-painted houses. A tree-lined main boulevard and streets paved with interlocking stones add to the orderliness.

If you're intrigued by this history, check out the **Ecomuseo Las Minas** (tel. 506/2662-0033, www.puebloantiguo.com, 8am-5pm Tues.-Fri., $5), displaying mining equipment at the entrance of an old mine. It is usually closed; call ahead to Centro Turístico Pueblo Antiguo (tel. 506/2662-0033), to which it belongs. It's near the hamlet of La Sierra, three kilometers (2 miles) east of Las Juntas. The center offers a Gold Mine Adventure down dank candlelit tunnels (helmets and flashlights provided, $20). **Mina Tours** (tel. 506/2662-0753, www.minatours.com) in Las Juntas also offers tours of a miners' cooperative; or book direct through the **Asociación Nacional de Mineros** (tel. 506/2662-0846), which has an office 500 meters (0.3 miles) east of town.

The road northeast from the triangular plaza leads into the Cordillera Tilarán via Candelaria and then (to the right) Monteverde or (to the left) Tilarán; a 4WD vehicle is recommended. In places the views are fantastic.

Getting There
Transportes Las Juntas (tel. 506/2258-5792 or 506/2695-5611) buses depart San José from Calle 14, Avenidas 1/3, at 10:45am and 5:30pm daily. Return buses to San José depart Las Juntas at 6:30am and 11:45pm daily. **Transportes Caribeños** (tel. 506/2669-1111) has a bus from Liberia at 4pm daily, returning at 5:30am daily.

Monteverde and Santa Elena

Monteverde, 35 kilometers (22 miles) north from the Pan-American Highway, means "Green Mountain," an appropriate name for one of the most idyllic pastoral settings in Costa Rica. Cows munch contentedly, and horse-drawn wagons loaded with milk cans still make the rounds in this world-famous community atop a secluded 1,400-meter-high (4,600-foot-high) plateau in the Cordillera de Tilarán. Monteverde is actually a sprawling agricultural community; the Reserva Biológica Bosque Nuboso Monteverde (Monteverde Cloud Forest Biological Reserve), which is what most visitors come to see, is a few kilometers southeast and higher up. A growing number of attractions are found north of Santa Elena, the main village, which has its own cloud-forest reserve. The two reserves are at different elevations and have different fauna and flora.

The reserves are within the **Zona Protectora Arenal-Monteverde** (Arenal-Monteverde Protected Zone). Created in 1991, it encompasses more than 30,000 hectares (74,000 acres) extending down both the Caribbean and Pacific slopes of the Cordillera de Tilarán, passing through eight distinct ecological zones, most notably cloud forest at higher elevations. Wind-battered elfin woods on exposed ridges are spectacularly dwarfed, whereas more protected areas have majestically tall trees festooned with orchids, bromeliads, ferns, and vines. Clouds sift through the forest primeval. February through May, quetzals are in the cloud forest. Later, they migrate downhill, where they can be seen around the hotels of Monteverde. Just after dawn is a good time to spot quetzals, which are particularly active in the early morning, especially in April and May.

The fame of the preserve has spawned an ever-increasing influx of tourists and a blossoming of attractions—the area is in danger of becoming overdeveloped and overpriced. The government's announcement, in 2013, that it would finally pave the road up to Monteverde will probably speed up the process.

ORIENTATION

The village of **Santa Elena** is the service center, with banks, stores, and bars. Populated by Tico families, Santa Elena is commonly considered to be Monteverde, although **Monteverde** proper is strung out along the road that leads up to the Reserva Biológica Bosque Nuboso Monteverde and is predominantly populated by the descendants of North American Quakers. Separating the two communities is the region of **Cerro Plano.**

★ MONTEVERDE CLOUD FOREST

The 14,200-hectare (35,090-acre) **Reserva Biológica Bosque Nuboso Monteverde** (Monteverde Cloud Forest Biological Reserve, tel. 506/2645-5122, www.reservamonteverde. com, 7am-4pm daily, adults $18, children and students $9), six kilometers (4 miles) east of Santa Elena, is owned and administered by the Tropical Science Center of Costa Rica. It protects more than 100 species of mammals, more than 400 species of birds, and more than 1,200 species of amphibians and reptiles. It is one of the few remaining habitats of all six indigenous species of the cat family: jaguar (on the lower slopes), ocelot, puma, margay, oncilla, and jaguarundi. Bird species include black guan, emerald toucanet, the critically endangered three-wattled bellbird, whose metallic "bonk!" call carries for almost three kilometers (2 miles), and 30 local hummingbird species. Hundreds of visitors arrive in hopes of seeing a resplendent quetzal; approximately 200 pairs nest in the reserve. Cognoscenti know that, ironically, the parking lot is perhaps the best place to see quetzals; in March 2014 it's where I saw a quetzal, perched like a

Monteverde and Santa Elena

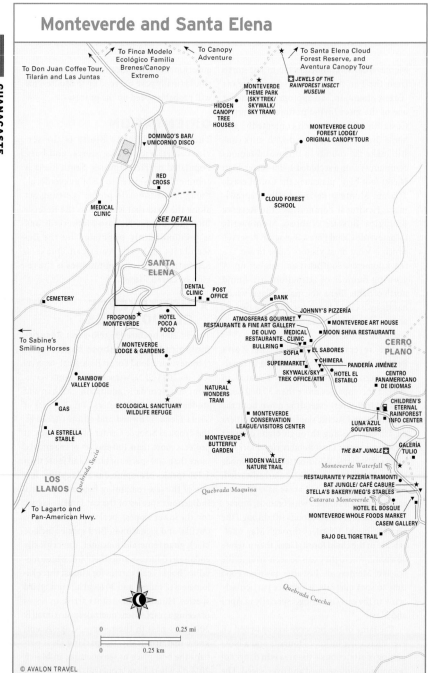

To Finca Modelo Ecológico Familia Brenes/Canopy Extremo

To Canopy Adventure

To Santa Elena Cloud Forest Reserve, and Aventura Canopy Tour

To Don Juan Coffee Tour, Tilarán and Las Juntas

JEWELS OF THE RAINFOREST INSECT MUSEUM

MONTEVERDE THEME PARK (SKY TREK/ SKYWALK/ SKY TRAM)

HIDDEN CANOPY TREE HOUSES

MONTEVERDE CLOUD FOREST LODGE/ ORIGINAL CANOPY TOUR

DOMINGO'S BAR/ UNICORNIO DISCO

RED CROSS

CLOUD FOREST SCHOOL

MEDICAL CLINIC

SEE DETAIL

SANTA ELENA

DENTAL CLINIC

POST OFFICE

BANK

CEMETERY

JOHNNY'S PIZZERÍA

FROGPOND MONTEVERDE

HOTEL POCO A POCO

ATMOSFERAS GOURMET RESTAURANTE & FINE ART GALLERY

MONTEVERDE ART HOUSE

MOON SHIVA RESTAURANTE

DE OLIVO RESTAURANTE

MEDICAL CLINIC

To Sabine's Smiling Horses

CERRO PLANO

BULLRING

MONTEVERDE LODGE & GARDENS

SOFIA

EL SABORES

CHIMERA

SUPERMARKET

PANDERÍA JIMÉNEZ

RAINBOW VALLEY LODGE

NATURAL WONDERS TRAM

SKYWALK/SKY TREK OFFICE/ATM

HOTEL EL ESTABLO

CENTRO PANAMERICANO DE IDIOMAS

GAS

ECOLOGICAL SANCTUARY WILDLIFE REFUGE

CHILDREN'S ETERNAL RAINFOREST INFO CENTER

LA ESTRELLA STABLE

MONTEVERDE CONSERVATION LEAGUE/VISITORS CENTER

LUNA AZUL SOUVENIRS

MONTEVERDE BUTTERFLY GARDEN

GALERÍA TULIO

THE BAT JUNGLE

HIDDEN VALLEY NATURE TRAIL

Monteverde Waterfall

LOS LLANOS

RESTAURANTE Y PIZZERÍA TRAMONTI

Quebrada Sucia

Quebrada Maquina

Catarata Monteverde

BAT JUNGLE/ CAFÉ CABURE

STELLA'S BAKERY/MEG'S STABLES

HOTEL EL BOSQUE

MONTEVERDE WHOLE FOODS MARKET

CASEM GALLERY

To Lagarto and Pan-American Hwy.

BAJO DEL TIGRE TRAIL

Quebrada Cuecha

0   0.25 mi

0   0.25 km

© AVALON TRAVEL

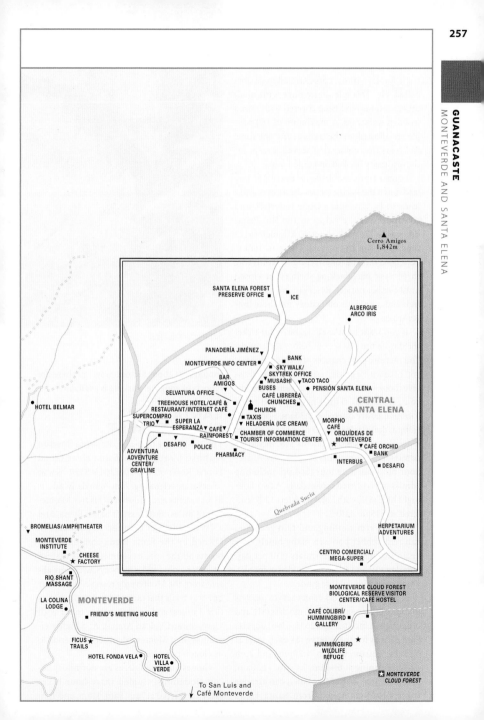

▲ Cerro Amigos
1,842m

SANTA ELENA FOREST
PRESERVE OFFICE ■   ■ ICE

ALBERGUE
ARCO IRIS ■

PANADERÍA JIMÉNEZ ▼
MONTEVERDE INFO CENTER ■   ■ BANK
■ SKY WALK/
SKYTREK OFFICE
BAR   ▼ MUSASHI ▼ TACO TACO
AMIGOS   BUSES
SELVATURA OFFICE   ● PENSIÓN SANTA ELENA
▼   CAFÉ LIBRERÉA
TREEHOUSE HOTEL/CAFÉ &   CHUNCHES
RESTAURANT/INTERNET CAFÉ ■   CENTRAL
SUPERCOMPRO   ● ■ CHURCH   SANTA ELENA
TRIO ▼ ■ ▼ ● TAXIS
SUPER LA   ▼ HELADERÍA (ICE CREAM)   MORPHO
ESPERANZA ▼ CAFÉ ▼   CAFÉ
RAINFOREST ■ CHAMBER OF COMMERCE   ▼ ORQUÍDEAS DE
▼ DESAFIO   ■ TOURIST INFORMATION CENTER   MONTEVERDE
■ POLICE   ★ ▼ CAFÉ ORCHID
ADVENTURA   PHARMACY ■   ■ BANK
ADVENTURE   INTERBUS ■   ■ DESAFIO
CENTER/
GRAYLINE

● HOTEL BELMAR

Quebrada Sucia

HERPETARIUM
ADVENTURES ■

▼ BROMELIAS/AMPHITHEATER
MONTEVERDE   CENTRO COMERCIAL/
INSTITUTE ■   MEGA-SUPER ■
★ CHEESE
FACTORY
RIO SHANT ●
MASSAGE
LA COLINA ●   **MONTEVERDE**   MONTEVERDE CLOUD FOREST
LODGE ★   BIOLOGICAL RESERVE VISITOR
■ FRIEND'S MEETING HOUSE   CENTER/CAFÉ HOSTEL ■
CAFÉ COLIBRÍ/
HUMMINGBIRD ■
FICUS ★   GALLERY
TRAILS   HUMMINGBIRD ★
HOTEL FONDA VELA ● ● HOTEL   WILDLIFE
VILLA   REFUGE
VERDE   ■★ MONTEVERDE
↓ To San Luis and   CLOUD FOREST
Café Monteverde

museum piece, almost within reach. Go early in the morning.

The reserve has 13 kilometers (8 miles) of trails for day visitors concentrated in an area called The Triangle. Parts ooze with mud; other sections have been covered with raised wooden walkways. A maximum of 180 people are allowed on the trails at any one time. Access is first come, first served, except for those already booked on guided tours.

Longer trails requiring an overnight stay lead down the Pacific slopes. **Sendero Valle** leads to La Cascada, a triple waterfall, and continues via the valley of the Río Peñas Blancas to Pocosol, about 20 kilometers (12 miles) south of La Fortuna. These are for experienced Indiana Jones-type hikers only (the three basic backpacking shelters are closed until further notice). Reservations are essential, and a guide is obligatory for these longer trails.

If you want to hike alone, buy your ticket the day before and set out before the crowds. You increase your chances of seeing wildlife if you hike with a guide; reservations are advisable (book online at www.reservamonteverde. com, from $18). Three-hour guided tours (*caminatas*) are offered at 7:30am, noon, and 1:30pm daily (minimum 3 people, maximum 9 people, adults $32, students $18, including admission); hourly tours are planned. A five-hour bird-watching tour ($64 pp, including admission) is offered at 6am daily. A two-hour night hike ($17, with hotel transfers $22) is offered at 6:15pm daily.

Bring warm clothing and rain gear. You can rent rubber boots in many hotels. The visitors center rents binoculars ($10 per day, plus deposit) and sells a self-guided pamphlet, a trail map, and wildlife guides.

A café at the visitors center serves omelets ($1.75), burgers, sandwiches, mochas ($1), and other fare. A bus (tel. 506/2645-6296) departs Santa Elena for the reserve ($1 each way) at 6:15am, 7:20am, 9:20am, 1:20pm, and 3pm daily, returning at 6:45am, 7:45am, 11:30am, 2pm, and 4pm daily. Most hotels can arrange transportation. A taxi from Santa Elena

resplendent quetzal

should cost about $10 one-way, but there are reports of gouging. Parking is available.

SANTA ELENA CLOUD FOREST

The 310-hectare (766-acre) **Reserva Bosque Nuboso Santa Elena** (Santa Elena Cloud Forest Reserve, tel. 506/2645-5390, www. reservasantaelena.org, 7am-4pm daily, adults $15, students and children $7) is five kilometers (3 miles) northeast of Santa Elena, and a 4WD vehicle is required to gain access. Owned by the Santa Elena community, it boasts all the species claimed by its eastern neighbor—plus spider monkeys, which are absent from the Monteverde reserve. It has four one-way trails that range 1.4 to 4.8 kilometers (0.9-3 miles) and an observation tower with views toward Volcán Arenal. At a higher elevation than Monteverde reserve, it tends to be cloudier and wetter.

Guides are available, as are dormitory accommodations. Guided three-hour hikes ($17) are offered at 7am, 9am, 11am, and 1pm

hikers in Monteverde Cloud Forest

Elena at 6:45am, 11am, and 2:30pm daily. A shared taxi ($2 pp) leaves Santa Elena village at 6:45am, 8am, 10:30am, 12:30pm, and 2pm daily, but you must book the day before. A regular taxi costs about $10 each way.

BOSQUE ETERNO DE LOS NIÑOS

Surrounding the Reserva Biológica Bosque Nuboso Monteverde on three sides, the **Bosque Eterno de Los Niños** (Children's Eternal Rainforest) is the largest private reserve in Central America. It is administered by the **Monteverde Conservation League** (tel. 506/2645-5003, www.friendsoftherainforest.org). The dream of a rainforest saved by children began in 1987 at a small primary school in rural Sweden. A study of tropical forests prompted nine-year-old Roland Teinsuu to ask what he could do to keep the rainforest and the animals that live in it safe from destruction. Young Roland's question launched a group campaign to raise money to help the league buy and save threatened rainforest in Costa Rica. Roland and his classmates raised enough money to buy six hectares (15 acres) of rainforest at a cost of $250 per hectare. Out of this initial success, a group of children dedicated to saving the tropical rainforest formed Barnens Regnskog (Children's Rainforest). The vision took hold, sweeping the globe, with contributions flocking in from the far corners. The original preserve, established

daily; there is also a 90-minute night tour at 7pm daily. You can buy trail maps and a self-guided trail booklet—and rent rubber boots ($1)—at the visitors center.

The reserve is the site of the **Monteverde Cloud Forest Ecological Center,** a farm that educates youngsters and local farmers on forest ecology and conservation.

Shuttles for ticket-holders leave Santa

The Disappearance of the Golden Toad

The Reserva Biológica Bosque Nuboso Monteverde owes its existence in part to a brilliant neon-orange arboreal toad—*sapo dorado* (*Bufo periglenes*)—discovered in 1964 and so stunning that one biologist harbored "a suspicion that someone had dipped the examples in enamel paint." The males are the orange ones; females, which are larger, are yellow and black with patches of scarlet. Monteverde is the only known home of this fabulous creature. But don't expect to see one; it is already extinct. Although in 1986 it could be seen in large quantities, by 1988 very few remained. No sightings have been made since 1996. These creatures may now exist only on the cover of tourism brochures, victims of a deadly fungus that has devastated the world's frog populations in recent decades.

near Monteverde in 1988, has grown to more than 22,000 hectares (54,000 acres).

It is accessed via the Bajo del Tigre (tel. 506/2645-5923, 7:30am-5:30pm daily, adults $20, children $12), off the main road, just above the CASEM Gallery. This section of the reserve is at a lower elevation than the Reserva Biológica Bosque Nuboso Monteverde and thus offers a different variety of plant and animal life. Quetzals are more easily seen here, for example, than higher up in the wetter, mistier cloud forest. Facilities include a Children's Nature Center, a self-guided interpretative trail, an arboretum, a visitors center, and a library. Guided two-hour tours ($20, with transfers $22) are offered at 5:30am (for bird-watchers), 8am, 2pm, and 5:30pm (a night tour) daily.

There are also two field stations: at Poco Sol, on the lower eastern slopes, with eight rooms (six with private baths) for 26 people as well as 10 kilometers (6 miles) of hiking trails; and San Gerardo, at 1,220 meters (4,000 feet) elevation, a 3.5-kilometer (2-mile) walk from the Santa Elena reserve, with accommodations for 26 people and six kilometers (4 miles) of trails. Guides are available by request.

SAN LUIS BIOLOGICAL RESERVE

Reserva Biológica San Luis (tel. 506/2645-8049, www.cct.or.cr, day visits $10, students $6, guided tour $20, horseback rides $10 per hour) is affiliated with the Tropical Science Center of Costa Rica and doubles as an integrated tourism, research, and education project on a 70-hectare (173-acre) farm and botanical garden at San Luis, eight kilometers (5 miles) southeast of Monteverde. The turnoff is immediately east of Hotel Fonda Vela on the road to the Monteverde reserve; it's a steep descent. Resident biologists work with members of the San Luis community to develop a model for sustainable development.

The station offers a wide range of activities: horseback rides, bird-watching, cloud-forest hiking (plus a hike to the San Luis waterfall), night walks, and hands-on laboratory study.

Open-air classes are given, including an intensive seven-day tropical biology course. You can even help farm or participate in scientific research.

It has a cozy wood-paneled bunkhouse—a former milking shed—with 30 bunks and shared baths, and four rooms with 2 to 12 beds each. It also has a four-room, 16-bed bungalow with private baths and verandas, plus 12 *cabinas* for 3 to 4 people each. Tico fare is cooked over a woodstove and served family-style. Lodging costs $49 pp in the dorm, $79 s or $144 d in the bungalow, and $102 s, $192 d in the cabins, which includes all meals and activities.

A taxi from Monteverde costs about $15.

WILDLIFE EXHIBITS
★ Jewels of the Rainforest Insect Museum

The Jewels of the Rainforest Insect Museum (tel. 506/2645-5929, www.selvatura.com, 7am-5pm daily, $15), at Selvatura, three miles northeast of Santa Elena, displays more than 50,000 insects, yet it's just a small fraction of Richard Whitten's findings from more than 50 years of collecting. It's the largest private collection of big, bizarre, and beautiful butterflies, beetles, and other bugs in the world. And it's surely is the most colorful—a veritable kaleidoscope of shimmering greens, neon blues, startling reds, silvers, and golds. Whitten began collecting "bugs" at a tender age; today his 1,900 boxes include more than one million specimens, many of them collected in Costa Rica. Part of the exhibit is dedicated to a collection of every known species in the country. Some beetles are bigger than your fist; some moths outsize a salad plate. Other exhibits include shimmering beetles displayed against black velvet, like opal jewelry, and boxes of bugs majestically turned into caskets of gems.

Covering 232 square meters (2,500 square feet), exhibits include a Biodiversity Bank with dozens of spectacular and informative displays; a wall of Neotropical Butterflies; a World of Beetles, from Tutankhamen scarabs to the giants of the beetle word; a Phasmid Room (stick insects and their relatives); and a Silk Room, displaying elegant moths. The dynamic displays combine art, science, music, and video to entertain and educate about insect mimicry, protective coloration and other forms of camouflage, prey-predator relationships, and more. A 279-square-meter (3,000-square-foot) auditorium screens fascinating videos.

Selvatura also has a hummingbird garden ($5), a vast domed butterfly garden ($15), and a reptile exhibit ($15). Guided nature hikes ($45) are offered.

★ The Bat Jungle

The Bat Jungle (tel. 506/2645-7701, www.batjungle.com, 9am-7:30pm daily, adults $12, students and children $10), between the gas station and the cheese factory, is the first in Costa Rica to provide an insight into the life of bats (Monteverde has at least 65 species). Eight species of live bats flit, feed, and mate within a sealed enclosure behind a wall of glass. Fascinating exhibits illuminate bat ecology and an auditorium screens documentaries. The guided tour is truly fascinating and illuminating. Guaranteed, you won't leave here without a deep admiration for these adorable and much misunderstood creatures. You can even don giant ears to get a sense for bats' supersize sonar hearing.

Monteverde Theme Park

The impressive Frog Pond of Monteverde, by which the Monteverde Theme Park (tel. 506/2645-6320, 9:30am-8:30pm daily, adults $12, children and students $10), on the south side of Santa Elena, is better known, displays 28 species of frogs and amphibians, from the red-eyed tree frog and transparent frogs to the elephantine marine toad, all housed in large, well-arranged display cases. It also has salamanders and a few snakes, plus termites and other bugs to be fed to the frogs, as well as a *mariposario* (butterfly garden, adults $12, children $10, $20 with Frog Pond). Evening visits are best, when the frogs become active.

Admission cost is valid for two entries, so you can see both daytime and nocturnal species.

Herpetarium Adventures

The Herpetarium Adventures (tel. 506/2645-6002, www.skyadventures.travel, 9am-8pm daily, adults $12, students $10, children $6, including guide), previously called the Serpentario, on the eastern fringe of Santa Elena village, lets you get up close and personal with an array of coiled constrictors and venomous vipers as well as their prey: frogs, chameleons, and the like. The dreaded fer-de-lance is here, along with 30 or so other species staring at you from behind thick panes of glass.

Monteverde Butterfly Garden

The Monteverde Butterfly Garden (tel. 506/2645-5512, www.monteverdebutterfly-garden.com, 8:30am-4pm daily, adults $15, students $10, children $5, including 1-hour guided tour), signed off the main road about one mile east of Santa Elena, features a nature center and three distinct habitats: a 450-square-meter (4,800-square-foot) netted butterfly flyway and two greenhouses representing lowland forest and mid-elevation forest habitats. Together they are filled with native plant species and hundreds of tropical butterflies representing more than 40 species. Fascinating guided tours begin in the visitors center, where butterflies and other bugs are mounted on display and rhinoceros beetles, stick insects, and tarantulas crawl around inside display cases. There's a computer station with interactive software about butterflies, plus an auditorium where videos are shown. Go mid-morning, when the butterflies become active (and most visitors are in the reserve).

Orquídeas de Monteverde

Orquídeas de Monteverde (Monteverde Orchid Garden, tel. 506/2645-5308, www.monteverdeorchidgarden.net, 8am-5pm daily, adults $10, students $7), in the heart of Santa Elena, took five years of arduous work to collate the results of the Monteverde Orchid Investigation Project, an ongoing effort to document and research local orchids. Short paths wind through the compact garden, displaying almost 450 species native to the region arranged in 22 groups ("subtribes"), each marked with an educational placard. Miniatures are preponderant, including the world's smallest flower, *Platystele jungermannioides,* about the size of a pinhead (fortunately, you are handed a magnifying glass upon arrival).

Finca Ecológica

Finca Ecológica (Ecological Sanctuary Wildlife Refuge, tel. 506/2645-5869, www.santuarioecologico.com, 7am-6pm daily, adults $10, students and children $8), on the same road as the Butterfly Garden, has six signed trails through the 48-hectare (119-acre) property, which has waterfalls. You have an excellent chance of seeing coatimundis, sloths, agoutis, porcupines, white-faced monkeys, butterflies, and birds. It offers a twilight tour (adults $25, students $20, children $15, including transfers) at 5pm daily.

Santamaría Night Walk

The great majority of critters in the cloud forest are nocturnal. To see them, take a guided tour at **Finca Agroturística Santamaría** (tel. 506/2645-6548, www.nightwalksantamarias.com, $22 including transfers), a great chance to spot sloths, snakes, and all manner of insects in this 10-hectare (25-acre) reserve to the northeast of Santa Elena.

FARM AND FOOD TOURS

Coffee is grown on the slopes just below Santa Elena and Monteverde; some three dozen small-scale coffee producers make up the Santa Elena cooperative. The **Don Juan Coffee Tour** (tel. 506/2645-7100, www.donjuancoffeetour.com, adults $30, children $12), offered at 8am, 10am, 1pm, and 3pm daily, provides an insight into coffee production.

The **El Trapiche Tour** (tel. 506/2645-7780, www.eltrapichetour.com, 10am and 3pm Mon.-Sat., 3pm Sun., adults $32, students $28, children $12) offers a more rounded experience that teaches about production of a wide range of crops, from coffee to sugarcane; the tour includes a ride in an ox-drawn cart. At **Finca Modelo Ecológica** (tel. 506/2645-5581, www.familiabrenestours.com, 6am and 3pm daily, adults $15, students and children $12) the Brenes family offers a tour of its

owner David Makynen at Monteverde Butterfly Garden

Costa Rica's Quaker Village

Monteverde was founded in 1951 by a group of 44 American Quakers—most from Fairhope, Alabama—who had refused to register for the draft as a matter of conscience. Led by John Campbell and Wilford "Wolf" Guindon, they chose Costa Rica for a new home because it had done away with its army. They built roads and cleared much of the virgin forest for dairy farming. They decided to make cheese because it was the only product that could be stored and moved to market without spoiling along a muddy oxcart trail. Cheese is still a mainstay of the local economy, and the Quaker organization is still active in Monteverde. It meets every Wednesday morning at the Friends Meeting House; visitors are welcome.

Don't expect to find the Quakers walking down the road dressed like the guy on the oatmeal box. *Cuaquerismo* (Quakerism) in Monteverde is a low-key affair.

organic dairy farm two kilometers (1.2 miles) north of Santa Elena.

La Lechería (Cheese Factory, tel. 506/2645-5436, 7:30am-5pm Mon.-Sat., 7:30am-4pm Sun.), in Monteverde, is famous for its quality cheeses. Production began in 1953 when the original Quaker settlers bought 50 Jersey cattle and began producing pasteurized Monteverde gouda cheese. The factory produces 14 types of cheese—from parmesan and emmentaler to Danish-style dambo and Monte Rico, the best-seller. Guided tours (tel. 506/2645-7090, www.monteverdecheesefactory.com, 9am and 2pm Mon.-Sat., adults $10, students and children $8) are offered.

ENTERTAINMENT AND EVENTS

Bromelias (tel. 506/2645-6272, 9am-5pm daily) hosts live music and occasional theater in the Monteverde Amphitheater, an open-air performance space. Bring a cushion to soften the iron-hard seating. In Santa Elena, **Restaurante Don Juan** (tel. 506/2661-7115) has live music upstairs (7pm Fri.-Sun.).

For a taste of local working-class color, wet your whistle at **Bar Amigos** (Monteverde, tel. 506/2645-5071, www.baramigos.com, noon-midnight daily), which has pool tables and karaoke; or at **Unicornios** (tel. 506/2645-6282, noon-midnight daily), a rough-and-tumble bar on the northwest side of Santa Elena. Both have pool tables. Unicornios has karaoke on Thursday. The

grooviest dance spot midweek is **Taberna** (tel. 506/2645-5883), on the east side of Santa Elena, with a nightly disco (free).

SPORTS AND RECREATION
Canopy Tours

An intriguing way to explore the Reserva Bosque Nuboso Santa Elena is by ascending into the forest canopy on a guided **Sky Walk** (tel. 506/2645-5238, www.skywalk.co.cr), which offers a monkey's-eye view of things. You walk along five suspension bridges and platforms and 1,000 meters (3,300 feet) of pathways that allow viewing from ground level to the treetops, where you are right in there with the epiphytes. Two-hour tours (adults $35, students $28, children $21) depart at 7:30am, 9:30am, 10:30am, 12:30pm, 1:30pm, and 3pm daily.

The same company offers a two-hour **Sky Trek** (adults $71, students $57, children $45) for the more adventurous. You'll whiz through the canopy in a harness attached to a zip line that runs between three treetop canopies, spanning two kilometers (1.2 miles). The tour starts with a ride on the **Sky Tram** cable car (which can only be taken in conjunction with the Sky Walk or Sky Trek).

Selvatura (tel. 506/2645-5929, www.selvatura.com, 7am-5pm daily), two kilometers (1.2 miles) north of Sky Walk, has a canopy exploration with three kilometers (2 miles) of suspended bridges ($30) and an 18-platform zip-line canopy tour (adults $45, students $40, children $30). Tours are at 8.30am, 11am, 1pm, and 2:30pm daily.

The **Aventura Canopy Tour** (tel. 506/2645-6388, www.monteverdeadventure. com), off the road to the Sky Walk, has 16 zip-line cables (tours at 8am, 11am, 1pm, and 3pm daily, adults $45, children $35) plus suspended walkways (adults $35, children $25).

The canopy tour craze began at Monteverde Cloud Forest Lodge, where **The Original Canopy Tour** (tel. 506/2645-5243, www. canopytour.com, adults $45, students $35, children $25) was created. Zip-line tours are offered at 7:30am, 10:30am, and 2:30pm daily. A thrilling beginning is the forest hike and a clamber up the interior of a hollow strangler fig to reach the first platform.

Extremo Canopy (tel. 506/2645-6058, www.monteverdeextremo.com) has a 16-cable zip-line tour (8am, 11am, and 2pm daily, adults $40, students $30, children $25), plus bungee jumping ($60), a Tarzan swing ($35), canyoneering and a Superman line ($45), and horseback rides ($30).

Horseback Riding

The following have stables and rent horses (usually $10-15 per hour) and offer guided tours: **La Estrella Stables** (tel. 506/2645-5075); **Sabine's Smiling Horses** (tel. 506/2645-6894, www.horseback-riding-tour. com); and **Terra Viva** (tel. 506/2645-5454, www.terravivacr.com), which also offers tours of its organic dairy farm and cloud-forest reserve with trails. I recommend **Desafío Adventure Company** (tel. 506/2645-5874, www.desafiocostarica.com) for horseback trips to La Fortuna ($65); the four-hour horseback ride from Monteverde to Río Chiquito is followed by a one-hour boat ride across Laguna de Arenal, then a 30-minute Jeep ride to La Fortuna.

SHOPPING

The **Artisans' Cooperative of Santa Elena and Monteverde** (CASEM, tel. 506/2645-5190, www.monteverdeinfo.com/casem,

the Sky Tram at Monteverde

8am-5pm Mon.-Sat., 10am-4pm Sun.) features the handmade wares of 140 local artisans. Monteverde boasts numerous excellent galleries. **Artes Tulio** (tel. 506/2645-5567, www. artestulio.wix.com, 9am-6pm daily) sells the exquisite creations of gifted artist Marco Tulio Brenes. **Sarah's Gallery** (tel. 506/2645-7624, www.monteverdeartistsarahdowell.blogspot. com), also in Monteverde, offers lovely paintings of local flora and fauna by Sarah Dowell.

Bromelias (tel. 506/2645-6272, 10am-5:30pm Fri.-Wed., 10am-10pm Thurs.) sells books and quality batiks, jewelry, and carvings. The most impressive selection is at the **Art House** (tel. 506/2645-5275, www.monteverdearthouse.com), serving as both a workshop and gallery for everything from papier-mâché to pottery. The **Hummingbird Gallery** (tel. 506/2645-5030, 8:30am-4:30pm daily), 100 meters (330 feet) below the entrance to the Reserva Biológica Bosque Nuboso Monteverde, is well stocked with souvenirs.

In Santa Elena, **Librería Chunches** (tel./

fax 506/2645-5147, 8am-6:30pm Mon.-Fri.) sells English-language magazines and newspapers, plus natural history books and laminated *Costa Rican Field Guides.*

ACCOMMODATIONS

Accommodations may be difficult to obtain in dry season, when tour companies block space; book well ahead.

Under $25

You can camp at ★ **Pensión Santa Elena** (tel. 506/2645-5051, www.pensionsantaelena. com, camping $7 pp, dorm 8-9 pp, private room $16-84 s/d, cabin $35-70 s/d), which offers plenty of facilities, such as Wi-Fi and a café, in the heart of Santa Elena. Beloved of budget travelers, Pensión Santa Elena is owned by super-friendly Texan siblings Randa and Shannon, who earn high marks from readers. It has 25 basic rooms of varying sizes (some are dark). Some have private baths; all have hot water. A two-story annex has three rooms, a bar, and a restaurant, and you get secure parking. The hotel provides free use of a kitchen, plus laundry service ($2), Internet access, and travel information.

$25-50

At the southern entrance to Santa Elena, **Rainbow Valley Lodge** (tel. 506/2645-7015, www.rainbowvalleylodgecr.com, $30-50 s, $35-60 d), run by a pleasant Minnesotan, has two spacious, cross-lit, and cross-ventilated rooms in a lovely lodge with awesome views across the forested valley toward Monteverde. The lower of the two units has no valley views, but monkeys frolic in the treetops at fingertip distance. Readers rave about Rolf, the owner.

I love the dramatic Thai-style frontage of all-log **La Colina Lodge** (tel. 506/2645-5009, www.lacolinalodge.com, low season bunks from $10 pp, shared baths $25 s/d, private baths $45 s, $55 d), in Monteverde, which has three wood-paneled rooms with private baths, plus nine rooms with shared baths with hot water. The rooms boast handcrafted furnishings and Guatemalan bedspreads. Rooms with

shared baths are small and dark. There's a TV room and a charming alpine restaurant.

$50-100

With easy access to Santa Elena, the splendid German-owned ★ **Albergue Arco Iris** (tel. 506/2645-5067, www.arcoirislodge.com, bunks from $27 s, $37 d, rooms from $67 s, $78 d) is run with Teutonic efficiency. It has six bunkrooms, 11 standard rooms, and two handsome stone-and-hardwood *cabinas* amid a spacious garden with deck chairs on a hillside backed by a two-hectare (5-acre) forest reserve. The *cabinas* feature terra-cotta tile floors and orthopedic mattresses with Guatemalan bedspreads. Best of all is the fabulous honeymoon suite with a kitchen, a sexy tiger-print bedspread in the upstairs bedroom, and gorgeous black-stone walls and sea-blue tiles in the bath with a two-person whirlpool tub. An airy restaurant offers breakfast only. Horses can be rented, and there's a library, laundry, and a safe.

Way up the hill close to the Monteverde reserve and exuding rusticity, **Hotel Villa Verde** (tel. 506/2645-4697, www.villaverdehotel.com, rooms $67 s, $90 d, villas $100 s, $120 d, including breakfast) has 16 cozy rooms with hardwood floors and five *cabinas* with roomy kitchenettes, a small lounge with a fireplace, and large bedrooms with four beds (one double, three singles). Villa suites have fireplaces and tubs, and voluminous tiled baths have hot water. The stone-and-timber lodge and its atrium restaurant offer a homey atmosphere and a game room. Horseback tours are offered.

$100-150

The nonsmoking **Monteverde Cloud Forest Lodge** (tel. 506/2645-5058, U.S. tel. 877-623-3198, www.cloudforestlodge.com, $90 s, $100 d), northeast of Santa Elena, earns raves from readers. It is surrounded by gardens set on a 25-hectare (62-acre) private forest reserve. The 18 wood-and-stone *cabinas* are clean and spacious, with large clerestory windows, peaked ceilings, and large baths. There's a large-screen TV and a VCR, plus free Wi-Fi. It has five kilometers (3 miles) of trails into forests, plus views of Nicoya from the deck. A daunting circular staircase leads to the entrance to the Sky Walk, at Santa Elena Cloud Forest Reserve.

The super-contemporary three-story **Hotel Poco a Poco** (tel. 506/2645-6000, www.hotelpocoapoco.com, low season from $99 s/d, high season from $134 s/d) is about 500 meters (0.3 miles) outside Santa Elena village center. Every year it seems to grow *poco a poco* (little by little), expanding from its original 5 rooms to 32 rooms with lively color schemes and sophisticated modern fittings, including cable TV, Wi-Fi, and DVD players (the hotel has a DVD library). It has an elegant restaurant, a spa, and a swimming pool—one of only two in Monteverde—that's heated and set in a flagstone sundeck with views.

Sufficiently alpine to make you want to yodel is the reclusive **Hotel Fonda Vela** (tel. 506/2645-5125, www.fondavela.com, rooms $105 s, $120 d, junior suites $140 s, $160 d), close to the Monteverde reserve. It has 20 standard rooms and 18 junior suites in nine buildings, all with rich hardwoods, picture windows, and recently upgraded furnishings that bring it stylishly into the 21st century. The suites are worth the splurge for their sitting rooms and large balconies. The landscaped grounds backed by forest are a delight for bird-watching.

Over $150

Earning high marks for its eco-consciousness and justifiably the latest addition to the Small Distinctive Hotels group, the family-run **Hotel Belmar** (tel. 506/2645-5201, www.hotelbelmar.net, low season $151-159 s/d, high season $189-199 s/d) is an ivy-clad Swiss-style grand dame with chalets that are the prettiest in Monteverde. Spacious rooms in the newer main building outshine the older cabins, not least for large baths with marble highlights; of its 28 comfortable rooms, four are family rooms. French doors in most rooms and lounges open onto balconies with views; a west-facing glass wall catches the sunset. The

lounge in the older building is a quiet spot for reading and for slide shows on Friday. The large restaurant has views. Hardy hikers can follow a trail to the mountain crest. Facilities include a whirlpool tub, a volleyball court, a pool table, and Internet access. Rates include tax.

The modern, eco-sensitive ★ **Monteverde Lodge & Gardens** (tel. 506/2645-5057, www.monteverdelodge.com, garden room $198 s/d, forest view $228 s/d year-round) is the best bargain in Monteverde, with spacious and elegant rooms that boast a classy chic that doesn't detract from the nature-lodge feel. Rooms feature large windows, two double beds with thick comforters and deluxe linens, plus phones, Wi-Fi, and well-lit solar-heated baths with stylish "salad bowl" sinks and large walk-in showers tiled with gray slate. Thoughtful touches include biscuits and coffee liqueurs by the bed at night. Opt for the upper Forest View rooms with balconies. A cavernous hotel entrance leads to an open-plan dining room and a cozy bar. The superb restaurant has a soaring beamed ceiling and wraparound windows overlooking beautifully landscaped grounds, where agoutis and other critters hang out. The bar has leather chairs, good for cuddling around an open hearth, and looks down on a large glass-enclosed whirlpool tub. The lodge is operated by Costa Rica Expeditions and is popular with bird-watching and nature groups. Rates include taxes.

Monteverde's largest, and some would argue most upscale, option is ★ **El Establo Hotel, Restaurant & Stable** (tel. 506/2645-5110, U.S. tel. 877-623-3198, www.hotelestablo.com, deluxe $216 s/d, suites $325 s/d year-round), which offers 155 standard rooms and junior suites, all with a stylish aesthetic. The original two-story wood-and-stone structure contains 20 standard rooms with cinderblock walls and wraparound windows; those on the ground floor open onto a wood-floored gallery lounge with deep-cushioned sofas and an open fireplace. Newer rooms are in a dramatic hillside annex (far enough that a shuttle ferries guests back and forth); all are junior suites with polished stone floors and exotic tile work, or upper-level carpeted suites with rattan furniture and king beds in lofts (plus double beds downstairs). You get rockers on your balcony, and there's a full-service spa, two restaurants, a swimming pool fit for a Balinese resort, and trails.

Monteverde hasn't been left out of the tree-house craze. Thus, ★ **Hidden Canopy B&B** (tel. 506/2645-5447, www.hiddencanopy.com, $225-445 s/d year-round) has four very private "tree-house chalets" accessed by lofty walkways. No ordinary tree houses, these chic and edgy all-wood units ooze class. The entire place is gorgeous, not least for its lush landscaped gardens. The ridge-top setting with vast views toward the Golfo de Nicoya is sublime. Two cabins are bi-level with two bedrooms. The others are single-story one-bedroom units; one is a honeymoon suite with a gas fire and a whirlpool tub. Owner Jennifer King also rents two rooms in the lodge, which has a fabulous lounge and a stone deck that's the setting for daily sunset teas. Furnishings include queen and king beds made of tree roots, with down comforters, and a hanging basket chair in which to soak up the forest views.

FOOD

I frequently dine at the **Morpho Café** (tel. 506/2645-7373, www.morphosrestaurant.com, 11am-9pm daily), in the heart of Santa Elena. It's known for its salads, sandwiches, great burgers, pastas, *casados* (set lunches, $4), and a house special of beef tenderloin with Monteverde blue cheese ($18). A copy-cat with a difference, the **Treehouse Café & Restaurant** (tel. 506/2645-5751, www.tree-house.cr, 11am-10pm daily), also in central Santa Elena, is built around a tree. Its menu ranges from burritos to fondues. My favorite? Chocolate fondue with brandy ($34 for 2 people).

The quaint, colorful **Dulce Marzo Bakery & Café** (tel. 506/2645-6568, 11am-7pm daily), in Cerro Plano, is good for wraps, sandwiches, and cookies. Chef Lisa Peters's peanut butter

cup specifically is to die for. For breakfast, try **Stella's Bakery** (tel. 506/2645-5560, 6am-6pm daily) in Monteverde. The rustic setting is perfect for enjoying granola with home-made yogurt ($2), pancakes, omelets, dough-nuts, sandwiches, and great milk shakes ($3).

For elegant dining, make a reservation at **Garden Restaurant** (tel. 506/2645-5057, 6am-8:20am, noon-2pm, and 6pm-8:30pm daily), at Monteverde Lodge, which dishes up superb gourmet cuisine. A typical dinner might include shredded duck empanadas ($6), roasted leek quiche ($8.50), and entrées of almond chicken curry with rice in a coconut cup ($13), followed by profiteroles ($7). It has a large wine list.

For fusion cuisine, make a beeline to ★ **Sofia** (tel. 506/2645-7017, knielsenmv@hotmail.com, 11:30am-9:30pm daily) in Cerro Plano, which serves gourmet Nuevo Latino dishes. Chef-owner Karen Nielsen whips up mean appetizers, such as a roasted eggplant, tomato, and goat cheese quesadilla, and black bean soup. For a main course, try the seafood chimichanga ($12) or plantain-crusted sea bass ($12). The bar serves very good mojitos, caipirinhas, and other cocktails ($5). Sofia has wine tastings and occasionally hosts live music such as choral and jazz. Karen also operates the chic fusion restaurant **Trio** (tel. 506/2645-7254, 11:30am-9pm daily) in Santa Elena. Decked out with an urbane chocolate, pea-green, and white decor, it has huge windows and a deck with forest views. Try the cream of carrot and sweet potato soup with coconut and tamarind ($4), followed by mojito shrimp ($12.50).

Karen also runs a gourmet yet casual tapas restaurant, **Chimera** (tel. 506/2645-7017, 11:30am-9:30pm daily), with an open kitchen; it's perfect if you want to share plates or have a light appetite. Everything here is organically grown. Choice selections include cold roasted eggplant ($3.50), coconut shrimp lollipops with mango-ginger sauce ($7.50), and smoked provolone with sun-dried tomato sauce ($3.50).

Restaurante y Pizzería Tramonti (400

meters/0.25 miles uphill from the gas station in Monteverde, tel. 506/2645-6120, www.tramonticr.com, 11:30am-9:45pm daily) offers good ambience along with excellent spaghetti dishes, carpaccio, lasagna, fried squid, and wood-fired pizzas ($5-15). While we're talking Italian, **Johnny's Pizzería** (1 kilometer/0.6 miles east of Santa Elena, tel. 506/2645-5066, www.pizzeriadejohnny.com, 11:30am-9:30pm daily), in Cerro Plano, is both classy and offers a wide-ranging pizza menu (small-large $4-10) plus pastas and daily specials such as smoked salmon and capers. It also has a tapas bar with nightly live music.

For a chocolaty treat or a delicious light lunch head to ★ **Café Caburé** (tel. 506/2645-5020, www.cabure.net, 8am-8pm Mon.-Sat.), at Paseo de Estella. Argentinean owner Susana Salas's eclectic menu offers chocolate-inspired dishes and drinks from around the world. You must try the passion fruit-, rum-, and vodka-flavored truffles. Salas also serves gourmet organic salads and wraps ($9.50). Caburé has Wi-Fi plus an excellent chocolate museum. Craving ice cream? Head to **Heladería Monteverde** (tel. 506/2645-6558, 10am-8pm daily), run by the cheese factory and serving 20 flavors of ice cream, such as blackberry and cherry. It's in the heart of Santa Elena.

INFORMATION AND SERVICES

The best starting point for visitor information is the impartial **Chamber of Commerce** (tel. 506/2645-6565, www.visitmonteverde.com, 8am-8pm daily) and, across the street, the **Monteverde Information Center** (tel. 506/2645-6559). Both are located in the center of Santa Elena. **Desafío Tours** (tel. 506/2645-5874, www.monteverdetours.com), in Santa Elena, also books tours and offers visitor advice. The **Monteverde Conservation League** (tel. 506/2645-5003, www.acmcr.org, 8am-5pm Mon.-Fri., 8am-noon Sat.), mid-way between Santa Elena and the Monteverde Cloud Forest Biological Reserve, is a great resource for information on ecological projects and the reserves.

The state-run **Centro Médico Monteverde** (tel. 506/2645-7080) clinic is on the west side of Santa Elena. In Cerro Plano, the **Consultorio Médico** (tel. 506/2645-7778, 24 hours daily) has a clinic and an ambulance. The **Red Cross** (tel. 506/2645-6128) is on the north side of Santa Elena. A private **dental clinic** (tel. 506/2645-7080) adjoins the post office.

The **police** (Guardia Rural, tel. 911 or 506/2645-6248) faces Super La Esperanza in Santa Elena. The **Banco Nacional** (tel. 506/2645-5027), in Santa Elena, is open 8:30am-3:30pm daily. The **post office** is on the east side of Santa Elena.

For Internet access, head to **Treehouse Internet** (tel. 506/2645-5751, 6am-11pm daily), or **Internet Pura Vida** (tel. 506/2645-5783, 10am-8pm daily), which also has laundry. **Las Delicias Campesinas** (tel. 506/2645-7032), in Cerro Plano, has self-service laundry ($6 per load).

The **Centro Panamericano de Idiomas** (50 meters/165 feet west of the gas station in Monteverde, tel./fax 506/2645-5441, www.cpi-edu.com) offers Spanish-language courses at its impressive facility. The **Monteverde Institute** (tel. 506/2645-5053, www.mvinstitute.org) hosts one-week arts workshops at the Monteverde Studios of the Arts (June-Aug.).

GETTING THERE AND AROUND

Beware touts who intercept arriving buses and cars to direct you to properties or businesses at which they'll receive commissions.

Transportes Monteverde (tel. 506/2645-5159, San José tel. 506/2222-3854) buses depart San José (4 hours, $5) from Calle 12, Avenidas 7/9, at 6:30am and 2:30pm daily; return buses depart Santa Elena at 6:30am and 2:30pm daily. The office in Santa Elena is open 5:45am-11:30am daily, as well as 1:30pm-5pm Monday-Friday and 1:30pm-3pm Saturday-Sunday. Buy your return bus ticket as soon as you arrive in Santa Elena. Buses also depart Calles 2/4 in Puntarenas at 7:50am, 1:50pm,

Between Monteverde and La Fortuna

For many travelers in Monteverde, the next destination of choice is La Fortuna (or vice versa). There are several ways of traveling between them. Most popular is a four-hour horseback ride from Monteverde to Río Chiquito, where you take a one-hour boat ride across Laguna de Arenal, then a 30-minute Jeep ride to La Fortuna. There are three different routes for the horseback ride. Several tour operators compete. Some have been accused of working their horses to death—literally—on the arduous San Gerardo Trail, on which horses that are often poorly fed exhaust themselves struggling through thigh-deep mud on the steep hills during wet season. The Río Chiquito route can also be tough on horses in wet season. The Lake Trail is the easiest on the horses. Check to see that the horses are not used both ways on the same day.

Alternatively, you can take a 90-minute Jeep ride to Río Chiquito, then continue on the one-hour boat ride across Laguna de Arenal and a 30-minute Jeep ride to La Fortuna.

and 2:15pm daily (you can pick it up at the Río Lagarto turnoff for Monteverde on the Pan-American Hwy.) and depart Monteverde at 4:30am, 6am, and 3pm daily. A bus departs Tilarán for Monteverde at 12:30pm daily, returning from Monteverde at 7am daily.

Interbus (tel. 506/4100-0888, www.interbusonline.com) and **Grayline Costa Rica** (tel. 506/2220-2393, www.graylinecostarica.com) operate shuttles between San José and Monteverde ($35) and key tourist destinations.

If you're **driving,** there are two turnoffs for Monteverde from Highway 1. The first is via Sardinal; the turnoff is at Rancho Grande, about 10 kilometers (6 miles) south of San Gerardo. The second is about seven kilometers (4.5 miles) north of San Gerardo (100 meters/330 feet before the bridge over the Río Lagarto), 37 kilometers (23 miles) north of Esparza. The roads lead 35 kilometers (22 miles) uphill along a gut-jolting dirt road as famous as the place it leads to. The drive takes 1.5 to 2 hours.

There is no local bus service except to the Reserva Biológica Bosque Nuboso Monteverde.

TILARÁN

Tilarán, about 23 kilometers (14 miles) east of Cañas and the Pan-American Highway, is the western gateway to Lake Arenal and Monteverde. This spruce little highland town is laid out in a grid around a pretty square and a park with cedars and pines in front of the small cathedral, **Catedral de San Antonio,** which has an amazing barrel-vaulted wooden ceiling. At 550 meters (1,800 feet) elevation, the air is crisp and stirred by breezes working their way over the crest of the Cordillera de Tilarán from Laguna de Arenal, five kilometers (3 miles) to the northeast. The countryside hereabouts is reminiscent of the rolling hill country of England.

The last weekend in April, Tilarán hosts a rodeo and a livestock show. On June 13, Tilarán celebrates San Antonio, the patron saint, with a bullfight and a rodeo.

Cataratas de Viento Fresco (tel. 506/2695-3434, www.vientofresco.net, 7:30am-5pm daily, adults $15, students $12), 11 kilometers (7 miles) east of Tilarán on the rough dirt road to Monteverde, has four 37-meter (120-foot) waterfalls, a waterslide, trails, and horseback riding ($55).

Accommodations and Food

A recommended bargain, **Hotel El Sueño** (tel. 506/2695-5347, standard $22 s, $32 d, deluxe $28 s, $38 d), one block north of the plaza, is a charming no-frills budget option. Sixteen rooms, all with TVs, fans, and hot water, surround a sunlit second-floor courtyard with fountain. Four more deluxe rooms have fridges and somewhat more ostentatious furnishings. The friendly owners provide fruit and toiletry baskets. Downstairs, the Restaurant El Parque has good seafood dishes. It has secure parking.

Understandably popular with tour groups, **Aroma Tico** (tel. 506/2695-3065, 6:30am-9:30pm daily), at the main entrance to town (the junction for Cañas and Laguna de Arenal), is a top choice for its clean ambience, hearty Tico fare, bargain buffet, and an excellent selection of souvenirs. Go on Sunday afternoon for live marimba music.

Information and Services

There are banks around the town square, which has public phones. **Café Internet Tica Explorer** (8:30am-10pm daily) is two blocks northeast of the plaza.

The **Red Cross** (tel. 506/2695-5256) is one block east of the church, and **Clínica Tilarán** (tel. 506/2695-5115) is open 24 hours daily. The **police station** (tel. 506/2695-5001) adjoins the bus station, 100 meters (330 feet) northwest of the plaza.

Getting There and Around

Auto Transportes Tilarán (tel. 506/2256-0105) buses depart San José (via Cañas, 4 hours, $3) from Calle 20, Avenida 3, at 7:30am, 9:30am, 12:45pm, 3:45pm, and 6:30pm daily. The bus continues to Nuevo Arenal. Local buses depart Cañas five times daily for Tilarán 5am-1:45pm; from La Fortuna at 8am and 4:30pm daily; from Santa Elena (Monteverde, tel. 506/2695-3102) at 4:30am and 12:30pm daily; and from Puntarenas at 11:45am and 4:30pm daily. Buses depart Tilarán for San José at 5am, 7am, 9:30am, 2pm, and 5pm daily; for Cañas six times 5am-3:30pm daily; for La Fortuna at 7am and 12:30pm daily; for Monteverde at 7am and 4pm daily; and for Puntarenas at 6am and 1pm daily.

There's a **gas station** two blocks northeast of the plaza. For taxis call **Unidos Tilarán** (tel. 506/2695-5324), or hail one on the west side of the plaza.

Cañas and Vicinity

As you continue northwest along Highway 1 from Cañas, the first impression is of a vast barren plain, burning hot in dry season, with palms rising like tattered umbrellas over the scrubby landscape, flanked to the east by the steep-sided volcanoes of the Cordillera de Guanacaste, from which rivers feed the marshy wetlands of the Tempisque Basin. Away from the main highway, the villages of whitewashed houses are as welcoming as any in the country. For the traveler interested in history or architecture, there are some intriguing sights, and the area is charged with scenic beauty.

CAÑAS

Cañas is a modest-size town and a pivotal point for exploring Parque Nacional Palo Verde (west) or Laguna de Arenal (east), and

for rafting trips on the Río Corobicí. Named for the white-flowered wild cane that still grows in patches hereabouts, Cañas is indisputably a cowboy town, as the many tanned *sabaneros* riding horses and shaded by wide-brimmed hats attest. Note the **Monumento a los Boyeros** (Ave. 5 and Hwy. 1), dedicated to yesteryear's oxcart drivers. Worth a stop is the main church—the **Parroquia de Cañas** (on the main plaza)—with its facade entirely inlaid with mosaic, the work of local conceptual artist Otto Apuy, who has graced the interior with psychedelic murals, including rainforest-themed stained-glass windows.

A paved road runs west from Cañas 14 kilometers (9 miles) to the village of **Bebedero,** a gateway to Parque Nacional Palo Verde; there's no bridge, but boats will take passengers across the wide Río Tenorio.

Cañas

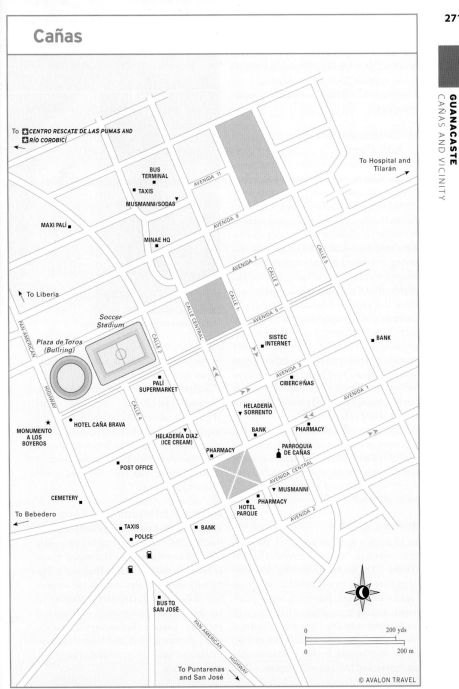

To ✚ CENTRO RESCATE DE LAS PUMAS AND
✚ RÍO COROBICÍ

To Hospital and Tilarán

BUS TERMINAL
■ TAXIS
MUSMANNI/SODAS ▼

AVENIDA 11

AVENIDA 9

MAXI PALÍ ■

MINAE HQ
■

AVENIDA 7

To Liberia

Soccer Stadium

CALLE 5

CALLE 3

CALLE 1

CALLE CENTRAL

AVENIDA 5

SISTEC INTERNET
■

■ BANK

Plaza de Toros (Bullring)

CALLE 2

PALÍ SUPERMARKET

AVENIDA 3

CIBERC@ÑAS
■

PAN-AMERICAN

HIGHWAY

MONUMENTO A LOS BOYEROS ★

● HOTEL CAÑA BRAVA

CALLE 4

HELADERÍA SORRENTO ▼

AVENIDA 1

HELADERÍA DIAZ (ICE CREAM)

BANK
■

PHARMACY ■

PHARMACY ■

PARROQUIA DE CAÑAS

POST OFFICE ■

AVENIDA CENTRAL

CEMETERY ■

▼ MUSMANNI

To Bebedero

■ TAXIS
■ POLICE

HOTEL PARQUE ● PHARMACY

AVENIDA 2

■ BANK

BUS TO SAN JOSÉ

PAN-AMERICAN HIGHWAY

0   200 yds
0   200 m

To Puntarenas and San José

© AVALON TRAVEL

Seven kilometers (4.5 miles) north of Cañas and one kilometer (0.6 miles) north of the Río Corobicí, a well-paved road, Highway 6, leads northeast 58 kilometers (36 miles) to Upala in the northern lowlands via Bijagua, in the low-lying saddle of the Tenorio and Miravalles volcanoes.

★ Centro de Rescate Las Pumas

Centro de Rescate Las Pumas (Las Pumas Rescue Center, tel. 506/2669-6044, www.centrorescatelaspumas.org, 8am-4pm daily, adults $10, students and children $5), five kilometers (3 miles) north of Cañas, was founded by the late Lilly Bodmer de Hagnauer, a Swiss-born environmentalist whose passion was saving and raising big cats: ocelots, jaguars, cougars, margays, jaguarundis, and oncillas (tiger cats). All six species are housed in large chain-link cages, but beware—there are no guardrails (nor guards), and the temptation to reach out to stroke a cat through the mesh is tempting but ill-advised. These are not house cats! Most of the animals were either injured or orphaned and have been reared by Lilly or her family, who still run the zoo. Those that can be released to the wild are rehabilitated in an area closed to the public.

Other species include deer, foxes, monkeys, peccaries, macaws, toucans, and dozens of parrots and other birds. The center also raises rabbits for sale. By selling only nonnative species, it hopes to help change the pet-keeping habits of Ticos.

★ Río Corobicí

Six kilometers (4 miles) north of Cañas, the Pan-American Highway crosses the Río Corobicí. The 40-kilometer-long (25-mile-long) river is fed by controlled runoff from Laguna de Arenal, providing water year-round, making it good for rafting. The trip is a relatively calm Class II run described as a "nature float." The river is lined with a riparian forest. Motmots, herons, crested caracaras, egrets, and toucans are common, as are

Mosaics adorn the Parroquia de Cañas.

howler monkeys, caimans, and iguanas basking on the riverbanks.

Safaris Corobicí (tel. 506/2669-6191, www.nicoya.com) has an office beside Highway 1, about 400 meters (0.25 miles) south of the river. It has guided floats on the river ($37-60), as does **Ríos Tropicales** (www.riostropicales.com), based at Restaurante Rincón Corobicí (tel. 506/2669-6262, www.rinconcorobici.com).

Accommodations and Food

You can camp at the budget **Hotel Capazuri** (tel. 506/2669-6280, camping $12 pp, rooms $25 pp), two kilometers (1.2 miles) north of town, on the east side of Highway 1. The friendly live-in owners rent out 19 rooms in two modern blocks; they vary in size, but all are clean and simply furnished, with fans and hot water. Capazuri has showers and toilets, plus a swimming pool, and hosts dances on Friday and Saturday evenings that are popular with locals.

Combining the atmosphere of a venerable cattle hacienda (which it is) and a stylish modern hotel, **Hacienda La Pacífica** (tel. 506/2669-6050, www.pacificacr.com, low season $53-59 s/d, high season $66-96 s/d, including breakfast) plays up its historic ambience in spacious rooms with high ceilings, wrought-iron candelabras, and huge colonial-style oak closets. Rooms have cable TV, Wi-Fi, and lovely modern baths. Alas, the mattresses and pillows are truly awful. But the delightfully rustic restaurant (7am-9pm daily, $5-15) serves an eclectic menu that includes cream of tomato soup, pastas, and tenderloin pepper steak. Most dishes are served with organic rice grown on the hacienda.

Restaurante Rincón Corobicí (tel. 506/2669-6262, www.rinconcorobici.com, 8am-6pm daily), beside the Pan-American Highway, is a pleasant place to eat, with good seafood dishes and a porch over the river where you can watch rafters go by. It prepares an excellent sea bass in garlic ($10); wash it down with superb lemonade.

You can't miss the huge signs on the Pan-American Highway advertising **Bar-B-Q Tres Hermanas** (tel. 506/2662-8584, www.bbqtreshermanas.com, 7am-9pm daily), about 20 kilometers (12 miles) south of town. Carnivores will devour the marinated and slow-grilled chicken, pork, and beef.

Information and Services

The **Comité de Cultura** (tel. 506/2669-0042), in the Edificio Palacio Municipal, on the north side of the main plaza, has visitor information. There are banks in the town center. The **post office** is on Avenida 3, about 30 meters (100 feet) west of Calle 4. The **police station** (tel. 506/2669-0057) is two kilometers (1.2 miles) south of town.

Internet Cibercañas (Ave. 3, Calles 1/3, tel. 506/2669-5232) is open 8:15am-9pm Monday-Saturday, 2pm-9pm Sunday. The **MINAE National Park Service headquarters** (tel. 506/2669-0533) is on Avenida 9, Calle Central.

Getting There

Empresa La Cañera (tel. 506/2258-5792) buses depart San José (3 hours, $3) for Cañas from Calle 14, Avenidas 1/3, five times daily 7:30am-6:30pm. **Empresa Reina del Campo** (tel. 506/2663-1752) buses depart Liberia nine times daily. Buses depart Cañas for San José from Calle 1, Avenidas 9/11, five times daily 5:30am-5pm.

Taxis Unidos de Cañas (tel. 506/2669-0898) has taxis on call.

MIRAVALLES VOLCANO

The small, nondescript town of Bagaces is on Highway 1, about 22 kilometers (14 miles) north of Cañas. Bagaces is the gateway to Parque Nacional Palo Verde (west) and Volcán Miravalles (east).

Highway 164 leads northeast from Bagaces and climbs steadily up the western shoulder of Volcán Miravalles (2,028 meters/6,654 feet), enshrined within the **Zona Protectora Miravalles** (Miravalles Protected Zone). The almost perfectly conical volcano is the highest in the Cordillera de Guanacaste. The western slopes are covered with savanna scrub; the northern and eastern slopes are lush, fed by moist clouds that sweep in from the Caribbean. The southern slopes are cut with deep canyons and licked by ancient lava tongues, with fumaroles spouting and hissing like mini Old Faithfuls. The forests, replete with wildlife, are easily accessed from the road. There are no developed trails or facilities for visitors, however, and no ranger station.

Highway 164 runs via the village of **Guayabo,** 21 kilometers (13 miles) north of Bagaces (it has a bank, an Internet café, and several *cabinas*). It is paved as far as **Aguas Claras** and extends beyond to the hamlet of San José in the northern lowlands. If you're souvenir shopping, call in at **Galería Tony Jiménez** (tel. 506/8821-8358, www.tonyjimenez.com), midway between Guayabo and Aguas Claras.

A loop road from Highway 164 leads east via the community of **La Fortuna de**

Bagaces to **Las Hornillas** (Little Ovens), an area of intensely bubbling mud pots and fumaroles expelling foul gases and steam. Here the Costa Rican Institute of Electricity (ICE) harnesses geothermal energy for electric power, with two plants that tap the superheated vapor deep within the volcano's bowels. You can visit the main geothermal plant, **Planta Miravalles** (tel. 506/2673-1111, ext. 232), about two kilometers (1.2 miles) north of Fortuna, by appointment.

★ Las Hornillas Volcanic Activity Center

The prime spot to enjoy the volcanic activity is the mesmerizing **Las Hornillas Volcanic Activity Center** (tel. 506/8839-9769, www. hornillas.com, 8am-5pm daily, $35), a "walkable live crater" two kilometers (1.2 miles) southeast of the ICE geothermal plant. Boardwalks lead through the crater itself, with mud pools and fumaroles hissing and bubbling all around. You can walk around at will and even take a therapeutic bath in warm mud, while a two-hour guided tour ($45) includes a tractor tour to waterfalls. A highlight is the 100-meter-long (330-foot-long) waterslide. It recently added three pedestrian swing bridges. It has showers and toilets, plus four cabins ($50 s, $100 d, including unlimited use of the facility).

★ Río Perdido Activity Center

"Wow" was my first reaction on seeing the deluxe **Río Perdido Activity Center** (tel. 506/2673-3600, www.rioperdido.com, 9am-5pm daily), which opened in 2013 in a previously unexplored river valley on the southern slopes of Volcán Miravalles. In fact, the name Río Perdido (Lost River) refers to its remote location near the hamlet of San Bernardo de Bagaces, northeast of Bagaces. It encompasses a 200-hectare (500-acre) semideciduous forest reserve atop the Río Blanco canyon, framed by 46-meter (150-foot) soaring rock walls.

At its core is a very sophisticated restaurant and spa, with stunning contemporary architecture and panoramic views through a curvilinear floor-to-ceiling wall of glass overlooking a swimming pool—one of three that grace the property. Gourmet nouvelle dining is strongly influenced by traditional Guanacastecan cuisine, courtesy of chef Andrés Flores, who is also a champion downhill biker. In fact, the center is billed not least as a bike park. Flores helped design the 19-kilometer (12-mile) network of dedicated bike trails ($12) that is a highlight of Río Perdido.

thermal swimming pool at Río Perdido Activity Center

You can also rent bicycles ($30-40) with advance notice, or sign up for a guided tour. Visitors also get to thrill to white-water rafting on the Río Blanco, or tubing on the Río Cuipilapa. The canyon is a setting for adrenaline-inducing aerial zip lines and Tarzan swing ("Canyon Adventure," $48). Plus you can go tubing ($40). The center's coup de grâce is probably its chic full-service spa for soothing away any aches after all the activity.

Accommodations and Food

The no-frills **Centro Turístico Yökö** (tel. 506/2673-0410, www.yokotermales.com, $40 s, $60 d) has 12 spacious, simply furnished, and perfectly comfortable cabins with verandas with volcano views, plus ceiling fans and large walk-in showers with hot spring water. It has a restaurant with a TV. Rates include breakfast and use of the facilities.

★ **Río Perdido Activity Center** (tel. 506/2673-3600, www.rioperdido.com, low season $200 s/d, high season $220 s/d) will delight sophisticates who appreciate fine contemporary taste. Its 20 stupendously stylish, postmodernist, modular, steel-shell bungalows are a city-slickers delight with glazed concrete floors, stainless steel highlights, glass walls, and lively yet calming Ikea-style furnishings, plus decks with hammocks. They're set well apart amid the dry forest, plus you get the superb restaurant, spa, and other facilities at hand.

Information and Services

A good resource is the **Cámara de Turismo Tenorio-Miravalles** (tel. 506/2466-8221, 9am-3pm daily), the local Chamber of Tourism, on the south side of Bijagua.

Getting There

Buses (tel. 506/2221-3318) for Guayabo depart San José from Calle 12, Avenidas 3/5, at 5:30am and 2pm daily and travel via Bagaces.

★ PALO VERDE NATIONAL PARK

Parque Nacional Palo Verde ($10), 28 kilometers (17 miles) south of Bagaces, protects 13,058 hectares (32,267 acres) of floodplain, marshes, and seasonal pools in the heart of the driest region of Costa Rica—the Tempisque basin, at the mouth of the Río Tempisque in the Golfo de Nicoya. The park derives its name from the *palo verde* (green stick) shrub that retains its bright green coloration year-round.

For half the year—November to March—no

mountain biker at Río Perdido Activity Center

rain relieves the heat of the Tempisque basin, leaving plants and trees parched and withered. Rolling, rocky terrain spared what is now the Lomas Barbudal reserve, in particular, from the changes wrought on the rest of Guanacaste Province by plows and cows. Here, the dry forest that once extended along the entire Pacific coast of Mesoamerica remains largely intact, and several endangered tree species thrive, such as Panamá redwood, rosewood, sandbox, and the *balas de cañón* (cannonball tree). A relative of the Brazil nut tree, the cannonball tree produces a pungent, nonedible fruit that grows to the size of a bowling ball and dangles from a long stem. Several evergreen tree species also line the banks of the waterways, creating riparian corridors inhabited by species not usually found in dry forests.

In all, there are 15 different habitats and a corresponding diversity of fauna. Plump crocodiles wallow on the muddy riverbanks, salivating, no doubt, at the sight of coatis, white-tailed deer, and other mammals that come down to the water to drink.

Parque Nacional Palo Verde is best known as a bird-watchers' paradise. More than 300 bird species have been recorded, not least great curassows and the only permanent colony of scarlet macaws in the dry tropics. At least 250,000 wading birds and waterfowl flock here in fall and winter, when much of the arid alluvial plain swells into a lake. Isla de Pájaros, in the middle of the Río Tempisque, is replete with white ibis, roseate spoonbills, anhingas, wood storks, jabiru storks, and the nation's largest colony of black-crowned night herons.

Three well-maintained trails lead to lookout points over the lagoons; to limestone caves; and to water holes such as Laguna Bocana, gathering places for a diversity of birds and animals. Limestone cliffs rise behind the old Hacienda Palo Verde, now the **park headquarters** (tel. 506/2200-0125, www.actempisque.webs.com or www.sinac.go.cr), eight kilometers (5 miles) south of the park entrance.

Dry season (Nov.-Apr.) is by far the best

white ibis, Palo Verde National Park

time to visit, although the Tempisque basin can get dizzyingly hot. Access is easier at this time of year, and deciduous trees lose their leaves, making bird-watching easier. Wildlife gathers by the water holes, and there are far fewer mosquitoes and other bugs. When the rains come, mosquitoes burst into action.

The park is contiguous to the north with the remote 7,354-hectare (18,172-acre) **Refugio de Fauna Silvestre Rafael Lucas Rodríguez Caballero,** a wildlife refuge, and beyond that, the 2,279-hectare (5,632-acre) **Reserva Biológica Lomas Barbudal** (Lomas Barbudal Biological Reserve, no tel., www.sinac.go.cr, donation). The three have a similar variety of habitats. The Lomas Barbudal park office (Casa de Patrimonio) is on the banks of the Río Cabuyo. Trails span the park from here. It's open on a 10-days-open, 4-days-closed schedule.

To the south, Parque Nacional Palo Verde is contiguous with **Refugio de Vida Silvestre Cipancí** (tel. 506/2651-8115), a national wildlife refuge that protects mangroves in 3,500 square kilometers (1,350 square miles) of riverside bordering the Ríos Tempisque and Bebedero. The banks of the Tempisque, which is tidal, are lined with archaeological sites.

Recreation

The **Organization of Tropical Studies** (OTS, tel. 506/2661-4717, www.ots.ac.cr) offers natural-history visits by advance reservation; guided walks cost $28-65, depending on the number of people. It also has birding and nocturnal walks ($30-80), plus boat tours ($45-57).

Tour companies in San José and throughout Guanacaste also offer river tours in Palo Verde, including **Aventuras Arenal** (tel. 506/2479-9133, www.aventurasarenal. com) from Bebedero. You can also explore Palo Verde from the Nicoya side of the Río Tempisque with **Palo Verde Boat Tours** (tel. 506/2651-8001, www.paloverdeboat-tours.com), departing Filadelfia and from **Hacienda El Viejo** (tel. 506/2665-7759, www. elviejowetlands.com), 17 kilometers (11 miles) southeast of Filadelfia.

Accommodations

The Parque Nacional Palo Verde administration building has a run-down campsite ($2) beside the old Hacienda Palo Verde. Water, showers, and barbecue pits are available. There is also a campsite seven kilometers (4.5 miles) east near Laguna Coralillo (no facilities). It is periodically closed, so call ahead to check. You may be able to stay with rangers in basic accommodations ($12) with advance notice; for information call the **Área de Conservación Tempisque** office (tel. 506/2695-5908, 8am-4pm daily) in Tilarán. Spanish-speakers might try the ranger station radio phone (tel. 506/2233-4160).

Visitors can also stay in a dormitory at the Organization of Tropical Studies' **Palo Verde Biological Research Station** (tel. 506/2661-4717, www.ots.ac.cr, reservations tel. 506/2524-0607, reservas@ots.ac.cr, low season $77 s, $148 d, high season $93 s, $186 d, including meals and a guided walk) on a space-available basis. Eight rooms have shared baths; five rooms have private baths.

The Reserva Biológica Lomas Barbudal has basic accommodations ($6 pp) and meals at the ranger station.

Information

The **Área de Conservación Arenal-Tempisque** (ACT, tel. 506/2671-1290, www. acarenaltempisque.org, 8am-4pm Mon.-Fri.) regional national parks office is opposite the junction for Palo Verde, next to the gas station on Highway 1, at the entrance to Bagaces.

Getting There

The main entrance to Parque Nacional Palo Verde is 28 kilometers (17 miles) south of Bagaces, along a dirt road that begins opposite the gas station and Área de Conservación Tempisque office on Highway 1. The route is signed; a 4WD vehicle is required, and high ground clearance is essential in wet season. No buses travel this route. A **Jeep taxi** from Bagaces costs about $30 one-way.

Coming from the Nicoya Peninsula, a **bus** operates from the town of Nicoya to Puerto Humo, where you can hire a boat to take you three kilometers (2 miles) upriver to the Chamorro dock, the trailhead to park headquarters; it's a two-kilometer (1.2-mile) walk, and it's muddy and swampy in wet season. Alternatively, you can **drive** from Filadelfia or Santa Cruz (on the Nicoya Peninsula) to Hacienda El Viejo; the park is four kilometers (2.5 miles) east from El Viejo, and the Río Tempisque two kilometers (1.2 miles) farther. A local boat operator will ferry you downriver to the Chamorro dock.

The unpaved access road for Reserva Biológica Lomas Barbudal is off Highway 1, at the Km. 221 marker near Pijijes, about 10 kilometers (6 miles) north of Bagaces. A dirt road—4WD recommended—leads six kilometers (4 miles) to a lookout point and then descends steeply from here to the park entrance. If conditions are particularly muddy, you can park at the lookout point and hike to the ranger station rather than face not being able to return via the dauntingly steep ascent from the ranger station in your vehicle. A Jeep taxi from Bagaces will cost about $50

round-trip. Palo Verde and Lomas Barbudal are also linked by a rough dirt road that is tough going in wet season.

Liberia and Vicinity

LIBERIA

Liberia, 26 kilometers (16 miles) north of Bagaces, is the provincial capital. It is also one of the country's most intriguing historic cities, with charming colonial structures made of blinding white ignimbrite, for which it is called the "white city." Many old adobe homes still stand to the south of the landscaped central plaza, with high-ceilinged interiors and kitchens opening onto classical courtyards. Old corner houses have doors—*puertas del sol*—that open on two sides to catch both morning and afternoon sun. Many of the historic houses along **Calle Real** (Calle Central, Aves. Central/8) have been restored, and at press time the street was due to be pedestrianized. The most interesting house is **Casa del Papel** (tel. 506/2666-0626), at the corner of Avenida 4, entirely covered with newspapers.

The leafy plaza hosts a modernist church—

Iglesia Inmaculada Concepción de María—and a colonial-era town hall flying the Guanacastecan flag. On the square's northwest corner, the old city jail, with towers at each corner, has metamorphosed into the **Museo de Guanacaste** (tel. 506/2665-7114, 8am-4pm Mon.-Sat., free). Still a work in progress, its contemporary interior has art spaces and performance venues.

At the far end of Avenida Central (also known as Ave. 25 Julio) is the recently restored **La Ermita La Agonía** (tel. 506/2666-0107, 2:30pm-3:30pm daily, other times by request, free). Dating from 1854, the church has a stucco exterior, simple adornments, and a small **Religious Art Museum.**

The town has long been a center for the local cattle industry. A **statue** at Avenida Central and Calle 10 honors the *sabaneros* (cowboys). The **Museo de Sabanero** (tel. 506/2666-0135, no set hours, by donation),

colonial-era building on Calle Real, Liberia

Liberia

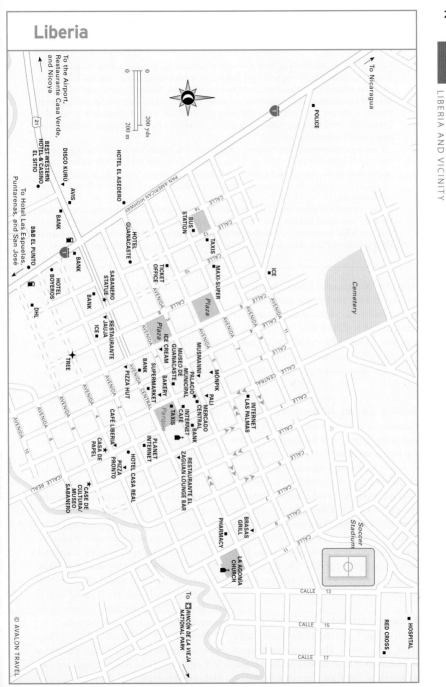

To Nicaragua

POLICE

To the Airport,
Restaurante Casa Verde,
and Nicoya

0   200 yds
0   200 m

21

BEST WESTERN
HOTEL & CASINO
EL SITIO

DISCO KURÚ

AVIS

BANK

B&B EL PUNTO

To Hotel Las Espuelas,
Puntarenas, and San José

BANK

HOTEL
BOYEROS

DHL

HOTEL EL ASEDERO

PAN-AMERICAN HIGHWAY

BUS
STATION

CALLE 14

CALLE 12

TAXIS

CALLE 10

HOTEL
GUANACASTE

MAXI-SUPER

TICKET
OFFICE

AVENIDA 5

SABANERO
STATUE

BANK

AVENIDA 3

Plaza

ICE

RESTAURANTE
JAUJA

Plaza

ICE CREAM

AVENIDA 1

TREE

AVENIDA 4

MUSEO DE
GUANACASTE

PALACIO
MUNICIPAL

MUSMANNI

BANK
CENTRAL

SUPERMARKET

AVENIDA 2

PIZZA HUT

BAKERY

MONPIK

PALI

MERCADO
CENTRAL

CALLE CENTRAL

INTERNET
LAS PALMAS

Cemetery

ICE

AVENIDA 6

AVENIDA 4

AVENIDA 2

CALLE 11

CALLE 9

CALLE 7

CALLE 5

CALLE 3

CALLE 1

INTERNET
CAFÉ

TAXIS

Parque

PLANET
INTERNET

CAFÉ LIBERIA

CASA DE
PAPEL

AVENIDA 6

AVENIDA 8

AVENIDA 10

CALLE REAL

PIZZA
PRONTO

HOTEL CASA REAL

CASE DE
CULTURA/
MUSEO
SABANERO

PHARMACY

RESTAURANTE EL
ZAGUAN LOUNGE BAR

BRASAS
GRILL

CALLE 1

CALLE 3

CALLE 5

CALLE 7

CALLE 9

CALLE 11

LA AGONIA
CHURCH

To
RINCÓN DE LA VIEJA
NATIONAL PARK

CALLE 13

CALLE 15

CALLE 17

Soccer
Stadium

RED CROSS

HOSPITAL

© AVALON TRAVEL

Costa Rican Rodeo

Fiestas populares (folk festivals), held throughout Guanacaste, keep alive a deep-rooted tradition of Costa Rican culture: *recorridos de toros* (bull riding), bronco riding, home-style Tico bullfighting, and *topes,* or demonstrations of the Costa Rican saddle horse. The bulls are enraged before being released into the ring, where *vaqueteros* are on hand to distract the wild and dangerous animals if a rider is thrown or injured. (Their title comes from *vaqueta,* a piece of leather originally used by cowboys on haciendas to make stubborn bulls move in the direction desired, much as the red cape is used by Spanish matadors.)

Cowboys ride bareback and hang onto angry, jumping, twisting bulls with only one hand (or "freestyle"—with no hands), although the *vaqueta* has given way to a red cloth (called a *capote* or *muleta*) or even the occasional clown. The *recorridos* also feature "best bull" competitions and incredible displays of skill—such as *sabaneros* (cowboys) who lasso bulls with their backs turned to the animals.

The events are a grand excuse for inebriation. As more and more beer is consumed, it fuels bravado, and scores of Ticos pour into the ring. A general melee ensues as Ticos try to prove their manhood by running past the bull, which is kept enraged with an occasional prod from an electric fork or a sharp instrument. The bull is never killed, but it's a pathetic sight nonetheless.

housed in the venerable Casa de la Cultura, honors the local cowboy tradition with saddles and other miscellaneous antiquities, scattered around as if in an attic. The building is a perfect example of a simple Liberian home with doors. It's maintained by volunteers of the Grupo Associación para la Cultura de Liberia.

Africa Safari Adventure Park

Guanacaste's savanna landscape is a perfect setting for **Africa Safari Adventure Park** (tel. 506/2666-1111, www.africasafaricostarica.com, 8am-6pm daily, adults $50, children $25), formerly Africa Mía, a private wildlife reserve at El Salto, nine kilometers (5.5 miles) south of Liberia. Elands, camels, ostriches, and zebras kick up dust alongside antelopes, giraffes, warthogs, and other creatures. The tour is in an open-air safari Jeep or a tractor-pulled trailer. The facility includes a gorgeous waterfall, and a snorkeling option is offered.

Entertainment and Events

The best time to visit is **Día de Guanacaste** (July 25), when the town celebrates Guanacaste's 1812 secession from Nicaragua, with rodeos, bullfights, parades, marimba music, and firecrackers. A similar passion is stirred for the Semana Cultural, the first week of September.

The Best Western Hotel & Casino El Sitio has a small **casino** (tel. 506/2666-1211, 4pm-5am Mon.-Sat.). The **Disco Kurú** (tel. 506/2666-0769, cover $5), across the street, pulses Thursday-Saturday and has karaoke Monday-Wednesday. **Restaurante El Zaguán** (Ave. Central, Calle 1, tel. 506/2666-2456, 11:30am-10pm Mon.-Fri., 7:30am-10pm Sat.-Sun.) hosts live music, from traditional guitar to electronica.

Café Liberia (Calle Real, Ave. 4, tel. 506/2653-1660, 10am-10pm daily), in a 120-year-old building declared a National Monument, is a fabulous venue for poetry readings, dance classes, and music lessons. Bohemians will appreciate the artistic events at **Hidden Garden Art Gallery** (tel. 506/2667-0592 or 506/8386-6872, http://hiddengarden.thevanstonegroup.com, 9am-3pm Tues.-Sat.), five kilometers (3 miles) west of the airport. The gallery displays works by almost 50 local artists, some renowned.

Multicines (tel. 506/2665-1515), in Plaza Liberia Shopping Center, one kilometer (0.6 miles) south of town, shows first-run Hollywood movies.

a saddlemaker store in Liberia

506/2665-2986, www.elpuntohotel.com, $60 s, $70 d), occupying a former school on the Pan-American Highway, 200 meters (660 feet) south of the main junction. Here, former classrooms have cleverly metamorphosed into six quirky, studio-style air-conditioned rooms furnished in colorful minimalist Ikea style, with upstairs lofts (which can get warm) and patios with lounge chairs. Gorgeous private baths feature organic toiletries and lots of steaming hot water. A common room has cable TV and Wi-Fi.

Out near the airport, the snazzy five-story **Hotel Hilton Garden Inn** (tel. 506/2690-8888, http://hiltongardeninn1.hilton.com, from $109 s/d) fits the usual Hilton mold and is by far the most sophisticated and stylish hotel in the area. State-of-the-art amenities in the comfy rooms include 32-inch high-definition TVs. It has a swimming pool, a gym, and a business center.

Accommodations

Backpackers and budget hounds will find the best bargain to be the lackluster **Hotel Guanacaste** (tel. 506/2666-0085, www.hi-guanacaste.com, dorms $8, private rooms $11-16 s, $26 d, including tax, 15 percent discount with HI card), affiliated with Hostelling International. Truckers prefer this popular option, with 27 simple dorms and private rooms with fans; some have private cold-water baths. There's table tennis, a restaurant, a TV lounge, Skype for free international calls, and secure parking. Camping ($5 pp) is available.

For comfort, opt for the **Best Western El Sitio Hotel & Casino** (tel. 506/2666-1211, U.S. tel. 800-780-7234, www.bestwestern.com, from $53 s/d), 150 meters (500 feet) west of Highway 1 on the road to Nicoya. This modern motel-type chain hotel has 52 predictably furnished rooms with private baths. There's a large swimming pool and a sundeck, plus a gift store and a tour desk.

For intimacy, the most appealing place is ★ **El Punto Bed & Breakfast** (tel.

Food

Liberia offers some tremendous options for dining, including **Restaurante Jauja** (tel. 506/2665-2061, www.restaurantejaujacr.com, 11am-11pm Mon.-Sat., 11am-11pm Sun.), with elegant rattan furnishings and an open patio with a huge tree. Go for the bargain-priced *plato ejecutivo* lunch ($5), nightly specials ($10) such as chicken salad, dorado with papaya sauce, and apple strudel with ice cream, and even sushi. It also has tremendous baked goods.

Taking Liberia into gourmet heights is ★ **Casa Verde** (tel. 506/2665-5037, 11am-9pm daily), alias The Greenhouse, in a dramatic modernist building two kilometers (1.2 miles) west of Liberia. This super-stylish restaurant boasts walls of glass, glazed concrete floors, and delicious fusion dishes, such as stroganoff ($13), baby-back ribs ($23), and Thai-style fish with curry coconut and onion ($13). For breakfast, how about pancakes, huevos rancheros, or a full Greenhouse breakfast ($10)? It even has a separate sushi bar and hosts a five-course dinner with live music on Friday nights. Fresh-squeezed juices are served in full carafes. The owners, Israel, from Venezuela, and Tanya, from New Zealand, have concocted a fantastic venue and in 2014 opened an equally chic adjoining lounge bar.

The best coffee shop around is **Café Liberia** (Calle Real, Ave. 4, tel. 506/2653-1660, 7am-10pm Mon.-Sat.), where new French owners serve delicious gourmet coffees in a treasure of a building; note the Raphael cherubs on the ceiling. It also serves a good ceviche and hosts live music.

Café Europa (tel. 506/2668-1081, www.panaleman.com, 6am-6pm daily), a German bakery two kilometers (1.2 miles) west of the airport, is a perfect spot to pick up succulent fresh-baked croissants, Danish pastries, pumpernickel breads, and much more. It has an airy spot to sit and munch, but it can get hot inside.

Information and Services

The **Red Cross** adjoins the **hospital** (Ave. 4, Calles Central/2, tel. 506/2666-0011). The **police station** (tel. 506/2666-5656) is on Avenida 1, one block west of the plaza. The **post office** is at Calle 8, Avenida 3.

The icy **Planet Internet** (Calle Central, Ave. Central/2, cell 506/2666-3737, 8am-10pm Mon.-Thurs., 8am-11pm Fri.-Sat.) charges $1 per hour. There's a **laundry** at Avenida Central, Calle 9.

Getting There and Around

SANSA (tel. 506/2229-4100, U.S./Canada tel. 877-767-2672, www.flysansa.com) and **Nature Air** (tel. 506/2299-6000, U.S. tel. 800-235-9272, www.natureair.com) offer scheduled daily service between San José and **Daniel Oduber Quirós International Airport** (LIR, tel. 506/2668-1032), 12 kilometers (7.5 miles) west of town. In addition to charter airlines, most major North American carriers have direct flights from the U.S. and Canada to Liberia. The airport has a bank as well as immigration (tel. 506/2668-1014) and customs (tel. 506/2668-1068) facilities.

Pulmitan (tel. 506/2222-1650) buses depart San José for Liberia (4 hours, $7) from Calle 24, Avenidas 5/7, hourly 6am-8pm daily. **Empresa Reina del Campo** (tel. 506/2663-1752) buses depart Puntarenas for Liberia (2.5 hours, $3) from the bus terminal nine times 5am-3pm daily. Buses from Nicoya and Santa Cruz depart for Liberia hourly 5am-8pm daily.

There are three gas stations at the junction of Highway 1 and Avenida Central.

To rent a car, I recommend **U-Save Car Rental** (tel. 506/2668-1516, www.usavecostarica.com), with an outlet near the airport. Several other car rental agencies are nearby. **Taxis** (tel. 506/2666-3330) gather at the northwest corner of the plaza, by the bus station, and at the airport.

★ RINCÓN DE LA VIEJA NATIONAL PARK

Parque Nacional Rincón de la Vieja, an active volcano in a period of relative calm, is the largest of five volcanoes that make up the Cordillera de Guanacaste. The volcano comprises nine separate craters, with dormant Santa María (1,916 meters/6,286 feet) the tallest; its crater harbors a forest-rimmed lake popular with tapirs. The main crater—Von Seebach—still steams; it features Linnet Bird Lagoon, to the southeast of the active volcano. Icy Lago Los Jilgueros lies between the two craters. The last serious eruption was in 1983, but the park occasionally closes temporarily due to volcanic activity. The national electricity company has a geothermal plant, **Planta Las Pailas,** just below the Las Pailas Ranger Station.

The 14,083-hectare (34,800-acre) Parque Nacional Rincón de la Vieja (www.sinac.go.cr) extends from 650 to 1,916 meters (2,133-6,286 feet) in elevation on both the Caribbean and Pacific flanks of the cordillera. The Pacific side has a distinct dry season (if you want to climb to the craters, Feb.-Apr. is best); by contrast, the Caribbean side is lush and wet year-round, with as much as 500 centimeters (200 inches) of rainfall annually on higher slopes. The park is known for its profusion of orchid species. More than 300 species of birds include quetzals, toucanets, the elegant trogon, three-wattled bellbirds, and the curassow. Mammals include cougars; howler, spider, and white-faced monkeys; and kinkajous, sloths, tapirs, tayras, and even jaguars.

Ranger Stations

There are two ranger stations, accessed by different routes from Liberia. The headquarters is at **Hacienda Santa María,** about 27 kilometers (17 miles) northeast of Liberia, which contains an exhibition room. The 19th-century farmstead was once owned by former U.S. president Lyndon B. Johnson, who sold it to the park service. However, the main access point to the park is the **Las Pailas Ranger Station** (tel. 506/2200-0399), on the southwestern flank of the volcano and from where the summit trail begins.

Hiking

The lower slopes can be explored along relatively easy trails that begin at, and connect, the two ranger stations. The **Sendero Encantado** leads through cloud forest full of *guaria morada* orchids (the national flower) and links with a 12-kilometer (7.5-mile) trail that continues to **Las Pailas** (The Cauldrons), 50 hectares (124 acres) of bubbling mud

volcanoes, boiling hot spring waters, vapor geysers, and **Las Hornillas fumaroles,** a geyser of sulfur dioxide and hydrogen sulfide. Be careful when walking around: It is possible to step through the crust and scald yourself, or worse.

Between the cloud forest and Las Pailas, a side trail (marked "Aguas Termales") leads to soothing hot-sulfur springs called **Los Azufrales** (The Sulfurs). The 42°C (108°F) hot spring waters form small pools where you may bathe and take advantage of their purported curative properties. Use the cold-water stream nearby for cooling off. Another trail leads to the **Hidden Waterfalls,** four continuous falls, three of which exceed 70 meters (230 feet), in the Agria Ravine.

You're restricted to hiking one trail at a time, and must report to the ranger station before setting out on each subsequent trail. If you don't report back, rangers set out to find you after a specified time.

The **summit hike** is relatively straightforward but challenging. You can do the round-trip to the summit and back in a day with a very early start. The trail begins at the Las Pailas Ranger Station (it's 4 hours from here), and snakes up the steep, scrubby mountainside. En route, you cross a bleak expanse of

hikers admiring a ficus, Rincón de la Vieja National Park

purple lava fossilized by the blitz of the sun. Trails are marked by cairns, though it is easy to get lost if the clouds set in; consider hiring a local guide. The upper slopes are of loose scree and very demanding.

It can be cool up here, but the powerful view and the hard, windy silence make for a profound experience. From on high, you have a splendid view of the wide Guanacaste plain shimmering in the heat like a dream world between hallucination and reality, and beyond, the mountains of Nicoya glisten like hammered gold from the sunlight slanting in from the south. On a clear day, you can see Gran Lago de Nicaragua. It's magical—you have only the sighing of the wind for company.

It will probably be cloudy. Bring waterproof clothing and mosquito repellent. The grasses harbor ticks and other biting critters, so wear long pants. Fill up with water at the ranger station, which sells maps ($2).

You must return the same day; no overnighting at the summit or along the trail is permitted. Be careful on your descent (3 hours).

Information and Services

The park is open 7am-5pm Tuesday-Sunday, and last entry is 3pm. Admission costs $10; you need to provide your passport number.

Camping is not permitted, except at Santa María Ranger Station ($2 pp), which has bath and shower facilities; bring a sleeping bag and mosquito netting. You can buy groceries at a small store immediately below the ranger station at Las Pailas.

Getting There

To the Santa María Ranger Station: The road begins in the Barrio Victoria suburb of Liberia (a sign on Hwy. 1 on the south side of Liberia points the way to Sector Santa María), where Avenida 6 leads east 25 kilometers (16 miles) past the ranger station entrance to the hamlets of San Jorge and Colonia Blanca (which can also be reached by a dirt road from Guayabo, north of Bagaces). The road is deeply rutted, and muddy in wet season; a 4WD vehicle is recommended. Santa María is linked to Las Pailas by a six-kilometer (4-mile) trail and by a dirt road that passes through private property ($1.50 toll).

To the Las Pailas Ranger Station: Las Pailas is reached off the Pan-American Highway via a dirt road that begins about six kilometers (4 miles) north of Liberia. The road leads past the village of Curubandé (at 10 kilometers/6 miles) to the gates of Hacienda Guachipelín cattle ranch (the gates are open during daylight hours; $1.50 toll, reimbursed if you stay here). The road leads three kilometers (2 miles) to Hacienda Lodge Guachipelín and, beyond, to Las Pailas Ranger Station. A bus departs Liberia for Curubandé and Hacienda Lodge Guachipelín at 4:15am, 12:45pm, and 4:15pm daily.

Lodges arrange transfers, and the Hotel Guanacaste in Liberia has transfers ($7 pp each way, minimum 3 people) at 7am and 4pm daily. A taxi from Liberia will cost about $30-40 each way.

AROUND RINCÓN DE LA VIEJA

Several nature lodges on the lower slopes of Rincón de la Vieja double as activity centers and accept day visitors.

Hacienda Lodge Guachipelín (tel. 506/2690-2900, www.guachipelin.com), a 100-year-old working cattle ranch east of Curubandé, 18 kilometers (11 miles) from Highway 1, has more than 1,000 hectares (2,400 acres) of terrain from dry forest to open savanna, plus a 1,200-hectare (2,965-acre) tree-reforestation project. Activities include guided horseback rides (adults $62, children $52), waterfall rappelling (adults $55, students $45, children $35), river tubing (adults $55, children $50, including horseback ride), plus the **Cañón Canopy Tour** (adults $50, students $40, children $30), where you can whiz across a canyon and between treetops from 10 platforms. A one-day Adventure Pass (adults $85, students $80, children $75) lets you partake in all the fun. Afterward you'll want to soothe away any aches at its **Simbiosis**

Volcanic Mud Springs & Spa (www.simbi-osis-spa.com), close to the Las Pailas Ranger Station. The lodge also has frogs, snakes, and butterfly exhibits (extra cost).

Buena Vista Mountain Lodge & Adventure Center (tel. 506/2690-1414, www.buenavistalodgecr.com), a 1,600-hectare (3,950-acre) ranch nestling high on the north-west flank of the mountain, offers guided hikes and horseback trips ($40-45), plus an 11-platform zip-line canopy tour ($40), an aerial trail with 17 hanging bridges ($25), and a 420-meter (1,380-foot) waterslide—like a toboggan run—ending with a plunge into a pool ($15). It also has frogs, snakes, and butterfly exhibits ($10), plus the deluxe **Tizate Wellness Garden Hot Springs & Spa,** with five hot spring pools linked by boardwalks and a sumptuous massage and treatment center. It's reached via the hamlet of Cañas Dulces, four kilometers (2.5 miles) east of Highway 1: The turnoff is 11 kilometers (7 miles) north of Liberia (don't mistake this for Cañas, farther south on Hwy. 1). Beyond Cañas Dulces, the road turns to dirt and climbs uphill 13 kilometers (8 miles) to Buena Vista.

One kilometer (0.6 miles) below Buena Vista Lodge, a side road leads three kilometers (2 miles) to **Hotel Borinquen Mountain Resort & Spa** (tel. 506/2690-1900, www.borinquenresort.com), an upscale moun-tain resort built around bubbling *pilas* (mud ponds) that feed the lovely **Amhra Sidae Spa,** which specializes in thermal treatments, including full-body mineral mud masks ($65). It has plunge pools (one hot, one tepid, one cold) and a beautiful landscaped swimming pool with a whirlpool tub. Borinquen also of-fers guided hiking (adults $20, children $10), horseback riding, a waterfall ride (by ATV $40, by horse $35), and a canopy adventure (adults $55, children $27.50). It is surrounded by primary forest accessed by trails (pass on the lame "ecotour"). One-day packages are available.

Buses depart Liberia daily for Cañas Dulces at 5:30am, noon, and 5:30pm daily, but you'll need a Jeep taxi to reach the two activity center-resorts.

Accommodations and Food

To escape the tour groups that often de-scend on the activity centers, my lodging of choice is the bargain-priced Belgian-run ★ **Aroma de Campo** (tel. 506/2665-0008, www.aromadecampo.com, $49 s, $67.50 d, in-cluding breakfast), a secluded hacienda-style

Horses get a daily hose-down at Hacienda Lodge Guachipelín.

bed-and-breakfast with four simple yet exquisitely romantic rooms, each in a rich, vibrant color scheme (avocado green, eggplant, papaya, or salmon), with gauzy drapes over the beds. It exudes a perfect combination of traditional architecture and a contemporary European aesthetic, such as glazed concrete floors. Quality meals are served family-style on the open-air patio with hammocks, Adirondack chairs, and lovely views. Wi-Fi is included.

Once merely a working cattle ranch, Hacienda Lodge Guachipelín (tel. 506/2666-8075, U.S./Canada tel. 877-998-7873, www.guachipelin.com, $81-173 s, $99-173 d year-round) has evolved into an eco-lodge that specializes in adventure tours. It boasts a gracious lobby with exquisite wrought-iron sofas, Internet access, and a bar overlooking a kidney-shaped pool under shade trees. The 34 older bedrooms are small and simply appointed but have fans and wide verandas; 18 newer units are slightly more elegant. Four junior suites in the old *casona* overlook the corral, where you can watch cattle and horses being worked. The stone and timber bar-restaurant (6am-10pm daily) at the entrance to the hacienda is open to the public and serves buffet dinners to the accompaniment of marimba players.

With a loftier perch than Hacienda Lodge Guachipelín, yet in a similar vein, the Buena Vista Mountain Lodge & Adventure Center (tel. 506/2665-7759, www.buenavistalodgecr.com, $65-80 s, $70-100 d year-round) has 77 rooms and rustic yet delightful cabins of stone and rough timbers, with pewter-washed floors and verandas looking down over lush lawns and, in some, a lake. You can admire the setting while soaking in a natural steam bath ringed by volcanic stone, and there's a bamboo sauna. It provides transfers from Cañas Dulces. A rustic restaurant serves buffet meals. You can camp for $10.

The upscale Hotel Borinquen Mountain Resort & Spa (tel. 506/2690-1900, www.borinquenresort.com, low season from $144 s, $159 d, high season from $166 s, $185 d), in colonial hacienda style, offers 39 spacious air-conditioned rooms (including graciously appointed deluxe rooms and junior suites) in single and duplex red-tile-roofed villas and bungalows spaced apart on the grassy hills. They're well lit and are graced by handmade furnishings, including wrought-iron candelabras and rustic antiques (take your pick of decor: pre-Columbian or Spanish colonial). Guests move around on electric golf carts. Facilities include a tennis court, a beauty salon, a gym, a spa, and a swimming pool with a swim-up bar.

The Far North

★ SANTA ROSA NATIONAL PARK

Founded in 1972, Parque Nacional Santa Rosa (www.sinac.go.cr) was the country's first national park. The 49,515-hectare (122,354-acre) park covers much of the Santa Elena peninsula and is part of a mosaic of ecologically interdependent parks and reserves—the 110,000-hectare (272,000-acre) Área de Conservación Guanacaste. Parque Nacional Santa Rosa is most famous for Hacienda Santa Rosa—better known as La Casona—the nation's most cherished historic monument. It was here in 1856 that the mercenary army of American adventurer William Walker was defeated by a ragamuffin army of Costa Rican volunteers.

The park is a mosaic of 10 distinct habitats, including mangrove swamp, savanna, and oak forest, which attract more than 250 bird species and 115 mammal species (half of them bats, including two vampire species), among them relatively easily seen animals such as white-tailed deer; coatimundis; howler, spider, and white-faced monkeys; and anteaters. In the wet season, the land is as green as emeralds, and the wildlife disperses. In dry season, however, wildlife congregates at watering holes and is easily spotted. Jaguars, margays, ocelots, pumas, and jaguarundis are here but are seldom seen. Santa Rosa is a vitally important nesting site for olive ridleys and other turtle species.

The park is divided into two sections: the more important and accessible Santa Rosa Sector to the south (the entrance is at Km. 269 on Hwy. 1, about 37 kilometers/23 miles north of Liberia) and the Murciélago Sector (the turnoff from Hwy. 1 is 10 kilometers/6 miles farther north, via Cuajiniquil), separated by a swath of privately owned land.

Santa Rosa Sector

From the entrance gate, the paved road leads six kilometers (4 miles) to **La Casona,** a magnificent colonial homestead (actually, it's a replica, rebuilt in 2001 after arsonists burned down the original) overlooking a stone corral where the battle with William Walker was fought. The fire destroyed the antique furnishings and collection of photos, illustrations, carbines, and other military paraphernalia commemorating the battle of March 20, 1856. Battles were also fought here during the 1919 Sapoá Revolution and in 1955. The garden contains rocks with petroglyphs.

The 1.5-kilometer (1-mile) **Naked Indian loop trail** begins just before La Casona and leads through dry forest with streams, waterfalls, and gumbo-limbo trees whose peeling red bark earned them the nickname "naked Indian trees." **Los Patos trail** has watering holes and is one of the best trails for spotting mammals.

The paved road ends just beyond the administration area, near La Casona. From here, a rugged dirt road drops steeply to **Playa Naranjo,** 13 kilometers (8 miles). A 4WD vehicle with high ground clearance is essential, but passage is never guaranteed, not least because the Río Nisperal can be impassable in wet season (the beach is usually off-limits

Aug.-Nov.). Park officials sometimes close the road and will charge you a fee if you have to be hauled out. Playa Naranjo is a beautiful kilometers-long pale-gray-sand beach that is legendary in surfing lore for its steep, powerful tubular waves and for **Witch's Rock,** rising like a sentinel out of the water. The beach is bounded by craggy headlands and frequently visited by monkeys, iguanas, and other wildlife. Crocodiles lurk in mangrove swamps at the southern end of the beach. At night, plankton light up with a brilliant phosphorescence as you walk the drying sand in the wake of high tide.

The deserted white-sand **Playa Nancite,** about one hour's hike over a headland from Estero Real, is renowned as a site for *arribadas,* the mass nestings of olive ridley turtles. More than 75,000 turtles will gather out at sea and come ashore over the space of a few days, with the possibility of up to 10,000 of them on the beach at any one time in September and October. You can usually see solitary turtles at other times August through December. Playa Nancite is a research site; access is restricted and permits are required, although anyone can get one from the ranger station or at the **Dry Tropical Forest Investigation Center** (Centro de los Investigaciones, tel. 506/2666-5051, ext. 233), next to the administrative center, which undertakes biological research. It is not open to visitors.

Playa Potrero Grande, north of Nancite, and other beaches on the central Santa Elena peninsula offer some of the best surf in the country. The makers of *Endless Summer II,* the sequel to the classic surfing movie, captured the Potrero Grande break on film perfectly. You can hire a boat at any of the fishing villages in the Golfo Santa Elena to take you to Potrero Grande or **Islas Murciélagos** (Bat Islands), off Cabo Santa Elena, the westernmost point of the peninsula. The islands are a renowned scuba site for advanced divers.

Murciélago Sector

The entrance to the Murciélago Sector of Parque Nacional Santa Rosa is 15 kilometers

Santa Rosa and Guanacaste National Parks

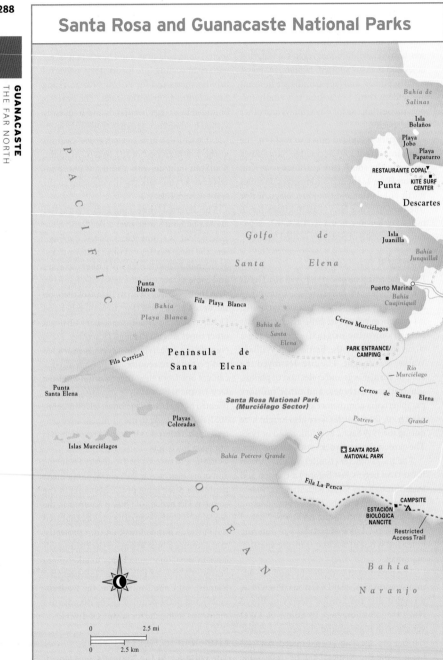

Bahía de
Salinas

Isla
Bolaños

Playa
Jobo

Playa
Papaturro

RESTAURANTE COPAL

KITE SURF
CENTER

Punta

Descartes

PACIFIC

Golfo   de

Santa   Elena

Isla
Juanilla

Bahía
Junquillal

Punta
Blanca

Fila Playa Blanca

Bahía
Playa Blanca

Bahía de
Santa
Elena

Cerros Murciélagos

Puerto Marina

Bahía
Cuajiniquil

PARK ENTRANCE/
CAMPING

Fila Carrizal

Peninsula   de

Santa   Elena

Río
Murciélago

Punta
Santa Elena

Santa Rosa National Park
(Murciélago Sector)

Cerros de Santa Elena

Playas
Coloradas

Islas Murciélagos

Bahía Potrero Grande

Potrero   Grande

Río

SANTA ROSA
NATIONAL PARK

Fila La Penca

OCEAN

CAMPSITE

ESTACIÓN
BIOLÓGICA
NANCITE

Restricted
Access Trail

Bahía

Naranjo

0   2.5 mi

0   2.5 km

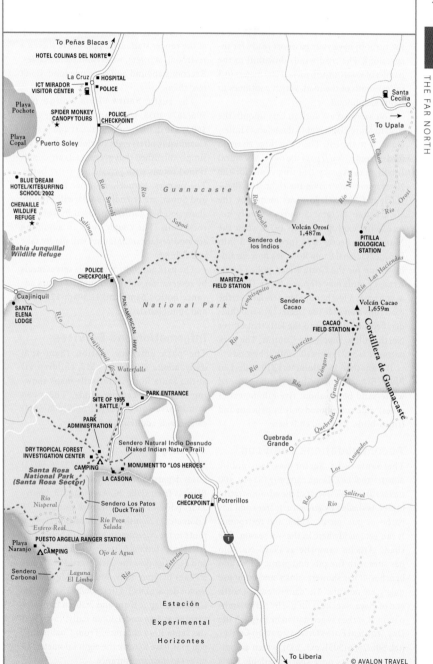

(9.5 miles) west of Highway 1, and 10 kilometers (6 miles) north of the Santa Rosa Sector park entrance (there's a police checkpoint at the turnoff; have your passport ready for inspection). The road winds downhill to the hamlet of **Cuajiniquil**, tucked 500 meters (0.3 miles) south of the road, which continues to Bahía Cuajiniquil.

You arrive at a Y-fork in Cuajiniquil; the road to Murciélago, eight kilometers (5 miles) along, is to the left. There are three rivers to ford en route. You'll pass the old U.S. Central Intelligence Agency training camp for the Nicaraguan Contras on the right. The site—Hacienda Murciélago—was owned by the Nicaraguan dictator Somoza's family before being expropriated in 1979, when the Murciélago Sector was incorporated into Parque Nacional Santa Rosa. It's now a training camp for the Costa Rican police force. Armed guards may stop you for an ID check as you pass. A few hundred meters farther, the road runs alongside the "secret" airstrip (hidden behind tall grass to the left) that Oliver North built to supply the Contras. The park entrance is 500 meters (0.3 miles) beyond.

It's another 16 kilometers (10 miles) to **Playa Blanca,** a beautiful horseshoe-shaped white-sand beach about five kilometers (3 miles) wide and enjoyed only by pelicans and frigate birds. The road ends here.

Accommodations and Food

The Santa Rosa Sector has two public **campsites.** La Casona campsite ($2 pp), 400 meters (0.25 miles) west of the administrative center, is shaded by *guanacaste* trees and has barbecue pits, picnic tables, and restrooms. It can get muddy here in the wet season. The shady Argelia campsite at Playa Naranjo has sites with fire pits and picnic tables and benches. It has showers, sinks, and outhouse toilets, but no water. The campsite at the north end of Playa Nancite is for use by permit only, obtained at the ranger station or through the **Dry Tropical Forest Investigation Center** (tel. 506/2666-5051, ext. 233), which accommodates guests on a space-available basis

(adults $15, scientists $10, students and assistants $6). Reservations are recommended.

In the Murciélago Sector, you can camp at the ranger station ($2 pp), where there's a restroom, showers, water, and picnic tables. Raccoons abound and scavenge food; don't feed them.

The rustic **Santa Elena Lodge** (tel. 506/2679-1038, www.santaelenalodge.com, $60 s, $80 d, including breakfast and tax), in Cuajiniquil, offers eight spacious and cozy yet simply furnished (but overpriced) air-conditioned rooms with private hot-water baths. The owners, Manuel, a former fisherman, and Sonia, are friendly. Sonia will proudly show you her garden enclosed by volcanic rock walls. The couple runs an adjoining seafood restaurant. Manuel will gladly take you fishing.

The park administration area serves meals by reservation only (minimum 2 hours advance notice, 6am-7am, 11:30am-12:30pm, and 5pm-6pm daily).

Information and Services

The park entrance station (8am-4pm daily, adults $10, surfers $15, children $1) at the Santa Rosa Sector sells maps showing trails and campgrounds. The **park administration office** (tel. 506/2666-5051) can provide additional information.

Getting There

Transportes Deldú (tel. 506/2256-9072) buses depart San José for La Cruz and Peñas Blancas from Calle 20, Avenidas 1/3, hourly 3am-7pm daily, passing the park entrance—35 kilometers (22 miles) north of Liberia—en route to the Nicaraguan border (6 hours, $5). Local buses linking Liberia with Peñas Blancas and La Cruz pass the park every 45 minutes 5:30am-6:30pm daily. Buses to Murciélago Sector depart Liberia (tel. 506/8357-6769) for Cuajiniquil at 5:30am and 3:30pm daily, returning at 7am and 4:30pm daily; catch it at the Santa Rosa entrance. From Cuajiniquil, you may have to walk the eight kilometers (5 miles) to the park entrance.

GUANACASTE NATIONAL PARK

Little-visited **Parque Nacional Guanacaste** (tel. 506/2666-7718 or 506/2666-5051, Sector Pocosol tel. 506/2661-8150, www.sinac.go.cr, by reservation only, $10) protects more than 84,000 hectares (208,000 acres) of savanna, dry forest, rainforest, and cloud forests extending east from Highway 1 to the top of Volcán Cacao at 1,659 meters (5,443 feet). The park is contiguous with Parque Nacional Santa Rosa to the west and protects the migratory routes of myriad creatures, many of which move seasonally between the lowlands and the steep slopes of Volcán Cacao and the dramatically conical yet dormant Volcán Orosi (1,487 meters/4,879 feet), whose rain-drenched eastern slopes contrast sharply with the dry plains.

It is one of the most closely monitored parks scientifically, with three permanent biological stations. The **Pitilla Biological Station** is at 600 meters (1,970 feet) elevation on the northeast side of Cacao amid the lush rain-soaked forest. It's a nine-kilometer (5.5-mile) drive via Esperanza on a rough dirt road from Santa Cecilia, 28 kilometers (17 miles) east of Highway 1. A 4WD vehicle is essential. **Cacao Field Station,** also called Mengo, sits at the edge of a cloud forest at 1,100 meters (3,600 feet) on the southwestern slope of Volcán Cacao. You can get there by hiking or taking a horse 10 kilometers (6 miles) along a rough dirt trail from Quebrada Grande; the turnoff from Highway 1 is at Potrerillos, nine kilometers (5.5 miles) south of the Parque Nacional Santa Rosa turnoff. You'll see a sign for the station 500 meters (0.3 miles) beyond Dos Ríos, which is 11 kilometers (7 miles) beyond Quebrada Grande. The road—paved for the first four kilometers (2.5 miles)—deteriorates gradually. With a 4WD vehicle you can make it to within 300 meters (1,000 feet) of the station in dry season, with permission; in wet season you'll need to park at Gongora, about five kilometers (3 miles) before Cacao, and proceed on foot or horseback.

Maritza Field Station is farther north, at about 650 meters (2,130 feet) elevation on the western side of the saddle between the Cacao and Orosi volcanoes. You get there from Highway 1 via a 15-kilometer (9.5-mile) dirt road to the right at the Cuajiniquil crossroads. There are barbed-wire gates; simply close them behind you. A 4WD vehicle is essential in wet season. The station has a research laboratory. From here you can hike to Cacao Field Station. Another trail leads to **El Pedregal,** on the western slope of Volcán Orosi, where almost 100 petroglyphs representing a pantheon of chiseled supernatural beings lie partly buried in the luxurious undergrowth.

Accommodations

You can camp at any of the field stations ($2 per day), which also provide Spartan dormitory accommodations on a space-available basis; for reservations, contact the park headquarters in Parque Nacional Santa Rosa, which can also arrange transportation. **Cacao Field Station** has a lodge with five rustic dormitories for up to 30 people. It has water, but no towels or electricity. **Maritza Field Station** is less rustic and has beds for 32 people, with shared baths, water, electricity, and a dining hall. The **Pitilla Biological Station** has accommodations for 20 people, with electricity, water, and basic meals. Students and researchers get priority. Rates for all are $15 for adult visitors, $10 for scientists, and $6 for students and assistants.

LA CRUZ AND VICINITY

La Cruz, gateway to Nicaragua, 19 kilometers (12 miles) north, is dramatically situated atop an escarpment east of Bahía de Salinas. A Costa Rican Tourist Board-run mirador (lookout) 100 meters (330 feet) west of the town plaza offers a spectacular view over the bay.

Bahía Salinas

From the mirador, a paved road drops to the flask-shaped Bahía Salinas, a windsurfing and kiteboarding mecca ringed by beaches backed by scrub-covered plains lined with salt pans

Restoring the Dry Forest

Parque Nacional Guanacaste includes large expanses of eroded pasture that were once covered with native dry forest, which at the time of the Spaniards' colonization carpeted a greater area of Mesoamerica than did rainforests. It was also more vulnerable to encroaching civilization. After 400 years of burning, only 2 percent of Central America's dry forest remained. Fires, set to clear pasture, often become free-running blazes that sweep across the landscape. If the fires can be quelled, trees can take root again.

For four decades, American biologist Daniel Janzen has led an attempt to restore Costa Rica's vanished dry forest to nearly 60,000 hectares (148,000 acres) of ranchland around a remnant 10,000-hectare (24,700-acre) nucleus. Janzen, a professor of ecology at the University of Pennsylvania, has spent six months of every year for more than 40 years studying the intricate relationships between animals and plants in Guanacaste.

A key to success is to nurture a conservation ethic among the surrounding communities. Education for grade-school children is viewed as part of the ongoing management of the park; all fourth-, fifth-, and sixth-grade children in the region get an intense course in basic biology. Many of the farmers who formerly ranched land are being retrained as park guards, research assistants, and guides.

Another 2,400-hectare (5,930-acre) project is centered on Reserva Biológica Lomas Barbudal in southern Guanacaste. Lomas Barbudal is one of the few remaining Pacific coast forests favored by the endangered scarlet macaw, which has a penchant for the seeds of the sandbox tree (the Spanish found the seed's hard casing perfect for storing sand, which was sprinkled on documents to absorb wet ink; hence its name).

and mangroves that attract wading birds and crocodiles. The beaches are of white sand fading to brown-gray along the shore of **Punta Descartes,** separating the bay from Bahía Junquillal to the south. High winds blow almost nonstop December-April, making this a prime spot for windsurfing.

The road, unpaved and in horrendous shape, leads past the hamlet of **Puerto Soley,** where the road splits. The right fork leads via **Playa Papaturro** to **Jobo,** a fishing village at the tip of Punta Descartes. Turn right in Jobo for **Playa Jobo** and **Playa la Coyotera.** The left fork leads to Bahía Junquillal; a 4WD vehicle is essential (this route was impassable during my last rainy-season visit due to mud and a washed-out bridge). En route, you'll pass **Refugio de Vida Silvestre Chenailles,** a private wildlife refuge not currently open to the public.

Refugio Nacional de Vida Silvestre Isla Bolaños (Bolaños Island National Wildlife Refuge) protects one of only four nesting sites in Costa Rica for the brown pelican, and the only known nesting site for the American oystercatcher. Frigate birds also nest on the rocky crag, about 500 meters (0.3 miles) east of Punta Descartes, during the January-March mating season. Visitors are not allowed to set foot on the island, but you can hire a boat and a guide in Puerto Soley or Jobo to take you within 50 meters (165 feet).

Recreation

Eco-Wind (tel. 506/2235-8810, www.ecoplaya. com, high season only) surf center at Eco-Playa Resort, at Playa Papaturro, and the **Kite Surf Center** (Blue Dream Hotel & Spa, tel. 506/8826-5221, www.bluedreamhotel.com) rent boards and offer classes and courses in windsurfing.

Ashore, adrenaline junkies can get their highs at **Spider Monkey Canopy Tour** (tel. 506/2679-8227), with its 11-cable zip line, on the road to Bahía Solanos.

Accommodations and Food

My favorite hostelry is **Amalia's Inn** (tel./fax 506/2679-9618, $25 pp), 100 meters (330 feet) south of the plaza. This charming place is operated by a friendly Tica and boasts a fabulous cliff-top perch with views over Bahía Salinas. Its eight rooms are large and cool, with tile floors, leather sofas, and striking paintings by the owner's late father, Lester Bounds. All have private baths. A pool is handy for cooling off, though the inn's setting is breezy enough. Breakfast and picnics are prepared on request.

The modern two-story **Blue Dream Hotel** (tel. 506/8826-5221, www.bluedream-hotel.com, Nov.-Sept., from $25 s, $35 d), at Playa Papaturro, specializes in windsurfing and has nine rooms, including a budget dorm room ($12 pp), with terra-cotta floors and sliding glass doors to terraces with views, plus four larger wooden rooms for three people. The restaurant serves Italian fare, including pizza, and jams in locals for postprandial pleasures such as videos and live music under the stars. Its room rates are inanely complicated, varying almost monthly. It closes for October.

Information and Services

There's a bank opposite the gas station on Highway 1 as you enter La Cruz. The **police station** (tel. 506/2679-9117), **Red Cross** (tel. 506/2679-9146), and **medical clinic** (tel. 506/2679-9116) are here too. There's an Internet café next to Amalia's Inn.

Getting There

Transportes Deldú (tel. 506/2256-9072) buses depart San José for La Cruz and Peñas Blancas from Calle 20, Avenidas 1/3, hourly 3am-7pm daily. Local buses depart Liberia for Peñas Blancas via La Cruz every 45 minutes 5:30am-6:30pm daily. You can buy bus tickets from the *pulpería* (tel. 506/2679-9108) next to the bus station. For a taxi, call **Taxi La Cruz** (tel. 506/2679-9112).

Buses (tel. 506/2659-8278) depart La Cruz five times daily for Puerto Soley and Jobo. A taxi from La Cruz will cost about $3 one-way to Puerto Soley, $8 to Jobo.

PEÑAS BLANCAS: CROSSING INTO NICARAGUA

Peñas Blancas, 19 kilometers (12 miles) north of La Cruz, is the border post for Nicaragua. Be careful driving the Pan-American Highway, which hereabouts is dangerously potholed and chockablock with articulated

fishing boats in Bahía Junquillal

trucks hurtling along. Steel yourself for a very lengthy and frustrating border-crossing process.

The bus terminal contains the Oficina de Migración (immigration office, tel. 506/2679-9025), a bank, a restaurant, and the **Costa Rican Tourism Institute** (ICT, tel. 506/2677-0138). Change money before crossing into Nicaragua (you get a better exchange rate on the Costa Rican side).

Transportes Deldú (tel. 506/2256-9072) buses depart San José for La Cruz and Peñas Blancas from Calle 20, Avenidas 1/3, hourly 3am-7pm daily. Local buses depart Liberia for Peñas Blancas via La Cruz every 45 minutes 5:30am-6:30pm daily.

Bahía Salinas

The Nicoya Peninsula

Look for ★ to find recommended sights, activities, dining, and lodging.

Highlights

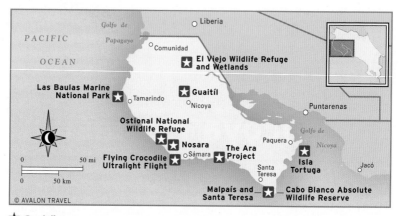

© AVALON TRAVEL

★ **Guaitíl:** Ancient pottery traditions are kept alive at this charming village, where you can witness ceramics being crafted in age-old fashion (page 308).

★ **El Viejo Wildlife Refuge and Wetlands:** The wetlands offer superb birding, hiking, and thrills, with a zip-line canopy tour as well as one of the largest sugar mills in Costa Rica (page 309).

★ **Las Baulas Marine National Park:** Surfers can enjoy consistent action while nature lovers can kayak or take boat trips in search of crocodiles, birds, and other wildlife in the reserve behind the beach. The seasonal highlight is a chance to witness giant leatherback turtles laying eggs (page 332).

★ **Ostional National Wildlife Refuge:** Site of a unique mass turtle nesting, this remote reserve has few services, but the experience of witnessing an *arribada* will be seared in your memory for the rest of your life (page 343).

★ **Nosara:** Beautiful beaches, cracking surf, plentiful wildlife, and a broad choice of accommodations combine to make Nosara a choice destination (page 345).

★ **Flying Crocodile Ultralight Flight:** Nothing short of space flight can beat the thrill of an ultralight flight along the Nicoya coastline (page 351).

★ **The Ara Project:** This breeding center propagates green and scarlet macaws for release into the wild (page 358).

★ **Isla Tortuga:** Stunning beaches, warm turquoise waters, and plenty of water sports await passengers on day cruises to this gorgeous little isle off southeast Nicoya (page 366).

★ **Cabo Blanco Absolute Wildlife Reserve:** This remote reserve is unrivaled for viewing wildlife, with all the main critters on show (page 371).

★ **Malpaís and Santa Teresa:** These burgeoning yet offbeat communities are the gateway to Playa Santa Teresa, the perfect spot to ride the waves and bag some rays (page 372).

The Nicoya Peninsula is a broad, hooked protuberance—130 kilometers (80 miles) long and averaging 50 kilometers (30 miles) wide—separated from the Guanacaste plains by the Río Tempisque and the Golfo de Nicoya. Known

for its magnificent beaches and a long dry season with sizzling sunshine, it's the epicenter of Costa Rican beach vacations. Most tourism activity is along the dramatically sculpted Pacific shoreline. Away from the coast, Nicoya is mostly mountainous.

Although each beach community has its own distinct appeal, most remain barefoot and traditional, appealing to laid-back travelers who can hang with the locals and appreciate the wildlife that comes down to the shore. This is particularly true of the southern beaches. Waves pump ashore along much of the coastline—a nirvana to surfers, who have opened up heretofore hidden sections of rainforest-lined shore. Newly cut roads are linking the last pockets of the once inaccessible Pacific coast, though negotiating the dirt highways is always tricky—and part of the fun.

Predominantly dry to the north and progressively moist to the south, the peninsula offers a variety of ecosystems, with no shortage of opportunities for nature-viewing; monkeys, coatis, sloths, and other wildlife species inhabit the forests along the shore. Two of the premier nesting sites for marine turtles are here. The offshore waters are beloved of scuba divers and for sportfishing, and water sports are well developed.

More than three-quarters of Costa Rica's coastal resort infrastructure is here, concentrated in northern Nicoya. Since the opening of the Daniel Oduber International Airport in 1996, scores of resort hotels and condo complexes have sprouted, tilting the demographics away from eco-conscious travelers and toward a high-end crowd. Aquifers are being drained, water pollution is rising, and wildlife is disappearing. Alarmed environmentalists say that an ecological disaster is playing out, due in part to government inaction in the face of developers who simply don't care. Another downside is skyrocketing crime.

Previous: Montezuma; Parroquia San Blas, Nicoya. **Above:** surfers at dusk on Playa Tamarindo.

The Nicoya Peninsula

■ FORD
□ FORD (OFTEN IMPASSABLE IN WET SEASON)

0   5 mi
0   5 km

OCEAN

FLYING CROCODILE ULTRALIGHT FLIGHT
Playa Sámara
Playa Carrillo
Carmen
CAMARONAL NATIONAL WILDLIFE REFUGE
Playa Camaronal
FORD
FORD
Sámara
Terciopelo
Santa Marta
Hojancha
CAFÉ PINILLA
Punta Islita
OPEN-AIR CONTEMPORARY ART MUSEUM
THE ART PROJECT
Playa Bejuco
Pueblo Nuevo
San Miguel
Playa San Miguel
JUNGLE BUTTERFLY FARM
Islita
Bejuco
FORD (IMPASSABLE CURRENTLY)
Congrejal (Soledad)
Río Ora
Zapotal
La Mansión
THE SANCTUARY AT TWO RIVERS RAINSONG WILDLIFE SANCTUARY
CABO BLANCO ABSOLUTE WILDLIFE RESERVE
Isla Cabo Blanco
Cabo Blanco
SANTA TERESA
MALPAÍS
Playa Santa Teresa
Playa Hermosa
Playa Manzanillo
Punta Coyote
Playa Coyote
Playa Caletas
Caletas-Ario Wildlife Refuge
Playa Bongo
Bajos de Ario
Bello Horizonte
FORD
FORD
Río Bongo
San Francisco de Coyote
La Y Griega
Jabillo
Quebrada Grande
Río Tabillo
Carmona
MONTEZUMA
MONTEZUMA WATERFALL CANOPY TOUR/MARIPOSARIO
MONTEZUMA GARDENS
Cabuya
NICOLAS WEISSENBURG ABSOLUTE RESERVE
Cóbano
Playa Montezuma
Playa Cocalito
Tambor
Río Frío
Cerro Frío
Zapote
Karen Mogensen Wildlife Refuge
San Ramón de Río Blanco
TANGO MAR COUNTRY CLUB
ISLA TORTUGA
Playa Tambor
Punta Tambor
Punta Piedra Amarilla
LOS DELFINES GOLF & COUNTRY CLUB
Pochote
HACIENDA LA ESPERANZA
Cerro Buenavista
Montaña Grande
Jicaral
Río Guarial
CURU NATIONAL WILDLIFE REFUGE
Paquera
Gigante
Río Ario
Le Panto
Isla Venado
21
Playa Naranjo
Ferry
Punta Coral
Isla San Lucas National Park
Isla Guayabo and Negritos Biological Reserves
PUNTARENAS
Costa del Pájaros
Isla Caballo
Isla Bejuco
Birds Island Biological Reserve
LA ENSEÑADA NATIONAL WILDLIFE REFUGE
Manzanillo
Gulfo de Nicoya
Puerto Moreno
LA AMISTAD DE TAIWAN BRIDGE
TB
Morales
Colorado
Las Juntas de Abaranges
Islas Guayabo
Ferry
Barranca
Puerto Caldera
PAN-AMERICAN HIGHWAY

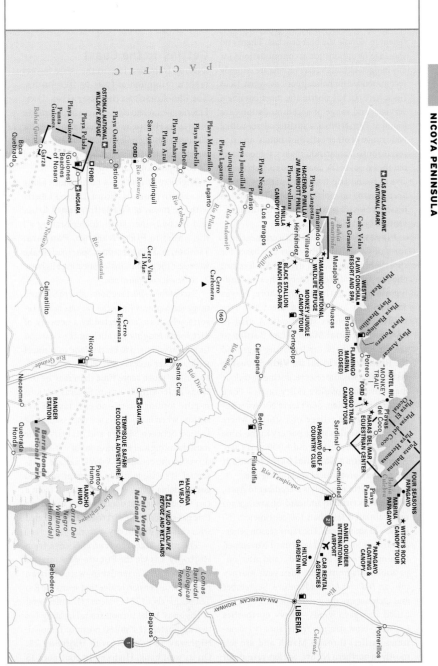

PLANNING YOUR TIME

Nicoya's beaches require a month to sample in earnest. One week to 10 days should be sufficient to sample the best beaches. There's no shortage of options for accommodations for any budget, although reservations are strongly recommended for holiday periods, when Ticos flock here. In the north, the most complete services and range of accommodations are found at Tamarindo, a surfing center with a wide range of other activities, hotels, and fine restaurants. Tamarindo makes a good base, but the layout of the coast roads is not conducive to round-trip travel. It's perhaps best to keep moving on, north or south. The section between Nosara and Sámara is a fabulous adventure by 4WD vehicle.

Playas del Coco and adjacent beach resorts of Ocotal and Hermosa are bases for sportfishing and scuba diving. Surfers can choose from dozens of beaches extending along the entire Pacific shore: Playas Tamarindo and Nosara are tops. Two nature experiences stand out: A visit to Parque Nacional Marino Las Baulas to see the leatherback turtles laying eggs, and the Refugio Nacional de Vida Silvestre Ostional, a wildlife reserve, during its unique mass invasions of olive ridley turtles. For a cultural immersion, don't leave Nicoya without visiting the village of Guaitíl, where Chorotega families make pottery in the same fashion their ancestors did 1,000 years ago. Nearby, Parque Nacional Barra Honda is the nation's preeminent spelunking site.

The best time to visit is December to April, when rain is virtually unheard-of; average annual rainfall is less than 150 centimeters (59 inches) in some areas. The rainy season generally arrives in May and lasts until November, turning dirt roads into muddy (and often impassable) quagmires that turn your journey into an *Indiana Jones* adventure. September and October are the wettest months. The so-called Papagayo winds—heavy northerlies (*nortes*)—blow strongly from January (sometimes earlier) through March and are felt mostly in northern Nicoya. Surfers rave about the rainy season (May-Nov.), when swells are consistent and waves—fast and tubular—can be 1.5 meters (5 feet) or higher.

Getting to the Coast

Driving from San José to the coast resorts takes a minimum of **four or five hours.** The **Pan-American Highway** (Hwy. 1) via Liberia gives relatively easy access to *northern* Nicoya via **Highway 21,** which runs west for 20 kilometers (12 miles) to Comunidad—gateway to **Bahía de Culebra,** the **Playas del Coco** region, and **Tamarindo.**

Highway 21 continues north-south along the eastern plains of Nicoya, linking Liberia with the towns of **Filadelfia, Santa Cruz,** and **Nicoya,** then south (deteriorating all the while) to **Playa Naranjo, Paquera, Tambor,** and **Montezuma.** Spur roads snake west over the mountains, connecting Highway 21 to beach communities.

Except for a short section south of Sámara, no paved highway links the various beach resorts, which are connected by a network of dirt roads roughly paralleling the coast; at times you will need to head inland to connect with another access road. Plan accordingly, and allow much more time than may be obvious by looking at a map. Several sections require fording rivers—no easy task in wet season, when many rivers are impassable (the section between Sámara and Malpaís is the most daunting and adventurous of wet-season drives in the country). A 4WD vehicle is essential. It's wise to fill up wherever you find gas available (often it will be poured from a can—and cost about double what it would at a true gas station). The dirt roads are blanketed with choking dust in dry season.

The main access to *central* Nicoya from **Highway 1** is via the **Puente de Amistad con Taiwan** (Friendship with Taiwan Bridge), a suspension bridge that spans the Río Tempisque about 27 kilometers (17 miles) west of Highway 1; the turnoff from Highway 1 is two kilometers (1.2 miles) north of Limonal. **Highway 18** connects with **Highway 21.** On its west bank, Highway 18 continues 15

Ferries to and from Nicoya

Two car-and-passenger ferries and a passengers-only ferry cross the Río Tempisque and Golfo de Nicoya, shortening the driving distance to or from the Nicoya Peninsula. In high season and on weekends, lines can get long, and you should get there at least an hour before departure times, which change frequently. Check ahead.

PUNTARENAS TO PAQUERA

Ferry Naviera Tambor (tel. 506/2661-2084, www.navieratambor.com) ferries departs Avenida 3, Calle 33, in Puntarenas for Paquera (pedestrians $2, car and passengers $229) every two or three hours—at 5am, 9am, 11am, 2pm, 5pm, and 8:30pm daily. Return ferries depart Paquera at 5:30am, 9am, 11am, 2pm, 5pm, and 8pm daily. Take this ferry to reach Montezuma and Malpaís.

A passengers-only *lancha* (water taxi, tel. 506/2661-0515) departs from Avenida 3, Calles 2/Central, in Puntarenas for Paquera (adults $1.25, bicycles and children $1) at 11:30am and 4pm daily. Return ferries depart Paquera at 7:30am and 2pm daily.

Buses (tel. 506/2642-0219) meet the ferries (except those arriving after 5pm) and depart Paquera for Cóbano at 6:15am, 8:30am, 10:30am, noon, 2:30pm, 4:30pm, and 6:30pm daily; and from Cóbano to Paquera at 3:45am, 5:45am, 8:30am, 10:30am, 12:15pm, 2:30pm, and 6:30pm daily.

PUNTARENAS TO NARANJO

Playa Naranjo is two-thirds of the way down the Nicoya Peninsula and makes a perfect landing point if you're heading to Sámara or Nosara. The **Coonatramar Ferry** (tel. 506/2661-1069, www.coonatramar.com) departs from Avenida 3, Calles 33/35, in Puntarenas for Playa Naranjo (adults $1.60, children $0.75, motorcycles $3, cars $10.50) at 6:30am, 10am, 2:30pm, and 7:30pm daily. The return ferry departs Playa Naranjo at 8am, 12:30pm, 5:30pm, and 9pm daily. Buy your ticket from a booth to the left of the gates at Naranjo, but be sure to park in line first. Buses to Jicaral, Coyote, Bejuco, Carmona, and Nicoya meet the ferry.

kilometers (9.5 miles) to a T-junction with Highway 21 at **Puerto Viejo;** the town of **Nicoya,** the regional capital, is 15 kilometers (9.5 miles) north of the junction.

Ferries link **Puntarenas** to **Naranjo** (for central beaches) and **Paquera** (for Montezuma and Malpaís).

Highway 21: Río Tempisque to Santa Cruz

BARRA HONDA NATIONAL PARK

The 2,295-hectare (5,671-acre) **Parque Nacional Barra Honda** (tel. 506/2659-1551 or 506/2659-1099, act.barrahonda@sinac.go.cr, 8am-4pm daily, $10), 13 kilometers (8 miles) west of the Puente de Amistad con Taiwan, is a rugged upland area known for its limestone caverns dating back 70 million years; 42 caverns have been explored to date,

and skeletons, utensils, ornaments, and petroglyphs dating back to 300 BC have been discovered. The deepest cavern thus far explored is the 240-meter-deep (790-foot-deep) Santa Ana Cave, known for its Hall of Pearls, full of stalactites and stalagmites.

The only caverns open to the public are **Terciopelo Cave** (children must be age 12 or older), with three chambers reached via an exciting 30-meter (100-foot) vertical ladder, then a sloping plane that leads to the bottom, 63 meters (207 feet) down; and **La Cuevita.** Within, Mushroom Hall is named for the shape of its calcareous formations; the Hall of the Caverns has large Medusa-like formations, including a figure resembling a lion's head. The columns known as The Organ produce musical tones when struck.

Some of the caverns are frequented by bats, including the Pozo Hediondo (Fetid Pit) Cave, which is named for the quantity of excrement accumulated by its abundant bat population (wear a mask to help protect against histoplasmosis). Blind salamanders and endemic fish species have also evolved in the caves.

Above ground, the hilly dry-forest terrain is a refuge for howler monkeys, deer, agoutis, peccaries, kinkajous, anteaters, and many bird species, including scarlet macaws. The park tops out at Monte Barra Honda (442 meters/1,450 feet), which has intriguing rock formations and provides an excellent view of the Golfo de Nicoya. Las Cascadas are strange limestone formations formed by calcareous sedimentation along a riverbed. A trail that begins 200 meters (660 feet) before Caverna Terciopelo leads through the limestone formations to **Mirador Nacaome,** offering a bird's-eye view over the landscape.

Guides and Tours

Cave descents (4 hours, $35 s, $52 d, including park entrance, guide, and cave equipment; price varies depending on number of participants) are allowed 8am-1pm daily, except during *semana santa* (the week before Easter). For cave descents, you must be accompanied by a guide from the **Asociación de Guías Especializados de Barra Honda** (tel. 506/2659-1551), which also has guided walks in dry season ($10 pp), plus nighttime tours (beginning at 4pm, 3-person minimum, $8 pp) to watch the bats exit Pozo Hediondo en masse. Budget at least four hours to visit the caves. You can drive to about 1.5 kilometers (0.9 miles) beyond the park entrance, after which you're on foot; it's hot and steep, and hungry mosquitoes await.

Reservations are required for the Sendero Las Cascadas, which leads to waterfalls, accessed only by guided tours.

Accommodations and Food

There's a campsite ($2 pp) at the ranger station, which also has simple cabins for volunteers willing to help with trail maintenance and other projects. It has basic showers and toilets plus picnic tables and water.

One kilometer (0.6 miles) before the park

limestone hillocks at Barra Honda National Park

entrance, Hotel Barra Honda (tel. 506/2659-1003, $15 s/d) is set in spacious tree-shaded grounds and has a simple open-air restaurant. It offers horseback rides. The 10 basic cabins have fans and spacious modern baths. Of similar standard, Las Cavernas Hotel (tel. 506/2659-1574, www.hotelcavernas.webnode.es, $12 pp), 400 meters (0.25 miles) from the park entrance, has five bare-bones rooms with cold-water private baths and a delightful cowboy-style restaurant and bar decorated with yokes and saddles. It has a small pool.

Café Kura (tel. 506/2659-2115, 1pm-4pm Tues. and Thurs.), about 800 meters (0.5 miles) before the park entrance, is a delightful surprise. This quaint open-air café sells ice cream, baked goods, sodas, coffees, and teas, enjoyed alfresco on a shady porch.

Getting There

The turnoff for the Nacaome (Barra Honda) ranger station is 1.5 kilometers (0.9 miles) east of Puerto Viejo and 15 kilometers (9.5 miles) west of the Tempisque Bridge. From here, an all-weather gravel road leads via Nacaome, gradually deteriorating all the while (a 4WD vehicle is recommended); signs point the way to the entrance, about six kilometers (4 miles) farther via Santa Ana.

A Tracopa-Alfaro (tel. 506/2222-2666) bus from San José to Nicoya will drop you at the turnoff for the park; Las Cavernas will send a pickup by prior arrangement. A bus departs Nicoya for Santa Ana and Nacaome at 12:30pm daily, plus 4pm on Monday, Wednesday, and Friday; you can walk to the park entrance. You can also enter the park from the east via a dirt road from Quebrada Honda, off Highway 21 immediately east of Nicoya township.

NICOYA

Nicoya, about 30 kilometers (18 miles) northwest of the Puente Amistad con Taiwan and 78 kilometers (48 miles) south of Liberia, is Costa Rica's oldest colonial city. Today, it bustles as the agricultural and administrative heart of the region. The town is named for a Chorotega cacique (chief) at the time of Spanish conquistador Gil González Dávila's conquest. The region's indigenous heritage is still apparent in the physical characteristics of the locals.

The only sight of interest is the Parroquia San Blas (tel. 506/2685-5109, 8am-4pm Mon.-Fri., 8am-noon Sat.), a church built in the 16th century, decorating the town's peaceful plaza. It contains a few pre-Columbian icons and religious antiques. Although it emerged from a restoration in 2010, the church was severely damaged by the September 2012 earthquake.

Accommodations and Food

The best budget bargain is Hotel Multiplaza (tel. 506/2685-3535, Calle 1, Aves. 5/7, $18 s, $30 d), which has 25 dark but spacious air-conditioned rooms with fans, comfy mattresses, and cable TV, but cold water only. There's a small café outside, and you're just steps from the town center.

The nicest place is Hotel Río Tempisque (tel. 506/2686-6650, www.hotelriotempisque.com, from $28 s, $46 d), on Highway 21, 800 meters (0.5 miles) north of the junction for Nicoya township, with 30 well-lit, spacious, air-conditioned cabins and 106 smaller rooms in tranquil gardens set back from the road. Each has two double beds, cable TV, a fridge, a coffeemaker, a microwave, a pleasing hot-water bath, and a blow-dryer. There's a swimming pool and a whirlpool tub in lush gardens.

The best bet in town is Café Daniela (Calle 3, Aves. Central/2, tel. 506/2686-6148, 7am-9pm daily), on the west side of the plaza. It serves excellent local fare, such as rice and garlic shrimp, and casados (set meals). Almost everything on the menu costs less than $8. There's a Musmanni bakery at Calle 1, Avenida 1.

Information and Services

The Costa Rican Tourism Board (ICT, tel. 506/2685-3260) has a small information bureau opposite the Universidad Nacional, 800 meters (0.5 miles) south of the town center.

Nicoya

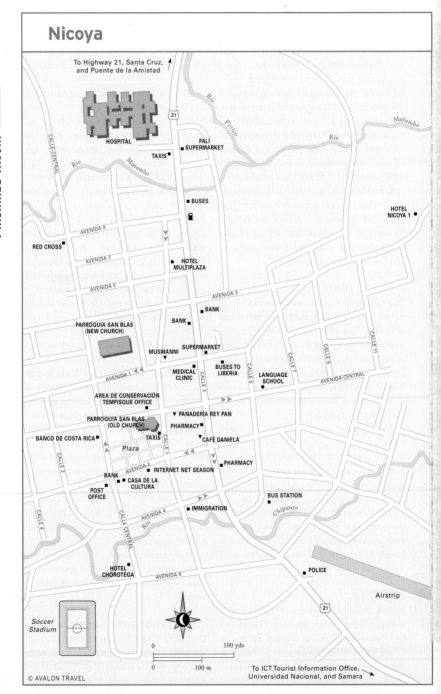

To Highway 21, Santa Cruz, and Puente de la Amistad

21

Río Perico

Río

Matambo

Río

HOSPITAL

PALÍ SUPERMARKET

TAXIS

CALLE CENTRAL

Río

Matambo

BUSES

HOTEL NICOYA 1

RED CROSS

AVENIDA 9

AVENIDA 7

HOTEL MULTIPLAZA

AVENIDA 5

AVENIDA 3

BANK

PARROQUIA SAN BLAS (NEW CHURCH)

BANK

MUSMANNI

SUPERMARKET

AVENIDA 1

MEDICAL CLINIC

BUSES TO LIBERIA

LANGUAGE SCHOOL

CALLE 3

CALLE 5

CALLE 7

CALLE 9

CALLE 11

AVENIDA CENTRAL

AREA DE CONSERVACIÓN TEMPISQUE OFFICE

PARROQUIA SAN BLAS (OLD CHURCH)

PANADERÍA REY PAN

PHARMACY

BANCO DE COSTA RICA

TAXIS

CAFÉ DANIELA

Plaza

CALLE

PHARMACY

CALLE 2

BANK

AVENIDA 2

INTERNET NET SEASON

POST OFFICE

CASA DE LA CULTURA

BUS STATION

CALLE 4

AVENIDA 4

Río

IMMIGRATION

Chipanzo

CALLE CENTRAL

HOTEL CHOROTEGA

AVENIDA 6

POLICE

Airstrip

Soccer Stadium

0   100 yds

0   100 m

21

To ICT Tourist Information Office, Universidad Nacional, and Samara

© AVALON TRAVEL

MINAE (tel. 506/2686-6760, fax 506/2685-5667, 8am-4pm Mon.-Fri.), on the north side of the plaza, administers the Área de Conservación Tempisque; it's not set up to serve visitors.

The **hospital** (tel. 506/2685-5066) is on the north side of town, and there are several medical clinics, plus a **Red Cross** (tel. 506/2685-5458). The **post office** is at Avenida 2, Calle Central. The **police station** (tel. 506/2685-5559) is 500 meters (0.3 miles) south of town on Calle 3. Banks include **Banco de Costa Rica,** on the west side of the plaza. You can make international calls from **Internet Net Season** (Ave. 2, Calles Central/1, tel. 506/2685-4045). **Inmigración** (Ave. 4, Calle 1, tel. 506/2686-4155, 8am-4pm Mon.-Fri.) can issue visa extensions.

Instituto Guanacasteco de Idiomas (tel. 506/2686-6948, www.spanishcostarica. com) offers Spanish-language instruction.

Getting There

Alfaro (tel. 506/2222-2666) buses depart San José for Nicoya (6 hours, $5) via Liberia from Calle 14, Avenidas 3/5, eight times daily 5:30am-6:30pm. **Transporte La Pampa** (tel. 506/2686-7245) buses serve Nicoya from Liberia, via Santa Cruz, five times daily.

Buses (tel. 506/2685-5032) depart Nicoya for San José from Avenida 4, Calle 3, for Playa Naranjo at 5:15am and 1pm daily; for Sámara 13 times 5am-9:45pm daily; and for Nosara at 5am, 10am, noon, and 3pm daily. Buses also serve other towns throughout the peninsula.

SANTA CRUZ

This small town, 20 kilometers (12 miles) north of Nicoya, is the "National Folklore City" and a gateway to Playas Tamarindo and Junquillal, 30 kilometers (19 miles) to the west. Santa Cruz is renowned for its traditional music, food, and dance, which can be sampled during the Fiestas Patronales de Santo Cristo de Esquipulas each January 15 and July 25.

The leafy **Parque Bernedela Ramos** boasts a Mayan-style cupola, lampshades with Mayan motifs, and monuments on each corner, including a "bucking bronco" in the northeast; a *campesina* (peasant woman), Bernedela, dressed in an apron and bearing the deed of the city founding in the northwest; the Chorotega cacique (chieftain) Diría in the southwest; and a tortilla maker in the southeast. On the east side, the ruins of an old church, toppled by an earthquake in 1950, stands next to its modern replacement

Parroquia San Blas, Nicoya

Festival of La Virgen de Guadalupe

Festival of La Virgen de Guadalupe, Nicoya

Try to visit Nicoya on December 12, when villagers carry a dark-skinned image of La Virgen de Guadalupe through the streets accompanied by flutes, drums, and dancers. The festival combines the Roman Catholic celebration of the Virgin of Guadalupe with the traditions of the Chorotega legend of La Yequita (Little Mare), a mare that interceded to prevent twin brothers from fighting to the death for the love of a princess. The religious ceremony is a good excuse for bullfights, explosive fireworks (*bombas*), concerts, and general merriment. Many locals get sozzled on *chicha*, a heady brew made from fermented corn and sugar, and drunk out of hollow gourds.

with a star-shaped roof and beautiful stained glass.

Accommodations and Food

A bargain, the motel-style **Hotel La Estancia** (tel./fax 506/2680-0476, with fans $20 s, $25 d, with a/c $25 s, $35 d) has 15 pleasing modern units with fans, TVs, and private baths with hot water. Spacious family rooms have four beds. Some rooms are dark. There is secure parking.

The nicest digs in town are at **Hotel La Calle de Alcalá** (tel. 506/2680-0000, www.hotellacalledealcala.com, from $52 s, $65 d), one block south of Plaza de los Mangos. This modest, mid-priced Spanish-run hotel boasts lively contemporary decor in 29 air-conditioned rooms with cable TV, Wi-Fi, and bamboo furnishings; the suite has a whirlpool tub. Rooms look out to an attractive swimming

pool with swim-up bar. There's secure parking. Its **Restaurante Mediterraneo** (7am-10pm daily) serves *típico* dishes and seafood such as octopus in garlic ($8), plus filet mignon ($12).

For a rustic dining ambience, try **Restaurante Juan Yi** (tel. 506/2680-3031, 11am-11pm Mon.-Sat., $2-10), facing Plaza de Buenos Aires, in an old farmhouse-style building decorated in farm implements. It serves shrimp, lobster, octopus, and other seafood.

The modern **Restaurante El Milenio** (tel. 506/2680-3237, 8am-10pm Mon.-Sat.), one block west of Parque de los Mangoes, offers seafood in a clean air-conditioned setting. For baked goods, try **Musmanni,** 50 meters (165 feet) north of the main plaza. The **Juice House,** on the southwest corner of Parque Central, sells 10 percent natural juices and smoothies.

Santa Cruz

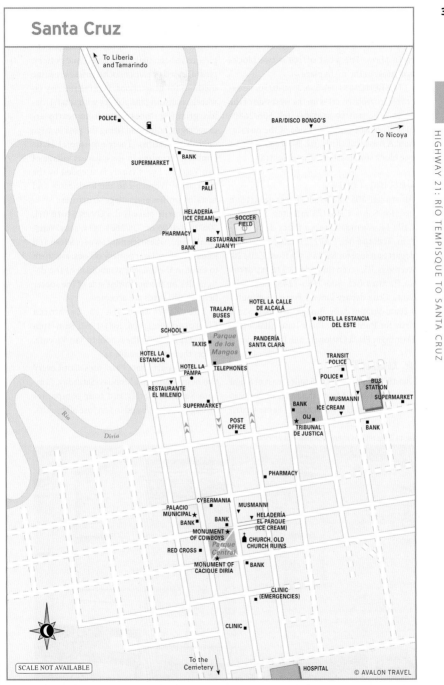

To Liberia and Tamarindo

POLICE ■

BAR/DISCO BONGO'S ▼

To Nicoya

BANK ■

SUPERMARKET ■

PALÍ ■

HELADERÍA (ICE CREAM) ▼

SOCCER FIELD

PHARMACY ●

BANK ■

RESTAURANTE JUAN YI

TRALAPA BUSES ■

HOTEL LA CALLE DE ALCALÁ ■

SCHOOL ■

HOTEL LA ESTANCIA DEL ESTE ●

Parque de los Mangos

TAXIS ■

PANDERÍA SANTA CLARA

HOTEL LA ESTANCIA ●

HOTEL LA PAMPA ●

TELEPHONES ■

TRANSIT POLICE ■

POLICE ■

BUS STATION

RESTAURANTE EL MILENIO ■

SUPERMARKET ■

BANK ■

MUSMANNI ICE CREAM ▼

SUPERMARKET

Río Diriá

POST OFFICE ■

OIJ ★

TRIBUNAL DE JUSTICA

BANK ■

PHARMACY ■

CYBERMANIA ■

MUSMANNI ▼

PALACIO MUNICIPAL ★

BANK ■

BANK ■

HELADERÍA EL PARQUE (ICE CREAM)

MONUMENT ★ OF COWBOYS

CHURCH, OLD CHURCH RUINS

RED CROSS ■

Parque Central

MONUMENT OF ★ CACIQUE DIRÍA

BANK ■

CLINIC (EMERGENCIES) ■

CLINIC ■

SCALE NOT AVAILABLE

To the Cemetery

HOSPITAL

© AVALON TRAVEL

Information and Services

There are **banks** on Highway 21 at the entrance to town and on the north side of the main plaza. The **post office** is two blocks northeast of the main plaza.

The **Red Cross** (tel. 506/2680-0330, santacruz@cruzroja.co.cr) is on the west side of the plaza. The **police station** (tel. 506/2680-0136) is on the northwest side of the bus station. A **medical clinic** (tel. 506/2680-0436) is one block southeast of Parque Central.

Getting There

Alfaro (tel. 506/2222-2666) buses depart San José for Santa Cruz (75 minutes, $5) from Calle 14, Avenida 5, seven times daily 6am-7pm. **Tralapa** (tel. 506/2221-7202) buses also depart San José for Santa Cruz from Calle 20, Avenidas 3/5, seven times daily. **Transportes La Pampa** (tel. 506/2686-7245) buses for Santa Cruz depart Liberia every 45 minutes 4:20am-9:15pm daily. Buses also depart Santa Cruz for Puntarenas, Playa Junquillal, Playa Flamingo, Playa Ostional, and Tamarindo.

★ GUAITÍL

Guaitíl, 12 kilometers (7.5 miles) east of Santa Cruz (the turnoff from the main highway is two kilometers/1.2 miles east of Santa Cruz), is a tranquil little village famous as a center for Chorotega ceramics. Many of the inhabitants—descendants of the Chorotega people—have been making their unique pottery, *piedra,* in red or black or ocher, using the same methods for generations, turning the clay on wheels, polishing the pottery with small jade-like grinding stones taken from nearby archaeological sites, and firing the pots in large open-hearth kilns. There are several artist families, including in the adjacent village of San Vicente. Every family is attended by the matriarch: Women run the businesses and sustain families and village structures.

My favorite place is the **Oven Store** (tel. 506/2681-1696 or 506/2681-1484, susy79ch@gmail.com), where friendly owners Susan and Jesús offer five-hour pottery classes; ask them to explain the ancient symbolism of the designs. It's on the northwest side of the soccer field. Credit cards are accepted.

The **Ecomuseo de la Cerámica Chorotega** (tel. 506/2681-1563, 8am-4pm Mon.-Fri.), behind the school in San Vicente, traces the ceramic tradition.

Buses depart Santa Cruz for Guaitíl every two hours 7am-7pm Monday-Saturday, 7am-2pm Sunday. Hotels and tour companies throughout Nicoya and in San José offer tours.

Santa Cruz retains many colonial-era wooden homes.

TEMPISQUE WETLANDS

The Río Tempisque estuary, at the head of the Golfo de Nicoya, is lined with mangrove forest and other important wetlands. Much of the western shore is protected within a series of reserves (most are within private haciendas) contiguous with Parque Nacional Palo Verde. Two points provide access, including **Puerto Humo,** a small village on the west bank of the Río Tempisque, about 12 kilometers (7.5 miles) north of Barra Honda; it's most easily reached from the town of Nicoya, 26 kilometers (16 miles) away. The bird-watching hereabouts is splendid, such as at **El Humedal Corral de Piedra** (Coral Stone Wetland, tel. 506/2659-8190), which protects 2,281 hectares (5,636 acres) of wetlands south of Puerto Humo, created in 2002 to protect the critically endangered jabiru stork.

Rancho Humo (tel. 506/2233-2233, www. ranchohumo.com), to the east of Puerto Humo, offers a chance to explore the wetlands and go bird-watching at this private reserve on the riverbank. In 2011 it opened an excellent visitors center with a lookout over the wetlands; it has spotting scopes. The 1,100 hectare (2,700-acre) facility offers a chance to hike various ecosystems, including dry forest, or take a guided tour using electric golf carts along 14 kilometers (9 miles) of manicured trails. **Aventuras Arenal** (tel. 506/2698-1142), in Puerto Humo, offers boat trips ($45 pp, with lunch).

A bus departs Nicoya township for Puerto Humo at 10am, 3pm, and 6pm daily.

★ El Viejo Wildlife Refuge and Wetlands

The 2,000-hectare (5,000-acre) **El Viejo Wildlife Refuge and Wetlands** (tel. 506/2665-7759, www.elviejowetlands.com, tours at 9am, 11am, 1pm, and 3pm daily), 17 kilometers (11 miles) southeast of Filadelfia, is an ideal place to explore the hinterlands of Parque Nacional Palo Verde and Río Tempisque. You can explore the wetlands— a superb birding venue—while hiking or in amphibious vehicles; explore Palo Verde on a boat tour (from $83); and thrill to a 12-platform zip-line canopy tour ($38). The refuge adjoins the owners' sugarcane estate, with one of the largest sugar mills in Costa Rica (it can be visited on the Trapiche Tour, $30, including lunch).

The beautiful colonial hacienda is now a restaurant that hosts traditional folk dances.

Guaitíl pottery is synonymous with Costa Rica's indigenous crafts.

PLAYA HERMOSA, PLAYA PANAMÁ, AND BAHÍA CULEBRA

Nicoya's most northerly beaches ring the horseshoe-shaped Bahía Culebra (Snake Bay), enclosed to the north by the Nacascolo Peninsula, and to the south by the headland of Punta Ballena. The huge bay is a natural amphitheater rimmed by scarp cliffs cut with lonesome coves sheltering gray- and white-sand beaches and small mangrove swamps. There are remains of a pre-Columbian indigenous settlement on the western shore of the bay at Nacascolo.

The north and south sides are approached separately. The north shore is reached from two kilometers (1.2 miles) north of Comunidad via a road immediately west of the Río Tempisque at Guardia. This road is a fast, sweeping, well-paved, lonesome beauty of a drive that dead-ends after 15 kilometers (9.5 miles) or so at the spectacular Four Seasons resort (not open to non-guests). En route you pass Witch's Rock Canopy Tour (tel. 506/2696-7101, www.

witchsrockcanopytour.com, 8am-5pm daily, last entry 3:30pm, $55), 18 kilometers (11 miles) from Guardia. It has 23 platforms over a 2.5-kilometer (1.5-mile) course with four hanging bridges and even a tunnel.

The south side of Bahía Culebra is reached via the road from Comunidad to Playas del Coco: The road divides two kilometers (1.2 miles) east of Playas del Coco; a turnoff leads three kilometers (2 miles) north to Playa Hermosa (separated from Playas del Coco by Punta Cacique), a pleasant curving gray-sand beach with good tide pools at its northern end. One kilometer (0.6 miles) north is Playa Panamá, a narrow gray-sand beach in a cove bordered by low scrub-covered hills—a bay within a bay. The beach is popular with Ticos, who camp along it. Weekends and holidays get crowded. The road dead-ends north of Playa Panamá atop the headland overlooking Bahía Culebra.

Recreation

Resort Divers de Costa Rica (tel. 506/2672-0000, www.resortdivers-cr.com), at the Hilton

sea snakes left high and dry on Playa Hermosa

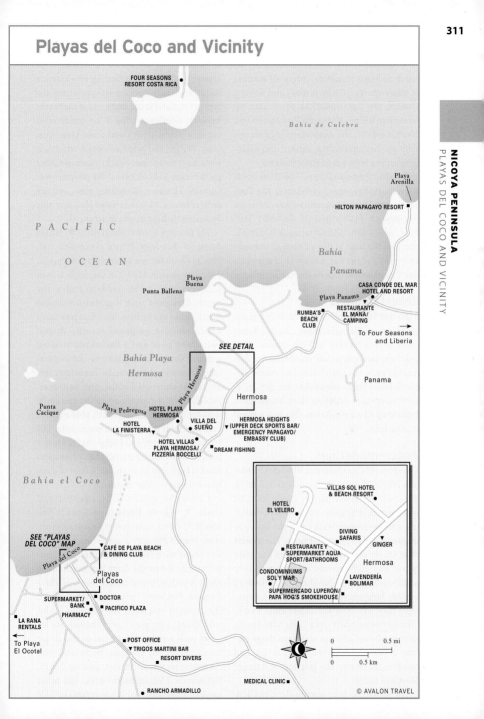

Playas del Coco and Vicinity

FOUR SEASONS
RESORT COSTA RICA

Bahía de Culebra

Playa
Arenilla

HILTON PAPAGAYO RESORT

PACIFIC

OCEAN

Bahía
Panama

Playa
Buena

Punta Ballena

CASA CONDE DEL MAR
HOTEL AND RESORT

Playa Panama

RUMBA'S
BEACH
CLUB

RESTAURANTE
EL MANÁ/
CAMPING

→
To Four Seasons
and Liberia

SEE DETAIL

Bahía Playa
Hermosa

Playa Hermosa

Hermosa

Panama

Punta
Cacique

Playa Pedregosa

HOTEL PLAYA
HERMOSA

HOTEL
LA FINISTERRA

VILLA DEL
SUEÑO

HERMOSA HEIGHTS
(UPPER DECK SPORTS BAR/
EMERGENCY PAPAGAYO/
EMBASSY CLUB)

HOTEL VILLAS
PLAYA HERMOSA/
PIZZERÍA BOCCELLI

DREAM FISHING

Bahía el Coco

VILLAS SOL HOTEL
& BEACH RESORT

HOTEL
EL VELERO

DIVING
SAFARIS

GINGER

SEE "PLAYAS
DEL COCO" MAP

Playa del Coco

CAFÉ DE PLAYA BEACH
& DINING CLUB

Playas
del Coco

RESTAURANTE Y
SUPERMARKET AQUA
SPORT/BATHROOMS

Hermosa

CONDOMINIUMS
SOL Y MAR

LAVENDERÍA
BOLIMAR

SUPERMARKET/
BANK

DOCTOR

PHARMACY

PACIFICO PLAZA

SUPERMERCADO LUPERÓN/
PAPA HOG'S SMOKEHOUSE

LA RANA
RENTALS

To Playa
El Ocotal

POST OFFICE

TRIGOS MARTINI BAR

RESORT DIVERS

0   0.5 mi

0   0.5 km

MEDICAL CLINIC

RANCHO ARMADILLO

© AVALON TRAVEL

Papagayo, offers surfing trips, sportfishing, snorkeling, and scuba trips.

Aqua Sport (tel. 506/2670-0050), on the beach at Playa Hermosa, offers all manner of water sports, plus boat tours and fishing. **Dream On** (tel. 506/8704-8210) also offers sportfishing. **Velas de Papagayo** (tel. 506/8384-1403, www.velasdepapagayo.com, $100 pp) has snorkeling, sunset, and nighttime sailing trips out of Playa Panamá.

Marina Papagayo (tel. 506/2690-3600, www.marinapapagayo.com), near the Four Seasons at Playa Manzanillo, has 180 slips. **Papagayo Fishing and Canopy** (tel. 506/2665-8458, info@papagayofloating. com), on the road to Playa Cabuyal, immediately north of the bay, has an 11-canopy zipline tour plus float trips on the Río Tempisque.

Entertainment

Villa del Sueño (tel. 506/2672-0026), at the south end of Playa Hermosa, has live bands three nights weekly in high season, plus guest appearances in low season. Sports fans might check out the charmless, overly air-conditioned **Upperdeck Bar** (tel. 506/2672-1276, noon-1am daily), in Hermosa Heights; **Embassy Club de Artes** also has a small cinema here.

Accommodations

The splendid Canadian-run **Villa del Sueño** (tel. 506/2672-0026, U.S. tel. 800-378-8599, www.villadelsueno.com, low season $60-139) is an exquisite Spanish colonial-style building a three-minute walk from the beach at the south end of Playa Hermosa. The owners offer six air-conditioned rooms in the main house and eight rooms in two two-story whitewashed stone buildings surrounding a lushly landscaped courtyard with a swimming pool. There are also condo units. Pastel-themed rooms boast terra-cotta tiled floors, lofty hardwood ceilings with fans, large picture windows, beautiful batik fabrics, and bamboo furniture. The gourmet restaurant hosts live music.

For views, the prize goes to the Canadian-

owned **Hotel La Finisterra** (tel. 506/2670-0227, U.S./Canada tel. 877-413-1139, www. lafinisterra.com, low season $85-130 s/d, high season $140-175 s/d, including breakfast), a handsome contemporary structure atop the breezy headland at the south end of the beach. Recently refurbished, the 10 air-conditioned rooms are now stylish and boast king beds, fans, Wi-Fi, and wide screened windows; some have forest (not beach) views. Another good reason to book here is the gourmet restaurant. There's a swimming pool, and the owners have a 38-foot sailboat (full-day tour $60); sportfishing tours are arranged.

My favorite hotel is the stylish ★ **Hotel Bosque del Mar Playa Hermosa** (tel. 506/2672-0046, www.hotelplayahermosa. com, low season $170-238 s/d, high season $226-294 s/d), at the southern end of the beach. Designed with a graceful Balinese motif, suites are in twin-level fourplex units built around a gorgeous amoeba-shaped swimming pool and a half-moon wooden sundeck shaded by a giant tree. Rooms feature deep-tone hardwoods, luxurious linens, coral stone-clad baths, and balconies, plus all the 21st-century amenities you could wish for. It has 38 junior suites, plus a deluxe four-bedroom spacious penthouse suite. The Niromi Restaurant and lounge-bar is a major plus. Almost entirely tree-shaded, this superb hotel is kept cool on even the hottest of days. Monkeys are regular visitors.

I love the marvelously situated and suave ★ **Hilton Papagayo Resort** (tel. 506/2672-0000, www.hiltonpapagayoresort. com, from $298 s/d), a sprawling all-inclusive resort with 202 rooms, suites, and bungalows nestled on the scarp face overlooking Playa Arenilla, immediately north of Playa Panamá. You sense the stylish sophistication the moment you enter the open-air lobby, with tantalizing views over the bay. Its infinity pool and handsome use of thatch are pluses, as are the gorgeous bedrooms with contemporary furnishings, quality linens, flat-screen TVs, in-room safes, and other modern amenities. Three restaurants include

The Gulf of Papagayo Project

In 1993 the Costa Rican Tourism Institute (ICT) began to push roads into the hitherto inaccessible Nacascolo Peninsula. The government also leased 2,000 hectares (4,900 acres) surrounding the bay as part of the ICT's long-troubled Gulf of Papagayo Tourism Project, begun in 1974 but left to languish until the early 1990s, when development suddenly took off exponentially with the enthusiastic backing of then-president Rafael Calderón Fournier.

The mini Cancún that began to emerge was intended to push Costa Rica into the big leagues of resort tourism. Headed by Grupo Papagayo, a conglomerate of independent companies headed by Mexico's Grupo Situr, the concession along 88 kilometers (55 miles) of coastline was planned as a 15-year development. Developers and environmentalists squared off over the project. An independent review panel expressed concern about illegal activities and environmental degradation. In March 1995, the former tourism minister and 12 other senior ICT officials were charged as allegations of corruption began to fly.

The Nacascolo Peninsula is an area of archaeological importance, with many pre-Columbian sites. When it was discovered that the bulldozers were plowing heedlessly, the government issued an executive decree declaring the peninsula a place of historic importance. To improve its image, the Grupo changed the name of the project to Ecodesarollo Papagayo, or Papagayo Eco-Development. Then the company went bankrupt, bursting the Papagayo bubble, and the bulldozers remained idle. In 1999 North American investors took over, and more conscientious development resulted in the 2004 opening of the Four Seasons Papagayo resort. Development is ongoing, but it has been a stop-and-go effort due to legal issues.

an Italian open-air dining room under soaring thatch, a thatched beachfront grill, and the chic La Consecha, serving gourmet fusion fare. There's a great spa.

The super-deluxe ★ **Four Seasons Resort Costa Rica at Peninsula Papagayo** (tel. 506/2696-0500, www.fourseasons.com/costarica, from $575 s/d), at the tip of Punta Mala, is considered the most deluxe resort in the country. Its 145 spacious guest rooms, including 25 suites, exude fine taste and boast every amenity you could hope for. Facilities include a gorgeous spa and an Arnold Palmer-designed 18-hole golf course (open to guests only). The setting is sublime, with two distinct beaches to each side of the tip of the peninsula that it occupies: One bayside, the other shelving into the Pacific Ocean.

Food

For simple surrounds on the sands, head to **Restaurante Aqua Sport** (tel. 506/2672-0050, 9am-9pm daily), a pleasing thatched restaurant at Playa Hermosa. It serves crepes,

ceviche, salads, a wide-ranging seafood menu, plus *típico* dishes, all for under $10.

You can walk in off the beach and enjoy open-air dining at the chic **Nimori Restaurant and Bar** (tel. 506/2672-0046, www.hotelplayahermosa.com, 7am-10pm daily), at the Hotel Playa Hermosa. The menu specializes in steaks from the owner's farm; try the lamb chops in mint sauce ($18), New York strip ($18), or coconut shrimp ($20). Nimori also serves salads, fast food, and pastas.

Gourmands rave about the Asian fusion fare at ★ **Ginger** (tel. 506/2672-0041, www.gingercostarica.com, 5pm-10pm Tues.-Sun., $5-20), beside the main road in the heart of Hermosa village. This chic contemporary tapas bar is run by Canadian chef Anne Hegney Frey. Striking for its minimalist design, with a trapezoidal bar, walls of glass, and a cantilevered glass roof, it also delivers fantastic food. Try the ginger rolls, fried calamari, or superb ginger ahi tuna. Two-for-one sushi rolls are served 5pm-10pm Friday. The bar is a local fave for its martinis and tropical cocktails.

For a meal with a view, head to **The Bistro** (tel. 506/2670-0227, noon-10pm daily) at Hotel La Finisterra, overlooking the south end of the beach. Here a creative French chef conjures way-better-than-average caesar salad ($3.50), ceviche Peruano ($5), filet mignon with peppercorn sauce ($10), and other mouthwatering fare. Friday is sushi night. It earns rave reviews and draws diners from afar.

Information and Services

Aqua Sport, on the beach at Playa Hermosa, has a public telephone, souvenir shop, and general store (6am-9pm daily). The **Emergencias Papagayo** (tel. 506/2670-0047) medical clinic is on the main road, alongside a laundry, **Lavandería Bolimar** (8am-5pm Mon.-Fri.). **Villa Acacia** (tel. 506/2672-1000, www.villacacia.com) has an Internet café.

Getting There

A **Tralapa** (tel. 506/2221-7202) bus departs San José for Playas Hermosa and Panamá (5 hours) from Calle 20, Avenidas 1/3, at 1:30pm daily. **Transportes La Pampa** (tel. 506/2686-7245) buses depart Liberia for Playa Hermosa eight times 4:30am-5:30pm daily. Buses depart Hermosa for San José at 5am daily, and for Liberia 6am-7:10pm daily.

A **taxi** from Coco will run about $5 one-way; from Liberia about $15.

PLAYAS DEL COCO

Playas del Coco, 35 kilometers (22 miles) west of Liberia, is one of the most accessible beach resorts in Guanacaste. The place can be crowded during weekends and holidays, when Josefinos flock here. A two-kilometer-wide (1.2-mile-wide) gray-sand beach—it is referred to in the plural, Playas del Coco—lines the horseshoe-shaped bay. Coco is still an active fishing village; the touristy area is to the east, and the laid-back fishing village is to the west. Playas del Coco is also a center for sportfishing and scuba diving, but these days it's best known as a party town.

Entertainment and Events

Coco is a lively spot and hosts a five-day *fiesta cívica* in late January, with bullfights, rodeos, and folk dancing.

The most fun spot is the open-air **Coconutz Sports Bar** (tel. 506/2670-1982, www.coconutz-costarica.com, 9am-midnight Sun.-Wed., 9am-1am Thurs.-Sat.), which

Four Seasons Resort Costa Rica at Peninsula Papagayo

Playas del Coco

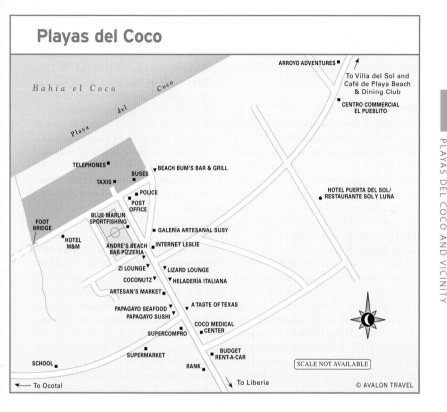

shows movies alfresco on a big screen and has live music (Thurs.-Sat.); NFL games are shown on Sunday. It serves pizza and Tex-Mex, including all-you-can-eat on Wednesday night.

The **Lizard Lounge** (tel. 506/2670-0307) has a pool table plus dancing nightly. Go for its happy hour (5pm-7pm daily) and theme nights: Wednesday is Italian night; Thursday is "ladies night"; and $2 shots are offered Friday-Saturday.

For a mellower vibe, head to the hip **Café de Playa** (tel. 506/2670-1621, www.cafedeplaya.com, 7am-midnight daily), a beach club where DJs spin tunes and special theme parties are hosted.

The **Coco Palms Beach Bar** (2pm-9pm daily), on the west side of the soccer field, is a nice spot for a quiet drink. The budget crowd gravitates to the simple beachfront **Beach Bum's Bar and Grill** (tel. 506/2670-0110),

done up in Rasta colors and with a rough-hewn wooden deck. It serves Caribbean fare, such as jerk pork and chicken.

Gamblers can try their hand with Lady Luck at the small **casino** in the Coco Beach Hotel (on the main street, tel. 506/2670-0494, 8pm-2am daily).

Recreation

Summer Salt Dive Center (tel. 506/2670-0308, www.summer-salt.com) has snorkel rental plus dive trips. **Sirenas Diving** (tel. 506/2670-0603, www.costaricadiving.net) has daily two-tank dive trips ($65), night and nitrox dives, and certification courses. Snorkelers can accompany dive boats ($30).

A fun day trip is to cruise the local beaches with **Arroyo Adventures** (tel. 506/2670-2153, www.grupomapache.com), which also offers sportfishing and boat trips; it's on the road to Café de Playa. At Sardinal, **Papagayo Golf and Country Club** (tel. 506/2697-0169, www.playgolfincostarica.com, 6:30am-5pm daily, low season $75, high season $100) has an 18-hole, par-72 course.

Accommodations

Backpackers have few choices except the beachfront **Hotel M&M** (tel. 506/2670-1212, www.hotelmym.com, $25-50 s/d, including breakfast), formerly Cabinas Mar y Mar. Recently expanded and upgraded, this lovely budget property is well-managed and has 17 simply but nicely furnished rooms with fans, cable TV, Wi-Fi, and private baths, but still with cold water only. Guests get use of a clean kitchen.

I love the Italian run **Hotel Puerta del Sol** (tel. 506/2670-0195, www.lapuertadelsol-costarica.com, low season $60 s, $80 d, high season $80 s, $100 d, including breakfast), an intimate hotel with a Mediterranean aesthetic. The 10 air-conditioned rooms feature tropical pastels, king beds, and wraparound sofas built into the soft-contoured walls. All have ceiling fans, TVs, phones, Wi-Fi, safes, fridges, coffeemakers, and patios. Two are suites with fridges, and casitas have full kitchens. There's a garden with a charming lap pool and gym. The restaurant excels.

Rancho Armadillo (tel. 506/2670-0108, www.ranchoarmadillo.com, low season $123-180 s/d, high season $180-246 s/d, including breakfast) is a Spanish colonial-style hacienda on a 10-hectare (25-acre) hillside finca 1.5 kilometers (0.9 miles) from the beach. Choose from six spacious air-conditioned suites and bungalows (sleeping up to four people), all with fans, magnificent hardwood furniture, hardwood floors, Guatemalan bedspreads, stained-glass windows, "rainforest" showers, coffeemakers, fridges, and cable TV. There's also a house for families or groups, plus an open-air kitchen beside the swimming pool, a gym, a mirador lounge with hammocks and rockers, and a library. Meals are offered by request. The estate is available for exclusive rental during peak season, with Rick, the owner and former professional chef, as chef.

Appealing to lovers of all things chic (and my favorite place to relax) is the ★ **The Suites at Café de Playa** (tel. 506/2670-1621, www.cafedeplaya.com, low season $160 s/d, high season $200 s/d), a hip contemporary-style club with a circular swimming pool, a "parachute" canopy over a wooden sundeck, an open-air sushi bar, plus lounge chairs on the beachfront lawn. It has a Hobie Cat and a yacht. Choose from five individually styled rooms with a super contemporary aesthetic. It's divine.

Food

You're spoiled for choice: **Papagayo Steakhouse & Seafood** (tel. 506/2670-0298, noon-10pm daily), with an open-air restaurant downstairs and an air-conditioned one upstairs, has a menu that includes sashimi, blackened Cajun-style catch of the day ($8-15), and sautéed Papagayo seafood au gratin in tarragon cream sauce. It's located 400 yards inland of the beach, on the main road. Next door, the same owners have opened the open-air **Papagayo Sushi,** where you can dine at a boat-turned-table it has a creative menu featuring sautéed black-tip shark, curry shrimp stir fry, and sushi and other Japanese fare.

A Taste of Texas (tel. 506/2670-2258, 10am-8pm daily), at Coco Beach Hotel on the main street, caters to the surf-and-turf crowd and is known for its barbecue burgers and awesome barbecue beef brisket.

Although barely more than a street-side shack close to the beach, ★ **Andres' Beach Bar & Pizzería** (tel. 506/2670-2052, 7am-11pm Tues.-Sun.) fires up killer thin-crust pizza. Andres also prepares sublime homemade pastas, plus specials such as lamb and steak dishes, even shepherd's pie, but stick with the prize-winning pizzas. For other Italian fare, head to **Restaurante Sol y Luna** (tel. 506/2670-0195, 5pm-10pm Wed.-Mon.) at Hotel Puerta del Sol; it serves homemade pastas ($5), cannelloni ($8), lasagna ($8), stuffed crepes, tiramisu, and daily specials, enjoyed amid exquisite Romanesque decor. It also serves cappuccinos and espressos, and has a large wine list and 15 types of beer.

For a truly classy ambience by the beach, check out **Café de Playa Beach & Dining Club** (tel. 506/2670-1621, www.cafedeplaya.com, 7am-midnight daily, $5-20). It serves great breakfasts and has a sushi bar, and the classy breeze-swept restaurant serves everything from salads and penne pasta to nouvelle seafood such as rum-sauce jumbo shrimp.

The chic **Citrón** (tel. 506/2670-0942, www.citroncoco.com, 1:30pm-11pm Mon.-Sat.), in Pacífico Plaza, also sets a tone for contemporary elegance. Chef David Posner conjures masterful Latin American fusion dishes amid surrounds that would fit well in New York or London. Anyone for rum-sautéed shrimp salad ($8), stir-fried poached sea bass ($14), or caramelized pork tenderloin ($12)? The same plaza hosts the super stylish **Congo Café Art Design Restaurant** (tel. 506/2670-2135, 8am-8pm Mon.-Sat., 8am-6pm Sun.), a superb place to start the day with gourmet coffee and tea, plus banana pancakes, omelets, and *típico* dishes. No surprise: It's also a gallery selling quality arts and crafts.

If the heat gets to you, the **Heladería Italiana** (tel. 506/8897-4463), in Pacífico Plaza, awaits with gelato at the ready.

Information and Services
The **post office** (8am-noon and 2pm-5:30pm Mon.-Fri.) and **police station** (tel. 506/2670-0258) face the plaza, which has public telephones.

Dr. Hanzel Larios Campos speaks English at **Coco Medical Clinic** (tel. 506/2670-1234) opposite the turnoff for Playa Ocotal; a **dental clinic** is next door. The **Red Cross** (tel. 506/2670-0190) is in Sardinal, eight kilometers (5 miles) east of Playas del Coco. Need a travel agent? Try **Swiss Travel** in Pacífico Plaza.

Getting There and Around
Pulmitan (tel. 506/2222-1650) buses depart San José for Playas del Coco (5 hours, $5.50)

from Avenida 5, Calle 24, at 8am, 2pm, and 4pm daily, returning at 4am, 8am, and 2pm daily. **Pulmitan** (tel. 506/2666-0458) buses depart Liberia for Coco eight times 5am-6:30pm daily. **Interbus** (tel. 506/4100-0888, www.interbusonline.com) operates minibus shuttles from San José ($40) and popular tourist destinations in Nicoya and Guanacaste. Carol at **J and C Tours** (tel. 506/8879-4029, www.jandctours.com) specializes in transfers by minivan and can arrange all manner of tours.

Taxis (tel. 506/2670-0303) park by the plaza. There's a gas station in Sardinal. **Adobe Rent-a-Car** (tel. 506/8811-4242, www.adobecar.com) has an office in Pacífico Plaza.

PLAYA EL OCOTAL
This secluded gray-sand beach is three kilometers (2 miles) southwest of Playas del Coco within the cusp of steep cliffs. It's smaller and more secluded than Coco, but it gets the overflow on busy weekends. The rocky headlands at each end have tide pools. Ocotal is a base for sportfishing and scuba diving. At Las Corridas, a dive spot only one kilometer (0.6 miles) from Ocotal, divers are sure of coming face-to-face with massive jewfish, which make this rock reef their home. Black marlin are occasionally seen.

Ocotal Diving Safaris (tel. 506/2670-0321, www.ocotaldiving.com), at El Ocotal Beach Resort and Marina, rents equipment and offers dive trips, including a free introductory dive daily, plus snorkeling and deep-sea fishing. **Rocket Frog Divers** (tel. 506/2670-1589, www.scuba-dive-costa-rica.com), also at Ocotal, competes.

Accommodations and Food
El Ocotal Beach Resort & Marina (tel. 506/2670-0321, www.ocotalresort.com, low season from $150 s, $175 s, high season from $160 s, $185 d), perfect for scuba divers, sportfishers, and lovers of sublime views, dominates Playa Ocotal. This gleaming white-washed structure stair-stepping the cliffs at

the southern end of the beach has 71 attractive air-conditioned rooms with fans and ocean views. Older rooms are in six duplex bungalows; newer rooms have their own whirlpool tub and sunning area. You can laze by any of three small pools, and there are tennis courts and horseback riding, plus a dive shop, sportfishing boats, and car rentals.

Your only food option (other than at El Ocotal Beach Resort) is the rustic and off-beat beachfront **Father Rooster Restaurant** (tel. 506/2670-1246, www.fatherrooster.com, 11am-10pm daily, $2-10) run by Steve, a friendly Floridian. This hip, happening party place serves seafood dishes, quesadillas, burgers, caesar salads, and huge margaritas ($5). It has a sand volleyball court, a pool table, darts, and occasional live music.

Playa Flamingo and Vicinity

South of Playas del Coco are a series of more-or-less contiguous beaches accessed by paved road via **Huacas,** reached from Highway 21 via Belén, 8 kilometers (5 miles) south of Filadelfia. At Huacas, turn right (north) for Playas Brasilito, Flamingo, Potrero, Penca, and Azúcar, where the road ends. If you don't turn right, the road continues straight for **Matapalo,** where you turn right for Playa Conchal, and left for Playa Grande.

If you have a spirit of adventure you can reach Playa Flamingo via a dirt road—the **Monkey Trail**—which begins three kilometers (2 miles) east of Playas del Coco and one kilometer (0.6 miles) west of Sardinal (8 kilometers/5 miles southwest of Comunidad, on Hwy. 21) and spills you out at the coast at Potrero. It can be a rough trip in wet season. About nine kilometers (5.5 miles) southwest from Sardinal is the **Congo Trail Canopy Tour** (tel. 506/2666-4422, congotrail@racsa. co.cr, 8am-5pm daily), where for $35 you can whiz between treetop platforms on a zip line, granting a monkey's-eye view with the howler monkeys (also called congos). It also has a butterfly farm, serpentarium, monkeys, and an aviary.

PLAYA CONCHAL AND BRASILITO

The hamlet of Brasilito, about three kilometers (2 miles) north of Huacas, draws a mix of offbeat travelers and sybarites and looks over **Playa Brasilito,** a light-gray stretch of sand that melds westward into **Playa Conchal**—one of Costa Rica's finest beaches. Alas, much of Conchal's white-as-snow sand has been hauled away by unscrupulous developers.

Playa Conchal lies in the crook of a scalloped bay with turquoise waters, a rarity in Costa Rica, and is backed by the Westin Playa Conchal Resort & Spa, a five-star hotel within the huge **Reserva Conchal** (tel. 506/2654-3000, www.reservaconchal.com) residential community. It encompasses the 40-hectare (99-acre) **Refugio Nacional de Vida Silvestre Mixto Conchal** (tel. 506/2654-4005, baquirre@reservaconchal.com), a national wildlife refuge that has been developed with trails and comprises dry forest and mangrove. It is large enough to support 20 mammal species, including ocelots, jaguarundis, white deer, and tamanduas.

Playa Conchal can also be accessed by road from the west via the hamlet of **Matapalo,** three kilometers (2 miles) west of Huacas, where a rough dirt road leads from the northwest corner of the soccer field four kilometers (2.5 miles) to the west end of Playa Conchal. A side road on the Matapalo-Conchal road leads west to **Playa Real,** a stunning little beauty of a beach nestled in a sculpted bay with a tiny tombolo leading to a rocky island. Venerable fishing boats make good resting spots for pelicans. ATVs on the beaches can destroy turtle nests, so stay off the sands!

Entertainment

It all happens at **Don Brasilito's** (tel. 506/2654-5310, www.donbrasilitos.com, 10am-2am daily), which is a worthy alternative for pizza. Located beside the plaza and beach, it shows sporting events on a 6.7-meter (22-foot) mega-screen, and has pool tables and a horseshoe court, plus Wi-Fi. It gets lively at night with live bands (including mariachis) and karaoke.

Sports and Recreation

Santana Tours (tel. 506/2654-4359), at Brasilito, offers horseback rides and scooter rental. There are water-sports concessions on Playa Conchal. You can buy day (8am-5pm) and night (6pm-1am) passes ($65) that permit nonguests to use the Westin resort facilities; a highlight is the **Reserva Conchal Golf Club** (golf@reservaconchal.com), with an 18-hole golf course designed by Robert Trent Jones Jr.; it is not open to walk-ins, but guests at local hotels can play by reservation.

Accommodations and Food

Perfect for budget travelers, the German-run **Hotel Brasilito** (tel. 506/2654-4237, www. brasilito.com, low season $34-74 s/d, high season $44-84 s/d), in a daffodil-yellow wooden home adorned with flower boxes a stone's throw from the beach, is laid-back, well-run, and has a varied selection of 15 simple rooms with fans (some are air-conditioned) and private baths with hot water. It has a terrific restaurant.

Gracious, bargain-priced, and family-run **Hotel Conchal** (tel. 506/2654-9125, www. conchalcr.com, low season from $55 s/d, high season from $85 s/d) is 200 meters (660 feet) inland of the beach at Brasilito. Risen like a Phoenix after a devastating fire in 2013, this charming hotel run by an English-Danish couple now boasts beautiful furnishings in nine tile-floored, air-conditioned rooms with wrought-iron beds (some are kings), ceiling fans, free Wi-Fi, and river-stone exteriors. They face a landscaped garden full of bougainvillea. The Robinson Crusoe-style upstairs lounge is a delightful space. A dive school is on-site.

For a more luxurious resort experience, check into the **Westin Playa Conchal Resort & Spa** (tel. 506/2654-3300, www. starwoodhotels.com, $302-1,185 s/d) at Playa Conchal. Spanning 285 hectares (704 acres) and surrounded by rippling fairways, the resort has 308 open-plan junior suites and two master suites in 37 two-story units amid

Playa Conchal

landscaped grounds behind the beach. All boast marble baths, mezzanine bedrooms supported by columns, and lounges with soft-cushioned sofas. The massive free-form swimming pool is a setting for noisy aerobics and games. It has three restaurants, two bars, a disco, a theater with nightly shows, tennis courts, and the championship golf course. The grounds are full of wildlife.

Laid-back to the max, Hotel Brasilito's breezy **El Oasis** (tel. 506/2654-4596, 7am-11pm daily), near the beach, is a cool place to chill, start the day with killer breakfasts such as grilled croissants and huevos rancheros ($3), or enjoy a varied lunch and dinner menu ranging from ceviche and barbecued shrimp to lasagna and grilled pork loin. Leave room for the chocolate brownie sundae. There's a large-screen TV for sports events.

Nearby, the oceanfront bougainvillea-festooned **Cameron Dorado** (tel. 506/2654-4028) is *the* place for seafood. Despite its tacky plastic furniture, it serves delicious dishes for under $10.

Information and Services

There is a **police station** (tel. 506/2654-4425) on the main road, facing the soccer field. The **Miracle Medical Center &** **Pharmacy** (tel. 506/2654-4996) is nearby, and there's a medical center (tel. 506/2654-5440) in nearby Huacas. For an **ambulance** call tel. 506/2654-5523; for **police,** call tel. 506/2654-5647.

Brasilito's **Café Internet Nany** (tel. 506/2654-4320, www.hotelnany.com) is at Apartotel & Restaurant Nany. **Books & More Books** (tel. 506/2653-7373), in Paseo del Mar commercial center, three kilometers (2 miles) south of Brasilito, sells guidebooks and novels in English.

PLAYA FLAMINGO

Playa Flamingo, three kilometers (2 miles) north of Brasilito, is named for the two-kilometer (1.2-mile) scimitar of white sand—one of the most magnificent beaches in Costa Rica—that lines the north end of Bahía Flamingo (there are no flamingos). Bookended by headlands, it is one of the most dramatically scenic of settings in all Costa Rica.

The area is favored by wealthy Ticos and expats (North Americans now own most of the land hereabouts), and expensive villas sit atop the headlands north and south of the beach, many with their own little coves as private as one's innermost thoughts.

tee time at Westin Playa Conchal Resort & Spa, Playa Conchal

Playa Flamingo and Vicinity

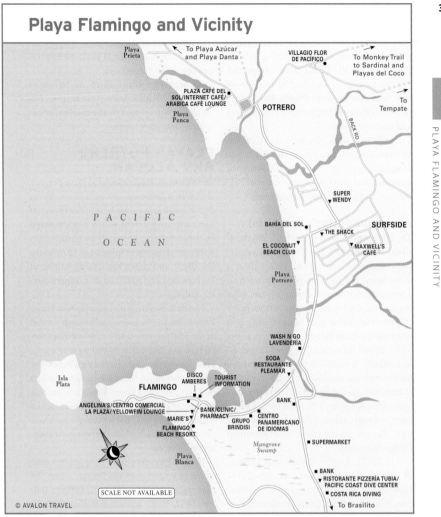

Playa Prieta · To Playa Azúcar and Playa Danta · VILLAGIO FLOR DE PACÍFICO · To Monkey Trail to Sardinal and Playas del Coco · PLAZA CAFÉ DEL SOL/INTERNET CAFÉ/ ARABICA CAFÉ LOUNGE · POTRERO · Playa Penca · BACK RD · To Tempate · SUPER WENDY · PACIFIC OCEAN · BAHÍA DEL SOL · THE SHACK · SURFSIDE · EL COCONUT BEACH CLUB · MAXWELL'S CAFÉ · Playa Potrero · WASH N GO LAVENDERÍA · SODA RESTAURANTE PLEAMAR · Isla Plata · DISCO AMBERES · TOURIST INFORMATION · FLAMINGO · BANK · ANGELINA'S/CENTRO COMERCIAL LA PLAZA/ YELLOWFIN LOUNGE · BANK/CLINIC/ PHARMACY · CENTRO PANAMERICANO DE IDIOMAS · MARIE'S · GRUPO BRINDISI · FLAMINGO BEACH RESORT · Mangrove Swamp · SUPERMARKET · Playa Blanca · BANK · RISTORANTE PIZZERÍA TUBIA/ PACIFIC COAST DIVE CENTER · COSTA RICA DIVING · To Brasilito

SCALE NOT AVAILABLE

© AVALON TRAVEL

Entertainment

The **Monkey Bar** (tel. 506/2654-4141) at the Flamingo Marina Resort, on the hill overlooking the marina, has a happy hour (5pm-7pm daily), live music on Friday, barbecue on Saturday, ESPN with pizza on Sunday, and Monday-night American football (in season). The always-lively bar at the **Mariner Inn** (tel. 506/2654-4081, 6am-10pm daily), in Flamingo, features cable TV and has live music at times.

Disco Amberes (tel. 506/2654-4011, http://amberescostarica.com, 6pm-2am Thurs.-Sat.), on the hill in Flamingo, has a spacious lounge bar, a lively disco, and a small casino. Live bands occasionally play. Video slots and card tables are also offered at **Flamingo Beach Resort** (tel. 506/2654-4444, 7pm-3am daily), on the beach.

Sports and Recreation

Grupo Brindisi (tel. 506/2654-5514, www.

brindisicr.com), 100 meters (330 feet) east of the marina at Flamingo, offers diving to Islas Murciélagos and has kayak-snorkeling trips, ATV tours, and sportfishing. Also in Flamingo, **Pacific Coast Dive Center** (tel. 506/2654-6175, www.pacificcoastdivecenter.com) offers diving, while **Manta Ray Sailing** (www.mantaraysailing.com) offers catamaran and snorkeling trips.

EcoTrans (tel. 506/2654-5151, www.ecotranscostarica.com), at the Flamingo Marina Resort, on the hill overlooking the marina, offers tours to Parque Nacional Palo Verde, Guaitíl, and other destinations.

Accommodations and Food

The **Flamingo Beach Resort** (tel. 506/2654-4444, U.S. tel. 877-856-5519, www.resort-flamingobeach.com, from $114 s/d) is a three-story, 120-room complex centered on a voluminous pool with a swim-up bar. After years in the doldrums, this beachfront property now boasts chic contemporary styling in spacious air-conditioned rooms and suites with fans and flat-screen TVs, free Internet access, minibars, and coffeemakers. Suites have kitchenettes and whirlpool tubs. It's chock-full of amenities, including three bars, two restaurants, tennis, a gym, a Turkish bath, a game room, a beauty salon, a dive shop, and a casino, plus you get the amenities of Flamingo village, steps away.

Almost a Costa Rican institution, ★ **Marie's Restaurant** (tel. 506/2654-4136, www.mariesrestaurantincostarica.com, 6:30am-9:30pm daily), at Flamingo, is under a huge *palenque* in Centro Comercial La Plaza. I've often started my day here with granola with yogurt and fresh fruit, or a great veggie omelet. Lunch and dinner brings fish-and-chips, chicken from the wood oven, rib-eye steak ($14), barbecue pork ribs ($12), and a large selection of sandwiches, plus ice cream sundaes, cappuccino, latte, mocha, and espresso.

Information and Services

There is a **visitor information center** (tel. 506/2654-4021, www.infoflamingo.com) in Centro Comercial La Plaza, above the marina; the plaza also has a bank, a clinic, and a pharmacy on the hill. **Wash N Go Lavanderí** is on the road to Potrero.

Centro Panamericano de Idiomas (tel. 506/2654-5002, www.cpi-edu.com), 100 meters (330 feet) east of the marina, offers Spanish-language courses.

PLAYAS POTRERO AND AZÚCAR

The **Monkey Trail** emerges at Playa Potrero, about 16 kilometers (10 miles) southwest of Sardinal and immediately northeast of Playa Flamingo, from which it is separated by Bahía Potrero. The gray-sand beach curls north for about three kilometers (2 miles) to the rustic and charming fishing hamlet of Potrero and is popular with campers during holidays.

North of Potrero, a dirt road leads to **Playa Penca,** backed by a mangrove estuary—that of the Río Salinas—and a rare saltwater forest replete with birdlife, including parrots, roseate spoonbills, and egrets. From Penca, the road snakes north three kilometers (2 miles) to Playa Azúcar (Sugar Beach), a narrow 400-meter (1,300-foot) spit of sun-drenched coral-colored sand that just might have you dreaming of retiring here. There's good snorkeling offshore.

Beyond Playa Azúcar, the rugged dirt road comes to an end at **Playa Danta,** where the first stage of the huge **Las Catalinas** (tel. 506/2654-4600, www.lascatalinascr.com) "township" development is now complete. The aim is to create a "Carmel or Positano in the Tropics," with civic buildings, hotels, plazas, and private homes. If the other stages come to fruition, it will be the first designed-on-a-drawing-board township in Costa Rica. A hilly hiking trail system—the **Sistema de Senderos de las Catalinas**—in the dry forest is already developed. **Ecuestrian Center La Fayette** (tel. 506/8347-2493), between Playas Penca and Danta, hosts riding lessons and shows.

Entertainment

At Potrero, **El Coconut Beach Club** (tel. 506/2654-4300, noon-midnight daily) is a stylish place to relax by the pool by day and to enjoy live music (5pm-7pm Sun.).

Accommodations and Food

For a reclusive beachfront resort, choose the gracious **Hotel Sugar Beach** (tel. 506/2654-4242, www.sugar-beach.com, low season $125-224 s/d, high season $158-280 s/d), enjoying a secluded setting on a rise amid 10 hectares (25 acres) of lawns and forests at Playa Azúcar. Choose from 16 rooms in eight handsome Spanish colonial-style duplexes, or 10 units connected by stone pathways. Also available are a three-bedroom beach house and an apartment suite. A large open-air restaurant overlooks the beach, and there's a small pool, horseback rides, and tours.

Inland of Playa Potrero and a favorite of expat locals, **Maxwell's Café** (tel. 506/2645-4319, www.maxwellscostarica.net, 8am-11pm Sun.-Fri.) is an open-air bar and grill serving American fare. Owners Mike and Kelly dish up nightly specials, such as meatloaf (Mon.), roast rosemary garlic chicken (Tues.), and roast pork (Wed.). It has Wi-Fi and a happy hour (6pm-7pm daily), plus karaoke on Tuesday. For something more chic and romantic, head to the open-air beachfront restaurant at **Bahía del Sol** (tel. 506/2654-4671, 6am-10pm daily, $5-20), also on Playa Potrero, specializing in seafood and continental cuisine; it has a *fiesta tropical* on Friday night, and karaoke on Saturday.

★ **Lola's Norte** (tel. 506/2652-9097, 8am-6pm Tues.-Sun.), at the end of the road in Playa Danta, is a re-creation of Lola's at Playa Avellanas, but without the pet pig that was *that* restaurant's main source of fame. This hip place is a perfect spot to relax in funky wooden beach chairs or loungers under shade trees or umbrellas after a satisfying meal of seared ahi salad, fish-and-chips, or delicious thin-crust pesto pizza.

Super Wendy (tel. 506/2654-4291), on the main road between Potrero and Flamingo, specializes in gourmet foodstuffs.

Information and Services

A **Welcome Center** (tel. 506/2654-5460) offers visitor information in the Plaza Casa del Sol, northwest of the Potrero village soccer field.

sailboats at dusk, Playa Potrero

GETTING THERE

Tralapa (tel. 506/2221-7202) buses depart San José for Playa Potrero (6 hours, $6) via Brasilito and Flamingo from Calles 20, Avenidas 1/3, at 8am, 10:30am, and 3pm daily, returning at 2:45am, 9am, and 2pm daily. **Transportes La Pampa** (tel. 506/2665-7530) buses depart Liberia for Brasilito, Flamingo, and Potrero eight times daily; and **Empresa El Folclórico** (tel. 506/2680-3161) buses depart Santa Cruz 13 times daily. **Grayline** (tel. 506/2220-2126, www.graylinecostarica.com) and **Interbus** (tel. 506/4100-0888, www.interbusonline.com) operate shuttles between Flamingo-Tamarindo and San José ($40).

To get to Flamingo from Playas Coco, Hermosa, or Panamá, take a bus to Comunidad, where you can catch a southbound bus for Santa Cruz or Nicoya; get off at Belén, and catch a bus for Flamingo.

For a taxi, call tel. 506/8836-1739. **Adobe Rent-a-Car** (tel. 506/8811-4242, www.adobecar.com) is in Paseo del Mar commercial center.

Tamarindo and Vicinity

Tamarindo, a former fishing village that has burgeoned into Guanacaste's most developed (some would say overdeveloped) resort, offers a scintillating prime beach, top surfing action, and a choice of accommodations from shoestring to sophisticated. Nearby, Parque Nacional Marino Las Baulas offers the best chance in the nation to witness the namesake endangered leatherback turtle laying eggs.

TAMARINDO

Playa Tamarindo, eight kilometers (5 miles) south of Huacas, is Nicoya's most developed beach resort and is especially popular with backpacking surfers. The gray-sand beach is about two kilometers (1.2 miles) long and very deep when the tide goes out—perfect for strolling and watching pelicans dive for fish. It has rocky outcrops, good for tide-pooling. Riptides are common, so ask locals in the

sunset at Playa Tamarindo

know for the safest places to swim. The Río Matapalo washes onto the beach at its northern end, giving direct access to Playa Grande in Parque Nacional Marino Las Baulas and to the Refugio Nacional de Vida Silvestre Tamarindo (Tamarindo National Wildlife Refuge) via the Estero Palo Seco; a boat will ferry you for $0.50. You can also wade across at low tide, although crocodiles are sometimes present, as they are in the mangroves at the eastern end of Playa Tamarindo.

To the south, separated from Playa Tamarindo by a headland, is more upscale **Playa Langosta,** a beautiful white-sand beach that stretches beyond the wide estuary of the Río Tamarindo for several kilometers.

Tamarindo has changed beyond recognition in the past decade, metamorphosing from a sleepy surfers' hangout to a full-blown resort with uncontrolled development. High-rise condominiums have arrived, as have shopping malls, plus prostitution and crime, including several murders of tourists. But most roads remain unpaved—dusty as hell in dry season and deplorably potholed with vast pools of mud in wet season. Fecal contamination of the ocean has reached dangerous levels.

Entertainment and Events

Tamarindo is known for its carefree party vibe. The **Crazy Monkey Bar,** at Best Western Tamarindo Vista Villas (tel. 506/2653-0114), on the hillside, shows Monday-night American football, with free shots at touchdowns; Friday is "ladies night," with free cocktails for women. Its two dance floors includes one for salsa.

The no-frills open-air **Pacífico Bar** (tel. 506/2653-4406), in the village center, is a happening spot on Sunday for reggae night. It has a pool table and music—but it also has a history of drawing an unsavory and raffish crowd, for example at Wednesday wet T-shirt contests.

Bar 1 (tel. 506/2653-2586, www.baronetamarindo.com, 6pm-2am daily), upstairs in Plaza Tamarindo, draws martini-sipping city-slickers. The open-air bar has hip black-and-white New York styling, plus there are pool tables, disco lighting, and a big screen for music videos. DJs spin on weekends, champagne "ladies night" is Tuesday, and Thursday offers free martinis for women in bikinis.

The only enclosed nightclub in Tamarindo is **Aqua Discoteque** (tel. 506/8411-2455, party@aquadiscoteque.com, 10pm-2:30am Mon. and Fri.-Sat.), 100 meters east of Hotel Tamarindo Diríaq, with sexy styling. Monday is "ladies night," with free drinks for women, and a wet T-shirt contest is held Friday.

At **El Gallito** (tel. 506/2653-2017), a Spanish tapas bar in Plaza Tamarindo, owners Ezequiel Marinoni (DJ Zeke) and Mauricio de Sostoa host punk rock on Monday, "ladies night" on Tuesday, hip-hop on Thursday, and a jumping house night on Saturday.

The hot sports bar of choice is **Sharky's** (tel. 506/8918-4976), 100 meters south of Plaza Colonial, with two big screens. It hosts theme nights, including karaoke on Tuesday, with free shots every time you sing; Saturday is '80s night, and women drink free 9pm-midnight.

The classy **Surf Club Sports Bar** (tel. 506/2653-1886, 5pm-10:30pm Mon. and Thurs.-Fri., 11am-10:30pm Sun.), in Playa Langosta, has pool tables and free Wi-Fi. Go on Friday for free pool and table soccer (6pm-9pm).

If you simply want to sip quality suds, check out **El Vaquero Bar** (tel. 506/2653-1262, 11am-midnight daily), serving fresh brews by Volcano Brewing Company. El Vaquero recently relocated from Lake Arenal to Witch's Rock Surf Camp, on the beach. It hosts live music at sunset Saturday and Sunday.

There are **casinos** at the Barceló Playa Langosta (8pm-3am daily) and Tamarindo Diría (6pm-11pm daily), in Plaza Colonial.

Costa Rica's annual **Credomatic Music Festival** is hosted in July and August at various venues in town.

Sports and Recreation

Arenas Adventures (tel. 506/2653-0108, www.tamarindoaventuras.com) specializes in ATV tours, but also has kayaking, waveboarding, and stand-up paddleboards.

Tamarindo

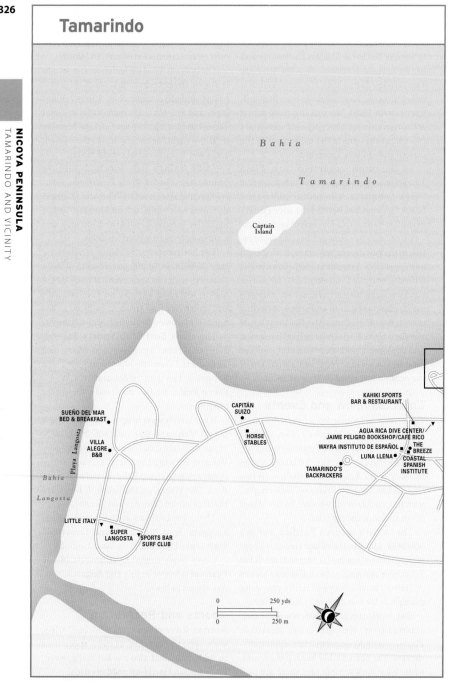

Bahía

Tamarindo

Captain
Island

Playa Langosta

Bahía

Langosta

KAHIKI SPORTS
BAR & RESTAURANT

SUEÑO DEL MAR
BED & BREAKFAST

CAPITÁN
SUIZO

AGUA RICA DIVE CENTER/
JAIME PELIGRO BOOKSHOP/CAFÉ RICO

VILLA
ALEGRE
B&B

HORSE
STABLES

WAYRA INSTITUTO DE ESPAÑOL

THE
BREEZE

LUNA LLENA

COASTAL
SPANISH
INSTITUTE

TAMARINDO'S
BACKPACKERS

LITTLE ITALY

SUPER
LANGOSTA

SPORTS BAR
SURF CLUB

0   250 yds

0   250 m

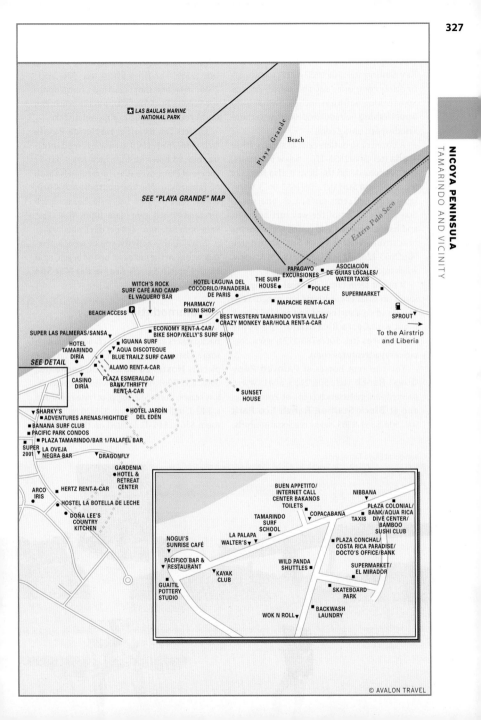

★ LAS BAULAS MARINE
NATIONAL PARK

Playa Grande Beach

Estero Palo Seco

SEE "PLAYA GRANDE" MAP

PAPAGAYO EXCURSIONES
ASOCIACIÓN DE GUÍAS LOCALES/
WATER TAXIS

WITCH'S ROCK SURF CAFÉ AND CAMP
EL VAQUERO BAR

HOTEL LAGUNA DEL COCODRILO/PANADERÍA DE PARIS

THE SURF HOUSE

POLICE

SUPERMARKET

BEACH ACCESS

PHARMACY/
BIKINI SHOP

MAPACHE RENT-A-CAR

SPROUT

SUPER LAS PALMERAS/SANSA

ECONOMY RENT-A-CAR/
BIKE SHOP/KELLY'S SURF SHOP

BEST WESTERN TAMARINDO VISTA VILLAS/
CRAZY MONKEY BAR/HOLA RENT-A-CAR

To the Airstrip
and Liberia

HOTEL TAMARINDO DIRIÁ

IGUANA SURF
AQUA DISCOTEQUE
BLUE TRAILZ SURF CAMP

SEE DETAIL

CASINO DIRIÁ

ALAMO RENT-A-CAR

PLAZA ESMERALDA/
BANK/THRIFTY
RENT-A-CAR

SUNSET HOUSE

SHARKY'S
ADVENTURES ARENAS/HIGHTIDE

HOTEL JARDÍN
DEL EDÉN

BANANA SURF CLUB
PACIFIC PARK CONDOS
PLAZA TAMARINDO/BAR 1/FALAFEL BAR

SUPER
2001

LA OVEJA
NEGRA BAR

DRAGONFLY

GARDENIA
HOTEL &
RETREAT
CENTER

ARCO
IRIS

HERTZ RENT-A-CAR

HOSTEL LA BOTELLA DE LECHE

DOÑA LEE'S
COUNTRY
KITCHEN

BUEN APPETITO/
INTERNET CALL
CENTER BAKANOS
TOILETS

NIBBANA

COPACABANA

PLAZA COLONIAL/
BANK/AQUA RICA
DIVE CENTER/
BAMBOO
SUSHI CLUB

TAMARINDO
SURF
SCHOOL

TAXIS

LA PALAPA
WALTER'S

PLAZA CONCHAL/
COSTA RICA PARADISE/
DOCTO'S OFFICE/BANK

NOGUI'S
SUNRISE CAFÉ

WILD PANDA
SHUTTLES

SUPERMARKET/
EL MIRADOR

PACIFICO BAR &
RESTAURANT

KAYAK
CLUB

SKATEBOARD
PARK

GUAITIL
POTTERY
STUDIO

WOK N ROLL

BACKWASH
LAUNDRY

Blue Dolphin Sailing (tel. 506/2653-0446, U.S./Canada tel. 855-842-3204, www.bluedolphinsailing.com) and Marlin del Rey Sailing (tel. 506/2653-1212, www.marlindelrey.com) offer day and sunset cruises. Sportfishing outfitters include Tamarindo Sportfishing (tel. 506/2653-0090, www.tamarindosportfishing.com).

A dozen or so outlets cater to surfers. Blue Trailz (tel. 506/2653-1705, www.bluetrailz.com) is considered the best; it also has bike tours. Iguana Surf (tel. 506/2653-0613, www.iguanasurf.net) rents surfboards, offers surf-taxi service to out-of-the-way surfing spots, and has surf lessons and courses, as does the beachfront Witch's Rock Surf Camp (tel. 506/2653-1262, U.S. tel. 888-318-7873, www.witchsrocksurfcamp.com).

It might seem tame after real surfing, but stand-up paddleboarding is fun nonetheless: You stand on a surfboard and paddle! Check it out with Costa Rica Stand-Up Paddle Adventures (tel. 506/8780-1774, www.costaricasupadventures.com).

You can rent horses at Painted Pony Guest Ranch (tel. 506/2653-8041, www.paintedponyguestranch.com), at Portegolpe; and at Black Stallion Ranch Eco Park (tel. 506/8869-9765, www.blackstallionhills.com) about three kilometers (2 miles) south of Tamarindo. The latter has sunset and barbecue rides, plus an 11-platform, 10-cable zip line ($55). The Bike Shop (tel. 506/2653-2136, www.bikeshoptamarindo.com), opposite Witch's Rock Surf Camp at the beach, can outfit you with a cruise or mountain bike.

Golfers can tee off at Hacienda Pinilla (tel. 506/2681-4500, www.haciendapinilla.com, 18 holes $150), which has a par-72 course at Playa Avenallas, immediately south of Tamarindo. The Langosta Beach Club, on the road to Playa Langosta, has a superb air-conditioned gym (8am-10pm Mon.-Fri., 9am-5pm Sat.-Sun., $10 per day), plus yoga.

After all this activity, you deserve a massage at one of the tables set up the beach, or at Hotel Capitán Suizo's Aroma del Mar Spa (tel. 506/2653-0075).

Accommodations
UNDER $25

Backpackers are spoiled for choice. Although some distance from the beach, my favorite place is Hostel La Botella de Leche (tel. 506/2653-2061, www.labotelladeleche.com, low season dorm $12-16 pp, private room $26 s, $40 d, high season dorm $13-20 pp, private room $36 s, $46 d), located on the southeast

surfers at Playa Tamarindo

side of town. One of the most popular surfers' and backpackers' spots in the country, it's run to high standards by a delightful Argentinean woman, Mariana "Mama" Nogaro; her son Wences offers surfing instruction. Painted like a Holstein cow, it has a laundry, a delightful lounge, a large common kitchen, plus surf rental, free Wi-Fi, and lockers. It has three dorms, plus six private rooms for up to four people. The equally impressive **Blue Trailz Surf Camp** (tel. 506/2653-1705, www.bluetrailz.com), opposite Hotel Tamarindo Diría, competes.

$50-100

French-run **La Laguna del Cocodrilo Hotel** (tel. 506/2653-0255, www.lalagunadelcocodrilo.com, low season $49-95 s/d, high season $65-122 s/d) is a perfect mid-priced option with a stupendous beachfront location: The garden merges into a lagoon with crocodiles. It has 10 air-conditioned rooms and two ocean-view suites, all with cable TV and minimalist but charming decor that includes terra-cotta tile floors, batik wall hangings, ceiling fans, and beautiful glazed baths. Some rooms have stone terraces facing the beach. It has a popular café-bakery, and free Wi-Fi.

Inland from the beach, the Italian-run, canary-yellow **Luna Llena** (tel. 506/2653-0082, www.hotellunallena.com, low season standard $75 s/d, bungalows $89, high season standard $90, bungalows $109) appeals for its tropical ambience. It offers air-conditioned rooms and bungalows around an alluring swimming pool with a swim-up bar and a raised wooden sundeck with a whirlpool tub. Stone pathways connect more spacious conical bungalows done up in lively Caribbean colors, with terra-cotta floors; a spiral staircase leads to a loft bedroom, and the semicircular baths are marvelous. There's a small restaurant and a laundry. Rates include tax and breakfast; the seventh night is free.

$100-150

For a long-term surf-camp stay, opt for the beachfront **Witch's Rock Surf Camp** (tel. 506/2653-1262, www.witchsrocksurfcamp. com, from $826 pp for 7 days), a lively place with great ambience. It has 18 clean, colorful, nicely appointed oceanfront hotel-style rooms, plus a swimming pool, game rooms, a thatched restaurant, a microbrewery, lockers, a surf shop, and surfing lessons. It specializes in one-week surf packages.

OVER $150

Down by the shores, **Hotel Tamarindo Diría** (tel. 506/2653-0031, www.tamarindodiria.com, $158-226 s/d year-round) ranks in the top tier of Costa Rica's large-scale beach resorts with its sensational location and eye-pleasing decor. The lobby, boasting Guanacastecan antique replicas and elegant rolled-arm chaises longues, opens to a horizon pool with fountains; the ocean beckons beyond. It has 239 pleasantly furnished air-conditioned rooms in varying styles, all with terra-cotta tile floors. Some have a whirlpool tub, and many are wheelchair-accessible. An airy restaurant opens onto an expansive bar and outside cocktail terrace. It has a kids pool, tennis courts, a casino, a golf driving range, and a boutique, plus sportfishing and tours.

Hotel Jardín del Edén (tel. 506/2653-0137, www.jardindeleden.com, low season $140-190 s/d, high season $170-260 s/d, including buffet breakfast) is located on a bluff overlooking Tamarindo. Truly a hillside "garden of Eden," it earns laurels for the chic decor in 40 recently refurbished rooms and two villas, all with high-speed Wi-Fi, hydro-massage tubs, and spacious terrace-porches offering ocean views. Rooms are themed in regional styles: Africa, Bali, Japan, Tunisia, Mexico. A pool with a swim-up bar, a whirlpool tub, and a sundeck with shady *ranchitos* are set in lush gardens, floodlit at night. The restaurant is one of the best in town.

For personalized service and intimacy, I love the ★ **Sueño del Mar Bed and Breakfast** (tel. 506/2653-0284, www.sueno-del-mar.com, low season $150-195, high season $195-295), a truly exquisite Spanish colonial house with six individually styled rooms cascading down a shaded alcove to a small landscaped garden and the sands at Playa Langosta. Rooms exude romantic ambience, with rough-hewn timbers, white-washed stone walls, terra-cotta tile floors, screened arched windows with shutters, and tasteful fabrics. Most have exquisite rainforest showers. The huge upstairs suite is a true gem, with all-around screened windows, mosquito netting on the four-poster log bed, and a Goldilocks'-cottage feel to the bath with a rainforest shower with gorgeous tile work. It also has a casita for four people. A small pool and a wooden sundeck adjoin a thatched *ranchito* with a hammock, perfect for enjoying cocktails and *bocas*. Complimentary snorkel gear, boogie boards, and bikes are available.

An awesome competitor to Sueño del Mar is the nearby **Villa Alegre** (tel. 506/2653-0270, www.villaalegrecostarica.com, low season $150-195, high season $170-230, including breakfast), a contemporary beachfront bed-and-breakfast run by Californians Barry and Suzye Lawson, who specialize in wedding and honeymoon packages. The main house has lofty ceilings, tile floors, a magnificent lounge with a library, and four air-conditioned bedrooms with French doors opening onto a private patio. The rooms are decorated with the globetrotting couple's mementoes. The Mexico and Russia rooms are wheelchair-accessible. Two casitas—one sleeping four people—each have a kitchen. A veranda overlooks a swimming pool with a thatched bar. The main reason to stay here, though, is the pampering attention of the Lawsons.

Seeking a self-catering rental? If minimalist modernism is your thing, check into one of the villas at **The Breeze** (U.S. tel. 305-964-5421 or 877-855-1767, www.thebreezetamarindo.com, low season from $175, high season from $250), on the southwest side of town, which will delight sophisticates with a taste for stylish contemporary design and decor, plus a flat-screen TV and high-speed Wi-Fi. It has one- and two-bedroom units, plus a seven-bedroom annex, and a split-level cascading pool.

My preferred place to rest my head is the Swiss-run ★ **Capitán Suizo** (tel. 506/2653-0075, www.hotelcapitansuizo.com, low season $210-605 s/d, high season $230-660), on the road to Playa Langosta, a deserving member of the Small Distinctive Hotels of Costa Rica. Beach-loving cognoscenti will appreciate the resort's casual sophistication. Even the local howler monkeys have decided this is the place to be. Pathways coil sinuously through a botanical fantasia to a wide sundeck and a large amoeba-shaped pool with a faux beach. The 22 lovely rooms and eight bungalows (some lack air-conditioning) have natural graystone floors and deep-red hardwoods, halogen lamps, and soft-lit lanterns; bungalows have mezzanine bedrooms with king beds and huge baths with rainforest showers and whirlpool tubs. The wood-paneled Honeymoon Suite has a king bed in its own loft. The bar and restaurant are among Tamarindo's finest, and Capitán Suizo has kayaks, boogie boards, a game room, and the Aromas del Mar Spa.

Food

Tamarindo has some of the most creative restaurateurs in the country. It's hard to keep up with the ever-evolving scene.

Start your day at the French-run beachfront **Panadería La Laguna del Cocodrilo** (tel. 506/2653-0255, 6am-7pm daily), which offers an all-you-can-eat buffet breakfast in the garden ($5). It also sells delicious croissants, chocolate éclairs, fruit tarts, baguettes, and bread, plus enchiladas and empanadas at lunch. For hearty gringo breakfasts, you can't beat the offbeat beachfront **Nogui Bar/ Sunrise Café** (tel. 506/2653-0029, 6am-9:30pm daily), which also has hearty seafood dinners and is a cool place to watch the sunset from the tin-shaded patio.

For a cool, unpretentious beach lunch spot, try **Nibbana** (tel. 506/2653-2222, www.nibbana-tamarindo.com, 7:30am-10:30pm daily), where chef-owner Fabien Mandréa prepares an eclectic menu that includes salads (Greek, Thai) and wraps such as Hawaiian chicken ($9.50) and turkey asiago

($9), seafood, and pizzas ($11-16), enjoyed alfresco beneath the palms.

Still in breakfast and lunch mode, I make a beeline to ★ **Sprout** (tel. 506/2653-2374, low season 10am-5pm daily, high season 7am-5pm daily), near the post office, east of town. U.S. expat owner Mike Finch serves awesome banana pancakes, chicken wraps, mahimahi and spiced-turkey sandwiches, gazpacho, curried chicken salads, and the like. Most dishes cost $6-8. Leave room for cheesecake or layered chocolate and coconut pudding. Yum! Wash it all down with a delicious fresh-fruit smoothie.

Romantics should consider dinner at the hip **El Jardín del Edén** (noon-10pm daily, lunch $6-13, dinner $15-60), at the hotel of that name, for its candlelit thatched setting on a bluff overlooking Tamarindo. It serves fusion dishes such as jumbo shrimp in whiskey and tenderloin in black-truffle sauce. Some of my favorite nouvelle dining is conjured at ★ **Capitán Suizo** (tel. 506/2653-0075, 7am-9:15pm daily), on the road to Playa Langosta. German chef Roland Brodscholl fuses European influences with fresh tropical produce. The creative menu includes a perfect papaya soup with curry, coriander, and ginger ($5.50), pumpkin gnocchi with tomato sauce and basil ($12), and tilapia in orange sauce ($15.50). The dinner menu changes daily. A guitar trio plays on Monday, marimba music is on Wednesday, and there's a beach barbecue on Friday.

Chef Tish Tomlinson is back at her world-renowned ★ **Dragonfly** (tel. 506/2653-1506, www.dragonflybarandgrill.com, 6pm-9:30pm Mon.-Sat. Nov.-Sept., cash only), where she continues to deliver mouthwatering fusion dishes, such as corn and jalapeño fritters ($6.50), apple citrus brined roast pork over rosemary infused white beans with chutney ($15), and ricotta and spinach ravioli ($13). You dine beneath canvas, but the place exudes romantic tropical elegance enhanced by strings of lights.

Cordon Bleu-trained Israeli chef Shlomy Koren serves up delicious Mediterranean dishes at ★ **Seasons by Shlomy** (tel. 506/8368-6983, www.seasonstamarindo.com, 6pm-10pm Mon.-Sat. Nov.-mid-Sept.), at Hotel Arco Iris, on the south side of town. The daily menu depends on what local produce is available. How about stuffed rigatoni with shrimp in a light creamy tomato sauce ($7.50) as an appetizer? And Middle Eastern-style chicken marinated in red wine and spices ($13)? It has a great wine selection and friendly, efficient service courtesy of some of the loveliest waitstaff around. Choose from a contemporary-styled interior or alfresco by the pool.

The first choice for sushi has to be **Bamboo Sushi Club** (tel. 506/8648-6912, 5pm-10pm Mon.-Sat.), a classy open-air sushi bar opposite waterfront Tamarindo Diría. Cool music and a romantic setting complement superbly fresh sashimi and *nigiri*. The 40-piece Love Boat is perfect for hungry couples.

Southerners missing their gravy and grits will feel right at home at **Doña Lee's Country Kitchen** (tel. 506/2653-0127, 6:30am-10pm daily) on the southeast side of town. Go on Monday night for American football on TV and barbecue ribs. It's also a great place for a full-plate gringo breakfast. Almost everyone who treks out to **Black Stallion Café & Surf Saloon** (tel. 506/8869-9765, www.blackstallionhills.com), in the hills about three kilometers (2 miles) south of Tamarindo, raves the barbecue ribs, chorizo sausages, and "ranch-style brunches" using fresh, organically raised veggies and free-range chickens. Go for the all-you-can-eat barbecue.

Information and Services

For visitor information, head to the U.S.-run **Costa Rica Paradise Tour Information** (tel. 506/2653-2251, www.crparadise.com, 8am-6pm daily), in Plaza Conchal. The *Tamarindo News*, distributed locally, is a great resource.

Jaime Peligro Bookshop (tel. 506/8820-9004, http://jaimepeligro.tamarindohomepage.com, 9am-7pm Mon.-Sat., noon-5pm Sun.), 100 meters west of Super 2001, sells used and new books and CDs and also has a book exchange.

In medical need? Call the **Coastal Emergency Medical Service** (tel. 506/2653-1974). There's a **pharmacy** (tel. 506/2653-0210) next to Hotel El Milagro. The **police station** (tel. 506/2653-0283) is near Tamarindo Vista Villas.

The many Internet cafés include **Bakanos Internet Call Center** (tel. 506/2653-0628, 9am-10pm daily), which doubles as an international call center; and **ILACNET** (tel. 506/2653-1740, 8am-7pm daily), in Plaza Conchal, which also hosts a bank (tel. 506/2653-1617) with an ATM, a post office, a doctor's office, and public toilets. The **Backwash Laundry** (tel. 506/2653-0870, 8am-8pm Mon.-Sat.) is 50 meters (165 feet) south.

The **Wayra Instituto de Español** (tel. 506/2653-0359, www.spanish-wayra.co.cr) offers Spanish-language courses.

Getting There and Away

SANSA (tel. 506/2229-4100, U.S./Canada tel. 877-767-2672, www.flysansa.com) and **Nature Air** (tel. 506/2299-6000, U.S. tel. 800-235-9272, www.natureair.com) operate scheduled daily service between Tamarindo airport and San José. The SANSA office is on the main street. A $3 departure tax is collected at the airport.

Alfaro (tel. 506/2222-2666) buses depart San José ($5) from Avenidas 5, Calles 14/16, at 11:30am and 3:30pm daily and travel via Liberia; **Tralapa** (tel. 506/2221-7202) buses depart San José from Calle 20, Avenidas 3/5, at 4pm daily. **Transporte La Pampa** (tel. 506/2686-7245) buses depart Liberia for Tamarindo nine times 5:30am-6pm daily, and from Santa Cruz six times 5:30am-7pm daily. Return buses depart Tamarindo for San José at 3:30am and 5:30am daily (Alfaro), and 7am daily (Tralapa); for Liberia nine times 3:30am-5:30pm daily; and for Santa Cruz at 6am, 8:30am, and noon daily.

Tamarindo Shuttle (tel. 506/2653-2727, www.tamarindoshuttle.com) charges $20 for door-to-door service from Liberia airport. **Grayline** (tel. 506/2220-2126, www.grayline-costarica.com) and **Interbus** (tel. 506/4100-0888, www.interbusonline.com), in Plaza Conchal, also offer airport shuttles.

There's no gas station, but the **Ferretería,** at the entrance to town, sells gas.

Getting Around

BlueTrailz (tel. 506/2653-1706, www.blue-etrailz.com) rents mountain bikes (2 hours $10, 24 hours $20). You can rent cars locally with **Thrifty Car Rental** (tel. 506/2653-0829) in Plaza Esmeralda, and **Hola Car Rental** (tel. 506/2653-2000) at Tamarindo Vista Villas.

★ LAS BAULAS MARINE NATIONAL PARK

Costa Rican beaches don't come more beautiful than **Playa Grande,** a seemingly endless curve of sand, varying from coral-white to gray, immediately to the north of Tamarindo and accessible by simply crossing the river estuary (or by driving via Matapalo).

The hamlet of **Comunidad Playa Grande** is on the main approach road, 600 meters (0.4 miles) inland from the beach. There's guarded parking ($2) at the main beach entrance; elsewhere car break-ins are an everyday occurrence. Don't leave anything in your vehicle.

A beach trail to the north leads along the cape through dry forest and deposits you at **Playa Ventanas,** with tide pools for snorkeling and bathing. Several robberies had occurred here at the shrub-enclosed end of the dirt road. Surf pumps ashore at high tide. Surfing expert Mark Kelly rates Playa Grande as "maybe the best overall spot in the country."

The sprawling woodsy community at the southern half of the beach is **Palm Beach Estates.** Inland of the southern half of the beach, a 400-hectare (988-acre) mangrove estuary is protected within **Refugio Nacional de Vida Silvestre Tamarindo** (Tamarindo National Wildlife Refuge, tel. 506/2296-7074) and features crocodiles, anteaters, deer,

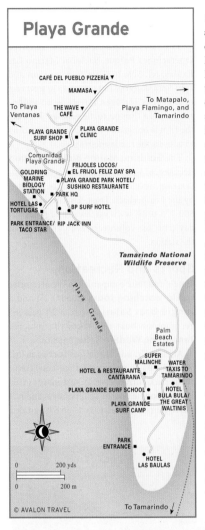

Playa Grande

CAFÉ DEL PUEBLO PIZZERÍA ▼
MAMASA ▼
→
To Matapalo,
Playa Flamingo, and
Tamarindo
To Playa
Ventanas
THE WAVE ▼
CAFÉ
PLAYA GRANDE
SURF SHOP ■
PLAYA GRANDE
■ CLINIC
Comunidad
Playa Grande
GOLDRING
MARINE
BIOLOGY
STATION
FRIJOLES LOCOS/
■ EL FRIJOL FELIZ DAY SPA
● PLAYA GRANDE PARK HOTEL/
SUSHIKO RESTAURANTE
■ PARK HQ
HOTEL LAS ●
TORTUGAS ■
■ BP SURF HOTEL
PARK ENTRANCE/
TACO STAR
RIP JACK INN

*Tamarindo National
Wildlife Preserve*

Playa Grande

Palm
Beach
Estates

SUPER
MALINCHE
HOTEL & RESTAURANTE
CANTARANA ●
WATER
■ TAXIS TO
TAMARINDO
PLAYA GRANDE SURF SCHOOL ●
●
HOTEL
BULA BULA/
■ THE GREAT
WALTINIS
PLAYA GRANDE
SURF CAMP

PARK
ENTRANCE ■
● HOTEL
LAS BAULAS

0   200 yds
0   200 m

© AVALON TRAVEL
To Tamarindo

1990 after a 15-year battle between developers and conservationists. The park is the result of efforts by Louis Wilson, owner of Hotel Las Tortugas, and his former wife, Marianel Pastor. The government agreed to support the couple's conservation efforts only if they could show that the site was economically viable as a tourist destination. The locals, who formerly harvested the turtles' eggs (as did a cookie company), have taken over all guiding; each guide is certified through an accredited course. However, much of the land backing the beach has been developed with condos, homes, and hotels. MINAE officials contemplated tearing down some of these for violating environmental laws, while the Óscar Arias administration considered eliminating the park. Meanwhile, fishing boats continue to trawl illegally and unpoliced within the sanctuary with longlines, which snag turtles. Alas, environmentalists are fighting a rear-guard action against developers and the shrimping industry, which are elbow-twisting the government to downgrade the park's status.

Turtle Viewing

Turtles call at Playa Grande year-round. The nesting season for the giant leatherback is **October to March,** when females come ashore every night at high tide. A decade ago, as many as 100 turtles might be seen in a single night; today, on a good night, a dozen might come ashore. Each female leatherback will nest as many as 12 times a season, every 10 days or so (usually at night to avoid dehydration). Most turtles prefer the center of the beach, just above the high-tide mark. Olive ridley turtles and Pacific green turtles can sometimes also be seen here May to August.

The beach is open to visitors by day at no cost, and by permit only with a guide at night in **nesting season** (6pm-6am, entrance $25, with guide; the fee is payable on leaving the beach if turtles have been seen); anyone found on the beach at night without a permit in nesting season faces a $1,000 fine (second offense; first offenders are escorted off the beach).

---

ocelots, and monkeys. Waterbirds and raptors gather, especially in dry season. The refuge's ranger station is about 500 meters (0.3 miles) upriver from the estuary.

The entire shoreline is protected within the 445-hectare (1,100-acre) **Parque Nacional Marino Las Baulas,** which guards the prime nesting site of the leatherback turtle on the Pacific coast, including 22,000 hectares (54,000 acres) out to sea. The beach was incorporated into the national park system in

Guides from the local community roam the beach and lead groups to nesting turtles; other guides spot for turtles and call in the location via walkie-talkies. Visitors are not allowed to walk the beach after dusk unescorted. Groups cannot exceed 15 people, and only 60 people are allowed onto the beach at night at each of two entry points (four groups per gate, with a maximum of eight groups nightly): one where the road meets the beach by the Hotel Las Tortugas, and the second at the southern end, by Villas Baulas. Reservations are mandatory, although entry without a reservation is possible if there's space in a group (don't count on it, as demand usually exceeds supply). You can make reservations up to eight days in advance, or 8am-5pm for a same-day visit. At certain times the waiting time can be two hours before you are permitted onto the beach; each night differs.

Resist following the example of the many thoughtless visitors who get too close to the turtles, try to touch them, ride their backs, or otherwise display a lack of common sense and respect. Flashlights and camera flashes are not permitted (professional photographers can apply in advance for permission to use a flash). And watch your step: Newly hatched turtles are difficult to see at night as they scurry down to the sea. Many are inadvertently crushed under visitors' feet.

The **park headquarters** (Centro Operaciones Parque Nacional Marino Las Baulas, tel. 506/2653-0470, 8am-noon and 1pm-5pm daily) is 100 meters (330 feet) east of Hotel Las Tortugas. It features an auditorium with a film on turtle ecology. Viewing the film is obligatory for everyone intending to witness the turtles nesting.

The **Goldring Marine Biology Station** (tel. 506/2653-0635, www.goldringmarinestation.org), next to Hotel Las Tortugas, is funded by the Leatherback Trust. **Earthwatch** (tel. 800-776-0188, www.earthwatch.org) has 10-day trips for volunteers, who are based at the station.

Sports and Recreation

Hotels and tour companies in the area offer **turtle-watching tours** (about $25) and a **Jungle Boat Safari** aboard a 20-passenger pontoon boat that takes you into the **Tamarindo Wildlife Refuge** ($30).

At Playa Grande, **Hotel Las Tortugas** (tel. 506/2653-0423, www.lastortugashotel.com), at the park entrance, rents surfboards ($15-35) and boogie boards ($10 per day) and has canoe tours of the estuary (solo $30, guided

sunset at Playa Grande

$55). **Pura Vida Café** (tel. 506/2653-0835) offers surf lessons ($50), as does **Frijoles Locos** (tel. 506/2652-9235, www.frijoleslocos.com), a well-stocked surf store at the entrance to Playa Grande.

Accommodations

For backpackers, I recommend **Playa Grande Surf Camp** (tel. 506/2653-1074, www.playagrandesurfcamp.com, dorm $18 pp, cabins $40.50 s/d), in Palm Beach Estates. It has three small but delightful air-conditioned wood-and-thatch cabins on stilts, plus two A-frames, including a dorm with screened windows. The courtyard has a pool and thatched shade areas with hammocks, plus there's Wi-Fi, board rental, and surf lessons.

For a touch of class, check into the **Playa Grande Park Hotel** (tel. 506/4700-7275, www.playagrandeparkhotel.com, $89-169 s/d), formerly the Playa Grande Surf Hotel, 400 meters (0.25 miles) inland of the beach near the park headquarters. This modern two-story Spanish colonial-style hotel is among the most stylish around, with a hip contemporary sophistication to its rooms and suites, all with flat-screen TVs, Wi-Fi, and air-conditioning. The Sushiko sushi restaurant is here.

If you *must* be by the beach, the **Hotel Las Tortugas** (tel. 506/2653-0423, www.lastortugashotel.com, low season economy $25-45 s/d, standard $50-60 s/d, suite $85, high season economy $50, standard $90, suite $120) has lost its edge but retains the advantage of abutting the sands and the park entrance, and has a great restaurant. Backpackers get eight "student" rooms with bunk beds and shared hot-water showers. The 12 other air-conditioned rooms vary markedly: Some look outdated and urgently need an upgrade. The hotel has a swimming pool, a whirlpool tub, and a palm-shaded corner with hammocks. The hotel rents surfboards and canoes for trips into the estuary and has horseback riding and a mangrove boat tour. It also rents apartments.

For low-key, laid-back cool, I like the **RipJack Inn** (tel. 506/2653-0480 or 800-808-4605, www.ripjackinn.com, low season from $70 s/d, high season from $90 s/d), with eight individually styled rooms, plus suites and bungalows, all with a crisp, clean, contemporary aesthetic. The open-air restaurant, **Upstairs at the RipJack,** serves nouvelle Costa Rican fare and has ocean views. Yoga fans will appreciate the yoga studio. Two adjoining neighbors offer a similar style, standards, and pricing: the rustic nine-room

entrance to Las Baulas Marine National Park

336

The Leatherback Turtle

baby leatherback turtles

The leatherback turtle (*Dermochelys coriacea*) is the world's largest reptile and a true relic from the age of the dinosaurs; fossils date back 100 million years. The average adult weighs about 450 kilograms (1,000 pounds) and is two meters (6.5 feet) in length, though males have been known to attain a staggering 900 kilograms (2,000 pounds). The leatherback is found in all the world's oceans except the Arctic.

Although it nests on the warm beaches of Costa Rica, the *baula*, as it is known locally, has evolved as a deep-diving cold-water critter; its great near-cylindrical bulk retains body heat in cold waters, and it can maintain a body temperature of 18°C (64°F) in near-frigid water. The leatherback travels great distances, feeding in the open ocean as far afield as subarctic waters, where its black body helps absorb the sun's warming rays. Like seals, the leatherback has a thick oily layer of fat for insulation. Its preferred food is jellyfish.

The females—which reach reproductive age between age 15 and 50—prefer to nest on steep beaches that have a deepwater approach, thus avoiding long-distance crawls. Nesting occurs during the middle hours of the night, the coolest hours. Leatherback eggs take longer to hatch— 70 days on average—than those of other sea turtles.

In other turtle species the bony exterior carapace is formed by flattened, widened ribs that are fused and covered with corneous tissues resembling the human fingernail, but the leatherback has an interior skeleton of narrow ribs linked by tiny bony plates all encased by a thick "shell" of leathery, cartilaginous skin. The leatherback's tapered body is streamlined for hydrodynamic efficiency, with seven longitudinal ridges that act like a boat's keel and long, powerful flippers for maximum propulsion. Leatherbacks have been shown to dive deeper than 1,300 meters (4,300 feet), where their small lungs, flexible frames, squishy bodies, and other specialist adaptations permit the animal to withstand pressures well over 10,000 kilopascals (1,500 psi).

The species is close to extinction. Contributions to help save leatherback turtles can be sent marked Programa de Tortugas Marinas to Karen and Scott Eckert, **Hubbs Sea World Research Institute** (2595 Ingraham St., San Diego, CA 92109, U.S. tel. 619-226-3870, www.hswri.org), or to the **Leatherback Trust** (161 Merion Ave., Haddonfield, NJ 08033, U.S. tel. 215-895-2627, www.leatherback.org).

Playa Grande Inn (tel. 506/2653-0719, www. playagrandeinn.com), and convivial **BP Surf Hotel** (tel. 506/8879-5643, www.bpsurfhotel.com).

I adore the ★ **Hotel Bula Bula** (tel. 506/2653-0975, U.S. tel. 877-658-2880, www. hotelbulabula.com, low season $85 s/d, high season $125 s/d), in lush gardens adjoining the mangrove estuary, two kilometers (1.2 miles) south of Las Tortugas. This attractive place is in the hands of two U.S. entrepreneurs, one a professional restaurateur. Although small, the 10 air-conditioned rooms are splashed with tropical ice-cream pastels and boast king beds with orthopedic mattresses, batik wall hangings, plus fans, fresh-cut flower arrangements, batik sarongs for use by the pool, and a shady balcony facing a swimming pool in a landscaped garden. It has a stage for live music. The excellent restaurant and bar (with Wi-Fi and loaner laptops) are popular with locals. A free water taxi to Tamarindo is available. It also has a beach house for rent.

Food

You don't have to leave the beach to eat. Just head to **Hotel Las Tortugas,** where the airy upstairs restaurant (7:30am-9:30pm daily) serves from an eclectic menu with local (such as grilled dorado) and gringo faves; leave room for the apple pie and ice cream.

Then there's **Mamasa** (tel. 506/5002-5468, www.mamasarestaurant.com, 10am-3pm daily, dinner 5:30pm-9pm Wed. and Sat. Jan.-Apr.) beckoning with eggs benedict, breakfast burrito, and granola parfait, or gourmet nouvelle creations at night; Wednesday is for tapas only. Owner Jamie Van Loan, from Fiji, is a professionally trained chef.

For more gourmet fare, head to **The Great Waltinis** (5:30pm-8:30pm Tues.-Thurs., 5:30pm-9pm Fri.-Sat.) restaurant at Hotel Bula Bula, two kilometers (1.2 miles) south of Las Tortugas. It serves international cuisine, including quesadillas, chicken wings, and shrimp and crab cakes, plus such superbly executed dishes as chicken *piccata* with white wine sauce and capers ($14), a 10-ounce New York strip prepared New Orleans-style ($16), and seared ahi tuna with wasabi and soy sauce ($12). Leave room for the "Siberia" chocolate drink-dessert. Avoid the superb oversize martinis if you're driving! Take the hotel's water taxi to and from Tamarindo.

Jason at **Playa Grande Inn** (tel. 506/2653-0719, www.playagrandeinn.com, 7:30am-10:30pm daily) serves great breakfasts and cooks *casados,* pulled-pork sandwiches, quesadillas, and pizzas (from $6).

Information and Services

In Playa Grande, the **Playa Grande Clinic** (tel. 506/8827-7774) is at the entrance to the hamlet when arriving from Matapalo.

Getting There

If driving from Flamingo, road access is via Matapalo, six kilometers (4 miles) east of Playa Grande (turn left at the soccer field in Matapalo). A rough dirt road also links Tamarindo and Playa Grande via Villareal. The Flamingo-bound buses from San José and Santa Cruz stop in Matapalo, where you can catch a taxi or the bus that departs Santa Cruz at 6am and 1pm daily; the return bus departs Playa Grande at 7:15am and 3:15pm daily.

Tamarindo Shuttle (tel. 506/2653-2727, www.tamarindoshuttle.com) charges $25 for door-to-door service from Liberia airport, and between Playa Grande and Tamarindo. A taxi from the airport will cost about $80.

The **Asociación de Guías Locales** (tel. 506/2653-1687, 7am-4pm daily) offers water-taxi service between Tamarindo and a dock on the estuary near the Hotel Bula Bula every two hours ($3).

PLAYAS AVELLANAS, LAGARTILLO, AND NEGRA

From Tamarindo, you must backtrack to Villarreal in order to continue southward via Hernández, three kilometers (2 miles) south of Villarreal. There's no shortage of cheap surfer and backpacker hostels. Theft and car break-ins are major problems at the string of beaches that unspool southward. Never leave items in your car.

Coral-colored **Playa Avellanas,** 12 kilometers (7.5 miles) south of Tamarindo, is renowned for its barrel surf at low tide and Little Hawaii (an open-face right break) at mid-tide. Between Tamarindo and Avellanas, most of the coastline backs onto **Hacienda Pinilla,** which covers 1,800 hectares (4,450 acres). This former cattle ranch is today an upscale residential resort, with a championship 18-hole golf course, a nature reserve, a stable for horse rides ($15-35), and a Marriott hotel, plus rental villas and condos.

Playa Lagartillo, beyond Punta Pargos, just south of Playa Avellanas, is another gray-sand beach with tide pools. Lagartillo is separated by Punta Pargos from **Playa Negra,** centered on the community of **Los Pargos,** one kilometer (0.6 miles) inland. Playa Negra is popular with the surfing crowd.

About five kilometers (3 miles) south of Los Pargos, the dirt road cuts inland about eight kilometers (5 miles) to the tiny hamlet of **Paraíso** (reached by paved road from Santa Cruz), where another dirt road leads back to the coast and dead-ends at **Playa Junquillal.** The narrow dirt coast road from Villareal becomes impassable in sections in the wet season, when you may have better luck approaching Playa Avellanas and Lagartillo from the south via Paraíso.

Sports and Recreation

You can rent surfboards at **Avellanas Surf School** (tel. 506/2653-1531, www.avellanas-surf-school.com).

Pargos Adventures (tel. 506/2652-9136), in Los Pargos, offers bike tours and surfboard rentals. **Los Pargos Surf Shop** (tel. 506/2653-4248) is 200 meters (660 feet) south.

Accommodations

If you like minimalist contemporary styling, you'll like **Las Avellanas Villas** (tel. 506/2652-9212, www.lasavellanasvillas.com, low season from $36 s/d, high season from $65 s/d, depending on length of stay), 300 meters (1,000 feet) inland of the beach at Playa Avellanas. The five self-contained cabins set amid spacious lawns have glazed concrete floors, slightly ascetic yet stylish furniture (including a double bed and a bunk), small kitchens, and heaps of light through cross-ventilated French doors opening to wooden decks. Daily yoga classes are offered.

In Los Pargos village, the best digs are at the Peruvian-run ★ **Café Playa Negra** (tel. 506/2652-9351, www.playanegracafe.com, low season from $35, $55 d, high season from $45 s, $65 d). This colorful and cozy, well-managed boutique option exudes tremendous ambience beyond the antique-style doors. It has six rooms (two with bunks) appointed with glazed concrete floors, plump sofas, mattresses atop poured concrete with Guatemalan bedspreads, sponge-washed walls, and hammocks on a broad veranda facing a gorgeous pool. Three rooms are air-conditioned; three have ceiling fans. It also has a full bar, board games, and a Peruvian restaurant.

★ **Hotel Restaurant Villa Deevena** (tel. 506/2653-2328, www.villadeevena.com, low season $85 s/d, high season $95 s/d), south and inland of Los Pargos, is indeed divine—in fact, it's the nicest place around. The six-room boutique hotel features faux-washed concrete walls and floors, poured-concrete fixtures, garden showers, deluxe linens, and an eye-pleasing simplicity that all combine to make this a choice place to stay. Bonus points for the swimming pool, restaurant, yoga, and pampering service.

None of the listings above are actually by the beach. For an oceanfront locate, check out **Hotel Playa Negra** (tel. 506/2652-9134, www.playanegra.com, low season $80-105s, $90-120 d, high season $90-115 s, $100-140 d), at Playa Negra, designed like a South African kraal. Its circular cabins are lovely, with simple yet colorful motifs. Air-conditioned suites have king beds; all have Wi-Fi. It has a pleasant beachfront restaurant, a games room, a swimming pool, and a surf shop.

If you dig large-scale resorts and have money to splurge, yours dreams may come true at the beachfront **JW Marriott Guanacaste Resort & Spa** (tel. 506/2681-2000, www.marriott.com, low season $209-519 s/d, high season $380-1,299 s/d), a sprawling resort and a world unto itself, enclosed within Hacienda Pinilla. Its 310 luxuriously appointed guest rooms, including 20 junior suites, all have lavish baths. The most sumptuous rooms have their own plunge pools. It also has a full-service spa, a huge infinity pool, and four restaurants. The inspiration is Old World colonial, reborn in contemporary style.

Food

At Playa Avellanas, ★ **Lola's on the Beach** (tel. 506/2652-9097, lolascostarica@me.com, 8am-6pm Tues.-Sun.) is a world-famous institution for the owner's now deceased giant pig—Lola—that used to take a daily dip in the ocean, But wait—Lolita, the new pet porker, carries on the tradition. This rustic beachfront restaurant, run by a U.S. transplant, is equally famous for its Hawaiian raw-fish salad and pizzas, to be enjoyed under palms at tables on the beach. It even has fish-and-chips. Laze around with a cold one or a rum-based smoothie on an Adirondack chair beneath a shade umbrellas.

Carlos at **Café Playa Negra** (tel. 506/2652-9351, www.playanegracafe.com, 7am-10am,

noon-4pm, and 5pm-9pm daily), on the main road to the beach in Playa Negra, conjures superb pancakes, french toast, quiches, sandwiches, ceviche, and salads, plus fusion entrées such as tuna teriyaki with mashed potatoes and sautéed veggies, and grilled mahimahi with sautéed shrimp in a pesto sauce with cherry tomatoes ($12). Oh, I forget to mention the killer *batidos* (shakes). Saturday is sushi night. The café also offers Internet connections ($2.50 per hour) and laundry service ($7.50 per load).

Also on the main road to the beach in Playa Negra, the simple open-air and thatched **Jalapeños Taco Grill** (tel. 506/2652-9270, 10am-8pm Mon.-Sat.), at Rocky Point Surf Lodge, satisfies with its $2 tacos, plus its mega-burritos and *casados,* including huge burrito breakfasts.

Gina's Sports Bar & Lounge (tel. 506/2653-0579, $5-12), at Los Pargos, has a state-of-the-art kitchen where the new owner-chef, Gina, prepares excellent international dishes, such as calzone, beef lasagna with salad ($9), blackened mahimahi with coconut-pineapple sauce ($12), and tuna with ginger sauce ($12) at giveaway prices. Its sports bar has big-screen TVs and pool tables; go Sunday daytime for U.S. football on TV with burgers and pasta, and Saturday and Sunday evening for live music.

Also competing in the fine-dining stakes is ★ **Hotel Restaurant Villa Deevena** (tel. 506/2653-2328, www.villadeevena.com), on the main road to the beach in Playa Negra, for the great setting and superb fusion dishes using fresh produce, all by owner-chef Patrick Jamon (formerly of the Regency Club, in Los Angeles). Start, perhaps, with a beet and goat cheese salad (Patrick makes the cheese himself), followed by rack of lamb Provençal or lobster ravioli. They host tapas nights and occasional parties. Budget about $40 per head for a three-course meal.

PLAYA JUNQUILLAL

Playa Junquillal, four kilometers (2.5 miles) southwest of Paraíso and 31 kilometers (19 miles) west of Santa Cruz, is a four-kilometer (2.5-mile) light-gray-sand beach with rock platforms and tide pools. Beware the high surf and strong riptides. The beachfront road dead-ends at the wide and deep Río Andumolo, whose mangrove estuary is home to birds and crocodiles.

Local youths called "Baula Boys" (after the Costa Rican name for the leatherback turtle) collect turtle eggs from nests to protect them in an incubation site on the beautiful beach. The program is run by the **Verdiazul Asociación Vida,** whose office is 50 meters (165 feet) inland of the beach.

Paradise Riding (tel. 506/2658-8162, www.paradiseriding.com) offers horse-riding trips. There's a **Welcome Center** (tel. 506/2658-7224) in Plaza Tierra Pacífica, as you enter Junquillal; a delicatessen and medical center are also here.

Accommodations and Food

Accommodations in Junquillal struggle to draw clientele, and the scene remains fluid.

A bargain-priced option, the modern **Guacamaya Lodge** (tel. 506/2658-8431, www.guacamayalodge.com, low season from $50 s, $55 d, high season from $60 s, $65 d), near the beach at the south end of town, is run by a Swiss couple. The huge open-air thatched bar-restaurant is a highlight. There's a clinical orderliness to the spacious, if simply appointed, *cabinas* and studio apartments, plus two two-bedroom villas, all of which are washed with plenty of sunlight. It has a sand volleyball court plus a tennis court.

Stealing the show is the very tropically themed **Mundo Milo Ecolodge** (tel. 506/2658-7010, www.mundomilo.com, low season $57-67 s/d, high season $67-77 s/d), a rustic yet gorgeous lodge run by Dutch expats Lieke and Michael, who designed the open-air lounge with "an African motif." The airy thatched Mexican- and African-style cabins have their own lovely themed aesthetic and oodles of comfort. The infinity pool is a plus. The restaurant draws folks from afar, especially for sushi on Tuesday evening.

Getting There

Buses depart Santa Cruz at 5am, 10am, 2:30pm, and 5:30pm daily. Return buses depart at 6am, 9am, 12:30pm, and 4:30pm daily.

turtle hatchery at Playa Junquillal

Junquillal to Carrillo

PLAYA LAGARTO TO SAN JUANILLO

South of Junquillal, the dirt road leads along a lonesome stretch of coast via Ostional to Nosara, 35 kilometers (22 miles) south of Junquillal. Driving south from Tamarindo or west from Santa Cruz on the Santa Cruz–Junquillal road, you must turn south four kilometers (2.5 miles) east of Paraíso—the turnoff is signed for Marbella, 16 kilometers (10 miles) along, and Nosara, then Sámara and Playa Carrillo. There are several rivers to ford, and a 4WD vehicle is essential.

Fabulous beaches lie hidden along this lonesome route, though they are out of sight of the road most of the way.

About 10 kilometers (6 miles) south of the junction, the road briefly hits the shore at **Lagarto** and **Playa Manzanillo** before curling inland to **Marbella,** where a side road runs down to **Playa Lagarcito** and black-sand **Playa Marbella** (also called Playa Frijólar); if you follow the sandy track the length of Playa Marbella, it ends beside the **Tiki Hut** bar and restaurant; Jeff, the owner, hails from California, and the place is the perfect hangout for surfers.

Six kilometers (4 miles) farther, you'll pass The Sanctuary residential resort at **Playa Azúl,** beyond which you'll ford a small river. About five kilometers (3 miles) farther south, a turnoff from the coast road leads to the fishing hamlet of **San Juanillo,** which has two beautiful white-sand beaches. Ostional is five kilometers (3 miles) farther south.

Paskis Adventures (tel. 506/2682-8103, http://paskisadventures.weebly.com), in San Juanillo, offers sportfishing and snorkeling and scuba diving trips (including scuba certification), and whale-watching and "swim with turtle" trips. Unfortunately, participants are encouraged to hold on to marine turtles. This is not good for the turtles and should be discouraged.

Accommodations and Food

Cabinas Cada Luna Café Bar (tel. 506/2682-8092, www.cadaluna.com, $28 s/d), on the dirt road to Playa Frijólar at Marbella, will appeal to young-at-heart travelers with

Fishers in simple craft bring home the catch at San Juanillo.

an appreciation for hip architecture. A young French couple run this bargain-priced beauty, with garden lounge and lots of poured concrete, although furnishings are Spartan. Its tapas bar (8am-10pm Sun.-Thurs., 8am-10pm Fri.-Sat.) draws the many expats who live hereabouts. It hosts an "electromoon" party each full moon.

At San Juanillo, the ever-expanding **Hotel Restaurant Playa San Juanillo** (tel. 506/2682-1311, www.playasanjuanillo.com, $55 s, $65 d) is a Swiss-run charmer with 10 simply appointed rooms with fans, heaps of hardwoods, and private baths. Its **Buddha Bar & Restaurant** serves vegetarian and seafood lunch and dinner, including fish sandwiches and pizzas, and has Wi-Fi and an espresso bar plus an open-air deck. Kick back in the Buddha Lounge and enjoy movies shown on a big screen; live music includes jazz, reggae, and salsa.

One of my all-time faves, especially when in a Swiss Family Robinson mood, is ★ **Tree Tops Bed & Breakfast** (tel./fax 506/2682-1334, www.costaricatreetopsinn.com, $135 s/d, including English breakfast), a secluded and rustic one-room bed-and-breakfast tucked above a cove at San Juanillo. Reservations are essential. This charming place is the home of former race-car champion Jack Hunter and his wife, Karen, delightful hosts who go out of their way to make you feel at home (they specialize in three- and five-day honeymoon packages). There's one basically furnished room with an orthopedic mattress, luxe linens, Wi-Fi, and an outdoor hot-water shower—appealing enough that almost every living Costa Rican president has stayed here. You're the only guest, here for spectacular solitude and a setting that includes a horseshoe reef with live coral (great for snorkeling) and a private beach for that all-over tan. Monkeys cavort in the treetops. The owners recently added two charming bungalows with the same back-to-basics decor and furnishings, plus fans and Wi-Fi, and outdoor showers. They offer excursions, including sportfishing; if you catch your own fish, Karen will prepare sushi. Karen is a self-trained gourmet chef capable of turning whatever ingredients are at hand into divine treats. I recently sampled a mango and chayote squash soup with coconut milk drizzled with chili oil; red and green leaf salad with avocado and heart of palm in balsamic with honey and vanilla; fresh red snapper with sherry and curry cream sauce with green rice, spinach, and coriander with veggies; plus coconut flan with coffee liqueur and

Tree Tops Bed & Breakfast, San Juanillo

grated orange and white chocolate, with fresh strawberries. Tree Tops is open to nonguests for three-course lunches (11am-2pm daily), and five-course dinners ($34 pp), including homemade ice cream, by reservation only one day in advance.

Tree Tops is just steps from San Juanillo hamlet and **Ancient People** (tel. 506/2862-5064, ancientpeople@gmail.com), a delightful open-air café with Wi-Fi, as well as a gift shop and an organic food store. The Israeli owners serve falafels and hummus—of course!—as well as smoked salmon wraps, coconut bars and chocolate brownies, plus ice creams and smoothies.

★ OSTIONAL NATIONAL WILDLIFE REFUGE

The 248-hectare (613-acre) **Refugio Nacional de Vida Silvestre Ostional** begins at Punta India, about two kilometers (1.2 miles) south of San Juanillo, and extends along 15 kilometers (9.5 miles) of shoreline to Punta Güiones, eight kilometers (5 miles) south of the village of Nosara. It incorporates the beaches of Playa Ostional, Playa Nosara, and Playa Güiones. The village of **Ostional** is midway along **Playa Ostional.**

The refuge was created to protect one of three vitally important nesting sites in Costa Rica for the *lora,* the olive ridley turtle (also called the Pacific ridley); the others are Playa Camaronal and Playa Nancite, in Parque Nacional Santa Rosa. A significant proportion of the world's olive ridley turtle population nests at Ostional, invading the beach en masse for up to one week at a time July-December. Peak season is August and September, starting with the last quarter of the full moon, and they arrive singly or in small groups at other times during the year.

If you time your arrival correctly, out beyond the breakers you may see a vast flotilla of turtles massed shoulder to shoulder, waiting their turn to swarm ashore, dig a hole in the sand, and drop in the seeds for tomorrow's turtles. The legions pour out of the surf in endless waves. It's a stupendous sight, this *arribada.* Of the world's eight marine turtle species, only the females of the olive ridley and its Atlantic cousin, Kemp's ridley, stage *arribadas,* and Ostional is the most important of these. Synchronized mass nestings are known to occur at only a dozen or so other beaches worldwide—in other parts of Central America, Suriname, and Orissa in India. So tightly packed is the horde that the turtles feverishly clamber over one another in their

coatimundis eating African date palms

Respite for the Ridley

Elsewhere in Costa Rica, harvesting turtle eggs is illegal and occurs in the dead of night. At Ostional it occurs legally and by daylight—the result of a bold conservation program that aims to help the turtles by allowing the local community to commercially harvest eggs in a rational manner.

Costa Rica outlawed taking turtle eggs nationwide in 1966, but egg poaching is a time-honored tradition. The coming of the first *arribada* (mass nesting) in 1961 was a bonanza to the people of Ostional. Their village became the major source of turtle eggs in Costa Rica. Coatis, coyotes, raccoons, and other egg-hungry marauders take a heavy toll on the tasty eggs too. Ironically, the most efficient scourges are the turtles themselves. Ridley turtles deposit millions of eggs at a time. Since the beach is literally covered with thousands of turtles, the eggs laid during the first days of an *arribada* are often dug up by turtles arriving later. As the newcomers dig, many inadvertently destroy the eggs laid by their predecessors, and the sand is strewn with rotting embryos. Even without human interference, only 1-8 percent of eggs in any *arribada* hatch.

Ridley turtles during an *arribada* at Playa Camaronal

By the early 1970s, the turtle population was below the minimum required to maintain the species. After a decade of study, scientists concluded that uncontrolled poaching would ultimately exterminate the nesting colony. They reasoned that a *controlled* harvest could actually rejuvenate the turtle population. Such a harvest during the first two nights of an *arribada* would improve hatch rates at Ostional by reducing crowded conditions and the number of broken eggs.

In 1987 the Costa Rican legislature approved a plan that legalized egg harvesting at Ostional. The unique legal right to harvest eggs is vested in members of the Asociación de Desarrollo Integral de Ostional (ADIO). The University of Costa Rica, which has maintained a biological research station at Ostional since 1980, is legally responsible for management and review. A quota is established for each *arribada*. Sometimes, no eggs are harvested. In the dry season (Dec.-May), as many as 35 percent of eggs may be taken; when the beach is hotter than Hades, the embryos become dehydrated, and the hatching rate falls below 1 percent. The idea is to save eggs that would be broken anyway or would have a low chance of hatching. By law, eggs may be taken only during the first 36 hours of an *arribada*. After that, the villagers protect the nests from poachers and the hatchlings from ravenous beasts.

The eggs are dealt to distributors, who sell on a smaller scale at a contract-fixed price to bakers (who favor turtle eggs over those of hens; turtle eggs give dough greater "lift") and bars, brothels, and street vendors who sell the eggs as aphrodisiac *bocas* (snacks). Net revenues from the sale of eggs are divided between the community (80 percent) and the Ministry of Agriculture. ADIO distributes 70 percent of its share among association members as payment for their labors, and 30 percent to the Sea Turtle Project and communal projects. Profits have funded construction of a health center, a house for schoolteachers, the ADIO office, and a Sea Turtle Research Lab.

Scientists claim that the project has the potential to stop the poaching of eggs on other beaches. It's a matter of economics: Poachers have been undercut by cheaper eggs from Ostional. Studies show that the turtle population has stabilized. Recent *arribadas* have increased in size, and hatch rates are up dramatically. Alas, illegal fishing still kills hundreds of turtles each year.

efforts to find an unoccupied nesting site. As they dig, sweeping their flippers back and forth, the petulant females scatter sand over one another and the air is filled with the slapping of flippers on shells. By the time the *arribada* is over, more than 150,000 turtles may have stormed this prodigal place and 15 million eggs may lie buried in the sand.

Leatherback turtles also come ashore to nest in smaller numbers October-January. Although turtles can handle the strong currents, humans have a harder time: Swimming is not advised. Howler monkeys, coatimundis, and kinkajous frequent the forest inland from the beach. The mangrove swamp at the mouth of the Río Nosara is a nesting site for many of the 190 bird species hereabouts.

The **Asociación de Desarrollo Integral de Ostional** (Ostional Integral Development Association, ADIO, tel./fax 506/2682-0470, adiotort@racsa.co.cr, www.arribadasostional. com), which oversees turtle welfare, seeks volunteers to assist with turtle programs.

Turtle Viewing

You must check in with ADIO before exploring the beach; their office is beside the road on the northwest corner of the soccer field. A guide from the **Asociación de Guías Locales** (tel. 506/2682-0428) is compulsory during *arribadas;* an entry fee ($10) is payable at the ADIO *puesto* (ranger station, tel. 506/2682-0400) at the southern end of the village. You will watch a video before entering the beach as a group. All vehicles arriving at night are required to turn off their headlights when approaching the beach. Flashlights and flash photography are also forbidden. Personal contact with turtles is prohibited, as is disturbing the markers placed on the beach.

Accommodations and Food

There are several budget accommodations in the village and along the shore, but by far the best is **Ostional Turtle Lodge** (tel. 506/2682-0131, www.surfingostional.com, $26-32 s, $40-54 d), on the south side of Ostional. Run by a conscientious and friendly owner, it continues to improve, and although simply appointed, the five cabins and rooms (with air-conditioning or fans) are kept spotless and have hot-water showers plus Wi-Fi; one room has a balcony and a kitchenette.

The nicest place is in the hills north of Ostional, where the former Brovilla Resort Hotel metamorphosed in late 2014 as **Camp Fit Costa Rica** (tel. 506/8519-6059, U.S. tel. 702-622-9655, www.campfitcostarica.com, call for rates), a fitness-oriented vacation retreat with a splendid setting with coast views. It focuses on all-inclusive packages for fitness groups. It has eight very eclectic types of rooms, cabins, and villas, and has a plunge pool and open-air terrace restaurant, plus tennis courts.

Information and Services

The *pulpería* at the northern end of the soccer field has a **public telephone.** There's a **police station** (tel. 506/8828-2892) in town.

Getting There

A **bus** departs Santa Cruz daily for Ostional (3 hours) at 12:30pm daily, returning at 5am daily; it may not run in wet season. You can take a **taxi** (about $8) or walk to Ostional from Nosara.

The dirt road between Ostional and Nosara, five kilometers (3 miles) south, requires you to ford (*vanar* in Spanish) the Río Montaña, about five kilometers (3 miles) south of Ostional, which can be impassable during wet season; sometimes a tractor will be there to pull you through for a fee. About one kilometer (0.6 miles) farther south, the road divides: The fork to the left (east) fords the Río Nosara just before entering the village of Nosara and is impassable in all but the most favorable conditions; the fork to the right crosses the Río Nosara via a bridge and the community of Santa Marta.

★ NOSARA

Nosara boasts three of the best beaches in Nicoya, each with rocky tide pools great for soaking. They're backed by hills smothered in

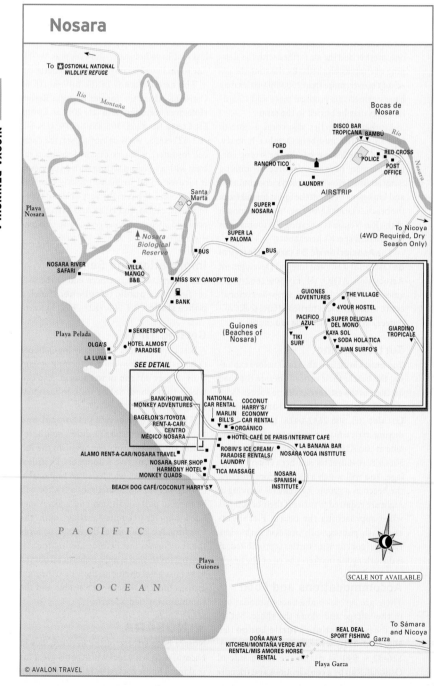

Nosara

To ✚ OSTIONAL NATIONAL WILDLIFE REFUGE

Río Montaña

Bocas de Nosara

Playa Nosara

Río Nosara

DISCO BAR TROPICANA BAMBÚ

FORD

RANCHO TICO

POLICE

RED CROSS

POST OFFICE

LAUNDRY

AIRSTRIP

Santa Marta

SUPER NOSARA

To Nicoya
(4WD Required, Dry Season Only)

↑ Nosara Biological Reserve

SUPER LA PALOMA

BUS

BUS

NOSARA RIVER SAFARI

VILLA MANGO B&B

MISS SKY CANOPY TOUR

BANK

Guiones (Beaches of Nosara)

GUIONES ADVENTURES

THE VILLAGE

4YOUR HOSTEL

PACIFICO AZUL

SUPER DELICIAS DEL MONO

GIARDINO TROPICALE

Playa Pelada

SEKRETSPOT

OLGA'S

HOTEL ALMOST PARADISE

LA LUNA

TIKI SURF

KAYA SOL

SODA HOLA TICA

JUAN SURFO'S

SEE DETAIL

BANK/HOWLING MONKEY ADVENTURES

NATIONAL CAR RENTAL

COCONUT HARRY'S/ ECONOMY CAR RENTAL

BAGELON'S/TOYOTA RENT-A-CAR/ CENTRO MÉDICO NOSARA

MARLIN BILL'S

ORGÁNICO

HOTEL CAFÉ DE PARIS/INTERNET CAFÉ

LA BANANA BAR

ROBIN'S ICE CREAM/ PARADISE RENTALS/ LAUNDRY

NOSARA YOGA INSTITUTE

ALAMO RENT-A-CAR/NOSARA TRAVEL

NOSARA SURF SHOP HARMONY HOTEL MONKEY QUADS

TICA MASSAGE

NOSARA SPANISH INSTITUTE

BEACH DOG CAFÉ/COCONUT HARRY'S

PACIFIC

Playa Guiones

SCALE NOT AVAILABLE

OCEAN

DOÑA ANA'S KITCHEN/MONTAÑA VERDE ATV RENTAL/MIS AMORES HORSE RENTAL

REAL DEAL SPORT FISHING

Garza

To Sámara and Nicoya

Playa Garza

© AVALON TRAVEL

moist tropical forest. **Playa Nosara** extends north from the estuary of the Río Nosara to Ostional; *arribadas* of olive ridley turtles occasionally occur. The sleepy village of **Bocas de Nosara** is five kilometers (3 miles) inland, five kilometers (3 miles) south of Ostional, on the banks of the river. It maintains a simple traditional Tico lifestyle but otherwise offers little appeal, except a lively disco and the airstrip.

Playa Pelada is tucked in a cove south of Punta Nosara; it has a blowhole at the south and a bat cave at the north end. The main beach, **Playa Güiones,** is separated from Playa Pelada by Punta Pelada and is a ruler-straight five-kilometer (3-mile) expanse of coral-white sand washed by surf. Hence Güiones is popular with surfers. Beware of the strong riptides!

Inland of Pelada and Güiones, a sprawling enclave of hotels, restaurants, and surf shops form the main resort area, **Güiones** (also known as Beaches of Nosara), four kilometers (2.5 miles) south of Bocas de Nosara village. Beaches of Nosara started three decades ago as a foreign residential community where about 200 homes are hidden amid the forest. The place is in the midst of a decade-long real estate boom that has had a devastating impact on local wildlife.

The roads of Pelada and Güiones are an intestinal labyrinth sure to turn you around, at least in your head.

Wildlife Refuges

About 40 hectares (100 acres) of wildlife-rich forest are protected in the private **Reserva Biológica Nosara** (tel. 506/2682-0035, www.lagarta.com) along the river; guided boat trips are offered. Guided nature walks are offered at 6:30am daily ($15 pp); self-guided walks ($6) can be enjoyed 6am-4pm daily.

Sibu Sanctuary (tel. 506/8413-8889, www.nosarasibusanctuary.com) takes in animals orphaned or injured by uninsulated power lines, vehicle strikes, and unleashed dogs. Run by Brenda Bombard, of Harbor Reef Hotel, it specializes in rescuing and aiding howler monkeys and is an extension of her Refugio Animals de Nosara—a 20-hectare (50-acre) finca that rehabilitates those animals that can be reintroduced to the wild. Tours are permitted by reservation ($50) and involve a good hike. Donations are urgently needed.

Entertainment and Events

The nightlife in Bocas centers on two rustic yet atmospheric bars beside the plaza: **Bambú,** with live marimba on Saturday, and

Playa Güiones is part of Ostional National Wildlife Refuge.

Disco Bar Tropicana (9:30pm-2:30am Fri.-Sat.), next door, which is the hot-ticket dance spot with a pack-'em-in disco on weekends. Its shuttle begins picking up guests at hotels in Güiones at 10:30pm and returns at 2am.

Tamer fare can be enjoyed at Café Lounge (tel. 506/2682-0080, cafeloungecr@hotmail.com), at Kaya Sol Surf Hotel, in Güiones, which shows movies at 3pm most days; by night DJ Darren Zman spins everything from reggae to electronica. Theme nights include Latin night on Friday, with free dance classes at 8pm. El Fenix (tel. 506/2686-0287), at Playa Pelada, also has nightly themes, including an all-you-can-eat sunset party on Thursday ($10, including free sangria).

At sunset, head to Playa Pelada for La Luna Bar and Grill (tel. 506/2682-0122, 11am-11pm daily, $5), an atmospheric place with cobblestone floors, bottle-green glass bricks, and a terrace hosting a Friday-night "multicultural party." It serves killer margaritas, plus lentil soup, sushi rolls, carpaccio, and more, and plays world music from Dylan to reggae.

On Wednesday, check out the live music (7pm) at Harbor Reef; and on Sunday nights, head to Pacífico Azul for barbecue and live blues.

Sports and Recreation

Fishing Nosara (tel. 506/2682-0606, U.S. tel. 904-591-2161, www.fishingnosara.com) offers sportfishing, while Nosara River Safari (tel. 506/2682-0610, www.nosararivsafari.com) has guided nature-focused boat trips into the estuary.

Inevitably, Nosara has a canopy tour at Miss Sky Canopy Tour (tel. 506/2682-0969, www.missskycanopytour.com, adults $60, children $40), with 21 zip-line runs. The longest is 750 meters (2,460 feet).

For horseback rides and ATV rentals, call Boca Nosara Tours (tel. 506/2682-0280, www.bocanosaratours.com); or Güiones Adventures (tel. 506/2682-5373, www.guionesadventures.com), specializing in ATV adventures. For screaming fun, rent a "Tom Car"

ATV from Howling Monkey Adventures (tel. 506/2682-0624, www.howlingmonkeyadventures.com); dress to get dirty!

Tica Massage (tel. 506/2682-0096, 9am-6pm daily) has treetop and garden rooms for walk-in massage.

SURFING

Nosara Surf Shop (tel. 506/2682-0113, www.safarisurfschool.com) has a Safari Surf School, including women's and children's clinics. It also sells and rents boogie boards and surfboards, as do Coconut Harry's Surf Shop and School (tel. 506/2682-0574, www.coconutharrys.com) and Juan Surfo's Surf Shop (tel. 506/2682-1081, www.surfocostarica.com). Nosara Surf Academy (tel. 506/2682-5082, www.nosarasurfacademy.com), at the Gilded Iguana in Güiones, has a surf school and offers sea kayaking. Drifters (tel. 506/2682-1380, www.drifterskayaking.com), at the mouth of Río Nosara, also rents kayaks.

YOGA

Nosara Yoga Institute (tel. 506/2682-0071, U.S. tel. 866-439-4704, www.nosarayoga.com) is dedicated to professional training and advanced career development for teachers and practitioners in the field of yoga and bodywork. Perched in the hills behind Playa Güiones, it's the perfect place to relax and recharge. The institute specializes in advanced techniques and offers intensive one- to four-week programs in yoga, meditation, and Pranassage (a private one-on-one yoga session), plus nature and health programs.

The Costa Rica Yoga Spa (tel. 506/2682-0192, U.S. tel. 888-533-6461, www.costaricayogaspa.com), north of the river at Bocas de Nosara, offers an alternative, and has inspirational ocean vistas. The Harmony Hotel's Healing Center (tel. 506/2682-4114), near the beach in Nosara, has free community yoga classes at 4pm each Wednesday.

Accommodations

Proof that even the budget-minded surf crowd has class, Kaya Sol Surf Hotel

(tel. 506/2682-1459, www.kayasol.com), at Güiones, offers something for every budget, including delightfully airy and welcoming dorms (low season $15-18 pp, high season $16-18 pp) with pastel color schemes and tin roofs, plus private economy rooms and an eclectic mix of more upscale options, from studios to chic beach villas (low season $40-230 s/d, high season $53-275 s/d). After the waves die down, it's time to lounge poolside with a chilled Imperial. Kaya Sol has one of the best restaurants and liveliest entertainment scenes in Nosara.

Hostel life went upscale in 2012 with the opening of **4 You Hostal** (tel. 506/2682-1316, www.4youhostal.com, dorm $18, private rooms $25, bungalow $40 s, $55 d)—a striking contemporary structure with clinically clean eight-bed dorms and three private rooms plus a bungalow, all with lovely minimalist furnishings. Relax in a garden that is a study in Zen-like serenity and harmony. It's run to high standards and gets great reviews.

Run by a delightful French-Portuguese couple, **Villa Mango B&B** (tel. 506/2682-1168, www.villamangocr.com, low season $49 s, $59 d, high season $74 s, $84 d, including breakfast and tax), in the hills at Pelada, is a bed-and-breakfast that enjoys views over Playa Güiones and will appeal to folk seeking an intimate family-like atmosphere. It has four bedrooms with parquet floors, raised wooden ceilings, and large picture windows, plus Wi-Fi. It has a kidney-shaped pool (monkeys and coatis come to drink!), plus a delightfully rustic restaurant and sundeck with bamboo rockers and hammocks.

The environmentally sound, if overpriced, **Harmony Hotel** (tel. 506/2682-4114, www.harmonynosara.com, $330-690 s/d, including breakfast), within spitting distance of the beach, is one of the class acts in Nosara. It offers 24 rooms with king beds and simple yet edgy furnishings as well as 11 one- and two-bedroom bungalows with decks and rinse showers in enclosed courtyards, plus private baths and hot water. Some units have air-conditioning; all have Wi-Fi. The landscaped grounds boast a curvaceous swimming pool, a tennis court, and a yoga gym, plus a large bar and restaurant with rattans and bamboos.

The chic **Nosara Suites** (tel. 506/2682-0087, www.nosarasuites.com, call for rates), owned by the French owners of Café de Paris (immediately south), are perfect for travelers for whom style is foremost in mind. These five trendy and individually themed loft-style apartments could fit in San Francisco or

A surfer and horseback riders enjoy Playa Güiones.

New York's SoHo. They offer fabulous views over Beaches of Nosara, and each has a spiral staircase to two or three bedrooms. The Café de Paris and other restaurants are a stone's throw away.

Food

In Playa Pelada, **Olga's** (tel. 506/2682-1116, 10am-10pm daily) is a rustic Tico-owned place, recommended for seafood ($5) and filling *casados,* plus pizza. A mobile disco sometimes sets up, and Olga's hosts occasional parties.

On the main road in the heart of Güiones, **Marlin Bill's** (tel. 506/2682-0458, 11am-2pm and 6pm-midnight daily, $3.50-13) offers great dining on a lofty, breeze-swept terrace with views. Lunch might include a blackened tuna salad or sandwich, french onion soup ($4), and brownie sundae or key lime pie. Pork loin chops, New York strip steak, and eggplant parmesan typify the dinner menu. The bar has a TV.

Fifty meters (165 feet) east of Marlin Bill's, in the heart of Güiones, **Orgánico** (tel. 506/2682-1434, 7:30am-7pm daily) has a great deli, including veggie and vegan foods, plus Middle Eastern specialties. At **Robin's Café** (tel. 506/2682-0617, www.robinsicecream. com, 8am-7pm Mon.-Sat., 10am-4:30pm Sun.), in Güiones, the namesake owner greets you with a smile at her ever-lively café, with Wi-Fi. It's a great place for sandwiches, wraps, salads, and homemade ice cream, including irresistible Mayan chocolate and a pineapple-ginger sorbet.

The French-run **Café de Paris** (tel. 506/2682-1036, 7am-11pm daily, $4-10), in the heart of Güiones, serves Gallic fare such as crepes and french toast, but also omelets, sandwiches such as chicken curry or turkey, and entrées such as penne pasta with creamed pesto fish and duck breast in green pepper sauce, plus wood-fired pizza.

Another great place to start the day, **Beach Dog Café** (tel. 506/2682-1293, 7am-3pm daily) serves fresh-baked breads, sandwiches, slow-cooked meats, filling burritos,

wraps, and smoothies. It's just steps from the beach at Güiones and has a terrific outdoor ambience. It offers free Wi-Fi and international calls.

Offering a tad of elegance, **Harmony Hotel** (tel. 506/2682-4114, www.harmonynosara.com, 7am-10:30am, noon-3:30pm, and 6pm-9pm daily, $5-15), near the beach in Nosara, is a winner for vegetarian and fusion cuisine such as coconut basil and ginger jumbo shrimp ($8), and a superb five-spice chicken risotto.

Information and Services

The Frog Pad (tel. 506/2682-4039, www.the-frogpad.com), in Villa Tortuga, in the heart of Güiones, has a book exchange, plus DVDs, videos, and board games. A stone's throw away there's a bank (7am-9pm daily) next to Café de Paris, which also offers Internet service, as do the **Seekretspot** (tel. 506/2682-1325, seekretspot@hotmail.com), an Internet and Italian café that doubles as an upscale hostel; and **The Frog Pad** (tel. 506/2682-4039, www.thefrogpad.com), nearer the beach in Güiones.

The private **Centro Médico Nosara** (tel. 506/2682-1212), in the heart of Beaches of Nosara, has dental services. There's a **Red Cross** (tel. 506/2682-0175) in Bocas de Nosara and a **clinic** (tel. 506/2682-0266) at the west end of Bocas de Nosara. The **police station** (tel. 506/2682-5126) is on the northeast side of the airstrip; the **post office** is next door.

Want to learn Spanish? **Nosara Spanish Institute** (tel. 506/2682-1460, www.nosaraspanishinstitute.com) can set you up.

Getting There

SANSA (tel. 506/2229-4100, U.S./Canada tel. 877-767-2672, www.flysansa.com) and **Nature Air** (tel. 506/2299-6000, U.S. tel. 800-235-9272, www.natureair.com) have twice-daily service between San José and Nosara's airstrip.

Alfaro (tel. 506/2222-2666 or 506/2682-0297) buses depart San José for Nosara (6

BAHÍA GARZA TO SÁMARA

The dirt road from Nosara leads south 26 kilometers (16 miles) to Playa Sámara via the horseshoe-shaped Bahía Garza, eight kilometers (5 miles) south of Nosara, rimmed by pebbly gray-sand **Playa Garza.** Beyond Garza, the road cuts inland from the coast, which remains out of view the rest of the way.

At **Barco Quebrado,** about 15 kilometers (9.5 miles) south of Nosara and 11 kilometers (7 miles) north of Sámara, the road divides: keep right for Sámara, or turn left for the road to Terciopelo and the town of Nicoya. Continuing south on the unpaved coast road, you pass **Playa Barrigona,** hidden from view (Mel Gibson recently sold a large property here), and pass through the hamlet of **Esterones,** where a side road leads two kilometers (1.2 miles) to **Playa Buena Vista,** where there are crocodiles in the river estuary at the south end.

On the way to Sámara, about one kilometer (0.6 miles) south of Esterones, you must ford the Río Buena Vista, which isn't always possible in wet season. In this case, backtrack to Barco Quebrado and head inland to Terciopelo and turn right on Highway 150.

★ Flying Crocodile Ultralight Flight

Want to try a flight in an ultralight plane? Head to Playa Buena Vista and the **Flying Crocodile Flying Center** (tel. 506/2656-8048, www.autogyroamerica.com), where Guido Scheidt, a licensed commercial pilot, will take you up in one of his state-of-the-art fixed-wing or autogiro ultralights. Choose from 20-minute ($110) trips to three-day tours (from $1,990) as far as the Osa Peninsula. Guido and his expert licensed flight instructors also offer tuition ($190 per hour).

Sports and Recreation

Mis Amores Horse Rental (tel. 506/2656-8011 or 506/8846-3502, misamores@ice.

Sámara seen from a Flying Crocodile ultralight flight

hours, $8) from Calle 14, Avenidas 3/5, daily at 5:30am; the return bus departs from Bocas del Nosara at 12:30pm. **Empresa Traroc** (tel. 506/2685-5352) buses depart Nicoya for Nosara six times 4:45am-5:30pm daily, returning at 5am, 7am, noon, and 3pm daily.

Interbus (tel. 506/4100-0888, www.interbusonline.com) operates minibus shuttles from San José ($45) and popular travel destinations in Nicoya and Guanacaste. Abel Avila Ugalde of **Vino Transportation** (tel. 506/2682-0879, abelavila1@yahoo.es) has personalized private shuttles.

Budget Rent-a-Car (tel. 506/2682-4114) is located at Harmony Hotel, near the beach in Nosara, and **Economy Rent-a-Car** (tel. 506/2299-2000) has an office on the main road next to Marlin Bill's.

There is no direct road link between Nosara and the town of Nicoya. You must drive south 15 kilometers (9.5 miles) to Barco Quebrado and turn inland; the dirt road meets the paved Nicoya-Sámara road (Hwy. 150) at Terciopelo.

co.cr), 400 meters (0.25 miles) north of Garza village, offers horseback rides. **Montaña Verde** (tel. 506/2682-0300, info@nosara-travel.com), next door, rents ATVs and has tours.

Accommodations and Food

You could fall in love with the German-run **Flying Crocodile Lodge** (tel./fax 506/2656-8048, www.flying-crocodile.com, low season $35-65 s, $41-85 d, high season $43-90 s, $70-100 d), between Esterones and Playa Buena Vista. This marvelous spot is an artistic vision with eight exquisite and eclectic cabins spaced well apart in beautifully maintained grounds. Each is splashed with lively tropical colors and murals and has hardwood floors, curving concrete bench seats with cushions, and showers boasting black stone floors. A pool has a waterslide and a swing, plus there are horses, mountain bikes, motorcycles, and 4WD vehicles. The Ultralight center is here.

    La Cocina de Doña Ana (tel. 506/2656-8085, cocinadonaana@gmail.com, 8am-9:30pm daily), atop Punta Garza, specializes in seafood (including ceviche) and *comida típica;* go for the fabulous setting between bays. It has Wi-Fi.

PLAYA SÁMARA

Playa Sámara, set in an attractive horseshoe-shaped bay with a light-gray beach about 15 kilometers (9.5 miles) south of Garza, is a popular budget destination for surfers and travelers in search of the offbeat. Unlike Nosara, it also draws heavily from a vacationing Tico clientele, due to its relative accessibility (it can be reached directly from Nicoya town by paved road—Highway 150—via Belén, and you can fly into nearby Playa Carrillo). For some reason, German and Swiss expats have settled here, forming their own community as hoteliers.

    The village backs the center of the beach, and it is separated by a cattle finca from **Cangrejal,** a funky hamlet at the north end of the beach. Playa Sámara extends south about two kilometers (1.2 miles) to the small ramshackle fishing community of **Matapalo.**

Entertainment

Small as it is, Sámara is happening once the sun goes down. The hottest nighttime venue is the beachfront **Tabanuco** (tel. 506/2656-0156, info.tabanuco@gmail.com, 1pm-2:30am Mon.-Sat.), which cranks up around 11pm. It's best-known for its Friday night reggae bash; Thursday is "ladies night" with free drinks

an ultralight flight with Flying Crocodile taking off

Playa Sámara to Carrillo

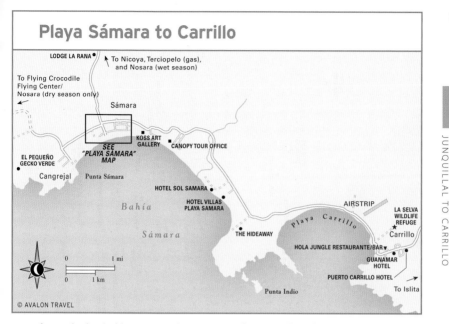

© AVALON TRAVEL

for *muchachas* (gals). A tree trunk grows up through the dance floor.

The mellow, open-air **La Vela Latina** (tel. 506/2656-2286, 11am-midnight daily) video-music bar, on the beach, shows big games on a big screen and plays cool music. Also on the beach, **Gusto Beach Sporting Club** (tel. 506/2656-0252) is a cool place to sip cocktails under the palms. A stone's throw away, **Lo Q Hay Pub** (tel. 506/2656-0811, 7pm-midnight daily) is another cool place to imbibe an ice-cold beer with your feet in the sand; go on "Taco Tuesday," when live music is hosted and there are taco and beer specials. Romantics can stare into each other's eyes over at the **Zen Den** (tel. 506/2656-2323, www.samarabeach.com/zenden, 6pm-2am daily), a chic and casual spot to pop the big question over sensual culinary treats.

Sports and Recreation

C&C Surf School (tel. 506/2656-0628 or 506/5006-0369, www.cncsurfsamara.webs.com), at the Tico Adventure Lodge, on the hillside about 100 meters (330 feet) from the beach, rents surfboards and offers lessons.

Blue Barrel Surf School (tel. 506/2656-0086, www.bluebarrelsurfschool.com) also has surf camps for kids. **Samara Tours** (tel. 506/2656-0920, www.samara-tours.com) can arrange sea kayaking, horseback rides, a dolphin-spotting tour, and more. **Wingnuts** (tel. 506/2656-0153, wingnutscanopytour@ hotmail.com, adults $55, children $35) has a 12-platform canopy tour.

You can rejuvenate at **Natural Center Gym Spa** (tel. 506/2656-2360, www.natural-centersamara.com), which has a gym, a bamboo massage hut, a whirlpool, and classes that include aerobics and tae kwon do. It also rents sea kayaks.

Accommodations

I like the bargain-priced **Tico Adventure Lodge** (tel. 506/2656-0628, www.ticoadventurelodge.com, low season from $25 s, $40 d, high season from $30 s, $50 d), on the hillside about 100 meters (330 feet) from the beach. It's made entirely of teak and offers nine rooms in a handsome sepia-toned two-story unit with glazed rough-hewn timbers. It also has apartments with kitchens, a treetop apartment, and

Playa Sámara

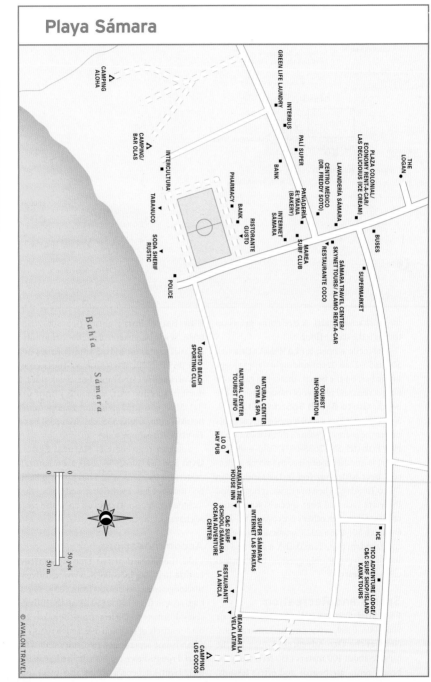

CAMPING ALOHA

GREEN LIFE LAUNDRY

INTERBUS

PALI SUPER

CAMPING/ BAR OLAS

INTERCULTURA

BANK

PLAZA COLONIAL/ ECONOMY RENT-A-CAR/ LAS DECLICIOUS (ICE CREAM)

LAVANDERÍA SÁMARA

CENTRO MÉDICO (DR. FREDDY SOTO)

PANADERÍA EL MANA (BAKERY)

PHARMACY

TABANUCO

BANK

INTERNET SÁMARA

RISTORANTE GUSTO

MAREA SURF CLUB

SÁMARA TRAVEL CENTER/ SKYNET TOURS/ ALAMO RENT-A-CAR

RESTAURANTE COCO

THE LOGAN

BUSES

SUPERMARKET

SODA SHERIF RUSTIC

POLICE

Bahía Sámara

GUSTO BEACH SPORTING CLUB

NATURAL CENTER GYM & SPA

NATURAL CENTER TOURIST INFO

TOURIST INFORMATION

LO Q HAY PUB

SAMARA TREE HOUSE INN

C&C SURF SCHOOL/SÁMARA OCEAN ADVENTURE CENTER

SUPER SÁMARA/ INTERNET LAS PIRATAS

RESTAURANTE LA ANCLA

BEACH BAR LA VELA LATINA

CAMPING LOS COCOS

ICE

TICO ADVENTURE LODGE/ C&C SURF SHOP/ISLAND KAYAK TOURS

0   0   0
0   50 yds
0   50 m

© AVALON TRAVEL

a villa for rent. The C&C Surf Camp is here, so it's popular with surfers.

Of the several German-run options, my fave is **Sámara Palm Lodge** (tel. 506/2656-1159, www.samarapalmlodge.com, low season from $55 s/d, high season from $65 s/d), on the road to Nosara. It exudes a suitably tropical theme with its tree-trunk supports, thatched roofs, wicker and bamboo furnishings, batik prints, and lush setting. Its nine spacious rooms get oodles of light and overlook a palm-fringed swimming pool. Some rooms have cable TV and are air-conditioned. Brigitte (Swiss) and Lothar (German) are friendly hosts at their thatch-fringed, wooden-decked poolside lounge-bar.

★ **Sámara Treehouse Inn** (tel. 506/2656-0733, www.samaratreehouse.com, low season $75-120 s/d, high season $89-135 s/d), on the beach in the heart of the village, is the nicest place in town. Made entirely of glossy hardwoods, the four thatch-fringed tree-house units with open patios (with hammocks and lounge chairs) face directly over the sands; each has a terra-cotta floor, a bamboo bed, and lively fabrics, plus a TV, a ceiling fan, a delightful modern bath faced with dark-blue tiles, and wall-of-glass ocean-view windows. It offers secure parking and a lovely circular pool in the landscaped forecourt, plus a fully equipped wheelchair-accessible ground-floor apartment.

For a fancy self-catering option (although you don't have to use the kitchen), check into ★ **The Logan** (tel. 506/2656-2435, www.the-logansamara.com, low season $115 s/d, high season $140 s/d), billing itself as an "eco-conscious luxury hotel." It is located 400 meters inland of the soccer field. I love staying here for its thoroughly 21st-century styling and relaxed, away-from-the-crowds intimacy. The 12 huge air-conditioned guest rooms are in irregular fourplex units and have huge baths, pleasant furnishings, Wi-Fi, and most other modern amenities. Meals are served, and there's a scimitar-shaped pool. The delightful owner, Rosy Ríos, is a perfect host.

One of my fave newcomers is **El Pequeño Gecko Verde** (tel. 506/2656-1176, www.gecko-verde.com, low season $85 s/d rooms, from $95 s/d bungalows, high season $105 s/d rooms, from $110 s/d bungalows), in the forested hills west of town. Set in lush gardens, its thatched bungalows are a tropical delight, not least for the exquisite decor and the stone-lined garden showers. You can splash around in a saltwater pool, and dine in an alfresco restaurant.

CAMPING
Camping and Bar Olas (tel. 506/2656-0187, camping $5 pp, huts $15 s, $25 d) offers a lively beachside bar and restaurant with shaded campsites with lockers. It also has basic palm-thatched A-frame huts with loft bedrooms.

Food
A great place to start the day is **Coco Mexican Restaurant** (tel. 506/2656-0665, 11am-midnight daily), located 100 meters inland of the soccer field. It has huge omelets and pancakes, plus lunchtime *casados* and sandwiches in addition to the usual Tex-Mex fare, such as shrimp-stuffed avocado ($6.50) Santa Fe chicken salad ($7.50), and Sinaloa chimichangas ($8.50). It has a big-screen TV, plus two-for-one margaritas during happy hour (5pm-7pm daily).

I like the creative menu at the thatched no-frills beachfront **Restaurante El Ancla** (tel. 506/2656-0716, 11am-11pm daily, $5-10), serving surf and turf, beef stroganoff, garlic sea bass, and calamari. Next door, **La Vela Latina** (tel. 506/2656-2286, 7:30am-10pm daily) has a modern look and a menu featuring seafood such as fried calamari with spicy sauce ($4.50) and mahimahi fillet ($12), burgers such as portobello mushroom and mozzarella ($9), and famous popcorn chicken. A side bar serves sushi. You can kick it in lounge chairs on the sand.

An Italian expat couple, Stefano and Stefania, run ★ **Ristorante Gusto** (tel. 506/2656-0252, noon-11pm daily), on the north side of the soccer field. Impeccable hosts, they serve creative Italian (such as pasta carbonara) and fusion dishes, such as tuna tartare or chicken curry in a coconut bowl, in a charming and stylish setting. Call in around sunset for the Italian aperitifs. The romantic mood is enhanced by a faux-washed floor inset with mosaics, plus cotton sails overhead and trendy music. It has Wi-Fi. The same owners also run **Gusto Beach Club** (tel. 506/2656-0252), a groovy place to dine under palm trees with the sand between your toes. It specializes in pizzas (Tues.-Sun.) with free drinks 6pm-9pm; it has a Wi-Fi zone, beach games, and showers. I enjoyed the pancake breakfast. Watch for specials, such as Wednesday 2-for-1 pasta and pizza, and free pizza when live bands play.

Across the street from Gusto Beach Club, **Natural Center** (tel. 506/2656-2360, www. naturalcentersamara.com, 7am-5pm Mon.-Sat.) has a natural foods café and store.

When things get too hot, head for ice cream at **Panadería y Heladería La Princesa** (tel. 506/8501-5624, 11am-7pm daily), a stone's throw west of Banco Nacional. The three lovely women who run this bakery and ice cream joint also make delicious breads, yummy soups, cinnamon rolls, and pumpkin pie, and serve hearty coffees.

Information and Services

Natural Center (tel. 506/2656-2360, www. naturalcentersamara.com) has a visitor information center. **Internet Las Piratas** (tel. 506/2656-2123, www.lospiratas-samara.com), on the beachfront road, has Internet service.

The **bank** is on the north side of the soccer field. The **police station** (tel. 506/2656-0436) is by the beach, near the soccer field.

Dr. Freddy Soto has a **medical clinic** (tel. 506/2656-0992) at the main crossroad in town; and there's a **pharmacy** (tel. 506/2656-0123) on the north side of the soccer field.

Lavandería Sámara (tel. 506/2656-3000, samaralaundry@yahoo.com, 8:30am-5:30pm Mon.-Sat.) offers same-day free delivery for laundry. **Green Life Laundry** is 100 meters (330 feet) west.

Intercultura & Sámara Language School (tel. 506/2656-0127, U.S./Canada tel. 866-978-6668, www.samaralanguageschool. com) offers Spanish-language courses.

Getting There

SANSA (tel. 506/2229-4100, U.S./Canada tel. 877-767-2672, www.flysansa.com) and **Nature Air** (tel. 506/2299-6000, U.S. tel. 800-235-9272, www.natureair.com) fly daily to Playa Carrillo. **Alfaro** (tel. 506/2222-2666 in San José, tel. 506/2685-0261 in Sámara) buses depart San José for Sámara (5 hours, $6.50) from Avenida 5, Calles 14/16, at noon and 6:30pm daily. **Empresa Rojas** (tel. 506/2685-5352) buses depart Nicoya for Sámara ($1.75) three blocks east of the park 13 times 5am-9:45pm daily. Buses depart Sámara for San José at 5:15am and 9:15am daily. **Interbus** (tel. 506/4100-0888, www.interbusonline. com) operates shuttles from San José ($40) and popular travel destinations in Nicoya and Guanacaste.

PLAYA CARRILLO

South of Sámara, the paved road continues over Punta Indio and drops down to coral-colored Playa Carrillo, five kilometers (3 miles) south of Sámara, one of the finest beaches in Costa Rica, arcing for three kilometers (2 miles) and virtually undeveloped. An offshore reef protects the bay. The fishing hamlet of Carrillo nestles around the estuary of the Río Sangrado, tucked behind a headland at the southern end of the bay.

To check out native animal species that are hard to see in the wild, follow signs to **La Selva Wildlife Refuge & Zoo** (tel. 506/2656-2236 or 506/8305-1610, 8am-7pm daily, adults $8 children, $5), inland at the southern end of the beach. This private Italian-run animal shelter has coatis, tamanduas, peccaries, agoutis, monkeys, snakes, and even jaguarundis, plus other cute and scary creatures. Guided tours are offered at feeding time, 9am and 5pm daily.

Café Internet Librería Onda Latina (tel. 506/2656-0434, ondalatinainternet@gmail.

com) is 100 meters (330 feet) uphill from Hotel Esperanza.

Carrillo Tours (tel. 506/2656-0543, www.carrillotours.com) offers kayaking on the Río Ora ($45). Kingfisher Sportfishing (tel. 506/2656-0091, www.costaricabillfishing.com) offers sportfishing.

Accommodations and Food

You don't have to be a surfer to dig Popo's (tel. 506/2656-2295, www.andreabrand.com/popos, low season from $40 s/d, high season from $45 s/d), an all-hardwood inn and former surf camp 400 meters inland of the shore that has gone upscale and has a cool welcoming tropical vibe. Choose from two rooms, two tree-house cabins, or a five-bedroom house, all set in lush gardens. All have hot-water baths and ceiling fans, and there's a lovely rusticity to the place, which is surrounded by foliage. It has kayak tours and the Blue Barrel Surf School.

For more contemporary styling and chic furnishings, check into Hotel Leyenda (tel. 506/2656-0381, www.hotelleyenda.com, low season from $107 s/d, high season from $169 s/d), two kilometers (1.2 miles) south of Carrillo. An inviting pool is set in lush gardens. Gorgeously furnished, its spacious rooms have kitchenettes plus ceiling fans and air-conditioning. Families can rent a VIP House (low season $420, high season $500) with its own pool. It provides shuttles to the beach and has a stylish restaurant, open on one side to the elements, serving seafood, pizza, pasta, and fast food.

About one kilometer (0.6 miles) farther south, and offering similar standards, Hotel El Sueño Tropical (tel. 506/2656-0151, www.elsuenotropical.com, $80-120 s/d) has a contemporary tropical motif and a lush landscaped setting surrounded by rainforest. It has 16 clean, simple, renovated bungalow rooms with terra-cotta tiles and air-conditioning, and an airy hilltop restaurant beneath a soaring *palenque* roof. There's a pool and a separate kids pool.

If you simply *must* have a beachfront locale, opt for the venerable Hotel Guanamar (tel. 506/2656-0054, www.guanamarhotel.com, from $80 s/d), a comfy family resort where the hillside setting guarantees fantastic views over the river estuary and cove. A large pool and sundeck are major pluses. Furnishings vary, and while they don't win any prizes, rooms are perfectly adequate and comfy. It offers kayaks.

Windstar cruise ship off Playa Carrillo

Getting There

The Nicoya-Sámara buses continue to Playa Carrillo. You can fly to Carrillo daily on **SANSA** (tel. 506/2229-4100, U.S./Canada tel. 877-767-2672, www.flysansa.com) and **Nature Air** (tel. 506/2299-6000, U.S. tel. 800-235-9272, www.natureair.com).

Playa Camaronal to Playa Manzanillo

The extreme southwest shore of the Nicoya Peninsula is one of the most remote coastal strips in Costa Rica. The beaches are beautiful, and the scenery at times is sublime.

Depending on weather conditions, the unpaved coast road south can deteriorate to a mere trail in places. In the words of the old song, there are many rivers to cross. The route can thwart even the hardiest 4WD vehicle in wet season, or after prolonged rains in dry season. For those who thrill to adventure, it's a helluva lot of fun. Allow a full day for this journey. Do not attempt the section south of Camaronal by ordinary sedan or at night, and especially not in wet season unless it's unusually dry—many travelers have had to have their vehicles hauled out of rivers that proved impossible to ford.

PLAYA CAMARONAL TO ISLITA

Immediately south of Carrillo, the Río Ora is an unbridged obstacle to reaching remote **Playa Camaronal,** about five kilometers (3 miles) south of Playa Carrillo. The paved road turns inland and begins to snake up into the mountains for Santa Marta (and beyond, Hojancha), where you turn south to cross the river (by bridge) and follow the signs for Punta Islita to return to Playa Camaronal.

Three-kilometer (2-mile) gray-sand Playa Camaronal is a popular nesting site for leatherbacks (Mar.-Apr.) and olive ridley turtles (year-round). It is earmarked as the **Refugio Nacional de Vida Silvestre Camaronal** (Camaronal Wildlife Refuge, tel. 506/2656-2050). An *arribada* occurred here for the first time in November 2006. Officially, you are supposed to visit by night only with a MINAE

guide ($10 pp). However, when I recently arrived at the onset of an *arribada,* I was horrified to find hundreds of people being allowed onto the beach uncontrolled. Children were even sitting on the turtles, while ignorant adults looked on and laughed. I was even offered eggs for sale. Don't molest the turtles!

From Camaronal, the dirt coast road (Hwy. 160) continues south nine kilometers (5.5 miles) to Playa Islita, a pebbly black-sand beach squeezed between soaring headlands that will have your 4WD vehicle wheezing in first gear. The community of Islita, in the valley bottom behind the shore, is enlivened by the **Museo de Arte Contemporáneo al Aire Libre** (Open-Air Contemporary Art Museum), with houses, tree trunks, and even the police station throughout the village decorated in bright paints and mosaics. The tiny **Casa Museo** (tel. 506/2656-2039, 8am-3pm daily, free) is catercorner to the police station and sells art by many of the four dozen or so community members who are now engaged in art. Joes Katnes, a Massachusetts transplant, has an art studio, **Galería Casa Estrella** (tel. 506/8648-0086, josephkaknes@gmail.com), opposite the church.

Hotel Punta Islita (tel. 506/2656-2020, www.hotelpuntaislita.com) has a canopy tour and offers a range of activities, from dolphin-watching excursions to horseback riding.

★ The Ara Project

Three decades ago, U.S. expats Richard and Margot Frisius initiated a breeding program for green and scarlet macaws at their home at Río Segundo de Alajuela, near San José. Although the Frisiuses have both died, a dedicated team of conservationists continue their legacy to help save these magnificent birds from extinction. In December 2013, **The Ara Project** (tel. 506/8389-5811 or 506/8730-0890, www.thearaproject.org, guided tours $20) relocated to Islita, where it has operated a macaw release program since 2011, on land leased from Hotel Punta Islita.

The breeding center breeds macaws for eventual release into the wild and features huge aviaries where pairs of breeding macaws are housed, plus flyways where they can fly and learn to flock. Volunteer field assistants are needed ($300 per month for lodging).

Accommodations and Food

The deluxe and utterly desirable ★ **Hotel Punta Islita** (tel. 506/2656-2020, www.hotelpuntaislita.com, low season from $177 s/d, high season from $280 s/d, 2-night minimum) commands a hilltop above Playa Islita and will appeal to romantics and anyone who enjoys sophistication. A highlight is the lobby lounge beneath a soaring thatched *palenque.* Open on three sides, it overlooks a sunken bar serving bathers in an infinity pool seemingly melding into the endless blues of the Pacific far below. Props from the movie *1492*—log canoes, old barrels and more—enhance the lovely ambience. The colony includes 20 bungalows in Santa Fe style, eight junior suites (each with a whirlpool spa on an ocean-view deck), and five two-bedroom casitas, all furnished in stylish contemporary fashion. A private forest reserve has trails, plus there's a canopy tour, a gym, a full-service spa, two tennis courts, a beach club with water sports, and a nine-hole golf course.

The elegant **Restaurante 1492** (tel. 506/2661-4044, 7am-10:30am, 12:30pm-3pm, and 6pm-10pm daily), at Hotel Punta Islita, is open to nonguests, as is the beach club, by request. The restaurant serves fusion delights such as bamboo-steamed mahimahi ($21) and tenderloin fillet ($28). The views are stunning.

The thatched **Restaurante Kmbute** (tel. 506/2656-1394), 200 meters (660 feet) south of Hotel Punta Islita, is set amid lawns and offers an airy roadside alternative to the hotel.

Information and Services

The **police station** (tel. 506/2656-2052) is beside the soccer field in Islita.

ISLITA TO PUERTO BEJUCO

South of Islita, the road climbs over Punta Barranquilla before dropping past gray-sand **Playa Corazalito** (reached by a side road).

Playa Bejuco

The dirt road then cuts inland to the village of Corazalito (with an airstrip) and continues south two kilometers (1.2 miles) to the hamlet of Quebrada Seca (also called Pilas de Bejuco), where another side road leads to the north end of undeveloped Playa Bejuco, a four-kilometer (2.5-mile) gray-sand beach backed by a large mangrove swamp replete with wildlife. Be warned that this section of the coast is subject to dangerous riptides; avoid swimming here.

The dirt road continues south from four kilometers (2.5 miles) to Pueblo Nuevo, connected to Highway 21 on the east side of the Nicoya Peninsula by a dirt road that clambers over the mountains to Carmona. A side road leads from Pueblo Nuevo to the funky fishing community of Puerto Bejuco, great for birdwatching (the village is hidden and unsigned). Pelicans, jabiru storks, and other wading birds are abundant, picking at the scraps as local fishers cut up their catch.

Less than one kilometer (0.6 miles) south of Pueblo Nuevo, Jungle Butterfly Farm (tel. 506/2655-8070, www.junglebutterfly-farm.com, 9am-4pm daily, adults $15, children $8) offers a treat. Entomologist Michael Malliet has developed scenic trails through his 19-hectare (47-acre) forested mountain-side property, which has a butterfly breeding and honey production facility. Monkeys and other critters abound. Night tours are offered by reservation.

Sports and Recreation

Rhodeside B&B and Café (tel. 506/2655-8006, $35 pp), one kilometer (0.6 miles) south of Pueblo Nuevo, offers horseback riding and has its own stable.

Accommodations and Food

Pennsylvania transplants Gwen and Edmund Rhodes make delightful hosts at the Rhodeside B&B and Café (tel. 506/2655-8006, www.rhodesidebedandbreakfast.com, low season $45 s/d, high season $60 s/d, including breakfast), one kilometer (0.6 miles) south of Pueblo Nuevo. They rent four spacious cross-ventilated rooms with ceiling fans; two have private baths, and two upstairs rooms share an outdoor shower. All share an upstairs kitchen with a terrace and ocean views, great for spotting monkeys.

The Espresso Café (7am-7pm daily) at Rhodeside B&B is a delightful spot for a cappuccino and baked goodies, or start the day with their yummy natural breakfast. Between the distant sound of the ocean, the nearby howler monkeys calling up the dawn, and the smell of fresh-brewed coffee, you couldn't want for more.

PLAYA SAN MIGUEL TO PUNTA COYOTE

Locals have labeled the blissfully crowd-free coastal zone south of Bejuco as Costa de Oro (Gold Coast). Cross the Río Bejuco (bridged) south of Pueblo Nuevo to arrive at the hamlet of San Miguel, midway along Playa San Miguel (also called Playa Jabillo), reached by a side road. The silver-sand beach is a prime turtle-nesting site; there's a ranger station at the southern end of the beach, plus a turtle hatchery. You can learn to surf at Flying Scorpion (tel. 506/2655-8080, www.theflying-scorpion.com), at Playa San Miguel. It also has horseback riding.

The beach runs south into Playa Coyote, a six-kilometer-long (4-mile-long) stunner backed at north and south ends by mangrove swamps. The beaches are separated by a river estuary. Playa Coyote is accessed by a side road off the coast highway; dirt roads extend north and south along the shore. The surfing is superb at high tide (a reef unfolds at low tide), with fine breaks.

The wide Río Jabillo pours into the sea at the south end of Playa Coyote, beneath the headland of Punta Coyote. The river and swamp forest force the coast road inland for six kilometers (4 miles) to the village of San Francisco de Coyote, connected by road inland over the mountains with Highway 21. Turn right in San Francisco to continue south; a bridge over the Río Jabillo permits passage even in the wettest of wet seasons.

Accommodations and Food

SAN MIGUEL

The German-run **Escorpión Volador** (Flying Scorpion, tel. 506/2655-8080, www. theflyingscorpion.com, low season from $45 s/d, high season from $55 s/d) rents five cozy seafront *cabinas,* a second-floor studio apartment, and five fully equipped houses. We're not talking luxury here, but perfectly adequate, simply appointed units for folks who like casual decor and ambience. Weimeraners abound underfoot!

Inland, with commanding coastal views, and the best place for miles, is the hilltop ★ **Cristal Azul** (tel. 506/2655-8135, U.S. tel. 888-822-7369, www.cristalazul.com, low season from $140 s/d, high season $225, including breakfast, 2-night minimum), run by Henner and Zene. The four thatched, glass-walled, air-conditioned rooms are gorgeous, with charcoal-gray floors, ceiling fans, fresh-cut flowers, handmade beds of glazed hardwood, and huge baths with outdoor garden showers. There's an infinity swimming pool and an open-air patio for enjoying hearty breakfasts with spectacular views. Henner is a professional skipper and offers sportfishing.

The owner of Escorpión Velador makes delicious omelets, french toast, and waffle breakfasts, served in the hotel's restaurant, **Rossi's Place** (7:30am-10:30am, 11:30am-3pm, and 6pm-9:30pm Thurs.-Tues., $2-12). A huge menu includes appetizers such as black bean soup, garlic fries, and nachos. For lunch, try the steak and onion *casado* ($7), poached shrimp ($15), or burgers, homemade pastas, pizzas, and ice cream.

SAN FRANCISCO DE COYOTE

Budget hounds have three options in San Francisco de Coyote, where **Cabinas Rey** (tel. 506/2655-1055, cabinasrey@yahoo.com, $10 s, $15 d) has simple rooms and, remarkably, a Wi-Fi hot spot in its **Soda Familiar,** serving filling meals, from sandwiches to *casados.* A more modern alternative, **Cabinas San Francisco** (tel. 506/2655-1334, www. cabsanfrancisco.webpin.com, $30 s, $40 d),

has spacious, modestly furnished air-conditioned family rooms, plus a swimming pool and secure parking. Both look onto the soccer field in the hamlet, as does **Café Sante** (tel. 506/2655-1307, 10am-4pm daily), a charming place to take a break and fuel up on a shake, cappuccino, sandwiches, banana bread, cakes, and fresh fruit smoothies—a great place to rehydrate when the dust and heat get to you. It has Wi-Fi.

Information and Services

Coyote Online (tel. 506/2655-1007, 2pm-6pm Mon.-Tues. and Thurs.-Fri.), in San Francisco de Coyote, has Internet service, including Wi-Fi and Skype.

PUNTA COYOTE TO PLAYA MANZANILLO

Uninhabited **Playa Caletas,** immediately south of Punta Coyote and some five kilometers (3 miles) south of San Francisco de Coyote, can also be reached from Highway 21 (on the east side of the Nicoya Peninsula) via Jabillo and the community of La y Griega. This kilometers-long, log-littered brown-sand beach has no settlements—it's just you and the turtles that come ashore to lay eggs. The beach is considered the second-most-important nesting site for leatherback turtles in the eastern Pacific Ocean from December to March. Olive ridleys also come ashore singly July to March, peaking in September and October. **Programa Restauración de Tortugas Marinas** (PRETOMA, tel. 506/2241-5227, www.pretoma.org) has a turtle hatchery here operated by **Turtle Trax** (tel. 506/2655-1197, www.turtle-trax.com), and as of 2015 had freed more than 235,000 hatchlings to the sea. Volunteers are needed.

Playa Caletas extends southward into Playa Bongo, Playa Ario, and Playa Manzanillo—together forming a 12-kilometer (7.5-mile) expanse of virtually inaccessible sand broken by the estuaries of the Río Bongo and Río Ario, inhabited by crocodiles. (Once while driving this road at night—in days when it could more easily be reached—I came around a

Punta Coyote to Playa Manzanillo

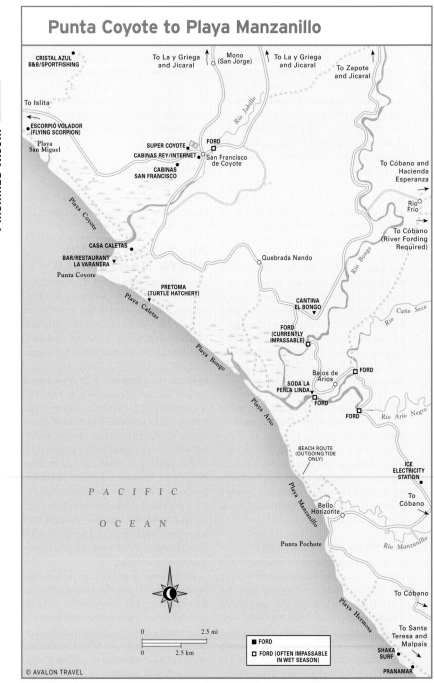

CRISTAL AZUL
B&B/SPORTFISHING

To La y Griega
and Jicaral

Mono
(San Jorge)

To La y Griega
and Jicaral

To Zapote
and Jicaral

Río Jabillo

To Islita

ESCORPIÓ VOLADOR
(FLYING SCORPION)

Playa
San Miguel

SUPER COYOTE

FORD

CABINAS REY/INTERNET

San Francisco
de Coyote

CABINAS
SAN FRANCISCO

To Cóbano and
Hacienda
Esperanza

Río
Frío

Playa Coyote

To Cóbano
(River Fording
Required)

CASA CALETAS

Río Bongo

BAR/RESTAURANT
LA VARANERA

Quebrada Nando

Punta Coyote

Caño Seco

Playa Caletas

PRETOMA
(TURTLE HATCHERY)

CANTINA
EL BONGO

Río

Playa Bongo

FORD
(CURRENTLY
IMPASSABLE)

Bajos de
Arios

FORD

SODA LA
PERLA LINDA

FORD

Playa Ario

FORD

Río Ario Negro

BEACH ROUTE
(OUTGOING TIDE
ONLY)

ICE
ELECTRICITY
STATION

PACIFIC

To
Cóbano

OCEAN

Playa Manzanillo

Bello
Horizonte

Punta Pochote

Río Manzanillo

To Cóbano

Playa Hermosa

To Santa
Teresa and
Malpaís

0   2.5 mi

0   2.5 km

FORD

FORD (OFTEN IMPASSABLE
IN WET SEASON)

SHAKA
SURF

PRANAMAR

© AVALON TRAVEL

bend to find a crocodile plodding across the road!) The entire coast zone here is within the 300-hectare (740-acre) **Refugio Nacional de Vida Silvestre Caletas-Ario** (Playa Caletas-Ario National Wildlife Refuge), extending seven kilometers (4.5 miles) out to sea.

The route between Caletas and Manzanillo is a true adventure, and a high-clearance 4WD vehicle is absolutely essential in wet season, when the Ríos Bongo, Caño Seco, and Ario are often impassable. In his case, you must drive over the mountains to Jicaral, on Highway 21, and then around the eastern seaboard of the Nicoya Peninsula via Paquera and Tambor, to reach Manzanillo—a five-hour journey.

South of Caletas, the marshy shore flats force the coast road inland. Keep straight via the hamlet of **Quebrada Nando** until you reach a major Y junction. Keep straight (left, heading south); if you miss the junction, you'll know it, as 400 meters (0.25 miles) farther south you'll soon come to a 90-degree left turn beside Cantina El Bongo. (If you turn right at the Y-fork, you'll arrive at the Río Bongo; at last visit the crossing was impossible and doesn't look like it will get any better any time soon.) Continue inland, uphill toward Jicaral, but after five kilometers (3 miles) turn east via a bridge over the Río Bongo for the hamlet of **Río Frío,** which is signed and is about three kilometers (2 miles) east of the bridge.

From here the going gets tricky. You can ask for directions at the general store at the T-junction beside the soccer field as you arrive in Río Frío. Keep straight to strike back toward the coast. After three kilometers (2 miles) you'll reach another T-junction; turn right. Five kilometers (3 miles) beyond, you'll twice ford the Río Caño Seco. Shortly beyond, you reach and need to ford the 30-meter-wide (100-foot-wide) Río Ario. These river crossings can be tricky, often with dangerously deep channels that may require scouting (they change yearly with each rainy season). If the way across isn't clear, wait for a local to show you the way.

After crossing the Río Ario, about five or so kilometers (3 miles) farther turn right at the Y-fork (the first junction you'll reach), just before the hamlet of **Betel.** The dirt road now winds downhill to **Bello Horizonte,** a small fishing hamlet inland of **Playa Manzanillo.**

South of Bello Horizonte, the coast road leads over **Punta Pochote** and alongside **Playa Hermosa** to Playa Santa Teresa and Malpaís. Choose between an easier, self-evident inland route, or a narrower track along the shore that is a devil in wet season.

Alternately, from Río Frío you can head due east for Cóbano, which is signed beside the soccer field in Río Frío. This route also requires you to ford the Río Ario. A second, unsigned route to Cóbano is signed in Río Frío for Bajo de Ario; after 1.5 kilometers (0.9 miles), turn left off this road at a Y junction, from where a really rugged, little-trafficked road leads to Cóbano and also involves fording the Río Ario.

Accommodations and Food

Part of a working cattle hacienda, the gorgeous ★ **Casa Caletas** (tel. 506/2655-1271, www.casacaletas.com, low season $130-165 s/d, high season $165-200) offers the best of all worlds: a superb location (on the south bank of the Río Jabillo atop Punta Coyote), divine comfort, an awesome aesthetic, and a relaxing no-pretensions ambience. Luxurious guest rooms feature travertine floors, halogen lighting, rustic glazed hardwood king beds with high-thread-count linens, and sliding glass doors with river-mouth views. Some have loft bedrooms. A hip breeze-swept bar under thatch opens to the sundeck with a kidney-shaped infinity pool, and the lounge with poured-concrete sofas is a delightful place to relax. It offers horseback rides and air-boat river trips.

GETTING THERE

SANSA (tel. 506/2229-4100, U.S./Canada tel. 877-767-2672, www.flysansa.com) and **Nature Air** (tel. 506/2299-6000, U.S. tel. 800-235-9272, www.natureair.com) fly daily to Islita from San José.

Empresa Arsa (tel. 506/2257-1835 or

506/2650-0179) buses depart Calle 12, Avenidas 7/9, in San José (4 hours, $6) at 6am and 3:30pm daily and travel via the Puntarenas-Playa Naranjo ferry and Jicaral to Coyote, Bejuco, and Islita, passing northbound through San Francisco de Coyote at about 11:30am and 10pm daily and Playa San Miguel about 30 minutes later. Return buses depart Bejuco at 2:15am and 12:30pm daily,

passing through Playa San Miguel around 3am and 1:15pm and San Francisco de Coyote 30 minutes later.

You can buy gas at the house of Ann Arias Chávez, on the southwest corner of the soccer field in Quebrada Seca; and at **Bar Restaurante La Conga** (tel. 506/2655-8005) in Pueblo Nuevo. Other folks sell gas from a can; just ask.

Southern Nicoya

HIGHWAY 21: CARMONA TO PLAYA NARANJO

Highway 21 connects communities along the eastern shore of the Golfo de Nicoya via Jicaral to Playa Naranjo, beyond which it swings south around the Nicoya Peninsula bound for Paquera, Montezuma, and Malpaís. The road has been graded and partially paved but can still be rough going, and it eats up the better part of a day.

Playa Naranjo is one of two terminals for the Puntarenas ferries (Coonatramar Ferry, tel. 506/2661-1069, www.coonatramar.com); use the Naranjo ferry to access the beaches of northern and central Nicoya only. If you're traveling from Puntarenas or the Pan-American Highway and aiming for Tambor, Montezuma, or Malpaís, you're best served by taking a ferry to Paquera, farther south. There's a gas station (Mon.-Sat.) and supermarket at Playa Naranjo.

If you're heading *north* from Playa Naranjo, at the village of **Lepanto,** six kilometers (4 miles) north of Naranjo, you can turn inland and drive to Montaña Grande for the **Karen Mongensen Wildlife Reserve,** protecting 900 hectares (2,200 acres) of wildlife-rich tropical moist forest. It's run by a local community organization, **Asociación Ecológica Paquera, Lepanto y Cóbano** (ASEPALECO, tel. 506/2650-0607, www.asepaleco.com). ASEPALECO offers horseback rides and hiking at the reserve's Cerro Escondido Lodge, which has an orchid

garden and a small eco-museum. The highlight is a hike to the 84-meter-tall (276-foot-tall) Velo de Novia (Bridal Veil) waterfall. To reach the lodge, you must mount a horse for the 90-minute ride. Alternatively, from Jicaral, eight kilometers (5 miles) north of Lepanto, turn west to Unií, then turn east for San Ramón de Río Blanco, 16 kilometers (10 miles) along, where you need to hike the three-kilometer (2-mile) trail to the lodge. It's wise to arrange a guide to meet you. ASEPALECO also arranges transfers on request. You can also take a bus to Jicaral, from where a Jeep taxi will cost about $15.

The road *south* from Playa Naranjo to Paquera has tortuous switchbacks. Prepare for a despairingly rugged ride; although sections have been graded and even paved, it was badly washed out in sections on my most recent drive. Still, you get some marvelous views out over the Golfo de Nicoya—including toward Isla Guayabo, which comes into view about six kilometers (4 miles) south of Playa Naranjo, where the road briefly meets the coast at **Gigante,** at the north end of **Bahía Luminosa,** also called Bahía Gigante. Offshore, **Reserva Biológica Isla Guayabo** and **Reserva Biológica Isla Los Negritos** protect nesting sites of the brown booby, frigate bird, pelican, and other seabirds as well as the peregrine falcon. They are off-limits to visitors. Dolphins and whales are often sighted offshore; January is the best month for whales.

Isla Chira

Costa Rica's second-largest island, Isla Chira floats below the mouth of the Río Tempisque, at the north end of the Golfo de Nicoya. It is surrounded by mangroves popular with pelicans and frigate birds, and it's uninhabited except for a few fishers, farmers, and others who eke out a living from *salinas* (salt pans). Roseate spoonbills and other wading birds pick among the pans—perfect for birders.

Isla de Chira Amistad Lodge (tel. 506/2661-3261, or c/o Costa Rican Association of Community-Based Rural Tourism, ACTUAR, tel. 506/2248-9470, www.actuarcostarica.com, $25 pp) offers a simple dorm and six quad rooms. ACTUAR offers one- and two-day packages ($62 and $122) with boat trips.

Isla San Lucas National Wildlife Refuge

The 615-hectare (1,520-acre) **Refugio Nacional de Vida Silvestre Isla San Lucas,** five kilometers (3 miles) offshore of Naranjo, seems a pleasant palm-fringed place where you might actually *want* to be washed ashore and languish in splendid sun-washed isolation. But at one time, a visit to Isla San Lucas amounted to an excursion to hell.

Until a few years ago, this was the site of the most dreaded prison in the Costa Rican penal system, with a legacy dating back 400 years. In the 16th century, the Spanish conquistador Gonzalo Fernández de Oviedo used San Lucas as a concentration camp for local Chara people, who were slaughtered on the site of their sacred burial grounds. The Costa Rican government turned it into a detention center for political prisoners in 1862. It closed in 1991. There are still guards here, but today their role is to protect the island's resident wildlife from would-be poachers. It also has eight pre-Columbian sites.

The overgrown prison now functions as a museum. Should you visit the grim bastion, the ghosts of murderers, miscreants, and maltreated innocents will be your guides. A cobbled pathway leads to the main prison building. The chapel has become a bat grotto, and only graffiti remains to tell of the horror and hopelessness, recorded by ex-convict José León Sánchez in his book *La isla de los hombres solos* (The Isle of the Lonely Men), available in English as *God Was Looking the Other Way.*

Bay Island Cruises (tel. 506/2258-3536, www.bayislandcruises.com) offers a package day trip, departing Puntarenas at 9:30am daily (and with the option of transfers from San José), including lunch at San Lucas Beach Club. **Coontramar** (tel. 506/2661-1069 ext. 113, www.coonatramar.com) also offers tours from Puntarenas.

Accommodations and Food

The nicest of several accommodations at Playa Naranjo is the modern Italian-owned **Hotel Playa Naranjo Inn** (tel. 506/2641-8290, www.hotelplayanaranjo.blogspot.com, with fan $40 s/d, with a/c $45 s/d), just 200 meters (660 feet) from the ferry terminal, with nine brightly decorated rooms fronted by a wide porch with hammocks. There's a pool, a thatched bar, and a pizza restaurant where movies are shown at 8pm daily.

The Karen Mongenson Reserve has a guest house, **Cerro Escondido Lodge** (c/o Costa Rican Association of Community-Based Rural Tourism, ACTUAR, tel. 506/2248-9470, www.actuarcostarica.com, 2-day packages $68), with four cozy wooden dorm-style cabins with solar power, plus private cold-water showers and verandas with magnificent forest views. It serves meals family-style in its open-air restaurant. It's great for an immersion in local country life.

PAQUERA TO TAMBOR
Paquera

Paquera, 24 kilometers (15 miles) south of Playa Naranjo, is where the Paquera ferry (Ferry Naviera Tambor, tel. 506/2661-2084, www.navieratambor.com) arrives and departs to and from Puntarenas. The ferry berth is three kilometers (2 miles) northeast of Paquera. Paquera has **banks** and a **gas station.**

Curú National Wildlife Refuge

The **Refugio Nacional de Vida Silvestre Curú** (tel. 506/2641-0100, www.curu.org, 7am-3pm daily, adults $10, children $5) is tucked into the fold of Golfo Curú, four kilometers (2.5 miles) southwest of Paquera. Privately owned, it forms part of a 1,500-hectare (3,700-acre) cattle finca, two-thirds of which is preserved as primary forest. The reserve includes 4.5 kilometers (3 miles) of coastline with a series of tiny coves and three beautiful white-sand beaches—Playas Curú, Colorada, and Quesera—nestled beneath green slopes. Olive ridley and hawksbill turtles nest on the crystalline beaches. Mangrove swamps extend inland along the Río Curú, backed by forested hills. Monkeys are almost always playing in the treetops by the gift store, and agoutis, sloths, anteaters, and even ocelots are commonly seen. The facility has a macaw reintroduction program and a reproduction and rehabilitation program for endangered spider monkeys; you can spy them living freely behind an electrified fence (the trail to the enclosure is boggy, so bring appropriate footwear).

Turismo Curú (tel. 506/2641-0004, www.turismocuru.com) has guided tours of the refuge, plus snorkeling trips to Isla Tortuga, and horseback riding.

Trails range from easy to difficult. You can rent horses ($10 per hour). Guided tours are offered; your tip is their pay. The bus between Paquera and Cóbano passes the unmarked gate; ask the driver to let you off.

★ Isla Tortuga

This stunningly beautiful 320-hectare (790-acre) island lies three kilometers (2 miles) offshore of Curú. Tortuga is as close to an idyllic tropical isle as you'll find in Costa Rica. The main attraction is a magnificent white-sand beach lined with coconut palms. Tortuga is a favorite destination of excursion boats that depart from Puntarenas; it's a superbly scenic 90-minute journey passing the isles of Negritos, San Lucas, Gitana, and Guayabo. En route you may spot manta rays or pilot whales. Even giant whale sharks have been seen basking off Isla Tortuga. You'll normally have about two hours on Isla Tortuga, with a buffet lunch, plus options for sea kayaking, snorkeling, volleyball, and hiking. It can get a bit crowded on weekends.

I recommend **Calypso Cruises** (tel.

white-faced monkey at Curú National Wildlife Refuge

506/2256-2727, U.S. tel. 866-887-1969, www. calypsocruises.com), which runs daily trips from Puntarenas aboard the luxurious *Manta Raya* catamaran, with a full bar, a fishing platform, and two whirlpool tubs. Trips depart from Puntarenas (adults $139, students $119, excluding transfers). The company also has cruises to its own **Punta Coral Private Reserve** (www.puntacoral.com), where snorkeling, sea kayaking, and other activities are offered. Monkeys and other animals abound in the adjacent forest, with trails. **Sun Trails Montezuma** (tel. 506/2642-0808, www.montezumatraveladventures.com) and **Zuma Tours** (tel. 506/2642-0024, www.zumatours. net) offer excursions from Montezuma.

Tambor

Tambor, 18 kilometers (11 miles) southwest of Paquera, is a small fishing village fronted by a gray-sand beach in **Bahía Ballena** (Whale Bay), a deep-pocket bay rimmed by **Playa Tambor** and backed by forested hills. I find the setting unappealing, but many readers report enjoying Tambor.

You can play a round of golf or tennis at the nine-hole **Tango Mar Golf Club** (tel. 506/2683-0001, www.tangomar.com, nonguests $20 green fee, golf cart $35, club rental $20). Tango Mar also offers tours, sportfishing, and horseback riding.

Seascape Kayak Tours (tel. 506/8314-8605, www.seascapekayaktours.com) offers sea kayaking to Curú, and multiday trips farther afield, November to April. **Pacific Coast Fishing Charters** (tel. 506/8346-2296, www.fishingtambor.wix.com) will take you sportfishing.

Accommodations and Food

If you need to bunk in Paquera for an early morning ferry, **Cabinas y Restaurante Ginana** (tel. 506/2641-0119, $35 s, $40 d) has 28 simply furnished rooms. Some are air-conditioned; all have private baths. There's a swimming pool and a restaurant.

Although overpriced, the architecturally dramatic **Tambor Tropical** (Tambor, tel. 506/2683-0011, U.S. tel. 866-890-2537, www. tambortropical.com, $160-220 s/d year-round) is a perfect place to laze in true tropical mode in the shade of a swaying palm. Twelve handcrafted two-story hexagonal *cabinas* (one unit upstairs, one unit down) face the beach amid lush landscaped grounds with an exquisite mosaic-lined pool and a whirlpool tub. The rooms boast voluminous baths with deep-well showers, wraparound balconies, and fully equipped kitchens. Everything is handmade of native hardwoods lacquered to a nautical shine. A restaurant serves international cuisine. Snorkeling and horseback riding are offered. Rates include breakfast.

For an intimate beachfront resort, top marks go to the romantic Belgian-run ★ **Tango Mar** (tel. 506/2683-0001, U.S. tel. 800-297-4420, www.tangomar.com, low season from $185 s/d, high season from $210 s/d), five kilometers (3 miles) southwest of Tambor. This stylish resort is backed by hectares of beautifully tended grounds below a forested cliff face. Its 25 rooms include five Polynesian-style thatched octagonal bamboo Tiki Suites raised on stilts, 18 spacious oceanfront rooms with large balconies, and 12 Tropical Suites with romantic four-poster beds with gauzy netting. You can also choose four- and five-person luxury villas. It has two swimming pools, a nine-hole golf course, stables, water sports, Internet access, plus massages and yoga. Rates include breakfast.

The **Restaurante Arrecife** (11am-2pm and 6pm-10pm daily low season, 11am-11pm daily high season, $4-9), in the Hotel Costa Coral, on the main highway in Tambor, is a good option for ceviche, a club sandwich, burgers, fettuccine, chicken with orange sauce, and sea bass with heart-of-palm sauce. Don your best clothes for a meal at the romantic and elegant thatched open-air **Cristóbal** (6:30am-10am, 11:30am-3:30pm, and 6:30pm-10pm daily, $5-25), at Tango Mar; it is open to nonguests and serves gourmet seafood and fusion dishes.

Information and Services

Internet Kara (tel. 506/2683-0001) and a **pharmacy** (tel. 506/2683-0581) are above the roadside **Toucan Boutique** in Tambor, where **Budget Rent-a-Car** (tel. 506/2683-0500) has a roadside office 400 meters (0.25 miles) east of the village.

Getting There

SANSA (tel. 506/2229-4100, U.S./Canada tel. 877-767-2672, www.flysansa.com) and **Nature Air** (tel. 506/2299-6000, U.S. tel. 800-235-9272, www.natureair.com) fly daily to Tambor from San José, with connecting service to other resorts. The Montezuma-bound buses pass by Curú and Tambor en route to and from Paquera.

MONTEZUMA

Montezuma, a funky and fascinating beach hamlet—and gateway to the Cabo Blanco Absolute Wildlife Reserve—tucked beneath cliffs at the far southwest corner of the Nicoya Peninsula, is popular with budget-minded backpackers and counterculture travelers, including a band of less-than-friendly faux-Rastafarians scrounging a living by juggling and selling hash pipes and funky jewelry. Business owners are prone to shut up shop on a whim—sometimes for days at a time, or longer.

The fantastic beaches east of Montezuma are backed by forest-festooned cliffs from which streams tumble down to the sands. Monkeys frolic in the forests. Beware of the riptides! The **Reserva Absoluta Nicolas Weissenburg** (Nicolas Weissenburg Absolute Reserve) was created in 1998 to protect the shoreline and forested hills to the east of Montezuma; it's strictly off-limits to visitors.

Montezuma is accessed from **Cóbano,** a crossroads village 25 kilometers (16 miles) southwest of Paquera and five kilometers (3 miles) north of Montezuma, and the main service center for the region (buses for Malpaís and the Paquera ferry arrive and depart from here). Montezuma is the gateway to the Reserva Natural Absoluta Cabo Blanco via **Cabuya,** a hamlet nine kilometers (5.5 miles) west of Montezuma (from Cabuya, a rough rock-and-dirt track leads seven kilometers (4.5 miles) north over the mountains to Malpaís, passable only in dry season; a 4WD vehicle is essential).

La Catarata Montezuma, a waterfall and swimming hole two kilometers (1.2 miles) southwest of town (the trail leads upstream

enjoying calm waters at Montezuma

from the Restaurante La Cascada), is dangerous. Do not climb or jump from the top of the fall. Several lives have been lost this way. The **Montezuma Butterfly Garden** (tel. 506/2642-1317, www.montezumagardens.com, 8am-4pm daily, $8), west of the village and 500 meters (0.3 miles) above the Montezuma Waterfall Canopy del Pacífico tour, has a netted garden and breeds morphos and other butterflies species.

You can contribute to the local community through **Proyecto Montezuma** (tel. 506/8314-0690, www.proyectomontezuma. com), which seeks volunteers, including to teach English and art to young children, or even trash removal.

Entertainment and Events

Although it may be hard to imagine, each November this tiny hamlet hosts the **Costa Rica International Independent Film Festival** (tel. 506/8320-5450, www.montezumafilmfestival.com), an international documentary film festival. **El Sano Banano** restaurant shows movies at 7pm nightly (free with dinner or minimum $6 order). Exotic in extremis, the **Anamaya Resort** (tel. 506/2642-1289, www.anamayaresort.com) hosts fire-dancing and special cabarets ($35, including dinner).

Sports and Recreation

Sun Trails Montezuma (tel. 506/2642-0808, www.montezumatraveladventures.com) offers all manner of activities, from ATV tours and horseback riding to its Montezuma Waterfall Canopy Tour ($40), which offers tours by zip line among the treetops at 8am, 10am, 1pm, and 3pm daily.

Montezuma Expeditions (tel. 506/2642-0919, www.montezumaexpeditions.com) similarly offers a wide range of tours and activities, as do **Zuma Tours** (tel. 506/2642-0024, www.zumatours.net), both of which also have trips to Isla Tortuga (low season $40 pp, high season $45 pp) and Reserva Natural Absoluta Cabo Blanco ($30).

Montezuma Yoga (tel. 506/2642-0076, www.montezumayoga.com), at Hotel Los Mangos, offers yoga classes at 9:30am Sunday-Friday. **Anamaya Resort** (tel. 506/2642-1289, www.anamayaresort.com) also hosts yoga and Zumba classes, as does **The Sanctuary at Two Rivers** (tel. 506/8718-7885, http://thesanctuarycostarica.com), a dedicated yoga retreat and teacher training center near Cabuya.

Montezuma Surf School (tel. 506/2642-1319, www.montezumasurfschool.com) offers lessons and gear rental, as does **Proyecto Montezuma** (tel. 506/8314-0690, www.proyectomontezuma.org), which also teaches English to the local community.

Accommodations

Budgeting backpackers should check in to **Luz en el Cielo Eco B&B Hostel** (tel. 506/2642-0030, www.luzenelcielo.com, dorm $15 pp year-round, cabins low season $50 s, $70d, high season $54 s, $78 d), in the heart of the village. This clean, well-run English-owned hostel has "standard" and "luxury" dorms, and three lovely, airy albeit simply furnished cabins, plus laundry, lockers, and a shared kitchen.

The best bet for location in this price range is beachfront **Hotel Moctezuma** (tel. 506/2642-0058, www.hotelmoctezuma.com, $15-35 s, $20-40 d), with 28 spacious and clean rooms; some have fans only, while others are air-conditioned and have TVs. It also has apartments. Sure, it's far from deluxe, but its in-town shorefront setting makes it the budget option of choice. Plus, its restaurants and bar sit directly over the beach.

For a peaceful out of town retreat, try **Nature Lodge Finca los Caballos** (tel. 506/2642-0124, www.naturelodge.net, low season $76-130 s/d, high season $98-168, including taxes), on a 16-hectare (40-acre) hillside ranch midway between Cóbano and Montezuma. Rooms feature beautiful coral-stone floors and river-stone showers with poured-concrete sinks, tasteful furnishings that include Indian bedspreads, and patios with hammocks and rockers. A fan-shaped infinity pool is inset in a multilevel wooden deck with poured-concrete, soft-cushioned sofas and lounge chairs for enjoying the fabulous forest and ocean views. There are trails and a small spa. Meals include a full breakfast in the open-air restaurant, which has Wi-Fi.

A relaxing and intimate inn by the shore, **Hotel Amor de Mar** (tel. 506/2642-0262, www.amordemar.com, low season $70-140, high season $90-130), 600 meters (0.4 miles) west of the village, enjoys a fabulous location on a sheltered headland, with a private tide pool and views along the coast in both directions. The two-story hotel is set in pleasant landscaped lawns, with hammocks beneath shady palms. It has 11 rooms (all but two have private baths, some with hot water), each unique in size and decor and made entirely of hardwoods. Check out its two beach houses.

If you're into upscale weeklong yoga retreats, check into ★ **Anamaya Resort** (tel. 506/2642-1289, www.anamayaresort.com, from $795 per week, including meals), atop the cliffs above Montezuma, where it offers sensational views. Each of the seven delightfully conceived *cabinas* and villas is unique, though all are decorated with luxurious Asian fabrics. The aesthetic throughout is superb. My favorite? The Bali Cabina, with floor-to-ceiling glass walls on three sides. An infinity pool overlooks the ocean, gourmet organic dishes highlight the restaurant menu (open to nonguests for dinner), and it hosts aerial dancing and even fire-dancing, plus movie nights and massage and other treatments.

The most romantic option is ★ **Ylang Ylang Beach Resort** (tel. 506/2642-0636, www.ylangylangresort.com, low season $140-275 s, $160-295 d, high season $140-330 s, $180-350 d), a 10-minute walk along the beach 800 meters (0.5 miles) east of the village. Owners Lenny and Patricia Iacono have created a totally delightful property spread across eight hectares (20 acres) of beachfront that is a lush fantasia of riotous foliage. It has three three-story suites (for up to four people) with kitchens; a three-bedroom apartment; eight concrete and riverstone bungalows; and deluxe tent cabins, all accessed by well-manicured paths lit at night. All have fans, private baths, fridges, coffeemakers, and Guatemalan bedspreads. The coup de grâce is an exquisite free-form pool in a faux-natural setting of rocks with water cascading and foliage tumbling all around.

Food

For breakfast, head to the **Bakery Café** (tel. 506/2642-0458, 6am-6pm Mon.-Sat.) for *gallo pinto,* banana bread, soy burgers, and tuna sandwiches served on a pleasant raised patio; or to ★ **El Sano Banano** (tel. 506/2642-0638, 7am-10pm Sun.-Wed., 7am-midnight Thurs.-Sat.), where I recommend the scrambled tofu breakfast. This popular natural-food restaurant serves garlic bread, pasta, yogurt, veggie curry, and nightly dinner specials. It also has fresh-fruit thirst quenchers and ice cream, and prepares lunches to go. Plus it has free movies at 7:30pm nightly.

I also like **Puggo's** (tel. 506/2642-0325, noon-11pm daily low season, 8am-11pm daily high season) for its colorful deck with Caribbean-style furnishings. It's a great venue for enjoying Greek or tuna salad ($6.50), Asian noodles, spiced kebabs, or Moroccan fish stew ($7). Fresh-baked focaccia comes with your meal. Its delicious lemon-and-mint smoothies are just the thing for hot days. Israeli owner Maya is a great host. Get there early to snag a seat.

Vegans will thrill to **Orgánico** (tel. 506/2642-1322, 10am-6pm Mon.-Sat. low season, 10am-8pm Mon.-Sat. high season), a bakery serving all-organic dishes. Choose from an Aztec bowl with quinoa and beans with green and pineapple salsa ($9) or lemongrass ginger curry with brown rice ($8). It also serves smoothies and ice cream, and has a pleasant, airy patio.

The best dining around is at ★ **Ylang Ylang** (tel. 506/2642-0068, 7am-9:30pm daily, $5-15), along the beach 800 meters (0.5 miles) east of the village, serving delicious fusion fare in utterly romantic surrounds, candlelit by night. The menu includes chilled gazpacho, fresh sushi, and Asian-inspired jumbo shrimp

Getting There

Buses (tel. 506/2221-7479 or 506/2642-0740) depart from Avenida 3, Calles 16/18, in San José at 6am and 2pm daily; minibuses meet the bus in Cóbano. Return buses depart Montezuma at 6am and 2:30pm daily, and buses from Cóbano depart for San José 30 minutes later. Local buses (tel. 506/2642-0219) for Montezuma depart Paquera seven times 6am-7pm daily. The bus for Paquera departs Montezuma six times 3:45am-4pm daily, and departs from Cóbano (from outside the Hotel Caoba) 15 minutes later.

Interbus (tel. 506/4100-0888, www.interbusonline.com) operates minibus shuttles from San José ($40), as does Montezuma Expeditions' **Tur Bus Shuttle** (tel. 506/2642-0919).

Most of the recreational tour companies offer **water taxis**. A **taxi** to Montezuma from Tambor airport costs about $25.

★ CABO BLANCO ABSOLUTE WILDLIFE RESERVE

This jewel of nature at the very tip of the Nicoya Peninsula is where Costa Rica's quest to bank its natural resources for the future began. The 1,250-hectare (3,089-acre) **Reserva Natural Absoluta Cabo Blanco** (tel. 506/2642-0093 or 506/2642-0096, cablanco@ns.minae.go.cr, 8am-4pm Wed.-Sun., adults $10, children $1)—the oldest protected area in the country—was created in October 1963 thanks to the tireless efforts of Nils Olof Wessberg, a Swedish immigrant commonly referred to as the father of Costa Rica's national park system (see David Rains Wallace's excellent book *The Quetzal and the Macaw: The Story of Costa Rica's National Parks*). Wessberg was murdered in the Osa Peninsula in the summer of 1975 while campaigning to have that region declared a national park. There is a plaque near the Cabo Blanco ranger station in his honor.

The reserve, which includes 1,800 hectares (4,450 acres) of ocean, is named Cabo Blanco (White Cape) after the vertical-walled island

northern tamandua, Cabo Blanco Absolute Wildlife Reserve

in pineapple and coconut sauce. It's a guaranteed gourmet treat.

Information and Services

Sun Trails Montezuma (tel. 506/2642-0808, 7am-9:30pm Mon.-Fri., 8am-9pm Sat.-Sun.), in the village center, has Internet service, but bring a sweater! There's an **ATM** next door.

The **police station** (tel. 506/2642-0770) and post office are 200 meters (660 feet) east of the **bank** in Cóbano; there are public telephones in front of the bank. The **medical clinic** (tel. 506/2220-0911 or 506/8380-4125) and **pharmacy** (tel. 506/2642-0685) are 100 meters (330 feet) south of the bank.

Librería Topsy (tel. 506/2642-0576, 8am-1pm Mon.-Fri., 8am-noon Sat.-Sun. low season, 8am-1pm and 3pm-5pm Mon.-Fri., 8am-noon Sat.-Sun. high season) has heaps of used books, plus an amazingly large selection of international newspapers and magazines, from the *New York Times* to the *Economist*.

at its tip, which owes its name to the accumulation of guano deposited by Costa Rica's largest community of brown boobies (some 500 breeding pairs). Two-thirds of the reserve is off-limits to visitors. One-third is accessible along hiking trails. **Sendero Sueco** leads to the totally unspoiled white-sand beaches of Playa Balsita and Playa Cabo Blanco, which are separated by a headland (you can walk around it at low tide). A coastal trail, **Sendero El Barco,** leads west from Playa Balsita to the western boundary of the park. Check tide tables with the park rangers before setting off—otherwise you could get stuck. Torrential downpours are common April to December.

Isla Cabuya, about 200 meters (660 feet) offshore, has been used as a cemetery for the hamlet of Cabuya, gateway to the reserve. You can walk out to the island at low tide.

The **ranger station** has self-guided trail maps. Camping is not allowed in the reserve.

Getting There

A **bus** departs Montezuma for Cabuya and Cabo Blanco ($1) at 8:15am, 10:15am, 2:15pm, and 6:15pm daily. The Cabuya-Montezuma bus departs at 7am, 9am, and 1pm daily. Collective taxis depart Montezuma for Cabo ($1.50 pp) at 7am and 9am daily, returning at 3pm and 4pm. A private **taxi** costs about $12 one-way.

Sun Trails Montezuma (tel. 506/2642-0802, www.montezumatraveladventures.com) has guided tours ($50) but also offers transfers ($6 round-trip).

★ MALPAÍS AND SANTA TERESA

The shoreline immediately north of Cabo Blanco is a lively surfers' paradise with some of the best surfing beaches in the country. The past few years have seen phenomenal tourism development, propelling the contiguous communities of Malpaís and Santa Teresa from offbeat obscurity to huge popularity. Dozens of hotels and restaurants have popped up out of nowhere, and land prices have skyrocketed.

A paved road that leads west 10 kilometers (6 miles) from Cóbano hits the shore at the hamlet of **Carmén,** known in the surfing realm as Malpaís. The tiny fishing hamlet of Malpaís is actually three kilometers (2 miles) south of Carmén, but no matter; this road dead-ends at the hamlet and turns inland, ending at the northern entrance gate to the Cabo Blanco reserve (there is no ranger station, hence no entrance fee). A rocky track

children celebrating Independence Day at Playa Santa Teresa

Malpaís and Santa Teresa

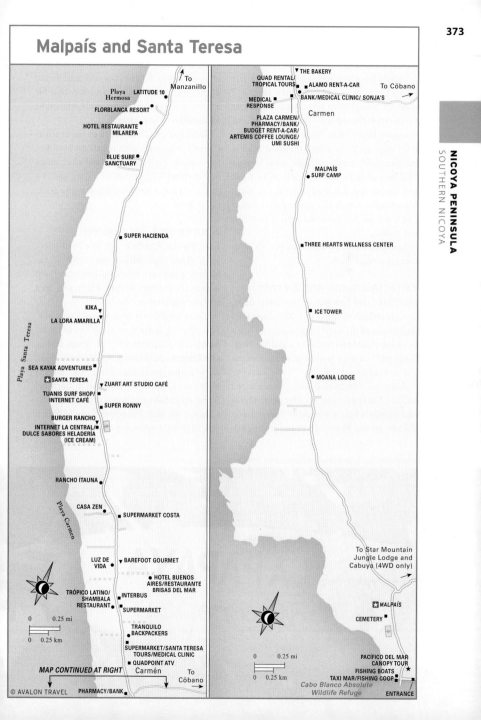

To Manzanillo

Playa Hermosa LATITUDE 10
FLORBLANCA RESORT
HOTEL RESTAURANTE MILAREPA
BLUE SURF SANCTUARY

SUPER HACIENDA

KIKA
LA LORA AMARILLA

Playa Santa Teresa

SEA KAYAK ADVENTURES
SANTA TERESA
ZUART ART STUDIO CAFÉ
TUANIS SURF SHOP/ INTERNET CAFÉ
SUPER RONNY
BURGER RANCHO
INTERNET LA CENTRAL/ DULCE SABORES HELADERÍA (ICE CREAM)

RANCHO ITAUNA

Playa Carmen

CASA ZEN
SUPERMARKET COSTA

LUZ DE VIDA
BAREFOOT GOURMET
HOTEL BUENOS AIRES/RESTAURANTE BRISAS DEL MAR
TRÓPICO LATINO/ SHAMBALA RESTAURANT
INTERBUS
SUPERMARKET
TRANQUILO BACKPACKERS
SUPERMARKET/SANTA TERESA TOURS/MEDICAL CLINIC
QUADPOINT ATV

0   0.25 mi
0   0.25 km

MAP CONTINUED AT RIGHT
Carmén
To Cöbano

© AVALON TRAVEL
PHARMACY/BANK

THE BAKERY
QUAD RENTAL/ TROPICAL TOURS
ALAMO RENT-A-CAR
To Cöbano
MEDICAL RESPONSE
BANK/MEDICAL CLINIC/ SONJA'S
PLAZA CARMEN/ PHARMACY/BANK/ BUDGET RENT-A-CAR/ ARTEMIS COFFEE LOUNGE/ UMI SUSHI
Carmen

MALPAÍS SURF CAMP

THREE HEARTS WELLNESS CENTER

ICE TOWER

MOANA LODGE

To Star Mountain Jungle Lodge and Cabuya (4WD only)

MALPAÍS
CEMETERY

0   0.25 mi
0   0.25 km

PACÍFICO DEL MAR CANOPY TOUR
FISHING BOATS
TAXI MAR/FISHING COOP
Cabo Blanco Absolute Wildlife Refuge
ENTRANCE

that begins 800 meters (0.5 miles) north of the dead-end links Malpaís with Cabuya; a 4WD vehicle is essential.

North from Carmén, the road parallels **Playa Carmén** and **Playa Santa Teresa**—together comprising several kilometers of coral-colored sand with pumping surf and dramatic rocky islets. Since forested mountains edge up to the coast, the coast road is the only road, with short side spurs to each side. Beyond Santa Teresa, the paving runs out and the narrow dirt road continues to Playa Manzanillo, where the going gets tougher and the road is a potholed bouillabaisse in wet season.

Local transportation is minimal. Most locals get around on ATVs.

Entertainment and Events

Malpaís Surf Camp (tel. 506/2640-0031, www.malpaissurfcamp.com), 200 meters (660 feet) south of the junction in Carmén, has a lively bar that shows surf videos and has Ping-Pong, table soccer, a pool table, and (occasionally) a mechanical bull.

Kika (tel. 506/2640-0408), an uninspired tiki bar, has open-mike Tuesday (8pm-10pm) and jumps when a live punk house band strikes up on Thursday (9pm-midnight).

When Kika closes, graduate next door to **Discotec La Lora Amarilla** (tel. 506/2640-0134), a no-frills nightclub that's *the* hot spot in Santa Teresa. It has a pool table and theme nights, including reggae and hip-hop on Thursday (midnight-3am) and Latin night on Saturday (10pm-3am).

Tabú (tel. 506/2640-0353), on the beach at Carmén, competes with reggae on Monday, Latin music on Wednesday, and electronica on Saturday. It has beach volleyball and is a mellower spot to watch the sunset with a cocktail in hand.

Sports and Recreation

Canopy del Pacífico (tel. 506/2640-0360, www.canopydelpacifico.com), with 11 cables and platforms, offers zip-line tours ($45) among the treetops at 9am, 11am, and 3pm daily by reservation.

There are a dozen or more surf shops, several offering tours, including **Tuanis Surf Shop** (tel. 506/2640-0370) in Santa Teresa, and **Malpaís Surf Camp** (tel. 506/2640-0031, www.malpaissurfcamp.com), 200 meters (660 feet) south of the junction in Carmén. Stand-up paddleboarding is now all the rage. Check it out with **Freedom Ride SUP** (tel. 506/2640-0521, www.sup-costarica.com).

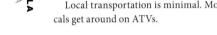

advertising surfboard repair at Playa Santa Teresa

Almost a dozen places rent ATVs and offer tours. Try **Quadtours Costa Rica** (tel. 506/2640-0178) and **Valerio's ATV** (tel. 506/2640-0736), in Carmén. **Sea Kayak Adventures** (tel. 506/2640-0853, www.pescatica.com), in Santa Teresa, lives up to its name, and **Bad Lands Bluewater Tackle** (tel. 506/2640-0449, www.badlandsbluewatertackle.com) offers sportfishing.

Star Mountain (tel. 506/2640-0101, www.starmountaineco.com) offers horseback riding in the mountains. Or enjoy a sailing trip with **Malpaís Sailing Tours** (tel. 506/2640-0454), then relax with a massage at **Sonja Spa** (tel. 506/2640-1060, jenifer106@hotmail.com), at Frank's Place, at the junction for Cóbano.

Accommodations

The area has dozens of great options in every price bracket.

UNDER $25

The area abounds with quality surfer and backpacker digs. One is **Tranquilo Backpackers** (tel. 506/2640-0589, www.tranquilobackpackers.com, dorms $11-13 pp, lofts $15 pp, private rooms $25-30 s/d), 800 meters north of the Carmén junction. Rooms are in a two-story New Mexico-style building with dangerously open rails on the balcony—take care up there! It has seven dorms with lofts and bunks, plus clean, airy, spacious private rooms with baths. There's an open-air lounge with hammocks, plus a kitchen, an Internet café, and parking.

$25-50

For a bargain, choose the calming **Casa Zen** (tel. 506/2640-0523, www.zencostarica.com, low season dorms $14 pp, rooms $30-50, high season dorms $16 pp, rooms $35-55 s/d), with an Indian motif, colorful cushions, chessboards, free movies at night, a great Thai restaurant, and four simply furnished spongewashed rooms (including two dorms) with batiks, ceiling fans, and shared baths. Located 1.5 miles north of the Carmén junction, Casa Zen also has an upstairs three-room apartment with a huge terrace with hammocks as well as a spa.

$50-100

The lovely **Ranchos Itauna** (tel./fax 506/2640-0095, www.ranchos-itauna.com, low season $80-90 s/d, high season $100-110 s/d, including tax), in Santa Teresa, is perfect if you're seeking laid-back tropical charm. Its run by an Austrian-Brazilian couple and offers four rooms in two octagonal two-story buildings with Wi-Fi, a fan, and a fridge. Two rooms have kitchens. The pleasing restaurant serves international cuisine, and the *rancho* lounge is a great place to chill.

Seeking chic sophistication in a boutique hotel? ★ **The Place** (tel. 506/2640-0001, www.theplacemalpais.com, rooms $70 s/d year-round, bungalows $95 s/d low season, $135 s/d high season), 0.4 miles south of the Carmén junction, is a romantic delight with an ultramodern style. The high point is a lovely jade-colored pool and open-air lounge with rattan pieces with leopard-skin prints. Reflecting the less-is-more philosophy, the rooms are simply yet fabulously furnished and include batiks. Even nicer, the bungalows have trendy cement floors, all-around floor-to-ceiling louvered French doors, and pink spreads enlivening whitewashed wooden walls. Each bungalow has its own style—I like the African villa.

For a wild escape try the **Star Mountain Jungle Lodge** (tel. 506/2640-0101, www.starmountaineco.com, year-round $69 s, $85 d), two kilometers (1.2 miles) northeast of Malpaís, on the track to Cabuya; the turnoff is 400 meters (0.25 miles) north of the soccer field in Malpaís. This gem is tucked in the hills amid an 80-hectare (198-acre) private forest reserve with trails. The four charming cross-ventilated *cabinas* are simply yet tastefully decorated and have Sarchí rockers on the veranda. A casita bunkhouse sleeps up to nine people. There's a pool, and guided horseback rides (2 hours, $30) are offered. Grilled meats and fish are prepared in a huge open oven. You'll need a 4WD vehicle to get here.

$100-150

The well-maintained U.S.-run **Santa Teresa Surf Camp** (tel. 506/2640-0049, www.santateresasurfcamp.com), set in neat gardens 0.5 miles south of the Carmén junction, specializes in weeklong surf packages (from $970 pp year-round). It offers wonderful air-conditioned studio apartments with Wi-Fi and beautiful color schemes; one spacious cabin has a sloping tin roof, ceiling fans, cement tile floors, and a kitchenette with a large fridge and large louvered windows opening to a terrace. Four other cabins have clean but shared outside baths with cold-water showers. It also has a beachfront two-bedroom house with cable TV, colorful walk-in showers, a large kitchen, and a wraparound veranda.

The Argentinean-run **Blue Surf Sanctuary** (tel. 506/2640-1001, www.bluesurfsanctuary.com, low season $125 s/d, high season $145 s/d), at the north end of Santa Teresa, has a cool vibe, not least due to its open kitchen-lounge with hammocks and sofas. Choose one of four individually themed raised villas with pendulous open-air queen lounge beds slung beneath. Lovely furnishings include dark contemporary hardwoods, indigenous pieces and fabrics, and gorgeous albeit small baths with mosaic tiles and large walk-in showers. It has a plunge pool and surf school. I like it! Equally lovely, and in similar style, is the English-run **Trópico Latino Lodge** (tel. 506/2640-0062, www.hoteltropicolatino.com, low season $100-370 s/d, high season $120-730 s/d, including tax), behind a rocky foreshore at Playa Santa Teresa. It offers spa and yoga sessions, plus it has a marvelous open-air restaurant and a gorgeous pool and a whirlpool tub by the beach.

Gorgeous decor seals the deal at the brilliantly conceived and executed Irish-owned ★ **Moana Lodge** (tel. 506/2640-0230, www.moanalodge.com, low season $95-250 s/d, high season $105-280 s/d), three miles south of the Carmén junction, where you'll likely find me resting my head. The African-themed lodge has 10 rooms and suites, some in huge colonial-style wooden cabins, featuring four-poster beds with cowhide drapes, fake zebra skins, leopard-print cushions, free Wi-Fi, and large well-lit baths with huge showers. The suite gets heaps of light through a glass wall. An open-air *rancho* with a poured-concrete sofa overlooks a large whirlpool tub and free-form pool in a stone-faced sundeck. Moana is really nice—and a bargain.

OVER $150

Intended to rent out in entirety and sleeping 8-12 people, the French-owned **Milarepa** (tel. 506/2640-0023, www.milarepahotel.com, low season $495, high season $1,000), at the north end of Playa Santa Teresa, has four Indonesian-style cabins spaced apart amid lawns inset with a lap pool. Two cabins are literally on the beach. They're made of bamboo and rise from a cement base, with a draped four-poster bed in the center of each villa and open-air bath-showers in their own patio gardens.

"Stunning" and "serene" are fitting descriptions for ★ **Florblanca Resort** (tel. 506/2640-0232, www.florblanca.com, low season $350-775 s/d, high season $400-925 s/d), perhaps the finest boutique beach resort in Nicoya. This gem enjoys an advantageous beachfront position at the north end of Santa Teresa. Fragrant plumeria and namesake *flor blanca* trees drop petals at your feet as you walk stone pathways that curl down through an Asian garden. The motif is Santa Fe meets Bali. Imbued with a calming Asiatic influence, its 10 luxury ocean-side villas stair-step to the beach and are furnished with quality rattan furnishings, tasteful art pieces, and king beds on raised hardwood pedestals. Each has a kitchenette, a vast lounge, and a stone-floored rainforest bath with separate showers and an oversize tub. Resort facilities include a deluxe spa plus a walk-in landscaped horizon pool, fed by a waterfall, with a swim-up bar. The superb oceanfront restaurant and sushi bar on their own are worth a visit. The resort offers yoga, kickboxing, and dance classes.

For the ultimate in reclusive privacy with pampering personalized service, check into

★ **Latitude 10** (tel. 506/2640-0396, www. latitude10resort.com, low season $245-430 s/d, high season $240-490 s/d), a super and super-exclusive adjunct with three junior suites and two beachfront master suites (actually, they're all private villas) hidden within its own forest garden. Villas are infused with Asian influences, including dark colonial plantation furnishings, glassless windows and French doors, lofty king beds with plump pillow-top mattresses, and fabulous open-air baths with rainforest showers. You get your own chef at the guests-only restaurant.

Shaka Beach Retreat (tel. 506/2640-1118, www.shakacostarica.com, $215 s, $320 d) surf camp and hotel, at Playa Hermosa, just north of Santa Teresa, specializes in weeklong surf and yoga packages and notably in surf camps for travelers with disabilities. In 2006 Shaka cofounder Christiaan Bailey, a surfer from Santa Cruz, California, suffered a spinal-cord injury while skateboarding. Remarkably, Christiaan continues to surf and has worked with board-maker Surftech to develop specialized boards for surfers with disabilities. Christiaan partnered with Florida surfer Frank Bauer to create Shaka Beach Retreat, a beautiful beachfront property built of hardwoods that is a fully ADA-compliant and wheelchair-accessible. Christiaan and a team of Shaka's coaches teach kids and adults with disabilities to swim and, yes, surf. Apart from their appealing aesthetic, the four spacious, air-conditioned villas have Wi-Fi, orthopedic mattresses, ceiling fans, and terraces.

CAMPING

The best of several places to camp is **Malpaís Surf Camp and Resort** (tel. 506/2642-0031, www.malpaissurfcamp.com, $10 pp to camp), 200 meters (660 feet) south of the junction in Carmén, which also has communal open-air *ranchos* ($15 pp) with camp beds beneath a tin roof with shared baths and toilets. It has gone more upscale of late and now has various poolside casitas ($95-150 s/d) with stone floors, tall louvered screened windows, and beautiful tile baths with hot water. There's a lively bar, a pool, and horse and surfboard rentals.

Food

Malpaís Surf Camp (7am-10pm daily), 200 meters (660 feet) south of the junction in Carmén, serves American breakfasts (from $5), plus lunch and dinner. It has an all-you-can-eat buffet ($9) at 6pm on Wednesday. **Casa Zen** (tel. 506/2640-0523, 7am-10pm

a gourmet *gallo pinto* breakfast at Latitude 10

daily), 1.5 miles north of the Carmén junction, is a marvelous Thai restaurant by night that serves American-style breakfasts ($5) such as veggie scramble and pancakes, along with lunches that include BLTs and tuna sandwiches. For dinner ($8), try the seared yellowfin tuna or red coconut curry. It has a highly ranked guesthouse.

For a great option for burgers, veggie dishes, kebabs, and slow-cooked chicken, try **Burger Rancho** (tel. 506/2640-0583, 10am-10pm daily), a tiny little spot that gets packed despite the road dust. It's opposite the soccer field in Santa Teresa.

I prefer to start my days at ★ **Zwart Art Studio Café** (tel. 506/2640-0011, 7am-10pm daily), coolly minimalist with all-white decor inside and out and a great place to watch the world go by. Opt for healthy granola with fruit, yogurt, and honey ($6), or raise your cholesterol with the buttermilk pancakes ($5). Whole-wheat sandwiches and burritos highlight the lunch menu; dinner might mean Greek salad with feta ($7.50) or fresh tuna with ginger dressing ($9.50). Follow it with a warm brownie and ice cream ($5). Plus there's great coffee and smoothies. Yum! Owner Margriet paints in an open studio beside her café.

You are spoiled for choice for unpretentious fine dining. For fresh seafood, my fave is **Product C** (tel. 506/2640-1026, www.product-c.com, 11am-7pm Tues.-Sat. Nov.-Aug.), in Plaza Comercial Playa Carmén. Canadian chef Damien Green is dedicated to serving sustainably caught fish and shrimp. Most dishes are pretty simple: fish tacos ($2), ceviche ($6), oyster on the half shell ($1.35 each), and smoked fish over rice with creamy dill sauce ($5). It's very inexpensive.

For superb fusion fare, head to ★ **Néctar** (tel. 506/2640-0232, www.florblanca.com, café 7am-3pm daily, sushi 3pm-6pm daily, full menu 6pm-9pm daily), at Florblanca, on the beach at the north end of Santa Teresa, where chef Spencer Graves conjures up fabulous Asian-Pacific-Mediterranean creations, including smoked trout, cream cheese, and

scallion *maki* appetizer ($7). Follow with Chinese five-spice marinated duck breast with caramelized red onion latkes and butter-wilted spinach ($20). The raised bar is a good place to enjoy top-quality sushi. A chef's five-course tasting menu is offered with 24 hours' notice. It plays cool music, from jazz to classical.

Chef Graves's rival is UK-born chef John Dewhurst, whose ★ **Buenos Aires** (tel. 506/2640-0941, 4pm-11pm Tues.-Sun., cash only) is an open deck at the eponymous hotel, high atop the hill away from all the dust. It has superb views and superb culinary sensations. The weekly menu might include an appetizer of fresh calamari with chipotle aioli ($7) or coconut-battered shrimp with ginger dipping sauce ($8); the main course could be sea bass with capers and olives in browned butter ($13) or beef tenderloin with brandy peppercorn sauce ($17). Wash it down with sangria or an electric-mint lemonade. Meals come with complimentary pita bread and three delicious dips.

The past few years have seen an explosion of sushi restaurants, including **Umi Sushi** (tel. 506/2640-0968, 11:30am-10pm daily), in Plaza Carmén. You can even wash down your miso soup and sashimi with an imported Sapporo beer.

Information and Services

There's a **bank** at Plaza Carmén, where **Carmén Connections** (tel. 506/8823-8600) is a tour information center.

There's a **medical clinic** (tel. 506/2220-0911) with ambulance service next to Frank's Place, at the junction for Cóbano; and **Dr. Jesús Moreno Rojas** (tel. 506/2640-0976) has an office across the street in Plaza Carmén, where there's a **pharmacy** (tel. 506/2640-0539). Tooth trouble? Head to **Dr. Manuel Vargas** (tel. 506/2640-0943), in Plaza Carmén.

There are half a dozen or so Internet cafés, including **Frank's Internet Café,** at the Carmén junction, and **Internet La Central** (tel. 506/2640-0762), opposite the soccer field in Santa Teresa.

Getting There

Transportes Hermanos Rodríguez (tel. 506/2642-0219) buses depart San José from Calle 16, Avenidas 1/3, at 7am and 3:30pm daily; return departures are at 7:30am and 3:30pm daily. Buses depart Cóbano for Malpaís at 10:30am and 2:30pm daily; return departures are at 7am and noon daily, connecting with onward buses to San José. **Montezuma Expeditions** (tel. 506/2642-0919, www.montezumaexpeditions.com) has a daily minibus shuttle from San José ($40), as does **Interbus** (tel. 506/4100-0888, www.interbusonline.com, $45).

You can rent an ATV, a virtual necessity in wet season, from **Quadpoint ATV** (tel. 506/2640-0965) and **Tropical Tours** (tel. 506/2640-0811, www.tropicaltours-malpais.com). **Alamo Rent-a-Car** (tel. 506/2640-0526) and **Budget Rent-a-Car** (tel. 506/2640-0500, www.budget.co.cr) have offices at Carmén. **Taíno Gas** (tel. 506/2640-0009), 500 meters (0.3 miles) north of the soccer field in Santa Teresa, is open 7am-6pm daily.

Taxi Mar (tel. 506/8837-2553) has water taxi shuttles to Sámara and elsewhere.

An ATV fords a river in southwest Nicoya.

The Central Pacific

The Central Pacific region comprises a thin coastal plain narrowing to the southeast and backed by steep-sided mountains cloaked in dense forest. The coast is lined by long gray-sand beaches renowned for fantastic surf. It is distinguished from more northerly shores by its wetter climate. The region becomes gradually humid southward, with the vegetation growing ever more luxuriant. It's no surprise, then, that this region has some of the nation's prime national parks.

Rivers cascade down from the mountains, providing opportunities to hike to spectacular waterfalls. The rivers slow to a crawl amid extensive mangrove swamps separated by miles-long sandy swaths punctuated by craggy headlands. One river, the Río Tárcoles, is home to a large population of crocodiles. The resort town of Jacó, the sportfishing town of Quepos, and more relaxed Manuel Antonio are now highly developed for tourism. South of Jacó, vast groves of African palms smother the coastal plains. Interspersed among them are orderly workers' villages, with gaily painted plantation houses raised on stilts.

Highway 34, the Costanera Sur, runs the length of the coast, linking the region with Puntarenas and Guanacaste to the north and Golfo Dulce and Osa southward. It is paved the entire way with the intent that Highway 34 will become the new Pan-American Highway, linking Nicaragua and Panamá, doing away with the need to head up over Cerro de la Muerte, thus shortening the route considerably.

PLANNING YOUR TIME

The Central Pacific zone is predominantly a beach destination. The area is easily explored along the coast highway, with side roads branching off into the mountains or beaches. Allocate at least one week to explore the entire region north to south. Three days is sufficient if you want to concentrate on either Manuel Antonio, Jacó, or Dominical—the three main destinations.

The most developed of the beach resorts is **Jacó**, long a staple of Canadian package

Look for ★ to find recommended
sights, activities, dining, and lodging.

Highlights

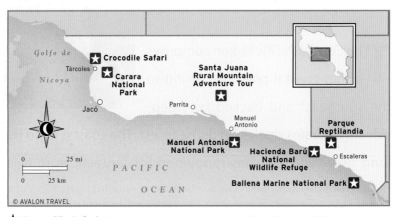

© AVALON TRAVEL

★ **Crocodile Safari:** You're sure to see crocs up close on a riverboat cruise up the Río Tárcoles, with fabulous bird-watching to boot. Your guide may even get out onto the muddy bank to feed a croc (page 386).

★ **Carara National Park:** This reserve, at the meeting point of moist and dry tropical ecosystems, is easily accessed. Monkey, sloth, and macaw sightings are virtually guaranteed (page 386).

★ **Santa Juana Rural Mountain Adventure Tour:** Head into the Fila Costeña mountains to visit a remote community whose various ecotourism projects will keep you active, entertained, and educated (page 401).

★ **Manuel Antonio National Park:** Popular and heavily visited, this small rainforest preserve offers diverse wildlife, good nature trails, beautiful beaches, and a small coral reef ideal for snorkeling (page 413).

★ **Hacienda Barú National Wildlife Refuge:** Wildlife abounds in this small reserve, which spans numerous ecosystems from mangroves to montane rainforest (page 418).

★ **Parque Reptilandia:** Dozens of snake species from around the world are displayed at this well-run reptile zoo, which even has a komodo dragon (page 419).

★ **Ballena Marine National Park:** Whales are present almost year-round in the waters off the Central Pacific, and whale-watching is now a popular activity—and the main reason to visit—Uvita (page 428).

charter groups but also an in-vogue destination for surfers, Tico youth, and sportfishing enthusiasts. If you like an active nightlife, this is also for you, but I find the place overrated; the beach is mediocre at best, and prostitution is overt. If quality is your gig, head to **Manuel Antonio,** combining great beaches, a vast choice of hotels, excellent restaurants, and guaranteed wildlife viewing in the tiny and, frankly, overcrowded national park. The gateway to Manuel Antonio is the nearby sportfishing town of **Quepos,** a secondary base popular with budget travelers and sportfishers.

From the Central Highlands, **Highway 3** (the old highway via Atenas; it's a steep switchback) and the faster **Autopista del Sol** (from San José) toll highway descend to **Orotina,** gateway to the Central Pacific. Six kilometers (4 miles) west of Orotina, Highway 3 and the Autopista del Sur merge with **Highway 27** (which runs west to Puntarenas) and **Highway 34** south to Jacó and Manuel Antonio.

Tárcoles to Playa Herradura

TÁRCOLES

Twenty-five kilometers (16 miles) south of Orotina, Highway 34 crosses the **Río Tárcoles.** The bridge over the river is the easiest place in the country to spot crocodiles, which bask on the mud banks below the bridge; don't lean over too far. If you park your car nearby, lock it and don't leave any contents in sight; theft has been an issue. A bigger threat is the danger of being hit by fast-moving trucks and buses as you walk along the bridge.

Crocodiles also gather at the mouth of the river, near the fishing village of Tárcoles; the turnoff is signed five kilometers (3 miles) south of the bridge. The estuary is also fantastic for bird-watching: More than 400 species have been identified. Frigate birds wheel overhead, while cormorants and kingfishers fish in the lagoons. Roseate spoonbills add a splash of color. Scarlet macaws fly overhead on their way to and from roosts in the mangrove swamps that extend 15 kilometers (9.5 miles) northward. **Mangrove Birding Tours** (tel. 506/2637-0472), by the river mouth, offers tours at 6am, 9am, noon, and 3pm daily. Luis Campos leads a two-hour **Mangrove Birding Tour & Photography Adventure** (tel. 506/2433-8278).

Opposite the turnoff for Tárcoles from Highway 34, a dirt road leads east and climbs steeply some eight kilometers (five miles) to the hamlet of **Bijagual.** About two kilometers (1.2 miles) along is the **Villa Lapas SkyWay** (tel. 506/2439-1816, www.villalapas.com, adults $20, children $10), a canopy tour with suspension bridges through the treetops offering fantastic views down over the coast. Buy tickets at the Villa Lapas Hotel, which also operates a zip line canopy tour (adults $35, children $17). Continuing uphill, you pass the signed trailhead to **Catarata Manantial de Agua Viva** (tel. 506/8831-2980, 8am-3pm daily, $20), a spectacular 183-meter-high (600-foot-high) waterfall, also known as the Bijagual Waterfall and supposedly the highest in the country. The best time to visit is in rainy season, when the falls are going full tilt. They don't cascade in one great plume but rather tumble down the rock face to natural pools, good for swimming. There are scarlet macaw nesting sites, and poison dart frogs hop along the paths. The trail is a stiff two-hour hike each way (take lots of water).

Two kilometers (1.2 miles) farther uphill brings you to **Pura Vida Botanical Garden** (tel. 506/2645-1001, www.puravidagarden.com, 8am-5pm daily, $20), a delight for the botanically minded. Manicured gravel trails through the gardens offer dramatic views over mountain ridges and the coast. A self-guided

Central Pacific

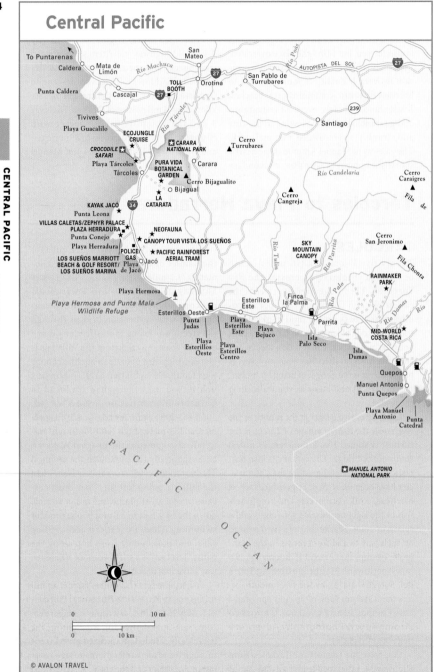

To Puntarenas
Caldera
Mata de Limón
Punta Caldera
Cascajal
San Mateo
Río Machuca
TOLL BOOTH
Orotina
San Pablo de Turrubares
AUTOPISTA DEL SOL
27
27
27
239
Santiago
Tivives
Playa Guacalilo
ECOJUNGLE CRUISE
CROCODILE SAFARI
Playa Tárcoles
Tárcoles
CARARA NATIONAL PARK
PURA VIDA BOTANICAL GARDEN
Carara
Cerro Turrubares
Río Tárcoles
Río Candelaria
Cerro Caraigres
Cerro Bijagualito
Bijagual
LA CATARATA
KAYAK JACÓ
Punta Leona
VILLAS CALETAS/ZEPHYR PALACE
PLAZA HERRADURA
Punta Conejo
Playa Herradura
LOS SUEÑOS MARRIOTT BEACH & GOLF RESORT/ LOS SUEÑOS MARINA
34
NEOFAUNA
CANOPY TOUR VISTA LOS SUEÑOS
PACIFIC RAINFOREST AERIAL TRAM
POLICE
GAS
Jacó
Playa de Jacó
Cerro Cangreja
Cerro San Jeronimo
Fila de
Fila Chonta
SKY MOUNTAIN CANOPY
Río Tulín
Río Parrita
RAINMAKER PARK
Río Palo
Playa Hermosa
Playa Hermosa and Punta Mala Wildlife Refuge
Esterillos Oeste
Punta Judas
Playa Esterillos Oeste
Esterillos Este
Playa Esterillos Este
Playa Esterillos Centro
Playa Bejuco
Finca la Palma
Parrita
Isla Palo Seco
Isla Dumas
MID-WORLD COSTA RICA
Río Damas
Río
Quepos
Manuel Antonio
Punta Quepos
Playa Manuel Antonio
Punta Catedral

PACIFIC OCEAN

MANUEL ANTONIO NATIONAL PARK

0   10 mi
0   10 km

© AVALON TRAVEL

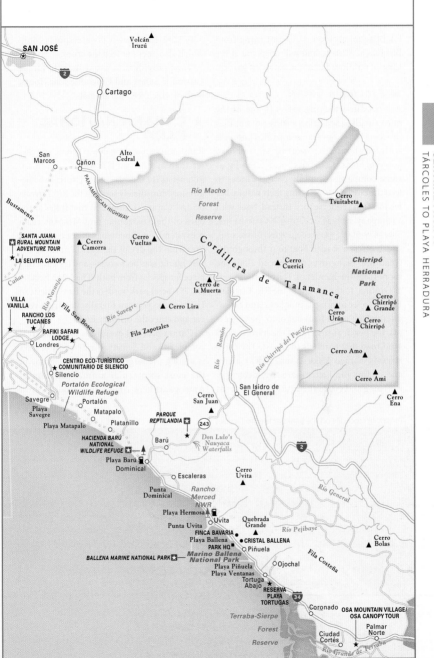

tour takes about one hour. It has a delightful restaurant overlooking the Bijagual Waterfall.

A bus (tel. 506/8831-2930) departs Orotina for Bijagual at noon daily, returning from Bijagual at 5:30am, and will drop you at the Catarata trailhead or at the botanical garden.

★ Crocodile Safari

A crocodile-watching safari is one of the most thrilling wildlife viewing possibilities in Costa Rica. Several companies compete with two-hour croc-spotting trips aboard pontoon boats ($25), but choose carefully, as some companies stupidly permit guides to feed the crocodiles, affecting their natural behavior. Don't endorse this! Instead, book with a company such as EcoJungle Cruises (tel. 506/2479-9002, www.ecojunglecruises.com), which offers a shaded boat tour through the Guacalillo mangroves that extend along the shore from the hamlet of Tivives, southwest of Orotina, to the mouth of the Río Tárcoles. Expect to see anhingas, monkeys, and crocodiles, which often haul out onto the tiny estuarine beach at the end of the hard-packed sand road that parallels the coast. The three largest—named Mike Tyson, Fidel Castro, and Osama Bin Laden—are five meters (16 feet) long and guard their turf and harems at recognized holes. Scarlet macaws hang out in the treetops. Morning is the best time to visit.

Alternately, try J.D.'s Watersports (tel. 506/2290-1560, www.jdwatersports.com), which also does not feed the crocs.

Tour providers to avoid include Jungle Crocodile Safari and Crocodile Man Tours, both of which feed the animals.

★ CARARA NATIONAL PARK

Rainforest exploration doesn't come any easier than at Parque Nacional Carara, 20 kilometers (12 miles) south of Orotina and beginning immediately south of the Río Tárcoles bridge. Carara is unique in that it lies at the apex of the Amazonian and Mesoamerican ecosystems—a climatological zone of transition from the dry of the Pacific north to the very humid southern coast—and it's a meeting place for species from both. The 5,242-hectare (12,953-acre) park borders the Pan-American Highway, so you can literally step from your car and enter the primary forest.

Carara protects evergreen forest of great complexity and density; the diversity of trees is among the largest in the world. Some of the most spectacular animals of tropical America are here: American crocodiles, great

American crocodile on the banks of the Río Tárcoles

hikers at Carara National Park

(0.6-mile) wheelchair-accessible trail with signs in braille that links to the Quebrada Bonita Trail. A map beside the ranger station indicates how to get to the 4.5-kilometer (2.8-mile) Laguna Meandrica Trail, which follows an old road paralleling the Río Tárcoles. Camping is not allowed. You can rent rubber boots ($2), and the **Asociación de Guías del Pacífico Central** (tel. 506/8723-3008, asoguipace@yahoo.com) hires out guides for $20 pp (ask for formal ID, as fake guides solicit services). Even if you want to explore on your own, it pays to have a guide, which can also be booked through **Costa Rica Expeditions** (tel. 506/2257-0766, www.costaricaexpeditions. com) or other tour operators.

Robberies have occurred here. Park by the visitors center and ask rangers about current conditions. The ranger station has secure lockers ($1).

Getting There
All buses traveling from San José or Puntarenas to Jacó and Quepos pass by the reserve.

PLAYA HERRADURA
A series of coves and beaches lines the coast south of Tárcoles, beginning with **Playa Malo,** a scenic bay fringed by a scalloped 800-meter (0.5-mile) white-sand beach. Fishing boats bob at anchor and are roosts for pelicans. At the south end rises the headland of Punta Leona, smothered with forest protected in a 300-hectare (740-acre) private nature reserve—part of a self-contained resort called Punta Leona.

South of Punta Leona the road climbs steeply before dropping down to Playa Herradura. At the crest of the rise is the entrance to **Villa Caletas** (tel. 506/2637-0505 or 506/2257-3653, www.villacaletas.com), a fabulous resort hotel atop a 500-meter (1,600-foot) headland with staggering views. You owe it to yourself to visit for lunch or dinner, or for a massage or treatment at the Serenity Spa. Every Saturday night Villa Caletas has music

anteaters, ocelots, spider monkeys, and poison dart frogs. Carara is also one of the best bird-watching locales in all of Costa Rica. Fiery-billed aracaris and toucans are common. So too are boat-billed herons. Around dawn and dusk, scarlet macaws—there are at least 400—can be seen in flight as they migrate daily between the wet forest interior and the coastal mangrove swamps (a macaw protection and reintroduction program has been very successful). The bridge over the Río Tárcoles is a good place to spot them as they fly over. Carara also has pre-Columbian archaeological sites.

Information and Services
The **Centro de Visitantes** (Visitors Center, tel. 506/2637-1080 or 506/2637-1054, 7am-4pm daily Dec.-Apr., 8am-4pm daily May-Nov., last entrance 3pm, $10) sits beside the coastal highway, three kilometers (2 miles) south of the Río Tárcoles. Here begins the Las Araceas Nature Trail, a one-kilometer (0.6-mile) loop, and a one-kilometer

concerts, particularly jazz and New Age, in a Greek amphitheater tucked into a cliff face.

About seven kilometers (4.5 miles) from both Tárcoles and Jacó is the turnoff for **Playa Herradura,** which in the past decade has exploded from obscurity into a burgeoning beach resort centered on the Los Sueón hotel and residential complex, with a golf course and a marina. The long gray-sand beach is swarmed by Ticos on weekends and holidays.

Shopping
One of the nation's top stores for quality indigenous art throughout South America, **Dantica Gallery** (tel. 506/2637-7572, 9am-7pm daily), in Plaza Herradura, has an irresistible collection of jewelry, masks, and other pieces from Costa Rica, Panamá, and Colombia.

Sports and Recreation
Costa Rica Dreams Sportfishing (tel. 506/2637-8942, U.S. tel. 732-901-8625, www.costaricadreams.com) offers half- and full-day sportfishing charters out of Los Sueños Marina. **Herradura Divers** (tel. 506/2637-7123, www.herraduradivers.com) offers scuba trips.

Kayak Jacó (tel. 506/2643-1233, www.kayakjaco.com) offers outrigger canoe and kayak trips, including inflatable kayaks, on the Río Dulce. It's at Playa Agujas, three kilometers (2 miles) south of Tárcoles.

A round of golf at Los Sueños's **Los Iguanas Golf Resort** (tel. 506/2630-9151, www.golflaiguana.com) costs $150 for nonguests, including a cart. Club rental costs $35. Go to **Villa Caletas** (tel. 506/2637-0505 or 506/2257-3653, www.villacaletas.com) for yoga at 7am and 4pm daily.

Inevitably, there's a canopy tour: **Canopy Vista Los Sueños** (tel. 506/2637-6020, www.canopyvistalossuenos.com, $60), with 15 platforms, 13 zip-line cables, and departures seven times daily. It has a serpentarium, a frog garden, and a butterfly garden. It's east of the main highway, not at Los Sueños Resort & Marina.

Accommodations
The swank **Los Sueños Marriott Beach & Golf Resort** (tel. 506/2630-9000, U.S. tel. 888-223-2427, www.marriott.com, from $179 s/d) megaresort and residential complex is centered on a championship golf course and draws a predominantly American clientele. At its heart is a four-story hotel in Spanish-colonial style—lots of red tile, natural stone,

Los Sueños Marina, Playa Herradura

and wrought iron—but nonetheless with an "Anywhere, USA" feel. Its 201 regally appointed air-conditioned rooms have all the expected amenities, and the resort boasts six restaurants, a casino, and a wide range of sports, shopping, and services. Costa Rica's largest marina is here, as is the golf course.

To feel like royalty, head to the palatial ★ **Hotel Villa Caletas** (tel. 506/2637-0505 or 506/2257-3653, www.villacaletas.com, low season $174-475 s/d, high season $205-545), a member of the Small Distinctive Hotels of Costa Rica and perhaps the finest boutique hotel in Costa Rica. Imagine a French colonial-style gingerbread villa—reached by a winding hillcrest driveway lined with Roman urns—and matching self-contained casitas overlooking the sea. Surround each with sensuous tropical greenery, then add sublime decor and stunning museum pieces, such as tasteful paintings, Renaissance antiques, giant clam shells, and Oriental rugs. You'll think you've entered the Louvre! It has 35 luxurious air-conditioned accommodations in eight categories, including eight bedrooms in the main house. Each is done up in warm tropical colors, with antique-style beds, Japanese-style lampshades, floor-to-ceiling French silk curtains and Indian bedspreads, cable TV,

minibars, and (in most) verandas opening onto stunning ocean vistas. Eight sumptuous and huge Junior Superior Suites have outdoor spas, and self-contained master-suite villas in their own private gardens have private parking and private entrances, whirlpool tubs with wraparound windows, infinity swimming pools, and bedrooms mirrored wall to wall for the ultimate romantic experience. Some are a hefty hike up and down stone-walled pathways. A shuttle runs down to the beach, with decks and a bar. Guests get golf privileges at the nearby Los Sueños Resort.

An extension of Villa Caletas, the adjoining ★ **Zephyr Palace** (www.zephyrpalace.com, $450-1,500 s/d, $7,500 for the entire place) is indisputably the most extravagant and deluxe hotel in the country. Inspired by imperial Rome and truly palatial, it has just seven individually themed suites, including an Imperial Suite with its own mirrored gymnasium and Turkish sauna. Other suites transport you to Africa, Egypt, and the Orient and reflect genius interior design. It has spectacular salons and state-of-the-art meeting rooms, plus a gorgeous infinity pool.

Food

Steve 'N' Lisa's Paradise Cove (tel.

Hotel Villa Caletas, Playa Herradura

506/2637-0655, 7am-10pm daily, $2-20), on the main highway, offers breezy patio dining and serves burgers, grilled chicken, and tuna-melt sandwiches; Wi-Fi is free.

The mountaintop ★ **Restaurante Mirador** (6pm-10pm daily high season, 6pm-10pm Fri.-Sun. low season, breakfast $10, lunch $22, 3-course dinner $35-45, 7-course $65) at Villa Caletas offers a sublime setting in which to enjoy chef Miguel Bolaños's gourmet nouvelle cuisine. Choose from à la carte dishes such as fire-grilled *chimichurri* vegetable rolls with tomato bruschetta and goat cheese ($13) and sea bass sashimi ($15); or entrées such as peach palm mahimahi with white wine ($26) or roasted lamb tenderloin ($29). The Mirador is slightly formal and aloof. More informal is the **Anfiteatro Sunset Restaurant** (7am-11pm daily), beneath the Mirador. Breakfast on the mountaintop with New Age music playing softly is a sublime way to start the day.

Information and Services

Plaza Herradura has a bank, as does the marina. Ocean Plaza, one kilometer (0.6 miles) inland of the beach, also has a bank, plus **Lava Max** (tel. 506/2637-8737) laundry. The **police station** is next to the gas station on Highway 34, one kilometer (0.6 miles) south of Plaza Herradura.

Getting There and Around

Los Sueños Marina (tel. 506/2643-4000) has a state-of-the-art dock with 200 slips. **National Rent-a-Car** (San José tel. 506/2242-7878) has an outlet at the marina.

Jacó and Vicinity

Jacó was the country's first developed beach resort, when it was put on the map by wintering Canadian charter groups. The snow-bird scene has been diluted by Ticos, as it's the closest beach resort to San José and therefore popular with a mix of Josefino families and young adults on a fling. It also draws surfers, the young offbeat party crowd, and North American anglers (and prostitutes seeking to be captain's mates). It gets packed on holidays and on weekends in dry season.

Highway 34 runs inland, parallel to Jacó, which lies 400 meters (0.25 miles) west of the highway and is linked by four access roads. The main strip in town—Avenida Pastor Díaz—runs south two kilometers (1.2 miles) to the suburb of Garabito. Everything lines the single main street, which parallels the beach for its full length.

Personally, I don't understand Jacó's appeal. Not least, the three-kilometer (2-mile) beach is ugly, and swimming is discouraged: Signs warn of dangerous rip currents, and the river estuaries at each end of the beach are said to be polluted. Meanwhile, city fathers have tried to spruce up Jacó's image by creating a lovely urban park—Parque Recreativo Municipal Johannes Dankers—on the main drag.

SIGHTS

If frogs and snakes interest you, check out **Neofauna** (tel. 506/2643-1904, 9am-4pm daily, $15), a small yet fascinating facility outside the entrance to the Waterfalls Canopy, four kilometers (2.5 miles) northeast of Jacó. It has educational tours of its exhibits.

ENTERTAINMENT

Jacó has no shortage of bar action. The scene is ever shifting. **The Beatle Bar** (tel. 506/2643-3211, 6pm-2:30am daily), next to Parque Recreativo, has pool tables, darts, table football, TV, and classic music (although its clientele includes a posse of sex workers). Its weekly pajama party (Tues.), bikini contests (Wed.), and pole-dancing contests (Fri.) give you an idea of what it's all about. Its

Jacó

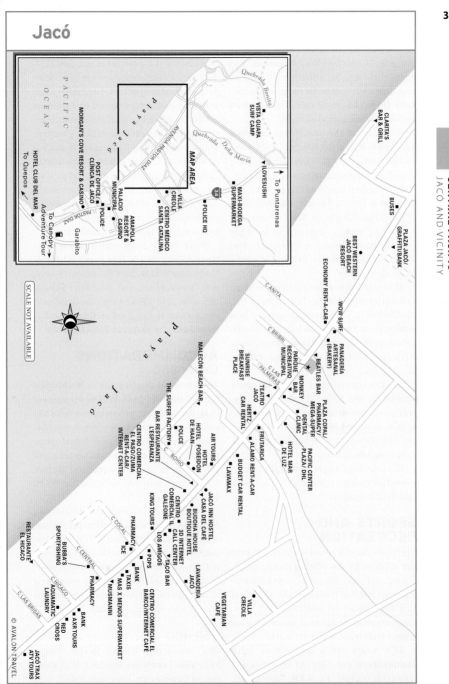

main competition is the **Monkey Bar** (tel. 506/2643-2357, 9pm-2:30am Tues.-Sun.), 100 meters south of The Beatle Bar, which packs 'em in for "Girls Gone Wild Weekends," and its upscale lounge-bar with DJs and live music, including a VIP tree-house room with leather sofas. Go for '80s music on Wednesday, with two-for-one margaritas all night.

Warm up at the beachfront **Clarita's Sports Bar & Grill** (tel. 506/2643-2615, www. claritashotel.com, 7am-10pm daily), popular with the expat crowd, not least for its Hooters-style bartenders. The Blind Pigs perform. **Sky Lounge & Sports Bar** (tel. 506/2643-1642) at Hotel Poseidon, in the heart of town, has a revolving menu of events: Monday-night football, tequila Tuesday, two-for-one beer on Thursday, and movies on Friday. I enjoyed a mean martini here!

More high-brow entertainment has come to town courtesy of the **Teatro Jacó** (tel. 506/2630-9812, www.teatrojaco.com), to host local English- and Spanish-language theatrical acts and bring international talent to town. It is located 100 meters south of, and opposite, Monkey Bar.

You can try your luck in the **Amapola Casino** (tel. 506/2643-2255, www.hotelamapola.com, 11am-3am daily), at the south end of Jacó, or nearby **Morgan's Cove Casino** (tel. 506/2643-3147, www.hoteljacocostarica. com, 2pm-3am daily).

The four-day **Jungle Jam** music festival (www.facebook.com/JungleJam) is held each year in mid-January.

SPORTS AND RECREATION

There's no shortage of tour agencies, many the size of phone kiosks, offering surfing, sportfishing, and everything else. Many local outfitters are based at Playa Herradura, north of Jacó. **King Tours** (tel. 506/2643-2441, www. kingtours.com) specializes in sportfishing but offers a wide range of activity tours.

ATV tours are a gas! Check with **Jaguariders** (tel. 506/2643-0180, www. jaguariders.com) or **AXR Tours** (tel.

506/2643-3130, www.axrjaco.com), which has one-hour to full-day tours by ATV and French-made AXR off-road vehicles.

Rainforest Adventures (tel. 506/2257-5961, www.rainforestadventure.com, 9am-4pm Mon., 6am-4pm Tues.-Sun.) offers a ride into the forest canopy aboard its Rainforest Aerial Tram (adults $60, children $30), comprising 18 wheelchair-accessible gondolas, with canvas awnings and guides. It also has a herbarium, a snake exhibit, plus waterfall climbing and rappelling. A $99 ticket gives access to everything. **Discovery Horseback Tours** (tel. 506/8838-7550, www.horseride-costarica.com), located three kilometers (2 miles) south of Jacó, offers horseback rides.

More than a dozen outlets on the main street cater to surfers. Take your pick! Two of the best are **W.O.W. Surf** (tel. 506/2643-3844, www.wowsurf.net) and **Jacó Surf School** (tel. 506/2643-1905, www.jacosurfschool. com). There is also good surfing, as well as related services, in nearby Playa Hermosa.

ACCOMMODATIONS
Under $50

The best surfer digs by a mile is ★ **Jacó Inn Hostel** (tel. 506/2643-1935, www.jacoinn. com, dorm $12 pp, private rooms from $25 s/d), a gorgeous home-away-from-home hostel on the main drag. This professional operation has clean dorms (men's and women's) and private rooms, plus a fully equipped kitchen, a TV lounge, secure lockers, and free Wi-Fi. It's a real beauty.

Another winner, **Buddha House** (tel. 506/2643-3615, www.hostelbuddhahouse. com, low season $25-70 s, $30-70 d, high season $30-80 s, $35-80 d), on the main drag next to Centro Comercial Il Galeone, also demonstrates how the hostel world has matured. It also has dorms and private rooms, lent ambience by a tropical color scheme.

$50-100

Of a dozen or more hotels in this price range, I like **Villa Creole** (tel. 506/2643-5151, www. hotelvillacreole.com, low season $60 s/d, high season $75 s/d, including tax) for its simple elegance in nine well-lit, air-conditioned rooms around a large pool with a water cascade and an orchid garden. The rooms have orthopedic mattresses, Guatemalan fabrics, kitchenettes, safes, patios, and stone-walled private baths, plus Wi-Fi. A minibus is on hand for tours, a *rancho* restaurant (high season only) serves gourmet French creole cuisine. It's on the east side of town, a 15-minute walk from the beach.

Popular with the party crowd, and one of the best beachfront options, **Clarita's Hotel** (tel. 506/2643-2615, www.claritashotel.com, low season $50-70 s/d, high season $60-80 s/d) has 16 rooms and one apartment. Rooms get lots of light, and the batik fabrics are a nice touch. Some rooms are air-conditioned; others have ceiling fans. Its bar-restaurant is one of the most colorful and lively in town, and it has a swimming pool with a swim-up bar.

In the heart of town, I like the French-Swiss-owned **Hotel Poseidon** (tel. 506/2643-1642, www.hotel-poseidon.com, low season $85 s/d, high season $115 s/d). The 14 large rooms are delightfully furnished, and baths have large mosaic-tiled showers. Upstairs air-conditioned rooms get the light; downstairs rooms (with fans only) are a bit dingy. Wi-Fi is included. There's a tiny pool with a whirlpool and a swim-up bar, plus an excellent restaurant and a lively rooftop bar.

$100-150

Surfers seeking serious tuition should book with **Vista Guapa Surf Camp** (tel. 506/2643-2830, www.vistaguapa.com, packages from $700 s, $1,200 d, including transfers, surf instruction, and meals), a dedicated surf camp 400 meters (0.25 miles) inland of the beach north of town, and owned by former Costa Rican surf champion Alvaro Solano. It offers six air-conditioned rooms on a ridge (a steep hike); all are spacious, with terra-cotta floors, safes, tall wooden beds, tiled baths, and glass French doors opening to decks with hammocks. Choose from two- to seven-night packages or specialized surfers' packages. Free

shuttles to and from San José are offered on Saturday.

Elegant and romantic, the contemporary **Hotel Club del Mar** (tel. 506/2643-3194, www.clubdelmarcostarica.com, low season $99-204 s/d, high season $159-349 s/d) nestles amid lawns beneath the cliffs at the southern end of Jacó, well away from the hubbub. It has eight hotel rooms, 22 spacious, conservatively furnished one- and two-bedroom condos, and a penthouse suite with a quasi-Asiatic motif. Three rooms are wheelchair-accessible. There's a pool and kids pool, plus a Serenity Spa.

FOOD

The place for breakfast is the **Sunrise Breakfast Place** (tel. 506/2643-3361, 6am-12:30pm daily), opposite Monkey Bar, serving waffles, eggs benedict ($7), omelets, and more. A worthy alternative, **The Coffee Shop** (Avenida Pastor Díaz, tel. 506/2643-3240, 7:30am-2pm Mon.-Fri.), next to Mango Surf Shop, also has omelets and pancakes.

My favorite lunch spot is the ★ **Taco Bar** (Calle Pops, tel. 506/2643-0222, noon-10pm Mon., 7am-10pm Tues.-Sun.), a delightful open-air Japanese-style restaurant with a great buffet, gourmet fish tacos, sashimi ($7), and citrus-teriyaki chicken ($8) on the menu. Wash it down with a mega-*batido* (shake) or natural lemonade, followed by a gourmet coffee. It also has granola and yogurt breakfasts ($5) and pancakes and fruit (Thurs.-Mon. $5.50, Tues.-Wed. $3), as well as daily specials. The tree-trunk stools and swing seats are pretty cool.

Another good choice is the elegant open-air **La Esperanza** (tel. 506/2643-3326, 10am-midnight daily, $4.50-12), centered on an octagonal bar under a skylight in the center of town. Its wide-ranging menu includes burgers, onion rings, chowders, ceviche, chicken in honey, and mussels in garlic and olive oil. You can't go wrong at **Clarita's Sports Bar & Grill** (tel. 506/2643-2615, 7am-10pm daily), beachside at the north end of town, for its omelets, burgers, burritos, and entrées ranging from teriyaki mahimahi ($9) to filet mignon ($15). Go for calypso on Saturday afternoon.

For delicious seafood, try the elegant beachfront **Restaurant Hicacos** (tel. 506/2643-3226, www.elhicaco.net, 11am-11pm daily), which has an all-you-can-eat lobster feast (6pm-10pm Wed.) with live calypso. It also hosts a live reggae band on Monday.

Another elegant favorite is **Hotel Poseidon Restaurant** (Calle Bohío, tel. 506/2643-1642, 7am-2pm and 6pm-10pm daily), with consistently good dishes such as marlin ceviche, a fabulous seared ahi tuna with mashed potatoes and crisp veggies, or filet mignon with béarnaise-jalapeño sauce ($15). Breakfasts include biscuits with gravy ($5) and bagel and eggs ($5).

Newcomer ★ **Graffiti** (tel. 506/2643-1708, www.graffiticr.com, 5pm-10pm Mon.-Sat.), a bistro tucked into the back of Plaza Jacó, exudes fantastic hip rustic decor. Its eclectic gourmet menu includes a tuna tartare tower, a cheddar burger, and a cacao- and coffee-encrusted filet mignon, but the menu follows the chef's whims. It has a wine bar, plus live music on weekends. I'll see you there!

For baked goods, try **Panadería Artesanal** (no tel.), on the main drag next to The Beatle Bar; **Musmanni** (tel. 506/2643-3248), on the main drag opposite Calle Central; or the clean and modern **Pachi's Pan** (tel. 506/2643-1153), across the street.

INFORMATION AND SERVICES

The private 24-hour **Centro Médico Santa Catalina** (tel. 506/2643-5059) is 400 meters (0.25 miles) east of the main drag in the center of town. The government's **Clínica de Jacó** (tel. 506/2643-3667) is behind the police station at the south end of town. The **Red Cross** (tel. 506/2643-3090) has ambulance service, as does **Emergencias 2000** (tel. 506/8380-4125), on Highway 21 midway between Herradura and Jacó. **Farmacia Fischel** (tel. 506/2643-2705), in Centro Comercial Il Galeone, is open 8am-10:30pm daily. **Dr. Darío Chaves** (tel. 506/2643-3221)

has a dental clinic; also try **VitalDent** (tel. 506/2643-4039), upstairs in Plaza Il Galeone.

There's a **police station** (tel. 506/2643-3011) on the beach, next to Hotel Balcón del Mar, and another in Garabito (tel. 506/2643-1213), adjoining the OIJ (tel. 506/2643-1723). The police headquarters is on Highway 34. The **post office** adjoins the police station in Garabito.

International Central (tel. 506/2643-2601, 7:30am-9pm daily), in Centro Comercial El Paso, is an international call center; as is **3-D Internet Call Center** (tel. 506/2643-3754), at Centro Comercial Il Galeone.

Dirty laundry? Clean up at **Aquamatic** (tel. 506/2643-2083, 7am-5pm Mon.-Sat.), at the south end of town; or **LavaMax,** on the main drag in the center of town.

GETTING THERE

Transportes Jacó (tel. 506/2223-1109 or 506/2643-3135) buses depart San José (2.5 hours, $2.75) from Calle 16, Avenida 3, at 6am and 7am and then every two hours until 7pm daily; buses return every two hours 5am-5pm daily. From Puntarenas, buses to Jacó depart seven times daily, arriving and departing from the Supermercado at the north end of Jacó. Buses also depart Quepos for Jacó six times daily. **Interbus** (tel. 506/4100-0888, www.interbusonline.com) and **Grayline** (tel. 506/2220-2126, www.graylinecostarica.com) operate minibus shuttles from San José ($35) and popular travel destinations.

Kevin's Transfers (tel. 506/8340-5182, www.kevinstransfers.com) and **CR VIP Transfers** (tel. 506/2643-6011, www.costaricaholidayrentals.com) offer personalized transfers. **Zuma Tours** (tel. 506/8849-8569, www.zumatours.net) offers water taxis between Jacó and Malpaís and Montezuma in Nicoya; plus Quepos, Manuel Antonio, and Uvita (one-way adults $40, children $30).

GETTING AROUND

Car rental companies in Jacó include **Europcar** (tel. 506/2643-2049); **Budget** (tel. 506/2643-2665), in Plaza de Jacó; and

Economy (tel./fax 506/2643-1719), toward the north end of town.

You can rent bicycles at Ciclo-Sport (tel. 506/8838-9178). Companies renting ATVs, motorcycles, and scooters include AXR Tours (tel. 506/2643-3130, www.axrjaco.com). For taxis, call Taxi Jacó (tel. 506/2643-3009).

PLAYA HERMOSA

Highway 34 south from Jacó crests a steep headland, beyond which Playa Hermosa (not to be confused with Playa Hermosa in Nicoya) comes into sight—an incredible view. The beach is 10 kilometers (6 miles) long and arrow-straight, with waves pummeling the shore, drawing surfers. The best time to visit is at 4pm Saturday for the weekly surf competitions (no fee, $300 prize), hosted by The Backyard.

Beginning some two kilometers (1.2 miles) south of the village, the Refugio de Vida Silvestre Playa Hermosa y Punta Mala (Playa Hermosa and Punta Mala Wildlife Refuge, tel. 506/2643-1066) protects the nesting grounds of four species of marine turtles. It's off-limits to visitors. The sandy beach road ends at the ranger station, which has a turtle hatchery open to view (free). Guided tours ($20) in nesting season, and of the mangroves at other times of year, are offered by reservation only.

Don't leave anything unattended in your vehicle; theft is a major problem along the beach.

Sports and Recreation

Discovery Horseback Tours (tel. 506/8838-7550, www.horseridecostarica.com), in Jacó, has guided tours, and Motoworld (tel. 506/2643-7111, www.mareabravacostarica.com), at Marea Brava Beachfront Suites & Villas, has motorcycle and ATV tours.

Las Olas Hotel (tel. 506/2643-7021, www.lasolashotel.com) offers surf tours and rents surfboards, snorkeling gear, and mountain bikes. Loma Del Mar Surf Camp (tel. 506/2643-2313, www.rovercam.com) also offers surf classes and board rentals. Surf camps include Waves Costa Rica (tel. 506/2653-4523, www.wavescr.com), Jim Hogan Surf Camp (tel. 506/2643-5167, www.jimhogansurfcamp.com), and Del Mar All Girls Surf Camp (tel. 506/2643-3197, www.costaricasurfcamp.com). Surprisingly, the only surf shop is CA Factory (tel. 506/2643-2871), two kilometers (1.2 miles) south of Playa Hermosa on the main highway. It rents and repairs boards and offers lessons.

turtle hatchery at Refugio de Vida Silvestre Playa Hermosa y Punta Mala

Chiclets Tree Tour (c/o Jacó Wave, tel. 506/2643-1880, www.jacowave.com) has a canopy tour that includes a daunting tree climb. Trips are offered at 7am, 9am, 1pm, and 3:30pm daily.

Accommodations

My budget pick, beloved of surfers, is the off-beat **Cabinas Las Arenas** (tel. 506/8729-4532, www.cabinaslasarenas.com, $39-57 s, $49-63 d), well run by a British-Canadian couple. The seven rooms are in a two-story unit, each with a fridge, a fan, a stove, and a private bath with hot water; some have cable TV and fridges. It has a simple, attractive bar-restaurant, and a river-stone courtyard on the beach. You can camp ($12 per tent).

Surfer dudes Jason and Jonathan run **Las Olas Hotel** (tel. 506/2643-7021, www.lasolashotel.com, rooms $45-75, cabins $100), a modern three-story structure with eight nicely kept rooms with kitchenettes and patios. There are also three two-story A-frame cabins, each with three bunks below and a double and single in the loft. There's a pool and a restaurant beachside for enjoying Taco Tuesdays, Pasta Sundays, and two-for-one tuna steak dinners on Wednesday.

For intimacy, opt for the modern **Hotel Fuego del Sol** (tel. 506/2643-6060, www.fuegodelsolhotel.com, low season from $73 s, $85 d, high season from $85 s, $97 d), a handsome two-story colonial-style structure in landscaped grounds. It has 17 spacious air-conditioned rooms and two suites, with cool tiles painted in tropical motifs, plus a pool with a swim-up bar, a gym, and a beachfront restaurant. It has a one-week surf camp.

The standout property, at the extreme north end of the beach, is the resort-style **Terraza del Pacífico** (tel. 506/2643-6862, www.terrazadelpacifico.com, low season from $101 s/d, high season from $128 s/d), which caters to the more upscale surf crowd. This Spanish colonial-style property has a superb beachfront location and 62 stylishly furnished air-conditioned rooms, all with Wi-Fi. The landscaped grounds boast a circular pool with a swim-up bar. There's a casino, a restaurant, and a bar. Rates include breakfast and tax.

Food

For a quick bite, the roadside **Jungle Surf Café** (no tel., 7am-9pm daily, $2-10) satisfies with Tex-Mex, "killer omelets," burgers, barbecue chicken, and filet mignon. Go for the fish tacos. Surf movies play on the TV at the bar.

The center of action is the **Backyard Bar** (tel. 506/2643-7011, 8am-10pm daily) at the Backyard Hotel, with a large international menu, including tapas, burgers, seafood, and steaks. It draws a crowd for live music and barbecue on Saturday (4pm-8pm), a nightly sunset happy hour (4:30pm-7:30pm), and free drinks for women on Friday (5pm-8pm). It sometimes has go-go dancers. Wednesday is "ladies' night" (10pm-1am), with "bonfire, dancing, and babes."

PLAYAS ESTERILLOS, PALMA, AND PALO SECO

The three Playas Esterillos extend for miles south of Hermosa. For years they remained off the tourism radar but are now catching on. Swimming here is high-risk due to riptides. Vehicular tracks run along the sands the length of each beach, but you'll need to backtrack to the coast highway to access the next beach.

Craggy Punta Judas separates Hermosa from **Playa Esterillos Oeste,** a favorite with surfers, and with Ticos on weekends. The seven-kilometer (4.5-mile) beach has tide pools at its northern end, where a **sculpture of a mermaid** sits atop the rocks and mollusk fossils are embedded in the rock strata. Farther south, **Esterillos Centro** is accessed by a separate road signed off Highway 34. **Playa Esterillos Este** (also called Playa Valencianillos), separated by a river from Esterillos Centro, is identical to its northerly siblings: kilometers long, ruler straight, with gray sand cleansed by high surf. The southern end of the beach is known as **Playa Bejuco,** reached via a separate access road.

Farther south, about four kilometers (2.5 miles) north of Parrita township, a dirt road leads west from the coast highway and zigzags through African palm plantations until you emerge at **Playa Palma,** separated from Bejuco by yet another river's mouth. Playa Palma extends south to the mouth of the Río Parrita, straddled inland by the small town of **Parrita**, 45 kilometers (28 miles) south of Jacó, and the main service center for a vast African oil palm ranches that extend south from here. A dirt road immediately south of Parrita leads eight kilometers (5 miles) to **Playa Palo Seco,** a black-sand beach. The local primary school maintains a turtle hatchery on the beach, which is backed by the mangrove swamps and braided channels of the Ríos Palo Seco and Damas.

Sports and Recreation

Sky Mountain (tel. 506/2778-3677, www.canopycostarica.com, $65), at La Chirraca, in the mountains about 20 kilometers (12 miles) north of Parrita, lets you whiz by zip line across a mountain gorge; it has 2,195 meters (7,200 feet) of zip lines. The views over the coast are stunning. It's within Reserva Ecológico Creando Naturaleza, with a stable for horseback rides ($50).

Del Pacífico (tel. 506/2778-7070, www.delpacifico.net) is a deluxe residential resort development at Esterillos Este, with a stable offering horseback rides.

Rainmaker Park (tel. 506/2777-3565, www.rainmakercostarica.org, 7am-5pm daily, $15) is a 540-hectare (1,334-acre) private rainforest reserve on the forested slopes of the Fila Chonta mountains, above the hamlet of Pocares, southeast of Parrita and seven kilometers (4.5 miles) inland of Highway 21. It pioneered the concept of suspension-bridge rainforest trails in Costa Rica with six hanging bridges (some span the rainforest canopy) stretched along a loop trail through a river canyon; 15 natural pools are good for bathing. Tours cost $25 guided, $15 self-guided. An early morning birding tour ($25) and a night tour ($35) are offered. A restaurant serves lunches ($5).

Accommodations and Food

There are about two dozen budget or otherwise ho-hum accommodations along the beaches. They mostly attract low- to mid-income Ticos and can get noisy on weekends.

At Esterillos Oeste, the nicest place is **Hotel La Dolce Vita** (tel. 506/2778-7015, www.resortladolcevita.com, low season from

Playa Esterillos Este

$47 s, $65 d, high season from $51 s, $75 d), with self-catering apartments in a motel-style building that extends inland from the beach, hence no ocean views. Rattan furniture attempts a hint at the tropics.

In Esterillos Centro, the place of choice is the French Canadian-run **Casa Amarilla** (tel. 506/2778-8408, U.S./Canada tel. 905-731-6501, www.vrbo.com/59476, low season $125 nightly, $790 per week, high season $155, $980 per week, 5-night minimum), a beautiful two-story home with a kidney-shaped pool. It has two rooms with full kitchens, spacious lounge-dining rooms, and lovely modern baths.

Esterillos Este has the broadest options. The lovely, intimate French-run **Bleu Azul** (tel. 506/2778-8070, www.bleuazul.com, low season $500 weekly, high season $625) has four nicely furnished studio apartments with batik bedspreads and balconies overlooking a circular pool. One is a two-bedroom unit sleeping four people. It specializes in surfing and offers surf lessons, plus massage.

Resorts at Esterillos Este are represented by the upscale beachfront **Hotel Monterey del Mar** (tel. 506/2778-8787, www.montereydelmar.com, low season $130-220 s/d, high season $145-245 s/d), popular with tour groups for its deluxe aesthetic. The 27 spacious rooms and suites are decked out with suave contemporary furnishings and modern amenities, including 32-inch flat-screen TVs. The open-air restaurant (torch-lit at night) is a highlight, plus it has a swimming pool and spa.

The most spectacular place for miles is ★ **Alma de Pacífica** (tel. 506/2778-7070, U.S. tel. 888-960-2562, www.almadelpacifico.com, low season $188-413 s/d, high season $260-485 s/d), sibling to Xandari Plantation near Alajuela. This colorful beachfront boutique hotel in Esterillos Este is set in gorgeous grounds that are themselves a work of art. The moment you enter, you'll understand why both *Condé Nast Traveler* and *Travel + Leisure* ranked this in their top 10 Central and South American Resorts. The vast villas are highlighted by signature waveform wooden ceilings, huge poured-concrete sofas with leather cushions, and gorgeous baths with colorful mosaic showers facing private patio gardens through walls of glass. All the accoutrements you could wish for are there, including thoughtful touches such as magazines, umbrellas, flashlights, and kitchenettes. The restaurant serves gourmet health-conscious fare, and the pool is inviting.

Nestled between beach and lagoon on Playa Palo Seco, the eco-themed **Clandestino Beach Resort** (tel. 506/2779-8807, www.clandestinobeachresort.com, low season $105-120 s, $130-145 d, high season $140-155 s, $165-180 d) makes a great first impression with its soaring *palenque* bar-restaurant and amoeba-shaped infinity pool. Oh-so-romantic and very tropical, there's nothing not to like, including rooms with bamboo furniture atop slate-gray tile floors. The restaurant is the nicest for miles, and the huge oceanfront swimming pool has a water cascade.

A half dozen simple restaurants are scattered along the beaches. The place to hang at Esterillos Oeste is **Restaurant Los Almendros** (tel. 506/2778-7322, 4pm-10pm daily), in a leafy patio garden. It serves local fare, plus Asian and Caribbean dishes. Nearby, **Soda Mary** (tel. 506/2778-7380) has a tour office and surfboard rentals, plus a camping area on lawns.

For gourmet and health-conscious fare, head for the open-air thatched restaurant at **Alma de Pacífica** (tel. 506/2778-7070, 6:30am-10pm daily), in Esterillos Este, which uses organic products grown in its own garden.

Quepos and Manuel Antonio

QUEPOS

The small yet booming port town of Quepos (pop. 12,000) is the gateway for travelers heading to Parque Nacional Manuel Antonio, seven kilometers (4.5 miles) south over a sinuous mountain road lined with hotels, restaurants, and bars. Banana plantations were established in the nearby flatlands in the 1930s, and Quepos rose to prominence as a banana-exporting port. The plantations were blighted by disease in the 1950s, and the bananas were replaced by African palms, which produce oil for food, cosmetics, and machines. The trees stretch in neatly ordered rows for miles north and south of Quepos.

Quepos is sportfishing central, and was so even before the 196-slip **Marina Pez Vela** (tel. 506/2777-9069, www.marinapezvela.

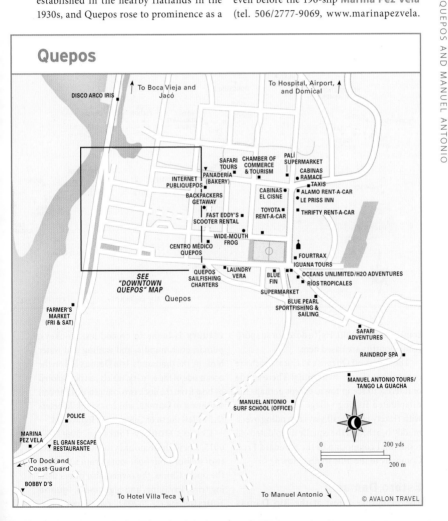

Quepos

© AVALON TRAVEL

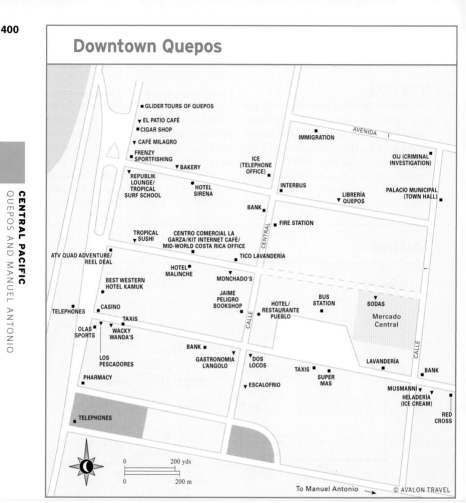

Downtown Quepos

GLIDER TOURS OF QUEPOS
EL PATIO CAFÉ
CIGAR SHOP
CAFÉ MILAGRO
FRENZY SPORTFISHING
BAKERY
REPUBLIK LOUNGE/ TROPICAL SURF SCHOOL
HOTEL SIRENA
BANK
TROPICAL SUSHI
CENTRO COMERCIAL LA GARZA/KIT INTERNET CAFÉ/ MID-WORLD COSTA RICA OFFICE
ATV QUAD ADVENTURE/ REEL DEAL
TICO LAVANDERÍA
HOTEL MALINCHE
MONCHADO'S
BEST WESTERN HOTEL KAMUK
JAIME PELIGRO BOOKSHOP
TELEPHONES
CASINO
TAXIS
HOTEL/ RESTAURANTE PUEBLO
BUS STATION
SODAS
Mercado Central
OLAS SPORTS
WACKY WANDA'S
BANK
LOS PESCADORES
GASTRONOMIA L'ANGOLO
DOS LOCOS
TAXIS
LAVANDERÍA
BANK
PHARMACY
SUPER MAS
ESCALOFRIO
MUSMANNI
HELADERÍA (ICE CREAM)
RED CROSS
TELEPHONES

IMMIGRATION
AVENIDA 1
OIJ (CRIMINAL INVESTIGATION)
ICE (TELEPHONE OFFICE)
INTERBUS
LIBRERÍA QUEPOS
PALACIO MUNICIPAL (TOWN HALL)
FIRE STATION
CENTRAL
CALLE
CALLE

0   200 yds
0   200 m

To Manuel Antonio →   © AVALON TRAVEL

com) opened in 2010. Half a dozen or so sport-fishing outfits are based here.

The waters off Quepos's El Cocal beach are contaminated—no swimming! There's little of interest to see in town, except perhaps the dilapidated fishing village of **Boca Vieja,** with rickety plank walkways extending over a muddy beach; and the equally dilapidated old residential compound of the Standard Fruit Company in the hills south of town.

Estero Damas

The mangrove forest at the **Río Damas** **estuary** is home to crocodiles, monkeys, pumas, coatimundis, and wading and water birds by the thousands. **Isla Damas** lies on the ocean side of the estuary, which can be explored by boat from the dock two kilometers (1.2 miles) southwest of **Damas,** which is four kilometers (2.5 miles) north of Quepos on Highway 34.

Chino's Monkey Tours (tel. 506/2777-0015, www.chinomonkeytours.com) offers two- to four-hour boat tours (from $25) from the dock; Chino, the owner, also offers fishing trips, kayaking, and night tours. **Iguana Tours** (tel. 506/2777-2052, www.iguanatours.

com) and **Kayak Lodge** (tel. 506/2777-6620) offer similar trips from their own dock; the turnoff from the highway is by the soccer field in Damas, where the **Hotel Kayak Lodge** (tel. 506/2777-6620, www.kayak-inn.com) offers kayaking tours of the mangroves.

Río Naranjo

Rancho Los Tucanes (tel. 506/2777-0775, www.rancholostucanes.com), near Londres on the banks of the Río Naranjo. about 10 kilometers (6 miles) east of Quepos, offers ATV tours, white-water rafting, and horseback rides to the 90-meter (300-foot) Los Tucanes waterfall in a private wildlife reserve.

En route you'll pass **Villa Vanilla** (tel. 506/2779-1155, www.rainforestspices.com), at Buena Vista, 10 kilometers (6 miles) east of Quepos, an organic spice farm with three kilometers (2 miles) of trails. It has fascinating two-hour educational tours (9am and 1pm Mon.-Sat., 9am Sun., $20) that include a hike to a massive ceiba tree.

Buses run from Quepos to Londres six times 4:30am-6pm daily.

★ Santa Juana Rural Mountain Adventure Tour

Deep in the Fila Chonta mountains, inland of Quepos, the community of Santa Juana is at the center of an ambitious ecological project established by Jim Damalas, owner of the Hotel Villas Si Como No in Manuel Antonio. Community members are engaged in ecotourism projects, such as breeding butterflies, reforestation, and growing and making products for use in local hotels. Meanwhile, the 1,000-hectare (2,470-acre) terrain is a pristine mountain sanctuary with trails, waterfalls, and natural swimming pools. The **Santa Juana Rural Mountain Adventure Tour** (tel. 506/2777-1043, www. sicomono.com, $125 pp) grants access and provides an educational "farm experience" (such as picking coffee or citrus) that includes a campesino lunch. An INBio biological station is planned, and there's a butterfly garden and a snake exhibit. The tour can be combined with a canopy zip-line safari.

Entertainment and Events

Quepos's three-week **Carnival** (mid-Feb.-early Mar.) offers plenty of entertainment.

For live music and impromptu dancing, try **El Gran Escape** (tel. 506/2777-0395, www. elgranescape.com, 8am-midnight daily), which also shows U.S. football games on the big screen and has happy hour 5pm-7pm daily.

white-faced monkey at Isla Damas

For dancing, locals gravitate to **Arco Iris** (tel. 506/2777-2061, 9pm-4am daily, $5), an air-conditioned disco on a barge north of the bridge in town; don't even think of getting here before midnight. The DJ spins everything from reggae to salsa.

A more discerning dance crowd heads to the upscale New York-style **Cuban Republik Lounge** (tel. 506/8394-7350, 6pm-2:30am daily, men $2, women free), on the bayfront road in town, a chic venue for sounds from Latin to electronic; Thursday is Latin night, Friday is "ladies' night." This is *the* place to get your groove on. Upstairs, **Mogambo Lounge** (tel. 506/2777-6310, 3pm-11pm) is a gay bar.

Hotel Kamuk (tel. 506/2777-0811, noon-3am daily), on the bayfront road in town, has a 24-hour casino.

Sports and Recreation

For guided horseback tours, try **Finca Valmy Tours** (tel. 506/2779-1118, www.valmytours.com); you can even overnight on a six-hour round-trip ride into the mountains and Santa María de Dota. **Fourtrax Adventures** (tel. 506/2777-1829, www.fourtraxadventure.com) and **ATV Quad Adventures** (tel. 506/2777-6600, www.atvquadadventure.com) specialize in ATV tours. You can rent boats from **Tres Niñas Boat Rental** (tel. 506/8305-0041, www.tresninasboatrental.com) for whale-watching and fishing.

Segway (tel. 506/2777-5151, www.segway-costa-rica.com), at Marina Pez Vela, offers tours around town and at Isla Cocal aboard Segways. Surfers are served by the **Tropical Surf School** (tel. 506/2774-0001, www.tropicalsurfschool.com).

For a one-stop adventure experience, head to **ADR Adventure Park** (tel. 506/2777-0082, www.adradventurepark.com), at San Antonio de Damas, with waterfall rappelling, a zip line, a waterfall zip line, a 4WD safari, and more. An all-day experience costs $130.

CANOPY AND CANYONEERING TOURS

For adrenaline-driven zip-line canopy tours, contact **Canopy Safari** (tel. 506/2777-0100, www.canopysafari.com) or **Titi Canopy Tour** (tel. 506/2777-3130, www.titicanopytour.com). If getting soaked while rappelling a waterfall sounds like fun, call **Quepos Canyoning** (tel. 506/2779-1127, www.quepocanyoning.com). **Midworld Costa Rica** (tel. 506/2777-7181, www.midworldcostarica.com), a 30-minute drive from Quepos, also has zip-lining, rappelling, a Superman line, a high ropes puzzle course, and ATVs on its own forest reserve in the mountains.

KAYAKING, RAFTING, AND WATER SPORTS

Iguana Tours (tel. 506/2777-2052, www.iguanatours.com) offer sea-kayaking trips, boat tours of the mangroves, river-rafting trips, and horseback rides. **H2O Adventures** (tel. 506/2777-4092, www.h2ocr.com), a franchise of Ríos Tropicales, has similar tours; **Quepoa Expeditions** (tel. 506/2777-0058, www.quepoa.com) has inflatable kayak ("rubber duckies") trips; and **Amigos del Río** (tel. 506/2777-0082, www.amigosdelrio.net) offers kayaking and white-water rafting on the Río Savegre. **Safari Mangrove Tours** (tel. 506/2777-7111, www.safariadventurescr.com) specializes in kayak trips to Damas.

Planet Dolphin (tel. 506/2777-1647, www.planetdolphin.com) has a boat tour in search of whales and dolphins ($65, includes snorkeling), plus a catamaran adventure to Parque Nacional Manuel Antonio ($65). **Sunset Sails Tours** (tel. 506/2777-1304, www.sunsetsailstours.com) and **Blue Pearl** (tel. 506/2777-2516, www.sailingtourmanuelantonio.com) offer sailing excursions by trimaran. For diving, contact **Oceans Unlimited** (tel. 506/2777-3171, www.oceansunlimitedcr.com).

SPORTFISHING

The Quepos region offers outstanding sportfishing for marlin and sailfish, December through August, while the inshore reefs are home to snapper, amberjack, wahoo, and tuna. The many operators in Quepos include: **Frenzy Sportfishing** (tel. 506/8851-0935, www.frenzysportfishing.com), **Quepos Sailfishing Charters** (tel. 506/2777-2025, www.queposfishing.com), **J. P. Sportfishing Tours** (tel. 506/2777-1613, www.jpsportfishing.com), **Reel Deal Sportfishing** (tel. 506/8869-2522, www.reeldealsportfishing.net), and **Bluefin Sportfishing** (tel. 506/2777-0000, www.bluefinsportfishing.com).

Shopping

Zoíla, a delightful Cuban, rolls excellent-quality cigars at **The Cigar Shoppe** (tel. 506/2777-2208, 7am-6pm Mon.-Sat.), next to Café Milagro on the bayfront road in town. **Jaime Peligro Books** (Calle Central, tel. 506/2777-7106, www.queposbooks.com, 9:30am-5:30pm Mon.-Sat.), one block west of the bus station, has a huge selection of used and some new books.

Accommodations

Hotels in town are about a 20-minute bus or taxi ride from Parque Nacional Manuel Antonio; the mountain road over the hill to the park is lined with more upscale hotels than are available in Quepos. Staying in town is cheaper and offers the benefit of services close at hand, but it is invariably noisy. There are dozens of options. The following are the pick of the litter.

Who can resist a place called ★ **Wide Mouth Frog** (tel. 506/2777-2798, www.widemouthfrog.org, dorm $11-13 pp, rooms with shared bath $30-40 s/d, rooms with private bath $40-50 s/d, cash only)? Two blocks east of the bus station, this clean backpacker haven—run to high standards by a Kiwi and a Brit—is a hip option, with a pool, a kitchen, games, parking, and more. It has two dorms and 22 private rooms, all with beautiful tiled showers. It charges $10 extra for air-conditioning. There's a TV room, free Wi-Fi, a laundry, and peaceful gardens.

I've laid my head more than once at **Cabinas El Cisne** (tel. 506/2777-2104, with fan $25 s, $35 d, with a/c $35 s, $45 d), one block north of the church, with secure parking. Chose from 12 cabins with fans, or 12 new and more spacious air-conditioned rooms in a three-story unit. Nearby **Cabinas Ramacee** (tel. 506/2777-0590) offers a near identical alternative.

The best bargain is the two-story white-and-blue ★ **Hotel Sirena** (tel. 506/2777-0572, www.lasirenahotel.com, low season $63-89 s, $73-99 d, high season $83-117 s, $93-127 d), with 10 double rooms (most with air-conditioning) with ceiling fans, whitewashed walls and a delightful contemporary aesthetic, including modern baths with glass-brick showers and coral-stone floors. It's perfectly located in the heart of town. The courtyard dining area has a sundeck and a pool. Wi-Fi is free.

The modestly classy **Best Western Hotel Kamuk** (tel. 506/2777-0811, www.kamuk.co.cr, low season $70-105 s/d, high season $80-130, including continental breakfast), on the bayfront road in town, has 44 spacious and elegant nicely furnished air-conditioned rooms, some with balconies, all with TVs and phones, all beautifully decorated in light pastels. The Miraolas Bar and Restaurant on the third floor has vistas. There's a small boutique, a pool, a classy bar, and small casino.

Food

Quepos has excellent options for dining. The *mercado central,* by the bus station, has budget *sodas* serving local dishes.

The place to start your day is Café Milagro's **El Patio Café** (tel. 506/2777-2272, www.cafemilagro.com, 6am-6pm daily), on the bayfront road in town, serving *gallo pinto,* granola with fruit and yogurt ($4), ice cream sundaes, homemade baked goods, sandwiches, raspberry iced mochas, lattes, and espresso to be enjoyed in a delightful airy space. Next door, the same owners have **Café Milagro** (tel. 506/2777-1707, 9am-5pm Mon.-Sat. low season, 6am-10pm daily high season), which roasts its coffee fresh and sells iced coffee, espresso, and cappuccino.

My favorite restaurant is ★ **El Gran Escape Restaurante** (tel. 506/2777-0395, www.elgranescape.com, 6am-11pm Wed.-Mon., $5-20), at a new location in Marina Pez Vela, serving salads, seafood, surf and turf, tuna melts, enchiladas, killer burgers, and coconut curry chicken, with large portions at bargain prices enjoyed in the open air. Tiny **Tropical Sushi** (tel. 506/2777-1710, 4:30pm-11pm daily) serves quality sashimi and sushi from Japanese-born chef Fuji's very capable hands. All-you-can-eat sushi is served 5pm-7pm daily.

For Mexican fare, head to **Dos Locos** (Calle Central, tel. 506/2777-1526, 7am-11pm Mon.-Sat., 11am-8pm Sun., $3-15), 50 meters west of the bus station, offering breakfast omelets, chimichangas, and chili con carne; my *burrito gigante* was superb. It has live music on Wednesday evening and Saturday afternoon. Mexican-themed **Monchado's** (tel. 506/2777-1972), one block north and east, competes with innovative and eclectic dishes that include an excellent tongue in salsa ($5.50); it has live music in high season.

Hugely popular, **Escalofrio** (Calle Central, tel. 506/2777-0833, 2:30pm-10pm Tues.-Sun.) is an atmospheric Italian restaurant open to the street and serving the to-be-expected dishes, including wood-fired pizza. You can also gorge on banana splits and shakes, but the main draw is its more than 20 homemade gelato flavors. It's divine and has free Wi-Fi.

You'll think you're in New York when you pop into **Gastronomía L'Angolo** (Calle Central, tel. 506/2777-4129, 8am-9pm Mon.-Sat.), a *real* Italian deli with hams and cheeses, plus paninis and pastas. It faces Escalofrio. For baked goods, head to **Musmanni** (tel. 506/2777-3055), at the southeast corner of the bus station.

Information and Services

The **Cámara de Comercio y Turismo** (tel. 506/2777-0749, www.camaradequepos.com),

one block north of the soccer field, represents local tourism companies and can provide information.

Hospital Dr. Max Teran V (tel. 506/2777-0020) is three kilometers (2 miles) south of Quepos on the Costanera Sur. In town, **Lifeguard Medical** (tel. 506/2220-0911) offers 24-hour emergency medical care. The **Red Cross** is one block east of the bus station. **Farmacia Quepos** (tel. 506/2777-0038) is open 8am-9pm daily.

The **police station** (tel. 506/2777-2117) is 100 meters (330 feet) south of the town center, en route to the dock; the OIJ (tel. 506/2777-0511) is two blocks northeast of the bus station. For immigration and visa issues, check with **Migración** (tel. 506/2777-0150, 8am-4pm Mon.-Fri.), 50 meters (165 feet) west of the OIJ.

The **post office** is on the north side of the soccer field. For Internet, head to **Internet Publiquepos** (tel. 506/2777-2161), one block northeast of the bus station; or **KIT Internet** (tel. 506/2777-7575) in Centro Comercial La Garza. Laundries include **Lavandería Casa Tica** (tel. 506/2777-2533, 8am-5pm Mon.-Sat.), adjoining the bus station.

Getting There and Away

Both **SANSA** (tel. 506/2229-4100, U.S./Canada tel. 877-767-2672, www.flysansa.com) and **Nature Air** (tel. 506/2299-6000, U.S. tel. 800-235-9272, www.natureair.com) have scheduled daily service to Quepos. SANSA offers hotel-airport transfers ($5 pp).

Transportes Delio Morales (tel. 506/2223-5567, Manuel Antonio tel. 506/2777-0318, www.autotransportesdm.com) buses depart San José for Quepos (direct, 4.5 hours, $7) from Calle 16, Avenida 3, six times daily 6am-7:30pm. Six slower buses also run daily. **Transportes Quepos** (tel. 506/2777-0743) buses depart Puntarenas six times daily 5am-4:30pm. **Interbus** (tel. 506/4100-0888, www.interbusonline.com) has shuttles between Quepos and San José as well as to other major travel destinations.

Getting Around

For taxis, call **Quepos Taxi** (tel. 506/2777-0425). Car rental agencies in town include **Alamo Rent-a-Car** (tel. 506/2242-7733, www.alamocostarica.com), **Budget** (tel. 506/2436-2000, www.budget.co.cr), and **Toyota** (tel. 506/2777-9196), which has an office at Marian Pez Vela.

QUEPOS TO MANUEL ANTONIO

Immediately southeast of Quepos, a road climbs sharply over the forested headland of Punta Quepos and snakes, dips, and rises south along a ridge for seven kilometers (4.5 miles) before dropping down to the evolving community of **Manuel Antonio.**

The hilltop 12-hectare (30-acre) **Manuel Antonio Nature Park and Wildlife Refuge** (tel. 506/2777-0850, www.sicomono. com, 8am-4pm daily), mid-way between Quepos and Manuel Antonio, is a project of Hotel Villas Si Como No and features multi-level trails that wind through a netted butterfly garden (adults $15, children $8), natural poison dart frog exhibits, and a crocodile and caiman lagoon (adults $20, children $15). The forested reserve is excellent for sighting monkeys and other endangered wildlife. Hourly guided nature walks ($10) are offered, as is a Jungle Night Walk (5:30pm daily, adults $39, children $29)—the trails use ultraviolet lighting to show off insect markings normally visible by night to other insects with ultraviolet vision. It has guided bird-watching tours by reservation at 4pm and 6pm daily.

Entertainment and Events

For drinks, the always-lively **Marlintinis** (tel. 506/2777-7474, www.marlintinisgrill.com, 11am-1am daily), about one mile south of Quepos, has live music and DJs, large-screen TVs, and great cocktails.

El Avión (tel. 506/2777-3378, 2pm-10pm daily), three miles south of Quepos, is named for the Fairchild C-123 transport plane now turned into a bar. It has live music Monday-Saturday. The aircraft-bar, opposite Casitas Eclipse, dates from 1954 and was used by the CIA to run arms to the Contras in Nicaragua in the 1980s. According to the posted spiel, when shot down by the Sandinistas, a sister C-123 was responsible for "breaking open the Contra affair that exposed the story and the Reagan administration's illegal and secret scheme."

The **Bat Cave** (tel. 506/2777-3489, 7pm-midnight daily) at La Mansion Inn, on the road to Playa Biesanz, is a piece of Tolkien fantasy, not least because it is entered by a Lilliputian door. This limestone cave-turned-bar has fish tanks inset in the walls, and a stupendous polished hardwood bar top. For live music, head to **Bambu Jam** (tel. 506/2777-3369, 6pm-10pm daily), with live Latin music Tuesday and Friday.

For cocktails, **Karolas** (tel. 506/2777-8880, 7am-10pm daily), at the beachfront Preserve at Los Altos, is the hippest lounge-bar around. This urbane open-air space draws a sophisticated crowd that prefers martinis to Budweiser. It has happy hour 4pm-7pm daily.

Football fans should head to **Billfish Sportbar** (tel. 506/2777-0411) at the Byblos Hotel, about 2.5 miles south of Quepos, which screens football games on Monday nights. Friday is "ladies night," with free drinks for women 8pm-midnight.

Gay and lesbian visitors enjoy sexy fun at **Liquid Lounge Disco** (tel. 506/2777-5158, 8pm-2am Tues.-Sun.), near the beach. Theme nights include oldies on Tuesday, margarita night on Wednesday, and Latin music on Sunday. Go on Friday for sexy live male and female dancers, and on Saturday when a DJ spins the hottest sounds. Everyone is welcome.

How about a movie in a surround-sound theater? Head to **Hotel Villas Si Como No** (tel. 506/2777-0777), about three miles south of Quepos, for dinner, and you'll also get free entrance to the movie at 8:30pm daily.

Sports and Recreation

Manuel Antonio Surf School (tel. 506/2777-4842, www.masurfschool.com) offers surf lessons; it has a beach outlet. The

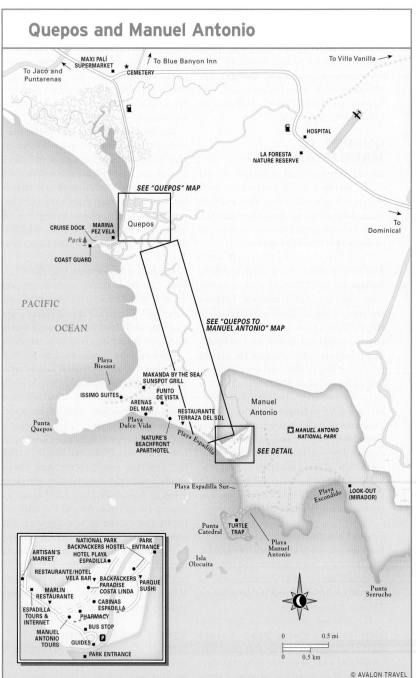

Quepos and Manuel Antonio

To Jacó and Puntarenas

MAXI PALÍ SUPERMARKET

To Blue Banyon Inn

★ CEMETERY

To Villa Vanilla

HOSPITAL

LA FORESTA NATURE RESERVE

SEE "QUEPOS" MAP

CRUISE DOCK
MARINA PEZ VELA
Quepos

Park

COAST GUARD

To Dominical

PACIFIC

OCEAN

SEE "QUEPOS TO MANUEL ANTONIO" MAP

Playa Biesanz

MAKANDA BY THE SEA/ SUNSPOT GRILL

ISSIMO SUITES

PUNTO DE VISTA

ARENAS DEL MAR

Punta Quepos

Playa Dulce Vida

RESTAURANTE TERRAZA DEL SOL

Manuel Antonio

NATURE'S BEACHFRONT APARTHOTEL

Playa Espadilla

■ MANUEL ANTONIO NATIONAL PARK

SEE DETAIL

Playa Espadilla Sur

Playa Escondido
LOOK-OUT (MIRADOR)

Punta Catedral
TURTLE TRAP

Isla Olocuita

Playa Manuel Antonio

Punta Serrucho

Detail inset:

ARTISAN'S MARKET

NATIONAL PARK BACKPACKERS HOSTEL
HOTEL PLAYA ESPADILLA

PARK ENTRANCE

RESTAURANTE/HOTEL VELA BAR

BACKPACKERS PARADISE COSTA LINDA

PARQUE SUSHI

MARLIN RESTAURANTE

CABINAS ESPADILLA

ESPADILLA TOURS & INTERNET

PHARMACY

MANUEL ANTONIO TOURS

BUS STOP

GUIDES

PARK ENTRANCE

0   0.5 mi

0   0.5 km

© AVALON TRAVEL

Quepos to Manuel Antonio

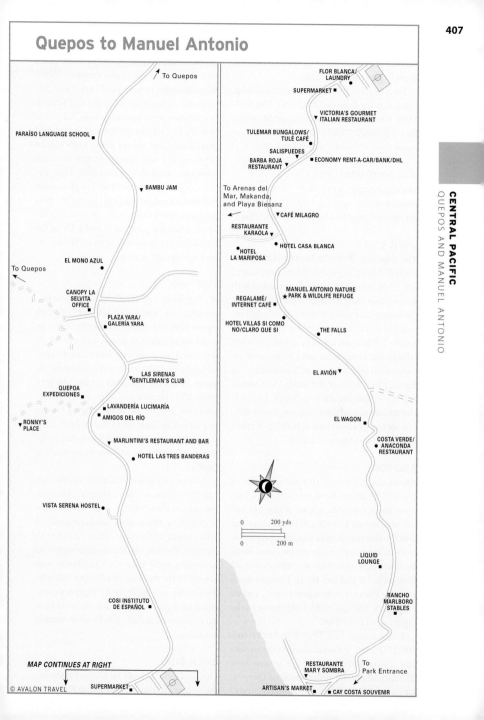

To Quepos

FLOR BLANCA/
LAUNDRY

SUPERMARKET ■

VICTORIA'S GOURMET
▼ ITALIAN RESTAURANT

PARAÍSO LANGUAGE SCHOOL ■

TULEMAR BUNGALOWS/
TULÉ CAFÉ

SALISPUEDES
BARBA ROJA
RESTAURANT ▼

■ ECONOMY RENT-A-CAR/BANK/DHL

▼ BAMBU JAM

To Arenas del
Mar, Makanda,
and Playa Biesanz

▼CAFÉ MILAGRO

RESTAURANTE
KARAOLA ▼

● HOTEL CASA BLANCA

● HOTEL
LA MARIPOSA

To Quepos

EL MONO AZUL ●

CANOPY LA
SELVITA
OFFICE ■

MANUEL ANTONIO NATURE
★ PARK & WILDLIFE REFUGE

REGALAMÉ/
INTERNET CAFÉ ■

PLAZA YARA/
GALERÍA YARA

HOTEL VILLAS SI COMO
NO/CLARO QUE SI

● THE FALLS

LAS SIRENAS
▼GENTLEMAN'S CLUB

EL AVIÓN ▼

QUEPOA
EXPEDICIONES ■

▼ RONNY'S
PLACE

LAVANDERÍA LUCIMARÍA ■
■ AMIGOS DEL RÍO

EL WAGON ■

COSTA VERDE/
● ANACONDA
RESTAURANT

▼ MARLINTINI'S RESTAURANT AND BAR

■ HOTEL LAS TRES BANDERAS

VISTA SERENA HOSTEL ●

0   200 yds

0   200 m

LIQUID
LOUNGE ■

RANCHO
MARLBORO
STABLES
■

COSI INSTITUTO
DE ESPAÑOL ■

MAP CONTINUES AT RIGHT

© AVALON TRAVEL

SUPERMARKET ■

RESTAURANTE
MAR Y SOMBRA ▼

To
Park Entrance

ARTISAN'S MARKET ■   ■ CAY COSTA SOUVENIR

CENTRAL PACIFIC
QUEPOS AND MANUEL ANTONIO

Tennis Club Quepos (tel. 506/8666-4212, www.tennisclubquepos.com), in the Palmas Pacífica residential resort, is open for nonresidents to play 6am-6pm daily.

For a relaxing massage or health treatment, check into the **Raindrop Spa** (tel. 506/2777-2880, www.raindropspa.com), or **Serenity Spa** (tel. 506/2777-0777, ext. 220, www.sicomono.com) at Hotel Villas Si Como No.

Accommodations

More expensive hotels have loftier, breezy perches on the road from Quepos. For budget options, head to Manuel Antonio village.

UNDER $25

The ridge-top ★ **Vista Serena Hostel** (tel. 506/2777-5162, www.vistaserena.com, dorms $10-16 pp, rooms $45-60 s/d) is a hostel with a view, deservedly beloved by backpackers for the loving care and all-in-the-family feel infused by owner Conrad and his mom. There's a cozy TV lounge, and a broad veranda has table soccer, hammocks, and a barbecue where communal feasts draw out "community" in the very best sense of the word. Vista Serena has Wi-Fi and free calls to North America. Dorms and almost luxurious apartment-style private rooms are clean and inviting. It offers its own Budget Mangrove Tour.

$50-100

About one kilometer (0.6 miles) south of Quepos, **El Mono Azul** (tel. 506/2777-1548, www.hotelmonoazul.com, low season $45-100 s/d, high season $50-120 s/d) has 20 clean and comfortable rooms in handsome condo-style units facing a small and pretty oval pool. Some have fans only; others are air-conditioned; all have cable TV and free Wi-Fi. There's a small gym, an Internet café, a game room, and an art gallery, and free movies are shown in the highly rated restaurant.

I like **Hotel Las Tres Banderas** (tel. 506/2777-1871, www.hoteltresbanderas.com, low season $60-150 s/d, high season $80-200 s/d), about 1.5 miles south of Quepos, for its friendly Polish owner Andrzej "Andy"

Nowacki. This two-story Spanish colonial-style property has 14 spacious air-conditioned rooms in three types, including three suites with glossy hardwoods and exquisite baths. Balconies open to both pool (front) and forest (rear). Suites have minibars and fridges. Two deluxe rooms have king beds. All rooms have Wi-Fi. You can opt for a fully equipped apartment (low season $200, high season $250), or the self-contained stone-walled cabin apartment (low season $200, high season $250). Meals are prepared at an outside grill and served on the patio beside the pool and large whirlpool tub. Trails lead into the forest. There's a game room and a TV in the bar, where live music is hosted on Sunday afternoons in high season.

$100-150

★ **The Falls** (tel. 506/2777-1332, www.fallsresortcr.com, low season $100-245 s/d, high season $149-350 s/d), named for the cascades in the lush gardens, is gorgeous. Luxuriously appointed with quality linens and tasteful white-and-chocolate color schemes, the rooms have king beds, flat-screen TVs with cable, DVD players, and terraces. Three luxury suites are connected by hanging bridges and served by their own infinity pool. Low-season rates are a steal for this exquisite property. It is located about three miles south of Quepos.

Perennially popular **Costa Verde** (tel. 506/2777-0584, www.hotelcostaverde.com, low season from $87 s/d, high season from $115 s/d), a three-story modern unit 3.5 miles south of Quepos, offers rooms with kitchens, studios, and studio apartments. Its most memorable feature is a penthouse suite housed in the fuselage of a Boeing 727, with the shower and toilet in the skipper's cockpit; at least you won't lack for overhead bins, but this wood-lined metal tube gets extremely hot inside.

OVER $150

The first deluxe hotel in Manuel Antonio, the venerable and ever-evolving **Hotel La**

Mariposa (tel. 506/2777-0355, U.S. tel. 800-572-6440, www.hotelmariposa.com, low season $160-335 s/d, high season $225-450 s/d), three miles south of Quepos, still has some of the best views in the area. It has 66 air-conditioned rooms. Eight vast standard rooms in the main house offer garden views from lower stories, and fabulous coastal views from upper rooms, enjoyed through picture windows and wraparound balconies, but I don't like their frumpy decor or the access by a frail metal spiral staircase. Ten split-level Mediterranean-style cottage-villas nestle on the hillcrest; each has a deck—with outside whirlpools in the junior suites—and a skylighted bath. Deluxe units have beam ceilings with fans and whirlpool bathtubs. Fifteen premier suites and a penthouse with walls of glass have striking contemporary furnishings. The restaurant serves French-inspired fare. It has two swimming pools, one an infinity pool, with swim-up bars, a massage room, and a gift store. A trail leads to the beach.

Readers report favorably on **Tulemar Bungalows** (tel. 506/2777-0580, www.tulemar.com, from $185 s/d), 2.5 miles south of Quepos, which claims its "own exclusive beach" with free kayaks and snorkeling, a forest reserve, and luxury ocean-view villas and bungalows in various sizes and styles. There's a small infinity pool with a bar, plus a shop and a snack bar.

Romantic deluxe villas are the theme at **Makanda by the Sea** (tel. 506/2777-0442, U.S. tel. 888-625-2632, www.makanda.com, low season $200-765 s/d, high season $300-1,165 s/d), with an enviable setting on the road to Playa Biesanz. Eleven elegant individually styled timber-beamed villas and studios line walkways that weave through a series of Japanese gardens designed into the hillside. All have king beds, vaulted ceilings, and minimalist decor that melds Milan with Kyoto. Wall-to-wall French doors open to wraparound verandas. The design extends to a pool suspended on the hillside, with a whirlpool tub and the exceptional Sunsport Poolside Bar and Grill. A complimentary breakfast is delivered to your door each morning. It's a long hike to the private beach, which lacks facilities, but I love the aesthetic here.

Issimo Suites (tel. 506/2777-4410, U.S./Canada tel. 888-400-1985, www.issimosuites.com, low season $189-525 s/d, high season $229-635 s/d) enjoys an enviable position with fantastic views on the road to Playa Biesanz. I love its contemporary style. Clad with coral-stone floors, the nine suites are gorgeous and

the airplane suite at Costa Verde hotel

have leopard-print spreads, wraparound sofas, and heaps of light pouring in through walls of glass opening to stone-paved balconies (the presidential suite even has its own patio pool). The restaurant has fabulous views, the lounge bar boasts a large-screen TV, and there's a deluxe spa plus a plunge pool used for dive training. Watch for special packages.

Eco-friendly **Arenas del Mar** (tel. 506/2777-2777, www.arenasdelmar.com, low season $270-530 s/d, high season $330-690 s/d) is the sole hotel in the area with both a forested hillside perch and direct beach access. The Asian-inspired lobby has a huge open-air bar and stylish restaurant (serving contemporary Costa Rican cuisine) opening to a free-form pool with a deck that has views over Playa Espadilla. Albeit small, the 38 one- and two-bedroom air-conditioned suites in seven three-story blocks have a stylish aesthetic, divinely comfortable beds, flat-screen TVs, Wi-Fi, ceilings studded with halogen lighting, and whirlpools inset in balconies—many with beach views. Families might opt for huge two-bedroom apartments. Its position overlooking *both* Playa Espadilla and Playa Dulce Vida is unbeatable. Golf carts ferry you up and down from the parking lot and to the hotel's beach club at Playitas, where some of the guest rooms are located. It's one of only a fistful of five-leaf hotels in the Certification for Sustainable Tourism program.

My favorite hotel remains ★ **Hotel Villas Si Como No** (tel. 506/2777-0777, U.S./Canada tel. 888-742-6667, www.sicomono.com, low season $225-350 s/d, high season $250-400 s/d), a lively, family-friendly resort hotel about three miles south of Quepos with 58 spacious and elegant suites with balconies and fantastic views. Eighteen deluxe wheelchair-accessible units have an even classier contemporary aesthetic, with king beds, oversize sofas, flat-screen TVs, and fabulous baths with huge walk-in showers. Three honeymoon suites have garden whirlpool tubs, and there's a three-bedroom penthouse suite plus apartment units. The ecologically state-of-the-art hotel has earned five leaves in the Certification for Sustainable Tourism campaign. A pool and sundeck feature a waterslide, cascades, a whirlpool, and a swim-up bar. A second pool is for adults only. Two restaurants are among Manuel Antonio's finest. There's also a state-of-the-art movie theater, a conference center, and an upscale spa. It runs its own tours, including the highly recommended Santa Juana Mountain Tour.

For better or worse, Manuel Antonio got

view of Manuel Antonio from Hotel Villas Si Como No

its first high-rise complex with the 2010 opening of the beachfront **The Preserve at Los Altos** (tel. 506/2777-1197, www.thepreserve-atlosaltos.com, from $850), about three miles south of Quepos. The units have a chic aesthetic, with pewter slate floors, marble counters, and a stylish chocolate, slate, and white color scheme. All floors have two units, each with direct elevator access. All are huge three-bedroom, 2.5-bath apartment suites with balconies, custom-designed handcrafted furniture, and full kitchens. Private chefs can be requested. The bi-level penthouse sleeps eight people and has a sensational master bath. An infinity pool and a sundeck stud spacious lawns with wonderful views down toward the ocean. It has a top-class gym, plus a rooftop hot tub and a private beach club. The Karolas restaurant is here.

The jaw-dropping ★ **Punto de Vista** (tel. 506/8841-8411, www.puntodevistacr.com, low season from $3,275, high season $3,975, for up to 12 people), about three miles south of Quepos, is an architectural mind-blower with a fine hillside venue. The inspired design is the work of the owner, architect David Konwiser, who created this five-story, 10-bedroom structure with nautically inspired walls of glass on three sides and a surfeit of marble, natural stone, and white cement. You'll dine alfresco on the rooftop deck (which has a triangular hot tub), and swim in an infinity pool illuminated by colored lights at night. World-renowned architect I. M. Pei has even vacationed here.

Food

The place for breakfast is **Café Milagro** (tel. 506/2777-0794, www.cafemilagro.com, 6am-10pm daily), about three miles south of Quepos, opposite Hotel Casa Blanca, with a full array of coffee drinks, pastries, sandwiches, and Nuevo Latino fusion dinners (at its **Bistro Latino,** also here) to be enjoyed on a tree-shaded patio; try the delicious shrimp in coconut-rum sauce with mango-infused rice.

Worth a short but rugged journey, **Ronny's Place** (tel. 506/2777-5120, www.ronnysplace.com, noon-10pm daily, $2-10), one kilometer (0.6 miles) west of Quepoa Expeditions, about two miles south of Quepos, is *the* place to enjoy simple but tasty local fare, including seafood, with a hilltop ocean view. Try the caramelized pumpkin in cane juice, best washed down with a piña colada served in a pineapple, or the house's famous sangria.

The rustic but hip *palenque* at **Bambu Jam** (tel. 506/2777-3369, 6pm-10pm daily), one kilometer (0.6 miles) south of Quepos, is a fabulous venue. The French-run restaurant serves the likes of beef stuffed with gorgonzola ($15) and mahimahi with almonds and lime ($12). Leave room for the profiteroles ($5).

For romantic elegance and tremendous nouvelle cuisine, head to the open-air ★ **Claro Que Seafood Grill** (tel. 506/2777-0777, 6:30pm-10:30pm daily) at Hotel Si Como No. I enjoyed fried squid ($6), roasted bell peppers, olives, and avocado salad ($7), stuffed ravioli with seafood and spinach ($10), and chocolate ice cream pie. Equally romantic by night is the ★ **Sunspot Grill** (tel. 506/2777-0442, low season noon-8pm, 11am-10pm daily high season), at the Makanda by the Sea hotel. This classy spot serves *bocas* such as calamari, mussels in chardonnay broth ($7-9), quesadillas, sandwiches, and huge salads for lunch. Dinner is a romantic candlelit gourmet affair; the menu includes gourmet pizzas, scallops with blackberry and balsamic reduction ($20), and divine focaccia with homemade herb butter. The extensive wine list includes many California reserves.

I enjoy the hip, torch-lit, open-air ambience and gourmet fusion fare at **Karolas** (tel. 506/2777-8880, 7am-10pm daily), in the gardens of the beachfront Preserve at Los Altos. The urbane decor includes pewter floors. Lunch might mean a chicken wrap ($8) or a burger. For my most recent dinner, I chose wisely: a superb tuna tartare appetizer ($7) followed by Thai chicken with rice and macadamia sauce ($12). Ocean views are a plus.

A Manuel Antonio institution since 1975, **Barba Roja** (tel. 506/2777-5159, www.

barbarojarestaurant.com, 4pm-10pm daily), about three miles south of Quepos, has superb ocean vistas and is known for great surf and turf. Nearby, **Salispuedes Tapas Bar** (tel. 506/2777-5019, 7am-10pm Wed.-Mon.) has a great ocean view and gets packed, especially at sunset. Shared plates include such treats as sashimi and *frijolitos blancos* (white beans stewed with chicken).

You could be forgiven for dining two nights in a row at **Victoria's Gourmet Italian Restaurant** (tel. 506/2777-5143, www.victoriasgourmet.com, 4pm-11pm Mon.-Sat.), about two miles south of Quepos, another fantastic option for the pasta grill, gourmet pizza, and divine Italian fare such as tuna chipotle and jumbo shrimp. The number-one Italian restaurant in town, it hosts live classical guitar.

There's even an Israeli restaurant, **El Wagon** (tel. 506/2777-0584) in an old railroad carriage opposite Hotel Costa Verde. Oddly, it pitches its Middle Eastern fare with English beer.

Information and Services

The **Cafetal Café** (tel. 506/2777-0777, 7:15am-10pm daily), next to Hotel Villas Si Como No, offers Internet service, including Wi-Fi, as does **Espadilla Tours & Internet** (tel. 506/2777-5334), by the beach. **Lavandería Lucimaria** (tel. 506/2777-2164), near Gaia Hotel, is a laundry.

Spanish-language programs are available at **La Academia de Español D'Amore** (tel. 506/2777-0233, www.academiadamore.com), about three kilometers (2 miles) south of Quepos; **Costa Rica Spanish Institute** (COSI, tel. 506/2777-0021, www.cosi.co.cr); and **El Paraíso Spanish Language School** (tel. 506/2777-4681, www.elparaisoschool.com).

MANUEL ANTONIO

Though the entire region south of Quepos is referred to as Manuel Antonio, the community of Manuel Antonio consists of a handful of hotels and restaurants backing **Playa Espadilla**—a two-kilometer (1.2-mile)

gray-sand scimitar that runs south to Parque Nacional Manuel Antonio. Crocodiles inhabit the lagoon at the north end of Playa Espadilla (they can sometimes be seen swimming in the bay), beyond which lies **Playita,** also called Playa Dulce Vida, a small beach framed by tall headlands. Other beaches are tucked into tiny coves, but the only one accessible to the public is **Playa Biesanz,** facing north toward Quepos. Beware of riptides!

Alas, development has gotten out of control. For example, a developer with land adjoining Hotel Arboleda has clear-cut the forest behind Playa Espadilla for condominiums called OceanAire; a pristine shorefront is now ruined.

Marlboro Stables (tel. 506/2777-1108), 200 meters (660 feet) before Playa Espadilla, offers guided horseback rides. **Farmacia La Económica** (tel. 506/2777-5370, 8am-8pm daily) is down by the beach in Manuel Antonio hamlet.

Accommodations

By Playa Espadilla, the best budget option is **Backpackers Paradise Costa Linda** (tel. 506/2777-0304, rooms $10 pp, apartments $40 s/d), 200 meters (660 feet) inland of Playa Espadilla. It has 22 basic rooms with shared and uninspiring outside toilets and showers, plus apartments with private baths. The handsome frontage belies the dour interior, although the restaurant is attractive. It has free Wi-Fi and an Internet café, plus laundry and luggage storage.

Offering one of Costa Rica's premier beachfront vistas, at Playa Espadilla the Canadian-run **Nature's Beachfront Aparthotel** (tel. 506/2777-1473, www.maqbeach.com, low season small studio $45 s, $49 d, luxury studio $89 s/d, high season small studio $49 s, $54 d, luxury studio $99 s/d) sits beachside at the bottom of a dirt road far from the main highway (you'll need wheels). It has four self-catering units, including three studios and a backpacker studio. An upstairs penthouse (low season $159 s/d, high season $189 s/d) sleeps eight and has a wraparound wall of glass, cable TV, and a huge terrace. It has added the Nature Villa ($120 s/d), overhanging the river.

A short stroll from the Playa Espadilla, the delightful **Cabinas Playa Espadilla** (tel. 506/2777-0903, www.espadilla.com, low season $88-99 s/d, high season $106-120 s/d) has 16 spacious units in three types, all with lots of glossy hardwood furnishings. It has gone more upscale in recent years, and the junior suites now boast deluxe decor. There's a swimming pool in beautifully landscaped grounds, plus secure parking. It has slightly larger, more upscale, and costlier rooms a stone's throw away at Hotel Playa Espadilla.

CAMPING

You can camp near the park entrance under shade trees on lawns at the back of the Hotel Manuel Antonio ($5 pp, showers $1); tents can be rented ($6).

Food

Down by Playa Espadilla, the simple **Marlin Restaurante** (tel. 506/2777-1134, 7am-10pm daily, $2-12) offers delicious breakfasts such as omelets ($6) or granola with yogurt and honey ($4), plus Tex-Mex, seafood, and steaks in a two-story structure with indoor and open-air

dining. It serves great margaritas and piña coladas and has happy hour 4:30pm-6:30pm daily. Nearby is **Restaurant Terraza del Sol** (tel. 506/2777-1015, 7am-7pm daily high season, 7am-7pm Wed.-Mon. low season), a delightful open-air place in colonial style at Hotel Arboleda; choose from American breakfasts ($8) and a wide-ranging dinner menu—from pastas and chicken woks to cordon bleu ($10).

Getting There

Public buses depart Quepos for Manuel Antonio and the national park ($0.60) every 30 minutes 7am-10pm daily and will pick you up (and drop you off) along the road if you flag them down. A metered taxi from Quepos to Manuel Antonio will cost about $7.

★ MANUEL ANTONIO NATIONAL PARK

Tiny it may be, but the 682-hectare (1,685-acre) **Parque Nacional Manuel Antonio** (7am-4pm Tues.-Sun., $10) epitomizes everything visitors flock to Costa Rica to see: stunning beaches, a magnificent setting with islands offshore, lush rainforest laced with a network of trails, and wildlife galore. Nowhere else in the nation guarantees so

surfboards for rent on Playa Espadilla, Manuel Antonio

much wildlife viewing in such a short time or such a small space.

Howler monkeys move from branch to branch, iguanas shimmy up trunks, and toucans and scarlet macaws flap by. About 350 squirrel monkeys live in the park, with another 500 on its outer boundaries. Capuchin (white-faced) monkeys and crab-eating raccoons welcome you on the beaches, where they will steal your belongings given half a chance. Some of the monkeys have become aggressive, and attacks on humans have been reported. It is illegal to feed the wildlife. If you're caught doing so, you may be ejected from the park.

Despite its diminutive size, Manuel Antonio is one of the country's most popular parks. Supposedly, the park service limits the number of visitors to 600 per day (800 on Sat.-Sun.), and the park is now closed on Monday. Nonetheless, at times the Sloth Trail can seem as crowded as New York's Grand Central Station. Consider visiting in the "green" or wet season.

Theft is a major problem on the beaches. Don't leave your things unguarded while you swim. There's parking by the creek near the park entrance ($4), but security is an issue; don't leave anything in your vehicle. Also beware the manchineel tree or "beach apple," in Spanish *manzanilla de la muerte*, common along the beaches. The apple-like fruits of the manchineel are highly toxic, and its sap irritates the skin.

Beaches and Trails

The park has four lovely beaches: **Espadilla Sur, Manuel Antonio, Escondido,** and **Playita.** The prettiest is Playa Manuel Antonio, a small scimitar of coral-white sand with a small coral reef. It's separated from Playa Espadilla Sur by a tombolo—a natural land bridge formed over eons through the accumulation of sand—tipped by **Punta Catedral,** an erstwhile island now linked to the mainland. Playa Espadilla Sur (also known as Second Beach) and Playa Manuel Antonio offer tide pools brimming with minnows and crayfish, plus good snorkeling, especially during dry season, when the water is generally clear.

At the far south end of Playa Manuel Antonio, you can see ancient turtle traps dug out of the rocks by the pre-Columbian Quepo people. Female sea turtles would swim over the rocks to the beach on the high tide. The tidal variation at this point is as much as three meters (10 feet); the turtles would be caught in

Manuel Antonio National Park

into humid tropical forest. Manuel Antonio's wildlife carnival is best experienced by following the **Sendero Perezoso** (Sloth Trail), named after the sloths that favor the secondary growth along the trail.

Guides

The **Asociación de Guías Naturalistas** (c/o Amigos del Parque, tel. 506/8894-1358) offers licensed guides (2-5 hours, $20 pp) at the two park entrances. A guide can spot and inform you about wildlife you're not likely to see without assistance, such as the superbly camouflaged and unusually immobile sloths.

Information and Services

The park is open 7am-4pm Tuesday-Sunday. There are two separate entrances, linked by a trail. The main entrance is 600 meters (0.4 miles) inland of Playa Espadilla, in the village. The second entrance is at the southern end of Playa Espadilla, where you wade across the shallow Río Camaronera; rowboats are on hand at high tide ($0.50), when you may otherwise be waist-deep.

Camping is not allowed in the park. There are no accommodations or snack bars, but there are showers by the beach and toilets on the Sendero Perezoso, near the **park headquarters** (tel. 506/2777-5185).

guapinol tree in Manuel Antonio National Park

the carved-out traps on the return journey as the tide level dropped. Olive ridley and green turtles still occasionally come ashore at Playa Manuel Antonio.

Between bouts of beaching, you can explore the park's network of trails, which lead

Savegre to Dominical

South of Quepos, Highway 34 leads, almost ruler-straight, 45 kilometers (28 miles) southeast to Dominical. It is now paved the entire way, and truck traffic has increased substantially. The first few miles south of town pass a sea of African palms.

SAVEGRE

Twenty-five kilometers (16 miles) southeast of Quepos, at the hamlet of Savegre, a rough dirt road leads inland six kilometers (4 miles) up the valley of the Río Savegre to the community of **El Silencio,** at the base of the mountains. Here, the local farmers cooperative operates the **Centro Eco-Turístico Comunitario de Silencio** (tel. 506/2290-8646 or 506/2787-5265, http://coopesilencio.com, www.turismoruralcr.com). It's a great spot for lunch and has a butterfly garden, well-marked trails, horseback rides (3 hours, $20), and rafting trips.

The **Río Naranjo** and **Río Savegre** flow down from the rainforest-clad mountains and eventually fan out into an estuary in Parque Nacional Manuel Antonio. In wet season both offer Class II-V white-water action. Tour operators in Quepos and San José offer rafting and kayaking, as does **Rafiki Safari Lodge** (tel. 506/2777-2250, www.rafikisafari.com), 16 kilometers (10 miles) beyond El Silencio and 19 kilometers (12 miles) from Highway 21. Rafiki also offers horseback rides and guided hikes. Indiana Jones types can sign up for the arduous Bushmaster hike-and-raft trip into the upper valley of the Río Savegre. It also has a tapir breeding and reintroduction program in the works; the tapirs will be released in a controlled environment that includes the lake beside the lodge, as in an African safari game park. You'll need a 4WD vehicle to get here.

Reserva Los Campesinos, near the hamlet of Quebrada Arroyo, is a 33-hectare (82-acre) reserve with a canopy walkway and trails that lead to the Los Chorros waterfall. Guided hikes, horseback rides, plus accommodations at a delightful albeit simple lodge are offered through **Costa Rican Association of Community-Based Rural Tourism** (ACTUAR, tel. 506/2248-9470, www.actuar-costarica.com).

Accommodations and Food
Albergue El Silencio (tel./fax 506/2779-9554, www.turismoruralcr.com, students $30, $40 s, $50 d) is a rustic lodge nestled on a breezy hill above Silencio village, with views down over a sea of palms. There are nine thatch-and-wood cabins (some with bunks) with lofts with two single beds, screened windows, and tiled private baths with cold water. Rates include breakfast.

Replicating a piece of Africa transplanted, ★ **Rafiki Safari Lodge** (tel. 506/2777-2250, www.rafikisafari.com, low season $159 s, $256 d, high season $189 s, $327 d, including all meals) is run by a hospitable South African family. It offers 10 genuine luxury African-safari four-person tents on stilts, with rough-hewn timber beds, gracious fabrics, wooden floors, huge skylighted baths with fire-heated hot-water showers, and large wooden decks. One is wheelchair-accessible; another is a honeymoon suite with stone-lined outdoor whirlpool tub. Quality international dining at the thatched Lekker Bar includes meats from a South Africa *braai* (barbecue). It has a waterslide into a springwater pool, and a lagoon great for bird-watching.

PLAYA MATAPALO
Playa Matapalo, five kilometers (3 miles) south of Savegre, is a beautiful gray-sand beach two kilometers (1.2 miles) east of the coast road; the turnoff is in the hamlet of

rafters passing through lowland rainforest on the Río Naranjo

Matapalo. Surf smashes ashore (swimmers should beware of riptides), and fishing from the beach is guaranteed to deliver a snapper or a snook. A sandy (or muddy) beach track leads north into the **Refugio de Vida Silvestre Ecológico Portalón** (Portalón Ecological Wildlife Refuge), where there's a marine turtle protection project (ASVO, tel. 506/2258-4430, www.asvocr.org) that welcomes volunteers.

Hop in the saddle with **Claudia Horseback Riding & Birding** (tel. 506/2787-5133), by the Centro Comercial Locos de Mar. The **Cabinas del Mar,** in the village, offers Internet service.

Accommodations and Food

Surfers gravitate to **Complejo Comercial Locos de Mar** (tel. 506/2787-5278, $12 pp), with simple rooms. It has a tiny open-air restaurant (7am-6pm daily), laundry, and a grocery.

Rafiki Beach Camp (tel. 506/2787-5014, www.rafikibeach.com, low season $85 s, $105 d, high season $100 s, $130 d), formerly Bahari Beach Hotel, offers tastefully furnished safari-style tent-bungalows atop platforms, with tile floors, full baths, and canopied patios looking over a lovely garden, an exquisite pool, and the beach. It also has air-conditioned rooms in the main building. The restaurant is equally airy and serves European classics plus seafood.

For more modern, air-conditioned, self-catering bungalows, opt for **Dreamy Contentment** (next door to Bahari, tel. 506/2787-5223, www.dreamycontentment.com, low season bungalows $50 s/d, house $150 s/d, high season bungalows $75 s/d, house $200 s/d).

In the hills, **El Castillo B&B** (tel. 506/8836-8059, low season $75 s/d, high season $95 s/d), two kilometers (1.2 miles) inland, is a beautiful modern two-story house with a huge columned atrium TV lounge with half-moon sofa that enjoys views through the arcing doorway. It has four bedrooms modestly furnished in rattan, with raised beamed ceilings. They open to a wraparound veranda. There's a spring-fed plunge pool. The turnoff is 500 meters (0.3 miles) north of Matapalo; you'll need a 4WD vehicle. Rates include breakfast.

South of Matapalo, the only option before Dominical is **Albergue Alma de Hatillo B&B** (tel. 506/8850-9034, www.cabinasalma.com, low season $55 s/d, high season $65 s/d), in Hatillo, a pleasant option run by a personable Polish woman, Sabina. She has eight simple rooms in three cabins furnished with custom-made bamboo furniture and original artwork, ceiling fans, coffeemakers, mini fridges, and hot showers.

Getting There

A bus departs San José for Dominical and Uvita at 3pm daily via Quepos (departing Quepos at 7pm) and passing Matapalo at 8:30am (Mon.-Fri.). An additional bus departs at 5am Saturday-Sunday (departing Quepos at 9:15am) and passes Matapalo at 10:45am. The northbound bus departs Uvita at 4:30am daily and Dominical at 6am, passing Matapalo at 6:30am. A second bus departs Uvita at 12:30pm Saturday-Sunday, and Dominical at 1:15pm, passing Matapalo at 2:30pm.

Costa Ballena

Completion of the Costanera Sur highway has opened up the lush, once-untrammeled section of coastline south of Dominical. The paved highway slices south along the forested coast past long beaches with pummeling surf. The pencil-thin coastal plain is backed by steep mountains perfect for hiking and horseback trips.

Alas, the boom in construction in the coastal mountains is threatening the coral reefs and Térraba-Sierpe mangroves with sediment and untreated waste, causing algal blooms.

DOMINICAL AND VICINITY

Dominical, 45 kilometers (28 miles) southeast of Quepos, is a tiny laid-back resort favored by surfers, backpackers, and the college-age crowd. The four-kilometer (2.5-mile) beach is beautiful albeit pebbly, and the warm waters attract whales and dolphins close to shore. Río Barú empties reportedly polluted waters into the sea near the beach north of the village, which is graced with murals. **Dominical**

Lifeguards (tel. 506/2787-0210) are on duty 8am-5pm daily, but swimming is dangerous because of riptides. The beach extends south five kilometers (3 miles) from Dominical to **Dominicalito,** a little fishing village in the lee of Punta Dominical.

If you overdose on the sun, sand, and surf, head into the lush mountains inland of Dominicalito, where a series of dirt roads lead steeply uphill to **Escaleras** (Staircases), a forest-clad region fantastic for horseback rides. Alternatively, head east on a paved road that leads to San Isidro, winding up through the valley of the Río Barú into the Fila Costanera mountains, where you may find yourself amid swirling clouds.

★ Hacienda Barú National Wildlife Refuge

The **Refugio Nacional de Vida Silvestre Hacienda Barú** (tel. 506/2787-0003, www. haciendabaru.com), one kilometer (0.6 miles) north of Dominical, was created from a 330-hectare (815-acre) private preserve. It protects three kilometers (2 miles) of beach

lifeguard at Playa Dominical

Dominical and Vicinity

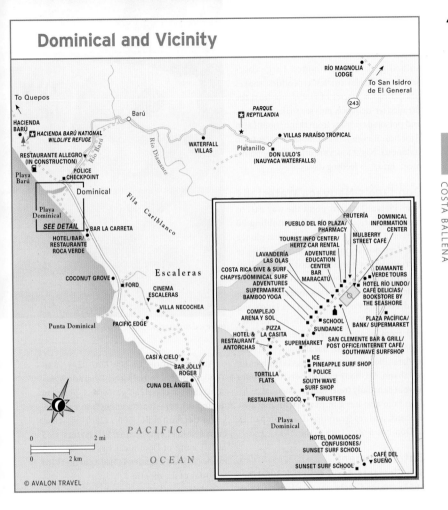

To Quepos

RÍO MAGNOLIA LODGE

To San Isidro de El General

243

Barú

PARQUE REPTILANDIA

HACIENDA BARÚ
HACIENDA BARÚ NATIONAL WILDLIFE REFUGE

WATERFALL VILLAS

Platanillo

VILLAS PARAÍSO TROPICAL

DON LULO'S (NAUYACA WATERFALLS)

RESTAURANTE ALLEGRO (IN CONSTRUCTION)

POLICE CHECKPOINT

Playa Barú

Río Barú

Río Diamante

Dominical

Playa Dominical

SEE DETAIL

BAR LA CARRETA

HOTEL/BAR/ RESTAURANTE ROCA VERDE

Fila Cariblanco

COCONUT GROVE

FORD

CINEMA ESCALERAS

VILLA NECOCHEA

Escaleras

Punta Dominical

PACIFIC EDGE

CASI A CIELO

BAR JOLLY ROGER

CUNA DEL ÁNGEL

PACIFIC

OCEAN

0   2 mi

0   2 km

FRUTERÍA   DOMINICAL INFORMATION CENTER

PUEBLO DEL RÍO PLAZA/ PHARMACY

TOURIST INFO CENTER/ HERTZ CAR RENTAL

MULBERRY STREET CAFÉ

LAVANDERÍA LAS OLAS

ADVENTURE EDUCATION CENTER

COSTA RICA DIVE & SURF

CHAPYS/DOMINICAL SURF ADVENTURES

BAR MARACATU

DIAMANTE VERDE TOURS

SUPERMARKET

HOTEL RÍO LINDO/ CAFÉ DELICIAS/ BOOKSTORE BY THE SEASHORE

BAMBOO YOGA

COMPLEJO ARENA Y SOL

SCHOOL SUNDANCE

PLAZA PACÍFICA/ BANK/ SUPERMARKET

PIZZA LA CASITA

HOTEL & RESTAURANT ANTORCHAS

SUPERMARKET

SAN CLEMENTE BAR & GRILL/ POST OFFICE/INTERNET CAFÉ/ SOUTHWAVE SURFSHOP

ICE

PINEAPPLE SURF SHOP

TORTILLA FLATS

POLICE

SOUTH WAVE SURF SHOP

RESTAURANTE COCO

THRUSTERS

Playa Dominical

HOTEL DOMILOCOS/ CONFUSIONES/ SUNSET SURF SCHOOL

CAFÉ DEL SUEÑO

SUNSET SURF SCHOOL

© AVALON TRAVEL

plus mangrove swamp and 40 hectares (100 acres) of primary rainforest: a safe haven for anteaters, ocelots, kinkajous, tayras, capuchin monkeys, and jaguarundis, among other creatures. More than 310 bird species have been recorded, including roseate spoonbills, curassows, and owls. Olive ridley and hawksbill turtles come ashore to nest at Playa Barú. Seven kilometers (4.5 miles) of trails (self-guided $7 pp; guided hike $30 four hours) lead through pasture, fruit orchards, cacao plantations, and forest. Petroglyphs (5-hour guided hike, $45) carved onto large rocks are the most obvious remains of what may be an ancient ceremonial site. Other highlights include a bird-watching tower, an orchid garden, a butterfly garden, and a turtle hatchery.

There's guided tree-climbing ($30) and a zip line ($40), plus early-morning bird-watching ($45, including breakfast), and A Night in the Jungle ($125), which ends at a fully equipped rainforest tent camp.

★ Parque Reptilandia

Well worth the drive, **Parque Reptilandia** (tel. 506/2787-0343, www.crreptiles.com,

9am-4:30pm daily, adults $10, children $5), near Platanillo, about 10 kilometers (6 miles) east of Dominical, is one of the best-laid-out animal parks in the country. Large cages and tanks display turtles, crocodiles, snakes (including 16 species of vipers, not least the dreaded fer-de-lance, plus sea snakes), lizards, and poison dart frogs from throughout Latin America. It even has a komodo dragon from Indonesia. Night tours are offered by appointment. Friday is feeding day.

Don Lulo's Nauyaca Waterfalls

Near Platanillo, signs point the way east to these magnificent waterfalls, tumbling 70 meters (230 feet) in two cascades that plunge into deep pools good for swimming. They're surrounded by tropical moist forest full of wildlife and accessed by trails. The falls, which are six kilometers (4 miles) east of the road, also go by other names: Don Lulo's and Santo Cristo. You can reach them on horseback from Escaleras or from **Don Lulo's** (tel. 506/2787-0541, www.cataratasnauyaca.com), at Platanillo, where a trail leads via the hamlet of Libano. Six-hour guided horseback tours leave at 8am daily (reservations essential, $60). Don Lulo also has a mini zoo with macaws, toucans, and *tepezcuintles*. Tour companies in Dominical offer trips to the falls.

Entertainment

San Clemente Bar & Grill (tel. 506/2787-0055), immediately south of the soccer field, has a pool table, table soccer, darts, Ping-Pong, and a large TV showing videos and sports events. Thursday is disco night. The happening scene is at **Maracatú** (tel. 506/2787-0091, www.maracatucostarica.com, 11am-midnight daily), facing the soccer field, which has an open jam on Sunday, and free drinks for women on Wednesday. **Tortilla Flats** (tel. 506/2787-0033), by the beach, has live Jams every Sunday.

Roca Verde (7am-2am daily), one kilometer (0.6 miles) south of Dominical, is an open-air bar with a large-screen TV; its Saturday night disco is legendary ($5).

red-eyed tree frog at Parque Reptilandia

At **Confusione** (tel. 506/2787-0244, 7am-11:30pm daily), in the Hotel Domilocos, accomplished classical guitarists perform during dinner—reason enough to eat here. **Cuna del Ángel** (tel. 506/2222-0704, www.cunadelangel.com), nine kilometers (5.5 miles) south of Dominical, has live classical music ($25, with dinner $45) at 8pm the third Saturday of the month.

Escaleras offers two great options. U.S. transplant Harley "Toby" Toberman presents classic movies at 5pm every Friday and Saturday at his **Cinema Escaleras** (also called Movie in the Jungle, Marina Vista 3, tel. 506/2787-8065, www.moviesinthejungle.com, Dec.-Apr.), although the cinema was taking a one-year hiatus for 2015. Movies are shown alfresco in a private villa, and Toby's wife, Kim, prepares popcorn. The scene gets started when everyone meets to enjoy the sunset and a dinner buffet. You'll need a 4WD vehicle to get here. After the movie, head downhill to **Bar Jolly Roger** (tel. 506/8706-8438, 4pm-10pm Mon.-Sat., $6), which serves hot wings and cold beer (choose from 22 labels) plus burgers. From opposite Hotel Cuna del Ángel, it's 1.7 kilometers (1 mile) up the dirt road to Escaleras.

Massage? Yoga? Belly-dancing classes? **Bamboo Yoga Play** (tel. 506/2787-0229), 100 yards west of the soccer field, has it all.

Sports and Recreation

Surfing is the name of the game. Outfits offering board rentals and gear include: **South Wave** (tel. 506/2787-0048, www.southwavecr.com); **Blowfish** (tel. 506/2787-0420); **Sunset Surf School** (tel. 506/8917-3143, www.sunsetsurfdominical.com), at Hotel Domilocos; **Green Iguana Surf Camp** (tel. 506/2787-0157, www.greeniguanasurfcamp.com), beachside at Dominicalito, which has weekly surf camp packages; and **Dominical Surf & Adventures** (tel. 506/2787-0431, www.dominicalsurfadventures.com), which also offers kayaking; as does **Pineapple Kayak** (tel. 506/8873-3283, www.pineapplekayaktours.com), also with paddleboarding.

Southern Expeditions (tel. 506/2787-0100, www.southernexpeditionscr.com) offers all manner of active excursions, from a crocodile night safari to scuba diving and whale-watching. **Tree of Life Tours** (tel. 506/9810-7620, www.treeoflifetours.com) offers guided hikes, rappelling, and horseback trips. **Rancho Savegre** (tel. 506/8834-8687, www.ranchosavegre.com) has beach and mountain horseback rides at 7:30am and 1:30pm daily ($58).

Accommodations

Theft is a major problem, and tents on the beach are routinely burglarized. Campers and hostellers should stick to **Hostel and Camping Antorchas** (tel. 506/2787-0459, camping $8 pp, cabins $10-18 pp), a bargain backpackers option 20 yards inland of the shorefront road with two-story shade platforms for tents and hammocks, plus three private rooms with double beds and shared baths, and a communal kitchen, laundry, parking, and cold-water showers. You can rent tents ($5 pp).

Surfers gravitate to **Tortilla Flats** (tel. 506/2787-0033, www.tortillaflatsdominical.com, low season $25-60 s/d, high season $30-110 s/d), on the shorefront road, not least for its cool bar. It has 18 modest beachside cabins and rooms—some in a two-story unit—with fans, hammocks on the patios, and private baths with hot water. An upstairs suite has a balcony. Nice! The restaurant is

whale breaching off Costa Rica's Pacific coast

a great breakfast and lunch spot for pancakes with bananas ($3), BLT sandwiches, and other fare.

I recommend the ever-improving **Hotel Arena y Sol** (tel. 506/2787-0140, www.arenaysol.com, low season $30 s, 45 d, high season $35 s, $55 d), 200 yards west of the soccer field, with clean dorms and cable TV in air-conditioned rooms; some rooms only have fans and are a tad small and dark, despite soothing tropical color schemes. It has a pool, an Internet café, a popular restaurant, and a supermarket, plus ATV rentals.

One of the nicest options, **Hotel Río Lindo** (tel. 506/8857-4937, www.riolindoresort-costarica.com, low season $65-90 s/d, high season $85-130 s/d) sits in gardens with hammocks and rockers at the northern entrance to Dominical. I like its pleasant B&B-style ambience. It has 10 air-conditioned rooms in three types. The standards are a bit bare for the price, but the suites are a better bargain with tasteful furnishings and flat-screen TVs. All have views over the handsome pool toward the river. The staff is friendly, plus there's a delightful café next door.

For a more intimate charmer, opt for the American-run **Coconut Grove** (tel. 506/2787-0130, www.coconutgrovecostarica.com, low season $75-130 s/d, high season $85-150 s/d), which sits in a cove two kilometers (1.2 miles) south of Dominical. It has two houses and four bungalows with kitchenettes, all with air-conditioning, wooden ceilings with fans, orthopedic mattresses, simple but pleasant furnishings, and verandas with rockers. The owners raise Great Danes. There's a small pool and a bar with hammocks.

Appealing to bird-watchers and nature lovers, **Hacienda Barú** (tel. 506/2787-0003, www.haciendabaru.com, low season $55-65 s/d, high season $80-90 s/d), one kilometer (0.6 miles) north of Dominical, has six modestly furnished two-bedroom cabins in a grassy clearing backed by forest; each has two doubles and one single bed, fans, hot water, a fridge, and cooking facilities, plus a patio. Six

newer rooms are simply furnished, but are spacious and comfy enough. There's a moderately priced thatch-fringed restaurant and a swimming pool.

IN ESCALERAS

Everything about ★ **The Necochea Inn** (tel. 506/8872-5782, www.thenecocheainn.com, low season $65-100 s/d, high season $75-125 s/d) is supremely tasteful. This luxuriously appointed bed-and-breakfast has six rooms with individual and eclectic decor, including hardwood floors and private balconies. Two rooms (one with a king bed) share a bath with a whirlpool tub and double sinks. A master suite also has a king bed, a whirlpool tub, a glass shower, and a wraparound deck with ocean views. The inn has a game room, a library, and a full bar, plus a pool with a sundeck that stair-steps to natural springs. Rates include a gourmet breakfast. The rooms are worth twice these rates.

Amiable Californian Susie and her affable Limey husband, George, are the reason enough to choose **Pacific Edge** (tel. 506/2787-8010, www.pacificedge.info, $70-100 s/d), reached via its own steep dirt road at Km. 148 on the highway. The coast vistas are awesome. It has four cabins stair-stepping down the lower mountain slopes; one is a two-bedroom, two-bath bungalow with a living room and a kitchen. Each cabin has a "half kitchenette," and there's a free-form pool and a deck with views. Susie whips up mean cuisine spanning the globe in her bamboo restaurant. No children under age 13.

Looking for your own exclusive villa? Barbara, an expat from North Carolina, plays wonderful host at **Casi el Cielo** (tel. 506/8813-5614, www.casielcielo.com, low season $3,500 per week, high season $4,500 per week), a gorgeous two-story, four-bedroom Tuscan-style villa perched hillside in Escaleras with magnificent views. It rents only as a whole house and comes fully staffed. Barbara specializes in groups and does not accept drop-ins; reservations are essential.

SOUTH OF DOMINICAL

The most deluxe option for miles is **Cuna del Ángel** (tel. 506/2222-0704, www.cunadelangel.com, low season $100-180 s/d, high season $127-233 s/d), nine kilometers (5.5 miles) south of Dominical. It's a member of the prestigious Small Distinctive Hotels of Costa Rica group (www.distinctivehotels.com), but personally I find the rambling architecture and classical decor uninspiring, and it gets road noise. And what's with all those angels? The 16 air-conditioned rooms have ceiling fans, Wi-Fi, minibars, safes, and blow-dryers. There's a full spa, an infinity pool, and a bar. The high point is the excellent open-air restaurant.

EAST OF DOMINICAL

For a truly Zen-like experience, lay your head at ★ **Waterfall Villas** (tel. 506/2787-4137, www.waterfallvillas.com, low season from $140-375 s/d, high season $165-430 s/d), in a forested riverside setting near Platanillo. Run by a delightful Tico-Californian couple, its Balinese-inspired aesthetic makes bold use of lava rock, river stones, and bamboo with a feng shui layout. Three villas have two huge individually decorated suites, each with stone-lined baths. All have forest-view balconies and gardens; two rooms have canopied bamboo king beds. An open lounge with huge bamboo sofas puts you up close and personal with the forest. Vegan meals are served. It's popular with yoga groups.

Farther uphill, **Río Magnolia Lodge** (tel. 506/8868-5561, www.riomagnolia.com, low season $160-225 s/d, high season $190-235 s/d) is in a stunning and reclusive mountain valley setting, near the hamlet of La Alfombra, 11 kilometers (7 miles) inland of Dominical. Canadian expats John and Maureen Patterson are your hosts at this magnificent lodge, with a vast stone-clad lounge with ocean views enjoyed from the deck or infinity pool. Choose from three large in-house rooms, with terracotta floors, stone-wall showers, canopy beds, and bamboo furnishings; or opt for one of four rustic yet cozy cabins. Maureen whips up gourmet fare. The lodge is backed by its own 100-hectare (250-acre) forest with trails for all abilities; it has horseback rides. Getting here down a steep and narrow track requires a 4WD vehicle.

Food

For breakfast I gravitate to the south end of Dominical and **Roca Verde** (tel. 506/2787-0036, 7am until the last guest leaves daily), serving excellent, filling *gallo pinto* or granola, fruit, and yogurt. Still, there's no denying that the coolest place around is **San Clemente Bar & Grill** (tel. 506/2787-0055, 7am-10pm daily, $2-8), immediately south of the soccer field, with a shaded open-air bar serving hearty breakfasts, including a filling Starving Surfers Special, plus burgers, Tex-Mex, and Cajun dishes (nachos and blackened chicken sandwiches), and a great tuna melt. Imagine grilled mahimahi with honey, rosemary, and orange sauce served with fresh vegetables.

Feel like Thai, Malay, or Indonesian fare in a romantic ambience? Head to **Coconut Spice** (tel. 506/2787-0073, 1pm-9pm Tues.-Sun.), on the river about 100 meters (330 feet) from the main entrance to Dominical. I recommend the spicy fish cake ($5) or Chiang Mai noodle soup ($9) appetizers, followed by prawns in coconut and pineapple sauce ($15).

For fine dining, head to Hotel Domilocos, where ★ **Confusione** (tel. 506/2787-0244, www.domilocos.com, 7am-10am and 6pm-110pm daily) combines elegance with mouthwatering dishes at fair prices. I enjoyed *funghi à la gorgonzola* ($6) and an exceptional penne with shrimp and capers in a white vodka sauce ($10). It also has seafood and steaks in a thousand variations. A classical guitarist plays on Friday and Sunday nights, and a violinist on Thursday and Saturday.

Competing with Domilocos for gourmet fare, **Palapas** (tel. 506/2787-8012, 6:30am-9:30am, 11am-5pm and 6pm-9pm daily), at Hotel Cuna del Ángel, nine kilometers (5.5 miles) south of Dominical, serves gourmet Italian-inspired cuisine and seafood. I enjoyed a delicious tomato-basil soup, and grilled corvina sea bass with creamy basil sauce and garlic mashed potatoes. The flambé desserts are to die for. Lunch is tremendous for salads and quiche.

Organic foods have come to town at **Maracatú Natural Restaurant** (tel. 506/2787-0091, 11am-9:30pm daily), facing the soccer field, serving salads, sandwiches, wraps, seafood specials, and Caribbean dishes. The bar stays open until midnight, and live music is sometimes featured.

You'll be amazed to find an entire Boeing 727 aircraft that doubles as the riverside **Charter** (tel. 506/2787-0172, 11am-10pm Mon.-Fri., 11am-11pm Sat.-Sun.), where the eclectic international menu spans penne shrimp in vodka and cream sauce to flavorful filet mignon. It's about two kilometers (1.6 miles) east of Dominical on the road to San Isidro.

The chicest place around, and the most romantic, is ★ **¿Por Que No?** (tel. 506/2787-0025, www.cpporqueno.com, 7am-1:30pm & 5pm-10pm Tues.-Sun.). It's essentially an open-air deck raised over the beach—an awesome locale to start your day or for sunset dining. Breakfast? Try the berry-stuffed french toast ($8), or spinach, cheese, and yuca scramble ($8). A typical dinner might mean roast pumpkin salad, pork ribs with pineapple barbecue sauce, plus a smoothie, or try the scrumptious wood-fired pizza ($20).

The Italian-run **Café en Sueño** (tel. 506/2787-0029), next to Hotel Domilocos, serves homemade pastries, plus mochas and cappuccino; as does **Café Delicias** (tel. 506/2787-0097, 7am-6pm Wed.-Sun.), on the north side of the soccer field, where pastries, cakes, cappuccinos, and sandwiches can be enjoyed in a lovely airy space.

Information and Services

A good information source is the **Dominical Information Center** (tel. 506/2787-0454, www.dominicalinformation.com), by the entrance to Dominical. **Bookstore by the Seashore** (no tel., 11am-4pm Mon.-Sat.) next to Café Delicias, is a great place to get the latest news. San Clemente Bar & Grill hosts a post office, DHL, and the **Dominical Internet Café** (tel. 506/2787-0191, 8:30am-8pm daily).

The **police station** (tel. 506/2787-0011) is at the southern end of the village; the **tourist police** (tel. 506/2787-0243) is also here. **Clínica González Arellano** (tel. 506/8358-9701) and **Farmacia Dominical** (tel. 506/2787-0454) adjoin each other in the Pueblo del Río complex, and the **Centro Médico** (tel. 506/2787-0326), with a 24-hour ambulance, is 50 meters (165 feet) to the south.

Adventure Education Center (tel. 506/2787-0023, www.adventurespanishschool.com) offers Spanish-language instruction.

Getting There and Away

Transportes Delio Morales (tel. 506/2777-0318) buses depart San José for Dominical (7 hours, $8) from Avenida 3, Calle 16, at 6am and 3pm daily, returning at 5am and 1pm daily.

Transportes Blanco (tel. 506/2771-4744) buses depart San Isidro de El General for Dominical at 7am, 9am, 1:30pm, and 4pm daily, returning at 6:45am, 7:15am, 2:30pm, and 3:30pm daily.

Southbound buses from Quepos depart for Dominical at 5am, 9:30am, 1:30pm, 4pm, and 7pm daily, returning at 8:30am and 3pm daily. Buses also serve Dominical from Ciudad Neily at 4:45am, 10:30am, and 3pm daily, returning at 6am, 11am, and 2:30pm daily.

The **gas station** is about one kilometer (0.6 miles) north of Dominical. You can rent cars with **Hertz** (www.hertzcostarica.com) and with **Solid Car Rental** (tel. 506/2787-0422, www.solidcarrental.com).

UVITA

South of Dominicalito, seemingly endless **Playa Hermosa** extends south to the headland of **Punta Uvita**, a tombolo (a narrow sandbar connecting an island to the mainland) jutting out west of the village of **Uvita**, 16 kilometers (10 miles) south of Dominical.

The Río Uvita pours into the sea south of Punta Uvita at **Bahía,** one kilometer (0.6 miles) east of the Costanera Sur and one kilometer (0.6 miles) south of Uvita; Bahía is an entry point to the northern end of Parque Nacional Marino Ballena. Thus, Uvita is really two villages in one: Uvita, straddling the river inland, and Bahía, closer to the ocean.

Crocodiles abound. A great place to see them is **Refugio Nacional de Vida Silvestre Rancho La Merced** (tel. 506/8861-5147, www.rancholamerced.com), a 365-hectare (900-acre) biological reserve on a cattle ranch that includes mangrove wetlands good for spotting all manner of wildlife. It offers horseback riding (7:30am-5pm daily, $45, sunset ride $60), self-guided hikes ($6, with guide $35), and bird-watching ($45), and you can even play Cowboy for a Day (half-day $45). More exciting is to overnight in a delightful old clapboard farmhouse or a modern cabin with a kitchenette. It serves meals family-style and has multiday packages.

If you're around town in February, check out **Best Fest** (www.thebestfestival.com) music festival, and the biennial **Envision Festival** (www.envisionfestival.com), which will appeal to fans of Big Man Festival with its weird pseudo-sacred performance art.

Sports and Recreation

Costa Canyoning (tel. 506/2743-8281, www.costacanyoning.com, $75) offers waterfall rappelling. **Dolphin Tour** (tel. 506/2743-8013, www.dolphintourcostarica.com) offers kayak, boat, and snorkel trips, as does **Ballena Aventuras** (tel. 506/2743-8362, www.bahiaaventuras.com), specializing in whale and dolphin trips.

Uvita Surf School (tel. 506/8586-8745, www.costaricasurfcamp.net) has surfing lessons. For diving, contact **Mad About Diving** (tel. 506/2743-8019, www.madaboutdivingcr.com).

Ultralight S.A. (tel. 506/2743-8037, www.ultralighttour.com, from $95) offers flights by ultralight planes. You can buzz around on an ATV with **Adventure Motorsports** (tel.

506/2743-8281, www.jungleatv.com); however, it does not issue helmets.

Accommodations

You can camp or sleep in a hammock at **Toucan Hotel** (tel. 506/2743-8140, www.tucanhotel.com, camping or hammocks $8 pp, dorm $12 pp, rooms $29-44 s/d), in Uvita. This well-run place, operated by a friendly American named Steven, also has three dorm rooms, plus seven air-conditioned rooms with private baths. Guests have free Internet access, laundry, a Sony PlayStation, and a TV, VCR, and DVD player. There's a communal kitchen, plus a restaurant and bar with a Caribbean-themed menu.

Backpacker fave **Flutterby House** (tel. 506/8341-1730, www.flutterbyhouse.com, loft or dorm $12, tree house $18, cabins $40-80 s/d), just 300 meters (1,000 feet) from the beach on the south side of Bahía, is a rustic counterculture delight with yurts and tepees. You can also camp or sling your hammock beneath a *rancho,* or opt for more welcoming accommodations in *cabinas* or tree houses. It has a communal kitchen and hot-water showers, plus surf rentals and lessons. The California sister duo owners run Flutterby House on sustainable principles, with a dose of fun.

There are about one dozen modest budget options in Bahía, including **Hotel Canto de Ballenas** (tel. 506/2743-8085, www.hotelcantoballenas.com, low season $33 s, $59 d, high season $39 s, $68 d), run by the rural cooperative Coopeuvita. It has 12 spacious, rustic cross-ventilated rooms in wooden huts with balconies slung with hammocks. Four are wheelchair-accessible. Rates include breakfast.

One of my favorite places hereabouts, ★ **Las Terrazas de Ballena** (tel. 506/2743-8034, www.terrazasdeballena.com, year-round $120-130 s/d, including tax) is tucked in the hills one kilometer (0.6 miles) inland of Uvita. Formerly Balcón de Uvita, this charming enclave around an old wooden home has a gorgeous Balinese aesthetic. It has three

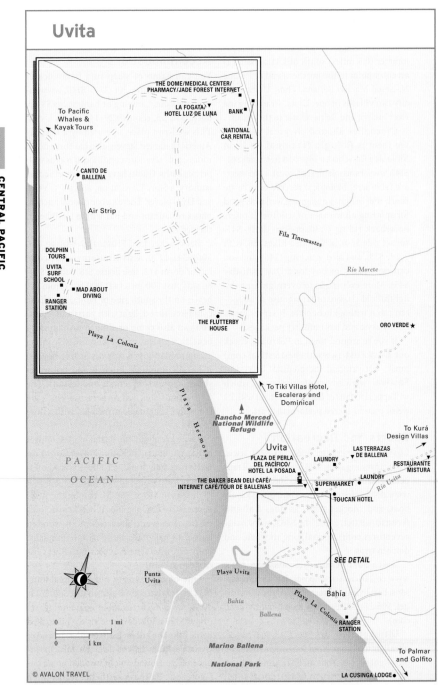

Uvita

THE DOME/MEDICAL CENTER/
PHARMACY/JADE FOREST INTERNET

To Pacific
Whales &
Kayak Tours

LA FOGATA/
HOTEL LUZ DE LUNA

BANK

NATIONAL
CAR RENTAL

CANTO DE
BALLENA

Air Strip

Fila Tinomastes

Río Morete

DOLPHIN
TOURS
UVITA
SURF
SCHOOL
MAD ABOUT
DIVING
RANGER
STATION

Playa La Colonia

THE FLUTTERBY
HOUSE

ORO VERDE ★

To Tiki Villas Hotel,
Escaleras and
Dominical

Playa Hermosa

Rancho Merced
National Wildlife
Refuge

Uvita

To Kurá
Design Villas

PACIFIC
OCEAN

PLAZA DE PERLA
DEL PACÍFICO/
HOTEL LA POSADA

THE BAKER BEAN DELI CAFÉ/
INTERNET CAFÉ/TOUR DE BALLENAS

LAUNDRY

LAS TERRAZAS
DE BALLENA

RESTAURANTE
MISTURA

LAUNDRY

SUPERMARKET

Río Uvita

TOUCAN HOTEL

SEE DETAIL

Punta
Uvita

Playa Uvita

Bahía

Bahía

Ballena

Playa La Colonia

RANGER
STATION

To Palmar
and Golfito

0   1 mi

0   1 km

Marino Ballena

National Park

LA CUSINGA LODGE ●

© AVALON TRAVEL

well-ventilated, stone-walled, thatched cabins with screened windows, orthopedic mattresses, huge walk-in showers with solar-heated water, and broad balconies with vast views; two have king beds. There's a marvelous candlelit restaurant, the exotic Buddha bar, and a sumptuous open-air lounge with hip rattan furniture and Wi-Fi. A guitar-shaped pool is inset in the stone sundeck. A 4WD vehicle is required.

Wow: ★ **Oxygen Jungle Villas** (tel. 506/8322-4773, www.oxygenjunglevillas.com, low season $198-215 s/d, high season $235-249 s/d) made a splash when it debuted in 2010 as one of Costa Rica's chicest resorts. This Balinese-style couples-only resort, set high amid a private rainforest reserve in the mountains backing Uvita, has 12 A-frame glass-walled luxury villas facing an infinity pool. These chic abodes purposely lack phones and other modern accoutrements, but you won't need them as you sink into blissful retreat. It has a clubhouse and a spa. A 4WD vehicle is required to get here.

Blowing away even Oxygen Jungle Villas, ★ **Kurà Design Villas** (tel. 506/8448-5744, www.kuracostarica.com, low season $550-620 s/d, high season $670-740 s/d), five kilometers inland, is a copycat version that ups the ante. Costa Rica has seen nothing quite as sexy as this. In fact, the two young owners, architect Martin Wells and his girlfriend, Alejandra Umaná, a biologist, describe their creation as having been "designed for sensuality." Imagine your single-room, open-plan villa (one of only six) as a cube of glass end-to-end and floor-to-ceiling and supported on a frame of steel girders enfolded in poured concrete. Stand-alone stone walls separated from the glass cube by water concourses frame the villa sides. The fourth wall (also of slate-gray concrete) holds the walk-in closet and toilet. A bamboo-lined ceiling brings the tropics indoors. Your king bed with luxurious linens seems to float in the center of the room atop a pewter-black slate floor. En suite baths include a walk-in, glass-enclosed, his-and-hers rain shower that opens directly onto an expansive balcony with spectacular views along the length of the Costa Ballena. The jaw-dropping minimalist architecture extends to the lounge and restaurant that looks over the travertine sundeck and L-shaped 19-meter-long (62-foot-long) saltwater infinity pool overhanging the ridge-top. Ascending the steep dirt-and-rock mountain road is a 4WD adventure.

Kurà Design Villas, Uvita

The Great Whale Parade

During summer and winter, you can count on humpbacks playing up and down the Pacific coast of the Americas. Increasingly, they're showing up off the coast of Costa Rica. Until recently, scientists believed that North Pacific humpbacks limited their breeding to the waters off Japan, Hawaii, and Mexico's Sea of Cortez. New findings, however, suggest that whales may get amorous off the coast of Costa Rica too. Whales seen December to March migrate from California waters, while those seen July to October come from Antarctica. Thus, two distinct populations of humpbacks exist here.

Food

Armando at **The Baker Bean Deli & Café** (tel. 506/2743-8990), on the main drag on the north side of town, bakes delicious empanadas, bagels with cream cheese, and other savory treats.

You'll want wheels to reach **Restaurante Mistura** (tel. 506/2743-8308 or 506/8855-8148), but it's more than worth the drive, signed past the Toucan Hotel. German expat Noah Poppe hosts special theme nights at this cool riverside spot beside a waterfall. Go on Friday for sushi. Once a month, Mistura hosts a full-moon party with a bonfire and live music. It has a swimming hole.

Luz de Luna (tel. 506/2743-8251, 5pm-9pm Mon. and Wed.-Fri., noon-9pm Sat.-Sun., $5-10), roadside in Uvita, has a delightfully rustic open-air ambience and serves wood-fired pizza.

Information and Services

You can pick up the local scoop and make bookings at **Uvita Tourist Information Center** (tel. 506/2743-8072 or 506/8843-7142, www.uvita.info), at the junction on the main drag in town. **Banco de Costa Rica** has a branch at the main junction in town. The **police station** (tel. 506/2743-8538) is also at the main junction.

Connect@2 Internet Café (tel. 506/8627-1012), beside Uvita Tourist Information Center, on the main drag in town, has Internet service, as does **Jade Forest Internet** (tel. 506/2743-8470), a stone's throw south at Dome Plaza. The **Consultorio Médico** (tel. 506/2743-8310),

next door, has a pharmacy. The **Servicios Médicos Bahía Ballena** (tel. 506/8839-4492 or 506/2743-8595), on the highway south of the bridge, offers 24-hour medical service, including dental care.

Getting There

The San José-Dominical buses continue to and from Uvita. **Transportes Musoc** (tel. 506/2771-4744) buses for Uvita depart San Isidro ($3) from Calle 1, Avenidas 4/6, at 9am and 4pm daily; return buses depart Bahía at 6am and 1:45pm daily. Local buses also serve Uvita from Dominical.

Taxi Uvita (tel. 506/2743-8044) has vehicles at the ready.

★ BALLENA MARINE NATIONAL PARK

Parque Nacional Marino Ballena (6am-6pm daily, $6) was created in 1990 to protect the shoreline of Bahía de Coronado and 4,500 hectares (11,000 acres) of water surrounding Isla Ballena. The park extends south for 15 kilometers (9.5 miles) from Uvita to Punta Piñuela, and about 15 kilometers (9.5 miles) out to sea. The bay is the southernmost mating site for humpback whales (Dec.-Apr.), which migrate from Alaska, Baja California, and Hawaii—hence the park's name.

It harbors within its relatively small area important mangroves and a large coral reef. Green marine iguanas live on algae in the saltwater pools. Olive ridley and hawksbill turtles come ashore May to November to lay their eggs; September and October are the best months to see them. Dolphins also frolic offshore.

Snorkeling is good close to shore during low tide (although sedimentation resulting from local construction has killed off much of the coral reef). Isla Ballena and the rocks known as Las Tres Hermanas (The Three Sisters) are havens for pelicans, frigate birds, and boobies. At the southern end, Playa Ventanas has caves accessible by kayak.

There are **ranger stations** at Uvita (Bahía), La Colonia, Playa Ballena, and Piñuela. **Park headquarters** (tel. 506/2786-5392), which has a small turtle hatchery, is at Playa Ballena, but the park is administered by **SINAC** (tel. 506/2786-7161) in Palmar Norte. All the ranger stations except Bahía permit **camping** and have showers and toilets.

Accommodations and Food

The German-run **Finca Bavaria** (tel. 506/8355-4465, www.finca-bavaria.de/eng, $64-84 s, $74-84 d), in the hills inland of Playa Ballena and 500 meters (0.3 miles) south of La Cusinga, offers five bungalows with a beautiful aesthetic that includes louvered glass windows, raised wooden ceilings, bamboo and rattan furnishings, halogen lamps, mosquito nets over the beds, and clinically clean baths with glass-brick showers. Trails lead through the forested 15-hectare (37-acre) property. Filling and delicious meals are served, washed down with chilled German beer served in steins. There's a swimming pool in the landscaped garden.

I'm enamored of **La Cusinga** (tel. 506/2770-2549, www.lacusingalodge.com, $181-294 s/d, including all meals), about five kilometers (3 miles) south of Uvita at Finca Tres Hermanas, a farm involved in reforestation and sustainable agriculture. It has huge and delightful albeit modestly appointed all-wood cabins with terra-cotta and river-stone floors, screened glassless windows, and exquisite stone-faced baths. Its Gecko Restaurant is fabulous, with staggering views, and trails lead through 250 hectares (618 acres) of primary forest (day visitors $5).

OJOCHAL AND VICINITY

South of Piñuela and Parque Nacional Marino Ballena, Playa Tortuga sweeps south to the mouth of the Río Térraba and the vast wildlife-rich mangrove swamps of the Delta del Térraba; the estuary of the Río Térraba is awesome for fishing for snapper, catfish, and snook. One kilometer (0.6 miles) south of **Tortuga Abajo,** and stretching inland from the highway, Ojochal has a large community

chilling at Punta Piñuela, Ballena Marine National Park

Ojochal

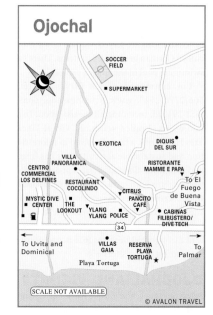

SOCCER FIELD

■ SUPERMARKET

▼ EXOTICA

DIQUIS DEL SUR •

VILLA PANORAMICA •
RISTORANTE MAMME E PAPA •

CENTRO COMMERCIAL LOS DELFINES

RESTAURANT COCOLINDO ▼

To El Fuego de Buena Vista

MYSTIC DIVE ■ CENTER

CITRUS ▼

PANCITO CAFÉ ▼

THE LOOKOUT

YLANG YLANG ▼

POLICE ▼

■ CABINAS FILIBUSTERO/ DIVE TECH

34

←
To Uvita and Dominical

VILLAS GAIA

RESERVA PLAYA TORTUGA ★

To Palmar →

Playa Tortuga

(SCALE NOT AVAILABLE)

© AVALON TRAVEL

of French Canadians and some of the best dining on the Pacific coast.

The Costanera Sur continues south via San Buena to Palmar Norte, gateway to the Golfo Dulce and the Osa region.

Reserva Playa Tortuga (tel. 506/2786-5200, www.reservaplayatortuga.org, 7:30am-4pm daily), at Tortuga Abajo, welcomes visitors, including volunteers willing to patrol beaches in turtle nesting season ($15 for 3 hours). It has a turtle hatchery and a netted butterfly facility, and it offers guided nature tours ($10-15).

Entertainment and Events

Adelante Hotel (tel. 506/2786-5304, www. adelantehotel.net), on the highway 500 meters (0.3 miles) north of Ojochal, is party central and hosts parties every first and third Friday of the month, plus poker tournaments on Monday.

Sports and Recreation

Mystic Dive Center (fax 506/2786-5217, www.mysticdive.com), in Plaza Maleku, offers dive trips, snorkeling, and fishing.

The confusingly named (it's nowhere near Osa) **Osa Canopy Tour** (tel. 506/2788-7555, www.osacanopytour.com, adults $55, students $45, children $35) has 11 zip lines, 15 platforms, and three rappels, plus waterfall rappelling. The office is at Km. 196 on the Costanera Sur, south of Ojochal. The tour, however, is at **Osa Mountain Village** (tel. 506/2772-5258, www.osamountainvillagecostarica.com), a sustainable farm community on a 383-hectare (946-acre) forest reserve.

Seemingly out of place in sleepy Coronado, five kilometers (3 miles) south of Ojochal, the classy **Baxter Bowl** (tel. 506/8570-7237, www.baxterbowlingcostarica.com) has 10-pin bowling.

Accommodations

Budget hounds should opt for **Adelante Hotel** (tel. 506/2786-5304, www.adelante-hotel.net, low season $20-80 s/d, high season $30-100 s/d), on the highway 500 meters (0.3 miles) north of Ojochal. Its colorful rooms exude romance, with indigenous fabrics and mosquito netting; it also has *cabinas* and a *casa prefábricada* (prefabricated house). This is one of the liveliest spots around, luring locals for its regular parties.

An adorable hilltop option, **The Lookout** (tel. 506/2786-5074, www.hotelcostarica.com, low season $79-110 s/d, high season $89-120), at Tortuga Abajo, exudes a bold and beautiful contemporary aesthetic. Paths weave through lush landscaped gardens to 12 bungalows with bright tropical color schemes, cool tile floors, raised wooden ceilings with fans, huge louvered glass windows, and terraces with hammocks. A mirador offers fantastic views over both the beach and the rainforest. Gourmet meals are prepared by a professional chef. There's also a spa.

Roadside at Tortuga Abajo, **Villas Gaia** (tel. 506/2786-5044, www.villasgaia.com, $75-135 s/d) offers14 colorful wooden *cabinas* dotting the forested hillside; they feature muted pastel decor and minimalist furnishings, orthopedic mattresses, and solar-heated hot water. One cabin is wheelchair-accessible. A sundeck and an open-sided thatched bar overhanging the pool boast views. The restaurant is recommended, and boat tours and various activities are offered.

The best bet in Ojochal is **Diquis el Sur** (tel. 506/2786-5012, www.diquiscostarica. com, $53-87 s/d), enjoying a breeze-swept hillside setting. This French Canadian-run option offers two twin-bedroom cabins amid tree-shaded lawns and lovely gardens. Cabins are cross-lit through huge louvered windows and feature handsome fabrics and modern baths. Meals are served under a lofty *palenque*. There's a nice pool and a sundeck, plus Internet access and a library.

Food

Ojochal is considered a gourmet ghetto in the tropics. The number of superb restaurants astounds for such an out-of-the-way place, with more added each year; check out the **restaurant association** (www.elsabordeojochal.com). It even hosts a Culinary Festival in January.

Where you find lots of French people, you find great bakeries. Start your day with fresh croissants and coffee at **Pancito Café** (tel. 506/8729-4115, 7am-3pm daily).

On the coast highway, **Roadhouse** (tel. 506/2786-5404, noon-9pm Sun.-Thurs., noon-10pm Fri.-Sat.), a charming wood-and-bamboo restaurant at Km. 169, at the entrance to the main park ranger station, is just the ticket for caesar salad ($7.50), grilled patty melts ($8.50), burgers, nachos, or even filet mignon ($18). It often has live music events.

Belying its boondocks locale, the open-air ★ **Restaurante Exótica** (tel. 506/2786-5050, exotica@racsa.co.cr, 5pm-9pm Mon.-Sat., $3-22), in Ojochal, is a hole-in-the-wall with world-class, world-spanning cuisine: Italian, Thai, Vietnamese, even Polynesian. You dine by candlelight at tables of hewn tree trunks. I enjoyed a green salad with raspberry vinaigrette, Tahitian fish carpaccio, fish fillet with banana curry sauce, and shrimp with Pernod Ricard and garlic sauce. It has Wi-Fi.

The sublime ★ **Citrus** (tel. 506/2786-5175, restocitrus@yahoo.ca, 11am-10pm Tues.-Sat.), riverside 400 meters inland of the coast road, sets a standard for sophisticated dining beyond San José. The stylish contemporary lounge has Balinese elements and rattan chairs beneath wrought-iron chandeliers. I salivated over a gazpacho ($7); other winning appetizers include a Caribbean seafood and coconut soup ($8.50). Entrées include filet mignon with white wine and wild mushroom sauce ($19) or sea bass in saffron and white wine sauce ($14.50). The wine list is equally impressive. It serves tapas throughout the day and holds monthly special events (including belly dancing and tango), plus a fresh produce market 9am-1pm every Tuesday.

Hans and Carole at **Ylang Ylang** (tel. 506/2786-5054, 5pm-9pm Wed.-Sat.), 100 meters west of the police station, serve impeccable Indonesian fare, including a Sunday buffet brunch (10:30am-3pm Sun.) alfresco atop tables hewn from tree trunks. À la carte dishes include treats such as beef stewed in coconut milk, Balinese-style sweet-and-sour pork, and tiger shrimp in coconut-tomato sauce. Leave room for lemon cake with coconut.

Information and Services

The **police station** (tel. 506/2786-5661) is on the left off the highway at the entrance to Ojochal. **Solid Car Rental** (www.solidcarrental.com) has an office in Diquis el Sur in Ojochal.

Golfo Dulce and the Osa Peninsula

Costa Rica's southwesternmost region is a distinct oblong landmass, framed on its east side by the Fila Costeña mountain chain and indented in the center by a vast gulf called Golfo Dulce. Curling around the gulf to the north is

the mountainous hook-shaped Osa Peninsula and, to the south, the pendulous Burica Peninsula. North and south of the gulf are two broad fertile plains smothered by banana and African date palm plantations—the Valle de Diquis, to the northwest, separating the region from the Central Pacific by a large mangrove ecosystem fed by the Río Grande de Térraba, and the Valle de Coto Colorado, extending south to the border with Panamá.

Nature lovers with a taste for the remote and rugged will be in their element. Star billing goes to the Osa Peninsula, smothered in a vast tract of pristine rainforest filled with the stentorian roar of howler monkeys, the screeches of scarlet macaws, and the constant dripping of water. Much of the rainforest—a repository for some of the nation's greatest wildlife treasures—is protected within a series of contiguous parks and reserves served by remote nature lodges.

The region is the largest gold source in the country, as it has been since pre-Columbian times. In the early 1980s gold fever destroyed thousands of hectares of the Osa forests, and the physical devastation was a deciding factor in the creation of Parque Nacional Corcovado. Rivers such as the Río Tigre and the Río Claro still produce sizeable nuggets; former gold miners have turned to ecotourism and today lead visitors on gold-mining forays.

The waters of the Golfo Dulce are rich in game fish, and the area is popular for sport-fishing. Whales occasionally call in, and three species of dolphin—bottle-nosed, black spotted, and spinner—frolic in the gulf, which is charged by luminescent plankton after sunset. Although the gulf is protected and relatively calm, surfers flock to the waves that wash the southeast tip of the Osa Peninsula and push onto the beaches of the Burica Peninsula, where indigenous communities exist in isolation in the mountains. Offshore, west of Corcovado, is craggy, desolate Isla del Caño,

---

Previous: horseback riders near Drake Bay; orchids at Casa Orquídeas. **Above:** red-lored Amazon.

Look for ★ to find recommended
sights, activities, dining, and lodging.

Highlights

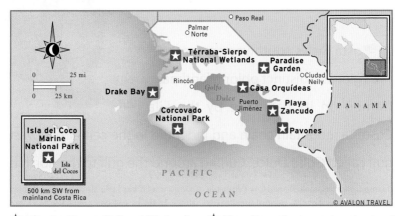

★ **Térraba-Sierpe National Wetlands:**
This vast mangrove ecosystem teeming with
wildlife can be explored by boat from Sierpe and
Ojochal (page 437).

★ **Drake Bay:** A dramatic setting close to
Corcovado and Isla del Caño adds to the appeal
of this hidden bay, where nature lodges specialize in sportfishing and diving. It's accessible by an
improved road, but drivers will still need to ford
three rivers (page 439).

★ **Corcovado National Park:** Jaguars,
tapirs, crocodiles, colorful snakes, monkeys, and
scarlet macaws are among the easily seen wildlife
in this rugged rainforest reserve (page 453).

★ **Casa Orquídeas:** Ron and Trudy McAllister
have spent more than two decades creating this
amazing botanical garden on the remote shores
of Golfo Dulce (page 459).

★ **Playa Zancudo:** A magnificent beach and
dramatic setting combine with low-key accommodations to provide a lazy, laid-back retreat
where all you need is swimwear and a hammock
(page 464).

★ **Pavones:** This surfers' paradise has it all:
great waves, stupendous palm-shaded beaches,
and plenty of budget options for eats and places
to rest your head (page 466).

★ **Isla del Coco Marine National Park:**
This remote isle is off-limits to all but experienced scuba divers, who come to commune
with whale sharks, rays, and hammerhead sharks
(page 469).

★ **Paradise Garden:** You'll learn fascinating
lore about plants, including their medicinal quali-
ties, at this tropical garden lovingly tended by its
North American creator and owner (page 470).

Golfo Dulce and the Osa Peninsula

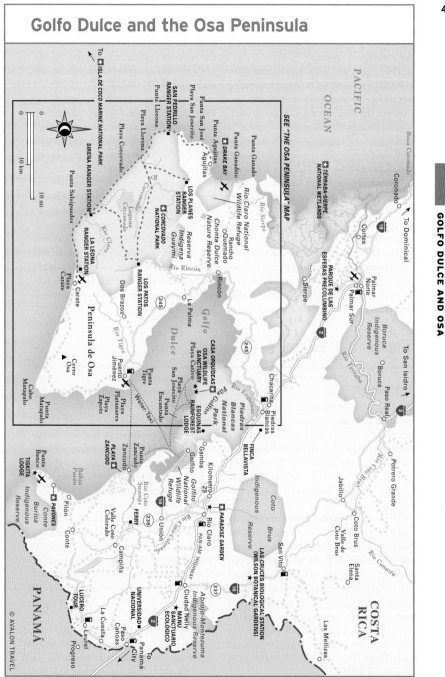

© AVALON TRAVEL

and way, way out to the southwest is the even more desolate Isla del Coco, an island whose surrounding waters are a venue for some of the world's finest diving.

This is one of Costa Rica's wettest regions. Be prepared for rain and a lingering wet season: the area receives 400 to 800 centimeters (160-315 inches) of rain annually. Violent thunderstorms move in October to December.

PLANNING YOUR TIME

Many visitors come to visit **Parque Nacional Corcovado** or **Drake Bay** and fly out after a brief two- or three-day stay. You'll short-change yourself with such a limited trip; allow at least one week.

Scheduled air service is offered to Ciudad Neily, Drake Bay, Palmar, and Puerto Jiménez (you can also charter flights to Corcovado), and Jeep taxis and local tour operators offer connecting service to almost anywhere you may then want to journey. If you're driving yourself, a 4WD vehicle is mandatory to negotiate the dirt roads of the Osa Peninsula and the Burica Peninsula. In wet season, the road to Corcovado can prove impassable to even the largest 4WD vehicles.

Accommodations tend to cater to nature lovers: take your pick of options ranging from safari-style tent-camps to deluxe eco-lodges. Dozens of nature lodges line the western shores of the Osa Peninsula and the contiguous Piedras Blancas, while beach options that primarily draw surfers and the student crowd tend toward the budget end of the spectrum.

Highway 2 (the Pan-American Highway) cuts a more or less ruler-straight line along the base of the Fila Costeña mountains, connecting the towns of Palmar (to the north) with Ciudad Neily and Paso Canoas (to the south), on the border with Panamá. The towns offer nothing of interest to travelers, other than as stops in times of need.

Valle de Diquis

PALMAR

The small town of Palmar is a service center for the banana and African date palm plantations of the Valle de Diquis and a major crossroads at the junction of the highways to and from Dominical and the Central Pacific coast (north), Golfito and the Osa Peninsula (south), and San Isidro and Valle de El General (east).

The town is divided into Palmar Norte and Palmar Sur by the Río Térraba. **Palmar Norte** is the main center, but there is nothing here to appeal to visitors. **Palmar Sur,** southwest of the bridge over the river, displays pre-Columbian granite spheres in the plaza alongside a venerable steam locomotive that once hauled bananas. They're now preserved in the **Parque Temático y Museo de las Esferas de Piedras** (Stone Sphere Museum and Theme Park, tel. 506/2786-7433, daily year-round, free).

Accommodations and Food

Cabinas Ticos Alemán (Calle 147, tel. 506/2786-6232, $18 s/d, with a/c and TV $25 pp), on the Pan-American Highway, has 25 basic but well-lit motel-style rooms with private baths; some have air-conditioning, TVs, and hot water, while others have cold water only. It has secure parking.

The nicest place in town is **Brunka Lodge** (Calle 149, Aves. 9/11, tel. 506/2786-7489, $36 s, $48 d). It has nicely furnished, well-lit rooms with modern baths, cable TV, fridges, and Wi-Fi. There's secure parking. Across the street, the open-air **Restaurante Diquis** is the nicest eatery in town and has a bakery.

Information and Services

There are two banks, a **post office** (Palmar Norte), and a **police station** (Palmar Sur, tel. 506/2786-6320). The regional **hospital** (tel.

antique steam train at Palmar Sur

boats to Drake Bay and for exploring the Delta de Térraba.

Parque de las Esferas Precolumbino, also called **Sitio Arqueológico Finca 6** (tel. 506/2100-6000, finca6@museocostarica. go.cr, guided tours 9am-4pm daily, $6), is an archaeological site displaying pre-Columbian stone spheres in situ. Located midway between Palmar Sur and Sierpe, the site—a former United Fruit Company banana plantation—contains the largest concentration of spheres still in their original astronomical alignments. The spheres, averaging nearly 1.5 meters (5 feet) in diameter and weighing several tons, were probably used to mark seasonal shifts and sacred architecture. It was named a UNESCO World Heritage Site in 2013.

There's a **police station** opposite Resturante La Perla.

★ Térraba-Sierpe National Wetlands

The 22,000-hectare (54,000-acre) **Humedal Nacional Térraba-Sierpe** is a vast network of mangrove swamps fed by the waters of the Río Térraba (to the north) and Río Sierpe (to the south), which, near the sea, form an intricate lacework of channels and tidal *esteros* (estuaries) punctuated by islets anchored by *manglares* (mangroves). The delta, which extends along 40 kilometers (25 miles) of shoreline, is home to crocodiles, caimans, and myriad birds.

Sports and Recreation

Tour Gaviotas de Osa (tel. 506/2788-1212, www.tourgaviotasdeosa.com), dockside in Sierpe, has mangrove and crocodile tours by day and night, plus fishing, hiking, and whale-watching trips. **Costa Rica Adventures** (tel. 506/2788-1603, www.osaexpeditions.com) competes.

Sierpe Divers (tel. 506/8720-0514), on the south bank of the river, offers diving trips.

Accommodations and Food

Sierpe has plenty of budget *cabinas*. **Cabinas Las Gaviotas de Osa** (tel. 506/2788-1163,

506/2788-8148) is in Cortés, an administrative town seven kilometers (4.5 miles) north of Palmar. **Café Internet B&F** (Calle 145, Aves. 7/9, Palmar Norte, tel. 506/2787-6167) is open 8am-8pm Monday-Saturday.

Getting There

SANSA (tel. 506/2229-4100, U.S./Canada tel. 877-767-2672, www.flysansa.com) and **Nature Air** (tel. 506/2299-6000, U.S. tel. 800-235-9272, www.natureair.com) both fly to Palmar Sur from San José daily.

Tracopa (tel. 506/2223-7685) buses depart San José for Palmar (6 hours, $8) from Calle 5, Avenidas 18/20, seven times daily. Buses for Sierpe ($1) leave from Supermercado Térraba in Palmar five times daily.

SIERPE

The end-of-the-road village of Sierpe, 15 kilometers (9.5 miles) due south of Palmar, is a hamlet on the banks of the Río Sierpe, trapped forlornly between date palm plantations and a swamp. Sierpe serves as departure point for adri-ahidalgo@hotmail.com, $12 pp) has six *cabinas* with fans and private baths with cold water only. Nearby, newer, and nicer, **Cabinas Sofia** (tel. 506/2788-1229, cabinassofia@gmail.com, $20 s/d) has simple air-conditioned riverside rooms plus Internet access.

"Utterly charming" sums up ★ **Veragua River House** (tel. 506/2788-1460, www.hotelveragua.com, $50 s/d), an old two-story house on the east side of the bridge. Converted by Italian-born artist Benedetto, it's like a piece of Siena transplanted, simply yet tastefully furnished with sponge-washed walls, old wicker and antiques, aging sofas, and Oriental throw rugs on the terra-cotta floors. The upper floor has a library-lounge. Three rooms in the house share a Victorian-style bath with a claw-foot tub. One of the rooms is in the loft, with dormer windows and a honeymoon feel. Four cabins in the garden are simpler yet still romantic; some have iron-frame beds. Guests share the kitchen and an outside rotisserie oven in a stone courtyard. Tours are offered. It also has a beach house ($120 for up to 5 people).

Eco-lodges accessed solely by boat include **Río Sierpe Lodge** (tel. 506/8702-5696, www.riosierpelodge.com, check website for package rates), 25 kilometers (16 miles) downriver from Sierpe near the river's mouth. It specializes in multiday packages, including fishing and diving. The 11 wood-paneled rooms are rustic but large, and each has a private bath with solar-heated water. Six additional rooms have lofts. An almost identical alternative is **Sabalo Lodge** (tel. 506/4001-7960, www.sabalolodge.com, from $125 s, $200 d, including transportation and meals), a family-run eco-lodge midway between Sierpe and Drake Bay.

For dining with a view you can't beat, **Kokopelli** (tel. 506/2788-1259), has a riverside deck and an eclectic menu that includes burgers and seafood.

Getting There

Buses and taxis (about $20) operate from Palmar Norte. Cabinas Las Gaviotas de Osa has water-taxi service to Drake Bay, Corcovado, and Isla del Caño.

Oxen are still used to harvest African date palms near Sierpe.

Osa Peninsula

CHACARITA TO RINCÓN

Access to the Osa Peninsula is via a single paved road that runs along the east coast to the village and service center of Puerto Jiménez and, beyond, Cabo Matapalo before curling west to dead-end at Carate, on the border of Parque Nacional Corcovado. The turn-off from the Pan-American Highway (Hwy. 2) is at **Chacarita,** about 32 kilometers (20 miles) southeast of Palmar and 26 kilometers (16 miles) northwest of Río Claro. There's a gas station at the junction. The only settlement of any significance along the route is **Rincón,** 42 kilometers (26 miles) south of Chacarita. At Rincón, the road divides: west for Drake Bay and east for Puerto Jiménez. The section between Chacarita and Rincón is badly deteriorated.

Accommodations and Food

Run by a delightful Tico family, **El Mirador Osa** (tel. 506/8823-6861, www.elmiradorosa.com, $30 pp, including breakfast and tax), midway between Chacarita and Rincón, straddles a ridge with glorious views over both the gulf and the forested Osa Peninsula. Five cozy, charming, if simple wooden cabins with kitchenettes, and meals (for hotel guests only) served in a homey family setting, make this a winner. It has Internet access and a small pool, and it offers tours.

The Swiss- and Tico-run **Suital Lodge** (tel. 506/8826-0342, www.suital.com, low season $45 s, $66 d, high season $51 s, $71 d), between Chacarita and Rincón, is a simple but pleasing wooden lodge with hillside vistas over the gulf. Its three spacious, cross-ventilated wooden cabins sit on stilts and have ceiling fans, mosquito nets, small terraces with rockers, and hot-water showers. Meals are served, and box lunches are prepared. There are four kilometers (2.5 miles) of trails, including one to the beach.

★ DRAKE BAY

On the north side of the Osa Peninsula, Drake Bay, pronounced "DRA-kay" locally, lies between the mouth of the Río Sierpe and the vastness of Parque Nacional Corcovado. It is a good base for sportfishing and scuba

Scuba divers set out from the Águila de Osa Inn at Drake Bay.

The Osa Peninsula

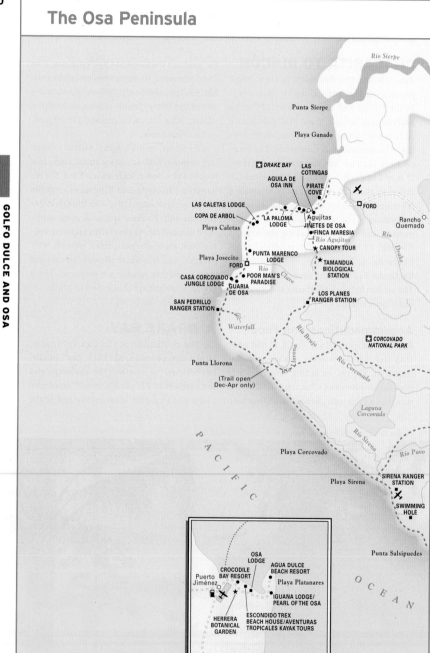

Rio Sierpe

Punta Sierpe

Playa Ganado

DRAKE BAY

LAS COTINGAS

AGUILA DE OSA INN

PIRATE COVE

FORD

Rancho Quemado

Rio Drake

LAS CALETAS LODGE

COPA DE ARBOL

LA PALOMA LODGE

Agujitas

JINETES DE OSA

FINCA MARESIA

Playa Caletas

Rio Agujitas

CANOPY TOUR

PUNTA MARENCO LODGE

Playa Josecito

FORD

Rio Claro

TAMANDUA BIOLOGICAL STATION

CASA CORCOVADO JUNGLE LODGE

POOR MAN'S PARADISE

GUARIA DE OSA

LOS PLANES RANGER STATION

SAN PEDRILLO RANGER STATION

Waterfall

Rio Brujo

Rio Corcovado

CORCOVADO NATIONAL PARK

Punta Llorona

(Trail open Dec-Apr only)

Rio Llorona

Laguna Corcovado

Rio Sirena

Rio Pavo

PACIFIC

Playa Corcovado

SIRENA RANGER STATION

Playa Sirena

SWIMMING HOLE

Punta Salsipuedes

OCEAN

OSA LODGE

CROCODILE BAY RESORT

AGUA DULCE BEACH RESORT

Puerto Jiménez

Playa Platanares

IGUANA LODGE/ PEARL OF THE OSA

HERRERA BOTANICAL GARDEN

ESCONDIDO TREX BEACH HOUSE/AVENTURAS TROPICALES KAYAK TOURS

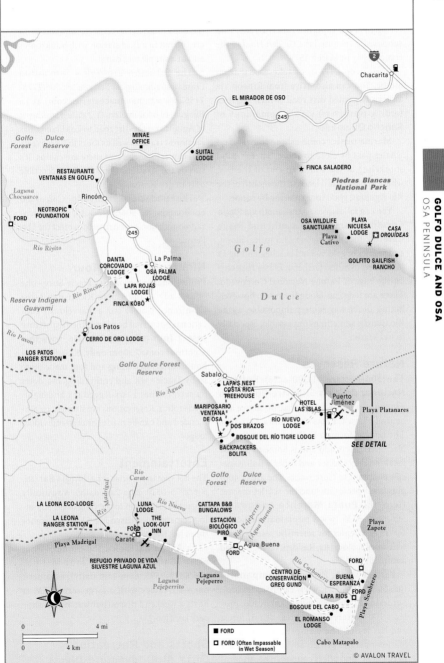

diving, and for hikes into nearby wildlife refuges and the national park. The bay is named for English sea captain Francis Drake, who supposedly anchored the *Golden Hind* in the tranquil bay in March 1579.

Most people fly in or take a boat from Sierpe. You can also drive from Rincón via a recently graded dirt road (which requires fording two rivers) via the community of **Rancho Quemado.**

Marine turtles come ashore to nest, and whales pass by close to shore. There's good snorkeling at the southern end of the bay, where a coastal trail leads to the mouth of the Río Agujitas, good for exploring by canoe.

You can follow a coast trail south via **Playa Cocalito** (immediately south) and **Playa Caletas,** four kilometers (2.5 miles) along, and a series of golden-sand beaches, ending 13 kilometers (8 miles) farther at **Playa Josecito** on the edge of Parque Nacional Corcovado. There are lodgings along the route; however, hiking all the way is often impossible, as the Río Claro is sometimes impassable, especially in wet season.

Nature Reserves

The 500-hectare (1,200-acre) **Refugio Nacional de Vida Silvestre Punta Río Claro** is a wildlife refuge that sits above and behind Playa Caletas and Punta Marenco. The reserve forms a buffer zone for Parque Nacional Corcovado and is home to all four local monkey species and other wildlife species common to Corcovado. The area's 400-plus bird species include the scarlet macaw. Here, the **Punta Marenco Lodge** (tel. 506/8877-3535, www.puntamarenco.com) serves as a center for scientific research and welcomes ecotourists. Resident biologists lead nature hikes ($35).

Farther south, **Proyecto Campanario** (tel. 506/2289-8694, www.campanario.org), bordering Parque Nacional Corcovado, protects 100 hectares (250 acres) of rainforest and has trails. The Campanario Biological Station operates principally as a "university in the field" and offers courses in neotropical ecology. There are four-day, three-night eco-camps and conservation camps for environmentally minded travelers. Accommodations are offered in a field station with bunkrooms and in a simple tent camp.

The **Estación Biológica Tamandúa** (Tamandúa Biological Station, tel. 506/2775-1456, www.tamanduacostarica.com) at La Bijagua, two kilometers (1.2 miles) southeast of Agujitas on the dirt road to Los Planos, has rainforest trails as well as tours to Corcovado. You can camp here, and there are cabins. It's run by the Arguijos family and is accessible only in dry season.

The **Fundación Corcovado** (Corcovado Foundation, tel. 506/2297-3013, www.corcovadofoundation.org) strives to protect the Osa Peninsula.

Nighttime Insect Tour

Professional entomologist Tracie Stice—the "Bug Lady"—and Costa Rican naturalist Gianfranco Gomez run a marvelously educational nocturnal bug hunt, the **Nighttime Insect Tour** (tel. 506/8701-7356, www.thenighttour.com, 7:30pm daily, $35). The 2.5-hour tour is fascinating and fun, made more so by Tracie's wit and enthralling anecdotes on such themes as six-legged sex and eight-eyed erotica. Reservations are strongly recommended and can be made through individual lodges.

Entertainment

The hot spot in Agujitas is **La Jungla Bar** (tel. 506/2775-0570, 2pm-2am daily). A rustically elegant bar is the yin to the yang of the adjoining cement-floor disco ($2-5), which sometimes has live music.

La Jungla has stolen the thunder from nearby **Bar y Restaurante Jade Mar** (tel. 506/8822-8595, 6am-1am daily), a modern open-air eatery with a large-screen TV. It hosts a weekend disco (but watch that slippery tile floor).

Sports and Recreation

Costa Rica Adventure Divers (tel.

506/2231-5806, U.S. tel. 866-553-7070, www. costaricadiving.com) is based at Jinetes de Osa hotel, at the southern edge of Agujitas, and has dive trips to Isla Caño. **Pirate Cove** (tel. 506/2234-6154 or 506/8393-9449, www.piratecovecostarica.com) also specializes in diving. The **Águila de Osa Inn** (tel. 506/2296-2190, www.aguiladeosa.com), at the mouth of the Río Agujitas, specializes in sportfishing and also has scuba diving and mangrove tours, and can arrange dolphin-spotting tours, birding ($35), mountain biking ($35), and kayaking.

The **Corcovado Canopy Tour** (tel. 506/8810-8908, www.corcovadocanopytour. com), at Los Planos, a 20-minute drive from Agujitas, has 14 platforms and 12 zip-line cables.

Accommodations

Hotels concentrate around **Agujitas,** the hamlet at the southern end of the bay. Isla del Caño dominates the view out to sea. Most lodges deal in multiday packages; one-night stays are rare because the bay is so difficult to reach. There are many more options than recommended here.

UNDER $25

Vista Drake Lodge (tel. 506/2775-1216, www.drakeview.com, $18 pp with a bed, $10 pp with your own tent, cabins from $20), atop a hill on the east side of the village, has three simple rooms plus three charming cabins, all with hot water and Wi-Fi. You can also camp: It has toilets and a cold-water shower, plus five roomy tents with beds or mattresses on decks. You can also bring your own tent.

Another great spot with a lovely garden on the north side of Agujitas is **Martina's Place Hostel** (tel. 506/8720-0801, www.puravidadrakebay.com, dorm $10 pp, rooms from $20 s, $30 d), with two dorms, simply furnished rooms with either shared or private bath, and a larger family room. You can use the family kitchen. German-born Martina prepares excellent meals.

$50-100

The hilltop **Cabinas Jade Mar** (tel. 506/8384-6681, www.jademarcr.com, rooms $45 s/d, cabins $55 s/d) can be recommended for the views. The seven clean wooden cabins are simple and vary in size. No frills here, but it does have Internet access and a popular restaurant.

Two kilometers (1.2 miles) inland along the road to Los Patos, ★ **Finca Maresia** (tel. 506/2775-0279, www.fincamaresia. com, $30-75 s, $40-90 d, including breakfast and tax) sets the standard for mid-range properties with its contemporary minimalist style. Run by a Spanish couple, it has seven wooden cabins in three types set on three hectares (7 acres), all with cement floors, glass walls, tin roofs, mosquito nets, Guatemalan bedspreads, and hip open baths with stylish accoutrements. Larger Japanese-style cabins have wraparound balconies. There's also a dorm. Finca Maresia is an absolute bargain.

$100-150

With a splendid waterfront setting, **Jinetes de Osa** (tel. 506/2231-5806, www.costaricadiving.com, low season $55-85 s, $65-96 d, high season $90-130 s, $96-140 d), at the southern edge of Agujitas, is a dedicated dive resort with nine rooms, each sleeping three people, with fans, cool tile floors, screened glassless windows, Guatemalan bedspreads, and spacious baths with hot water.

Also specializing in diving, **Pirate Cove** (tel. 506/2234-6154 or 506/8393-9449, www. piratecovecostarica.com, low season $125 s, $190 d, high season $135 s, $210 d), overlooking the mouth of the Río Drake, north of Agujitas, has a delightful ambience. The lodge has eight elegant wooden cabins set amid landscaped grounds and connected by wooden walkways. It also has simpler yet cozy "bungalows." Each has two beds with orthopedic mattresses, mosquito netting, and a deck with a hammock. Dining is family-style on a shaded deck. Contact the lodge for rates.

OVER $250

The class act in Agujitas is the American-run ★ **Águila de Osa Inn** (tel. 506/2296-2190 or 506/8840-2929, www.aguiladeosa.com, 2-night package from $521 s, $886 d, including all meals and two tours), at the mouth of the Río Agujitas. The 11 stone-faced deluxe rooms and two suites are spacious and have cathedral ceilings with fans, screened glass-less windows, bamboo beds with Guatemalan bedspreads, and exquisite baths with huge walk-in showers with piping-hot water. Junior suites, farther up the hill, have magnificent views and wraparound verandas with hammocks. The focal point is the circular open-air restaurant and bar-lounge. It specializes in diving and sportfishing.

Cross the creaky suspension footbridge over the Río Agujitas to reach the serenely landscaped ★ **Villas La Paloma Lodge** (tel. 506/2293-7502, www.lapalomalodge.com, 3-night package low season from $820 pp, high season from $990 pp, including transfers, all meals, and tours), which perches atop a cliff overlooking Playa Cocalito and offers a superb view of Isla del Caño. Seven spacious bungalows—furnished with hammocks on the balcony—and five comfy cabins perched on stilts have ceiling fans, orthopedic mattresses, private baths with solar-heated water, and balconies. A 2009 upgrade added stylish Balinese furnishings, faux-wicker chairs, and blood-red loungers. The club-house is a perfect spot for family-style dining. There's a small pool with a bar. Hikes and horseback rides are offered, as are boat trips to Isla del Caño and sportfishing, and there's a fully stocked dive shop.

For a private house rental, check out **Drake's Bay Beach House** (U.S. tel. 954-493-8426, www.drakesbaybeachhouse.com, low season $159, $999 per week, high season $199, $1,254 per week), which sleeps six people. Opposite Café PuraVida and sitting atop a hill, it offers sublime views, refreshing breezes, and an eco-sustainable design. It has a covered deck and comes with a maid and a handyman.

BETWEEN AGUJITAS AND CORCOVADO

I like the rustic yet Swiss-clean (and Swiss-Tico-run) **Las Caletas Lodge** (tel. 506/8826-1460, www.caletas.co.cr, Nov.-Aug., $75-95 s/d, including meals and taxes), at Playa Las Caletas. The lodge is open on three sides, with open-air family dining and lovely views beyond the manicured lawns. The five simply

Villas La Paloma Lodge

appointed one- or two-story cabins are cross-ventilated with screened windows and have tiled hot-water baths and hammocks on balconies. There are also two tent-cabins ($65 pp).

At Playa San Josecito, a Tico named Pincho Amaya and his expat wife, Jenny, run **Poor Man's Paradise** (tel. 506/2788-1442, www.mypoormansparadise.com, 3-day packages from $325 pp, including meals, boat transfers, and tours). They have two rooms, plus 12 tent-cabins, all with shared baths. You can also camp ($10 pp, meals extra). Meals are served in an airy *rancho*. Electricity is shut off at 9pm. Pincho offers sportfishing and tours.

Perfect for honeymooners and solitude-seekers, the gorgeous ★ **Drake Bay Rainforest Chalet** (tel. 506/8701-7462, www.drakebayholiday.com, 3-night package from $1,150 pp, including round-trip airfare from San José) is tucked up along the Río Agujitas, a 20-minute walk from Playa Cocalito. This open-plan mahogany chalet with a full kitchen and a full entertainment system (including satellite TV) has vast picture windows and a gracious aesthetic, including rattan furniture and romantic mosquito netting over the king bed.

By far the most luxurious place in the region is ★ **Casa Corcovado Jungle Lodge** (tel. 506/2256-8825, U.S. tel. 888-896-6097, www.casacorcovado.com, 3-day package from $695 s, $1,190 d), run by Chicago expat Steven Lill, who has conjured a wonderful hilltop resort from a defunct cacao plantation close to the northern border of Corcovado National Park. There are 14 thatched, conical *cabinas* (including two "honeymoon" units) with hardwood four-poster beds and mosquito nets, ceiling fans, twin-level ceilings, and huge showers with hot water and designer fixtures. There's a lounge and a library, plus a mirador bar. Trails lace the 120-hectare (300-acre) property. A small spring-fed pool provides cooling dips. It has guided hikes, sea kayaking, and scuba diving. The restaurant serves gourmet cuisine, family-style. This calming counterpoint to the tangle of Corcovado on its doorstep is one of only 11 hotels in the country to earn five leaves in the Certification for Sustainable Tourism program.

In 2011, California entrepreneur Jay Tress opened **Copa de Arbol** (tel. 506/8935-1212, www.copadearbol.com, low season $220-240 d, high season $270-290 d, with meals), a lovely two-story lodge made entirely of fallen timber and bamboo about two miles west of Agujitas. Its 10 air-conditioned rooms, stilt-cottages, cabins, and a duplex each have ceiling fans, huge windows, and stylish contemporary baths. Guests get use of boogie boards, kayaks, and mountain bikes. Trails lead into the hotel's own forest reserve.

Another lovely, airy option, **Guaria de Osa** (U.S. tel. 908-998-1920 or 510-235-4313, www.guariadeosa.com, $150 pp), built from reclaimed hardwoods at Playa Rincón de San Josecito, is also within walking distance of the national park. It's centered on a three-tier Balinese-style lodge called Lapa Lapa; the top tier serves as an observation perch and meditative space. It has five rooms, two cabins, and five "tentaloos"—upscale safari tents with wooden floors and a shared bathhouse with exquisite tile. Delicious meals are served in a handsome restaurant. It specializes in yoga and has a garden and nursery growing native trees and fruits.

Food

Martina Wegener prepares ceviche and cooks up fresh seafood, burgers, pastas, and fajitas at **Café Pura Vida** (tel. 506/8720-0801, www.puravidadrakebay.com, 8am-8pm daily), in the heart of Agujitas. You sit on tree stumps beneath shade in her garden.

For cheap local fare, head to **Soda Mar y Bosque** (tel. 506/8313-1366, 6:30am-9pm daily) serving bargain-priced *gallo pinto* and *casados* (set lunches).

A hotel-restaurant standout, **Jinetes de Osa** (tel. 506/2231-5806, www.costaricadiving.com), at the southern edge of Agujitas, has a rustic but attractive open-air bar that serves Costa Rican cuisine as well as great burgers and hot dogs.

Information and Services

In Agujitas, the *pulpería* (tel. 506/2771-2336) has a public phone. The **Hospital Clínica Bíblica** is by the beach in Agujitas, and the **police station** (tel. 506/8988-4098) is next to the soccer field. **Soda Mar y Bosque** (tel. 506/8313-1366) has laundry service.

Getting There

Both **SANSA** (tel. 506/2229-4100, U.S./Canada tel. 877-767-2672, www.flysansa.com) and **Nature Air** (tel. 506/2299-6000, U.S. tel. 800-235-9272, www.natureair.com) provide scheduled flights to the Drake Bay airport, north of Agujitas.

A **bus** for Agujitas departs Rincón at 11am daily, and from Agujitas for Rincón at 3:45am daily. The **Sierpe Shuttle** (tel. 506/8586-8920, www.supershuttlecr.com) offers twice-daily service to and from San José and other points.

A **water taxi** ($20 pp) departs Sierpe for Agujitas at 11:30am and 3:30pm daily, and from Agujitas for Sierpe at 7:30am and 2:30pm daily. The trip takes one hour down the rainforest-draped Río Sierpe. Lodges arrange transfers for guests.

The dirt road from Rincón to Agujitas requires fording three rivers; a 4WD vehicle is essential, not least to tackle the steep and muddy sections in wet season, when you'll need a high-clearance vehicle. You'd be wise to wade the rivers to check the depth and the shallowest route across, especially the wide Río Drake.

RINCÓN TO PUERTO JIMÉNEZ

At **La Palma,** 11 kilometers (7 miles) south of Rincón, turn left for Puerto Jiménez. To the right, the gravel and mud road leads 12 kilometers (7.5 miles) up the Valle del Río Rincón to the **Estación Los Patos** ranger station, easternmost entry point to Parque Nacional Corcovado. Eventually you find yourself driving along a riverbed to reach the park; the drive is not possible in wet season.

CoopeUnioro, at Los Patos, is a local cooperative of former gold miners who offer guided tours. Pre-Columbian people sifted gold from the streams of the Osa millennia ago, but it wasn't until the 1980s that gold fever struck. After gold panners—*oreros*—found some major nuggets, prospectors poured into the region. At the boom's heyday, at least 3,000 miners were entrenched in Parque Nacional Corcovado. Because of the devastation they wrought—dynamiting riverbeds, polluting rivers, and felling trees—the park service and civil guard ousted the miners in 1986. Most *oreros* have turned to other ventures—not least ecotourism—but it is not unusual to bump into a lucky (or luckless) *orero* celebrating (or commiserating) over a beer in a bar.

Finca Köbö (tel. 506/8398-7604, www.fincakobo.com), four kilometers (2.5 miles) south of La Palma on the road to Puerto Jiménez, is worth a visit. This self-sufficient organic farm grows cacao, fruits, and vegetables, and has trails through 30 hectares (74 acres) of primary rainforest. A chocolate tour is offered ($32), as is kayaking and even a night tour in the forest. It's also a nice place to stay ($33 s, $60 d), with a lovely upscale rustic ambience. Six bedrooms above the lounge have fans, mosquito nets, and hot water, plus hammocks on the veranda. It serves hearty meals using products from the organic garden.

About 25 kilometers (16 miles) southeast of La Palma, four kilometers (2.5 miles) before Puerto Jiménez, a turnoff to the right follows the Río Tigre 14 kilometers (9 miles) west to **Dos Brazos,** another old gold-mining center, one kilometer (0.6 miles) from the eastern border of Parque Nacional Corcovado.

Accommodations

Tucked in the forest, the charming **Danta Corcovado Lodge** (tel. 506/2735-1111, www.dantalodge.com, from $108 s/d, including meals), about two kilometers (1.2 miles) west of La Palma on the Los Patos road, is a Goldilocks and the Three Bears-style lodge of rough-hewn timbers and cut logs. Run by the local community, it has exquisite, albeit simply appointed, rooms, plus two tin-roofed, cement-floor cabins; the latter have lovely outside showers and modern toilets. A lagoon contains caimans. Horseback riding, bird-watching, and hiking tours are offered. Bring insect repellent.

About as rustic as it gets, **Bolita Rainforest Hostel** (tel. 506/8877-7334, www.bolita.org, camping or dorm $12 pp), at Dos Brazos, rents foam mattresses to campers and has dorms and solar-heated showers. Set amid its own 61-hectare (150-acre) patch of rainforest, it has 13 kilometers (8 miles) of trails. It's a tough 700-meter (0.4-mile) hike from the end of the road, and you have to cross the river, which can be impassable in wet season. It's closed off-season.

Also at Dos Brazos and requiring a river crossing, the rustic wood-and-stone tin-roofed **Bosque del Río Tigre Sanctuary & Lodge** (tel. 506/8824-1372 or 506/8383-3905, www.osaadventures.com, low season $146 s, $254 d, high season $168 s, $286 d, including meals) adjoins a 13-hectare (31-acre) private nature reserve and has four bedrooms, plus a cabin with a private bath. Bird-watching is a specialty. A nighttime frog walk, mangrove kayaking, and other activities are offered, as are package rates.

To live like Tarzan and Jane, but in style, opt for a night atop a 70-meter-tall (230-foot-tall) *guanacaste* tree at ★ **Lapa's Nest Costa Rica Tree House** (tel. 506/8372-3529, U.S. tel. 508/714-0622, www.treehouseincostarica.com, low season $1,800 per week, high season $2,275 per week), in the foothills above the hamlet of Barrio Bonito, 13 kilometers (8 miles) north of Puerto Jiménez. The six-level, four-bedroom, two-bath house has a living room, a kitchenette, gas-heated hot water, Wi-Fi (most of the time), a flat-screen TV, and wonderful 360-degree ocean views. With luxurious Egyptian cotton sheets it makes "Swiss Family Robinson's tree house look like the slums," says owner and creator Michael Cranford. If you literally want to live with the monkeys, this is it. The tree house is the highlight of **Lapa's Retreat,** a villa with eight rental rooms and a huge mezzanine lounge. It's part Gaudí, part Tolkien in inspiration and makes fabulous use of natural timbers and river stone, with open walls and a pool. Michael's rainforest reserve has trails (tree-house guests get a private naturalist guide plus a maid). Advance reservations are required; no walk-ins. To reach it, turn west at the soccer field in Barrio Bonito, about four kilometers (2.5 miles) west of the Dos Brazos turnoff, and follow the Río Agujitas for two kilometers (2.5 miles)—but it's wise to ask Michael for exact directions.

Getting There

Puerto Jiménez-bound buses pass through La Palma. Buses serve Dos Brazos from Super 96 in Puerto Jiménez at 5:45am, 11am, and 4pm daily; return buses depart Dos Brazos at 6am, noon, and 5pm daily.

PUERTO JIMÉNEZ

This small laid-back town serves as the gateway to Parque Nacional Corcovado and is popular with the backpacking crowd and surfers. Locals have colorful tales to tell of gambling and general debauchery during the gold-boom days in the 1980s, when the town briefly flourished, prostitutes charged by the ounce, and miners bought bottles of whiskey just to throw at the walls.

A mangrove estuary lies northeast of town, fed by the **Río Platanares.** There's a chance of seeing caimans, monkeys, freshwater turtles, rays, even river otters and crocodiles—and scarlet macaws can be seen and heard squawking in the treetops and flying overhead. The mangroves extend east to **Playa Platanares** (also called Playa Preciosa), a gorgeous kilometers-long swath of sand about five kilometers (3 miles) east of town. A reef lies offshore in jade-colored waters, the forest behind the beach abounds with wildlife, and the views across the gulf are fantastic. Five species of marine turtles come ashore to lay eggs on the beach, notably May-December. There's a **turtle hatchery** (*vivero*); nocturnal

Puerto Jiménez

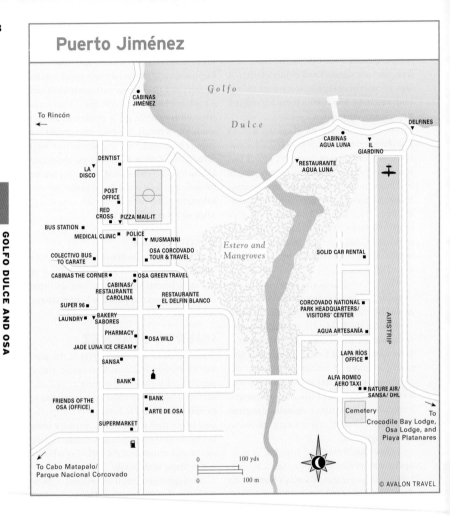

To Rincón

Golfo Dulce

CABINAS JIMÉNEZ

DELFINES

CABINAS AGUA LUNA

IL GIARDINO

RESTAURANTE AGUA LUNA

DENTIST

LA DISCO

POST OFFICE

RED CROSS   PIZZA MAIL-IT

BUS STATION

MEDICAL CLINIC   POLICE

MUSMANNI

Estero and Mangroves

COLECTIVO BUS TO CARATE

OSA CORCOVADO TOUR & TRAVEL

SOLID CAR RENTAL

CABINAS THE CORNER   OSA GREEN TRAVEL

CABINAS/ RESTAURANTE CAROLINA

RESTAURANTE EL DELFIN BLANCO

SUPER 96

CORCOVADO NATIONAL PARK HEADQUARTERS/ VISITORS' CENTER

LAUNDRY   BAKERY SABORES

AIRSTRIP

PHARMACY   OSA WILD

AGUA ARTESANÍA

JADE LUNA ICE CREAM

LAPA RÍOS OFFICE

SANSA

BANK

ALFA ROMEO AERO TAXI

NATURE AIR/ SANSA/ DHL

FRIENDS OF THE OSA (OFFICE)

BANK

ARTE DE OSA

Cemetery

To Crocodile Bay Lodge, Osa Lodge, and Playa Platanares

SUPERMARKET

To Cabo Matapalo/ Parque Nacional Corcovado

0   100 yds

0   100 m

© AVALON TRAVEL

turtle tours can be arranged (no flashlights are permitted).

A huge area around Platanares is being protected and reforested back to its natural state by philanthropist billionaire Paul Tudor-Jones, who even bought out local tuna- and shrimp-fishing rights to restore the gulf populations. Meanwhile, **Herrera Gardens & Conservation Project** (tel. 506/2735-5267, 6am-5pm daily, self-guided tour $5, 2-hour guided tour $15) is a 103-hectare (255-acre) swatch of rainforest with gardens plus 15 kilometers (9.5 miles) of forest trails good for bird-watching and wildlife-spotting. The gardens are a mosaic given to specific botanical themes, such as heliconias and medicinal herbs. It even has some tree platforms. Tour operators in town arrange visits, or visitors can drop in; the entrance is opposite Crocodile Bay Lodge, east of the town.

Entertainment

Backpackers gravitate to watch surf videos and play table soccer and pool at the open-air bar at **Cabinas Iguana Iguana** (tel. 506/2735-5158, 4pm-2am daily).

The hot spot in town is **La Disco** (tel. 506/2735-6060), which revs into high gear on weekends. On Friday nights, head out to **Pearl of the Osa** (tel. 506/8848-0752, www.iguanalodge.com), at the Iguana Lodge at Playa Platanares. Bring your dance shoes for sexy salsa, merengue, and *cumbia* dancing, fueled by a live band—the Villalobos Brothers—and killer cocktails. Look out for The Bone Rollers, an eclectic group of musically gifted expats who crank out everything from punk rock to Santana.

Sports and Recreation

Osa Travel (tel. 506/5014-1818, www.osa-travel.com) offers active adventures from snorkeling and sea kayaking to a zip-line canopy tour, operated by **Aventuras Bosque Mar** (tel. 506/2735-5752), eight kilometers (5 miles) south of Puerto Jiménez. **Aventuras Tropicales** (tel. 506/2735-5195, www.aventurastropicales.com), on the road to Platanares, offers a similar menu and even has a Crocodile by Candlelight tour. California expat Andy Pruter offers the most rad tours through his **Everyday Adventures** (tel. 506/8353-8619, www.psychotours.com), alias Psycho Tours. You can also thrill to a rope climb up a giant strangler fig ($85), then leap from a platform 20 meters (66 feet) above the ground. The waterfall rappels ($85) will get your heart racing.

Osa Wild (tel. 506/8765-3330, www.osawildtravel.com) offers community-rooted tours that include rural homestays and cultural immersion.

Crocodile Bay Resort (tel. 506/2735-5631, U.S. tel. 800-733-1115, www.crocodile-bay.com), about one kilometer (0.6 miles) east of town, and **La Islas Lodge** (tel. 506/2735-5510, www.lasislaslodge.com), about two kilometers (1.2 miles) west of town, specialize in sportfishing.

Pollo's Surf School (tel. 506/8366-6559, www.pollosurfschool.com) offers lessons.

Shopping

You can buy souvenirs anywhere, but a visit to **Jagua Artesanía** (tel. 506/2735-5267, 7am-5pm daily), by the airstrip, will have you pulling out your wallet posthaste. Owner Karen Herrera has Boruca masks and a great collection of jewelry, much of it indigenous, plus blown glass. **Arte de Osa** (tel. 506/2735-5429, 8am-5pm daily) is a worthy alternative.

Accommodations

Sparse it may be, but **The Corner** (tel.

A water taxi awaits customers in Puerto Jiménez.

506/2735-5328, www.jimenezhotels.com/cabinasthecorner, with cold water $8 s, with hot water $12 s, $18 d) has clean digs that include a dorm and five rooms, all with fans and private baths. It has laundry and rents tents ($8) and bikes ($1.50).

Cabinas Marcelina (tel. 506/2735-5286, fax 506/2735-5007, www.jimenezhotels.com/cabinasmarcelina, with fan $25 s, $40 d, with a/c $36 s, $50 d), 200 meters (660 feet) south of the soccer field, offers six simply furnished clean and charming rooms with private baths and fans.

Although pricey considering its meager furnishings, the beachfront **Agua Luna Restaurant and Cabinas** (tel. 506/2735-5393, www.jimenezhotels.com/cabinasagualuna, from $35 s, $45 d) is one of the nicer places and has clean simply furnished, air-conditioned rooms with large windows, TVs, and private baths; six rooms have hot water.

The nicest *cabinas* in town are at the well-run shorefront ★ **Cabinas Jiménez** (tel. 506/2735-5090, www.cabinasjimenez.com, from $40 s, $55 d), offering bay vistas. Kept spick-and-span, these lovely air-conditioned cabins in various types all come with fans, mini fridges, safes, Guatemalan bedspreads, and porches with chairs for enjoying the views. It also has a choice of superb bungalows and a wooden *rancho,* as well as Wi-Fi and a swimming pool.

Sportfishing fans should book at either **Las Islas Lodge** (tel. 506/2735-5242, www.lasislaslodge.com, low season from $65 s/d, high season from $95 s/d, including breakfast and tax), about two kilometers (1.2 miles) west of town; or at **Crocodile Bay Resort** (tel. 506/2735-5631, U.S. tel. 800-733-1115, www.crocodilebay.com, low-season from $65 s/d, high season from $95 s/d), about one kilometer (0.6 miles) east of town. Both specialize in sportfishing packages and have spacious, graciously furnished air-conditioned rooms.

Hands down the nicest place for miles, the beachfront ★ **Iguana Lodge** (tel. 506/8848-0752, www.iguanalodge.com, low season from $145 s/d, high season from $180 s/d), at Playa Platanares, boasts a luxurious aesthetic courtesy of nature-loving live-in owners Loran and Toby Cleaver, from Colorado. It has two types of lodging. First, to one side, four hardwood casitas raised on stilts amid the forest have louvered windows on all sides, plus broad verandas. Shared showers and baths (candlelit at night) are located nearby. Newer, more luxurious cabins have private baths. To the other side, a wooden lodge has eight upstairs Iguana Club Rooms done up in sumptuous tropical fashion, with divinely comfy king beds, ceiling fans, halogen lighting, and gorgeous modern baths with huge walk-in showers. A simply furnished three-bedroom house—Villa Kula—includes a master suite with its own wraparound veranda (3-night minimum, low season $499, high season $650). There are two deluxe cabins, along with a Balinese-inspired yoga deck, a gym, and a 20-meter (66-foot) lap pool with a huge hot tub. Gourmet meals are served family-style; there's also a simpler beachfront restaurant and bar.

Food

The breakfast spot of choice, **Restaurante Carolina** (tel. 506/2735-5185, 6am-10pm daily, $2-10), 100 yards south of the soccer field, serves a good granola with fruit and yogurt, plus other American-style breakfasts. It has cheap *casados* for lunch, and the inexpensive menu includes chicken cordon bleu and fettuccine alfredo.

Pizza Mail-It (tel. 506/2735-5483, 4pm-10:30pm daily), next to the post office, has a delightful, relaxed open-air terrace. Italian expats Nadia and Fabio Colvatti are great hosts and make a fantastic thin-crust pizza, plus homemade calzones and pastas. *Delicioso!* Italian expats have also brought gourmet fare to town at the waterfront **Il Giardino** (tel. 506/2735-5129, www.ilgiardinoitalianrestaurant.com, 10am-10pm Mon.-Fri.), with a huge menu of Mediterranean favorites using fresh homemade pastas.

Worth the drive to Playa Platanares is ★ **Pearl of the Osa** (tel. 506/8848-0752, www.iguanalodge.com, 11am-8:30pm daily,

$2-15) at Iguana Lodge, with a beautiful hardwood bar and spacious shaded patio with hammocks. It serves ceviche, chicken fingers, burritos, burgers, tuna melts, *casados,* and seafood dishes. Nonguests can also make reservations for gourmet family-style dinners at the lodge's fine-dining Iguana Rancho, with its revolving menu of regional specials such as ginger chili-grilled mahimahi, and Vietnamese shrimp and chicken satay. Friday night is pasta night, with live music and dancing.

Information and Services

Osa Travel (tel. 506/2735-5649, www.osatravel.com) and Osa Corcovado Tours & Travel (tel. 506/8632-8150, www.soldeosa.com) offer visitor information. The Osa Conservation Area headquarters (tel. 506/2735-5580, corcovado@minae.go.cr, 7:30am-noon and 1pm-5pm Mon.-Fri.), beside the airstrip, has a visitor information office; you must register here if you're visiting Parque Nacional Corcovado on your own.

There's a medical clinic (tel. 506/2735-5203), a Red Cross (tel. 506/2735-5109), and police station (tel. 506/2735-5114), all 50 meters (165 feet) southwest of the soccer field. Dentist Dr. Muñoz (tel. 506/2735-6303) speaks English.

The Banco Nacional is at the south end of town. The post office is on the west side of the soccer field. Wash clothes at Lavandería Puerto Jiménez (tel. 506/8548-0730, 8am-6pm Mon.-Sat.), two blocks south of the bus station.

Getting There and Around

SANSA (tel. 506/2229-4100, U.S./Canada tel. 877-767-2672, www.flysansa.com) and Nature Air (tel. 506/2299-6000, U.S. tel. 800-235-9272, www.natureair.com) have scheduled daily flights to Puerto Jiménez from San José and Drake Bay. Alfa Romeo Aero Taxi (tel. 506/8632-8150, www.alfaromeoair.com) has an office at the airstrip.

Transportes Blanco (tel. 506/2257-4121 or 506/2771-4744) buses depart San José for

Puerto Jiménez (8 hours, $10) from Calle 14, Avenidas 9/11, at noon daily, and from San Isidro de El General at 6:30am and 3:30pm daily. Transporte Térraba (tel. 506/2783-4293) buses depart Ciudad Neily ($4) at 6am and 2pm daily. Buses depart Puerto Jiménez for San José at 5am daily; for San Isidro at 5am and 1pm daily; and for Ciudad Neily at 5:30am and 2pm daily.

Water taxis (tel. 506/2775-0472 or 506/8896-7519), or *lanchas,* run from the *muelle* (dock) in Golfito for Puerto Jiménez (1.5 hours, $6) at 6am, 11am, and 3pm daily, and return at 6am, 8:45am, 11am, and 2pm daily. Private boats can be hired for the journey ($10).

Taxis await customers on the main street. Solid Car Rental (tel. 506/2735-5777) has an office by the airstrip.

PUERTO JIMÉNEZ TO CARATE

The southeast shore of Osa is lined with hidden beaches—Playa Tamales, Playa Sombrero—in the lee of craggy headlands, notably Cabo Matapalo at the southeast tip of the Osa Peninsula about 18 kilometers (11 miles) south of Puerto Jiménez. Surfers flock for the powerful two-meter (6-foot) waves, especially in summer.

The rough dirt road peters out 43 kilometers (27 miles) from Puerto Jiménez at Carate, consisting of an airstrip and a small *pulpería* (grocery). About three kilometers (2 miles) before Carate, you pass Laguna Pejeperrito, good for spotting crocodiles, caimans, and waterfowl. The drive to Carate takes about two hours in good conditions. It gets gradually narrower, bumpier, and muddier. Several rivers need fording and can be impassable in wet season: A high-clearance 4WD vehicle is essential, but even that is no guarantee of passage. The Río Agua Buena is the real challenge, but even the narrow and seemingly innocuous Río Carbonera, which pours into the sea near Matapalo, has washed vehicles downriver after torrential rains.

You can charter an airplane to Carate, but

the airstrip sometimes floods in wet season. A *colectivo* truck (tel. 506/2837-3120) runs from Puerto Jiménez (2 hours, one-way $8 pp) at 6am and 1:30pm daily, departing Carate for Puerto Jiménez ($7) at 8:30am and 4pm daily. It stops at Matapalo ($4). You can also rent a Jeep taxi ($80-100 per carload).

Accommodations
CABO MATAPALO

Near Matapalo, surfers and backpackers can flop at the eclectic **Buena Esperanza** (tel. 506/2735-5531, martinatica@hotmail.com, $25 pp), also called Martina's, beloved for its colorful Moroccan-style decor. Windowless open-sided *cabinas* have low cement walls with wraparound sofas with batiks and cushions, sponge-washed concrete floors, and rough-hewn beds with mosquito nets. Toilets and outdoor showers are shared and have cold water only. Rates include breakfast. Its offbeat bar-restaurant (9am-midnight daily) serves international cuisine (such as Thai and Mexican) at budget prices.

Several world-renowned eco-lodges line the route, among them the Spanish- and German-run **El Remanso Lodge** (tel. 506/2735-5569, www.elremanso.com, low season from $195 s, $260 d, high season $265 s, $340 d, including meals), atop Cabo Matapalo. It runs entirely on its own hydroelectric power and offers seven spacious and airy cabins with sponge-washed concrete floors and a gorgeous aesthetic that includes soft-contoured concrete bed bases, batik covers, hammocks, and wall-to-wall louvered windows. It also has a two-story group cabin for four people, plus a six-bedroom house, plus an open-air restaurant, a deck with plunge pool, and a zip line.

A deluxe gem, ★ **Bosque del Cabo** (tel. 506/2735-5206, www.bosquedelcabo.com, low season from $190 s, $320 d, high season from $225 s, $360 d) nestles atop the cliff of Cabo Matapalo within its own forest reserve and centered on a stylish *palenque* restaurant and lounge-bar. Set in landscaped grounds are seven thatched cliff-top *cabinas* with superb ocean views. Screened open-air showers

have their own little gardens; verandas have hammocks. Three splendid deluxe cabins each have terra-cotta floors, a king bed with a mosquito net, chic decor, and lofty rough-hewn stable doors that open to a wraparound veranda with sublime ocean vistas. Then there's the Casa Blanca and Casa Miramar, exquisitely decorated two-bedroom villas. Budget travelers get two much simpler cabins, accessed by a muddy forest trail and a suspension bridge. There's a cooling-off pool, a yoga platform, and a zip-line canopy tour.

Also on a ridge near Cabo Matapalo, the eco-conscious ★ **Lapa Ríos** (tel. 506/2735-5130, www.laparios.com, low season from $410 s, $600 d, high season from $540 s, $860 d, including all meals and tours) overcharges for its world fame. Sixteen romantic, luxuriously appointed bungalows reached by wooden stairways feature gleaming hardwood floors, screened windows, gorgeous stone-lined baths, patio gardens complete with outdoor showers, and louvered French doors opening to private terraces. There's a small pool with a sundeck and a bar. The property is backed by a 400-hectare (990-acre) private reserve. Rainforest hikes and other excursions are offered. Lapa Ríos offers superb gourmet dishes in its thatched **Restaurante Brisas Azul** (7am-8:30am daily, $5-25), which has a spiral staircase winding up from the restaurant to a mirador (lookout platform). It's worth the drive just for the carrot cake!

CARATE

Seeking a safari-style experience? **La Leona Eco-lodge** (tel. 506/2735-5704, www.laleonaeco-lodge.com, from $95 s, $178 d, including two meals), just 200 meters (660 feet) from the La Leona ranger station, is a simple tent camp with 17 tent-cabins on wooden platforms, each with two small mattress-beds. Some share a bathhouse with four baths and showers; others have private baths.

In the hills above Carate, the superb **Luna Lodge** (tel. 506/4070-0010, U.S. tel. 888-760-0760, www.lunalodge.com, low season $135-245 s, $250-390 d, high season $150-290 s,

Abusing the Osa

The Osa region has had a tormented history in recent decades at the hands of gold miners, hunters, and loggers. Half of the land that now forms Parque Nacional Corcovado, for example, was obtained in a land trade from a logging company. The opening of a road linking Rincón with Drake Bay in 1997 resulted in a cutting frenzy within the forest reserves (it is claimed that the road was put in as a result of lobbying by loggers). In 1997 a moratorium on logging in Osa was issued following a grassroots campaign by local residents, but laws go unenforced. The loggers are accused of being mafiosi who pay locals to allow illegal logging on their land, while people who speak out against them often end up being intimidated into silence or even killed.

The Osa Peninsula was even slated to get Central America's largest woodchip mill, courtesy of Ston Forestal, a Costa Rican subsidiary of the paper giant Stone Container Corporation of Chicago. The chip mill would have dramatically increased truck traffic and caused excessive pollution that would have threatened the marinelife of the Golfo Dulce. Community efforts to fight the project forced Ston Forestal to shelve its project.

Hunting by Ticos of tapirs, jaguars, peccaries, and other big mammals continues under the nose of—and even in collusion with—park staff. *Oreros* occasionally show up in Puerto Jiménez with ocelot skins and other poached animals for sale. Scarlet macaw nests are routinely poached. The turtle population continues to be devastated by the local populace, who poach the nests simply because there is nobody to stop them. Poison is being used to harvest fish from coastal breeding lagoons such as Peje Perro and Pejeperrito. And the system of issuing wildlife permits is routinely abused by people who obtain a permit for "rescuing" a specific animal, then use the permit to trade other animals. It's a lucrative trade: Local expats claim that some of the money finds its way to low-paid park rangers, who turn a blind eye.

The **Comité de Vigilancia de los Recursos Naturales** (COVIRENA), a branch of the park service, exists in eight indigenous communities around Osa to combat logging and poaching. **Fundación Corcovado** (tel. 506/2297-3013, www.corcovadofoundation.org) and **Friends of the Osa** (tel. 506/2735-5756, www.osaconservation.org) work to save Corcovado's wildlife.

$270-450 d, including meals) is centered on a massive thatched *rancho* lounge-restaurant offering fabulous views. Eight circular bungalows have exquisite rainforest baths with shower-tubs in their own gardens. Or choose one of five safari-style budget tents reached by a stiff uphill climb. A wellness center offers yoga, tai chi, and massages, plus there's a solar-heated pool. To get here, you have to crisscross the Río Carate several times, beginning at Carate; the river is often impassable.

Luna Lodge's nearby and near-identical twin, **Finca Exótica** (tel. 506/2735-5230, www.fincaexotica.com, low season tents $70 s/d, cabins $140 s, $230 d, high season tents $80 s/d, cabins $155 s, $250 d, including all meals) also offers lovely A-frame safari-style open-air thatched cabins plus safari-style tents (most with private outdoor showers). Plus there's a fully equipped two-story cabin for rent. It has a yoga platform and its own private rainforest refuge.

★ CORCOVADO NATIONAL PARK

Parque Nacional Corcovado is the largest stronghold of Pacific coastline primary rainforest, which has been all but destroyed from Mexico to South America. Its 41,788 hectares (103,260 acres) encompass eight habitats, from mangrove swamp and *jolillo* palm grove to montane forest. The park protects more than 400 species of birds (20 exist only here), 116 species of amphibians and reptiles, and 139 of mammals—representing 10 percent of the mammals in the Americas.

Its healthy population of scarlet macaws

(about 1,200 birds) is the largest concentration in Central America. Corcovado is one of very few places in the country harboring squirrel monkeys, and one of the last stands in the world for the harpy eagle. Four species of sea turtles—green, olive ridley, hawksbill, and leatherback—nest on the park's beaches. Plus, the park supports a healthy population of tapirs and big cats, which like to hang around the periphery of the Laguna de Corcovado. Corcovado also has a large population of peccaries. Alas, the park's mammal population is under intense pressure from illegal hunting and logging.

The Osa Peninsula bears the brunt of torrential rains April to December. It receives up to 400 centimeters (157 inches) per year. The driest months, January to April, are the best times to visit.

The park has four main entry points: **La Leona,** on the southeast corner near Carate (the ranger station is about two kilometers/1.2 miles from Carate); **Los Patos,** on the northeastern boundary; **San Pedrillo,** at the northwest corner, 18 kilometers (11 miles) south of Drake Bay; and you can also fly into the park headquarters at **Sirena,** midway between La Leona and San Pedrillo. All entry points are linked by trails. Entrance costs $10, prepaid at Banco Nacional, and the maximum stay is four nights.

Hiking Trails

Corcovado has a well-developed trail system, although the trails are primitive and poorly marked. Several short trails make for rewarding half- or full-day hikes. Longer trails grant an in-depth backpacking experience in the rainforest. Allow three days to hike from one end of the park to the other, which can be done in dry season only.

As of 2014, all visitors must be accompanied by an ICT-certified guide.

FROM LA LEONA

It's 15 kilometers (9.5 miles) from the La Leona ranger station (the southern entrance) at Carate to Sirena. The coast trail follows the beach for most of the way. Allow up to eight hours. Beyond Punta Salsipuedes, the trail cuts inland through the rainforest. You must cross some rocky points that are cut off by high tide: Don't try this at high or rising tide. Consult a tide table before you arrive.

FROM SIRENA

One trail leads northeast to Los Patos via the Laguna de Corcovado—great for wildlife

hiking to San Pedrillo waterfall, Corcovado National Park

viewing. Another trail—only possible at low tide—leads 23 kilometers (14 miles) to the San Pedrillo ranger station, at the northern boundary. There are three rivers to wade. The trick is to reach the Río Sirena and slightly shallower Río Llorona before the water is thigh-deep. Here, watch for crocodiles (and for sharks around high tide). Don't let me put you off; dozens of hikers follow the trail each week. Halfway, the trail winds steeply into the rainforest and is often slippery. The last three kilometers (2 miles) are along the beach. The full-day hike takes you past La Llorona, a 30-meter (100-foot) waterfall that cascades spectacularly onto the beach. Tapirs are said to come down to the beach around sunrise, but you must remain silent at all times, as the animals are timid and easily scared away.

FROM SAN PEDRILLO
You can enter the park at San Pedrillo via the coast trail that leads south from Drake Bay, where lodges will also run you by boat. From the ranger station, a moderately demanding two-kilometer (1.2-mile) hike leads inland to a spectacular waterfall. Be careful; the rocks near its base are very slippery. It has pools beneath a cascade, good for bathing. This is the most visited station due to its proximity to Drake Bay lodges, and the waterfall trail can be crowded in high season.

FROM LOS PATOS
The trail south from Los Patos climbs steeply for six kilometers (4 miles) before flattening out for the final 14 kilometers (9 miles) to the Sirena Research Station. The trail is well marked but narrow, overgrown in parts, and has several river crossings where it is easy to lose the trail on the other side. You must wade. Be especially careful in rainy season, when you may find yourself hip-deep. There are three small shelters en route. A side trail will take you to the Laguna de Corcovado. Allow up to eight hours.

Accommodations
A basic bunkhouse with foam mattresses (but no sleeping bags or linens) is available at **Sirena** ($8 pp), where there are showers and water. Rangers will cook meals by prior arrangement (breakfast $15, lunch and dinner $20), but you have to supply your own food.

Camping is allowed only at ranger stations ($4 pp). Rangers can radio ahead to the various stations within the park and book you in for dinner and a tent spot. No-see-ums, pesky microscopic flies you'll not soon forget, infest

bathers at San Pedrillo cascades, Corcovado National Park

the beaches and come out to find you at dusk. Take a watertight tent, a mosquito net, and plenty of insect repellent.

Reservations are required for all overnight stays, made through the park headquarters in Puerto Jiménez (tel./fax 506/2735-5036, pncorcovado@gmail.com). Thirty days' notice is recommended due to limited space; prepayment is required through Banco Nacional.

Getting There

You can charter **Alfa Romeo Aero Taxi** ($500, up to 5 people) to fly you to Sirena from Puerto Jiménez; otherwise you'll have to hike in from Carate or one of the other access points. Boats from Marenco and Drake Bay will take you to either San Pedrillo or Sirena.

ISLA DEL CAÑO BIOLOGICAL RESERVE

Reserva Biológica Isla del Caño ($10) is 17 kilometers (11 miles) off the western tip of the Osa Peninsula, directly west of Drake Bay. It is of interest primarily for its importance as a pre-Columbian cemetery. Many tombs and artifacts—pestles, corn-grinding tables, and granite spheres (*bolas*)—are gathering moss in the rainforest undergrowth. Isla del Caño gets struck by lightning more often than any other part of Central America, and for that reason was considered sacred by pre-Columbian people, who used it as a burial ground. The 300-hectare (740-acre) island is ringed with secluded white-sand beaches that attract olive ridley turtles. Among its residents are boa constrictors (the only venomous snakes here are sea snakes), giant frogs, a variety of hummingbirds, and three mammal species: the opossum; the paca, which was introduced; and a species of bat. Surprisingly, only 13 terrestrial bird species are found here. Snorkelers can see brilliant tropical fish and moray eels among the coral beds. Offshore waters teem with dolphins and whales.

A wide and well-maintained trail leads steeply uphill from the ranger station. Contact the **Osa Conservation Area headquarters** (Puerto Jiménez, tel./fax 506/2735-5036, pncorcovado@gmail.com) for information. Most lodges in the region offer day trips; it's forbidden to stay overnight.

Baird's tapir

The March of the Soldier Crabs

If you think you see the beach moving, it's not the heat nor last night's excess of *guaro* messing with your mind. Daily, whole columns of seashells—little whelks and conchs of green and blue and russet—come marching down from the roots of the mangroves onto the sand. Scavengers only two centimeters (1 inch) long, soldier crabs are born and grow up without protective shells. For self-preservation they squeeze into empty seashells they find cast up on the beach. Although they grow, their seashell houses do not; thus whole battalions of crabs continually seek newer and larger quarters. When threatened, a soldier crab pulls back into its shell, totally blocking the entrance with one big claw.

Golfo Dulce

The Golfo Dulce region fringes the huge bay of the same name, framed by the Osa Peninsula to the west and the Fila Costeña mountains to the north. The region is centered on the town of Golfito, on the north shore of the gulf. The bay is rimmed by swamp, lonesome beaches, and remote tracts of rainforest accessible only by boat. Humpback whales and dolphins are frequently seen in the bay.

Río Claro, 64 kilometers (40 miles) southeast of Palmar and about 15 kilometers (9.5 miles) west of Ciudad Neily, is a major junction at the turnoff for Golfito from Highway 2. It's about 23 kilometers (14 miles) to Golfito from here. Río Claro has restaurants, a gas station, and taxi service.

PIEDRAS BLANCAS NATIONAL PARK

Centered on the village of La Gamba, this rainforest zone was split from Parque Nacional Corcovado in 1999 and named a national park in its own right. Land within the bounds of Parque Nacional Piedras Blancas is still privately owned, and logging permits issued before 1991 apparently remain valid. The Austrian government underwrites local efforts to save the rainforest. A cooperative provides income for local families whose members are employed at Esquinas Rainforest Lodge (which has kilometers of forest trails) and on fruit farms and a botanical garden; it also has a *tepezcuintle* (lowland paca) breeding program. Guides ($15) can be hired for hiking. The "Rainforest of the Austrians" also operates La Gamba Biological Station in conjunction with the University of Vienna. There's no ranger station.

The turnoff from the Pan-American Highway is at Km. 37, midway between Piedras Blancas and Río Claro. La Gamba is six kilometers (4 miles) from the highway, and a 4WD vehicle is not required. You can also get there via a very rough dirt road that leads north from Golfito, which requires a high-clearance 4WD vehicle.

Playa San Josecito, about 10 kilometers (6 miles) northwest and a 25-minute boat ride from Golfito, is a wide, lonesome, pebbly brown-sand beach. The rainforest sweeps right down to the shore, as it does a few kilometers north at Playa Cativo. The beaches can be accessed by boat and are popular day trips from Golfito.

Fundación Santuario Silvestre de Osa (Osa Wildlife Sanctuary, tel. 506/8861-1309, www.osawildlife.org, Dec.-Apr.), at Playa Cativo, is a nonprofit animal rescue shelter run by Earl and Carol Crews and spanning 304 hectares (751 acres). You're welcomed by howler and spider monkeys, scarlet macaws flap and squawk in the treetops, and don't be surprised if a baby tamandua climbs up your leg and onto your shoulders. Tours are given

Golfito

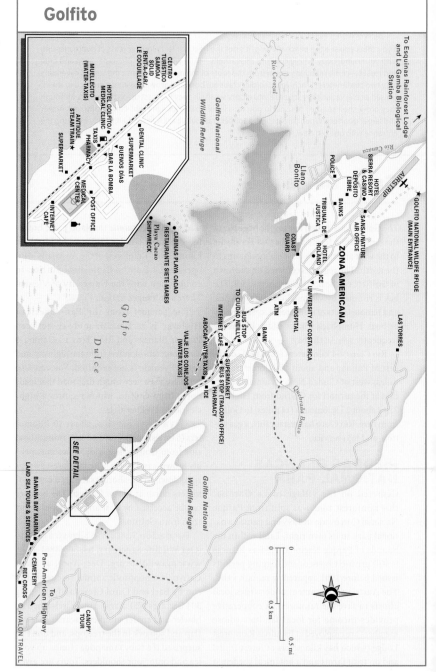

To Esquinas Rainforest Lodge and La Gamba Biological Station

Río Coroval

Golfito National Wildlife Refuge

Llano Bonito

POLICE

HOTEL SIERRA RESORT & CASINO

DEPÓSITO LIBRE

SANSA/NATURE AIR OFFICE

Río Cámara

AIRSTRIP

GOLFITO NATIONAL WILDLIFE RFUGE (MAIN ENTRANCE)

TRIBUNAL DE JUSTICA

BANKS

ZONA AMERICANA

COAST GUARD

HOTEL ROLAND

ICE

UNIVERSITY OF COSTA RICA

LAS TORRES

ATM

HOSPITAL

BANK

BUS STOP TO CIUDAD NEILLY

INTERNET CAFÉ

ABOCAP (WATER TAXIS)

VIAJE LOS CONEJOS (WATER TAXIS)

SUPERMARKET

BUS STOP (TRACOPA OFFICE)

PHARMACY

ICE

Quebrada Banco

Golfo Dulce

CABINAS PLAYA CACAO

RESTAURANTE SIETE MARES

Playa Cacao

SHIPWRECK

SEE DETAIL

Golfito National Wildlife Refuge

BANANA BAY MARINA

LAND SEA TOURS & SERVICES

CEMETERY

RED CROSS

To Pan-American Highway

CANOPY TOUR

To Pan-American Highway

0   0.5 km

0   0.5 mi

© AVALON TRAVEL

Detail

CENTRO TURISTICO SAMOA/SOLID RENT-A-CAR/LE COQUILLAGE

MUELLECITO (WATER-TAXIS)

HOTEL GOLFITO/MEDICAL CLINIC

TAXIS

ANTIQUE STEAM TRAIN

SUPERMARKET

DENTAL CLINIC

SUPERMARKET

PHARMACY

BUENOS DIAS

BAR LA BOMBA

MEDICAL CENTER

POST OFFICE

INTERNET CAFÉ

at 9:30am, 11:30am, and 1:30pm daily by reservation only. A full day's advance notice is required to visit; children under age five are not permitted, and interns are sought.

★ Casa Orquídeas

Casa Orquídeas (tel. 506/8829-1247, 8am-5am Sat.-Thurs., self-guided tour $5 pp, guided tour $8 pp, 3-person minimum) has nearly five hectares (12 acres) of private botanical gardens at the northwest end of Playa San Josecito. This labor of love culminates the 20-odd-year efforts of Ron and Trudy MacAllister. Ornamental plants, including 100 species of orchids, attract zillions of birds. Two-hour guided tours are offered 8:30am-11am Thursday and Sunday. Tour operators throughout Golfo Dulce offer tours to the garden; otherwise take a water taxi from Golfito or any of the local lodges.

Accommodations

The reclusive stone-and-timber **Esquinas Rainforest Lodge** (tel. 506/2741-8001, www. esquinaslodge.com, low season $130 s, $210 d, high season $160 s, $260 d, including 3 meals and taxes), at La Gamba, is a great base for exploring the forest. Its five duplex cabins are connected by a covered walkway to the main lodge, which features an open-walled lounge with forest views. Guest rooms have screened glassless windows, and porches with rockers and hammocks. Facilities include a bar, a gift shop, a library, and a thatched dining room, plus a naturally filtered swimming pool. Excursions are offered.

U.S.-British expats Harvey and Susan are your amiable hosts at **Finca Saladero** (tel. 506/8761-0425, www.fincasaladero.com, camping $10 s/d, low season $95-170 s, $150-240 d, high season $95-200 s, $150-260 d), a laid-back bay-front lodge with wide sloping lawns fronting its own rainforest reserve near the mouth of the Río Esquinas. The duo permit camping and offer safari-style deluxe tent-cabins; a quaint little screen cabin; a simple bungalow; a delightful tree house; and lovely two-story beach house. The couple make gourmet meals, served family-style in the open-air lodge.

Fronted by a beach and backed by a mountainous private rainforest reserve, the splendid ★ **Playa Nicuesa Rainforest Lodge** (tel. 506/2222-0704, U.S./Canada tel. 866-504-8116, www.nicuesalodge.com, mid-Nov.-Sept., low season $230-280 s, $380-830 d, high season $280-305 s, $250-920 d), at Playa Nicuesa, is a perfect base for adventures.

a close encounter with wildlife at Fundación Santuario Silvestre de Osa

Crafted entirely of multihued hardwoods, the two-story open-atrium eco-lodge is a stunner. Four hexagonal cabins and a four-room guesthouse feature a quasi-Japanese motif, canopied beds, ceiling fans in open-beam roofs, and full-length wraparound louvered doors, plus open baths with outdoor showers. The open-air upstairs lounge-cum-dining room looks over the lush grounds, candlelit at night. It has family programs, and yoga is offered on the beachfront deck. River otters and caimans frequent the lagoon, accessed by kayaks.

GOLFITO

Golfito, a sportfishing center and the most important town in the Pacific southwest, is for travelers who love forlorn ports. This one is a muggy, funky, semi-down-at-the-heels place born in 1938, when the United Fruit Company moved its headquarters here after shutting down operations on the Caribbean coast. By 1955 more than 90 percent of the nation's banana exports were shipped from Golfito. The United Fruit Company pulled out in 1985 after a series of crippling labor strikes.

orchid at Casa Orquídeas

The town sprawls for several kilometers along a single road on the estuary of the Río Golfito. First entered, to the southeast, is the **Pueblo Civil,** the run-down working-class section full of tumbledown houses, many hanging on stilts over the water. The Pueblo Civil extends northwest to the compact town center, an area of cheap bar life, with an uninspired plaza. About two kilometers (1.2 miles) farther is the **Muelle de Golfito,** the banana-loading dock (also called Muelle Bananero) at the southern end of the **Zona Americana,** a more tranquil and orderly neighborhood where the administrative staff of United Fruit used to live in brightly painted two-story wooden houses set in manicured gardens. Here, too, is the **Depósito Libre,** a duty-free shopping compound that lures Ticos in droves on weekends, when the town's dozens of cheap *cabinas* fill up. Golfito was declared a duty-free port in 1990—an attempt to offset the economic decline that followed United Fruit's strategic retreat. The

biggest boost may be if the proposed Golfito Marina Village (www.golfitomarinavillage.com) gets built.

The vision of Golfito improves dramatically from across the bay at **Playa Cacao,** literally at the end of the road, five kilometers (3 miles) southwest of Golfito; the winding narrow dirt road can be a challenge in wet season. Popeye the Sailor would have felt at home here; funky charm was never funkier or more charming.

The 1,309-hectare (3,234-acre) **Refugio Nacional de Vida Silvestre de Golfito,** a wildlife refuge created to protect the city's watershed, is a primary rainforest covering the steep mountains immediately east and north of town. The main entrance and park office (tel. 506/2775-2620, 8am-4pm Mon.-Fri.) is via the dirt road that curls around the south end of the airstrip; it's signed. This trail leads to a waterfall. Alternately, a trail that begins behind the Banco Nacional, across from the Plaza Deportes soccer field in the Pueblo Civil, leads about nine kilometers (5.5 miles) uphill to Las Torres radio station. Don't hike this alone due to possibility of muggings; hire a guide such as Pedro Caballo (tel. 506/2775-2240).

Entertainment

On the waterfront in the center of Golfito, **Centro Turístico Samoa** (tel. 506/2775-0233, www.samoadelsur.com, 10am-2am daily) has a dartboard (a darts club meets on Monday nights), table soccer, and a pool table, plus music at a bar shaped like a sailing ship with a busty mermaid prow. **Bar La Bomba,** upstairs opposite the gas station, is another lively, colorful bar with karaoke. Expatriate gringos gravitate toward **Latitude Ocho,** opposite Hotel Costa Surf. **Hotel Roland** (tel. 506/2775-0180), by the Depósito Libre, offers a snazzier alternative. Nearby, the **Casino Golfito** (tel. 506/2775-0666) is open 6pm-2am daily.

Sports and Recreation

Prime season for sailfish is December to May; for marlin, June to September; and for snook, May to September. **Banana Bay Marina** (tel. 506/2775-1111, www.bananabaymarina.com), one kilometer (0.6 miles) south of the town center, offers sportfishing packages and charters, as does **Captain Bobby McGuinness** (tel. 506/2775-0664, www.4costaricafishing.com), who holds more than 140 world records.

Accommodations

The town is awash in budget—and often grim—accommodations not worth recommending.

The **Hotel y Restaurante el Gran Ceibo** (tel. 506/2775-0403, $20-50 s/d), where the road from the Pan-American Highway meets the shore at the entrance to Golfito, has 27 simple rooms in modern two-story and one-story units. All have cool tile floors, TVs, and clean baths. There's a good restaurant and a nice poolside breakfast area, plus a swimming pool and a kids pool. Road noise is a problem. The lively bar draws a young crowd. It has no frills, but it's adequate.

Close to the heart of town is **Hotel Centro Turístico Samoa** (tel. 506/2775-0233, www.samoadelsur.com, low season $40-45, high season $55, up to 4 people), on the waterfront. It has 17 well-kept *cabinas* with fans and TVs. There's an excellent restaurant, the liveliest bar in town, and a swimming pool.

My favorite place in town is the contemporary **Banana Bay Marina** (tel.

Golfo Dulce

A Life in the Trees

A tree house is one thing. But a tree-house community? Yes. Although still in its formative years, **Finca Bellavista** (U.S. tel. 301/560-7160, www.fincabellavista.net, $50-250 s/d) is a 142-hectare (350-acre) eco-sustainable residential community. It will eventually have almost 100 tree houses linked by suspension bridges and by 23 zip lines connecting platforms throughout the property.

Billed as "off the ground, off the grid, and out of this world," this one-of-a-kind community was cofounded in 2006 by Colorado escapees Erica and Matt Hogan, who claim (only half tongue-in-cheek) that the idea was inspired by the Ewoks in the *Return of the Jedi* movie. The Hogans bought what was originally a 25-hectare (62-acre) plot to save it from being cleared for timber. Then they decided to create a community where ecologically minded property owners could live together and steward a managed rainforest environment. Individual lots are sold to buyers who must commit to covenants that protect the environment and the sustainable nature of the project.

If you want to go out on a limb, some units are available to rent, each distinct in design, including a one-bedroom "jungalow" and the octagonal El Castillo Mastate, with a treetop master suite and a kitchen. Some units are up to 20 minutes' walk from base camp. Finca Bellavista has TVs and phones, but not in the rental units, some of which have only minimal solar powered electricity. But you do get access to a community kitchen and dining area, and an open-air *rancho*, the setting for yoga. High-speed Internet and Wi-Fi are available. Trails lead through the rainforest to swimming holes and waterfalls.

This is a work in progress, and construction noise could be part of the deal. Plus, expect tough up-and-down climbing on trails in the rain. A 4WD vehicle is a wise idea for getting here. A two-night minimum stay is required. Reservations are obligatory: No drop-ins or unscheduled visitors are permitted.

506/2775-0838, www.bananabaymarinagolfito.com, low season rooms $75 s/d, suite $100 s/d, high season rooms $95 s/d, suite $135 s/d), overhanging the waters one kilometer (0.6 miles) south of the town center. It offers three standard air-conditioned rooms and a gorgeous master suite, all with gracious mint-and-sea-green decor, ceiling fans, and large baths with walk-in showers. It has a lively bar and restaurant, an Internet café, and the best sportfishing marina in town.

At Playa Cacao, **Rancho Tropical** (U.S. tel. 800-705-3474, www.fishgolfito.com, package rates vary), alias Fish Golfito, is another dedicated sportfishing ranch and has three simply but charmingly furnished cabins by the shore. All have cable TV, DVD players, coffeemakers, and fridges, and you get use of a small swimming pool and a hillside hot tub. It has two 31-foot Bertrams for fishing.

Land-Sea Services (tel./fax 506/2775-1614, www.golfitocostarica.com) offers vacation rentals, including furnished air-conditioned waterfront villas and apartments with gulf views.

Food

In the town center, the clean, air-conditioned **Buenos Días** (tel. 506/2775-1124, 6am-10pm daily), on the main road, serves U.S.-style breakfasts, green salads, and local lunches at bargain prices. For the tastiest Tico fare, you can't beat **Restaurante La Cubana** (tel. 506/8313-1411, 7am-10pm Wed.-Mon.), an open-air *soda* above the main drag downtown.

For elegance and variety, head to **Banana Bay Marina** (tel. 506/2775-0838, 6am-10pm daily, $5-15), one kilometer (0.6 miles) south of the town center, where the menu includes spicy Louisiana gumbo and pork loin with mushroom pasta and veggies. Or try the chic restaurant at **Casa Roland Marina Resort** (tel. 506/2775-0180, 7am-10am and noon-10pm daily), in Zona Americana, serving such nouvelle delights as jumbo shrimp with whiskey and honey mustard ($20) or beef tenderloin over a portobello mushroom and goat cheese ($22).

For inexpensive seafood, I opt for the open-air **Le Coquillage** (6am-11:30pm daily) at Centro Turístico Samoa, which also offers a wide menu, from burgers and pizzas to paella. Portions are filling, and the corvina *al ajillo* (garlic sea bass, $6) is splendid.

Information and Services

Land-Sea Services (tel./fax 506/2775-1614, www.golfitocostarica.com, 7:30am-5pm Mon.-Fri.), on the waterfront at Km. 2, is a one-stop, full-service visitor information and reservation center, with laundry, Internet access, a book exchange, and international phone service. **Banana Bay Marina** (tel. 506/2775-0838, 6am-10pm daily), one kilometer (0.6 miles) south of the town center, has an Internet café; and there's another downtown opposite Hotel Delfina, which hosts the **Lavandería Cristy** (tel. 506/2775-0043), a 24-hour laundry.

The **Hospital de Golfito** (tel. 506/2775-0011) is in the Zona Americana; the **Consultorio Médico** (tel. 506/8832-5800) is by the soccer field. **Dr. Victor Morales Berrocal** (tel. 506/2775-0540) has a dental clinic 100 meters (330 feet) north of the gas station.

The **police station** (tel. 506/2775-1022) is on the west side of the Depósito Libre. There are three banks in the Depósito Libre, and a Banco Nacional in the Zona Americana. The **post office** is on the northwest side of the soccer field, in Pueblo Civil.

The **immigration office** (tel. 506/2775-0487, 7am-11am and 12:30pm-4pm Mon.-Fri.) is beside the *muelle* (dock).

Getting There

Both **SANSA** (tel. 506/2775-0303 or 506/2229-4100, U.S./Canada tel. 877-767-2672, www.flysansa.com) and **Nature Air** (tel. 506/2299-6000, U.S. tel. 800-235-9272, www.natureair.com) operate scheduled flights to Golfito.

Tracopa (tel. 506/2221-4214 or 506/2775-0365) buses depart San José (8 hours, $8) via San Isidro from Calle 5, Avenidas 18/20, thrice daily 7am-10:15pm. Buses depart for Ciudad Neily hourly, and to Zancudo from the *muellecito* (the little dock immediately north of the gas station in the center of Golfito) at 1:30pm daily; and for Puerto Jiménez from the *muelle* at 11am daily.

Water taxis (*lanchas*) depart the *muellecito* to Puerto Jiménez ($5-12 pp each way, depending on the boat) six times daily, and to Playa Cacao ($1 pp each way), Playa Zancudo

Golfito's Zona Americana has many old wooden homes.

($5 pp each way), plus Playa San Josecito and other destinations. Fares are based on a full boat. **Viajes Los Conejos** (tel. 506/2775-2329) operates water taxis to Playa Cacao from near the *muelle bananero* commercial dock; and **Association ABOCOP** (tel. 506/2775-0712) operates from the dock.

You can rent cars with **Solid Car Rental** (tel. 506/2775-3333, www.solidcarrental.com), in the Hotel Centro Turístico Samoa.

Getting Around

Buses (155 colones/$0.30) run between the two ends of town 5:30am-10pm daily. *Colectivos* (shared taxis) also cruise up and down and will run you anywhere in town for $1-2, picking up and dropping off passengers along the way. You can call for a **taxi** (tel. 506/2775-2242 or 506/2775-1170) or flag one down along the main road.

The Burica Peninsula

The rugged Burica Peninsula, on the east side of Golfo Dulce, forms the southernmost tip of Costa Rica. Its dramatically beautiful coast is washed by surf. To the northeast, the Valle de Coto Colorado is planted with banana and date palm trees stretching to the border with Panamá.

★ PLAYA ZANCUDO

Playa Zancudo, 10 kilometers (6 miles) from Golfito as the crow flies, strung below the estuary of the Río Coto Colorado, is one of my favorite offbeat spots. The ruler-straight gray-sand beach (littered with coconuts and flotsam) stretches about six kilometers (4 miles) along a slender spit backed by the mangroves of the **Río Coto swamps,** fed by the estuarine waters of the Río Coto Colorado. Waterfowl abound. With luck you may see river otters, crocodiles, and caimans basking on the riverbanks. The fishing is good in the freshwater (there are several docks on the estuary side) and in the surf at the wide river mouth. High surf comes ashore, but surfers shun Zancudo in favor of nearby Pavones. At dusk and during full moon, the no-see-ums are voracious.

The hamlet of **Zancudo** is near the river mouth at the north end of the spit, reached along a sandy roller-coaster road. Hotels and restaurants are strung along five kilometers (3 miles). The road ends here, by the estuary, making Zancudo one of the most reclusive spots in the country, with killer sunsets thrown in.

Entertainment

The bar at **Cabinas Sol y Mar** (tel. 506/2776-0014, www.zancudo.com), two kilometers (1.2 miles) north of Soda Tranquilo, is a local meeting spot and hosts live acoustic music (Thurs.), volleyball (Sat.), and horseshoes (Sun. afternoon and Wed. evening). Rough-around-the-edges **El Coquito** (tel. 506/2776-0010), in the village, is favored by locals for dancing.

Sports and Recreation

Zancudo Lodge (tel. 506/2776-0008, U.S. tel. 800-854-8791, www.thezancudolodge.com) specializes in sportfishing. **Zancudo Boat Tours** at Cabinas Los Cocos (tel. 506/2776-0012, www.loscocos.com) has kayak trips and boat trips up the Río Coto.

Accommodations

Accommodations are strung out along the five-kilometer (3-mile) spit; there are many more options than listed here.

I like **Cabinas Sol y Mar** (tel. 506/2776-0014, www.zancudo.com, low season $20-27 s/d, high season $33-50 s/d) for its pleasant casual ambience and landscaped grounds. The five economy *cabinas* have Wi-Fi and are tastefully furnished with ceiling fans and private skylighted hot-water baths; river rocks surround the showers. It also has duplex and "nonduplex" cabins, plus a thatched three-story house designed with no dividing walls for free air flow (sleeps 4, $800 per month). There's volleyball and other games at the small but always lively thatched bar, plus great food. You can camp ($4 pp).

Another popular option is **Cabinas Los Cocos** (tel. 506/2776-0012, www.loscocos. com, $70 s/d), about 600 meters (0.4 miles) north of Sol y Mar, with four attractive self-catering oceanfront units amid landscaped grounds. One is a thatched hardwood unit with a double bed downstairs and another in the loft; two others are refurbished banana-company properties shipped from Palmar. Each has a kitchenette, mosquito nets, inside and outside showers, and a veranda with ham-mocks. Delightful owners Susan and Andrew Robertson also operate Zancudo Boat Tours.

For an intimate air-conditioned option, I recommend ★ **Oceano** (tel. 506/2776-0921, www.oceanocabinas.com, low season $40 s/d, high season $60 s/d), run by Canadians Kevin and Elena. The two tiled rooms with ceiling fans have simple yet adorable decor and fur-nishings, including mosquito nets over the beds, plus cable TV. Umbrellas, flashlights, and toiletries are among the thoughtful extras provided. Free Internet access, bicycle use, and breakfast are included. The restaurant is hip.

The only upscale lodging around is **Zancudo Lodge** (tel. 506/2776-0008, U.S. tel. 800-854-8791, www.thezancudolodge. com, $250-525 s/d), at the far north end of Zancudo. Sportfishing is a forte. Its 19 junior suites (most in a two-story unit set around lawns with palms and a swimming pool) have beautiful hardwood floors, glossy hard-wood furnishings, and Wi-Fi throughout. For more room, check into one of the two ocean-front suites. There's a beachfront restaurant and bar.

Food

For the best dining around, head to **Oceano** (tel. 506/2776-0921, www.oceanocabinas. com, 11am-close daily high season, 11am-close Tues.-Sun. low season), where you eat at tree-trunk tables under thatch. Start the day with huevos rancheros, waffles, and omelets ($2.50-4); lunch and dinner means ceviche or pizza. Be sure to leave room for the awesome brownie sundae!

The breakfast menu ($3-6) at **Cabinas Sol y Mar** (7am-9pm daily, $3-13), two kilo-meters (1.2 miles) north of Soda Tranquilo,

Playa Zancudo

includes omelets, french toast, home fries, home-baked breads and muffins, and coffee from a real espresso machine. The lunch and dinner menu ($3-12) features Thai dishes and barbecue. A nightly special could mean pork chops in teriyaki sauce or tuna with capers, rice, chayote squash, and green beans with roasted pepper sauce ($6). It's popular for its Monday- and Friday-night barbecues.

Information and Services

The **police station** (tel. 506/2776-0212) is on the north side of Zancudo village.

Getting There and Around

A **bus** departs from the municipal dock in Golfito for Zancudo ($2) at 2pm daily and travels via Paso Canoas and Laurel. The return bus departs Zancudo at 5:30am daily.

The paved road to Zancudo begins about eight kilometers (5 miles) south of the Pan-American Highway, midway along the road to Golfito; the turn is signed at Únion. In 2010 a wheezing ferry that once transported you across the Río Coto, 18 kilometers (11 miles) beyond El Rodeo, was replaced by a bridge. On the south bank, the intermittently paved road, usually in horrendous condition, runs five kilometers (3 miles) to a Y junction, called La Cruce, at Pueblo Nuevo; turn right for Zancudo and Pavones and continue about 10 kilometers (6 miles) to a T-junction at Conte. Turn right here; Zancudo, in 18 kilometers (11 miles), and Pavones, in 22 kilometers (14 miles), are signed. One kilometer (0.6 miles) along, this road divides; take the right-hand fork for Zancudo, and the left for Pavones. The **Mini-Super Tres Amigos** (Mon.-Sat.) and **Super Bella Vista** (tel. 506/2776-0101), in Zancudo, sell gas.

A *lancha* (water taxi) departs Golfito's *muellecito* (dock) for Zancudo ($5 pp) at noon daily, returning from Zancudo at 7am daily. You can also charter a *lancha* (up to 6 passengers, $50); call the **Asociación de Boteros** (tel. 506/2775-0357). **Zancudo Boat Tours** at Cabinas Los Cocos also has water-taxi service to Golfito or Puerto Jiménez ($20 pp, $50 minimum). **Super Bella Vista** (tel. 506/2776-0101), in Zancudo, has taxi service.

★ PAVONES

From Conte, a bumpy potholed road clambers over the hills south of Zancudo and drops to Punta Pilón and the fishing hamlet of Pavones, a legend in surfing circles for one of the longest waves in the world—more than a kilometer (0.6 miles) on a good day. The waves are at their best May-November, during rainy season, when surfers flock for the legendary very fast and very hollow tubular left. Riptides are common, and swimmers should beware. A narrow coast road with river fords also connects Zancudo directly to Pavones.

South from Pavones, the dirt road crosses the Río Claro and follows the dramatically scenic and rocky coast about five kilometers (3 miles) to the tiny community of **Punta Banco.** About two kilometers (1.2 miles) south of Punta Banco, you reach the end of the road. From here, the Burica Peninsula sweeps southeast 50 kilometers (31 miles) to Punta Burica along a lonesome stretch of coast within the mountainous **Reserva Indígena Guaymí.**

Yoga enthusiasts can sign up for workshops and summer retreats with **The Yoga Farm** (no tel., www.yogafarmcostarica.org), above Punta Banco on the rough dirt road to the Guaymí reserve.

Tiskita Ecolodge & Private Biological Reserve

Farm, nature lodge, exotic-fruit station, biological reserve, seaside retreat: **Tiskita Lodge** (tel. 506/2296-8125, www.tiskita.com) is all these and more. Overlooking Punta Banco, one kilometer (0.6 miles) north of the village, Tiskita offers sweeping panoramas. The rustic old lodge is surrounded by 150 hectares (370 acres) of virgin rainforest laced by trails; one leads sharply uphill to a series of cascades and pools. Wildlife abounds. Owner Peter Aspinall's pride and joy is his tropical-fruit farm, which contains the most extensive collection of tropical fruits in Costa Rica. Peter is also involved in a scarlet macaw release program. Guided nature walks, horseback rides, and bird-watching hikes are offered.

Punta Banco Sea Turtle Restoration Project

Endangered olive ridley turtles (plus hawksbill and green turtles in lesser numbers) lay their eggs along these shores, predominantly August to December. The locals long considered them a resource to be harvested for eggs and meat. In 1996 the **Programa Restauración de Tortugas Marinas** (PRETOMA, tel. 506/2241-5227, www.pretoma.org) began a program to instill a conservation ethic in the community. It initiated a program to collect and hatch turtle eggs and release the hatchlings directly into the ocean, dramatically increasing their chances of survival. Poaching of nests has been reduced from 100 percent of nests in 1995 to less than 20 percent, and the hatcheries now achieve a better than 80 percent hatching rate for translocated eggs.

Sports and Recreation

Alexander Outerbridge and Amy Khoo run **Sea Kings Surf Shop** (tel. 506/2776-2015, www.surfpavones.com), which rents boards, and **Shooting Star Studio** (www.yogapavones.com), offering yoga classes. **Venus Surf Adventures** (tel. 506/2776-2014, www.venussurfadventures.com) also rents boards and offers surf camps and lessons.

Accommodations

In Pavones, there are almost a dozen budget options on the north side of the soccer field, and more within shouting distance. By far the most appealing is the endearing **Cabinas & Café de la Suerte** (tel. 506/2776-2388, www.cafedelasuerte.com, $35-70 s/d), behind the café in the heart of Pavones. It has four colorful air-conditioned rooms with Guatemalan bedspreads, fans, and Wi-Fi. One has a double bed and a bunk.

A popular budget option and a favorite of surfers, the Dutch-run **Rancho Burica** (tel.

506/2776-2223, www.ranchoburica.com, dorm $15 pp, rooms $30-70 s/d, including breakfast and dinner), at the end of the road in Punta Banco, offers a range of options. Set in trim gardens, seven simple cabins have huge cold-water showers and large porches, and there's a thatched dorm, plus simply yet pleasantly furnished cabins. Barbecues are made on the grill, guests have kitchen privileges, and there's a fishing boat for trips.

The most popular surfer lodge is **La Ponderosa Beach & Jungle Resort** (tel. 506/2776-2076, U.S. tel. 954-771-9166, www.laponderosapavones.com, cabins $60-140 s/d, cash only), 2.5 miles north of Punta Banco, run by Angela and Marshall McCarthy. Set in five hectares (12 acres) of gardens, it offers six two-story cabins with varnished hardwoods, fans, screened windows, and modern tiled baths with hot water; four have air-conditioning and two are suites. A dining room serves burgers, seafood, and more. It has a lounge with a bar, a TV, a sand volleyball court, and a swimming pool. It also rents a five-bed villa ($200) and an upscale two-bedroom house with a king bed and a kitchen ($250). Trails lead to a waterfall.

"Eclectic" and "Tolkienesque" perfectly describe **Castillo de Pavones** (tel. 506/2776-2191, www.castleofcostarica.com, $150-250 s/d, including breakfast), in the hills behind Pavones. The rooms here will bring a smile to your face. This three-story stone-and-timber lodge has six huge individually themed suites with king beds hewn of lofty tree trunks, and quaint black stone-lined baths with waterfall sinks, whirlpool tubs, and homemade organic toiletries. The bi-level restaurant is a winner.

Families or a group of friends should try for the Colorado-style ★ **Casa Siempre Domingo Bed and Breakfast** (tel. 506/2776-2185, www.casa-domingo.com, call for rates), a deluxe breeze-brushed lodge nestled on the hillside 400 meters (0.25 miles) inland, 1.5 kilometers (0.9 miles) south of the Río Claro. A mammoth cathedral ceiling soars over the lounge and the dining room, done up in evocative tropical style, with plentiful bamboo and rainforest prints. It has four rooms and the entire house can be rented as a single unit.

Joseph Robertson and his girlfriend, Shirley, are great hosts at **Rancho Cannatella** (tel. 506/2776-2251, www.pavonesranchocannatella.com, $25-35 pp), two kilometers (1.2 miles) south of Pavones. This lovely four-bedroom villa with wings flanking a free-form pool can be rented in its entirety ($450), but the air-conditioned rooms (which vary) are also rented individually; one has a king bed and a rainforest shower. There's also a simple wooden cabin. Joseph will teach you stand-up paddle surfing, and kayaks and snorkeling gear are available.

For an immersion in nature, check into ★ **Tiskita Lodge** (tel. 506/2296-8125, www.tiskita.com, call for rates), in the hills above Punta Banco. It's centered on a charming old farmhouse that serves as lounge and dining room. There are 16 spacious rooms in nine rustic, sparsely furnished, but huge and comfortable wooden cabins in a combination of double, twin, and bunk beds (with rather soft mattresses). Each cabin has screened windows, a wide veranda with a hammock and an Adirondack chair, plus a stone-lined outdoor bath with a shower and solar-heated water. "Country-style" meals are served family-style at set times (don't be late), and packed lunches are provided for hikers. It has a small swimming pool and a rustic bar. Three- to seven-day packages are offered, and the lodge is reserved for groups only June-August.

Food

The best place to start your day is **Café de la Suerte** (tel. 506/2776-2388, www.cafedelasuerte.com, 8am-5pm Mon.-Sat.), on the plaza in Pavones. Run by a delightful Argentinean woman, this simple open-air vegetarian restaurant serves granola with yogurt and fruit, plus sandwiches, hummus, omelets, cappuccinos, and fruit shakes.

I love the hip vibe at **La Manta Club** (tel. 506/2776-2281, food noon-10pm daily, drinks noon-1am daily, $2-12), on the beachfront in Pavones. Sloping timber frames support a soaring thatched roof—a great space for lazing to cool music while savoring fish tacos, falafels, hummus, shish kebabs, ice cream, and iced drinks. Movies are shown on a big screen at 6pm daily.

Restaurante La Bruschetta (tel. 506/2776-2174, 11am-10pm daily, $5-15), between Pavones and Punta Banco, is an exquisite open-air Italian restaurant serving hand-tossed wood-oven pizzas and pastas (gnocchi, lasagna), plus salads and burgers served on the open-air terrace.

Information and Services

The public phone (tel. 506/2770-8221) is at Soda La Plaza, beside the soccer field in Pavones. Nearby, **Clear River Sports & Adventure** (tel. 506/2776-2016, 8:30am-4:30pm daily) has an Internet café with Skype.

There's a **police station** (no tel.) on the north side of the soccer field in Pavones. The nearest **Red Cross** station is at Conte.

Getting There

A private airstrip allows direct access to Tiskita by chartered **plane** (55 minutes from San José).

Buses depart Golfito for Pavones and Punta Banco at 10am (Pavones only) and 3pm daily, returning at 5am (from Rancho Burica) and 12:30pm (from Pavones only) daily.

The coast road that leads south from Pavones ends at the mouth of the Río Claro, one kilometer (0.6 miles) south of the village. To cross it and continue to Punta Banco, back up and turn inland at Escuela Las Gemelas, then right at Super Mares; you'll cross a bridge, then drop back down to the coast.

A private **water-taxi** charter from Golfito will cost about $65 one-way. A **Jeep taxi** from Golfito to Pavones will cost about $75.

★ ISLA DEL COCO MARINE NATIONAL PARK

The only true oceanic island off Central America, **Parque Nacional Marino Isla del Coco**—500 kilometers (300 miles) southwest of Costa Rica—is a 52-square-kilometer (20-square-mile) mountainous chunk of land, called Cocos Island in English, that rises to 634 meters (2,080 feet) at Cerro Iglesias. Declared a UNESCO World Heritage Site in 1997, the island is the northernmost and oldest of a chain of submarine volcanoes stretching south along the Cocos Ridge to the equator, where several come to the surface as the Galápagos Islands. These islands were formed by a hot spot, which pushes up volcanic material from beneath the earth's crust. The hot spot deep inside the earth remains stationary, while the sea floor moves over it. Over time, the volcanic cone is transported away from the hot spot and a new volcano arises in the same place.

Cliffs reach higher than 100 meters (330 feet) around almost the entire island, and dramatic waterfalls cascade onto the beach. Cocos's forested hills supposedly harbor gold doubloons. More than 500 expeditions have sought in vain to find the Lima Booty—gold and silver ingots that mysteriously disappeared while en route to Spain under the care of Captain James Thompson. The pirate William Davies supposedly hid his treasure here in 1684, as did Portuguese buccaneer Benito "Bloody Sword" Bonito in 1889. The government has placed a moratorium on treasure hunts.

Isla del Coco is inhabited only by national park guards who patrol the park equipped with small Zodiac boats. The only safe anchorage for entry is at Bahía Chatham, on the northeast corner, where scores of rocks are etched with the names and dates of ships dating back to the 17th century.

There are no native mammals. The surrounding waters, however, are home to four unique species of marine mollusks. The island has one butterfly and two lizard species to call its own. Three species of birds are endemic: the Cocos finch, Cocos cuckoo, and the Ridgeway or Cocos flycatcher. Three species of boobies—red-footed, masked, and brown— live here too. Isla del Coco is also a popular spot for frigate birds to roost and mate, and white terns may hover above your head. Feral pigs, introduced in the 18th century by passing sailors, today number about 5,000 and have caused substantial erosion.

Access to the island is restricted. The waters around the island are under threat from illegal longline fishing. The **Fundación Amigos de la Isla del Coco** (Friends of Cocos Island, FAICO, tel. 506/2256-7476, www.cocosisland.org) works to protect the area from illegal fishing.

Diving

The island is one of the world's best diving spots, famous for its massive schools of white-tipped and hammerhead sharks, eerie manta rays, pilot whales, whale sharks, and sailfish. Snorkelers swimming closer to the surface can revel in moray eels and colorful reef fish.

Cocos is for experienced divers only. Drop-offs are deep, currents are continually changing, and beginning divers would freak out at the huge shark populations. Converging ocean currents stir up such a wealth of nutrients that the sharks have a surfeit of fish to feed on, and taking a chunk out of a diver is probably the last thing on their minds.

Two dive vessels operate out of Los Sueños Marina. The *Okeanos Aggressor* (U.S. tel. 866-348-2628, www.aggressor.com) is a 34-meter (112-foot) fully air-conditioned 10-stateroom ship with complete facilities for 21 divers. It offers 8- and 10-day trips. **Undersea Hunter** (tel. 506/2228-6613, U.S. tel. 800-203-2120, www.underseahunter.com) operates 10- and 12-day Isla del Coco trips using the 18-passenger MV *Sea Hunter* and the 14-passenger MV *Undersea Hunter.*

Information and Services

For information, contact **MINAE** (tel. 506/2291-1215 or 506/2291-1216, isla.coco@

sinac.co.cr, www.isladelcoco.go.cr), the government department that administers national parks, or the ranger station (tel.

506/2542-3290). There are no accommodations on the island, and camping is not allowed.

Ciudad Neily and Vicinity

CIUDAD NEILY

Ciudad Neily squats at the base of the Fila Costeña mountains, beside the Pan-American Highway, 18 kilometers (11 miles) northwest of Panamá and 15 kilometers (9.5 miles) east of the town of Río Claro and the turnoff for Golfito. Ciudad Neily is surrounded by banana and date palm plantations and functions as the node for plantation operations. There is nothing to hold your interest, although you are likely to see indigenous women in colorful traditional dress.

North from Ciudad Neily, a road switchbacks steeply uphill 31 kilometers (19 miles) to San Vito and the Valle Coto Brus, in south-central Costa Rica. South from town, a road leads through a sea of African palm plantations to the airstrip at Coto 47.

★ Paradise Garden

A decade of labor and love has gone into creating Paradise Garden (tel. 506/2789-8746, 8am-3pm Mon.-Sat.), immediately west of Río Claro (the poorly marked turnoff is on the west side of the Río Lagarto bridge, opposite the Arrocera El Ceibo rice factory; the garden is 200 meters/660 feet north of the turnoff). Owner Robert Beatham, from Maine, started the garden as a hobby; today he produces 16 tons of African palm fruits per month. But it's the heliconias, gingers, and dozens of other species that delight, while Robert's immense knowledge keeps you wide-eyed in awe. Lunch is served as Robert expounds about the various fruits, seeds, and nuts used in the meal and introduces you to local remedies (such as the "wandering jew" plant, purportedly good for treating diabetes).

Accommodations and Food

There's no shortage of budget hotels in town. One of the best bets is Cabinas Heileen (tel. 506/2783-3080, $18 pp, with TV $23 pp), in a nicely kept home festooned with epiphytes. Its 10 simple but clean rooms have fans and private baths with cold water (one room has hot water); five rooms have TVs.

The nicest place in town is Hotel Andrea (tel. 506/2783-3784, www.hotelandreacr.com, with fans $32 s, $38 d, with a/c $40 s, $45 d), with 35 rooms in a handsome two-story colonial-style property festooned with hanging plants, 50 meters (165 feet) west of the bus station. Rooms are clean, with tile floors and modest furnishings. All have TVs and hot water, and 14 have air-conditioning. It has secure parking and the most elegant restaurant in town (6am-10:30pm daily, $1.50-15), serving pancakes and honey, huevos rancheros, omelets, onion soup, shrimp salad, pastas, and filet mignon.

The clean, modern Restaurante La Moderna (tel. 506/2783-3097, 7am-11pm daily, $2-12), one block east of the plaza on the main street of Ciudad Neily, has an eclectic menu ranging from burgers and pizza to ceviche and típico dishes.

Information and Services

The hospital (tel. 506/2783-4111) is 1.5 kilometers (0.9 miles) southeast of town on Highway 2. Consultorio Médico (tel. 506/2783-3840, 8am-8pm Mon.-Sat.) and Pharmacy Kayros adjoin each other on the main street. The Red Cross (tel. 506/2783-3757) is on the northeast side of town, opposite the police station (tel. 506/2783-3150).

Ciudad Neily

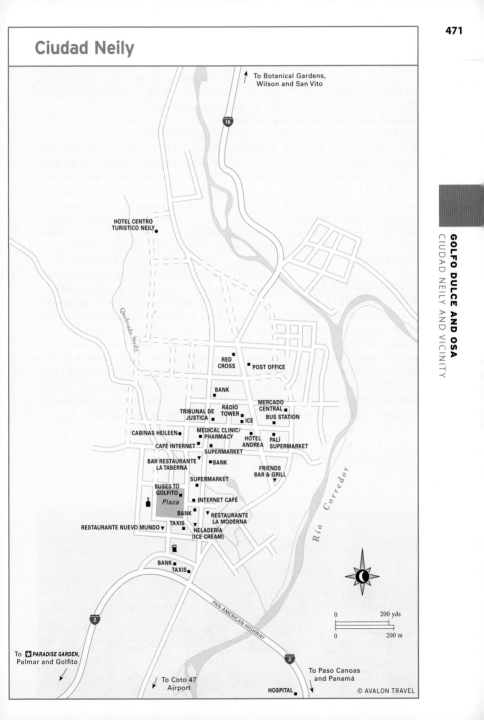

To Botanical Gardens, Wilson and San Vito

16

HOTEL CENTRO TURISTICO NEILY

Quebrada Neily

RED CROSS

POST OFFICE

BANK

MERCADO CENTRAL

TRIBUNAL DE JUSTICA

RADIO TOWER

ICE

BUS STATION

CABINAS HEILEEN

MEDICAL CLINIC/ PHARMACY

HOTEL ANDREA

PALÍ SUPERMARKET

CAFÉ INTERNET

SUPERMARKET

BAR RESTAURANTE LA TABERNA

BANK

FRIENDS BAR & GRILL

SUPERMARKET

Río Corredor

BUSES TO GOLFITO

Plaza

INTERNET CAFÉ

BANK

RESTAURANTE LA MODERNA

TAXIS

RESTAURANTE NUEVO MUNDO

HELADERÍA (ICE CREAM)

BANK

TAXIS

PAN-AMERICAN HIGHWAY

0   200 yds

0   200 m

2

To PARADISE GARDEN, Palmar and Golfito

To Coto 47 Airport

2

To Paso Canoas and Panamá

HOSPITAL

© AVALON TRAVEL

There are three banks in the center of town. The **post office** (tel. 506/2783-3500) is on the northeast side of town.

Getting There

The airport is four kilometers (2.5 miles) south of town, at Coto 47. **SANSA** (tel. 506/2229-4100, U.S./Canada tel. 877-767-2672, www.flysansa.com) has scheduled flights to Coto 47.

Tracopa (tel. 506/2221-4214) buses for Ciudad Neily (8 hours) depart San José from Calle 5, Avenidas 18/20, four times daily 5am-6:30pm, and from San Isidro (tel. 506/2771-0468) four times daily 4:45am-3pm. For taxis, call **Taxi Ciudad Neily** (tel. 506/2783-3374).

PASO CANOAS AND VICINITY

There's absolutely no reason to visit ugly Paso Canoas unless you intend to cross into Panamá. Endless stalls and shops selling duty-free goods are strung out along the road that parallels Panamá's perfectly paved and marked highway (there's no barrier, so be careful that you don't cross into Panamá accidentally, which is easily done). Avoid Easter week and the months before Christmas, when Paso Canoas is a zoo.

The border road runs south to the town of **Laurel,** a regional center for the banana industry with lots of old wooden plantation homes, and then to Conte.

Practicalities

Among the better places to overnight is the modern motel-style **Cabinas Alpina** (tel. 506/2732-2612, basic rooms $8 pp, nicer a/c rooms upstairs $20 s/d), two blocks south of the bus terminal in Paso Canoas, offering rooms away from the bustle, plus secure parking. The most upscale option is **Hotel Los Higuerones** (tel. 506/2732-2157, www.hotelloshiguerones.com, $40 s, $50 d), a classical-themed hotel set in secure landscaped grounds on the south side of town, and a veritable oasis amid the chaos of this unsightly town. Its 39 air-conditioned rooms have cable TV, and you get Wi-Fi on the porch.

The **Costa Rican Tourist Board** (CIT, tel. 506/2732-2035, 7am-10pm Mon.-Fri.) has an information bureau at the border post. **Customs and immigration** (tel. 506/2732-2150) are opposite the bus terminal 100 meters (330 feet) west of the border post.

African date palm groves around Ciudad Neily

South-Central Costa Rica

Look for ★ to find recommended sights, activities, dining, and lodging.

Highlights

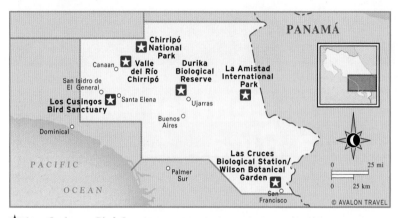

★ **Los Cusingos Bird Sanctuary:** Birdwatchers worldwide know this forest reserve, where visitors can thrill to sightings of more than 300 species (page 478).

★ **Valle del Río Chirripó:** Tucked into a fold of the Talamanca Mountains, this scenic valley is the gateway to Parque Nacional Chirripó (page 481).

★ **Chirripó National Park:** Hiking to the summit of Costa Rica's highest mountain requires no more than stamina and offers the reward of sensational views (page 486).

★ **Durika Biological Reserve:** High on the mountain slopes abutting Parque Internacional La Amistad, this eco-sensitive commune provides a unique experience in a rustic communal lifestyle. Getting there is a challenge (page 490).

★ **Las Cruces Biological Station:** This reserve and research station has kilometers of nature trails through humid montane ecosystems, offering magnificent wildlife viewing. The highlight is the **Wilson Botanical Garden,** a jewel among tropical botanical gardens (page 494).

★ **La Amistad International Park:** This park, shared with Panamá, is the ultimate in rugged, remote mountain terrain. It's most easily accessed from the south; here, trails lead into a private cloud-forest reserve (page 496).

The south-central region is the Cinderella of Costa Rican tourism. A larger proportion of the region is protected as national park or forest reserve than in any other part of the country. Much remains inaccessible and unexplored.

Herein lies the beauty: Huge regions such as Parque Nacional Chirripó and Parque Internacional La Amistad harbor incredibly diverse populations of Central American flora and fauna.

The region is dominated to the east by the massive and daunting Talamanca massif, rising to 3,819 meters (12,530 feet) atop Cerro Chirripó. Slanting southeast and paralleling the Talamancas to the west is a range of lower-elevation mountains called the Fila Costeña. Between the two lies the 100-kilometer-long by 30-kilometer-wide (60- by 20-mile) Valle de El General, extending into the Valle de Coto Brus to the south. The valley is a center of agriculture, with pineapples covering the flatlands of the Río General, and coffee smothering the slopes of Coto Brus (much of the land once planted in coffee has been replaced by cattle). The rivers that drain the valley merge to form the Río Grande de Térraba, which slices west through the Fila Costeña to the sea.

The region is home to the nation's largest concentration of indigenous people. In the remote highland reaches, and occasionally in towns, you'll see indigenous Guaymí and Boruca women dressed in traditional colorful garb.

The regional climate varies with topography. Clouds moving in from the Pacific dump most of their rain on the western slopes of the Fila Costeña, and the Valle de El General sits in a rain shadow. To the east, the Talamanca massif is rain-drenched and fog-bound for much of the year. Temperatures drop as elevation climbs, and atop the Talamancas temperatures approach freezing.

PLANNING YOUR TIME

The region is linked to San José by the Pan-American Highway (Hwy. 2), which runs south from Cartago, climbs over the Cerro de la Muerte—a daunting and dangerous drive—and descends to San Isidro (also known

Previous: Chirripó Valley and Talamanca Mountains; Sara Longwing butterfly. **Above:** The Boruca people are famous for their balsa devil masks.

South-Central Costa Rica

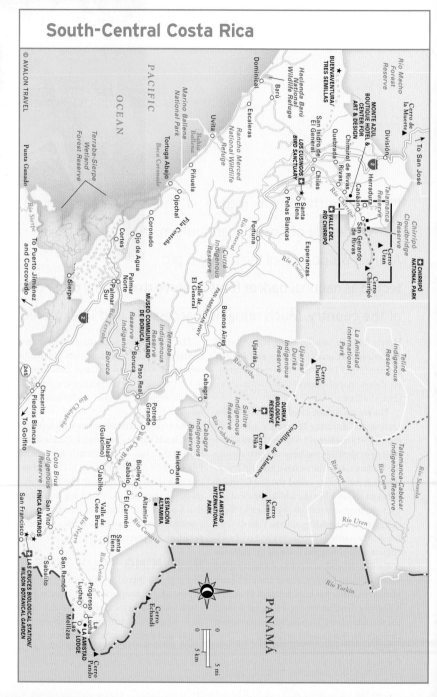

© AVALON TRAVEL

as Pérez Zeledón) in the Valle de El General. South of Buenos Aires, the Pan-American Highway exits the valley via the gorge of the Río Grande de Térraba, linking it with the Golfo Dulce region. Another road transcends the Fila Costeña and links San Isidro de El General with Dominical on the Central Pacific coast. Most visitors pass through the area in two or three days, which is a sufficient amount of time to see the highlights, including the delightful mountain village of **San Gerardo de Dota.** However, a week would not be too long, with the towns of **San Isidro** and **San Vito** as your bases.

Much of the mountain terrain is within indigenous reserves, such as **Reserva Indígena Boruca,** which welcomes visitors. It is also the source of the fantastic carved masks prominent in quality souvenir stores. Visitor facilities are minimal.

Organized activities in the region are minimal, with the exception of **whitewater rafting** on the Ríos Chirripó and General. **Selva Mar** (tel. 506/2771-4582, www.exploringcostarica.com) acts as a tour information center and reservation service for the region.

San Isidro and Vicinity

CERRO DE LA MUERTE TO SAN ISIDRO

From the 3,491-meter (11,453-foot) summit of Cerro de la Muerte, about 100 kilometers (60 miles) south of San José, the Pan-American Highway drops steeply to San Isidro, in the Valle de El General. When the clouds part, you are rewarded with a fabulous vista, the whole Valle de El General spread out before you. The route is often fog-bound, and there are many large trucks (some without lights). Frequent landslides, fathoms-deep potholes, and too many accidents for comfort are among the dangers—take extreme care, and avoid this road at night.

A statue of Christ balances precariously above a 100-meter (330-foot) sheer cliff face. The impressive **La Piedra de Cristo** (Km. 104), by artist Francisco Ulloa, was erected in 1978 above the highway two kilometers (1.2 miles) north of San Rafael.

Mirador Vista del Valle (Km. 119, tel. 506/2200-5465, www.valledelgeneral.com, $35) has a zip-line tour with 10 platforms, seven cables, and a rappel.

Accommodations and Food
If you're stuck on the mountain, **Mirador Vista del Valle** (Km. 119, tel. 506/2200-5465, www.valledelgeneral.com, $55 s/d) has eight simple wooden *cabinas* (overpriced, I think) with modern baths. It has a delightfully rustic restaurant named for its stunning view, plus a canopy zip line, bird-watching, and fishing.

For a homey feel and personalized attention, check in with Canadian-German couple, Lisa and Rolf Zersch, who lovingly tend their bed-and-breakfast home, **Bosque del Tolomuco** (tel. 506/8847-7207, www.bosquedeltolomuco.com, $65-75 s/d, including breakfast and taxes), at Km. 118. Their charming inn, set in lush landscaped gardens, has five cozy wooden cabins with modern baths. The lounge is heated by a roaring wood-burning stove. It has Wi-Fi. Dinners are served by appointment. There's a heated swimming pool, and trails lead into a private forest; you can see as far as the Osa Peninsula on a clear day from atop the mountain.

A small, traditional *trapiche* (ox-driven sugar mill) is still in operation at **El Trapiche de Nayo** (tel. 506/2771-7267, trapichenayo@costarricense.cr), immediately below La Piedra de Cristo. The delightful rustic restaurant serves delicious traditional meals.

SAN ISIDRO DE EL GENERAL

San Isidro, regional capital of the Valle de El General, is an agricultural market town, gateway to Parque Nacional Chirripó and Dominical, and a base for white-water rafting.

The handsome modernist concrete **Catedral de San Isidro de Labrador,** on the east side of the plaza, has lovely stained-glass windows. Otherwise there is little to see in town.

Nature Reserves and Farms

La Gran Vista Agroecological Farm (tel. 506/8924-8983, www.lagranvista.com), at El Peje de Repunta, 15 kilometers (9.5 miles) south of San Isidro, teaches sustainable agricultural practices to local farmers. It relies on travelers for volunteer labor. Accommodations are in dorms ($20 pp, including all meals) with hot showers. A minimum weeklong stay is recommended.

Three Seeds Eco-Education Camp (tel. 506/8512-0234, www.experiencecostarica.org, $60 pp, students $25, volunteers $20, including meals) is about 35 kilometers (22 miles) northwest of town, in the Río División valley. At this organic farm, you can volunteer to teach English to local children through hands-on activities, including on the farm and in the kitchen. The kids (and you) learn about organic farming and sustainable living practices in an experiential setting. It adjoins the Reserva Forestal Los Santos, perfect for nature hikes ($25) and horseback rides ($50). An orientation tour costs $10.

★ Los Cusingos Bird Sanctuary

The 142-hectare **Los Cusingos Bird Sanctuary** (contact the Centro Científico Tropical, tel. 506/2738-2070 or 506/8659-2228, www.cct.or.cr, 7am-4pm Mon.-Sat., 7am-1pm Sun., $13), in Quizarrá de Pérez Zeledón, is on the lower slopes of Chirripó, near the small community of Santa Elena, 15 kilometers (9.5 miles) southeast of San Isidro.

red-capped manakin at Los Cusingos Bird Sanctuary

The former home of the late Dr. Alexander Skutch (coauthor with Gary Stiles of *Birds of Costa Rica*) now lies within the Alexander Skutch Biological Corridor. Run by the Centro Científico Tropical (Tropical Science Center), the reserve is surrounded by primary forest, home to more than 300 bird species. You can tour Skutch's simple clapboard home, retained as it was when he and his wife lived here. An hour-long trail, muddy and slippery in parts, leads to a rock carved with pre-Columbian petroglyphs. Guides can be hired; or go with ornithologist Pieter Westra of **Aratinga Tours** (tel. 506/2574-2319, www.aratinga-tours.com).

You get here via General Viejo: five kilometers (3 miles) east of San Isidro from the San Gerardo de Rivas road, then south for Peñas Blancas; or from Highway 2 via Peñas Blancas, then north for General Viejo. Turn east for Quizarrá-Santa Elena, two kilometers (1.2 miles) north of Peñas Blancas, then follow the signs for Quizarrá.

San Isidro de El General

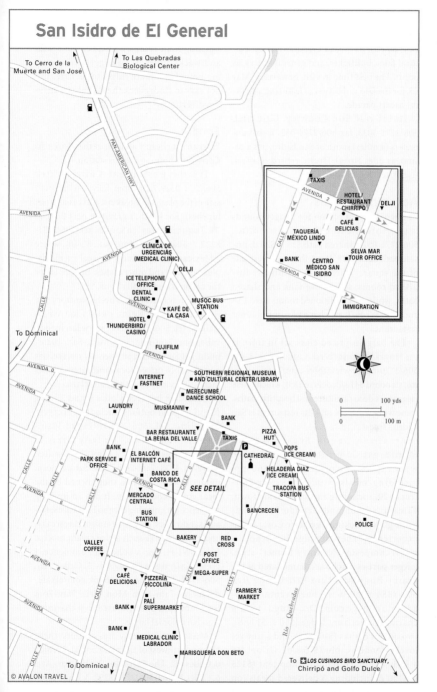

To Cerro de la
Muerte and San José

To Las Quebradas
Biological Center

PAN-AMERICAN HWY

AVENIDA 1

CALLE 10

AVENIDA 5

CLÍNICA DE
URGENCIAS
(MEDICAL CLINIC)

DELJI

ICE TELEPHONE
OFFICE

DENTAL
CLINIC

AVENIDA 3

KAFÉ DE
LA CASA

MUSOC BUS
STATION

HOTEL
THUNDERBIRD/
CASINO

To Dominical

FUJIFILM

AVENIDA 1

AVENIDA 0

AVENIDA 2

INTERNET
FASTNET

SOUTHERN REGIONAL MUSEUM
AND CULTURAL CENTER/LIBRARY

MERECUMBÉ
DANCE SCHOOL

LAUNDRY

MUSMANNI

BANK

PIZZA
HUT

BAR RESTAURANTE
LA REINA DEL VALLE

TAXIS

POPS
(ICE CREAM)

BANK

EL BALCÓN
INTERNET CAFÉ

CATHEDRAL

PARK SERVICE
OFFICE

CALLE 8

CALLE 6

CALLE 4

BANCO DE
COSTA RICA

AVENIDA 4

HELADERÍA DIAZ
(ICE CREAM)

AVENIDA 6

MERCADO
CENTRAL

SEE DETAIL

TRACOPA BUS
STATION

BUS
STATION

BANCRECEN

POLICE

VALLEY
COFFEE

AVENIDA 8

BAKERY

RED
CROSS

POST
OFFICE

CALLE 2

CAFÉ
DELICIOSA

PIZZERÍA
PICCOLINA

MEGA-SUPER

CALLE 3

AVENIDA 10

PALÍ
SUPERMARKET

FARMER'S
MARKET

BANK

Río Quebradas

BANK

CALLE 4

MEDICAL CLINIC
LABRADOR

MARISQUERÍA DON BETO

To Dominical

To ✚ LOS CUSINGOS BIRD SANCTUARY,
Chirripó and Golfo Dulce

0   100 yds

0   100 m

Detail:

TAXIS

AVENIDA 2

HOTEL/
RESTAURANT
CHIRRIPÓ

DELJI

CALLE 0

CAFÉ
DELICIAS

TAQUERÍA
MÉXICO LINDO

SELVA MAR
TOUR OFFICE

BANK

CENTRO
MÉDICO SAN
ISIDRO

AVENIDA 4

IMMIGRATION

© AVALON TRAVEL

Entertainment and Events

The town comes alive in late January and early February for its **Fiesta Cívica,** when agricultural fairs, bullfights, and general festivities occur. The best time to visit, however, is May 15, for the **Día del Boyero,** featuring a colorful oxcart parade.

Hotel del Sur Country Club (tel. 506/2771-3033, fax 506/2771-0527), six kilometers (4 miles) south of San Isidro, has a casino, as does **Hotel Thunderbird** (Calle 4, Ave. 3, tel. 506/2770-6230).

Accommodations

In town, the best option for budget hounds is the **Hotel/Restaurante Chirripó** (tel. 506/2771-0529, shared bath $16 s, $20 d, private bath $22 s, $28 d), on the southwest side of the square, offering 41 minimally furnished rooms; some have fans and shared baths, while air-conditioned rooms have TVs and even Wi-Fi. It also has a pleasing outdoor restaurant.

The bargain-priced class act in town is the **Hotel Thunderbird** (Calle 4, Ave. 3, tel. 506/2770-6230, www.tbrcr.com/hotelcostarica, standard $41 s/d, deluxe $83), which offers elegant art deco furniture and beautiful baths, some with whirlpool tubs. Its restaurant is San Isidro's finest.

At **Three Seeds Eco-Education Rainforest Camp** (tel. 506/8371-5869, www.experiencecostarica.org, $60 pp, including meals, students $25, volunteers $20, including meals), outside town, Tamara Newton and Geraldo Saenz welcome guests seeking a genuine Costa Rican experience. They arrange local homestays, campesino (country farmer) style. Larger parties can be accommodated at the nearby **Buenaventura Eco-Lodge** (tel. 506/8884-6560, www.buenaventura-eco-adventurelodge.com, Dec.-Aug.), with a charming riverfront lodge ($50 s, $100 d), two quaint casitas ($100 s/d), and a tiny yet lovely wooden cabin ($75 s/d). Or opt for a fully equipped mountaintop tent ($125 s, $150 d, including 3 delivered meals) on a summit with spectacular views. It primarily caters to "theme" groups, including Burning Man camps, so expect some wild and wacky times. It's a rugged drive over fog-bound mountain ridges to get here, and not easy to find; check the website for driving directions.

Food

You can eat cheaply at *sodas* at the **Mercado Central,** adjoining the bus station.

Try the **Restaurant Chirripó** (tel. 506/2771-0529, 7am-10pm daily), on the south side of the plaza, for breakfast and *casados* (set lunches). For lunch, I gravitate next door to ★ **Taquería México Lindo** (tel. 506/2771-8222, 9:30am-8pm Mon.-Sat., $2-10), where a Mexican cook produces the real enchilada, plus burritos and other dishes. Be sure to try the coconut and vanilla flans.

The always packed and lively two-story **Bar Restaurante La Reina del Valle** (Ave. 0, Calle 0, tel. 506/2771-4860, www.lareinadelvalle.com, 7am-midnight Mon.-Sat., 10am-midnight Sun.), with an open-air terrace, has a reasonably priced local and international menu, and views over the main plaza.

Avenida 8 between Calles 0 and 2 has a fistful of good options, including **Pizzería Piccolina** (tel. 506/2772-1975, 10:30am-10:30pm Thurs.-Tues.) for tasty pizzas. A stone's throw away is **Valley Coffee** (tel. 506/2771-1738, 7am-7pm Mon.-Sat.), a clean, modern, well-lit coffee shop owned by the local coffee cooperative. It has an inviting ambience for enjoying combo breakfasts, salads, sandwiches, crepes, tiramisu, cheesecake, and coffee drinks such as ice cream mocha. It has Wi-Fi. For a bohemian ambience, I prefer **Kafé de la Casa** (Ave. 3, Calle 4, tel. 506/2770-4816, www.facebook.com/elkafedelacasa, 7am-8pm Mon.-Fri., 7am-7pm Sat., 7am-3pm Sun.), housed in a charming wooden colonial home.

Musmanni bakery has outlets three blocks southwest of the plaza and at Avenida 0, Calles 0/2. The **Feria del Productor** (Ave. 6, Calles 3/5, tel. 506/2771-8292, 3:30am-10pm

Wed.-Thurs., 6am-2pm Fri.) farmers market is perhaps the best-organized market in Costa Rica; more than 300 farmers sell their fresh produce.

Information and Services

Selva Mar (Calle 1, Aves. 2/4, tel. 506/2771-4582, www.exploringcostarica.com) offers visitor information and acts as a reservation service. The hospital (tel. 506/2771-3122) is on the southwest side of town. Medical centers include Centro Médico San Isidro (Ave. 4, Calles Central/1, tel. 506/2771-4467), Hospital Clínica Labrador (Calle 1, Avenidas 8/10, tel. 506/2771-7115), and Clínica de Urgencias (Hwy. 1, Ave. 5, tel. 506/2772-7070), with a 24-hour pharmacy.

The post office (tel. 506/2770-1669) is three blocks south of the plaza, on Calle 1. The police station (tel. 506/2771-3608) is hidden south of the river on Avenida 0. The town's many Internet cafés include Balcón Internet Café on Avenida 4.

Getting There

Musoc (tel. 506/2222-2422) buses for San Isidro depart Calle Central, Avenida 22, in San José hourly 5:30am-5:30pm daily, plus express service at 1pm and 4pm daily. Return buses (tel. 506/2771-0414) depart San Isidro from Highway 2, at the junction of Avenida 0, hourly 5:30am-5:30pm daily. Tracopa (tel. 506/2221-4214) buses depart Calle 5, Avenidas 18/20, in San José 14 times 5am-6:30pm daily, returning 5pm-8:30pm daily.

The regional bus station in San Isidro is at Calle Central and Avenidas 4/6. Transportes Blanco (tel. 506/2771-2550) buses depart for San Isidro from both Quepos and Dominical five times daily; from Puerto Jiménez at 1pm daily; from San Vito four times daily; and from Uvita at 6am and 1:45pm daily. Buses depart San Isidro for Dominical and Quepos four times daily; for Puerto Jiménez at 6:30am daily; for San Gerardo de Rivas at 5:30am and 4:30pm daily; for San Vito four times daily; and for Uvita at 9am and 4pm daily.

Chirripó and Vicinity

★ VALLE DEL RÍO CHIRRIPÓ

The Valle del Río Chirripó cuts deeply into the Talamancas northeast of San Isidro, fed by waters cascading down from Cerro Chirripó, Costa Rica's highest mountain at 3,819 meters (12,530 feet). The hard-to-find, unmarked turnoff from the highway is 200 meters (660 feet) south of the bridge on the south side of San Isidro. The river is favored for trout fishing, and for kayaking and rafting, with enormous volumes of water. Contact Costa Rica Expeditions (tel. 506/2257-0766, www.costaricaexpeditions.com) for rafting tours and trips. The drive offers spectacular scenery.

Rivas, a little village six kilometers (4 miles) east of San Isidro, is famous for the roadside Piedra de los Indios (Indian Rock), carved with pre-Columbian motifs. It's 100 meters (330 feet) north of Rancho La Botija

(tel./fax 506/2770-2146, www.rancholabotija.com, 9am-5pm Tues.-Sun., adults $5, children $3), where trails lead to even more impressive giant rocks carved with petroglyphs. This coffee and fruit finca also has a 150-year-old *trapiche* (sugar mill) and an atmospheric café. Trail tours (9am Tues.-Sun., $5) are offered.

Passing through the hamlets of Chimirol and Canaan, 18 kilometers (11 miles) northeast of San Isidro, you arrive at San Gerardo de Rivas. This quaint village, on the southwest flank of Chirripó at 1,300 meters (4,260 feet) elevation, is the gateway to Parque Nacional Chirripó. The setting is alpine, the air crisp. The scent of pines and the sound of rushing streams fill the air. The locale is perfect for hiking and bird-watching. Quesos Canaan (tel. 506/2742-5125, origith@hotmail.com, 8am-4pm daily), in the village of Canaan, is a small family-run farm

Chirripó and Vicinity

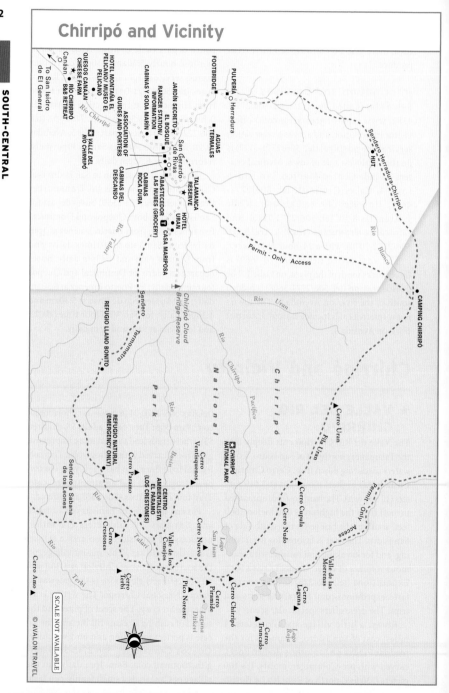

To San Isidro
de El General

Canáan

QUESOS CANAAN
CHEESE FARM

RIO CHIRRIPO
B&B RETREAT

HOTEL MONTAÑA EL
PELICANO/ MUSEO EL
PELICANO

CABINAS Y SODA MARIN

VALLE DEL
RÍO CHIRRIPÓ

ASSOCIATION OF
GUIDES AND PORTERS

JARDIN SECRETO
EL BOSQUE

RANGER STATION
INFORMATION

San Gerardo
de Rivas

CABINAS DEL
DESCANSO

CABINAS
ROCA DURA

ABASTECEDOR
LAS NUBES (GROCERY)

CASA MARIPOSA

HOTEL
URAN

FOOTBRIDGE

PULPERIA
Herradura

AGUAS
TERMALES

TALAMANCA
RESERVE

Sendero Herradura-Chirripó

HUT

Río Blanco

Permit - Only Access

CAMPING CHIRRIPÓ

Río Chirripó

Río Uran

Chirripó Cloud
Bridge Reserve

Río Lori

Sendero
Termometro

REFUGIO LLANO BONITO

Río

Bosin

Río Chirripó
Pacífico

Río Uran

C h i r r i p ó

N a t i o n a l

P a r k

Cerro Uran

Fila Uran

Cerro Cupula

Cerro Nudo

Permit - Only Access

Valle de las
Morrenas

REFUGIO NATURAL
(EMERGENCY ONLY)

Sendero a Sabana
de los Leones

Cerro Paramo

Cerro
Crestones

Río

Talari

CENTRO
AMBIENTALISTA
EL PARAMO
(LOS CRESTONES)

Valle de los
Conejos

Cerro
Ventisqueros

CHIRRIPÓ
NATIONAL PARK

Cerro Nuevo

Lago
San Juan

Cerro
Pirámide

Cerro Chirripó

Cerro
Laguna

Lago
Roja

Río
Terbi

Cerro
Terbi

Cerro
Crestones

Pico Noreste

Laguna
Ditkevi

Cerro
Truncado

Cerro Amo

SCALE NOT AVAILABLE

© AVALON TRAVEL

where you can milk the cows and learn about cheese-making. **Samaritan Xocolata** (tel. 506/8820-7095, www.samaritanxocolata.com) makes artisanal chocolates and bonbons flavored with blackberry, *guanábana* (soursop), guava, coffee, and more. A factory tour ($25 pp) is offered with 48 hours' notice. **Lácteos La Pardita** (tel. 506/2771-0608) produces "Crema Don Paneco" coffee liqueur that tastes even better than Baileys!

A side road in San Gerardo follows the Río Blanco upstream west three kilometers (2 miles) to the hamlet of **Herradura,** from where a more arduous trail to Cerro Chirripó and Cerro Urán begins. In 2008 floods wiped out the bridge, and the hamlet is accessible only by a footbridge. En route you'll pass the **Aguas Termales** (tel. 506/2742-5210, 7am-6pm daily, $5), a peaceful spot with landscaped hot spring pools, hugely popular with locals on weekends. Horticulturalists on a busman's holiday will appreciate **Jardín Secreto** (tel. 506/2742-5086, 8am-5pm daily, $3), a lovely little garden with orchids, heliconias, and bromeliads on display.

The **Cámara de Turismo** (Chamber of Tourism, tel. 506/2742-5050, www.sangerardocostarica.com) is a good information resource.

El Pelicano Galería de Arte

The small **El Pelicano Galería de Arte** (tel. 506/2742-5050, www.hotelelpelicano. net, 8am-8pm daily, free), on a coffee finca between Canaan and San Gerardo, displays the eclectic and unique works of local artist Rafael Elizondo Basulta. Crafted from stones and natural timbers, the exhibits include a five-meter (16-foot) snake hewn from a branch. My favorite is a half-scale motorcycle made from 1,000 twigs and other pieces of wood. Rafael's stone sculptures are displayed in the beautifully landscaped garden. With luck you may be invited into his charming house to see the tree trunks hewn magically into a storage cupboard and even a wooden fridge.

Private Reserves

About 800 meters (0.5 miles) above the soccer field in San Gerardo, the dirt road divides: To the right, it clambers steeply for about one kilometer (0.6 miles) to the trailhead to Parque Nacional Chirripó.

En route, you'll pass **Talamanca Reserve** (tel. 506/2742-5080, www.talamancareserve. com), a 2,000-hectare (5,000-acre) reserve that has miles of trails—some for hikers (but steep), others for ATVs ($50 for 2 hours, with guide). One follows a river to a cascade and swimming holes. Horseback rides and guided walks ($15-45) from two to six hours are offered. Use of the facility is included in the rates for overnight guests. Trails here offer the best views of Chirripó, with Los Crestones clearly visible on fine days.

The dirt road continues in deteriorating condition past the Parque Nacional Chirripó trailhead 1.5 kilometers (0.9 miles) to **Chirripó Cloudbridge Reserve** (no tel., www.cloudbridge.org), a private reserve and reforestation project with 12 kilometers (7 miles) of trails and more than a dozen waterfalls, plus a meditation garden. Entry is by donation; simply sign in and set off.

Accommodations

Midway between San Isidro and Rivas, **Rancho la Botija** (tel. 506/2770-2147, www. rancholabotija.com, $41 s, $68 d) is bargain-priced. The four simple cabins with wooden walls and bamboo ceilings offer a rustic, romantic charm. Eight newer cabins are more spacious and have Wi-Fi; four have TV, and two cater to travelers with disabilities. It has a swimming pool and trails.

The calming **Talari Mountain Lodge** (tel. 506/2771-0341, www.talari.co.cr, low season $55 s, $80 d, high season $59 s, $84 d), near Rivas, is a small resort nestled over the Río Chirripó on an eight-hectare (20-acre) property with orchards good for bird-watching. All rooms offer great mountain views from the terraces. There's a swimming pool and a restaurant where Jan, the Dutch owner, plays jazz on the piano. Guided hiking and bird-watching are offered.

In San Gerardo, **Cabinas del Descanso** (tel. 506/2742-5099, www.hoteleldescansocr.com, tents $5, dorms $15 pp, *cabinas* $20-50 pp), 200 meters (660 feet) uphill from the ranger station, has a tiny dorm with bunks and shared baths, plus nine *cabinas* with double beds and hot water (two rooms have private baths). It also permits camping (there are cold-water showers) and has Internet and laundry. A rustic restaurant serves filling *típico* meals. The Elizondo family leads treks (including bird-watching), offers trout fishing, and will drive you to the park entrance.

Want to be close to the Chirripó trailhead? The marvelous ★ **Casa Mariposa** (tel. 506/2742-5037, www.hotelcasamariposa.net, dorm $15 pp, private rooms from $38 d) backpacker hostel is built into the boulders and has rock-face rooms that offer tremendous ambience for budget digs. It has five dorms, plus laundry, Internet, storage, and a fabulous soaking tub built into the rocks (as is the dorm's outdoor communal toilet and shower). The owners, California transplants John and Jill, have added a larger cross-ventilated cabin ($30-45 s, $36-52 d) with a screened wall offering views over the river valley. Next door,

Hotel Urán (tel. 506/2742-5004, www.hoteluran.com, from $21 pp) offers 10 well-kept rooms, barracks-style, in a modern wooden two-story structure with a tin roof and shared baths with hot water. It has a *pulpería* (grocery) and a clean, airy restaurant (4:30am-8pm daily). A larger room has four beds and a private bath.

Set in lush landscaped gardens, **Talamanca Reserve** (tel. 506/2742-5080, www.talamancareserve.com, standard $69 s/d, junior suites $79 s/d, cabin suites $150), on the road to Chirripó, causes a double-take. Built in dramatic contemporary style, it has modestly furnished rooms with lovely sunlit baths; junior suites are preferable. It has a great restaurant serving the best gourmet food around, an Internet café, and miles of ATV and hiking trails.

Río Chirripó B&B and Retreat (tel. 506/2742-5333, www.riochirripo.com, $97 s/d, includes all meals and tax) enjoys an exquisite setting in a ravine beneath huge granite boulders one kilometer (0.6 miles) above Canaan. Run by American expat Frank Faiella and his Costa Rican girlfriend, Oriana, this intimate mountain lodges boasts a Santa Fe aesthetic. Its heart is a huge lounge (with Wi-Fi) in a circular *ranchito* with soaring *palenque*

bell at Río Chirripó B&B and Retreat, San Gerardo de Rivas

gourmet dinner at Monte Azul

CHIRRIPÓ AND VICINITY

the walls; many pieces were created on-site through Monte Azul's artist-in-residence program. Four luxury riverfront suites have glass-wall frontages with patios overlooking gorgeous tropical gardens. Within, the hip aesthetic includes two-tone checkered tile floors, Kohler bath fixtures, Ikea-style kitchens, top-of-the-line imported mattresses and linens, and custom-designed furniture. A chic open-air restaurant serves gourmet American-Asian fusion dishes using organic produce from the hotel's garden. Dinner is always a three-course daily menu, such as chayote soup, beet and goat cheese salad, and pork loin with green curry.

Food

Cabinas y Soda Marín (tel. 506/2742-5091, 5am-7:30pm daily), next to the ranger station, and **Bar/Restaurant El Bosque** (c/o tel. 506/2771-4129), next door, each have no-frills restaurant serving filling *comida típica*; El Bosque also has a *pulpería* (general store) where you can buy food for the hike up Chirripó. For rustic charm, try the restaurant at **Cabinas Roca Dura** (7am-10pm daily), built atop boulders; it serves typical Costa Rican dishes, plus burgers and sandwiches. Close to the Chirripó trailhead, the restaurant at **Hotel Urán** (tel. 506/2742-5004) opens at 4:30am to serve early-bird hikers.

The **Talamanca Reserve** café-restaurant (tel. 506/2742-5080, www.talamancareserve.com, 8am-10pm daily), on the road to Chirripó, is the place for everything from pancakes, omelets, eggs, and smoked ham for breakfast to bowls of chili, chicken fingers, and triple-decker sandwiches. Dinner leans toward gourmet. I enjoyed a steaming bowl of garbanzos and a superb dish of sautéed liver with onion and green peppers with mashed potato. It also sells ice cream and cappuccinos.

Information and Services

Talamanca Reserve, on the road to Chirripó, has an Internet café (8am-10pm daily) and a book exchange.

roof, Aztec motifs, New Mexican throw rugs, Guatemalan wall hangings, sofa seats with batik cushions, and open walls with mountain vistas. Oriana makes fabulous meals, and the dining area is swarmed by bougainvillea. Eight small, rustic wooden cabins hang over the river, boasting earth-tone color schemes, Guatemalan bedspreads, balconies, and walk-in showers. You can also rent a more spacious casita ($140 s, $190 d). The B&B has a swimming pool, a heated riverside whirlpool tub, and a yoga gym.

Exuding class, and one of my favorite hotels in all of Costa Rica, ★ **Monte Azul: Boutique Hotel + Center for Art & Design** (tel. 506/2742-5222, www.monteazulcr.com, 2-night minimum, $439 s, $498 d, including all meals) is set on its own 125-hectare (309-acre) reserve at Chimirol de Rivas. This art-themed, smoke-free hotel is the brainchild of Carlos Rojas, a Costa Rica-born artist-turned-art dealer, and his partner Randy Langendorfer. Contemporary art festoons

Getting There

Buses (tel. 506/2742-5083) depart San Isidro for San Gerardo de Rivas at 5am and 2pm daily, returning at 7am and 4:30pm daily. Be sure to specify San Gerardo de Rivas, not San Gerardo de Dota.

If you're **driving,** the unsigned turnoff for Rivas and San Gerardo is one kilometer (0.6 miles) south of San Isidro. A 4WD taxi from San Isidro will cost about $20.

★ CHIRRIPÓ NATIONAL PARK

Parque Nacional Chirripó ($15 for 2 days, $15 per extra day) protects 50,150 hectares (124,000 acres) of high-elevation terrain surrounding Cerro Chirripó, Costa Rica's highest peak at 3,819 meters (12,530 feet). The park is contiguous with Parque Internacional La Amistad to the south; together they form the Amistad-Talamanca Regional Conservation Unit. Flora and fauna thrive here relatively unmolested by humans. One remote section of the park is called Savanna of the Lions, after its large population of pumas. Tapirs and jaguars are common, though rarely seen; the forests also protect several hundred bird species. Cloud forest, above 2,500 meters (8,200 feet) elevation, covers almost half the park, which features three distinct ecological zones. The park is topped off by subalpine rainy *páramo,* marked by contorted dwarf trees and marshy grasses.

Cerro Chirripó was held sacred by pre-Columbian people. Community leaders and shamans performed rituals atop the lofty shrine; lesser mortals who ventured up Chirripó were killed.

Just as Edmund Hillary climbed Everest "because it was there," so Chirripó lures the intrepid who seek the satisfaction of reaching the summit. Many Ticos choose to hike the mountain during Easter week, when the weather is usually dry. Avoid holidays, when the huts may be full. The hike from San Gerardo ascends 2,500 meters (8,200 feet) and is no Sunday picnic but requires no technical

crystal-clear stream on Cerro Chirripó

expertise. The trails are well marked but steep and slippery.

The park service is pushing the lesser-known Herradura trail (minimum 3 days, 2 nights), via Paso de los Indios, with the first night atop Cerro Urán.

The weather is unpredictable; dress accordingly. When the bitterly cold wind kicks in, the humidity and wind-chill factor can drop temperatures to freezing. Rain is always a possibility, even in "dry season," and a short downpour usually occurs mid-afternoon. Fog is almost a daily occurrence at higher elevations, often forming in midmorning. Temperatures can fall below freezing at night. February and March are the driest months.

The mountain plays host to the annual **Carrera Internacional Campo Traviesa de Chirripó** (www.carrerachirripo.com) each February, a rugged race to the top and back.

Guides and Equipment

No guides are required for hiking the Termómetro trail, but they are compulsory

Climbing Chirripó

descending Cerro Chirripó

You can do the 16-kilometer (10-mile) hike to the summit in a day, but it normally takes two days (three days round-trip). Call MINAE (tel. 506/2742-5083, Mon.-Fri.), the government department that administers national parks, three days in advance to register, and pay your deposit at Banco Nacional; if you arrive without reservations, pay your fee at the ranger station at San Gerardo. There are distance markers every two kilometers. Pack out all your trash and bury human waste.

DAY 1

Today is 14 kilometers (9 miles), mostly steeply uphill. Less-fit hikers should begin not long after dawn, as it can take 12 hours or even longer in bad conditions (fitter hikers should be able to hike this section in 6 to 7 hours). You can hire local porters to carry your packs to base camp.

From the soccer field in San Gerardo, walk uphill about 600 meters (0.4 miles) to the Y fork; turn right, cross the bridge, and follow the rocky track one kilometer (0.6 miles) uphill. The trailhead is well signed on the right, 100 meters (330 feet) above Albergue Urán (you can drive up to this point with a 4WD vehicle; several homesteads advertise parking for a small fee). There's a stream 500 meters (0.3 miles) beyond Refugio Llano Bonito, beyond which you begin a grueling uphill stretch called La Cuesta del Agua; allow at least two hours for this section. The climb crests at Monte Sin Fé (Faithless Mountain). You'll see a rudimentary wooden shelter at the halfway point, beyond which you pass into dwarf cloud forest adorned with old man's beard.

About six kilometers (4 miles) below the summit is a cave large enough to sleep five or six people, if rains dictate. From here a two-kilometer (1.2-mile) final climb—La Cuesta de los Arrepentidos (Repentants Hill)—takes you to Centro Ambientalista El Páramo lodge, beside the Río Talari beneath an intriguing rock formation called Los Crestones. It has heating, but be prepared for a cold night anyway.

DAY 2

Today, get up and onto the trail by dawn to make the summit before the fog rolls in. It's about a 90-minute hike from the hut via the Valle de los Conejos (Rabbits Valley). On clear days, the view is awesome. With luck, you'll be able to see both the Pacific and the Caribbean.

You can head back to San Gerardo the same day, or contemplate a round-trip hike to Cerro Ventisqueros, the second-highest mountain in Costa Rica (by permit only); the trail begins below the Valle de los Conejos. Another trail through the Valle de las Morenas, on the northern side of Chirripó, is off-limits without a permit, as is the Camino de los Indios, a trail that passes over Cerro Urán and the far northern Talamancas.

for the Herradura trail. The communities of San Gerardo and Herradura run an association of guides and porters (*arrieros,* tel./fax 506/2742-5225); its office is 50 meters (165 feet) below Cabinas El Descanso. Prices are fixed at $60 per day, with a 16-kilogram (35-pound) limit per porter. If you want to attempt the Herradura trail, check with the *pulpería* (tel. 506/2742-5066) in Herradura.

You can rent tents, stoves, sleeping bags, and other equipment at Roca Dura and Cabinas del Descanso; stoves are permitted only within the Los Crestones hut. Be sure to bring the following:

- Warm clothes—preferably layered clothing for varying temperatures and humidity. A polypropylene jacket remains warm when wet.

- Rain gear; a poncho is best.

- Sturdy hiking boots.

- A warm sleeping bag, good to 0°C (32°F).

- A flashlight with spare batteries.

- A compass and a map.

- Water. There is no water supply for the first half of the hike.

- Food, including snacks. Dried bananas and peanuts are good energy boosters.

- A bag for garbage.

- Wind and sun protection.

Accommodations

There's a cave refuge halfway up the mountain, and an open-air hut, **Refugio Llano Bonito,** with a one-night limit ($5). The main lodge—**Centro Ambientalista El Páramo** (tel. 506/2206-5080, $10 pp), "Los Crestones"—is 14 kilometers (9 miles) from the trailhead and has four bunks (with foam pads) in each of 15 rooms, and shared baths with lukewarm showers, a communal kitchen, and solar-powered electricity 6pm-8pm daily. You can reserve meals; otherwise, you need to cook for yourself.

Camping is not permitted except at **Camping Chirripó,** 10 kilometers (6 miles) from the trailhead on the Herradura trail (8 people maximum; reservations required).

Information and Services

The **ranger station** (tel. 506/2742-5083 or 506/2200-5348, 6:30am-4:30pm daily) in San Gerardo has toilets. If you plan on going solo, consider buying the 1:50,000 topographical survey map (sections 3444 II San Isidro and 3544 III Durika) in advance; if you plan on hiking to nearby peaks, you may also need sections 3544 IV Fila Norte and 3444 I Cuerici, available in San José from the **Instituto Geográfico Nacional** (tel. 506/2523-2959, Plaza González Víquez, Mon.-Fri. 8am-4pm).

Only 40 visitors are allowed within the park at any one time. Only 10 spaces daily are available for people arriving without reservations; the other 30 spaces are for people with reservations. Reservations (tel. 506/2742-5083) are accepted Monday-Friday only, to be prepaid via the Banco Nacional. Experienced hikers recommend showing up anyway, as there are usually some no-shows.

Costa Rica Trekking Adventure (tel. 506/2771-4582, www.chirripo.com), in San Isidro, offers guided treks.

La Amistad International Park and Vicinity

The 193,929-hectare (479,208-acre) Parque Internacional La Amistad "friendship" park is shared with neighboring Panamá. Together with the adjacent Parque Nacional Chirripó, the Reserva Biológica Hitoy-Cerere, Parque Nacional Tapantí, Zona Protectora Las Tablas, Parque Nacional Barbilla, Estación Biológica Las Cruces, and a handful of indigenous reservations, it forms the 600,000-hectare (1.5-million-acre) Amistad Biosphere Reserve, a UNESCO World Heritage Site also known as the Amistad-Talamanca Regional Conservation Unit.

The park transcends the Cordillera Talamanca, rising from 150 meters (500 feet) above sea level on the Caribbean side to 3,819 meters (12,530 feet) atop Cerro Chirripó. The Talamancas comprise separate mountain chains with only a limited history of volcanic activity; none of the mountains is considered a volcano. La Amistad's eight ecological zones form habitats for flora and fauna representing at least 60 percent of the nation's various species, including no fewer than 450 bird species (not least the country's largest population of resplendent quetzals and 49 species found only here), as well as the country's largest density of tapirs, jaguars, harpy eagles, ocelots, and many other endangered species. Cloud forests extend to 2,800 meters (9,200 feet), with alpine *páramo* vegetation in the upper reaches.

Most of this massive park remains unexplored. It has few facilities, and trails are unmarked and often barely discernible. Hike with a local guide. The park, which extends the entire length of the South Central region, has five official entry points, one accessed via Buenos Aires, one via Helechales, one via Altamira, and two via San Vito. Admission is $6.

LA AMISTAD INTERNATIONAL PARK–NORTH

The gateway to the northern section of Parque Internacional La Amistad (tel. 506/2771-3155) is Buenos Aires, a small

park rangers at La Amistad International Park

agricultural town in the midst of an endless green ocean of *piñas*. The nondescript town, 63 kilometers (39 miles) south of San Isidro de El General, is the main base for exploring Parque Internacional La Amistad. The air for miles around Buenos Aires is redolent of sweet-smelling pineapples, the economic mainstay of the Valle de El General. The mountains around Buenos Aires are home to several indigenous groups.

A dirt road that begins in Buenos Aires leads north 10 kilometers (6 miles) to the hamlet of **Ujarrás,** beyond which the boulder-strewn dirt road continues four kilometers (2.5 miles) to **Balneario de Aguas Termales** (also called Rocas Calientes), where hot spring water pours forth amid a rock landscape. A trail from Ujarrás crosses the Talamancas via Cerro Abolado and the valley of the Río Taparí, ending in the Reserva Biológica Hitoy-Cerere on the Caribbean side. It's a strenuous, multiday endeavor. Do not attempt this hike without a local guide. The **Talamanca Association of Ecotourism and Conservation** (ATEC, tel./fax 506/2750-0191 www.ateccr.org), based in Puerto Limón, on the Caribbean coast, offers 6- to 15-day guided Transcontinental Hikes ($750) from Ujarrás to the Caribbean side or vice versa.

Another dirt road that begins at the gas station at **Brujo,** 10 kilometers (6 miles) southeast of Buenos Aires, leads into the mountains and the **Reserva Indígena Cabagra** (Cabagra Indigenous Reserve). The gas station's **Restaurante Brujo** (tel. 506/2730-1645) serves an excellent buffet.

Southeast from Buenos Aires, the Pan-American Highway follows the Río General 25 kilometers (16 miles) to its confluence with the Río Coto Brus at Paso Real.

★ Durika Biological Reserve

Founded in 1989 as Finca Anael, the **Reserva Biológica Durika** (tel./fax 506/2730-0657, www.durika.org) is a 700-hectare (1,730-acre) farm reserve operated by the Fundación Durika, an outgrowth of a self-sufficient agricultural community of 100 or so members who work on conservation, protecting and reforesting a mountain reserve that comprises various types of forest, including cloud forest. The community operates an authentic ecotourism project that welcomes visitors. A guide is assigned to you. Besides the opportunity to milk the goats, make yogurt

newborn goat at Durika Biological Reserve

and cheese, try your hand at carpentry, and participate in organic farming, you can attend classes in martial arts, meditation, and art. Guided hikes, including one to an indigenous village, plus a five-day camping trip to the summit of Cerro Durika, are available.

Durika has accommodations, including a dorm ($15 pp) and nine simple cabins ($48 s, $80 d) with private baths, but you'll need to bring your own sleeping bag. Rates include transfers and vegetarian meals.

To get here from Buenos Aires, follow the Ujarrás signs to Rancho Cabecar restaurant, then take the right at the Y fork (Durika is signed) and continue uphill 15 kilometers (9.5 miles) until you see the entrance for the farm. Jeep taxis operate from Buenos Aires. This drive is not for the faint-hearted. The first 12 kilometers (7 miles) or so are a breeze, then suddenly the narrow, rocky, muddy track plunges into a canyon and begins a long, dauntingly steep, narrow, snaking ascent that requires you to floor the gas at all times, come what may. It could well be the single most challenging drive in the nation.

Accommodations and Food

There are several modest *cabinas* in Buenos Aires and at Ujarrás. The nicest digs are **Cabinas Kamarachi** (tel. 506/2730-5222, $25 s, $35 d), one kilometer (1.2 miles) off Highway 2 on the road into Buenos Aires. It has 20 air-conditioned rooms in a two-story block with cable TV, secure parking, and a small air-conditioned restaurant.

Information and Services

There are two banks on the plaza in Buenos Aires. The **police station** (tel. 117 or 506/2730-0103) is one block northeast of the plaza; the **Red Cross** (tel. 506/2730-0078) is on the north side of the plaza.

Getting There

Tracopa (tel. 506/2221-4214) buses to Buenos Aires depart San José (4.5 hours) from Calle 5, Avenidas 18/20, at 8:30am and 2:30pm daily; there are also indirect buses. **Transportes**

Gafeso buses depart San Isidro for Buenos Aires every 30 minutes 6am-5pm daily.

Buses depart Buenos Aires for Potrero Grande at 6:30am and noon daily; you can get a Jeep taxi from there. Buses also serve Ujarrás from Buenos Aires.

RÍO GRANDE DE TERRABA VALLEY

Southwest of Buenos Aires, at **Paso Real** (there is no community as such), the Río El General and Río Coto Brus merge to form the **Río Grande de Terraba,** which swings west and runs through a ravine in the Fila Costeña mountains, connecting the Valle de El General to Palmar and the Golfo Dulce region; the Pan-American Highway follows the river.

Boruca Indigenous Reserve

About 10 kilometers (6 miles) south of Paso Real, a dirt road leads sharply uphill and runs along a ridge (offering fantastic views) to **Reserva Indígena Boruca,** in the Fila Sinancra, comprising a series of indigenous villages scattered throughout the mountains. The main village is **Boruca,** a slow-paced hamlet set in a verdant valley in the heart of the reserve. There's an excellent little **Museo Comunitario Boruca** (tel. 506/2514-0045, www.boruca.org, 9am-4pm daily, free) honoring the local culture; signs are in English, German, and Spanish. It's funded by the sale of beautiful carved balsa-wood masks, natural cotton weavings made on back-strap looms, and other traditional crafts made by artisans of the Flor Co-operativa (Sô Cagrú, "masked warrior" in the local language), headed by Mileny González (tel. 506/2730-5178, laflordeboruca@gmail.com).

Community tours offer an opportunity to learn about traditional weaving and the creation of "warrior" masks meant to scare away evil spirits. To see masks being made, seek out Ismael González Lázaro, or Santos Lázaro Lázaro (tel. 506/8941-6349, santoslazarol@gmail.com), head of the **Taller Familiar de Artesanías Independiente Boruca,** an artisans' cooperative. Try to visit for the Festival de los Diablitos (Dec. 30-Jan. 2).

Kan Tan Educational Finca (tel. 506/2225-6397) works to sustain local indigenous culture and foster a sustainable lifestyle, and has had great success in saving the Boruca tongue from extinction.

The Bar, Soda y Cabinas Boruca (no tel., $10 pp) has five basic rooms with private cold-water baths. You can also stay with local families by prior arrangement. Lourdes Frasser (tel. 506/2730-2453, artelocagru@yahoo.es) has a thatched guest rancho with a bamboo-enclosed outside toilet and shower.

Buses depart Buenos Aires for Boruca (1.5 hours) at 11am and 1:30pm daily. The return bus departs Boruca at 6:30am and 1pm daily.

LA AMISTAD INTERNATIONAL PARK-CENTRAL

The Valle de Coto Brus is drained by the Río Coto Brus and its tributaries, which merge into the Río Grande de Terraba, spanned by a bridge one kilometer (0.6 miles) south of Paso Real. From here, Highway 237 leads to San Vito, the regional capital, on a ridge at the head of the valley. It's one of the most scenic drives in the country. The valley is a center for coffee production. The summits of Cerro Kamuk (3,549 meters/11,644 feet) and Cerro Fabrega (3,336 meters/10,945 feet) loom massively overhead.

Three kilometers (2 miles) southeast of the bridge over the Río Grande de Terraba, a dirt road off Highway 237 leads north five kilometers (3 miles) to Potrero Grande and then another 12 kilometers (7.5 miles) uphill to Helechales and the Estación Tres Colinas ranger station for Parque Internacional La Amistad. A 4WD vehicle is required; it's tough going.

About 18 kilometers (11 miles) southeast of the Río Grande de Terraba, another rough dirt road begins at Guácimo (also known as Las Tablas) on Highway 237 about three kilometers (2 miles) north of Jabillo; it leads 21 kilometers (13 miles) via the hamlets of

El Carmén and Altamira to the Parque Internacional La Amistad headquarters at Estación Altamira (tel. 506/2730-9846, adults $10, children $1), on the edge of the cloud forest. This is the main access point to the park. Neither the road nor Altamira are marked on most road maps. Turn left about three kilometers (2 miles) above El Carmén; it's easy going to Altamira, beyond which it's signed via a steep and rugged two-kilometer (1.2-mile) 4WD climb. The Altamira ranger station has a small ecology museum. Trails include Sendero Valle del Silencio, a six-hour, 20-kilometer (12-mile) hike into the cloud forest, good for spotting quetzals.

The dirt road that begins at Guácimo divides after three kilometers (2 miles). Take the right fork for El Carmén; the left fork offers a more direct route to Altamira via the hamlet of Biolley (a 4WD vehicle is essential), a center of coffee production (in winter picking season, Guaymí laborers flock in from Panamá, brightening the scene with their gaily colored dresses). Two trails into Parque Internacional La Amistad begin about two kilometers (1.2 miles) above Biolley, where Finca Palo Alto (tel. 506/2743-1063, www.hotelfincapaloalto.com) is a farm with cattle, horses, and goats. The charming owner hosts educational day visits and leads guided horseback and hiking trips to high-altitude waterfalls.

To learn about and sample coffees from around the world, stop in at Finca Coffea Diversa (www.coffeadiversa.net), just below the Estación Altamira ranger station. It claims to be the largest varietal coffee garden in the world, with more than 200 coffee species amid flowering shrubs. It is still a work in progress.

The Asociación de Productores Orgánicos La Amistad (La Amistad Organic Producers Association, tel. 506/2743-1184) at Altamira and the Asociación de Mujeres de Biolley (Biolley Women's Association) operate guide services.

Accommodations

Estación Altamira, the main access point

Fiesta de los Diablitos

artisans at Boruca

Every year on December 30, a conch shell sounds at midnight across the Fila Sinancra. Men disguised as devils burst from the hills into Boruca and go from house to house, performing skits and receiving rewards of tamales and *chicha*, the traditional corn liquor. Drums and flutes play while villagers dressed in burlap sacks and traditional balsa-wood masks perform the Fiesta de los Diablitos. Another dresses as a bull. Plied with *chicha*, the *diablitos* chase, prod, and taunt the bull. Three days of celebrations and performances end with the symbolic killing of the bull, which is then reduced to ashes on a pyre. The festival reenacts the battles between indigenous forebears and Spanish conquistadors with a dramatic twist: The native people win.

to the park, has a camping area ($6 pp) with toilets and showers, drinking water, and a picnic area; you'll need to bring stoves and food. There's also a basic three-room dorm ($6 pp); reservations are required. There's even a TV lounge with sofas.

In El Carmén, Marialeno Garbanzo Camacho is the gracious owner of **Soda y Cabinas La Amistad** (tel. 506/2743-1080, $12 pp), next to the police station. She has eight simple, clean rooms with fans and shared outside baths with hot water. The *soda* (6am-9pm daily) serves filling *casados*.

At Biolley, **Finca Palo Alto** (tel. 506/2743-1063, www.hotelfincapaloalto.com, dorm $6 pp, rooms $50 pp, including all meals) has six rustic wooden cabins with modern baths and TVs, plus male and female dorms with narrow bunks for 26 people. This place has a real campesino ambience, and filling meals are served in the country-style outdoor restaurant.

Getting There
Tracopa (tel. 506/2771-3297) buses depart Buenos Aires for San Vito via El Carmén and Biolley at 11:30am daily; the Buenos Aires-bound bus departs San Vito at noon daily.

SAN VITO AND VICINITY
San Vito is a pleasant hill town that nestles on the east-facing flank of the Fila Costeña, overlooking the southern end of the Valle de Coto Brus, at 990 meters (3,250 feet) above sea level. The town was founded by Italian immigrants in the early 1850s. The tiny park at the top of the hill in the heart of town has a life-size statue of two children under

an umbrella dedicated to "La Fraternidad Italo-Costarricense."

Finca Cántaros (tel./fax 506/2773-5530, www.fincacantaros.wordpress.com, 8:30am-5pm daily, $5), a 9.5-hectare (23-acre) reserve three kilometers (2 miles) southeast of San Vito, is centered on a beautifully restored farmhouse converted into a gallery with beautiful indigenous crafts, plus a library. Self-guided trails lead to Laguna Zoncho, which attracts waterfowl, and into forest good for spotting such rare local inhabitants as the collared trogon, orange-collared manakin, and streaked saltator. Rest spots offer lovely views over San Vito. Recent archaeological finds include stone petroglyphs and a metate, on display.

Cooprosanvito (tel. 506/2773-3932, www.cooprosanvito.com), the local coffee cooperative, offers a tour of its *beneficio* (processing facility), ending with a tasting. **Desafío Tour** (tel. 506/2773-5810) also offers a coffee tour, plus horseback riding and ATV tours.

★ Las Cruces Biological Station

Estación Biológica Las Cruces (tel. 506/2773-4004, www.ots.ac.cr), six kilometers (4 miles) south of San Vito, is a nature lover's delight. The center, in the midst of a 325-hectare (800-acre) forest reserve proclaimed part of La Amistad Biosphere Reserve, is run by the Organization of Tropical Studies (OTS). New plants are propagated for horticulture, and species threatened with habitat loss and extinction are maintained for future reforestation efforts.

The reserve is in mid-elevation tropical rainforest along a ridge of the Fila Zapote at 1,900 meters (3,200 feet) elevation. During the wet season, heavy fog and afternoon clouds spill over the ridge, nourishing a rich epiphytic flora of orchids, bromeliads, ferns, and aroids. The forest is a vital habitat for pacas, anteaters, opossums, kinkajous, porcupines, armadillos, sloths, tayras, monkeys, deer, small cats, more than 45 species of bats, and some 800 species of butterflies. Bird-watching at Las Cruces is especially rewarding: More than 400 species have been recorded.

The highlight is the 12-hectare (30-acre) **Wilson Botanical Garden** (8am-5pm daily, adults $8, children free) established in 1963 by Robert and Catherine Wilson, former owners of Fantastic Gardens in Miami. Both are now buried on the grounds. The garden was inspired by the famous Brazilian gardener Roberto Burle-Marx, who designed

The Guaymí are the largest of Costa Rica's indigenous groups.

much of the garden following his vision of parterres as a palette. Approximately 10 kilometers (6 miles) of well-maintained trails (and many more in the forest reserve) meander through the Fern Grove, Orchid Grotto, the largest palm collection in the world, heliconia groves, and other locales. The garden also has an open-air cactus exhibit, plus greenhouses of anthuriums, ferns, elkhorns, and more. More than 2,000 native plant species are on display, and a bird-watching tower has been added.

Guided walks, including night tours and early birding walks, as well as meals are available by reservation; and you can buy self-guided-tour booklets in the store.

Accommodations and Food

Finca Cántaros (tel./fax 506/2773-5530, www.fincacantaros.com) has camping ($6 pp), with showers, toilets, and use of a simple outdoor grill and kitchen converted from cattle stalls.

The nicest place in San Vito is Hotel El Ceibo (tel./fax 506/2773-3025, $35 s, $45 d), with 40 modern air-conditioned rooms with fans and private baths with hot water, a large restaurant, a lounge with a TV, and a small bar. The hotel's restaurant (7am-10pm daily) serves the likes of cannelloni, lemon scaloppini, and fresh tuna spaghetti.

Las Cruces (reservations tel. 506/2524-0628 or 506/2773-4004, www.ots.ac.cr, low season $77 s, $148 d, high season $98 s, $186 d, including meals, taxes, and a guided walk), six kilometers (4 miles) south of San Vito, will accept drop-in overnighters on a space-available basis. It has 12 spacious and cozy rooms with picture windows opening to verandas with views, and Wi-Fi throughout. Dining is family-style at set hours. Discount rates apply for researchers, volunteers, and students. Walk-in backpackers can bunk in well-run dorms with showers and toilets.

Personal service and great breakfasts are the name of the game at the bargain-priced ★ Casa Botania (tel. 506/2773-4217, www.casabotania.com, from $55 s, $65 d), an exquisite new B&B opposite Finca Cántaros, about two kilometers (1.2 miles) from Las Cruces. The fantastic views down the Valle de Coto Brus are reason enough to stay here; so too is the filling breakfast that has to be seen to be believed. Pepe and Kathleen, a Tico-Belgian couple, play gracious hosts. Choose from either of two cabins or a master bedroom, all elegantly appointed and with Wi-Fi. Three-course prix fixe gourmet dinners ($20) are served. Nonguests are welcome to dine by reservation; the alfresco restaurant has stunning views.

Pizzería Lilliana (tel. 506/2773-3080, 10am-10pm daily), 50 meters (165 feet) west of the plaza in San Vito, is recommended for Italian fare, with fresh homemade pasta, gnocchi, and lasagna. Owner Liliana Sorte d'Almazio was one of the first settlers of San Vito, arriving in 1955.

Information and Services

The hospital (tel. 506/2773-3103) is one kilometer (0.6 miles) south of town, on the road to Ciudad Neily. The Red Cross (tel. 506/2773-3196) is on the northwest side of town.

There are two banks on the main street. Internet cafés include Cybershop (tel. 506/2773-3521, 8am-7pm Mon.-Fri., 8am-6pm Sat.), 200 meters (660 feet) west of the gas station; and El Kiosko (tel. 506/2773-5040, 7am-6pm Mon.-Fri.), next to the ICE building, on the small park. The post office is 200 meters (660 feet) up the hill north of the main bus station; continue another two kilometers (1.2 miles) for the police station (tel. 506/2773-3225).

Getting There

Tracopa (tel. 506/2221-4216, in San Vito tel. 506/2771-0468) buses depart San José from Calle 5, Avenidas 18/20, four times daily 6am-4pm. Buses from San Isidro depart for San Vito five times daily. Buses depart Terminal Cepul for Ciudad Neily, Las Mellizas, and Las Tablas. San Vito-Ciudad Neily buses will drop you off at Estación Biológica Las Cruces; they operate from San Vito eight times daily.

Tracopa buses from San José also pass via Las Cruces four times daily.

★ LA AMISTAD INTERNATIONAL PARK–SOUTH

Northeast of San Vito, the Talamancas are protected within Parque Internacional La Amistad, which provides splendid options for spotting quetzals, pumas, and other rare wildlife. The **Estación Pittier** (tel./fax 506/2773-4060), at Progreso, about 30 kilometers (19 miles) northeast of San Vito, has an exhibition room and a mirador, plus basic facilities.

At Sabalito, six kilometers (4 miles) east of San Vito, turn left at the gas station and continue straight until reaching Las Mellizas, where the paved road ends. A left turn here (a 4WD vehicle is required for this rocky skunk of a road) leads one kilometer (0.6 miles) to **La Amistad Lodge** (tel. 506/2228-0405, www.haciendalaamistad.com), a 1,215-hectare (3,000-acre) coffee farm—Agroindustrias Las Mellizas—within Zona Protectora Las Tablas. The private wildlife reserve adjoins Parque Internacional La Amistad. Horseback rides and guided hikes are offered. The lodge is in the heart of Guaymí territory and is also a great birding site (Roberto Montero, the owner, is a birder), with such species as the scaly-breasted leaf-tosser, the three-wattled bellbird, and the solitary eagle.

From La Amistad Lodge, a trail leads to the remote **Estación Las Tablas.** It's a rugged 10-kilometer (6-mile) hike or drive in a 4WD vehicle (conditions permitting); continue uphill from the lodge and take the right fork beyond the gates. You can camp ($6 pp) here, but there are no facilities.

Also adjoining is **Las Alturas de Cotón** (www.lasalturas.com), a conservation and eco-sustainable farming research center and wildlife refuge with large-growth primary forest good for birding. The Organization of Tropical Studies (OTS) administers the Las Alturas Biological Station here, which has dorm accommodations; contact Las Cruces Biological Station (tel. 506/2773-4004, www.ots.ac.cr). Day-visits can be arranged by permit.

You can also enter Parque Internacional La Amistad via the equally remote **Estación La Escuadra** ranger station, at Agua Caliente, in the Cotón valley some 30 kilometers (19 miles) northeast of San Vito and reached via the communities of Juntas, Poma, and Santa Elena; a 4WD vehicle is required.

Getting There

Buses depart San Vito for Cotón at 3pm daily, for Progreso and Las Mellizas at 9:30am and 2pm daily, for Las Tablas at 10:30am and 3pm daily, and for Santa Elena at 10am and 4pm daily. **Jeep taxis** will run you there in dry season from San Vito (about $75 round-trip).

Background

The Landscape

Travelers moving south overland through Central America gradually have their choice of routes whittled away until they finally reach the end of the road in the swamps and forests of Darien, in Panamá, where the tenuous land bridge separating the two great American continents is nearly pinched out and the Pacific Ocean and the Caribbean Sea almost meet. Costa Rica lies at the northern point of this apex—a pivotal region separating two oceans and two continents vastly different in character.

The region is a crucible. There are few places in the world where the forces of nature so actively interplay. Distinct climatic patterns clash and merge; the great landmasses riding atop the Cocos and Caribbean Plates jostle and shove one another, triggering earthquakes and spawning volcanic eruptions; and the flora and fauna of the North and South American realms—as well as those of the Caribbean and the Pacific—come together and play Russian roulette with the forces of evolution. The result is an incredible diversity of terrain, biota, and weather concentrated in a country that, at 50,895 square kilometers (19,651 square miles), is barely bigger than the state of New Hampshire.

Lying between 8 and 11 degrees latitude north of the equator, Costa Rica sits wholly within the tropics, a fact quickly confirmed on a rainy afternoon in the middle of the rainy season on the Caribbean lowlands or the Nicoya or Osa Peninsulas. Elevation, however, tempers the stereotypical tropical climate. In fact, the nation boasts more than a dozen distinct climatic zones.

GEOGRAPHY
A Backbone of Mountains

Costa Rica sits astride a jagged series of volcanoes and mountains, part of the great Andean-Sierra Madre chain that runs the length of the western littoral of the Americas. The mountains rise in the nation's northwestern corner as a low, narrow band of hills. They grow steeper and broader and ever more rugged until they gird Costa Rica coast to coast at the Panamanian border, where they separate the Caribbean and Pacific from one another as surely as if these were the Himalayas.

Volcanic activity has fractured this mountainous backbone into distinct cordilleras. In the northwest, the Cordillera de Guanacaste rises in a leap-frogging series of volcanoes, including Rincón de la Vieja and Miravalles, whose steaming vents have been harnessed to provide geothermal energy. To the southeast is the Cordillera de Tilarán, dominated by Arenal, one of the world's most active volcanoes. To the east is the Cordillera Central, with four great volcanoes—Poás, Barva, Irazú, and Turrialba—within whose cusp lies the Meseta Central, a high plateau ranging in elevation from 900 to 1,787 meters (2,950-5,863 feet). To the south of the valley rises the Cordillera Talamanca, an uplifted mountain region that tops out at the summit of Cerro Chirripó (3,819 meters/12,530 feet), Costa Rica's highest peak.

Meseta Central

The Meseta Central (meaning "central tableland," but really it's a valley), the heart of the nation, is a rich agricultural valley cradled by the flanks of the Cordillera Talamanca to

---

the south and by the fickle volcanoes of the Cordillera Central to the north and east. San José, the capital, lies at its center. At an elevation of 1,150 meters (3,773 feet), San José enjoys a springlike climate year-round.

The Meseta Central measures about 40 kilometers (25 miles) north to south and 80 kilometers (50 miles) east to west and is divided from a smaller valley by the low-lying Cerros de la Carpintera that rise a few miles east of San José. Beyond lies the somewhat smaller Valle del Guarco, at a slightly higher elevation. To the east the turbulent Reventazón—a favorite of white-water enthusiasts—tumbles to the Caribbean lowlands. The Río Virilla exits more leisurely, draining the San José valley to the west.

Northern Zone and Caribbean Coast

The broad wedge-shaped northern lowlands are cut off from the more densely populated Meseta Central by the Cordillera Central. The plains or *llanuras* extend along the entire length of the Río San Juan, whose course demarcates the Nicaraguan border. Farther south the plains narrow to a funnel along the Caribbean coast, framed by the steep eastern slopes of the central mountains, which run along a northwest-southeast axis. Numerous rivers drop quickly from the mountains to the plains. Beautiful beaches line the Caribbean coast, which sidles gently south.

Pacific Coast

Beaches are a major draw on Costa Rica's Pacific coast, which is deeply indented by two large gulfs—the Golfo de Nicoya (in the north) and Golfo Dulce (in the south), enfolded by the hilly, hook-nosed peninsulas of Nicoya and Osa, respectively. Mountains tilt precipitously toward the Pacific, and the slender coastal plain is only a few kilometers wide. North of the Golfo de Nicoya, the coastal strip widens to form a broad lowland belt of savanna—the Tempisque basin. The basin is drained by the Río Tempisque and narrows northward until hemmed in near

the Nicaraguan border by the juncture of the Cordillera de Guanacaste and rolling, often steep, coastal hills that follow the arc of the Nicoya Peninsula.

A narrow, 64-kilometer-long (40-mile-long) intermontane basin known as the Valle de El General nestles comfortably between the Cordillera Talamanca and the coastal mountains—Fila Costeña—of the Pacific southwest.

GEOLOGY

Costa Rica lies at the boundary where the Pacific's Cocos Plate—a piece of the earth's crust some 510 kilometers (320 miles) wide—meets the crustal plate underlying the Caribbean. The two are converging as the Cocos Plate moves east at a rate of about 10 centimeters (4 inches) per year. It is a classic subduction zone in which the Caribbean Plate is forced under the Cocos. Central America has been an isthmus, a peninsula, and even an archipelago in the not-so-distant geological past. Costa Rica has one of the youngest surface areas in the Americas—only three million years old—because the volatile region has only recently been thrust from beneath the sea.

In its travels eastward, the Cocos Plate gradually broke into seven fragments, which today move forward at varying depths and angles. This fracturing and competitive movement causes the frequent earthquakes with which Costa Ricans contend.

The most devastating earthquakes generally occur in subduction zones, when one tectonic plate plunges beneath another. Ocean trench quakes off the coast of Costa Rica have been recorded at 8.9 on the Richter scale and are among history's most dramatic, heaving the sea floor sometimes tens of meters. This is what happened when a powerful 7.4 earthquake struck Costa Rica on April 22, 1991. That massive quake, which originated near the Caribbean town of Pandora, caused the Atlantic coastline to rise permanently—in parts by as much as 1.5 meters (5 feet), thrusting coral reefs above the ocean surface and reducing them to bleached skeletons. And a 6.2 earthquake that struck near Poás volcano on January 8, 2009, triggered massive landslides that killed dozens of people.

Volcanoes

Costa Rica lies at the heart of one of the most active volcanic regions on earth and is home to 7 of the isthmus's 42 active volcanoes, plus 60 dormant or extinct ones. Some have the look classically associated with volcanoes—a graceful symmetrical cone rising to a single crater. Others are sprawling, weathered mountains whose once-noble summits have collapsed into huge depressions called calderas (from the Portuguese word for "cauldron").

In 1963 Volcán Irazú (3,412 meters/11,194 feet) broke a 20-year silence, disgorging great clouds of smoke and ash. The eruptions triggered a bizarre storm that showered San José with 13 centimeters (5 inches) of muddy ash, snuffing out the 1964 coffee crop but enriching the soil of the Meseta Central for years to come. The eruption lasted for two years, then abruptly ceased.

Volcán Poás (2,692 meters/8,832 feet) has been particularly violent during the past 30 years. In the 1950s the restless 6.5-kilometer-wide (4-mile-wide) giant awoke with a roar after a 60-year snooze, and it has been huffing and puffing ever since. Eruptions then kicked up a new cone about 100 meters (330 feet) tall. Two of Poás's craters now slumber under blankets of vegetation (one even cradles a lake), but the third crater belches and bubbles persistently.

Volcán Arenal (1,624 meters/5,328 feet) gives a more spectacular light-and-sound show. After a four-century-long Rip van Winkle-like dormancy, this 4,000-year-old juvenile began spouting in 1968, when it laid waste to a 10-square-kilometer (4-square-mile) area. Arenal's activity, sometimes minor and sometimes not, continues unabated; it erupted spectacularly in August 2000, killing two people, and then delivered small eruptions virtually daily until 2010, when it suddenly stopped spewing. In 2013 it awoke from slumber again, as did Volcán Turrialba, which at press time had sustained stop-and-go eruptions resulting in several evacuations of local inhabitants.

Several national parks have been created around active volcanoes. Atop Poás's crater rim, for example, you can gape down into the great well-like vent and see pools of molten lava bubbling menacingly, giving

Arenal Volcano

off diabolical fumes and emitting explosive cracks, like the sound of distant artillery.

CLIMATE

Costa Rica lies wholly within the tropics, yet boasts at least a dozen climatic zones and is markedly diverse in local microclimates. Most regions have a rainy season (May-Nov.) and a dry season (Dec.-Apr.). Rainfall almost everywhere follows a predictable schedule. In general, highland ridges are wet, and windward sides are always the wettest.

The terms "summer" (*verano*) and "winter" (*invierno*) are used by Ticos to designate their dry and wet seasons, respectively. Since the Tican "summer" occurs in what are winter months elsewhere in the northern hemisphere (and vice versa), it can be confusing.

Temperature

Temperatures, dictated more by elevation and location than by season, range from tropical on the coastal plains to temperate in the interior highlands. Mean temperatures average 27°C (81°F) at sea level on the Caribbean coast and 32°C (90°F) on the Pacific lowlands. In the highlands, the weather is refreshingly clear and invigorating. San José's daily temperatures are in the low 20s Celsius (70s Fahrenheit) almost year-round, with little monthly variation, and there's never a need for air-conditioning. A heat wave is when the mercury reaches above 27°C (81°F). Nights are usually 16-21°C (61-70°F) year-round, so bring a sweater.

Temperatures fall steadily as elevation climbs, about 1°C for every 100-meter gain (1°F per 200 feet). They rarely exceed a mean of 10°C (50°F) atop Cerro Chirripó, at 3,819 meters (12,530 feet), the highest mountain, where frost is frequent and enveloping clouds drift dark and ominous among the mountain passes.

Sunrise is around 6am and sunset about 6pm throughout the year, and the sun's path is never far from overhead, so seasonal variations in temperatures rarely exceed 5 degrees Celsius (9 degrees Fahrenheit) in any given location. Everywhere, March to May are the hottest months, with September and October not far behind. Cool winds bearing down from northern latitudes lower temperatures during December, January, and February, particularly on the northern Pacific coast, where certain days during summer (dry season) months can be surprisingly cool. The most extreme daily fluctuations occur during the dry season, when clear skies at night allow maximum heat loss through radiation. In the wet season, nights are generally warmer, as the heat built up during the day is trapped by clouds.

Rainfall

Rain is a fact of life in Costa Rica. Annual precipitation averages 250 centimeters (98 inches) nationwide. Depending on the region, the majority of this may fall in relatively few days. The Tempisque basin in Guanacaste, for example, receives as little as 48 centimeters (19 inches), mostly in a few torrential downpours. The mountains, by contrast, often exceed 385 centimeters (152 inches) per year, sometimes as much as 760 centimeters (300 inches) on the more exposed easterly facing slopes.

Generally, rains occur in the early afternoons in the highlands, mid-afternoons in the Pacific lowlands, and late afternoons (and commonly during the night) in the Atlantic lowlands. Sometimes it falls in sudden torrents called *aguaceros*, sometimes it falls hard and steady, and sometimes it sheets down without letup for several days and nights.

Dry season on the Meseta Central and throughout the western regions is December through April. In Guanacaste, the dry season usually lingers slightly longer; the northwest coast (the driest part of the country) often has few rainy days even during wet season. On the Atlantic coast, the so-called dry season starts in January and runs through April.

Be prepared: 23 hours of a given day may be dry and pleasant; during the 24th, the rain can come down with the force of a waterfall. The sudden onset of a relatively dry period, called *veranillo* (little summer), sometimes occurs in July and August or August and September, particularly along the Pacific coast.

Seasonal patterns can vary, especially in years when the occasional weather phenomenon known as El Niño sets in. For example, 2008 was the wettest year ever recorded—torrential rainfall struck the entire country, causing horrendous flooding and landslides. Rarely do hurricanes strike Costa Rica, although Hurricane César came ashore on July 27, 1996, killing 41 people and trashing the Pacific southwest.

ENVIRONMENTAL ISSUES
Deforestation

One hundred years ago, rainforests covered two billion hectares (5 billion acres), 14 percent of the earth's land surface. Now less than half remains, and the rate of destruction is increasing: An area larger than the U.S. state of Florida is lost every year. Today, the rainforests resound with the carnivorous buzz of chain saws.

It's a story that has been repeated again and again during the past 400 years. Logging, ranching, and the development of large-scale commercial agriculture have transformed much of Costa Rica's wildest terrain. Cattle ranching has been particularly wasteful. Large tracts of virgin forest were felled in the 1930s through the 1960s to make way for cattle, stimulated by millions of dollars of loans provided by U.S. banks and businesses promoting the beef industry to feed the North American market.

Throughout the 1980s, Costa Rica's tropical forest was disappearing at a rate of at least 520 square kilometers (200 square miles) per year—faster than anywhere else in the western hemisphere and, as a percentage of national land area, reportedly nine times faster than the rainforests of Brazil. By 1990 less than 1.5 million hectares (3.7 million acres) of primal forest remained, about 20 percent of its original extent.

By anyone's standards, Costa Rica has since led the way in moving Central America

away from the soil-leaching deforestation that plagues the isthmus (when humans cut the forest down, the organic matter-poor soils are exposed to the elements and are rapidly washed away by the intense rains, and the ground is baked by the blazing sun to leave an infertile wasteland). The country has one of the world's best conservation records: About one-third of the country is under some form of official protection. The nation has attempted to protect large areas of natural habitat and to preserve most of its singularly rich biota. But it is a policy marked by the paradox of good intent and poor application.

Many reserves and refuges are poorly managed, and the Forestry Directorate, the government office in charge of managing the country's forest resources, has been accused of failing to fulfill its duties. In the 1970s, the Costa Rican government banned export of more than 60 diminishing tree species, and national law proscribes cutting timber without proper permits. It happens anyway, much of it illegally, with logs reportedly trucked into San José and the coastal ports at night. Wherever new roads are built, the first vehicles in are usually logging trucks.

It's a daunting battle. Every year giant agribusinesses expand their fruit farms, depleting the forests that once covered 80 percent of Costa Rica. Fires set by ranchers lap at the borders of Parque Nacional Santa Rosa, and oil-palm plantations squeeze Manuel Antonio against the Pacific. In 2009 the administration of President Óscar Arias planned on downgrading the status of Leatherback Turtle Marine National Park to curry favor with the fishing and shrimping industry. (Arias also championed a proposed gold mine near the Nicaraguan border.)

Reforestation and Protection

Part of the government's answer to deforestation has been to promote reforestation, mostly through a series of tax breaks, leading to tree farms predominantly planted in nonnative species such as teak. These efforts, however, do little to replace precious native hardwoods or to restore complex natural ecosystems, which take generations to reestablish. Nonetheless, dozens of dedicated individuals and organizations are determined to preserve and replenish core habitats. Privately owned forests constitute the majority of unprotected primary forest remaining in Costa Rica outside the national parks. Scores of private reserves have been created to prove that rainforests can produce more income from ecotourism than if cleared for cattle. As a result of all these efforts, forest cover increased to 51 percent of the nation by 2005, up from only 21 percent in 1987, according to MINAE, while illegal logging is down significantly. (However, MINAE now seems to include even the most marginal forest types.) President Óscar Arias determined to make Costa Rica the first carbon-neutral country in the world by 2021.

Ironically, a conservationist ethic is still weak among country-based Costa Ricans. The majority of ecological efforts, including that which resulted in the creation of the national park system, are the result of initiatives by foreign residents.

Meanwhile, the **Bandera Azul Ecológica** (Ecological Blue Flag) program has had tremendous success in cleaning up Costa Rica's beaches. Modeled on the ICT's successful Certification for Sustainable Tourism, the program assesses the cleanliness of individual beaches and their communities, who have been provided an incentive to clean up their act and stay clean. That said, an alarming 97 percent of the nation's sewage flows untreated into rivers and the ocean.

National Parks

While much of Costa Rica has been stripped of its forests, the country has managed to protect a larger proportion of its land than any other country in the world in national parks. In 1970 there came a growing acknowledgment that something unique and lovely was vanishing, and a systematic effort was begun to save what was left of the wilderness. That year, the Costa Ricans formed a national park

system that has won worldwide admiration. Costa Rican law declared inviolate 10.27 percent of land. Today, one-third of land is legally set aside as national parks and forest reserves, "buffer zones," wildlife refuges, and indigenous reserves. Throughout the country, representative sections of all the major habitats and ecosystems are protected. The government's national parks are under the jurisdiction of the **Sistema Nacional de Áreas de Conservación** (National Conservation Areas System, SINAC, Ave. 15, Calle 1, San José, tel. 506/2522-6500, www.sinac.go.cr), which is responsible to the Ministerio de Ambiente y Energía (Ministry of the Environment and Energy, MINAE, www.minae.go.cr). SINAC protects more than 70 areas—including 26 national parks, 4 biological reserves, 3 forest reserves, 23 wildlife refuges, and various wetlands that can be visited—in 11 conservation areas. Dozens more reserves are in private hands.

However, SINAC remains severely hampered by underfunding. The government has also found it impossible to pay for land set aside as national parks (15 percent of national parks, and much more of reserves, are private property with payments outstanding). And budgetary constraints have traditionally prevented the severely understaffed parks service from hiring more people. Thus, poaching continues inside national parks, often with the connivance of rangers and corrupt parks service officials.

Much of the praise heaped on SINAC actually belongs to individuals (preponderantly foreigners), private groups, and local communities whose efforts—often in the face of bureaucratic opposition—have resulted in creation of many of the wildlife refuges and parks for which SINAC takes credit. (The creation of the national park system itself was the product of lobbying by a foreigner, Olaf Wessberg, as related in David Rains Wallace's *The Quetzal and the Macaw*.) The current focus is on integrating adjacent national parks, reserves, and national forests into Regional Conservation Areas (RCAs) to create corridors where

Natural Parks and Protected Areas

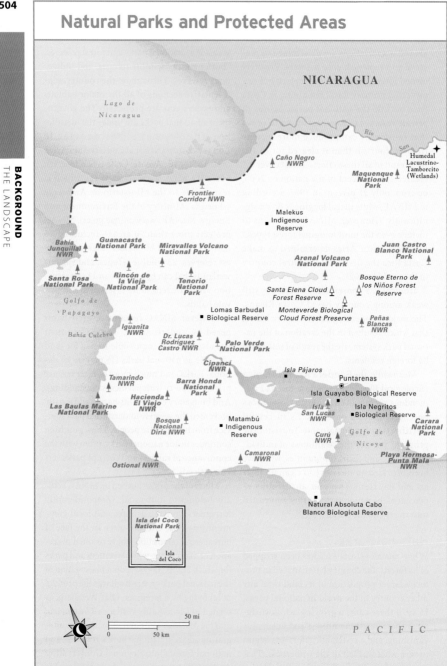

NICARAGUA

Lago de Nicaragua

Río

Caño Negro NWR

Humedal Lacustrino-Tamborcito (Wetlands)

Maquenque National Park

Frontier Corridor NWR

Malekus Indigenous Reserve

Bahía Junquillal NWR

Guanacaste National Park

Miravalles Volcano National Park

Arenal Volcano National Park

Juan Castro Blanco National Park

Santa Rosa National Park

Rincón de la Vieja National Park

Tenorio National Park

Bosque Eterno de los Niños Forest Reserve

Golfo de Papagayo

Santa Elena Cloud Forest Reserve

Bahía Culebra

Iguanita NWR

Lomas Barbudal Biological Reserve

Monteverde Biological Cloud Forest Preserve

Peñas Blancas NWR

Dr. Lucas Rodríguez Castro NWR

Palo Verde National Park

Cipancí NWR

Isla Pájaros

Puntarenas

Tamarindo NWR

Barra Honda National Park

Isla Guayabo Biological Reserve

Las Baulas Marine National Park

Hacienda El Viejo NWR

Isla San Lucas NWR

Isla Negritos Biological Reserve

Carara National Park

Bosque Nacional Diría NWR

Matambú Indigenous Reserve

Curú NWR

Golfo de Nicoya

Ostional NWR

Camaronal NWR

Playa Hermosa-Punta Mala NWR

Natural Absoluta Cabo Blanco Biological Reserve

Isla del Coco National Park

Isla del Coco

0   50 mi

0   50 km

PACIFIC

Caribbean Sea

Juan

Barra del Colorado NWR

Tortuguero National Park

Matina-Pacuare Forest Reserve

Puerto Limón

Rara Avis Biological Reserve

Braulio Carrillo National Park

Nairi-Awari (Barbilla) Indigenous Reserve

Limoncito NWR

Turrialba Volcano National Park

KeKôldi Indigenous Reserve

Bajo Chirripó Indigenous Reserve

Tayni Indigenous Reserve

Cahuita National Park

Poás Volcano National Park

Irazú Volcano National Park

Barbilla National Park

Gandoca-Manzanillo NWR

Prusia Forest Reserve

Guayabo National Monument

Hitoy-Cerere Biological Reserve

Bribri de Talamanca Indigenous Reserve

SAN JOSÉ

Telire Indigenous Reserve

Cabecar de Talamanca Indigenous Reserve

Quitirrisi Indigenous Reserve

Tapantí-Macizo de la Muerte National Park

PANAMÁ

Río Macho Forest Reserve

Chirripó National Park

La Amistad International Park

La Cangresa National Park

Los Quetzales National Park

Salitre Indigenous Reserve

Los Santos Forest Reserve

Ujarrás Indigenous Reserve

Cabagra Indigenous Reserve

Manuel Antonio National Park

Térraba Indigenous Reserve

Guaymi (Coto-Brus) Indigenous Reserve

Ballena Marine National Park

Boruca Indigenous Reserve

LAS CRUCES AND WILSON BOTANICAL GARDEN

Humedad Térraba-Sierpe (Wetlands)

Piedras Blancas National Park

Golfito NWR

Golfo Dulce Forest Reserve

Guaymi (Abrojos-Montezuma) Indigenous Reserve

Guaymi de Osa Indigenous Reserve

Golfo Dulce

Caño Island Biological Reserve

Corcovado National Park

Golfo Dulce Forest Reserve

Guaymi (Conte-Burica) Indigenous Reserve

OCEAN

© AVALON TRAVEL

wildlife can move with greater freedom over much larger areas.

If you need specialized information on scientific aspects of the parks, contact the Conservation Data Center, **Instituto Nacional de Biodiversidad** (INBio, tel. 506/2507-8100, www.inbio.ac.cr). Entrance for walk-in visitors varies from $6 to $15, valid for 24 hours only; most parks cost $10. You will need permits for a few of the biological reserves; these can be obtained in advance from SINAC.

You can volunteer with **ProParques** (tel./fax 506/2263-4162, www.proparques.org), a private foundation that works to support and strengthen operation of the national park system.

International Parks

Wildlife doesn't observe political borders; birds migrate, plants grow on each side. Park management increasingly requires international cooperation through the creation of transnational park networks, with neighboring countries viewing the rivers and rainforests along their borders not as dividing lines but as rich tropical ecosystems that they share.

The idea fruited in Central America as the Paseo Pantera, dedicated to preserving biodiversity through the creation of a contiguous chain of protected areas from Mexico to Colombia. This cooperative effort has since evolved into the multinational Mesoamerican Biological Corridor project. The intent is for the isthmus to once again be a bridge between continents for migrating species.

The most advanced of the transfrontier parks is Parque Internacional La Amistad, created in 1982 when Costa Rica and Panamá signed a pact to join two adjacent protected areas—one in each country—to create one of the richest ecological biospheres in Central America. UNESCO cemented the union by recognizing the binational zone as a biosphere reserve.

Plants

In 1947 biologist L. H. Holdridge introduced a system of classifying vegetation types or "zones" according to a matrix based on combinations of temperature, rainfall, and seasonality. Each zone has a distinct natural vegetation and ecosystem. Costa Rica has 12 such zones, ranging from tidal mangrove swamps to subalpine *páramo* with stunted dwarf plants atop the high mountains.

Costa Rica's tropical location, in combination with its remarkable diversity of local relief and climates, has resulted in the evolution of a stupendously rich biota. Some habitats, such as the mangrove swamps, are relatively simple. Others, particularly the ecosystem of the tropical rainforests of the Caribbean lowlands and the Nicoya and Osa Peninsulas, are among the most complex on the planet.

The lowland rainforests have strong affinities with the *selva* (rainforest) of South America and form a distinctive assemblage of species in which the large number of palms, tree ferns, lianas, and epiphytes attest to the constant heat and humidity of the region. The impressive tropical rainforest of eastern Costa Rica and the Nicoya and Osa Peninsulas gives way on the Central Pacific to a dry evergreen forest at lower elevations and dry deciduous forest farther north. Above about 1,000 meters (3,300 feet), the species are fewer and the affinities with North America are stronger. In the Cordillera Talamanca, conifers of South American provenance are joined by North American oaks. Above the tree line, approximately 3,000 meters (9,800 feet), hikers familiar with the mid-elevation flora of the high Andes of Peru and Ecuador will find many similarities in the shrubby open landscape of Costa Rica's cordillera.

The forests and grasslands flare with color.

heliconia

meters (13 feet) tall, with fiddleheads large enough to grace a cello. Others are epiphytes, arboreal "nesters" that take root on plants but that are not parasitic.

The epiphytic environment is extremely poor in mineral nutrients. The bromeliads—brilliantly flowering, spiky-leafed "air" plants—have developed tanks or cisterns that hold rainwater and decaying detritus in the whorled bases of their tightly overlapping stiff leaves. The plants gain nourishment from dissolved nutrients in the cisterns. Known as tank epiphytes, they provide trysting places and homes for tiny aquatic animals high above the ground.

All plants depend on light to power the chemical process by which they synthesize their body substances from simple elements. Height is therefore of utmost importance. When an old tree falls, the strong unusual light triggers seeds that have lain dormant, and banana palms and ginger plants, heliconias and cecropias—all plants that live in the sunshine on riverbanks or in forest clearings—burst into life and put out big broad leaves to soak up the sun. Another prominent plant is the poor man's umbrella (*sombrilla del pobre*), whose giant leaves make excellent impromptu shelters.

TROPICAL RAINFOREST

Once upon a time, before the freezing embraces of the most recent ice age, thick evergreen forests blanketed much of the world's warm, humid surface. Today's tropical rainforests—the densest and richest proliferation of plants ever known—are the survivors of these primeval rainforests of ages past.

These forests, the largest of which is Brazil's Amazon rainforest, are found in a narrow belt that girdles the earth at the equator. In the tropics, constant sunlight, endless rains, and high temperatures year-round spell life. The steamy atmosphere and fast nutrient turnover have promoted favorable growth conditions and intense competition, allowing the forest flora to evolve into an extraordinary multitude of different species, exploiting to the full

Begonias, anthuriums, and "blood of Christ," named for the red splotches on the underside of its leaves, are common. My favorite plant is the "hot lips" (*labios ardientes*), sometimes called "hooker's lips" (*labios de puta*), whose bright-red bracts remind me of Mick Jagger's famous pout. The vermilion *poró* tree (the bright flame-of-the-forest), pink-and-white meadow oak, purple jacaranda, and the almost fluorescent-yellow *corteza amarilla* all add their seasonal bouquets to the landscape. The morning glory spreads its thick lavender carpets across lowland pastures, joined by carnal red passionflowers (their unromantically foul smell is a crafty device to enlist the help of flies in pollination).

Costa Rica is a nation of green upon green upon green, including more than 9,000 species of higher plants and no less than 2,000 species of bromeliads. Of heliconias (members of the banana family) there are some 30 species. It has many more species of ferns—about 800—than all the rest of North America, including Mexico. Ferns grow sometimes four

Orchids

It's appropriate that the orchid is the national flower of Costa Rica: The country has more than 1,400 identified species. Countless others await discovery. At any time of year you're sure to find dozens of species in bloom, from sea level to the highest subfreezing reaches of Chirripó. There is no best time for viewing orchids, although the beginning of both the dry season (May) and the wet season (Dec.) are said to be particularly favorable. Orchid lovers should head for the cloud forests; there the greatest diversity exists in humid mid-elevation environments where they are abundant as epiphytes (constituting 88 percent of orchid species).

Orchids are not only the largest family of flowering plants, they're also the most diverse—come around with magnifying glass in hand and you'll come across species with flowers less than one millimeter (four-hundredths of an inch) across. Others, like the native *Phragmipedium caudatum,* have pendulant petals that can reach more than half a meter (20 inches). Some flower for only one day; others last several weeks.

Houlletia tigrina

Orchids have evolved a remarkable array of ingenious pollination techniques. Some species attract insects by sexual impersonation. One species, for example, produces a flower that closely resembles the form of a female wasp—complete with eyes, antennae, and wings. It even gives off the odor of a female wasp in mating condition. Male wasps, deceived, attempt to copulate with it. In their vigor, they deposit pollen within the orchid flower and immediately afterward receive a fresh batch to carry to the next false female. Male bees and other insects are known to use the pollen of orchids as a perfume to attract females.

Guile seems to be the forte of orchids. One species drugs its visitors. Bees clamber into its throat and sip a nectar so intoxicating that they become inebriated, lose their footing, and slip into a small bucket. Escape is offered up a spout—the proverbial light at the end of the tunnel. As the drunken insect totters up, it has to wriggle beneath an overhanging rod, which showers its back with pollen.

An annual orchid show is held each March at Instituto Nacional de Biodiversidad (INBio), near San José. Gardens dedicated to orchids include the **Botanical Orchid Garden** (La Garita, tel. 506/2487-8095, www.orchidgardencr.com, 8:30am-4:30pm Tues.-Sun., adults $12, children $6) and **Jardín de la Guaríoa** (Palmares, tel. 506/2452-0091, 7am-6pm daily May-June, $4).

every conceivable niche. Tropical rainforests contain more than half of all living things known to science.

Only superficially does the rainforest resemble the fictional jungles of Tarzan. Yes, the foliage can indeed be so dense that you cannot move without a machete. But since only about 10 percent of the total sunlight manages to penetrate through the forest canopy, the undergrowth is generally correspondingly sparse, and the forest floor is surprisingly open and relatively easy to move around in. The plants array their leaves to avoid leaf shade; others are shaded purple underneath to help reflect back the light passing through the leaf; the "walking palm" literally walks across the forest floor in search of light on its stilt-like roots.

The stagnant air is loaded with moisture. To a visitor, the tropical rainforest always seems the same: uniform heat and stifling 90 percent humidity. But this is true only near

Flange roots offer extra support in thin soils.

of flora congregate neatly into distinctive plant "neighborhoods" with few other species interspersed, in the rainforest you may pass one example of a particular tree species, then not see another for 800 meters (0.5 miles). In between, however, are hundreds of other species. In the rainforest, life is piled on life—literally. The firm and unyielding forest floor is a "dark factory of decomposition," where bacteria, mold, and insects work unceasingly, degrading the constant rain of leaf litter and dislodged fruits into nutrient molecules.

Fungi proliferate as well. They are key to providing the nourishment vital to the rainforest's life cycle. While a fallen leaf from a North American oak may take a year to decompose, a leaf in the tropical rainforest will fully decay within a month. The trees suck up the minerals and nutrients through a thick mat of rootlets that grow close to the surface of the inordinately thin soil. To counteract their inherent instability, many species grow side buttresses: wafer-thin flanges that radiate in a ring around the base of the tree like the tail fins of rockets.

For every tree in the rainforest, there is a clinging vine fighting for a glimpse of the sun. Instead of using up valuable time and energy in building their own supports, these clutching vines and lianas rely on the straight, limbless trunks typical of rainforest tree species to provide a support in their quest for sunlight. They ride piggyback to the canopy, where they continue to snake through the treetops, sometimes reaching lengths of 300 meters (1,000 feet). One species spirals around its host like a corkscrew; another cements itself to a tree with three-pronged tendrils.

The bully of the forest, however, is the strangler fig, which isn't content to merely coexist. While most lianas and vines take root in the ground and grow upward, the strangler figs do the opposite. After sprouting in the forest canopy from seeds dropped by birds and bats, the strangler fig sends roots to the ground, where they dig into the soil and provide a boost of sustenance. Slowly but surely—it may take a full century—the roots grow and

the ground. High in the tops of the trees, where the sun comes and goes, breezes blow and moisture has a chance to be carried away, the swings in temperature between day and night are as much as 15 degrees Celsius (27 degrees Fahrenheit), and the humidity may drop from 95 percent, its fairly constant nighttime level, to as low as 60 percent as the sun rises and warms the forest. Thus, within 30 vertical meters (100 feet), two distinctly different climates prevail. Tropical rainforests are places of peace and renewal, like a vast vaulted cathedral—mysterious, strangely silent, and of majestic proportions.

Botanists have distinguished 30 or so different types of rainforest. Tropical evergreen rainforest exists in areas of high rainfall, at least 200 centimeters (79 inches), and regular high temperatures averaging no less than 25°C (77°F). In Costa Rica, the lush tropical evergreen rainforest of the Caribbean lowlands gives way on the Pacific side to a seasonally dry evergreen forest in the well-watered south.

While in temperate forests distinct species

envelop the host tree, choking it until it dies and rots away, leaving a hollow, trellised, free-standing cylinder.

The vigorous competition for light and space has promoted the evolution of long, slender, branchless trunks, many well over 35 meters (115 feet) tall, and flat-topped crowns with foliage so dense that rainwater from driving tropical downpours often may not reach the ground for 10 minutes. This great vaulted canopy—the clerestory of the rainforest cathedral—is the rainforest's powerhouse, where more than 90 percent of photosynthesis takes place. Above this dense carpet of greenery rise a few scattered giants towering to heights of 70 meters (230 feet) or more.

The scaffolding of massive boughs is colonized at all levels by a riot of bromeliads, ferns, and other epiphytes. As they die and decay, they form compost on the branch capable of supporting larger plants that feed on the leaf mold and draw moisture by dangling their roots into the humid air. Soon every available surface is a great hanging gallery of giant elk-horns and ferns, often reaching such weights that whole tree limbs are torn away and crash down to join the decaying litter on the forest floor.

Sit still awhile, and the unseen beasts and birds will get used to your presence and emerge from the shadows. Enormous morpho butterflies float by, flashing like bright neon signs. Is that vine really moving? More likely it's a brilliantly costumed tree eyelash viper, so green it is almost iridescent, draped in sensuous coils on a branch.

Scarlet macaws and lesser parrots plunge and sway in the high branches, announcing their play-acting with an outburst of shrieks. Arboreal rodents leap and run along the branches, searching for nectar and insects, while insectivorous birds watch from their vantage points for any movement that will betray a stick insect or leaf-green tree frog to scoop up for lunch. Legions of monkeys, sloths, and fruit- and leaf-eating mammals also live in the green world of the canopy. Larger hunters live up there too. In addition to the great eagles plunging through the canopy to grab monkeys, there are also tree-dwelling cats. These superbly athletic climbers are quite capable of catching monkeys and squirrels as they leap from branch to branch and race up trunks. There are also snakes here, some twig-thin, such as the chunk-headed snake with catlike eyes, which feasts on frogs and lizards and nesting birds.

Come twilight, the forest soaks in a brief moment of silence. Slowly, the lisping of insects begins. There is a faint rustle as nocturnal rodents come out to forage in the ground litter. All around, myriad beetles and moths take wing in the moist velvet blanket of the tropical night.

TROPICAL DRY FOREST

Before the arrival of the Spanish in the early 16th century, dry forests blanketed the Pacific coastal lowlands from Panamá to Mexico. Fires set by the Spanish and by generations of farmers and ranchers thereafter spread savannas across the province. Three decades ago, the dry forests had dwindled to some 2 percent of their former range—a mere 520 square kilometers (200 square miles) of Costa Rica in scattered patches centered on the lower Río Tempisque in Guanacaste. Far rarer than rainforests, they are significantly more endangered, especially by fires, which eviscerate whole forest patches, opening holes in which weeds and other ecological opportunists rush in. Eventually savanna comes to replace the forest. The fate of even the preserved dry-forest parcels hinges on the success of two ambitious conservation projects that are exemplars of forest restoration: one focusing on educating children and former farmers about the value of the dry forest, and one studying and promoting the scarlet macaw, vital to the survival of the sandbox tree.

Unlike Costa Rica's rainforests, the rare tropical dry forest is relatively sparsely vegetated, with far fewer tree species and only two strata. Canopy trees have short, stout trunks with large, flat-topped crowns, rarely more than 15 meters (50 feet) above the ground.

Beneath is an understory with small open-top crowns, and a layer of shrubs with vicious spines and thorns. Missing are the great profusion of epiphytes and the year-round lush evergreens of the rainforest.

From November through March, no rain relieves the parching heat. Then the deciduous dry forests undergo a dramatic seasonal transformation—the purple jacaranda, pink-and-white meadow oak, yellow *corteza amarilla,* scarlet *poró,* and the bright orange flame-of-the-forest explode in Monet colors in the midst of a drought.

MANGROVE ESTUARIES

Costa Rica's shorelines are home to five species of mangroves. These pioneer land builders thrive at the interface of land and sea, forming a stabilizing tangle that fights tidal erosion and reclaims land from the water.

Mangroves are what botanists call halophytes, plants that thrive in salty conditions. Costa Rica's rivers deposit silt and volcanic ash onto the coastal alluvial plains. The nutrient-rich mud generates algae and other small organisms that form the base of the marine food chain. Their sustained health is vital to the health of other marine ecosystems.

The nutrients the mangroves seek lie near the surface of the acid mud, deposited by the tides. There is no oxygen to be had in the mud, hence there is no point in the mangroves sending down deep roots. Instead, they send out aerial roots, maintaining a hold on the glutinous mud and giving the mangroves the appearance of walking on water. They draw oxygen from the air through small patches of spongy tissue on their bark.

The irrepressible, reddish-barked, shrubby mangroves rise from the dark water on interlocking stilt roots. Brackish streams and labyrinthine creeks wind among them like snakes, sometimes interconnecting, sometimes petering out in narrow cul-de-sacs, sometimes opening suddenly into broad lagoons.

Mangrove swamps are esteemed as nurseries of marinelife and as havens for waterbirds—cormorants, frigate birds, pelicans, herons, and egrets—that feed and nest here by the thousands, producing guano that makes the mangroves grow faster.

A look down into the water reveals luxuriant life: oysters and sponges attached to the roots, small stingrays flapping slowly over the bottom, and tiny fish in schools of tens of thousands. Baby black-tipped sharks and other juvenile fish also spend much of their early lives among mangrove roots, shielded

Mangroves thrive in brackish water.

by the root maze that keeps out large predators. Raccoons, snakes, and arboreal creatures also inhabit the mangroves. There is even an arboreal mangrove tree crab (*Aratus pisonii*), which eats mangrove leaves and is restricted to the very crowns of the trees by the predatory activities of another arboreal crab, *Goniopsis pulchra*.

Mangroves are aggressive colonizers, thanks to one of nature's most remarkable seedlings. The heavy, fleshy mangrove seeds, shaped like plumb bobs, germinate while still on the tree. The flowers bloom for a few weeks in the spring and then fall off, making way for a fruit. A seedling shoot soon sprouts from each fruit and grows to a length of 15 to 30 centimeters (6-12 inches) before dropping from the tree. Falling like darts, at low tide they land in the mud and put down roots immediately. Otherwise, a seaborne seedling may drift for hundreds of miles. Eventually, it touches the muddy floor and anchors. By its third year a young tree starts to sprout its own forest of arching prop roots; in about 10 years it has fostered a thriving colony of mangroves, which edge ever out to sea, forming a great swampy forest. As silt builds up among the roots, land is gradually reclaimed from the sea. Mangroves build up the soil until they strand themselves high and dry. In the end they die on the land they have created.

Animals

Anyone who has traveled in the tropics in search of wildlife can tell you that disappointment comes easy. But Costa Rica is one place that lives up to its reputation. Costa Rica is nature's live theater—and the actors aren't shy. The scarlet macaws are like rainbows, the toucans and hummingbirds like the green flash of sunset. The tiny poison dart frogs are bright enough to scare away even the most dim-witted predator. And the electric-blue morphos, the neon narcissi of the butterfly world, make even the most jaded of viewers gape in awe.

Then there are all the creatures that mimic other things and are harder to spot: insects that look like rotting leaves, moths that look like wasps, the mottled, bark-colored *machaca* (lantern fly), and the giant *Caligo memnon* (cream owl) butterfly, whose huge open wings resemble the wide-eyed face of an owl.

Much of the wildlife is glimpsed only as shadows. Well-known animals that you are not likely to see are the cats—pumas, jaguars, margays, and ocelots—as well as tapirs and white-lipped peccaries. With patience, however, you can usually spot monkeys galore, as well as iguanas, quetzals, and sloths that get most of their aerobic exercise by scratching their bellies and look, as someone has said, like "long-armed tree-dwelling Muppets."

Identifying the species is a prodigious task, which every day turns up something new. Insects, for example, make up about half of the estimated 500,000 to one million plant and animal species in Costa Rica. The country is home seasonally to more than 850 bird species—10 percent of all known bird species (the United States and Canada combined have less than half that number). There are 5,000 different species of grasshoppers, 160 known amphibians, 220 reptiles, and 10 percent of all known butterflies (Parque Nacional Corcovado alone has at least 220 different species).

EARLY MIGRATIONS

About three million years ago, the Central American isthmus began to rise from the sea to form the first tentative link between the two Americas. Going from island to island, birds, insects, reptiles, and the first mammals began to move back and forth between the continents. During this period, rodents of North

America reached the southern continent, and so did the monkeys, which found the tropical climate to their liking.

In due course, South America connected with North America. Down this corridor came the placental mammals to dispute the possession of South America with the marsupial residents. Creatures poured across the bridge in both directions. The equids used it to enter South America, the opossums to invade North America. Only a few South American mammals, notably armadillos, ground sloths, and porcupines, managed to establish themselves successfully in the north. The greatest migration was in the other direction. The mammals soon came to dominate the environment, diversifying into forms more appropriate to the tropics. In the course of this rivalry, many marsupial species disappeared, leaving only the tough, opportunistic opossums.

The isthmus has thus served as a "filter bridge" for the intermingling of species and the evolution of modern, distinctive Costa Rican biota, resulting in a proliferation of species that is vastly richer than the biota of either North or South America.

MAMMALS

Given the rich diversity of Costa Rica's ecosystems, it may come as a surprise that only 200 mammal species—half of which are bats—live here. Several species of dolphins and seven species of whales are common in Costa Rican waters, but there are no seals. And the only endemic marine mammal species of any significance is the endangered manatee. Before people hunted them to extinction, there were many more mammal species. Even today, all large—and many small—mammal populations are subject to extreme pressure from hunting or habitat destruction.

The mostly nocturnal and near-blind **nine-banded armadillo** (*cusuco*) will be familiar to anyone from Texas. The animal can grow to almost one meter (3 feet) long. They are terrestrial dwellers that grub about on the forest floor, feeding on insects and fungi. The

female lays a single egg that, remarkably, divides to produce identical triplets. Its smaller cousin, the **naked-tailed armadillo,** is far less frequently seen. The dog family is represented by the brown-gray **coyote** and nocturnal **gray fox,** both found mostly in the dry northwest. The marsupials—mammals whose embryonic offspring crawl from the birth canal and are reared in an external pouch—are represented by nine species of **opossums.** The blunt-nosed, short-spined, **prehensile-tailed porcupine** (*puerco espín*) is nocturnal and arboreal and rarely seen. There are also two species of **rabbits** (*conejos*).

Anteaters

Anteaters are common in lowland and middle-elevation habitats throughout Costa Rica. Anteaters are purists and subsist solely on a diet of ants and termites, plus a few unavoidable bits of dirt. There is no doubt about what the best tool is for the job—a long tongue with thousands of microscopic spines. The anteater's toothless jaw is one long tube. When it feeds, using its powerful forearms and claws to rip open ant and termite nests, its thong of a tongue flicks in and out of its tiny mouth, running deep into the galleries. Each time it withdraws, it brings with it a load of ants, which are scraped off inside the tunnel of its mouth and swallowed, ground down by small quantities of sand and gravel in its stomach.

The most commonly seen of Costa Rica's three anteater species is the tree-dwelling **lesser anteater** (called tamandua locally), a beautiful creature with a prehensile tail and the gold-and-black coloration of a panda bear. It can grow to 1.5 meters (5 feet) and weigh up to eight kilograms (18 pounds). The critically endangered **giant anteater,** with its huge bushy tail and astonishingly long proboscis, is now restricted to the Nicoya and Osa Peninsulas. It can grow to two meters (6.5 feet) long, and when threatened rears itself on its hind legs and slashes wildly with its claws. At night you may, with luck, see the strictly arboreal cat-size **silky anteater,** which can hang from its strong prehensile tail.

Bats

The most numerous mammals by far are the bats; there are 109 species in Costa Rica. You may come across them slumbering by day halfway up a tree or roosting in a shed or beneath the eaves of your lodgings. In true Dracula fashion, most bats are photophobic: They avoid bright light. They also suspend foraging completely while the moon is at its peak, probably for fear of owls. Many bat species—like the giant **Jamaican fruit bat** (called *murciélago frutero*), with a wingspan of more than 50 centimeters (20 inches)—are frugivores (fruit eaters) or insectivores. Quite harmless to people, they play a vital role in pollination, seed dispersal, and mosquito control.

The three species of **vampire bats** (Ticos call them *vampiros*)—which belong to neotropical regions, not Transylvania—are a different matter: They inflict an estimated $100 million in damage on domestic farm animals throughout Central and South America by transmitting rabies and other diseases. Two species feed on birds; the third on mammals, with a modus operandi almost as frightening as the stuff of Bram Stoker's *Dracula*. It lands on or close to a sleeping mammal, such as a cow. Using its two razor-sharp incisors, it punctures the unsuspecting beast and, with the aid of anticoagulant saliva, merrily squats beside the wound and laps up the blood while it flows.

The most interesting of bats, however, and one easily seen in Drake Bay and Tortuguero, is the **fishing bulldog bat** (*murciélago pescador*), with its huge 60-centimeter (24-inch) wingspan and great gaff-shaped claws with which it hooks fish.

Cats

Costa Rica boasts six endangered members of the cat family. All are active by day and night but are rarely seen. Cats are primarily solitary and nocturnal and spend the greater part of the day sleeping or hidden in dense vegetation. Although they are legally protected, hunting of cats still occurs in Costa Rica.

However, the main threat to the remaining populations is deforestation.

One of the most abundant of cats is the **jaguarundi** (called *león breñero* locally), a spotless dark-brown or tawny critter about the size of a large house cat. It has a long slender body, short stocky legs (its hind legs are taller than its forelegs), long tail, and a venal face with yellow eyes suggesting a nasty temperament. It is more diurnal than its cousins and is sometimes seen hunting in pairs, preferring lowland habitats.

The **puma** (*león*) also inhabits a variety of terrains, though it is rarely seen. This large cat—also called the "mountain lion"—is generally dun-colored, though coloration varies markedly among individuals and from region to region.

The spotted cats include the cute-looking, house-cat-sized **margay** (*caucel*) and its smaller cousin, the **oncilla.** Both wear an ocher coat spotted with black and brown spots, like tiny leopards. Their chests are white. The solitary and strongly nocturnal margay, which can weigh up to six kilograms (13 pounds), has a very long tail in relation to its body size, which, combined with its ability to turn its hind feet by 180 degrees, provides monkey-like climbing abilities. It is found only in primary or very little-disturbed forests. The oncilla or tiger cat has black ears and is distinguished from the margay by its face, closely resembling that of a domestic cat, its shorter tail, and more slender body shape. This solitary animal prefers montane cloud forest.

The most commonly seen cat is the **ocelot** (*manigordo*), which is well distributed throughout the country and among various habitats. The ocelot is the biggest of Costa Rica's "small" cats—males can weigh up to 15 kilograms (33 pounds), the females up to 11 kilograms (24 pounds)—and has short, dense fur with brown spots and rosettes with black edges, arranged in parallel rows along its body length, with a background of grayish-yellow. It has a characteristic white spot on each ear, and black stripes on both cheeks and forehead.

Worshiped as a god in pre-Columbian civilizations, the **jaguar** is the symbol of the Central American rainforest. *Panthera onca* (or *tigre* to locals) was once abundant throughout Central America. Today, this magnificent and noble beast is an endangered species, rare except in parts of the larger reserves: Santa Rosa, Tortuguero, and Corcovado national parks, and the Cordillera Talamanca. When roads penetrate the primeval forest, the jaguar is among the first large mammals to disappear. While a few of the famous black "panther" variety exist, most Central American jaguars are a rich yellow, spotted with large black rosettes. Jaguars are the largest and most powerful of the American members of the cat family—a mature jaguar measures over two meters (6.5 feet), stands 60 centimeters (24 inches) at the shoulders, and weighs up to 90 kilograms (200 pounds). The animal's head and shoulders are massive, the legs relatively short and thick. An adept climber and swimmer, the beast is a versatile hunter, at home in trees, on the ground, and even in water. Like all wild cats, jaguars are extremely shy and attack humans very rarely.

Deer

Costa Rica has two species of deer: the **red brocket deer** (called *cabro de monte*), which favors the rainforests, and the larger, more commonly seen **white-tailed deer** (*venado*), widely dispersed in habitats throughout the country, but especially Guanacaste. The former is slightly hump-backed and bronze. The latter varies from gray to red, normally with a white belly and a white dappled throat and face.

Manatees

Anyone venturing to Parque Nacional Tortuguero or Refugio Nacional de Vida Silvestre Gandoca-Manzanillo will no doubt hope to see a **West Indian manatee** (*manati*). This herbivorous marine mammal looks like a tuskless walrus, with small round eyes, fleshy lips that hang over the sides of its mouth, and no hind limbs, just a large,

flat, spatulate tail. The animals, sometimes called sea cows, can grow to four meters (13 feet) long and weigh as much as a ton. Now endangered throughout their former range, these creatures once inhabited brackish rivers and lagoons along the whole coast of Central America's Caribbean shoreline. Today, only a few remain in the most southerly waters of the United States and isolated pockets of Central America and the Caribbean isles. Tortuguero, where the animals are legally protected, has one of the few significant populations. They are not easy to spot, because they lie submerged with only nostrils showing. Watch for rising bubbles in the water: Manatees suffer from flatulence, a result of eating up to 45 kilograms (100 pounds) of water hyacinths and other aquatic flora daily.

Monkeys

Costa Rica has four species of monkeys: the white-faced (or capuchin), howler, spider, and squirrel. Along with approximately 50 other species, they belong to a group called New World monkeys. They inhabit a wide range of habitats, from the rainforest canopy to the scrubby undergrowth of the dry forests, though each species occupies its own niche and the species seldom meet. Together, they are the liveliest and most vocal rainforest tenants. Beyond the reach of most predators, they have little inhibition in announcing their presence with their roughhousing and howls, chattering, and screeches.

The distinctive-looking **capuchin,** or white-faced monkey (*mono cara blanca*), is the smartest and most inquisitive of Central American simians. It derives its name from its black body and monk-like white cowl. They're the little guys favored by organ grinders worldwide. Capuchins range widely throughout the wet lowland forests and the deciduous dry forests of the northwest Pacific below 1,500 meters (4,900 feet) elevation. Two excellent places to see them are Santa Rosa and Manuel Antonio national parks, where family troops are constantly on the prowl. These opportunistic feeders are fun to watch as they search under logs and leaves or tear off bark as they seek out insects and small lizards. Capuchins also steal birds' eggs and nestlings. While their taste is eclectic, they are fussy eaters: They'll meticulously pick out grubs from fruit, which they test for ripeness by smelling and squeezing.

The howler (*mono congo*) is the most abundant as well as the largest of Central American monkeys; it can weigh up to five kilograms (11 pounds). It inhabits both lowland and montane forests throughout Costa Rica and can be found clinging precariously to existence in many relic patches of forest. The stentorian males greet each new day with reveille calls that seem more like the explosive roars of lions than those of small arboreal leaf-eaters. The hair-raising vocalizations can carry for almost 1,500 meters (1 mile) in even the densest rainforest. The males sing in chorus again at dusk (or whenever trespassers get too close) as a spacing mechanism to keep rivals at a safe distance. Their Pavarotti-like vocal abilities are due to unusually large larynxes and throats that inflate into resonating balloons. Females generally content themselves with loud wails and groans—usually to signal distress or call a straying infant. This noisy yet sedentary canopy browser feeds on leaves and fruit.

The smallest and most endangered Costa Rican primate, the squirrel monkey (*mono titi*) grows to 25 to 35 centimeters (10-14 inches), plus a tail up to 45 centimeters (18 inches). Fewer than 2,000 individuals are thought to exist. It is restricted to the rainforests of the southern Pacific lowlands. Always on the go, day and night, they scurry about in the rainforest understory and forest floor on all fours. Squirrels are more gregarious than most other monkeys; bands of 40 individuals or more are not uncommon. The golden-orange *titi*, with its face of white and black, is the arboreal goat of the forest. It will eat almost anything: fruit, insects, small lizards. The *titi* is well on its way to extinction.

The large, loose-limbed spider monkey (*mono colorado*)—the supreme acrobat of the forest—was once the most widespread of the Central American monkeys. The last few decades have brought significant destruction of spider monkey habitats, and land clearance and hunting have greatly reduced spider monkey populations throughout much of their former range. These copper-colored acrobats can attain a length of 1.5 meters (5 feet). They have evolved extreme specialization for a highly mobile arboreal

capuchin monkeys

lifestyle. Long slender limbs allow spider monkeys to make spectacular leaps. But the spider's greatest secret is its extraordinary prehensile tail, which is longer than the combined length of its head and body. The underside is ridged like a human fingertip for added grip at the end of treetop leaps (it is even sensitive enough for probing and picking). You might see individuals hanging like ripe fruit by their tails. Gregarious by night (they often bed down in heaps), by day they are among the most solitary of primates. The males stay aloof from the females. While the latter tend to their young, which they carry on their backs, the males are busy marking their territory with secretions from their chest glands.

Peccaries

These myopic, sharp-toothed wild pigs are potentially aggressive creatures whose presence in the rainforest may be betrayed by their pungent, musky odor and by the churned-up ground from their grubbing. Gregarious beasts, they forage in herds and make a fearsome noise if frightened or disturbed. Like most animals, they prefer to flee from human presence. Occasionally, however, an aggressive male may show his bravado by threatening to attack you, usually in a bluff charge. Attacks by groups of a dozen or more peccaries sometimes occur. Rangers advise that if attacked, you should climb a tree or stand absolutely still. Don't try to frighten them away—that's a sure way to get gored.

The more common **collared peccary** (*saino*) is marked by an ocher-colored band of hair running from its shoulders down to its nose; the rest of its body is dark brown. The larger **white-lipped peccary** (*cariblanco*), which can grow to one meter (3 feet) long, is all black or brown, with a white mustache or "beard."

Raccoons

Raccoons, familiar to North Americans, are present throughout Costa Rica, where they are frequently seen begging tidbits from diners at hotel restaurants. The **northern raccoon** (*mapache* to Ticos) is a smaller but otherwise identical cousin of the North American raccoon and can be found widely in Costa Rica's lowlands, predominantly in moist areas. Its cousin, the darker-colored **crab-eating raccoon,** is found only along the Pacific coast.

A relative, the long-nosed **coatimundi** (called *pizote* locally), is found throughout the country. Coatis wear many coats, from yellow to deepest brown, though all are distinguished by faintly ringed tails, white-tipped black snouts, and panda-like eye rings. They are gregarious critters and often seen in packs.

Another raccoon family member is the small and totally nocturnal **kinkajou** (known to Ticos as the *martilla*), with its large limpid eyes and velvet-soft coat of golden brown. It's a superb climber (it can hang by its prehensile tail) and spends most of its life feeding on fruit, honey, and insects in the treetops. Its smaller cousin is the much rarer grayish, bug-eyed **olingo** (*cacomistle*), with panda-like white spectacled eyes and a bushy white tail ringed with black hoops.

Rodents

The **agouti** (*guatusa* to Ticos) is a brown cat-size rodent related to the guinea pig. It inhabits the forests up to 1,980 meters (6,500 feet) elevation and is often seen by day feeding on the forest floor on fruits and nuts (the wet-forest agoutis are darker than their chestnut-colored dry-forest cousins). It looks like a giant tailless squirrel with the thin legs and tiptoeing gait of a deer, but it sounds like a small dog. They are solitary critters yet form monogamous pairs.

Agoutis have long been favored for their meat and are voraciously hunted by humans. Their nocturnal cousin, the **paca** (called *tepezcuintle* by locals), also makes good eating. It can grow to one meter (3 feet) long and weigh 10 kilograms (22 pounds), three times larger than the agouti; it is favored by a wide variety of predators. It is brown with rows of white spots along its side. Both are easily captured because of the strong anal musk they use to scent their territories and because of their habit of running in circles. If you disturb one in the forest, you may hear its high-pitched alarm bark before you see it.

Costa Rica also has five squirrel species and about 40 species of rats, mice, and gophers.

Sloths

Ask anyone to compile a list of the world's strangest creatures, and the sloth (locally called *perezoso,* which means "lazy"), a creature that moves with the grace and deliberation of a tai chi master, would be right up there with the duck-billed platypus. There are six distinct species, of which Costa Rica has two: the **three-fingered sloth** (*Bradypus variegatus,* called locally *perezoso de tres dedos*) and the nocturnal **Hoffman's two-fingered sloth** (*Choloepus hoffmanni,* called *perezoso de dos dedos*). The animals are commonly called "three-toed" and "two-toed," but in fact both species have three toes. The two species are only faintly related and belong to two different families. Both grow to the size of a medium-size dog. The three-fingered sloth has a small head and a flat face with a snub nose; the two-fingered sloth has a tapered nose. Both have beady eyes and seemingly rudimentary ears (its reputation for poor hearing is entirely incorrect). Sloths have long arms with curving claws that hook over and grasp the branches from which they spend almost their entire life suspended upside down. The creatures spend up to 12 hours daily sleeping curled up with their limbs drawn close together and their heads tucked between the forelimbs.

The sloth's shaggy fur harbors algae, unique to the beast, that make sloths greenly inconspicuous—wonderful camouflage from prowling jaguars and keen-eyed eagles, their chief predators. Communities of moths live in the depths of the fur and feed on the algae as well.

There's a very good reason sloths move at a rate barely distinguishable from rigor mortis. A sloth's digestion works as slowly as its other bodily functions, and food remains in its stomach for up to a week. Hence it has evolved a large ruminant-like stomach and intestinal tract to process large quantities of relatively indigestible food. To compensate, it has sacrificed heavy muscle mass—and, hence, mobility—to maximize body size in proportion to weight. Sloths need warm weather to synthesize food. During long spells of cold weather, the animals may literally starve to death.

Sloths live 20 years or longer and reach sexual maturity at three years. Females screech to draw males, which have a bare orange patch on their back with unique sexual markings. Females give birth once a year and spend half their adult lives pregnant. When the juvenile reaches six months, the mother simply turns tail on her youngster, which inherits her home range of trees.

An easy way to find sloths is to look up into the green foliage of cecropia trees, one of the sloth's favorite food staples. The sight of a sloth languishing in open cecropia crowns is a heavenly vision to harpy eagles, which swoop in to snatch the torpid creature like plucking fruit.

Tapirs

Another symbol of the New World tropics is the strange-looking **Baird's tapir** (locally *danta*), a solitary, ground-living, plant-eating, forest-dwelling, ungainly mixture of elephant, rhinoceros, pig, and horse. The tapir uses its short, highly mobile proboscis—an evolutionary forerunner to the trunk of the elephant—for plucking leaves and shoveling them into its mouth. Tapirs live in dense forests and swamps and rely on concealment for defense. They are generally found wallowing up to their knees in swampy waters, to which they rush precipitously at the first sign of danger. This endangered species is the largest indigenous terrestrial mammal in Central America. Like its natural predator, the jaguar, the tapir has suffered severely at the hands of humans. The animal was once common in Costa Rica and ranged far and wide in the lowland swamps and forests. Hunters have brought it to the edge of extinction. Today, tapirs are

neotropical river otter in Río Sarapiquí

de agua, or water dog, to locals) grow as long as one meter (3 feet) and are commonly seen in lowland rivers, especially in Tortuguero.

A cousin, the sleek, long-haired, chocolate-brown **tayra** (locals call it *tolumuco*)—a one-meter-long (3-foot-long) giant of the weasel family—resembles a mix of grison and otter. It is often seen in highland habitats throughout Costa Rica.

SEALIFE

Costa Rica is as renowned for its marinelife as for its terrestrial and avian fauna—most famously, perhaps, for the billfish (marlin and sailfish) that cruise the deep blue waters offshore, and for tarpon and snook, feisty estuarine and wetland game fish. The former swim seasonally in the warm waters off the Golfo de Papagayo and Golfo Dulce; the latter are concentrated in the waters of the Río Colorado and Caño Negro.

Sharks are forever present in Costa Rican waters. They seem particularly to favor waters in which marine turtles swim. Isla del Coco is renowned for its schools of hammerhead sharks, as well as giant whale sharks (the world's largest fish), which can also be found hanging out with giant groupers, jewfish, and manta rays in the waters around the Islas Murciélagos, off the Santa Elena Peninsula in Guanacaste.

Whales—notably **humpbacks**—can be seen predictably along the west coast of Costa Rica December-October, when they migrate from both Antarctic and North Pacific waters to mate and give birth in the warm waters off the Costa Ballena.

BIRDS

With approximately 850 recorded bird species, the country boasts one-tenth of the world's total. More than 630 are resident species; the others are travelers who fly in for the winter. Birds that have all but disappeared in other areas still find tenuous safety in protected lands in Costa Rica, although many species face extinction from deforestation.

It may surprise you to learn that in a land

found only in national parks and reserves where hunting is restricted, with the greatest density in Parque Nacional Corcovado.

Weasels

Costa Rica boasts seven members of the weasel family. The most ubiquitous is the **skunk** (*zorro* in local parlance), one of the most commonly seen mammal species, of which Costa Rica has three species. The black **striped hog-nosed skunk,** with its bushy white tail and white stripe along its rump, will be familiar to North Americans. The smaller **spotted skunk** and **hooded skunk** are more rarely seen. Their defense is a disgusting scent sprayed at predators from an anal gland.

Costa Rica is also home to the badger-like **grison,** another member of the weasel family that can weigh three kilograms (6.5 pounds) and is often seen hunting alone or in groups in lowland rainforest during the day. The grison is gray, with a white stripe running across its forehead and ears, white eye patches, and a black nose, chest, and legs. **Otters** (*perro*

Shopping with a Conscience

Think twice before buying something exotic: The item may be banned by U.S. Customs and, if so, you could be fined. Even if it's legal to import, consider whether your purchase is an ecological crime. In short, shop with a conscience. Don't buy:

- Combs, jewelry, or other items made from tortoise shells.

- Coral, coral items, and shells. Costa Rica's coral reefs are gradually being destroyed, and every shell taken from a beach is one less for the next person to enjoy.

- Jewelry, artwork, or clothes made of or decorated with feathers.

- Furs from jaguars, ocelots, and other animals in danger of extinction. Such furs are illegal.

- Tropical hardwood products, unless labeled as having been made from fallen timber.

with so many exotic species, the national bird is the relatively drab *yiquirro*, or clay-colored thrush (it was previously called the clay-colored robin), a brown-and-buff bird with brick-red eyes. You may hear the male singing during the March-May breeding season when, according to campesino folklore, he is "calling the rains."

The four major avifaunal zones roughly correspond to the major geographic subdivisions of the country: the northern Pacific lowlands, the southern Pacific lowlands, the Caribbean lowlands, and the interior highlands. Guanacaste's dry habitats (northern Pacific lowlands) share relatively few species with other parts of the country. This is a superlative place, however, for waterfowl: The estuaries, swamps, and lagoons that make up the Tempisque basin support the richest freshwater avifauna in all Central America, and Parque Nacional Palo Verde, at the mouth of the Río Tempisque, is a bird-watcher's mecca. The southern Pacific lowland region is home to many South American neotropical species, such as jacamars, antbirds, and, of course, parrots.

Depending on the season, location, and luck, you can expect to see many dozens of species on any one day. Many tour companies offer guided bird-study tours, and the country is well set up with lodges that specialize in bird-watching programs. But the deep heart of the rainforest is not the best place to look for birds: You can't see very well amid the complex, disorganized patterns of shadow and light. For best results, find a large clearing on the fringe of the forest, or a watercourse where birds are sure to be found in abundance. The most diverse avifauna is found in the wet lowlands and forested foothills. The **Organization of Tropical Studies** (www. ots.ac.cr) offers half- and full-day birding workshops.

Anhingas and Cormorants

The **anhinga** (*pato aguja* to locals) and its close cousin, the **olivaceous cormorant** (*cormorán*), are sleek, long-necked, stump-tailed waterbirds with the pointy profile of a Concorde. Although they dive for fish in the lagoons and rivers of the lowlands and are superb swimmers, their feathers lack the waterproof oils of other birds. Thus you can often see them after a dousing, perched on a branch, sunning themselves in a vertical position with wings spread. These birds have kinked necks because they spear fish using the kink as a trigger.

Aracaris and Toucans

The bright-billed toucans—"flying bananas"—are a particular delight to watch as they pick fruit with their long beaks, throw it in the air, and catch it at the back of their throats. Costa Rica's six toucan species are among the most flamboyant of all Central American birds.

The gregarious **keel-billed toucan** (*tucán pico iris*) inhabits lowland and mid-elevation forests throughout the country, except the Pacific southwest. This colorful stunner has a jet-black body, blue feet, a bright yellow chest and face, beady black eyes ringed by green feathers, and a rainbow-hued beak tipped in scarlet. Its similarly colored cousin, Swainson's or **chestnut-mandibled toucan** (Ticos call it *dios tedé*, onomatopoeia for the sound it makes; a fight is on to officially rename it the "black-billed toucan"), is the largest of the group—it grows to 60 centimeters (24 inches) long and has a two-tone yellow-and-brown beak. It is found in moist forests below 600 meters (2,000 feet) elevation, notably along the coastal zones, including the Pacific southwest.

There are also two species of toucanets, smaller cousins of the toucan: the green **emerald toucanet**, a highland bird with a red tail; and the black **yellow-eared toucanet**, found in the Caribbean lowlands.

Aracaris (*tucancillos*) are smaller and sleeker relatives, with more slender beaks. Both the **collared aracari** (a Caribbean bird) and **fiery-billed aracari** (its southern Pacific cousin) boast olive-black bodies, faces, and chests, with a dark band across their rust-yellow underbellies. The former has a two-tone yellow-and-black beak; the latter's beak is black and fiery orange.

Birds of Prey

Costa Rica has some 50 raptor species: birds that hunt down live prey and seize it with their talons. The various species have evolved adaptations to specific habitats. For example, the large **common black hawk** (*gavilán cangrejero*, or "crab-hunting hawk" to Ticos) snacks on crabs and other marine morsels. And the **osprey** is known as *águila pescadora* ("fishing eagle") locally for scooping fish while on the wing. That lunatic laughter that goes on compulsively at dusk in lowland rainforests is the **laughing falcon** (*guaco*).

The endangered neotropical **harpy eagle** (*águila arpía*), the largest of all eagles at one meter (3 feet) long, is renowned for twisting and diving through the treetops in pursuit of sloths and monkeys. Sightings in Costa Rica—where in recent years it has been relegated to the Nicoya and Osa Peninsulas and more remote ranges of the Talamancas—are extremely rare. Costa Rica's two species

chestnut-mandibled toucan at La Paz Waterfall Gardens

of caracaras—the **crested caracara** and **yellow-headed caracara**—are close cousins to the eagles, although like vultures they also eat carrion. You'll often see these large, fearsomely beaked, goose-stepping, long-legged birds picking at roadkill.

Costa Rica also has eight species of hawks; they are physically robust, with broad wings and short wide tails, compared to the sleeker kites, which have longer slender tails and wings. The most ubiquitous hawk is the small gray-brown **roadside hawk** (*gavilán chapulinero*).

Egrets, Herons, and Relatives

Some 25 or so stilt-legged, long-necked wading birds are found in Costa Rica. Most common is the snowy white **cattle egret.** It favors cattle pastures and can often be seen hitching a ride on the backs of cattle, which are happy to have it pick off fleas and ticks. The males have head plumes, which, along with the back and chest, turn tawny in breeding season. The species is easily mistaken for the **snowy egret,** a larger though more slender bird wearing "golden slippers" (yellow feet) on its black legs. Largest of the white egrets is the **great egret,** which grows to one meter (3 feet) tall.

There are three species of brown herons—called "tiger herons" (*garza tigre*)—in Costa Rica, most notably the **bare-throated tiger heron.** The **little blue heron,** commonly seen foraging alongside lowland watercourses, is a handsome blue-gray with purplish head plumage (the female is white, with wings tipped in gray). The northern lowlands are also a good place to spot the relatively small **green-backed heron.** The dun-colored **yellow-crowned night heron** is diurnal, not nocturnal as its name suggests. It is unmistakable, with its black-and-white head crowned with a swept-back yellow plume. Another instantly identifiable bird is the stocky gray **boat-billed heron,** named for the keel shape of its abnormally wide, thick bill.

Storks—notable for their fearsomely heavy, slightly upturned bills—also inhabit the lowland wetlands, notably in Caño Negro and Palo Verde national parks, where the endangered **jabiru** can be seen. This massive bird—it grows to over one meter (3 feet) tall—wears snow-bright plumage, with a charcoal head and a red scarf around its neck. Its relative, the **wood stork,** is also white, but with black flight feathers and a featherless black head.

The **roseate** spoonbill (*espátula rosada*) is the most dramatic of the waders, thanks to its shocking-pink plumage and spatulate bill. Costa Rica also has three species of **ibis.**

Hummingbirds

Of all the exotically named bird species in Costa Rica, the hummingbirds beat all contenders. Their names are poetry: the **green-crowned brilliant, purple-throated mountain-gem, Buffon's plumeleteer,** and the bold and strikingly beautiful **fiery-throated hummingbird.** More than 300 species of New World hummingbirds constitute the family Trochilidae (Costa Rica has 51). The fiery-throated hummingbird is a glossy green, shimmering iridescent at close range, with a dark blue tail, a violet-blue chest, a glittering coppery orange throat, and a brilliant blue crown set off by velvety black on the sides and back of the head. Some males take their exotic plumage one step farther and are bedecked with long streamer tails and iridescent mustaches, beards, and visors.

These tiny high-speed machines are named because of the hum made by the beat of their wings. At up to 100 beats per second, the hummingbirds' wings move so rapidly that the naked eye cannot detect them. They are often seen hovering at flowers, from which they extract nectar (and often insects) with their long, hollow, and extensile tongues, which are forked at the tip. Alone among birds, they can generate power on both the forward and backward wing strokes, a distinction that allows them to fly backward. Nests are often no larger than a thimble and eggs are no larger than coffee beans.

Motmots

The motmot is a sickle-billed bird that makes its home in a hole in the ground. Motmots have a pendulous twin-feathered tail with the barbs missing three-quarters of the way down, leaving two bare feather shafts with disc-shaped tips. According to Bribrí legend, the god Sibo asked all the creatures to help him make the world. They all chipped in gladly except the motmot, who hid in a hole. Unfortunately, the bird left his tail hanging out. When the other birds saw this, they picked the feathers from the motmot's tail but left the feathers at the tip. When the world was complete, Sibo gave all the tired animals a rest. Soon the motmot appeared and began boasting about how hard he had labored. But the lazy bird's tail gave the game away, so Sibo, who guessed what had happened, admonished the motmot and banished him to live in a hole in the ground.

Of the nine species of motmot in tropical America, six live in Costa Rica. You'll find them from humid coastal southwest plains to the cool highland zone and dry Guanacaste region. Two commonly seen species are the **blue-crowned motmot** and **turquoise-browed motmot**.

Owls

Costa Rica's 17 species of owls are nocturnal hunters, more often heard than seen. An exception is the large dark-brown **spectacled owl** (*bujo de anteojos*), which also hunts by day.

Parrots

If ever there were an avian symbol of the neotropical zone, it must be the parrot. This family of birds is marked by savvy intelligence, an ability to mimic the human voice, and uniformly short, hooked bills hinged to provide the immense power required for cracking seeds and nuts. Costa Rica claims 16 of the world's 330 or so species, including six species of parakeets and two species of macaws, the giants of the parrot kingdom. Parrots are predominantly green, with short, truncated tails (parakeets and macaws, however, have long tails), and varying degrees of colored markings. All are voluble, screeching raucously as they barrel overhead.

Although **macaw** is the common name for any of 15 species of these large long-tailed birds found throughout Central and South America, only two species inhabit Costa Rica: the scarlet macaw (*lapa roja*) and the great green or Buffon's macaw (*lapa verde*). Both bird populations are losing their homes to deforestation and poaching. The largest of the neotropical parrots, macaws have harsh, raucous voices that are filled with authority. They are gregarious and rarely seen alone. They are usually paired male and female—they're monogamous for long periods; some pair for life—often sitting side by side, grooming and preening each other, and conversing in rasping loving tones, or flying two by two. Macaws usually nest in softwood trees where termites have hollowed out holes. They rarely eat fruit but prefer seeds and nuts, which they extract with a hooked nutcracker of such strength that it can split a Brazil nut—or a human finger.

The **scarlet macaw** can grow to 85 centimeters (33 inches) in length. It wears a dazzling rainbow-colored jacket of bright yellow and blue, green, or scarlet. Although the scarlet macaw ranges from Mexico to central South America and was once abundant on both coasts of Costa Rica, today it is found only in a few protected areas on the Pacific shore, and rarely on the Caribbean side. Until recently only three wild populations of scarlet macaws in Central America were thought to have a long-term chance of survival—at Parque Nacional Carara and Parque Nacional Corcovado in Costa Rica, and at Parque Nacional Coiba, an island in Panamá. The bird can also be seen with regularity at Parque Nacional Palo Verde and more rarely at Parque Nacional Manuel Antonio and Parque Nacional Santa Rosa, although these populations are below the minimum critical size. An estimated 400 scarlets live at Carara and as many as 1,000 at Corcovado. Following

Saving the Macaw

Several conservation groups are working to breed green and scarlet macaws for reintroduction to the wild in an effort to reestablish viable populations of these critically endangered birds and to link up the various isolated populations.

Zoo Ave (tel. 506/2433-8989, www.zooave.org), at La Garita, west of Alajuela, has an extensive macaw breeding program, and has released over 100 macaws to Parque Nacional Piedras Blancas.

The Ara Project (tel. 506/8339-4329 or 506/8339-2407, www.thearaproject.org) is a macaw-breeding program at Islita, on the Nicoya Peninsula. Here, the Beirute family and a dedicated staff breed and raise green and scarlet macaws using special techniques and cages. The first scarlet macaws were released in 1999. Dozens of scarlet macaws have since been released at Tiskita, near Pavones; about 85 percent have survived, and the various released populations are intermingling. Additional releases are planned near Dominical and in southwest Nicoya. The first 11 captive-bred green macaws were released on the southern Caribbean in 2011, where The Ara Project has opened a second facility. Donations are needed, as are volunteer workers.

ASOPROLAPA (tel. 506/8980-0594, http://delfines.com/costa-rica-photos/asoprolapa), based at the Barceló resort at Tambor, also breeds scarlet macaws for release.

a decade of reintroduction of human-bred scarlet macaws to the wild, populations are rebounding throughout their range.

The **Buffon's macaw,** or great green macaw, is slightly larger than the scarlet. It has a body of multiple shades of green that are slightly iridescent around the neck, a pinkish-white face that flushes when the bird is excited, teal-blue wingtips, and a red tail. About 50 breeding pairs of Buffon's macaw are thought to exist in the wild, exclusively in the Caribbean and northern lowlands. The bird relies on the *almendro* tree—a heavily logged species—for nest sites, and calls have gone out for a ban on logging *almendros*. Its population is increasing slowly thanks to environmental efforts, including the release of macaws bred by the Ara Project.

Seabirds and Shorebirds

Costa Rica has almost 100 species of seabirds and shorebirds, including a wide variety of gulls. Many are migratory visitors, more abundant in winter months.

The large, pouch-billed **brown pelican** (*pelicano*) can be seen up and down the Pacific coast (and in lesser numbers on the Caribbean). **Boobies** inhabit several islands off Nicoya, as do the beautiful red-billed,

fork-tailed **royal tern** and a variety of other seabirds. **Oystercatchers** and **sandpipers,** often seen in vast flocks, and other shoreline waders frequent the coastal margins.

Frigate birds, with their long scimitar wings and forked tails, hang like kites in the wind all along the Costa Rican coast. Despite the sinister look imparted by its long hooked beak, the frigate bird is quite beautiful. The adult male is all black with a lustrous faint purplish-green sheen on its back (especially during the courtship season). The female, the much larger of the two, is easily distinguished by the white feathers that extend up her abdomen and breast, and the ring of blue around her eyes. Superb stunt flyers, frigate birds often bully other birds on the wing, pulling at the tails of their victims until the latter release or regurgitate a freshly caught meal (bird-watchers have a name for such thievery: kleptoparasitism). Frigate birds also catch much of their food themselves. You may see them skimming the water and snapping up squid, flying fish, and other morsels off the water's surface. They must keep themselves dry, as they have only a small preen gland, insufficient to oil their feathers; if they get too wet they become waterlogged and drown.

Tanagers and Other Passerines

Costa Rica boasts 50 species of tanagers—small, exorbitantly colored birds that favor dark tropical forests. The tanagers' short stubby wings enable them to swerve and dodge through the undergrowth as they chase after insects. Among the most astonishing is the **summer tanager,** flame-red from tip to tail. The black male **scarlet-rumped tanager** also has a startlingly flame-red rump; his mate is orange and olive-gray. The exotically plumed **blue-gray tanager** is as variegated in turquoise and teal as a Bahamian sea, while the **silver-throated tanager** is lemon yellow.

Tanagers belong to the order Passeriformes—"perching birds" or passerines—that includes about half of all Costa Rica's bird species. It is a taxonomically challenging group, with members characterized by certain anatomical features: notably, three toes pointing forward and a longer toe pointing back. **Sparrows, robins,** and **finches** are passerines, as are **antbirds** (30 species), **blackbirds** (20 species), **flycatchers** (78 species), **warblers** (52 species), and **wrens** (22 species).

Trogons

Costa Rica has 10 of the 40 species of trogons: brightly colored, long-tailed, short-beaked, pigeon-size, forest-dwelling tropical birds. Most trogons combine bodies of two primary colors—red and blue, blue and yellow, or green and some other color—with a black-and-white striped tail. The **orange-bellied trogon,** for example, is green with a bright-orange belly beneath a sash of white.

Many bird-watchers travel to Costa Rica simply to catch sight of the **quetzal,** or resplendent trogon. What this bird lacks in physical stature it makes up for in audacious plumage: vivid, shimmering green that ignites in the sunshine, flashing emerald to golden and back to iridescent green. The male sports a fuzzy punk hairdo, a scintillating crimson belly, and two brilliant green tail plumes up to 60 centimeters (24 inches) long, sinuous as feather boas. The female lacks the elaborate plumage.

Early Maya and Aztecs worshiped a god called Quetzalcoatl, the Plumed Serpent that bestowed corn on humans, and depicted him with a headdress of quetzal feathers. The bird's name is derived from *quetzalli,* an Aztec word meaning "precious" or "beautiful." The Maya considered the male's iridescent green tail feathers worth more than gold. Quetzal plumes and jade, which were traded throughout Mesoamerica, were the Maya's most precious objects. It became a symbol of authority vested in a theocratic elite, much like only Roman nobility was allowed to wear purple silks. Its beauty was so fabled and the bird so elusive and shy that early European naturalists believed the quetzal was a myth of the indigenous people.

The male proclaims its territory each dawn through midmorning and again at dusk with a telltale melodious whistle—a hollow, high-pitched call of two notes, one ascending steeply, the other descending—repeated every 8-10 minutes. Narcissistic males show off their tail plumes in undulating flight, with spiraling skyward flights presaging a plummeting dive with their tail feathers rippling behind, all part of the courtship ritual.

Nest holes, often hollowed out by woodpeckers, are generally about 10 meters (33 feet) from the ground. By day, the male incubates the eggs while his 60-centimeter (24-inch) tail feathers hang out of the nest. At night, the female takes over.

The movement of quetzals follows the seasonal fruiting of different laurel species. Everywhere throughout its 1,600-kilometer (1,000-mile) range from southern Mexico to western Panamá, the quetzal is endangered by the loss of its cloud-forest habitat.

Waterfowl

Costa Rica lies directly beneath a migratory corridor between North and South America, and in the northern lowland wetlands, the air is always full of **blue-winged** teals, shoveler ducks, and other waterfowl settling and taking off. Most duck species are winter migrants from North America. Neotropical species include **black-bellied whistling ducks** and **Muscovy ducks.**

The wetlands are also inhabited by 18 species of the order Gruiformes: rails, bitterns, and their relatives, with their large, widesplayed feet good for wading and running across lily- and grass-choked watercourses. Many are brightly colored, including the **purple gallinule,** cloaked in vivid violet and green, with a yellow-tipped red bill. The yellow-beaked, black-and-brown **northern jacana** is easy to see, especially in the canals of Tortuguero, hopping around atop water lilies thanks to its long slender toes—hence its nickname, the "lily-trotter." The female jacana is promiscuous, mating with many males, who take on the task of nest-building and brooding eggs that may have been fertilized by a rival. Tortuguero is also a good place to spot the **sungrebe,** a furtive brown waterbird with a black-and-white striped neck and head and a red beak. Males carry young chicks in a fold of skin under their wings.

Vultures

Costa Rica has four species of vultures (*zopilotes*). You can't help but be unnerved at the first sight of scrawny black vultures swirling overhead on the thermals as if waiting for your car to break down. They look quite ominous in their undertaker's plumage, with bald heads and hunched shoulders. The red-headed **turkey vulture** is common in all parts of Costa Rica below 2,000 meters (6,500 feet) elevation, noticeably so in moister coastal areas where it hops around on the streets of forlorn towns such as Golfito. The stockier **black vulture** has a black head. Both are otherwise charcoal colored. Count yourself lucky to spot the rarer **lesser yellow-headed vulture,** with its namesake yellow head; or the mighty **king vulture,** which wears a handsome white coat with black wing feathers and tail, and a wattled head variegated in vermilion and yellow.

Other Notable Birds

The **three-wattled bellbird,** which inhabits the cloud forests but also migrates to coastal lowlands, is rarely spotted in the mist-shrouded treetops, although the male's eerie call, like a hammer clanging on an anvil, haunts the forest as long as the sun is up. It is named for the strange wattles that dangle from its bill. Its population is declining alarmingly.

In the moist Caribbean lowlands (and occasionally elsewhere) you may spot the telltale pendulous woven nests—often one meter (3 feet) long—of **Montezuma oropendolas,** a large bronze-colored bird with a black neck, head, and belly, a blue-and-orange bill, and bright yellow outer tail feathers. The birds nest in colonies. The **chestnut-headed oropendola** is less commonly seen.

The great **curassow,** growing as tall as one meter (3 feet), is almost too big for flight and tends to run through the undergrowth if disturbed. You're most likely to see this endangered bird in Corcovado or Santa Rosa national parks.

All four New World species of kingfishers inhabit Costa Rica: the large **red-breasted kingfisher;** the slate-blue **ringed kingfisher,** which can grow to 40 centimeters (16 inches); its smaller cousin, the **belted kingfisher;** and the **Amazon kingfisher** and smaller **green kingfisher,** both green with white and red underparts.

The **common pauraque** (*cuyeo*) is a member of the nightjar family—nocturnal birds that in flight are easily mistaken for bats. They like to sit on the dusty roads at night, where they are well camouflaged, causing a heck of a scare as they lift off. Another neotropical nightjar is the odd-looking **great potoo** (*nictibio grande*), a superbly camouflaged bird that perches upright on tree stumps and holds its head haughtily aloft. Its squat cousin, the **common potoo,** resembles an owl.

REPTILES

Costa Rica is home to more than 200 species of reptiles, half of them snakes.

Crocodiles and Caimans

Many travelers visit Costa Rica in the hope of seeing American crocodiles and the croc's diminutive cousins, caimans. Both species are easily seen in the wet lowlands. They are superbly adapted for water. Their eyes and nostrils are atop their heads for easy breathing and vision while otherwise entirely submerged, and their thick muscular tails provide tremendous propulsion.

The **American crocodile**—one of four species of New World crocodiles—can easily be seen in dozens of rivers throughout the lowlands and estuaries along the Pacific coastline. Sections of the Río Tárcoles have as many as 144 crocodiles per kilometer, far higher than anywhere else in Costa Rica. The creatures, which can live 80 years or more and reach six meters (20 feet) in length, spend much of their days basking on mud banks, maintaining an even body temperature, which they regulate by opening their gaping mouths. To the crocodile (*cocodrilo*), home is a "gator hole" or pond, a system of trails, and a cave-like den linked by a tunnel to the hole. The croc helps maintain the health of aquatic water systems by weaning out weak and large predatory fish. Mating season begins in December. For all their beastly behavior, crocodiles are devoted parents. Eggs are laid March-May, during dry season. The mother will guard the nest and keep it moist for several months after laying. When they are ready to hatch, the hatchlings pipe squeakily, and she uncovers the eggs and takes the babies into a special pouch inside her mouth. She then swims away, with the youngsters peering out between a palisade of teeth. The male assists, and soon the young crocs are feeding and playing in a special nursery, guarded by the two watchful parents (only 10 percent of newborn hatchlings survive).

Despite being relics from the age of the dinosaurs, croc brains are far more complex than those of other reptiles. They are sharp learners (in the Tempisque basin, crocs have been seen whacking tree trunks with their tails to dislodge chicks from their nests). They also have an amazing immune system that can even defeat gangrene.

At night, they sink down into the warm waters of the river for the hunt. The American crocodile is generally a fish-eater, but adults are known to vary their diet with meat, even taking cattle carelessly taking a drink at the river's edge ... so watch out! Crocs cannot chew; they simply snap, tear, and swallow. Powerful stomach acids dissolve everything, including bones. It would be a horrible way to go.

No more than two meters (6.5 feet) long, the **spectacled caiman** (*guajipal* locally) is still relatively common in parts of wet lowland Costa Rica on both the Atlantic and Pacific coasts. Palo Verde and Tortuguero are both good places to spot them in small creeks, *playas,* and brackish mangrove swamps, or basking on the banks of streams and ponds.

Caiman or croc? It's easy to tell. The former is dark brown with darker bands around its tail and holds its head high when sunning. The much larger crocodile is an olive color with black spots on its tail.

Iguanas and Lizards

The most common reptile you'll see is the dragon-like tree-dwelling iguana, which can grow to one meter (3 feet) in length. You'll spot them in all kinds of forest habitats, but particularly in drier areas below 760 meters (2,500 feet) elevation. There's no mistaking this reptile for any other lizard. Its head is crested with a frightening wig of leathery spines, its heavy body encased in a scaly hide, deeply wrinkled around the sockets of its muscular legs. Despite its menacing *One Million Years B.C.* appearance, it is a nonbelligerent vegetarian.

There are two species in Costa Rica: the green and the spiny-tailed iguana. The **green iguana** (*Iguana iguana*), which is a dull olive color (adults) to bright green (juveniles), with a black-banded tail, can grow to two meters (6.5 feet) long. The males turn a bright orange when they get ready to mate in November or December and choose a lofty perch from which to advertise their prowess as potential lovers. Females nest in holes in the ground, then abandon their eggs. Male iguanas are territorial and defend their turf aggressively against competitors. Campesinos, for reasons you may not want to think about, call the green iguana the "tree chicken."

The smaller, gray or tan-colored **spiny-tailed iguana** (*Ctenosaura pectinata*)—known locally as *iguana negra* or *garrobo*—has a tail banded with rings of hard spines that it uses to guard against predators by blocking the entrance to holes in trees or the ground.

Another miniature dinosaur is *Basiliscus basiliscus,* or **Jesus Christ lizard,** a Pacific lowland dweller common in Santa Rosa, Palo Verde, and Corcovado national parks. These use water as their means of escape, running across it on hind legs (hence their name).

To learn more, visit the website of the **Green Iguana Foundation** (www.iguanaverde.com).

Snakes

The 138 species of snakes make up more than half of all reptile species in the nation. Wherever you are in the country, snakes are sure to be around. They are reclusive, however, and it is a fortunate traveler indeed who gets to see in the wild the fantastically elongated **chunk-headed snake,** with its catlike elliptical eyes, or the slender, beak-nosed, bright green **vine snake.** Among the more common snake species you are likely to see are the wide-ranging and relatively benign **boas.** Boas are aggressive when confronted: Although not venomous, they are quite capable of inflicting serious damage with their large teeth.

Only 18 species of snakes in Costa Rica are venomous (nine are *very* venomous). The **coffee palm viper** is a heat-seeking missile that can detect differences of 0.0003°C

per meter. The small yet potentially deadly **eyelash vipers** are superbly camouflaged—yellow, green, mottled brown, gray, or chocolate to suit their environment—and often remain immobile for days on end, awaiting passing prey.

The all-black *zopilota* eats only other snakes and prefers the fearsome **fer-de-lance** (locally called *terciopelo,* Spanish for "velvet"), which is much feared for its aggressiveness and lethal venom—it accounts for 80 percent of all snakebites (and snakebite mortalities) in Costa Rica. One of several Central American pit vipers, the fer-de-lance can grow to a length of three meters (10 feet) and is abundant throughout the country, except in Nicoya, particularly in overgrown fields and river courses in drier lowland regions. Tiny juvenile fer-de-lance are just as deadly and are almost impossible to see as they rest in loose coils of black and brown on the forest floor. Give the fer-de-lance a wide berth; it stands its ground and will bite with little provocation. Its equally large cousin, the **bushmaster,** is the most venomous of all vipers (humans suffer a 75 percent fatality rate if bitten), but it is relatively sheepish.

Among the more colorful snakes are the four species of **coral snakes,** with small heads, blunt tails, and bright bands of red, black, and yellow or white. These highly venomous snakes (often fatal to humans) exhibit a spectacular defensive display: They flatten their bodies and snap back and forth while swinging their heads side to side and coiling and waving their tails.

In the Pacific Ocean, you may sometimes encounter venomous pelagic **sea snakes,** yellow-bellied and black-backed serpents closely related to terrestrial cobras and coral snakes. This gregarious snake has developed an oar-like tail to paddle its way through the ocean. Its venom is among the most deadly toxins known, but they are known to have bitten humans only rarely.

Turtles

Five of the world's seven species of marine

turtles nest on Costa Rica's beaches, and you can see turtles laying eggs somewhere in Costa Rica virtually any time of year.

Parque Nacional Tortuguero, in northeastern Costa Rica, is one of fewer than 30 places in the world that the **green turtle** considers clean enough and safe enough to lay its eggs. Although green turtles were once abundant throughout the Caribbean, today there are only three major sites in the region where they nest: one on Aves Island, 62 kilometers (39 miles) west of Montserrat; a second at Gandoca-Manzanillo; and the third on the endless beach between Tortuguero and Pacuare, also the most important nesting site for leatherback turtles in Costa Rica.

On the Pacific coast, the most spectacular nestings are at Playa Nancite in Parque Nacional Santa Rosa, Refugio Nacional de Vida Silvestre Ostional, and recently at Playa Camaronal, where tens of thousands of **olive ridley turtles** (*lora*) come ashore July-December in synchronized mass nestings known as *arribadas*. Giant **leatherback turtles** (*baula*) nest at Playa Grande, near Tamarindo, October-April and in lesser numbers at several other beaches. Hawksbills, ridleys, leatherbacks, Pacific greens, and occasionally loggerheads (primarily Caribbean nesters) appear in lesser numbers at other beaches along the Pacific coast.

Most of the important nesting sites in Costa Rica are now protected, and access to some is restricted. Turtle populations continue to decline because of illegal harvesting and environmental pressure, and all species are now critically endangered. Despite legislation outlawing the taking of turtle eggs or disturbing nesting turtles, nest sites continue to be raided by humans, encouraged by an ancient Mayan legend that says the eggs are aphrodisiacs. Mother Nature poses her own challenges: Coatis, dogs, raccoons, and peccaries dig up nest sites to get at the tasty eggs. Gulls and vultures pace the beach hungrily awaiting the hatchlings; crabs lie in wait for the tardy; and hungry jacks, barracudas, and sharks come close to shore for the feast. Of the hundreds of eggs laid by a female in one season, only a handful will survive to reach maturity.

Turtles have hit on a formula for outwitting their predators, or at least for surviving despite them. Each female turtle normally comes ashore two to six times each season and lays an average of 100 eggs on each occasion.

Most females make their clumsy climb up the beach and lay their eggs under the cover and cool of darkness (loggerheads and ridleys often nest in the daytime). They normally time their arrival to coincide with high tide, when they do not have to drag themselves puffing and panting across a wide expanse of beach. Some turtles even die of heart attacks brought on by the exertions of digging and laying.

Once she settles on a comfortable spot above the high-tide mark, the female scoops out a large body pit with her front flippers. Then her dexterous hind flippers go to work hollowing out a small egg chamber below her tail and into which white, spongy, golf ball-size spheres fall every few seconds. After shoveling the sand back into place and flinging sand wildly around to hide her precious treasure, she makes her way back to sea.

The eggs normally take six to eight weeks to hatch, incubated by the warm sand. Some marvelous internal clock arranges for most eggs to hatch at night when hatchlings can make their frantic rush for the sea concealed by darkness. Often, baby turtles will emerge from the eggs during the day and wait beneath the surface of the beach until nightfall. They are programmed to travel fast across the beach to escape hungry mouths. Even after reaching the sea they continue to swim frantically for several days—flippers paddling furiously—like clockwork toys. No one knows where baby turtles go. They swim off and generally are not seen again until they appear years later as adults.

Turtles are great travelers capable of amazing feats of navigation. Greens, for example, navigate across up to 2,400 kilometers (1,500 miles) of open sea to return, like salmon, to the same nest site, guided presumably by stars and currents and their own internal compass.

When near nesting sites, respect the turtles' need for peace and quiet. Nesting turtles are very timid and extremely sensitive to flashlights, sudden movements, and noise, which will send a female turtle in hasty retreat to the sea without laying her eggs. Sometimes she will drop her eggs on the sand in desperation, without digging a proper nest.

Freshwater turtles (*jicoteas*) are also common in Costa Rica, particularly in the Caribbean lowlands, where they are easy to spot basking on logs.

INSECTS

Butterflies, moths, ants, termites, wasps, bees, and other tropical insects have evolved in astounding profusion. There are so many species, no one knows their true numbers.

Ants

Ants, which number several thousand species, are the most abundant insects (one hectare of rainforest contains an average of nine million ants). Although related to bees and wasps, like butterflies they pass through four life stages: egg, larva, pupa, and adult. They are fully social creatures, each ant entirely dependent on its siblings so that the colony acts as a single organism. They are also almost completely blind and for communication rely on the chemicals—pheromones—that they release to alert each other to danger and food sources.

Each colony is dependent on the queen ant, whose sole task is to produce eggs (thus most colonies die when the queen, which can live up to 20 years, dies). Only the queen, who may boast 1,000 times the body weight of a minor worker, is fertile. Once a year, usually at the beginning of rainy season (around May and June), the queen produces a unique brood of about 50,000 eggs; approximately one-fifth are fertilized and will become new queens, and the others will become males. The entire colony doubles its efforts to care for and feed the large larvae. On maturity, males and queens develop wings and, on a particular

weather cue, set out to form a new colony. Males exist only to fertilize the queen and then die.

Army ants march through the forest with the sole intent of turning small creatures into skeletons in a few minutes. They're like a wolf pack, but with tens of thousands of miniature beasts of prey that merge and unite to form one great living creature. While the ants advance across the forest floor driving small creatures in front of them, humans and other large creatures can simply step aside and watch the column pass by; this can take several hours. Even when the ants raid human habitations, people can simply clear out with their food stock while the ants clean out the cockroaches and other vermin. The army ants' jaws are so powerful that indigenous people used them to suture wounds: the tenacious insect is held over a wound and its body squeezed so that its jaws instinctively clamp shut, drawing the flesh back together. The body is then pinched off.

The most noticeable ant is the **leafcutter ant** (*Atta cephalotes*), a mushroom-farming insect that carries upright in its jaws a circular green shard scissored from the leaves of a plant. They are found in forests throughout Costa Rica. At some stage in your travels you're bound to come across a troop of workers hauling their cargo along rainforest pathways as immaculately cleaned of debris as any swept doorstep. The nests are built below ground, sometimes extending over an area of 200 square meters (2,100 square feet), with galleries to a depth of six meters (20 feet). The largest nests provide homes for single colonies of up to five million insects. Trails span out from the nests, often for 100 meters (330 feet) or more. The worker ants set off from their nests day and night in long columns to demolish trees, removing every shoot, leaf, and stem section by tiny section and transporting them back to their underground chambers (about 15 percent of total leaf harvesting in Costa Rica is the work of leafcutter ants).

They don't eat this material. Instead, they chew it up to form a compost on which they cultivate a nutritional bread-like fungus whose tiny white fruiting bodies provide them with food. So evolved has this symbiosis become that the fungus has lost its reproductive ability (it no longer produces sexual spores) and relies exclusively on the ants for propagation. When a new queen leaves her parent colony, she carries a piece of fungus with her with which to start a new garden. The cutting and carrying are performed by intermediate-size workers (*medias*) guarded by ferocious-looking "majors," or soldier ants, about two centimeters (1 inch) long and with disproportionately large heads and jaws that they use to protect the workers—usually fighting to the death—from even the largest marauder. They also work to keep the trails clear. Beneath ground, tiny "minors" (*minimas*) tend the nest and mulch the leaves to feed the fungus gardens.

Butterflies

With nearly 1,000 identified species (approximately 10 percent of the world total), Costa Rica is a lepidopterist's paradise. You can barely stand still for one minute without checking off a dozen dazzling species: metallic gold Riodinidae; delicate black-winged *Heliconius* splashed with bright red and yellow; orange-striped *paracaídas;* and the deep neon-blue flash of morphos fluttering and diving in a ballet of subaqueous color.

Some butterflies are ornately colored to keep predators at bay. The bright-white stripes against black on the **zebra butterfly** (like other members of the heliconia family), for example, tell birds that the butterfly tastes acrid. There are even perfectly tasty butterfly species that mimic the heliconia's colors, tricking predators into disdain. Others use their colors as camouflage so that at rest they blend in with the green or brown leaves or look like the scaly bark of a tree. Among the most intriguing are the **owl-eye butterflies,** with their 13-centimeter (5-inch) wingspans and startling eye spots. The blue-gray *Caligo memnon*, the cream owl butterfly, is the most spectacular of the owl eyes: the undersides of

its wings are mottled to look like feathers, and two large yellow-and-black "eyes" on the hind wing, which it displays when disturbed, give it an uncanny appearance of an owl's face.

The Narcissus of the Costa Rican butterfly kingdom is the famous **blue morpho.** There are about 50 species of morphos, all in Central and South America, where they are called *celeste común.* The males of most species are bright neon blue, with iridescent wings that flash like mirrors in the sun. This magnificent oversize butterfly grows to 13-20 centimeters (5-8 inches). The morpho is a modest, nondescript brown when sitting quietly with its wings closed. But when a predator gets too close, it flies off, startling its foe with a flash of its beautiful electric-blue wings. The subspecies differ in color: In the Atlantic lowlands, the morpho is almost completely iridescent blue; one population in the Meseta Central is almost completely brown, with only a faint hint of electric blue. One species, commonly seen gliding around in the forest canopy, is red on the underside and gray on top. Show people have always used mirrors to produce glitter and illusion. The morpho is no exception. Look through a morpho butterfly's wing toward a strong light and you will see only brown. This is because the scales *are* brown. The fiery blue is produced by structure, not by pigment. Tiny scales on the upper side of the wing are set in rows that overlap like roof shingles. These scales are ridged with minute layers that, together with the air spaces between them, refract and reflect light beams, absorbing all the colors except blue.

The best time to see butterflies is in the morning, when they are more active, although a few species are more active at dawn and dusk. In general, butterfly populations are densest in June and July, corresponding with the onset of the rainy season on the Pacific side. Like birds, higher-elevation species migrate up and down the mountains with changes in local weather. The most amazing migration—unsurpassed by any other insect in the neotropical region—is that of the black and iridescent green Uraniidae, in which millions of individuals pass through Costa Rica heading south from Honduras to Colombia.

AMPHIBIANS

Costa Rica hosts approximately 160 species of amphibians, primarily represented by the dozens of species of frogs and toads. That cat-like meow? That's Boulenger's *Hyla,* one of Costa Rica's more than 20 kinds of toxic frogs. That insect-like buzz is probably two bright-red poison dart frogs wrestling belly-to-belly for the sake of a few square meters of turf. And the deafening choruses of long loud whoops that resound through the night in Nicoya and the adjacent lowlands of Guanacaste? That's an orgiastic band of orange and purple-black Mexican burrowing toads getting it on.

Of all Central America's exotic species, none are more colorful than the **poison dart frogs,** from which indigenous people extract deadly poisons to tip their arrows. Frogs are tasty little fellows to carnivorous amphibians, reptiles, and birds. Hence, in many species, the mucous glands common to all amphibians have evolved to produce a bitter-tasting poison. In Central and South America at least 20 kinds of frogs have developed this defense still further: Their alkaloid poisons are so toxic that they can paralyze a large bird or small monkey immediately. Several species—the Dendrobatidae—produce among the most potent toxins known. Some species' eggs and tadpoles even produce toxins, making them unpalatable, like bad caviar.

Of course, it's no value to an individual frog if its attacker dies *after* devouring the victim. Hence poison dart frogs have developed conspicuous, striking colors—bright yellow, scarlet, purple, and blue, the colors of poison recognized throughout the animal world—and sometimes "flash colors" (concealed when at rest but flashed at appropriate times to startle predators) that announce, "Beware!" These confident critters don't act like other frogs either. They're active by day, moving boldly around the forest floor.

In April and May, toads go looking for love in the rain pools of scarlet bromeliads that festoon the high branches. Here, high in the trees, tadpoles of arboreal frogs wriggle about. Many species, particularly the 39 species of hylids, spend their entire lives in the tree canopies, where they breed in holes and bromeliads. The hylids have enlarged suction-cup pads on their toes. They often catch their prey in midair leaps, and the suction discs guarantee surefooted landings. Others deposit their eggs on vegetation over streams; the tadpoles fall when hatched. Others construct frothy foam nests, which they float on pools, dutifully guarded by the watchful male.

History

EARLY HISTORY

When Spanish explorers arrived in what is now Costa Rica at the dawn of the 16th century, they found the region populated by several poorly organized, autonomous indigenous groups living relatively prosperously, if wantonly at war, in a land of lush abundance. In all there were probably no more than 200,000 indigenous people on September 18, 1502, when Columbus put ashore near modern-day Puerto Limón. Although human habitation can be traced back at least 10,000 years, the region had remained a sparsely populated backwater separating the two areas of high civilization: Mesoamerica and the Andes. Although these people were advanced in ceramics, metalwork, and weaving, there are few signs of large complex communities, little monumental stone architecture lying half-buried in the luxurious undergrowth, and no planned ceremonial centers of comparable significance to those located elsewhere in the isthmus.

The region was a potpourri of distinct

cultures divided into chiefdoms. In the east along the Caribbean seaboard and along the southern Pacific shores, indigenous groups shared distinctly South American cultural traits. These groups—the Caribs on the Caribbean and the Borucas, Chibchas, and Diquis in the southwest—were seminomadic hunters and fishers who raised squash, *pejibaye* (bright orange palm fruits), and yuca and other tubers supplemented by shrimp, lobster, other crustaceans, and game. They chewed coca and lived in communal village huts surrounded by fortified palisades. The matriarchal Chibchas and Diquis had a highly developed system of slavery and were accomplished goldsmiths. They were also responsible for the perfectly spherical granite balls (*bolas*) of unknown purpose found in large numbers at burial sites in the Río Térraba valley, Isla del Caño, and the Golfito region. The people had no written language, and their names are of Spanish origin—bestowed by colonists, often reflecting the names of chiefs.

The most advanced indigenous groups lived in the Central Highlands. Here were the Corobicí people and the Nahuatl people, who had recently arrived from Mexico at the time that Columbus stepped ashore. The largest and most significant of Costa Rica's archaeological sites found to date is here, at Guayabo, on the slopes of Volcán Turrialba.

Perhaps more important (little architectural study has been completed) was the Nicoya Peninsula in northwest Costa Rica. In late prehistoric times, trade in pottery from the Nicoya Peninsula brought this area into the Mesoamerican cultural sphere, and a culture developed among the Chorotega people that in many ways resembled the more advanced cultures farther north. The Chorotegas were heavily influenced by the Olmec culture and may have even originated in southern Mexico before settling in Nicoya early in the 14th century (their name means Fleeing People). They developed towns with central plazas; brought with them an accomplished agricultural system based on beans, corn, squash, and gourds; had a calendar; wrote books on deerskin parchment; and produced highly developed ceramics and stylized jade figures depicting animals, humanlike effigies, and men and women with oversized genitals, often making the most of their sexual apparatuses. Like the Olmecs, they filed their teeth; like the Maya and Aztecs, the militaristic Chorotegas kept slaves and maintained a rigid class hierarchy dominated by high priests and nobles. Human sacrifice was

pre-Columbian gold ornament, Museo del Oro Precolombino

a cultural mainstay. Little is known of their belief system, although the potency and ubiquity of phallic imagery hints at a fertility-rite religion. Shamans were an important part of each community's political system.

Alas, the pre-Columbian cultures were quickly choked by the stern hand of gold-thirsty colonial rule—and condemned also that the European God might triumph over local idols.

COLONIALISM
The First Arrivals

When Columbus anchored his storm-damaged vessels—*Capitana, Gallega, Viscaína,* and *Santiago de Palos*—in the Bay of Cariari, off the Caribbean coast, on his fourth voyage to the New World in 1502, he was welcomed and treated with great hospitality by indigenous people, who had never seen Europeans before. The dignitaries from the indigenous communities appeared wearing much gold, which they gave Columbus. "I saw more signs of gold in the first two days than I saw in Española during four years," his journal records. He called the region La Huerta (The Garden). The great navigator struggled home to Spain in worm-eaten ships (he was stranded for one whole year in Jamaica) and never returned. The prospect of vast loot, however, drew adventurers whose numbers were reinforced after Vasco Núñez de Balboa's discovery of the Pacific in 1513. To these explorers, the name Costa Rica would have seemed a cruel hoax. Floods, swamps, and tropical diseases stalked them in the sweltering lowlands, and fierce elusive native people harassed them maddeningly.

In 1506, Ferdinand of Spain sent a governor, Diego de Nicuesa, to colonize the Atlantic coast of the isthmus he called "Veragua." He ran aground off the coast of Panamá and was forced to march north. Antagonized indigenous bands used guerrilla tactics to slay the strangers and willingly burned their own crops to deny them food. Nicuesa set the tone for future expeditions by foreshortening his own cultural lessons with the musket ball.

Things seemed more promising when an expedition under Gil González Dávila set off from Panamá in 1522 to settle the region. It was Dávila's expedition—which reaped quantities of gold—that won the land its nickname of Costa Rica, the "Rich Coast." The local people never revealed the whereabouts of the fabled mines of Veragua; most likely it was placer gold found in the gold-rich rivers of the Nicoya and Osa Peninsulas.

Later colonizing expeditions on the Caribbean failed as miserably as Dávila's. When two years later Francisco Fernández de Córdova founded the first Spanish settlement on the Pacific at Bruselas, near present-day Puntarenas, its inhabitants all died within three years.

For the next four decades Costa Rica was virtually left alone. The conquest of Peru by Francisco Pizarro in 1532 and the first of the great silver strikes in Mexico in the 1540s turned eyes away from southern Central America. Guatemala became the administrative center for the Spanish Main in 1543, when the captaincy-general of Guatemala, answerable to the viceroy of New Spain (Mexico), was created with jurisdiction from the Isthmus of Tehuantepec to the neglected lands of Costa Rica and Panamá.

Prompted by an edict of 1559 issued by Philip II of Spain, the representatives in Guatemala thought it time to settle Costa Rica and Christianize the natives. Barbaric treatment and European epidemics—ophthalmia, smallpox, and tuberculosis—had already reaped the indigenous people like a scythe and had so antagonized the survivors that they took to the forests and eventually found refuge amid the remote valleys of the Cordillera Talamanca. Only in the Nicoya Peninsula did there remain any significant indigenous population, the Chorotegas, who soon found themselves chattel on Spanish land under the *encomienda* (serfdom) system.

Settlement

In 1562, Juan Vásquez de Coronado—the true conquistador of Costa Rica—arrived as governor. He treated the surviving indigenous people more humanely and moved the few existing Spanish settlers into the Meseta Central, where the temperate climate and rich volcanic soils offered the promise of crop cultivation. Cartago was established as the national capital in 1563.

After the initial impetus given by its discovery, Costa Rica lapsed into a lowly Cinderella role in the Spanish empire. Land was readily available, but there was no indigenous labor to work it. The colonists were forced to work the land themselves (even the governor, it is commonly claimed, had to work his own plot of land to survive). Without gold or export crops, trade with other colonies was infrequent at best. The Spanish found themselves impoverished in a subsistence economy. Money became so scarce that the settlers eventually reverted to the indigenous method of using cacao beans as currency. A full century after its founding, Cartago could boast little more than a few score adobe houses and a single church, which all perished when Volcán Irazú erupted in 1723.

Gradually, however, towns took shape. Cubujuquie (now Heredia) was founded in 1717, Villaneuva de la Boca del Monte (San José) in 1737, and Villa Hermosa (Alajuela) in 1782. Later, exports of wheat and tobacco placed the colonial economy on a sounder economic footing and encouraged the intensive settlement that characterizes the Meseta Central today.

In other colonies, Spaniards married indigenous people and a distinct class system arose, but people of mixed blood (mestizos) represent a much smaller element in Costa Rica than they do elsewhere on the isthmus. All this had a leveling effect on colonial society. As the population grew, so did the number of poor families who had never benefited from the labor of *encomienda* indigenous people or suffered the despotic arrogance of criollo (Creole) landowners. Costa Rica, in the traditional view, became a "rural democracy," with no oppressed mestizo class resentful of the maltreatment and scorn of the Creoles.

Removed from the mainstream of Spanish culture, the Costa Ricans became individualistic and egalitarian.

Not all areas of the country, however, fit the model of rural democracy. Nicoya and Guanacaste on the Pacific side were administered quite separately in colonial times from the rest of Costa Rica. They fell within the Nicaraguan sphere of influence, and large cattle ranches or haciendas arose. The cattle-ranching economy and the more traditional class-based society that arose persist today. On the Caribbean side of Costa Rica, cacao plantations became well established. Eventually large-scale cacao production gave way to small-scale sharecropping, and then to tobacco as the cacao industry went into decline. Spain closed the Costa Rican ports in 1665 in response to English piracy, thereby cutting off seaborne sources of legal trade. Smuggling flourished, however, for the largely unincorporated Caribbean coast provided a safe haven to buccaneers and smugglers, whose strongholds became 18th-century shipping points for logwood and mahogany.

EMERGENCE OF A NATION
Independence

Independence of Central America from Spain came on September 15, 1821. Independence had little immediate effect, however, for Costa Rica had required only minimal government during the colonial era. In fact, the country was so out of touch that the news that independence had been granted reached Costa Rica a full month after the event. In 1823 the other Central American nations proclaimed the United Provinces of Central America, with their capital in Guatemala City. A Costa Rican provincial council, however, voted for accession to Mexico.

The four leading cities of Costa Rica felt as independent as had the city-states of ancient Greece, and the conservative and aristocratic leaders of Cartago and Heredia soon found themselves at odds with the more progressive republican leaders of San José and Alajuela.

The local quarrels quickly developed into civic unrest and, in 1823, to civil war. After a brief battle in the Ochomogo Hills, the republican forces of San José were victorious. They rejected Mexico, and Costa Rica joined the federation with full autonomy for its own affairs. Guanacaste voted to secede from Nicaragua and join Costa Rica the following year.

From this moment on, liberalism in Costa Rica had the upper hand. Elsewhere in Central America, conservative groups tied to the church and the erstwhile colonial bureaucracy spent generations at war with anticlerical and laissez-faire liberals, and a cycle of civil wars came to dominate the region. By contrast, in Costa Rica colonial institutions had been relatively weak, and early modernization of the economy propelled the nation out of poverty and laid the foundations of democracy far earlier than elsewhere on the isthmus. While other countries turned to repression to deal with social tensions, Costa Rica turned toward reform.

Juan Mora Fernández, elected the federalist nation's first chief of state in 1824, set the tone by ushering in a nine-year period of progressive stability. He established a sound judicial system, founded the nation's first newspaper, and expanded public education. He also encouraged coffee cultivation. The nation, however, was still riven by rivalry, and in September 1835 the War of the League broke out when San José was attacked by the three other towns. They were unsuccessful, and the national flag was planted firmly in San José.

Braulio Carrillo, who seized power as a benevolent dictator in 1835, established an orderly public administration and new legal codes to replace colonial Spanish law. In 1838, he withdrew Costa Rica from the Central American federation and proclaimed independence. The Honduran general Francisco Morazán invaded and toppled Carrillo in 1842. Morazán's extranational ambitions and the military draft and direct taxes he imposed soon inspired his overthrow; he was executed within the year.

Coffee Is King

The reins of power were taken up by a new elite, the *cafetaleros* (coffee barons) who in 1849 announced their ascendancy by conspiring to overthrow the nation's enlightened president, José María Castro. They chose as Castro's successor Juan Rafael Mora, a powerful *cafetalero*. Mora is remembered for the remarkable economic growth that marked his first term and for "saving" the nation from the imperial ambitions of the American adventurer William Walker during his second term. Still, his compatriots ousted him from power in 1859. After failing in his own coup against his successor, he was executed—a prelude to a second cycle of militarism.

The Guardia Legacy

The 1860s were marred by power struggles among the coffee elite, supported by their respective military cronies. General Tomás Guardia, however, was his own man. In April 1870 he overthrew the government and ruled for 12 years as an iron-willed military strongman backed by a powerful centralized government of his own making.

True to Costa Rican tradition, Guardia proved himself a progressive thinker and a benefactor of the people. His towering reign set in motion forces that shaped the modern liberal-democratic state. Hardly characteristic of 19th-century despots, he abolished capital punishment, managed to curb the power of the coffee barons, and, ironically, tamed the use of the army for political means. He used coffee earnings and taxation to finance roads and public buildings. And in a landmark revision to the Constitution in 1869, he made "primary education for both sexes obligatory, free, and at the cost of the nation."

During the course of the next two generations, militarism gave way to peaceful transitions to power. In 1917, democracy faced its first major challenge. At that time, the state collected the majority of its revenue from the less wealthy. President Alfredo González Flores's bill to establish direct, progressive taxation based on income and his espousal

The William Walker Saga

Born in Nashville in 1824, William Walker graduated from the University of Pennsylvania as an MD at the age of 19. He tried his hand unsuccessfully as a doctor, lawyer, and writer, and even joined the miners and panners in the California Gold Rush. Somewhere along the line he became filled with grandiose schemes of adventure and an arrogant belief in the "manifest destiny" of the United States to control other nations.

He dreamed of extending the glory of slavery and forming a confederacy of Southern U.S. states to include the Spanish-speaking nations. To wet his feet, he invaded Baja California in 1853 with a few hundred cronies bankrolled by a pro-slavery group called the Knights of the Golden Circle. Forced back north of the border by the Mexican army, Walker found himself behind bars for breaking the Neutrality Act. Acquitted and famous, he attracted a following of kindred spirits to his next wild cause.

During the feverish California gold rush, eager fortune hunters sailed down the East Coast to Nicaragua, traveled up the Río San Juan and across Gran Lago de Nicaragua (Lake Nicaragua), and then were carried by mule the last 19 kilometers (12 miles) to the Pacific, where with luck a San Francisco-bound ship would be waiting. In those days, before the Panamá Canal, wealthy North Americans were eyeing southern Nicaragua as the perfect spot to build a passage linking the Pacific Ocean and the Caribbean Sea. The government of Nicaragua wanted a hefty fee.

Backed by North American capitalists and the tacit sanction of President James Buchanan, Walker landed in Nicaragua in June 1855 with a group of mercenaries and the ostensible goal of molding a new government that would be more accommodating to U.S. business interests. But Walker, it seems, had secret ambitions—he dreamed of making the five Central American countries a federated state with himself as emperor. After subduing the Nicaraguans, he had himself "elected" president of Nicaragua and promptly legalized slavery there.

Next, Walker looked south to Costa Rica. In March 1856, he invaded Guanacaste. President Mora called up an army of 9,000. Armed with machetes and rusty rifles, they marched for Guanacaste and routed Walker and his cronies, who retreated pell-mell. Eventually, the Costa Rican army cornered Walker's forces in a wooden fort at Rivas, in Nicaragua. A drummer boy named Juan Santamaría bravely volunteered to torch the fort, successfully flushing Walker out into the open. His bravery cost Santamaría his life; he is now a national hero and a symbol of resistance to foreign interference.

With his forces defeated, Walker's ambitions were temporarily scuttled. He was eventually rescued by the U.S. Navy and taken to New York, only to return in 1857 with even more troops. The Nicaraguan army defeated him again, and Walker was imprisoned. Released three years later and unrepentant, he seized a Honduras customs house. In yet another bid to escape, he surrendered to an English frigate captain who turned him over to the Honduran army, which promptly shot him, thereby bringing to an end the pathetic saga.

of state involvement in the economy had earned the wrath of the elites. They decreed his removal. Minister of War Federico Tinoco Granados seized power. Tinoco ruled as an iron-fisted dictator, but Costa Ricans were no longer prepared to acquiesce to oligarchic restrictions. Women and high-school students led a demonstration calling for his ouster, and Tinoco fled to Europe.

There followed a series of unmemorable administrations. The apparent tranquility was shattered by the Great Depression and the social unrest it engendered. Old-fashioned paternalistic liberalism had failed to resolve social ills such as malnutrition, unemployment, low pay, and poor working conditions. The Depression distilled all these issues. Calls grew shrill for reforms.

CIVIL WAR
Calderón

The decade of the 1940s and its climax, the civil war, marked a turning point in Costa Rican history: from paternalistic government by traditional rural elites to modern, urban-focused statecraft controlled by bureaucrats, professionals, and small entrepreneurs. The dawn of the new era was spawned by Rafael Calderón Guardia, a profoundly religious physician and a president (1940-1944) with a social conscience. In a period when neighboring Central American nations were under the yoke of tyrannical dictators, Calderón promulgated a series of farsighted reforms, including founding the University of Costa Rica.

Calderón's social agenda was hailed by the urban poor and leftists and despised by the upper classes, his original base of support. His early declaration of war on Germany, seizure of German property, and imprisonment of Germans further upset his conservative patrons, many of whom were of German descent. World War II stalled economic growth at a time when Calderón's social programs called for vastly increased public spending. The result was rampant inflation, which eroded his support among the middle and working classes. Abandoned, Calderón crawled into bed with two unlikely partners: the Roman Catholic Church and the communists (the Popular Vanguard Party). Together they formed the United Social Christian Party.

The Prelude to Civil War

In 1944, Calderón was replaced by his puppet, Teodoro Picado Michalski, in an election widely regarded as fraudulent. Picado's uninspired administration failed to address rising discontent throughout the nation. Intellectuals, distrustful of Calderón's "unholy" alliance, joined with businesspeople, campesinos, and labor activists and formed the Social Democratic Party, dominated by the emergent professional middle classes allied with the traditional oligarchic elite. The country was thus polarized. Tensions mounted.

Street violence finally erupted in the run-up to the 1948 election, with Calderón on the ballot for a second presidential term. When he lost to his opponent Otilio Ulate (the representative of Acción Democrática, a coalition of anti-Calderonistas), the government claimed fraud. The next day, the building holding many of the ballot papers went up in flames, and the Calderonista-dominated legislature annulled the election results.

Don Pepe: "Savior of the Nation"

Popular myth suggests that José María ("Don Pepe") Figueres Ferrer—a 42-year-old coffee farmer, engineer, economist, and philosopher—raised a "ragtag army of university students and intellectuals" and stepped forward to topple the government that had refused to step aside for its democratically elected successor. In actuality, Don Pepe's "revolution" had been long in the planning; the 1948 election merely provided a good excuse.

Don Pepe, an ambitious and outspoken firebrand, had been exiled to Mexico in 1942. He returned to Costa Rica in 1944, began calling for an armed uprising, and arranged for foreign arms to be airlifted in to groups trained by Guatemalan military advisors. In 1946 he participated with a youthful Fidel Castro in an aborted attempt to depose General Trujillo of the Dominican Republic.

In 1948, back in Costa Rica, Figueres formed the National Liberation Armed Forces. On March 10, 1948, he made his move and plunged Costa Rica into civil war: the "War of National Liberation." Supported by the governments of Guatemala and Cuba, Don Pepe's insurrectionists captured the cities of Cartago and Puerto Limón from Calderonistas (the government's army at the time numbered only about 500) and were poised to pounce on San José when Calderón surrendered. The 40-day civil war claimed more than 2,000 lives, mostly civilians.

CONTEMPORARY TIMES
Foundation of the Modern State

Don Pepe became head of the Founding Junta of the Second Republic of Costa Rica. He consolidated Calderón's progressive social

Minor Keith and the Atlantic Railroad

Costa Rica became the first Central American country to grow coffee when seeds were introduced from Jamaica in 1808. Coffee flourished and transformed the nation. It was eminently suited to the climate (the dry season made harvest and transportation easy) and volcanic soils of the Central Highlands. There were no rival products to compete for investments, land, or labor. And the coffee bean—*grano de oro*—was exempt from taxes. Soon, peasant settlements spread up the slopes of the volcanoes and down the slopes toward the coast.

By 1829, coffee had become the nation's most important product. Foreign money was pouring in. The coffee elite owed its wealth to its control of processing and trade rather than to direct control of land. Small farmers dominated actual production. Thus no sector of society failed to advance. The coffee bean pulled the country out of its miserable economic quagmire and placed it squarely on a pedestal as the most prosperous nation in Central America. Nonetheless, in 1871, when President Guardia decided to build a railroad to the Atlantic, coffee for export was still being sent via mule and oxcart 100 kilometers (60 miles) from the Meseta Central to the Pacific port of Puntarenas, then shipped (via a circuitous three-month voyage) around the southern tip of South America and up the Atlantic to Europe.

Enter Minor Keith. In 1871, at the age of 23, Minor came to Costa Rica at the behest of his brother Henry, who had been commissioned by his uncle, Henry Meiggs, to oversee the construction of the Atlantic Railroad linking the coastal port of Limón with the coffee-producing Meseta Central. By 1873, when the railroad should have been completed, only one-third of it had been built and money for the project had run out. Henry Keith promptly packed his bags and went home.

The younger brother, who had been running the commissary for railroad workers in Puerto Limón, picked up the standard and for the next 15 years applied unflagging dedication to achieve the enterprise his brother had botched. He renegotiated the loans and raised new money. He hired workers from Jamaica and China, and drove them—and himself—like beasts of burden.

The workers had to bore tunnels through mountains, bridge rivers, hack through rainforests, and drain the Caribbean marshlands. During the rainy season, mudslides would wash away bridges. And malaria, dysentery, and yellow fever plagued the workers (the project eventually claimed more than 4,000 lives). In December 1890, a bridge high over the turbulent waters of the Río Birris finally brought the tracks from Alajuela and Puerto Limón together.

For Keith, the endeavor paid off handsomely. He had wrangled from the Costa Rican government a concession of 324,000 hectares (800,000 acres) of land (nearly seven percent of the country's territory) along the railroad track and coastal plain, plus a 90-year lease on the completed railroad. And the profits from his endeavors were to be tax-free for 20 years.

Keith planted his lands with bananas, and Costa Rica became the first Central American country to grow them. Like coffee, the fruit flourished. Exports increased from 100,000 stems in 1883 to more than one million in 1890, when the railroad was completed. By 1899 Keith, who went on to marry the daughter of the Costa Rican president, had become the "Banana King," and Costa Rica was the world's leading banana producer.

Along the way, the savvy entrepreneur had wisely entered into a partnership with the Boston Fruit Company, the leading importer of tropical fruits for the U.S. market. Thus was born the United Fruit Company, which during the first half of the 20th century was to become the driving force and overlord of the economies of countries the length and breadth of Latin America.

reform program and added his own landmark reforms: He banned the press and the Communist Party, introduced suffrage for women and full citizenship for blacks, revised the Constitution to outlaw a standing army, established a presidential term limit, and created an independent Electoral Tribunal to oversee future elections.

On a darker note, Calderón and many of his followers were exiled to Mexico, special tribunals confiscated their property, and in a sordid episode, many prominent left-wing officials and activists were abducted and murdered. Supported by Nicaragua, Calderón twice attempted to invade Costa Rica and topple his nemesis but each time was repelled. Eventually he was allowed to return and even ran for president unsuccessfully in 1962.

Then, Figueres returned the reins of power to Otilio Ulate, the actual winner of the 1948 election. Costa Ricans later rewarded Figueres with two terms as president, 1953-1957 and 1970-1974. Figueres dominated politics for the next two decades. A socialist, he founded the Partido de Liberación Nacional (PLN), which became the principal advocate of state-sponsored development and reform. He died a national hero on June 8, 1990.

The Contemporary Scene

Social and economic progress since 1948 has helped return the country to stability, and though post-civil war politics has reflected the play of old loyalties and antagonisms, elections have been free and fair. The country has ritualistically alternated presidents between the PLN and the Social Christians. Successive PLN governments have built on the reforms of the Calderonista era, and the 1950s and 1960s saw a substantial expansion of the welfare state. The intervening conservative governments have encouraged private enterprise and economic self-reliance.

By 1980, the bubble had burst. Costa Rica was mired in an economic crisis: epidemic inflation; crippling currency devaluation; soaring oil bills and social welfare costs; plummeting coffee, banana, and sugar prices; and disruptions to trade caused by the Nicaraguan war. On July 19, 1979, the leftist Sandinistas toppled Nicaragua's Somoza regime. Thousands of Nicaraguan National Guards and right-wing sympathizers fled to Costa Rica, where they were warmly welcomed by wealthy ranchers sympathetic to the right-wing cause. By the summer of 1981, the anti-Sandinistas had been cobbled into the Nicaraguan Democratic Front (FDN), headquartered in Costa Rica, and the U.S. CIA was beginning to take charge of events.

Costa Rica's foreign policy underwent a dramatic reversal as the former champion of the Sandinista cause found itself embroiled in the Reagan administration's vendetta to oust the Sandinista regime.

In May 1984, events took a tragic turn at a press conference on the banks of the Río San Juan held by Edén Pastora, the U.S.-backed leader of the Contras. A bomb exploded, killing foreign journalists; Pastora escaped. General consensus is that the bomb was meant to be blamed on the Sandinistas; the CIA has been implicated.

In February 1986, Costa Ricans elected as their president a relatively young sociologist and economist-lawyer, Óscar Arias Sánchez. Arias's electoral promise had been to work for peace. Immediately, he put his energies into resolving Central America's regional conflicts. Arias's tireless efforts were rewarded in 1987, when his peace plan was signed by the five Central American presidents—an achievement that earned Arias the 1987 Nobel Peace Prize.

In February 1990, Rafael Ángel Calderón Fournier, a conservative lawyer, won a narrow victory. He was inaugurated 50 years to the day after his father, the great reformer, had been named president. Restoring Costa Rica's economy to sound health was Calderón's paramount goal. Under pressure from the World Bank and the International Monetary Fund, Calderón initiated a series of austerity measures aimed at redressing the country's huge deficit and national debt. In March 1994, in an intriguing historical quirk, Calderón, son of the president ousted by Don Pepe Figueres in 1948, was replaced by Don Pepe's youthful son, José María Figueres, a graduate of West Point and Harvard University. The Figueres administration (1994-1998), however, was bedeviled by problems, including the collapse of the Banco Anglo Costarricense in 1994, followed in 1995 by inflation, a massive teachers' strike, and antigovernment demonstrations. A slump in tourism and Hurricane César, which ripped through the Pacific southwest in 1996, causing $100 million in damage, worsened the country's plight. Ticos took some solace in the gold medal—the first ever for a Costa Rican—won at the 1996 Olympics by swimmer Claudia Poll. And President Bill Clinton's visit to Costa Rica in May 1997 during a summit of Central American leaders heralded a new era of free trade.

In 2000 a series of strikes by government employees erupted into the worst civil unrest since the 1970s, as an attempt by the government to break up the country's 50-year-old power and telecommunications monopoly resulted in nationwide street protests that brought the country to a halt. In 2003 the Supreme Court voted to reverse the 1969 law barring presidents from running for office again within an eight-year period following the end of their single term. In 2006 the nation reelected former president Óscar Arias as president. His administration was considered less corrupt by far than its predecessors, and perhaps more effective. Arias's campaign in favor of the Central America Free Trade Agreement (CAFTA) treaty paid off when voters approved it in 2007.

The lingering 2008 rainy season was the wettest ever recorded, resulting in extensive flooding and landslides nationwide. When a moderate earthquake of 6.2 on the Richter scale shook the Volcán Poás region in January 2009, saturated hillsides gave way, destroying the village of Cinchona and killing dozens of people.

In March 2010, Arias's hand-picked successor, Laura Chinchilla, his minister of justice and a former vice president, was elected in a landslide victory and took office as the country's first female president. In November 2010, the perpetual feud with neighboring Nicaragua over sovereignty of the Río San Juan turned ugly when Nicaraguan troops occupied Costa Rican soil, ostensibly to protect dredgers led by ex-Sandinista guerrilla Edén Pastora. Nicaraguan president Daniel Ortega refused to honor a decision by the Organization of American States that ordered Nicaragua to withdraw. In mid-2011 Chinchilla issued an executive order for construction of a road along the length of Río San Juan, parallel to the Nicaraguan border. Construction of "Ruta 1856 Juan Rafael Mora Porras," named for the president who expelled the Nicaraguan invasion of 1856, was immediately initiated without appropriate environmental impact studies. It has since become a quagmire of corruption and incompetence.

On September 5, 2012, the largest recorded earthquake in Costa Rica's history struck off the Nicoya Peninsula. Fortunately, the epicenter of the 7.6 Richter jolt was sufficiently deep that relatively little damage was done, although it shook the entire nation.

In February 2014, voters elected Luis Guillermo Solís, of the leftist Citizens Action Party, as president—the first president in half a century not from the two main political parties. At press time he appeared to be the first president in just as long to actually be running a clean government in which corruption is no longer tolerated, and which is committed to fighting social and economic inequality.

Government and Economy

GOVERNMENT

Costa Rica is a democratic republic, as defined by the 1949 Constitution. As in the United States, the government is divided into independent executive, legislative, and judicial branches, with separation of powers.

The executive branch comprises the president, two vice presidents, and a cabinet of 17 members called the Consejo de Gobierno (Council of Government). Legislative power is vested in the Asamblea Legislativa (Legislative Assembly), a unicameral body composed of 57 members. *Diputados* are elected for a four-year term and a maximum of two nonconsecutive terms. The assembly can override presidential decisions by a two-thirds majority vote. The power of the legislature to go against the president's wishes is a cause of constant friction, and presidents have not been cowardly in using executive decrees.

The Asamblea Legislativa also appoints Supreme Court judges for minimum terms of eight years. Twenty-four judges now serve on the Supreme Court. These judges, in turn, select judges for the civil and penal courts. The courts also appoint the three "permanent" magistrates of the Special Electoral Tribunal, an independent body that oversees each election and is given far-reaching powers. Control of the police force reverts to the Supreme Electoral Tribunal during election campaigns to help ensure constitutional guarantees.

The nation is divided into seven provinces—Alajuela, Cartago, Guanacaste, Heredia, Limón, Puntarenas, and San José—each ruled by a governor appointed by the president. The provinces are subdivided into 81 *cantones* (counties), which, in turn, are divided into a total of 421 *distritos* (districts) ruled by municipal councils.

Little Costa Rica is big on government. Building on the reforms of the Calderonista era, successive administrations have created an impressive array of health, education, and social-welfare programs while steadily expanding state enterprises and regulatory bodies, all of which spell a massive expansion of the government bureaucracy that pays the salaries of approximately one in four employed people. Costa Rica's government employees have nurtured bureaucratic formality to the level of art.

Political Parties

The largest party is the Partido de Liberación Nacional (PLN, National Liberation Party), founded by the statesman-hero of the Civil War, "Don Pepe" Figueres. The PLN, which roughly equates with European social democratic parties and welfare-state liberalism in the United States, has traditionally enjoyed a majority in the legislature, even when an opposition president has been in power. Its support is traditionally drawn from among middle-class professionals, entrepreneurs, and small farmers. PLN's archrival, the Partido de Unidad Social Cristiana (PUSC, Social Christian Unity Party), formed in 1982, represents more conservative interests.

In addition, a number of less influential parties represent all facets of the political spectrum, notably the Partido Acción Ciudadana (PAC, Citizen Action Party), formed in 2002 by former Justice Minister José Miguel Villalobos, who resigned from the Abel Pacheco government to protest corruption. Most minor parties form around a candidate and represent personal ambitions rather than strong political convictions. A small number of families are immensely powerful, regardless of which party is in power, and it is said that they pull the strings behind the scenes.

Elections

Costa Rica's national elections, held every four years on the first Sunday in February, reaffirm the pride Ticos feel for their democratic

Costa Rica's Vital Statistics

- **Area:** 50,664 square kilometers (19,561 square miles)
- **Population:** 4,755,000 (July 2014 estimate)
- **Annual population growth:** 1.24 percent
- **Annual birth rate:** 16.08 per 1,000
- **Mortality rate:** 4.49 per 1,000
- **Infant mortality rate:** 8.7 per 1,000
- **Life expectancy:** 78.23 years
- **Literacy:** 96.3 percent
- **Highest point:** Cerro Chirripó, 3,819 meters (12,530 feet)
- **Religion:** 73.6 percent Roman Catholic
- **GDP/GDP per capita:** $61.43 billion (2013 estimate)/$12,900 (2013 estimate)
- **Population below the poverty line:** 24.8 percent

system. In the rest of Central America, says travel writer Paul Theroux, "an election can be a harrowing piece of criminality; in Costa Rica [it is] something of a fiesta." Schoolchildren decked out in party colors usher voters to the voting booths. The streets are crisscrossed with flags, and everyone drives around honking their horns, throwing confetti, and holding up their purple-stained thumbs to show that they voted. Cynics point out that most of the hoopla is because political favors are dispensed on a massive scale by the victorious party, and that it pays to demonstrate fealty.

Costa Rican citizens enjoy universal suffrage, and citizens are automatically registered to vote on their 18th birthday. Since 1959 voting has ostensibly been compulsory for all citizens ages 18 to 70, although 32 percent abstained from voting in the 2014 presidential election. All parties are granted equal airtime on radio and television, and campaign costs are largely drawn from the public purse: Any party with 5 percent or more of the vote in the prior election can apply for a proportionate share of the official campaign fund, equal to 0.5 percent of the national budget. Don't expect to buy a drink in the immediate run-up to an election: Liquor and beer sales are banned for the preceding three days.

Armed Forces and Police

Costa Rica has no army, navy, or air force. The nation disbanded its military forces in 1949, when it declared itself neutral. Nonetheless, Costa Rica's police force has various powerfully armed branches with military capabilities. The government has made serious efforts in recent years to purge the force of systemic corruption. Major investment, including new cars and equipment and better training, has resulted in a noticeably more professional police force in recent years, notably in the tourist and transit divisions. However, the local constabulary is underpaid, little educated, and patently ineffective.

Corruption

Despite the popular image as a beacon of democracy, nepotism and cronyism are entrenched in the Costa Rican political system, and corruption is part of the way things work. The political system is too weak to resist the "bite," or bribery, locally called *chorizo* (a poor grade of bacon). Corruption is so endemic that a board game, suitably called *Chorizo*, was launched in 2000.

Abel Pacheco's much-troubled government witnessed the resignation of 13 ministers, some allegedly due to financial irregularities, and former presidents Miguel Ángel Rodríguez, Rafael Ángel Calderón, and José Figueres have been indicted on corruption charges since leaving office.

ECONOMY

Costa Rica's economy this century has, in many ways, been a model for developing nations. Highly efficient coffee and banana industries have drawn in vast export earnings, and manufacturing has grown modestly under the protection of external tariffs and the expanding purchasing power of the domestic market. Since the late 1970s, Costa Rica has moved progressively toward a more diversified trading economy; coffee, bananas, sugar, and beef, which together represented almost 80 percent of exports in 1980, earn less than 40 percent today. Tourism is the number-one income earner, followed by technology, then agriculture.

Agriculture

Everywhere you go in the Central Highlands, a remarkable feature of the land is almost complete cultivation, no matter how steep the slope. Nationwide, some 11 percent of the land area is planted in crops; 46 percent is given to pasture. Agriculture's share of the economy, however, continues to slip.

Despite Costa Rica's reputation as a country of yeoman farmers, land ownership has always been highly concentrated, and there are areas, such as Guanacaste, where rural income distribution resembles the inimical patterns of Guatemala and El Salvador. The top 1 percent of farm owners own more than one-quarter of the agricultural land.

The mist-shrouded slopes of the Meseta Central and southern highlands are adorned with green undulating carpets of coffee—the *grano de oro,* or golden bean—the most important crop in the highlands. In the higher, more temperate areas, flowers grow under hectares of plastic sheeting, and dairy farming is becoming more important in a mixed-farming economy that has been a feature of the Meseta since the end of the 19th century.

Vast banana plantations (and increasingly African date palms) swathe the Caribbean plains and Golfo Dulce region. Cacao, once vital to the 18th-century economy, is on the rise again in the Caribbean. And pineapples are important throughout the Northern Zone and Valle de El General. Costa Rica is the world's leading pineapple exporter; in 2009 pineapples surpassed bananas and coffee as the country's most important crop.

BANANAS

Bananas have been a part of the Caribbean landscape since 1870, when American entrepreneur Minor Keith shipped his first fruit stems to New Orleans. In 1899 his Tropical Trading & Transport Company merged with the Boston Fruit Company to form the United Fruit Company, which soon became the overlord of the political economies of the "banana republics." By the 1920s much of the rainforest south of Puerto Limón had been transformed into a vast sea of bananas. The banana industry continues to expand to meet the demand of a growing international market, and plantations now cover about 50,000 hectares (124,000 acres); Costa Rica exported 1.9 million tons of bananas in 2012, up 28 percent over 2009, representing almost 10 percent of national export earnings.

The banana companies have cut back production in recent years due to overproduction, but the country is still the second-biggest exporter of bananas in the world, after Ecuador.

CATTLE

By far the largest share of agricultural land—70 percent—is given over to cattle pasture. Costa Rica is a leading beef exporter. Guanacaste remains essentially what it has been since mid-colonial times—cattle country—and three-quarters of Costa Rica's 2.2 million head of cattle are found here. They are mostly humpbacked zebu. Low-interest loans in the 1960s and 1970s encouraged a rush into cattle farming for the export market, prompting rapid expansion into new areas such as the Valle de El General and more recently the Atlantic lowlands.

The highland slopes are munched on by herds of Charolais, Hereford, Holstein, and Jersey cattle raised for the dairy industry.

COFFEE

Costa Rica earned $308 million from coffee exports in 2013 (54 percent went to the United

Bananas: Green or Not?

Banana production is a monoculture that causes ecological damage. Banana plants deplete ground nutrients quickly, requiring heavy doses of fertilizer to maintain productivity. Eventually the land is rendered useless for other agricultural activities. Fertilizers washed down by streams have been blamed for the profuse growth of water hyacinth and reed grasses that now clog the canals and wildfowl habitats, such as the estuary of the Río Estrella. And silt washing down from the plantations is acknowledged as the principal cause of the death of the coral reef within Parque Nacional Cahuita and, more recently, in Gandoca-Manzanillo.

Bananas are also prone to disease and insect assault. Pesticides such as the nematicide DBCP, banned in the United States but widely used in Costa Rica, are blamed for poisoning and sterilizing plantation workers and for major fish kills in the Tortuguero canals. Plus, caimans and other aquatic creatures near banana plantations show a high concentration of chemicals in their systems.

Campaigns by local pressure groups and the threat of international boycotts have sparked a new awareness among the banana companies. A project called Banana Amigo recommends management guidelines. Companies that follow the guidelines are awarded an Eco-OK seal of approval to help them export bananas; companies continuing to clear forests are not.

Banana producers assert that the industry provides badly needed jobs. Environmentalists claim that devastating environmental effects are not worth the trade-off for a product for which demand is so fickle. Multinational corporations are hardly known for philanthropy either. Workers' unions, for example, have historically been pushed out of the banana fields. Some banana companies have been accused of operating plantations under virtual slave-labor conditions. The Limón government and environmentalists have also denounced British company Geest's clear-cutting of forests separating the national parks Barra del Colorado and Tortuguero.

In recent years, the banana companies have scaled back due to overcapacity, and the first people to lose out have been the independent small-scale producers, many of them poor campesinos who had been induced to clear their forests and raise bananas for sale to the big banana companies, who are no longer buying.

States), down almost one-third over the prior year (the 2013-2014 crop was the lowest in four decades) and well behind export of bananas and pineapples. Some 53,000 farmers grow coffee. Beans grown here are ranked among the best in the world. Costa Rica's highlands possess ideal conditions for coffee production. The coffee plant loves a seasonal, almost monsoonal climate with a distinct dry season; it grows best in well-drained, fertile soils at elevations between 800 and 1,500 meters (2,600-4,900 feet) with a narrow annual temperature range—natural conditions provided by much of the country. The best coffee is grown near the plant's uppermost altitudinal limits, where the bean takes longer to mature.

The first coffee beans were brought from Jamaica in 1779. Within 50 years, coffee had become firmly established; by the 1830s it was the country's prime export earner, a position it occupied until 1991, when coffee plunged to third place in the wake of a precipitous 50 percent fall in world coffee prices and the onset of the tourism boom. The 2012-2013 harvest plunged 10 percent due to lower yields caused by the "coffee rust" fungus.

The plants are grown in nurseries for their first year before being planted in long rows that ramble invitingly down the steep hillsides, their paths coiling and uncoiling like garden snakes. After four years, they fruit. In April, with the first rains, small white blossoms burst forth and the air is laced with perfume not unlike jasmine. By November the glossy green bushes are plump with shiny red berries—the coffee beans—and the seasonal labor is called into action.

The hand-picked berries are trucked to

beneficios (processing plants), where they are machine-scrubbed and washed to remove the fruity outer layer and dissolve the gummy substance surrounding the bean (the pulp is returned to the slopes as fertilizer). The moist beans are then blow-dried or laid out to dry in the sun in the traditional manner. The leather skin of the bean is then removed by machine, and the beans are sorted according to size and shape before being vacuum-sealed to retain the fragrance and slight touch of acidity characteristic of the great vintages of Costa Rica.

Industry

Manufacturing accounts for about 40 percent of GNP. This is due almost entirely to Costa Rica's newfound favor as a darling of high-tech industries. The 1997 arrival of Intel, the computer-chip manufacturer, which accounted for a remarkable one-third of Costa Rica's exports by value in 2009, presaged the evolution of a "Silicon Valley South." Motorola, 3Com, Abbott Laboratories, and Hewlett Packard have since built assembly plants, and Amazon brought a big chunk of its customer-service business here in 2010. The nation has also staked a claim as a world center for the Internet gaming industry (online casinos).

Local manufacturing is still largely concerned with food processing, although pharmaceutical and textile exports have risen dramatically in recent years. The state has a monopoly in key economic sectors such as energy, telecommunications, and insurance.

Tourism

Tourism is the nation's prime income earner. According to the Instituto Costarricense de Turismo (ICT, the Costa Rica Tourism Board), Costa Rica closed out 2013 with 2.43 million tourist arrivals, generating about $2 billion, up from two million in 2010. Fully 40 percent came from the United States. About 100,000 workers are directly employed in tourism-related activities; another 400,000 are indirectly employed.

The majority of tourists cite natural beauty as one of their main motivations for visiting Costa Rica, and one-third specifically cite ecotourism. Costa Rica practically invented the term—defined as responsible travel that contributes to conservation of natural environments and sustains the well-being of local people by promoting rural economic development. The government has since positioned Costa Rica as a comprehensive destination for the whole family, and for medical tourism.

People and Culture

Costa Rica has a population of about 4,755,000, more than half of whom live in the Meseta Central. Approximately 350,000 live in the capital city of San José, with about three times that number in the metropolitan region; 60 percent of the nation's population is classed as urban.

DEMOGRAPHY

Costa Rica is the most homogeneous Central American nation in terms of race as well as social class. The census classifies 94 percent of the population as "white" or "mestizo" and less than 3 percent as "black" or "Indian."

Exceptions are Guanacaste, where almost half the population is visibly mestizo, a legacy of the more pervasive unions between Spanish colonists and Chorotega people through several generations; and the population of the Atlantic coast province of Puerto Limón, which is one-third black, with a distinct culture that reflects its West Indian origins.

Immigrants from many nations have been made welcome over the years. Between 1870 and 1920, almost 25 percent of Costa Rica's population growth was due to immigration, notably Germans and Italians, plus Chinese contract laborers brought in to work on the

Atlantic Railroad. More recently, tens of thousands of Central American immigrants from El Salvador, Guatemala, and Nicaragua provide cheap labor for the coffee fields: As many as 450,000 *nicas* (Nicaraguans) live in Costa Rica, and the majority are considered "illegals" not protected by law.

Afro-Caribbean People

Costa Rica's approximately 40,000 black people are the nation's largest minority. Most black Costa Ricans trace their ancestry back to the 10,000 or so Jamaicans hired by Minor Keith to build the Atlantic Railroad, and to later waves of immigrants who came to work the banana plantations in the late 19th century. In the 1930s, when "white" highlanders began pouring into the lowlands, black people were quickly dispossessed of land. Late in that decade, when the banana blight forced the banana companies to abandon their Caribbean plantations and move to the Pacific, "white" Ticos successfully lobbied for laws forbidding the employment of *gente de color* in other provinces, one of several circumstances that kept blacks dependent on the United Fruit Company, whose labor policies were often abhorrent. Many converted their subsistence plots into commercial cacao farms. In 1949 the new Constitution ended apartheid, allowing black people to travel beyond Siquirres and enter the highlands.

Today, race relations are relatively harmonious. On the Caribbean coast, they have retained much of their traditional Jamaican culture, including religious practices rooted in African beliefs about transcendence through spiritual possession (*obeah*), their cuisine (such as "rundown"), the rhythmic lilt of their antiquated-sounding English, and the deeply syncopated funk of their music.

Indigenous People

Costa Rica's indigenous people have suffered abysmally in decades past and still remain a marginalized populace. Today, approximately 65,000 people from eight ethnic groups manage to eke out a living on 22 reservations and adjacent territories. The Chorotega people live in northern Nicoya; the Maleku people live on the northern slopes of the Cordillera Guanacaste and Cordillera de Tilarán, principally near San Rafael de Guatuso; the Huetar people live in the Meseta Central, near Santiago de Puriscal; the Bribrí, Boruca, and Cabecar peoples live on the slopes of

A Boruca woman spins cotton for weaving.

the Cordillera Talamanca; and the Guaymí people live in the extreme southwest and the Talamancas.

In 1977 a law was passed that prohibited nonindigenous people from buying, leasing, or renting land within the reserves. Although various agencies continue to work to promote education, health, and community development, the indigenous people's standard of living is appallingly poor, alcoholism is endemic, health and educational facilities are sparse, and the communities remain subject to exploitation. Banana and mining companies have gradually encroached, pushing campesinos onto marginal land. The National Commission for Indigenous Affairs (CONAI) has proved ineffective in enforcing protections, not least against the pernicious encroachment of evangelists. Virtually all groups have been converted to Christianity, and Spanish is today the predominant tongue.

Fortunately, recent years have seen a resurgence of cultural pride, assisted by tourism efforts that are opening the reserves to respectful visitation.

WAY OF LIFE

Most Costa Ricans—Los Costarricense, or Ticos—insist that their country is a "classless democracy." There is considerable social mobility, and no race problem. A so-called middle-class mentality runs deep, including a belief in the Costa Rican equivalent of the American conviction that through individual effort, sacrifice, and a faith in schooling, any Costa Rican can climb the social ladder and better himself or herself.

Despite its relative urban sophistication, Costa Rica remains a predominantly agrarian society, and despite the high value Ticos place on equality and democracy, their society contains all kinds of inequities. Urbanites, like city dwellers worldwide, condescendingly chuckle at rural "hicks." And the upwardly mobile "elite," who consider menial labor demeaning, indulge in conspicuous spending and, sometimes, snobbish behavior. Overt class distinctions are kept within bounds by a delicate balance between "elitism" and egalitarianism unique in the isthmus; even the president is inclined to mingle in public in casual clothing and is commonly addressed in general conversation by his first name or nickname.

Although comparatively wealthy compared to most Latin American countries, by developed-world standards most Costa Ricans are poor; the average income in the northern

Costa Ricans have been rated the happiest people in the world.

lowlands is barely one-seventh of that in San José. Many rural families still live in simple huts of adobe or wood, and at least one-fifth of the population are *marginados* who live in poverty. More than half of rural homes lack clean drinking water, while almost one-third of urban homes lack clean water. Child labor exploitation is also a major issue, as is sexual crimes against minors.

However, that all paints far too gloomy a picture. In a region where millions starve, the Costa Ricans are comparatively well-to-do. Most Costa Ricans keep their proud little bungalows tidy and bordered by flowers, and even the poorest are generally well groomed and neatly dressed.

The Tican Identity

Costa Ricans' unique traits derive from a profoundly conscious self-image, which orients much of their behavior both as individuals and as a nation. The Ticos—the name is said to stem from the colonial saying "we are all *hermaniticos*" (little brothers)—feel distinct from their neighbors by their "whiteness" and relative lack of indigenous culture. Above all, the behavior and comments of most Ticos are dictated by *quedar bien*, a desire to leave a good impression. Like the English, they're terribly frightened of embarrassing themselves and of appearing rude or vulgar. They often prefer to lie rather than telling you an unpleasant truth, which is considered rude and to be avoided.

Ticos are also hard to excite. They lack the volatility, ultranationalism, and deep-seated political divisions of their Latin American brethren. It is almost impossible to draw a Tico into a spirited debate or argument. They are loath to express or defend a position and simply walk away from arguments. Former president Figueres once accused Ticos of being as domesticated as sheep; they are not easily aroused to passionate defense of a position or cause. As such, resentments fester and sneaky retributions—such as arson—are common. Many North American and European hoteliers and residents bemoan the general passivity that often translates into a lack of initiative. Nonetheless, they are savvy businesspeople with a bent for entrepreneurship.

The notion of democracy and the ideals of personal liberty are strongly cherished. Costa Ricans are intensely proud of their accomplishments in this arena and gloss over endemic theft, corruption, and fraud. There is only a limited sense of personal responsibility among Ticos, who display a limited regard for the law. Their Bud Light culture has been called the "white bread" of Latin America.

The cornerstone of society is the family and the village community. Social life still centers on the home. Nepotism—using family ties and connections for gain—is the way things get done in business and government. But traditional values are severely challenged. Drunkenness among the working classes is common. Drug abuse has intruded, and Costa Rica has become a major trading zone for cocaine traffic. And though many Ticos display a genuine concern for conservation, that ethic is still tentative among the population as a whole.

Machismo and the Status of Women

By the standards of many Latin American countries, the nation is progressive and successful in advancing the equal rights of women. Women outnumber men in many occupations, notably in university faculties; a woman was elected president in 2010; and there have been several women as vice president. Nonetheless, low-level occupations especially reflect wide discrepancies in wage levels for men and women. The greater percentage of lower-class women remains chained to the kitchen sink and rearing children. Gender relationships, particularly in rural villages, remain dominated to a greater or lesser degree by machismo and *marianismo*, its female equivalent: Women are supposed to be bastions of moral and spiritual integrity while accepting men's infidelities.

The Latin male expresses his masculinity in amorous conquests, and the faithful husband and male celibate is suspect in the eyes of his friends. But hip urban Ticas have forsaken old-fashioned romanticism for a latter-day liberalism. Even in the most isolated rural towns, dating in the Western fashion has displaced the *retreta*—the circling of the central plaza by men and women on weekend evenings—and chaperones, once common, are now virtually unknown.

In fact, almost 10 percent of all Costa Rican adults live together in "free unions," one-quarter of all children are *hijos naturales* (born out of wedlock), and one in five households is headed by a single mother. *Compañeras,* women in consensual relationships, enjoy the same legal rights as wives. Many rural households are so-called queenbee (all-female) families headed by an elderly matriarch who looks after her grandchildren while the daughters work. Divorce is common and easily obtained under the Family Code of 1974, although desertion remains as it has for centuries "the poor man's divorce."

Health

Perhaps the most impressive impact of Costa Rica's modern welfare state has been the truly dramatic improvements in national health. Infant mortality has plummeted from 25.6 percent in 1920 to only 8.7 percent in 2013. And the average Costa Rican today can expect to live to a ripe 78.3 years—about as long as the average U.S.-born American.

One key to the nation's success was the creation of the Program for Rural Health in 1970 to ensure that basic health care would reach the farthest backwaters. Costa Rica assigns about 10 percent of its GNP to health care, provided free of cost to all citizens. A private medical system performs at levels akin to the United States, at far lower cost.

Education

The country boasts 96.3 percent literacy, the most literate populace in Central America. Nonetheless, according to United Nations statistics, about 40 percent of Costa Rican teenagers drop out of school by the sixth grade or never gain access secondary education. Many rural schools are underfunded and lacking in basic facilities.

Costa Rica has four state-funded schools of higher learning, and opportunities abound for adults to earn the primary or secondary diplomas they failed to gain as children. The University of Costa Rica (UCR) enrolls some 35,000 students, mostly on scholarships. In addition, there are also scores of private "universities," although the term is applied even to the most marginal cubbyhole college.

Religion

More than 90 percent of the population is Roman Catholic, the official state religion, but Protestant missionaries have made a dent recently, notably among indigenous people. Nonetheless, the country has always been relatively secular, and the church has not attained undue political power. Every village has its own saint's day, and every taxi, bus, government office, and home has its token religious icons. *Semana santa* (Holy Week), the week before Easter, is a national holiday, and communities throughout Costa Rica organize processions.

Resignation to the imagined will of God is tinged with fatalism. In a crisis Ticos will turn to a favorite saint to request a miracle. Folkloric belief in witchcraft is still common; Escazú is renowned as a center for *brujas* (witches).

THE ARTS

Historically, Costa Rica has been relatively impoverished in the area of indigenous arts and crafts. The country, with its relatively small and heterogeneous pre-Columbian population, had no unique cultural legacy that could spark a creative synthesis where the modern and the traditional might merge. And social tensions, often catalysts to artistic expression, felt elsewhere in the isthmus were lacking. In recent years, however, artists across the spectrum have found new confidence, and the arts are flourishing.

decorating traditional Guaitíl pottery

Art

Escazú, in particular, has been a magnet for artists. Here, in the late 1920s, Teodorico Quirós and a group of contemporaries provided the nation with its own identifiable art style—the Costa Rican "landscape" movement—which expressed in stylized forms the personality of little mountain towns with cobblestone streets, adobe houses, and a backdrop of volcanoes. One of the finest examples of sculpture from this period, the chiseled stone image of a mother and child, can be seen outside the Maternidad Carit maternity clinic in southern San José. Its creator, Francisco Zuñigo, Costa Rica's most acclaimed sculptor, left for Mexico in a fit in 1936 when the sculpture, titled *Maternity,* was lampooned by local critics.

By the late 1950s, many local artists looked down on the work of the prior generation as the art of casitas (little houses) and were indulging in more abstract styles. Today, Costa Rica's homegrown art is world-class. **Costa Rica Art Tours** (www.costaricaarttour.com)

offers day-long visits to various leading artists' studios, including that of Rodolfo Stanley (www.artestanley.com), whose works seemingly combine those of Henri de Toulouse-Lautrec with Paul Gauguin.

Crafts

The Boruca people are known for their devil masks and balsa ornamental masks featuring colorful wildlife and indigenous faces. At Guaitíl, in Nicoya, the Chorotega people's tradition of pottery is booming, flooding souvenir stores nationwide with quintessential Costa Rica pieces. In Escazú, master craftsman Barry Biesanz crafts subtle, delicate bowls and decorative boxes from carefully chosen blocks of tropical hardwoods.

Many of the best crafts in Costa Rica come from Sarchí, known for its *carretas* (oxcarts) and rockers. Although full-size oxcarts are still made, today most of the *carretas* are folding miniature trolleys that serve as liquor bars or indoor tables, and half-size carts used as garden ornaments or simply to accent a corner of a home. The carts are decorated with geometric mandala designs and floral patterns that have also found their way onto wall plaques, kitchen trays, and other craft items.

Literature

In literature, Costa Rica has never fielded figures of the stature of Latin American writers such as Gabriel García Márquez, Pablo Neruda, or Jorge Luis Borges. Indeed, the Ticos are not at all well-read and lack a passionate interest in literature. Only a handful of writers make a living from writing, and Costa Rican literature is often belittled as the most prosaic and anemic in Latin America. Lacking great goals and struggles, Costa Rica was never a breeding ground for the passions and dialectics that have spawned literary geniuses elsewhere.

Costa Rica's early literary figures were mostly essayists and poets: Roberto Brenes Mesen and Joaquín García Monge are the most noteworthy. Even the writing of the

The Oxcarts of Sarchí

Sarchí is famous as the home of gaily decorated wooden *carretas* (oxcarts), the internationally recognized symbol of Costa Rica. The carts once dominated the rural landscape of the Central Highlands when, at the height of the coffee boom and before the construction of the Atlantic Railroad, oxcarts were used to transport coffee beans to Puntarenas, on the Pacific coast. In their heyday, some 10,000 cumbersome, squeaking *carretas* had a dynamic impact on the local economy, spawning highway guards, smithies, inns, teamsters, and crews to maintain the roads.

artisan working on an oxcart wheel, Fábrica de Carretas Eloy Alfaro, Sarchí

In the rainy season, the oxcart trail became a quagmire. Carretas thus featured spokeless wheels to cut through the mud without becoming bogged down. Today's *carretas* bear little resemblance to the original rough-hewn, cane-framed vehicles. Even then, though, the compact wheels—about 120-150 centimeters (4-5 feet) in diameter—were natural canvases awaiting an artist. Enter Trinidad Arguedaz Saens, the wife of Fructuoso Barrantes (a cart maker in San Ramón), with a paintbrush and a novel idea. She enlivened her husband's cart wheels with a geometric starburst design in bright colors set off by black and white. Soon every farmer in the district had given his aged *carreta* a lively new image.

By 1915 flowers had bloomed beside the pointed stars. Faces and even miniature landscapes soon appeared. And annual contests (still held today) were arranged to reward the most creative artists. The *carretas* had ceased to be purely functional. Each cart was also designed to make its own "song," a chime produced by a metal ring striking the hub nut of the wheel as the cart bumped along. Once the oxcart had become a source of individual pride, greater care was taken in their construction, and the best-quality woods were selected to make the best sounds.

The *carretas*, forced from the fields by the advent of tractors and trucks, are almost purely decorative now, but the craft and the art form live on in Sarchí, where artisans still apply their masterly touch at two *fábricas de carretas* (workshops), which are open to view. A finely made reproduction oxcart can cost up to $5,000.

1930s and 1940s, whose universal theme was a plea for social progress, lacked the verisimilitude and rich literary delights of other Latin American authors. Carlos Luis Fallas's *Mamita Yunai,* which depicts the plight of banana workers, is the best and best-known example of this genre. Modern literature still draws largely from the local setting, and though the theme of class struggle has given way to a lighter approach, it still largely lacks the depth and subtlety of the best of Brazilian, Argentinean, and Colombian literature. An outstanding exception is Julieta Pinto's *El Eco de los Pasos,* a novel about the 1948 civil war.

Music and Dance

The country is one of the southernmost of the "marimba culture" countries using the African-derived marimba (xylophone). The guitar is also a popular instrument, especially as an accompaniment to folk dances such as the *punto guanacasteco,* a heel-and-toe stomping dance for couples, officially decreed the national dance.

Guanacaste is the heartland of Costa Rican

folkloric music and dancing. Here, even such pre-Columbian instruments as the *chirimia* (oboe) and *quijongo* (a single-string bow with gourd resonator) are still used. Dances usually deal with the issues of enchanted lovers (usually legendary coffee pickers) and are based on the Spanish *paseo,* with pretty maidens in frilly satin skirts and white bodices circled by men in white suits and cowboy hats, accompanied by tossing of scarves, fanning of hats, and lusty yelps from the men.

When it comes to dancing, Ticos prefer the hypnotic Latin and rhythmic Caribbean beat and bewildering cadences of *cumbia, lambada,* merengue, salsa, and soca, danced with sure-footed erotic grace. The Caribbean coast is the domain of calypso and reggae. Says *National Geographic:* "To watch the viselike clutching of Ticos and Ticas dancing...is to marvel that the birthrate in this predominantly Roman Catholic nation is among Central America's lowest."

On the Caribbean, the *cuadrille* is a maypole dance in which each dancer holds one of many ribbons tied to a pole: As they dance they braid their brightly colored ribbons.

Theater

Costa Rica supports a thriving acting community. In fact, Costa Rica supposedly has more theater companies per capita than any other country in the world. The streets of San José are lined with tiny theaters—everything from comedy to drama, avant-garde, theater-in-the-round, mime, and even puppet theater. Performances are predominantly in Spanish. The English-speaking Little Theater Group is Costa Rica's oldest theatrical troupe; it performs in its own theater in Escazú.

Essentials

Transportation

GETTING THERE
Air

About 20 international airlines provide regular service to Costa Rica. Most flights land at **Juan Santamaría International Airport** at Alajuela, 19 kilometers (12 miles) northwest, and 20 minutes by taxi, from San José. An increasing number of flights land at **Daniel Oduber International Airport,** 12 kilometers (7.5 miles) west of Liberia in Guanacaste. **Tobías Bolaños Airport,** 6.5 kilometers (4 miles) southwest of San José, is for domestic flights only.

RESERVATIONS AND FARES

To get the cheapest fares, make your reservations as early as possible (several months ahead is ideal), especially during peak season, as flights often sell out. Central American carriers are usually slightly cheaper than their U.S. counterparts but often stop at cities en route. Low-season and midweek travel is often cheaper, as are stays of more than 30 days. Travel during Christmas, New Year's, and Easter usually costs more.

If making your reservation online, such as through **Expedia** (www.expedia.com), **Orbitz** (www.orbitz.com), or **Priceline** (www.priceline.com), compare quotes at different sites, as they vary even for the same flight. Alternatively, use a Costa Rica travel specialist, such as **Costa Rica Experts** (U.S. tel. 800-827-9046, www.costaricaexperts.com). International specialists in low fares include **STA Travel** (U.S. tel. 800-781-4040, www.statravel.com), which has offices worldwide.

FROM THE UNITED STATES

U.S. flights are either direct or have stopovers in Central America. Fares typically range about $500-1,000 depending on the season and city of origin. **American Airlines** (tel. 800-433-7300, www.aa.com), **Delta** (tel. 800-221-1212, www.delta.com), **Frontier** (tel. 800-432-1359, www.flyfrontier.com), **JetBlue** (tel. 800-539-2583, www.jetblue.com), **Southwest Airlines** (tel. 800-435-9792, www.southwest.com), **Spirit Air** (tel. 800-772-7117, www.spiritair.com) and **United** (tel. 800-864-8331, www.united.com) fly to San José and/or Liberia. **TACA** (tel. 800-400-8222, www.taca.com), a consortium of Central American carriers, including Costa Rica's LACSA, offers daily flights from Dallas, Los Angeles, Miami, New York City's JFK, Orlando, and San Francisco.

FROM CANADA

TACA (tel. 800-400-8222, www.taca.com) flies between Toronto and San José, as does **Air Canada** (tel. 888-247-2262, www.aircanada.com). **Charters** may need to be booked through a travel agent: **Signature Vacations** (tel. 866-324-2883, www.signature.ca) flies to Liberia; **Air Transat** (tel. 877-872-6728, www.airtransat.com) flies to San José.

FROM LATIN AMERICA AND THE CARIBBEAN

Aeroméxico (tel. 800-021-4000, www.aeromexico.com) flies between Mexico City and San José. **TACA** (tel. 800-400-8222, www.taca.com) serves Costa Rica from all the Central American nations and most countries in South America.

ESSENTIALS
TRANSPORTATION

FROM THE UK AND EUROPE

Costa Rica is served by **British Airways** (tel. 44/844-493-0787, www.british-airways.com), and **Virgin Atlantic** (tel. 44/344-209-7777, www.virgin-atlantic.com) flies to the United States, where you can connect to another carrier serving Costa Rica.

Air Berlin (tel. 49/30-3434-3434, www.airberlin.com), **Air France** (tel. 33/9-69-39-02-15, www.airfrance.fr), **Condor** (tel. 49/180-5-707-202, www.condor.com), **KLM** (tel. 31/20-474-7747, www.klm.com), and **Iberia** (tel. 34/902-400-500, www.iberia.com) are among the European carriers that fly to Costa Rica.

Land
BUS

The overland route from North America is an attractive alternative for travelers for whom time is no object. Allow at least one week. Obtain all necessary visas and documentation in advance. You can travel from **San Diego** or **Texas** to Costa Rica by bus for as little as $100 (with hotels and food, however, the cost can add up to more than flying direct). Book as far ahead as you can—the buses often sell out well in advance. You will need to provide a passport and visas when buying your ticket.

Buses serve **Mexico City** from the U.S. border points at Mexicali, Ciudad Juárez, and Laredo. From **Nicaragua,** cross-border buses depart from Peñas Blancas every hour for Rivas, a small town about 40 kilometers (25 miles) north of the border.

CAR

Many people drive to Costa Rica from the United States via Mexico, Guatemala, Honduras, and Nicaragua. It's a long haul, but you can follow the **Pan-American Highway** all the way from the United States to San José. It's 3,700 kilometers (2,300 miles) minimum, depending on your starting point. Experienced travelers recommend skirting El Salvador and the Guatemalan highlands in favor of the **Pacific coast road.** Allow three weeks at a leisurely pace. You should plan your itinerary to be at each day's destination before nightfall (80 percent of insurance claims are a result of nighttime accidents).

You'll need a passport, visas, a driver's license, and your vehicle's registration. It's also advisable to obtain tourist cards (good for 90 days) from the consulate of each country before departing. A U.S. driver's license is good throughout Central America, although an **International Driving Permit**—issued through AAA—is recommended. You'll need to arrange a transit visa for Mexico in advance, plus car entry permits for each country. AAA can provide advice on *carnets* (international travel permits).

A separate vehicle liability insurance policy is required for each country. Most U.S. firms will not underwrite insurance south of the border. **Sanborn's** (U.S. tel. 800-222-0158, www.sanbornsinsurance.com) specializes in insurance coverage for travel in Mexico and Central America.

Upon arrival in Costa Rica, foreign drivers must buy **insurance stamps** for a minimum of one month (approximately $20 per month). There's also a $10 **road tax** (good for three months) payable upon arrival in Costa Rica. **Vehicle permits** are issued at the border for stays up to 30 days. You can extend this to six months at the Instituto Costarricense de Turismo. Once in Costa Rica, you can drive for up to 90 days on your foreign license.

GETTING AROUND
Air

Traveling by air in Costa Rica is easy and economical, a quick and comfortable alternative to often long and bumpy road travel. Flights to airstrips around the country are rarely more than 40 minutes from San José. Book well in advance. The domestic airline **SANSA** (tel. 506/2229-4100, U.S./Canada tel. 877-767-2672, www.flysansa.com), a division of Grupo TACA, uses 22- to 35-passenger Cessnas. Reservations have to be paid in full and are nonrefundable. You can check in at the airport or SANSA's San José office (no tel.) at Avenida las Américas and Calle

40, which provides a free minibus transfer to Juan Santamaría Airport. SANSA's baggage allowance is 11 kilograms (24 pounds). Schedules change frequently, especially between seasons. The privately owned **Nature Air** (tel. 506/2299-6000, U.S. tel. 800-235-9272, www.natureair.com) flies to 14 destinations, including Nicaragua and Panamá, from Tobías Bolaños Airport, three kilometers (2 miles) west of downtown San José. Its rates are higher than SANSA's. Baggage limit is 12 kilograms (26 pounds).

CHARTERS

You can charter small planes to fly you to airstrips throughout the country. The going rate is about $300-500 per hour per planeload (usually for up to 4-6 people). You'll have to pay for the return flight too if there are no passengers returning from your destination. Luggage space is limited. **Aerobell** (tel. 506/2290-0000, www.aerobell.com) is recommended for small plane or helicopter charter. **Aerodiva** (tel. 506/2296-7241, www.aerodiva.com) also offers helicopter tours and charters.

Bus

Buses serve even the remotest towns: Generally, if there's a road, there's a bus.

Popular destinations are served by both fast buses (*directo*) and slower buses (*normal* or *corriente*), which make stops en route. Most buses serving major towns from San José are modern air-conditioned buses with toilets. In the boondocks, local buses are usually old U.S. high school buses with butt-numbing seats. You can travel to most parts of the country for less than $10.

Buy **tickets** (*boletos*) in advance for long-distance travel; for local buses, you pay when getting aboard. Get there at least an hour before departure or your reservation may not be honored. Long-distance buses have storage below; local buses do not. Travel light; a soft duffel is preferable, so you can tuck it under your seat or carry it on your lap. Theft is endemic—keep your baggage with you.

Bus stops (*paradas*) are marked, and you can usually flag down rural buses anywhere along their routes. Long-distance buses don't always stop when waved down. To get off, shout "*¡Pare!*" (PA-ray). Many buses don't run during Easter week. You can check schedules online at www.thebusschedule.com.

TOURIST BUSES

Interbus (tel. 506/4441-0888, www.interbusonline.com) operates scheduled shuttles

Nature Air plane at Tortuguero

between major tourist destinations, plus airport transfers. Complete listings of routes, schedules, and fares are available online. **Grayline Fantasy Bus** (tel. 506/2220-2126, www.graylinecostarica.com) offers a similar service to destinations throughout Costa Rica. **Costa Rica Shuttle** (tel. 506/4000-1040, www.costaricashuttle.com) and **Coach Costa Rica** (tel. 506/2229-4192, www.coachcostarica.com) offer customized shuttle service nationwide using minivans, as does **SuperShuttle** (tel. 506/4033-7549, www.supershuttlecrc.om).

Car and Motorcycle

Rent a car if you want total freedom of movement. Costa Rica has 30,000 kilometers (19,000 miles) of highway, 20 percent of it paved. MOPT, the Ministry of Public Transport, has invested considerably in road improvements in recent years, particularly in the highlands. However, beyond the Central Highlands, roads generally deteriorate with distance and can shake both a car and its occupants until their doors and teeth rattle. Parts of the country are often impenetrable by road during the rainy season, when flooding and landslides are common and roads get washed out. Hitchhiking is far from safe and I do not recommend it. Women should never hitchhike alone.

TRAFFIC REGULATIONS AND TRAFFIC POLICE

You must be at least 21 years old and hold a passport to drive in Costa Rica. Foreign driver's licenses are valid for 90 days upon arrival. For longer, you'll need a Costa Rican driver's license; apply at **Consejo de Seguridad Vial** (COSEVI, Ave. 20, Calle 11, San José, tel. 506/2257-7200). The **speed limit** on highways is 80 kilometers per hour (50 mph), and 60 kilometers per hour (40 mph) on secondary roads. Speed limits are vigorously enforced. Costa Rican drivers typically flash their high beams at other drivers to warn of traffic police ahead. Seat belt use is mandatory, and motorcyclists must wear helmets. Insurance—a

state monopoly—is also mandatory; car rental companies sell insurance with rentals.

It is illegal to:

- enter an intersection unless you can exit.
- make a right turn on a red light unless indicated by a white arrow.
- overtake on the right—you may pass only on the left.

Traffic police patrol the highways. In the past they've been fond of rental cars (the "TUR" on rental car license plates gives the game away) in the hope of extorting bribes, although such instances now seem rare. If you're stopped, the police will request to see your license, passport, and rental contract. *Tránsitos* use radar guns, and you will get no special treatment as a tourist if you're caught speeding. Speeding fines are paid at a bank; the ticket provides instructions. Delinquent fines are reported to the immigration authorities, and people have been refused exit from the country. Normally, the car rental agency will handle the tickets, although you pay the fine.

Never pay a fine to police on the road. The police cannot legally request payment on-site. If he (I've never seen a female traffic cop) demands payment, note the policeman's name and number from his MOPT badge (he is legally required to show this *carnet* upon request) and call tel. 800-800-0645 or report the incident to the **Oficina de Recepción de Denuncias** (Office for the Reception of Complaints, tel. 506/2295-3272 or 506/2295-3273, 24 hours daily) or the closest OIJ office.

Local phone numbers for **traffic police** (tel. 117 or 506/2255-3562) are listed at www.transito.go.cr.

DRIVING SAFETY

Tico males display unbelievable recklessness, often driving at warp speed, flouting traffic laws, holding traffic lights in disdain, crawling up your tailpipe at 100 kilometers per hour (60 mph), and overtaking on blind corners with a total disregard for anyone else's safety. Costa Rica's road fatality statistics are sobering.

Roads usually lack sidewalks, so pedestrians—and even livestock—walk the road. Be particularly wary at night. And drive mountain roads with extra caution: They're often blocked by thick fog, floods, and landslides.

Potholes are a problem. Hit a big one and you may damage a tire or even destroy a wheel. Vehicles often swerve into your path to avoid potholes. And slower-moving vehicles ahead of you often turn on their left-turn indicator to signal that you can overtake—a dangerous practice that is the cause of many accidents with vehicles that really are turning left. Consider driving with your lights on at all times to ensure being seen.

ACCIDENTS AND BREAKDOWNS

The law states that you must carry **fluorescent triangles** in case of a breakdown. Locals, however, generally pile leaves, rocks, or small branches in the road or at the roadside to warn approaching drivers of a car in trouble. If your car is rented, call the rental agency: It will arrange a tow. Otherwise call tel. 800-800-8001 for roadside assistance.

After an accident, never move the vehicles until the police arrive. Get the names, license plate numbers, and *cedulas* (legal identification numbers) of any witnesses. Make a sketch of the accident. And call the *tráfico* (traffic police, tel. 117 or 506/2255-3562); local numbers are listed at www.transito.go.cr. Do not offer statements to anyone other than the police. In case of injury, call the **Red Cross** (tel. 128 or 911 or 506/2410-0599, www.cruzroja. or.cr). Try not to leave the accident scene, or at least keep an eye on your car: The other party may tamper with the evidence. And don't let honking traffic pressure you into moving the cars.

Show the *tráfico* your license and vehicle registration. Make sure you get them back: They are not allowed to keep any documents unless you've been drinking. If you suspect the other driver has been drinking, ask the *tráfico* to administer a Breathalyzer test (*alcolemia*). Nor can the *tráfico* assess a fine. The police will issue you a green ticket or "summons." You must present this to the nearest municipal office (*alcaldía*) or traffic court (*tribunal de tránsito*) within eight days to make your *declaración* about the accident. Wait a few days so that the police report is on record. Don't skip this! The driver who doesn't show is often found at blame by default. Then take your driver's license, insurance policy, and a police report to the **INS** (Ave. 7, Calles 9/11, San José, tel. 506/2287-6000 or 800-800-8000, ext. 1, www.ins.go.cr), the state insurance monopoly, to process your claim. Car rental companies will take care of this if your car is rented.

CAR RENTALS

The leading U.S. car rental companies have franchises in Costa Rica, although they are not always as reliable as their U.S. parents. There are many local rental companies (some reputable, some not), with slightly cheaper rates. Several agencies have offices at or near Juan Santamaría Airport, plus representatives in popular resort towns.

I highly recommend **U-Save** (tel. 506/2430-4647, U.S./Canada tel. 800-497-3659, www.usavecostarica.com). The staff and service have proved consistently professional each time I've used it, its vehicles have always been in good repair, and it has the lowest rates. Other agencies include **Alamo** (tel. 506/2233-7733, www.alamocostarica.com), **Budget** (tel. 506/2436-2000, www.budget.co.cr), **Europcar** (tel. 506/2440-9990, www.europcar.co.cr), and **Hertz** (tel. 506/2221-1818, www.hertzcostarica.com).

Regardless of where you plan to go, rent a 4WD vehicle. If you don't, you'll regret it. A 4WD vehicle is essential for off-the-beaten-path destinations.

The minimum age for drivers ranges 21-25, depending on the agency. You'll need a valid driver's license plus a credit card. Without a credit card, you'll have to pay a hefty cash deposit. Most agencies offer discounts during the low season (May-Oct.) and for making your reservations from abroad before departure. Stick shift is the norm; you'll pay extra for automatic. Reserve as far in advance as possible, especially in dry season and for Christmas and holidays. Take a copy of your reservation with you. And be prepared to dispute mysterious new charges that may be tagged on in Costa Rica.

Economy cars such as the Toyota Yaris begin at about $75 per day, $240 per week in high season with unlimited mileage. Small 4WD models such as the Suzuki Jimmy begin at about $60 per day, $360 per week in high season, with unlimited mileage. A midsize 4WD such as the Suzuki Gran Vitara will cost about $80 per day, $480 per week in high season. A full-size 4WD such as the superb Mitsubishi Montero will cost about $100 per day, $600 per week in high season.

Readers constantly write to report of scams pulled by unscrupulous agencies. Always leave one person with the car when you return it to the car rental office, especially if unforeseen billing problems arise; there are numerous examples of renters having their belongings stolen from the vehicle while their attention is distracted. And thieves have been known to slash tires or deflate them while you're picking up or dropping off your car; while you're occupied changing the tire, the thieves pounce and strip your vehicle of its contents, then drive off. A sudden flat tire should be treated as a set-up for a potential robbery. Drive to a secure place before stopping, otherwise you may find that you've been followed by robbers pretending to be good Samaritans. It's a major problem in Costa Rica.

MOTORCYCLES

Motorcycling in Costa Rica is not recommended except for experienced riders, as road conditions can be challenging. A valid motorcycle license is required, and you must be 25 years old. **Wild Rider Motorcycles** (tel. 506/2258-4604, www.wild-rider.com) rents three types of dirt bikes. The company also has organized tours, as does **Costa Rica Motorcycle Tours & Rental** (tel. 506/2225-6000, www.costaricamotorcycletours.com).

INSURANCE

Insurance is mandatory, and you will need to accept the obligatory collision damage waiver (CDW) charged by car rental companies. If you make a reservation through a rental agency abroad and are told the rate includes insurance, or that one of your existing policies will cover it, get it in writing. Otherwise, once you arrive in Costa Rica, you may find that you have to pay the mandatory insurance fee on top of your quoted rate. The insurance does not cover your car's contents or personal possessions or a deductible. Each company determines its own deductible—ranging $500-1,000—even though the INS sets this at 20 percent of damages. Rates range from $15 per day for smaller vehicles to $20 daily for larger vehicles.

Inspect your vehicle for damage before departing. Note even the smallest nick and dent on the diagram you'll be presented to sign. Don't forget the inside, as well as the radio antenna, and check that all the switches and buttons function. Most agencies provide 24-hour road service.

GASOLINE

Unleaded gasoline is either high-octane "super" or lesser-octane "regular." Many service stations (*bombas* or *gasolineras*) are open 24 hours; in rural areas they're usually open dawn to dusk only, and they're often far apart. Gasoline prices fluctuate, but at press time were about 760 colones per liter ($5.40 per U.S. gallon). In the boondocks, there's sure to be someone nearby selling from their backyard stock at a premium.

MAPS AND DIRECTIONS

The past few years have seen signposts erected in major cities and along major highways, but don't count on a sign being there when you need it. In towns, many signs point the wrong way: they were placed by crews who hadn't the foggiest idea which street was a *calle* and which an *avenida*. Ticos often use left-pointing arrows to indicate straight ahead.

Fording Rivers

fording a river on the road to Corcovado National Park

Every year, more bridges are built over rivers that once had to be forded, but in certain parts of the country—notably southwest Nicoya and the Osa Peninsula—there are still enough rivers without bridges to add spice to your driving adventure. Usually these are no problem in dry season, but wet season is another matter. Many unwary foreigners misjudge the crossing, swamp the engine, and have to be towed out. Do not expect the car rental agency to be sympathetic; you will have to pay for the damage. It is not unknown for cars to be washed away.

If the river is murky, wade across on foot first to gauge the depth and force of the river, which may be strong enough to whip your wheels from under you. Check for the placement of the engine's air filter to ensure that it won't swamp. Even if the engine won't swamp, you need to check the height of the door sills. Sure, your car might make it across without stalling, but do you really want six inches of muddy water inside the car? Keep the windows down and the doors unlocked.

Look for the tire tracks of other vehicles. It usually pays to follow them. Sometimes you may need to drive along the riverbed to find the exit, rather than it being a straight-across route. It's often best to wait for a local to arrive and show the way. Be patient.

OK, ready to go? There's a technique to fording rivers successfully. First, enter the river slowly. Many drivers charge at the river, causing a huge wave that rides over the hood and drowns the engine. It pays to inch across gently, not least because a shallow crossing often betrays a hidden channel, usually near the bank, where the water runs deep and into which it is easy to plunge nose-first just as you think you've made it across. Still, once you enter the water, keep your foot on the gas.

You'll need the best road map you can obtain. I recommend the ***Costa Rica Nature Atlas-Guidebook,*** which has detailed 1:200,000 road maps that are mostly accurate, but not entirely. You can rent a GPS unit from most car rental agencies.

Taxi

Taxis are inexpensive by U.S. standards, so much so that they are a viable means of touring for short trips, especially if you're traveling with two or three others. A white triangle on the front door contains the taxi's license plate number. Taxi drivers are required by law to use their meters (*marías*). Many drivers don't use them, and instead use all manner of crafty lines to charge you, the gullible tourist, extra. Insist on it being used, as Costa Rican taxi drivers are notorious for overcharging. Don't be afraid to bargain.

Outside San José, you'll usually find taxis around the main square of small towns. Generally, taxis will go wherever a road leads. Most taxis are radio dispatched. Jeep taxis are common in more remote areas. Outside cities, few taxis are metered, and taxi drivers are allowed to negotiate their fare for any journey over 15 kilometers (9.5 miles). Check rates in advance with your hotel concierge.

Visas and Officialdom

DOCUMENTS AND REQUIREMENTS
Passports, Visas, and Tourist Cards

All citizens of the United States, Canada, Western European nations, Australia, and New Zealand need a valid **passport** to enter Costa Rica. No **visas** are required. Tourist cards are issued during your flight or at the immigration desk on arrival and permit stays of 90 days. Citizens of China and most Asian, Middle Eastern, and African countries are either limited to entry for up to 30 days or need a visa (see www.migracion.go.cr/visas/directrices.doc).

Make photocopies of all documentation and keep them with you, separate from the originals. A recent attempt to crack down on illegal immigration has resulted in many innocent tourists being carted off to jail to face a bureaucratic minefield.

You can request a **tourist card extension** (*prórroga de turismo*) monthly for up to 60 days ($3) from the immigration office (Migración, Hwy. 166, La Uruca, tel. 506/2299-8026, www.migracion.go.cr, 8:30am-3:30pm Mon.-Fri.) and regional immigration offices around the country. You'll need three passport-size photos, a certified copy of your outbound ticket, a certified copy of all pages in your passport, and a written statement of the reason for your extension. Be sure to begin the process before your 30 or 90 days are up. Since you'll need to allow three days minimum—plus an additional four days or more if you are asked to submit to a blood test for HIV—it may be just as easy to travel to Nicaragua or Panamá for 72 hours and then reenter with a new visa or tourist card.

Immunizations

No vaccinations are required to enter Costa Rica unless entering from a yellow fever zone, such as Colombia, in which case, a certificate for immunization is ostensibly required, but rarely asked for. If you plan on staying beyond the 30 or 90 days, you may be required to show proof that you are free from HIV. The **Ministerio de Salud** (Ministry of Health, Calle 16, Aves. 6/8, San José), can perform an HIV test.

EMBASSIES

The following embassies are located in San José: **United States** (Blvd. Rohrmoser, tel. 506/2519-2000, ext. 4, for after-hours emergencies tel. 506/2220-3127, http://sanjose.usembassy.gov), **Canada** (Oficentro Ejecutivo La Sabana, Edificio 5, Sabana Sur, tel. 506/2242-4400, www.canadainternational.gc.ca/costa_rica), and **United Kingdom** (Centro Colón, Paseo Colón, Calles 38/40, tel. 506/2258-2025, pager 506/2225-4049, www.britishembassycr.com).

CUSTOMS AND DEPARTURE TAXES

Travelers exiting Costa Rica by air are charged $29 (or its equivalent in colones), but since December 2014 this is priced into your airline ticket; no tax is imposed for transit stays of less than 12 hours.

Returning Home

U.S. residents can bring home $800 of purchases duty-free. You may also bring in one quart of spirits plus 200 cigarettes (one carton). Live animals, plants, and products made from endangered species will be confiscated by U.S. Customs. Tissue-cultured orchids and other plants in sealed vials are OK. Canadian residents are allowed an exemption of C$750 annually for goods purchased abroad, plus 1.14 liters of spirits and 200 cigarettes. UK residents are permitted to import goods worth up to £390, plus 200 cigarettes, 50 cigars, and two liters of spirits.

CROSSING INTO NICARAGUA AND PANAMÁ

You cannot cross into Nicaragua or Panamá with a rental car; you can only do so with your own vehicle. If it has Costa Rican plates, you'll need a special permit from the **Registro Nacional** (tel. 506/2202-0800, www.registronacional.go.cr). It's good for 15 days and must be obtained in person from the main office in Curridabat, San José. There's also a Registro Nacional in Liberia. Visa requirements are always in flux, so check in advance with the Nicaraguan or Panamanian embassy.

Nicaragua

Citizens of Canada, the United States, and most European and Central and South American nations do not need visas to enter Nicaragua. A **tourist visa** is issued at the border ($10 Mon.-Fri., $11 Sat.-Sun., good for 3 months). You can cross into Nicaragua for 72 hours and renew your 30- or 90-day Costa Rican visa if you want to return to Costa Rica to stay longer. A 72-hour transit visa for Nicaragua costs $1.

BORDER CROSSINGS

Peñas Blancas: Most people arriving from Nicaragua do so at Peñas Blancas, in northwest Costa Rica. This is a border post, not a town. The Costa Rican and Nicaraguan posts are contiguous. The border (Costa Rican Immigration, tel. 506/2677-0064) is open 6am-8pm daily. There are no signs telling you how to negotiate the complicated procedures; hence touts will rush up to you offering assistance when you arrive. First you must get an exit form, which you complete and return with your passport. Then walk 600 meters (0.4 miles) to the border, where your passport will be validated (it must have at least six months remaining before it expires). Southbound, you may be required to pay an exit fee ($2) leaving Nicaragua, plus a $1 stamp; the Costa Rica tourist card is free. If you're asked for proof of an onward ticket when entering Costa Rica, you can buy a bus ticket—valid for 12 months—back to Nicaragua at the bus station at Peñas Blancas. If you're driving south, your car will be fumigated upon entering Costa Rica ($4). Northbound, on the Nicaraguan side, go to the immigration building, where you'll pay $10 for a 30-day tourist visa, plus a $1 municipal stamp, and if you're driving, an additional $25 for your car. Then complete a customs declaration sheet, present it with your passport, and proceed to the customs inspection, in the next building along. Then take your papers to the gate for final inspection. The wait in line can be several hours. Count on at least an hour for the formalities, and be sure to have all the required documents in order or you may as well get back on the bus to San José.

Cross-border buses ($1) depart from here every hour for Rivas, a small town about 40 kilometers (25 miles) north of the border. *Colectivo* (shared) taxis also run regularly between the border and Rivas, the nearest Nicaraguan town with accommodations. Buses fill fast—get here early. The bus terminal contains the **Oficina de Migración** (immigration office, tel. 506/2679-9025), a bank, a restaurant, and the **Costa Rican Tourism Institute** (ICT, tel. 506/2677-0138). Change money before crossing into Nicaragua; you get a better exchange rate on the Costa Rican side. **Transportes Deldú** (tel. 506/2256-9072) buses depart San José for La Cruz and Peñas Blancas (6 hours, $8) from Calle 20, Avenidas

1/3, hourly 3am-7pm daily. Local buses depart Liberia for Peñas Blancas via La Cruz every 45 minutes 5:30am-6:30pm daily.

Los Chiles: Since 2014 you can cross at Tablillas, seven kilometers (4.5 miles) north of Los Chiles, where there's an **Oficina de Migración** (immigration office, by the wharf, tel. 506/2471-1233, 8am-6pm daily). The Nicaraguans have built a bridge over the Río San Juan. Foreigners can also cross into Nicaragua by a *colectivo* (shared water taxi) that departs Los Chiles for San Carlos de Nicaragua ($10 pp) at 11am (it departs when full, which often isn't until 1:30pm) and 2:30pm daily.

BUSES

Ticabus (Ave. 3, Calles 26/28, reservations tel. 506/2248-9636, terminal tel. 506/2223-8680, www.ticabus.com) has express service to and from San José and Nicaragua ($32) and El Salvador ($58) daily; and regular service for Nicaragua ($21), El Salvador ($53), and Guatemala ($74) thrice daily; as does **Transnica** (Calle 22, Aves. 3/5, tel. 506/2223-4242, www.transnica.com).

Panamá

Citizens of Canada, the United States, and most European and Central and South American nations do not need visas to enter Panamá. A **tourist visa** ($5, good for 30 days) is issued at the border.

BORDER CROSSINGS

Paso Canoas: The main crossing point is on the Pan-American Highway. The border posts have been open 24 hours, but hours are subject to change (at press time, they were open 6am-10pm daily). If you don't have a ticket out of the country, you can buy a Tracopa bus ticket in David to Paso Canoas and back. A bus terminal on the Panamanian side offers service to David, the nearest town (90 minutes), every hour or two until 7pm daily. Buses leave from David for Panamá City (7 hours; last bus 5pm daily). Panamanian border guards may require proof that you have a ticket out of the

country; there have been reports of disreputable guards at Paso Canoas causing problems for tourists. It's best to buy your return ticket in advance in Costa Rica.

First, get a Costa Rica exit visa from *migración* (tel. 506/2732-2150) by the Tracopa bus terminal 400 meters (0.25 miles) west of the border post, where you can buy your Panamá tourist card. No rental vehicles are permitted, and private cars are usually fumigated ($5). Still, it's very easy to accidentally drive through this border post without realizing it. The post is crowded, confusing, and has no barriers. I've done it twice, and no one stopped me. Simply turn around and drive back.

Sixaola: This rather squalid village on the Caribbean coast sits on the north bank of the Río Sixaola. Its counterpart is Guabito, on the Panamanian side of the river. The two are linked by a bridge. The Costa Rican Customs and Immigration offices (tel. 506/2754-2044, 7am-5pm daily) are on the west end of the bridge. Time in Panamá is one hour later than in Costa Rica. The Panamanian office (tel. 507/759-7952), on the east end of the bridge, is open 8am-6pm daily.

Minibuses operate a regular schedule from Guabito to Changuinola (16 kilometers/10 miles) and Almirante (30 kilometers/19 miles). Taxis are available at all hours to Changuinola ($8), from where you can take a water taxi to Bocas del Toro ($5) or fly or catch a bus onward to the rest of Panamá.

Río Sereno: There's another crossing between Costa Rica and Panamá, at the remote mountain border post of Río Sereno, east of San Vito, in the Pacific southwest. Costa Rican Immigration (tel. 506/2784-0130) and Panamanian Immigration (tel. 507/722-8054) are 50 meters (165 feet) apart and open 8am-5pm daily.

BUSES

Southbound, **Tracopa** (tel. 506/2221-4214, www.tracopacr.com) buses leave from Avenida 5, Calle 14, in San José for Paso Canoas five times daily, and for David in Panamá (8 hours,

$9) twice daily, in each direction. **Ticabus** (reservations tel. 506/2248-9636, terminal tel. 506/2223-8680, www.ticabus.com) buses depart Avenida 4, Calles 9/11, in San José for Panamá City twice daily (executive $37; regular $26). **Transporte Mepe** (tel. 506/2257-8129) buses depart the Gran Caribe terminal in San José for Sixaola and Changuinola (8 hours, $10) at 10am daily. Return buses depart Changuinola at 10am daily.

Recreation

Costa Rica has scores of tour operators offering a complete range of options. I recommend **Costa Rica Expeditions** (tel. 506/2257-0766, www.costaricaexpeditions.com/resourcelibrary), a pioneer in natural history and adventure travel in Costa Rica; it has a complete range of tour packages. Other recommended tour operators include **Costa Rica Sun Tours** (tel. 506/2296-7757, www.crsuntours.com), **Ecole Travel** (tel. 506/2234-1669, www.ecoletravel.com), and **Horizontes Nature Tours** (tel. 506/2222-2022, www.horizontes.com).

BICYCLING

The occasional sweat and effort make Costa Rica's spectacular landscapes and abiding serenity all the more rewarding from a bicycle saddle. Sure, you'll work for your reward. But you'd never get so close to so much beauty in a car. Away from the main highways, roads are little traveled. However, there are no bike lanes, potholes are a persistent problem, and traffic can be hazardous on the steep and winding mountain roads. Leave your touring bike at home: Bring a mountain bike or rent one once you arrive. A helmet is essential.

Costa Ricans are fond of cycling (both road racing and mountain biking), and bicycle racing is a major Costa Rican sport, culminating each November in the grueling **La Ruta de los Conquistadores** (tel. 506/2225-8295, www.adventurerace.com), which crosses the mountain chain from sea level to over 3,000 meters (9,800 feet) elevation.

Airlines generally allow bicycles to be checked free if they're properly packaged. The following Costa Rican Tour companies are recommended: **Bike Arenal** (tel. 506/2479-9020, www.bikearenal.com) and **Coast to Coast Adventures** (tel. 506/2280-8054, www.ctocadventures.com). In the United States, **Backroads** (U.S. tel. 510-527-1555 or 800-462-2848, www.backroads.com) also has guided tours.

BIRD-WATCHING

Few places in the world can boast so many different bird species in such a small area. However, bird-watching requires some knowledge of where you are going, what you're looking for, and the best season. No self-respecting ornithologist would be caught without his copy of *A Guide to the Birds of Costa Rica* by F. Gary Stiles and Alexander Skutch; *Birds of the Rainforest: Costa Rica* by Carmen Hidalgo; or *A Travel and Site Guide to Birds of Costa Rica* by Aaron Sekerak. Even with these in hand, your best bet is to hire a qualified guide or to join a bird-watching tour. I recommend **Karla Taylor** (tel. 506/8915-2386, www.tortugerovillage.com/karlataylortraveladvisor). Another standout is eagle-eyed **Pietra Westra** (tel. 506/2574-2319, www.aratinga-tours.com). He leads bird-watching tours in fluent English, Dutch, or Spanish; his website provides an excellent primer on birds.

Dozens of companies offer bird-watching tours, including **Costa Rica Expeditions** (tel. 506/2257-0766, www.costaricaexpeditions.com) and **Horizontes** (tel. 506/2222-2022, www.horizontes.com). In the United States, **Cheeseman's Ecology Safaris** (U.S. tel. 408-741-5330 or 800-527-5330, www.cheesemans.com), **Field Guides** (U.S. tel. 512-263-7295 or 800-728-4953, www.fieldguides.com), and **Holbrook Travel** (U.S. tel.

800-451-7111, www.holbrooktravel.com) offer bird-watching tours to Costa Rica. In Europe, Journey Latin America (UK tel. 44/20-3432-9175, www.journeylatinamerica.co.uk) offers a 16-day bird-watching tour.

CANOPY TOURS

Hardly a month goes by without another canopy tour opening in Costa Rica. No experience is necessary for most such treetop explorations, which usually consist of a system of treetop platforms linked by horizontal transverse zip lines (cables) that permit you to "fly" through the treetops. The originator of the concept, the Original Canopy Tour (tel. 506/2291-4465, www.canopytour.com), has four facilities: at Monteverde, Liverpool (near Limón), Drake Bay, and Mahogany Park (near Orotina). There is no government regulation, and not all operators use safe practices. Several people have been killed or seriously injured. We cannot guarantee the safety of any particular operation. If you have doubts, pass.

CRUISE TOURS

Natural-history cruise touring is a splendid way to explore Costa Rica's more remote wilderness sites. Normally you'll cruise at night so that each morning when you wake, you're already anchored in a new location. You spend a large part of each day ashore on guided natural-history hikes or recreational-cultural excursions. Most vessels cruise the Pacific coast. Lindblad Expeditions (U.S. tel. 212-765-7740 or 800-397-3348, www.expeditions.com) and National Geographic Expeditions (U.S. tel. 888-966-8687, wwww.nationalgeographicexpeditions.com) offer weeklong itineraries combining Costa Rica and Panamá aboard the 64-passenger *National Geographic Sea Lion*. I escort two trips each winter; join me (www.christopherbaker.com). Windstar Cruises (U.S. tel. 877-827-7245, www.windstarcruises.

com) uses its luxurious 148-passenger *Wind Song* for nine-day itineraries December to March down the Pacific Coast and combining Panamá and Costa Rica.

GOLF

Costa Rica claims half a dozen championship courses: a Robert Trent Jones Jr. stunner at the Westin Playa Conchal Resort & Spa, at Playa Conchal in Nicoya; the Marriott Los Sueños course, at Playa Herradura in the Central Pacific; Los Delfines Golf & Country Club, at Playa Tambor in Nicoya; Parque Valle del Sol, at Santa Ana, west of San José; the Arnold Palmer-designed course at Four Seasons, at Bahía Culebra in Nicoya; and the championship course at Hacienda Pinilla, also in Nicoya.

HIKING

Hiking tours with a professional guide can be arranged through nature lodges or local tour operators. The hardy and adventurous might try a strenuous hike to the peak of Cerro Chirripó, Costa Rica's tallest mountain. Hiking in the more remote parks may require a high degree of self-sufficiency. If you plan on hiking in the Talamancas or other high mountain areas, you're advised to at least obtain topographical maps from the Instituto Geográfico Nacional (National Geographic Institute, Ave. 20, Calles 9/11, tel. 506/2523-2000 or 506/2523-2619, 7am-noon and 12:45pm-3:30pm Mon.-Fri.), but I strongly recommend hiring a guide. Rain gear and a warm sweater or jacket are essential for hiking at higher elevations.

Coast to Coast Adventures (tel. 506/2280-8054, www.ctocadventures.com) specializes in hiking trips. In the United States, Mountain Travel-Sobek (U.S. tel. 510-594-6000 or 888-831-7526, www.mtsobek.com), and Wildland Adventures (U.S. tel. 206-365-0686 or 800-345-4453, www.wildland.com) all offer hiking programs in Costa Rica.

HORSEBACK RIDING

Horseback riding is very popular in Costa Rica, where the campesino culture depends on the horse for mobility. Wherever you are, horses are sure to be available for rent.

In Santa Ana, about nine kilometers (5.5 miles) west of San José, **Club Hípico la Caraña** (tel. 506/2282-6106, www.lacarana. com) provides riding instruction. Scores of ranches nationwide offer trail rides, notably in Guanacaste, where city slickers longing to be the Marlboro Man can pay perfectly good money to get coated with dust and manure alongside workaday cowboys. **Equitour** (U.S. tel. 307-455-3363 or 800-545-0019, www.ridingtours.com) has 8- to 11-day riding adventures in Costa Rica.

FISHING

Fishing expert Jerry Ruhlow (tel. 800-308-3394, www.costaricaoutdoors.com) has a column on fishing in the weekly *Tico Times*. Carlos Barrantes has a tackle shop, **La Casa del Pescador** (Calle 2, Aves. 18/20, San José, tel. 506/2222-1470). In the United States, **Rod & Reel Adventures** (U.S. tel. 800-356-6982, www.rodreeladventures. com) and **Sportfishing Worldwide** (U.S. tel. 513-984-8611 or 800-638-7405, www.

sfww.com) offer fishing packages to Costa Rica.

Deep-Sea Fishing

When your fishing-loving friend tells you all about the big one that got away in Costa Rica, don't believe it. Yes, the fish come big in Costa Rica. But hooking trophy contenders comes easy; the fish almost seem to line up to get a bite on the hook. The country is the world's undisputed sailfish capital on the Pacific, and the tarpon capital on the Caribbean. Fishing varies from season to season, but hardly a month goes by without some International Game Fish Association record being broken. Boat charters run around $400-650 per half day, $850 for a full day, for up to four people, with lunch and beverages included.

The hard-fighting blue marlin swims in these waters year-round, although this "bull of the ocean" is most abundant in June and July, when large schools of tuna also come close to shore. June-October is best for dorado. Yellowfin tuna offer a rod-bending challenge also June-October. Wahoo are also prominent, though less dependable. Generally, summer months are the best in the north; winter months are best in the south.

Tamarindo is the most prominent fishing

hiking to San Pedrillo waterfall, Corcovado National Park

center in the northern Pacific. However, northern Guanacaste is largely unfishable December-March because of winds: Boat operators move boats south to Playa Herradura and Quepos during the windy season, when the Central Pacific posts its best scores. To the south, Golfito is the base for another popular fishing paradise, the Golfo Dulce.

Inland and Coastal Fishing

Part of the beauty of fishing Costa Rica, says one angler, is that "you can fish the Caribbean at dawn, try the Pacific in the afternoon, and still have time to watch a sunset from a mountain stream." More than a dozen inland rivers provide action on rainbow trout, *machaca* (Central America's answer to American shad), drum, *guapote, mojarra* (Costa Rica's bluegill with teeth), and *bobo* (a moss-eating mullet). A good bet is the Río Savegre and other streams around San Gerardo de Dota. Laguna Caño Negro and the waters of the Río San Juan present fabulous potential for snook and tarpon. Laguna de Arenal is famed for its feisty rainbow bass (*guapote*).

A freshwater fishing license is mandatory. The closed season runs September to December. Lodges and outfitters provide the license, as does the Banco Nacional de Costa Rica (Ave. 1, Calle 2/4, San José).

Costa Rica's northeastern shores, lowland lagoons, and coastal rivers offer the world's hottest tarpon for the light-tackle enthusiast. When you tire of wrestling these snappy fighters, you can take on snook—another worthy opponent. Fall is the best time to get a shot at the trophy snook that return to the beaches around the river mouths to spawn. Tarpon are caught year-round. Snook season runs from late August into January, with a peak August-November. November to January, the area enjoys a run of *calba,* the local name for small snook that average two kilograms (4.5 pounds) and are exceptional sport on light tackle. Jacks are also common year-round in Caribbean waters.

HANG-GLIDING AND AERIAL TOURS

Ballooning is offered by **Serendipity Adventures** (tel. 506/2558-1000, U.S./Canada tel. 877-507-1358, www.serendipity-adventures.com). **Helitours by AeroDiva** (tel. 506/2296-7241, www.aerodiva.com) offers helicopter tours. **Ultralight S.A.** (tel. 506/2743-8037, www.ultralighttour.com) offers autogiro and other ultralight flights at Flying Crocodile Lodge, in Playa Sámara at Bahía (near Uvita).

KAYAKING AND CANOEING

Sea kayaking is quickly catching on in Costa Rica, and no wonder. The sea kayak's ability to move silently means you can travel unobtrusively, sneaking up close to wild animals without freaking them out. The one- and two-person craft are remarkably stable and ideally suited for investigating narrow coastal inlets and flat-water rivers larger vessels cannot reach.

In San José, you can rent kayaks, canoes, and camping equipment from **Mundo Aventura** (tel. 506/2221-6934, www.maventura.com). **Ríos Tropicales** (tel. 506/2233-6455, U.S. tel. 866-722-8273, www.riostropicales.com) and **Kayak Jacó** (tel. 506/2643-1233, www.kayakjaco.com) offer kayaking trips. In the United States, **BattenKill Canoe** (U.S. tel. 802-362-2800 or 800-421-5268, www.battenkill.com) offers canoeing trips to Costa Rica, as do **Canoe Costa Rica** (tel. 506/2282-3579, U.S. tel. 732-736-6586, www.canoecostarica.com) and in Canada, try **Galaiano Kayaks** (Canada tel./fax 250-539-2442, www.seakayak.ca).

MOTORCYCLE TOURING

Motorcycle enthusiasts haven't been left out of the two-wheel touring business. **Wild Rider** (tel. 506/2258-4604, www.wild-rider.com) uses scramblers for its tours. **Costa Rica BMW Motorcycle Tours** (tel. 506/2225-6000, www.costaricabmwtours.com) offers 7- and 10-day trips.

In the United States, **Moto-Discovery Tours** (U.S. tel. 830-438-7744 or 800-233-0564, www.motodiscovery.com) runs eight-day guided tours in Costa Rica.

SCUBA DIVING

Costa Rica's diving is all about pelagic areas. If you're looking for coral, you'll be happier in Belize or the Bay Islands of Honduras. Visibility, unfortunately, ranges only 6 to 24 meters (20-80 feet), but water temperatures are a steady 24-29°C (75-84°F) or higher. In San José, **Mundo Aquático** (tel. 506/2224-9729, www.mundoacuaticocr.com), 25 meters (80 feet) north of Mas X Menos in San Pedro, rents and sells scuba gear. The only hyperbaric chamber is at Cuajiniquil, in Guanacaste.

Pacific Coast

Most dive-site development has been along the Pacific coast. You'll see little live coral and few reefs. In their place, divers find an astounding variety and number of fish, soft corals, and invertebrates. Most diving is around rock formations. Visibility can often be obscured, particularly in rainy season (May-Nov.), but on calm days you may be rewarded with densities of marinelife that cannot be found anywhere in the Caribbean.

Favored dive destinations in the Pacific northwest include Islas Murciélagos and the Catalinas. Both locations teem with groupers, snappers, jacks, sharks, and giant mantas as well as indigenous tropical species. Morays peer out from beneath rocky ledges. Giant jewfish, turtles, and eagle rays are common. Great bull sharks congregate at a place called "Big Scare." The two island chains are challenging because of their strong currents and surges.

The Punta Gorda dive site, six kilometers (4 miles) west of Playa Ocotal, is known for thousands of eagle rays and whale sharks. Divers also report seeing black marlins cruising gracefully around pinnacle rocks. Uvita, midway down the Pacific coast, has a small coral reef, as does Isla del Caño, just off the

Osa Peninsula. About two kilometers (1.2 miles) out from Caño is a near-vertical wall and parades of pelagic fish, including manta rays. The island is served by dive boats out of Drake Bay and Golfito. Charters can also be arranged out of Quepos.

Isla del Coco is the Mount Everest of dive experiences in Costa Rica. Its reputation for big-animal encounters—whale sharks, hammerheads (sometimes schooling 500 at a time), and mantas—have made it renowned. Isla del Coco is 500 kilometers (300 miles) southwest of mainland Costa Rica, necessitating a long sea journey on a live-aboard dive vessel.

Caribbean Coast

The Caribbean coast has yet to develop a serious infrastructure catering to sport divers, although dive operators can be found in Cahuita, Puerto Viejo, and Manzanillo. At Cahuita is Costa Rica's most beautiful—but much damaged—coral reef, extending 500 meters (0.3 miles) out from Cahuita Point. Two old shipwrecks—replete with cannons—lie on the Cahuita reef, seven meters (23 feet) down. The Gandoca-Manzanillo Wildlife Refuge protects a southern extension of the Cahuita reef, and one in better condition. The best time for diving is during the dry season (Feb.-Apr.), when visibility is at its best. Check with park rangers for conditions, as the area is known for dangerous tides.

SURFING

Surfing is one of Costa Rica's main assets, drawing tens of thousands of boarders each year. Long stretches of oceanfront provide thousands of beach breaks. Rivers offer river-mouth breaks, particularly on the Pacific coast. The coral reefs on the Caribbean coast, says Costa Rican surf expert Peter Brennan, "take the speed limit to the max." If the surf blows out or goes flat before you are ready to pack it in for the day, you can simply jump over to the other coast, or—on the Pacific—head north or south. If one break isn't working, another is sure to be cooking. You rarely see monster-size Hawaiian-type waves, but they're nicely shaped, long, and tubular.

All the major surf beaches have surf shops where board sales and rentals are offered. And there are plenty of surf camps. Many hotels and car rental companies offer discounts to surfers. Generally, your double board bag flies free (or for a small fee) as a second piece of checked luggage on international airlines. Airlines require that you pack your board in a board bag. Within Costa Rica, Nature Air permits short boards, but not long boards, for a $40 fee. **Costa Rican Surf Report** (www.crsurf.com) is a great information source. In Costa Rica, look for *Surfos,* a slick biannual magazine available free. Board rentals and repairs, plus surfing lessons, are available at all the main surfing beaches.

WHITE-WATER RAFTING

White-water rafting is the ultimate combination of beauty and thrill—an ideal way to savor Costa Rica's natural splendor. Because the land is so steep, streams pass through hugely varied landscapes within relatively short distances. You'll tumble through a tropical fantasia of feathery bamboo, ferns, and palms, a roller-coaster ride amid glistening forest full of the chattering of monkeys and birds.

Rafters are required to wear helmets and life jackets, which are provided by tour operators. Generally, all you need to bring is a swimsuit, a T-shirt, and tennis shoes or sneakers. Sunscreen is a good idea, as you are not only in the open all day but also exposed to reflections off the water. Most operators provide a special waterproof bag for cameras. One-day trips start at about $75.

Planning Your Time

Generally, May-June and September-October are the best times for high water. Rivers are rated from Class I to VI in degree of difficulty, with Class V for true experts only. The **Río Chirripó** (Class III-IV) runs down the slopes of the southwest Pacific and is recommended for two- to four-day trips. The river, which tumbles from its source on Cerro Chirripó, has been compared to California's Tuolumne and Idaho's Middle Fork of the Salmon, with massive volumes of water and giant waves. The **Río Corobicí** (Class II), in Guanacaste, provides more of a float trip and makes an ideal half-day trip for families, with superb wildlife-viewing and calm waters. It is runnable year-round.

windsurfer at Lake Arenal

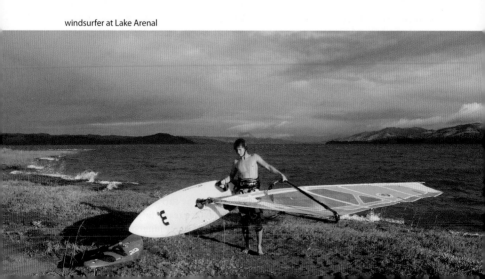

The high-volume **Río General** is famous for its dramatic gorges, challenging rapids, and big waves ideal for surfing. **Río Naranjo** and **Río Savegre,** in the mountains above Manuel Antonio on the Central Pacific coast, are real corkers in high water, with swirling Class IV action.

For an in-depth immersion in nature, the **Río Pacuaré** (Class III-IV) is the best choice as it slices through virgin rainforest, plunging through mountain gorges to spill onto the Caribbean plains near Siquirres. Toucans, monkeys, and other animals galore make this journey unforgettable. Overhead loom cliffs from which waterfalls drop into the river. Steep drops produce big waves. The best months are June and October. The **Río Reventazón** (Class II-V) tumbles out of Lake Angostura and also cascades to the Caribbean lowlands in an exciting series of rapids. Beginners can savor Class II and III rapids on the "mid-section," the most popular run for one-day trips. The Guayabo section offers Class IV-V runs. Constant rainfall allows operators to offer trips year-round; June and July are the best months. The **Río Sarapiquí** (Class III) runs along the eastern flank of the Cordillera Central and drops to the Caribbean lowlands.

In Costa Rica, the preeminent operator is **Ríos Tropicales** (tel. 506/2233-6455, www. riostropicales.com), which runs the Ríos Corobicí, Sarapiquí, Reventazón, General, and Pacuaré. Numerous regional companies also offer white-water trips.

WINDSURFING

Strong winds sweep the coast of the Pacific northwest in summer; Bahía Salinas is recommended and has two windsurfing centers. Inland, Laguna de Arenal is paradise, with 23- to 35-km/h (14-22-mph) easterly winds funneling through a mountain corridor year-round. Strong winds rarely cease during the dry season (Dec.-Apr.). The lake is one of the best all-year freshwater windsurfing spots in the world, with two dedicated windsurfing centers.

Conduct and Customs

It is a rare visitor to the country who returns home unimpressed by the Costa Ricans' cordial warmth and hospitality. However, Ticos have a hard time speaking forthrightly. They can't say no and would prefer to tell you what they think you might want to hear rather than the truth. Thus, when a Tico makes a promise, don't expect him or her to come through, to show up for a date or appointment, or even to return a call. And don't expect an apology; you usually receive an excuse. Ticos have been called icebergs for their tendency to conceal the real meaning of what they say or feel below the surface.

Nor should you count on a Tico's punctuality. Most businesses are efficient and operate *hora americana,* punctually, but many other Ticos still tick along on turtle-paced *hora tica. ¿Quien sabe?* ("Who knows?") is an oft-repeated phrase. So too *¡Tal vez!* ("perhaps") and, of course, *¡Mañana!* ("tomorrow").

Making friends with Ticos usually takes considerably longer than it does in North America or Britain. Family bonds are so strong that foreigners often find making intimate friendships a challenge.

All the above trends are beginning to break down as the younger generation adopt more relaxed, forthright, and more confident "North American" attitudes and behaviors.

Young female travelers should be prepared to receive *piropos*—effulgent, romantic, but often vulgar compliments. Dressing conservatively can help thwart unwanted advances. Since 2005 it has been illegal for men to pay unwelcome compliments to women on the street.

Ethical Tourism

- Travel with a spirit of humility and a genuine desire to meet and talk with local people.

- Be aware of the feelings of others. Act respectfully and avoid offensive behavior.

- Cultivate the habit of actively listening and observing rather than merely hearing and seeing. Avoid the temptation to "know all the answers."

- Realize that others may have concepts of time and attitudes that are different—not inferior—to those you inherited from your own culture.

- Instead of looking only for the exotic, discover the richness of another culture and way of life.

- Learn local customs and respect them.

- Remember that you are only one of many visitors. Don't expect special privileges.

- When bargaining with merchants, don't take advantage of the poor. Pay a fair price.

- Keep your promises to people you meet. If you cannot, don't make the promise.

- Spend time each day reflecting on your experiences in order to deepen your understanding. Is your interaction beneficial for all involved?

- Be aware of why you are traveling in the first place. If you truly want a "home away from home," why travel?

FESTIVALS, EVENTS, AND HOLIDAYS

Local fiestas called *turnos* are found nationwide, notably in Guanacaste and Nicoya, highlighted by rodeos, fireworks, and firecrackers (*bombetas*). Individual towns also celebrate their patron saint's day: Highlights usually include a procession, benign bullfights, rodeos, dancing, and parades. The *Tico Times* (www.ticotimes.net) provides weekly listings of festivals and events nationwide. The website www.whereincostarica.com is another excellent resource.

Costa Rica is a Roman Catholic country, and its holidays (*feriados*) are mostly religious. Most businesses, including banks, close on official holidays. The country closes down entirely during the biggest holiday time, Easter Holy Week (*semana santa*), Wednesday through Easter Sunday—a good time to see colorful religious processions. Buses don't run that week on Holy Thursday or Good Friday. Banks and offices are closed. Hotels and rental cars are booked solid months in advance as everyone heads for the beach. Avoid the popular beaches during Easter week. Most Ticos now take the whole Christmas (*navidad*) holiday week through New Year as an unofficial holiday.

Official Holidays
January 1: New Year's Day
March/April: Easter Week
April 11: Juan Santamaría Day
May 1: Labor Day
May 29: Corpus Christi Day
July 25: Annexation of Guanacaste Day
August 15: Mother's Day
September 15: Independence Day
November 2: All Soul's Day
December 25: Christmas Day

Festivals and Events
JANUARY
Alajuelita: Fiesta Patronales—parade and pilgrimage (week of Jan. 15).
Palmares: Folk dances, music, rodeos (early Jan.).
Santa Cruz: Fiestas de Santa Cruz—folk dances, music, rodeos, bullfights (week of Jan. 15).

Jacó: Jungle Jam—multiday live music festival (mid Jan.).

FEBRUARY

Puntarenas: Carnival—parade floats, music, and dancing (first two weeks).
Uvita: Best Fest—music festival hosting performers from throughout the Americas (early Feb.).

MARCH

Alajuela: Festival Imperial—the nation's biggest rock festival (every two years).
Escazú: Día del Boyeros—oxcart parade with music, dancing, and competitions (2nd Sun.).
Cartago: Holy pilgrimage to Ujarrás (mid-Mar.).
San José: National Orchid Show.

APRIL

Alajuela: Juan Santamaría Day—parade with marching bands (Apr. 11).
San José: University Week—concerts, exhibits, parades (last week); Festival de Salsa—concerts, dance parties.

MAY

Puerto Limón: May Day—cricket matches, music, and dancing (May 1).
Zarcero: Tourist Fair (mid-month).

JUNE

Monteverde: Tourist Fair (late June).

JULY

Liberia and Santa Cruz: Guanacaste Day—folkloric dancing, music, rodeos, and bullfights (July 25).
Puntarenas: Virgin of the Sea Festival—boat regatta, parades, music, fireworks (Sat. closest to July 16).

AUGUST

Cartago: Día del Virgen de los Ángeles—religious processions (Aug. 2).
Nationwide: Credomatic International

Music Festival—concerts ranging from classical to jazz.
Puerto Limón: Festival Afrocultural—celebration of Afro-Caribbean culture.
Turrialba: National Adventure Tourism Festival—competitions and demonstrations of kayaking, rafting, mountain biking (end of Aug.).

SEPTEMBER

Nationwide: Día de Independencia—parades, marching bands, music and dance (Sept. 15).

OCTOBER

Puerto Limón: Carnival—music, dancing, parades (mid-Oct.).
San José: Feria Indígena—celebration of indigenous culture.
Upala: Fiesta del Maíz—parades and music in celebration of maize (corn).

NOVEMBER

Nationwide: All Soul's Day—church processions (Nov. 2); Encuentro Nacional de la Mascarada Tradicional—clowns and masks.
San José: International Festival of the Arts—dance troupes, theater, experimental music, puppets, jazz, folklore, and classical music; Oxcart Parade—boyeros camp and hold a song festival in Parque la Sabana, followed by a parade down Paseo Colón (last Sun.).

DECEMBER

Nationwide: Immaculate Conception—fireworks (Dec. 8); Los Posadas—caroling house to house (December 15 onward); Topes Caballos—horse parades, including downtown San José (Dec. 26).
Boruca: Fiesta de los Negritos—costumed dancing (Dec. 8); Fiesta de los Diablitos—indigenous festival, masked dancing, fireworks (Dec. 30).
Nicoya: Fiesta de la Yegüita—processions, bullfights, fireworks, and concerts (Dec. 12).
San José: Festival of Lights—parade with floats adorned with lights, plus fireworks (2nd week).

Accommodations and Food

Accommodations run the gamut from cheap *pensiones,* beachside *cabinas,* and self-catering *apartotels* to rustic nature lodges, swank mountain lodges, and glitzy resort hotels with casinos. The term *cabina*—literally, cabin— is a loose term used throughout Costa Rica to designate budget accommodations, and as often as not refers to hotel rooms as well as true cabins.

Many readers have written to complain about rude behavior by hotel owners or their staff, who are unfortunately quite unresponsive to complaints. To get the most out of your trip, adjust your expectations before departing.

Unless you're staying in the upscale hotels, you may need to bring your own shampoo, washcloths, and sink plug. The cheapest accommodations usually have communal baths, and in hot lowland areas, often cold-water showers only; often shower units are powered by electric heating elements, which you switch on for the duration of your shower. Beware: It's easy to give yourself a shock from any metal object nearby; hence these systems have the nickname "suicide showers." In places where trying to flush your waste paper down the toilet may cause a blockage, waste receptacles are provided for toilet paper. Use the basket unless you want a smelly backup.

Ensure that the door is secure and that your room can't be entered through the window.

Reservations

Reservations are strongly advised for dry-season months (Dec.-Apr.). Christmas, Easter week, and weekends are particularly busy. Don't rely on mail to make reservations; it could take several months to confirm. Instead, book online, call direct, or have your travel agent make reservations. It may be necessary to send a deposit, without which your space may be released to someone else. Take a copy of your reservation with you, and reconfirm a few days before arrival.

Hotels' failure to honor reservations is a common complaint. If you make a reservation by phone, be sure to follow up by email,

relaxing at Kurà Design Villas, Uvita

Certificate for Sustainable Tourism

The Certificate for Sustainable Tourism (CST, tel. 506/2299-5800, www.turismo-sostenible.co.cr) seeks to categorize and certify hotels and other tourism entities according to the degree to which they comply to a model of sustainability. It is now the standard by which to compare hotels (and other services) according to rational criteria. Unscrupulous companies ("greenwashers") can no longer jump on the ecotourism bandwagon by simply adopting a self-appointed label.

Hotels are graded according to environmental, socioeconomic, and other attributes, with 150 variables judged by independent investigators on a level of one to five. Entities are then awarded one to five "leaves" according to the total score. CST certification is now so widely recognized and coveted that hoteliers have been provided a real incentive to improve their practices, with an eye toward earning maximum leaves and therefore a competitive advantage. Hotels are reevaluated every two years, and can be demoted. At press time, 30 hotels nationwide had earned the full five leaves. Check the website for a list by region.

as you may need that paper trail. Discounts or refunds are rarely offered, regardless of circumstances.

Rates

Many hotels have separate rates for low ("green") season (May-Oct.) and high season (Nov.-Apr.), often with premium rates during Christmas, New Year, and Easter. Couples requesting a *cama matrimonial* (to sleep in one bed) will often receive a discount off the normal double rate. A 16.3 percent tax is added to your room bill at most hotels. Some hotels charge extra (as much as 6 percent) for paying by credit card. Every attempt has been made to ensure that prices given here are accurate at press time.

ACCOMMODATIONS
Camping

Several national parks have basic camping facilities. Camping is illegal on beaches, although that doesn't stop many Costa Ricans.

You'll need a warm sleeping bag and a waterproof tent for camping in the mountains. You'll also need a mosquito net and plenty of bug repellent. Avoid grassy pastures: They harbor chiggers and ticks. And don't camp near riverbanks, where snakes congregate and flash floods may occur. Theft is a problem. If possible, camp with a group of people so one person can guard the gear.

Apartotels and Villas

A hybrid of hotels and apartment buildings, *apartotels* resemble motels on the European and Australian model and offer rooms with kitchens or kitchenettes (pots and pans and cutlery are provided) and sometimes small suites furnished with sofas and tables and chairs. Weekly and monthly rates are offered. *Apartotels* are popular with families and Ticos.

Scores of private homes and villas are available for rent nationwide. A good resource is **Escape Villas** (U.S. tel. 888-771-2976, www.villascostarica.com).

Homestays and Bed-and-Breakfasts

Many Costa Rican families welcome foreign travelers into their homes as paying guests—an ideal way to experience Tico hospitality and to bone up on your Spanish. "Guesthouse" refers to a bed-and-breakfast hotel in a family-run home where you are made to feel like part of the family, as opposed to hotels that include breakfasts in their room rates. Many local hosts advertise in the *Tico Times*.

Bell's Home Hospitality (tel. 506/2225-4752, www.homestay-thebells.com) is a good starting point.

Hotels

Costa Rica's hotels run the gamut from beach

resorts, mountain lodges, and haciendas-turned-hotels to San José's plusher options. Many upper-end hotels can hold their own on the international hotel scene. Others can't justify their rates; where this is the case, I've said so.

Small Distinctive Hotels of Costa Rica (tel. 506/2258-0150, www.distinctive-hotels.com) is an association of nine of the finest hotels in the country. The **Charming & Nature Hotels of Costa Ricap** (www.charmingnaturehotels.com) is a consortium of small German- and Swiss-owned properties. The **Costa Rican Hotel Association** (tel. 506/2220-0575, www.costaricanhotels.com) represents more than 250 hotels.

Motels

As throughout Latin America, "motels" are explicitly for lovers. Rooms are rented out by the hour. If mirrors over the bed and adult videos piped in 24-7 are your thing, fine!

Nature Lodges

Costa Rica is endowed with mountain and rainforest lodges, from basic to luxurious. Most have naturalist guides and arrange nature hikes, horseback riding, and other activities. **Cooprena** (tel. 506/2290-8646, www.turismoruralcr.com) is a cooperative of rural community organizations that promotes rustic eco-lodges.

Hostels

Costa Rica boasts dozens of excellent backpacker hostels. Hostelling International is represented in Costa Rica by the **Hostel Casa Yoses** (Ave. 8, Calle 41, San José, tel. 506/2234-5486, www.hihostels.com).

FOOD AND DRINK
Costa Rican Cuisine

Costa Rican cuisine is simple, and spices are shunned. *Comida típica,* or native cuisine, relies heavily on rice and beans, and "home style" cooking predominates. *Gallo pinto,* the national dish of fried rice and black beans, is ubiquitous, including as a breakfast

a health-conscious salad at Río Perdido, Guanacaste

(*desayuno*) staple. Many meals are derivatives, including *arroz con pollo* (rice and chicken) or *arroz con tuna.* At lunch, *gallo pinto* becomes the *casado* (literally "married"), a cheap set lunch plate of rice and beans supplemented with cabbage-and-tomato salad, fried plantains, and meat. Vegetables do not form a large part of the diet.

Food staples include *carne* (beef, sometimes called *bistec*), *pollo* (chicken), and *pescado* (fish). Beef and steaks are quite lean—Costa Rican cattle is grass-fed and flavorful. Still, don't expect your tenderloin steak (*lomito*) to match its North American counterpart.

Seafood is popular—especially sea bass (*corvina*), mahimahi, shrimp (*camarones*), and lobster (*langosta*). Light and flavorful tilapia (African bass) is increasingly popular, especially served with garlic (*al ajillo*). Marlin and sailfish are regional specialties at local restaurants. Ceviche is also favored, using the white meat of corvina steeped in lemon juice mixed with dill or cilantro and finely cut red peppers.

Guanacaste province is noted for its local specialties, especially dishes based on corn.

Eating in Costa Rica doesn't present the health problems that plague the unwary traveler elsewhere in Central America, but you need to be cautious. Always wash vegetables in water known to be safe, and peel any fruits you eat. Otherwise, stick to staples such as bananas and oranges.

Sodas, open-air lunch counters, serve inexpensive snacks and meals. In San José, restaurants serve the gamut of international cuisine at reasonable prices. Hoteliers and gourmet chefs have opened restaurants of note in even the most secluded backwaters. On the Caribbean coast, the local cuisine reflects its Jamaican heritage with spiced specialties such as johnnycakes, curried goat, curried shrimp, and pepper-pot soup.

Many bars serve *bocas*—savory tidbits ranging from ceviche to *tortillas con queso* (tortillas with cheese)—with drinks. Some provide them free, as long as you're drinking. Turtle (*tortuga*) eggs are a popular dish in many working-class bars. Most towns have Saturday-morning street markets (*ferias de agricultor*). Even the smallest hamlet has its *pulpería* or *abastecedor*—local grocery store.

Fruit

Costa Rica grows many exotic fruits. The bunches of vermilion fruits on the stem sold at roadside stalls nationwide are *pejibayes.* You scoop out the boiled avocado-like flesh; its taste is commonly described as between that of a chestnut and a pumpkin. The *pejibaye* palm (not to be confused with the *pejibaye*) produces the *palmito* (heart of palm), used in salads. *Guayabas* (guavas) come into season September-November; their pink fruit is used for jams and jellies. The *marañón,* the fruit of the cashew, is also commonly used in *refrescos. Mamones* are little green spheres containing grapelike pulp. And those yellow-red egg-size fruits are *granadillas* (passion fruit). One of my favorites is the star fruit, or *carambeloa,* with the flesh of a grape and the taste of an orange.

Succulent *sandías* (watermelons) should not be confused with the lookalike *chiverre,* whose "fruit" resembles spaghetti. *Piña* (pineapple) is common. So too are *melón* (cantaloupe) and mangos. Papayas come in two forms: the round yellow-orange *amarilla* and the elongated red-orange *cacho. Moras* (blackberries) are most commonly used for fruit shakes.

Imperial is Costa Rica's most popular beer.

Eating Costa Rican

arreglados: sandwiches or tiny puff pastry stuffed with beef, cheese, or chicken. Greasy!

arroz con pollo: a basic dish of chicken and rice.

casado: set lunch, usually consisting of *arroz* (rice), frijoles (black beans), *carne* (beef), *repollo* (cabbage), and *plátano* (plantain). Avocado (*aguacates*) or egg may also be included.

ceviche: marinated seafood, often chilled, made of corvina (sea bass), *camarones* (shrimp), or *conchas* (shellfish). Normally served with lemon, chopped onion, garlic, and sweet red peppers.

chorreados: corn pancakes, often served with sour cream (*natilla*).

elote: corn on the cob, either boiled (*elote cocinado*) or roasted (*elote asado*).

empanadas: turnovers stuffed with beans, cheese, meat, or potatoes.

enchiladas: pastries stuffed with cheese and potatoes and occasionally meat.

gallo: tortilla sandwiches stuffed with beans, cheese, or meat.

gallo pinto: the national dish (literally "spotted rooster"), made of lightly spiced rice and black beans. Traditional breakfast (*desayuno*) or lunch dish. Sometimes includes *huevos fritos* (fried eggs).

olla de carne: soup made of squash, corn, yuca (a local tuber), chayote (a local pear-shaped vegetable), *ayote* (a pumpkin-like vegetable), and potatoes.

palmitos: succulent hearts of palm, common in salads.

patacones: thin slices of deep-fried plantain, a popular Caribbean dish.

pescado ahumado: smoked fish.

picadillo: a side dish of ground meat.

sopa de mondongo: soup made from tripe.

sopa negra: a creamy soup, often with a hard-boiled egg and vegetables soaking in the bean broth.

tamales: steamed cornmeal pastries stuffed with corn, chicken, or pork, and wrapped in a banana or corn leaf. A popular Christmas dish.

tortillas: Mexican-style corn pancakes or omelets.

cono capuchino: an ice-cream cone topped with chocolate.

dulce de leche: a syrup of boiled milk and sugar; also thicker, fudge-like *cajeta*—delicious!

flan: cold caramel custard.

mazamorra: cornstarch pudding.

melcocha: candy made from raw sugar.

milanes: chocolate candies.

pan de maíz: sweet cornbread.

queque seco: pound cake.

torta chilena: multilayered cake filled with *dulce de leche*.

Drink

Costa Rica has no national drink, perhaps with the exception of *horchata*, a cinnamon-flavored cornmeal drink. Coffee is traditionally served very strong and mixed with hot milk. When you order coffee with milk (*café con leche*), you'll generally get half coffee, half milk. If you want it black, you want *café sin leche* or *café negro*.

North American sodas are popular and widely available, as are their Tico equivalents. *Refrescos* are energizing fruit sodas and colas.

Batidos are fruit shakes served with water (*con agua*) or milk (*con leche*). *Agua dulce* is boiled water with brown sugar—energy for field workers. Roadside stalls also sell *pipas*, green coconuts with the tops chopped off. You drink the refreshing cool coconut water from a straw—perfect for fighting off dehydration.

Imperial is the most popular local brew. Tropical is a low-calorie light beer. Heineken is also brewed here under license. Bavaria is a flavorful dark beer (*negra*), and real ale lovers will appreciate two delicious brews by Costa

Rica Craft Brewing Co. (www.beer.cr). Even the poorest campesino can afford the native red-eye, *guaro*, a harsh, clear spirit distilled from fermented sugarcane. My favorite drink? *Guaro* mixed with Café Rica, a potent coffee liqueur. Imported alcohol is expensive. Chilean and Argentinean wines are widely available and inexpensive.

Travel Tips

OPPORTUNITIES FOR STUDY AND EMPLOYMENT
Student Cards

An **International Student Identity Card** issued by the International Student Travel Federation (www.isic.org) entitles students ages 12 to 26 to discounts on transportation, entrance to museums, and other savings. When purchased in the United States ($25), ISIC even includes $3,000 in emergency medical coverage, limited hospital coverage, and access to a 24-hour toll-free emergency hotline. Students (and educators under 26) can obtain ISICs at any student union. Alternately, contact the **Council on International Educational Exchange** (www.ciee.org), which issues ISICs and also arranges study vacations in Costa Rica. In Canada, cards can be obtained from **Travel Cuts** (Canada tel. 416-614-2887 or 866-246-9762, www.travelcuts.com). In the United Kingdom, students can obtain an ISIC from any student union office.

Travel and Work Study

The **University of Costa Rica** offers special *cursos libres* (free courses) during winter break (Dec.-Mar.). It also grants "special student" status to foreigners. Contact the Oficina de Asuntos Internacionales (tel. 506/2207-5080, www.ucr.ac.cr). The **University for Peace** (tel. 506/2205-9000, www.upeace.org) and **Organization for Tropical Studies** (tel. 506/2524-0607, U.S. tel. 919-684-5774, www.ots.duke.edu) also sponsor study courses. **EcoTeach** (U.S. tel. 800-626-8992, www.ecoteach.com) places students on environmental projects in Costa Rica.

Work-abroad programs are also offered through **CIEE's Work Abroad Department** (U.S. tel. 888-268-6245, www.ciee.org), which publishes *Work, Study, Travel Abroad* and *The High School Student's Guide to Study, Travel, and Adventure Abroad.*

Holbrook Travel (U.S. tel. 800-451-7111, www.holbrooktravel.com) offers an eight-day Tropical Education Program in Costa Rica for students and teachers. The **School for Field Studies** (U.S. tel. 978-741-3567 or 800-989-4418, www.fieldstudies.org) has summer courses in sustainable development.

Transitions Abroad (U.S. tel. 413-992-6482, www.transitionsabroad.com) provides information for students wishing to study abroad, as does **Studyabroad.com** (U.S. tel. 484-766-2920, www.studyabroad.com).

Language Study

Costa Rica has dozens of language schools. Most programs include homestays with Costa Rican families—a tremendous (and fun) way to boost your language skills and learn the local idioms. Many also feature workshops on Costa Rican culture, dance lessons, and excursions. Courses run an average of 2 to 4 weeks.

The following language schools are recommended:

- **Centro Panamericano de Idiomas** (tel. 506/2265-6306, www.cpi-edu.com).

- **Costa Rica Language Academy** (tel. 506/2280-1685, U.S. tel. 866-230-6361, www.spanishandmore.com).

- **Institute for Central American Development Studies** (tel. 506/2225-0508, www.icads.org). Weds Spanish tuition to learning about social conditions, environmental issues, and politics.

- **Intensa** (tel. 506/2281-1818, U.S. tel. 866-277-1352, www.intensa.com).

- **Spanish Abroad** (U.S. tel. 602-778-6791 or 888-722-7623, www.spanishabroad.com). The largest language school in Costa Rica, with nine locals nationwide and classes starting every Monday year-round.

- *Speak Spanish like a Costa Rican,* by Christopher Howard, is a book and 90-minute audio recording.

ACCESS FOR TRAVELERS WITH DISABILITIES

Few allowances have been made in infrastructure for travelers with disabilities, although wheelchair ramps are now appearing on sidewalks, and an increasing number of hotels provide facilities for the physically challenged.

In the United States, the **Society for Accessible Travel & Hospitality** (U.S. tel. 212-447-7284, www.sath.org) and the **American Foundation for the Blind** (U.S. tel. 212-502-7600 or 800-232-5463, www. afb.org) are good resources. **Flying Wheels Travel** (U.S. tel. 507-451-5005 or 877-451-5006, www.flyingwheelstravel.com) is a travel agency for individuals with physical disabilities.

Travelers with disabilities can learn to surf at **Shaka Beach Retreat** (tel. 506/2640-1118, www.shakacostarica.com), at Playa Hermosa, just north of Malpaís in southwest Nicoya. Shaka's staff is trained to work with individuals with a range of challenges, from autism and amputations to muscular dystrophy. Surf camps are offered free of charge to selected nonprofit organizations, such as **Wheels for Humanity** (www.ucpwfh.org) and the **Association of Amputee Surfers** (www. ampsurf.org).

TRAVELING WITH CHILDREN

Generally, travel in Costa Rica with children poses no special problems, and virtually everything you'll need for children is readily available. Ensure that your child has vaccinations against measles and rubella (German measles), as well as any other inoculations your doctor advises. Bring cotton swabs, adhesive bandages, and a small first-aid kit with any necessary medicines for your child. The **Hospital Nacional de Niños** (Children's Hospital, tel. 506/2523-3600, www.hnn.sa.cr) is at Paseo Colón, Calle 14, in San José.

Children under age two travel free on airlines; children ages 2-12 are offered discounts. Children are also charged half the adult rate at many hotels; others permit free stays when kids are sharing parents' rooms. Baby foods and milk are readily available. Disposable diapers, however, are expensive (consider bringing cloth diapers; they're better ecologically). If you plan on driving around, bring your child's car seat—they're not offered with rental cars.

Single parents traveling alone with children need a notarized letter of permission from the other parent; otherwise you may not be allowed onto your departing flight.

Rascals in Paradise (U.S. tel. 415-273-2224, www.rascalsinparadise.com), **Wildland Adventures** (U.S. tel. 206-365-0686 or 800-345-4453, www.wildland.com), and **Country Walkers** (U.S. tel. 800-234-6900, www. countrywalkers.com) offer family trips to Costa Rica.

WOMEN TRAVELING ALONE

The majority of Tico men treat foreign women with great respect. Still, Costa Rica is a *machismo* society, and the art of gentle seduction is to Ticos a kind of sport and a trial of manhood. Men might hiss in appreciation from a distance like serpents, and call out epithets such as *"guapa"* ("pretty one"), *"machita"* (for blonds), or *"mi amor."* Be aware that many Ticos think a gringa is an "easy" *conquista.* The wolf-whistles can grate, but sexual assault of female tourists is rare—though it does happen.

Take effusions of love with a grain of salt;

while swearing eternal devotion, your Don Juan may conveniently forget to mention he's married. And when he suggests a nightcap at some romantic locale, he may mean a love motel. On the Caribbean coast, "Rent-a-Rastas" earn their living giving pleasure to women looking for love beneath the palms. Come prepared: Carry condoms; don't rely on the man.

If you're not interested in love in the tropics, unwanted attention can be a hassle. Pretend not to notice. Avoid eye contact. An insistent stare—*dando cuervo* (making eyes)—is part of their game. You can help prevent these overtures by dressing modestly. There have been reports of a few taxi drivers coming on to women passengers. Though this is the exception, where possible take a hotel taxi rather than a street cab. And beware of illegal unmarked "taxis" that may be cruising for single women. Avoid deserted beaches, especially at night.

Women Travel: Adventures, Advice, and Experience, by Niktania Jansz and Miranda Davies, offers practical advice for women travelers, as does *Gutsy Women,* by Marybeth Bond.

In Costa Rica, **CEFEMINA** (Centro Feminista de Información y Acción, tel. 506/2224-3986, www.cefemina.com), the **Women's Club of Costa Rica** (tel. 506/2282-6801, www.wccr.org) and the **Instituto Nacional de Las Mujeres** (National Institute of Women, tel. 506/2255-1368, www.inamu.go.cr) are good resources.

SENIOR TRAVELERS

Useful resources include **AARP** (U.S. tel. 888-687-2277, www.aarp.org), whose benefits include discounts on airfares, hotels, car rentals, etc., plus group tours for seniors.

ElderTreks (U.S. tel. 416-588-5000 or 800-741-7956, www.eldertreks.com) and **Elderhostel** (U.S. tel. 800-454-5768, www.roadscholar.org) offer tours to Costa Rica for seniors.

Thinking of retiring in Costa Rica? I recommend the Live or Retire in Paradise Tour offered by Christopher Howard (tel. 506/8849-0081 or 800-365-2342, www.liveincostarica.com), author of *The New Golden Door to Retirement and Living in Costa Rica,* and *Living Abroad in Costa Rica* (www.moon.com) by Erin Van Rheenen. The **Association of Residents of Costa Rica** (tel. 506/2233-8068, www.arcr.net) serves the interests of foreign residents as well as those considering living in Costa Rica.

GAY AND LESBIAN TRAVELERS

On the books, Costa Rica is tolerant of homosexuality and has laws to protect gays from discrimination; despite being a Roman Catholic nation, homosexual sex is legal. There is general tolerance among educated urbanites, but Costa Rica remains a *machismo* society, and in recent years has witnessed violent antigay demonstrations. There is less tolerance of lesbians.

Useful resources include the **International Gay and Lesbian Association** (U.S. tel. 212-620-7310, www.gaycenter.org); **Costa Rica Gay Map** (www.costaricagaymap.com); and the **International Gay & Lesbian Travel Association** (U.S. tel. 954-630-1637, www.iglta.org). *Gente 10* (www.gente10.com) is a gay magazine published in Costa Rica.

Colours Destinations (U.S. tel. 954-241-7472 or 866-517-4390, www.gaytravelcostarica.com) offers tours to Costa Rica. *Odysseus: The International Gay Travel Planner* lists worldwide hotels and tours and publishes travel guides for gays and lesbians. In Costa Rica, try **Gay Travel Costa Rica** (tel. 506/2241-3220, www.costaricagaytraveler.com); **Costa Rica Gay Vacation** (www.costaricagayvacation.com); and **Gaytours Costa Rica** (tel. 506/8305-8044, www.gaytourscr.com).

Health and Safety

Sanitary standards in Costa Rica are high, and the chances of succumbing to a serious disease are rare. As long as you take appropriate precautions and use common sense, you're not likely to incur serious illness. If you do, you have the benefit of knowing that the nation has a good health-care system. There are English-speaking doctors in most cities.

BEFORE YOU GO

Dental and medical checkups may be advisable before departing home, particularly if you have an existing medical problem. Take along any medications, including prescriptions for glasses and contact lenses; keep prescription drugs in their original bottles to avoid suspicion at customs. If you suffer from a debilitating health problem, wear a medical alert bracelet. A basic health kit is a good idea. Pack the following (as a minimum) in a small plastic container: alcohol swabs and medicinal alcohol, antiseptic cream, adhesive bandages, aspirin or painkillers, diarrhea medication, sunburn remedy, antifungal foot powder, calamine, antihistamine, water-purification tablets, surgical tape, bandages and gauze, and scissors.

The U.S. **Centers for Disease Control and Prevention** (U.S. tel. 800-232-4636, www.cdc.gov) issues the latest health information and advisories by region. Information on health concerns can be answered by the **U.S. Department of State's Citizens Emergency Center** (U.S. tel. 202-501-4444 or 888-407-4747, http://travel.state.gov) and the **International Association for Medical Assistance to Travelers** (IAMAT, U.S. tel. 716-754-4883, www.iamat.org). In the United Kingdom, you can get information, inoculations, and medical supplies from the **MASTA Travel Clinics** (www.masta-travel-health.com).

Medical Insurance

Travel insurance is strongly recommended.

Travel agencies can sell you travelers health and baggage insurance as well as insurance against cancellation of a prepaid tour. Travelers should check to see if their health insurance or other policies cover medical expenses while abroad. The following U.S. companies are recommended for travel insurance: **Travelers** (U.S. tel. 888-695-4625, www.travelers.com) and **TravelGuard International** (U.S. tel. 800-826-4919, www.travelguard.com). The **Council on International Education Exchange** (www.ciee.org) offers insurance to students.

In the United Kingdom, the **Association of British Insurers** (UK tel. 44/20-7600-3333, www.abi.org.uk) provides advice for obtaining travel insurance. Inexpensive insurance is offered through **Endsleigh Insurance** (UK tel. 800-028-3571, www.endsleigh.co.uk).

Costa Rica's social security system, the **Instituto Nacional de Seguros** (INS, tel. 506/2287-6000, www.ins.go.cr), has a comprehensive travel insurance program for foreigners. You can choose coverage between $1,000 and $20,000 for up to 12 weeks. You can buy coverage at travel agencies or the INS.

Vaccinations

Epidemic diseases have mostly been eradicated throughout the country. Consult your physician for recommended vaccinations. Travelers planning to rough it should consider vaccinations against tetanus, typhoid, and infectious hepatitis.

MEDICAL SERVICES

In **emergencies,** call 911. Alternately, call 128 for the Red Cross, which provides ambulance service nationwide.

The state-run social security system (INS) operates full-service hospitals and clinics nationwide. Foreigners receive the same emergency service as Costa Ricans in public hospitals, and no one is turned away in an emergency (however, a $39 fee applies; a typical overnight with care costs about $350). Private hospitals offer faster and superior treatment to public hospitals (a large deposit may be requested on admittance). Private doctor visits usually cost $25-50. Hospitals and clinics accept payment by credit card. U.S. insurance is not normally accepted, but you can send your bill to your insurance company for reimbursement. Every community has at least one pharmacy (*farmacia* or *botica*).

Medical Evacuation

Traveler's Emergency Network (U.S. tel. 800-275-4836, www.tenweb.com) and **International SOS Assistance** (U.S. tel. 713-521-7611 or 800-523-8930, www.internationalsos.com) provide worldwide ground and air evacuation and medical assistance, plus access to medical facilities around the world.

Many medical and travel insurance companies also provide emergency evacuation coverage.

HEALTH PROBLEMS

Even the slightest scratch can fester quickly in the tropics. Treat cuts promptly and regularly with antiseptic and keep the wound clean.

Diseases

Malaria is a limited risk in the lowlands only, especially the Caribbean lowlands south of Cahuita. Consult your physician for the best type of antimalarial medication. Begin taking your tablets a few days (or weeks, depending on the prescription) before arriving in an infected zone, and continue taking the tablets for several weeks after leaving the malarial zone. Malaria symptoms include high fever, shivering, headache, and sometimes diarrhea.

The best mosquito repellents contain DEET (diethylmetatoluamide). Avon's Skin-So-Soft oil is such an effective bug repellent that U.S. Marines use it by the truckload. Use mosquito netting at night in the lowlands. A fan and mosquito coils (*espirales*) also help keep mosquitoes at bay. Coils are available from *pulperías* and supermarkets (don't forget the metal stand—*soporte*—for them).

Outbreaks of **dengue fever** have occurred in recent years, notably around Puntarenas, the Caribbean coast, and the Golfito region. Transmitted by mosquitoes, the illness can be fatal; death usually results from internal hemorrhaging. Its symptoms are similar to malaria, with additional severe pain in the joints and bones (it is sometimes called "breaking bones disease"). Unlike malaria, dengue is not recurring.

Rabies, though rare, can be contracted through the bite of an infected dog or other animal. It is always fatal unless treated.

Hepatitis is epidemic throughout Central America, although only infrequently reported in Costa Rica. Main symptoms are stomach pains, loss of appetite, yellowing skin and eyes, and extreme tiredness. Hepatitis A is contracted through unhygienic foods or contaminated water; salads and unpeeled fruits are major culprits. A gamma globulin vaccination is recommended. The much rarer hepatitis B is usually contracted through unclean needles, blood transfusions, or unprotected sex.

Insects and Arachnids

Spiders, scorpions, no-see-ums—it's enough to give you the willies! Check your bedding before crawling into your bed, which you should move away from the wall if possible. Always shake out your shoes and clothing before putting them on. Repellent sprays and lotions are a must, especially in the rainforest, marshy areas, and coastal lowlands. Bites can easily become infected in the tropics, so avoid scratching. A baking-soda bath can help relieve itching if you're badly bitten, as can antihistamine tablets, hydrocortisone, and calamine lotion.

Chiggers (*coloradillas*) inhabit grasslands, particularly in Guanacaste. Their bites itch like hell. Mosquito repellent won't deter them. Nail polish apparently works on the bites by suffocating the beasts. **Ticks** (*garrapatas*) hang out near livestock. They bury their heads into your skin. Remove them with tweezers—grasp the tick's head parts as close to your skin as possible and pull gently but steadily. Wear long pants and your socks in your shoes when hiking in grassland.

Tiny, irritating **no-see-ums** (sandflies about the size of a pinpoint, known locally as *purrujas*) inhabit many beaches and marshy coastal areas; avoid beaches around dusk. They're not fazed by bug repellent with DEET, but Avon's Skin-So-Soft works great. Sandflies on the Atlantic coast can pass on leishmaniasis, a debilitating disease; seek urgent treatment for nonhealing sores.

Avoid **bees'** nests. Africanized bees have infiltrated Costa Rica, and they're very aggressive and will attack with little provocation.

Many bugs are local. The bite of a rare kind of insect found along the southern Caribbean coast and locally called **papalamoya** produces a deep and horrible infection that can even threaten a limb. It may be best to have such infections treated locally, and certainly promptly; doctors back home or even in San José might take forever to diagnose and treat the condition.

Intestinal Problems

Water is safe to drink almost everywhere. To play it safe, however, drink bottled mineral water (*agua mineral* or *soda*). Remember, ice cubes are water too, and don't brush your teeth using suspicious water.

Food hygiene standards in Costa Rica are generally high. However, the change in diet may cause temporary **diarrhea** or **constipation.** Most cases of diarrhea are caused by microbial gut infections resulting from contaminated food. Don't eat uncooked fish or shellfish, uncooked vegetables, unwashed salads, or unpeeled fruit. Diarrhea is usually temporary, and many doctors recommend letting it run its course. Otherwise use Lomotil (cophenotrope), and drink lots of liquid to replace the water and salts lost. Avoid alcohol and dairy products. If conditions persist, seek medical help.

Diarrhea accompanied by severe abdominal pain, blood in your stool, and fever is a sign of **dysentery.** Seek immediate medical diagnosis. Tetracycline or ampicillin is normally used to cure bacillary dysentery. More complex professional treatment is required for amoebic dysentery. The symptoms of both are similar. **Giardiasis,** acquired from infected water, causes diarrhea, bloating, persistent indigestion, and weight loss. Again, seek medical advice. **Intestinal worms** can be contracted by walking barefoot on infested beaches, grass, or earth.

Snakebite

Snakes are common in Costa Rica. Fewer than 500 snakebites are reported each year, and less than 3 percent of these are fatal. Always watch where you're walking or putting your hands; many snakes are arboreal. Never reach into holes or under rocks, debris, or forest-floor leaf litter without first checking to see what might be slumbering there. Be wary in long grass. Avoid streams at night. If you spot a snake, keep a safe distance, and give the highly aggressive fer-de-lance a very wide berth.

If bitten, seek medical attention without delay. Rural health posts and most national park rangers have antivenin kits. Commercial snakebite kits are normally good only for the specific species for which they were designed, so it will help if you can definitively identify the critter. But don't endanger yourself further trying to catch it.

If the bite is to a limb, immobilize the limb and apply a tight bandage between the bite and the body. Release it for 90 seconds every 15 minutes. Ensure you can slide a finger under the bandage; too tight and you risk further damage. Do not cut the bite area in an attempt to suck out the poison. Recommendations to use electric shock as snakebite treatment have been discredited.

Sunburn and Skin Problems

Don't underestimate the tropical sun! It is intense and can burn you through light clothing or while you're lying in the shade. Use a sunscreen or sunblock—at least SPF 15 or higher.

Zinc oxide provides almost 100 percent protection. Use an aloe gel after sunbathing. Calamine lotion and aloe gel will soothe light burns; for more serious lobster-pink burns, use steroid creams.

Sun glare—especially prevalent if you're on water—can cause **conjunctivitis** (eye infection). Sunglasses will protect against this. **Prickly heat** is an itchy rash, normally caused by clothing that is too tight or in need of washing. This, and **athlete's foot,** are best treated by airing out the body and washing your clothes.

Drink plenty of water to avoid dehydration. Leg cramps, exhaustion, and headaches are possible signs of dehydration.

SAFETY CONCERNS

Costa Rica's many charms can lull visitors into a false sense of security. However, burglary is rampant and crimes against tourists have risen alarmingly, including armed carjackings, home invasions, gang muggings, "express kidnappings" (individuals are abducted and forced to withdraw funds from ATMs), spiked drinks in bars, and thieves who slash car tires and then assist in repair while an accomplice steals items from the vehicle.

Passport theft is also a serious problem. Car break-ins have become pandemic along the Nicoya shoreline, particularly at the most popular surf beaches. And armed robberies of tour buses have occurred in recent years, particularly in the Northern Lowlands. One-third of thefts reported by tourists occurred on public transportation.

Most crime is opportunistic, and thieves seek easy targets. Don't ride buses at night, be careful in parks, and watch for traffic at all times. Outside the city, be savvy of some basic precautions. Hikers straying off trails can easily lose their way. Atop mountains, sunny weather can turn cold and rainy in seconds, so dress accordingly. Be extra cautious when crossing rivers; a rainstorm upstream can turn the river downstream into a raging torrent without warning.

Precautions

The Instituto Costarricense de Turismo publishes a leaflet—"Let's Travel Safe"—listing precautions and a selection of emergency phone numbers. It's given out free at airport immigration counters. The ICT operates a 24-hour toll-free tourist information line (tel. 800-012-3456) for emergencies.

A few common-sense precautions are in order. Make photocopies of all important documents. Carry these with you and leave the originals in the hotel safe if possible. If this isn't possible, carry the originals with you in a secure inside pocket. Don't put all your eggs in one basket! Prepare an "emergency kit" to include photocopies of your documents and an adequate sum of money in case your wallet gets stolen. If you're robbed, immediately file a police report. You'll need this to make an insurance claim.

Don't wear jewelry, chains, or expensive watches. Never carry more cash than you need for the day. The rest should be kept in the hotel safe. For credit card security, insist that imprints are made in your presence. Make sure any incorrectly completed imprints are torn up. Destroy the carbons yourself. Don't let store merchants or anyone else walk off with your card. Keep it in sight!

Never leave your purse, camera, or luggage unattended in public places. Always keep a wary eye on your luggage, and never carry your wallet in your back pocket. Carry bills in your front pocket beneath a handkerchief. Carry any other money in a money belt, inside pocket, a "secret" pocket sewn into your pants or jacket, or in a body pouch or an elastic wallet below the knee. Spread your money around your person.

Don't carry more luggage than you can adequately manage. Limit your baggage to one suitcase or duffel. Have a lock for each luggage item. Purses should have a short strap (ideally, one with metal woven in) that fits tightly against the body and snaps closed or has a zipper. Always keep purses fully zipped and luggage locked.

Don't trust locals to handle your money,

Prostitution

Prostitution is legal in Costa Rica, drawing male tourists whose presence has earned Costa Rica a controversial reputation. Many Costa Rican men use prostitutes as a matter of course, and almost every town and village has a brothel—San José has dozens. The government issues licenses for brothels and prostitutes. Statistics suggest that most of the estimated 15,000 prostitutes who work nationwide are not registered. Many fall into the profession after a childhood of trauma and sexual abuse—a widespread problem within Costa Rican society.

Sex is legal at the age of 16 in Costa Rica but prostitution under age 18 is not, and under Costa Rican and international law, foreigners can be prosecuted for having sex with anyone under 18 (estimates suggest that as many as 3,000 prostitutes nationwide may be underage).

The Costa Rican government has launched a major campaign to eradicate child prostitution and to prosecute foreigners having sexual relations with minors. The **Patronato Nacional de la Infancia** (tel. 506/2523-0700, www.pani.go.cr) is a government-sponsored organization to fight sexual exploitation of children. **Fundación Paniamor** (tel. 506/2234-2993, www.paniamor. org) is a tourism-community organization that works to eradicate sex with minors.

Casa Luz (tel. 506/2255-3322, in the U.S. c/o Samaritan's Purse, U.S. tel. 800-665-2843, www. casaluz.org) is a home for young mothers who have been physically or sexually abused and are at high risk. By providing shelter, emotional support, educational and vocational development, parental skills, and spiritual counseling, the goal is for the young mothers and their children to be able to live socially healthy lives. It is run by a nonprofit association operated by the owners of the Hotel Grano de Oro, San José. Donations are welcome.

If you know of anyone who is traveling to Costa Rica with the intent of sexually abusing minors, contact **Interpol** (children@interpol.int, www.interpol.int); the **Task Force for the Protection of Children from Sexual Exploitation in Tourism** (www.world-tourism. org); or the **U.S. Customs's International Child Pornography Investigation and Coordination Center** (U.S. tel. 800-843-5678, www.cybertipline.com).

and don't exchange money before receiving the services or goods you're paying for. Be particularly wary after getting money at a bank. And be cautious at night, particularly if you intend to walk on beaches or park trails, which you should do with someone trusted wherever possible. Stick to well-lit main streets in towns.

Don't leave anything of value within reach of an open window. Make sure you have bars on the window and that your room is otherwise secure (bringing your own lock for the door is a good idea). Don't leave anything of value in your car, nor leave tents or cars unguarded. Be especially cautious if you have a flat tire, as many robberies involve unsuspecting travelers who are robbed while changing a tire by the roadside. The ICT advises driving to the nearest gas station or other secure site to change the tire. And never permit a Costa Rican male to sit in the back seat of a taxi while you're in the front; there have been several reports of robberies in taxis in which the driver has worked in cahoots with an accomplice, who strangles the victim from behind.

Never allow yourself to be drawn into arguments (Costa Ricans are usually so placid that anyone with a temper is immediately to be suspected). And don't be distracted by people spilling things on you. These are ruses meant to distract you while an accomplice steals your valuables. Remain alert to the dark side of self-proclaimed good Samaritans.

If Things Go Wrong

In an emergency, call 911 for an English-speaking operator for fire, police, or ambulance, or contact one of the following:

· **Tourist police:** tel. 506/2286-1473
· **Fire:** tel. 118

- **Red Cross ambulance:** tel. 128 or 506/2233-7033

If things go wrong, contact the **Victims Assistance Office** (in the OIJ Bldg., Aves. 4/6, Calles 15/17, San José, tel. 506/2295-3271 or 506/2295-3643, 7:30am-noon and 1pm-4pm Mon.-Fri.). You might also contact your embassy or consulate. The *Handbook of Consular Services* (Public Affairs Staff, Bureau of Consular Affairs, U.S. Department of State, Washington, DC 20520) provides details of such assistance. Friends and family can also call the Department of State's **Overseas Citizen Service** (U.S. tel. 888-407-4747, outside U.S. tel. 202-501-4444, www.travel. state.gov) to check on you if things go awry. The **U.S. State Department** (www.state. gov) also publishes travel advisories warning U.S. citizens of trouble spots. The **British Foreign and Commonwealth Office** (UK tel. 20-7008-1500, www.fco.gov.uk) has a similar service.

To report issues relating to drugs, contact the **Policía de Control de Drogas** (tel. 800-376-4266, www.msp.go.cr). Report theft or demands for money by traffic police to the **Ministerio de Obras Públicas y Transportes** (Ministry of Public Works and Transportation, Calle 9, Aves. 20/22, tel. 506/2227-2188 or 506/2523-2000). For other complaints about the police, contact the **Office for the Reception of Complaints** (tel. 506/2295-3643, 24 hours daily).

Riptides

Riptides (channels of water pulling out to sea at high speed) cause the deaths by drowning of dozens of people every year in Costa Rica. Tides change from extremely low to extremely high, and the volume of water pouring onto or off the beach can be immense. The period two hours before and two hours after low tide are the most dangerous. Riptides are often identifiable by their still surface where surf is otherwise coming ashore. If you get caught in one, swim parallel to the shore; if you try to swim directly back to shore, you will be unsuccessful, and you'll tire yourself out and possibly drown.

police station, Tortuguero

Information and Services

MONEY

Costa Rica's currency is the **colón** (plural colones), which is written "¢" and sometimes colloquially called "peso." Notes come in the following denominations: 1,000, 2,000, 5,000, 10,000, and 50,000 colones; coins come in 5, 10, 25, 50, 100, and 500 colones. You may hear cash referred to colloquially as *efectivo* or *plata*. *Menudo* is loose change.

Most businesses accept payment in **U.S. dollars,** as do taxis. Other international currencies are generally not accepted. Many shopkeepers won't accept notes that are torn, however minute the tear, but will dispense such notes to you without guilt.

At press time the official **exchange rate** had stabilized at approximately 534 colones to the dollar. All prices in this book are quoted in U.S. dollars unless otherwise indicated.

Changing Money

You can change money at the two international airports upon arrival. Legally, money may be changed only at a bank or hotel cash desk. Banks are normally open 9am-4pm Monday-Saturday, but hours vary. Foreign-exchange departments are often open longer. Don't expect fast service. At some banks you may have to stand in two lines: one to process the transaction, the other to receive your cash. Ask to make sure you're in the correct line. Most hotels will exchange dollars for colones for guests; some will do so even for nonguests.

Many hustlers offer money exchange on the street, although this is strictly illegal and dangerous—the Judicial Police receive between 10 and 15 complaints a day from tourists who've been ripped off while changing money on the street.

Credit and Debit Cards

Most larger hotels, car rental companies, and travel suppliers, as well as larger restaurants and stores, will accept payment by credit card.

A service charge may be added. You can also use your credit cards to get cash advances at banks (minimum $50); some banks will pay cash advances in colones only. Most banks accept **Visa;** very few accept **MasterCard.** You can reach the major credit card companies from within Costa Rica by calling the following numbers: **American Express** (tel. 800-012-3211), **MasterCard** (tel. 800-011-0184), **Visa International** (tel. 800-011-0030). The **Credomatic office** (Calle Central, Aves. 3/5, tel. 506/2295-9898, www.credomatic.com, 8am-7pm Mon.-Fri., 9am-1pm Sat.) is authorized to assist with American Express, Visa, and MasterCard replacement.

At least one bank in every major town now has a 24-hour **ATM** (*cajero automático*) for credit and debit card withdrawals. You'll need your PIN number. Stick to regular banking hours if possible in case of problems (such as the *cajero* not returning your card). Always use a well-lit ATM in a secure location.

Tipping

Taxi drivers do not normally receive tips. Nor is tipping in **restaurants** the norm—restaurants automatically add both a 13 percent sales tax and a 10 percent service charge to your bill. Add an additional tip as a reward for exceptional service. **Bellboys** in classy hotels should receive $0.50-1 per bag, and **chambermaids** should get $1 per day. **Tour guides** normally are tipped $1-2 pp per day for large groups, and much more, at your discretion, for small, personalized tours. Again, don't tip if you had lousy service.

COMMUNICATIONS AND MEDIA

Telephones

Local phone calls within Costa Rica are extremely cheap. Calls from your hotel room are considerably more expensive (and the more expensive the hotel, the more they jack up the fee). There are no area or city codes; simply dial the eight-digit number.

The Costa Rica country code is 506. When calling Costa Rica from North America, dial 011 (the international dialing code), then 506, followed by the eight-digit local number. For outbound calls from Costa Rica, dial 00, then the country code and local number. For an English-speaking international operator, dial 116, also used to make collect calls (reversing the charges) or to charge to a credit card.

Public phone booths are found throughout the nation. In more remote spots, the public phone is usually at the village *pulpería,* or store. Most public phone booths use phone cards, in which the cost of your call is automatically deducted from the value of the card. Buy them at ICE phone agencies, banks, calling card vending machines, and stores—look for the Kölbi *tarjetas telefónicas* sign; cards are sold in various denominations from $1 to $20. Follow the instructions on the card.

CELL PHONES

Four companies compete for cell phone service in Costa Rica. ICE's Kölbi (www.kolbi.cr) has the largest coverage. TuYo Movil (www.tuyomovil.com) also uses the Kölbi network. Claro (www.claro.cr) and Movistar (www.movistar.cr) have less extensive coverage.

You can buy a SIM card in Costa Rica from any of the above carriers, but you will need to ensure that your phone is unlocked to be able to use it; most U.S. cellphones are locked to a specific carrier, such as Verizon. Cell Phones Costa Rica (tel. 506/2293-5892, www.cellphonescr.com) offers cellular phone rentals.

Publications

Costa Rica has three major dailies. *La Nación* (www.nacion.co.cr) is an excellent newspaper, up to international standards, with broad-based coverage of national and international affairs. *La República* and *La Prensa Libre* are lesser alternatives. *El Día* and the mass-market *Diario Extra* are sensationalist rags with reports on sex, mayhem, and gore.

Available online only, the English-language *Tico Times* (www.ticotimes.net) diligently covers environmental issues, tourism, and cultural events. *Costa Rica Traveler* (www.crtraveler.com) is a glossy bimonthly focused on tourism. The bimonthly *Costa Rica Outdoors* (www.costaricaoutdoors.com) is dedicated to fishing and outdoor sports.

MAPS AND VISITOR INFORMATION
Visitor Information Offices

The Instituto Costarricense de Turismo (ICT, Costa Rican Tourism Institute, www.visitcostarica.com) has a 24-hour toll-free visitor information line (U.S. tel. 800-343-6332) in the United States. The ICT head office (tel. 506/2299-5800) is on the north side of the General Cañas highway, in the La Uruca district of San José. It has regional offices, and also publishes excellent brochures for each of the national parks.

Maps

The best all-around map is the 1:350,000 scale *National Geographic Adventure Map,* published by the National Geographic Society. Another good road map is a topographical 1:500,000 sheet published by ITMB Publishing (U.S. tel. 604-273-1400, www.itmb.com). The Neotropic Foundation (tel. 506/2253-2130, www.neotropica.org) publishes a superb topographical map with nature reserves and parks emphasized. All are sold at gift stores throughout Costa Rica, as is the *Costa Rica Nature Atlas,* with detailed 1:200,000 scale maps and accounts of national parks and other sites.

WEIGHTS AND MEASURES

Costa Rica operates on the metric system. Liquids are sold in liters, fruits and vegetables by the kilogram. Some of the old Spanish measurements still survive in vernacular usage. Street directions, for example, are often given as 100 *varas* (the Spanish "yard," equal to 84 centimeters or 33 inches) to indicate a city block. See the chart at the back of this book for metric conversions.

Time

Costa Rica time is equivalent to U.S. Central Standard Time—six hours earlier than Greenwich mean time, one hour earlier than New York in winter, and two hours later than California in winter. Costa Rica has no daylight saving time; during those periods, it is two hours earlier than New York. There is little seasonal variation in dawn (approximately 6am) and dusk (6pm).

Business Hours

Businesses are usually open 8am-5pm Monday-Friday. A few also open Saturday morning. Lunch breaks are often two hours; businesses and government offices may close 11:30am-1:30pm. Bank hours vary widely, but in general are between 8:15am or 9am and 3pm or 3:45pm. Most shops open 8am-6pm Monday-Saturday. Some restaurants close Sunday and Monday. Most businesses also close on holidays.

Electricity

Costa Rica operates on 110 volts, 60 hertz AC nationwide. Some remote lodges are not connected to the national grid and generate their own power. Check in advance to see if they run on direct current (DC) or a nonstandard voltage. Two types of plugs are used, the same as in the United States: two flat parallel pins and three pins. It's a good idea to get a two-prong adapter; most hardware stores in Costa Rica—*ferreterías*—can supply them.

Resources

Glossary

abastacedor: small grocery

alacrán: scorpion

a la leña: oven-roasted

albergue: hostel

almuerzo ejecutivo: business lunch (set menu)

apartado: post office box (abbreviated "Apdo.")

apartotel: self-catering hotel with kitchen units

arribada: mass arrival of marine turtles

arroz con pollo: rice with chicken

autopista: expressway

avenida: avenue

balneario: swimming pool

barrio: district

batido: milk shake

beneficio: coffee-processing factory

biblioteca: library

boca: bar snack

bola: ball (refers to the large granite balls from Golfo Dulce)

boyero: oxcart driver

cabina: refers to any budget accommodations

cafetalero: coffee baron

calle: street

campesino: small-scale farmer or peasant

campo: countryside

canton: county

carreta: traditional oxcart

carretera: road

casado: set lunch (literally, "married")

casita: small house, cottage

cayuco: canoe

cerveza: beer

chorizo: corruption, bribery; a poor grade of bacon

circunvalación: ring road

cocodrilo: crocodile

colón: Costa Rican currency

comida típica: local food

cordillera: mountain chain

costeños: coastal people

danta: tapir

empanada: stuffed turnover

encomienda: feudal servitude

estero: estuary

farandula: bohemian in-crowd

fiesta: party

fiesta cívica: civic *fiesta*

finca: farm

gallo pinto: rice, beans, and fried egg

gasolinera: gas station

grano de oro: coffee bean

guaro: a cheap liquor

guayaba: guava

hacienda: large farmstead, cattle ranch

helado: ice cream

hornilla: geysers

hospedaje: lodging

invierno: "winter" (refers to summer wet season)

lancha: motorized boat, ferry

lapa roja: scarlet macaw

lapa verde: green macaw

lavandería: laundry

manglar: mangrove

manigordo: ocelot

manzanillo: manchineel tree

mapache: northern raccoon

marisquería: seafood restaurant or outlet

mercado: market
mirador: lookout point
mola: stitched appliqué fabric
mono carablanca: capuchin monkey
mono colorado: spider monkey
mono congo: howler monkey
mono titi: squirrel monkey
murciélago: bat
museo: museum
orero: gold-miner
palenque: thatched roof
palmito: heart of palm
panga: small motorized boat
parada: bus stop
páramo: high-altitude savanna
pastelería: bakery
pejibaye: bright-orange palm fruit
peña: an intellectual soirée where poems are read, music played, and bonhomie shared

pensionado: pensioner
perezoso: sloth
pila: mud pond
pizote: coatimundi
plato fuerte: main dish
playa: beach
pulpería: small grocery
purruja: no-see-um, tiny insect
ranchito: open-sided thatched structure
refresco: soda pop or fruit juice
sabanero: cowboy
selva: rainforest
soda: simple eatery, usually open to the street
tamandua: lesser anteater
tepezcuintle: a large rodent, also called a paca
terciopelo: fer-de-lance, a fearsome snake
Tica: female Costa Rican

Spanish Phrasebook

PRONUNCIATION GUIDE
Vowels

a as in "father," but shorter
e as in "hen"
i as in "machine"
o as in "phone"
u usually as in "rule"; when it follows a 'q' the 'u' is silent; when it follows an 'h' or 'g' it's pronounced like 'w,' except when it comes between 'g' and 'e' or 'i,' when it's also silent

Consonants

c as 'c' in "cat" before 'a,' 'o,' or 'u'; like 's' before 'e' or 'i'
d as 'd' in "dog," except between vowels, then like 'th' in "that"
g before 'e' or 'i' like the 'ch' in Scottish "loch"; elsewhere like 'g' in "get"
h always silent
j like the English 'h' in "hotel," but stronger
ll like the 'y' in "yellow"
ñ like the 'ni' in "onion"
r always pronounced as strong 'r'

rr trilled 'r'
v similar to the 'b' in "boy" (not as English 'v')
y similar to English, but with a slight "j" sound. When *y* stands alone it is pronounced like the 'e' in "me."
z like 's' in "same"
b, f, k, l, m, n, p, q, s, t, w, x, z as in English

NUMBERS

0 *cero*
1 *uno* (masculine), *una* (feminine)
2 *dos*
3 *tres*
4 *cuatro*
5 *cinco*
6 *seis*
7 *siete*
8 *ocho*
9 *nueve*
10 *diez*
11 *once*
12 *doce*
13 *trece*
14 *catorce*

15 *quince*
16 *dieciseis*
17 *diecisiete*
18 *dieciocho*
19 *diecinueve*
20 *veinte*
21 *vientiuno*
30 *treinta*
40 *cuarenta*
50 *cincuenta*
60 *sesenta*
70 *setenta*
80 *ochenta*
90 *noventa*
100 *cien*
101 *cientouno*
200 *doscientos*
1,000 *mil*
10,000 *diez mil*

DAYS OF THE WEEK

Sunday *domingo*
Monday *lunes*
Tuesday *martes*
Wednesday *miércoles*
Thursday *jueves*
Friday *viernes*
Saturday *sábado*

TIME

What time is it? *¿Qué hora es?*
one o'clock *la una*
two o'clock *las dos*
at two o'clock *a las dos*
ten past three *las tres y diez*
6am *las seis de la mañana*
6pm *las seis de la tarde*
today *hoy*
tomorrow, morning *mañana, la mañana*
yesterday *ayer*
week *semana*
month *mes*
year *año*
last night *la noche pasada* or *anoche*
next day *el próximo día* or *al día siguiente*

USEFUL WORDS AND PHRASES

Hello. *Hola.*
Good morning. *Buenos días.*
Good afternoon. *Buenas tardes.*
Good evening. *Buenas noches.*
How are you? *¿Cómo está?*
Fine. *Muy bien.*
And you? *¿Y usted?* (formal) or *¿Y tú?* (familiar)
So-so. *Así así.*
Thank you. *Gracias.*
Thank you very much. *Muchas gracias.*
You're very kind. *Usted es muy amable.*
You're welcome *De nada.* (literally, "It's nothing.")
yes *sí*
no *no*
I don't know. *No sé* or *no lo sé*
It's fine; OK *Está bien.*
good; OK *bueno*
please *por favor*
Pleased to meet you. *Mucho gusto.*
Excuse me. (physical) *perdóneme*
Excuse me. (speech) *discúlpeme*
I'm sorry. *Lo siento.*
Good-bye. *Adiós.*
See you later *hasta luego* (literally, "until later")
more *más*
less *menos*
better *mejor*
much *mucho*
a little *un poco*
large *grande*
small *pequeño*
quick *rápido*
slowly *despacio*
bad *malo*
difficult *difícil*
easy *fácil*
He/She/It is gone, as in "She left," "He's gone" *Ya se fue.*
I don't speak Spanish well. *No hablo bien español.*
I don't understand. *No entiendo.*

How do you say ... in Spanish? *¿Cómo se dice ... en español?*

Do you understand English? *¿Entiende el inglés?*

Is English spoken here? (Does anyone here speak English?) *¿Se habla inglés aquí?*

TERMS OF ADDRESS

I *yo*
you (formal) *usted*
you (familiar) *tú*
he/him *él*
she/her *ella*
we/us *nosotros*
you (plural) *ustedes*
they/them (all males or mixed gender) *ellos*
they/them (all females) *ellas*
Mr., sir *señor*
Mrs., madam *señora*
Miss, young woman *señorita*
wife *esposa*
husband *marido* or *esposo*
friend *amigo* (male), *amiga* (female)
sweetheart *novio* (male), *novia* (female)
son, daughter *hijo, hija*
brother, sister *hermano, hermana*
father, mother *padre, madre*

GETTING AROUND

Where is ...? *¿Dónde está ...?*
How far is it to ...? *¿Qué tan lejos está a ...?*
from ... to ... *de ... a ...*
highway *la carretera*
road *el camino*
street *la calle*
block *la cuadra*
kilometer *kilómetro*
north *el norte*
south *el sur*
west *el oeste*
east *el este*
straight ahead *al derecho* or *adelante*
to the right *a la derecha*
to the left *a la izquierda*

ACCOMMODATIONS

Can I (we) see a room? *¿Puedo (podemos) ver una habitación?*
What is the rate? *¿Cuál es el precio?*
a single room *una habitación sencilla*
a double room *una habitación doble*
key *llave*
bathroom *retrete* or *lavabo*
bath *baño*
hot water *agua caliente*
cold water *agua fría*
towel *toalla*
soap *jabón*
toilet paper *papel sanitario*
air conditioning *aire acondicionado*
fan *abanico, ventilador*
blanket *cubierta* or *manta*

PUBLIC TRANSPORTATION

bus stop *la parada de la guagua*
main bus terminal *la central camionera*
airport *el aeropuerto*
ferry terminal *la terminal del transbordador*
I want a ticket to ... *Quiero un tique a ...*
I want to get off at ... *Quiero bajar en ...*
Here, please. *Aquí, por favor.*
Where is this bus going? *¿Dónde va este guagua?*
round-trip *ida y vuelta*
What do I owe? *¿Cuánto le debo?*

FOOD

menu *carta, menú*
glass *taza*
fork *tenedor*
knife *cuchillo*
spoon *cuchara, cucharita*
napkin *servilleta*
soft drink *refresco*
coffee, cream *café, crema*
tea *té*
sugar *azúcar*
drinking water *agua pura, agua potable*
bottled carbonated water *club soda*
bottled uncarbonated water *agua sin gas*
beer *cerveza*
wine *vino*

milk *leche*
juice *jugo*
eggs *huevos*
bread *pan*
watermelon *patilla*
banana *plátano*
apple *manzana*
orange *naranja*
meat (without) *carne (sin)*
beef *carne de res*
chicken *pollo*
fish *pescado*
shellfish *camarones, mariscos*
fried *frito*
roasted *asado*
barbecue, barbecued *barbacoa, al carbón,* or *a la parrilla*
breakfast *desayuno*
lunch *almuerzo*
dinner (often eaten in late afternoon) *comida*
dinner, or a late-night snack *cena*
the check *la cuenta*

MAKING PURCHASES

I need ... *Necesito ...*

I want ... *Deseo ...* or *Quiero ...*
I would like ... (more polite) *Quisiera ...*
How much does it cost? *¿Cuánto cuesta?*
What's the exchange rate? *¿Cuál es el tipo de cambio?*
Can I see ...? *¿Puedo ver ...?*
this one *ésta/ésto*
expensive *caro*
cheap *barato*
cheaper *más barato*
too much *demasiado*

HEALTH

Help me, please. *Ayúdeme por favor.*
I am ill. *Estoy enfermo.*
pain *dolor*
fever *fiebre*
stomachache *dolor de estómago*
vomiting *vomitar*
diarrhea *diarrea*
drugstore *farmacia*
medicine *medicina*
pill, tablet *pastilla*
birth-control pills *pastillas anticonceptivas*
condoms *condones, gomas*

Suggested Reading

GENERAL

Baker, Christopher P. *Enchanting Costa Rica.* Oxford, UK: John Beaufoy, 2015. This coffee-table book spans the entire country, highlighting the best of all aspects and regions.

Koutnik, Jane. *Costa Rica: A Quick Guide to Customs and Etiquette.* Portland, OR: Graphic Arts Books, 2005. Concise yet detailed insight into the local culture.

Ras, Barbara, ed. *Costa Rica: A Traveler's Literary Companion.* San Francisco: Whereabouts Press, 1994. Twenty-six stories by Costa Rican writers that reflect the ethos of the country.

HISTORY, POLITICS, AND SOCIAL STRUCTURE

Biesanz, Richard, et al. *The Ticos: Culture and Social Change in Costa Rica.* Boulder, CO: Lynne Reinner, 1999. This essential work for understanding Tico culture is an updated version of its popular forerunner, *The Costa Ricans.*

Daling, Tjabel. *Costa Rica in Focus: A Guide to the People, Politics, and Culture.* Northampton, MA: Interlink, 2001. A general and insightful review of national culture.

Molina Jiménez, Ivan, and Steven Palmer, eds. *The Costa Rica Reader: History, Culture, Politics.* Durham, NC: Duke University Press, 2004. Essential background reading and the most thoughtful and readable academic account of the nation.

LIVING IN COSTA RICA

Howard, Christopher. *The New Golden Door to Retirement and Living in Costa Rica,* 17th ed. San José: C.R. Books, 2014. A splendid comprehensive guide to making the break.

Van Rheenen, Erin. *Moon Living Abroad in Costa Rica.* Berkeley, CA: Avalon Travel Publishing, 2013. The definitive guide to living in Costa Rica also includes highly useful information for travelers passing through.

NATURE AND WILDLIFE

Allen, William. *Green Phoenix: Restoring the Tropical Forests of Guanacaste.* Oxford, UK: Oxford University Press, 2006. A wonderful read, this powerfully engaging book tells the story of the remarkable and successful efforts to resurrecting Costa Rica's ravaged dry forests.

Beletsky, Les. *The Ecotravellers' Wildlife Guide to Costa Rica.* San Diego: Academia Press, 2002. A superbly illustrated volume for nature lovers.

Boza, Mario, and A. Bonilla. *The National Parks of Costa Rica.* Madrid: INCAFO, 1999. Available in both hardbound coffee-table and less-bulky softbound versions, as well as in a handy pocket-size edition. Lots of superb photos. Highly readable.

Carr, Archie F. *The Windward Road.* Gainesville, FL: University of Florida Press, 1955. A sympathetic book about the sea turtles of Central America.

DeVries, Philip J. *The Butterflies of Costa Rica and Their Natural History.* Princeton, NJ: Princeton University Press, 1987. A well-illustrated and thorough lepidopterist's guide.

Emmons, Louise H. *Neotropical Rainforest Mammals—A Field Guide.* Chicago: University of Chicago Press, 1997. A thorough yet compact book detailing mammal species throughout the neotropical region.

Fogden, Michael, and Patricia Fogden. *Hummingbirds of Costa Rica.* Richmond Hill, Canada: Firefly Books, 2006. Lavishly illustrated coffee-table book.

Fogden, Michael, and Susan Fogden. *Photographic Field Guide to the Birds of Costa Rica.* Sanibel Island, FL: Ralph Curtis Publishing, 2005. Superbly illustrated pocket-size guide.

Garrigues, Richard, and Robert Dean. *The Birds of Costa Rica: A Field Guide.* Ithaca, NY: Cornell University Press, 2014. A splendidly illustrated guide written by one of Costa Rica's foremost ornithologists.

Henderson, Carrol L. *Field Guide to the Wildlife of Costa Rica.* Austin: University of Texas Press, 2002. This weighty tome provides a thorough layman's treatment of individual wildlife species, but it's a bit too bulky for the road. Most species are shown in color photographs.

Hepworth, Adrian. *Costa Rica: A Journey through Nature.* San José, Costa Rica: Zona Tropical, 2014. This coffee-table book features fine photography off wildlife.

Janzen, Daniel, ed. *Costa Rican Natural History.* Chicago: University of Chicago Press, 1983. Weighty and large-format, it's the bible for scientific insight into individual species of flora and fauna. With 174 contributors.

Perry, Donald. *Life Above the Jungle Floor.* New York: Simon & Schuster, 1986. A fascinating account of life in the forest canopy, relating Perry's scientific studies at Rara Avis.

Savage, Jay M. *The Amphibians and Reptiles of Costa Rica.* Chicago: University of Chicago Press, 2005. The most comprehensive treatment of amphibian and reptile ecology, with in-depth information on 396 species.

Stiles, F. Gary, and Alexander Skutch. *A Guide to the Birds of Costa Rica.* Ithaca, NY: Cornell University Press, 1989. A superbly illustrated compendium for serious bird-watchers.

Wainwright, Mark. *The Natural History of Costa Rica: Mammals.* San José, Costa Rica: Zona Tropical, 2003. A splendid companion for naturalists, with identifying charts and lots of esoteric information.

Wallace, David R. *The Quetzal and the Macaw: The Story of Costa Rica's National Parks.* San Francisco: Sierra Club Books, 1992. An entertaining history of the formation of Costa Rica's national park system.

Zuckowski, Willow. *A Guide to Tropical Plants of Costa Rica.* San José, Costa Rica: Zona Tropical, 2006. Beautifully illustrated field guide.

Zuckowski, Willow, and Turid Forsyth. *Tropical Plants of Costa Rica: A Guide to Native and Exotic Flora.* Ithaca, NY: Cornell University Press, 2007. More than 500 photographs.

Internet Resources

COSTA RICA TRAVEL

Costa Rica Travel App
www.christopherpbaker.com/costa-rica-travel-app
With the *Costa Rica ¡Pura Vida!* travel app in your pocket, you can travel "on the go," quickly finding the best lodgings, restaurants, beaches, and experiences. This app shows only the best of Costa Rica, from Volcán Arenal to zip-line adventures. It's available for the iPhone, iPod, iPad, and Android devices. It's a perfect companion to *Moon Costa Rica.*

Costa Rica Outdoors
www.costaricaoutdoors.com
The first-stop site for anglers and active travelers.

Costa Rica Expeditions
www.costaricaexpeditions.com/resourcelibrary
One of the leading travel operators specializing in nature adventures.

Small Distinctive Hotels of Costa Rica
www.distinctivehotels.com
For travelers with a taste for elegance, this site represents nine of the most endearing hotels in the country.

SANSA
www.flysansa.com
Costa Rica's state-owned regional airline, with online reservations and links to the websites of affiliate Central American airlines.

Nature Air
www.natureair.com
Website of the privately owned airline, serving Costa Rica and Panamá.

SINAC
www.sinac.go.cr
Website of the Sistema Nacional de Áreas de Conservación, with information on individual national parks and wildlife reserves. In Spanish only.

Essential Costa Rica
www.visitcostarica.com
The official website of the Costa Rican Tourism Board offers search capability plus online reservations.

ECOTOURISM

International Ecotourism Society
www.ecotourism.org
The website serves anyone interested in responsible travel.

SustainableTrip.org
www.sustainabletrip.org
The Rainforest Alliance's eco-index of sustainable tourism.

Certification for Sustainable Tourism
www.turismo-sostenible.co.cr
Overseen by the Costa Rican Tourism Institute (ICT), the website lets you differentiate tourism-sector businesses based on the degree to which they comply with a sustainable model of tourism.

Conservation Organizations

Conservation International (U.S. tel. 703-341-2400 or 800-429-5660, www.conservation.org) supports conservation projects worldwide.

The Monteverde Conservation League (tel. 506/2645-5003, www.acmcr.org) promotes reforestation projects and works to assist farmers of the Monteverde region to increase productivity in a sustainable manner.

Nature Conservancy (U.S. tel. 703-841-5300 or 800-628-6860, www.nature.org) identifies species in need of protection and acquires land to protect them.

Fundación Neotrópica (Neotropic Foundation, tel. 506/2253-2130, www.neotropica.org), promotes sustainable development and conservation among local communities.

Organization for Tropical Studies (OTS, U.S. tel. 919-684-5774, www.ots.ac.cr) is dedicated to biological research. It offers rainforest ecology workshops in Costa Rica, where it has research facilities and lodges open to the public.

Rainforest Alliance (U.S. tel. 212-941-1900 or 888-693-2786, www.rainforest-alliance.org) works to save rainforests worldwide.

Sea Turtle Conservancy (STC, U.S. tel. 352-373-6441, www.conserveturtles.org) works to protect turtle populations and accepts donations and volunteers.

Titi Conservation Alliance (tel. 506/2777-2306, www.monotiti.org) works to protect the endangered squirrel monkey.

World Wildlife Fund (U.S. tel. 202-293-4800, www.wwf.org) works to protect endangered wildlife worldwide.

Index

List of Maps

Also Available

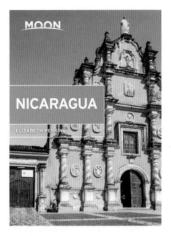

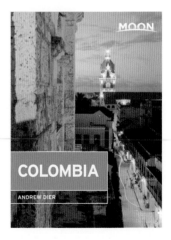

MAP SYMBOLS

═══════ Expressway	○ City/Town	✈ Airport	⚓ Golf Course
─────── Primary Road	◉ State Capital	✗ Airfield	🅿 Parking Area
·········· Secondary Road	⊛ National Capital	▲ Mountain	▲ Archaeological Site
- - - - - Unpaved Road	★ Point of Interest	✛ Unique Natural Feature	⚲ Church
─────── Feature Trail	• Accommodation		⛽ Gas Station
- - - - - Other Trail	▾ Restaurant/Bar	🏞 Waterfall	Glacier
············ Ferry	■ Other Location	▲ Park	Mangrove
═══════ Pedestrian Walkway	Δ Campground	⛺ Trailhead	Reef
▥▥▥▥ Stairs		⛷ Skiing Area	Swamp

CONVERSION TABLES

°C = (°F − 32) / 1.8
°F = (°C x 1.8) + 32
1 inch = 2.54 centimeters (cm)
1 foot = 0.304 meters (m)
1 yard = 0.914 meters
1 mile = 1.6093 kilometers (km)
1 km = 0.6214 miles
1 fathom = 1.8288 m
1 chain = 20.1168 m
1 furlong = 201.168 m
1 acre = 0.4047 hectares
1 sq km = 100 hectares
1 sq mile = 2.59 square km
1 ounce = 28.35 grams
1 pound = 0.4536 kilograms
1 short ton = 0.90718 metric ton
1 short ton = 2,000 pounds
1 long ton = 1.016 metric tons
1 long ton = 2,240 pounds
1 metric ton = 1,000 kilograms
1 quart = 0.94635 liters
1 US gallon = 3.7854 liters
1 Imperial gallon = 4.5459 liters
1 nautical mile = 1.852 km

MOON COSTA RICA

Avalon Travel
a member of the Perseus Books Group
1700 Fourth Street
Berkeley, CA 94710, USA
www.moon.com

Editor: Nikki Ioakimedes
Series Manager: Kathryn Ettinger
Copy Editor: Christopher Church
Graphics Coordinator: Lucie Ericksen
Production Coordinator: Lucie Ericksen
Cover Design: Faceout Studios, Charles Brock
Moon Logo: Tim McGrath
Map Editor: Mike Morgenfeld
Cartographer: Brian Shotwell
Indexer: Rachel Kuhn

ISBN-13: 978-1-63121-139-3
ISSN: 1082-4847

Printing History
1st Edition — 1994
2nd Edition — December 2015
5 4 3 2 1

Front cover photo: toucan © Christopher P. Baker
Title page photo: traditional painted ox-cart © Christopher P. Baker
Back cover photo: surfer at sunset, Playa Grande, Nicoya Peninsula © Christopher P. Baker
All interior photos: © Christopher P. Baker

Printed in China by RR Donnelley.

All recommendations, including those for sights, activities, hotels, restaurants, and shops, are based on each author's individual judgment. We do not accept payment for inclusion in our travel guides, and our authors don't accept free goods or services in exchange for positive coverage.

Although every effort was made to ensure that the information was correct at the time of going to press, the author and publisher do not assume and hereby disclaim any liability to any party for any loss or damage caused by errors, omissions, or any potential travel disruption due to labor or financial difficulty, whether such errors or omissions result from negligence, accident, or any other cause.